The First Team and the Gua

The First Team
and the
Guadalcanal Campaign

Naval Fighter Combat
from August to November 1942

JOHN B. LUNDSTROM

NAVAL INSTITUTE PRESS · ANNAPOLIS, MARYLAND

Naval Institute Press
291 Wood Road
Annapolis, MD 21402

First Naval Institute Press paperback edition, 2005
ISBN 978-1-59114-472-4

The Library of Congress has cataloged the hardcover edition as follows:
Lundstrom, John B.
    The first team and the Guadalcanal campaign : naval fighter combat from
August to November, 1942 / John B. Lundstrom.
        p. cm.
    Includes bibliographic references and index.
    ISBN 1-55750-526-8 (alk. paper)
    1. World War, 1939–1945—Aerial operations, American. 2. World War,
1939–Naval operations, American. 3. Guadalcanal Island (Solomon
Islands), Battle of, 1942–1943. I. Title.

D790.L79   1993
940.54′4923—dc20

                                                    93-8184

Printed in the United States of America on acid-free paper ∞
12 11 10 09   9 8 7 6 5 4 3

To Sandy and Rachel, who make it all possible

Contents

Foreword

John B. Lundstrom's *First Team and the Guadalcanal Campaign* is an enthralling, well-documented, nonjudgmental sequel to *The First Team*. Like his initial volume, it presents in intimate detail the intense, punishing combat action as it occurred, offering valuable insights into those difficult early flattop engagements in support of our tenuous foothold on Guadalcanal.

One of the most fascinating chapters of the carrier war in the Pacific was the magnificent exploits of a small number of naval aviators who played a vital role in helping bring to a standstill the powerful Japanese thrust in the southern Solomons. Orphaned by costly carrier sea battles, including the sinking of the *Wasp* and *Hornet* and battering of the *Enterprise,* these much-needed fliers and their aircraft were gratefully welcomed ashore to operate alongside their Marine and Army Air counterparts from a rough-and-ready jungle airfield located precariously near the front lines on Guadalcanal. They provided a terrific boost to the beleaguered shore-based contingents holding the line. After a crucial three-month series of bitter, retaliatory air battles, this CACTUS Air Force succeeded; a determined enemy was forced to abandon its plans to retake Guadalcanal.

Because our air and ground efforts were defensive in nature, it is difficult to assess fairly the general progress of our carrier operations during this period. They had little going for them, but this special breed swallowed hard and made sure that it would be enough to stem the tide until America's industrial might made possible the scheduled 1943 phase-in of the new *Essex-* and *Independence*-class carriers with their improved fighter aircraft. Many of our imaginations were captured by the impressive enemy plane tallies compiled by shore-based Marine fighter pilots Joe Foss, John Smith, Bob Galer, and Marion Carl at Guadalcanal. It seems fitting to note also that with a little more ammo and alert fighter help "Swede" Vejtasa, one of VF-10's unsung heroes, might have run his score to an even dozen in one day off the "Big E" at the Battle of Santa Cruz, instead of having to settle for only a "miserly" seven on that one flight.

Realizing that statistics do not always tell the whole story in regard to the loss ratio in fighter-to-fighter combat, it would be prudent to recognize that in most of our early engagements our fighters were outnumbered. Battle losses tended to even out by the end of 1942, when the availability of fighter aircraft on our side improved substantially. As regards the change of quality of naval carrier pilots, Japan's pilot training program did not meet its mass-production requirements. When the war began, their pilots were trained to a high degree of combat efficiency. But after heavy attrition and the destruction of the best carrier squadrons, there were insufficient quality replacements to remain combat ready. Japanese carrier aviation never seemed to recover from the heavy casualties suffered in 1942. This produced a new uncertainty in subsequent aerial combat, of course: not knowing if one was going to face a wily veteran or a raw recruit.

Many lessons were learned from the experiences of the First Team in the early days of the war. With the distinct advantage of a dominant fighter aircraft, those of us who followed in Hellcats and Corsairs had all the confidence in the world to fly "aggressive-smart" against a highly dedicated enemy. Our First Team predecessors—with special credit to our fighter leaders, Jimmy Thach, Jimmy Flatley, and "Butch" O'Hare—have earned our heartfelt thanks.

Cdr. Alex Vraciu, USN (Ret.)

Preface

The present work concludes the history of U.S. naval fighter combat during the first year of the Pacific War, December 1941 through November 1942. Unlike the first six months, the carriers enjoyed no sudden, stunning victories such as in June at Midway. Both the U.S. and Japanese naval aviators had taken the measure of each other. There would be no surprises now; the struggle entered a new phase. Instead of conducting a mobile defense, the U.S. flattops had to support the first Allied amphibious offensive in the southern Solomon Islands. The initial seizure on 7–8 August 1942 of a foothold on Guadalcanal occurred rather easily, but the Japanese reacted fiercely. The U.S. Pacific Fleet strained its resources to the limit trying to protect and supply the Marines, sailors, and soldiers who tenaciously held that narrow coastal area. During the course of the Guadalcanal campaign, the U.S. carriers fought two frustrating and costly battles with their Japanese counterparts. Tactical defeats became transformed into strategic victories afterward only because the Japanese did not or could not continue to advance against Guadalcanal. Stripped from flattops that were either blasted under the sea or sent home for repairs, carrier aviators fought from a primitive jungle airfield alongside their Marine and Army Air Force counterparts. American sea, land, and air power proved just enough to increase Japanese attrition and force them to cut their losses and evacuate Guadalcanal. The course of the Pacific War had turned against Japan for good.

The aim of this work is to use the detailed experiences of the naval fighting squadrons to illuminate the general progress of carrier operations. Unlike the dive and torpedo bombers, the fighters fought largely a defensive war. They protected the task forces and acted as escorts on strike missions, with the attack planes entrusted to their care. Their effectiveness and numerical strength largely determined where the carriers could go and how long they could stay there, elements of extreme strategic importance not often properly considered when evaluating carrier commanders such as VAdm. Frank Jack Fletcher. Unlike the carrier battles of 1943–45, where the U.S. naval fighter squadrons enjoyed both qualitative and numerical superiority, the offensive of 1942 had to be prosecuted in fighters inferior in performance to the Japanese. Gunnery training and tactical doctrine proved to be the decisive factors.

Also unlike the first six months of the war, carrier fighters also served in the unfamiliar role of shore-based interceptors to help the Marine and Army fighters of the so-called CACTUS Air Force whittle down masses of enemy aircraft assailing Guadalcanal. Their success helped turn the tide of battle.

The focus here is on the carrier fighters rather than the other types of aircraft. The available sources, including extensive Japanese records, permit detailed reconstruction of the carrier battles from the viewpoints of both opponents. The activities of the naval fighters at CACTUS are also extremely well documented, in unfortunate contrast to those of the Marines. Therefore they can serve as a rare case study for a general understanding of fighter operations from Guadalcanal.

As with the first volume, who, as well as how and why, has become a vital consideration. In a long air campaign of rarely matched ferocity, the many American and Japanese aviators chronicled in these pages fought battles that will long inspire the naval traditions of their nations. For the first time specific opponents can be identified and their particular deeds described. Wartime animosity has faded, and the brave aviators of both sides can be remembered and honored.

Acknowledgments

An enduring pleasure of my research has been associating with the many veterans, historians, and archivists who have so greatly assisted my work. Simply mentioning some of them under "Acknowledgments" is certainly an inadequate demonstration of my indebtedness to all of them.

As I finished *The First Team* and turned to its sequel covering Guadalcanal, I was fortunate to receive the cooperation of many participants, whose names appear in the section on sources. I deeply regret that a good number did not live long enough to see this book come to press.

In their accessibility, assistance, and encouragement, several veterans contributed significantly. My first mentor was Capt. Howard W. Crews, whose knowledge, clear judgment, and sense of humor proved invaluable. He introduced me to other VF-5 stalwarts, including RAdm. Leroy C. Simpler, Capt. Walter E. Clarke, Cdr. Frank O. Green, Cdr. John M. Wesolowski, and Lt. Cdr. John P. Altemus. Already helping with the first volume, Capt. Gordon E. Firebaugh of VF-6 has continued his staunch support. Other VF-6ers requiring special mention are Capt. Howell M. Sumrall, Capt. Paul Mankin, and Lt. Cdr. Richards L. Loesch. My principal contacts in VF-71 were Capt. Roland H. Kenton, Cdr. David V. Senft, and Lt. Cdr. Thaddeus J. Capowski, and in VF-72 Cdr. Philip E. Souza and Cdr. George L. Wrenn. For VF-10 Capt. Stanley W. Vejtasa, Cdr. Raleigh E. Rhodes, and Lt. Cdr. Albert E. Mead have been of particular help.

Aside from the fighter pilots, several other participants need to be mentioned here. Torpedo Ten is blessed with an excellent reunion organization, which provided me addresses for Thomas C. Nelson, Michael Glasser, and Thomas Powell. William Shinneman, brother of VT-10 radioman Charles Shinneman, graciously shared his excellent research on VT-10 at Santa Cruz. Cdr. Hal Buell of VS-5 and VB-10, author of the superb memoir *Dauntless Helldiver,* has offered much insight into air operations. Dr. Norman Haber, a VP-24 PBY pilot, provided key documents and recollections. Two *Enterprise* Santa Cruz veterans, Capt. John H. Griffin, FDO, and Capt. James G. Daniels, Air Group Ten LSO, have given documents and recollections of great worth. Capt. Lewis C. Mattison, CACTUS FDO, provided his fine personal diary kept on Guadalcanal.

Exploring the close alliance of carrier aviators with Marine Corps squadrons at Guadalcanal has resulted in many valued associations with numerous Marines. Chief among them is Rex Hamilton, a VMF-223 ground crewman at CACTUS and now an indefatigable historian. He opened the way to veterans of VMF-223, VMF-224, VMF-212, and VMF-121. I would thank in particular Brig. Gen. Frederick R. Payne (VMF-212), Col. Frank C. Drury (VMF-212), Col. Jack E. Conger (VMF-212), Col. Dean S. Hartley (VMF-224),

Col. Roger Haberman (VMF-121), Col. Jefferson DeBlanc (VMF-112), Col. Carl M. Longley (VMO-251), and Lt. Col. Wendell V. Garton (VMO-251). Lt. Col. Dennis Byrd, who was Lt. Col. Dick Mangrum's radioman with VMSB-232 at Guadalcanal, has labored long to write a history of MAG-23 at CACTUS. He generously shared his findings with me.

I was fortunate to meet several ex–Imperial Japanese naval aviators who fought in the battles I describe. They were Abe Zenji, Arima Keiichi, Sakai Saburō, Komachi Sadamu, and Ishikawa Shirō. The unique perspective of their recollections much enhanced this book.

The families of deceased aviators have also significantly aided this research by providing diaries and other valuable documents. In particular I would like to mention the families of VAdm. James H. Flatley, Cdr. James A. Halford, Lt. Cdr. Foster Blair, Col. John L. Smith, Lt. Col. Harold W. Bauer, and Maj. Gen. Shingō Hideki for their kind response to my inquiries.

For me personally, perhaps the great unforeseen result of *The First Team* has been deep friendships established with other historians. James C. Sawruk is now my closest collaborator in researching Pacific War aviation. A tireless researcher, he has uncovered a tremendous amount of new information. The same can certainly be said of Robert J. Cressman, noted author and historian with the Naval Historical Center. Richard B. Frank, author of the superb *Guadalcanal*, generously shared his translations of Japanese sources and his unsurpassed insight into the campaign. Dr. Steve Ewing, curator of the USS *Yorktown* (CV-10), Helen McDonald of the Admiral Nimitz Museum, Capt. Earle Rogers of the National Aviation Museum Foundation, Capt. E. T. Wooldridge of the National Air and Space Museum, and Daniel Martinez of the USS *Arizona* Memorial invited me to symposia and encouraged my work. Author Michael Wenger has helped me understand photo interpretation. Aviation historians Henry Sakaida, Barrett Tillman, Mark Horan, Lawrence Hickey, Frank Olynyk, Robert Lawson, John Kreis, Thomas F. Gates, Eric Hammel, and the late Richard M. Hill also contributed materially to this research.

Three individuals provided me the Japanese documents that contributed greatly to the value of this work. They are Dr. Izawa Yasuho, renowned Japanese naval historian, Osamu ("Sam") Tagaya, a young American aviation historian, and Dr. David C. Evans of the University of Richmond. Without their kindness this book could not have been written. Bunichi Ohtsuka, Dr. Akira Funahashi, Herbert Kadowaki, D. Y. Louie, and Ray Cheung provided expert translations.

Several archives contributed the documents used as the framework of this book. At the Naval Historical Center, I would like to thank in particular Dr. Dean C. Allard, the director of naval history, who has long supported my work, B. F. Cavalcante, Kathy Lloyd, Michael Walker, and photo archivist Charles Haberlein. At the Marine Corps Historical Center, J. M. Miller, curator of personal papers, has been of special help. At the National Archives I would like to thank Richard Boylan and Richard von Doenhoff.

Last, I desire to notice those who have contributed to the production of this work. My fine editor, Therese Boyd, has labored through the long text. Rose Henderson drew the Wildcat side views, and Joanne Peterson copied some of the photos. My wife, Sandy Lundstrom, drew the maps and diagrams, with drafting equipment thoughtfully provided by Bernard Weber, and along with our daughter Rachel, she has shown unusual patience and understanding when I spent so much time on this book.

Special Note

All distances are given in nautical miles. Degrees of bearing are True, unless noted "M." (for Magnetic). For operations in the vicinity of the Solomons, all times have been converted to Zone minus 11. For other geographical locations, local times are indicated.

Japanese names are rendered in proper usage with surnames first and given names second. The only exceptions are for Japanese Americans and in the citation of Japanese authors for books published in the West.

In dealing with Japanese aircraft types, the Allied code names such as ZEKE, BETTY, KATE, and VAL are not used except when a particular type is first mentioned in the text. These names appeared after the period covered in this book and hence are anachronistic. In their place I have provided the proper Japanese terminology for the main combat types as well as Japanese model and year descriptions.

MAIN AIRCRAFT TYPES AND TERMS

English	Japanese	Abbreviation
Carrier fighter	*kanjō sentōki*	*kansen*
Carrier (dive) bomber	*kanjō bakugekiki*	*kanbaku*
Carrier (torpedo) attack plane	*kanjō kōgekiki*	*kankō*
Land attack plane (medium bomber)	*rikujō kōgekiki*	*rikkō*

JAPANESE AIRCRAFT MENTIONED IN TEXT

Imperial Navy

Aichi D1A1 Type 96 carrier bomber	[no nickname]
Aichi D3A1 Type 99 carrier bomber	[VAL]
Aichi E13A1 Type 0 reconnaissance seaplane	[JAKE]
Kawanishi E7K2 Type 94 reconnaissance seaplane	[ALF]
Kawanishi H6K4 Type 97 flying boat	[MAVIS]
Kawanishi H8K1 Type 2 flying boat	[EMILY]
Mitsubishi A5M4 Type 96 carrier fighter	[CLAUDE]
Mitsubishi A6M2 Type 0 carrier fighter, Model 21	[ZEKE]
Mitsubishi A6M3 Type 0 carrier fighter, Model 32	[HAMP]
Mitsubishi F1M2 Type 0 observation seaplane	[PETE]
Mitsubishi G4M1 Type 1 land attack plane	[BETTY]

Nakajima A6M2-N Type 2 sea fighter   [RUFE]
Nakajima B5N2 Type 97 carrier attack plane   [KATE]
Nakajima E8N1 Type 95 reconnaissance seaplane   [DAVE]
Nakajima J1N1-C Type 2 land reconnaissance plane   [IRVING]
Yokosuka D4Y1-C Type 2 carrier reconnaissance plane   [JUDY]
Imperial Army Air Force
Mitsubishi Ki-46 Type 100 command reconnaissance plane   [DINAH]

To help understand the hierarchy of command among the active aviators in the air groups and squadrons, I have cited U.S. Naval Academy graduates by the year of their graduating class. The Imperial Navy referred to the graduating classes of the Naval Academy at Eta Jima by number rather than year. The specific classes mentioned with their number and year of graduation are:

58th Class	1930	62nd Class	1934	66th Class	1938
59th Class	1931	63rd Class	1936	67th Class	1939
60th Class	1932	64th Class	1937	68th Class	1940
61st Class	1933	65th Class	1938	69th Class	1941

Abbreviations and Special Terms

AA	Antiaircraft
AAF	U.S. Army Air Forces
ACTG	Advanced carrier training group
ACV	Auxiliary aircraft carrier (in 1943 CVE—escort carrier)
Air Group	Unit with two or more squadrons
AirSoPac	Aircraft, South Pacific Force
AK	Cargo ship
AlNav	All Navy
Angels	Fighter director term for altitude
AP	Transport ship
APD	Destroyer transports
A-V(N)	Naval Aviator (Reserve)
A-V(S)	Aviation Service Officer (Reserve)
Bandit	Enemy aircraft
BB	Battleship
Bogey	Unidentified aircraft
BSIPDF	British Solomon Islands Protectorate Defence Force
BuAer	Bureau of Aeronautics
Buntaichō	Division officer (command echelon in Imperial Navy)
Buster	Fighter director term, to proceed at best sustained speed
BUTTON	Espiritu Santo
CA	Heavy cruiser
CAG	Commander, Air Group
CAP	Combat air patrol
CACTUS	Guadalcanal
CEAG	Commander, *Enterprise* Air Group
CHAG	Commander, *Hornet* Air Group ("Sea Hag")
Chūtai	A unit of six to nine aircraft
Chūtaichō	Commander of a *chūtai*
CG	Commanding General
CinCPac	Commander-in-Chief, U.S. Pacific Fleet
CL	Light cruiser
CL(AA)	Light cruiser—antiaircraft
CNO	Chief of Naval Operations
CO	Commanding Officer

ComAirCACTUS	Commander, Aircraft, CACTUS
ComAirFor	Commander, Air Force, Pacific Fleet
ComAirLant	Commander, Aircraft, Atlantic Fleet
ComAirPac	Commander, Aircraft, Pacific Fleet
ComAirSoPac	Commander, Aircraft, South Pacific Force
ComCarPac	Commander, Carriers, Pacific Fleet
ComCruPac	Commander, Cruisers, Pacific Fleet
ComFAirWest	Commander, Fleet Air, West Coast
ComGenCACTUS	Commanding General, CACTUS
CominCh	Commander-in-Chief, U.S. Fleet
ComPatWing	Commander, Patrol Wing
ComSoPac	Commander, South Pacific Area and Force
ComSoWesPacFor	Commander, Southwest Pacific Force
CRAG	Carrier Replacement Air Group
CSAG	Commander, *Saratoga* Air Group
CTF	Commander, Task Force
CTG	Commander, Task Group
CTU	Commander, Task Unit
CV	Carrier
CVL	Light carrier
CWAG	Commander, *Wasp* Air Group
CXAM	Type of radar
D.	Died
DD	Destroyer
DesDiv	Destroyer Division
DesRon	Destroyer Squadron
DFC	Distinguished Flying Cross
Division	A unit of four to nine planes
FD	Fighter director
FDO	Fighter director officer
FG	Fighter group (USAAF)
FO	Flight Officer
FS	Fighter squadron (USAAF)
Hey Rube	Fighter director term ordering return to base
Hikōchō	Air Officer
Hikōkitai	Air group (such as attached to a ship)
Hikōtaichō	Air group officer (command echelon, Imperial Navy)
IAP	Inner Air Patrol
IFF	Identification, Friend or Foe
IJN	Imperial Japanese Navy
JCS	Joint Chiefs of Staff
Kanbaku	*Kanjō bakugekiki*: carrier (dive) bomber
Kankō	*Kanjō kōgekiki*: carrier (torpedo) attack plane
Kansen	*Kanjō sentōki*: carrier fighter
KIA	Killed in action
Kidō Butai	Carrier striking force (literally, mobile force)
Kōkūtai	Naval air group (land-based)
LSO	Landing Signal Officer
(M.)	Magnetic
MAG	Marine Air Group
MarDiv	Marine Division

MAW	Marine Air Wing
MCAS	Marine Corps Air Station
MIA	Missing in action
NA	Imperial Japanese Naval Academy at Eta Jima
NAP	Naval Aviation Pilot
NAS	Naval Air Station
OpNav	Chief of Naval Operations
OpPlan	Operations Plan
PPC	Patrol plane commander
RAAF	Royal Australian Air Force
RAF	Royal Air Force
RANVR	Royal Australian Navy Volunteer Reserve
Res.	Reserve
Ret.	Retired
rikkō	*Rikujō kōgekiki*: land attack plane (medium bomber)
RINGBOLT	Tulagi
ROSES	Efate
SCAP	Screen combat air patrol
SecNav	Secretary of the Navy
Section	A unit of two to four planes
Shōtai	A unit of two to four planes (usually three)
Shōtaichō	Commander of a *shōtai*
SoPac	South Pacific Area and Force
SNLF	Special Naval Landing Force
Special Duty	Officer promoted from enlisted man (*tokumu*)
Squadron	A unit of six to thirty-six planes
SWPA	Southwest Pacific Area
(T.)	True
Tally ho	Fighter pilot term for making in intercept
TBS	"Talk between ships"
TF	Task force
TG	Task group
TU	Task unit
USAAF	U.S. Army Air Forces
USMC	U.S. Marine Corps
USMCR	U.S. Marine Corps Reserve
USN	U.S. Navy (referring to personnel—regular Navy)
USNA	U.S. Naval Academy, Annapolis
USNR	U.S. Naval Reserve
VB	Bombing, dive bomber (often used for any bomber)
Vector	Direct out on a magnetic heading
VF	Fighting, fighter
VGS	Escort scouting
VMF	Marine fighting, fighter
VMJ	Marine utility (transport)
VMO	Marine observation
VMSB	Marine scout bomber
VOS	Observation float plane
VP	Patrol, patrol plane (usually flying boat)
VR	Reconnaissance plane
VS	Scouting, scout plane (usually dive bomber)

VSB	Scout bomber (dive bomber)
VT	Torpedo, torpedo plane
VTB	Torpedo bomber
XO	Executive Officer
YE	Homing signal and transmitter
Zed Baker	Homing signal receiver (ZB)

RANKS USED IN TEXT

Commissioned

USN and IJN		USAAF and USMC	
Adm.	Admiral	Gen.	General (USAAF only)
VAdm.	Vice Admiral	Lt. Gen.	Lieutenant General
RAdm.	Rear Admiral	Maj. Gen.	Major General
—	—	Brig. Gen.	Brigadier General
Capt.	Captain	Col.	Colonel
Cdr.	Commander	Lt. Col.	Lieutenant Colonel
Lt. Cdr.	Lieutenant Commander	Maj.	Major
Lt.	Lieutenant	Capt.	Captain
Lt. (jg)	Lieutenant (junior grade)	1st Lt.	1st Lieutenant
Ens.	Ensign	2d Lt.	2nd Lieutenant
WO	Warrant Officer (IJN)		
Gun.	Gunner	Mar. Gun.	Marine Gunner (USMC only)
Mach.	Machinist		
Rad. Elec.	Radio Electrician		

Enlisted Ratings

The most commonly mentioned USN enlisted ratings (petty officers) are as follows:

Aviation Ordnance Man	Chief (ACOM), AOM1c, AOM2c, AOM3c
Aviation Machinist's Mate	Chief (ACMM), AMM1c, AMM2c, AMM3c
Aviation Pilot	Chief (CAP), AP1c, AP2c
Aviation Radioman	Chief (ACRM), ARM1c, ARM2c, ARM3c
Radioman	Chief (CRM), RM1c, RM2c, RM3c

Nonrated men, USN

Seaman, 1st Class	Sea1c
Seaman, 2nd Class	Sea2c

Imperial Japanese naval enlisted ranks (Aviation Branch)

Flight Chief Petty Officer	CPO (after 1 November 1942)
Flight Petty Officer, 1st Class	PO1c
Flight Petty Officer, 2nd Class	PO2c
Flight Petty Officer, 3rd Class	PO3c (to 1 November 1942)
Flight Leading Seaman	LdgSea (after 1 November 1942)
Flight Superior Seaman	SupSea (after 1 November 1942)
Flight Seaman, 1st Class	Sea1c
Flight Seaman, 2nd Class	Sea2c

The First Team and the Guadalcanal Campaign

PART I

Amphibious Offensive

CHAPTER 1

The New Mission

SQUARING AWAY AFTER MIDWAY

To Lt. William N. Leonard, USN, a fighter pilot with the well-traveled Fighting Squadron Forty-two (VF-42), the news received on 19 June 1942 at Naval Air Station (NAS) Kaneohe Bay seemed tantamount to "being ordered into heaven." Only two weeks after the stunning carrier victory in the Battle of Midway, seventy-four battlewise but tired fighter, dive-bomber, and torpedo pilots from the *Yorktown* (CV-5) and *Enterprise* (CV-6) air groups received long-awaited furloughs of 30 days leave before reassignment. It seemed the crowning touch after months of hard campaigning capped by a superb but costly victory. To return home in the euphoria following Midway meant being treated as "conquering heroes."[1]

Certainly the rest was well deserved, for these particular carrier pilots had accrued the most combat experience in the fleet. In December 1941 the *Enterprise* Air Group stumbled into the buzzsaw of the Pearl Harbor attack. After a number of false starts, the U.S. Pacific Fleet launched from February to April 1942 a series of pioneering carrier raids against Japanese island strongholds in a valiant but vain effort to arrest the enemy's southward advance. Led by VAdm. William F. Halsey, Jr., the *Enterprise* (with VF-6) struck first at the Marshalls, Wake, and Marcus islands. Later she escorted the *Hornet* (CV-8) with VF-8, loaded with Lt. Col. James "Jimmy" Doolittle's sixteen Army B-25 medium bombers, to within 650 miles of Japan for the celebrated April Tokyo raid. During the same period the *Yorktown* (with VF-42) attacked the southern Marshall and Gilbert islands and, in concert with the *Lexington* (CV-2) with VF-3, raided Lae and Salamaua in Papua, New Guinea. Subsequently, the *Yorktown* patrolled the beautiful Coral Sea, the key to Australia and New Zealand.

The late spring of 1942 brought two desperate carrier battles. On 7–8 May the Allies and Japan clashed in the Coral Sea for the first carrier duel in history. As part of a two-pronged offensive against New Guinea and the Solomons, three Japanese flattops (*Shōkaku, Zuikaku,* and *Shōhō*) protected an invasion convoy bound for Port Moresby. Adm. Chester W. Nimitz, Commander-in-Chief, Pacific Fleet (CinCPac), opposed them with RAdm. Frank Jack Fletcher's Task Force 17 (TF-17) centered around the *Yorktown* (with VF-42) and *Lexington* (with VF-2). At the cost of the gallant *Lex,* a destroyer, and a fleet oiler, as well as a bomb blast in the *Yorktown*'s middle, the Americans sank the light carrier *Shōhō,* pounded the *Shōkaku* with three bombs, and gutted the *Zuikaku* Air Group as well. Forced to withdraw the convoy, Japan suffered its first strategic setback of the war.

In early June a much more formidable force, led by four big carriers and supported by most of the Combined Fleet, threatened tiny Midway, only 1,100 miles northwest of the Hawaiian Islands. The beleaguered Pacific Fleet countered with the *Enterprise* (with VF-6) and *Hornet* (with VF-8) under RAdm. Raymond A. Spruance. Scarred from her Coral Sea wounds, Fletcher's *Yorktown* sortied from Pearl with a rebuilt air group, whose fighting squadron, VF-3, comprised mostly VF-42 veterans. On 4 June, American carrier strikes fatally damaged all four enemy carriers: the *Akagi*, *Kaga*, *Sōryū*, and *Hiryū*, but took fearful losses in return. Crippled by *Hiryū* aircraft, the *Yorktown* capsized on 7 June as a result of a submarine attack.

How did the U.S. Pacific Fleet's fighting squadrons fare in the first six months of the war? From 1 February to 4 June USN fighter pilots shot down seventy-four Japanese aircraft (seventeen fighters, fourteen medium bombers, sixteen dive bombers, fourteen torpedo planes, seven float planes, and six flying boats). In return, sixteen VF pilots died on combat missions and two in operational accidents. Of great concern was the performance of the Grumman F4F-4 Wildcat, the standard carrier fighter, especially when compared to its deadliest foe, the Mitsubishi A6M2 Type 0 carrier fighter, Model 21. Slower than the Zero in level speed and climb, as well as much less maneuverable, the tubby little Wildcat nevertheless held the edge in firepower and protection. Some veteran fighter pilots and many senior officers complained bitterly of the F4F-4's shortcomings. Yet in the direct confrontations between the two fighters, fifteen Zeros succumbed as opposed to ten F4Fs (seven pilots killed). To those who would next take the Wildcat into combat, the controversy seemed meaningless. Nothing better than the F4F-4 loomed immediately on the horizon, and they were determined to make the best of it.

Several fresh carrier squadrons reached Pearl Harbor during the Battle of Midway and gave the Pacific Fleet the opportunity to reorganize its carrier air groups. Thus Admiral Nimitz released the pilots with the most service, but the new groups retained a leaven of combat veterans. The Pacific Fleet now controlled four carriers, at Pearl Harbor the *Saratoga* (CV-3), *Enterprise,* and *Hornet,* and at San Diego the *Wasp* (CV-7) newly arrived from the Atlantic. Victory at Midway affected the balance of power in the Pacific, but no one at Pearl realized how soon the high command might take advantage of it.

CARRIERS FOR THE SOUTH PACIFIC

Tuesday, 23 June 1942, the day after Bill Leonard and his associates so gratefully boarded the transport *Mount Vernon* for the voyage home, did not start out as a watershed for the headquarters of the U.S. Pacific Fleet at Pearl. Admiral Nimitz was returning after a routine inspection of isolated Palmyra Island in the Central Pacific. For the past 10 days the fleet had enjoyed its first quiet period since the outbreak of war, and the carrier air groups anticipated an untroubled interval to complete their reorganization.

Any Midway-induced complacency that remained at CinCPac headquarters dissipated on 23 June upon receipt of an information message from Washington prefaced: "Handle this with the greatest of secrecy." In it Adm. Ernest J. King, Commander-in-Chief of the U.S. Fleet (CominCh), informed Gen. Douglas

MacArthur, Allied Supreme Commander of the Southwest Pacific Area (SWPA), of Joint Chiefs of Staff (JCS) interest in a possible offensive by the British Eastern Fleet against Timor or some other "suitable place" in the Dutch East Indies. That would coincide with the "seizure and occupation of Tulagi," a fine harbor in the southern Solomon Islands which the Japanese utilized as an advanced seaplane base. The Joint Chiefs set a target date of 1 August, less than six weeks off.[2]

The Pacific Fleet staff looked southward to their principal trouble spot, the Solomon chain of islands between the main Japanese base at Rabaul and the line of communication from the West Coast to Australia and New Zealand. The Allies held New Caledonia and the New Hebrides, but in May had lost Tulagi, their toehold in the Solomons. Ernie King predicated his Pacific strategy on a step-by-step advance from the New Hebrides up through the Solomons to recapture Rabaul. The instrument of this offensive was to be a component of Nimitz's Pacific Fleet and Pacific Ocean areas, known as the South Pacific Area (SoPac) under its commander (ComSoPac), VAdm. Robert L. Ghormley. He had only assumed command on 19 June.

Only the day before the message from Washington arrived, Nimitz had outlined for Ghormley a plan for utilizing the four carriers in the South Pacific. Between 15 July and 24 August two CV task forces would patrol SoPac waters, to be joined briefly by the other two carriers before the first pair started back north to Pearl. At that time, Nimitz had advised, during the four-day overlap when SoPac wielded all four carriers, Ghormley might initiate some sort of offensive operation. Now the die had been cast sooner than anyone had expected.[3]

The Joint Chiefs' recommendation for a South Pacific offensive stemmed from MacArthur's 8 June proposal offered in the wake of the overwhelming carrier victory at Midway. His primary strategic task was to hold eastern New Guinea to protect the approaches to northern Australia. Now he suggested that SWPA execute a surprise amphibious landing against Rabaul, the key enemy base on New Britain in the Bismarck Archipelago at the head of the Coral Sea. The actual assault troops and most of the naval support, including two carriers, had to come from Nimitz's Pacific Fleet. MacArthur's hastily conceived plans, the scope of which he later tried to diminish, riveted JCS attention on the Southwest Pacific as the locus of the first Allied counteroffensive of the Pacific War. Loath to place strong naval forces under a general whose competence to handle sea power he doubted, King recommended the capture of Tulagi rather than the far more ambitious and dangerous direct assault against Rabaul. Indications from ULTRA decrypts of Japanese naval communications outlined plans for reinforcing the region and fueled CominCh concern for a speedy attack.[4]

On 24 June King showed he meant business by directing that two carrier task forces be placed on 12-hour notice. For the impending South Pacific operations Nimitz turned first to the old giant *Saratoga*, busy with an aircraft ferry mission to Midway. As flagship of TF-11, she would sail early the next month for the South Pacific. At San Diego, the smaller *Wasp*, flagship of TF-18 under RAdm. Leigh Noyes, received orders to escort a convoy of five transports carrying the 2nd Marines and scheduled to depart on 1 July. In mid-July Noyes would join TF-11 in the South Pacific. Thus CinCPac laid initial plans for carrier support in the upcoming Solomons offensive. Meanwhile, the much-traveled *Enterprise* and the *Hornet* required time to work up their new squadrons.

On 30 June, in preparation for the upcoming offensive, Pearl Harbor witnessed a sort of musical chairs among the carrier task force commanders. The new

lineup was: TF-11 on the flagship *Saratoga,* commanded by RAdm. Frank Jack
Fletcher; TF-16 on the *Enterprise,* commanded by RAdm. Thomas C. Kinkaid;
and TF-17 on the *Hornet,* commanded by RAdm. Aubrey W. Fitch.

In the absence of VAdm. Bill Halsey, sick since 26 May, RAdm. Frank Jack
Fletcher became the senior Pacific Fleet carrier commander. Although he was a
nonaviator and a surface warfare expert, no one else had accumulated as much
carrier combat experience. For the past seven months Fletcher had borne tremendous responsibility with almost constant action: the abortive Wake Island
relief expedition (December 1941), two carrier raids (February in the Marshalls
and Gilberts, March against Lae and Salamaua), and overall command in the first
two battles, Coral Sea and Midway. Both victories cost two carriers.

Plain and unpretentious, a warm individual, Fletcher had strength of character
and a careful approach to war. Although naturally excitable, he was not rash, but
acted aggressively when he saw the need. Despite what his critics have said, his
innate caution never degenerated to timidity. RAdm. William Ward Smith, his
cruiser commander at Coral Sea and Midway, described him well: "Frank Jack
was a man's man. He made quick decisions, usually the right ones." Nimitz
reiterated his recommendation for Fletcher's immediate promotion to vice admiral and chose him to go south to command the carriers during the Tulagi
offensive.[5]

With Fletcher bound for southern waters, two carrier task forces would remain behind for training. Pending Halsey's return to active duty, RAdm. Thomas

VAdm. Frank Jack Fletcher in his cabin in the *Saratoga,* 17 Sept. 1942. (USN via Dr.
Steve Ewing)

C. Kinkaid, his able cruiser commander, took over TF-16 with his flag on the *Enterprise*. A veteran of Coral Sea and Midway, Kinkaid shone forth with clear judgment and strong professionalism. The senior naval aviator on duty at Pearl, RAdm. Aubrey W. Fitch relieved RAdm. Marc A. Mitscher on the *Hornet* as commander of TF-17. As events transpired, Fitch could not remain with TF-17 for long. He was too valuable ashore handling the administration of Carriers, Pacific Fleet (CarPac), overseeing the organization of all the carrier and Marine squadrons. Fortunately for the war effort, he soon escaped Pearl for a very important combat aviation assignment in SoPac.

CARRIER AIRCRAFT

Each U.S. carrier wielded an air group of four squadrons: fighting (VF) equipped with fighters, two identical dive-bombing units separately designated scouting (VS) or bombing (VB), and finally torpedo bombing (VT). Normal complements numbered twenty-seven Grumman F4F-4 Wildcat fighters in the VF squadrons, eighteen Douglas SBD-3 Dauntless scout bombers in each dive-bombing squadron, and eighteen of the newly arrived Grumman TBF-1 Avengers per VT squadron. The carrier air group commanders flew TBFs or, in one case, an SBD.

The flattop's offensive punch rested with her dive bombers and torpedo bombers. The dependable Douglas SBD-3 Dauntless scout bomber, capable of delivering a heavy bomb in a steep dive, emerged as the victor of Midway. Its actual performance figures appear less than spectacular. The two-seat SBD lugged a powerful 1,000-pound bomb (maximum strike radius about 250 miles) or a 500-pounder on scouting missions out to perhaps 325 miles. Defensively the pilot wielded two .50-caliber machine guns firing forward and his radioman a twin .30-caliber flexible mount. The Grumman TBF-1 Avenger torpedo bomber, which replaced the obsolescent Douglas TBD-1 Devastators slaughtered at Midway, was far more likely to survive the perilous delivery of a torpedo at low altitude within 1,500 yards of its target. Remarkable for such a big plane (wingspan 54 feet, weight 15,905 pounds fully loaded, and crew of three or four), the Avenger proved an excellent carrier aircraft—relatively fast (235 knots), long ranged, and rugged. Either one Mark XIII aerial torpedo (unfortunately unreliable), two 1,000-pound or four 500-pound bombs rested fully enclosed in a spacious bomb bay. The TBF enjoyed a combat radius slightly superior to the Dauntless. It featured a powered dorsal turret with a single .50-caliber machine gun, a .30-caliber stinger in the ventral radio compartment, and another single .30-caliber "peashooter" for the pilot. The Avenger proved such an upgrade from the TBD that the carrier commanders needed to learn its full potential.[6]

A workhorse (if not a thoroughbred), the Grumman F4F-4 Wildcat would continue to equip the carrier fighting squadrons for the next nine months. Its putative successor, the much more powerful bent-wing Vought XF4U-1 Corsair, first flew in May 1940, but suffered a long and troubled gestation. Indeed, the first production F4U-1s only appeared in July 1942. Meanwhile, the Navy hedged its bets with another excellent Grumman product, the XF6F-1 Hellcat, which made its maiden flight on 25 June 1942.[7]

Powered by a twin-bank Pratt & Whitney R-1830-86 radial engine rated at 1,200 horsepower and with a two-stage supercharger, the F4F-4 Wildcat attained a top speed of about 278 knots (320 MPH) at 18,800 feet. Initial climb rate was 2,190 feet per minute, time to 10,000 feet 5.6 minutes (average 1,786 FPM), and to

20,000 feet 12.4 minutes (average 1,613 FPM). Official range was 720 miles at 140 knots, offering, with internal fuel, an effective combat radius of about 175 miles. Tired of waiting for the Bureau of Aeronautics to develop drop tanks for the F4Fs, in the spring of 1942 NAS Pearl Harbor devised a 42-gallon belly tank that resembled a bathtub. The bureau's product, 58-gallon wing tanks, appeared in late summer of 1942. Both systems provided vital auxiliary fuel required to fly longer escort missions. The F4F-4 featured six wing-mounted Browning .50-caliber machine guns with 240 rounds per gun, enough for 18 seconds of firing. Well protected, the Wildcat enjoyed pilot armor and self-sealing fuel tanks. Although underpowered for its weight (7,975 pounds fully loaded), the F4F-4 boasted rugged construction, excellent protection, a moderately fast dive with good high-speed control, and a stable gun platform. Its drawbacks in comparison to its principal opponent, the Mitsubishi A6M2 Zero fighter, included inferior climb and acceleration, a slightly slower top speed, and much less maneuverability at low and medium speeds. Yet the Wildcat fought its nemesis to a draw in the first two carrier battles of the war through tactical skill rather than mechanical performance. When flown intelligently, the Wildcat possessed the tools to beat the Zero.

If the F4F-4 was a winner, the same could not be said for its photo-reconnaissance version, the F4F-7, being supplied in limited numbers to carrier utility units for use by the VF squadrons. Basically, the F4F-7 was a stripped-down version of the fixed wing F4F-3 transformed into a camera-equipped flying fuel tank. Fully loaded with 685 gallons of fuel, the beast topped 10,300 pounds and required special wind conditions just to get aloft. Fuel supplanted all the armament and protection, with only a fuel dump system for defense. Even so, top speed reached only 270 knots (310 MPH), slower than its prospective opponents. Estimated range was 3,700 miles; indeed the F4F-7 flew nonstop from coast to coast in 11 hours. As one expert on the Wildcat quipped, "At one time an endurance of 24 hours was claimed for the airplane, which must have brought great joy to everyone except the prospective pilot." At San Diego Lt. Louis H. Bauer's VF-2 detachment rendered a scathing verdict of the F4F-7. Its prospective pilots, certain members of the VF squadrons who had taken aerial photography courses at Quantico, felt little reason to love the photo Wildcat.[8]

REBUILDING THE CARRIER AIR GROUPS

Restoring the carrier groups in Hawaii to full combat effectiveness proved difficult due to severe losses at Midway and to the departure of so many veteran pilots.[9] At Midway the three torpedo squadrons (VT-3 from the sunken *Yorktown*, VT-6 from the *Enterprise*, and the *Hornet*'s VT-8) suffered virtual annihilation. Only VT-8 easily reformed around the nucleus led by Lt. Harold H. Larsen (USNA 1935). The two *Enterprise* dive-bombing squadrons (VB-6 and VS-6) also sustained terrible losses. By contrast, the three fighting squadrons (VF-3 *Yorktown*, VF-6 *Enterprise*, and VF-8 *Hornet*) came through tolerably well, but they still required complete reorganization by Capt. James M. Shoemaker, acting administrative head of CarPac.

In early June, two former Atlantic Fleet squadrons, VF-5 and VF-72, deployed to Hawaii along with the VF-2 Detachment from the West Coast. Despite the losses at Midway, ComCarPac suddenly enjoyed a surfeit of VF squadrons and pilots, including about twenty graduates from the Advanced Carrier Training

Group (ACTG) at San Diego. Lacking sufficient numbers of trained torpedo pilots, Shoemaker tapped surplus fighter pilots to fill out the VT squadrons. Most went to Torpedo Six, now re-formed under Lt. Edwin B. Parker (USNA 1935), former executive officer (XO) of VT-5. Indeed, by 25 June, no fewer than ten of eighteen VT-6 pilots had transferred in from fighters. That day the Hawaiian VF squadrons numbered 123 pilots:

Unit	Commanding Officer	Location	Pilots	F4F-4s
VF-3	Lt. Cdr. Edward H. O'Hare	NAS Maui	24	23
VF-5	Lt. Cdr. Leroy C. Simpler	*Saratoga*	31	27
VF-6	Lt. Louis H. Bauer	NAS Kaneohe Bay	31	27
VF-72	Lt. Cdr. Henry G. Sanchez	NAS Maui	19	28
VF-8	Lt. Cdr. Samuel G. Mitchell	NAS Maui	18	17
			123	122

CarPac fighter strength also included at San Diego, VF-71 under Lt. Cdr. Courtney Shands (USNA 1927) with the *Wasp* Air Group and newly formed VRF-10 (Lt. Cdr. James H. Flatley, Jr., USNA 1929), part of Carrier Replacement Air Group Ten.

Given her assignment, priority went to venerable *Saratoga*, still the longest warship in the world. Commissioned in 1927, the *"Sara,"* like sister *Lexington*, comprised a 900-foot flight deck perched high on a converted battlecruiser hull. At full load she displaced 48,500 tons, far bigger than the other carriers, and she could reach 33.5 knots. Torpedoed by a submarine in January 1942, the *Saratoga* underwent a full refit at Bremerton, Washington, and emerged with strengthened antiaircraft (AA) armament. Under her new commanding officer, the able Capt. Dewitt W. ("Duke") Ramsey (wings 1917 as Naval Aviator No. 45), the *Saratoga* arrived too late to fight at Midway.[10]

The *Saratoga* Air Group under Cdr. Harry D. ("Don") Felt (USNA 1923) comprised perhaps the most experienced squadrons remaining in the Pacific Fleet. Two were original *Saratoga* outfits: Bombing Squadron Three (VB-3) under Lt. Cdr. Dewitt W. Shumway (USNA 1932), proud *Yorktown* veterans who sank the carrier *Sōryū*, and Scouting Squadron Three (VS-3) led by Lt. Cdr. Louis J. Kirn (USNA 1932). Kirn's outfit had trained from February to May at

The *Saratoga* with air group on board, August 1942. (NA 80-G-12246)

NAS San Diego. Lieutenant "Swede" Larsen's Torpedo Eight derived from old VT-8 based on the *Hornet*, whose crews had remained behind at Norfolk as the first to work up the new Grumman TBF-1 Avengers.

Fighting Five, known as the "Striking Eagles," boasted a long and distinguished history. Formed in August 1927 as VF-3B ("B" for Battle Fleet as opposed to "S" for Scouting Fleet), it served from 1928 to 1936 on the *Lexington*, the old *Langley* (CV-1), and the recently commissioned carrier *Ranger* (CV-4). Redesignated VF-5 on 1 July 1937, the squadron switched to the *Yorktown* commissioned that September. In the spring of 1941 when the *Yorktown* deployed to the Atlantic Fleet, VF-5 went ashore at NAS Norfolk to exchange its Grumman F3F-2 biplanes for Grumman F4F-3A Wildcats. After duty on board the *Ranger*, VF-5 joined the *Wasp* in October for neutrality patrols in the North Atlantic. Again cast onto the beach in February 1942, VF-5 received folding-wing F4F-4 Wildcats at Norfolk. Hoping finally to catch up with the *Yorktown*, the squadron reached Pearl Harbor on 29 May, too late to make her last voyage. On 7 June VF-5 embarked on the *Saratoga* and on 18 June became her fighting squadron.

VF-5 fortunately possessed a strong nucleus of nine senior pilots, most with the squadron for two years or more. The commanding officer (CO), Lt. Cdr. Leroy C. Simpler (USNA 1929), earned his wings in 1931 and that May joined VS-5S on the light cruiser *Marblehead* (CL-13). His next duty was definitely out of the ordinary, on the great dirigible USS *Macon*, which operated Curtiss F9C-2 "trapeze" fighters from a hangar set in her keel. Simpler survived her watery demise on 12 February 1935. From 1936 to 1938 he again piloted float planes, this time from the heavy cruiser *Augusta* (CA-31) in the Asiatic Fleet. In June 1940 he became VF-6 flight officer on the *Enterprise*, and that November transferred to the *Yorktown*'s VF-5, taking over as CO in February 1942. A steady, able, and respected leader, cheerful and easygoing, Roy Simpler led a remarkably contented and efficient squadron.

Lt. Richard E. ("Chick") Harmer (USNA 1935), VF-5's XO, completed flight training in early 1939 and the next summer switched from scout bombers to VF-5. The flight officer, Lt. David C. Richardson (USNA 1936), earned his wings in early 1940 and joined VF-5. A classmate, Lt. James J. Southerland II (USNA 1936), known to all as "Pug" for his boxing skills, was engineering officer. In spring 1942, VF-5 received two ex-lawyers recently commissioned as A-V(S) lieutenants, Alexander F. Barbieri and William S. Robb. They fearlessly employed their administrative skills to handle the paperwork. Simpler later quipped that when necessary they even "bossed" him around. Glenn C. Poston, ACMM, a superb leading chief who ultimately wore the four stripes of a captain, supervised the ground echelon.[11]

Except for the short voyage out to Midway, VF-5 had seen no carrier duty since February. Many young pilots had only just qualified with carrier landings or still faced that ordeal. At NAS Kaneohe Bay a landing signal officer (LSO) brought them in one at a time for mock carrier landings. One pilot greatly puzzled the LSO by responding very strangely or not at all to the directions he waved with his wands. Instead of watching the LSO, the wayward pilot had been responding to the frantic arm signals of a colorfully dressed, rotund Hawaiian woman who controlled vehicular traffic crossing the runway.[12] On 22 June, VF-5 departed on board the *Saratoga* for the trip out to Midway. Save for a few gunnery practice flights, the cruise was uneventful, if uncomfortable due to the heat and the *Sara*'s poor ventilation. If only they knew what "hot waters" she would next traverse.

Second of the Pacific Fleet carriers assigned to the upcoming SoPac offensive, the *Wasp* displaced 21,000 tons at full load. With an overall length of 741 feet, she was considerably smaller than the *Yorktown*-class carriers, yet she wielded an air group nearly as large. The cost came at significantly less internal protection, and at 29.5 knots she was nearly four knots slower. Her design featured an innovative folding deck edge number 1 elevator located portside forward in the leading catapult bay. Commissioned in April 1940, she spent all of her time in the Atlantic and in the second half of 1941 undertook several arduous neutrality patrols directed against German U-boats and surface raiders.

The *Wasp*'s resident fighting squadron, VF-71, did not always serve on board due to the Atlantic Fleet's policy of air group rotation. Formed in July 1939 as VB-7, the squadron became VF-71 on 1 July 1940 and sported as its insignia Thor, the Norse war god. Like the *Ranger*'s air group, the *Wasp* Air Group originally comprised two fighting squadrons and two scouting squadrons in place of the conventional group of single VF, VB, VS, and VT squadrons. (A torpedo squadron, VT-7, first appeared in 1942.) Thus VF-71 alternated service on board the *Wasp* with its twin, VF-72. December 1941 found VF-71 shore-based, waiting for its folding-wing F4F-4s, but it soon took VF-5's place on board the *Wasp*. ComAirLant (Commander, Aircraft, Atlantic Fleet) greatly reinforced VF-71 with sixteen pilots drawn from VF-72, VF-41 on the *Ranger,* and VF-5, giving it thirty-seven pilots and twenty-nine F4F-4s, the first VF squadron to attain such numbers.

On 22 March 1942 the *Wasp* left Casco, Maine, bound for the great British naval base at Scapa Flow in northern Scotland. Most of the air group staged into the Royal Naval Air Station at Hatson, but the *Wasp* retained nineteen F4Fs for combat air patrol (CAP). Up the river Clyde at Glasgow she embarked forty-seven Royal Air Force (RAF) Spitfire V fighters meant for besieged Malta. That entailed traversing the Straits of Gibraltar into the confines of the western Mediterranean. At dawn on 20 April, the *Wasp* launched the Spitfires from 50 miles north of Algiers, then dashed back through the straits. Two weeks later she returned with an identical cargo, this time protected by twenty VF-71 F4Fs. On 9 May, the *Wasp* and the British carrier *Eagle* sent sixty Spitfires winging toward Malta. One RAF pilot aborted, but executed a fine hookless landing back on board the *Wasp*, for which the group presented him with a pair of naval aviator wings. During her two forays into the Mediterranean, the *Wasp* encountered no Axis aircraft, although VF-71 eagerly looked for a fight. On 11 May Prime Minister Winston Churchill congratulated the carrier: "Who said a *Wasp* could not sting twice."[13] She quickly reclaimed her air group and set sail for Norfolk, where Capt. Forrest P. Sherman relieved Capt. John W. Reeves, Jr.

On 5 June the *Wasp* headed south from Norfolk, passed through the Panama Canal on the 11th, and reached San Diego eight days later. Her air group flew ashore to North Island. Soon after, Rear Admiral Noyes boarded his new flagship to form TF-18. A late-blooming naval aviator like King, Halsey, and Fitch, Noyes happily escaped shore duty in Washington and Pearl Harbor for a carrier command. The first task involved re-equipping VS-71 and VS-72 with SBDs and VT-7 with TBFs. Lt. Cdr. Wallace M. Beakley (USNA 1924), the group commander (CWAG), initiated what the VS-71 war diary described as "a high pressure training schedule which crowded a month's training into a week's time." On 22 June the *Wasp* got underway for five days of day and night carrier qualification or refresher landings, interrupted only by a short interval ashore. Despite several accidents, no one was hurt and the wrecked planes were replaced. On 27 June, after sending her air group ashore, the *Wasp* again docked at San Diego.[14]

VF-71's senior officers were, for the most part, highly experienced. After leaving Annapolis in 1927, red-haired Courtney Shands received his wings in February 1930 and served in battleship and cruiser float planes with two intervals ashore (1932–34 and 1937–39) as a flight instructor. In July 1939 he became flight officer of VF-7 (later VF-72) and in July 1941 fleeted up to command of VF-72, only to transfer in March 1942 to VF-71. His XO, Lt. Cdr. Robert L. Strickler (USNA 1932), graduated from Pensacola in 1936 and spent two years with VF-4B on the *Ranger*, followed by a year in VO-3 with the battleship *New Mexico* (BB-40). From June 1939 to August 1941, he instructed at Pensacola, then became XO of VF-71. Much alike in personality and style, Shands and Strickler were quiet, capable, conservative, and dedicated naval aviators, who enjoyed the respect and loyalty of the squadron.

Third in the VF-71 hierarchy, Lt. Carl W. ("Pat") Rooney (USNA 1934) was a relative newcomer to aviation, having reported in April 1941 straight from Pensacola. For a time he brandished his Academy discipline as the bane of the junior ensigns. Perhaps the most flamboyant officer, Lt. Hawley ("Monk") Russell had a different background from the others. Instead of attending the "trade school," he completed the original Aviation Cadet program in December 1936 and served nearly two years with VO-4B on board the battleship *West Virginia* (BB-48). In late 1938, he became an instructor at Pensacola, and in early 1942 joined VF-71.

The two sisters, *Enterprise* and *Hornet*, rested in temporary reserve at Pearl. The incomparable "Big E" was the Pacific Fleet's most battlewise carrier and victor over the *Akagi*, *Kaga*, and *Hiryū* at Midway. Commissioned in May 1938, she displaced 25,500 tons at full war load, her overall length was 809 feet, and her top speed was 33 knots. The *Hornet*, commissioned in October 1941, was larger at 29,114 tons maximum load and slightly longer, 824 feet. During full power trials in September 1941, she registered 33.84 knots, considerably faster than her designed speed of 32.5 knots. Distinguished for her role in taking Lt. Col. James Doolittle's B-25 Mitchells to within strike range of Tokyo, the *Hornet* nevertheless smarted over lost opportunities at Midway and eagerly sought revenge.

The *Enterprise* Air Group changed greatly after Midway. Its CO, Lt. Cdr. Clarence Wade McClusky (USNA 1926), a true hero of the Midway victory, went home for a rest. His old classmate, Lt. Cdr. Maxwell F. Leslie (USNA 1926), former VB-3 CO on the *Yorktown* and another hero of the battle, replaced him. The two dive-bombing squadrons were Bombing Six (VB-6) under Lt. Ray Davis (USNA 1933) and, from the old *Yorktown*, Scouting Five (VS-5) led by Lt. Turner F. Caldwell (USNA 1935). Lt. Cdr. Charles M. Jett (USNA 1931) rebuilt VT-3 from almost nothing. Leslie worked hard to mold his scratch air group into a team, aided immeasurably in his task by "The Big E" 's new air officer, Cdr. John G. Crommelin, Jr. Eldest of five famous brothers, "Uncle John" was a highly respected naval aviator, much experienced in fighters. An acknowledged gunnery expert, he took an especially strong interest in the *Enterprise*'s fighting squadron, a much reworked VF-6.

Formed in 1935 as VF-1B (VF-8B in 1936–37 and VF-6 from 1 July 1937), the old "Shooting Star" squadron was now stretched mighty thin. Almost all of the veterans of the early raids and Midway either went home or transferred to VF-5. On 19 June only thirteen pilots remained, of whom only one, Lt. (jg) Howard L. Grimmell, Jr., had served with VF-6 more than three weeks. Seven were Naval Aviation Pilots (NAP), who had earned their wings as petty officers. They hailed from VF-2, the famed enlisted squadron, and only joined VF-6 on temporary duty. The wonder was that VF-6 remained in existence at all after ComCarPac decided to incorporate the entire VF-2 Detachment into its ranks. On 19 June Lt. Louis H. Bauer (USNA 1935) reported as the new CO of VF-6 and brought with him eleven more NAPs. By all rights the squadron should have become Fighting Two, as nineteen of twenty-five pilots either hailed from VF-2 or had orders there. Unfortunately ComCarPac, misinterpreting Admiral King's orders, decreed that VF-2 would be rebuilt as part of Carrier Replacement Air Group Ten forming at NAS San Diego. The number change proved only temporary, but the old VF-2 disappeared forever. The NAPs were disappointed not to retain their old number, but they still chafed to fight.[15]

Lt. Louis Hallowell Bauer, VF-6's new skipper, completed flight training in March 1939. Reporting to VF-2 on board the *Lexington,* he matured as a fighter leader in a squadron that painted the Efficiency "E" on all eighteen aircraft. By December 1941 he was flight officer under the able Lt. Cdr. Paul H. Ramsey (USNA 1927) and his brilliant XO, Lt. James H. Flatley, Jr. Without seeing combat, Bauer joined Flatley's VF-2 Detachment formed in February to cover the wounded *Saratoga*'s voyage back to the West Coast and took over in late March. Re-equipped with F4F-4s, the VF-2 Detachment rode the *Sara* in May to Pearl, where Bauer expected to reform VF-2 as XO to Lt. Cdr. Donald A. Lovelace (USNA 1928). However, Lovelace died in a 30 May crash on the *Yorktown.* A quiet, confident leader, Lou Bauer was meticulous in his approach to flying. His squadron included some of the most experienced fighter pilots in the Navy.

Fighting Six XO Lt. John Louis ("Whitey") Mehlig (USNA 1937) had only just completed ACTG and was handicapped by a lack of flight time. Another fledgling "trade school" graduate, Lt. Vincent P. de Poix (USNA 1939), accompanied Mehlig to VF-6. In contrast the other department heads included lieutenants (junior grade) Harold E. Rutherford, Gordon E. Firebaugh, and Theodore S. "Dick" Gay, all former "Chiefs of Fighting Two" with many hundreds of hours in fighters. In VF-6 flying experience counted more than rank, and aloft Bauer did not hesitate to place even senior officers under those far junior to them.[16]

After observing some of his new replacement pilots in the air, Bauer was dissatisfied with their inadequate ACTG gunnery training, where one young ensign fired only 300 rounds per gun. On 28 June the *Enterprise*'s Capt. George D. Murray fired off a blistering letter to ComCarPac. In turn, Vice Admiral Halsey's headquarters recommended on 6 July that ACTG afford its fighter trainees 20 hours of fixed gunnery Individual Battle Practice (IBP) flying the standard firing passes, followed by 10 hours using camera guns. The fleet squadrons no longer had time to teach basic aerial gunnery techniques.

The other three fighting squadrons in Hawaii, VF-3, VF-72, and VF-8, all relocated to NAS Maui, where they could train without interference from the many aircraft crowding the skies above Oahu. ComCarPac decided a different fate for each squadron.

Already earmarked as the *Hornet*'s fighter squadron in place of hapless VF-8, VF-72 waited ashore for sailing orders. The squadron originated on 1 July 1939 as VF-7, its insignia appropriately a fighting "Blue Wasp" for the *Wasp.* Only on 1 July 1940 did it become VF-72. During 1941, VF-72 made cruises both on the *Wasp* and the *Ranger* in the Atlantic Fleet, but the outbreak of war found it at NAS Norfolk. On 19 December, it re-embarked on the *Ranger* for four months of rugged duty in the North Atlantic, then went ashore to re-equip with folding-wing F4F-4s. Along with VF-5 and the VT-8 Detachment, VF-72 rode a convoy out to Pearl and accompanied the *Saratoga* out to Midway and back.[17]

Lt. Louis Bauer, CO of VF-6, receives the Navy Cross from Admiral Nimitz, 15 Oct. 1942. (NA 80-G-17230)

Lt. Cdr. Henry G. ("Mike") Sanchez (USNA 1930) completed flight training in 1932 and spent nearly three years on the *Langley* with VF-3S (the Striking Eagles, later VF-5). After a tour ashore, he joined the Asiatic Fleet aircraft tender *Heron* (AVP-2) in 1937 and in 1939 became an instructor at NAS Pensacola. In October 1941 he reported to VF-72, and on 21 March 1942 succeeded Shands as CO. A fiery, rather choleric leader, he nevertheless ran an efficient squadron. His XO, Lt. Edward W. ("Red") Hessel (USNA 1937) earned his wings in June 1940 and joined VF-72 that December.

The lack of carrier decks transformed VF-3 and VF-8 into training units quite useful for providing replacement pilots a final check-out before being posted to squadrons afloat. Could ComCarPac afford both in that role?

Originally the *Saratoga*'s fighting squadron, VF-3 (insignia: Felix the Cat) had boarded the *Lexington* in late January 1942 bound for the South Pacific. The CO was Lt. Cdr. John S. ("Jimmy") Thach (USNA 1927), soon renowned as the fleet's outstanding fighter leader in the first six months of war. On 20 February VF-3 repulsed two level bombing attacks against the *Lex,* and Lt. Edward H. O'Hare (USNA 1937) earned the Medal of Honor. In late March, after transferring twelve pilots to VF-2 on the *Lex,* Thach and his enlisted echelon went ashore at Kaneohe. In late May, sixteen veterans from VF-42 and some rookies joined VF-3 now on board the *Yorktown.* The squadron won great honor at Midway, but the loss of the *Yorktown* dispersed the team.

Formed in September 1941 as an original component of the *Hornet* Air Group, VF-8 suffered through a decidedly mixed performance at Midway. Four pilots bravely defended the *Yorktown,* but tragic incompetence during the great mission against the Japanese carriers put CO Lt. Cdr. Samuel G. Mitchell (USNA 1927) and nine others into the water. Two never returned. On 18 June, VF-8 reassembled twenty-five pilots and twenty-seven F4F-4s. The next day Shoemaker ordered the squadron to turn ten F4Fs over to VF-72, and in the next several days VF-8 lost five pilots to other duty (three to torpedo squadrons).

In late June, things seemed more or less static for VF-72 and VF-8, but VF-3 underwent some changes. By 24 June its strength climbed to twenty-four pilots and twenty-three F4F-4s. That day, Lieutenant Commander O'Hare relieved Thach, who went home for a well-deserved rest. Although unhappy VF-3 would remain ashore in the foreseeable future, "Butch" O'Hare nevertheless adapted remarkably well to his new job of teaching fledgling fighter pilots their trade. Like Thach, he established close ties with the Army Air Forces's fighter squadrons defending the Hawaiian Islands and even arranged for Capt. John C. Wilkins from the 46th Fighter Squadron (FS) to join VF-3 on temporary duty. Wilkins fared so well that O'Hare created a special program to train Army fighter pilots with VF-3.[18]

REINFORCING THE FIGHTING SQUADRONS

The *Saratoga*'s top priority brought about a new look for her fighting squadron, one that ultimately affected all VF squadrons in Hawaii. The morning of 29 June VF-5 flew twenty-four F4Fs into Ewa. The pilots greatly looked forward to a promised 48-hour liberty at the Royal Hawaiian Hotel on Waikiki Beach. They made the best of it. The subsequent mayhem greatly resembled the post-Midway bash so aptly described by torpedo pilot Ens. Frederick Mears:

> The routine of the returning airmen for the next few nights consisted of their tramping from room to room hunting for liquor, talking, arguing, fighting, and breaking the furniture. Some few were feeling tender enough to want to find a girl, but for the most part their emotions were released in being just as mean as they could. [The hotel], which was blacked out, had dim and eerie lights in the hallways, and the scene took on a kind of savage aspect, as though the natives were celebrating a ritual.[19]

Ens. John P. Altemus, a VF-5 pilot, noted in his diary, "people were fighting all up & down the hall & the din & uproar was terrific" and added details of numerous altercations. The pilots let off steam and felt better.[20]

On 1 July, during night field carrier landing practice at Kaneohe Bay, one of the VF-6 rookies died in a tragic accident. About 2115, Ens. Sylvester Hopfensperger's F4F crashed 500 yards off shore and immediately sank. Only after questioning Lt. Richard J. Teich did the review board piece together what happened. Teich flew Consolidated PBY-5 Catalina flying boats with Patrol Squadron 91 (VP-91) and practiced night landings in Kaneohe Bay. He spotted the lights of three F4Fs take off from Kaneohe and swing into the landing circle, but noticed the trailer did not follow the two. For a time the water reflected its running lights, but they disappeared after a sudden splash and a brief bright flash. The board theorized that Hopfensperger, watching the lights of Teich's PBY above him, did not realize his F4F had assumed a deadly nosedown attitude aimed straight for the water.[21]

While VF-5 took its ease, ComCarPac received authorization to reinforce its operating strength from twenty-seven to thirty-six fighters, a 100 percent increase over the allowance only three months before.[22] Shoemaker saw this as the best answer to the crying need for additional fighters on board the carriers. He stripped VF-3 and VF-8 at Maui of the required pilots and aircraft. On 2 July O'Hare transferred four Midway veterans for temporary duty with VF-5, while Mitchell's VF-8 provided five pilots and nine F4F-4s (half his aircraft). To make room on board the *Saratoga* for nine additional F4F-4s, VT-8 was supposed to operate only twelve TBF-1s instead of sixteen, but this decrease never came to pass.

Shoemaker so favored the idea of thirty-six-plane carrier VF squadrons that he immediately remodeled VF-72 and VF-6 to the same configuration,[23] which meant the end of VF-8 as well as a much reduced VF-3. On 4 July VF-8 sent eleven pilots and its last nine F4F-4s to VF-72, but Sanchez still counted only thirty-one pilots, too few to man his assigned thirty-six F4F-4s. Only Mitchell and two other pilots remained with VF-8, but in mid-July they left as well, Mitchell to the *Hornet* as an assistant air officer. On 22 August, Lt. John Carlin, squadron A-V(S) officer, finally decommissioned the squadron for the unmourned demise of VF-8.

To fill out VF-6, Shoemaker again victimized Butch O'Hare's VF-3. Summoning Lt. Albert O. Vorse, Jr. (USNA 1937), the XO and a Coral Sea veteran with 2.5 kills to his credit, he asked whether Vorse wanted to go to sea with another squadron. Eager to get back into action, "Scoop" immediately volunteered and joined VF-6 on 6 July along with seven more pilots and nine F4F-4s from VF-3. He became VF-6 operations officer, but no doubt would have taken over the squadron in place of his inexperienced classmate, John Mehlig, had something happened to Bauer.[24] Among the other transferees was Ens. Robert A. M. ("Ram") Dibb, who as Thach's wingman at Midway flew the famous weave in combat and downed one Zero. VF-6 now comprised thirty-seven pilots and thirty-six F4F-4s.

All of the recent reassignments set the VF pilots talking. Celebrating the Fourth of July at dinner, VF-5 ensign pilots George J. Morgan and John Altemus unmercifully teased one of their buddies, Ens. Foster J. ("Crud") Blair, by insisting that he would be transferred to Torpedo Eight—a fate greatly feared by the hot fighter pilots. "The poor guy was really worried," Altemus confided to his diary. That evening a Marine Corps messenger unexpectedly appeared at the Ford Island bachelor officers' quarters (BOQ) with orders detaching Morgan, Altemus, and two other pilots (not Blair) to dreaded VT-8. Altemus was so scared that he could not sleep. The next morning, VF-5 discovered a hoax neatly engineered by Chick Harmer, the XO, at Blair's instigation. Greatly relieved but very embarrassed, Morgan and Altemus suffered "an awful kidding from the whole squadron."[25] That day Simpler took VF-5 back to Ewa to prepare for the final sailing orders.

CHAPTER 2

South to Guadalcanal

On 2 July, while Admiral Nimitz conferred with Admiral King at San Francisco, the Joint Chiefs issued the basic directive for the South Pacific offensive. Task One (code-named PESTILENCE), set to begin about 1 August ("D-day"), called for the occupation of the Santa Cruz Islands (southeast of the Solomons) and the capture of Tulagi (operation code-named WATCHTOWER). Task Two involved taking Lae, Salamaua, and other positions in northeast New Guinea, followed by Task Three, the capture of Rabaul itself.[1]

In the absence of Nimitz at San Francisco, the staff received permission to delay TF-11's sailing until after 6 July. That enabled RAdm. Frank Jack Fletcher, the carrier commander, and RAdm. Richmond Kelly Turner, the designated amphibious force commander, to meet on the 5th, discuss arrangements for air support in detail, and brief Nimitz upon his return. Deciphered enemy radio messages revealed a Japanese airfield under construction at Lunga Point on Guadalcanal, the big island 20 miles south of Tulagi, and hinted at a greater build-up in the South Pacific. CinCPac needed to strike before that airfield could be completed. Hence Guadalcanal became the prime objective.

The Pacific Fleet planners did not count on surprise, but thought they would have to fight their way in. They predicated the offensive on intensive bombing by General MacArthur's heavy and medium bombers that would neutralize Japanese land-based aviation operating from Rabaul on New Britain and Buka north of Bougainville and clear the way for the invasion. "If this operation is a success, the task is a cinch. If not, we may lose a carrier."[2] They expected the carriers to provide fighter cover for the transports for three days—the two days leading up to the invasion and D-day itself (as it was later called). The 1st Marine Division (1st MarDiv) would storm ashore on Tulagi and at Lunga. Turner declared he would unload and withdraw the transports the night of D-day. The carriers were to cover their retirement if possible. A defense battalion with heavy equipment would later be brought in and the airfield at Lunga readied as quickly as possible to receive American planes. Thus, in order to stage aircraft into Guadalcanal, construction of an airfield on Espiritu Santo in the New Hebrides, about 550 miles southeast of Tulagi, became vital.

Obviously every single carrier fighter would be needed, not only to protect the flattops and escort strikes, but also to support the amphibious forces operating well to the north. That became the controversial aspect of the operation. Fortunately, Turner reported to Fletcher that at San Francisco Nimitz advised that RAdm. Thomas Kinkaid's TF-16 with the *Enterprise* would also be joining the fight. On 6 July Nimitz flew back from San Francisco, reviewed the minutes of the conference, and issued the final orders directing Fletcher's TF-11 with the *Saratoga* to sail on 7 July.[3]

After meeting with MacArthur in Australia, VAdm. Robert Ghormley informed King and Nimitz on 8 July that unloading the transports would take from 36 hours to four days. To provide close air support for such an extended period would expose the carriers to enemy land-based air attack. Ghormley thought it "extremely doubtful" that the flattops could furnish continuous fighter protection to the invasion area, especially in the face of vigorous counterattacks. Consequently MacArthur and he jointly recommended that the Tulagi offensive be postponed until Allied land-based air in the region received powerful reinforcements and new air bases were built in the Santa Cruz Islands and the New Hebrides.[4]

The Joint Chiefs, however, would brook no delay. On 10 July King ordered the Tulagi operation to proceed as planned. Ghormley replied that MacArthur's Allied Air Force must interdict the enemy air bases at Rabaul and at Lae in Papua. For his own part, Nimitz recognized that the lack of available land-based air power was a major flaw in WATCHTOWER, but he felt compelled to proceed no matter what. He worried (correctly) that the Japanese were about to consolidate their hold on the Solomons. The CinCPac Greybook noted, "It is now a race to see whether or not we can kick them out in time, and with present forces," which was why Nimitz committed three of four carriers to the Solomons. Whether he could afford them being crippled or sunk is another matter.[5]

Now that preparations for an offensive in the South Pacific were underway, it became necessary to organize the forces and get them to the target area, preferably without being detected by the enemy. At the risk of some repetition, the simplest way to deal with the South Pacific odyssey of the carrier task forces is to cover each in turn.

TASK FORCE 18

Rear Admiral Leigh Noyes, commanding TF-18 from the *Wasp*, learned on 27 June of orders to sail on 1 July from San Diego. He would escort a convoy of five transports carrying the 2nd Marines and join Fletcher's TF-11 southeast of Christmas Island.[6] He sailed on 30 June, re-embarked the *Wasp* Air Group, and arranged to meet the convoy after it sailed the next day. The *Wasp* Air Group comprised four squadrons with seventy-one aircraft:

CWAG	Lt. Cdr. Wallace M. Beakley	Flew VT-7 TBF
VF-71	Lt. Cdr. Courtney Shands	30 F4F-4s
VS-71	Lt. Cdr. John Eldridge, Jr.	15 SBD-3s
VS-72	Lt. Cdr. Frank Turner[a]	15 SBD-3s
VT-7	Lt. Henry A. Romberg	10 TBF-1s
Utility Unit		1 J2F-5

[a]Soon relieved by Lt. Cdr. Ernest M. Snowden (USNA 1932)

On the evening of 1 July, TF-18 (*Wasp*, heavy cruiser *Quincy* [CA-39], light AA cruiser *San Juan* [CL-54], seven destroyers, and five transports) assembled off San Diego and set course on 230 degrees at 13 knots. The flattop took station astern of the rest of the ships, making it easier for her and her plane guard destroyers to conduct flight operations. Capt. Forrest Sherman kept the air group busy on patrol and with training exercises. The succeeding days were uneventful. On 3 July Noyes learned that TF-11 would be late, and soon the rendezvous was rescheduled for 19 July southwest of Tongatabu in the Tonga group. During the voyage south one day merged with the next as the weather grew hotter.

The morning of 10 July, TF-18's Shellbacks prepared to cross the equator with the customary celebrations to welcome King Neptune and his entourage on board. This being the *Wasp*'s first trip across the planet's belt line, the lowly Pollywogs greatly outnumbered the Shellback veterans. Just after noon, the Royal Family appeared on number 2 elevator. Assisted by the Shellbacks they gave the neophytes a proper initiation to Neptune's kingdom by forcing them to run the gauntlet and suffer the indignation of the Royal Barber, who slopped gold paint on their scalps. All in all the crew enjoyed a fine Neptune party.[7]

Early on 13 July, as the *Wasp* neared Samoa from the northeast, loud scraping noises from the starboard high-pressure steam turbine forced the engineers to shut down, lock the system, and use only the port engine. The crippled carrier dropped far behind the rest of the convoy and only that evening attained 15 knots to regain position. Noyes informed CinCPac and ComSoPac of the *Wasp*'s difficulties and plans to undertake repairs at Tongatabu. At 0130, 14 July, the engineers completed lifting the casing of the starboard turbine and discovered badly damaged impulse blades. They removed all the blades for repair, a massive job for a warship at sea.[8]

The damaged *Wasp* plodded southward toward Tongatabu. On 16 July, Lieutenant Commander Beakley brought three VS-71 SBDs to the Army airfield there. For TF-18, the date line erased 17 July, and during the rainy afternoon of the 18th, the ships anchored off Nukualofa Roads. The VS-71 war diary noted "the view from the ship lived up to all expectations. The first trip ashore, however, dispelled any illusions of grandeur and romance which we had about the islands." Most conspicuously absent were bevies of Polynesian beauties. Queen Salote, the Tongan monarch, bade the young women hide in the hills. The 19th brought gale-force winds gusting to 67 knots, but the carrier rode the storm well. Below decks her engineers completed rebuilding the starboard turbine on 20 July.

Sherman scheduled full power trials for the morning of 21 July. Once at sea the *Wasp* took the opportunity to launch sixteen VF-71 F4Fs and six SBDs to Tongatabu field. The rebuilt blades performed well, as she worked up toward 25 knots, but her engineers strongly recommended that the whole assembly be replaced at Pearl Harbor as soon as feasible. Noyes praised the crew for a magnificent job. On the 23rd, TF-18 steamed south to join TF-11 the next day. Led by Lieutenant Commander Shands, the *Wasp* aircraft flew out to the ship. Ens. Samuel W. Forrer, his wingman, arrived in spectacular fashion. He had stowed as much fresh produce from Tongatabu as he could fit in his cockpit, and when he landed, he hit the barrier, flipping the F4F over and loosing a mass of fruit, which showered the upside-down pilot and spilled over the deck. Later that evening, the *Wasp* recovered her SBDs and headed for the rendezvous with Fletcher's TF-11. She finally caught up with the Pacific Fleet.[9]

TASK FORCE 11

The morning of 7 July, the *Saratoga*, flagship of Rear Admiral Fletcher's TF-11, departed Pearl Harbor on what appeared to casual observers as merely another short training cruise with gunnery exercises off Hawaii.[10] Only a few knew she was bound for the first Pacific Fleet counteroffensive of the war. Accompanying the *Sara* were the four heavy cruisers *Astoria* (CA-34), *New Orleans* (CA-32), *Minneapolis* (CA-36), and the *Vincennes* (CA-44), seven destroyers, three oilers, and Transport Division 12 with four old four-stack destroyers converted to fast transports (APDs). At sea the ships conducted gunnery and other exercises.

Eighty miles out from NAS Pearl Harbor, the *Saratoga* Air Group found the ships late that afternoon. Still so close to Pearl, the *Sara*'s fighter director officer (FDO), Lt. Cdr. Calvin E. Wakeman, took the opportunity to break radio silence and work with VF-5 on interception tactics. During the subsequent recoveries, several pilots tallied their first carrier landings. Counting planes hoisted on board, the *Saratoga* Air Group comprised:

CSAG	Cdr. Harry D. Felt	1 SBD-3
VF-5	Lt. Cdr. Leroy C. Simpler	36 F4F-4s
VB-3	Lt. Cdr. Dewitt W. Shumway	18 SBD-3s
VS-3	Lt. Cdr. Louis J. Kirn	18 SBD-3s
VT-8	Lt. Harold H. Larsen	16 TBF-1s
Utility Unit		1 F4F-7

The total reached ninety, far stronger than in the earlier battles.

The next morning the task force practiced supporting an amphibious landing against a hostile shore. The cruisers bombarded the firing range at Cape Kahae on the southeast tip of Hawaii. To one airborne onlooker their eight-inch shell bursts appeared as unimpressive "small puffs" (he would think differently at Guadalcanal on the receiving end of a similar bombardment).[11] VF-5 strafed the beaches. The SBDs dropped live 500-pounders into an old crater, releasing considerable smoke. Lt. (jg) Frank O. Green of VF-5 toured the *Sara*'s F4F-7 photo plane on a five-hour hop. The takeoff gave him "quite a thrill," when his right wing dropped abruptly due to improperly balanced wing tanks.[12]

For those not in the know, the big surprise occurred the afternoon of 8 July. Instead of swinging back toward Pearl, TF-11 assumed course 210 degrees toward the South Pacific. Rumors abounded of possible targets, but no matter the outcome, VF-5 knew their cruise through equatorial waters in poorly ventilated *Saratoga* would certainly be hot. By 11 July they drew near Palmyra and the equator—the realm of King Neptune. Forestalled by her earlier torpedo hit, the *Sara* faced her first wartime line crossing, and the crew intended to make the most of it. The nine VF-5 Shellbacks conspired that morning in Chick Harmer's room, but the Pollywogs intruded for a "good scrap." During the afternoon the Pollywogs reported to the flight deck in their cold-weather flying suits, where Dave Richardson in shorts led them in calisthenics. Other miscreants searched for King Neptune with coke bottles taped together as binoculars or used their noses to push cans of shoe polish down the wooden flight deck.[13]

That evening, Lt. (jg) James C. Smith of VF-5 touched down for the *Saratoga*'s 61,000th landing, duly rewarded with the traditional cake presented by Congressman Melvin Maas, a retired Marine colonel. VF-5 handled more serious business in their ready room, learning for the first time the objectives of Tulagi and Guadalcanal. Together with the *Wasp* Air Group, they would attack ground targets and fly CAP over the invasion forces. Before turning in, the VF-5 Shellbacks broke up a Pollywog meeting, but found their own bunks overturned. During the night Frank Green and accomplices rang the rooms of the squadron

VF-5, July 1942. *Top row* (*l to r*): Price, Reiplinger, Altemus, Gunsolus, Eichenberger, Innis, Gray, Kleinmann, Morgan, Roach, Dufilho, Smith. *Center row:* Currie, Robb, Wesolowski, Starkes, Davy, Holt, Daly, Presley, McDonald, Tabberer, Barbieri, Haynes, Bass, Blair, Bright. *Bottom row:* Kleinman, Stover, Crews, Brown, Southerland, Harmer, Simpler, Richardson, Green, Jensen, Clarke, Stepanek. (Capt. H. W. Crews)

Shellbacks every half hour. About noon on 12 July the task force crossed the line northeast of Canton Island, while King Neptune and his associates held court on the flight deck. The Pollywogs ran the customary gauntlet to be "washed" and "shampooed" and made presentable to the royal visitors. Now everyone ranked as a Shellback. For the *Sara*'s crew and aviators, the good-natured, amusing line-crossing hijinks provided an excellent boost for morale and a way to let off steam before combat.

Searing heat punctuated by periods of humid, squally, gusty weather marked the next few days as TF-11 closed Samoa from the northeast. On 15 July the VF-5 officers assembled for a squadron photograph, always an event marked by ominous undertones. As Frank Green noted in his diary, "Here is the hope that we can all assemble for the same type of picture after the excitement." (The next such VF-5 photo session took place at the end of September on Guadalcanal with many new faces.) The next day, Fletcher learned that SoPac postponed the operation to 7 August. He also received his belated promotion to vice admiral, to date from 26 June. Green watched in fascination as the new three-star admiral played darts with Congressman Maas.[14]

During the *Wasp*'s turbine travail, Fletcher marked time south of Tongatabu and caught the fringe of the gale that battered the islands. The *Saratoga*, now rolling and pitching, was not an easy vessel on which to weather a storm. A nagging run of minor accidents dogged VF-5's almost daily CAPs or inner air patrols (IAPs). On 14 July Johnny Altemus bounced twice, put F-8 sideways into the wire crash barrier, and nearly went overboard. The F4F was repairable. Four days later, as the *Saratoga* pitched steeply Crud Blair's prop brushed the barrier.[15]

On 16 July Ghormley broadcast a summary of his Operations Plan (OpPlan) 1-42 covering Task One. He unexpectedly assigned Fletcher in tactical command as CO of the Expeditionary Force (TF-61) with control over the carrier Air Support Force (Task Group 61.1) and Turner's SoPac Amphibious Force (TG-61.2). Unfortunately Fletcher was not in a position to participate a great deal in the planning, as he rode the *Saratoga* on radio silence to the South Pacific, while Turner flew from island to island to organize the amphibious force. Perforce Fletcher left the details to Turner.[16]

The morning of 20 July, with seas still rough, sixteen VF-5 F4Fs departed for gunnery exercises. At 1048, while landing, Ens. Wayne C. Presley came in hot and high and floated his F4F into the barrier. He was unhurt, but the F4F was wrecked. With the deck tied up, Ens. Roy M. Gunsolus, another VF-6 transferee, ran out of fuel and ditched F-36 off the *Sara*'s port quarter. Despite a fractured vertebra and severe head injuries, he escaped the sinking Wildcat and reached the destroyer *Phelps* (DD-360). A week later, when retrieved by the *Sara,* he still looked "terrible." Mechanical trouble compelled Ens. Melvin C. Roach to request a deferred forced landing. Next, Ens. Frank J. ("Rip") Reiplinger came nose high and slow, wobbled at the cut and dropped hard to the deck, where the landing gear folded "like an accordion," according to Foster Blair. Low on fuel, a grateful Roach landed safely. After VF-5's fiasco, one TBF touched down, bounced, and kept on coming up deck, forcing "Fog" Green and others standing forward beyond the LSO platform to duck.

Lieutenant Commander Simpler assembled all his pilots in the ready room for serious talk about the loss of three F4Fs. As Green wrote, "all agreed we should have it out of our system," but that was not to be. At 1728, upon returning from an afternoon IAP, Ens. Charles E. Eichenberger's F-28 floated up the deck, tore the tops off two barriers, then flopped onto the back of Ens. Charles D. Davy's F-19 being parked forward. The propeller sliced through the turtleback only 18 inches behind Davy's cockpit. Davy turned "white as a sheet, and no one blamed him for it." At the same time a snapped cable from a torn-up barrier broke the jaw of Marine Pfc. J. G. Williams. The day's toll for a shell-shocked VF-5 amounted to five aircraft (three totaled or lost), the "worst showing I have ever seen Fighting Five put on," according to Green.[17]

In the wardroom the next day, group commander Felt gave all the pilots the "straight dope" by laying out the plans for "Dog-Day," not only the invasions of Tulagi and Guadalcanal, but even tasks Two and Three against Rabaul. He told them that any aviators who went down were not to approach the Solomon natives, as intelligence was uncertain how they would react. Everyone was primed on the stories of cannibals in the Solomons and especially kidded the rotund Roach about avoiding the cook pot.

On 24 July, as TF-11 waited for Noyes and the *Wasp,* VF-5 suffered another tragedy. At 0608, before the morning patrols departed, the *Sara* happened to roll heavily, throwing John I. Brunnell, AMM2c, a VF-5 plane captain, into a spinning prop. He died at 1420 from massive head injuries, the squadron's first wartime fatality. At his burial at sea, Simpler tossed a wreath onto the waves. The accident dampened an otherwise happy reunion with Wally Beakley, former VF-5 skipper and now the *Wasp* Air Group commander, who that day brought Noyes over to confer with Fletcher. TF-11 and TF-18 finally united south of Tongatabu. Now it was necessary to meet the third carrier task force.

TASK FORCE 16

After TF-11 sailed south, two carrier task forces remained at Pearl Harbor. Rear Admiral Kinkaid settled into TF-16 flagship *Enterprise,* while newly promoted

RAdm. Thomas Kinkaid on the *Enterprise*, 22 July 1942. (NA 80-G-11651)

RAdm. George D. Murray, her former CO, relieved RAdm. Aubrey Fitch as CTF-17 on board the *Hornet*. Of the two carrier air groups, only "The Big E" 's was ready for sea. Unbeknownst to them, Nimitz had decided to send Kinkaid south to reinforce Fletcher.[18]

On 8 July TF-16 left for a short training cruise, its first outing since returning from Midway. The *Enterprise*'s new CO, Capt. Arthur C. Davis, wanted to qualify the new air group. LSOs Lt. Robin M. Lindsey and Lt. Cleo J. Dobson faced a long day recovering the whole group at least twice. That included the new

TBFs, which hitherto had not landed on board the *Enterprise*. To Dobson the Avenger looked "as big as the side of a house," but behaved like a "good carrier plane."[19] The only severe mishap occurred when Lt. Rubin H. Konig (USNA 1938) came in with his right wing low, then bounced and slid over the side. He and his crew survived. Lt. Lou Bauer took thirty-two VF-6 F4Fs out to the ship. On 9 July, off Maui, twenty-eight F4Fs and thirty-three SBDs bombed a towed sled, and the next day the *Enterprise* practiced spotting and launching deckload strikes. The first comprised eight VF and twenty-two scout bombers (VSB), the second twenty-two VF and fifteen VSB for simulated attacks on shore targets. After this very useful training, the *Enterprise* sent her air group on 11 July to Marine Corps Air Station (MCAS) Ewa and docked at Pearl.

Beginning at 0907 on 15 July Kinkaid's TF-16 filed out of Pearl Harbor. Along with the *Enterprise* came the first of the new fast battleships, the *North Carolina* (BB-55), whose massive bulk proved especially reassuring. TF-16 also comprised the *Portland* (CA-33), light AA cruiser *Atlanta* (CL-51), and seven destroyers.

Thirty VF-6 fighters strafed a towed sled and afterward flew exercises conducted by the *Enterprise*'s new FDO, Lt. Henry A. Rowe. To improve fighter direction, Capt. Ralph A. Ofstie, CinCPac air staff officer, had suggested to Nimitz that Rowe, XO of the Fighter Director School, gain practical experience afloat. A graduate of both the RAF and Royal Navy fighter director schools, Rowe had also flown from British carriers. He joined "The Big E"'s regular FDO, Lt. Cdr. Leonard J. Dow, TF-16 staff communications officer, who was not exactly happy to see him after having handled the *Enterprise*'s fighter direc-

LSOs Robin Lindsey and Cleo Dobson bring one of the new VT-3 TBFs on board the *Enterprise*, 16 July 1942. (NA 80-G-10455)

tion since before the Pearl Harbor attack. Dow concerned himself primarily with the functioning of the radar and other electronic measures, while Rowe handled the CAP. This day Rowe deployed the CAP to meet a simulated dive-bombing attack.[20]

At 1215, the TBFs of VT-3 led the group landings, but Harold M. O'Leary, AP1c, in F-32 interrupted the proceedings. During the strafing runs, a generator in his plane had failed and knocked out the motor controlling the propeller pitch. O'Leary also ran the main fuel tank dry (the gauge was faulty). At 1235 he lowered his gear and flaps, chased the last of the TBFs out of the landing circle, and turned for a long approach to the ramp. He never made it. Five hundred yards out, the Wildcat flopped into the water. The destroyer *Ellet* (DD-398) rescued O'Leary unhurt. Later that afternoon, an SBD with a VF-6 pilot passenger flew back to NAS Pearl Harbor to fetch another fighter. Both landed back on board at 1914 and restored VF-6 to thirty-six F4Fs. The air group comprised:

CEAG	Lt. Cdr. Maxwell F. Leslie	Flew VT-3 TBF
VF-6	Lt. Louis H. Bauer	36 F4F-4s
VB-6	Lt. Ray Davis	19 SBD-3s
VS-5	Lt. Turner F. Caldwell	18 SBD-3s
VT-3	Lt. Cdr. Charles M. Jett	16 TBF-1s
Utility Unit		1 F4F-7

Like the other carriers, the *Enterprise* used the voyage south as a long-needed opportunity to train. VF-6 flew more gunnery and strafing missions, as well as

VF-6, July 1942. *Top row (l to r)*: Cline, Born, Grimmell, Brewer, Barnes, Brooks, Sumrall, Mankin, Mehlig, Achten, O'Leary, Nagle, Wileman, Rutherford, Rouse. *Center row:* Willis, Stephenson, Gay, Loesch, Johnson, Firebaugh, Register, Lindsey, Rhodes, March, Reid, Disque, Wallace. *Bottom row:* Warden, Allard, Hartmann, Dibb, Bauer, Cook, Halford, de Poix, Shoemaker, Vorse, Runyon. (USN)

practicing intercept tactics. TF-16 crossed the equator at midday on 19 July, but the line-hardened *Enterprise* dispensed with ceremony. Late the next afternoon 10 miles west of the ships, Ens. James C. Dexter of VB-6, a Midway veteran, towed a gunnery sock for eighteen F4Fs and six other SBDs. Somehow he became disoriented and flew away from the ships. Kinkaid broke radio silence to try to make contact, but even if Dexter copied the messages, he did not use his radio. He evidently tried for the nearest land, the Phoenix Islands, but he and his radioman were never found.

In his posthumously published memoir, Ens. Frederick Mears well described "The Big E" 's voyage south:

> Living on a carrier became very satisfactory to us after a week or two out. There were eating and sleeping and smoking and the weather to think about. There was time to enjoy the smaller luxuries—a cigar, eliminating, a hot shower, or spitting down wind . . . Women—all of them—for most of the men aboard tended to merge into a rosy composite of Hedy Lamarr and the Virgin Mary, and in this abstraction they seemed their most delightful.

> There were health and high spirits out there, but the cares of money and the feverishness of business were no longer. The days slid by. Life was natural. And there were always the clean strong wind and the restless sea.[21]

By 23 July TF-16 drew close enough to Tongatabu to fly two VT-3 TBFs and the F4F-7 photo plane to the Army field, where the crews spent a pleasant night downing the Army's potent Australian beer. They were the only ones from the *Enterprise* to see much of the island this trip. The next morning she entered Nukualofa harbor, but tarried only a few hours and was soon bound for the great rendezvous to the south.

THE GREAT RENDEZVOUS

On 26 July some 350 miles south of Fiji, all of the WATCHTOWER task forces made contact for the first time. Fletcher's TF-11 (*Saratoga*) and Noyes's TF-18 (*Wasp*) with their transports had already joined. Now Kinkaid's TF-16 with the *Enterprise* and more transports appeared to the northeast, while the balance of Turner's TG-61.2 (or TF-62) creased the southern horizon. His Amphibious Force was escorted by the cruisers and destroyers of TF-44 under RAdm. Victor A. C. Crutchley, V.C., Royal Navy, commanding the Australian Squadron. Together the eighty-two ships formed a massive array, a wonder to all observers. It was a tremendous achievement given the very short time for preparation. TF-61 spent the rest of 26 July getting organized while proceeding slowly north toward Fiji.

The morning of the 27th, while TF-61 flirted with the date line 100 miles south of Koro in the Fiji Archipelago, senior officers arrived on the *Saratoga* to discuss final plans for the 7 August landings.[22] Beakley flew Noyes to the *Saratoga*. From the destroyer *Balch* (DD-363) came Kinkaid's *Enterprise* party. Kelly Turner, RAdm. John S. McCain, Commander, Aircraft, South Pacific Force (ComAir-SoPac), and Maj. Gen. Alexander Archer Vandegrift (commanding the 1st Mar-Div), riding the destroyer *Hull* (DD-350) from Fiji, had the most unforgettable entrance. With both crews watching, the *Hull*'s motor whaleboat brought the VIPs to her port sea ladder. Despite calm seas, the *Sara* ("this tub," according to one of her complement) rolled briskly. As McCain took hold of the ladder, she acted true to form and drenched him to his waist, christening one "mad little admiral," as Vandegrift wryly noted.[23]

The other passengers transferred by breeches buoy to this memorable conference, which began around 1130 and lasted for three hours. It was practically a reunion of the Annapolis Class of 1906 to which Noyes, Fletcher, and McCain all belonged. Significantly, another classmate, Ghormley, chose not to appear but in his place sent his chief of staff, RAdm. Daniel J. Callaghan.

The proceedings turned stormy, with much give and take between Fletcher and Turner over several aspects of the operation, most notably the hasty nature of such an undertaking with drastic shortages of fuel oil and almost everything else. The decision urged by Fletcher over Turner's objections was that all of TF-61, less five cargo ships screened by Crutchley's TF-44, would follow Turner's transports southward by D+2.[24]

The central weakness of Operation WATCHTOWER was the question of air support, both on carriers and land-based. The primary limitations were geographic. The Guadalcanal-Tulagi area lay far out of support range of the nearest Allied airfields in the New Hebrides, over 600 miles from Efate (ROSES) and 550 from the soon to be completed field on Espiritu Santo (BUTTON). Tontouta Field on New Caledonia was even farther away. Yet the entire area fell within air strike range of Rabaul.

The main dispute between Turner and Fletcher concerned how long the carrier force (TG-61.1) should remain exposed to air and submarine attack in Guadalcanal waters while offering air support, specifically fighters, to cover the unloading of the transports and cargo ships. On 20 July, Turner had radioed from New Zealand an outline of his plans for the Amphibious Force. He counted on the carriers to provide the equivalent of one VF and three VSB squadrons for air support, with an additional squadron of each type also available for the first two hours of Dog-Day. During daylight, approximately half this strength was to remain employed over the transport area. To control these fighters, Turner recommended an FDO be installed in the flagship of the cruiser-destroyer screening group. So far so good.[25]

Five days later Turner advised Fletcher that if the actual Tulagi-Guadalcanal landings proceeded well, he would, by the night of D+1 (8 August), have sent to the rear all of the transports and "about all of the Pacific Fleet combatant ships," which included the Santa Cruz Occupation Force, tentatively set to depart the evening of D-day. This schedule was in line with his previous projections. However, he stressed, "the great difficulty is going to be with the five cargo vessels." He could give no definite time estimate for unloading them other than three to six days with the promise to do his best. Turner concluded, "We will need air protection during this entire period,"[26] and vehemently argued for the carriers to remain in support until all of the cargo ships had unloaded.

Fletcher consulted Noyes and his air experts, also his own air operations officer, Lt. Cdr. Oscar Pederson, former *Yorktown* Air Group commander. To provide such air support, particularly with the short-ranged fighters, the carriers needed to remain within 60 miles or so of Tulagi and of necessity within the southward arc. That pinned TF-61 to a narrow area of operation, severely restricting its mobility and greatly increasing the risk of land-based air attack from Rabaul and Bougainville. Enemy submarines also posed a real danger with such prolonged loitering. As emphasized above, Fletcher learned from Turner that almost the entire Amphibious Force would very likely retire from the invasion area by the evening of D+1. Evidently Fletcher did not think it was worth risking the carriers to protect the five cargo ships for an indeterminate period while they completed their unloading. He felt the preservation of his carriers, which he considered the major strategic asset of the Pacific Fleet, must be his paramount goal. According to Kinkaid, Fletcher went as far as "calculated risk warranted."[27]

At the 27 July conference on the *Saratoga*, Fletcher's declaration stunned Turner, Vandegrift, and Callaghan. The Marine, for one, felt betrayed. Casting aspersions on Fletcher's fortitude, he later described the task force commander as looking "nervous and tired." He was surprised Fletcher "appeared to lack knowledge of or interest in the forthcoming operation," less inexplicable when one understands how little opportunity Fletcher had to participate in the actual planning.[28] Kinkaid summarized the conference well: "Turner asked for a lot of things, much of which he didn't get, because they were not in the realm of the possible."[29] Despite a rather acrimonious debate, Turner could not sway Fletcher to agree to stay until all the cargo ships had unloaded. As events later showed, he apparently felt his senior would bend to his wishes. But Fletcher meant what he said; only the absent Ghormley could have changed his mind.

The second obstacle proved to be the lack of land-based planes to send immediately to Guadalcanal once the airfield became operational. Vandegrift was originally promised his own land-based air by D+3 (10 August), but he would not get it. King's directive of 24 June specified that CinCPac provide two Marine fighting squadrons (VMF) and two Marine scouting squadrons (VMSB), in addition to Marine Observation Squadron 251 (VMO-251) with F4F-3P Wildcat photo fighters already in the South Pacific.[30] For WATCHTOWER, Nimitz earmarked Col. William J. Wallace's newly organized Marine Air Group 23 (MAG-23) with VMF-223, VMF-224, VMSB-231 and VMSB-232 at Ewa. Most unfortunately, a desperate shortage of pilots prevented any MAG-23 squadrons from riding either the *Saratoga* or the *Enterprise* to the South Pacific.[31]

The available fighters at the nearest SoPac bases were: at Efate, VMF-212 commanded by Maj. Harold W. Bauer ("Indian Joe" or "Joe"), with eighteen F4F-3As; and at Tontouta, VMO-251 commanded by Lt. Col. John N. Hart, with sixteen F4F-3Ps, and 67th FS commanded by Capt. Dale D. Brannon, with thirty-eight P-400s. VMO-251 awaited the completion of the airfield at Espiritu Santo to move there in early August. (Actually the field at Espiritu Santo was ready by 30 July, which McCain later called a "truly remarkable achievement."[32])

Turner's original idea, communicated on 21 July, involved staging VMF-212's F4F-3As and VMO-251's F4F-3Ps through Espiritu Santo to Guadalcanal once its field could take them. He hoped also to deliver as soon as possible VMSB-231 and VMSB-232 and park VMF-223 at Santo and VMF-224 on Efate. However, even from Santo, VMF-212 and VMO-251 could not actually fly to Guadalcanal, much less support that location. Neither possessed belly tanks, not even the photo squadron earmarked for long-range reconnaissance missions. Transport by Fletcher's carrier was not the answer, either. On the 22nd, McCain pointed out there was no way to embark VMF-212 and VMO-251 on board, as few Marine pilots were carrier-qualified. He thought it best to leave these two squadrons in their present locations and commit the MAG-23 squadrons directly to Guadalcanal.[33]

On 22 July, CinCPac designated VMF-223 and VMSB-232 as the MAG-23 first echelon to depart Pearl about 1 August on the auxiliary carrier *Long Island* (ACV-1),[34] while VMF-224 and VMSB-231 would leave about 15 August. At the 27 July conference someone suggested that the carriers fly fighter belly tanks to Espiritu Santo or Efate, which could allow VMO-251 and VMF-212 to reach Guadalcanal. If the tanks proved unsuitable, later the *Long Island* would have to ferry the Marine fighters to Guadalcanal.[35]

On 28 July, Fletcher's carriers marked time south of the Fijis, while Turner's

Amphibious Force closed Koro, the site for the rehearsal scheduled for the 30th. The next day the *Wasp* sent a small party to the destroyer *Aaron Ward* (DD-483) for eventual transfer to the YOKE Squadron, which was designated to attack Tulagi. They included VF-71 XO Lt. Cdr. Robert Strickler, Lt. (jg) Michael Elin, a VF-71 pilot, and Lt. William O. Adreon, a VS-71 A-V(S) officer, making up one of two air control groups for the invasion. Lt. Cdr. William E. Townsend of the *Enterprise*'s Air Department led the other to Turner's flagship *McCawley* (AP-10) in the X-RAY Squadron (heading for Guadalcanal). That morning the *Saratoga* detached a junior FDO, Lt. Robert M. Bruning, Jr., to Crutchley's Screening Group, which would be staying past D+1 according to Turner's plan. He went to the *Chicago* (CA-29) rather than the flagship, heavy cruiser *Australia,* due to unfamiliarity with Royal Australian Navy radar, plotting techniques, and communications.[36]

That afternoon low visibility separated the three carrier task forces. Fletcher needed to rendezvous them without breaking radio silence. Lt. (jg) Carl Starkes of VF-5 volunteered to find TF-16 and endured 40 miles of thick, low clouds. Missing the *Enterprise,* he used instruments to grope back through the soup. Ahead loomed the task force. Starkes swooped low over the *Sara* and dropped a message stating he could not find the *Enterprise*. A vigorously flashing signal light led him to think the message went astray, so he released a copy. Suddenly he realized with growing embarrassment that he was buzzing the *Enterprise*. She re-spotted her flight deck and instructed the F4F to land. Facing grinning greeters, Starkes gave the *Saratoga*'s position. "The Big E" responded with messages for Fletcher and also something less welcome: two SBDs to lead Starkes home. In the next morning news summary, her air officer observed, "A child who knows not its own mother is not so smart." That chide was nothing in comparison to the ribbing Starkes faced from his VF-5 buddies.[37]

The 29th of July brought daunting news. According to one report, observers counted six land-based Zeros using the Lunga airfield. That meant possible heavy air opposition and stressed the need for surprise to torch the bandits on the ground. A photo-reconnaissance mission when the weather cleared would determine whether Zeros were indeed at Lunga.

Early on 30 July the three carriers readied practice air strikes and CAPs as part of the Amphibious Force rehearsal at Koro Island. At 0530 the *Wasp* dispatched Shands with sixteen VF-71 F4Fs against "Tulagi," while Simpler left the *Saratoga* with twelve VF-5 F4Fs to strafe "Lunga." The predawn high humidity gave VF-5 mechanics fits; five F4Fs would not start. Lt. Howard W. Crews took aloft the *Saratoga* Utility Unit's F4F-7 photo plane to patrol for five hours over the practice area. From the *Enterprise,* Lt. Lou Bauer's VF-6 F4Fs flew CAPs and exercised with Lieutenant Bruning, screen FDO on board the *Chicago,* while SBDs and TBFs flew practice air support missions. At Koro the transports debarked troops into landing boats. For the Amphibious Force the exercise seemed not very useful—Vandegrift called it "a bust"—but the carriers valued the test of the basic air plan.

The next two days the carriers loitered south of Fiji waiting for the entire task force to reassemble. Finally, on the evening of 1 August, TF-61 and TF-62 joined 100 miles south of Fiji and started westward at 15 knots toward the Solomons.

On the afternoon of 2 August the question of carrier air support rose anew. Advised by Callaghan that Fletcher planned to withdraw the carriers prior to day D+3, Ghormley stressed the need for "providing continuous VF support" to the invasion forces. The rest of the message likely caused Fletcher to shake his head in disbelief. Ghormley asked him to consider, if the Lunga airfield was ready, leaving

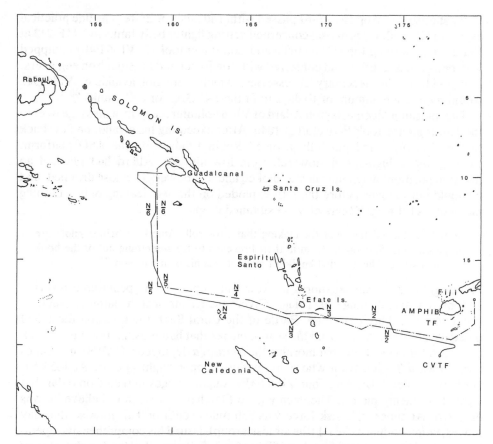

TF-61 (Carriers) and TF-62 (Amphibious Force) approach the target area.

two of his three VF squadrons (roughly sixty fighters) there when he withdrew the carriers. ComSoPac added that Major Bauer's eighteen VMF-212 F4F-3A Wildcats at Efate required belly tanks to fly to Guadalcanal. Therefore, the carriers should deliver belly tanks on D+4 (11 August) to Efate to allow VMF-212's Wildcats to stage on D+6 (13 August) to Guadalcanal. Subsequently, on her arrival in the Solomons, the *Long Island* would bring the MAG-23 first-echelon aircraft straight to Lunga, then recover the carrier fighters and fetch them to their carriers. Ghormley advised that if enemy carriers appeared in the area, the fighters at Lunga "would be released to you immediately."[38]

Many ready objections rose to Ghormley's proposal. First, the Amphibious Force made only rudimentary provision for air support facilities and an aviation headquarters for the Lunga airfield. Where were sixty-odd carrier fighter pilots to secure the gasoline, bullets, and other supplies to operate from Guadalcanal? Were they supposed to service each other's aircraft? As for the *Long Island,* she was still at Pearl Harbor and needed two weeks even to reach Guadalcanal. A converted flattop with a tiny flight deck, she could barely handle one VF squadron at a time. Landing on board was risky, and a bad accident could tie up her flight deck and prevent any more aircraft from coming on board. What was Fletcher supposed to do without two-thirds of his fighters? In such a weakened condition (a "strip tease," according to VAdm. George Dyer[39]), the carriers must strictly avoid the risk of enemy air attacks. Fletcher made no recorded answer to this ludicrous proposal.

By sunrise on 3 August, TF-61 passed within 40 miles of Efate. The one practical aspect of Ghormley's proposal concerned getting fighter belly tanks to VMF-212 at Efate. That morning John Crommelin and Lou Bauer took six VF-6 F4Fs equipped with belly tanks to Efate and conferred with Joe Bauer and his squadron engineers. Even with all the necessary accessories, which were not available, VMF-212 would require a minimum of 10 days to fit the F4F-3As for belly tanks.[40]

That morning Mach. Clayton Allard of VF-6 volunteered to fly a message over to the *Saratoga* and took F-10 aloft at 1040. After executing his errand, he flew back to the *Enterprise* and playfully zoomed Robin Lindsey on the LSO platform. Reefing into a high-speed slow roll from low altitude, Allard had reached an inverted position, when the engine smoked and lost power. The nose dropped, and he could not recover before the F4F exploded on the sea, leaving only a burning patch of fuel. Ensign Mears of VT-3 summed it up:

> Nobody criticized the pilot for making that slow roll. American fighter pilots are supposed to have enough steam in their breeches to try something out of the book once in a while. The fact that he didn't make it was his own business.[41]

The morning of 4 August, north of New Caledonia, TF-61 penetrated possible extreme air search range of Tulagi. Given enemy air search patterns (such as encountered in May during the Battle of the Coral Sea), the invasion force had timed its move hoping to avoid the search planes that had presumably started back on their return legs. Late that morning the *Saratoga* deployed a CAP 30 to 35 miles north toward Tulagi, from where an enemy snooper might appear. At 1355 Lt. Herbert S. "Pete" Brown's four VF-5 F4Fs sought a bogey detected on radar, but sighted no enemy planes. The enemy gave Fletcher no reason to believe he was detected. At sunset the task force was 530 miles south of Tulagi. Also that day Noyes, commanding TG-61.1 (the air task group), issued his comprehensive operations order, an intricate schedule of flights for 7–8 August. Lt. (jg) Frank Green of VF-5 voiced the thoughts of many pilots when he wrote in his diary, "I am afraid it will be fouled up long before the day is over."[42]

Also on the 4th, McCain informed ComSoPac of the impossibility of fitting belly tanks on VMF-212's F4F-3As so they could fly to Guadalcanal. Prompted by the aggressive Joe Bauer, he laid out a scheme to deploy VMF-212 at Lunga. He advised that Fletcher leave one whole fighting squadron at Lunga and dispatch fourteen more F4F-4s with belly tanks to Efate for VMF-212. That would allow Bauer to proceed to Guadalcanal. The fourteen Navy fighter pilots at Efate could either fly Marine F4F-3As out to the carriers, or better yet, ride carrier SBDs or TBFs back to their ship. McCain wanted some Marine fighters to stay at Efate, as he had spare pilots to man them. Later, the *Long Island* could exchange VMF-223 for the Navy VF squadron left at Guadalcanal. Again SoPac's plan to place fighters at Lunga proved totally impractical. As events transpired, the Lunga airfield barely supported the thirty-one aircraft of MAG-23 when they finally arrived on 20 August, let alone a squadron and a half of fighters. These proposals only underlined the failure to prepare land-based aircraft and support facilities to operate immediately from Guadalcanal.[43]

At noon on 5 August, TF-61 turned north toward Tulagi. This day TF-61 also avoided detection, and by sunset Tulagi lay less than 400 miles away. During the day the carrier air groups learned to their pleasure that U.S. Army reconnaissance planes saw no enemy land-based planes at Lunga.[44]

Thursday, 6 August, was to be the crucial day of the approach. It appeared that the Japanese Solomons search umbrella could hardly be avoided. Most fortunately, dawn brought a deep fog and haze—ideal for an unseen passage to the target. This was a great relief, as TF-61 expected to have to fight its way through Japanese air strikes to gain the objective, something often forgotten when considering the "inevitable" Allied success at Guadalcanal. At 0800 Noyes assumed tactical command of the carrier force and specified launch points and times for the next day. That morning TF-61 launched no searches, so as not to alert the Japanese of the presence of carrier planes. Two flights each of ten VF-6 F4Fs flew intermediate air patrol 40 miles ahead of the ships. During the afternoon the VF-5 CAP tried unsuccessfully to find four bogeys that had appeared on radar screens. At 1410 one closed within 21,000 yards, but visibility barely exceeded one mile. No frantic warnings sounded on known enemy radio frequencies, so TF-61 again remained undetected. This gave the Allies an unforeseen but tremendous advantage at the outset of the battle.

In fact, three Japanese flying boats had left Tulagi at dawn and split up to cover the F Kō Sector. Each was to proceed south 400 miles before turning left on a 60-mile dogleg, then start back toward base to complete the wedge-shaped flights. About 0800, on its outbound leg the aircraft in the center passed very close to TF-61, but missed it in the overcast. The westernmost aircraft flew only 370 miles on its outbound leg before bad weather turned it directly back to base. Had conditions allowed it to fly the mission as briefed, it too would likely have spotted the invaders. Thus, under normal circumstances two of the flying boats would have given the alarm.[45] The afternoon radar contacts must have been American land-based search planes.

By sunset, the south coast of Guadalcanal loomed only 85 miles northeast and Tulagi another 50 miles beyond. After dark, carrier deck crews began spotting first-wave aircraft on the flight decks, while below the crew cleared for action. All bedding was piled on deck in the middle of compartments, and inflammables placed in steel lockers and cabinets. Aviators tried to get some rest before their wake-up calls early on the morning of 7 August. The three carriers wielded 237 aircraft of which 234—98 fighters, 96 dive bombers, and 40 torpedo bombers—were operational. They were ready to execute the first Allied counteroffensive of the Pacific War.

CHAPTER 3

"Sock 'em in the Solomons!"

THE INITIAL STRIKES

During the predawn hours of 7 August, VAdm. Frank Jack Fletcher's TF-61 drew near to Guadalcanal. Undetected by the Japanese, the first Allied amphibious assault of the Pacific War was about to commence.[1] Cutting around the west coast, RAdm. Kelly Turner's invasion convoy split into two parts. The YOKE Squadron continued north of Savo Island and then turned east toward Tulagi, while the X-RAY Squadron followed the shoreline to Lunga. Southwest of the island, the three carriers of TG-61.1, under the tactical command of Rear Admiral Noyes, feverishly prepared the first strike wave planes parked on blacked-out flight decks. The Air Operations Plan called for simultaneous surprise dawn attacks by ninety-three aircraft (forty-four VF, forty-eight VSB, and one VT) against Tulagi and Guadalcanal to destroy aircraft and gun positions (see table 3.1).[2] The *Enterprise's* first deckload also included eight VF-6 F4Fs under Lt. (jg) Theodore Gay to fly screen CAP (SCAP) over the cruisers and transports.

Aircrews manned planes around 0500, as idling engines dotted the decks with bright blue exhaust flames, making it hard to accustom eyes to the darkness. Sufficient light from a quarter moon demarcated the horizon—a relief for rookies not relishing their first predawn takeoffs. Heavy clouds, however, towered northeast toward Guadalcanal, and the seas were rough. Promptly at 0530 at Point VICTOR (bearing 240 degrees, 95 miles from Tulagi), the *Saratoga* turned into the wind. Deployed abreast at five-mile intervals, the *Enterprise* north and the *Wasp* to the south of the *Sara*, the three flattops worked up to high speed, an "inspiring sight" according to Kinkaid.[3] No lights showed other than aircraft exhaust. The *Wasp* aircraft were to form up to the southwest, *Saratoga's* ahead, and "The Big E" 's to the northeast.

At 0535, the *Enterprise* launched the first plane, a VF-6 F4F. The other two flattops followed suit, F4Fs first, then SBDs. Noyes permitted the pilots only tail lights for five miles, where they could switch on their running lights to aid rendezvous. Tail lights and aircraft exhausts appeared all around the ships. Taking off from the *Saratoga*, Ens. William R. Bell stalled his VS-3 SBD and tragically disappeared in the dark waters. Almost inevitably, given the inexperienced pilots, darkness, and three carriers in close proximity, the various flight echelons so neatly defined in the OpPlan became intermixed. Pilots joined the wrong formations, or flights split into small groups. Everyone blamed someone else. Ac-

TABLE 3.1
Air Operations Plan against Tulagi and Guadalcanal

Against Tulagi (16 VF, 24 VSB, 1 VT)		
Wasp Air Group		
	Lt. Cdr. Wallace M.Beakley[a]	1 TBF-1
VF-71	Lt. Cdr. Courtney Shands	16 F4F-4s
VS-71	Lt. Cdr. John Eldridge, Jr.	15 SBD-3s
Enterprise Air Group		
VS-5	Lt. Turner F. Caldwell	9 SBD-3s
Against Guadalcanal (20 VF, 24 VSB)		
Saratoga Air Group		
	Cdr. Harry D. Felt[a]	1 SBD-3
VF-5	Lt. Cdr. Leroy C. Simpler	12 F4F-4s
VS-3 and VB-3	Lt. Cdr Louis J. Kirn	23 SBD-3s
Enterprise Air Group		
VF-6	Lt. Louis H. Bauer	8 F4F-4s

[a]Strike coordinator (group commander)

cording to the *Wasp* people, *Saratoga* planes tore through their formation. A VS-71 pilot, Ens. Robert A. Escher, accidentally dumped his bomb due to an electrical malfunction, and the blinding flash of the explosion caused *Enterprise* planes to scurry to avoid collisions. So as not to waste any more time, flight leaders gathered whom they could and headed out toward assigned targets. Plagued with a bum compass, Lou Bauer located no one from his VF-6 flight, circled until dawn, and made his own way to Guadalcanal. In many small elements the strike planes cut around the island's western tip to avoid detection instead of flying the direct route over its mountainous spine. The subsequent simultaneous attacks are best described according to the target areas.

Tulagi Attack

In the murk Courtney Shands, VF-71's skipper, garnered eleven of the sixteen *Wasp* F4Fs. Rounding Guadalcanal, he took precautions against possible antiaircraft (AA) fire from Savo by diving to 50 feet. ORANGE BASE (Turner's flagship, the *McCawley*) radioed that enemy planes were taking off from the Lunga airfield. Shands tried in vain to raise his air controller, PURPLE BASE, then queried Roy Simpler of VF-5 to see if he needed help over Lunga. Fortunately, it was a false alarm. Shortly after 0600 the transports of the YOKE Squadron loomed in the darkness ahead. After passing without challenge, VF-71 concentrated on the target. Tucked within a large inlet of Florida Island, Tulagi and associated islets seemed to slumber, but at 0613 gun flashes from Group X-RAY warships pounding Lunga 18 miles south shattered the stillness.

Ahead of VF-71 a cluster of red flares arced in belated warning. About 900 Japanese sailors occupied Tulagi and its satellite islands across the harbor, as well as a few sites on Florida's south coast. The small linked islets of Gavutu and Tanambogo, 3,000 yards east of Tulagi, served as the principal seaplane base for the Yokohama Air Group under Capt. Miyazaki Shigetoshi, a naval aviator since 1922. The highly experienced Yokohama crews had flown daily long-range searches over the region since late January and fought American carriers in February and during the May Coral Sea battle. Four Kawanishi H6K4 Type 97 flying boats [MAVIS] swung at moorings along Tanambogo's north shore, while in the quiet waters off Tulagi's east coast, gasoline barges serviced the other three for a dawn takeoff.

The Yokohama group also boasted a flight of new Nakajima A6M2-N Type 2 sea fighters [RUFE] led by Lt. Satō Riichirō (NA 66-1938).[4] An amphibious version of the standard A6M2 Zero carrier fighter, the Type 2 featured one large main float and two smaller stabilizing floats under the wings. Retaining enough performance to cause bombers a great deal of trouble, they provided fighter defense for advanced seaplane bases. Organized in February 1942 with twelve Type 2s, the detachment reached Rabaul in early June and deployed on 5 July to Tulagi. In the past weeks, Satō fought a number of sharp actions with Allied bombers and lost three pilots and four planes. Now six Type 2s drifted in line just off Halavo, a small village on a peninsula of Florida a mile east of Tanambogo. Two others under repair reposed ashore on Tanambogo.[5]

As Shands neared Tulagi, he deployed his four divisions according to plan. The following VF-71 pilots were present (with claims):[6]

1st Division		
F-30	Lt. Cdr. Courtney Shands	1 VP, 4 float VF
F-5	Ens. Samuel W. Forrer	1 VP, 3 float VF
F-26	Ens. Don G. Reeves	2.5 VP
F-20	Ens. Raymond F. Conklin	2.5 VP
2nd Division		
F-25	Lt. S. Downs Wright	3 VP
F-23	Ens. Roland H. Kenton	3 VP
3rd Division		
F-9	Lt. Charles S. Moffett	—
F-19	Ens. William M. Hall	—
F-21	Ens. Thomas M. Purcell, Jr.	—
4th Division		
F-22	Lt. (jg) Clark H. Gates	—
F-3	Ens. Norman J. Laskey	—

Gates and Laskey climbed to 5,000 feet to protect the strafers, and Moffett's 3rd Division peeled off to the left toward the little Florida village of Haleta west of Tulagi. Meanwhile, Shands's 1st Division skirted Tulagi's northwest tip, while Downs Wright's pair angled south toward Gavutu and Tanambogo.

Barreling in at barely 50 feet, Shands paralleled Tulagi's east coast into the main harbor seeking aircraft, motor torpedo boats, gun positions—anything that might interfere with the landing soon to take place. Pale light reflecting off the water revealed several dark objects floating off tiny Makambo Island. Shands led Sam Forrer sharply left to strafe them. Walking their .50-caliber tracers into two of the floaters rewarded both with instant results when their targets spouted bright flames. The glare illuminated a number of four-engine flying boats. Don Reeves and Ray Conklin quickly joined in. Soon four pyres burned brilliantly on the water. Conklin later described how his victim flamed up so fast, it was like "flying through a prairie fire."[7] The flickering light silhouetted more flying boats, one taxiing to take off. Reeves and Conklin cut short that Kawanishi's cruise, then torched another pair. Altogether the 1st Division left seven fires around Makambo Island: all three Type 97s and four auxiliaries that serviced them.

To the east Wright discovered the other nest of four flying boats anchored in a semicircle around Tanambogo's north coast. On the first pass he and Roland Kenton set on fire four targets: a mixture of flying boats, lighters, and fuel barges gray and indistinct in the darkness except for the dazzling flames. Coming around

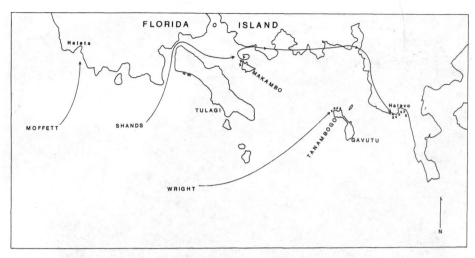

VF-71 strafing attacks, 0610–0620.

again, Wright sank a silver rubber boat full of flight personnel who bravely set out northeast from Gavutu. In the meantime, Kenton burned two more floating objects. Together they tallied six flying boats, but in fact they destroyed all four remaining Type 97s.

At about 0620 Shands and Forrer flew east over Florida past the fires of Tanambogo toward Port Purvis harbor beyond Halavo. In the growing light, Shands spotted the line of six sea fighters (he thought seven) moored close together about 30 feet off the Halavo shore. Several of their pilots were running across the beach or swimming through the surf to man planes. Shands and Forrer took great care in firing quick bursts to preserve their ammunition and get all the targets. In succession they pressed their runs low over the water, roared above the float planes, then nosed up sharply to clear palm trees on the hills overlooking the beach. One after another the Type 2s exploded in flames. With his final burst Shands torched the last, while Forrer silenced a 13-mm machine-gun nest. Soon, other VF-71 pilots flamed a truck hauling gasoline drums down to the beach. The Tulagi air detachment was out of business.

Moffett's three Wildcats made three strafing runs against an enemy camp just north of Haleta, shot up some shacks, and sent troops (more likely villagers) scurrying for cover. Waiting above, Gates and Laskey noticed no enemy planes (none got off), so they joined the others in blasting likely targets around the harbor. Lieutenant Commander Beakley, the group commander, surveyed the area now dotted with fires and thick, black smoke. Off Gavutu, another new arrival, Lt. (jg) Charles W. Tucker, from Gates's VF-71 division, assailed what looked like the hull of a beached submarine, but was actually the destroyer *Kikuzuki* sunk on 4 May by the *Yorktown* Air Group.

Nine VS-71 SBDs, under Lt. Cdr. John Eldridge (USNA 1927), along with nine VS-5s and a VS-3 stray led by Turner Caldwell, followed Shands and Beakley to Tulagi. Starting in while the fighters finished up, they encountered only weak AA. The VS-71 war diarist noted sarcastically that the F4Fs posed more of a danger than did the enemy: "[We] cleared out to keep from getting shot down by our own fighters who were going wild and shooting at everything in sight."[8] Could this someone have been jealous over VF-71's accomplishments?

Most of the VF-71 F4Fs left for home about 0700, their only damage a single

Lt. Cdr. Courtney Shands (center), VF-71 CO, with Capt. Forrest Sherman (*l*), Lt. Cdr. John Shea, and Cdr. Michael Kernodle (*r*), in the *Wasp*'s air plot, 7 Aug. 1942. (NA 80-G-12784)

bullet hole through Conklin's wing. All but Reeves returned without incident.The others feared he had gone down northwest of Guadalcanal, but Reeves, low on gas, took refuge on the *Enterprise,* which refueled him and sent him home. The SBDs also suffered no real harm. The Japanese bluejackets disappeared underground to await the Marines now disembarking from their transports.

VF-71 destroyed every enemy plane they saw with credits of thirteen flying boats and seven float fighters. In fact, all three Type 97 flying boats at Makambo and the four off Tanambogo burned and sank. VF-71 also strafed gas lighters and motor boats, which in the poor light looked like seaplanes, especially when they exploded and burned as readily. Shands and Forrer finished all six sea fighters so providentially served up at Halavo, and subsequent action destroyed the pair on Tanambogo.

Shaken by the surprise attack, the garrison prepared to resist to the end. Miyazaki's last radio message ended with: "We will defend to the last man. Pray for our success."[9] On Tulagi the 84th Guard Force numbered a few hundred Special Naval Landing Force troops. Armed mainly with light weapons, Yokohama Air Group personnel and some construction troops gave an excellent account of themselves in two fierce days of fighting on Gavutu and Tanambogo. On 8 August Miyazaki and several pilots died attacking two Marine tanks on Tanambogo. With about forty men Satō fled Halavo before the Marines landed on Florida. Roaming the inland mountains, they hid out until 19 September, when a patrol from the 2nd Marines surprised their camp and killed Satō and fifteen others. Native police later picked off the surviving stragglers.[10]

Guadalcanal Dawn

Roy Simpler's VF-5 flight came through the confused launch nearly intact, eleven of twelve.[11] To make up the difference, Gun. Charles E. Brewer of VF-6 tagged along. Simpler approached the target as briefed by way of the west coast, turned right at Cape Esperance, and led the F4Fs into a shallow, high-speed dive toward the Lunga Point airfield. Out in front, the heavy cruiser *Quincy* cut loose with her eight-inch guns against shore installations, soon also pounded by three more cruisers and one destroyer. The shock of the bombardment ran most of the Japanese into the hills.

The 8th Fleet's Guadalcanal garrison comprised the 11th and 13th naval construction battalions and 247 bluejackets from the 84th Guard Force, total 2,800 men (mostly Korean laborers). Defensive armament included an assortment of two 75-mm mountain guns, a triple 25-mm cannon mount, two 13-mm AA machine guns, and even two radar sets. These weapons were, for the most part, neither mounted nor effectively manned. Base headquarters, the guard force, and the 13th Construction Battalion camped west of the Lunga River, and the 11th to the east. Only the 13th had mustered before dawn. They crossed the Lunga and planned to make the airfield operational that very day (so close was WATCH-TOWER's timing). Two days before, they had completed a runway 800 by 60 meters (2,624 by 197 feet) and declared it suitable for fighters. Within a week the field was to be ready to handle twenty-seven fighters and twenty-seven medium bombers, and by mid-September no fewer than forty-five fighters and sixty bombers—formidable numbers indeed.

At first Simpler's 1st Division, Lt. Walter E. Clarke's 3rd, and Lt. Richard Gray's 5th concentrated on the airstrip. Off to the north was the encouraging glow of fires ignited by VF-71 at Tulagi. The 13th Battalion immediately took cover in makeshift air-raid shelters. Roaring low over the field, the F4Fs shot up all likely structures, including the future aviation headquarters (later dubbed "The Pagoda") and six hangars. They encountered virtually no resistance or even signs of life. Lt. (jg) E. T. ("Smokey") Stover observed red tracers floating lazily from his guns toward the target, but none from the other way. Simpler's wingman, Ens. John M. Wesolowski, wrecked a truck tearing across the field and helped scatter a herd of goats or cows, mistaken at first for enemy troops (which led to his being dubbed the "Bull-shooter"). Off Kukum at Lunga Point, ensigns Wayne Presley and Mel Roach set ablaze a small schooner frantically trying to clear out. The destroyers *Selfridge* (DD-357) and *Dewey* (DD-349) finished the job. The intense fire bespoke a highly flammable cargo, almost certainly gasoline. Don Felt called on the radio: "Hey Roy, get out from over Lunga airfield. We're coming down."[12] His twenty-six VB-3, VS-3, and VS-71 Dauntlesses wanted their crack at the target.

VF-6's rendezvous proceeded less smoothly than VF-5's. The skipper never joined, and most of the others flew out in two groups: five (plus one from VF-5) under Mach. Doyle C. Barnes for ground attack and seven with Lt. (jg) Dick Gay for the first of many CAPs over the screening force. Barnes shot up shacks and piers along the Lunga beach and holed several small boats. Resistance appeared negligible. Actually no Japanese dared remain near the beach, but withdrew deep into the coconut groves fringing the shore. Five errant F4Fs (four VF-71 and Bauer of VF-6) also harassed the Lunga area.

By 0700 most F4Fs were well on their way back to the carriers. Felt remained at Lunga as strike coordinator. Ground-support flights continued to plaster the area. After 0900 when the 1st MarDiv stormed ashore on RED Beach east of

Lunga, no Japanese came out to fight. The bombardments and air strikes scattered the enemy forces. Nearest to RED Beach, Capt. Monzen Kanae of the 11th Construction Battalion reluctantly reported that his men "had gotten out of hand."[13] Some of the garrison streamed westward to regroup on the far bank of the Mantanikau River, and the rest cowered in the coconut groves away from the beaches.

SUPPORTING THE LANDINGS

After launching the dawn strikes, the carriers settled into the routine dictated by the OpPlan's intricate flight schedule. They flew carrier CAP, SCAP, ground support, searches, and IAP on lookout for submarines. Almost constant flight operations occurred, as the carriers landed and immediately reserviced aircraft for later missions. Deck crews re-spotted planes several times an hour. TG-61.1 generally held east-southeasterly courses parallel to Guadalcanal's south coast. Light winds forced many 25-knot spurts that consumed fuel oil at prodigious rates.

That morning the CV CAP comprised sixteen to twenty-four fighters drawn from all three VF squadrons for patrols of about two hours. Lt. Hank Rowe, RED BASE FDO on the *Enterprise,* assumed control. The CV CAP occasionally checked out suspicious radar contacts, but spotted no enemy planes. Its only

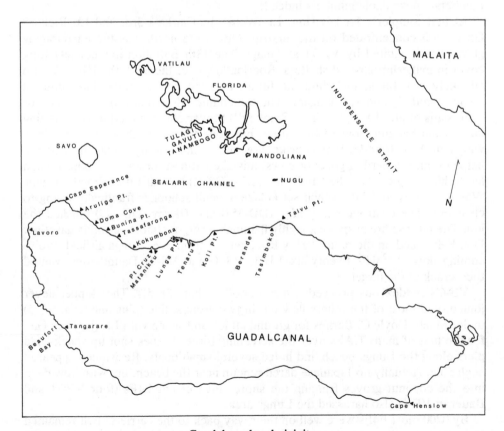

Guadalcanal and vicinity.

morning mishap took place at 0617, when Lt. James Southerland's VF-5 division took off from the *Saratoga*. On his way up deck, the wind lofted Ens. Charles Eichenberger's right wing, so that his left wing scraped the deck along the port catwalk. It struck a gun mount and flipped the F4F over on its back, spinning it inverted into the water. Eichenberger looked like a goner. Only water pouring into the cockpit revived him. To everyone's surprise and relief, he escaped the sinking Wildcat and reached the destroyer *Phelps* with only minor (but painful) injuries. The squadron had fashioned chest straps from SNJ safety belts, and that precaution saved Eichenberger. Despite repeated fleet requests, BuAer had failed to issue standard chest straps for the F4Fs.

The fighters also flew SCAP over the cruisers, destroyers, and transports between Tulagi and Guadalcanal. That meant flights of 60 miles or more to and from station, which limited the amount of time they could spend on duty. The SCAP comprised eight to sixteen F4Fs from VF-5 and VF-6 directed by BLACK BASE (on the heavy cruiser *Chicago* in TG-62.6, the cruiser-destroyer screening force) under the FDO, Lt. Robert Bruning from the *Sara*.

The carriers provided a steady stream of ground-support flights to bomb and strafe strong points hindering the Marine advance. In the Group YOKE (Tulagi-Florida) sector, the Marines landed first at Haleta (0740), then on Tulagi itself (0800) where initial opposition was heaviest, Halavo at 0845, and late that morning on Gavutu, where resistance was also fierce. Lt. Cdr. Robert Strickler's PURPLE BASE on board the transport *Neville* (AP-16) controlled the air-support flights in that sector. For seven hours, Lieutenant Commander Beakley, the *Wasp* group commander, helped select and direct aircraft to specific targets and also took important photographs. From Turner's flagship *McCawley* south across the channel, Lt. Cdr. William Townsend's ORANGE BASE directed air-support flights against Lunga. Felt stayed on station until relieved at 0900 by "The Big E" 's Max Leslie. Through Townsend, Turner kept too close a leash on Tulagi air-support operations and did not give Strickler the latitude to command he deserved.

SBDs and occasionally bomb-armed TBFs handled most of the air-support flights. Beginning about dawn, VF-71 also flew five ground-support missions (twenty sorties), about one an hour, until Noyes canceled those scheduled after 1200. These flights loitered in their assigned sector until the strike coordinator designated a specific target. At 0845 Lt. Hawley ("Monk") Russell and Ens. Frederick L. Huss strafed Tanambogo's north coast to help suppress small arms fire. An hour later Lt. George S. Leonard's division worked over vehicles seen moving in a coconut grove near Kukum, and Lt. (jg) Fred C. Hamilton set two trucks ablaze. At 1040 Lt. Carl Rooney's four fighters likewise blasted suspected enemy troop positions near Kukum and along the Lunga River. However, the last two missions received no targets at all. Despite heavy resistance at Tulagi and Gavutu, the invasions appeared to be going quite well. Everyone wondered when the Japanese air force would counterattack.

"REPEL AIR ATTACK"—PHASE ONE

The 5th Air Attack Force

The 5th Air Attack Force conducted naval air operations in the Bismarck Archipelago and eastern New Guinea, certainly the Imperial Navy's most active com-

RAdm. Yamada Sadayoshi, CO of the 5th Air Attack Force. (NHC, Capt. Roger Pineau Collection)

bat theater. Correspondingly, its excellent CO, RAdm. Yamada Sadayoshi, who completed flight training in 1919, was perhaps the senior Japanese naval aviator then holding a combat command. Organized around the headquarters of the 25th Air Flotilla (its administrative title), the 5th reported to "Base Air Force" (11th Air Fleet), the Navy's principal land-based aviation command, under VAdm. Tsukahara Nishizō. The 5th operated primarily from two land bases, Rabaul on New Britain and Lae in Papua, from the seaplane base at Tulagi, and prepared additional advance fields at Buna in Papua and on Guadalcanal.[14]

Since its creation in April Yamada's 5th Air Attack Force battled a seemingly endless supply of Royal Australian (RAAF) and U.S. Army Air Force (USAAF) squadrons based at Port Moresby and northeast Australia. Although his primary task was to support the advance against Port Moresby and the consolidation of Japanese positions in the Solomons, Yamada also prepared for possible offensives against New Caledonia, Fiji, and even distant Samoa, which led to the selection of Guadalcanal as the site of an advanced airfield.

Considerably weaker than the preinvasion Allied estimates of sixty fighters, sixty bombers, and thirty flying boats, the 5th Air Attack Force nonetheless was formidable. Operational air strength the morning of 7 August comprised thirty-nine fighters, thirty-two medium bombers, sixteen dive bombers, six sea fighters, and eleven flying boats, counting the Tulagi force that would soon be destroyed. Around Rabaul itself, the fighters and carrier bombers operated from Lakunai Field (Rabaul East set on a small peninsula east of the village proper), the land attack planes at Vunakanau (Rabaul West), and the flying boats in Simpson harbor (see table 3.2).

The principal strike capability rested with the 4th Air Group's twin-engine naval medium bombers, known as "land-attack planes" (*rikujō kōgekiki*, abbreviated *rikkō*, also *chūkō* for "medium attack"). Formed in February 1942 at Truk, the valiant 4th bore the brunt of attack missions in the theater and consequently sustained heavy losses. The CO was Capt. Moritama Yoshiyotsu, a non-

TABLE 3.2
5th Air Attack Force Operational Air Strength, 7 August 1942

Unit (Force)	Group and Commander	Strength	
		Authorized (14 July 1942)	Actual (Operational)
No. 1	Tainan Air Group	60 Zero 21 fighters	24
	Capt. Saitō Masahisa	8 Type 98 land recon planes	2
		4 transport planes	?
	Attached	3 Type 2 land recon planes	2
No. 2	4th Air Group	48 Type 1 land attack planes	32
	Capt. Moritama Yoshiyotsu		
No. 3	2nd Air Group	16 Zero 32 fighters	15
	Cdr. Yamamoto Sakae	16 Type 99 carrier bombers	16
No. 4	Flying Boat Detachments		
	Capt. Tai Haruaki (of the *Akitsushima*)		
	Detachment, Yokohama Air Group	3 Type 97 flying boats	2
	Detachment, 14th Air Group	2 Type 2 flying boats	2

aviator, as were most naval air group commanders. Tactically the group flew three flights (*chūtais*), each consisting of nine Type 1 land attack planes.[15]

Introduced in 1941, the Mitsubishi Type 1 land attack plane, Model 11 (later called BETTY by the Allies) became renowned for its extremely long range: 1,540 miles with normal fuel and payload and up to 3,256 miles under special conditions. This meant a combat radius of 700 miles or more, but with a modest payload of 800 kilograms of bombs or one aerial torpedo. Two 14-cylinder 1,530-HP radial engines gave a top speed of 231 knots at 4,200 meters (13,800 feet). The crew numbered seven or eight: two pilots, two or three observers, one or two radiomen, and a flight engineer. Usually the senior observer, not the pilot, commanded the aircraft. Defensive armament comprised four 7.7-mm Type 92 machine guns (nose, dorsal blister, port and starboard fuselage blisters) and one 20-mm Type 99 cannon in the tail. The Type 1's generally fine performance, especially its outstanding range, came at the price of no armor or self-sealing fuel tanks. That rendered it vulnerable to antiaircraft fire and enemy fighters. Its elongated fuselage with bulbous nose and large cockpit elicited the nickname "flying cigar" (*hamaki*), ironic because its tendency to catch fire in combat gave new meaning to that sobriquet.[16]

One of the worst surprises for the Allies in the early phases of the Pacific War, the Imperial Navy's Mitsubishi A6M2 Type 0 carrier fighter, Model 21 (later ZEKE to the Allies) equipped both carrier- and land-based fighter units. The *Reisen* (Zero fighter) uniquely combined superb combat performance (especially maneuverability, climb, and acceleration), a reasonably strong armament, and phenomenal range. Very light, only 5,313 pounds at normal load, the Model 21 was powered by a 940-HP, 14-cylinder Sakae radial engine for a top speed of 288 knots at 4,500 meters (14,764 feet) and a climb to 5,000 meters (16,404 feet) of 5 minutes, 50 seconds. The Zero wielded a mixed armament of two Type 97 7.7-mm machine guns mounted over the engine (680 rounds per gun) and two Type 99 20-mm cannons in the wings (only sixty rounds each). Internal fuel tanks held 525 liters (138.7 gallons), invariably supplemented with a 330-liter (87.2-gallon) drop tank. A maximum range of 1,675 miles meant a combat radius of nearly 600 miles, the longest for a single-engine fighter until the North American P-51 Mustang. In common with other Japanese aircraft, the Zero lacked pilot armor and self-sealing fuel tanks. Despite these crucial drawbacks, the high caliber of the Imperial Navy's fighter pilots and the superb performance of the Zero itself rendered combat losses very light.[17]

The Tainan Air Group, fighter component of the 25th Air Flotilla, enjoyed perhaps the highest reputation in the Navy.[18] Its ranks included many of the top-scoring aces. Organized in October 1941 mainly from China veterans, the group swept all opposition out of the skies over the Philippines and the Dutch East Indies. Transferred on 1 April to the newly formed 25th, the group operated from Rabaul and the forward base at Lae, only 180 miles north of Port Moresby, for constant combat with a tenacious enemy. The CO, Capt. Saitō Masahisa, was an old fighter pilot. His impetuous air officer, Cdr. Kozono Yasuna, led an infamous August 1945 revolt to protest the decision to surrender. The *hikōtaichō* (group leader), Lt. Cdr. Nakajima Tadashi (NA 58-1930), was one of the most senior officers still flying combat. Four flight leaders (*buntaichō*) and fifty-one other pilots, mostly noncommissioned, filled out the group. Lacking enough aircraft, Saitō used six rather than the standard nine-plane *chūtais*. With so many veterans and few aircraft, the junior enlisted men rarely flew combat unless they demonstrated real ability.

On 6 August the converted carrier *Yawata Maru* ferried to Rabaul East the 2nd Air Group led by Cdr. Yamamoto Sakae, another pioneer naval pilot (wings 1923). Formed on 31 May 1942, the 2nd comprised separate carrier bomber (*kanbaku*) and carrier fighter squadrons. The first numbered sixteen Aichi D3A1 Type 99 carrier bombers [VAL] led by the *hikōtaichō*, Lt. Inoue Fumito (NA 59-1931), while the fighter squadron flew fifteen new Mitsubishi A6M3 Type 0, Model 32 carrier fighters [HAMP]. Characterized by shorter, squared-off wings for faster, more controlled diving speed, the Zero 32 featured a bigger 1,130-HP engine with two-stage supercharger. Effective range, however, was about 20 percent less than the Model 21. Thus this theater valued Zero 32s more as interceptors for base defense than as long-range escort fighters. (On 29 July the tanker *No. 2 Nisshin Maru* had delivered to Rabaul twenty crated Zero 32s, which were gradually assembled for the units there.) The fighter *buntaichō*, Lt. Kurakane Akira (NA 63-1936), had survived being shot down on 1 February by Lt. (jg) Wilmer E. Rawie of VF-6 during the *Enterprise*'s Marshalls Raid.[19]

On 3 August Japanese scout planes discovered a small Allied airfield at Rabi on Milne Bay, New Guinea's easternmost tip. Greatly concerned about his advance fields at Lae and Buna, Yamada recalled all Zeros to Rabaul and organized an "all-out attack" against Rabi scheduled for 7 August. Lt. Egawa Renpei (NA 62-1934) was to take twenty-seven Type 1 land attack planes and nine Tainan Zeros to bomb the airfield. Before dawn on the 7th, ground crews at Vunakanau and Lakunai fields worked to arm and fuel the assigned aircraft.

As the Allies attacked that day, Yamada, faced with a totally new threat from an unexpected quarter, canceled the Rabi mission and at 0835 ordered an immediate strike against the enemy invasion force off Tulagi. One of the last radio messages reported one battleship, one carrier, three cruisers, fifteen destroyers, and many transports. Yamada relied on his morning search to pinpoint these ships. The 4th Air Group retained the payloads intended for Rabi: two 250-kilogram and four 60-kilogram high-explosive "land" bombs per aircraft. Against ships the *rikkō* crews much preferred using aerial torpedoes, but Yamada could not risk the time necessary to rearm with torpedoes, for fear that an enemy air attack would catch his bombers on the ground. This entailed a difficult level bombing run in the face of AA and fighters. Later that morning, as soon as they could be fueled and armed, the 2nd Air Group would follow with nine unescorted Type 99 carrier bombers to bomb enemy transports off Tulagi.

At Lakunai in the shadow of a large volcano, the Tainan fighter pilots gathered around headquarters to be briefed. Not long before the scheduled departure for Rabi, they learned the new target was Guadalcanal. The news elicited gasps of amazement and eager looks at charts. Lunga Point was all of 560 miles southeast of Rabaul, the farthest combat mission yet asked of the long-legged Zeros. In December 1941, after vigorous training, the Tainan pilots had effectively escorted strikes from Taiwan to Manila in the Philippines, some 500 miles. Now they faced a mission 10 percent longer. (By comparison, Berlin lay about 460 miles from bases in eastern England.)

Yamada wanted all twenty-four operational Zero 21s to escort the land attack planes, but Saitō persuaded him to reduce the number to eighteen, organized in three six-plane *chūtais* under Nakajima, who revised the flight schedule to include the best pilots. Indeed, four later ranked among the Imperial Navy's ten top fighter aces. According to the plan of attack, the 2nd *Chūtai* under Lt. Kawai Shirō (NA 64-1937), the senior *buntaichō,* would proceed ahead of the main body as the "air control force" to surprise enemy interceptors, while Nakajima's other two *chūtais* flew close cover. Fuel posed the crucial problem. Contrary to the usual practice, the pilots could not jettison their belly tanks before battle, because they needed all of their fuel to get back. Saitō directed those unable to make Rabaul to take refuge 160 miles south at the small, abandoned airstrip on Buka, where the ex-destroyer *Akikaze* would service aircraft.

At 0950 eighteen heavily laden Zeros began taking off from Lakunai, and under Nakajima's watchful eye formed up for the long climb to escort altitude. PO1c Ōki Yoshio, a *shōtai* (section of three planes) leader in Kawai's 2nd *Chūtai,* regretfully aborted when his landing gear did not retract. From Vunakanau, Egawa's twenty-seven *rikkōs* took to the skies at 1006 and deployed into three tight, nine-plane Vee-of-Vees, with following aircraft stepped up behind the leaders. The formation resembled a giant arrowhead pointed at the enemy.[20]

The fighters moved into their escort slots: Nakajima's 1st *Chūtai* behind and to the right of the bombers, and the 3rd *Chūtai* under Lt. (jg) Sasai Junichi (NA 67-1939), a talented young fighter leader, in the corresponding slot on the left quarter. Kawai's 2nd *Chūtai* climbed above the others. No land-based Zeros carried radio receivers or transmitters; the pilots considered them unreliable and too heavy to justify their presence. They relied on visual signals, and each *chūtai* guarded a specific sector where they were to return after countering enemy interceptors.

Flying as 2nd *Shōtai* leader in Sasai's 3rd *Chūtai* on the left was PO1c Sakai Saburō, then the Imperial Navy's top scoring ace with some forty-eight aerial victories. A pilot since November 1937, when he graduated first in his class (earning the emperor's silver watch), Sakai saw extensive combat in China, the Philippines, and the East Indies. For the last four months he had fought a wild succession of air battles against Allied land-based air units defending Port Moresby. Now with professional interest he contemplated fighting U.S. carrier pilots and wondered how good they really were. Cruising southward along Bougainville's west coast, the hot tropical sun beat through his canopy, so he sought to slake his thirst with a bottle of soda water from his lunch kit. In the *rikkōs,* the crews likewise enjoyed their meals. Opening the bottle, Sakai accidentally sprayed carbonated beverage all over his cockpit. Chagrined, he wiped the sticky liquid from his windscreen, unaware that far below someone counted the planes and radioed a warning to the Guadalcanal invaders.

The Japanese Strike Back

For the three U.S. carriers, the morning of 7 August proved by far the most hectic in memory. Strike planes and fighters shuttled back and forth from the invasion areas and CAP stations, as carrier captains tried to hold to Noyes's intricate schedule of flights. Around 1130, TF-61 copied three messages that disrupted the routine. In the first CinCPac warned, based on deciphered enemy messages, that Rabaul was sending eighteen bombers and seventeen fighters to strike the invasion forces off Guadalcanal. Sixty miles south-southwest of Lunga, Fletcher's carriers also came within range of the Japanese strike. Nine minutes later, CinCPac warned with another ULTRA of Japanese submarines bound for Tulagi.[21] Close on its heels came a plain-language message on a special emergency frequency: "From STO, 24 bombers headed yours."[22] The call sign identified the sender as PO Paul E. Mason, RANVR, a bespectacled Australian planter stationed on Malabita Hill near Buin in southern Bougainville, about 300 miles northwest of Lunga. He was part of an invaluable surveillance network set up before the war by the Royal Australian Navy.

Knowing the enemy was coming did not make it much easier to provide an adequate air defense, particularly as TF-61 fighters protected two threatened locations 60 miles apart. The three precious flattops took top priority. At 1130 the CV CAP numbered twenty-four F4Fs, and the carriers readied twenty-four more to relieve them. No longer earmarked for ground-support missions, most of VF-71 could reinforce the CV CAP. The situation over the transports was not as good. At 1130 the SCAP stood at fourteen F4Fs (eight VF-5, six VF-6), but by 1300 all would have departed for lack of fuel. In the next 90 minutes only eight F4Fs were to replace them. Ground-support missions could tie up the flight decks when it became necessary to scramble fighter reinforcements. Given the tricky mechanics of carrier operations, the flattops simply could not launch or recover aircraft on demand, as the Japanese learned to their dismay in the Battle of Midway. The SCAP needed up to 30 minutes to reach station, and dwindling fuel often forced the F4Fs to leave early.

The *Saratoga*'s next scheduled fighter launch at 1203 involved eight VF-5 F4Fs (Lieutenant Harmer) on CV CAP and Lt. Pete Brown's four on SCAP. Captain Ramsey thought it advisable to reinforce Brown, so he ordered Lieutenant Southerland's SCARLET 2 division with four F4Fs to depart 75 minutes early. A messenger found Pug Southerland and his pilots enjoying a quick lunch in the wardroom after two CAP missions that hectic morning. Hurrying to the ready room, Southerland warned his boys that a fight appeared imminent, and on impulse buckled on his Colt .45 pistol. The sixteen F4Fs, all equipped with belly tanks, took off at 1203. On board the *Enterprise,* Lou Bauer made ready to head out on SCAP with six, including a pair to relieve the section escorting Max Leslie, the X-RAY strike controller over Lunga. The only other fighters in the invasion area, Monk Russell's four VF-71 F4Fs on ground support, received no assignments and circled as a sort of CAP.

Bauer's RED 1 division reached station around 1230, and BLACK BASE soon had work for him. Ground clutter and a parade of SBDs and TBFs only partially equipped with IFF hampered Bob Bruning's efforts as FDO. Nevertheless, when

The *Enterprise*'s flight deck, 7 Aug. 1942. (USN via Dr. Steve Ewing)

the *Chicago*'s radar displayed a large bogey Bruning directed Bauer northwest on 310 degrees (M.), Angels 8 (8,000 feet). About 1300, while still east of rugged Savo Island Bauer heard orders to steer 205 degrees (M.), that is, south-southeast over western Guadalcanal and back toward the carriers about 25 miles off shore. At 1300 he overheard RED BASE detach four CV CAP fighters (Dick Gay's RED 3) north to Guadalcanal, and could not fathom why he was sent south. Requesting a repeat, he again heard 205. Puzzled, he obeyed orders and soon discerned the task force. RED BASE told him to orbit overhead.

Later, an irate Bauer complained that had his division held its initial favorable position, it would have hurt the enemy a long way out. He blamed BLACK BASE. Yet Bruning never sent those controversial orders; it was RED BASE that brought Bauer back. Rowe feared the enemy might turn south toward the carriers still southwest of Guadalcanal and tried to coordinate an intercept by Bauer and Gay. The enemy, however, continued toward Guadalcanal. About 1300, VF-5 pilots heard BLACK BASE vector "Red Affirm" (the VF-6 pilots) on 300 degrees (M.), 36 miles, for a "look see" at a "bogey."[23] Had Bauer still been orbiting Savo, he would have run right into the incoming Japanese.

Meanwhile, "The Big E" followed the flight schedule and at 1311 launched Lt. (jg) Gordon Firebaugh's Flight 321: four F4Fs for SCAP and two to escort the group commander over Lunga. Fourteen VT-3 TBFs cleared the flight deck for rapid recoveries and takeoffs. The *Wasp* readied sixteen VF-71 F4Fs to reinforce the CV CAP and launched them at 1319, expanding the CV CAP to about forty fighters. Finally realizing that no bogeys threatened the carriers, Rowe released Lt. Pat Rooney's eight VF-71 F4Fs north to Tulagi. Unlike the VF-6 reinforcements, they would arrive too late.

Into the "Japanese Meatgrinder"

Bauer's involuntary departure left the air defense of TF-62 solely to eight VF-5 pilots patrolling at 12,000 feet:

SCARLET 2		
F-12	Lt. James J. Southerland II[a]	2 bombers
	Ens. Robert L. Price[a]	MIA
	Lt. (jg) Charles A. Tabberer[a]	MIA
	Ens. Donald A. Innis	1 Zero damaged
SCARLET 8		
	Lt. Herbert S. Brown, Jr.	1 Zero damaged
	Ens. Foster J. Blair	1 bomber damaged
	Lt. (jg) William M. Holt[a]	MIA
	Ens. Joseph R. Daly[a]	2 bombers

[a]Shot down

Evidently Bruning did not position them higher because of a thick cloud layer that extended above 13,000 feet.[24]

From the northwest the strike group, guided by the island signposts, approached Guadalcanal. The 4th Air Group cruised at 5,000 meters (16,404 feet). Over New Georgia Nakajima's twelve direct-cover Zeros behind the bombers ascended to 6,000 meters (19,684 feet), while Kawai's five went even higher (8,500 meters/27,880 feet). Ahead across brilliant blue water past the Russell Islands rose the jagged peaks of Guadalcanal and Savo, its small companion. Until this point Egawa had received no search reports locating enemy carriers. With the target in sight, Kawai pushed his fighters ahead of the main body to hunt Grummans. Nearer to Guadalcanal gaps in the clouds revealed a large number of distant black specks: enemy warships off the long north coast. Their strength, fifty-plus, amazed the Japanese. Screened by the clouds, Kawai missed the F4Fs on patrol below, but alertly doubled back in a fast, shallow glide toward the main body. The 4th Air Group itself nosed down into a gentle descent to gain speed and release bombs from just beneath the overcast. The three nine-plane *chūtais* had deployed as follows (see figure).

Concerned because he could not see the direct-escort Zeros, Egawa radioed PO2c Sekine Shōji's *rikkō* flying at the back of the 3rd *Chūtai*. Sekine replied he could not see the fighters either. Even so Egawa instructed his command pilot, WO Nishimura Kiyoshi, to set up the bomb run against the ships off Lunga Point.

Just after 1300, Bruning piped up to vector SCARLET 6 (Jensen) out on 310 degrees (M.), Angels 12 (12,000 feet). Southerland stepped in for the absent Jensen and took the steer. Brown followed a few miles behind, but out of sight due to the overcast. The cloud base looming directly above made interception difficult. Roy Simpler aptly remarked: "The day was one of heavy cumulus clouds that hung in huge lumps—the kind that you can ride around the corner and anything could be right smack in front of you."[25]

At 1315, near Savo, Southerland heard orders to swing left 10 degrees. Suddenly the land attack formation descended through the clouds astonishingly close, the nearest *rikkō* barely 500 yards from his left wing. He excitedly counted twenty-seven medium bombers arrayed in tight formation only a few hundred feet above and sang out on the radio:

Horizontal bombers, three divisions, nine planes each, over Savo, headed for transports. Angels 12. This division from Pug: drop belly tanks, put gun switches and sight lamps on. Let's go get 'em boys.[26]

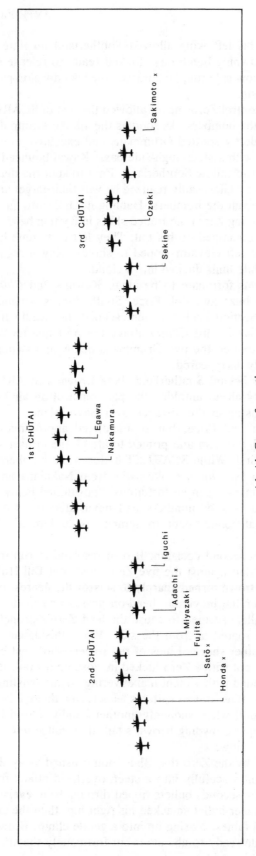

4th Air Group formation.

Bombers crowding his left wing allowed Southerland no time to climb for a proper run. Their yawning bomb bays looked ready to release deadly cargoes. Dropping into a left low-side run, he harassed the lead division passing before his sights with snap bursts.

Kawai's five air-control Zeros never allowed the rest of SCARLET 2 to follow their leader against the bombers. As soon as the 4th Air Group dropped through the overcast, they alertly spotted Grummans and executed an especially adroit ambush. Screaming with a steep high-side pass, Kawai bounced the three F4Fs after they turned left to follow Southerland. First to spot the deadly threat from above, Don Innis, the trailer, sadly realized he was their target and that they had already cut him off from the bombers. Hauling his F4F into an abrupt climbing turn to scissor the diving Zeros, he traded shots in fleeting head-ons with all five attackers, before one camped on his tail. They left forty-nine holes in his F4F and the fabric of the left elevator ripped to shreds. Kawai regained altitude to renew the attack, while Innis ducked into a cloud.

"Stinky" Innis was fortunate to be alive. Kawai's 2nd *Chūtai* cut through SCARLET 2 like a buzzsaw. Bob Price, Southerland's wingman, and "Tab" Tabberer, the 2nd Section leader, never escaped the deadly trap beneath the enemy escorts. In Sasai's 3rd *Chūtai* above the port quarter of the bombers, Sakai momentarily spotted the two Grummans below and swung out to attack, but the enemy swiftly disappeared.

Following not far behind Southerland, Pete Brown's SCARLET 8 searched the clouds. Suddenly ahead unfolded the panorama of an air battle: "Fighters diving, turning, smoking in the distance over Savo Island."[27] Brown charged in to help Tabberer and Price, but soon noticed approximately fifty enemy bombers about level with him and primed to attack the cruiser screen. Protecting the ships came first. While SCARLET 8 closed the bombers, the other five Zeros of the Tainan 1st *Chūtai* broke away from Nakajima and assaulted the new batch of Grummans again so fortuitously positioned below. Realizing that inferior altitude and lack of numbers had devastated the CAP, Simpler likened their piecemeal commitment to scraps tossed into a "Japanese meat-grinder."[28]

Faced with a split-second decision, Brown resolved to run interference with his wingman Crud Blair against the five Zeros and sent Bill Holt's 2nd Section after the bombers. Brown turned sharply to scissor the nearest bandit coming in at the same level for the inevitable head-on passes and made the most of his opportunity. His bullets seemed to cause the lead Zero's propeller to slow, but the next Mitsubishi roared in from the side. When this Japanese disappeared, Brown received another shock. Lines of red tracers shot past both sides of his cockpit. In a tough spot with a Zero tucked in close on his tail, Brown rolled out of his climb and evaded with violent maneuvering. While twisting, climbing, and scissoring the Zeros, Blair stayed with his leader, saw the one latch onto his tail, and prepared to shoot, when suddenly another bandit chased him as well. He drove off the interloper crowding Brown's tail, then rolled into a swift split-S to the cradle of clouds below.

Even while beset by the Zero that Blair soon brushed away, Brown glimpsed another Japanese roll gracefully into a steep overhead attack from about 1,500 feet above. For a few seconds bullets ripped through from every direction. With a puff of smoke a tracer bullet smacked his right hip, then the cockpit exploded and filled with acrid fumes. Nosing up into a gentle climb, Brown cranked back his canopy and made ready to abandon, but fortunately the smoke cleared. He checked his bloody hip and leg.

The Japanese who executed the adroit overhead (and wounded Brown with a full-deflection shot as later investigation determined) drew alongside his victim's wing. The two pilots carefully looked each other over and, pleased with himself, the Japanese grinned and waved. The odds are strong that Brown's able and amiable opponent was PO1c Nishizawa Hiroyoshi, Nakajima's wingman and one of the brightest stars in the Tainan galaxy of fighter aces. Before his death on 26 October 1944, he is thought to have made about eighty-seven kills, the top Japanese score. The skill and unusual behavior of Brown's assailant was totally in character for Nishizawa, a wild man aloft. Whether Nishizawa's or not, the Zero pushed a little ahead as the F4F lost speed. Trying hard to return the compliment, Brown triggered a burst that caused the Wildcat to stall and spin. Nosing down, he fired at another Zero before gaining the clouds. Growing weak from loss of blood and nursing a shot-up airplane, Pete Brown still faced the ordeal of trying for home plate.

While Brown's section absorbed all the Zeros on the right side, Holt and wingman Joe Daly attained proper attack position high over the left side of the bombers. Sighting Grummans diving at them, Sasai's 3rd Tainan Chūtai scattered, but Holt and Daly concentrated on the 2nd Chūtai under Lt. Fujita Bakurō (NA 65-1938) on the left. Several rikkōs spouted tracers trailed by thin lines of gray smoke, as Daly poured bullets into one of the outside bombers. At such close range his slugs had to be striking home, but he detected no damage. Holt did not score either. After pulling out, the two F4Fs climbed into position for another run. These tactics—long, steep attacks against the bombers with recovery far below to zoom up for another try—proved quite puzzling to the Japanese.

In the meantime, Southerland had climbed and shifted his point of aim for long-range sniping of the right division, the nine of the 3rd Chūtai under Lt. (jg) Ozeki Toshikatsu (NA 67-1939). As he crossed over from right to left, his momentum drew him close to Fujita's 2nd Chūtai on the left. He singled out the Type 1 of PO2c Satō Tamotsu, Fujita's left wingman, riddled the cigar-shaped fuselage forward of the open bomb bay, and caused flame to blossom forth. Roaring into a high-side run from left of the bombers, Blair watched Southerland's victim nose down in flames for the U.S. Navy's first aerial victory of the Guadalcanal landings.

Southerland banked left and down, but before he scooted out of range sharpshooting Japanese gunners scored. A bullet cracked the Wildcat's bullet-proof glass windscreen, while the fuselage reeked with the unmistakable smell of incendiary rounds behind the cockpit. Not certain how long he could remain airborne, Southerland crossed over to right of the bombers for another shallow low-side attack, this time against the outside Vee of Ozeki's 3rd Chūtai. Selecting the right trailer, he pumped the rest of his bullets into PO1c Sakimoto Yoshiyuki's right wing and engine. The Type 1 commenced smoking and fell back, but Southerland could not finish it off. Indeed, his own mount inspired little confidence. As he dived away, he noticed his fuselage trailed smoke. With a damaged plane and no ammunition, he figured it was time to go.

As the VF-5 pilots worked over the bombers, black shell bursts sought Egawa's formation. Crutchley's warships had watched the oncoming attackers and noticed Satō's burning aircraft fall east of Savo. Gun directors swiftly determined the correct altitude and shot on target. Several Type 1s sustained damage. Shrapnel ripped the right engine of Egawa's left wingman, PO1c Nakamura Asayoshi, and started tearing the powerplant apart. Kneeling over the bombsight in the lead rikkō's glassed-in nose, the enlisted bombardier aimed at cruisers maneuvering swiftly below and hoped to trap at least one within the tight forma-

tion bomb pattern. At 1320, from 3,700 meters (12,139 feet) he toggled his payload, at which time the other bombardiers also released. The 156 bombs exploded together in spectacular fashion between the cruisers and the Group
X-RAY transports anchored southeast near Lunga Point. A disgusted Sakai
watched the huge columns of water erupt wide of the targets. Even so, Egawa's
crews claimed one destroyer sunk and damage to a transport.

Immediately after the bombing, the Wildcats reappeared. Blair observed two
Grummans assailing the 4th Air Group. One was Daly, who was doing quite well
with high-astern, low-deflection approaches despite the dangerous tail stingers.
Coming around for his second pass, Daly noticed Nakamura's AA-stricken Type
1 drop out of the lead division and followed through by setting ablaze two *rikkōs*
in the rear rank. Daly later remarked, "Their tail gunners had put quite a few
holes in my wings and tail surfaces, but had done no serious damage."[29] Blair
also saw Daly's two targets take many hits.

SCARLET 8 enjoyed a good time against the 4th Air Group. Holt and Daly
badly damaged at least three land attack planes from the last rank. PO2c Sekine
(in Ozeki's 3rd *Chūtai* on the right) glanced behind to see Grummans racing in
like "attacking dogs."[30] In the 2nd *Chūtai* on the left, fighters set afire PO2c
Iguchi Masayoshi's right engine, but he kept his place in formation. Then it was
Sekine's turn. Bullets holed one of his wing fuel tanks, which sprayed gasoline,
but the white stream soon stopped. One other Type 1 (either PO1c Honda Shigeo
or PO1c Adachi Umeo from the 2nd *Chūtai*) took hits as well, but no *rikkōs*
actually went down at this time.[31]

The 1st *Chūtai* Zeros quickly regrouped. Blair saw one F4F (Holt) brush a
Zero off the other's tail (Daly). After three attacks, only two of Daly's guns still
worked. Even so, he opted for just one more run. Glimpsing two fighters closing
from astern, he thought for a second they were welcome reinforcements, but
realized that they moved too fast for F4Fs. As he tried to scissor, still another
Zero caught him by surprise:

> The whole plane shook as a 20-millimeter shell exploded beneath the cockpit. The
> next second I was sitting in a flame. My clothes were on fire; my pants and shirt
> were burning: I could see nothing but red fire all around me. I remember vividly the
> thought that ran through my head: "Sonny boy, you're not going to get out of this;
> this is it!"[32]

With flames engulfing the cockpit (20-mm rounds ripped open the self-sealing fuel
tank), Daly pushed back the canopy, released his safety belt, and hurtled into the
open at 13,000 feet. Fearful of being strafed, he held off pulling his ripcord. After
a Zero flashed past, he dropped into the cloud bank. A minute or so later he
finally popped his chute at 7,000 feet and splashed off Berande Point some 15
miles east of RED Beach. Masts from Group X-RAY vessels barely creased the
horizon. Daly discovered his face, wrists, knees, and ankles were badly burned.
In shock, he thought the saltwater "felt wonderfully soothing." With a slow
breaststroke he swam toward distant Guadalcanal.

Nakajima's pilots also blasted Bill Holt out of the sky. Daly last noticed him
during the initial run against the bombers, but Blair had seen Holt sticking with
Daly throughout much of the fight. To this day no one knows for certain what
befell him.[33] In the meantime Blair set to work from below and behind against
the trailer on the right. This was Sakamoto from the 3rd *Chūtai*, already beset by
Southerland. Fire erupted in its bomb bay, but Blair was not at leisure to watch
its fate. Two Zeros suddenly snared him in the midst of red tracers, holed his
right wing, and ran him down into the clouds.

Despite the kills his escort tallied, Nakajima was furious that his pilots left the 4th Air Group unattended. Again the lack of radios severely hampered his tactical control. Their mission essentially wasted, the land attack planes continued east past Lunga into heavy cloud cover. Egawa arranged for a careful formation turn left (north) toward Malaita Island. He radioed base that two enemy heavy cruisers, three destroyers, and about twenty-five transports were anchored off Tulagi, but no carriers were in sight.

The 4th Air Group endured one more sally from VF-5. After escaping the melee that nearly destroyed SCARLET 2, Don Innis attained 20,000 feet and noticed the bombers passing east of RED Beach. As the *rikkōs* completed their left turn to head north over the channel, he rolled into a steep overhead run and fired off all of his remaining ammunition during the long diving attack. Two Zeros chased him down into the overcast. After a brief game of tag, Innis turned south for home.

Southerland versus Sakai

One of the escorts who dodged SCARLET 8's surprise attack, Sakai Saburō, rejoined *chūtai* leader Sasai, but his own wingmen, PO2c Kakimoto Enji and PO3c Utō Kazushi, had disappeared. Searching the skies, he finally saw far behind and below a lone Grumman battling three Zeros, two of which appeared to be his errant wingmen. Shockingly, the enemy pilot actually chased the three Japanese. His boys needed help! Flying up alongside Sasai, Sakai signaled by hand for permission to dive in.[34]

Pug Southerland of VF-5 flew the Wildcat that Sakai viewed with such amazement. A few minutes before over Savo, PO3c Yamazaki Ichirōbei from Kawai's 2nd *Chūtai* suddenly latched onto the F4F at 11,500 feet for short, sharp firing passes from behind. Cranking down his seat to take full advantage of the armor plate behind the cockpit, Southerland manually recharged his guns hoping they had jammed rather than run dry. He later wrote:

> A Zero was attacking at this time from my starboard quarter so I pushed over as though diving to escape him, then pulled out immediately, cracking my flaps and whacking off my throttle. He overran as I'd hoped and made a climbing turn to the left. I turned inside easily and had the aviator's dream; a Zero at close range perfectly lined up in my sights for about a ¼ deflection shot. However, I pressed my trigger without result and realized sadly that I'd have to fight the rest of the battle without guns.[35]

To survive, he depended on his wits and the stoutly made Wildcat.

Kakimoto and Utō soon joined Yamazaki's assault. Southerland quickly analyzed their tactics. Two fighters worked their runs from opposite flanks, while the third waited to take its turn. He devised his own counter:

> This consisted merely of determining which of the two Zeros, attacking almost simultaneously on either quarter, was about to open fire first, and turning sharply toward him as he opened up. This gave him a full deflection shot so he invariably underled me, riddling my fuselage aft but doing little serious damage. This quick turn also placed the second plane directly behind me so that I was well protected by my armor plate. When runs were not exactly simultaneous, I would rely chiefly on my armor, placing the attackers directly aft in succession as they made their runs.

While 7.7-mm bullets thudded into his armor plate, Southerland coolly and carefully executed his defensive maneuvers. Numerous times Zeros overran after flashing in from astern and pulled out directly ahead of the much slower, twisting

Wildcat. That gave Sakai the impression that the Grumman "chased" his men. He assessed the American pilot as "very skilled." Southerland was just trying to stay airborne long enough to reach RED Beach and bail out. Gradually losing altitude, he led his pursuers southeast away from the other Japanese.

Diving in, Sakai cut loose at 600 meters (1,968 feet), an especially long range, to distract the enemy pilot. Noticing a fourth Zero enter the fight, Southerland countered with a sharp left turn to offer only a full-deflection angle, then reversed and climbed as if to counterattack. Surprised when the F4F uncannily snapped into a right turn to disrupt his aim, Sakai thought the American now stalked him from underneath—his own favorite tactic. Chagrined, he rolled out, chopped his speed, and hauled into a tight left turn. Unlike the three other foes, he intended to use the Zero's fabulous maneuverability to fly onto the Grumman's tail rather than merely make firing passes. In the contest of turns, Southerland kept trying to turn into his new opponent, but Sakai was not shooting just yet. With a series of tight left spirals, he cut inside the F4F's turns and gradually worked his way onto its tail. It was hard work. Sakai admired the "terrific man behind that stick." In his own right, Southerland contended with a failing airplane and other Zeros as well.

When the rugged hills loomed below, Southerland realized the spirals had used up nearly all his altitude. After the fifth one he surprised Sakai by breaking out into level flight. Sakai knew he had his man. Easily slipping onto Southerland's tail, he swiftly scanned the sky, then resumed the business at hand. The Grumman's well-finished appearance impressed him, and he snapped a photo with his hand-held Leica camera. From 50 meters he fired a deadly burst of 200 7.7-mm rounds, but the imperturbable Grumman flew along as before. Sakai described it as dotted with holes, with the rudder "ripped to shreds, looking like an old torn piece of rag." Momentarily distracted, he was startled when the F4F slowed up and his Zero overran uncomfortably in front of its guns. No bullets came. Sakai dropped back until he flew wing to wing with his opponent, then pushed open his canopy for a look.

All this time Southerland made ready to abandon, calmly working though his checklist: disconnect radio cord, undo safety belts, and open the canopy. He quickly assessed the state of faithful F-12:

> My plane was in bad shape but still performing nicely in low blower, full throttle, and full low pitch. Flaps and radio had been put out of commission . . . The after part of my fuselage was like a sieve. She was still smoking from incendiary but not on fire. All of the ammunition box covers on my left wing were gone and 20-mm explosives had torn some gaping holes in its upper surface . . . My instrument panel was badly shot up, goggles on my forehead had been shattered, my rear view mirror was broken, my plexiglass windshield was riddled. The leak proof tanks had apparently been punctured many times as some fuel had leaked down into the bottom of the cockpit even though there was no steady leakage. My oil tank had been punctured and oil was pouring down my right leg.

Roy Grumman's products were sturdy. As Sakai remarked, no Zero could have survived anywhere near this kind of punishment.

Carefully observing the American pilot, Sakai described him as a big man with a round face, some seven to eight years older than himself (actually Pug was five years older), and wearing a blood-stained khaki flight suit. As Pug changed the stick from his right to his left hand and undid the belts, Sakai thought him hunched over like a man at prayer. The American even appeared to give him a weak wave. Sakai felt a strange empathy for his wounded opponent so obviously at his mercy. For the first time in his many combats, he perceived one of his adversaries as a human being brought to grief by his efforts. Yet Sakai felt great excitement about victory over such a worthy foe.

Sakai again dropped behind the Grumman. As it heaved into a shallow climb, he brought its engine into his sights and squeezed off five or six cannon rounds. Where they struck, "a burst of flame and smoke exploded outward from his engine." Southerland later recounted:

> At this time a Zero making a run from the port quarter put a burst in just under the left wing root and good old 5-F-12 finally exploded. I think the explosion occurred from gasoline vapor. The flash was below and forward of my left foot. I was ready for it . . . Consequently I dove over the right side just aft of the starboard wing root, head first. My .45 holster caught on the hood track, but I got rid of it immediately, though I don't remember how.

After exiting his F4F at extremely low altitude, Southerland managed to open his chute and drifted toward the trees.

Sakai saw his tenacious opponent hanging in his chute straps, then lost him to view. Noticing that he himself had gone "much too low for safety," he regained altitude and soon encountered his joyous companions. Sakai, Utō, and Yamazaki shared the tough Grumman kill, certainly one of the most memorable and best documented fights between Wildcats and Zeros.

Southerland set down among the trees with surprising ease. Fearing a strafing run by his opponents, he had loosened his straps on the way in and, once he landed, took off running "100 yards away in 9 seconds flat." Under cover he sat down to collect his wits: "My first grateful thought was to thank God that I was alive. I can guarantee that this was a wholly unexpected outcome of the battle." He counted eleven wounds, the worst on his right foot, and burns on his arms, but decided, "not bad at all, considering!" Figuring he touched down about 10 miles east of Cape Esperance and four miles in from the beach, he started downhill for the coast. Hoping to stay on high ground, he soon realized he would have to traverse the jungle. On the way he neatly avoided a Japanese observation post in a tree and worked his way through the undergrowth toward the water's edge.

The SBDs Fight

After the Tainan Zeros destroyed five of eight VF-5 Wildcats, several battled ground-support planes operating between Tulagi and Guadalcanal. At approximately 1320 Beakley ordered Eldridge's eight VS-71 SBDs to bomb two positions off the Florida coast a few miles southeast of Tulagi. Eldridge (USNA 1927) and wingman Lt. Dudley H. Adams (USNA 1939) toggled their bombs against tiny Bungana Island, then heard the call, "Bombers above!"[36] Beakley exhorted them to break off and intercept the enemy. Lt. (jg) William P. Kephart, leading Eldridge's 2nd Division, radioed his men to jettison their 500-pound bombs and climb. They slipped into loose-line astern, joined by Eldridge and Adams.

At 7,500 feet the six SBDs met a reception committee chaired by Sasai. Spotting the enemy carrier bombers soon after Sakai left to fight Southerland, Sasai, PO1c Ōta Toshio, and PO2c Endō Masuaki tore after the lead SBDs with swift high-sides. Kephart responded with a twisting dive to the left, which shook off the three trailers: Eldridge, Adams, and Ens. Jacob S. Paretsky (VS-72). The three Zeros managed a quick series of passes against the lead Dauntlesses before Kephart reached safety in the overcast, then they climbed back into the sun toward the 4th Air Group making the big turn northwest over Florida Island. While Sasai assailed Kephart, two Zeros from Kawai's 2nd *Chūtai,* PO2c Tokushige Norio and a teammate (possibly PO2c Nishiura Kunimatsu), jumped "Dud" Adams from above and behind. His radioman Harry E. Elliott, ARM3c, held them off until all three trailing SBDs split up and got clear. The five Japanese claimed four Curtiss "SBC" (*sic*) carrier bombers (Sasai 1, Endō 2, and Tokushige 1), but neither side sustained any losses.[37]

Sakai, Kakimoto, Utō, and Yamazaki, the victors over Southerland, cut across Sealark Channel toward Tulagi to rejoin the land attack planes. While they passed through a cloud layer at 7,000 feet, a bullet lanced through Sakai's rear canopy glass and barely missed him. Startled and angry at being caught unaware, he looked back to spot an audacious carrier bomber off his port quarter. After evading Tokushige, Dudley Adams of VS-71 had run across Sakai's flight and actually stalked the four Zeros ascending through the clouds. Swiftly Sakai and his three friends climbed above and easily drew away from their much slower opponent. Now safe, Sakai turned the tables with a high-side run, and his first bursts forced the SBD to stall and fall away toward the water. Gunfire killed Harry Elliott and painfully wounded Adams. At 1337 he ditched 71-S-10 astern of the Screening Group. The *Dewey* left the X-RAY transports and rescued him eight minutes later.

Following the rude interruption, Sakai resumed his flight toward the 4th Air Group. Ahead at 7,800 feet he noticed what appeared to be eight Grumman fighters in tight formation almost begging to be ambushed. Unfortunately for him the targets proved to be Lt. Carl H. Horenburger's eight VB-6 and VS-5 SBDs still toting their 500-pound bombs. They observed Zeros and closed formation even more to meet their attack. Too late did Sakai realize his disastrous mistake, but he had committed to a low-deflection stern attack into the muzzles of sixteen .30-caliber machine guns. With no other choice, he pressed his run to the limit against the right side of the shallow Vee. Kakimoto followed closely, but the other two broke off in time. The radiomen caught the lead Zero in a wicked cross fire. One bullet shattered the windscreen, tore into Sakai's head, and temporarily blinded him. Thrown into inverted flight, his smoking Zero passed up over the formation and rolled into a straight dive toward the water. Kakimoto dipped beneath for a pass against the left side, but broke off when the eight SBDs flew into a cloud bank.

Utō tried to overtake his leader, but soon decided Sakai had suffered mortal wounds. Despite a bullet-grazed skull, near blindness, and excruciating pain, Sakai pulled out low alone over the waves and set course for home. His flight later reported the destruction of two carrier bombers (one each to Sakai and Kakimoto), but Flight 319 sustained only slight damage. The eight SBD crews felt equally certain they finished one Zero, but that error rose only from the immense courage of Sakai Saburō, who despite disabling wounds reached Lakunai Field on his own.[38]

Parthian Shots

By 1330 the escort Zeros had knocked all the SCARLET F4Fs out of action. Ten VF-6 and eight VF-71 F4Fs raced north from TG-61.1, but only the *Enterprise* fighters would harass the withdrawing Japanese. The first to arrive after the bombing were the four of VF-6's RED 3 division:

—	Lt. (jg) Theodore S. Gay, Jr.	2 bombers probable
F-35	Lt. Vincent P. de Poix	1 bomber, 1 bomber damaged
F-4	Mach. Howell M. Sumrall	1 bomber damaged
F-11	Mach. Julius A. Achten[a]	1 Zero damaged

[a]Shot down

Traversing Guadalcanal's mountainous spine, RED 3 saw numerous black dots from five-inch AA shells bursting over the channel. Strung out loosely at 16,000 feet they headed out over the water toward Tulagi. Lieutenant de Poix happened to sight the Japanese bomber formation about 4,000 feet below crossing over Florida. They moved swiftly northwest, stepping out at nearly 180 knots.[39]

Around 1345 RED 3 caught up with the *rikkō* as they ventured out over Indispensable Strait toward Santa Isabel. The 4th Air Group flew the customary tight Vee-of-Vees. No escort Zeros appeared, although about eight (Nakajima's 1st *Chūtai,* along with Kawai and PO1c Yoshida Mototsuna from the 2nd) lurked nearby. From ahead de Poix rolled in for a high-opposite attack, while Gay crossed over to the left to bracket the formation, then dropped into a steep high-side run against the 2nd *Chūtai.* Only when Gay dived did he notice two Zeros 800 yards behind and about 1,000 feet beneath the bombers—a strange escort slot. He ignored them and followed through with his attack. Sumrall and Achten swung into high-side passes from right of the bomber formation.

To RED 3, the bombers looked so close together, wing tips nearly touching, that seemingly their .50-caliber slugs could not miss. Sumrall watched the red bands of de Poix's tracers smother a Type 1 in the lead division and elicit smoke. Unfortunately his own gunsight malfunctioned, so he aimed with his tracers and smoked the port engine of the number 2 *rikkō* in the lead division. Following through, he sliced his bullets through the wing of a bomber in the third division, while Achten poured heavy fire into another. RED 3 thought they hurt several bombers, but none left formation.

Eager for a second try, Gay reefed around for a low-side run from starboard against a straggler with only one engine—PO1c Sakamoto's 3rd *Chūtai* Type 1, already winged by Pug Southerland and Crud Blair. This time he witnessed positive results, when the target lost power and trailed smoke. In the meantime, de Poix had reversed course with a hard, flat turn and overtook the same *rikkō* from astern. He did not relent until it flamed in dramatic fashion. The 3rd *Chūtai rikkō* crews tried frantically to alert the two Zeros trailing the formation out to the left. Several gunners even loosed lines of tracers out ahead of them. Finally the two Tainan pilots woke up to the danger and roared after the two Grummans, but it was too late for Sakamoto's burning *rikkō.* It flopped over on its left side and plunged into the sea. One Tainan pilot raced after Gay, the other chased de Poix. PO2c Sekine thought they finished the Grummans, but both F4Fs escaped below into a convenient mass of clouds.[40]

Sumrall and Achten most definitely would have joined the party, but more of the escorts showed up. About to make his second pass against the bombers, Sumrall glimpsed one Zero climbing rapidly toward him, too fast for him to press his attack. Despite a split-S to the left, the Zero was on him before he could get away. With fine deflection shooting, the Japanese riddled his F4F with 7.7-mm bullets and punched two 20-mm shells through the left fuselage star, which made a mess of the radio and filled the cockpit with thick fumes. Opening the canopy soon cleared the atmosphere, but Sumrall unhappily found himself in the midst of four 1st *Chūtai* Zeros jockeying for the kill. They had him dead to rights with no chance to fight back. He nosed down steeply to gain speed and aimed for the sanctuary of a convenient cloud. The Zeros did not follow.

Even before Achten pulled out of his first run, two Zeros jumped him from above and behind. The leader erred in gaining too much speed (a typical mistake), overran the target, and recovered in range of Achten's guns. Profiting from the sudden opportunity, he shot into the Mitsubishi, which faltered, then spun toward the water. Perhaps this was PO1c Yamashita Sadao's Zero, struck by four bullets without causing vital damage. The wingman gave Achten no time to savor his victory, but charged close up his tail and ran him into cloud cover. Achten did not escape unscathed. Oil streamed from his torn-up wing cooler, which was proving to be the Wildcat's Achilles' heel. Within a few minutes the engine froze, but he used his fleeting flight time to recross Florida toward Tulagi harbor. At 1350 he coaxed F-11 into a successful deadstick ditching astern of the *San Juan* with Group YOKE, who provided a landing boat for a warm welcome on board the transport *Neville*.

Gay radioed a superfluous order for RED 3 to return to base. His division was out of the fight, confronted at tactical disadvantage by the surprisingly resilient Tainan escorts. Ultimately RED 3 claimed one bomber (by de Poix) and five other probables, including a fighter by Achten. Sekine's account shows that de Poix indeed finished off Sakamoto's battered Type 1.

Even as eight Zeros repulsed RED 3, RED 5 came on fast:

F-25	Lt. (jg) Gordon E. Firebaugh[a]	—
F-22	William J. Stephenson, AP1c[a]	MIA
F-21	Mach. William H. Warden[a]	—
F-34	Ens. Robert M. Disque	1 bomber
F-29	Rad. Elec. Thomas W. Rhodes	1 Zero
F-26	Lee Paul Mankin, AP1c	1 bomber; 1 Zero damaged

[a]Shot down

Bustering north from the carrier, Firebaugh climbed steadily at maximum sustained speed, swiftly reached Lunga, and caught sight of the bomber formation still far ahead over Florida. Rad. Elec. "Dusty" Rhodes disobeyed orders by staying instead of peeling off at Lunga to escort Leslie's TBF. Under the circumstances, he heard nothing more about it.[41] Counting the distant black dots, Firebaugh advised BLACK BASE: "32 bombers at Angels 17 bustering northwest." To still-climbing RED 5, the land attack planes appeared far above at 17,000 feet. It was an optical illusion. Actually the 4th Air Group held steady at about 12,000 feet, but moved at 180 knots, quite fast for twin-engine bombers. Bruning approved Firebaugh's request to pursue beyond the 35-mile limit. Only their extra fuel afforded RED 5 this capability.

Well after 1400, following a run of nearly 150 miles from the task group, Firebaugh eased into attack position 2,000 feet above and 6,000 yards right of the bombers as they drew abreast of small San Jorge Island off Santa Isabel's long southern coast. Getting there cost the last of the fuel in the 42-gallon belly tanks. Surveying the situation, Firebaugh noticed only three Zeros cruising in a Vee to the left of and 2,000 feet below the bombers. Actually all sixteen Zeros (less the critically wounded Sakai) had reassembled near the bombers. Nakajima, Nishizawa, and Sea1c Yoshimura Keisaku flew the three rear guard fighters. Eight more under Sasai (3rd *Chūtai*) and WO Takatsuka Toraichi (1st *Chūtai*) fell in ahead of the *rikkōs*, while Kawai's five 2nd *Chūtai* Zeros resumed the top cover. Flight 321 indeed faced formidable opposition.

Firebaugh's VF-6 division, July 1942 (*l to r*): Stephenson, Warden, Firebaugh, and Disque. (USN)

Assessing the tactical situation, Firebaugh instructed Bill Warden and Dusty Rhodes to drop belly tanks and attack the bombers, while he dealt with the three bandits in the clean-up spot astern. As Firebaugh's section rolled in to attack, the quarry instantly swung right and climbed steeply to scissor. Gaining altitude astonishingly fast, the three Zeros met Firebaugh halfway. He lined up for a head-on run against the leader and cut loose at 500 yards. The .50-caliber slugs appeared to tear off pieces of its cowling, so he "nudged the nose down a little" to dive beneath his opponent. To his left, Stephenson's F4F fell off into a shallow dive with a Zero, guns smoking, tucked up close on its tail. Firebaugh maneuvered to shoot Stephenson's assailant, but the third Japanese surprised Firebaugh with an excellent display of deflection shooting. A "well concentrated burst" of 7.7-mm slugs tore into the cockpit barely ahead of his right knee and ripped through the instrument console. Momentarily stunned by the noise and shattered glass, he snapped into a tight right turn to scissor. A menacing line of eight Zeros passed beneath, but the bandit who so neatly ambushed him was not in sight. At a 45-degree angle Stephenson's F4F plunged straight into the water.

While the lead section battled the three trailing Zeros, the other four VF-6 pilots crossed to the left against the bombers. Warden radioed that his belly tank failed to release, so Firebaugh told him to stay out of the fight. Wingman "Deke" Disque joined Rhodes and Paul Mankin for high-side runs from left of the now unprotected bombers. Rhodes and Disque blazed away at several *rikkōs* in Fujita's closely spaced 2nd *Chūtai* and caused one Type 1 in the rear rank to fall slowly behind the others. Mankin flew top cover for the other two, when his belly tank would not jettison either. After his run, Rhodes immediately swung back to find Firebaugh.

Disque's second high-side against the 4th Air Group forced another *rikkō* to drop out of formation. The third time he set afire one of the stragglers, which

"immediately trailed a long bright orange flame with black smoke streaming behind it." Entranced by the sight and oblivious of return fire, he pulled alongside
the stricken bomber and thought, "If my dad could only see this."[42] Mankin
noticed the other cripple: "Look down there, Deacon. There's one lone bomber,
and I am going to get him." Warned it might be a trap, he replied, "If it's a
decoy, it's too bad for the decoy."[43] Drop tank and all, he rolled into a high-side
run. The port engine nacelle flamed up, and the bomber nosed down toward the
water. The two VF-6 pilots finished off PO1c Honda and PO1c Adachi from the
2nd *Chūtai*.

For several minutes Disque and Mankin enjoyed the 4th Air Group all to
themselves. Finally a Zero appeared from nowhere and charged up behind
Disque. Mankin warned, "There's a Zero on your tail!"[44] Disque countered by
scissoring for a head-on shot, but saw the enemy dive away. Using his tracers
Mankin adroitly brushed the Zero off his teammate's tail (although it turned too
tightly for him to hit) and chased the enemy fighter a short while. Its pilot was
none other than Nakajima, who later recounted with considerable anger how one
Grumman forced him off the tail of its teammate. He was furious that the other
escorts did not regroup to protect the bombers.

In fact the Zeros had become embroiled in a big fighter action with three RED
5 Wildcats. Sasai and Takatsuka split forces, each *chūtai* to take on a single
Grumman. Struggling with his belly tank, Warden lost track of the other F4Fs
until he located Firebaugh far below in deep trouble. Sasai's four 3rd *Chūtai*

On 10 Aug. 1942 Rad. Elec. Thomas Rhodes of VF-6 sits in F-29 in the *Enterprise*'s
hangar deck. Bullet damage from 7 August can be seen on the turtleback behind the
cockpit. (NA 80-G-12981)

Zeros latched onto Warden, who scissored each opponent as he came in. They destroyed one of his vulnerable wing coolers, so he broke off the fight. Two Zeros pursued, but sheered off by the time he reversed course to confront them. Warden flew back into the midst of the 3rd *Chūtai* and barely escaped again, this time with only three guns working. With his overheated engine running very roughly, Warden resumed his homeward flight.

By the time Rhodes returned to the right, Firebaugh had disappeared, but he did witness an airplane splash. Takatsuka's four Zeros bounced the lone Grumman, but one incautiously recovered out in front of its guns. Ripping the Zero convincingly, Rhodes felt certain it later splashed, but Takatsuka extinguished a fire before it consumed his plane. His teammates shot up the Grumman and chased it out of the area. Rhodes radioed for help, but no one came to his aid. With a sour engine and only three guns, Warden happened to sight below a Zero "cold nosing" a Wildcat. From long range he bluffed the Japanese by shooting tracers out ahead of him. The gambit cost all his remaining ammunition, but happily the Mitsubishi pulled off at the first glimpse of tracers. Rhodes lost track of his rescuer in the clouds, but a few minutes later noticed an F4F drop dead-stick into the sea north of the Russell Islands. It was Warden, whose powerplant finally seized. The impact threw his head into the instrument panel and gashed his forehead, but he revived quickly enough to free his life raft before F-21 went under. On one low pass, Rhodes elicited a wave from the unknown pilot. With fuel getting low, he turned home.

Eventually Kawai's five 2nd *Chūtai* Zeros flying top cover finished off Firebaugh, but not cheaply. They first appeared high on his starboard beam. Highly skilled (over 1,300 hours just in fighters), he knew what he must do merely for a chance to survive. With care he watched the lead Mitsubishi commit itself to a firing pass and draw into range. At that instant he turned sharply into it to "bitch" its run by offering only a full-deflection shot. Thus Firebaugh countered the same way as did Southerland earlier. Kawai missed and dived on past. Using tactics similar to Jimmy Thach's first countermove at Midway, Firebaugh swiftly reversed his turn to shoot the lead bandit before it climbed away, but Kawai was too fast for him. The next Tainan pilot punched holes in the twisting F4F, but Firebaugh took his revenge. Again reversing his initial turn, he caught the Mitsubishi pulling out ahead and scored with a strong burst. In dramatic fashion the Zero flipped over and spiraled in a right turn all the way to the water, killing Kawai's senior wingman, PO1c Yoshida Mototsuna, an ace with twelve kills.

The third Zero to attack (PO3c Yamazaki, Southerland's first opponent, if the *chūtai* maintained proper order) executed a steep high-side run, but this time defense availed little against excellent marksmanship. Explosive 20-mm shells and 7.7-mm slugs ripped through the length of the F4F's rear fuselage. A massive jolt, almost as if the airplane smashed into a brick wall, threw Firebaugh around the cockpit. The F4F now flew very tail-heavy, and no wonder. Shot out of the turtleback behind the cockpit, the yellow raft draped itself grotesquely over the tail surfaces.

Despite the condition of his aircraft, Firebaugh battled his adversaries, who politely took turns for runs from above and behind instead of jumping his tail. The 2nd *Chūtai* again suffered for these tactics. PO2c Nishiura Kunimatsu, in the fifth Zero to attack, overshot as the Grumman twisted in its counter, and ended up in front of it. Firebaugh quickly riddled the unfortunate *Reisen*. The next assailant (possibly Kawai making his second pass) set the F4F's cockpit ablaze, igniting gasoline leaking from a prior 20-mm hit in the main fuel tank. Getting clear of the airplane at about 3,000 feet, Firebaugh suffered severe burns, but fearing attack he did not pull his ripcord until close to the sea. Beneath him his faithful Wildcat splashed, then he, too, slammed into the water with a blow that took his breath away and injured his spine. A few seconds later Nishiura's Zero struck the sea nearby. On Santa Isabel, coastwatcher Geoffrey Kuper noticed four planes (two F4Fs and two Zeros) fall off tiny Eugene (Nainubhana) Island near Point Mufu.

As Firebaugh struggled out of his harness, Yamazaki and Tokushige buzzed him at 300 feet but, content to look him over, they departed northwest. He faced a long swim to Santa Isabel, whose mountains darkened the northern horizon. Gone were his flying goggles, torn away by a bullet that creased his left temple. His face, neck, and wrists stung from flash burns; flame had also seared his ankles and knees. Weakened by his wounds, a wrenched back, and near exhaustion, Firebaugh determined to reach safety. Two Wildcats, Disque and Mankin, passed overhead too high to see him floating alone on the vast sea.

Flight 321 provided the toughest opposition the Japanese strike faced that day. Disque and Mankin received credit for a bomber apiece, Rhodes a VF, and Mankin one damaged. Firebaugh's two kills did not appear in the initial reports (although he later received credit for three Zeros); neither did any claims by Warden. The cost, however, was high: three F4Fs (one pilot killed).

Despite fierce opposition, Japanese losses proved surprisingly light. Four land attack planes fell to enemy fighters. PO1c Nakamura bellied his AA-crippled *rikkō* onto a beach in northern Buka, while PO1c Miyazaki Noboru crashed his stricken bomber at Rabaul. Thus six *rikkōs* were written off, nineteen others holed. The 4th Air Group lost twenty-eight men, but claimed one destroyer sunk, a transport damaged, and fifteen Grummans. By 1730 ten fighters had set down at Rabaul after eight hours aloft. They included Sakai and also Nishizawa, who became enraged after Sakai failed to rendezvous. Frantically seeking more opponents to fight or even ram, he started home only after cooling down. Five others (one totaled) took refuge at Buka. Two pilots were missing: PO1c Yoshida and PO2c Nishiura. Permanently blinded in one eye, Sakai did not fight for nearly two years. In a mission renowned even for them, the Tainan pilots claimed thirty-six Grumman fighters (including seven unconfirmed) and seven carrier bombers (see table 3.3).

Thirty-four U.S. planes (eighteen F4F-4s, sixteen SBD-3s) fought this extraordinary air battle, the first between U.S. carrier planes and land-based Zeros. Official credits numbered seven "Mitsubishi 97" twin-engine bombers, five probables, and two Zeros. Nine F4Fs (exactly half) and one dive bomber went down; three fighter pilots and one radioman died in action. The few American aircraft actually brought into battle greatly impressed their opponents, whose claims led some to reckon upwards of ninety intercepting Grummans. Even the Japanese official history states that they battled sixty-two U.S. Navy fighters.[45]

The 50 percent losses suffered by the USN fighters proved extremely significant. The aviation professionals pointed to such reasons as poor initial positioning and remained confident of their airplanes and tactics. However, nonaviator Fletcher later remarked, "Nobody mentions the matter, for fear of bringing down the wrath of the aviators upon them, the Japanese Zero's all wore Seven League Boots [and] our aviators gave them a lot of g.d. respect."[46] This was not exaggerated. For example, on 13 August Lou Bauer radioed to Pearl Harbor a routine summary of how VF-6's machine guns and ammunition functioned. Although pleased at the ruggedness and overall protection afforded by the F4F-4,

TABLE 3.3
Claims by Tainan Air Group, 7 August 1942

1st *Chūtai*			
1st *Shōtai*		2nd *Shōtai*	
Lt. Cdr. Nakajima Tadashi	—	WO Takatsuka Toraichi	4 VF(1)
PO1c Nishizawa Hiroyoshi	6 VF	PO1c Yamashita Sadao	2 VF[c]
Sea1c Yoshimura Keisaku	5 VF(2)	PO2c Matsuki Susumu	3 VF(1), 1 VF[c]
2nd *Chūtai*			
1st *Shōtai*		2nd *Shōtai*	
Lt. Kawai Shirō	1 VF	PO1c Ōki Yoshio[b]	—
PO1c Yoshida Mototsuna[a]	—	PO2c Tokushige Norio	4 VF(1), 1 VB
PO3c Yamazaki Ichirōbei	1 VF, 1VF[c]	PO2c Nishiura Kunimatsu[a]	—
3rd *Chūtai*			
1st *Shōtai*		2nd *Shōtai*	
Lt. (jg) Sasai Junichi	3 VF(1), 1 VF,[c] 1VB(1)	PO1c Sakai Saburō	1 VF,[c] 2 VB
PO1c Ōta Toshio	2 VF, 2VF[c]	PO2c Kakimoto Enji	1 VF, 1VB
PO2c Endō Masuaki	1 VF, 2 VB	PO3c Utō Kazushi	2 VF, 2 VF[c]

[a]Missing in action
[b]Aborted the mission
[c]Shared victory

he rather dramatically concluded, "Pilots are anxiously awaiting faster and better fighters. Repeat pilots are anxiously awaiting faster and better fighters."[47] For Fletcher and others this crucial first engagement of carrier fighters with land-based Zeros helped set the pattern for the entire campaign.

INTERMISSION

During the air battles over Guadalcanal and Tulagi, Fletcher's three carriers labored to provide all available F4Fs, while still holding closely to scheduled ground support and search flights. At 1330, the *Enterprise* hurriedly assembled "Special Flight Z": six F4Fs on CV CAP and four for the screen. The *Saratoga* scrambled eleven VF-5 F4Fs (eight for SCAP), while 15 minutes later the *Enterprise* relaunched Don Runyon's six F4Fs for Guadalcanal. Thus by 1400, forty-four F4Fs (some low on fuel) protected the CVs, and eighteen the invasion forces.

During the frantic CAP launchings, numerous planes, including battle survivors, awaited open flight decks. In the worst shape, VF-5's Pete Brown, wounded in the hip by an incendiary, nearly fainted from loss of blood, but kept himself awake with a phial of ammonia. Noticing the *Sara*'s deck now free, he painfully cranked down the landing gear and started in without flaps. Coached by the steady hands of LSO Lt. William Godwin, he landed safely, lifted himself out onto the right wing, but collapsed into the arms of Irvin Howe, PhM1c. While undergoing emergency treatment in the VF-5 ready room, he said of the Zeros, "There was a million of 'em!"[48] Stinky Innis and Crud Blair, two more battle-scarred participants, soon found the *Saratoga*. Their outrageous nicknames must have brought them luck, for of eight VF-5 pilots, only they and Brown reached home plate. The squadron yeoman, Harvey W. Ward, Y2c, took down statements from the three and was summoned to flag plot to read them to

Fletcher and Ramsey. Blair noted in his diary that Ward "had a cup of coffee with the Old Boy & everything."[49]

Although Rooney's eight VF-71 F4Fs missed the enemy raiders, the mission proved costly. While on the downwind leg of his landing approach, Lt. Wilson G. Wright III (USNA 1939) had his Curtiss-Hamilton electric propeller control lock in full high pitch. He poured on the power, but could not stay aloft very long. After LSO Lt. David McCampbell gave him a wave-off, he tried a 180-degree turn to set down ahead of the *Wasp*. At 1438, F-18 stalled and spun in from 50 feet. Its left wing slapped the waves and cartwheeled the airplane, but an improvised chest belt saved "Wee Gee" Wright from injury. He soon boarded the destroyer *Lang* (DD-399).[50] A minute later Fred Hamilton suffered serious head injuries when his F4F flipped over while landing on the *Wasp*. F-23 was a total loss, soon jettisoned. Hamilton later convalesced in the States.

"REPEL AIR ATTACK"—PHASE TWO

At 1400, after the Japanese planes departed Turner suddenly warned of attacking enemy dive bombers. Shortly thereafter TF-61 copied another, apparently garbled, message: "25 planes about 8000 feet disappearing bearing 100 degrees."[51] The erroneous reference to short-range dive bombers certainly set the carrier admirals wondering whether Japanese flattops lurked in the area, despite radio intelligence that located them all in home waters. They placed Lunga far out of range of any such aircraft coming from Rabaul.

Turner's message proved prophetic by 45 minutes. From desperation or careful deliberation, Yamada ordered Lieutenant Inoue's nine 2nd Air Group Type 99 carrier bombers on an unescorted mission against transports off Tulagi. Unable to carry auxiliary fuel, they could not fly 560 miles to the target and return. That meant water landings off Shortland south of Bougainville, where the seaplane tender *Akitsushima* and one four-engine Kawanishi H8K1 Type 2 flying boat would be waiting. Thus Yamada knew he would lose all nine planes, but hopefully not their crews as well. What would he gain from it? Not much it seems, because the land-based Type 99s customarily carried only two light 60-kilogram bombs, a much smaller payload than the 250-kilogram bombs used by carrier-based dive bombers. Sixties could not inflict any real damage on ships.[52]

Inoue's nine 2nd Air Group carrier bombers departed Rabaul at 1045. Slowly climbing to 3,000 meters (9,840 feet), they followed the northern boundary of the island chain, which effectively shielded them from coastwatchers and TF-62's land-locked radars. Around 1430 Inoue turned south over Florida to find the ships off Tulagi. Cloud cover blocked his view of Group YOKE, so he continued south over the channel toward the more distant X-RAY ships. Finally nearing the Guadalcanal coast, he waved his 3rd *Shōtai* under WO Ōta Gengo against the warships off to the west and led his six east toward the transports anchored off RED Beach. His opposition would be fifteen VF-5 and VF-6 F4Fs in four scattered flights on SCAP.[53]

With the three F4Fs (another had aborted) from VF-6's "Special Flight Z," Scoop Vorse circled 11,000 feet over the western flank of Group X-RAY. Suddenly Ōta's three carrier bombers appeared not far below. Shaking off his amazement, Vorse abruptly rolled into a dive for a flat-side run, but the two wingmen failed to keep contact and missed out on the fight. Vorse's gambit turned into a tail chase of the trailer, PO2c Iwaoka Minoru. Ōta aimed for the *Mugford* (DD-

Wasp flight deck crews lift Lt. (jg) Fred Hamilton's F-23 (BuNo. 5103), wrecked in a landing accident on 7 Aug. 1942. (NA 80-G-12623)

389), the most westerly destroyer in the antisub screen. At 1457, one of her lookouts, lying on his back on the roof of the number 2 five-inch gun house, saw two dive bombers with fixed landing gear (Ōta and his number 1 wingman, PO2c Takahashi Kōji) emerge out the clouds astern. To the bridge he yelled, "Planes! They've got wheels."[54] A few seconds later two more bandits appeared: Iwaoka with Vorse right behind. Lt. Cdr. Edward W. Young, the *Mugford*'s skipper, ordered right full rudder.

Crossing over the *Mugford*, the two lead Type 99s rolled into their dives from off her starboard quarter. Ōta's two 60-kilogram bombs raised splashes to starboard, but one of Takahashi's landed aft on the superstructure just forward of the number 3 five-inch gun. The blast killed twenty-one men (including fourteen blown overboard), wrecked the aft deck house, and rendered number 3 and 4 guns temporarily inoperable. Vorse stayed right with Iwaoka in the third *kanbaku*, because Sea1c Nakamoto Seiki, his pilot, never popped his dive brakes. Smoking but not showing flames, the *kanbaku* plunged straight into the water. Vorse leveled out at 2,000 feet and sought the other two hawks, but they eluded him and escaped to the west.

Meanwhile, Inoue's six carrier bombers angled eastward at about 10,000 feet toward the X-RAY transports. Coming toward them at 7,000 feet were SCARLET 5's six VF-5 F4Fs under Lt. Richard Gray. For some reason he skylarked much lower than his assigned altitude of 10,000 feet and was far out of position to the east. Suddenly Lt. Hayden Jensen, leading the third section, happened to sight off to the right about eleven enemy dive bombers emerge unannounced 3,000 feet above. Some of them split off to the west, but about five now headed in

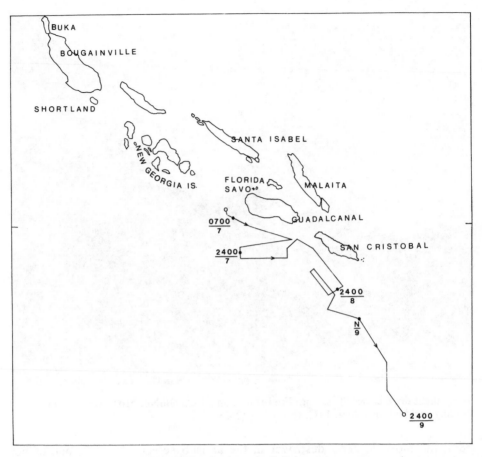

TF-61 (Carriers) track, 7–9 August.

his direction. Racing ahead of the others and waggling his wings to sound the alarm, he led Gray's F4Fs in a full power climb against the "hawks" as they passed overhead to the east. From 13,000 feet, but several miles north, Lt. David Richardson, VF-5 flight officer, and Ens. Charles Davy almost simultaneously spotted the bandits. Slanting down, they realized they would be fortunate to reach the enemy before they dived.

Climbing furiously, the SCARLET 5 F4Fs soon overtook the "rather slow" fixed landing gear dive bombers, but lost one of their number on the way. Testing his guns, Frank Green discovered they would not work and pulled off to clear them. The battle left him behind. Lt. Marion W. Dufilho, his section leader, certainly understood. A VF-3 wingman in the famous 20 February fight over the *Lex,* malfunctioning guns kept him out of action, while Butch O'Hare, his section leader, earned the Medal of Honor. With enemy fighters closing in, Inoue realized his slow *kanbakus* would never reach the transports. He led the string of six Type 99s into a wingover to reverse course and go after the nearest warship, a light cruiser, he thought, but actually the destroyer *Dewey* in the antisub screen just west of the transports.

While the ships fired impartially at every plane within range, Jensen was the first to reach the Japanese seconds before Inoue pushed over. Rolling in with a shallow side attack, he tagged one Aichi in WO Nakagaki Seisuke's 2nd *Shōtai*. The target shook and shuddered from bullet strikes and separated from the others. Jensen followed the damaged *kanbaku* down toward the water and stayed with it despite its "erratic attempts at evasion."

By the time some of the other fighters caught up, the carrier bombers had pushed over in the midst of black five-inch AA shell bursts and ribbons of tracers into their dives against the *Dewey*. Lt. (jg) Carl Starkes spiraled down with the enemy, shooting whenever one flashed through his sights, as did Marion Dufilho. Next in, Ens. Mark K. Bright overran one dive bomber in the middle of the string and found himself directly behind the one ahead, the number 3 in Inoue's 1st *Shōtai* commanded by PO3c Tokiwa Shūzō, the observer in the rear seat. Bright loosed a long burst, answered by Tokiwa's 7.7-mm Lewis gun with a line of tracers that floated slowly past the diving F4F. Suddenly the Aichi caught fire in the belly between the landing gear, and soon the whole aircraft streamed fire. In the meantime, Gray lunged at the last dive bomber, but broke off to guard against a second wave. Richardson and Davy could not overtake the trailer and, like Gray, stayed high looking for more bandits.

Inoue and his number 1 wingman, PO3c Satō Seiji, pressed their dives against the *Dewey* and pulled out low over the water. One bomb landed only 15 feet to starboard. Behind them Nakagaki, the 2nd *Shōtai* leader, and one other *kanbaku* likewise released their payloads and pulled out. Nearby, the third member of the *shōtai* suffered damage from the attentions of Jensen, Starkes, Dufilho, and Bright in brief flurries, and also from a new cast of characters, which entered stage right. From radio chatter Mach. Don Runyon's four VF-6 F4Fs learned that foxes had raided the hen house. Adroitly skirting AA bursts, they picked out several enemy planes retiring south at low altitude toward Lunga Point. Runyon tried cornering one with a high-side, but saw no effect. Torched by Howard S. Packard, AP1c (2nd Section leader), the stricken Type 99 crashed off the beach at Lunga.

Shortly after shooting at the *kanbaku,* which finally went down off Lunga, Carl Starkes tangled with Inoue and Satō (1st *Shōtai*), who worked a neat little routine against him. Whenever he attacked, the leader countered with a steep, climbing turn, while the wingman cut inside and threatened from underneath. Unable to separate the pair, Starkes fruitlessly shot off the rest of his bullets. He chased them westward past Cape Esperance and last saw them disappear over the Coral Sea.

Nakagaki and the other member of the 2nd *Shōtai* were not so lucky. Harried by F4Fs, one of them flew south over the Lunga coast and inland toward the mountains. Dufilho latched onto its tail at 50 yards. Oil thrown up from the engine obscured his windshield and compelled him to lean out of the left side of the cockpit in order to sight in his guns. Suddenly 7.7-mm slugs from the rear gunner shattered the heavy plexiglass windshield and filled the cockpit with shards, cutting Dufilho in the neck and right shoulder. He sheered off without seeing the Type 99 take any apparent damage. Packard charged the same dive bomber, but Runyon got there first with a low-opposite run. At the same time Ens. Joseph D. Shoemaker, Packard's wingman, roared in from the side. Boxed in by three F4Fs, the Type 99 dropped into a ravine about four miles south of Lunga, credit Runyon.

Like hounds chasing a fox, the CAP ran down the last member of the ill-fated 2nd *Shōtai* along the north coast of Guadalcanal. Both Bright (VF-5) and Runyon (VF-6) thought they splashed it over the channel a few miles west of Lunga, but the Japanese got away. A few minutes later Shoemaker and Ens. Harry A. March, the two VF-6 wingmen, tangled with the lone *kanbaku* out toward Savo.

Shoemaker broke right for an orthodox high-side run, but March ignored the rear gunner, bored in from astern, and felt certain *he* flamed the aircraft. Trailing all of them, Hayden Jensen of SCARLET 5 watched the four F4Fs make passes at the same target, which emitted whitish smoke as if from a broken oil line. He gradually overtook that Type 99, opened fire at 350 yards, and watched flame erupt from the bottom of its fuselage. The aircraft plowed into the water, leaving only a small amount of wreckage, including both wheels, floating on the sea.

In a spirited battle, the VF-5 and VF-6 pilots claimed fourteen dive bombers, five more than the Japanese had.[55] The 2nd Air Group survivors claimed one light cruiser set afire and another heavily damaged. They also saw two of their number succumb to fighters. Shipboard observers later confirmed this assessment with two dive bombers splashing near the destroyers. Vorse (VF-6) accounted for Iwaoka with Ōta's 3rd *Shōtai*, and VF-5 finished Tokiwa from Inoue's 1st *Shōtai*. Later at low altitude VF-5 and VF-6 fighters picked off the entire 2nd *Shōtai* of Nakagaki, PO2c Kuroda Hideichi, and PO3c Ōmoto Masaru. Inoue estimated that sixteen Grummans had overwhelmed Nakagaki. The remaining four Type 99s flew all the way to Shortland as briefed. At 1700 Ōta and Takahashi set down in the water together and swam to the nearby Type 2 flying boat. A little later the *Akitsushima* picked up Inoue and his observer, PO2c Matsui Katsu, but could not find PO3c Satō and his observer, Sea2c Norota Toshio, who ditched nearby. Thus the 2nd Air Group lost nine Type 99 carrier bombers and a dozen brave men.

THE FIGHTERS REGROUP

Dive bombers in the second strike suggested a possible nearby enemy carrier. Fletcher thought it sufficient to scout carefully the next morning, but Kinkaid advised an immediate search. Noyes felt (correctly) that the enemy planes came from a land base and only staged through the auxiliary fields at Buka or Bougainville. However, he agreed with Kinkaid's caution and diverted one SBD strike eastward away from Tulagi with negative results. He also arranged for a comprehensive search the next day.

The carriers kept on with their vital but exhausting flight operations. No flattops had ever worked so hard as the *Saratoga*, *Enterprise*, and *Wasp* did. More VF-6 warriors returned after battling the enemy at long range. From RED 3 Gay landed on the *Enterprise*, while Vince de Poix took refuge on the *Wasp*. At 1513 Howell Sumrall brought his shot-up Wildcat on board "The Big E," followed 15 minutes later by Dusty Rhodes. They knew nothing of the rest of Flight 321 except that one unidentified plane splashed and an F4F ditched.

Deke Disque and Paul Mankin made their way back from distant Santa Isabel, but got lost south of Guadalcanal. Finally around 1615 after anxious searching with fuel nearly gone, they sighted the *Sara*'s angular silhouette, but she could not take them. Disque peeled off for the *Wasp*. While still in the arresting gear, his engine died from fuel starvation. Mankin headed directly to the *Enterprise* as she started a 180-degree turn to starboard out of the wind. Reluctant to ditch with belly tank still attached, Mankin ignored Crommelin's red flag flapping from Pri-Fly. Without benefit of LSO, he cut inside her turn and touched down. According to Kinkaid watching from the flag bridge, it was "as pretty a landing as I have ever seen."[56] Mankin counted upon his brakes to stop if the arresting wires were not rigged, but they were and he thankfully snagged one. Opposite the island, he, too, ran out of fuel. Only Bauer's emphasis on fuel conservation saved the two pilots on such a long chase. An hour later the *Wasp* relaunched Disque, but de Poix stayed the night.

East of the transports, badly wounded Joe Daly of SCARLET 8 made little progress swimming south toward Guadalcanal. Three destroyers passed within a mile, but missed his frantic waving. Finally a Curtiss SOC-1 cruiser float plane on antisub patrol happened to fly overhead. Ens. John W. Baker of Observation Squadron Four (VCS-4) on the *Chicago* recognized a swimmer and set down to investigate. Wary of ambush, he pulled his .45-caliber pistol. Daly's burns darkened his face, making him look Japanese, but his joyous greeting identified him well enough. When he clambered on board the "Seagull," his left leg would not bear his weight. Shell fragments had severed a nerve, restored only after extensive treatment. Baker lifted him into the rear cockpit onto the radioman's lap and intended to set down near the *Vincennes*, the first cruiser he encountered. However, his passenger seemed stable enough to go all the way to the *Chicago*, which lifted the SOC on board at 1615.

For the most part the afternoon CAPs proceeded routinely, but not without danger. Around 1540 Monk Russell's four VF-71 F4Fs patrolled the thickening clouds over the channel. Finally over Tulagi he waggled his wings and dived against nine suspicious aircraft. Not until they started their runs did the F4Fs discover friendlies, namely VS-5 SBDs. After some difficulty the F4Fs reassembled, minus Ens. Thaddeus J. Capowski in F-13.

After the brush with the SBDs, the skies seemed totally empty, so Capowski turned south.[57] No ships hove into sight (he was too far west). When F-13 unaccountably gobbled fuel, he returned to Guadalcanal. Still west of Lunga, his engine quit at 800 feet, so he aimed for the tree line along the beach and eased between two palms. At the last instant he brought up his left arm to protect his face, but passed out when the F4F slammed into a tree. He awoke suspended upside down out of the cockpit. F-13 hung steeply inverted, its nose buried in the ground, and fuselage ripped just behind the cockpit. The impact broke four ribs and punctured his left lung. Not until almost dark could he lower himself to the ground. The crash occurred between Kokumbona and the Mantanikau River, far behind Japanese lines.

About 1630 the *Saratoga* recovered Joe Shoemaker (who fought dive bombers), Patrick Nagle, and Earl Cook from Runyon's VF-6 flight. Strangely, with sunset only 50 minutes off, she relaunched them an hour later for SCAP over Lunga. Shoemaker soon dropped out when his engine acted up and around 1800 met up with Dick Gay's VF-6 CV CAP flight about 18 miles southwest of the ships. Meanwhile, Pat Nagle and Earl Cook surprised Bob Bruning, the BLACK BASE FDO, who immediately ordered them back, but it was too late to get home before dark.

At 1830 Cook warned the *Enterprise* that Nagle, for unknown reasons, had ditched about 20 miles southeast of Guadalcanal, but he could not tell whether the pilot escaped the sinking plane. He asked the ship to "spring" him, that is, give him a direction to fly. He thought he was northeast of the task force. Hank Rowe told him to climb to 7,000 feet, as the F4F needed at least that much altitude to pick up the YE homing beacon and hopefully also register on radar. Unfortunately Cook could not tune his radio homer. Radar never had him, so Rowe instructed him to fly southwest. Noyes permitted the carriers to show deck lights, but Cook needed to be below the clouds at 4,000 feet to see them. Lookouts watched in vain. At 1915 Cook advised he had turned on his landing lights to ditch. "Letting down out of gasoline" was the last heard from F-17.[58]

Both Pat Nagle and Earl Cook set down at night on a lonely sea, and no one knew whether they even survived. A special search the next day failed to locate either man. Several aspects of their flight remain puzzling. Why less than an hour before sunset did the *Saratoga* send the F4Fs 60 miles north for SCAP? Second, why did they ditch so soon? Perhaps Nagle suffered mechanical difficulty, but Cook actually reported running out of gas less than two hours after the *Saratoga* supposedly topped off his tanks with enough juice for four hours or more. Were they indeed sent off without being refueled?

THE CASTAWAYS

As of nightfall, four fighter pilots known to have survived the day's fierce battles still had not reached safety.[59] On western Guadalcanal, Pug Southerland of VF-5 walked down from the hills toward the beach. In a deserted enemy encampment, he found a handy signaling device, the reflector of an old flashlight. Later, he waded into the water to tend his wounds. Only the right foot still troubled him badly. Soon, with his reflector and by waving his yellow Mae West, he attracted the attention of several SBDs and sent by semaphore an "SOS," followed by "Send Cruiser Scout." One pilot dropped a smoke bomb before departing. Southerland spent a "very cold and windy" night on the beach awaiting rescue.

Several miles east, Thad Capowski from VF-71 crawled 200 painful yards down to the shore. His left side felt as if it were on fire, and he was drenched with sweat. Unbuckling his pistol belt, he waded into the water to cool himself off, but when he emerged, he could not find his gun. Near midnight he noticed an armed Japanese soldier stride toward him. To his amazement the sentry never glanced down, but walked on past only 10 feet away. Capowski scooted back to the palms and stayed under cover.

More than 40 miles northwest of Guadalcanal, two pilots from VF-6 spent the night of 7-8 August trying to reach shore. Bill Warden enjoyed good weather, calm seas, and a providential current that drifted his life raft south toward the Russell Islands. He wended his way through the reefs and before first light landed on Pavuvu Island, where he decided to wait until dawn before exploring the vicinity.

Farthest away of all the downed Navy pilots, Gordon Firebaugh doggedly swam north toward the darkening coast of Santa Isabel. Slowed by wounds and burns, he divested himself of his flight suit, shoes, gun belt, and leaking Mae West. By sundown the tops of palm trees loomed far ahead, and after dark he gratefully pulled himself ashore on a sandy beach. Too exhausted to move, he dug himself into the sand, but soon regained his wind and explored the moonlit shore. His refuge was a small island. A shed with a rain gutter and barrel provided the "sweetest water" he had ever drunk, so finally he slept.

TF-62 exerted much effort to find the missing aviators. Probably warned by the SBD that sighted Southerland, Turner ordered the destroyer minesweeper *Hovey* (DMS-11) to scout "Point Santa Cruz" on Guadalcanal. She cruised only a mile offshore and sent an armed landing party ashore. Not finding anyone, the boat returned at 1725. Shortly thereafter, she received orders along with the *Southard* (DMS-10) to proceed west of Savo and north of the Russells to look for lost VF-6 pilots. The two vessels fruitlessly searched until 0822 the next morning. The afternoon of the 8th the *Southard* resumed her search, this time off Cape Esperance, but again with negative results.

SUMMARY AND UPDATE FOR 7 AUGUST

The evening of 7 August marked the end of the first day of Operation WATCH-TOWER. At 2130, Turner provided a lengthy summary of Dog-Day operations.[60] With surprising ease the Marines landed on Guadalcanal and were poised to assault the airfield, the primary objective of the whole campaign. On Tulagi and tiny Gavutu bitter fighting raged, with Tanambogo yet to be taken. However, no one doubted their swift recapture from an isolated garrison. Turner requested "maximum VF coverage and 2 VSB squadrons" for the 8th, as well as searches to seek any enemy surface forces approaching from the west. He advised, "Early morning 8th expect to send out Santa Cruz [Ndeni] occupation force less *President Jackson* [AP-37], *Wilson* [DD-408], plus *McCawley, Fuller* [AP-14], *Heywood* [AP-12], *Trever* [DMS-16], *Mugford,* some other APs later in day." This was in line with previously discussed plans to withdraw most of TF-62 on D+1.

Late that night Turner learned from Vandegrift of heavy casualties at Tulagi and Gavutu. Consequently he decided, without consulting Ghormley or Fletcher, to cancel the Ndeni occupation by turning over most of the assigned troops to the Marine commander at Tulagi. At 0217, 8 August, he radioed Ghormley and Fletcher: "Owing to reinforcements Florida area will not commence retirement *as planned*" (emphasis added).[61] Neither addressee received this message straightaway. Turner's communications were extremely poor, and this message only appears in the CinCPac message log dated 11 August.

On board the three carriers, exhausted aviators gratefully rested, while squadron support personnel labored to ready as many aircraft as possible for another punishing day of operations. During the day the flattops had conducted an amazing 704 takeoffs and 686 landings. The three VF squadrons (5, 6, and 71) sustained by far the heaviest loss: fifteen out of ninety-nine F4Fs. The enemy shot down nine; five more ditched or crashed, and another was jettisoned. Another five were badly damaged. Twelve VF pilots failed to return (ultimately six survived). Despite some rocky moments, the SCAP successfully protected TF-62. Only the *Mugford* sustained damage. Yet they took grievous losses (50 percent in one battle) for two basic reasons: poor initial positioning (below their opponents) and piecemeal commitment. Nowhere did the fighters achieve any real concentration of numbers, and the Zeros swarmed on their isolated groups. At a time when most F4F pilots experienced their first combat, they dueled the celebrated Tainan Air Group, the enemy's finest. Yet this was only Round 1 in a long, deadly slugging match for Guadalcanal.

As noted previously, the Southwest Pacific Area's suppression of Japanese air strength at Lae and Rabaul was vital to WATCHTOWER.[62] MacArthur's intelligence estimated 150 enemy aircraft were based at Vunakanau Field and 50 more at Lakunai. Maj. Gen. George C. Kenney, newly arrived commander of the SWPA Allied Air Force (soon to be designated the Fifth Air Force), hoped to plaster Vunakanau Field with up to twenty Boeing B-17E heavy bombers, the AAF's greatest concentration yet in the Southwest Pacific. Unfortunately Rabaul lay far out of fighter escort range, so the Fortresses would go in alone.

At 1220 on 7 August Lt. Col. Richard H. Carmichael led thirteen B-17s from the 19th Bombardment Group against Rabaul, but eighteen Zeros (fifteen 2nd and three Tainan) barred the way. The 19th Group attacked with great bravery, reported bombing revetments and runways, and claimed seven Zeros. Enemy fighters flamed Capt. Harl Pease's B-17, and he earned a posthumous Medal of Honor.[63] Initial strike assessments were vague, indicating only that the B-17s had bombed the airfield. The raid cost Yamada no planes, either CAP or *rikkōs* on the ground, and crews repaired the runways before Egawa returned.

Yamada prepared to renew the assault the next day. Aside from the sixteen seaplanes destroyed at Tulagi, four land attack planes, six carrier bombers, and two Zeros failed to return, and two land attack planes and three carrier bombers ditched or crash-landed. Late that afternoon the Misawa Air Group's 2nd *Chūtai* under Lt. Ikeda Hiromi (NA 65-1938) brought nine Type 1 *rikkōs* from Tinian, with the balance (eighteen) and Vice Admiral Tsukahara set to follow the next day. In a message later deciphered by Allied intelligence, Yamada reported thirty operational land attack planes available for the 8th. When Kenney learned of it, he told MacArthur his B-17s had destroyed or damaged the other hundred or so he believed were there. In his memoirs he boasted that they destroyed 75 of 150 enemy bombers parked wing tip to wing tip on Vunakanau Field. In fact, virtually no land attack planes even remained at Vunakanau; they were busy elsewhere. It was a ridiculous claim, a disservice to those who made the attack.[64]

That afternoon VAdm. Mikawa Gunichi, 8th Fleet commander, sortied with five heavy cruisers, two light cruisers, and a destroyer, bound for a night surface raid on Tulagi. If unmolested during daylight on 8 August, he could deliver his attack after midnight on the 9th.

CHAPTER 4

D plus One

Overnight on 7/8 August, Vice Admiral Fletcher's TG-61.1 steamed to its next assigned operating area 20 miles south of Cape Henslow on Guadalcanal's southeast coast. Prevailing winds again dictated easterly courses and high speeds for flight operations. Although the designated dawn launch point was 110 miles east-southeast of the previous dawn, the carriers remained well within land-based air-strike range of Rabaul. Fletcher certainly anticipated an all-out air attack. With the Marine successes, the need for ground-support flights lessened, but he still faced the vital task of protecting both his carriers and the transport force 60 to 100 miles away.[1]

The afternoon of the 7th, Rear Admiral Noyes had issued orders for the next day calling for the *Wasp* to search north toward Rabaul seeking enemy carriers and the whole *Saratoga* group to be held in reserve for possible attack. The *Enterprise,* with the help of the *Wasp,* drew the onerous task of maintaining the CV CAPs and SCAPs, quite hard without *Sara's* F4Fs. Complications arose even before Noyes could implement his plan. Concerned that evening over enemy ground resistance, Rear Admiral Turner had contacted Commander Felt, who directed the Group YOKE support flights, and requested a dawn strike against Tanambogo. Since Captain Ramsey could not contact Noyes on the *Wasp* due to radio silence, he decided to ignore orders and furnish the ground-support flight himself. Before daybreak on 8 August the *Sara* dispatched about half her air group (Felt with eighteen SBDs and nine TBFs) for Turner's mission. At the same time twelve *Wasp* SBDs searched 280 to 040 degrees to 220 miles. Forty miles north of Santa Isabel, Lt. Cdr. Ernest Snowden, VS-72 CO, splashed an Aichi E13A1 Type 0 reconnaissance seaplane [JAKE] from the heavy cruiser *Kako* with VAdm. Mikawa's force. Obviously an angry man, Snowden gunned down one crewman who had parachuted into the water.[2]

The CAPs took a little longer to deploy, but by 0800 sixteen F4Fs circled the carriers, and the same number went out on SCAP. Again violating orders, the *Saratoga* contributed four F4Fs for each duty assignment, including a flight led personally by Lt. Cdr. Leroy Simpler to check out Guadalcanal for some sign of his missing pilots. At 0800 "The Big E" launched a special search of six SBDs to look for Pat Nagle and Earl Cook lost the previous night. Both mercy missions were unfortunately negative.

Trying to man both CAP stations, RED BASE ran short of fighters. Limited fuel capacity forced frequent rotations of the CAP. At 0758 Rear Admiral Kinkaid requested permission from Noyes for eight VF-5 F4Fs on the 0830–1030 CV CAP, but Noyes swiftly disapproved and reminded Kinkaid of the orders to hold the *Sara* in reserve. By 0925 when Noyes finally discovered that she had actually launched aircraft, he was not pleased and told Ramsey to "refer conflicting request [for fighter support] to me."[3] A half hour later, RED BASE again asked Ramsey for eight fighters. Expecting Noyes's approval, at 0952 (before the *Wasp* could reply) he launched eight F4Fs for CV CAP. At 1015 that launch drew the following from an exasperated Noyes:

> Invite your attention to present situation if enemy CV should be located and I ordered your attack group launched. Your VF should also be ready for launching for actual bombing attack till noon.[4]

Certainly the *Saratoga* could not comply with the air task group commander's orders. Ramsey swiftly recalled his fighters, set about landing the SBDs and TBFs dispatched earlier that morning, and prepared a strike escorted by F4Fs fitted with belly tanks. While recovering, re-spotting, refueling, and rearming these aircraft, the *Sara* could execute no missions on demand. Evidently Ramsey felt quite strongly that no enemy carriers prowled the Solomons and did not desire his air strength tied up needlessly. His surmise, if not his actions, was proven correct at 1041 when the last of the *Wasp* search reported negative results. Ramsey strongly recommended that the chief FDO serve on the air task force flagship to eliminate such confusion as occurred on 8 August.

THE JAPANESE ATTACK

Conscious of opportunities lost on 7 August, Rear Admiral Yamada determined to strike hard and fast. Because of the many carrier aircraft his aviators said they encountered (and shot down), he judged two, possibly three enemy carriers lurked northeast or east of Tulagi. He carefully organized a comprehensive search of the whole southern Solomons and planned to hit the enemy with all available land attack planes armed with torpedoes. Monitoring the situation from Tinian, Vice Admiral Tsukahara agreed, adding that the enemy carriers must be within 150 miles of Tulagi.

By 0630, three *rikkōs* and two flying boats left on search missions. An hour later Lt. Kotani Shigeru (NA 62-1934), senior *buntaichō* of the 4th Air Group, led twenty-six Type 1 land attack planes aloft from Vunakanau. The 4th contributed seventeen Type 1s making up Kotani's 1st *Chūtai* and Lieutenant Fujita's 2nd *Chūtai*, while the 3rd *Chūtai* comprised Lieutenant Ikeda's nine Misawa Type 1s. They departed at 0800, and ten minutes later fifteen Tainan Zero fighters under Lt. Inano Kikuichi (NA 64-1937) joined up. Only two of the fifteen pilots, PO1c Yamashita Sadao and PO2c Kakimoto Enji, had flown the 7 August strike.[5] Proceeding southeast at low altitude along the Solomons chain, Kotani monitored the search radio frequency in hopes of learning where the enemy carriers operated. If within range, he would attack, but his alternate target was the invasion force off Tulagi. Soon three 4th Air Group Type 1s turned back, leaving twenty-three *rikkōs* (fourteen 4th, nine Misawa) and the fifteen Zeros.

The Allies already knew the Japanese were coming. From Pora Pora in extreme northern Bougainville (400 miles northwest of Lunga) Lt. W. J. ("Jack") Read, RANVR, guarded Buka Passage. At 0942 a large formation of enemy bombers, very low, rattled his hilltop jungle hideout. Fifteen minutes later he flashed a warning of forty large twin-engine bombers flying northwest to southeast. Relayed by another coastwatcher, the message reached Rear Admiral Crutchley's heavy cruiser *Australia* a half hour later. Turner ordered TF-62 to get underway.[6] Screened by its cruisers and destroyers, each transport squadron headed for the center of the channel to maneuver freely to evade air attacks. The *Chicago* logged Read's message at 1044. Lieutenant Bruning, BLACK BASE FDO, estimated enemy planes could reach Tulagi in about a half hour.

Five minutes after the *Chicago* was warned, so was Fletcher. At that time the fighter situation was:

	SCAP	CV CAP	On deck
VF-71	7 (Russell)	—	9 (Shands)
	8 (Rooney-en route)		
VF-6	3 (Runyon)	8 (Gay)	15 (Bauer)
VF-5	—	—	27 (Simpler)

Lieutenant Rowe, the RED BASE FDO, suggested that all available VF-5 F4Fs (twenty-seven) plus half the VF-71 F4Fs on deck leave immediately for Tulagi, while all of VF-6 plus the remaining VF-71 F4Fs fly CV CAP. At 1101 the *Enterprise* launched VF-6 skipper Lou Bauer with thirteen F4Fs for CV CAP. Finally convinced the morning search was negative, Noyes released VF-5 at 1105. Incredibly poor fleet communications so characteristic of the whole operation prevented the *Saratoga* from receiving his approval until 1135—a crucial delay for the RED BASE plan to defend the transports.

Although Bruning, the *Chicago*'s FDO, did not have the incoming raid on radar, he expected it very soon. Therefore he sent the eighteen SCAP F4Fs (fifteen VF-71, three VF-6) up to 17,000 feet to ensure altitude superiority. Yet the enemy did not show up when expected. Their fuel dwindling, the fighters waited a half hour for the Japanese to appear. At 1130 the *Wasp* reluctantly recalled her fifteen F4Fs and at 1140 scrambled Lt. Cdr. Courtney Shands with nine F4Fs to relieve them, but 30 minutes would elapse before they could arrive. Until then only Mach. Don Runyon's three VF-6 F4Fs protected the entire invasion force. To empty her flight deck, the *Wasp* sent thirteen VS-72 SBDs aloft as antitorpedo plane patrol. Fletcher and Noyes had no idea whether the Japanese would attack the carriers or the transports off Guadalcanal.

Thirty minutes ticked by before the *Saratoga* scrambled any VF-5 F4Fs for the incoming raid. In the meantime, Ramsey ordered all twenty-seven F4Fs brought up on deck. For a time confusion reigned, as the Air Department respotted all the SBDs and TBFs to free up the fighters for launch. Given the limited hangar access, this became a lengthy process. To VF-5's anger, deck crews removed belly tanks from some F4Fs, whose pilots complained to Cdr. Edgar A. Cruise, the air officer. He agreed, but the tanks had to be replaced below deck. In fighters originally assigned as escorts, radio transmitters and receivers needed to be reset from attack to CAP frequencies, but it took three or four changes for the proper settings. The pilots were even uncertain which planes to man.[7] At 1141 the *Saratoga* finally launched Simpler's eight F4Fs. John Wesolowski, the skipper's wingman, lost his belly tank on deck, but kept on anyway. Nine minutes later Chick Harmer followed with six more. RED BASE sent all fourteen fighters 70 miles north at 16,000 feet to surmount the cloud cover. Thus twenty-three *Wasp* and *Saratoga* F4Fs bustered north to reinforce Runyon's trio.

TF-62 moved out to the center of the channel at 13.5 knots, and the transports deployed by squadrons into parallel columns surrounded by the screen. To the north the YOKE Squadron escort comprised three heavy cruisers, one light cruiser (AA), and eleven destroyers, while three heavy cruisers, one light cruiser, and nine destroyers protected the X-RAY transports. Nothing as yet turned up on radar. Perhaps the enemy had turned south toward the carriers after all. At 1155 TF-62 lookouts suddenly spied to the east a gaggle of medium bombers at 2,000 feet cutting around the east tip of Florida Island.

Because the search reported no enemy carriers, Kotani continued on at slow cruise to Tulagi. Around 1050 the Kawanishi H8K1 Type 2 flying boat on the 130-degree line from Rabaul passed within a few miles of TG-61.1, but never saw it. By keeping north of the Solomons (and hoping until the last moment to learn of enemy carriers northeast of Tulagi), Kotani had inadvertently avoided radar detection when mountains on Santa Isabel and Florida shielded his advance. As the strike charged west toward the YOKE Group, Lt. Yamashita Jōji (NA 66-1938) raced ahead with five 2nd *Chūtai* Zeros for air control duty. Kotani's twenty-three land attack planes nosed down toward the water. His 1st *Chūtai* (seven *rikkōs*) was in the center. Fujita's seven fanned out southward with five 3rd *Chūtai* Zeros under Lt. (jg) Hayashitani Tadashi (NA 67-1939). Ikeda's nine Misawa Type 1s opened out to the north, protected by Inano's five Tainan fighters.

The YOKE Squadron cut loose with heavy AA fire at torpedo bombers now skimming above the waves at between 150 feet and 10 feet. To the southwest, Turner's flagship *McCawley* led the X-RAY Squadron into two 30-degree turns away from the incoming Japanese. In their four divisional columns steaming abreast, the ships resembled a school of fish, but they possessed a strong bite. Bunches of black shell bursts and bright red lines of tracers seemingly disoriented the humped-back Mitsubishis (so appearing because of bomb-bay doors removed to accommodate torpedoes). According to eyewitnesses, "the fire of all these ships was so extensive and of such volume that the Japanese pilots showed utter confusion and state of mind and reacted accordingly."[8]

In response to the fire, Kotani swung the whole force south away from the YOKE ships to take on the X-RAY Squadron. The three *chūtais* broke formation so the *shōtai* leaders could select individual ship targets. Gunfire, which included the cruiser eight-inchers, dropped one *rikkō* after another. Some foolhardy Japanese actually flew among and hopped over the ships or maintained highly vulnerable parallel courses. Few aircraft ever released torpedoes, and at least eight crashed in flames. Apparently only three Type 1s, probably from Kotani's 1st *Chūtai*, passed entirely through the X-RAY Squadron, and screening ships claimed two of them before they could get away. Ikeda's 3rd (Misawa) *Chūtai* maneuvered north and Fujita's 2nd south outside the formations. One flaming Mitsubishi barely missed the stern of the *Vincennes*, while another barged through the rigging of the transport *Barnett* (AP-11) before splashing alongside. At 1202, a Type 1 plowed into the boat deck abaft the stack of the *George F. Elliott* (AP-13) and set her afire. Only the hapless destroyer *Jarvis* (DD-393) took a "fish," which struck her forward on the starboard side.

After bombing tiny Mbangi Island in Tulagi harbor, John Eldridge's 1st Division of six VS-71 SBDs withdrew southeast at low altitude. Above at 3,000 feet, about a half dozen aircraft approached from the northeast. He supposed them *Enterprise* SBDs, but they were bandits: Yamashita's five Tainan Zeros. The lead *shōtai* never saw enemy planes and kept going west, but PO1c Ōki Yoshio and PO3c Kimura Yutaka bounced the 1st Section of Eldridge's 2nd Division under Lt. Porter W. Maxwell. In a fight much like Sasai's on the previous day, the two Zeros flashed through several runs without causing any damage, held at length by tracers from the three SBD radiomen.

Meanwhile, Lt. (jg) Robert L. Howard, 2nd Section leader of VS-71's 2nd Division, glimpsed the Misawa land attack planes skirt south around Group YOKE.[9] Oblivious to AA fire, he worked out an attack on one bomber, but his two .50s would not shoot. After pulling off to clear them, he sheepishly realized that in his excitement he had never charged them. After beating up Maxwell's section, Ōki and Kimura latched onto Howard's lone SBD. Lawrence P. Lupo, Sea2c, the radioman, responded enthusiastically to a series of four stern attacks. At last Kimura reefed in a tight climbing turn for a head-on approach, but Howard raked his Zero with a strong burst. Catching fire as it went past, the Mitsubishi fell off to the left and plowed into the water among some small boats near Florida. Ōki saw his wingman go down, then raced up Howard's tail to duel with Lupo at close range. Not only did Lupo drive off the Zero, but he perforated his own vertical stabilizer as well. 71-S-15 returned to base sporting ten bullet holes, including two in the right main fuel tank, but neither Howard nor Lupo was hurt. Ōki claimed three SBDs for the *shōtai*.

The second air battle broke out in the center of Sealark Channel, where three VF-6 F4Fs circled 17,000 feet over the X-RAY Squadron. From radio chatter Don Runyon learned of torpedo planes at low level and rolled into a high-speed dive. On the way down he spotted several medium bombers ("Type 97s") retiring westward after runs against the southern flank of the X-RAY Squadron. Making a respectable 200 knots, five Type 1s from Fujita's 2nd *Chūtai* dipped as low as 20 feet. At 1205, Runyon's shallow side attack missed against one *rikkō*, but from astern wingman Will Rouse evaded tracers from the 20-mm tail stinger and flamed the Mitsubishi. After his first pass, Runyon maneuvered head-on against a second Type 1, concentrated his bullets in the vulnerable engines and cockpit, and shot it down.

Pressing his luck with another scary attack up the tail of a third land attack plane, Rouse also set this target ablaze. From ashore at Lunga, correspondent Richard Tregaskis witnessed its end:

> Our fighter planes dived into the foray. I saw one of them rout a Jap plane out of the fracas and chase it fiercely, with the Jap apparently in panicky flight toward the western tip of Guadalcanal. I heard the popping and rattling of the American's machine guns, continuing for seconds on end, and suddenly the Jap began to trail smoke. Then fire came at the root of the smoke plume, and the plane, falling, traced a gorgeous, steadily brightening curve across the sky. I watched, fascinated, while the plane arched into the water, and the slow white fountain of a great splash rose behind it, and then the white turned into brilliant orange as the plane exploded and sent a sheet of flame backfiring a hundred feet into the sky.[10]

Covering Fujita's Type 1s, Lieutenant (jg) Hayashitani's 3rd *Chūtai* Zeros had split up when his wingmen PO2c Suzuki Masanosuke and PO3c Arai Masami chased two Curtiss SOC cruiser float planes over Lunga. Later they strafed small boats off the beach. The inexperienced Hayashitani, who only completed operational training in late June, ran into real opposition. He jumped Rouse's F4F after the third bomber went down, but teammate "Dutch" Shoemaker distracted him. Hayashitani rolled out of the way, only to fall to the alert Runyon's swift head-on attack. Spec. Duty Ens. Yamakawa Noboru and PO2c Ichiki Toshiyuki from the 2nd *Shōtai* sparred with one F4F, claimed as an unconfirmed kill by Yamakawa.

Meanwhile, Shoemaker added to the score by splashing a fourth bomber with a side attack. The VF-6 pilots noticed another *rikkō* escape to the west.

In the short action off Lunga, the three F4Fs of *Enterprise* Flight 309 dispatched four Type 1s from the 4th Air Group and one Tainan Zero. Rouse accounted for two bombers, Runyon one bomber and one fighter, and one bomber fell to Shoemaker. From the 2nd *Chūtai* only PO2c Hatakeyama Hikafusa's *rikkō* remained. His crew had watched Grummans gun down all three planes from the 2nd *Shōtai*: Res. Ens. Sasaki Takafumi, PO1c Kaneko Shōji, and PO1c Imai Shōichi.[11]

The entire attack lasted only 10 minutes, and the scattered Japanese survivors fled west at high speed. At 1345 some passed over Vice Admiral Mikawa's cruiser force off Choiseul Island southeast of Bougainville and received waves of encouragement. The 5th Air Attack Force was shocked at how few Type 1s turned up. Of the twenty-three that reached the target, no fewer than seventeen (eleven 4th Air Group, six Misawa) went down, most from Turner's remarkably effective AA fire. All five surviving *rikkōs* (three 4th Air Group, two Misawa) were badly shot up, and one other Misawa aircraft had crashed. Besides the eighteen *rikkōs*, the mission cost 125 bomber crewmen dead or missing, including all the officers: the heaviest single loss of land attack planes during the whole Guadalcanal campaign.

Those who returned bore tales of incredible success: four large cruisers, three light cruisers, two destroyers, and three transports sunk, and severe damage to a

Mach. Don Runyon, Howard Packard, AP1c, Ens. Joe Shoemaker, and Ens. Will Rouse (*l to r*) of VF-6 stand in front of F-31 (BuNo. 5126), 10 Aug. 1942. (NA 80-G-11092)

Ditched Type 1 land attack plane alongside the *Bagley*, 8 Aug. 1942. Japanese crewmen had fired their pistols at the destroyer before being killed. (NA 80-G-K303)

large cruiser, a destroyer, and six transports. Yamada himself reduced this hysterical tally to one CA, one DD, and nine APs sunk, three CLs and two unknown ships badly damaged—still far wide of the mark. In fact the strike severely damaged one transport (which later sank) and one destroyer. The 4th Air Group claimed four of ten enemy fighters. Seven Tainan Zero pilots tallied three SBD carrier bombers (two shared) and one unconfirmed Grumman, for the loss of Hayashitani and Kimura. PO1c Ōki's fighter took slight damage.

Several wrecked, half-sunken bombers floated near the X-RAY Squadron, whose destroyers steamed over to investigate. Nearing a tailless Type 1, the *Bagley* (DD-386) noticed its crew sitting on the wing, who opened fire with pistols, then turned the weapons on themselves. Because of severe wounds and shock, other Japanese aviators proved more amenable to being taken prisoner. The *Blue* (DD-387) picked up four, the *Selfridge* and *Mugford* two each, and DMS *Trevor* another.

DECISION TO WITHDRAW

While Turner's TF-62 so handsomely repulsed the enemy air attack, the carriers sent help and solidified their own defense. At 1202 the *Saratoga* requested permission to launch all remaining VF-5 F4Fs to help BLACK BASE. Spurred on by a voice message reporting forty attacking torpedo planes, Noyes swiftly agreed. All twenty-five operational VF-5 fighters raced toward Tulagi, but would be too late to catch the enemy. They saw one transport ablaze, a tincan in obvious distress, two ditched bombers still afloat, and numerous oily patches burning on the water, the pyres of enemy planes. Still greatly concerned, Noyes reinforced the CV CAP, so by 1234 TG-61.1 wielded thirty-four F4Fs on CV CAP, thirty-four F4Fs on SCAP, three (Runyon's flight) returning from SCAP, and four still on board the *Enterprise*. Everyone waited to see if the Japanese would find the carriers. At 1249 Runyon's three F4Fs landed on board "The Big E" and reported what happened to the transport force.

By 1315 it began to look as if the Japanese might not come after all. Since the CAP fighters simply could not stay aloft very long, Rowe suggested that the *Wasp* recall all of her F4Fs (VF-71 lacked belly tanks), while the other two carriers maintain six F4Fs on CV CAP and six on SCAP, and land the rest for refueling. After a great deal of re-spotting of SBDs and TBFs, the *Sara* took on board Richardson's eleven fighters at 1328, and 45 minutes later cleared her deck by launching thirty-one SBDs and five TBFs as IAP. With her one effective elevator, the old warrior just could not conduct flight operations as swiftly as her more modern counterparts. To free her deck for fighters, the *Enterprise* sent nine SBDs aloft and also dispatched fourteen TBFs to search 270 to 090 degrees, 260 miles westward and 220 miles east. By 1406 the *Wasp* had landed all twenty-four F4Fs.

Only VF-5 had trouble coming back. Wesolowski's lost belly tank forced him to take refuge on the *Wasp*. At 1505 four of Harmer's six SCARLET 4 F4Fs landed, but the *Sara* unexpectedly displayed the red flag halting recovery. Low on gas, Lt. Howard Crews and Ens. Foster Blair did not care for the frantic wave-offs. The ship soon recanted and recovered Crews, but again turned out of the wind before the startled Blair could follow. At 1526 his tanks ran dry, and he flopped into the sea. The destroyer *MacDonough* (DD-351) soon rescued him unhurt but quite angry. An SBD pilot wisecracked on the radio, "How do you want us to make these water landings, by sections or divisions?"[12] A half hour later the *MacDonough* transferred Blair by breeches buoy back to the *Sara*, where he let all and sundry know of his displeasure. Finally on the afternoon of 11 August, "Bat" Cruise, the air officer, poked his head into the VF-5 ready room and apologized to Crud by saying, "Sorry, I miscounted."[13]

Specific details regarding the enemy torpedo attack slowly filtered through TG-61.1. As was typical, the *Saratoga* did not receive Kinkaid's 1316 summary of Runyon's debriefing until 1510. In the meantime, Fletcher queried his commanders about the forty enemy bombers reported at Tulagi: "Were planes actually carrying torpedoes?"[14] He soon learned affirmative. At this point he did not know how badly hurt was the enemy, but only that on two succeeding days they struck hard and far from their base, despite MacArthur's vaunted air interdiction of Rabaul.

The long-held fears of enemy air power seemed confirmed. Notwithstanding brave bomber crews, MacArthur obviously accomplished little against Rabaul. Fortunately the Japanese had not found TG-61.1, but Fletcher could not count on that not happening. During the last two days his fighters had taken quite a beating, with combat and operational losses totaling sixteen destroyed and five others badly damaged and not immediately flyable. Short of returning to Pearl Harbor, the prospects of replacing pilots and aircraft were nil. Even there few fighter replacements could be found. Not having received Turner's message from the previous night canceling the withdrawal of the transports, Fletcher had every reason to believe Turner would pull out most of TG-61.2 that evening as previously planned. He considered the various factors involved in protecting the cargo ships and the Screening Group from air attack and obviously thought the risk to the carriers overshadowed everything else. They must be preserved to deal with the enemy carriers soon expected from Japan.[15]

Consequently Fletcher decided to seek ComSoPac permission to withdraw one day early, rather than staying to D+2 (9 August) as he stated at the Koro conference.[16] At 1525, he queried Noyes, who was in tactical command:

> In view of possibility of torpedo plane attack and reduction of our fighter strength I intend to recommend immediate withdrawal of carriers. Do you agree? In case we continue present operation I believe same area should be used tomorrow. What do you think?

Noyes replied, "Affirmative to both questions,"[17] so Fletcher advised Ghormley and Turner at 1807:

> Total fighter strength reduced from 99 to 78. In view of large number of enemy torpedo and bomber planes in area, recommend immediate withdrawal of carriers. Request you send tankers immediately to rendezvous decided by you as fuel running low.[18]

Fletcher added the part about fueling because both of his task group commanders had emphasized that oil was a problem. While awaiting Ghormley's decision, Fletcher headed southeast on 140 degrees, speed 15 knots, but would remain in the waters west of San Cristobal until he learned what he would be doing on the 9th.

A report from one of MacArthur's search planes, logged on the *Saratoga* about 1845, noted three enemy cruisers, three destroyers, and two seaplane tenders or gunboats in the central Solomons and on course for Guadalcanal. They did not seem to be anything Crutchley's Screening Group could not handle. At any rate sundown prevented the carriers from loosing any kind of strike. At 2140 the *Enterprise* reported her afternoon search spotted no enemy ships, but apparently the enemy had not continued south. Actually one VT-3 TBF passed within 30 miles of Mikawa's cruiser force over the horizon. At 2330, TG-61.1 changed course to 230 degrees, and 90 minutes later came right to 320 degrees bound for the previous day's operating area. This would enable Fletcher to support TF-62 for the final day should Ghormley decline his request. At 0330, 9 August, Fletcher was awakened to the word that ComSoPac set a fueling rendezvous for the 10th and approved retiring the carriers. At 0430 TG-61.1 resumed course 140 degrees. Hearing of no real difficulties, Fletcher expected that most of the transports had safely pulled out that evening.[19]

In reality, things were anything but safe for Turner's TF-62. He had not withdrawn *any* of his ships. Overnight he had learned that unloading of supplies had not proceeded well. After regrouping from the noon air attack, the transports did not resume unloading supplies until about 1700. A little over an hour later, Turner received as an informational addressee Fletcher's message asking Ghormley's permission to withdraw the carriers one day early. He was surprised, angry, and unprepared, although he had continually advised Fletcher that the transports would be departing on D+1. Word of the approaching enemy cruisers, destroyers, and supposed seaplane tenders did not worry him unduly, as he thought them bound for Rekata Bay on Santa Isabel to set up a seaplane base. He requested Rear Admiral McCain's B-17s to bomb Rekata the next day. Of far more concern was the lack of fighter support on 9 August to protect his ships from expected enemy air attack. He (but not Fletcher) knew the landing of supplies had turned into a fiasco, that the transports, as well as the cargo ships, had not unloaded all the supplies or even disembarked all the troops.[20]

At 2045 Turner called an immediate conference of senior commanders on board the *McCawley*. Crutchley rode over on his flagship *Australia,* thus weakening the cruiser covering force. Before Turner, Crutchley, and Vandegrift adjourned near to midnight, they reluctantly decided that the transports should depart beginning 0630 the next day. Obviously the Marines felt abandoned. They had expected the unloading would proceed until D+4 (11 August), with air cover for that whole time. The problem arose from unexpected difficulty in unloading supplies, for which Turner and Vandegrift, but not Fletcher, were ultimately responsible. At 0105, 9 August, Turner radioed Fletcher: "Absence air support require me to withdraw all ships tomorrow temporarily from this area to avoid unwarranted loss." Like so many other of Turner's messages gone astray because of abominable communications, Fletcher did not receive it straightaway. The *Wasp* copied only a garbled version, and not until 1009, 9 August, did she forward it to the flagship.[21]

At about 0145 that same day, Mikawa's eight warships tore into the Screening Group deployed on both sides of Savo Island and within an hour left four Allied heavy cruisers sinking. The heavy cruiser *Chicago* and one destroyer sustained severe damage. Despite the presence of Allied radar, the Japanese showed themselves far superior in night combat. Their gunfire and especially their "Long Lance" torpedoes were deadly. In return, Mikawa's ships received only slight damage. Fearing carrier air attack after dawn, he did not press eastward against the transports, but instead shaped course for home, running at 30 knots back up the central Solomon waters soon dubbed "The Slot." The Battle of Savo Island resulted in a stunning, bitter Allied defeat.

One fighter pilot who reluctantly experienced the battle at first hand was VF-5's Joe Daly, burned on 7 August and rescued by the *Chicago*'s cruiser float plane. He awoke on the 8th to discover his lips were "greatly swollen, so that I had to drink my meals through a tube, and my eyes were so puffed up and stuck together that I couldn't see."[22] That day, with the *Chicago* securely buttoned up under air attack, he realized how easily he could be trapped should she sustain any real damage. Early the next morning came the surprise clanging of general quarters and the sound of battle. The *Chicago* took one devastating torpedo in the bow and several large shells, fortunately none near sickbay. She remained afloat. Daly often wondered what would have happened if he chanced to be on board one of the other four heavy cruisers, all of which sank. As a squadronmate commented, "Sometimes even being rescued can be dangerous."[23]

Word of the night battle off Savo filtered only sporadically to TG-61.1. Radio communications remained inexplicably poor, but neither did Turner report his difficulties in timely fashion. Kinkaid later wrote that TF-61 was "completely uninformed regarding surface actions in Iron Bottom Sound during their progress."[24] Around 0300 the *Enterprise* monitored a so-called flash report indicating something amiss. However, Kinkaid assumed Fletcher knew of the report and would act if warranted. The *Wasp* also intercepted some sort of message. Three times Captain Sherman asked permission of Noyes to run northwest at high speed and launch a predawn strike at the enemy force engaging Turner. Privy to Ghormley's consent to withdraw the carriers, Noyes felt the reasons had not altered and denied the request.[25] Yet Fletcher and the *Sara* remained ignorant of the action off Guadalcanal until 0500 or later on the 9th.[26]

After dawn, TG-61.1 proceeded with scheduled air operations. At 0500 the *Saratoga,* the duty carrier, launched eight SBDs for a search astern to 175 miles, which took some of them back over the Guadalcanal area. Other than spotting the damaged destroyer *Jarvis* limping around the island's west tip, the search proved negative. At 0612 the *Enterprise* sent two SBDs to Guadalcanal to drop aerial photographs for 1st MarDiv headquarters. While circling Lunga Point, they copied a message from an exasperated Turner, who had already postponed to late afternoon the withdrawal of his transports in order to land more vital supplies for the Marines: "Appreciate knowing Admiral Fletcher's plan by message drop."[27] At 0839 the *Wasp* passed this transmission on to the flagship. Like the *Sara*'s search, the returning *Enterprise* SBDs reported nothing unusual in Guadalcanal waters.

Later that morning the *Saratoga* monitored messages from coastwatchers on Bougainville reporting enemy planes bound for Guadalcanal. Lt. Nakamura Tomoo (NA 59-1931), *hikōtaichō* of the Misawa Air Group, led seventeen Type 1 land attack planes and fifteen Zero fighters in search of the American carriers. He did not find them, but settled for the unfortunate *Jarvis,* thought to be a light cruiser. The wounded destroyer put up a gallant fight, shot down two bombers, and crippled a third before sinking with all hands.

At 1114 Fletcher reassumed tactical command of the carriers and instructed Noyes to "double CAP and stand by for enemy attack." He finally received Turner's 0841:

> Unable to depart as planned because insufficient supplies have been landed. Request cover for attack on enemy surface force this area.[28]

Wasp plane handlers park VF-71 F4Fs on deck, 9 Aug. 1942. In the foreground is F-2 (BuNo. 5031), wrecked in an accident in mid-August. (NA 80-G-14027)

From several confused messages, Fletcher now realized something bad had befallen Turner, but he still lacked details. At 1150 he consulted ComSoPac:

> Am receiving despatches from Turner describing losses in cruisers in engagement
> which continues to westward. Are you receiving them?[29]

Actually things were very unusual at Guadalcanal. Crutchley's Screening Group
regrouped after terrific losses, while Turner's transports, still laden with vital
supplies and nearly 1,400 Marines, prepared to depart that afternoon. The 1st
MarDiv was on its own, at least for the time being.

Fletcher considered turning back to Guadalcanal to support Turner, but realized that by this time any Japanese ships had long withdrawn far up the Slot.
Pursuit meant the danger of a major air strike from Rabaul. He correctly guessed
a Japanese strike group sought his carriers. Also he worried about the high-speed
operations any protracted pursuit would entail, as fuel was becoming a severe
problem. At 1515 he radioed Ghormley a summary of Turner's fragmentary messages and added, "Movements require protection which I am unable to provide.
Direct Turner to make report directly to you, info to me."[30] Under the circumstances it is questionable whether Fletcher was ever able to exercise command as
the overall expeditionary commander.

That evening Ghormley ordered Fletcher to provide Turner with such air
cover as practicable without interfering with the refueling. He also informed
Pearl that the carriers were "short of fuel," but said nothing about the danger of
air attack or the heavy losses in fighters—important omissions that would subsequently cause Fletcher much trouble. Ghormley still had not established direct
contact with Turner, but summarized some of his messages. He noted all ships
would retire "until such time as I have shore based aircraft in such strength that I
can protect my line of communication to Guadalcanal and supply Guadalcanal
with sufficient aviation for effective defense."[31]

Fletcher's recommendation to withdraw his carriers from Guadalcanal waters
to protect them from land-based air attack and submarines remains that embattled admiral's most controversial decision. Turner, the Marines, and virtually
every historian, commentator, and journalist who has written of Guadalcanal
have condemned the move.[32] They accuse Fletcher of literally abandoning the
1st MarDiv to an uncertain fate, as if he ran all the way to San Francisco rather
than temporarily withdrawing southeast into safer waters. RAdm. Samuel Eliot
Morison downplayed the risks of air and submarine attacks and quipped that had
Fletcher stayed just south of Guadalcanal on 9 August, he would at most have
suffered "sunburn."[33] Virtually none of the commentators noted Turner's constant plans to pull out the transports and most of the Screening Group on D+1,
upon which Fletcher based his own plans, or Fletcher's failure to receive the
crucial message early on 8 August announcing that Turner had altered his intention to leave.

Interestingly, many of Fletcher's fellow carrier commanders agreed, at least in
principle, with his desire to retire the carriers from Guadalcanal waters as soon
as possible after the landings. Both Noyes and Kinkaid concurred with the need
to withdraw.[34] In September 1942, after being relieved of his command Fletcher
wrote a lengthy letter to Admiral Nimitz elucidating a number of lessons and
opinions regarding carrier combat. He stressed the necessity of not risking the
carriers by tying them to the defense of specific points. The key question was the
necessity for land-based aviation to take over that defense.[35] On 9 October Vice
Admiral Halsey concurred and added:

Land plane bases and the operating units thereon should be available in supporting positions *before* the operation is undertaken at all. It is only by this provision in advance that the risking of carriers in restricted covering positions can be avoided.[36]

In January 1943 Halsey commented further on the same question:

While overcaution is to be avoided, it should still be borne in mind that Midway remains the classic example of what can happen to a large powerful invasion force bent on carrying out its mission without benefit of land based air support.[37]

Adding to the righteous indignation over Fletcher is the defeat at Savo Island. His critics cannot overtly blame the surprise on him, for if he did not appreciate the threat posed by Mikawa, neither did Turner. From the benefit of hindsight, they see no reason why he could not have pursued Mikawa and at least revenged Savo. Fletcher's own point of view on this matter appeared in his preliminary report on 9 September 1942:

With the [carrier] task forces in the position they would have been, had they remained in this area [southeast of Guadalcanal], and with sufficient fuel available to operate independently at high speed, it is barely possible that with definite information the enemy might have been located after conducting a search the next morning. However, an attack force would have had to be launched from a minimum distance of 200 miles, and with the carriers in a position much further to the northwest than they would be expected to operate.[38]

The critics also stress Fletcher's supposedly characteristic obsession over fuel. They gleefully compute the number of barrels of fuel oil on hand to decide that TF-61 faced no fuel crisis at all, hence no need to pull out. Of course they ignore the fact that Fletcher himself never had the luxury of counting every barrel in every ship, but perforce took the word of his subordinates. That there was serious worry over fuel cannot, however, be doubted, for Noyes, Kinkaid, and ship captains from TF-11 warned that high-speed spurts due to low wind conditions cost the escorts much more fuel than previously estimated. Later, in assessing the battle, Nimitz wondered if it would have been possible to withdraw and fuel just one of the three carrier groups at a time and retain the other two to provide the requisite air support. The idea had occurred to Fletcher, but he rejected it because the other two carrier task group commanders had both reported grave shortages of fuel.[39]

In fact, Fletcher's principal concern was preserving his carrier strength, both decks and aircraft, until he confronted the Japanese carriers that he knew would surely hurry southward from home waters.[40] His carriers, incredibly valuable strategic assets, comprised the only force that could deal with their enemy counterparts. This was just the beginning of what Fletcher felt would be a long, bloody campaign to hold Guadalcanal. Aside from the *Hornet* in reserve at Pearl, no additional fleet carriers joined the Pacific Fleet until at least late spring 1943. Without the carriers and their aircraft, which Fletcher has been accused of overprotecting, the Japanese would certainly have recaptured Guadalcanal.

FOUR FIGHTER PILOTS SURVIVE

Now that the carriers have left Guadalcanal waters for a time, it is appropriate to resume chronicling the individual experiences of the four fighter pilots, who had ditched, crashed, or parachuted behind enemy lines on 7 August. As with the 1st

MarDiv marooned at Guadalcanal and Tulagi, their immediate survival depended on their own ingenuity.[41]

At dawn on 8 August, Pug Southerland of VF-5 limped eastward along the coast toward Lunga Point. After passing through several unoccupied villages, he discovered a seemingly more practical mode of transportation, a large canoe. The leaky old vessel swiftly filled with water and forced his return to the beach. Around noon, while scouting the abandoned village of Ruijo and its small Catholic chapel, Southerland encountered two Guadalcanalese. Pidgin English revealed their names as Jonas and Joseph. A native of Malaita, Jonas was a servant of Australian coastwatcher SubLt. F. Ashton ("Snowy") Rhoades, RANVR.[42] While parleying, the three witnessed the Japanese air attack against the X-RAY Squadron, a marvelous spectacle, but not to the natives. They retraced their steps west to Mamara village, where Southerland ate and relaxed while his hosts took good care of him. After midnight on the 9th, Southerland and the villagers heard the rolling thunder of distant naval gunfire, and dawn revealed that the cruisers and destroyers had pulled out. The two natives now hesitated to risk a trip to Kukum. Southerland spent the day resting while the inhabitants dropped in to meet him. All were quite friendly, with one exception: an ancient, white-haired man who upon leaving muttered something like, "Used to eat white man, now don't [know] what to do."[43]

At dawn on 10 August Southerland, Jonas, and two others paddled east in a large canoe past a Japanese camp near the mouth of the Mantanikau River and soon reached their goal. A party of soldiers in green fatigues accosted them, leading Southerland for the moment to fear they were the enemy, but he soon recognized Marines. Col. Leroy Hunt of the 5th Marines was happy to meet Jonas and his friends. Off Point Santa Cruz Japanese machine-gun bullets holed the canoe carrying Jonas and his party, and they were captured. Jonas quickly managed to escape. On 12 August Southerland went out in a Catalina PBY-5A amphibian, the first plane to land at Lunga airfield.

Thad Capowski from VF-71 made his own way back unaided. At dawn on 8 August he found he could walk short distances if he braced his chest with his arms. Hampered by injuries, he spent the day moving slowly eastward, evading enemy troops despite more close encounters. After crossing a shallow stream he ran into a coral reef fringing the coast, which meant hard going, but Japanese lurked inland. That evening he reached a cove just west of Point Cruz. Nearby was the Japanese camp complete with fence and lookout posts. Capowski fashioned a raft of branches to cross the mouth of the lagoon, but it would not float. Dejected, he curled up in a ball and endured a rainstorm.

Like Southerland, Capowski was startled after midnight by the sound of what he thought was distant thunder but was actually naval gunfire. At dawn he watched the enemy encampment, as about 100 men from the guard detachment and 300-odd more from the two dispersed naval construction battalions lined up for the morning roll call.[44] An hour later the lagoon area was totally bereft of enemy troops, so he chanced crossing the outside fringe of coral and sand and swam the mouth of the cove. Ahead was a wide, sandy beach, not good for concealment, but the sight of ships ahead off Lunga Point cheered him. The Japanese, too, marched eastward, but fortunately on inland trails. Expecting Mikawa's victorious ships to assault the Allied beachhead, Capt. Monzen Kanae advanced eastward to strike the American flank and support the landings. When he discovered Allied, not Japanese, ships off shore, he called off the "attack," and his troops dejectedly stumbled back to their stronghold west of the Mantanikau River.

In the meantime, Capowski worked his way across the sandbars off the mouth of the Mantanikau River. It was nerve-wracking to walk out on the exposed beach, but he stayed as close to the water's edge as he could and missed detection by enemy troops retreating under the trees. To his right he glimpsed some movement in a grove of palms and waded into the water. A figure dressed in green like the others he had seen motioned for him to come out. He thought the "Japanese" would finish him off, but one said, "What outfit are you from, buddy?" Capowski could not talk. Exhausted and confused, he still thought he was about to die. Finally one man handed him a bottle of soda water, and he realized they were U.S. Marines. An officer asked him if he had seen the enemy, and he described the Japanese camp. The patrol took him to the first-aid post at Kukum. Thad Capowski spent five more days in the hospital, then on 15 August left on a destroyer transport to convalesce at Noumea.

The morning of 8 August Gordon Firebaugh of VF-6 awoke on small Eugene Island, inhabited only by cattle. Point Mufu on Santa Isabel proper lay four miles away. He spent the day gathering materials to make a raft, including wood from a small lean-to and shed. That night he also watched the distant spectacle off Savo. The next morning he floated across the channel to north of Point Mufu and started walking north along the beach, when two natives appeared. One spoke English and introduced himself as Silas. They escorted Firebaugh to their village and treated him hospitably.

A stranger's presence on Santa Isabel was already known to the only coastwatcher left there. A runner in an Australian bush hat brought a note:

> To the aviator shot down. Whether you be ally or otherwise, report to me immediately.
>
> Geoffrey Kuper
> Base Defence Officer, Santa Isabel.

Firebaugh felt unable to walk the four hours the man said it would take to reach the coastwatcher's location. With a pencil thoughtfully provided by the messenger, he scribbled on the note, "I am unable to travel," and signed his name, rank, serial number, and branch of service. Kuper arrived that afternoon, a personable, good-looking man whom Firebaugh "liked immediately." The son of a German planter and a Malaitan woman, he had trained as a native medical practitioner. A large dugout canoe delivered Firebaugh to his vessel, the schooner *Joan,* hidden in a stream up the coast. There he met Kuper's pretty young wife Linda and relaxed a bit. Very curious about the United States, she enjoyed asking him questions about home.

The morning of 10 August Kuper radioed the coastwatcher on Florida Island of Firebaugh's rescue and asked for a seaplane to pick up his guest. That was not feasible, so Kuper decided to take the pilot to Tulagi himself. For the next three days Firebaugh tended his burns, while Kuper prepared for the hazardous voyage. The evening of the 14th, the *Joan* worked her way downriver and southeast along the west coast of Santa Isabel. She ran aground numerous times. A Chinese friend brought a small chicken for the cook pot, but as Firebaugh wrote, "our tough little rooster contributed little more than flavor to our dinner." At a village near the southern tip of the island, they loaded fuel, then started across Indispensable Strait toward Florida.

At dawn on 16 August, with the *Joan* still west of Florida, a B-17 heavy bomber buzzed the suspicious little vessel that flew no flag. Firebaugh hurriedly semaphored "US Navy, US Navy." Soon a Navy Higgins boat arrived to escort her into Tulagi harbor, where they were greeted warmly by the Marines, including Brig. Gen. William Rupertus. Firebaugh was safe, but his wrenched back prevented a speedy recovery from his wounds and injuries. That afternoon he bade farewell to the Kupers, who returned to Santa Isabel. Much later he wrote, "Other than my genuine thanks there was nothing I could do for this daring and courageous Coastwatcher and tears filled my eyes as he departed, just as they do now." It was a sentiment echoed later by numerous other Allied aviators whom Kuper rescued during the Solomons Campaign.[45]

Fellow VF-6 pilot Bill Warden needed almost two months to report back. He also enjoyed the help of coastwatchers. The morning of 8 August he brought his rubber boat ashore on the Russell Islands about 35 miles northwest of Guadalcanal. No one was home; at least none of the natives made their presence known to him. He spent six days checking out the two main islands, Pavuvu and Banika, and found water in an abandoned plantation house. Tiring of his emergency rations and coconuts, Warden set out on 14 August to row his raft east toward Guadalcanal. By evening he drew within sight of shore and later that night landed at Nugu Point near the northwest tip. Reassured that he was an American because of a star stitched on his raft, friendly natives took him to a village on Tiaro Bay. The next day he met coastwatcher Leif Schroeder, who had come down from Savo. While walking to an inland hideout, Warden fell and badly injured his right arm, so Schroeder brought him to a cave occupied by fellow coastwatcher "Snowy" Rhoades.

Worried about Warden's arm, Rhoades sent word to Father Emery de Klerk, a Dutch missionary priest whose station lay south at Tangere on Beaufort Bay. On 21 August he arrived, treated the injured limb, and took Warden back to Tangere to join missionaries fleeing the Japanese-occupied villages on the north and west coasts. Father de Klerk arranged for their evacuation. On 8 September he set out with Warden and eleven natives over a rugged trail heading northeast across Guadalcanal. After traversing extremely rough terrain, on 11 September the party reached Nala village high in the mountainous center of the island for a distant view of the Battle of the Ridge.

Crossing enemy lines to the north coast proved impossible, so the party trekked north to a camp on "Gold Ridge." There de Klerk left Warden with Lt. Donald S. Macfarlan and SubLt. Ken Hay (both RANVR) and returned to Tangere to see to his refugees. They arranged on 1 October for a group of native police to take Warden to the American perimeter. After an arduous two-day march, the party reached the coast east of Marine lines, where a Higgins boat conveyed them to Lunga. On 4 October, Bill Warden reached Espiritu Santo by R4D transport plane. The last orphan of 7 August had returned.

CHAPTER 5

The Waiting Game

THE CARRIERS REFUEL

Through 9 August and into the next afternoon, Vice Admiral Fletcher's TG-61.1 with the three carriers steamed south looking to fuel southwest of Espiritu Santo. He expected fueling would take three or four days. The carrier aviators welcomed the rest. Constant flight operations on 7, 8, and 9 August brought near exhaustion. On the 10th some pilots enjoyed their first full meal in four days. The squadrons used the respite to repair aircraft affected by the wear and tear of the past several days. The heavy ships completed fueling on the 12th—only the tincans needed topping off to prepare TF-61 for action.

For the carrier admirals the sojourn in relatively safe waters allowed for a reassessment of the situation, especially after learning of the disastrous losses sustained in the Battle of Savo Island. Bereft of carrier air support, Rear Admiral Turner's Amphibious Force fell back to Noumea, leaving the 1st MarDiv isolated on Guadalcanal and Tulagi. The Marines mopped up resistance on Tanambogo and consolidated their hold on Lunga. After overrunning the airstrip on the 8th, Major General Vandegrift dubbed it "Henderson Field" in honor of Maj. Lofton R. Henderson, the brave CO of VMSB-241 lost at Midway. As of 10 August he estimated Henderson Field could handle thirty-eight fighters and nine dive bombers with some machine-gun ammunition, 400 drums of aviation gasoline, and oil, but there were no ground crews to service them. The 3rd Defense Battalion did not get to land its SCR-270-B radar, so some technicians fiddled with the captured Japanese radar sets.[1]

The afternoon of 11 August Vice Admiral Ghormley outlined Fletcher's basic tasks, giving him the primary mission to destroy enemy carriers, but also to:

a. cover the Espiritu Santo–Noumea line of communication;
b. support Guadalcanal and Tulagi against enemy ships;
c. cover the movement of friendly ships to Guadalcanal.[2]

Rear Admiral McCain's Aircraft, South Pacific Force (AirSoPac) PBYs and B-17s hoped to give Fletcher at least 24 hours warning of the approach of enemy landing forces threatening Guadalcanal. However, Lt. Cdr. Oscar Pederson, TF-61 air operations officer, summarized the basic dilemma:

> The lack of air facilities at Guadalcanal required the carriers to be in position to furnish support; the lack of facilities also by necessity forced the long range

searches to the northward to be conducted from Espiritu Santo and Vanikoro some 400–600 miles away. This shortened the margin of warning we could receive of any impending attack and forced the carriers to operate closer to Guadalcanal in the more dangerous waters between the Solomons and the Santa Cruz Islands.[3]

Air reconnaissance and interdiction of enemy air bases by General MacArthur's air force were especially vital. So far results on that score seemed meager.

For estimates of enemy intentions, TF-61 relied upon ULTRA intelligence analysts at Pearl Harbor, Brisbane, and Washington. CinCPac cautioned of a striking force being organized in Japan around the fleet carriers *Shōkaku* and *Zuikaku,* light carriers *Ryūjō* and *Hōshō,* an unnamed converted carrier, and four battleships. Nimitz thought they would require seven to ten days to reach the Solomons and again urged ComSoPac to use every possible means to strengthen the hold on Guadalcanal and Tulagi. In the interim he stressed that SoPac must prevent Japanese troops from landing on Guadalcanal and expected Ghormley would commit Fletcher's carriers to its defense.[4]

To reinforce SoPac, Nimitz arranged for Rear Admiral Murray's TF-17 with the *Hornet* to depart Pearl on 17 August. Concerned that sending all the carriers south increased the risk to Hawaii, Admiral King preferred they be rotated in and out of the South Pacific. He desired one CV task force to remain within 1,200 miles of Pearl Harbor except under "extraordinary circumstances." No doubt thinking the Guadalcanal situation to be an "extraordinary circumstance," Nimitz replied that he required maximum carrier strength in SoPac, at least until Ghormley could spare the *Wasp.*[5]

Looking from the *Wasp* to the *Saratoga* and the *Enterprise* beyond, 12 Aug. 1942. VF-71 Wildcat F-8 (BuNo. 5033) went down with the *Wasp* on 15 September. (USN)

The 12th offered the *Saratoga* Air Group plenty of distractions. To get back into fighting trim, Don Felt chased his flyers topside for calisthenics and a lap around the flight deck. However, VF-5 enjoyed two pleasant surprises. The *Phelps* delivered a bruised, but cheerful, "Ike" Eichenberger, who miraculously survived his 7 August crash, followed that evening by word of Pug Southerland safe on Guadalcanal. Johnny Altemus wrote in his diary: "I cannot describe what a lift that wonderful piece of news has given me."[6]

The next afternoon tricky winds bedeviled the VF-6 CAP pilots. A gust lofted Larry Grimmell's F4F after touchdown, causing it to snag the number 5 wire and collapse the right wheel. A far more spectacular accident soon occurred. Coming in slightly fast, Scoop Vorse set down without difficulty, but his tail hook skipped over several wires. Another ill-timed blow lifted Vorse high enough to ensnare his wheels atop the number 1 wire barrier. Somersaulting the barrier, the F4F ended up on its back, but Vorse emerged unhurt, if a bit shaken. Although in sad shape with vertical stabilizer, rudder, turtleback, and windshield flattened, F-33 was later rebuilt. That night in consolation VF-6 received the great news that Gordon Firebaugh, missing since 7 August, had reached Santa Isabel.[7]

That same evening, Fletcher copied an urgent message from Efate telling of a surface ship shelling the island. Such Japanese boldness seemed remarkable, but soon the location was corrected to Tulagi. The *I-122*, one of several submarines reconnoitering Iron Bottom Sound, surfaced off Tulagi and exchanged fire with guns ashore. Breaking off the fueling of his destroyers, Fletcher bent on 20 knots on 330 degrees the rest of that day and most of the 14th, so as by dawn, 15 August, to be 120 miles south of San Cristobal. The absence of further alarms, however, led him to deduce correctly that the foray was nothing more than a raid. TF-61 returned south, and by daybreak on the 15th drew 400 miles southeast of Tulagi. Steaming on fueling courses while topping off oil tanks increased the distance by sunset beyond 500 miles.

Soon after dark, Fletcher swung northwest to support a convoy of four APDs bound for Guadalcanal. He planned to patrol between Espiritu Santo and San Cristobal, so as to move north toward Guadalcanal during the day and retire southward at night. That conformed to his basic doctrine of avoiding enemy searches until the Japanese actually committed themselves against Guadalcanal. Ideally his movements never placed TF-61 more than 12 hours from air striking range of the island.

Hoping for more direct assistance, Kelly Turner informed Ghormley on 15 August of the conditions he felt must be met to ensure the safety of ships supplying Guadalcanal, code-named CACTUS. They included carrier fighter patrols over Lunga with squadron-sized missions from 1030 to 1630, when enemy air attacks were most likely. Implementing such CAPs meant keeping the carriers directly south of Guadalcanal, with all of the problems encountered during the initial landings and now even greater risks from enemy air and submarine attacks. Given the strategic and tactical situation, his plan was unrealistic, but it underscored the crucial failure to provide for land-based air power at Guadalcanal.

PLANS TO RETAKE GUADALCANAL

To the Japanese high command, the invasions of Tulagi and Guadalcanal proved a nasty surprise. Early on 8 August, Adm. Yamamoto Isoroku, Commander-in-Chief Combined Fleet, outlined the naval forces to be used to eject the enemy from the Solomons. He massed his "decisive battle forces," VAdm. Kondō Nobutake's 2nd Fleet (Advance Force) and the new 3rd Fleet (Carrier Striking Force) under VAdm. Nagumo Chūichi, and created the Support Force under Kondō's overall command. Their mission was to "support" the "cleaning out" of enemy forces on Guadalcanal. That task accomplished, Port Moresby would be the next objective.

To Imperial General Headquarters (IGHQ), however, the Solomons invasion seemed more of a nuisance than a threat, particularly after the exaggerated air claims on 8 August and the only-too-true Savo victory. At first they failed to perceive the landings as a legitimate counteroffensive, but worried more about delays to their own offensive already underway against Port Moresby. Therefore IGHQ assigned only about 9,000 troops to reconquer the Solomons: army detachments under Col. Ichiki Kiyonao (2,400) and Maj. Gen. Kawaguchi Kiyotake (6,000), and the navy's Yokosuka 5th Special Naval Landing Force (600). Rather optimistically they even hoped some of these men could be earmarked immediately for the Port Moresby operation. More concerned, especially after 11 August when analyzing the grave danger should the Allies operate aircraft from Guadalcanal, Yamamoto considered it absolutely vital to deny them that now valuable strategic asset.

Set to sail on 11 August, Kondō's Advance Force comprised the five heavy cruisers of the 4th (*Atago, Takao,* and *Maya*) and 5th cruiser divisions (*Myōkō* and *Haguro*), escorted by the 2nd and 4th destroyer squadrons. He also received the old (and slow) battleship *Mutsu,* while the seaplane carrier *Chitose* (flagship of the 11th Seaplane Tender Division) provided air support. Kondō would coordinate his planning with the Rabaul admirals: Vice Admiral Tsukahara, now commanding the whole Southeast Area as well as Base Air Force, and Vice Admiral Mikawa, CO of the 8th Fleet (Outer South Seas Force).[8]

REBUILDING THE JAPANESE CARRIER FORCE

The second half of Kondō's Support Force was Nagumo's 3rd Fleet (formerly 1st Air Fleet), the carrier striking force (*Kidō Butai*—"Mobile Force").[9] In the past few months the *Kidō Butai* sustained devastating losses in ships, aircrew, and aircraft. The Battle of the Coral Sea (7–8 May 1942) cost the light carrier *Shōhō* sunk, the big carrier *Shōkaku* hurt by three bombs, and the *Zuikaku* many planes. Air losses numbered about 69 planes (19 Mitsubishi Model 21 Zero fighters, 19 Aichi D3A1 Type 99 carrier bombers, and 31 Nakajima B5N2 Type 97 carrier attack planes [KATE]). Less than a month later, at Midway four more fast carriers, the *Akagi, Kaga, Soryū,* and *Hiryū,* slipped beneath the waves with their entire air complement of about 228 planes (73 Zero fighters, 72 Type 99 carrier bombers, 81 Type 97 carrier attack planes, and 2 experimental Yokosuka D4Y1 Type 2 reconnaissance planes [JUDY]), as well as 21 Zero fighters from the land-based 6th Air Group earmarked for Midway. Thus carrier aircraft losses in the two battles numbered upwards of 297, with severe aircrew casualties, particularly among leaders. Three group and seven squadron commanders perished.[10] Most of the surviving aviators had been fighting since the Pearl Harbor attack and desperately needed rest.

Thus by late June Nagumo's 1st Air Fleet comprised only five flattops, with another nearing completion. Only three of six were designed as carriers from the keel up. They were the superb *Shōkaku* and *Zuikaku* commissioned in 1941 (each

25,675 tons, 34 knots) and the older (1934) light carrier *Ryūjō* (10,600 tons, 29 knots). The *Zuihō* (11,262 tons, 28 knots) was a converted sub tender, the *Junyō* and *Hiyō* (each 24,100 tons, 25 knots) both transformed from passenger liners. None was as efficient as a specially designed flattop. Under repair since 17 May at Kure, the *Shōkaku* would be ready by late July, and the *Hiyō* neared completion. In the meantime the *Zuikaku* operated in the western Inland Sea along with the *Ryūjō*, *Junyō*, and *Zuihō*.

Greater emphasis after Midway on fighters and carrier bombers increased the aircraft complement of these six carriers to 300 (141 VF, 90 VB, and 69 VT), mostly by adding 39 fighters and subtracting 5 carrier attack planes: *Shōkaku*, *Zuikaku* (each 27 VF, 27 VB, 18 VT); *Zuihō* (21 VF, 6 VT); *Junyō*, *Hiyō* (each 21 VF, 18 VB, 9 VT); and *Ryūjō* (24 VF, 9 VT). In contrast the six big carriers that assailed Pearl Harbor the previous December wielded no fewer than 414 aircraft: 135 VF, 135 VB, and 144 VT.

On 14 July, in a major reorganization of the entire Combined Fleet, Nagumo's 1st Air Fleet became the 3rd Fleet. The 5th Carrier Division (*Shōkaku*, *Zuikaku*, *Zuihō*) was renumbered the 1st under Nagumo's direct control, while RAdm. Kakuta Kakuji's 4th Carrier Division (*Ryūjō*, *Junyō*, and *Hiyō*) changed to the 2nd. The 3rd Fleet also received the two fast battleships *Hiei* and *Kirishima* (11th Battleship Division) and four heavy cruisers, *Kumano* and *Suzuya* (7th Cruiser Division) and *Tone* and *Chikuma* (8th Cruiser Division). Yamamoto acknowledged that the failure both to provide close support to the carriers and to detect approaching enemy aircraft helped bring defeat at Midway. As integral components, these ships would help correct those errors. In early August Nagumo's flagship *Shōkaku* and also the *Kirishima* received the Type 21 *Gō Dentan* (air search radar), Model 1, a later version of the air search radars originally installed in May on the old BBs *Ise* and *Hyūga*.

For the Guadalcanal counteroffensive Yamamoto at first allocated only the 1st Carrier Division (*Shōkaku*, *Zuikaku*, and *Ryūjō*) with 177 aircraft (78 VF, 54 VB, and 45 VT). The other three flattops needed at least another month to prepare. In contrast with the good old days, Nagumo's new *Kidō Butai* was considerably weaker than the opposition. Even to bring his three carrier air groups to authorized strength required stripping the *Junyō*, *Hiyō*, and *Zuihō* of fighters and carrier bombers. They lacked 29 fighters and 16 carrier bombers, although retaining 15 more carrier attack planes than authorized.

Lt. Cdr. Nakajima Tadashi described the fine new CO of the flagship *Shōkaku* as "slender, gentle in appearance, and soft-spoken."[11] Yet Capt. Arima Masafumi's mild exterior concealed a will of steel. Unusually aggressive in battle, he did not hesitate to differ with Nagumo. On 15 October 1944, ten days before the first Divine Wind Kamikaze attacks in the Philippines, Rear Admiral Arima died leading a strike against U.S. carriers off Luzon. Completely reorganized, the *Shōkaku* Air Group, as befitted the fleet flagship, carried the senior *hikōtaichō* (group leader) for each aircraft type. Seeing his first combat of the war, Lt. Cdr. Seki Mamoru (NA 58-1930) commanded the group and also the *Shōkaku* Carrier Bomber Squadron, now increased to twenty-seven dive bombers (three *chūtais* each of nine planes). His classmate, Lt. Cdr. Murata Shigeharu, led the *Shōkaku* Carrier Attack Squadron with three *chūtais* each of six planes. The most illustrious pilot with the fleet, Murata had commanded the torpedo planes that crippled the U.S. battleline at Pearl Harbor.

The *Shōkaku* Carrier Fighter Squadron increased from twenty-one to twenty-seven Zero fighters in three nine-plane *chūtais*. Two officers and eight men remained from the old squadron. The new CO, Lt. Shingō Hideki (NA 59-1931), had served from December 1941 through March 1942 as *hikōtaichō* of the crack Tainan Air Group in the Philippines and the East Indies. His senior *buntaichō*, Lt. Ibusuki Masanobu (NA 65-1938), came from the *Akagi*, as did eight others. Prior to sailing, Shingō detached some rookies to train with the *Junyō* and borrowed Lt. Shigematsu Yasuhiro (NA 66-1938) and two other ex-*Hiryū* pilots.

The *Zuikaku*'s CO, Capt. Nomoto Tameteru, was a nonaviator like Arima. Her air group retained only one officer, a junior *buntaichō*, from the previous complement. The new group commander, Lt. Takahashi Sadamu (NA 61-1933), also led the twenty-seven-strong *Zuikaku* Carrier Bomber Squadron, while Lt. Imajuku Shigeichirō (NA 64-1937) took over the *Zuikaku* Carrier Attack Squadron's eighteen planes. Lt. Shirane Ayao (NA 64-1937), new CO of the *Zuikaku* Carrier Fighter Squadron, already boasted a renowned combat record not only with the *Akagi*, but also in China. His twenty-seven-plane squadron received only one other *buntaichō*, fresh caught from flight training, but included two highly capable warrant officers: Sumita Tsuyoshi and Osanai Suekichi (ex-*Akagi*), both flying since 1935. Along with Sumita, ten pilots remained from the old *Zuikaku* squadron. Relatively few carrier veterans (three *Kaga*, one *Shōkaku*) joined, but other commands furnished five experienced pilots. Shirane also loaned out his rookies and received Lt. Hidaka Saneyasu (NA 66-1938) and two other seasoned *Zuihō* pilots.

Capt. Katō Tadao, a naval aviator since 1921, commanded the *Ryūjō*. Like the other carriers, she received virtually a new set of officers, but also a new mission as a fighter carrier. Lt. Nōtomi Kenjirō (NA 62-1934), a highly respected fighter pilot who led the *Shōhō* Air Group at Coral Sea, took over as *hikōtaichō* and leader of the reinforced *Ryūjō* Carrier Fighter Squadron, now with twenty-four Zeros. His fighter *buntaichō* was ex-*Kaga* Lt. Iizuka Masao (NA 66-1938). Again the squadron strongly relied on two warrant officers, Shigemi Katsuma and Maruyama Akira, while the rest of the pilots, mostly highly experienced, included a few Midway veterans. The *Ryūjō* Carrier Attack Squadron, now under Lt. Murakami Binichi (NA 66-1938), shrank from twenty to nine Type 97 *kankōs*.

On 16 August the *Kidō Butai* sailed from Kure with the *Shōkaku*, *Zuikaku*, and *Ryūjō*, the 11th Battleship Division (*Hiei* and *Kirishima*), the 8th Cruiser Division (*Tone* and *Chikuma*), light cruiser *Nagara* (flagship, 10th Destroyer Squadron), and ten destroyers. En route to Truk, the group leaders hoped to conduct carrier landing qualifications and tactical work. The same day, in a move that would prove most unfortunate for CACTUS, the Japanese began changing their Naval Code Book D and started to shut the door, for the time being, to eavesdropping by Allied codebreakers.[12]

AIRCRAFT FOR CACTUS

By sunrise 16 August, Fletcher's TF-61 neared the end of its northward patrol 300 miles southeast of Guadalcanal and reversed course so as not to penetrate the Shortland air umbrella. That evening Ghormley provided King and Nimitz with a summary of his plans. The *Long Island* with the two MAG-23 squadrons reached Fiji on 13 August, and Ghormley hoped to deliver her cargo to Guadalcanal about the 18th or 19th, with TF-61 in support. He acknowledged that Fletcher's carriers constituted the ''principal defense'' for the entire region which in turn protected vital sea lanes from the U.S. to New Zealand and Australia. The two Japanese task forces with an estimated four carriers and four bat-tleships posed the greatest threat to Guadalcanal. Ghormley estimated they could attack CACTUS as early as 19 August:

> Regard next few days highly critical and might be dangerous if carriers expend fighter planes in support of Guadalcanal garrison and destroyers are expended es-corting and screening under enemy shore based aircraft. As of August 8 fighter planes on board carriers had already been reduced from 99 to 78. No replacements available this area.[13]

Ghormley dismissed Turner's recommendation for standing carrier fighter CAPs over Guadalcanal and hoped to preserve his carrier fighter strength before the coming carrier battle. Indeed Fletcher already assessed his carriers as short forty-eight planes (twenty-six fighters, eighteen dive bombers, and four torpedo planes), with no replacements in sight.[14]

At Fiji the *Long Island*'s CO, Cdr. James D. Barner, advised McCain that VMF-223 pilots were not carrier-qualified. Without additional training, Barner doubted that they could even take off safely from his small carrier. A dismayed Ghormley complained, "I need fighter planes on Guadalcanal now." McCain recommended the *Long Island* sail to Efate and exchange pilots with Lieutenant Colonel Bauer's more experienced VMF-212. Barner reached there on the 17th.[15]

Daylight 17 August found TF-61 about 275 miles southeast of Guadalcanal and as usual ending its northward nightly run. Fletcher came around toward Espiritu Santo to rendezvous with the oilers *Platte* (AO-24) and the *Kaskaskia* (AO-27) for a final drink of oil before the expected arrival of the Japanese striking force. On board the *Enterprise,* VF-6 learned to its delight of another orphan of 7 August, when coastwatchers reported finding Mach. Bill Warden. On the *Sara-toga,* VF-5 paused from crafting wicked-looking survival knives to take part in a ship-wide quiz contest. Dressed as a cheerleader in red helmet, a plane spotter's yellow jersey, and blue trunks, the comely Crud Blair led the VF-5 team sporting mortarboards and gowns. They won the first round, enlivened by the antics of a lieutenant from Communications, who, miffed by a judge's ruling, stalked out.[16]

West of Espiritu Santo, the two oilers topped off TF-11 and TF-18 on 18 August. When the *Sara*'s turn came, VF-5 detached wounded Lt. Pete Brown to the *Platte* for passage home. Fog Green tried without success to get some candy sent back along with the *Sara*'s mail, the first she received in six weeks. Newly returned Lt. Bob Bruning, former BLACK BASE FDO on board the *Chicago,* told of the wounded Joe Daly's heroics on 7 August. At Noumea Daly had trans-ferred to the hospital ship *Solace* (AH-5). The *San Juan* delivered Lt. Cdr. Wil-liam Townsend's ORANGE BASE air control team to the *Enterprise,* and they included a familiar face, Mach. Joe Achten. In the confusion, no one had in-formed VF-6 of his rescue, so his reappearance was a pleasant surprise.

That afternoon Beakley flew Noyes to the *Saratoga* for a personal conference with Fletcher. They had much to talk over, as things were heating up in the Solomons. The first order of business was to escort the *Long Island* to within ferry range of Guadalcanal to deliver the two Marine squadrons to Henderson Field. CinCPac intelligence warned of Japanese moves. The day before, two enemy convoys supposedly departed Truk. One carried "Jap Marines" (SNLF) and the other was loaded with Army "shock troops" from the old Midway attack force. They rendezvoused with three heavy cruisers, two or three light cruisers, and several destroyers. Several more heavy cruisers and destroyers operated separately as a covering force. Nimitz cautioned, "Attack day can be as early as 20 August but actual date not indicated." ULTRA offered no data on the Japanese carriers, but thought they might be in home waters.[17]

Naval cryptanalysts at Pearl, Brisbane, and Washington had indeed picked up key elements of the "KI Operation." As of 18 August several Japanese task forces were in or north of the Solomons. Vice Admiral Mikawa gave RAdm. Tanaka Raizō's 2nd Destroyer Squadron responsibility for delivering the troops and materiel to Guadalcanal. Six destroyers, packed with the 1st Echelon (916 men) of the army's Ichiki Detachment (the Army "shock troops" mentioned in the CinCPac estimate), sped down from Rabaul. On 16 and 17 August Tanaka's Reinforcement Force departed Truk in two echelons. The first comprised two slow army transports carrying 1,000 men of the Ichiki Detachment's 2nd Echelon escorted by light cruiser *Jintsu* and two "patrol boats" (converted old destroyers). Two more patrol boats screened the Navy transport *Kinryū Maru* with 500 sailors of the Yokosuka 5th Special Naval Landing Force. After joining forces on the 19th, Tanaka planned to deliver the troops the evening of 21 August ("V Day") at Taivu Point, 20 miles east of Lunga. Mikawa led the covering force of four heavy cruisers and two destroyers. Due to the convoy's slow speed, Tsukahara postponed the landings to 22 August. He hoped to have the whole Kawaguchi Detachment on Guadalcanal by the 28th.

Fletcher arranged to meet the *Long Island* on the 19th about 450 miles southeast of Guadalcanal. She sailed from Efate with her flight deck packed with the thirty-one aircraft of VMF-223 and VMSB-232 and planned to launch them the afternoon of 20 August from southeast of San Cristobal. Vandegrift recommended they arrive after the usual Japanese noontime raid, which meant exposing the *Long Island* within air search range of Shortland.

That evening ComSoPac broadcast OpPlan 2-42 outlining CinCPac's estimates. The presence of enemy carriers was "not definitely indicated, but highly probable." Ghormley expected TF-61 to "destroy hostile vessels prior to arrival and while at CACTUS," and arranged to reinforce Fletcher on 21 August with Crutchley's TF-44 (CA *Australia,* CL *Hobart,* and three U.S. destroyers). Ghormley also queried Nimitz whether the dispatch of Murray's TF-17 from Pearl canceled the intended relief of TF-18. Concerned about the *Wasp*'s unreliable propulsion system, Nimitz directed her return to Pearl at the "earliest date consistent with the military situation existing on the arrival of TF-17." He did authorize Ghormley to retain her air group as replacements.[18]

For the KI Operation, Base Air Force prepared an elaborate air search of the waters east and south of the Solomons. At 1020 on 20 August WO Taguchi Iwao's Kawanishi Type 97 flying boat from the 14th Air Group radioed "Enemy sighted" and placed one cruiser and two destroyers bearing 118 degrees and 500 miles from Shortland base. At 1130 he piped up with the discovery of an enemy carrier, one cruiser, two destroyers, and other ships about 250 miles south of Guadalcanal and headed north-northeast at 14 knots.[19] Taguchi had indeed discovered TG-2.6 with the *Long Island*. By 1200 she had closed within 40 miles of San Cristobal. All nineteen F4F-4s of VMF-223 and twelve SBD-3s of VMSB-232 got away after 1330 without difficulty. Setting down at Henderson Field, they received a joyous welcome from their fellow Leathernecks.

At 1334 a V-slash on the *Enterprise*'s A-scope radar screen pinpointed a bogey bearing 185 degrees, distance 25 miles. RED BASE broke radio silence to loose VF-71 F4Fs after the intruder. However, Ens. Harlan J. Coit, flying a VS-71 SBD on antisub patrol, beat the CAP to it. Spotting an enemy plane, Taguchi broke off snooping the *Long Island,* hightailed it north past the eastern tip of

San Cristobal, and thereby missed the launch. However, his tail gunner adroitly punched a 20-mm round through the SBD's left fuselage between Coit and rear seat man George Yanik, ARM3c. That persuaded Coit to break off. The CAP never overtook the fleeing Kawanishi, while Taguchi thought he escaped an enemy "two-place fighter."[20]

Taguchi's carrier sighting, the first since June, generated quite a reaction among the Japanese admirals. Base Air Force quickly plotted the target at 220 miles southeast of Tulagi and 800 miles from Rabaul, regrettably out of strike range. Mikawa thought the Americans hunted the Guadalcanal reinforcement convoy, so at 1457 he ordered Tanaka to turn south-southeast toward Rabaul. At the same time Tsukahara simply told Tanaka to retire north. He hoped the carrier force would pursue, so he could counterattack the next day. Bewildered, Tanaka split the difference by steaming northwest. Kondō's Support Force was not a factor; his Advance Force swung at anchor at Truk, and Nagumo's *Kidō Butai* was still far north of there.

While the Japanese high command contemplated the presence of one American carrier 200 miles southeast of Guadalcanal, a second soon appeared, this time in the D1 sector (118 degrees) adjacent to Taguchi. At 1340 on his return leg PO1c Shakata Shōichi, commanding another 14th Air Group Type 97 flying boat, discovered one carrier, four cruisers, and nine destroyers 240 miles southeast of Tulagi. He added at 1415 that the ships were retiring southeast at 18 knots. Debriefing the two crews back at Shortland, Base Air Force placed the two carrier contacts 70 miles apart. Taguchi's crew described "their" carrier as having no island structure, while Shakata noted that the carrier he spotted certainly featured a superstructure. Headquarters correctly assumed the presence of at least two enemy carriers some 250 miles southeast of Tulagi. Bound for Truk with the Combined Fleet Main Force, Admiral Yamamoto at first decided the Americans stalked the 2nd Echelon convoy north of the Solomons. At 1720 he ordered Kondō to consolidate his Support Force, hasten south to the waters immediately north of Guadalcanal, and protect Tanaka. That evening Kondō sortied from Truk. Roughly 200 miles north of Truk, Nagumo canceled his planned stopover in order to rendezvous with Kondō at 0900, 21 August, 120 miles east of Truk.[21]

Yamamoto changed his mind that evening, after the Japanese Guadalcanal garrison radioed that twenty enemy carrier aircraft had landed at the Lunga airfield. Swiftly deciding the enemy carriers no longer threatened the troop convoy, at 2242 he ordered all commands to destroy the Lunga airfield through air attack and ship bombardments and deny its use to the Allies. Thus Yamamoto set the entire course of the campaign. For 21 August, Base Air Force orchestrated another comprehensive search to locate enemy carriers and set up an attack. To permit the Support Force to move into position, Tsukahara also postponed to 24 August the arrival of Tanaka's 2nd Echelon Convoy at Taivu Point.

GROPING IN THE DARK

21 August

The 20th was an especially important day in the Guadalcanal campaign. Now the 1st MarDiv had an air force of its own. The night of 20/21 August, Vandegrift's 1st Marines repulsed the first of many enemy counterattacks, when Ichiki's 1st Echelon of 900 men rashly tried forcing its way across the Ilu River toward the airfield. The harsh sounds of battle off to the east surprised the newly arrived Marine aviators at Henderson Field. The fierce action lasted well into the 21st and killed over 700 Japanese, including Ichiki. CinCPac had stressed enemy destroyers could be used to run troops to Guadalcanal and concluded, "Carrier aircraft must be employed to prevent landing particularly if attempted prior to arrival [of] enemy carriers."[22] Vandegrift seconded CinCPac's caution:

> Strength of enemy force uncertain. If not prevented by surface craft enemy can continue night landings beyond range of action and build up large forces. Request every means available be used to prevent this.[23]

Overnight TF-61 retired southeast at 25 knots while escorting the *Long Island* out of the area. At 0552, before dawn, Fletcher learned from CACTUS of two enemy destroyers landing more troops. At 0640 he altered course to 295 degrees, speed 20 knots, to close Guadalcanal now about 400 miles northwest and do his best to support CACTUS. At 0854 he informed Noyes and Kinkaid of plans to strike at 1330 if enemy ships remained off CACTUS. He needed AirSoPac searches to identify and pinpoint these forces. So far only the seaplane tender *Mackinac* (AVP-13) sounded an alarm. At 0820 she warned of being bombed at Ndeni in the Santa Cruz Islands, but quickly sent a correction. Her assailants were two *Wasp* search SBDs, one of which dropped its bomb in error.[24]

At the same time a powerful strike sought the American carriers. At 0807 Lieutenant Nakamura departed Rabaul with twenty-six torpedo-armed land attack planes (seventeen Misawa, nine 4th Air Group), escorted by thirteen Tainan Air Group Zeros under Lieutenant Kawai. Tsukahara reiterated orders for Tanaka to land the troops on 24 August. Southeast of Truk, Kondō's Advance Force joined briefly with Nagumo's *Kidō Butai,* then separated to refuel on southerly courses. Nagumo advised that as of 2000, 23 August, his three carriers would be 130 miles northeast of Ontong Java and prepared to support the landings on the 24th.

At 1045 WO Tokunaga Yasuichi's Yokohama Air Group Type 97 flying boat encountered five ships, types unknown, on the D2 line 530 miles southeast of Shortland. They held course 250 degrees at 20 knots. About 15 minutes later the intruder itself was snooped by Lt. Robert M. Ware (USNA 1937), flying a VS-72 SBD on IAP. He first noticed the big four-engine Type 97 cruising at low level about a mile ahead, but it swiftly climbed into patches of broken clouds. Pouring on the power, Ware discovered a speed advantage of only 20 knots over the fleeing Kawanishi. At 1116 Tokunaga informed base, "We are engaged in aerial combat." Ware loosed long-range bursts from his twin .50s as the two adversaries entered some clouds, then resumed firing when they broke into the clear at 3,000 feet. He held down the trigger until within 50 feet of his massive target and flamed its port outboard engine. After the Type 97 descended to 1,000 feet, the left wing burned completely off, dropping the fiery wreckage into the sea 15 miles northeast of TF-61. Wally Clarke's eight VF-5 Wildcats raced hard to get into the action, but found only a pillar of smoke and a burning patch on the water. A pontoon and wing section replete with red ball insignia dramatically floated back to the surface. Score another kill for VS-72. In return Ware sustained two 7.7-mm hits in his engine. The two aggressive *Wasp* scouting squadrons (71 and 72) now tallied three aerial victories, while a highly frustrated VF-71 had yet to score one. The SBDs were certainly rubbing it in. In his diary Blair spoke for many VF pilots: "Wish the damn scouts would tend to their own business."[25]

About the same time Tokunaga's crew died, Fletcher received a welcome

A fine study of a VS-72 SBD Dauntless (BuNo. 03341), 24 Aug. 1942. VS-71 placed a horizontal white line underneath the number. This aircraft ended up in the *Hornet*'s VB-8 after the loss of the *Wasp*. Renumbered B-7, it was flown on 26 October by Lt. (jg) Joe Auman against the *Shōkaku*. (NA 80-G-19393 via R. J. Cressman)

reinforcement in the form of Crutchley's TF-44, which enhanced TF-61's surface-attack capability. He also learned that the morning search found no enemy ships around Guadalcanal, so he eased back to a more economical 15 knots. At 1214 came word from AirSoPac that Ens. Theodore S. Thueson of VP-23 discovered four enemy cruisers and one destroyer up near Ontong Java, about 300 miles northwest of Tulagi. They were Mikawa's Outer South Seas Force covering the approach of the 2nd Echelon Convoy slowly steaming south from Truk.

Anticipating an enemy night bombardment of CACTUS, Fletcher advised Noyes and Kinkaid at 1435 that prior to dawn on the 22nd TF-61 would close Cape Henslow on Guadalcanal's southeast coast. Believing the enemy knew his approximate position, he protected the advancing carriers against a night surface ambush by deploying a vanguard 20 miles out in front. The *Minneapolis, New Orleans, San Francisco* (CA-38), *Salt Lake City* (CA-25), and six destroyers under RAdm. Carleton H. Wright accelerated ahead with orders to rejoin at 0630 and 50 miles south of Guadalcanal.

Ghormley certainly approved of TF-61 operating so close to CACTUS. That afternoon he specifically ordered Fletcher and McCain to support the arrival on 22 August of the cargo ships *Alhena* (AK-26) and *Fomahault* (AK-22) at Tulagi and Guadalcanal. He desired "maximum practicable air cover" until they could retire early the next day. By sunset on the 21st Fletcher neared San Cristobal, and at 2250 he warned Ghormley of the snoopers encountered on the 20th and 21st, which certainly indicated the enemy had sighted his carriers. He also commented that SoPac radio communications had not improved, which meant that contact reports were received "very late." Therefore he considered it inadvisable to send his cruisers and destroyers nightly to Guadalcanal. Assessing his own situation, he advised that TF-61 "must retire on 24th for fuel and redistribution of provisions."[26]

For the Japanese waiting for their offensive to unfold, 21 August became a highly frustrating day. From Warrant Officer Tokunaga's last messages, Base Air Force deduced the American carrier force still remained more than 800 miles from Rabaul, out of possible air attack range. After combing the waters south of Guadalcanal, Lieutenant Nakamura came to the same conclusion. At 1140 he turned the bombers back and released the thirteen escort Zeros to patrol over Lunga. There Kawai flushed four VMF-223 F4Fs led by the CO, Capt. John L. Smith. MAG-23's first air battle resulted in two F4Fs badly damaged without Japanese loss, but Smith felt the skirmish "did a great deal of good." Impressed the Wildcats could still fly after being so badly shot up, he later noted that "our pilots had a great deal of confidence in the Grumman type airplane."[27]

22 August

Before sunrise, TF-61 left San Cristobal astern, bound for the waters directly south of Guadalcanal. Wright's vanguard of four cruisers and six destroyers forged 20 miles ahead, and at dawn Fletcher expected to wade into enemy ships off Guadalcanal. The *Alhena* and *Fomahault* had anchored at Lunga, and to cover them two tincans headed into the channel. Apprised the previous day of their approach, Mikawa thoughtfully provided the destroyer *Kawakaze* to greet them. At 0400 she surprised and fatally torpedoed the hapless destroyer *Blue,* then got clean away before dawn.

Noyes had designated the *Saratoga* as the duty carrier for searches and CAP and the *Enterprise* as morning relief, and had put the *Wasp* in reserve ready for action. Therefore at 0600 from about 50 miles south of Guadalcanal, the *Sara* launched fourteen SBDs to scout west and north to 200 miles. Commander Felt dropped in at CACTUS for a short visit to assess the feasibility of operating carrier planes from Henderson Field. After flight operations, TF-61 swung around to 120 degrees, 15 knots, to avoid the particularly dangerous waters west of Guadalcanal. A half hour later Wright's vanguard caught up from astern. Surprisingly the morning search proved negative except for the *Kawakaze* retiring at high speed 75 miles north of Tulagi. Two SBDs tested their skills against the agile tincan, but missed. Given the lack of targets, Fletcher advised at 1020 that he would hold his present southeasterly course until noon, then turn east. By the next dawn he wanted to be just east of Malaita, where he could seek enemy forces possibly swooping down from Truk.

Meanwhile, at 1018 the *Enterprise*'s radar found a bogey lurking 55 miles northwest, estimated altitude 8,000 feet. Heavy rain squalls dotted the immediate area, much affecting visibility and radio reception. While RED BASE fruitlessly contacted eight VF-6 F4Fs on CAP, the flattop scrambled twelve VF-6 F4Fs waiting on alert. At 1025 Lieutenant Rowe raised Scoop Vorse's RED 5, one of the newly launched divisions, and vectored them out on 270 degrees at 10,000 feet. Carefully working out a possible intercept, he turned RED 5 due south. Above and ahead Vorse soon spotted a four-engine Kawanishi flying boat flown by PO1c Shakata of the 14th Air Group, who was again handling the D1 sector from Shortland. Unlike on the 20th, however, his luck had run out.[28]

Vorse and wingman Ens. Richards "Dix" Loesch ascended over the Kawanishi, while Lt. (jg) Howard "Larry" Grimmell and Ens. Francis R. "Cash" Register charged in for opposite runs. Scoop beat everyone to the punch. At 1035 he rolled F-4 into an overhead pass and triggered a short burst of 100 rounds right on target. Fueled by leaking gasoline, the Type 97's fuselage flamed dramatically. By the time Loesch opened up, the Kawanishi was already a goner. Fire spread to the midsection, collapsed the large parasol wing, and broke up the plane in midair. One crewman jumped minus parachute. In sudden, stunning defeat, Shakata never sent a message, but TF-61 clearly overheard the victor's dialogue on the fighter director (FD) circuit:[29]

> RED 5: We shot him down in flames.
> RED BASE: Good going.
> RED 5: Look at her burn. There, his wings came off about 7000 feet. That's the prettiest picture I've seen in a long time.
> RED BASE: Atta boy. Good for you!

Among the excited listeners was VF-5 sitting in their ready room on board the *Saratoga*. They cheered as they heard the news. For them the last two weeks had been a struggle against boredom, as TF-61 shuttled to and fro west of the New Hebrides. Many pilots had not even flown in the last 10 days. Now with VS-72's victory the previous day and RED 5's kill, action seemed imminent.

After clearing the east tip of San Cristobal, Fletcher turned northwest at 1930 toward the waters east of Malaita. A few minutes later he informed ComSoPac that in view of the impending battle he wanted to fuel his entire force on 25 August if possible from three oilers. In turn, his message crossed an important dispatch from ComSoPac, which again delayed the schedule for the enemy attack against CACTUS, this time to between 23 and 26 August. Within 600 miles of Kavieng on New Ireland, CinCPac intelligence placed one, possibly two, Japanese battleships, ten heavy and five light cruisers, as well as numerous destroyers and submarines, but *no* carriers. They reckoned enemy land-based air strength in the region at 60-plus fighters and 80 to 100 bombers. Ghormley thought the presence of enemy carriers "possible but not confirmed" and relayed CinCPac's incorrect judgment that the Japanese had not spotted TF-61 in the past 10 days. He concluded:

> Important fueling be conducted soonest possible and if practical one CV TF at a time retiring for that purpose your 211120 [21 August]. Am sending *Platte* and *Cimarron* [AO-22] from ROSES daylight tomorrow.[30]

From Shakata's failure to return, Base Air Force deduced that an enemy carrier force operated in the D1 sector. The only other sighting that day occurred in the adjacent sector, where Warrant Officer Taguchi picked up the *Alhena* and *Fomahault* withdrawing south. Because of bad weather Base Air Force canceled the usual bombing raid against Guadalcanal. At noon on the 22nd, Tanaka's 2nd Echelon convoy, zigzagging at 9 knots, was 350 miles north of Guadalcanal, and the other forces took position to protect it. Kondō's Support Force drew up on both of Tanaka's flanks: the Advance Force 120 miles northwest and Nagumo's *Kidō Butai* 200 miles northeast of the convoy. They refueled while steaming slowly southward into the prevailing trade winds. Mikawa's Outer South Seas Force moved out ahead of the convoy. His main force (heavy cruisers *Chōkai*, *Kinugasa*, and destroyer *Isonami*) broke off to refuel at Shortland, temporarily leaving the 1st Section of the 6th Cruiser Division (*Aoba* and *Furutaka*) and two destroyers to cover the convoy.

Tsukahara urged Combined Fleet to order Nagumo's carriers to knock out the Guadalcanal airfield on 23 August and on the 24th provide close air support over Taivu Point. Vigorously seconding the request, Tanaka also desired air cover for

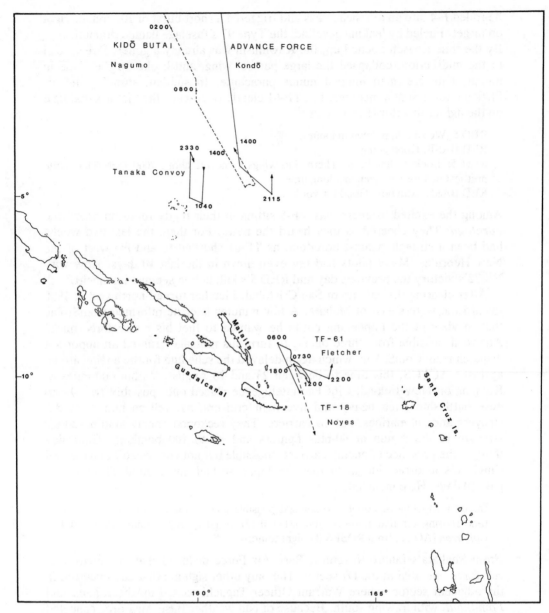

Task force operations (main forces only), 23 August.

his final approach. However, Yamamoto preferred not to risk the premature exposure of the *Kidō Butai,* but did authorize a carrier strike on the 24th, if necessary. That sealed the *Ryūjō*'s fate.

23 August

The night of 22/23 August, TF-61 advanced northwest beyond San Cristobal and paralleled the east coast of Malaita.[31] Fletcher planned to run north until dawn, then retire southeast to await the results of the morning searches. He achieved good position from which to find and flank an enemy force threatening Guadalcanal from the north. At the same time he felt growing concern over the vital need to refuel his carrier task groups in the next few days. He signaled Noyes on the *Wasp* that if no important contacts appeared during the day, he was to take TF-18 south that evening to rendezvous with the oilers.

On 23 August, the *Enterprise* took over as duty carrier, handling the morning searches and the first CAP. The *Wasp* became her relief, while the *Saratoga* Air Group remained poised to launch a full strike. At 0555 the *Enterprise* dispatched fifteen SBDs and nine TBFs to search the northern semicircle out to 180 miles. A few minutes later, Cdr. Walter G. "Butch" Schindler, TF-61 staff gunnery officer and Fletcher's trusted emissary, left the *Saratoga* with two VT-8 TBFs bound for Henderson Field. Following up Felt's visit the previous day, Schindler arranged for the field to receive a carrier strike group should one need to take refuge there. The presence of a functioning airfield on Guadalcanal offered Fletcher considerable flexibility in planning air operations. At 0621, with the first launches completed, he changed course southeast to await the results of his own and McCain's AirSoPac searches. By 0940, the carrier missions proved negative except for two submarine contacts by SBDs, but bad weather prevented adequate coverage to the northwest. Therefore Fletcher could not rule out the presence of enemy ships in that crucial quadrant.

Beginning at 0942 TF-61 copied sighting reports from an AirSoPac PBY Catalina about 300 miles to the northwest. Lt. Leo B. Riester of VP-23 discovered eight enemy ships (reported as two heavy cruisers, three destroyers, and four transports) on course 190 degrees, speed 17 knots. This vital contact offered the first tangible clue to the offensive that everyone feared. Fletcher felt this enemy force indeed threatened Guadalcanal, but not before the next day. Currently out of strike range, it would likely remain so, if TF-61 continued withdrawing southeast. Especially concerned about whether enemy carriers lurked nearby, Fletcher's first inclination was to hold course until sunset and remain ready to strike should any Japanese flattops turn up.

Riester most definitely ferreted out Tanaka's 2nd Echelon Convoy, which noted the skulking so-called Consolidated at 0930. At that time Tanaka had closed within 300 miles of Guadalcanal. Worried about American carriers, Mikawa again ordered Tanaka to retire northward until the situation cleared. He complied at 1040 and anxiously awaited the day's actions by Base Air Force and Nagumo's *Kidō Butai*. However, Tsukahara's searchers turned up nothing but the fact that the land attack plane flying the 115-degree line from Rabaul failed to return. Perhaps it succumbed to poor weather or engine failure, for no one claimed it. Storms again prevented Tsukahara from bombing Lunga.

Meanwhile, from far to the northeast of the 2nd Echelon Convoy Nagumo planned to run the carrier force south all night so as by 0600 on 24 August to arrive east of Malaita and only 200 miles north-northeast of Guadalcanal. Kondō's Advance Force would conform and at that time be 60 miles northeast of the *Kidō Butai*. From there the cruiser float planes searching 300 miles eastward could guard Nagumo's left flank. With so many aircraft criss-crossing the eastern Solomons, Kondō and Nagumo fully expected to find any American carriers opposing the invasion convoy. Aware of Yamamoto's directive to strike Guadalcanal if Base Air Force failed to knock out American air strength there, the 3rd Fleet staff prepared a contingency plan. Nagumo instructed RAdm. Hara Chūichi, 8th Cruiser Division CO, to prepare to take the *Ryūjō*, flagship *Tone*, and two destroyers south against Lunga. Recently frozen out of carrier command, the aggressive Hara (nicknamed "King Kong") had led the 5th Carrier Division from Pearl Harbor through the Coral Sea battle.

Soon Fletcher changed his mind about retiring southeast away from Malaita. At 1140 he learned from a B-17 of another enemy force, reported as two transports and two destroyers, in Faisi harbor off southern Bougainville. They appeared to be the second element of a two-pronged attack converging on Guadalcanal, but actually were Mikawa's minesweepers and destroyers refueling at Shortland. At 1203 Fletcher proposed to Noyes, the air task force commander, to reverse course to head northwest. Going after Riester's convoy now seemed the best course of action. At the same time Kinkaid asked permission to press ahead with TF-16, strike the convoy himself, and recover aircraft before dark. Fletcher refused, because he desired the *Enterprise* to search again that afternoon, while the *Saratoga* handled the invasion force.

At 1341 TF-61 came around to 310 degrees, speed 15 knots. Thirty-one SBDs (fifteen VB-3, fifteen VS-3, and CSAG) and six VT-8 TBFs were poised on the *Sara*'s flight deck. In the wardroom (which served as the VSB/VT ready room), Felt happily announced to his pilots, "Let's go boys! No carriers have been found. We will attack the cruisers."[32] Fletcher provided no escort fighters. First of all, he thought there was no defending CAP, and second, the mission might be a long one. Indeed, he instructed Felt to land at Guadalcanal by sunset, spend the night, and return the next morning to the *Saratoga* east of Malaita. The old warship buzzed with excitement as the strike made ready to take off, while the envious VF-5 pilots waited in their ready room. At 1440 Felt's thirty-seven planes departed to the northwest into increasingly dirty weather.

Again Ghormley would have approved of TF-61's actions. At 1431 he sounded the alarm over direct, immediate threats to CACTUS. Enemy ships could arrive by midnight. He told Fletcher to prepare to send a surface force to destroy them. Deeply concerned, Vandegrift committed his entire air strength, nine VMSB-232 SBDs, one VT-8 TBF, and twelve VMF-223 F4Fs under Maj. Dick Mangrum against the same cruiser-transport force sought by Felt's *Saratoga* flyers. Unfortunately for SoPac, the afternoon's activities did not proceed as hoped. The *Enterprise* afternoon search located nothing except for another surfaced submarine, while storms blanketing the critical northwest sectors again prevented proper investigation beyond 145 miles. Hunting the convoy through the same thick clouds and squalls, Felt's strike vouchsafed no reports at all. At 1730 Vandegrift advised SoPac that weather had forced Mangrum to turn back. At twilight Felt's raiders turned up over Henderson Field after a fruitless search and harrowing flight to Guadalcanal. The *Saratoga* flyers needed another 30 minutes to get down, but aided by Marine flares all landed safely, despite potshots from Japanese machine guns. Butch Schindler greeted Felt and the squadron leaders on the field.

From east of Malaita, TF-61 withdrew southeast during the night. Fletcher now faced the decision whether or not to detach TF-18 to refuel according to Ghormley's directive. He reviewed the situation. It was growing imperative to initiate the lengthy process of refueling the carrier task forces one at a time, as ComSoPac ordered. The day's searches failed to detect any sign of carriers. Also that afternoon Fletcher received the daily CinCPac intelligence bulletin. In contrast with the previous week's vague estimates on enemy carrier movements, the Pearl Harbor analysts now placed the *Shōkaku* and *Zuikaku* as en route from Japan to Truk, the *"Hitaka"* (*Hiyō*), *"Hayataka"* (*Junyō*), *Zuihō,* and *Ryūjō* as still in the homeland.[33]

Thus intelligence at the highest level seemed to agree with search reports that the coast was clear: no enemy carriers were *south* of Truk. Indeed, CinCPac indicated the striking force might still be well north of there. For the next few days enemy carriers appeared to pose no immediate threat to TF-61 or Guadalcanal. At 1823 Fletcher directed Noyes to proceed southeast, fuel TF-18 the next day north of Espiritu Santo, and hasten northward as soon as possible. With him went the *Wasp* (twenty-six fighters, twenty-six dive bombers, and eleven torpedo planes), two heavy cruisers, one light cruiser (AA), and seven destroyers. With the comfortable advantage of hindsight, critics take Fletcher to task for not delaying TF-18's fueling. They feel he should somehow have deduced the presence of enemy carriers, despite the fact neither ULTRA nor sighting reports placed them there. Perhaps CTF-61 needed a crystal ball. If so, others did also. In an intelligence bulletin issued 18 hours later (1323, 24 August, Z − 11), CinCPac analysts firmly placed the *Shōkaku* and *Zuikaku* in Truk waters and all the other carriers (except for the CVE *Kasuga Maru* transporting planes) in home waters.[34]

In fact, intelligence described what appeared to be the only immediate threat against CACTUS. Based on PBY sightings, it comprised two heavy cruisers, five destroyers, and six transports able to arrive in the next 12 hours and land troops at Lunga. Fletcher thought the *Enterprise* and *Saratoga* with 153 aircraft (57 fighters, 68 dive bombers, and 28 torpedo planes, including the *Saratoga* strike group at Henderson Field) could handle these forces on the 24th. Once Noyes rejoined, another task force could take his place and fuel. Just before midnight Fletcher learned why Felt's strike group missed the target. A long-delayed AirSoPac report noted that the convoy had changed course at 1300 (actually long before) and steamed north out of range.

At Henderson Field, the *Saratoga* flyers spent an interesting night with the Marines. At air headquarters, the famous "Pagoda," Felt conferred with Vandegrift, who was determined to attack the enemy invasion convoy no matter when it arrived. Like the Marines, the *Saratoga* contingent would execute night attacks if the Japanese showed up before dawn. Given the time needed to refuel the planes, Schindler advised Fletcher it was necessary to delay from 0800 to 1100 the strike group's intended arrival back at the *Sara*. Marine ground crews dispersed the aircraft over the darkened field, and helped by the eager but untrained CUB-1 bluejackets, they started the laborious refueling. Aircrews sat by their planes all night and bummed food from friendly Marines.[35]

For the Japanese, 23 August proved much less exciting. Afternoon searches from both Nagumo and Kondō yielded negative results. Nagumo knew the Allies had not sighted his ships, and he wanted to preserve that happy state of affairs by not closing prematurely to within air range of Guadalcanal and Efate. At 1740 he advised that unless otherwise instructed, he would run north all night (150 miles), then at 0700 resume heading southeast. Unwittingly he had already closed within 300 miles of TF-61. Like Fletcher he played hide-and-seek until he located the opposing carriers. Kondō soon reversed course in order to keep station on Nagumo. By 0700 on the 24th he expected to be 150 miles southeast of the *Kidō Butai*, allowing him to fulfill his task of flank guard. Tsukahara directed the 2nd Echelon convoy to arrive at Taivu Point on the 24th as planned. Tanaka pointed out the delay caused by his northward run during most of the 23rd put the convoy so far north of Guadalcanal that he could not reach there on the 24th. Faced with the facts, Tsukahara had to agree. Reluctantly he again postponed the landings, this time to 25 August.

The stage was now set for the series of naval actions that would come to be known to the Allies as the Battle of the Eastern Solomons and to the Japanese as the Second Solomons Sea Battle (Savo was the first). Due to the unfortunate detachment of the *Wasp,* TF-61 was now weaker in air strength (153 to 177) than the *Kidō Butai.*

TABLE 5.1
Carrier Aircraft Strength, 24 August 1942, 0500

Task Force 61, VAdm. Frank Jack Fletcher
Task Force 11, VAdm. Fletcher
USS *Saratoga*

	On board ship	At Henderson Field
CSAG Cdr. Harry D. Felt	0	1 SBD-3
VF-5 Lt. Cdr. Leroy C. Simpler	27 F4F-4s (27)	0
	1 F4F-7 (1)	0
VB-3 Lt. Cdr. Dewitt W. Shumway	2 SBD-3s (0)	15 SBD-3s
VS-3 Lt. Cdr. Louis J. Kirn	0	15 SBD-3s
VT-8 Lt. Harold H. Larsen	6 TBF-1s (6)	7 TBF-1s
Utility Unit	1 F4F-7 (1)	

Task Force 16, RAdm. Thomas C. Kinkaid
USS *Enterprise*

CEAG Lt. Cdr. Maxwell F. Leslie	Flew VT-3 TBF
VF-6 Lt. Louis H. Bauer	29 F4F-4s (28)
VB-6 Lt. Ray Davis	17 SBD-3s (17)
VS-5 Lt. Turner F. Caldwell	18 SBD-3s (16)
VT-3 Lt. Cdr. Charles M. Jett	15 TBF-1s (15)
Utility Unit	1 F4F-7 (1)

Kidō Butai (3rd Fleet), VAdm. Nagumo Chūichi
1st Carrier Division, VAdm. Nagumo

Shōkaku
Air Group Commander	Lt. Cdr. Seki Mamoru[a]	
Carrier Fighter Squadron	Lt. Shingō Hideki[a]	27 Zero VF (26)
Carrier Bomber Squadron	Lt. Cdr. Seki	27 Type 99 VB (27)
Carrier Attack Squadron	Lt. Cdr. Murata Shigeharu[a]	18 Type 97 VT (18)

Zuikaku
Air Group Commander	Lt. Takahashi Sadamu[a]	
Carrier Fighter Squadron	Lt. Shirane Ayao[b]	27 Zero VF (25)
Carrier Bomber Squadron	Lt. Takahashi	27 Type 99 VB (27)
Carrier Attack Squadron	Lt. Imajuku Shigeichirō[b]	18 Type 97 VT (18)

Ryūjō
Air Group Commander	Lt. Nōtomi Kenjirō[a]	
Carrier Fighter Squadron	Lt. Nōtomi	24 Zero VF (23)
Carrier Attack Squadron	Lt. Murakami Binichi[b]	9 Type 97 VT (9)

[a] *Hikōtaichō*
[b] *Buntaichō*

PART II

Battle of the Eastern Solomons

CHAPTER 6

Sinking the *Ryūjō*

THE MORNING SEARCHES

For nine days Vice Admiral Tsukahara's Southeast Area Force and Vice Admiral Mikawa's Outer South Seas Force had labored to deliver 3,000 reinforcements safely to Guadalcanal. As of midnight, 24 August, only 320 miles (36 hours) separated Rear Admiral Tanaka's slow convoy with 1,500 troops from their objective of Taivu Point 20 miles east of Lunga. Three widely dispersed task forces protected his flank. Together they comprised three aircraft carriers, a seaplane carrier, two battleships, eleven heavy and three light cruisers, and twenty-four destroyers—a significant portion of the Combined Fleet.

At 2200, 23 August, Admiral Yamamoto from flagship *Yamato* 180 miles south of Truk issued the overall directive for the 24th. Base Air Force bombers were to plaster the Guadalcanal airfield. Advancing southward from waters east of the convoy, Vice Admiral Kondō's Support Force (2nd and 3rd fleets) also would strike Guadalcanal should the morning search not locate American carriers, the more vital target. At 0145 Vice Admiral Nagumo implemented the contingency plan, which called for Rear Admiral Hara's so-called Detached Force (heavy cruiser *Tone*, light carrier *Ryūjō*, and destroyers *Tokitsukaze* and *Amatsukaze*) to race south of the *Kidō Butai* and get out in front of Tanaka's convoy in the direction of Guadalcanal. Hara departed at 0400. By 1200 he was to be 200 miles north of Lunga. In the event the search found no enemy carriers, the *Ryūjō* would bomb and strafe the airfield. Hara could either recover the planes or route them to Buka, but at Captain Katō's urging, he decided to retrieve planes before withdrawing north to refuel.

At 0600 the *Kidō Butai* swung southeast on 150 degrees, speed 15 knots. About 120 miles to the southeast, Kondō's Advance Force (2nd Fleet) matched the maneuver and guarded Nagumo's eastern flank. Both admirals thought any enemy carriers present would be lurking far to the south. At 0615 the *Shōkaku* and *Zuikaku* dispatched nineteen Type 97 carrier attack planes for a precautionary 250-mile search of the eastern semicircle (000–190 degrees), while Kondō sent seven seaplanes out ahead for his morning search. At the same time, Nagumo instructed the *Shōkaku* and *Zuikaku* to prepare three deckload air-attack waves. The first two comprised fifty-four carrier bombers and twenty-four fighters, and the third, the follow-up, thirty-six carrier attack planes and twelve fighters.[1] This was in line with 3rd Fleet's new policy of holding the torpedo planes in reserve until the others had softened up the targets. Although logical given heavy torpedo plane losses at Midway, it certainly did not sit well with Lieutenant Commander Murata, the aggressive carrier attack *hikōtaichō*.

For 24 August Tsukahara organized a maximum effort for Base Air Force. At 0625 two Yokohama Type 97 flying boats and two new Type 2 flying boats (one Yokohama, one 14th Air Group) left Shortland to cover the D sector (092–122 degrees). Radius was 700 miles with a 60-mile left dogleg. At the same time the Misawa Air Group provided four Type 1 land attack planes for the E sector (092–132 degrees), distance 800 miles from Rabaul. At 0830 twenty-four Type 1 land attack planes and fourteen Zeros departed Rabaul to bomb Guadalcanal.

The predawn hours of 24 August found Vice Admiral Fletcher's truncated TF-61 operating east of Malaita and about 170 miles east of Tulagi. After detaching Rear Admiral Noyes's TF-18 with the *Wasp*, he retained carriers *Saratoga* (his flagship) and *Enterprise* (TF-16 flagship for Rear Admiral Kinkaid). The previous afternoon, Commander Felt's thirty-one *Saratoga* SBD dive bombers and six TBF torpedo planes missed Tanaka's reinforcement convoy in the murky skies north of Guadalcanal and took refuge at Henderson Field for the night. Fletcher had expected those thirty-seven planes back by 0830, but they were delayed, greatly reducing TF-61's attack strength. While awaiting their return, he arranged for his own search and monitored the radio network for sightings from AirSoPac B-17s and PBYs. At 0555 the *Saratoga* put eight VF-5 F4Fs aloft on CAP, while the *Enterprise* dispatched twenty SBDs to look over the northern semicircle (270–090 degrees, 200 miles) and three more on IAP. Fletcher later directed the *Enterprise* to handle searches and IAPs the rest of the day, while the *Sara* recovered her Guadalcanal strike. Felt's raiders would be readied for immediate launch if the enemy again turned up.

While TF-61 cleared for action, the AirSoPac search planes spread out over the waters north of the Solomons.[2] In the western arc of the semicircle, 11th Bomb Group B-17s flew up the Slot toward Bougainville. Anchored at the advance base at Ndeni, Santa Cruz Islands, the tender *Mackinac* dispatched six VP-23 Consolidated PBY Catalina flying boats north to cover the crucial sector 306 to 348 degrees to 650 miles. All of them contacted the enemy. Because their reports (at least those Fletcher actually received) strongly influenced the battle, it is useful to list the individual aircraft:

Call sign	Sector	Plane No.	Patrol Plane Commander
1V37	306–313°	23-P-1	Ens. Theodore S. Thueson
3V37	313–320°	23-P-3	Lt. Joseph M. Kellam
5V37	320–327°	23-P-5	Ens. Gale C. Burkey
7V37	327–334°	23-P-7	Ens. James A. Spraggins
8V37	334–341°	23-P-8	Lt. (jg) Robert E. Slater
9V37	341–348°	23-P-9	Lt. Leo B. Riester

For TF-61 the morning proceeded without incident and with excellent weather. At 0947 the *Enterprise* reported her dawn search as negative except for another submarine bombed at 0630. To clear her deck for recovery, she launched eight VF-6 F4Fs (Ens. George W. Brooks) on CAP, six VT-3 TBFs as IAP, and eight SBDs as intermediate air patrol also on the lookout for I-boats. By 1010 she had retrieved the twenty search SBDs.

The first AirSoPac ship sightings started filtering in about 0935, when the *En-*

terprise copied a message from 5V37 (Ens. Gale C. Burkey's 23-P-5), which located one carrier, two cruisers, and four destroyers at latitude 4°40′ S, longitude 161°15′ E, and on course 180 degrees. At 0945 when Kinkaid asked Fletcher by TBS ("talk between ships") if he had received it, he heard a negative and provided it, although apparently TF-61 did not copy the call sign. That offered the first indication an enemy carrier might be nearby. At 281 miles northeast of TF-61, it lay out of attack range for the time being, so authentication and possible amplification of this contact could wait. Even so, at 1012 Fletcher told Kinkaid to ready a strike group as soon as possible and report when ready.

At 1003 B-17 22V40 discovered a heavy or light cruiser running southeast between Santa Isabel and New Georgia. Two minutes later PBY 1V37 (Ensign Thueson's 23-P-1 from Ndeni) advised it had encountered three Zeros at 0900. Since 1V37 was closest to the island chain itself, the sighting did not necessarily mean carrier-based fighters. Fletcher's staff reasoned that the PBY might have

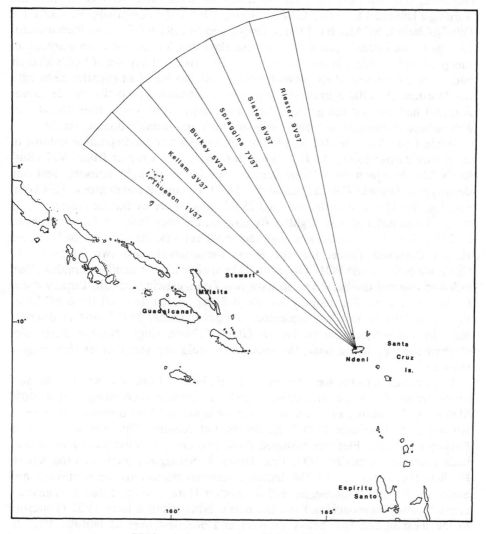

PBY search sectors from Ndeni, 24 August.

run afoul of Zeros from Buka. Actually, Thueson had spotted float planes bound for Tanaka's convoy or its close escort of cruisers.

A few minutes later Lt. Leo Riester (9V37) in the easternmost sector sighted two heavy cruisers and two destroyers, which opposed with AA fire. They were the vanguard of Kondō's Advance Force, and the seaplane carrier *Chitose* stung back with her Mitsubishi F1M2 Type 0 observation seaplanes [PETE]. Three of the nimble biplanes riddled 23-P-9 and killed the copilot, Ens. Robert S. Wilcox III. At 1030 Riester radioed, "Attacked by aircraft planes fighting type Zero."[3] Twenty minutes later Lt. (jg) Robert E. Slater, flying PBY 23-P-8 in the sector immediately west of Riester, also advised he had fought enemy planes. To Fletcher the presence of fighters so remote from island bases meant carriers, but he was wrong. In fact Riester misidentified the kind of aircraft that intercepted him, while Slater failed to specify any type at all.

While pondering these early reports, Fletcher was heartened to see the *Saratoga*'s errant strike group arrive from Guadalcanal. Felt brought twenty-nine SBDs (two others stayed for the time being at Henderson Field) and seven TBFs (including one that flew there on the 22nd). To make room on deck, at 1030 the *Saratoga* launched her third CAP of twelve VF-5 F4Fs comprising SCARLET 3 (Wally Clarke), SCARLET 5 (Dick Gray), and SCARLET 7 (Dave Richardson). Lt. (jg) Frank Green's plane captain remarked that he had not even warmed up this particular Wildcat in the last ten days! By 1100 all thirty-six of Felt's aircraft had roosted on board, their crews bubbling with stories of an eventful night with the Marines. At 0200 a brief shelling from a submarine (actually the destroyer *Kagerō*) had livened things up. Tired and happy to be back, they found "an atmosphere of quiet excitement" on board their comfortable floating airport.[4]

While Felt's flyers settled in, Fletcher received his first indisputable sighting of an enemy carrier force. At 1110 the *Saratoga* copied a report from 5V37 (Burkey's 23-P-5) which placed one carrier, two heavy or light cruisers, and one destroyer at latitude 4°40′ S, longitude 161°20′ E, course 180 degrees. This composition was identical to that relayed 75 minutes before by the *Enterprise,* while the positions differed only slightly. By now the distance from TF-61 had dropped to 245 miles. Actually Burkey had sent both reports. At 0955 he had greeted Hara's Detached Force, but the *Ryūjō* impolitely loosed two Zeros (PO1c Okugawa Noboru and PO1c Okumura Takeo) after him. A nearby cumulus cloud failed to conceal the big PBY, so with two Zeros clawing his tail, Burkey dived for the wave tops. Surprisingly his adroit flying fended them off for a full hour. Finally at 1105 he lost his tormentors in heavy clouds. 23-P-5 sustained amazingly light damage, only twelve to fifteen 7.7-mm slugs. Neither Zero pilot claimed the wily flying boat; the most they could say was that its right engine smoked.[5]

More contacts to the west followed closely behind Burkey's. At 1116 the *Saratoga* received via the *Mackinac* a garbled message recounting that at 1050 Slater's 8V37 spotted one cruiser (heavy or light) and four unidentified ships at latitude 5° S, longitude 162°05′ E, course 140 degrees. This was not far from Burkey's sighting. Fletcher assumed these two groups would soon join, if they hadn't already. Actually 7V37, Ens. James A. Spraggins, originated the report. He flew the sector 327 to 334 degrees, between Burkey to the southwest and Slater to the north. Spraggins either spotted Hara's *Ryūjō* force or Tanaka's convoy slowly approaching from the north. Nine minutes later 1V37 (Thueson) to the west placed two heavy cruisers and one destroyer at latitude 5°12′ S, longitude 158°50′ E, course 355 degrees, speed 20 knots. This was northeast of

Burkey's carrier. In fact Thueson revealed the Close Cover Force that protected Tanaka's transports.

Given a carrier and a rich supporting cast to westward, Kinkaid chafed to unleash the *Enterprise* Air Group. At 1129 he signaled Fletcher:

> Fighter and attack group ready, 20 VF, 25 SBD with 1,000 pound bombs, 8 VTB with 2 500 pound bombs each, 1 VTB group commander with belly tank. Plan to use 8 VTB and 12 VSB for afternoon search. Recommend sector 290–090 radius 250 miles.[6]

Not prepared to concentrate on just the one reported carrier, Fletcher waited to see if more turned up. Later he described his course of action:

> In order to verify these [search] reports and guard against a repetition of the attack made under similar circumstances on the 23rd which never found its objective, I reluctantly ordered Commander Task Force SIXTEEN to immediately launch a search covering the arc 290°–090° to a distance of 250 miles.[7]

His "reluctance" stemmed from the necessity of devoting twenty potential strike planes to cover such a wide search area. The Battle of the Coral Sea also came to mind. On 7 May he had destroyed the light carrier *Shōhō,* only to discover soon after that two big enemy carriers also operated within range. At 1140 he directed Kinkaid to launch his recommended search as soon as possible.

At 1150 Lt. Cdr. Calvin Wakeman, SCARLET BASE FDO (call sign "Eppie," his nickname) on board the *Saratoga,* broke radio silence when radar detected an intruder to the southwest. He dispatched Dave Richardson's SCARLET 7 out on 260 degrees (M.) at 12,000 feet and at 1157 turned them right to 290 degrees, warning of the bogey 15 miles ahead. Two minutes later and about 30 miles from the ships, one SCARLET 7 pilot sang out, "On our port bow, Dave." Asked "up or down?," he replied, "Tally ho 1 Kawanishi." Richardson discerned the flying boat two miles ahead and more than 1,000 feet above.[8]

SCARLET 7 had flushed WO Ata Kiyomi's experimental Kawanishi H8K1 Type 2 flying boat [EMILY]. The Yokohama crew hunted southeast along the 122-degree line from Shortland. Spotting Grummans, Ata swung southwest, gained a few thousand more feet, then nosed over into a fast, shallow dive aiming for a cloud layer. The big, slab-sided Type 2 quickly attained over 225 knots, forcing the CAP to go over 300 just to catch it. Richardson told Frank Green's section to dip underneath the clouds, so they followed the Kawanishi into the murk, while he and Ens. Foster Blair patrolled atop of the cloud layer. Finally at 1205 and about 50 miles from the ships, Green noticed the enemy emerge in the clear at 500 feet and warned Richardson. Throttles blocked forward, Green and Ens. Don Innis dived in first with a "sort of high-side" from the port beam. Swiveling around, the Type 2's 20-mm tail turret blazed away while still out of range. Green retaliated, but underled the unexpectedly swift target. His bullets clipped the tail gunner and sprinkled the sea behind the patrol plane. Innis seemed on target, but saw no evident damage.

Richardson waved Blair out to the side, then dropped toward the Type 2's starboard quarter. Ignoring angry "red flashes" from the 20-mm dorsal turret, he walked his bullets into the fuselage. Meanwhile, Blair followed through with a high-side pass from the starboard side. For an instant Green thought Blair's F4F had caught fire, but it was only smoke from its guns. Set afire in the port inboard engine, the Kawanishi whipped into a steep left wingover and plowed into the water with a "terrific explosion." At 1211 Richardson exulted, "I got him Hank. Bingo!" "Hank" was Lt. Henry Rowe, RED BASE FDO, whom Richardson wrongly thought controlled the intercept. Not offended, Wakeman replied, "Nice going Dave." Shortland copied no messages from Ata, and even TF-61 doubted this snooper ever sighted it. To Blair's later displeasure, Richardson received full credit for the kill, a sleek, modern aircraft tentatively identified as a Sikorsky S44 or S45 flying boat.[9]

At 1204 Fletcher inquired of Kinkaid what strike group he would have after sending out his afternoon search. He instructed *Enterprise* to take over fighter direction and be prepared to recover and service the dozen *Saratoga* fighters launched at 1110. Thirty minutes later Kinkaid replied that after the search departed and the planes in the air were recovered, the *Enterprise* could provide by 1330 an attack group of twenty fighters, twelve dive bombers (1,000-pound bombs), six TBFs with torpedoes, and the group commander's aircraft. At 1244 Fletcher replied, "Will hold your attack group in reserve for possible second carrier. Do not launch attack group until I direct you."[10]

From 1235 to 1247 the *Enterprise* launched forty-five aircraft. Sixteen F4Fs—RED 1 (Lieutenant Bauer), RED 2 (Machinist Barnes), RED 3 (Lieutenant [jg] Gay), and RED 4 (Machinist Runyon)—reinforced the CAP, while the afternoon search comprised sixteen SBDs (eight VB-6, eight VS-5) and seven VT-3 TBFs on the northern semicircle (290–090 degrees). Six SBDs (three VB-6, three VS-5) took over as relief IAP.

While these flight operations took place, VF-5 destroyed another snooper. At 1245 Wakeman alerted Dick Gray's SCARLET 5. This time he vectored the CAP south on 185 degrees (M.), altitude 7,000 feet. Five minutes later he told them to orbit, because the bogey approached from 12 miles ahead. At 1253 and 20 miles out from the ships, Gray noticed an aircraft wave-hopping at 200 feet and called, "Tally ho. It appears to be a B-17." Wakeman queried the identification, and at 1255 Gray announced, "Yeah, he's a Jap bomber." The four F4Fs nosed over, and the startled Japanese turned left to evade. SCARLET 5 had ambushed PO1c Takahashi Sachito's Misawa Air Group Type 1 land attack plane flying the 115-degree line from Rabaul. Gray's high-side run deteriorated into a stern attack, but he set the *rikkō* aflame. Ens. Mark Bright followed him in, while Lt. Marion Dufilho and Ens. Leon Haynes approached from high-astern. By the time the last F4F quit shooting, the bomber splashed only seven miles from TF-61, whose lookouts witnessed the action. Some speculated (incorrectly) that the enemy plane carried a torpedo. Although Gray declared in his report, "All four of us shot him down," like Richardson he later received sole credit for a "4-engined patrol plane [*sic*]."[11]

At 1307 the *Enterprise* turned into the wind to recover Red Brooks's eight VF-6 CAP F4Fs, six VT-3 TBFs from IAP, and the eight SBDs of the Intermediate Air Patrol. The twelve F4Fs of the *Saratoga*'s third CAP, namely Clarke's SCARLET 3, Gray's SCARLET 5, and Richardson's SCARLET 7, also flopped down on "The Big E." Felt's strike group covered the *Saratoga*'s flight deck, and she did not want to break the spot. It was an important step in increasing air flexibility among the carriers. Fog Green, for one, minded not at all and enjoyed the wardroom lemonade, which was "not the cheap imitation that we have been getting [on the *Sara*]."[12]

This time Fletcher felt certain the last snooper had reported his position (although Rabaul never heard from Takahashi). No doubt the major counteroffensive against Guadalcanal was well underway, mounted by a large force of warships spread across a frontage of 60 miles. The transports discovered the previous day were probably sheltered behind them. As yet the search had turned

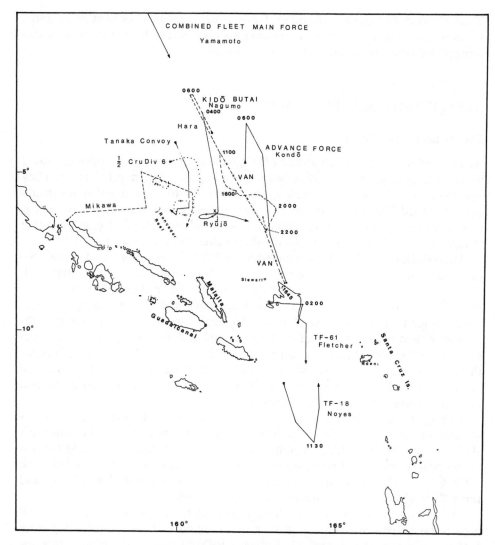

Task force operations, 24 August.

up only one enemy carrier. One flattop did not seem sufficient for an operation of this scope. Despite the rosy ULTRA estimates, Fletcher decided the Japanese very likely had stashed two or more carriers nearby, but so far the searches failed to find them. He intended for Kinkaid to:

1. have the *Enterprise* maintain CAP, IAP, and take over fighter direction;
2. ready a strike group in case a second enemy carrier was discovered within range;
3. service and direct the 12 VF-5 F4Fs as desired.

At the same time the *Saratoga* was to:

1. hold her strike group ready to launch;
2. prepare to service fighters until the strike group returned;
3. arm remaining TBFs (those not scheduled for the strike) with torpedoes to join the *Enterprise*'s follow-up strike.

Thus Fletcher laid out his afternoon battle plan. He waited as long as he dared for new search reports before committing his main strength against the lone carrier spotted three hours before by Ensign Burkey.

ATTACK AND COUNTERATTACK

The Ryūjō Bombs CACTUS

At 1320, while the *Saratoga* awaited the go-ahead to launch her strike her radar detected a large group of bogeys bearing 350 degrees, distance 112 miles. They appeared to fly 220 degrees, that is, away from TF-61, and at 103 miles disappeared toward CACTUS. To find out who they were and what they were doing, it is necessary to follow the operations of Rear Admiral Hara's Detached Force (*Ryūjō, Tone, Tokitsukaze,* and *Amatsukaze*) after Burkey departed at 1105.

At 1200, Hara reached the scheduled point 200 miles north of Guadalcanal. No one had found any American carriers, so the *Ryūjō* prepared to go through with the Lunga attack. She divided fifteen Zero fighters and six Type 97 carrier attack planes into two strike waves. Lt. Murakami Binichi, CO of the *Ryūjō* Carrier Attack Squadron, led the first of six *kankō*, each carrying six 60-kilogram high-explosive land bombs, escorted by WO Shigemi Katsuma's six Zeros. The second wave ("Raiding Force") comprised nine Zeros under Lt. Nōtomi Kenjirō, the group commander. Primarily a "fighter aircraft carrier," the *Ryūjō* packed such a small offensive punch that her mission to knock out gun positions and aircraft at Lunga seems a useless gesture.[13]

To prepare for flight operation, the *Ryūjō* lowered her four large radio masts situated on both sides of the flight deck to permit the six Type 97s and Shigemi's six Zeros to take off at 1220. Nōtomi's nine Zeros followed, and at 1248 the last of the twenty-one planes departed south. Her deck clear, the *Ryūjō* landed three CAP fighters (WO Maruyama Akira's 16th *Shōtai*), which placed nine Zeros and three Type 97 carrier attack planes on board (see table 6.1).

Hara withdrew north, but only temporarily, as he tarried in the same general area to be able to recover the strike group four hours later. At 1341 Japanese lookouts discerned Lt. Joseph M. Kellam's PBY 23-P-3 [3V37] on its return leg after checking out the sector immediately south of Burkey's. At 1405 Kellam announced the sighting of two heavy or light cruisers, one carrier, and two destroyers at latitude 5°40′ S, longitude 162°20′ E, course 140 degrees. Within a few minutes Fletcher had the message in hand—only the second sighting report of an enemy carrier provided him so far that day. Its call sign came through as 1V37 (Thueson) in the next sector west. This new carrier appeared to be the one reported hours before by Burkey, but since she was 60 miles northeast of where Fletcher expected the first one to be, she might be another carrier altogether. Actually both PBYs had located the *Ryūjō*, but Fletcher could not know that for certain.

1V37's report caused great concern because TF-61 had already shot its bolt. At 1340 the *Sara* launched her fourth CAP of twelve VF-5 F4Fs: SCARLET 1 (Lieutenant Commander Simpler), SCARLET 4 (Lieutenant Harmer), and SCARLET 6 (Lieutenant Jensen), and Felt followed with thirty SBDs (CSAG, fifteen VS-3, fourteen VB-3) and eight VT-8 TBFs. One TBF later aborted. Again because of the range to the target, Fletcher decided not to provide fighter escort.

TABLE 6.1
Ryūjō Strike Group

	First Wave	
	Carrier Attack Force (6 Type 97s)	
1st *Shōtai*	2nd *Shōtai*	
Lt. Murakami Binichi (P)	Lt. (jg) Satō Keizō[a] (O)	
WO Takehira Shinkichi (O)	PO1c Nemoto Masao[a] (O)	
PO1c Satō Takamori[c] (P)	PO2c Kikuda Harasada[a] (O)	
	Direct Escort (6 Zeros)	
12th *Shōtai*	17th *Shōtai*	
WO Shigemi Katsuma	PO1c Yoshizawa Tomio	
PO1c Shikada Tsugio	PO2c Nojima Jinsaku[a]	
PO3c Morita Toyoo	Sea1c Yoshida Ippei	
	Second Wave	
	Raiding Force (9 Zeros)	
11th *Shōtai*	13th *Shōtai*	14th *Shōtai*
Lt. Nōtomi Kenjirō	PO1c Okugawa Noboru	PO1c Kurihara Hiroshi
PO1c Okumura Takeo[b]	PO2c Hōjō Hiromichi	PO2c Yotsumoto Chiune
Sea1c Banno Takao	Sea1c Ishihara Shūji[a]	Sea1c Sanada Eiji

Note: Aircraft commanders: P = pilot; O = observer. All other aircraft ditched, crews saved.
[a] Shot down
[b] Missing in action, recovered
[c] Crash-landed at Ndai Island, recovered

Felt headed out against Burkey's old contact of one CV, two CAs, four DDs, using an outbound leg of 320 degrees and 216 miles, gambling that the ships held their reported course and speed. Now 1V37's sighting report placed the same target or perhaps another fully 60 miles northeast of Felt's objective. The *Saratoga* tried but could not raise Felt to advise him of the new position.

Cruising at about 3,000 meters (9,840 feet), the *Ryūjō*'s two attack waves discerned first Malaita, then Florida and Guadalcanal beyond. At 1415 Murakami shuffled his carrier attack planes into the special arrowhead formation for horizontal bombing, with his wingman WO Takehira Shinkichi (the most experienced bombardier) in the lead. Shigemi's six Zeros cruised in tight formation only 500 meters to their right. On schedule the main body nosed down into a shallow dive, while Nōtomi's nine Raiding Force Zeros dived swiftly to strafe the airfield just after the bombs struck.

CACTUS control at Henderson Field enjoyed no radar surveillance capability as yet, so Lt. Col. Charles Fike, the MAG-23 XO, relied on CAPs during so-called Tojo Time, when an enemy raid was most likely. At 1415 four VMF-223 Grumman F4F-4 Wildcats of the 3rd Division circled 12,000 feet over Sealark Channel: Capt. Marion E. Carl and Technical Sgt. Johnny D. Lindley; 2nd Lt. Fred E. Gutt and Mar. Gun. Henry B. Hamilton (VMF-212). A dozen more F4Fs from VMF-223 and also some Bell P-400 Airacobra fighters from the AAF's 67th FS waited on alert at Henderson Field.

On patrol Marion Carl observed the incoming Japanese strike north out over the channel toward Tulagi and alerted CACTUS. The Pagoda crew sounded the air-raid siren and hoisted the black flag signifying Condition RED. Spurred on by the sound of incoming enemy planes, the pilots ran for the waiting fighters, gunned their engines, and bounced along the taxiways to the runway. In no particular order, ten Marine Wildcats took to the air:

VMF-223	VMF-212 (attached to 223)
Capt. Rivers J. Morrell	2nd Lt. John H. King
2nd Lt. Cloyd R. Jeans	2nd Lt. Lawrence C. Taylor
2nd Lt. Zenneth A. Pond	2nd Lt. John M. Massey
2nd Lt. Kenneth D. Frazier	2nd Lt. Robert F. McLeod
2nd Lt. Elwood R. Bailey	
2nd Lt. Robert R. Read	

At the 67th's hangar, Capt. Dale D. Brannon and 2nd Lt. Deltis H. Fincher manned two ready P-400s. Those pilots who got away early climbed after the bombers, but Nōtomi's raiders cut off the others.[14]

Carl led his four F4Fs over what he thought were unescorted bombers. At 1423 he and Johnny Lindley peeled off into steep overhead attacks against the six planes trailing on the right and struck swiftly. Carl claimed one "bomber," but actually he had bounced Shigemi's six fighters cramped in tight formation and finished PO2c Nojima Jinsaku's 17th *Shōtai* Zero. Surprised by two Grummans, PO1c Yoshizawa Tomio and Sea1c Yoshida Ippei from the 17th quickly evaded. Carl and Lindley split up, and both regained altitude for follow-up attacks. At 1425 "Tex" Hamilton, a highly experienced NAP, mixed in with Shigemi's 12th *Shōtai* Zeros for an extended dogfight, while Fred Gutt took after Murakami's Type 97s ready to drop their payloads.

At 1428 spotters from the 3rd Defense Battalion placed six twin-engine (*sic*) bombers bearing 315 degrees at 8,200 feet, and the four 90-mm AA guns of Battery E started pounding away at them.[15] At 1430 Murakami's six bombardiers released their thirty-six 60-kilogram bombs. Their tight bomb pattern, leaving "fairly regular lines of large craters churned into black earth,"[16] bracketed the 90-mm battery area but inflicted no real damage.

As the bombs exploded, Nōtomi's nine Zeros roared low over Lunga for simultaneous strafing attacks from three directions. Directly over the field, Nōtomi's own 11th *Shōtai* caught "Rapid Robert" Read's F4F shuffling along at 500 feet just after he lifted off. Wounded in the head and right shoulder, Read limped north and finally ditched his battered Wildcat about two miles short of Florida Island. The next day friendly natives brought him safely to Tulagi. While trying to evade ground fire, Sea1c Ishihara Shūji, number 3 in PO1c Okugawa's 13th *Shōtai*, ran afoul of Brannon and Fincher in the two P-400s. They swiftly torched the Zero. In return Okugawa and PO2c Hōjō Hiromichi ripped the two long-nosed "Bell fighters" and claimed one. After some anxious moments, Fincher evaded the Mitsubishi shooting up his tail. Meanwhile, PO1c Kurihara Hiroshi (14th *Shōtai* leader) sustained AA hits in his fighter, but kept on going. His number 2, PO2c Yotsumoto Chiune, barely avoided an exploding fuel dump.

Out to the north toward Malaita, about six *Ryūjō* Zeros fought a low-level running battle against the two P-400s and three of the newly scrambled F4Fs. Bob McLeod of 212 winged PO1c Okumura Takeo, Nōtomi's wingman, who crash-landed his stricken fighter on Guadalcanal. Meeting up with Japanese troops, he later joined another tough bunch, the Tainan Air Group, for further Guadalcanal adventures. In turn the Japanese shot down 2nd Lt. Elwood Bailey of VMF-223. Although seen to bail out over Tulagi, he never came back.

After releasing bombs, Murakami's six carrier attack planes swung in a wide

180-degree turn to retire northward. From overhead, Carl's scattered division resumed mauling the bombers as they headed out. At the same time more Marines, including Morrell, Jeans, Frazier, Pond, King, and Taylor, climbed into the fight as fast as their straining Wildcats allowed. All took their turns at the bombers. At 1433 Carl's beautiful overhead pass notched his second kill, a bomber on the left side, while Ken Frazier blasted another on the right. Within a minute, a third Type 97 burst into flames. The five direct-escort Zeros, soon joined by Kurihara and Yotsumoto from the Raiding Force, rallied to protect their charges. After pulling out of his second pass, Carl brushed a Zero off Lindley's tail. Another Japanese peppered Gutt's fuselage and wounded him in the left arm and leg. He escaped by diving away. After sharing a bomber with "Rex" Jeans, "Red" Taylor of 212 fell to an enemy fighter. At the same time John King singled out one bomber "flying along like a fat and happy goose," which "exploded at the first burst."[17] Zeros subsequently chased him into a cloud and kept him there for a time.

Thus despite the escorts, from 1423 to 1450 ten Marines claimed eleven bombers and five fighters from the main body for the loss of one F4F shot down. Together they destroyed the entire 2nd Carrier Attack *Shōtai:* Lt. (jg) Satō Keizō (NA 67-1939), PO1c Nemoto Masao, and PO2c Kikuda Harasada, as well as PO2c Nojima's Zero. PO1c Satō Takamori's Type 97 dropped out with heavy damage. The other pair of Type 97s and seven Zeros gratefully withdrew.

Landing back at Henderson Field after what for most was their first battle, the CACTUS fighter pilots appeared "hilariously elated." Confusion as to the details of the fight pretty much set the tone for this immensely perplexing air battle. Perhaps prompted by inaccurate ground-spotter reports, some Marines erroneously remembered fighting twin-engine bombers as well as the single-engine jobs. Correspondent Dick Tregaskis described Ken Frazier: "He could not say surely how many enemy bombers there had been or whether they were one or two motored craft."[18] Actually, bad weather had forced back the morning strike of twenty-four Type 1 land attack planes and fourteen Zeros before they ever neared Guadalcanal. By 1130 they were back on the ground at Rabaul.

Marine claims that day ultimately totaled eleven single and twin-engine bombers and six Zero fighters. The 67th FS added another Zero, while the 3rd Defense Battalion tallied one enemy plane, type not indicated. CACTUS lost three F4Fs shot down (Lawrence Taylor, Elwood Bailey, and Robert Read, who was the only survivor). Fred Gutt left the island for a time because of wounds. Japanese claims numbered fifteen Grumman and Bell fighters (including two unconfirmed), but three *Ryūjō* Type 97 carrier attack planes and three Zeros went down over the target, with PO1c Okumura the only survivor. PO1c Satō set down his stricken Type 97 *kankō* off Ndai Island north of Malaita, and the next day the destroyer *Mochizuki* rescued the crew. Considering the lack of real damage to the field and Japanese losses, the strike was certainly a failure. Even worse, it placed the *Ryūjō* in a precarious position.

The Loss of the Ryūjō

Soon after Hara received word of the Lunga bombing, his Detached Force was snooped almost simultaneously by three separate *Enterprise* search sections. About 1440, Lieutenant Commander Jett and wingman Ens. Robert J. Bye, flying two VT-3 TBFs in the 320 to 330 degrees sector, sighted ahead on the horizon one carrier and three destroyers, with two more cruisers about two miles off her starboard beam. Jett sent a contact report and spiraled north to gain position for a horizontal bombing run against the CV.[19]

At the same time Lt. Stockton Birney Strong (USNA 1937) and Ens. Gerald S. Richey with two VS-5 SBDs closed Hara from the next sector north. They even saw Jett and Bye climb away. Unable to catch them, Strong closed within five miles of the carrier, sent a contact report, but withdrew without attacking. He later vowed never to repeat that mistake. From the southwest, Ens. John H. Jorgenson's mismatched search pair (his VS-5 SBD and Ens. Harold L. Binga-man's VT-3 TBF) sighted the same four ships, reported as a CV and three DDs. At low altitude they drew near the CV before the CAP scared them off.[20]

Meanwhile Jett and Bye had worked up to 12,000 feet while circling out to the west, when at 1455 the Japanese finally spotted them. Misidentifying the two TBFs as B-17s, the *Amatsukaze* directed 12.7-cm AA fire in their path, and the *Tone* and *Tokitsukaze* joined in. Belatedly, the *Ryūjō* swung into the wind to launch PO1c Sugiyama Teruo's three 18th *Shōtai* Zeros and one Type 97 carrier attack plane for antisub patrol. At 1458, as the carrier evaded with a sharp turn to starboard, Jett and Bye together dropped four 500-pound bombs in a tight group. They detonated in her wake as virtually one splash 150 meters astern. Sugiyama raced after the two misidentified Avengers, but could not catch them.

Reaching Fletcher at 1500, Jett's contact report placed one carrier, one heavy cruiser, one light cruiser, and three destroyers at latitude 6°25' S, longitude 161° E. Ten minutes later another message noted the enemy course as 270 degrees, speed 20 knots, and added that the carrier's deck was empty of planes. Fletcher thought Jett's contact must be the same force previously reported by 5V37 (Burkey) and probably 1V37 (actually Kellam's 3V37). Yet it was farther north than he expected and at 260 miles even more distant. The *Enterprise* had prepared a strike of eleven SBDs and seven TBFs, escorted by fifteen F4Fs, which Kinkaid wanted to use against this target. He requested a northwesterly Point Option course to continue closing and shorten their return flight. Fletcher disagreed and maintained for the time being the Point Option course to the east. However, he told Kinkaid to await his order to launch the strike group to attack and then spend the night at Guadalcanal.

If the *Enterprise* aviators grew frustrated, their feelings were nothing compared with those of one Japanese destroyer skipper. Cdr. Hara Tameichi, CO of the *Amatsukaze*, watched in growing disbelief at his perceived incompetence of the *Ryūjō*'s Air Department. After 1500, with no evident move to reinforce the CAP after Jett's near misses, he sent a rather unprecedented message to his old Academy classmate, Cdr. Kishi Hisakichi, the *Ryūjō*'s XO: "Fully realizing my impertinence, am forced to advise you my impression. Your flight operations are far short of expectations. What is the matter?" Kishi replied, "Deeply appreciate your admonition. We shall do better and count on your cooperation."[21] Perhaps spurred by Hara's rocket, the *Ryūjō* soon launched her 16th *Shōtai*, reduced to PO1c Miyauchi Yukuo's two Zeros when Warrant Officer Maruyama's fighter had to be scratched.

Now with increased Japanese alertness, two VT-3 TBFs on the dogleg of their search ran afoul of the *Ryūjō* force. Lt. John N. Myers (USNA 1938) and Mach. Harry L. Corl (one of VT-3's three Midway survivors) flew south of Jorgenson and Bingaman. Around 1500 one heavy cruiser (with one stack) appeared ahead. Myers and Corl eased up to 10,000 feet for a horizontal bombing run, while their intended target, the *Tone*, quickly boosted speed, zigzagged, and cut loose with her guns. Nearing the bomb point, Myers happened to notice a carrier about 10 miles away and turned to go after her but almost at the same time two Zeros suddenly appeared. PO1c Miyauchi and PO3c Yoshiwara Isamu (16th *Shōtai*) broke up the bomb run. One of them zoomed in with a head-on run against Corl, then both concentrated on Myers, who evaded. Yoshiwara stayed with Myers, while Miyauchi hastened after Corl. Myers last saw the other TBF disappear below with a Zero close on its tail, but could do nothing because Yoshiwara ran him out of the area.

Diving through the clouds, Corl momentarily escaped his pursuer, then tried radioing the *Enterprise,* but with no success. Near to the water Miyauchi showed up again, this time joined by Sea1c Kotani Kenji (a *Hiryū* veteran and number 3 in the 18th *Shōtai*). Together they blasted Corl's TBF into the sea. The radioman/turret gunner, Delmar D. Wiley, RM3c, lived through the crash. For 15 harrowing days he drifted in his life raft northwest and fetched up on isolated Carteret Island, 40 miles northeast of Buka and far behind Japanese lines. Not until 11 April 1943 after many adventures did Del Wiley reach safety at Guadalcanal.[22]

Time expired for the *Ryūjō,* when at 1536 Felt's *Saratoga* strike group finally sighted the target to the northwest. On the way out, Felt took his twenty-nine SBDs (CSAG, fifteen VS-3, thirteen VB-3) to 15,000 feet while Lt. Bruce Harwood's seven VT-3 TBFs cruised 3,000 feet below.[23] Felt monitored Jett's sighting report at 1518, which placed the carrier farther north than expected, and turned north briefly before swinging west again. A bum radio forced him to relinquish the lead to Lt. Cdr. Louis Kirn, VS-3 CO. Anxious eyes scanned the sea, finally to be rewarded by the glorious sight of distant wakes and tiny enemy ships.

Felt decided to approach the target from the northeast and signaled his tactical deployment: Kirn's VS-3, Lt. Cdr. Dewitt Shumway's 1st Division of VB-3, and six TBFs to attack the carrier, the remaining six SBDs and one TBF against the swift cruiser. The cry of the lookouts, "Many enemy planes approaching," finally apprised the force of its great danger. Captain Katō swung the *Ryūjō* into the wind to scramble the 15th *Shōtai* (Lt. Iizuka Masao and PO1c Tomoishi Masateru), raising to seven the number of Zeros aloft. Two Type 97 carrier attack planes sat aft on her flight deck, while Warrant Officer Maruyama's malfunctioning Zero was struck below. Already spread widely across the sea, the cruiser and two destroyers eventually opened to intervals of 5,000 meters. That gave them plenty of freedom for evasive maneuvers, but availed little defense for the carrier.

At 1550 Kirn's squadron pushed over from 14,000 feet against the *Ryūjō.* No Zeros intervened, yet Katō's shiphandling definitely bothered VS-3. He continued circling sharply starboard, with splashes from big thousand-pound bombs erupting all around the carrier. Shumway's VB-3 1st Division followed VS-3 down, also faced no fighters on the way in, but likewise scored no hits. Two pairs of Zeros, PO1c Sugiyama and PO3c Bandō Makoto (18th *Shōtai*) and PO1c Miyauchi and PO3c Yoshiwara (16th *Shōtai*), comprised a belated reception committee for Shumway, when they tore into the VB-3 SBDs near the water. Ens. William A. Behr came in for particular attention from two Japanese who thoroughly riddled his Dauntless.

From overhead Felt watched about ten bombs fall wide of the mark. Greatly concerned, he abruptly ordered all remaining aircraft to concentrate against the carrier. He waited until he thought the last of his dive bombers had gone ahead, then dived himself against the *Ryūjō.* Carefully observing her flight deck, he was positive no bombs had struck her previous to his thousand-pounder, which he reckoned as a direct hit portside aft. Instead it probably was a very near miss. Fortuitously VB-3's 2nd Division of six SBDs led by Lt. Harold S. Bottomley (USNA 1937) aborted their runs against the *Tone*, braved attacks by the four Zeros, then followed through with three hits on the carrier. Officially Katō reported no direct bomb hits (certainly incorrect), but noted several damaging near misses that breached the *Ryūjō*'s hull. However, it is believed at least three bombs did strike home: two on the starboard deck edge (one forward, the other aft) and a third far abaft on the starboard side.

While the SBDs made their drops, the seven VT-8 TBFs executed fast, shallow dives from 12,000 feet.[24] Bruce Harwood's five split for an anvil attack against the *Ryūjō*, while ensigns Corwin F. Morgan and Robert A. Divine tackled the "light cruiser," actually the heavy cruiser *Tone*. Near sea level Lieutenant Iizuka, PO1c Tomoishi (15th *Shōtai*), and Sea1c Kotani (18th) opposed the torpedo planes. Jinking in and out for a good shot at the smoke-enshrouded *Ryūjō*, Harwood's three-plane section launched their fish at her starboard bow. They claimed one certain and two probable hits. In fact, one torpedo slammed into her starboard side aft, knocked out both the fire and engine rooms, and crippled steering control. Two more TBFs missed from off her port bow, as did Morgan and Divine against the *Tone*, although they claimed one hit.

Although harassed by CAP Zeros, all thirty-six *Saratoga* strike planes took course for home, confident they had destroyed a carrier. They reported one torpedo hit on a light cruiser and two aircraft shot down: a torpedo plane (the Type 97 on antisub patrol) by Lt. Fred J. Schroeder of VS-3 and a Zero by Joseph V. Godfrey, ARM3c, in Ens. Alden W. Hanson's VB-3 SBD. In return Iizuka's seven CAP Zeros emerged unscathed (as did the Type 97 that reached Buka) and claimed fifteen (one unconfirmed) carrier bombers and attack planes.

At 1608 Hara ordered his ships to retire north, but the *Ryūjō* was finished. Felt could not resist staying behind alone until 1620 to watch her plight: "Carrier continued to run in circles to the right pouring forth black smoke which would die down and belch forth in great volume again."[25] On fire from the deadly 1,000-pound bomb hits and riven by a torpedo in her starboard engine room, the stricken carrier coasted to a stop and soon listed 23 degrees to starboard. At 1600 Katō had belatedly ordered Lieutenant Nōtomi to take his strike group to Buka, However, his *Ryūjō* planes soon arrived overhead to witness the horrifying sight of their carrier spouting flames and thick, black smoke. Now they lacked the fuel to reach a friendly base. The same fate now threatened Don Felt and his raiders, for the mighty *Kidō Butai* had already hurled two powerful air strikes against TF-61.

CHAPTER 7

Riposte—The *Kidō Butai* Attack on Task Force 61

LOCATING THE AMERICAN CARRIERS

While the *Saratoga* unleashed Commander Felt's strike group against the *Ryūjō*, an especially ominous event took place. Believing its location already vouchsafed to the Japanese, TF-61 failed to realize the significance of one more snooper. At 1338 RED BASE mustered the eight VF-6 F4Fs of Bauer's RED 1 and Barnes's RED 2 to 300 degrees (M.) at 15,000 feet. Rowe warned at 1345, "Bogey close in back of you."[1] Three minutes later he loosed them along 230 (M.) in pursuit and for the next several minutes contrived to place the F4Fs ahead of the wily Japanese (for it could only be an enemy plane).

Bauer sighted nothing, but Tom Barnes enjoyed better luck. At 1355, Ens. Douglas M. Johnson spotted the interloper at 3,000 feet over Stewart Island (35 miles northwest of TF-61). A minute later Barnes radioed base: "Bogey is bandit, apparently a slow seaplane type." The quarry, an Aichi E13A1 Type 0 reconnaissance seaplane, disappeared into a cloud. Skillfully piloted, it rolled and cavorted through the sky. Gun. Chuck Brewer, the 2nd Section leader, killed the gunner on his second run, and finally at 1400 Barnes set the float plane on fire 28 miles from the ships: "Tally ho, bomber in water, Bingo! Got him Chuck, landed in the water. RED 2, 1 bogey down."

At 1403 the *Enterprise* launched RED 5 (Vorse), half of RED 7 (Rutherford), and half of SCARLET 5 (Gray and Fog Green from SCARLET 7), total eight F4Fs, to strengthen the CAP. The enemy would indeed attack during their watch.

Unlike Fletcher, Nagumo did not need to juggle confusing and sometimes conflicting sighting reports. He had only one, which cost the three brave men of Spec. Duty Ens. Fukuyama Kazutoshi's *Chikuma* number 2 aircraft, the Type 0 reconnaissance seaplane shot down by RED 2. The all-important message was: "Spotted large enemy force. Being pursued by enemy fighters, 1200 [Z − 9, local time 1400]."[2] Fukuyama flew the Vanguard Force late-morning search launched at 1100. Originally the staff assigned six float planes to cover a sector 060 to 150 degrees, but at the last minute they fortuitously added Fukuyama on the 165-degree line. The *Chikuma* blinkered his report up the line to the *Shōkaku*, and Nagumo had the message in hand at 1425. It gave no position, but revealed an enemy CAP, which could only have come from a carrier. From Fukuyama's flight time and search schedule, the staff estimated the target bore 153 degrees, distance 260 miles. In this game of high stakes hide-and-seek, Nagumo thought he knew the enemy's location and would attack.

Throughout the day the air groups of the *Kidō Butai* tensely awaited word of an enemy carrier force. Remembering Midway quite well, they did not want to be caught again by surprise with fueled and armed aircraft on board. Flagship *Shōkaku* had retained all her operational aircraft: twenty-six Zero fighters, twenty-seven Type 99 carrier bombers, and eighteen Type 97 carrier attack planes. At 1435 Lieutenant Shingō, the fighter squadron CO, took three Zeros aloft on CAP. Lieutenant Commander Seki, the group commander, prepared the first deckload strike of eighteen carrier bombers and Lieutenant Shigematsu's nine 3rd *Chūtai* Zeros. The *Zuikaku* (with twenty-five Zeros, twenty-seven Type 99 carrier bombers, and eighteen Type 97 carrier attack planes) had already furnished three CAP Zeros. Three more departed at 1430. Her contribution to Seki's first strike numbered nine carrier bombers under Lt. Ōtsuka Reijirō (NA 66-1938), a Coral Sea veteran, and six Zeros led by Lt. Hidaka Saneyasu.

At 1450 the *Shōkaku* sent aloft the first of Seki's twenty-seven planes, while the *Zuikaku* followed suit at 1500 with her nine carrier bombers and six Zeros. The forty-two aircraft soon departed southeast on 153 degrees and climbed toward high altitude. Meanwhile, the carriers brought the second strike wave up on deck. The carriers retained the eighteen carrier attack planes in reserve for a possible follow-up torpedo strike.

Southeast of Nagumo, American PBY flying boats repeatedly snooped Kondō's Advance Force, which parried with the *Chitose*'s Type 0 observation seaplanes. Now the wide-ranging *Enterprise* afternoon search showed up. About 1430, VB-6 XO Lt. John T. Lowe (USNA 1934) and Ens. Robert D. Gibson counted three heavy cruisers, several destroyers, and other ships on course 180 degrees, speed 20 knots. The two SBDs circled eastward to check out the area, tapped out a contact report, then attacked with their 500-pounders. At 1447 they scored near misses against heavy cruiser *Maya* of Kondō's 4th Cruiser Division.[3]

Just as Seki departed the *Kidō Butai,* the pugnacious *Enterprise* search pulled off another surprise attack. Around 1445, Lt. Ray Davis, VB-6 skipper, and Ens. Robert C. Shaw noticed an enemy task force far to the northwest. While they maneuvered to bomb one of the lead "light cruisers" (actually a destroyer), Davis saw in the distance a very large carrier with many planes spotted on deck. The two SBDs happened to fly between Nagumo's carriers and Abe's Vanguard Force 40 miles ahead. Eager to get that flattop, Davis swung upwind while climbing to 14,000 feet and adroitly evaded detection by the CAP. Only at the last minute did *Shōkaku* lookouts discern two enemy carrier bombers poised to attack.

In their inexperience the Japanese had committed a serious error. The *Shōkaku*'s radar indeed detected two incoming planes, but word did not reach her bridge in time to act. This marked the first time that Japanese shipborne radar contacted hostile aircraft, but no one warned the nine Zeros on CAP. The only fighters to spot the enemy were Shigematsu's nine *Shōkaku* escort Zeros in the process of leaving the area. They faced a great dilemma, whether to stay with the strike or pursue the attackers back toward the ships. Finally five of the nine broke away from the strike group: the whole 19th *Shōtai* under PO1c Matsuda Jirō and two from PO1c Ōmori Shigetaka's 18th *Shōtai*. Only PO3c Komachi Sadamu from the 18th remained with Shigematsu's own 17th *Shōtai*, thus reducing the *Shōkaku* escorts to four.[4]

At 1515 and still unseen by the CAP, Davis and Shaw pushed over from 14,000 feet, but Captain Arima ordered right full rudder just in time to throw off their aim. One 500-pound bomb missed the *Shōkaku*'s starboard side by only 10 meters (but killed six of her crew); the second exploded 10 meters beyond. The CAP never caught up with the attackers, but some of the erstwhile escort Zeros did. Davis wrongly believed AA brushed one overeager Zero off his tail.[5]

A similar snafu soon bedeviled the American side. Davis's careful contact reports gave the enemy strength ("2 CV's with decks full"), position and course, and a bombing report. Exceptionally poor radio reception prevented the *Enterprise* and the *Saratoga* from copying these messages in full, but they did hear enough to indicate the presence of two enemy carriers. Most important, neither the originator's identity nor the enemy positions came through. Thus Fletcher was denied a great opportunity to send a follow-up strike against Nagumo.

Davis and Shaw certainly shook up the *Kidō Butai*. From 1520 to 1530, the *Shōkaku* scrambled eleven Zeros (all she had) and the *Zuikaku* four more, raising the CAP to twenty-nine fighters (nineteen *Shōkaku*, including the five ex-escorts, and ten *Zuikaku*). At 1550 Nagumo alerted Abe's Vanguard Force 40 miles ahead to finish off the enemy task force that night. Between 1550 and 1600 the two carriers dispatched Takahashi's second strike group of eighteen *Zuikaku* carrier bombers and nine from the *Shōkaku* led by Lt. Yamada Shōhei (NA 65-1938). Nine Zeros (six *Zuikaku*, three *Shōkaku*) under Lieutenant Shirane, CO of the *Zuikaku* Carrier Fighter Squadron, escorted the strike. While Takahashi formed up, the *Hiei* observation seaplane in the sector immediately adjacent to Fukuyama's lost *Chikuma* number 2 plane provided a vital contact. Its crew placed enemy carriers at latitude 9°30' S, longitude 163°20' E, course 130, speed 20 knots. Thus advised, Takahashi started southeast on 150 degrees and expected to find the target about 1800, around sundown. At 1600, Nagumo swung left from 150 to 100 degrees to steam east at 24 knots and await the results of his two strikes.

ATTACK ON TASK FORCE 16

The Defense Prepares

On board the *Saratoga*, Fletcher remained unaware of the Japanese main force of two carriers poised only 250 miles north. Even so, he maintained a wary stance. Leslie's strike group spotted for launch tied up the *Enterprise*'s flight deck, so at 1450 sixteen VF-6 F4Fs (Bauer's RED 1, Barnes's RED 2, Gay's RED 3, and Runyon's RED 4) "pancaked" for fuel on the *Saratoga*, free since Felt's departure. Increased coordination of air operations between carriers meant it was no longer unusual for one flattop to service another's aircraft.

A search PBY inadvertently stirred up the CAP. At 1502 RED BASE assigned Dick Gray's SCARLET 5 division to check out a low-altitude bogey bearing 340 degrees (M.), later adding Scoop Vorse's RED 5 to the hunt. At 1514 Gray radioed, "Bogey appears to be a PBY." At 1520 the *Enterprise* launched Dave Richardson's SCARLET 7 and Brooks's RED 6.[6] By mistake Mark Bright of VF-5 joined on Brooks, giving him five F4Fs and Richardson only three. The PBY behaved suspiciously by deliberately approaching the task force. At 1530 RED BASE sent Vorse out on 300 (M.) to investigate this supposedly friendly plane now located between the two task forces. "Get right on him Scoop," Rowe warned. At 1535, Vorse identified the bogey as a PBY, but Rowe told him to stay

Lt. Scoop Vorse's four VF-6 F4Fs inspect Lt. Joe Kellam's PBY just prior to the attack on TF-16. The destroyer is the *Benham*. Photo taken from the *Portland*. (NA 80-G-299831)

with it anyway. Looking over the Catalina at low altitude, Vorse thought the crew looked Caucasian, not Japanese, who were rumored to have captured PBYs in the East Indies. At 1540 he finally relented: "Hey, looks OK, Hank."

The troublesome interloper was Joe Kellam's 23-P-3. Unsure whether base ever copied his original contact reports of the *Ryūjō* force, he flew up astern of the *Enterprise* and flashed by blinking light, "Small enemy carrier bearing 320 True distance 195 miles," and gave its course and speed, along with the position of another force of three CL, two DD, and three AP, 50 miles from first contact. "Are you through with us?" he asked, and she flashed an "R" for Roger. Not entirely convinced the Catalina was friendly, Fletcher was later assured by Air-SoPac that the mystery PBY was indeed a *Mackinac* plane.[7]

While this contretemps occurred, the admirals considered whether to loose the *Enterprise*'s strike group against Jett's contact. When Kinkaid opined the contact seemed sound, Fletcher replied at 1536, "If you consider contact good send your boys in."[8] At 1543 he added that it seemed to be the same the PBY reported. The *Enterprise* made ready to dispatch her strike. At 1600 the TF-61 CAP numbered twenty-four F4Fs aloft and twenty-nine on deck (see table 7.1).

As of 1600 Fletcher's TF-11 held course 070 degrees, with TF-16 deployed 10

TABLE 7.1
Task Force 61 CAP, 1600, 24 August 1942

TF-16	TF-11
Aloft over the *Enterprise*	Aloft over the *Saratoga*
4 F4Fs RED 5 (Vorse)[a]	4 F4Fs SCARLET 1 (Simpler)[b]
5 F4Fs RED 6 (Brooks)[b]	4 F4Fs SCARLET 4 (Harmer)[b]
2 F4Fs RED 7 (Rutherford)[c]	2 F4Fs SCARLET 5 (Gray)[b]
	3 F4Fs SCARLET 7 (Richardson)[c]
On deck (intended strike escort)	On deck
2 F4Fs 2nd Section RED 7 (de Poix)	3 F4Fs SCARLET 6 (Jensen)
5 F4Fs SCARLET 3 (Clarke)	3 F4Fs SCARLET STANDBY (Smith)
	About to take off from the *Saratoga*
	4 F4Fs RED 1 (Bauer)
	4 F4Fs RED 2 (Barnes)
	4 F4Fs RED 3 (Gay)
	4 F4Fs RED 4 (Runyon)

[a] 8,000 feet
[b] 10,000 feet
[c] 15,000 feet

miles northwest. The *Saratoga* turned southeast into the wind to launch Bauer's sixteen VF-6 F4Fs (RED 1, 2, 3, and 4), and Commander Cruise, the air officer, alerted aircrews to taxi five VT-8 TBFs and two VB-3 SBDs forward once the fighters got away. The clear deck would allow her to land SCARLET 1, 3, and 5, all quite low on fuel. On the *Enterprise* plane handlers readied Leslie's group of eleven SBDs, eight TBFs, and seven F4Fs, while air plot worked out the details.

At 1602 the *Enterprise*'s CXAM radar suddenly displayed a large return bearing 320 degrees, 88 miles (at the same time the more distant *Saratoga* had it at 103 miles). It swiftly faded from both screens. This looked like the real thing. Lieutenant Commander Pederson, TF-61 air ops officer, described how Fletcher and the staff felt upon learning this news:

> To say the least we were in a bad predicament—all of our attack planes were committed on missions with the main enemy force still unlocated and his planes coming in to attack us. The best we could do was to get ready for an air attack and hope for the best.[9]

Hank Rowe, the RED BASE FDO, requested the *Sara* to launch all available fighters and sent ten F4Fs (Brooks's RED 6, Rutherford's RED 7, and Richardson's SCARLET 7) northwest on 320 degrees (M.) for a distant intercept. Both radars in fact detected Seki's first strike group (twenty-seven carrier bombers, ten fighters) at almost the same instance that the *Hiei* observation seaplane advised him of the corrected enemy position. Seki altered course slightly from 153 to 160 degrees and resumed scanning the horizon.

At 1604 a second radar contact bearing 315 degrees, 42 miles, complicated matters. It appeared to be small, perhaps an enemy seaplane or returning *Enterprise* searcher. To check it out, Rowe turned ten F4Fs (Brooks, Rutherford, and Richardson) left to 280 (M.) and also alerted Vorse's four RED 5 F4Fs on 310 (M.) at 8,000 feet. At 1608 he placed the bogey 30 miles ahead. To back up the fourteen F4Fs already committed, he tapped Bauer's newly launched sixteen VF-6 F4Fs. They had not formed up together, but flew separate divisions. Rowe hustled them north-northwest: Bauer's RED 1 and Barnes's RED 2 on 290 (M.) at 8,000 feet, RED 3 (Gay) and RED 4 (Runyon) on 280 (M.) at 4,000 feet.

Fletcher instructed TF-16 to close TF-11 immediately and at 1610 ordered Kinkaid to launch his attack. After Bauer departed, the *Saratoga* continued clearing her flight deck of fueled and armed aircraft: six VF-5 F4Fs (Jensen's SCARLET 6 and a SCARLET standby section led by Jim Smith), followed by Swede Larsen's five VT-8 TBFs and two stray VB-3 SBDs. Larsen had expected to circle the task force out of gun range. However, at the last minute, the ship told him to attack the enemy carrier previously reported by Jett of VT-3. Running out on deck, he ejected one of his pilots from a TBF. After takeoff, the *Sara* instructed him to join the *Enterprise* strike group about to be launched.

RED BASE carefully maneuvered the CAP divisions to entrap the smaller contact. At 1615 and 25 miles northwest of the ships, Vorse eyeballed the culprit, a returning VT-3 search plane with its IFF transmitter turned off. Two minutes later Rowe recalled all the fighters except for Vorse, Brooks's RED 6, and Rutherford's RED 7. The last two flights he sent an additional 20 miles due north aiming for a distant intercept.

At 1618 the large bogey reappeared on the *Enterprise*'s radar, still on 320 degrees, but now only 44 miles and closing. Noting the time the bogey remained in the null areas of the wave lobes, the radar operator checked the fade chart and calculated its altitude as 12,000 feet. Far from foolproof, in this instance the estimate proved much too low. Rowe responded by swinging RED 7 left to 300 degrees (M.) "Many bogeys ahead." Sounding the call, "Get up high," he also committed his principal reserve of sixteen F4Fs (RED 1, 2, 3, and 4) northwest on 300 degrees (M.) at 12,000 feet. Of sixteen VF-5 F4Fs circling the *Saratoga*, Simpler's SCARLET 1 with four made ready to pancake for fuel. That left twelve (SCARLET 4, 5, 6, and Standby). SCARLET BASE told all others with enough "juice" to remain airborne, to which Harmer of SCARLET 4 replied he had sufficient fuel to stay up. No CAP directly covered TF-16, whose defense now depended upon the separate flights of fighters searching northwest.

The CAP as finally deployed comprised an outer shell of eleven F4Fs (RED 5, 6, and 7) 40 or more miles northwest, supported by sixteen more (RED 1, 2, 3, and 4) en route. Fifteen VF-5 F4Fs (SCARLET 4, 5, 6, 7, and Standby) remained in reserve near the ships. They could be reinforced to twenty-six by the seven escort fighters (SCARLET 3 and 2nd Section of RED 7) on the *Enterprise* and Simpler's SCARLET 1 on the *Sara*. Thus TF-61 wielded fifty-three Wildcats, seemingly enough to do the job if they could overwhelm the enemy strike before it attacked.

At 1620, while RED BASE arrayed the defense, a relieved Seki spotted enemy ships in "ring formation" about 40 miles ahead and to his left. Visibility that day was excellent. After sighting the U.S. ships, he turned east to approach the target from the north. On the way in he observed a second enemy carrier force to the southeast beyond the first and knew he must deal with it as well. At 1627 the practiced hand of Spec. Duty Ens. Nakasada Jirō, Seki's observer, tapped out *"to-tsu-re,"* short for *"totsugeki junbi taikei tsukure* [assume attack formation]." According to plan, Shigematsu's four *Shōkaku* Zeros, all that remained of the original nine-plane "air control force," moved out ahead to deal with waiting Grummans. That left Hidaka's six *Zuikaku* fighters as direct cover for Seki's twenty-seven carrier bombers.

Seki's original right turn to 160 degrees 20 minutes before had registered on the *Enterprise*'s radar plot. It led RED BASE to believe the enemy strike had edged southward and now threatened TF-16 from the west. Rowe had only seconds to work out a countermove, so he swung Bauer's RED 1, 2, 3, and 4 left onto a heading of 270 degrees (M.) to position these sixteen F4Fs ahead to block the strike. Next he steered the eleven F4Fs making up the outer shell (40-plus miles to the northwest) left on 300 (M.). Seki soon passed Brooks and Rutherford without being seen. By rushing westward, RED 1, 2, 3, and 4 now risked not intercepting the strike altogether.

The two carriers completed their preparations for battle. At 1625 the *Sara* recovered SCARLET 1, whose pilots jumped out to help the plane handlers push the four F4Fs back toward the stern.[10] Back in their cockpits, they waited anxiously for the fueling detail to fill the tanks. At the same time "The Big E" committed the seven F4Fs of Clarke's SCARLET 3 and de Poix's 2nd Section of RED 7 with orders to circle TF-16 at 15,000 feet. Since they were originally slated for escort duty, their radios operated on the search-and-attack rather than the CAP frequency, which precluded the pilots from hearing the FDO.

Spurred on by enemy aircraft now 27 miles and closing, the *Enterprise* started launching Leslie's unescorted strike group. In addition to CEAG's TBF, it comprised Lieutenant Caldwell's eleven SBDs (seven VS-5, four VB-6), and seven VT-3 TBFs under XO Lieutenant Konig. Kinkaid sent them against Jett's 1440 contact of one CV, one CL, and two DD now perhaps as far as 260 miles away. Caldwell and Konig formed their flights without being able to rendezvous before the enemy strike came in. Leslie lifted last of all at 1638, only three minutes before the lead dive bomber pushed over against the *Enterprise*. In the hangar deck Crud Blair (SCARLET 7) waited in his F4F to be pushed onto the number 2 elevator to go up to the flight deck. When General Quarters sounded, the plane handlers "left me like a hot potato." Soon Blair jumped out of the Wildcat and hastened up the ladders to the VF-6 ready room.[11]

First Contact

While bustering west and clawing for height, Tom Barnes's RED 2 spotted enemy planes about 25 miles northwest of TF-16 at 1629. Out ahead to their right, they discovered Seki's trailing element, Ōtsuka's nine *Zuikaku* carrier bombers, headed in the opposite direction. Letting down from 5,000 meters (16,400 feet) in a shallow dive, the raiders had very nearly slipped unseen past RED 2. Brewer, 2nd Section leader, transmitted the vital sighting report:

> At 1 o'clock above this is RED 2, Tally ho! There are about 1 or 2 . . . 9 bogeys unidentified about 12,000 feet, 300 . . . Many ahead of those . . . bogey bears 350, 20 [miles] Angels 12. They're dive bombers. [signed] Chuck.

Caught below and now rapidly drawn behind the Japanese, RED 2 reefed around to chase them. As combat has demonstrated many times, the Grumman F4F-4 Wildcat broke no records as a swift climber.

RED BASE immediately assumed that all sixteen of Bauer's F4Fs contacted the enemy. At 1630 Rowe exhorted, "Don't let them get away, Lou!" With only RED 1 in hand, Bauer saw only empty sky, as did Dick Gay's RED 3 and Don Runyon's RED 4. Only Barnes pursued in a long struggle to overtake the enemy. Fletcher's air defense unraveled when Seki penetrated the outer CAP shell unscathed.

Two minutes after his first contact report, Brewer followed with "Some at one o'clock—some directly above us 8 o'clock. They look like Zeros. RED BASE from Chuck, astern about 20 miles, Angels 13.'' He added, ''They disappeared. Keep a good lookout.''

''They'' were Lieutenant Shigematsu's *Shōkaku* 17th *Shōtai* on air control duty. An ex-*Hiryū* fighter leader, he had survived two escort missions at Midway. PO1c Muranaka Kazuo and Sea1c Hayashi Shigeru were also *Hiryū* veterans, while PO3c Komachi, a brash six-footer who had fought with the *Shōkaku* at the Coral Sea, had latched on from the 18th *Shōtai*. Hunting southward, Shigematsu passed over RED 2 without seeing them, but stalked the Grummans that had caught his eye.

Scoop Vorse's four RED 5 F4Fs happened to be Shigematsu's quarry.[12] After checking out the errant TBF, they reached 8,000 feet, then at 1633 noticed enemy planes ahead and off to the north:

> About 36 bombers, course 120.
> Any fighters? Are they ours?
> Hey Scoop, on our right.
> Get in back of them. Let's go get them.
> Get up there.

Vorse sandwiched his two greenies, Dix Loesch and Cash Register, between himself and Mach. Howell (''Muscles'') Sumrall, a tough, experienced NAP. Just a minute after RED 5's first report, Sumrall warned of trouble overhead: ''Zero right above us, Scoop.'' Shigematsu profited from his overaggressive performance on 4 June at Midway when he jumped six *Enterprise* SBDs at low altitude, but left the *Hiryū* carrier bombers unprotected. Reluctant now to relinquish altitude advantage unless the Grummans directly threatened his charges, he interposed his *shōtai* between them and the strike group. Using ''stick-together'' tactics, RED 5 climbed in formation but could not catch the dive bombers as they approached TF-16 from the north. Shigematsu kept 4,000 feet between himself and the F4Fs.

After a minute or two of wary observation, Hayashi, the trailing *Shōkaku* pilot, grew impatient and overeager for a kill. Sumrall saw the last Zero in line roll over on its back several times to keep the F4Fs in view. ''I knew he was looking for a straggler,'' he later recounted, ''so I straggled.''[13] As the F4Fs passed 10,000 feet, Hayashi waggled his wings and rolled into a steep dive. Sumrall waited until the Zero committed itself to attack, then dropped his right wing and applied full left rudder. This maneuver yanked the F4F out of its old flight path and ruined Hayashi's shot. As the Zero flashed past, Sumrall sharply reversed his turn back to the right. A snap burst kept the Japanese diving. When Hayashi finally did recover below and ahead of the F4F, Sumrall was ready. He nosed over, swiftly closed, and triggered a burst through the Mitsubishi's fuselage and wingroot. Among other things his incendiaries set the belly tank on fire. Bright red flames streamed from beneath the fighter.

Register, Sumrall's exuberant wingman flying ahead of him, thought the bandit jumped him instead of the trailer. He countered with a steep wingover, opened fire about the time Sumrall torched Hayashi's Zero, but believed he inflicted the fatal hits. Against the rules he broke away from the other F4Fs to follow the burning Zero. An irritated Sumrall radioed him to rejoin. Closer to the descending Mitsubishi than Sumrall, only Register saw Hayashi finally bail out at 6,000 feet. Everyone else, including the 17th *Shōtai*, thought the pilot was a goner. While trying to overtake Vorse and Loesch now far ahead, Sumrall watched the pilotless Zero glide steadily downward at a shallow angle toward the water. As its speed built up, the nose lifted, and more burning fuel poured out from the underside in a long trail of fire. Finally it struck the sea. Many in TF-16 witnessed its meteoric demise, recorded at 1640 as a dive bomber splashing about six miles northwest of the ships. Miraculously, Hayashi survived, circumstances not known. Shigematsu described this fight as involving six Grummans at 2,500 to 3,000 meters (8,200 to 9,840 feet).[14]

Keeping a wary eye on the other three bandits, Vorse and Loesch gained more height while following the dive bombers. Above 18,000 feet they appeared to outclimb and even overtake the Zeros, but with Seki nearing his dive point over the *Enterprise*, Shigematsu ended the climbing duel and chased after his charges. From 20,000 feet Vorse and Loesch likewise dived toward the task force.

The 17th *Shōtai* soon encountered the still-climbing Sumrall below them, and the sight was too much for Komachi. He roared in with a steep high-side run. Sumrall saw the bandit still a good distance away, but noticed another F4F already pursuing this attacker. That was Vorse, whom Loesch warned at 1642: "Scoop, drop your belly tank before you attack." Sumrall decided to play decoy, flying straight and level, and hoped the other Wildcat would bag the Zero in time.

Vorse's low-side run caught the enemy by surprise. He fired into its fuselage and reported flames behind the cockpit. Although not on fire, Komachi tried climbing steeply away, but the F4Fs had the speed to stay with him. Loesch took his licks as well. Finally the Zero shuddered as it neared a stall in the thin air. Komachi deliberately dropped into a spin and whirled down playing a dead duck quite convincingly. He pulled out at around 1,000 meters. Vorse and Loesch were too busy to follow. In a short, sharp sequel, Shigematsu and Muranaka ripped through RED 5 and forced Vorse, Loesch, and Sumrall to separate and run. They fought no more that day. No Zeros or F4Fs fell in this particular skirmish, which Shigematsu ascribed to six Grummans at between 4,000 and 5,000 meters (13,120 to 16,400 feet) and north of target. He and Muranaka ended up northwest of the ships and somewhat lower than before.

Other CAP divisions, some still ahead of the Japanese and others frantically trying to catch up, made visual contact with the incoming enemy strike group. While returning on station over the *Saratoga*, Richardson's SCARLET 7 (three VF-5 F4Fs) saw distant enemy dive bombers off to the side. Climbing at full power above 15,000 feet, SCARLET 7 spread out in line-astern—quite vulnerable when at 1638 Hidaka's six *Zuikaku* Zeros on direct cover surprised them with steep high-side attacks from out of the sun. Each pair ganged up on a single F4F, so SCARLET 7 could not coordinate its defense. Hoping for a head-on shot, Richardson turned up into his two assailants to scissor, but they flashed past before the F4F could even swing all the way around. He dropped about 4,000 feet, corkscrewing to clear his tail. By the time he regained altitude, everyone else had disappeared. Two opponents overhauled Lee Haynes from astern, then recovered out ahead to come around for head-on runs. Coral Sea veteran Haynes thought sloppy pullouts marred the Japanese attacks. After the initial flurry, one Zero parked on his tail and compelled him to dive out. Quickly zooming back into the fight, he used four working .50s to blast that Zero (or another), which nosed over and disappeared below 6,000 feet. Haynes rejoined Richardson, but neither observed Marion Dufilho after the initial ambush.[15]

Dick Gray's bobtailed SCARLET 5 also fought in this sector, most likely against some of the same opponents. After the *Saratoga* refused their request to land for fuel, Gray and Green climbed northwest. Spotting dive bombers, Green broke off to chase them (his experiences are covered below), but at the same time Gray observed a Zero peel off at 18,000 feet against one of the SCARLET 7 F4Fs. With a high-side, he started down after the Japanese, who countered by a chandelle. At the top of its climbing turn, the Mitsubishi rolled out and spun, so Gray claimed it. Another bandit forced him to dive to 10,000 feet, and he fought no more.[16]

The whole battle would cost Hidaka's *Zuikaku chūtai* three of six Zeros, but no one can say when they went down. Almost certainly none succumbed in the fights with SCARLET 7 and SCARLET 5, and five of six *Zuikaku* pilots disengaged quickly. They later caught up with their own carrier bombers in the skies over TF-16. In the first action, however, the *chūtai* certainly accounted for Marion Dufilho. A personable 1938 Annapolis graduate, Dufilho met his end in a fight much like the one he survived on 8 May at the Coral Sea flying the *Lexington*'s CAP in VF-2.

At 1638, while Shigematsu held off RED 5 and Hidaka overwhelmed SCAR-

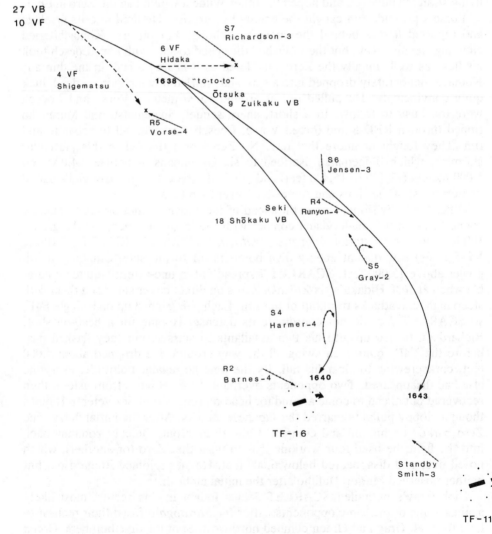

Japanese first-strike deployment and CAP interceptions.

LET 7, Seki deployed his group to attack the carriers 15 miles and 25 miles to the south. Nakasada sent *"to-to-to,"* short for *"zengun totsugeki seyo* [all forces attack]." The eighteen *Shōkaku* carrier bombers swung sharply south to assail the nearer carrier (the *Enterprise*), while Ōtsuka's nine *Zuikaku* carrier bombers continued southeast to confront the second one (the *Saratoga*). Both *kanbaku* flights opened formation and let down toward pushover points 3,500 meters (11,480 feet) over their respective targets. Henceforth the two attacks will be discussed separately, but in the end they comprised two distinct waves against TF-16.

"The enemy planes are directly overhead now!"

First Wave

Seki aimed his eighteen *Shōkaku* carrier bombers toward the *Enterprise*'s port quarter, as she turned away starboard to 170 degrees. By waggling his wings, he had strung the two nine-plane *chūtais* into one long column with intervals of about 100 meters between aircraft. The lead *chūtai* comprised his own 20th *Shōtai* and the six 2nd *Chūtai* Type 99s under Lt. Yoshimoto Kazuo (NA 66-1938). Behind them came the 1st *Chūtai* under Lt. Arima Keiichi (NA 64-1937), the senior *buntaichō*. The crews well understood that they represented Japan's first real chance to avenge Midway, but it would not be easy. Although Grummans had not barred the way, they now massed ahead and in pursuit.[17]

Despite nearly dry tanks, Chick Harmer's four SCARLET 4 F4Fs firewalled throttles, ascending from 5,000 to 14,000 feet while hastening northwest toward the *Enterprise*. About five miles astern of TF-16, they could see hawks slanted down in shallows dives, but still slightly above the F4Fs. Straining to catch the dive bombers, SCARLET 4 flew a constant right-hand turn curving in behind the Japanese. Finally Harmer overtook the lead group (seven to nine planes, he estimated) just after the first one nosed over steeply.[18]

Prepared by radar warnings, TF-16 made ready to repel an air attack. The nine warships assumed the circular 1-Victor formation around the *Enterprise,* with heavy cruiser *Portland* on her port bow, the CL(AA) *Atlanta* on her starboard bow, and six destroyers evenly deployed on a 1,800- to 2,000-yard radius from the carrier. The battleship *North Carolina* brought up the rear 500 yards farther astern of the circle. Kinkaid bent on 27 knots (top speed for the battlewagon) and prepared for more. More than VF filled the crowded skies around TF-16. Three VS-5 SBDs flew IAP, at least half of the twenty *Enterprise* search SBDs and TBFs had returned, while two strike groups with thirteen SBDs and thirteen TBFs sought to join up and clear the area as expeditiously as possible.

RED BASE did its best to interpose the CAP between the ships and the incoming raiders. The lack of radio discipline by some inexperienced VF pilots handicapped the defense. Ens. George P. Givens, a junior FDO, helped plot during the attack:

> My best memory is of "Ham" Dow sweating like a Turk while he attempted to break into the many, many radio transmissions that were on the fighter frequency. Bear in mind that if two transmitters open up at the same time in the same general area, you get nothing but a squeal on the air. That happened several times on this particular day . . . *Good radio discipline* is essential. Messages should be brief and the transmitter should get off the air as soon as possible.[19]

Of all times, the *Enterprise*'s fire control radar malfunctioned, preventing her

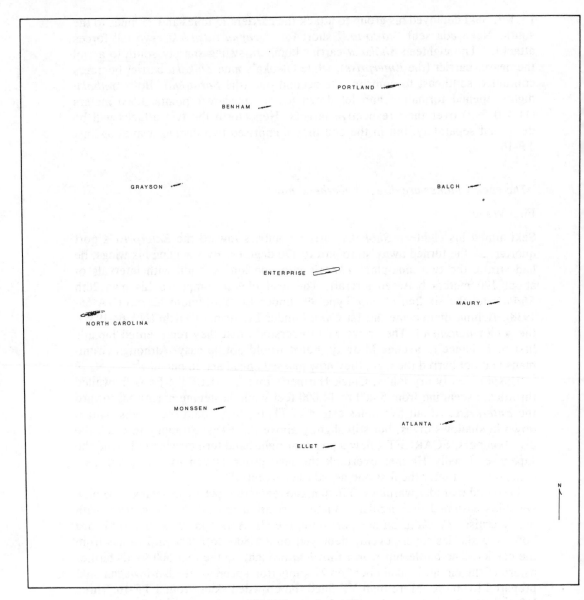

TF-16 formation, 1640.

gunners from tracking the incoming strike planes. Topside observers peered into the setting sun, which caused great difficulty in picking out targets, but the fiery trail of Hayashi's Zero alerted them. First lookouts on a destroyer noticed sunlight reflecting off the polished wing of an enemy plane. Finally at 1640, Marine 1st Sgt. Joseph R. Schinka, a portside 20-mm battery commander on "The Big E," caught sight of a puff of smoke high off the port bow and glimpsed a dive bomber coming in. He yelled to one of his gunners to open fire, a single ribbon of tracers and smoke. The *Enterprise*'s five-inchers joined in, along with other guns bearing in that sector. The *Atlanta* cut loose her massive five-inch battery and, according to Fred Mears, "the battleship accompanying our carrier lit up like a

Christmas tree. Black and white puffs of smoke covered the late afternoon sky.''[20]

At 1641 the first of the carrier bombers reached the dive point high over the *Enterprise*'s port bow and pushed over, while SCARLET 4 struggled to catch them. To Harmer's displeasure, wingman Ens. John McDonald impatiently jumped the enemy leader rather than following with his run in proper sequence. Plunging into intense AA fire, McDonald latched onto Seki at 8,000 feet and stuck with him all the way down to 1,500. Captain Davis turned radically away to starboard to avoid bombs, and the screen conformed to his movements. Seki's 250-kilogram bomb fell wide aport of the swiftly turning flattop. When told in error by *Enterprise* observers that the lead dive bomber splashed, McDonald claimed it. However, Seki cleared the ships, but McDonald's earnest attentions certainly distracted him.

With a steep above-rear attack, Harmer himself took on the second VB to dive: PO1c Imada Tetsu's number 2 of the 20th *Shōtai* (pilot PO1c Kamijima Hajime). Chasing the Type 99 into fierce AA fire, Harmer traded bursts with Imada manning the single Type 92 7.7-mm flexible Lewis machine gun. He thought he silenced the rear gunner and perhaps finished off the plane. Again a SCARLET 4 pilot did not score, but neither did the Japanese. Evidently releasing his bomb higher than he intended, Kamijima missed badly. He joined Seki just above the waves. Meanwhile, Harmer circled lower hoping to catch another dive bomber on its way out.

Lt. Howard Crews, Harmer's 2nd Section leader, dropped straight down on PO1c Sasaki Mitsuo's number 3 Aichi. His first shots tore into its wings and fuselage; from closer range a two-second burst struck cowling and engine. With the AA getting "thick," Crews pulled out at 3,000 feet and never saw what befell the dive bomber. Perhaps wounded, Sea1c Akutagawa Takeshi, Sasaki's pilot, tripped his bomb release prematurely, then spun in vertical tight spirals toward the water. His bomb raised a great splash 200 yards from the *E*'s port quarter, and the flaming Type 99 struck the water 600 yards from her port beam. Last of the SCARLET 4 F4Fs to intercept, Ens. Benjamin ("Mole") Currie, Crews's wingman, tried to follow the lead Type 99s down, but his twisting dive prevented him from taking any shots.

SCARLET 4 disrupted the attack of Seki's 20th *Shōtai* and accounted for one dive bomber. Not bothered by fighters, Yoshimoto, PO1c Someno Fumio, PO3c Tanaka Hirokichi, and Spec. Duty Ens. Saitō Chiaki from the 2nd *Chūtai* dived beginning at 1642 in short intervals against the *Enterprise*'s port beam and quarter. Most of their bombs fell short of the target, leaving "dirty brown circles" after the splashes subsided. One after another the pilots pulled out low toward the *Grayson* (DD-435) steaming off the carrier's port quarter and the *North Carolina* falling farther astern. On the way out several crews left their calling cards with the *Grayson*. Machine-gun bullets and fragments from bursting five-inch AA shells combined to wound eleven sailors on the tincan.

During the dives of Seki's lead carrier bombers, the four VF-6 F4Fs of Tom Barnes's RED 2 finally caught up with the trailers after a long stern chase.[21] Drawing nearer, they noticed the last nine Type 99s (Arima's 1st *Chūtai*) had opened into loose, ragged order as the crews awaited their turn to go in. At 1640 RED 2's battle cry, "OK, let's go give them hell," rang out on the radio. The four F4Fs split up. Barnes and wingman Ram Dibb bounced the rear of Arima's 1st *Chūtai* waiting to dive. At 14,000 feet Dibb smoked one Type 99, but the highly regarded Barnes did not survive the first pass when a deadly five-inch shell burst scored a direct hit. At 1642.5 observers on the destroyer *Balch* noticed one plane, its wings and tail blown off, plummet into the water 2,000 yards off the port quarter. Dibb remained at 14,000 feet looking for other bombers.

Douglas Johnson also stayed high to challenge the waiting 1st *Chūtai*, but his section leader, Chuck Brewer, had other ideas. Diving steeply, he pursued the last two members of Seki's lead *chūtai*, PO1c Yasuda Nobuyoshi and PO2c Kitamura Kenzō from the 28th *Shōtai*. The two had pushed over almost simultaneously against the *Enterprise*. Lines of tracers torched Yasuda's plane and compelled pilot PO2c Shirai Gorō to drop his bomb too high for accuracy. It raised a geyser off the carrier's starboard bow, and the burning Type 99 hit the water 1,000 yards farther out. Brewer caught up with the trailer, Kitamura, when the pilot, PO2c Miki Isamu, maneuvered to give Kitamura a better shot with the free gun against the Grumman threatening astern. Brewer riddled the dive bomber but relented at 4,000 feet to escape massive gunfire from the ships. He pulled out at high speed and ran for safer air. Kitamura's Type 99 staggered in the midst of shell bursts and tracers from the ships. At 2,000 feet Miki released his bomb and followed it down, hoping to crash his fatally stricken Aichi onto the *Enterprise*'s flight deck. The bomb narrowly missed the carrier amidships to starboard. Diving erratically, the flaming carrier bomber "screamed past sky control in a fiery blur" and plowed into the sea just to port as the *Enterprise* heeled sharply away. Japanese witnesses mistakenly thought that Kitamura's *kanbaku*, with bomb still attached, had flown into the target.[22]

From over the port quarter of the turning *Enterprise*, Arima weighed in immediately behind ill-fated Yasuda and Kitamura. He saw the fighters intercept the planes ahead, several of which blossomed bright red flames. Antiaircraft fire unlike anything he ever encountered in China seemed to envelop his aircraft. After pushing over into the dive, Arima called out the changing altitudes to his pilot, PO1c Furuta Kiyoto, as the Aichi's broad dive brakes caught the thickening air. He was surprised by the forest of tracers easily visible in daylight. Shrapnel noisily rattled through the wings and fuselage, but inflicted no fatal damage. The highly experienced Furuta loosed his bomb and recovered low over the water.[23] Arima saw it strike the carrier's flight deck for the first hit ever scored on "The Big E." At 1644 his 250-kilogram "ordinary" (semi-AP) bomb penetrated the starboard forward corner of her number 3 elevator aft. It sliced through to the third deck before detonating in the chief's quarters, causing extensive damage and loss of life.[24]

The first 21st *Shōtai* wingman, PO1c Koitabashi Hiroshi (pilot PO1c Akimoto Tamotsu), also executed a superb, determined dive. His 242-kilogram high-explosive "land" bomb with contact fuses slammed into the *Enterprise* less than 30 seconds after the first hit. It also landed aft in a powerful explosion near the number 3 elevator, but only 11 feet in from the starboard deck edge. Flame engulfed the starboard aft five-inch gun platform, set off the ready ammunition, killed all thirty-eight men in the gun crews, and ignited serious fires that threatened the five-inch magazine. As the other 21st *Shōtai* wingman, PO2c Iida Yoshihiro, dived in flames from off the *Enterprise*'s starboard quarter, 20-mm rounds touched off the payload directly over the carrier. "The whole plane disintegrated [in] a tremendous burst in mid air and nothing but small pieces came fluttering down, just like confetti on Wall Street."[25]

The 22nd *Shōtai* of Lt. (jg) Motoyama Hiroyuki (NA 67-1939), PO2c Tsuchiya Ryōroku, and PO2c Horie Kazumi followed the 21st in. Either Motoyama or

A *Shōkaku* Type 99 carrier bomber, believed to be PO2c Iida Yoshihiro's, an instant before it disintegrated above the *Enterprise,* 24 Aug. 1942. Censors have removed her radar antenna from the photo. (NA 80-G-11894)

Tsuchiya achieved a close miss to starboard which drenched the *Enterprise*'s island. Last of all, Horie's Type 99 sustained hits above the release point which staggered the aircraft. Yet the 242-kilogram land bomb fell free from the demolished plane and at 1646 struck the *Enterprise* amidships just abaft the center elevator. The fierce explosion blew a 10-foot hole in the flight deck and wreaked more havoc topside. Horie's aircraft plunged into the sea off her starboard bow. Motoyama and Tsuchiya made their way out at low altitude. That ended the first attack wave against the *Enterprise.*

WO Aragane Masaki's 23rd *Shōtai* trailed the rest of squadron. Whether due to RED 2's F4Fs, AA, or poor positioning, he led his planes against the battleship *North Carolina* as she dropped farther astern when the other ships accelerated southward away from her. At 1643 her lookouts picked out approximately ten aircraft high off the starboard bow. A minute later Aragane, PO3c Murakami Shingi, and PO3c Aoki Toyojirō, pursued by RED 2 pilot Doug Johnson, executed their dives in close succession.[26] They resulted in near misses, two to port and one to starboard of the battlewagon, but AA tagged one carrier bomber that splashed 1,500 yards off her starboard quarter. Either AA or Johnson (he claimed one VB just after pullout) brought down another toward the *Enterprise*'s port quarter. The third Type 99 survived a low-level barrage laid by five-inchers from the *North Carolina* and the *Atlanta,* only later to fall to fighters. No Japanese lived to report attacking the battleship. AA fire also riddled Johnson's wings and sheered off the radio antenna.

Japanese carrier bomber diving against the *Enterprise*, 24 Aug. 1942, as seen from the *Portland*. (NA 80-G-299801)

Thus of the eighteen *Shōkaku* Type 99 carrier bombers, fifteen assailed the *Enterprise* and three the *North Carolina*. Senior *Enterprise* LSO Robin Lindsey had carefully watched their dives against his ship:

> These Jap planes launched about the most beautiful awe-inspiring attack I have ever seen. It was almost suicidal in fact, they came so low. They used a roll-over approach, a rather shallow dive . . . about 60 to 55 degrees . . . . came down and released about a thousand feet and were pulling out at 200 feet.[27]

Seki and his men paid for their daring. Up to this point seven Type 99s fell to fighters or AA. Those who eventually returned claimed six bomb hits on a "new" carrier and did secure three.

Eleven *Shōkaku kanbaku* survived the actual dives but, as will be shown, they faced far from an easy time getting away. Eight F4Fs (SCARLET 4 and RED 2) intercepted their attack and lost one from VF-6 (Doyle Barnes) to AA. The absence of Zeros in direct escort made the CAP's job easier, as Shigematsu had his hands full with Vorse's RED 5. Even so, the *Shōkaku* crews badly hurt "The Big E" with their accurate dive bombing. Could the other Japanese finish her?

Second Wave

At 1638 Lieutenant Ōtsuka's nine *Zuikaku* carrier bombers broke off eastward to attack the second enemy carrier force (TF-11 with the *Saratoga*) 10 miles southeast of the first. Moments before, Hidaka's six *Zuikaku* Zero escorts had bounced Richardson's SCARLET 7, but left Ōtsuka temporarily undefended. Unlike Seki, Ōtsuka would have to fight his way to the target, as Wildcats soon swarmed all over his *chūtai*. Letting down from 5,000 meters (16,400 feet) toward the pushover point, he opened formation from a Vee-of-Vees out to a column of three *shōtai* Vees.

The three SCARLET 6 F4Fs, Hayden Jensen, and ensigns John M. Kleinman and Carl Starkes were the first to challenge Ōtsuka.[28] When first alerted, they had attained 10,000 feet, but received no specific vectors thereafter. From radio chatter Jensen knew the enemy was coming, so he sallied northwest, and at 1632 spotted enemy dive bombers farther out ahead to his left. While still out ahead of them, Jensen sought altitude superiority at 20,000 feet.

About 10 miles northeast of TF-16, SCARLET 6 moved into attack position. Jensen executed a high-side run against the "second group," presumably the 2nd *Shōtai* under Lt. (jg) Nakamura Gorō (NA 67-1939) in the middle of the column. He blasted one wingman, who fell out of formation and burst into flames. During his run, Ōtsuka opened the column of Vees into the final attack formation, a long string of single aircraft. Jensen took advantage of the looser enemy disposition by dropping back for a "lazy side run" against the trailer. He flamed the last plane just as Starkes passed over in a high-side pass, then worked his way up the string from astern. Jensen blew the next Type 99 out of line for his third kill. Meanwhile, Starkes rushed through four quick passes against the dwindling line and claimed two bombers shot down in flames. Kleinman, the other wingman, likewise attacked several times and also tallied two bombers. So far SCARLET 6 boasted seven victories.

The *Zuikaku* carrier bombers also attracted another CAP division, Don Runyon's RED 4, furiously racing the enemy back to the ships. Runyon cut inside Ōtsuka's turn to interpose RED 4 between the hawks and TF-16 and bounced Ōtsuka a minute after SCARLET 6 started in. Thus many F4Fs unwittingly attacked in concert. About the time Runyon barreled in, Ōtsuka evidently concluded that the heavy fighter opposition would prevent his reaching the more distant target. Instead, he supported Seki's attack against the nearer carrier by swinging sharply right to take on the *Enterprise* from the northeast.

From 20,000 feet, Runyon executed a crisp high-side run out of the sun, singled out and swiftly torched one target, then recovered on the same side to soar sunward again. Again he scored, and as an added dividend forced two more dive bombers to turn tail and run. Wingman Howard Packard missed on his first pass and regained altitude for a second go. Mach. Beverly W. "Bill" Reid's fate remains unknown, but wingman Joe Shoemaker made a number of runs against the dive bombers.[29]

Finally catching up with the melee, four *Zuikaku* Zeros jumped the scattered SCARLET 6 Wildcats. A split-S delivered Jensen from a bad situation. Coming out of his fifth pass against the bombers, Starkes saw a Zero beat up an F4F, possibly Jensen, so he roared up close astern of the Mitsubishi and claimed it. Another bandit forced him to dive away. An enemy fighter (erroneously identified as an Me-109) clumsily recovered in front of Kleinman, who retaliated and thought he damaged the interloper. Another Zero sat on his tail, and he dived on out. A *Zuikaku* Zero executed a similar attack against Runyon climbing for his third pass against the bombers. It leveled out below and ahead of the F4F, so Runyon nosed over, touched the trigger, and exploded the Zero in flames. His next low-side run set afire a third dive bomber, but again a Zero intervened and recovered clumsily from its pass. He sent it diving away trailing smoke. In short order Don Runyon had finished three dive bombers and one fighter without so much as a bullet hole in return.

Several other F4Fs added to the agony of Ōtsuka's long run to the target.

Chasing dive bombers as they circled east, Frank Green of SCARLET 5 soon found himself in the midst of the SCARLET 6–RED 4 melee. Ahead three different F4Fs battled one bomber, but even so it kept on chugging. Green took over and smoked it with a long burst. The Type 99 burst into flames, no doubt claimed by all four Americans. Green silenced the rear gunner of another Type 99, whose pilot reacted with the "slickest maneuver." With exceptional maneuverability, the VB turned directly onto Green's tail and loosed "two small streams of smoke," but the bullets lacked enough deflection to hit. Green dived away.[30]

Bustering north from TF-11, the VF-5 standby division of Jim Smith, Ike Eichenberger, and Ens. Horace Bass joined the melee just as the *Zuikaku* carrier bombers entered TF-16's AA fire.[31] Either *Zuikaku* Zeros or AA accounted for Smith and Bass, as well as Bill Reid of Runyon's RED 4. Ship observers noticed a dogfight develop off the port bow, from which one enemy plane and one F4F fell out of control. Wrapped in flames and wings badly damaged, a second F4F plunged vertically into the water 4,000 yards off the *Balch*'s port beam.

The eight F4Fs who opposed the *Zuikaku* flight most likely destroyed two *Zuikaku* carrier bombers (including Ōtsuka's) and perhaps one fighter. The high number of CAP claims (ten VB, two VF) resulted mainly from concurrent attacks against the same targets. Many pilots thought they alone finished the few planes that went down. Even so, by killing Ōtsuka the CAP effectively broke up the *Zuikaku* attack. Under intense fighter opposition, the surviving *Zuikaku* crews split into two groups, each seeking a different target.

Lookouts on the *North Carolina* laboring far astern of the carrier spotted six incoming planes. Four were *Zuikaku* carrier bombers who chose the battleship instead of the carrier. Around 1645 Howard Packard of RED 4 overtook this flight deployed in line astern and essayed three quick overhead runs against alternate targets. Only one Type 99 smoked. During Packard's third run, a Zero forced him to break off and run. The four dive bombers rolled in against the battlewagon, which was aiming most of her massive five-inch AA battery ahead over the *Enterprise*. Thus the *Zuikaku* crews faced mostly 20-mm cannons, ineffective at longer ranges. Joe Shoemaker of Runyon's RED 4 followed one dive bomber down, but overran because of too much speed and missed. He shot at another during its dive with no visible effect. At 1646, one after another, four bombs raised geysers alongside the *North Carolina*, while the carrier bombers cleared the immediate area without reforming. As with the *Shōkaku* crews, no *Zuikaku* aviators would live to tell of assaulting the battleship.

Of the eight SCARLET 4 and RED 2 pilots who, a minute or so before, had battled Seki's *Shōkaku* carrier bombers, only Ram Dibb from RED 2 now prowled high over the *Enterprise*. Gingerly navigating his way through black AA bursts at 12,000 feet, he saw a Zero pass overhead, stalked it from behind, and triggered a burst that missed. The Japanese countered with two swift passes that forced Dibb to relent and dive out. Descending in a controlled power spin, he recovered in the opposite direction, but his pursuer did not follow.

Three *Zuikaku kanbaku* bombed the *Enterprise*. PO2c Koretsune Goichi (2nd *Shōtai*) lost contact with the rest of his section. At 1646 he dived against what he described as the "rear aircraft carrier," but missed.[32] The fallen Ōtsuka's two wingmen, PO1c Shirakura Kōta (pilot PO1c Igata Sakuo) and PO2c Maeno Hiroshi (pilot Sea1c Ōkawa Toyonobu) attacked in unison. Observer Maeno personally saw little of his *chūtai*'s ordeal during the hellish approach and never realized his leader had shifted to the first carrier task force. Very probably the two were the pair of dive bombers forced by Runyon to break off. After continuing southwest past the ships, they reversed course to threaten the *Enterprise*'s starboard quarter, as she heeled sharply starboard while swinging hard aport. The two Type 99s pushed over almost simultaneously at 1647. Eichenberger, only survivor of the ill-fated VF-5 standby division, latched onto Shirakura's tail at 12,000 feet and held fast all the way down to 4,000 feet before relenting. Later he saw that particular hawk fly into the water. Shirakura's 250-kilogram "ordinary" bomb gave Lindsey a special thrill:

> It is really horrifying to watch the Jap dive bombers come down, because you felt rather helpless, especially about the next to the last plane [that] came down, and I would just see my name written on the nose of that bomb. It looked like it was coming to light right in my lap . . . It fell a little short of my Landing Signal Platform, just missed the ramp by about a foot and went into the water underneath the Landing Signal Platform and caved in the side of the ship . . . Although it did not puncture the hull [it] sent up a column of water so hard it blew up the deck about two feet.[33]

Maeno's bomb fell 300 yards aport of the carrier.

Recovering low, Shirakura ran afoul of RED 2's redoubtable Ram Dibb, driven down by a *Zuikaku* Zero. Toward the end of the battle and in the midst of fierce AA close to the *Enterprise,* Dibb smoked a dive bomber that lurched into the sea 500 yards off the *Grayson*'s port bow. He immediately pursued another Type 99, but it evaded with a tight turn. Out of ammunition and with a shot-up mount, Dibb cleared the area. So too did Maeno, his erstwhile second target, who also saw Shirakura splash. Maeno claimed hits on an enemy carrier for his fallen comrade and himself, the last Japanese to assault TF-16.

From collating reports, some tentative statements regarding the attack on TF-16 can be made. Up to this point twenty-seven F4Fs (twelve VF-6, fifteen VF-5) engaged the enemy strike, estimated by the Americans to number thirty-six dive bombers and twelve fighters. Their victory credits so far numbered seventeen VB and seven VF: (VF-5 ten VB, three VF; VF-6 seven VB, four VF). CAP losses totaled five F4Fs and pilots (three VF-5, two VF-6). AA gunners claimed twenty-seven enemy planes: *Enterprise* fifteen, *North Carolina* seven, *Portland* one, *Balch* two, *Monssen* one, and *Grayson* one. Of twenty-seven carrier bombers, two fell prior to pushing over, about eighteen attacked the *Enterprise* and seven the *North Carolina*. Their losses up to this point amounted to ten (seven *Shōkaku*, three *Zuikaku*), most likely six to fighters and four by AA. One *Shōkaku* Zero (whose pilot, Hayashi, survived) and probably one *Zuikaku* fighter also succumbed.

The Japanese Fight Their Way Out

Apparently eleven *Shōkaku* and six *Zuikaku* carrier bombers, three *Shōkaku* and five *Zuikaku* Zeros survived the bomb runs against TF-16. However, many enemy aircraft barred the way out, including CAP F4Fs, IAP SBDs, returning search planes low on fuel, and strike planes. The first encounters in this phase of the battle took place at low altitude near TF-16. A set sequence of events cannot be given, necessitating an episodic treatment.

Fighting Five

Chick Harmer (VF-5's XO) and wingman John McDonald of SCARLET 4 had contested the attacks of the lead pair of *Shōkaku* carrier bombers. After chasing Seki's wingman Imada into fierce AA, Harmer circled the black blizzard of shell bursts looking to ambush other dive bombers emerging lower down. Against one his above-rear run silenced the rear gunner, but the pilot reefed steeply in front, forcing him to roll out of the way. Seeing a large splash he thought perhaps that Aichi had succumbed. The next dive bomber turned the tables by charging hard up Harmer's tail at 500 feet. Exhibiting excellent marksmanship, its pilot riddled the F4F's fuselage and cockpit with sixteen to twenty 7.7-mm slugs and severely wounded Harmer in both thighs and the left ankle. More bullets bounced harmlessly off the armor plate behind his seat. Hurt and flying a battered airplane about to run out of gas, Harmer veered southeast toward the *Saratoga*. Meanwhile "Jughead" McDonald caught a carrier bomber that tried S-turns at 50 feet to avoid his tracers, but to no avail, as his full-deflection shot flamed the VB.

Mole Currie, also SCARLET 4, splashed a dive bomber withdrawing low over the water. After battling bombers and diving to escape their escorts, SCARLET 6's Carl Starkes leveled out at 1,000 feet right ahead of a full *shōtai* of three Type 99s heading out at low altitude. He damaged one, but did not see it crash. His opponents were probably Yoshimoto, Someno, and Saitō, of the *Shōkaku* 2nd *Chūtai*. If so, it was the first of several battles they survived to reach home safely.

Unable to intercept the dive bombers, more VF-5 pilots got into the act shortly afterward. At 1636 Simpler's four SCARLET 1 F4Fs scrambled from the *Saratoga* without waiting to rendezvous and watched the battle develop in front of them. Black shell bursts and lines of red tracers almost hid the dive bombers from view and also burned the tails of more than a few F4Fs, including SCARLET 1. Simpler was most impressed with the five-inch fire put up by the *North Carolina*, which shifted her barrage around like a "big detached block of black air."[34] He wondered how many of his boys fell to this "friendly fire."

At the same time a formation of B-17 bombers passed high overhead bound for the reported enemy carrier. Thinking they were enemy planes, Simpler rapidly gained altitude. To his dismay he encountered no opponents; neither did "Weasel" Wesolowski nor Mel Roach. Wayne Presley noticed a chute descend near the water. At 1650, TF-16 observers likewise sighted the white canopy about five miles southeast. The identity of the parachutist is still unknown. As Presley flew over to investigate, an approaching dive bomber lined up for a head-on run. While Presley shot back, the *kanbaku* dipped its nose and without visible evidence of damage dropped into the sea.[35]

In another sector, SCARLET 3's five F4Fs led by Walter Clarke broke formation as they tried to catch the enemy over TF-16. With wingmen George Morgan and Don Innis, Clarke never did overtake any Japanese. His second section of Smokey Stover and Ens. Mortimer C. "Junior" Kleinmann had attained 17,500 feet during the attack. Suddenly a lone *Zuikaku* Zero (Dick Gray's opponent?) bounced them and recovered below and ahead. They dropped belly tanks and bracketed the target, but the Japanese was having none of that. In a wild, five-minute chase the two F4Fs shot up a storm (Kleinmann using all his ammunition) without harming the Zero.[36]

Fighting Six

Chuck Brewer of RED 2, one of the CAP pilots who risked AA to dive along with the *Shōkaku* carrier bombers, later picked up a Type 99 flying right over the waves. He lined up a long opposite run, but in the process a Zero jumped his tail. Coolly Brewer nailed the *kanbaku*, then turned tightly to get out of the fighter's line of fire. He chopped his throttle, pulled up sharply, then swung around for a head-on run. After flashing past, Brewer quickly reversed course and used a full-deflection shot to finish off the Zero.

Hastening eastward after missing the initial interceptions, RED 3 (Dick Gay, Wes Lindsey, Joe Achten, and Deke Disque) observed their own ships maneuvering under attack. White splashes from near misses surrounded the *Enterprise,* while streaks of bright orange flames and black smoke marked the demise of aircraft. Astern of the carrier the *North Carolina* seemed smothered in her own gun flashes. From 14,500 feet Gay noticed what looked like three Zeros a few thousand feet below, one of which was menacing a lone F4F. RED 3 abruptly rolled over and dived to the rescue.[37]

Several minutes before, Cash Register had foolishly followed Hayashi's flaming Zero and lost contact with the rest of RED 5. Now as he climbed to find his teammates, an enemy fighter jumped him from above. With a tight wingover to the left, Register forced the bandit (he wrongly identified it as an Me-109) to overshoot and make a clumsy pullout. The Japanese rolled out to the left, unwittingly out in front of RED 3's swiftly diving F4Fs. Alarmed, the Zero reefed into a climbing right turn directly through Register's close-range, full-deflection burst, but avoided the red bands of tracers by reversing his turn ("like a cartwheel"). Gay finally burned the Zero, which fell away. Wingman Wes Lindsey also took a shot. Thus three pilots (Register, Gay, and Lindsey) each laid claim to this one fighter.

While Gay and Lindsey assisted Register, Joe Achten tackled the second Zero. Trying hard to stay with his section leader's violent game of "crack the whip," Deke Disque heard what sounded like "a handful of gravel thrown against the side of a tin barn,"[38] only now the "tin barn" was his airplane. To avoid more damage, he tightened his turn. Even so, the third Zero ripped his fuselage with excellent deflection shooting. Among other things, bullets holed the vacuum tank controlling the flaps. Coming out of his turn, Disque observed a Zero (Achten's original target) bank sharply right and accelerate away. From almost head-on, his run caused the Mitsubishi to stream black smoke, roll over, and drop toward the water. Achten pursued Zero number 3, Disque's assailant, but could not catch it.

It appears that the *Zuikaku* Zero that had jumped Register possibly fell to Gay, but the other two adversaries were familiar ones: Shigematsu and Muranaka from the *Shōkaku* 17th *Shōtai.* Neither Japanese succumbed in the sharp tussle with RED 3, although somewhere along the line one Zero sustained damage. Shigematsu later noted a skirmish against four Grummans between 3,000 and 3,500 meters (9,840 to 11,450 feet) southwest of the ships. Finally calling it a day, he led Muranaka out to the west.

Meanwhile, Disque lost track of the rest of RED 3, but noticed another friendly plane in trouble below. Back after sighting the *Ryūjō* force, Ens. Harold Bingaman of VT-3 found TF-16 under attack. He circled south hoping to keep clear of the fight, but three *Zuikaku* Zeros cornered him at low altitude. A frustrated VF pilot (original orders VF-42), Bingaman scissored each in turn, but the TBF lacked the performance and firepower (just a single .30-caliber forward) to match its opponents. While jinking and weaving, he tried to give turret gunner Paul Knight, ARM3c, good shots at the enemy.[39]

Bullets from one Zero's long above-rear pass raised a flurry of white splashes on the sea beneath Bingaman's TBF. Suddenly Disque intervened from above, and the Japanese took alarm with an Immelmann turn to evade. Simultaneously Knight triggered a long burst with his single .50, and Disque opened fire. The Zero spun rightward and plowed into the water. At the same time another *Zuikaku* pilot scored critical hits on the TBF, forcing Bingaman to set down on the water. The crew had time to retrieve the large life raft before the Avenger sank. They rowed westward toward Stewart Island, observed a few minutes before the fight, and made landfall about eight hours later. On 27 August Lt. (jg) George Clute of VP-11 rescued them unharmed.

Bingaman's crew never saw an F4F join their fight, and Disque soon became too busy to notice what happened to the Avenger. He climbed, scanned the area, then observed a Zero, probably one of the three that had worked over Bingaman, hug the waves. Hurtling down, Disque, as he later wrote, "camped on his tail and let him have everything I had."[40] "Everything" made no difference against the imperturbable Mitsubishi which gradually accelerated away. Disque last saw it pass over the northern horizon.

Another CAP division that missed the initial interception was Lou Bauer's RED 1. They witnessed a spectacular AA show blossom far ahead, but arrived too late for the dive-bomber attack. Flying at 6,000 feet, Bauer kept an eye out for enemy torpedo planes yet to appear, but about five miles north of the ships, a lone carrier bomber headed out at 2,000 feet. Bauer gathered wingman Ens. Will Rouse and with a high-side run smoked the Type 99. It stalled in a climbing turn and pitched into the sea. The 2nd Section of ensigns Jim Halford and Hank Hartmann stayed above as top cover. Most likely Bauer finished off the last *Shōkaku kanbaku* that had bombed the *North Carolina*.

Soon after Bauer splashed the dive bomber, he sighted a Zero flying alone at low altitude. His bullets holed its fuel tank, which gushed a white trail of raw gasoline. In defense, the Japanese nosed down to wave-top level and ran at high speed. Watching from above and three miles off, Halford converted altitude into knots to pursue the fleeing Zero. His first burst at long range seemed to rattle the enemy pilot, who responded with S-turns to evade tracers, a poor maneuver under the circumstances. By cutting his speed, the Japanese allowed the F4F to narrow the gap. After 10 minutes, Halford overtook and destroyed the hapless *Zuikaku* fighter. Witnessing the kill, Bauer thought the Japanese pilot demonstrated his inexperience by not simply escaping flat out in level flight. At 1715 RED 1 spotted another parachutist (not the same one seen earlier by Wayne Presley of SCARLET 1) and notified base. Again his identity is a mystery.[41]

SBDs and TBFs

Task Force 16 ordered the dive bombers and torpedo planes in the vicinity to "keep clear during the attack," but that proved difficult for the IAP, returning search planes, and the newly launched strike groups dotting the skies. Too busy fighting F4Fs, most Zeros did not bother with the SBDs and TBFs (Bingaman was an exception), but withdrawing carrier bombers shared some adventures with them.

Ensigns Howard R. Burnett, George Glen Estes, and Walton A. "Red" Austin of VS-5 flew the TF-16 IAP hunting I-boats. When the AA barrage opened, the three SBDs quickly moved northward out of range and spread out to watch for torpedo planes. An old hand at this, Austin had survived the *Yorktown*'s 8 May antitorpedo plane patrol at the Coral Sea. Soon "Redbird" Burnett latched onto a pair of carrier bombers coming out low. Overhauling the trailer, he pressed his assault until the Type 99 splashed and fruitlessly chased the survivor 60 miles. Estes watched Burnett depart and later saw black smoke out that way. Against another carrier bomber Estes countered with a head-on run, and his tracers disappeared into its belly. If not destroyed, the enemy certainly remembered the occasion. Of more concern, Estes wondered what befell his aggressive friend Burnett.[42]

Like Bingaman, several VT-3 TBFs newly back from the search had anticipated landing back on board "The Big E." Ens. Fred Mears heard orders for SBDs to intercept torpedo planes, so he broke formation to get in on the fun. Soon two carrier bombers (he thought they were Zeros) chased him back to the bosom of his mates—Jett and a third TBF. One Type 99 gave up, but the second buzzed through no fewer than seven firing passes against the three TBFs, but inflicted only minor damage. Its delay in getting clear probably spelled death from CAP F4Fs. Mears himself felt a bit chastened by the experience.

Circling alone northwest of the task force, Ens. Robert Bye, Jett's wingman, challenged two *Zuikaku* carrier bombers with his single .30-caliber popgun. They split up and ran, making Bye feel pretty good, until three more Japanese showed up. At that point, he called it quits. In another fight, Lt. John Myers of VT-3, who escaped the *Ryūjō* CAP Zeros, ran afoul of a *Zuikaku* Zero 25 miles west of TF-16. Its pilot poured four 20-mm shells and fifty to one hundred 7.7-mm slugs into the tough Avenger, shot bombardier Charles R. Beatty, ARM2c, through both feet, and slightly wounded Douglas L. Anderson, ARM1c, the radioman/gunner. A little later the battered TBF with its "tail section half gone" joined the circling VT-3 formation. To Mears the irrepressible Myers "grinned and put his fingers to the corners of his eyes, the slant-eye Jap sign."[43]

The strike certainly disrupted the *Enterprise* strike group struggling to form up at low altitude. A carrier bomber accosted Mach. John R. Baker's VT-3 TBF, whose turret gunner, Carl R. Gibson, ARM3c, claimed its destruction. While Max Leslie circled at 500 feet, the *North Carolina*'s AA pinked his TBF, so he complimented her accuracy. His turret gunner, Gerald G. Aulick, ARM1c (a VT-5 veteran), drove off a nasty Type 99. By the time Leslie cleared the task force, his group had departed without him.

During the second phase of the fighting, eleven fresh F4Fs (three VF-5, eight VF-6) entered the lists. Claims racked up in this portion of the battle amounted to: VF-5 (3 VB); VF-6 (2 VB, 8 VF); SBDs and TBFs (3 VB). It appears the Japanese lost four carrier bombers (three *Shōkaku*, one *Zuikaku*) and two *Zuikaku* Zeros, although some planes crippled earlier might also have succumbed.

Distant Skirmishes

Away from TF-16, the outer CAP F4Fs and more returning search-and-strike planes dogged the way of the thirteen-odd Type 99s still aloft:

1. Seki with three (2 *Shōkaku*, 1 *Zuikaku*)
2. Arima with three *Shōkaku*
3. Yoshimoto with three *Shōkaku* and one *Zuikaku*, with another *Zuikaku* nearby
4. One unknown *Zuikaku* crew
5. Koretsune (*Zuikaku*)

Shōkaku Zero pilots Shigematsu and Muranaka flew westward together, but Komachi was alone in the rendezvous area west of the ships. Hidaka, PO3c Tochi Hajime, and Sea1c Egawa Yoshio from the *Zuikaku* had long since split up. The clearest way to describe the distant altercations is to follow the fortunes of separate Japanese flights as seen primarily through the reports of their enemies.

Retiring northward, Seki's flight of three encountered Lt. Raymond P. Kline (USNA 1939) of VB-6, who claimed the trailer. However, Seki's force retired unscathed. At 1655 they crossed the flight path of another pugnacious VB-6 SBD search pilot, Lt. Carl Horenburger, who led the 7 August flight that nearly finished off Sakai Saburō. Returning from a northeasterly search sector, he traded successive head-on runs with two dive bombers before all went their separate ways.

Other Japanese were not so fortunate as Seki. Yoshimoto's three *Shōkaku* Type 99s and one from the *Zuikaku* (with another *Zuikaku kanbaku* nearby) cleared the target to the west before wheeling north for home. At 1710 and perhaps 75 miles northwest of TF-16, this small band clashed with a mixed flight of thirteen *Saratoga* SBDs (ten VS-3, three VB-3) led by VS-3 skipper Lou Kirn. Flying home after bombing the *Ryūjō,* Kirn's bunch knew of the attack on TF-16. Indeed, a few minutes before they flushed a lone Zero withdrawing at high speed, but could not catch it. Now Kirn discovered the four Type 99s approaching nearly head-on at 500 feet, just above his thirteen SBDs deployed in a Vee-of-Vees. He maneuvered his center section directly beneath the oncoming enemy planes giving pilots and radiomen alike good shots at these juicy targets. The lead pilots blazed away with their .50s on the way in, and as Yoshimoto's four Type 99s flashed overhead (clearing Kirn by a mere 20 feet), the radiomen took over with their twin .30s. Together they produced a "high volume of fire," as Kirn later related the story. To him this was the "most interesting time of the whole day."[44]

After bombing the *Enterprise,* PO1c Akimoto Tamotsu, pilot of *Shōkaku* Type 99 carrier bomber EI-232, looks at the camera. The aircraft commander, PO1c Koitabashi Hiroshi, mans the 7.7-mm Lewis gun in the rear cockpit. Beyond is EI-235, but the crew cannot be identified. This is a frame from a motion picture taken by Lt. Arima Keiichi.
(Arima Keiichi via the Admiral Nimitz Museum and Dr. Steve Ewing)

TABLE 7.2
Claims for Strike Aircraft Destroyed by Task Force 16

	VF Aloft	VF, VB, VT Engaged	Shot down	Claims		
				VB	VF	VT
VF-5	25	19	3	14	3	—
VF-6	28	24	2	12	12	2
VB-6	—	2	—	1	—	—
VB-3 and VS-3	—	13	—	4	—	—
VS-5	—	2	—	1	—	—
CEAG	—	1	—	1	—	—
VT-3	—	7	1	1	1	—
	53	68	6	34	16	2

TABLE 7.3
1st Strike Group, Lt. Cdr. Seki Mamoru

Shōkaku Carrier Bomber Squadron
(27 Type 99 carrier bombers)

20th *Shōtai*	27th *Shōtai*	28th *Shōtai*
Lt. Cdr. Seki Mamoru (P)	Lt. Yoshimoto Kazuo (P)	Spec. Duty Ens. Saitō Chiaki (O)
PO1c Imada Tetsu (O)	PO1c Someno Fumio (O)	PO1c Yasuda Nobuyoshi[a] (O)
PO3c Sasaki Mitsuo[a] (O)	PO2c Tanaka Hirokichi[a] (O)	PO2c Kitamura Kenzō[a] (O)

1st *Chūtai*

21st *Shōtai*	22nd *Shōtai*	23rd *Shōtai*
Lt. Arima Keiichi (O)	Lt. (jg) Motoyama Hiroyuki[a] (O)	WO Aragane Masaki[a] (P)
PO1c Koitabashi Hiroshi (O)	PO2c Tsuchiya Ryōroku (O)	PO3c Murakami Shingi[a] (O)
PO2c Iida Yoshihiro[a] (O)	PO2c Horie Kazumi[a] (O)	PO3c Aoki Toyojirō[a] (O)

Zuikaku Carrier Bomber Squadron

1st *Shōtai*	2nd *Shōtai*	3rd *Shōtai*
Lt. Ōtsuka Reijirō[a] (O)	Lt. (jg) Nakamura Gorō[a] (P)	WO Sano Susumu[a] (O)
PO1c Shirakura Kōta[a] (O)	PO2c Koretsune Goichi[d] (O)	PO1c Kobayashi Tadafumi[a] (P)
PO2c Maeno Hiroshi[c] (O)	Sea1c Kawaguchi Toshimitsu[a] (O)	PO3c Matsumoto Yoshiichirō[a] (P)

Escort Fighters (10 Zeros)

17th *Shōtai* (*Shōkaku*)	14th *Shōtai* (*Zuikaku*)	15th *Shōtai* (*Zuikaku*)
Lt. Shigematsu Yasuhiro	Lt. Hidaka Saneyasu	PO1c Makino Shigeru[a]
PO1c Muranaka Kazuo	PO2c Sakaida Gorō[a]	PO3c Tochi Hajime[c]
PO3c Komachi Sadamu[c]	PO2c Ōkubo Toshiharu[a]	Sea1c Egawa Yoshio
Sea1c Hayashi Shigeru[b]		

Note: Aircraft commanders: P = pilot; O = observer
[a] Failed to return
[b] Shot down and survived
[c] Ditched—crew recovered
[d] Ditched at Malaita

TABLE 7.4
CAP Divisions and Claims in the Attack on Task Force 16

Fighting Five

SCARLET 1
Lt. Cdr. Leroy C. Simpler	
Ens. John M. Wesolowski	
Ens. Wayne C. Presley	1 VB
Ens. Melvin C. Roach	

SCARLET 3
Lt. Walter E. Clarke	
Ens. George F. Morgan	
Ens. Donald A. Innis	
Lt. (jg) Elisha T. Stover	
Ens. Mortimer C. Kleinmann, Jr.	

SCARLET 4
Lt. Richard E. Harmer	1 VB
Ens. John B. McDonald, Jr.	2 VB
Lt. Howard W. Crews	
Ens. Benjamin F. Currie	1 VB

SCARLET 5
Lt. Richard Gray	1 VF
Lt. (jg) Frank O. Green	

SCARLET 6
Lt. Hayden M. Jensen	3 VB
Ens. John M. Kleinman	2 VB
Lt. (jg) Carlton B. Starkes	3 VB

SCARLET 7
Lt. David C. Richardson	
Lt. Marion W. Dufilho[a]	
Ens. Leon W. Haynes	1 VF

SCARLET STANDBY
Lt. (jg) James C. Smith[a]	
Ens. Charles E. Eichenberger	1 VB
Ens. Horace A. Bass, Jr.[a]	

Fighting Six

RED 1
Lt. Louis H. Bauer	1 VB
Ens. Wildon M. Rouse	
Ens. James A. Halford, Jr.	1 VF
Ens. Henry E. Hartmann	

RED 2
Mach. Doyle C. Barnes[a]	
Ens. Robert A. M. Dibb	2 VB
Gun. Charles E. Brewer	2 VB, 1 VF
Ens. Douglas M. Johnson	1 VB

RED 3
Lt. (jg) Theodore S. Gay, Jr.	1 VF
Ens. Charles W. Lindsey	1 VF
Mach. Julius A. Achten	1 VF
Ens. Robert M. Disque	2 VF

RED 4
Mach. Donald E. Runyon	3 VB, 1 VF
Howard W. Packard, AP1c	
Mach. Beverly W. Reid[a]	
Ens. Joseph D. Shoemaker	

RED 5
Lt. Albert O. Vorse, Jr.	1 VF
Ens. Richards L. Loesch, Jr.	
Mach. Howell M. Sumrall	1 VF
Ens. Francis R. Register	2 VF

RED 6
Ens. George W. Brooks	1 VB, 1 VT
Ens. Harry A. March	1 VT
Ens. Mark K. Bright (VF-5)	1 VB
Rad. Elec. Thomas W. Rhodes	1 VT
Lee Paul Mankin, Jr., AP1c	2 VB

RED 7, 1st Section
Lt. (jg) Harold L. Rutherford
Ens. William W. Wileman

RED 7, 2nd Section
Lt. Vincent P. de Poix
Lt. (jg) Howard L. Grimmell, Jr.

[a] Missing in action

Doubtless it was interesting for Yoshimoto's crews as well, especially when some SBDs broke off from the flanking sections to press individual attacks. Lt. Ralph Weymouth (USNA 1938) and Lt. (jg) Alan S. Frank of VS-3, as well as VB-3's Lt. (jg) Robert K. Campbell and Ens. Alden W. Hanson all claimed kills. Kirn himself reported seeing three splashed dive bombers, with the fourth trailing smoke.[45] However, *no* Japanese went down at this time, but their ordeal was far from over.

Originally dispatched for a distant intercept, Red Brooks's RED 6 (four VF-6, 1 VF-5) went nearly 100 miles out on 330 degrees (M.).[46] Learning the enemy had slipped past, Brooks reversed course and bustered southeast at 11,000 feet. Around 1715 he glimpsed eight enemy planes just 50 feet above the water and headed north. From his lofty perch, the Japanese appeared to be an odd mixture of dive bombers and torpedo planes in several flights. Actually RED 6 discovered Yoshimoto's four Type 99 carrier bombers being pursued by the four *Saratoga* SBDs. By the time the F4Fs descended to effective attack range, the SBDs had departed. Brooks and wingman Harry March charged Yoshimoto's three *Shō-kaku* carrier bombers, which evaded with shallow turns. Brooks reported downing one torpedo plane and one dive bomber, while March fired off all 1,440 rounds to claim another torpedo plane. However, all three Type 99s escaped and reported a scrap with eight Grummans.

On the way down Dusty Rhodes, Paul Mankin, and VF-5's Mark Bright separated from RED 6's lead section. They saw (and later reported) only two or three enemy dive bombers, certainly no torpedo planes.[47] Bright watched Rhodes assail one VB and joined with a high-side run of his own. However, his guns misfired, so he pulled off to recharge them. Coming around for a second pass, he noticed Rhodes's target had already dropped into a fatal stall. The Type 99 spun leftward into the water. In the meantime, Rhodes's guns also jammed, but he could not fix them. While the first dive bomber succumbed, Mankin raked another with a low-deflection shot from close astern and "burned him good."[48] Thus both *Zuikaku* crews flying near Yoshimoto went down in flames.

RED 6's interception remains the most mysterious episode of the Battle of the Eastern Solomons. Back on board the *Enterprise,* the skirmish somehow got blown way out of proportion. Everyone wondered about the strange absence of Japanese torpedo planes, hitherto the enemy's most effective carrier-killers. Actually no Japanese carrier attack planes even flew the mission. To account for their nonappearance, an air battle of mythic proportions gradually grew out of the stories of a certain participant which became better at each retelling. By the time Max Leslie's air group report appeared in September, RED 6 had battled an entire enemy twelve-plane torpedo squadron guarded by Type 99 dive bombers and Zeros. According to Leslie, RED 6 "immediately closed on the enemy who promptly dispersed and gave every evidence of *abandoning* their mission."[49] The best that can be said of this incident is that the leader, although an experienced pilot, fought his first combat and very likely was confused by the bizarre behavior of his opponents, which no one realized was a mixture of friendly and enemy planes.

Brooks and Rhodes flew back independently, but Mankin, Bright, and March joined on each other. A few minutes later they noticed a lone carrier bomber, perhaps a cripple, hugging the waves. March had saved no ammunition, but Bright and Mankin retained plenty. Despite their high-side runs from the left, the Type 99 adroitly spiraled upward to "bitch" their lunges. Neither F4F could jump its tail. Every time the *kanbaku* turned, Mankin nosed down, but could not shoot. For three more criss-crosses, the Japanese showed "remarkable evasive action," but Mankin, as he later wrote, finally "wised up." Now ready for the gambit, he scored telling hits as the Type 99 crossed ahead. It continued in front of Bright, who "chopped gun and sat on his tail for about a 20–25 second burst." When Mankin swung around for an above-rear approach, the Aichi pulled up steeply, then fell away. Its sharply pointed left wing sliced through the waves, but to his surprise the Type 99 did not cartwheel, but settled back on its wings into the sea. Mark Bright received credit for this, the seventeenth and final carrier bomber shot down from the first strike.[50]

The last encounter between American planes and the first strike group occurred around 1744. After the attack Arima, the *Shōkaku* 1st *Chūtai* leader, and his faithful wingman Koitabashi had taken station just northwest of the task force to help guide fighters back to base. Soon another *Shōkaku* Type 99 joined up. In the distance they watched the *Enterprise* continue to burn. A quarter hour or more later, four Grummans took notice of the three bandits and chased them westward away from the ships. At 1744 Lou Kirn's thirteen *Sara* SBD spotted three more enemy planes about five miles east and changed course to fight. Arima would have none of it and detoured around the formation. Several SBDs broke off to pursue, and one, Ens. Roger C. Crow of VS-3, reported smoking one dive bomber. He rashly chased the enemy flight about 25 miles north, only to discover he had run dry of bullets. Arima's conscientious attention to the duty of homing possible lost fighters explained why he was still so close to TF-16 an hour after the attack.[51]

In the last phase of the action, the five RED 6 pilots claimed four dive bombers and two torpedo planes, and the *Sara*'s SBDs added four more dive bombers to the tally. Actually three *Zuikaku* carrier bombers went down, which left only two remaining from Ōtsuka's ill-fated *chūtai*.

For the whole action against TF-16, U.S. claims for strike aircraft destroyed in aerial combat totaled fifty-two (fifteen more than the Japanese had) (see table 7.2). At the same time the Japanese claimed twelve Grummans (one unconfirmed) (see tables 7.3 and 7.4).

CHAPTER 8

Mutual Retreat

THE CARRIERS REGROUP

After the bombing, alarms of incoming torpedo planes beset both TF-16 and TF-11. At 1650 Ham Dow warned, "All combat planes from RED BASE, keep sharp lookout for TB attack now." Three minutes later he urged, "All RED and SCARLET planes get over the ship," and added, "Don't bother those getting away."[1] The reports proved false, although the CAP had to check them out.

At 1651 the *Enterprise*'s radar screen flashed real danger in the form of a large group of bogeys bearing 265 degrees, 50 miles, and headed southwest. In fact, TF-16 had detected Lieutenant Takahashi's second strike group of twenty-seven carrier bombers and nine Zeros hunting the American carriers. Later they happened to fly over Lou Kirn's formation, who counted eighteen VB, nine VT, and three VF. Had Takahashi only seen and followed the SBDs, he would have sighted TF-16 a few minutes later. One Japanese contact plane already had TF-16 in view. At 1650 the *Chikuma* number 5 aircraft radioed the position of the enemy task force seen dealing "fierce AA" to Seki's first-wave attackers. Its report definitely placed the American carriers east of Takahashi, but he copied neither the original message nor the *Kidō Butai*'s rebroadcast. Some second-wave crews heard both messages, but wrongly assumed Takahashi, too, received them. It proved to be the crucial Japanese mistake of the battle.

With so many aircraft (fighters and returning strike planes alike) low on fuel it became imperative for the carriers to recover them. Still afire aft, the *Enterprise* coped with malfunctioning number 2 and 3 elevators along with damaged arresting gear. The F4Fs flocked toward the *Saratoga* now open for business. Down to fumes, RED 5's Scoop Vorse hastened over to TF-11, but at 1700 his engine died from fuel starvation. He ditched close astern of the carrier, and the *Phelps* soon took him on board. From 1701 to 1740, twenty-seven F4Fs (fourteen VF-6, thirteen VF-5) took refuge on board the *Sara:*

VF-5	VF-6
SCARLET 3: Stover, Kleinmann	RED 2: Dibb, Brewer, Johnson
SCARLET 4: Harmer, McDonald, Crews, Currie	RED 3: Gay, Lindsey, Achten
SCARLET 5: Gray, Green	RED 4: Runyon, Packard, Shoemaker
SCARLET 6: Jensen, Kleinman, Starkes	RED 5: Sumrall, Register, Loesch
SCARLET 7: Richardson, Haynes	RED 7: Rutherford, Wileman

The only mishap, a spectacular one, befell Chick Harmer, the wounded VF-5 XO in a badly shot-up mount. After touchdown, the Wildcat bounded up, flipped over on its back, and wrapped itself in the wire barrier. Harmer escaped further injury, and without much delay flight deck crews pushed the smashed F4F over the side. While the pilots crowded into the VF-5 ready room, the *Sara*'s Air Department worked frantically to rearm and refuel some F4Fs to fly relief CAP. At 1740, TF-16 rejoined TF-11, and seven minutes later the *Saratoga* launched eleven VF-6 fighters (Gay's RED 3, Runyon's RED 4, RED 5 under Sumrall, and Rutherford's RED 7) and Crews's four VF-5 F4Fs. Thereafter she held a southeasterly course to land more aircraft.

Throughout the recovery and servicing of the CAP, the *Enterprise* FDOs anxiously watched the radar plot for news of bogeys to the west. At 1715 a frustrated Ham Dow lashed out on the fighter circuit: "All planes from RED BASE. Please keep quiet. There may be more bogeys and we have to give orders, so keep quiet."

At 1730, Takahashi's second wave muffed the second golden opportunity to learn the American position. Seki's post-strike report, rebroadcast by the *Shōkaku*, placed two enemy carriers, two battleships, six heavy cruisers, one light cruiser, and twelve destroyers bearing 075 degrees, 200 miles from Tulagi. Again Takahashi missed this all-important communication, but others in his strike group did not. At 1743 he reached the position where he expected to find the enemy carriers (actually 83 miles due south of TF-16), but saw only open water. Takahashi searched westward in vain until sunset. At 1827 U.S. radar last showed the strike 70 miles southwest and heading away to the northwest.

Thus Japanese blunders spared the *Enterprise* a devastating blow; if it had transpired, she would have been nearly helpless. At first she appeared much improved after her rough pounding. Kinkaid notified Fletcher at 1740 of two bomb hits aft and some underwater damage, but concluded "damage apparently light."[2] She expected to recover her own planes and worked up to 24 knots, while repair crews hastily patched the holes in her flight deck. Kinkaid detailed the *Grayson* at 1735 to proceed northwest 40 miles and stand by to pick up any crews unable to reach the carriers. At 1749 the *Enterprise* started landing aircraft. The pilots approached the ramp in more of a port arc rather than straight in to avoid the bulged area starboard aft on the flight deck. In the next 21 minutes Robin Lindsey brought in thirty-three planes, including twenty SBDs (seven VB-6, thirteen VS-5), four VT-3 TBFs, and nine F4Fs (RED 6: Brooks, March, Rhodes, Mankin, and Bright of VF-5; RED 1: Hartmann; RED 3: Disque; RED 7: de Poix, Grimmell).

While landing fighters, the *Enterprise* suffered a crash that resembled Harmer's accident on the *Saratoga*. Making his approach without flaps, Disque was waved off as too "hot." The next time he overcompensated, came in low and slow to cut down his speed, and took his cut rather far astern. The F4F floated over the deck without snagging a wire, clipped the barrier with its landing gear, and ended up on its back. Despite the plane's crushed vertical stabilizer, rudder, turtleback, and windshield, Disque was unhurt but shaken. He fell on his head when he released his seat belt. The battered Wildcat was preserved to study the effects of gunfire on its structure.[3]

At 1810, the *Enterprise* briefly suspended landings for a quick re-spot to launch five RED 6 F4Fs for CAP. At 1813, while recovering Ensign Behr's shot-up VB-3 SBD, she unexpectedly lost all steering control. Sounding her siren, she careened through the screen and nearly collided with the *Balch* before Captain

Davis rang "All stop." Fletcher alerted SoPac that she might require a tug. Soon she circled at 10 knots, while her engineers worked frantically to restore the steering motors shorted out by water and foamite used to fight the fires from the second bomb hit. In the meantime two SBDs (Gibson of VB-6, Jorgenson of VS-5) and one VT-3 TBF (Bye) ditched out of fuel, but destroyers soon picked up their crews. With great relief, Davis finally regained control at 1853. In the interim, Takahashi's second wave would have found easy pickings.

With the *Enterprise* again out of action, the *Saratoga* moved to the fore. From 1805 to 1855, she landed the *Ryūjō* strike of twenty-eight SBDs and seven TBFs, John Myers of VT-3, and all thirty-one F4Fs (eighteen VF-6, thirteen VF-5) aloft. Yet to return were the strikes launched just before the enemy attacked. The *Grayson* searched to the west looking for downed aircrews. She was to rejoin TF-16 the next day.

The dusk carrier landings proceeded quite well, with much credit due to the *Sara*'s fine LSO Bill Godwin. Only another of the famous somersaulting fighters marred the performance. After dark Dix Loesch of RED 5, returning from his second CAP of the evening, approached a bit too high and brushed the barrier with his wheels. The inverted Wildcat flopped into the open number 1 elevator pit, but its wings blocked the fall, leaving the fuselage suspended upside down over the open elevator well. Loesch had cut his scalp on the exposed deck edge and hung head down until the elevator was raised high enough for someone to help him from his cockpit. The battered F4F went over the side, and the equally ill-used pilot repaired to sickbay. The wound took numerous stitches to close, and Loesch felt the shaved scalp and scar "looked like hell." For the next several days he took to wearing a cap even in the *Sara*'s wardroom, which was considered bad manners. Other officers would come up behind the ensign and flip off his cap, only to replace it when they saw his scalp.[4]

THE FOLLOW-UP STRIKES

Three separate strikes departed TF-61 when the Japanese attacked. Lieutenant Larsen with five VT-8 TBFs and Lt. (jg) Robert M. Elder's two VB-3 SBDs went out separately on 340 degrees, but joined at 1710.[5] Taking the lead, Elder worked up to 9,000 feet, while Larsen cruised at 7,000. About 15 minutes later they reached the target area, but saw nothing. Heavy clouds decreased visibility, so Larsen directed that they search north. He made the correct decision. At 1735, VT-8 spotted four heavy cruisers, six light cruisers, and about eight destroyers on course 150 degrees, speed 15 to 20 knots—Vice Admiral Kondō's Advance Force. The seaplane carrier *Chitose,* stopped while recovering aircraft, quickly sounded the alarm. She sent three Type 0 observation seaplanes to chase three enemy "attack planes" (apparently the two SBDs). At 1740 the TBFs dropped their fish from the port side of Kondō's four heavy cruisers deployed abreast. VT-8 thought perhaps one CA in the center took a torpedo, but no ships were damaged.

After the torpedo runs only three VT-8 TBFs rejoined. Alone, Lt. (jg) Edward L. ("Frenchie") Fayle circled the enemy task force trying to get his bearings, but ran into trouble in the form of two *Shōkaku* Zeros flown by PO1c Iwaki Yoshio and PO2c Ōhara Hiroshi. After separating from Lieutenant Ibusuki, the 14th *Shōtai* leader, they spotted Fayle's TBF, which Ōhara uncertainly described as a "multi-engine land plane." The lead Japanese punched holes into the Avenger's

TABLE 8.1
Final Distribution of Fighter Pilots and Planes

Ship	Aircraft	Losses
Saratoga		
S1: Simpler, Wesolowski, Presley, Roach	4	—
S3: Clarke, Morgan, Stover, Kleinmann	4	—
S4: Harmer, McDonald, Crews, Currie	3	1 F4F jettisoned (Harmer)
S5: Gray, Green, Bright	3	—
S6: Jensen, Kleinman, Starkes	3	—
S7: Richardson, Innis, Haynes	3	1 F4F (Dufilho)
Standby: Eichenberger	1	2 F4F (Smith, Bass)
Fighters out of commission	2	
	23	
R1: Bauer, Rouse, Halford	3	—
R2: Dibb, Brewer, Johnson	3	1 F4F (Barnes)
R3: Gay, Lindsey, Achten	3	—
R4: Runyon, Packard, Shoemaker	3	1 F4F (Reid)
R5: Sumrall, Register, Loesch	2	1 F4F ditched (Vorse)
		1 F4F jettisoned (Loesch)
R6: Brooks, March, Rhodes, Mankin	4	—
R7: Rutherford, Wileman	2	—
	20	
Enterprise		
R1: Hartmann	1	—
R3: Disque	1	(F4F inop.)
R7: de Poix, Grimmell	2	(de Poix's F4F inop.)
Fighter out of commission	1	—
	5	
S7: Blair	1	

right wing and fuselage and shattered the plexiglass of the turret, but Edward Velazquez, ARM3c, the gunner, took his revenge. He set Iwaki's Zero on fire and killed the ace, whose eight kills included some against VT-8 at Midway. Later Ōhara claimed his mysterious opponent but, far from gone, Fayle turned south for CACTUS. He ran out of fuel short of his destination and ditched off Nura Island northeast of Guadalcanal. On 29 August the destroyer minelayer *Gamble* (DM-15) recovered the men. Ens. John Taurman's VT-8 TBF fetched up on San Cristobal, and its crew was rescued on the 28th.[6]

Elder and Ens. Robert T. Gordon of VB-3 only glimpsed the Advance Force briefly through the clouds, but they latched onto a "battleship" (actually the *Chitose*) well astern of the others. Diving from 12,500 feet, the two SBDs severely damaged the *Chitose* by near misses portside aft (which destroyed three Type 0 reconnaissance seaplanes). She soon retired to Truk for repairs.

Army Air Force B-17s from the 11th Bomb Group likewise looked over this sector. Departing Espiritu Santo at 1305, they separated into two flights. After overflying TF-61 during the Japanese attack, Maj. J. Allan Sewart's 2nd Division of four Flying Fortresses encountered at 1750 Rear Admiral Abe's Vanguard Force about 30 miles ahead of Nagumo's main body. Their payloads missed the destroyer *Maikaze,* but the big bombers continued north to within sight of the Japanese carriers. There they skirmished with three *Shōkaku* Zeros from Nagumo's scattered CAP of twenty-three (nineteen *Shōkaku,* four *Zuikaku*). PO1c Ogihara Tsuguo and PO2c Sasakibara Masao (both 13th *Shōtai*) and PO1c Taniguchi Masao (18th) fought four B-17s without visible results, although two Zeros took slight damage. For his own part Sewart suffered no losses and reported hits with 500-pound bombs on an enemy "carrier." His gunners claimed five Zeros.

Searching out to the west, Caldwell's eleven *Enterprise* SBDs failed to join Konig's TBFs (reduced to six when one aborted). Max Leslie trailed them all. Bound for Jett's old (1500) contact report of the *Ryūjō* force, their mission was already extraneous, because Felt's *Saratoga* strike finished off the *Ryūjō*. Wrapped in smoke, she listed badly, while the two destroyers picked up her crew and ditched aviators from the Guadalcanal attack force and CAP. Near to sundown at 1810, Maj. Ernest R. Maniere's 1st Division with three 11th Bomb Group B-17s claimed one 300-pound bomb hit on the stricken carrier. Three *shōtai* leaders, Lieutenant Iizuka (15th), PO1c Sugiyama (18th), and from the strike, PO1c Yoshizawa (17th), combined to shoot up one B-17, reported as a joint kill. No Army planes splashed, but 1st Lt. Robert E. Guenther's Fortress crashed at Espiritu Santo, killing him and four of the crew.

After dark Hara ordered the *Ryūjō* scuttled. Loaded with survivors, the *Tone, Tokitsukaze,* and *Amatsukaze* steamed eastward to rejoin the *Kidō Butai.* The *Ryūjō* lost all but one carrier attack plane from her original complement of twenty-four Zeros and nine Type 97s. A Zero pilot, Sea1c Takaoka Matsutarō, also died on the ship. A distant witness to her destruction, Rear Admiral Tanaka's Reinforcement Convoy likewise received orders to withdraw north.

Only increasing darkness and rapidly worsening weather greeted the *Enterprise* strike in the target area. About 275 miles out, Konig's six VT-3 TBFs briefly sighted ship wakes at 1835, only to discover Roncador Reef north of Santa Isabel. Konig told his crews to dump torpedoes and turn for home. He never knew of the orders to fly to Henderson Field. Caldwell broke off the fruitless search with no qualms about turning south for CACTUS. The island lay 50 miles closer than the carrier and was not likely to sail off in an unknown direction. His eleven SBDs reached there safely at 2020, a most welcome reinforcement for MAG-23. After missing his strike in the target area, Leslie turned back alone.

THE BATTLE WINDS DOWN

At 1919, Kinkaid's TF-16 with the wounded *Enterprise* came around to 180 degrees and retired south at 25 knots. Ready for more night operations, Fletcher's TF-11 held course southeast into the wind. At 1930 the *Saratoga* recovered her mini-strike of Larsen's three VT-8 TBFs and Elder's two VB-3 SBDs. About 1930 Fletcher finally learned to his great consternation of Ray Davis's vital 1530 sighting report of the two large enemy carriers, obviously the source of the strike against TF-16. That meant three or possibly four opposing carriers, including the one badly damaged or sunk by the *Saratoga* afternoon strike. Under the circumstances he felt compelled to break off the action. First of all, the battered *Enterprise* must reach safer waters. Second, TF-11 required fuel before returning north to support Rear Admiral Noyes's TF-18 with the *Wasp.* Having fueled that day, Noyes pounded north at maximum sustained speed to "stand toward Guadalcanal" and break up attempted enemy landings.

At 2128 while proceeding south, the *Enterprise* was surprised when six Avengers from her dusk strike appeared overhead instead of flying to CACTUS as instructed. Of course Konig, the VT-3 flight leader, never got the word, and found the carrier only because of the skill of his radioman, David H. Lane, ARM2c. Despite poor radio reception, Lane copied "The Big E" 's YE homing signal.[7] Kinkaid courageously turned on the truck lights to aid the landings. One TBF got on board safely, but Ens. Edward B. Holley plowed spectacularly into the number 2 crane abaft the island. He and his crew emerged unhurt, but wreckage fouled the deck. The other four TBFs located the *Saratoga,* which likewise showed lights and brought them on board at 2152 without incident. Last to land was Max Leslie at 2303 on the *Saratoga.* TF-11 followed an hour behind TF-16, as both forces withdrew south.

Japanese aviators also faced perilous night landings. From 1835 to 1850, the *Shōkaku* recovered ten CAP Zeros, but PO3c Ishizawa Yoshihide landed in the water for lack of fuel, unusual for the long-legged A6M2s. Planes from Seki's first strike force began to turn up at 1900. Most experienced a difficult return leg, as the carriers were not where expected. Finally they located the Vanguard Force, which placed the carriers another 60 or so miles behind. PO2c Maeno Hiroshi's *Zuikaku* carrier bomber set down near the Vanguard, as did PO3c Tochi Hajime's *Zuikaku* escort Zero. The *Chikuma* picked up the crews. In the meantime the *Shōkaku* brought on board eight of her carrier bombers and Shigematsu's two fighters, as well as four more CAP Zeros and two *Zuikaku* first-strike Zeros. One of the last to land was Arima, whose battered Type 99 ran out of fuel while taxiing up the deck.[8]

Flying back alone, PO3c Komachi Sadamu anxiously searched the skies with no success. At dusk with fuel running low, he finally discovered two destroyers and set down alongside with a perfect water landing. To his surprise they promptly disappeared, too busy to stop and pick up a lone pilot. Floating nearby, Komachi noticed his empty belly tank, which he had been unable to jettison in combat. Sheered off during the ditching, it now looked like a handy life preserver. However, it was too slippery even to grasp. For eight long hours he drifted in his life jacket. Finally another batch of destroyers happened by. One shined a searchlight and noticed Komachi's furious waving. This time they picked him up.[9]

Plagued by radio trouble, PO2c Koretsune Goichi's Type 99 never tried for the *Zuikaku,* but flew to Malaita instead. The pilot, PO2c Hikiune Yukio, set down at Cape Astrolabe on the extreme northern tip. Nearby at Afufu, they joined a party of Japanese coastwatchers, later wiped out by Marines on 5 November. Allied coastwatchers recovered Koretsune's diary.[10]

Japanese first-strike losses therefore comprised nineteen carrier bombers (seventeen shot down, two ditched) and six Zeros (four shot down, two ditched)— twenty-five out of thirty-seven planes. At 1928 after debriefing Seki, Nagumo announced three bomb hits scored against an *Enterprise*-class carrier. Soon afterward he read Maeno's report of two more hits supposedly on a different carrier.

At 2000 the *Shōkaku* finally allowed her last three CAP Zeros on board, but four more from the *Zuikaku* circled in the darkness. At the same time Nagumo advised Yamamoto and Kondō that his carriers would head north after recovering the strikes. He believed the enemy force fled at 25 knots southward out of reach, but the *Shōkaku*'s Captain Arima disagreed and recommended vigorous pursuit. Five minutes later Kondō broadcast his orders, noting that an enemy withdrawal rendered a night battle no longer possible. Therefore the Advance Force and Vanguard Force would pursue only until midnight and to the last known position of the American task force to finish off any crippled carriers. If none turned up, the whole Support Force would retire north to fuel.

While the opposing commanders radioed their plans, planes from the frustrated second strike found the *Kidō Butai*. Starting at 2015, the *Zuikaku* recovered sixteen of Takahashi's carrier bombers, all six of Shirane's fighters, and the last four CAP Zeros. PO2c Matsushita Hisao's carrier bomber went missing. The *Amatsukaze* rescued the crew of another that ditched.[11] To his regret, Takahashi learned of the missed opportunities to finish off the enemy carriers. At the same time the *Shōkaku* recovered three Zeros and three carrier bombers from her second strike force, but six other Type 99s failed to return. Two hours later, after Nagumo turned on searchlights, three of them found their way home and landed, but the whole 25th *Shōtai*, led by Lt. (jg) Ikeda Hiroto (NA 68-1940), never turned up. Thus the second strike cost four more carrier bombers missing and one ditched. Listening in to the homing efforts, U.S. intelligence analysts wrongly thought many more Japanese aircraft disappeared while looking for their carriers.

Kondō's lookouts made no contacts before the stipulated time, so at 0000, 25 August, he changed course to the north. Thus both the American and Japanese combatants quit the battle area. At 0145, Combined Fleet reported the results of the "2nd Solomons Sea Battle": two enemy carriers set afire and the rest sent packing. However, the basic objective of landing the troops on Guadalcanal remained to be accomplished.

MARINE AIR GROUP 23 REPULSES TANAKA

By 25 August the heavy ships of both sides, Fletcher's TF-61 and Kondō's Support Force, withdrew in opposite directions. In addition to the *Ryūjō*, the Japanese sustained the severe loss of carrier planes: thirty-two Zero fighters, twenty-four carrier bombers, and eight carrier attack planes, total sixty-four aircraft. As of the morning of the 25th, the *Kidō Butai*'s two carriers wielded only forty-one flyable fighters, twenty-five carrier bombers, and thirty-four carrier attack planes. TF-61's plane losses on the 24th proved much lighter than the Japanese, only sixteen: seven (five F4Fs, two TBFs) shot down, six (one F4F, two SBDs, and three TBFs) ditched, and three (two F4Fs, one TBF) lost in crashes. Fletcher believed his aircraft severely damaged, if not sank, a light carrier, but that at least two more carriers, supported by powerful surface forces, opposed the *Saratoga* and the damaged *Enterprise*. Noyes's TF-18 with the *Wasp* served as Guadalcanal's sole carrier support until TF-11 could refuel and join on the 26th.[12]

The two principal Japanese fleet commanders, Kondō and Nagumo, thought they inflicted heavy damage on the American force, including two carriers left burning. Balancing that was the loss of the *Ryūjō* and her planes, as well as severe casualties among the *Shōkaku* and *Zuikaku* air groups. Now they, too, must fuel and wait to see what happened to the Guadalcanal reinforcement operation. Vice Admiral Mikawa (8th Fleet), the local commander, originally ordered Rear Admiral Tanaka's Reinforcement Convoy to postpone the scheduled landings. Yet learning of the supposed drubbing inflicted on the enemy carriers, he changed his mind and sent Tanaka again steaming south, although this time virtually naked without support from other forces.

Major General Vandegrift's 1st MarDiv on CACTUS watched to see if the enemy landing force fought its way to Guadalcanal. The night of 24/25 August Henderson Field was a busy place. First, Turner Caldwell's eleven *Enterprise* SBDs showed up in the darkness; then, after midnight, three destroyers bombarded Lunga but inflicted little real damage. Major Mangrum took six SBDs from VMSB-232 and Flight 300 aloft to harass them. About 0100 Vandegrift learned from ComSoPac of enemy carriers still bound for the north tip of Malaita, possibly to "hit your position at daylight."[13] Around 0340, five seaplanes from Mikawa's cruisers bombed Lunga.

Noyes's TF-18 with the *Wasp* (twenty-six F4F-4s, twenty-six SBD-3s, and eleven TBF-1s), had weathered a frustrating 24 August, fully aware of the desperate battle taking place a few hundred miles north. At 0630, they had contacted the oilers about halfway between San Cristobal and Espiritu Santo and commenced fueling. The only mishap of the day involved Lt. (jg) Robert Howard's VS-71 SBD, which developed engine trouble and flopped down alongside the *Alhena*. At 1530, TF-18 completed fueling and took course 340 degrees at 22 knots. Noyes and Forrest Sherman feared pushing the *Wasp*'s fragile propulsion plant any harder than that. Learning of the *Enterprise*'s damage, Noyes changed course so as by dawn to be within air support range of her last known position.[14]

After midnight on 25 August TF-16 with the *Enterprise* passed east of TF-18, followed an hour later by Fletcher's TF-11. Finally the *Grayson* pounded south after being buzzed by Kondō's night seaplane trackers. Noyes reduced speed to 20 knots and considered how he might best support CACTUS. A half hour before sunrise, TF-18 reached the waters east-southeast of Malaita and came around to 130 degrees into the wind for a CAP and a 200-mile dawn search of the northwest quadrant. The SBDs flew single-plane sectors to conserve aircraft for the strike group held for instant departure should enemy ships turn up.

The AirSoPac night search detected considerable enemy activity. At 2015, 24 August, Ens. William C. Corbett's 23-P-11 discovered seven enemy ships, later identified as one carrier and six other vessels. At 0430 word of this sighting reached CACTUS as one CV, one CL, five DD 180 miles north of Guadalcanal, course 190 degrees, speed 17 knots. Vandegrift decided on a dawn strike against this enemy carrier force which so directly threatened his forces. At 0600 MAG-23 launched Mangrum's eight SBDs (five Marine, three Navy) and a strong escort of ten VMF-223 F4Fs under John Smith. The fighters lacked belly tanks which greatly reduced the time they could stay with the SBDs.

Despite search reports of a carrier, only Tanaka's Reinforcement Convoy remained north of Guadalcanal. Two of three destroyers that had shelled Lunga joined at 0740, giving him one light cruiser, seven destroyers, and four patrol boats escorting the three transports. By 0800 they had closed to within 150 miles of Guadalcanal and continued southeast to land troops that night.

Mangrum's strike group vainly sought the enemy carrier force, but Smith's F4Fs had to break off. Later, north of Malaita they encountered WO Fujiwara Tomosaburō's Yokohama Type 97 scouting the D2 line (107 degrees) from Shortland. Although Capt. Rivers Morrell and 2nd Lt. Rex Jeans claimed the Kawanishi, Fujiwara staggered home and ran the riddled aircraft aground before it sank from battle damage. One crewman died from wounds.[15]

Meanwhile, Mangrum's SBDs happened upon Tanaka's convoy. At 0805 1st Lt. Lawrence Baldinus laid his thousand-pounder forward on flagship *Jintsu* and forced her to limp back to Truk. Two minutes later, Ens. Christian Fink of VB-6 blasted the transport *Kinryū Maru*. She burned and later was scuttled. Mangrum scored a damaging near miss on the *Boston Maru*. At 1015 Capt. Walter E. Chambers's flight of three 11th Bomb Group B-17s sank the destroyer *Mutsuki* while she rescued survivors. With his convoy in a shambles, a dazed Tanaka ordered all forces to withdraw. That postponed the Guadalcanal reinforcement mission for the time being. Mangrum's strike transformed an indecisive clash of carriers into an Allied tactical victory.

TF-18 delivered more parting shots. The morning search was a nervous time, as Noyes did not know quite what to expect. At 0657 about 150 miles northwest of the force, VS-71's Lt. (jg) Chester V. Zalewski noticed a twin-float seaplane cruising at 1,500 feet. It fled toward some clouds, but Zalewski's below-rear attack swiftly flamed it. One crewman jumped from the burning plane and never opened his chute. "Feeling pretty good over his achievement," as Zalewski later wrote, he resumed his search. At 0825, only 30 miles from home plate, he spotted a similar seaplane approaching about 500 feet above. This time he torched the enemy plane before the crew could react, and again a hapless Japanese jumped before his flaming aircraft crashed into the sea. The sharpshooting Zalewski destroyed two Type 0 reconnaissance seaplanes commanded by WO Nakamura Saburō and WO Adachi Hisaji from heavy cruiser *Atago* (Kondō's flagship). Lt. Roy E. Breen, Jr. (USNA 1939), of VS-72, shot up a third enemy seaplane, another Type 0 from the *Myōkō,* only 30 miles from TF-18. The Japanese got away, but only after Breen expended all his bullets.[16]

Other than raising havoc with Kondō's morning search, the *Wasp*'s SBDs sighted no ships, because the Japanese drew northward out of range. From the AirSoPac morning search reports, Noyes learned of more ships too distant to attack. More accessible targets appeared to westward. At 1007 Lt. James J. Murphy in 23-P-1 sighted Tanaka's battered invasion convoy, with the *Kinryū Maru* being abandoned. A little later, CACTUS announced Mangrum's attack.

Hoping his forces would renew battle that morning, an impatient Nimitz sent the following to Ghormley and Fletcher: "Realize situation still critical but exchange of damage to date seems to be in our favor . . . Let's finish off those carriers."[17] Fortunately the Japanese had withdrawn out of reach of the outmatched *Wasp.*

Noyes turned northwest, and at 1326 the *Wasp* dispatched Lieutenant Commander Beakley with twenty-four SBDs and ten TBFs on a search/attack mission against the convoy. While they took off, a 14th Air Group Kawanishi Type 2 flying boat (Spec. Duty Ens. Itō Tatsuhisa) snooped TF-18 and at 1345 reported one carrier, two cruisers, and six destroyers ("whether enemy's or ours unknown") bearing 110 degrees and 514 miles from Shortland. Easing into position several miles to abeam as the *Wasp* planes climbed to 12,000 feet, Itō shadowed the strike group as it headed west toward his base. After about 40 minutes, the big Type 2 flying boat had foolishly closed within 3,000 yards of the nearest *Wasp* planes, which had finally noticed it. VS-71's 2nd Division of Lt. Morris R. Doughty, Ens. Howard N. Murphy, Lt. (jg) Charles H. Mester, and Ens. Robert A. Escher climbed above the target and rolled into a rear attack. The Japanese gunners could not prevent Doughty from igniting the right inboard engine. In deep trouble, Itō reefed the Kawanishi into a chandelle, but the other three SBDs quickly charged in from the rear. At 9,000 feet the Type 2 shed its wings in a fiery explosion. VS-71 scored a remarkable victory against a tough, swift target. Since 8 August the two *Wasp* scouting squadrons, 71 and 72, shot down six enemy aircraft, while a frustrated VF-71 had yet to even see an enemy plane aloft.[18]

Beakley carefully searched the designated area, but sighted no enemy ships. He then flew southwest toward Santa Isabel to check out Rekata Bay on the north coast, a suspected lair for enemy float planes, but none was there. Disappointed, he directed his planes to jettison payloads and turned southeast for home. In the meantime Noyes steamed northwest to shorten the return flight.

From 1737 to 1806, just before sundown, the *Wasp* landed her strike and CAP fighters, then retired southeast to join TF-11. That afternoon a CACTUS follow-up strike of nine SBDs also sought the convoy, but found only an oily patch of water. On the way back they roughed up the *Mochizuki* north of Isabel.

To Combined Fleet it now seemed that two Americans carriers, albeit damaged, might still be around. Overnight submarines *I-17* and *I-15* had each sighted a retiring enemy carrier force, but could not attack. After learning of the mauling of Tanaka's convoy, Yamamoto sent the *Zuikaku* and three destroyers southwest as a covering force. From the northwest he approached the area with his Main Force: the new super battleship *Yamato*, converted carrier *Taiyō* (ex-*Kasuga Maru* with a few Zeros on board), and two destroyers. Within 400 miles north of Guadalcanal, he turned northeast toward Kondō's Support Force. Despite the setback, the Japanese vowed to renew the Guadalcanal reinforcement mission.

On 25 August, first TF-16 and then TF-11 drew oil from the *Platte, Cimarron,* and *Sabine* (AO-25) about 150 miles northwest of Espiritu Santo. Fletcher queried Kinkaid about the condition of the *Enterprise*. In addition to heavy casualties (seventy-four dead, sixty-three wounded), he cited damage to two elevators and the arresting gear. Although her propulsion system was fine, a flooded compartment prevented radical high-speed maneuvers. She retained six fighters, twenty-one dive bombers, and three torpedo planes. Davis thought his flattop could operate about fifty planes in an emergency. Kinkaid recommended "when practicable" she be detached to Noumea for temporary repairs.[19]

That afternoon the two carriers sorted out their air groups. The *Saratoga* kept seventeen VF-6 F4Fs and six VT-3 TBFs from the *Enterprise*. That meant dismembering Fighting Six. The VF-6 pilots temporarily attached to VF-5 were:

Lt. (jg) Harold E. Rutherford, NAP, USN	Ens. Joseph D. Shoemaker, A-V(N)
Lt. (jg) Howard L. Grimmell, Jr., A-V(N)	Ens. Francis R. Register, A-V(N)
Ens. Harry A. March, Jr., A-V(N)	Mach. Howell M. Sumrall, NAP, USN
Ens. William W. Wileman, A-V(N)	Mach. Julius A. Achten, NAP, USN
Ens. James A. Halford, Jr., A-V(N)	Gun. Charles E. Brewer, NAP, USN
Ens. Robert A. M. Dibb, A-V(N)	Howard S. Packard, AP1c, NAP, USN
Ens. Wildon M. Rouse, A-V(N)	Lee Paul Mankin, AP1c, NAP, USN
Ens. Richards L. Loesch, Jr., A-V(N)	Robert H. Nesbitt, AP1c, NAP, USN

Fourteen VF-6 pilots with nine F4Fs stayed on the *Enterprise*:

Lt. Louis H. Bauer, USNA 1935	Ens. Douglas M. Johnson, A-V(N)
Lt. John H. Mehlig, USNA 1937	Ens. George W. Brooks, NAP, USN
Lt. Vincent P. de Poix, USNA 1939	Mach. Donald E. Runyon, NAP, USN
Lt. (jg) Theodore S. Gay, Jr., NAP, USN	Rad. Elec. Thomas W. Rhodes, NAP, USN
Ens. Henry E. Hartmann, A-V(N)	Harold M. O'Leary, AP1c, NAP, USN
Ens. Robert M. Disque, A-V(N)	Clark A. Wallace, AP1c, NAP, USN
Ens. Charles W. Lindsey, A-V(N)	Stanley W. Tumosa, AP2c, NAP, USN

The destroyer *Maury* (DD-401) fetched personal belongings and pay records for the *Enterprise* aviators transferred from their carrier. In return the *Saratoga* sent VF-5 pilots Lt. (jg) Edward G. Stepanek and ensigns Charles D. Davy, Frank J. Reiplinger, and John P. Altemus to ride "The Big E" back to Pearl for further training. VF-5 retained thirty-eight pilots for its forty operational F4F-4s.

That day VF-5 orphan and notorious raconteur Crud Blair returned to the

Saratoga brimming with stories of being stranded on the *Enterprise* during the bombing. Warned of his arrival, all the pilots stuffed their ears with cotton. Rushing into the VF-5 ready room eager to let fly, he halted and disappointedly mumbled, "Aw fellas," as everyone broke up laughing. Actually he had a most interesting tale to tell, having witnessed the whole bombing attack from a ringside seat in "The Big E" 's port catwalk.[20]

The evening of 25 August Fletcher added BB *North Carolina,* CL(AA) *Atlanta,* and three destroyers from TF-16, then at 2346 sent Kinkaid southeast toward Efate and further orders from Ghormley. In the meantime TF-11 completed fueling and at 2330 turned north to join TF-18 southeast of Malaita.[21]

SUMMING UP THE BATTLE

Fletcher and his staff labored to make sense of the plethora of sighting and strike reports and to assess the enemy's strength and losses. Upon reflection it appeared that on the 24th the enemy comprised at least two and very possibly three separate carrier task forces, totaling four flattops.[22] Felt's raiders pounded what Fletcher later designated "Task Force A," containing one carrier, believed to be the *Ryūjō.* At the very least this carrier either sank or sustained severe damage after taking one torpedo and four 1,000-pound bombs. When found by the *Saratoga* aviators, she retained only a few planes on deck, and the staff speculated she launched the late afternoon strike that missed TF-61.

Fletcher dubbed "B" the task force found by Ray Davis which comprised the two big carriers *Shōkaku* and *Zuikaku.* He felt this force loosed the eighty or so planes that beat up the *Enterprise* and thought that Larsen's mini-strike sparred with the advance screen of this force.

Evidence appeared of yet another carrier operating southeast of "Task Force B." Fletcher called this phantom group "Task Force C." Specifically his report cited the message from "9V37" (Lieutenant Riester's 23-P-9) which identified intercepting planes as "Zeros." It also noted "1V37's" 1405 report of a carrier which proved so disturbing just after the *Saratoga* dispatched Felt's strike. He thought perhaps the CACTUS-bound strike detected on *Saratoga*'s radar originated from this force. Finally he cited the report from the evening of the 24th by B-17s that identified their target as a carrier.

For a considerable amount of time even ULTRA could not settle the question of how many enemy carriers were present. The day after the battle, the HYPO analysts admitted their bafflement:

> Success of a large task force including carriers in reaching the Solomons without detection by R.I. indicates that radio security practices of the Japs are effective insofar as concealing actual movements is concerned.[23]

They decided that the initial inclusion of the carrier forces in the local communication net meant their actual rather than future presence in the South Pacific. Even nailing down the loss of the *Ryūjō* proved difficult. The cryptanalysts were not certain until 9 January 1943, when they deciphered a Japanese naval message from 10 November 1942 removing her from the Navy List. Even so, Pederson noted in 1943, "The consensus of those of us who were there is that there were 4 Jap carriers." Of course only three Japanese flattops fought in the Eastern Solomons. The presence of "Task Force C" resulted from misidentification and incorrect navigation.[24]

No matter how many Japanese carriers were present, and despite the Allied strategic victory, many, including Nimitz, thought Fletcher could have done better. They believed that TF-11 with the *Saratoga* should not have retired the evening of the 24th to refuel, but should have remained north to pound the exposed Japanese heavy forces supposedly still advancing the next day. Ironically Nimitz accepted the overexaggerated claims of Japanese aircraft destruction and believed that combat and operational losses on the 24th had gutted their carrier air groups, supposedly leaving easy pickings for the *Saratoga* and *Wasp* flyers. The final CinCPac report estimated the enemy lost two full carrier groups (eighty planes), plus another twenty-five land- and seaplanes, with possibly *another* carrier air group gone missing the night of the 24th because it failed to find its flattop. Of course Japanese plane losses numbered far fewer than Nimitz thought. With Japanese carrier fighter and torpedo plane strength largely untouched, the situation was much less sanguine for TF-61.[25]

FIGHTER LESSONS FROM THE EASTERN SOLOMONS

Soon after the battle, both the carriers and their air groups compiled voluminous reports analyzing 24 August and seeking ways to improve performance. The single overriding complaint concerned communications, namely poorly functioning radios, delayed contact reports, malfunctioning IFF gear, and other shortcomings in passing vital information to those who needed to know. Captain Davis of the *Enterprise* described communications as "weak to the point of danger." Kinkaid called them the "greatest weakness." Fletcher reiterated his request for UHF radios to be furnished for aircraft.

Related to the problem of communications was the quality of fighter direction for the combat air patrol. On the *Enterprise,* the two FDOs Dow and Rowe decried the lack of radio discipline on the fighter circuit, for which Rowe later blamed training methods.[26] According to Davis, the many radio transmissions during the attack resulted in "intolerable confusion." Numerous seemingly useless fighter pilot transmissions quoted out of context echoed loudly in post-battle analyses and subsequent histories.

Some commanders disagreed with placing all of the blame on the pilots. The most vocal was Roy Simpler, CO of VF-5. (Lou Bauer of VF-6 apparently shot his bolt in the fighter direction controversy of 7 August.) Simpler criticized the FDOs for not massing the CAP prior to the enemy's approach, for using the generic term *bomber,* which led to confusion as to whether they meant horizontal or dive bombers, and for attempting to overcontrol the many small flights. He thought it better simply to report the enemy's range, bearing, and altitude and let the fighters go from there. He had a point. In addition to the drawbacks of estimating altitudes, the CXAM radar also had problems determining reasonable bearings for the contacts. Often the blips on the A-scope were so big as to obscure the exact bearing of the bogey.

Standing up for his pilots, Simpler did not buy the overcrowded radio circuit excuse. He felt it unreasonable to expect sixty-odd VF to maintain radio silence in battle. Besides,

> a bit of exuberance improperly expressed doe[s] not harm the circuit unless it is already overloaded (which has always been the case in the past) and may have great morale value.[27]

He recommended each CV's CAP operate on a different radio frequency (something Rowe certainly seconded). Captain Ramsey also thought the furor was overblown:

> Although numerous transmissions by VF pilots were the result of inexperience and excitement, the volume of inter-plane traffic, in light of the number of fighters engaged and their wide dispersal cannot be considered as abnormal. Furthermore, it is apparent that conversations in the main served to provide useful information for attack purposes.[28]

He recommended that interplane communications, such as between section leader and wingman, use a different frequency than the main FD circuit. In turn Fletcher summed up fighter direction as "not entirely satisfactory although much better than previously experienced."[29] The intercept of lone shadowers continued to improve, but the carriers still seemed at a loss trying to defeat enemy strike groups with the CAPs alone.

The carrier commanders appeared satisfied with the Grumman F4F-4 Wildcat, although the Japanese Zero still excelled in performance. Several officers commented on the visible deterioration of enemy pilot skills. Some old and bitter controversies never came up. For example, the reduced ammunition supply of the six-gun F4F-4s appeared not to be a problem. Only a few VF pilots ran dry of bullets. However, the F4F-4's limited range still caused worry, despite the belly tanks. The fleet anxiously awaited the arrival of the gull-wing Vought F4U-1 Corsairs, and some fighter leaders also desired a special carrier-based interceptor (foreshadowing the Grumman F8F Bearcat).

Simpler bluntly proposed creation of a fighter "wing" by placing *all* of the fighters on one carrier under one command. He did not elaborate on the idea, but others did. Ramsey suggested that one flattop of a two- or three-ship carrier task force might carry only fighters earmarked for the CAP, but the others would retain strike planes and fighters necessary for escorts. Such ideas already struck a chord at higher levels. In his endorsement to the *Saratoga* report, Fletcher revealed that in July he gave "serious consideration" to placing all 100 TF-61 fighters on one carrier, but discarded it due to the time necessary to effect such a drastic reorganization of the air groups.[30] It would seem that concern over what would happen if such a unique flattop were sunk or crippled also played a role.

Nevertheless, Fletcher strongly advocated the use of a "fighter carrier" if enough other CVs were available to accomplish the offensive mission. In addition to defensive drawbacks, he felt the lack of fighters for escort adversely affected the strike missions, particularly with torpedo planes. Some commentators, notably Arthur Davis, stressed the mythical 24 August repulse of the enemy torpedo planes by RED 6 and recommended employing torpedo planes mainly in limited roles, such as moonlight strikes or finishing off cripples. Fletcher strongly disparaged the use of torpedo planes as horizontal or glide bombers against ships in lieu of carrying torpedoes. His fears for the misuse of VT would become real in the autumn of 1942.

On 10 September, when TF-16 reached Pearl Harbor, Kinkaid independently echoed Fletcher's concerns over fighter strength.[31] Heretofore the Pacific Fleet depended chiefly on surprise to compensate for numerical or materiel inferiority, but in the face of Japanese land-based air cover, Kinkaid warned that happy event could no longer be expected. He desired forty rather than thirty-six fighters per carrier for "normal operations," and against soft targets that could even be reduced. However, strong opposition demanded the number of fighters per carrier be raised to sixty. Furthermore, given an amphibious operation such as Guadalcanal-Tulagi, where the carriers were expected to substitute for friendly land-based air support, Kinkaid wanted one carrier equipped with 100 or more fighters. Only such strength would permit adequate air coverage of the landings and protection of the carrier task forces.

The question of carrier fighter strength was far from settled. The fact that so many commanders advocated greatly increased numbers of fighters tends to vindicate Fletcher's decision to withdraw the carriers on 9 August. To them at least, fighter losses as high as the 20 percent suffered on 7–8 August augured significantly to the campaign as a whole. It was vital to balance the offensive power vested in dive bombers and torpedo planes with the need for defense in the form of fighters. Certainly new fighters superior to the F4F-4 Wildcats would help.

CHAPTER 9

"Let's not let this offensive die on the vine"

GAIN ONE, LOSE ONE

On the evening of 26 August Vice Admiral Fletcher's TF-11 with the *Saratoga* met Rear Admiral Noyes's TF-18 (*Wasp*) east of San Cristobal, while Rear Admiral Kinkaid's TF-16 with the damaged *Enterprise* headed southeast toward the waters between Efate and New Caledonia.[1] Only a portion of her air group remained on board; the rest either served on the *Saratoga* or had deployed to Guadalcanal. There Lieutenant Caldwell's Flight 300 now had ten SBD dive bombers after losing one on the 25th. The morning of the 27th ComSoPac ordered TF-16 to Tongatabu via waters south of Fiji to avoid possible enemy activity. Kinkaid arranged to send most of his planes to Efate, where the F4F-7 photo plane already roosted, delivered the previous day by John Crommelin. The *Enterprise* dispatched fourteen SBDs of VB-6 and VS-5 under Lieutenant Davis and five VT-3 TBFs led by Lieutenant Commander Jett. During takeoffs two overloaded TBFs flown by Jett and Ensign Holley ditched, but the other seventeen aircraft reached Efate safely. "The Big E" retained eight F4Fs (six operational) under VF-6 CO Lou Bauer and VS-5 XO Birney Strong's eight SBDs (seven VS-5 and one VB-3).

To follow the experiences of the *Enterprise* and VF-6 a bit further—she reached Tongatabu on 30 August, where experts from the repair ship *Vestal* (AR-4) inspected the damage. Accompanied by the *Portland*, the *San Juan*, four destroyers, and a fleet oiler, Kinkaid sailed on 3 September for Pearl Harbor. On 10 September after a routine voyage, the *Enterprise* maneuvered directly into drydock number 1. Lou Bauer transferred the remnants of VF-6 to NAS Kaneohe Bay to begin rebuilding with new pilots and planes. On the voyage back the squadron had amused itself by painting tombstones on the tails of their Wildcats to represent the victory tallies. In September and October circumstances militated against VF-6 from securing enough F4Fs to fly and train the new squadron, especially after Jim Flatley's new VF-10 was earmarked to take their place on "The Big E."

On 27 August Fletcher's TF-61 with the *Saratoga* and *Wasp* retired to familiar waters between San Cristobal and Santa Cruz, from where it could support CACTUS when necessary. TF-61 would remain in that area until effecting rendezvous with Rear Admiral Murray's TF-17 with the *Hornet* en route from Pearl Harbor. Twice as TF-61 traversed the Japanese sub scouting line *Wasp* SBDs attacked I-boats, vividly demonstrating that pig boats were on the prowl.[2]

Mach. Don Runyon stands next to the tail of VF-6 F4F F-13 (BuNo. 5193) on the *Enterprise*, 9 Sept. 1942. On the trip back to Pearl Harbor, VF-6 painted the tails of its Wildcats with a special tombstone insignia denoting 41 victories in the Solomons. (NA 80-G-11103)

Lieutenant Commander Shands, VF-71's CO, regularly assigned young ensigns to take turns leading CAP divisions and working with the FDO. At 1430 the *Saratoga*'s radar located a bogey. In this instance Lieutenant Commander Wakeman tapped four VF-71 rookies under Ens. David V. Senft. Sallying out at 4,500 feet into skies punctuated by low, broken clouds, he suddenly beheld a flying boat exiting a cloud about 500 feet above. At 1429 Spec. Duty Lt. (jg) Hayashi Chōjirō, the veteran commander of the 14th Air Group's experimental Type 2 flying the 123-degree line from Shortland, had warned of enemy ships. Distracted by the VF-71 fighters, he could not follow up with their composition and location. Instead, he turned sharply left and nosed down into a shallow high-speed dive. Finally at 1435 he got off a warning of attacking enemy planes. Meanwhile, Senft fairly shouted into the microphone that he was going after the snooper.

All four VF-71 Wildcats "bent" their throttles over the quadrants in pursuit of the speedy flying boat. Senft and Ens. Millard C. Thrash closed from the right, while ensigns William M. Hall and Earl H. Steiger branched off left to bracket the target. While still out of range, its tail turret spat bright red but ineffectual

Ensigns Earl Steiger and William Hall, VF-71, 27 Aug. 1942, after downing Spec. Duty Lt. (jg) Hayashi's Type 2 flying boat. (NA 80-G-12997)

20-mm tracers. Just as Senft sighted in his guns, Hayashi reefed into another tight left turn to evade. This drew the big Type 2 right in front of Hall and Steiger, who cut loose at 800 yards. At 1445 the big wing caught fire in the center section, then simply folded up and broke off. Senft finally caught up and fired into the fuselage. The F4Fs passed through thick smoke from the burning Type 2, which fell in flames.

VF-71 had finally notched its first aerial victory. An excited Senft radioed, "Scratch one more bastard," or words to that effect, which earned him a stiff reprimand from Shands. The pilots submitted a detailed report that included a drawing of a Type 2 flying boat, reasonably accurate even down to the tail number, reported as "W-25" (actually W-45). Bill Hall received full credit for the kill.[3] That evening four F4Fs from the *Saratoga* flew over to the *Wasp* and restored VF-71 to thirty planes, while VF-5 retained thirty-six Wildcats.

The evening of 27 August Vice Admiral Ghormley issued another basic directive for the carriers. Spurred by CominCh, he voiced concerns about a possible "end run" by Japanese carriers against his right flank (Espiritu Santo–Fiji–Samoa). Therefore he wanted TF-61 as far east as it could go and still support CACTUS, so Fletcher was to stay south of latitude 10° S (which passed just south of Guadalcanal) unless an especially important target appeared within range. At the same time Major General Vandegrift warned that the Japanese apparently continued their program of destroyer troop runs to Guadalcanal. That tactic was difficult for CACTUS to counter, except by relatively short-ranged SBD attacks. Vice Admiral Mikawa's Outer South Seas Force (8th Fleet) used destroyers and barges to shuttle the 2nd Echelon of the Ichiki Detachment and the Kawaguchi Brigade to Guadalcanal. Simultaneously, in New Guinea the 17th Army loosed the South Seas Detachment (a reinforced regiment) over the incredibly rugged Owen Stanley Mountains to assault Port Moresby, while Mikawa conducted an amphibious assault (the RE Operation) against the Allied air base near Rabi on Milne Bay. The night of 25 August, 1,150 SNLF and naval construction troops landed at Lehoea just east of Rabi, but unexpectedly stiff Allied resistance required they be swiftly reinforced.

At 0713, 29 August, Murray's TF-17 with the *Hornet* met TF-61 50 miles east of San Cristobal and restored Fletcher's strength to three carriers.[4] Left at Pearl Harbor in July after the departure of the *Saratoga* and the *Enterprise* task forces, the *Hornet* Air Group took the opportunity to train ashore and on several exercises at sea. On 30 July Rear Admiral Fitch went ashore as acting Commander, Carriers, Pacific Fleet (ComCarPac). Taking his place as CTF-17 was newly promoted RAdm. George Murray, the *Enterprise*'s captain during the early raids and at Midway. The most experienced aviator with the carriers, Murray earned his wings in 1915 as Naval Aviator No. 22. His flag captain, Charles P. Mason, wore the golden wings nearly as long (1917, Naval Aviator No. 52).[5]

The *Hornet*'s fighting squadron was Lieutenant Commander Sanchez's VF-72. In early July the great reshuffle of fighter pilots and planes left him with thirty-one pilots and thirty-six F4F-4s, so VF-72 operated twenty-seven fighters and kept the other nine as spares. On 11 July eight more pilots reported from Butch O'Hare's VF-3, including Lt. Alberto C. Emerson, who took over as XO–Flight Officer. Quite unusual for a 1942 fighter pilot, "Ace" Emerson (also dubbed "Silver" because of his prematurely gray hair) had enlisted in the Naval Reserve in 1931 and the next year earned his wings at NAS Pensacola. After several tours of active duty with an observation float plane (VOS) squadron and as an instructor, he became a regular lieutenant (junior grade) in March 1941 and later ex-

RAdm. George Murray, taken 1941 when he was a captain and in command of the *Enterprise*. (NA 80-G-338815)

celled as the *Yorktown*'s hangar deck officer at Coral Sea and Midway. Emerson was a much respected, aggressive leader.[6]

During July, VF-72 ended up with thirty-seven pilots, including Capt. John Wilkins, the first carrier-qualified Army fighter pilot. After a short training cruise VF-72 re-embarked on the *Hornet*. From NAS Pearl Harbor Sanchez drew another F4F-4 and a F4F-7 photo plane for a total of thirty-eight aircraft. The squadron engineers likewise received twenty new F4F-4s, stripped the wings, and hoisted them into the *Hornet*'s hangar overhead.

VF-72, August 1942: *Top row (l to r):* Merritt, Sorensen, Gallagher, Jennings, Ford, Sutherland, Emerson, Wilkins, Johnson, Holland, Franklin, McClintock, Freeman, Weimer. *Center row:* Savage, Bagley, Hessel, Phillips, Wrenn, Carey, Kiekhoefer, Montgomery, Rynd, Dalton, Landry, Morris, Blake, Robbins. *Bottom row:* Fairbanks, Hughes, Souza, Bliss, Luebke, Roberts, Sanchez, Formanek, Cook, Bower, Moran, Lowndes, Dietrich. (RAdm. W. W. Ford)

As of 17 August the *Hornet* Air Group comprised:

CHAG	Cdr. Walter F. Rodee	1 TBF-1
VF-72	Lt. Cdr. Henry G. Sanchez	37 F4F-4s, 1 F4F-7
VB-8	Lt. Cdr. Alfred B. Tucker III	16 SBD-3s
VS-8	Lt. Cdr. William J. Widhelm	16 SBD-3s
VT-6	Lt. Edwin B. Parker	16 TBF-1s

To test doctrine ComCarPac instructed the *Hornet* Air Group to operate with thirty-two fighters, an ad hoc scout-bomber squadron of twenty-four SBDs under Lieutenant Commander Tucker (USNA 1931) and thirteen torpedo planes (CHAG and twelve VT-6), retaining the other aircraft as spares. Murray and Mason experimented with deckload strikes to increase flexibility and reduce launch times, a big problem at Midway. Sanchez organized VF-72's fighters into eight-plane flights to be deployed in the following manner: number 1 on CAP, number 2 with a first-wave deckload strike on the flight deck, number 3 in the hangar with the second wave, and number 4 as reserve CAP.[7]

Departing Pearl Harbor on 17 August, TF-17 comprised the *Hornet,* RAdm. Howard H. Good's heavy cruisers *Northampton* (CA-26) and *Pensacola* (CA-24), the light AA cruiser *San Diego* (CL-53), and six destroyers. Murray was to report to ComSoPac when crossing the equator at 174° W (northeast of Canton Island). Only the tragic death of Tucker, VB-8's highly regarded CO, marred an otherwise routine voyage. On 19 August during a search mission, his SBD inexplicably broke out in flames, and he bailed out. His wingman alerted Murray, who sent a destroyer to make the rescue. However, Tucker could not be found. Lt. Cdr. William J. Widhelm assumed command of the ad hoc VSB squadron, while Lt. James E. Vose (USNA 1934), VB-8 XO, took over Bombing Eight.[8]

After TF-17 joined on 29 August, Fletcher moved south toward Espiritu Santo. He reverted to his earlier policy of advancing north during the night and running back south in daylight. The three carriers had 215 operational aircraft: 98 VF, 75 VB, and 42 VT. (See table 9.1 for TF-61.)

Early on 30 August ComSoPac directed TF-61 to retire one carrier task force on 2 September to Noumea for provisions, while oilers met the other two carrier task forces the same day. Greatly concerned about the Milne Bay operation, Ghormley protested MacArthur's request for naval support, especially the return of Rear Admiral Crutchley's TF-44 still on loan from SWPA. He desired TF-61

TABLE 9.1
Task Force 61, 29 August 1942

	TG-61.1	TG-61.2	TG-61.3
	Fletcher	Murray	Noyes
CVs	*Saratoga*	*Hornet*	*Wasp*
BB	*North Carolina*	—	—
CAs	*Minneapolis*	*Northampton*	*San Francisco*
	New Orleans	*Pensacola*	*Australia*
CLs	—	—	*Hobart*
			Phoenix
CL(AAs)	*Atlanta*	*San Diego*	—
DDs	7	7	7

"centrally located," able to deploy to any point between Milne Bay and Samoa. Land-based air was key to halting Japanese infiltration:

> It is hoped that the resolute use of our defensive positions and land based aviation may create a favorable situation wherein I can decisively employ the carrier task forces, whether on my extended front or to the westward. It is hoped my freedom of action will not be circumscribed by restrictive tasks or missions.[9]

Unfortunately, SoPac's land-based air was weak. At CACTUS Vandegrift reported only eight F4Fs and fourteen P-400s in commission and pleaded, "Cannot additional planes be sent at once?"[10]

On 30 August Admiral King suggested a compromise whereby TF-44 would be released as soon as possible to MacArthur's control. Later that day Ghormley directed Fletcher to detach Crutchley with CA *Australia,* CLs *Hobart* (RAN) and *Phoenix* (CL-46), and four destroyers to Brisbane. As the *Wasp* had not provisioned since late June, TF-18 left southwest at midnight for Noumea.[11]

The rest of Fletcher's TF-61 patrolled the waters between San Cristobal and the Santa Cruz Islands. Early on 31 August, it completed a normal night run northwest toward San Cristobal and at 0639 reversed course southeast into the wind. At 0741 as TF-61 steadied on 180 degrees at 13 knots, the *MacDonough,* on the *Saratoga*'s starboard bow, made a sonar contact dead ahead at 3,500 yards. Suddenly a periscope popped out only 10 yards away. She quickly rolled two depth charges, but too late. A torpedo wake pointed directly at the carrier. Captain Ramsey immediately ordered right full rudder and rang for full speed, but the massive *Sara* reacted "sluggishly." At 0748 a torpedo from Cdr. Yokota Minoru's *I-26* struck her starboard side just aft the island, injuring twelve, including Fletcher. Playing acey-deucy in the ready room, Howard Crews of VF-5 later wrote, "Our game terminated with a dull thud and the ship heaved a couple of times like some old antiquated street car lurching along an equally old track." According to Frank Green, the *Sara* "went into a fit and fairly lifted itself out of the water and then shook itself good." After assuring himself she was not sinking, he went to his stateroom to pack a small kit of clothes and other necessaries and "made it my belongings." Lee Haynes, another VF-5 pilot, found the experience quite familiar, because he was on board on 11 January when she was "smacked" the first time.[12]

By 0753 the *Saratoga* drifted dead in the water and listed 4 degrees to starboard. Seawater filled one fireroom and partially flooded another, short-circuiting her turbo-electric drive. By 0836 heroic efforts by her engineers brought 6 knots, but at 1053 while she turned into the wind to launch aircraft, the quirky propulsion system again quit. The *Minneapolis* rigged a tow line, and by 1236 the *Saratoga* was again underway. The tow and two of her own engines brought her up to 10 knots, just enough with the "brisk" wind to launch planes. At 1330 Lieutenant Commander Kirn led twenty SBDs (ten VS-3, ten VB-3) and nine VT-8 TBFs 347 miles southeast to Espiritu Santo and Bomber Field No. 1, where they enjoyed the hospitality of Lieutenant Colonel Hart's VMO-251. The *Sara*'s launch of aircraft while under tow was aptly described as a "unique performance."[13]

Warned of the *Sara*'s misfortune, Ghormley ordered Fletcher to proceed to Tongatabu. At 1637 she resumed steaming under her own power. Murray's TF-17 left at 1900 for the previously designated refueling rendezvous. At 2130 Fletcher advised ComSoPac that the *Saratoga* was now capable of 14 knots, noted that thirty-six fighters remained on board, and requested another fueling rendezvous for 2 September, hopefully from the oiler that carried the mail.[14]

CACTUS AIRCRAFT CONTROVERSY

One man's misfortune can mean another's gain. Like an heir discovering a deceased rich uncle, RAdm. John McCain, the wizened, astute ComAirSoPac, looked hungrily at the carrier aircraft newly roosted at Espiritu Santo. The evening of 31 August he advised:

> Recommend all remaining planes which are not required for security of ship be flown off Efate tomorrow Tuesday—particularly as many fighters as can be spared. Fighters should be equipped with belly tanks. TBFs loaded with torpedoes if practicable. Spare pilots, flight crews, engineers, ordnance men plus personal effects and as many critical operating spares as practicable be sent in via DD.[15]

McCain desired VS-3 and VT-8 at Espiritu Santo, and VB-3 and VF-5 at Efate.

On 1 September the *Saratoga* sent three more VT-8 TBFs to Espiritu Santo. In VF-5 rumors ran rampant. One had them being committed piecemeal as replacements to CACTUS. The next morning came the parting of the ways, when Fletcher decided to send twenty-eight F4Fs to Efate, leaving nine to protect the ships. Some pilots were assigned, others volunteered, and some cut cards to see who would go. Eleven pilots remained on board as the VF-5 Detachment:

Lt. Richard E. Harmer, USNA 1935	Ens. Robert A. M. Dibb,[a] A-V(N)
Lt. Richard Gray, USNA 1936	Gun. Charles E. Brewer,[a] NAP, USN
Lt. (jg) Harold E. Rutherford,[a] NAP, USN	Mach. Howell M. Sumrall,[a] NAP, USN
Lt. (jg) Carlton B. Starkes, A-V(N)	Mach. Julius A. Achten,[a] NAP, USN
Ens. Wayne C. Presley, A-V(N)	Howard S. Packard,[a] AP1c, NAP, USN
Ens. Leon W. Haynes, A-V(N)	

[a]Fighting Six

Lieutenant Bill Robb's party of 101 VF-5 enlisted men transferred to the *Monssen* (DD-436) and *Grayson* bound for Efate, where they would service VF-5's fighters, while Lt. Alex Barbieri's forty-five enlisted men and the squadron's heavy gear would be dropped off at Tongatabu. The morning of the 2nd, twenty-eight F4Fs under Lieutenant Commander Simpler took off for Efate about 100 miles southwest. That afternoon Lieutenant Larsen brought fifteen TBFs and two SBDs back to load torpedoes and other gear, then returned to Espiritu Santo. One SBD ditched on takeoff. Thus a total of twenty-eight F4Fs, twenty-two SBDs, and fifteen TBFs deployed ashore.

The *Saratoga* Air Group appeared at a very crucial time for the defense of SoPac. It had become quite obvious, at least to the local commanders, that the aircraft committed to embattled Guadalcanal proved totally inadequate to ensure its security. Even before the landings, Maj. Gen. Millard F. Harmon, SoPac Commanding General (CG), strongly urged the War Department to send additional planes, including at least two squadrons of the Lockheed P-38F Lightning fighters that enjoyed the high-altitude performance so highly sought for CACTUS. His recommendations received vigorous agreement from Undersecretary of the Navy James V. Forrestal, on an inspection trip to SoPac.[16]

On 31 August McCain himself sent an important missive to CinCPac and Com-

SoPac, which estimated that CACTUS required no fewer than forty high-altitude fighters for an adequate defense. He assessed the VF already there: "P-400s no good at altitude and disheartening to brave men who fly them. F4F-4 more successful due in part to belly tanks on Zeros in part to cool maneuvering and expert gunnery."

Like Harmon, McCain desired two P-38 squadrons and immediate replacement of the P-400s. "The situation admits of no delay whatever." Stuck on their ships, the carrier air groups could not be expected to help defend CACTUS. The stakes were high: "Guadalcanal can be a sinkhole for enemy air power and can be consolidated, expanded and exploited to the enemy's mortal hurt."[17]

With rhetoric indicative of their respective personalities, Ghormley and Turner fully concurred with McCain's cogent appraisal. To ComSoPac the "retention of CACTUS is more vital to the prosecution of the war in the Pacific than any other commitment." Turner, the ex–Naval War College strategist, likened Guadalcanal to an "unsinkable aircraft carrier," which could be built into "an invincible fleet."[18]

The most important response to McCain came on 2 September from Admiral Nimitz, who advised CominCh:

> All aircraft that can be spared from *Enterprise* and *Saratoga* are being transferred to ComSoPac for use in present campaign. Employment of carrier aircraft and pilots from shore bases necessary because of lack of suitable Army type planes for GUADALCANAL fighting but such use carrier pilots most uneconomic from military viewpoint aid our present shortage trained carrier air groups.

Nimitz was aware of the growing deficit of F4F Wildcats in Hawaii and on the West Coast. They were short seventy-five fighters, and new deliveries by 15 September would provide only sixteen. He repeated the litany of requests for Army aircraft and concluded with the plea: "Let's give GUADALCANAL the wherewithal to live up to its name. Something for the Japs to remember forever."[19]

The fighter alarums from the South Pacific proved most unwelcome in Washington. Gen. Henry H. "Hap" Arnold, commanding the USAAF, noted in his memoirs: "As soon as General Harmon began yelling about the poor performance of the P-39's, Admirals Ghormley and Nimitz took up Harmon's battle cry and shouted to high heaven until every brass hat in Washington heard the echoes." Immersed in preparations for the strategic air offensive in Europe and the North African invasion (Operation TORCH), Arnold bristled at the detrimental comments against the P-39s. He noted MacArthur's SWPA showed a four-to-one victory ratio of P-39s over Zeros and judged the P-39 superior to the Grumman F4F Wildcat and perfectly adequate for SoPac, a secondary theater. Besides, he wanted all of his P-38s in Europe, for the real air war.[20]

THE DEPARTURE OF A CARRIER ADMIRAL

SoPac bid adieu to the *Saratoga* for the time being and permanently to VAdm. Frank Jack Fletcher. TF-11 reached Tongatabu on 6 September (three days after the *Enterprise* departed), sailed on the 12th, and reached Pearl Harbor on the 21st. There the VF-5 pilots were reassigned, and the VF-6 veterans rejoined Lieutenant Bauer at Kaneohe.

Relieved as Commander, Cruisers, Pacific Fleet (ComCruPac), Fletcher left Oahu on 27 September for a well-deserved rest at home. Before departing, he wrote his valedictory, the summary of carrier lessons previously cited when discussing the withdrawal of TF-61 on 9 August.[21] Although he was a nonaviator, Fletcher's unequaled carrier combat experience the past nine months (the attempted Wake Island relief, the early raids, Coral Sea, Midway, the Guadalcanal landings, and Eastern Solomons) certainly gave value to his observations.

Nimitz forwarded Fletcher's letter to Vice Admiral Halsey for his comments.[22] In general Halsey agreed, but two opinions proved distinctly controversial. In the first Fletcher recommended turning away when spotted by enemy snoopers, but Halsey snorted that ships could not run from airplanes. Second, Fletcher urged concentrating carrier task forces quite close together for mutual support and protection. That permitted massing the CAP on defense. Certainly he thought of Coral Sea, where the *Lexington* and *Yorktown* operated together, almost in one screen, as contrasted with Midway, where TF-17 with the *Yorktown* fought alone away from TF-16 (*Enterprise* and *Hornet*).

That did not sit well with the carrier experts. In his report for Eastern Solomons, Captain Davis of the *Enterprise* declared that operations by more than two carrier task forces had proved too unwieldy. He wanted to separate the CV task forces by 15 to 20 miles and attributed the *Saratoga*'s escaping attack on 24 August to that interval. Kinkaid concurred with Davis. In his endorsements of their reports, Fletcher declared such a separation (15 to 20 miles) of "little consequence" in evading the attacks.[23] He correctly assumed that TF-61's CAP, not the separation, forestalled Lieutenant Ōtsuka's assault on the *Saratoga*. In fact, he thought that up to four carrier task forces could maneuver safely together. Their concentrated air power would offset any drawbacks faced in operating in such close proximity. In this regard he showed greater foresight than the aviators.

Halsey considered Fletcher's concentration of the carriers to be "fraught with grave danger." In the teeth of enemy attacks he preferred dispersion rather than concentration. His "ideal" situation allowed two carrier task forces to be "tactically concentrated" until they detected or suspected an inbound enemy strike. In that event they were to separate to a distance equal to twice the actual limit of visibility, so that one Japanese strike could not spot both CVs. Unfortunately Halsey did not address the problems of coordinating operations of separate forces under radio silence or the poor communications so inherent in recent actions.

Neither Fletcher's nor Halsey's concepts prevailed in the next carrier battle, Santa Cruz on 26 October. TF-61 would fight as at Eastern Solomons, with the two carrier task force deployed only 10 miles apart. The question of carrier task force strength and operating procedure sparked intense debate in 1943 during planning to employ the many carriers under construction during the crucial Guadalcanal campaign.

A rather hostile CominCh kept Fletcher in Washington for a short time before naming him commandant of the 13th Naval District at Seattle. In October 1943 he took over the North Pacific Area and orchestrated attacks on the Kuriles and the occupation of northern Japan. History has come down hard against Frank Jack Fletcher's competence as a carrier leader, but once his decisions are studied in light of what he himself knew at the time, a far different picture emerges.

NOYES TAKES OVER

The trip to New Caledonia proved a bit dicey for TF-18, because the destroyers were so low on fuel. On 3 September a portion of the *Wasp* Air Group flew to Tontouta Field, and TF-18 entered Noumea. Cross-winds bedeviled VF-71 while landing at Tontouta. One F4F ground-looped into a fire truck. The *Wasp* aviators found conditions there understandably primitive, with tents and poor food, but they bristled when local Army officers neglected to invite Lieutenant Commander Shands to share their screened-in mess. The *Wasp* squadrons stood down for a few days, and the crews enjoyed liberty at Noumea.

The evening of 3 September Leigh Noyes made his arrival call to his old Annapolis classmate Robert Ghormley on flagship *Argonne* (AG-31). This was the first time that ComSoPac actually met with one of his carrier commanders. An associate of Ernie King, Captain Noyes earned his wings in March 1937 and subsequently commanded the *Lexington,* before becoming chief of staff of King's Aircraft, Battle Force in 1938–39. In December 1941 he was serving as director of naval communications and joined the Pacific Fleet in March as Halsey's shore representative for Carriers, Pacific Fleet. A mild-mannered, good-natured, meticulous leader, Noyes would command TF-61 less than a week before tragedy intervened.

Noyes found his old friend still very worried about his right flank (Espiritu Santo–Fiji–Samoa). On 26 August the Japanese finally completed the long-anticipated capture of Ocean and Nauru islands, and Ghormley wondered what their striking force was doing. ULTRA was no help. Actually the Japanese carriers swung at anchor at Truk. Ghormley much preferred TF-61 east of the Santa Cruz Islands to threaten the enemy's left flank and keep them east of enemy submarines operating west of the Ndeni–Espiritu Santo line (longitude 166° E). This meant no direct carrier support for CACTUS, but Ghormley judged this acceptable for the present.

On 3 September while fueling 250 miles southeast of Espiritu Santo, George Murray's TF-17 received the fruit of Ghormley's deliberations. He was to stay south of latitude 12° S (120 miles further south than the 27 August directive) and east of the Ndeni–Espiritu Santo line (longitude 166° E) unless "promising targets" appeared within striking range. The effect was to keep the carriers well southeast of the Solomons.[24]

Just as futile as the KI Operation was the Japanese assault against the Milne Bay airfields. On 29 August the 8th Fleet landed a second force of 750 men, but they could not advance. The Allied garrison stood up bravely to the Japanese, and their air superiority over the battlefield greatly contributed to Japan's defeat. On 4 September Mikawa ordered the Rabi force evacuated by sea, and beginning the next day about 1,300 men re-embarked.

Murray completed fueling and moved northwest. Despite ComSoPac strictures, he was determined to sweep toward the southern Solomons. By sundown, 4 September, TF-17 had closed within 75 miles of Vanikoro (Santa Cruz Islands) only 30 miles south of ComSoPac's northerly limit. Early the next morning Murray moved west across Ghormley's western boundary, and by 0800 on 6 September was fully 250 miles west of the Ndeni–Espiritu Santo line. From within 75 miles of Rennell Island, he started back southeast at 15 knots, but not soon enough to escape a very serious incident. At 1245 the *Hornet* sent aloft an IAP of three VT-6 TBFs. Just six minutes later, both the aft lookout and, coincidentally,

Ens. Henry A. "Al" Fairbanks of VF-72 spied a torpedo wake off her starboard quarter. At the same time Ens. John Cresto on IAP spotted what he thought was a submarine conning tower break the surface between the plane guard destroyer and the battleship *North Carolina* and dropped a 325-pound depth charge. Through the greatest of good luck it touched off not only one torpedo warhead, but also another 100 yards away. The third fish missed the carrier altogether. Cdr. Tsuneo Shichiji of the *I-11* only heard this contretemps and assumed he put two fish into a *Yorktown*-class carrier. He avoided subsequent attacks by TF-17 destroyers and aircraft.[25]

The afternoon of 7 September, as TF-17 moved southeast toward Espiritu Santo, Murray informed ComSoPac of the submarine attack, his position, and his belief that the enemy had detected him. He added that the directive was too restrictive and recommended that TF-17 be allowed to operate within 300 miles of CACTUS and southeast of there as necessary. Even before ComSoPac could respond, TF-17 suffered another sub contact. At 1730 Lt. John F. "Jock" Sutherland's four VF-72 F4Fs strafed a submerging I-boat not far from the ships. "Astounded" that Murray had deliberately contravened his orders by proceeding west of the Ndeni–Espiritu Santo line, Ghormley "invited" his attention to the 3 September directive and icily suggested that TF-17 move east of that boundary at good speed.[26]

The night of 7/8 September TF-17 steamed northeast toward the Santa Cruz Islands through waters previously teeming with enemy submarines, and only about sundown on 8 September crossed 166° E to end the offensive patrol. Murray now headed south to fuel 125 miles northeast of Espiritu Santo. ComAirSoPac eagerly awaited the *Hornet*'s cargo of twenty F4F-4s. On 9 September she flew thirty-four aircraft to Espiritu Santo for an overnight stay to clear sufficient

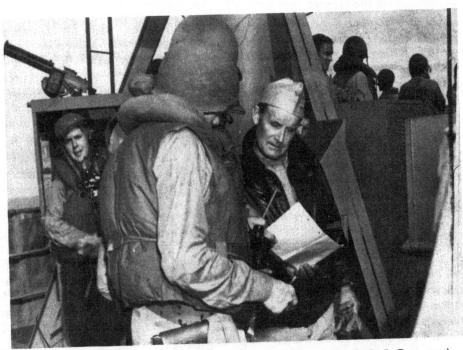

RAdm. Leigh Noyes on the *Wasp*'s bridge, August 1942. (USN via R. J. Cressman)

room to assemble the F4F-4s for AirSoPac. The next day VF-72 ferried nineteen Wildcats and the one F4F-7 to Espiritu Santo and rode the other *Hornet* planes back. TF-17 fueled and awaited TF-18 en route from Noumea.[27]

On 8 September Noyes nosed TF-18 out of Noumea and cut around the southern tip of New Caledonia bound northeast toward Espiritu Santo. During the *Wasp*'s sojourn in port, she received welcome reinforcements of four more VF-5 F4Fs (flown from Efate by VF-71 pilots) and for VS-71 and VS-72 six *Enterprise* SBDs with VB-6 crews. In return the *Wasp* aviators left inoperable at Tontouta two F4Fs and three SBDs. The group now comprised:

CWAG	Lt. Cdr. Wallace M. Beakley	Flying VT-7 TBF
VF-71	Lt. Cdr. Courtney Shands	32 F4F-4s (28)[a]
VS-71	Lt. Cdr. John Eldridge	14 SBD-3s (14)
VS-72	Lt. Cdr. Ernest M. Snowden	14 SBD-3s (14)
VT-7	Lt. Edward V. Wedell, A-V(N)	10 TBF-1s (10)

[a]Numbers in parentheses are those operable.

As TF-18 escorted the CTF-62 flagship *McCawley,* Kelly Turner flashed to Noyes a draft operations plan to bring the 7th Marines to Guadalcanal. He desired two additional land-based VF and two VSB squadrons sent to CACTUS, and if AirSoPac could not furnish them, "presumably the carriers will help." In addition he requested that TF-61: a) furnish VF to CACTUS if AirSoPac could not; b) maintain constant antisub patrol off Malaita–San Cristobal; and c) attack enemy naval forces threatening the convoy. After consulting with Forrest Sherman, Noyes replied that tasks (a) and (b) were impossible. Certainly he could spare no fighters, and second, he would not tie down the carriers in one restricted area for the time needed to fly the antisub patrols.

Turner fired off an acrid reply leaving no doubt his opinion of Noyes differed little from his pungent feelings about Fletcher. The *McCawley* and the New Zealand light cruiser *Leander* left that evening for Espiritu Santo. A perplexed Noyes summarized the exchange for Ghormley so he would not "misunderstand" his position and concluded, "I had not thought that anyone even considered it wise to land any aircraft from these remaining carriers."[28]

On 9 September Ghormley issued SoPac OpPlan 3-42 with the basic task organization: TF-61 (Carriers) under Noyes, TF-62 (Amphibious Force) under Turner, TF-63 (AirSoPac) under McCain, and TF-64, the new SoPac Screening and Attack Force, under Rear Admiral Wright. Worried about subs, Ghormley again cautioned Noyes to keep south of latitude 12° S and east of the Ndeni–Espiritu Santo line. At 0800 on 11 September, TF-18 joined Murray's TF-17 fueling northeast of Espiritu Santo, and Noyes assumed command of both task forces. He planned to move east of the Santa Cruz Islands to flank the next enemy advance against Guadalcanal, which according to CinCPac and SoPac intelligence reports appeared imminent.[29]

PART III

Fighting Five at CACTUS

CHAPTER 10

The Japanese Offensive

GREETINGS AT HENDERSON FIELD

For five days VF-5 camped on tiny Irikiki Island in Efate's Vila harbor awaiting orders. On 4 September torrential rains transformed the bivouac into a quagmire. Bored from sitting around in damp tents, Dave Richardson and Howard Crews braved the weather for a ride to Vila and tramped through the mud to island HQ. They hoped for the latest war news on the desperate battles being fought all over the world, but that day's headline proclaimed the latest sexual escapade of actor Errol Flynn.[1] Finally on 7 September things cleared up enough to resume flying. That day AirSoPac called for six VF-5 F4Fs and pilots to prepare to go to CACTUS. Roy Simpler thought it vital to maintain the integrity of his four-plane fighting teams. Determined to lead the first echelon, he took eight F4Fs (his 1st and Wally Clarke's 3rd divisions) to Espiritu Santo the next day and met with Capt. Matthias B. Gardner, the able AirSoPac chief of staff. After some fast talking, he received permission to take all eight Wildcats to Guadalcanal when called. Given heavy VF losses at CACTUS, that summons would surely come soon. On 10 September Edward L. Bell, AMM1c, led six VF-5 specialists to CACTUS to get acquainted with conditions there.

Because of heavy plane losses, Rear Admiral McCain decided to send all twenty-four VF-5 fighters to Guadalcanal. Surprise orders received after breakfast on the 11th sent Richardson's Efate contingent scurrying to bid farewell to Lt. Hayden Jensen's 6th Division left behind for lack of airplanes. They flew sixteen F4Fs north to join Simpler at Espiritu Santo. Around noon all twenty-four F4Fs (each with a belly tank) departed Santo for the 500-mile flight northwest to Guadalcanal. A B-17 Flying Fortress served as guide past San Cristobal at the bottom of the Solomons chain into the waters so familiar from the 7–8 August invasion. Little had VF-5 thought that dawn of 7 August when strafing the unfinished jungle airstrip that five weeks later they would fight there under conditions far different from comfortable old *Sara*.

After nearly four hours, VF-5 arrived over Lunga and while circling to land readily noted the vast change of facilities. Now there existed two airfields, both oriented southwest to northeast toward the prevailing winds blowing in from the sea. Laid on a gravel base, Bomber Field No. 1 (Henderson Field, the former Japanese strip) measured 3,800 by 150 feet, with dispersal and taxi ways along its northern edge. Cut palms and blasted stumps revealed where a detail of Lt. Cdr.

Henderson Field from the south, about 23 Aug. 1942. The Pagoda is in the center, and the Lunga River on the left. (NA 80-G-16312)

J. Paul Blundon's 6th Naval Construction Battalion had begun clearing an additional 1,300 feet. The Seabees also arranged for proper drainage, which the enemy had neglected. As yet, steel Marston mats only covered unstable spots in the center of the field. Numerous airplane wrecks now decorated the "boneyard" on the south edge of the runway. A few days before VF-5's arrival, Blundon's Seabees cut by hand the high grass of a meadow located about a mile to the east. Using captured equipment they rolled the 18-inch high grass and tamped it down. Fighter Field No. 1 (prosaically the "cow pasture" or "sod field") extended about 4,600 feet long and 300 feet wide. Beginning 9 September the Marine fighting squadrons operated from there.

Control told the twenty-four F4Fs to land at the main field, where rugged Marines ("with tears in their eyes") waved them to the cleared zone for wide dispersal. VF-5 brought smiles of relief to Major General Vandegrift and the rest of the division. For the first time SoPac committed a whole carrier squadron to CACTUS, helping to demonstrate to skeptical Leathernecks that the Navy meant to hold the island. At the same time VF-5 was very proud to fight alongside the Marines.

WITH THE FIRST MARINE AIR WING

Newly promoted Maj. Gen. Roy S. Geiger, CO of the 1st Marine Air Wing (1st MAW), controlled all aviation on Guadalcanal (ComAirCACTUS) under Vandegrift (ComGenCACTUS). Earning his wings in 1917 as Marine Aviator No. 5,

TABLE 10.1
Fighting Five

1st Division	2nd Division
Lt. Cdr. Leroy C. Simpler, USNA 1929	Lt. (jg) Howard L. Grimmell, Jr.,[a] A-V(N)
Lee Paul Mankin,[a] AP1c, USN	Ens. James A. Halford, Jr.,[a] A-V(N)
Ens. John M. Wesolowski, A-V(N)	Ens. Harry A. March, Jr.,[a] A-V(N)
Robert H. Nesbitt,[a] AP1c, USN	Ens. Joseph D. Shoemaker,[a] A-V(N)
3rd Division	4th Division
Lt. Walter E. Clarke, A-V(N)	Lt. Howard W. Crews, USN
Ens. George J. Morgan, A-V(N)	Ens. Benjamin F. Currie, A-V(N)
Lt. (jg) Elisha T. Stover, A-V(N)	Ens. Richards L. Loesch, Jr.,[a] A-V(N)
Ens. Mortimer V. Kleinmann, Jr., A-V(N)	Ens. Wildon M. Rouse,[a] A-V(N)
5th Division	7th Division
Lt. (jg) Frank O. Green, A-V(N)	Lt. David C. Richardson, USNA 1936
Ens. Donald A. Innis, A-V(N)	Ens. Charles E. Eichenberger, A-V(N).
Ens. Mark K. Bright, A-V(N)	Ens. William W. Wileman,[a] A-V(N)
Ens. Melvin C. Roach, A-V(N)	Ens. Francis R. Register,[a] A-V(N)

6th Division (remaining on Efate)
Lt. Hayden M. Jensen, USN
Ens. Foster J. Blair, A-V(N)
Ens. John B. McDonald, Jr., A-V(N)
Ens. John M. Kleinman, A-V(N)

[a] Joined VF-5 from VF-6 on 25 August 1942

Geiger fought in World War I, and by 1940 rose to be one of the senior Marine air commanders. Two Marine historians aptly described his qualities:

> What this new commanding officer with his frank, brusque ways and cold stare added to the Henderson tradition was a vast experience and an unflinching spirit. It served him and those under him very well.[2]

The highly capable Col. Louis E. Woods headed the staff, which included the wing intelligence officer (W-2), Lt. Col. John C. Munn. Of the operational headquarters, only Col. William J. Wallace's MAG-23 had reached CACTUS. No stranger to naval aviators, Wallace took VS-14M on board the *Saratoga* in 1931 for the first Marine carrier duty. Senior MAG-23 staff were Lt. Col. Charles L. Fike, XO; Lt. Col. Raymond C. Scollin, Operations; and Lt. Col. Walter L. J. Bayler, Communications. The 1st MAW and MAG-23 HQs moved into the "Pagoda," the Oriental-esque wooden building erected by the former tenants on a small hill about 200 yards north of the Henderson Field runway.

Geiger's air force comprised a motley crew of Marine, Navy, and Army aviators, the main reason why Japan had not yet retaken Guadalcanal. They comprised two elements: attack planes for search and strikes, and fighters primarily on defense. The main offensive punch rested with the twenty-odd operational SBD-3 Dauntless dive bombers flown by:

VMSB-232	Lt. Col. Richard C. Mangrum
VMSB-231	Maj. Leo R. Smith
Flight 300 (VS-5, VB-6)	Lt. Turner F. Caldwell
VS-3 Detachment	Lt. Robert M. Milner

Constant flying and combat whittled down the SBDs, but in the past three weeks they accounted for one large transport, a destroyer, and numerous barges, as well as other damaged vessels. Their crews waited in ready tents pitched near the dispersal circle north of Pagoda Hill.[3]

An unlikely but valuable addition to the strike force proved to be Maj. Dale Brannon's 67th FS flying Bell P-400 fighters.[4] They set up shop in an old Japanese hangar near the southwest corner of Henderson Field. An inferior export version of the P-39, the P-400 (Airacobra I) possessed good speed (355 MPH at 13,000 feet), heavy armament (one 20-mm cannon, two .50- and two .30-caliber machine guns), and reasonable protection. Yet its 1,150-HP Allison engine lacked a turbo-supercharger, resulting in poor high-altitude performance—academic because the 67th had no bottles for the high-pressure British-type oxygen system. Air combat showed the P-400s to be "klunkers," no match for Zeros. Nevertheless the "Game Cock Squadron" fought tenaciously and claimed five Zeros and a flying boat, but at the cost of six aircraft (two pilots). By 11 September only three P-400s remained flyable. Yet the newly dubbed "Jagstaffel" (*sic*) found its forte in low-level ground and antishipping attacks, which they accomplished with a vengeance.

Formed on 1 May 1942, Maj. John Smith's VMF-223 and Maj. Robert Galer's VMF-224 constituted the main CACTUS fighter force.[5] Few pilots joined the squadrons before early July. Other than those with the dubious benefit of combat with VMF-221 at Midway, most were recent flight school graduates. The senior officers were:

	VMF-223	VMF-224
CO	Maj. John L. Smith[a]	Maj. Robert E. Galer[a]
XO and FO	Maj. Rivers J. Morrell, Jr.[a]	Maj. John F. Dobbin[a]
EO	Capt. Marion E. Carl	Maj. Kirk Armistead[a]

[a]Newly promoted to date from 7 August 1942

VMF-223 had arrived on 20 August from the escort carrier *Long Island,* followed 10 days later by VMF-224 from Espiritu Santo.

From 21 August to 11 September the Japanese raided Guadalcanal ten times with 149 fighter, 160 land attack (medium bomber), and six carrier attack (torpedo) sorties. Their losses to all causes amounted to:

	Shot down	Force-landed
Zero fighters	17	2
Land attack planes	11	4
Carrier attack planes	3	1

Marine kill credits against these attacks numbered seventy-seven: twenty-nine Zero fighters, thirty-seven medium bombers ("Improved Mitsubishi 97s"), and eleven single-engine VT. During the same time period the Marines lost twenty-seven of forty-four F4F-4s (see table 10.2). Seven pilots (four 223, three 224) died in battle, and accidents claimed two from 224. By the evening of 11 September, VMF-223 retained thirteen pilots and seven F4Fs, VMF-224 fourteen pilots and ten Grummans. Even so, only about a dozen aircraft could still fly; the rest had already been stripped for spare parts.

The Marine squadrons relied on their own trusted ground echelons to service their aircraft. They worked around the hangars on the south edge of the main field, while the pilots waited near Fighter 1. The men of CUB-1 under Cdr. James P. Compton, the naval base CO, assisted all of the squadrons. His first echelon

TABLE 10.2
Losses on Guadalcanal, 21 August–11 September 1942

	Combat				
	Shot down	Damaged and totaled	Bombed	Noncombat	Total
VMF-223	7	4	3	4	18
VMF-224	4	0	0	5	9

under Ens. George W. Polk had arrived on 15 August. CUB-1 and the Seabees expanded and ran the CACTUS air facilities.[6]

John L. Smith, the superb skipper of VMF-223, greeted VF-5 at Henderson Field. Despite his rather acerbic personality, his remarkable leadership and skill with his pilots (mostly green second lieutenants) enabled VMF-223 to perform far above its nominal level of training and experience. With thirteen victories of his own, "Smitty" certainly spoke with authority. In a quiet, informal way he summarized the situation and outlined the tactics he and Bob Galer used to counter the almost daily enemy raids. Beginning with Smith's initial talk, and then through others more gradually, VF-5 learned the peculiar circumstances of flying and fighting from CACTUS.[7]

The early warning network of Australian coastwatchers stationed on key islands in the northern and central Solomons proved especially vital for air defense. On 16 August Lt. Cdr. Hugh A. Mackenzie, RANVR, the Deputy Staff Intelligence Officer (DSIO) for the British Solomon Islands Protectorate, set up a radio station at Lunga to monitor the coastwatcher warnings and relay them to Vandegrift and Geiger. (See table 10.3 for those coastwatchers of primary interest to CACTUS as of 12 September.) Constantly watching for ships, aircraft, and any other signs of enemy activity, they reported anything sighted promptly to Mackenzie.[8]

Until 2 September, MAG-23 depended on the coastwatchers and their own lookouts for warning of enemy attack. Finally a big SCR-270-B air search radar from the 3rd Defense Battalion, emplaced near aviation headquarters at the main field, maintained a constant radar watch. Its extreme range of 150 miles meant that, depending on their altitude, it could detect enemy strike groups still over New Georgia. Climate, of course, greatly affected reliability, and topography blanked out coverage in some sectors, but when combined with the coastwatchers, radar offered vital early warning of enemy air attack.

The Marines employed three conditions of readiness: GREEN, YELLOW, and RED. GREEN was the all-clear. If MAG-23 detected or suspected an inbound raid, the Pagoda watch (four enlisted men) cranked a siren and ran up a red flag for Condition YELLOW. That meant the enemy was perhaps an hour away. On YELLOW the pilots hurried to their planes and took off. Condition RED, signaled by a black flag and the siren, strongly urged all to take cover immediately.

Renowned as the "last man off Wake Island," Lieutenant Colonel Bayler, MAG-23 communications officer, also handled fighter direction. Working from a one-ton truck (RECON BASE) equipped with a transmitter/receiver stripped from a wrecked Grumman, he plotted contacts on a pilot's navigation board. At Condition YELLOW, the FD team drove east from the Pagoda to "Secondary Control," another small hill immediately south of the fighter strip and a good

Maj. John Smith, the brilliant CO of VMF-223, at Henderson Field on 10 Oct. 1942, the day he scored his nineteenth victory. (NA 80-G-20665)

place from which to observe the skies over the perimeter. There they plugged into the radio warning circuit and received updates from the radar post.

Unlike a carrier FDO, Bayler rarely employed a standing CAP. For one thing the 1st MAW lacked the aircraft and gasoline for such a luxury. Generally the fighters scrambled on alert and needed 35 to 40 minutes for a formation climb to 30,000 feet to ensure altitude advantage. Coincidentally this corresponded with the time the Japanese took to close Guadalcanal after being sighted by Maj. Donald Kennedy on New Georgia and/or appearing on radar. Bayler also coped

TABLE 10.3
Coastwatchers of Primary Interest to CACTUS, 12 September 1942

Call Sign	Name and Location	Distance from Lunga
BTH	Lt. W. J. Read, RANVR North Bougainville (Buka Passage)	400 miles
LQK	PO Paul E. Mason, RANVR South Bougainville (Buin area)	300
ZGJ5	Maj. Donald G. Kennedy, BSIPDF Southeast New Georgia (Segi)	140
Unattached K	Sgt. Geoffrey Kuper, BSIPDF South Santa Isabel	75
VQJ10	SubLt. F. Ashton Rhoades, RANVR West Guadalcanal (Lavoro)	25
VQJ8	Lt. Donald S. Macfarlan, RANVR Central Guadalcanal (Gold Ridge)	15

with generally unreliable aircraft radio communications, particularly beyond 5 or 10 miles. Ground returns from the surrounding mountains blanked out radar within 25 miles of base. Therefore he tried no distant intercepts or fancy tactics, but just positioned the fighters above and ahead of the incoming bombers.[9]

This first evening, VF-5 lacked the time to absorb their oral instructions on air fighting CACTUS-style, but the Japanese would administer the first quiz the next day. Before sundown the pilots took a closer look at their new home. To disperse his fighter strength, Geiger kept VF-5 on Henderson Field instead of combining them with the Marines at Fighter 1. The most visible landmark around the main

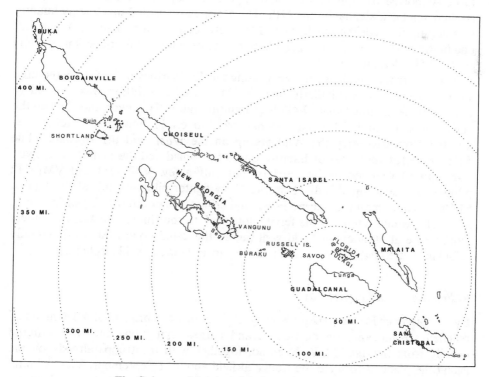

The Solomon Islands, with distances from Lunga.

field was the Pagoda, where VF-5 assembled between alerts. South of the runway, four (out of the original six) tall, rickety hangars stood where the Marine ground crews had set up shop along with a Marine field kitchen. Shallow bomb craters dotting the landscape proved useful for storage and as foxholes. That evening, after a meal of fish and beans, VF-5 drew folding cots, blankets, mosquito netting, and several tents each holding six to eight men. The one given to Frank Green's group sported thirty or more shrapnel holes, handy for star gazing. The first night most of the pilots slept out in the open near the field, but two days later they moved into the coconut grove's aviator camp about a mile north.

From the *Enterprise*'s Flight 300, Ens. Hal Buell of VS-5 wandered over for a pleasant reunion with several VF-5 pilots with whom he had completed flight training. He noted in his diary:

> I was glad to see this Navy fighter outfit come in yet hate to see so many of my friends also caught in this place. It is going to be tough if any of these good pals get it here.[10]

His friends would soon learn why he looked so tired and gaunt. Once the sun set, there was little to do but stay put. Nervous sentries discouraged anyone from wandering around in the darkness.

Worries about the Japanese Offensive

The morning of 11 September, rear admirals Turner and McCain flew into CACTUS to confer with Vandegrift about landing the 7th Marines, which needed a week to reach Guadalcanal. Would the 1st MarDiv still hold Lunga when they arrived? The latest intelligence estimate warned that a powerful Japanese landing force supported by four carriers had apparently departed Truk on the 9th and could reach Guadalcanal by the 12th. The Marines suspected that enemy infantry was cutting through the jungle east of the perimeter. As a precaution Vandegrift dug in the Marine raiders and parachute troops on a long, bare ridge immediately south of Henderson Field.[11]

Turner's tentative plans for transporting the 7th Marines to CACTUS required strong air support, particularly fighters. The obvious solution was to send to CACTUS the nineteen spare F4F-4s at Espiritu Santo. However, they lacked the belly tanks demanded by the 500-mile trip, so on 11 September McCain requested Noyes to ferry the Wildcats up on the *Wasp* and the *Hornet*. While TF-61 refueled southeast of Espiritu Santo he considered the matter. The spare F4Fs must be landed on his carriers, but only a few VMO-251 and VMF-212 pilots were carrier-qualified. Therefore Navy fighter pilots would ride TBFs and SBDs to Santo, man the Marine F4Fs, and bring them out to the ships. The TBFs and SBDs would fetch Marine ferry pilots back to the ships. The Marine fighters must arrive at Henderson Field well before the usual noon raid, so they could refuel in time to fight. That meant a dawn carrier launch on 13 September.

Riding the "Guadal Highway"

By 7 September Major General Kawaguchi's reinforced brigade of 6,000 men had reached Guadalcanal on destroyers and barges, but along the way suffered heavily from the 1st MAW. Even so, together with the troops already on the island, he planned to seize the Lunga airfield about 11 September. Vice Admiral Tsukahara's Base Air Force sought air superiority over the southern Solomons.

For the past week his planes had operated mainly over eastern New Guinea, raiding Port Moresby and Milne Bay in support of the 17th Army's South Seas Detachment advancing from Buna south over the steep Owen Stanley Mountains toward Port Moresby. Now its air cover would be cut drastically, as attention centered on Guadalcanal. The Japanese suffered greatly from the lack of land-based air strength for simultaneous advances on multiple lines from Rabaul.

Beginning on 9 September Base Air Force resumed daily raids against Guadal-canal to knock out defending air power and isolate the garrison. That day Vice Admiral Kondō's Support Force, made up of the 2nd and 3rd fleets (which in-cluded the *Shōkaku, Zuikaku,* and the newly arrived *Zuihō*), sortied from Truk to prowl north and east of the Solomons. Combined Fleet expected Kawaguchi to eliminate the threat of enemy land-based air at Guadalcanal, so Kondō could battle American carriers relieving their garrison. Greatly underestimating enemy strength on Guadalcanal, the Japanese hoped for quick land victory and a speedy deployment of aircraft to the Lunga air base.

The composition of Base Air Force in the New Britain, New Guinea, and Solomons area had altered considerably since early August.[12] Now on 12 Sep-tember two air attack forces operated under Tsukahara's direct control (see table 10.4). The six air groups and several detachments at Rabaul had a paper strength

TABLE 10.4
Base Air Force, 12 September 1942

		Strength	
Unit (Force) Group		Authorized (14 July 1942)	Estimated
5th Air Attack Force			
RAdm. Yamada Sadayoshi (CO, 25th Air Flotilla)			
No. 1	Tainan Air Group	60 Zero 21 fighters	20
	Capt. Saitō Masahisa	8 Type 98 recon planes	1
	Attached: 24th Air Flotilla	4 transport planes	2
	Fighter Detachment	3 Type 2 land recon planes	2
No. 2	4th Air Group	48 Type 1 land attack planes	12
	Capt. Moritama Yoshiyotsu		
No. 3	2nd Air Group	16 Zero 32 fighters	8
	Cdr. Yamamoto Sakae	16 Type 99 carrier bombers	5
No. 4	Tōkō Air Group	16 Type 97 flying boats	11
	Capt. Wada Saburō		
	Attached: Yokohama Air Group (remnants)		
	Type 2 Flying Boat Detachment	3 Type 2 flying boats	3
6th Air Attack Force			
VAdm. Yamagata Seigō (CO, 26th Air Flotilla)			
"A"	Kisarazu Air Group	36 Type 1 land attack planes	12
	Capt. Fujiyoshi Naoshiro		12
"B"	Misawa Air Group	36 Type 1 land attack planes	
	Capt. Sugawara Masao		
"C"	6th Air Group Advance Detachment	18 Zero 21 fighters	12
	Lt. Kofukuda Mitsugi	12 Zero 32 fighters	11
	Attached: 24th Air Flotilla Detachment	10 Type 1 land attack planes	6
	Lt. Andō Nobuo (Chitose Air Group)		

(using 14 July 1942 tables of organization) of 277 aircraft, but on 12 September only about 117 (93 operational) were actually present:[13]

---

45 Mitsubishi A6M2 Type 0, Model 21 fighters [ZEKE] and Mitsubishi A6M3 Type 0, Model 32 fighters [HAMP]
5 Aichi D3A1 Type 99 carrier bombers [VAL]
1 Mitsubishi C5M2 Type 98 land reconnaissance plane [BABS]
2 Nakajima J1N1-C Type 2 land reconnaissance planes [IRVING]
30 Mitsubishi G4M1 Type 1 land attack planes [BETTY]
8 Kawanishi H6K4 Type 97 flying boats [MAVIS]
2 Kawanishi H8K1 Type 2 flying boats [EMILY]

The Imperial Naval Air Force lacked the crews and airplanes to bring these units up to anywhere near authorized strength. Beginning in late August substantial reinforcements entered the pipeline, mostly to operate from Guadalcanal when recaptured. On 12 September Lt. Doki Osamu (NA 62-1934) reached Rabaul with a *chūtai* of nine Type 1 land attack planes from the Kanoya Air Group. The rest of the group and the 1st Air Attack Force (21st Air Flotilla) HQ would follow in a few days. Detachments from other groups were also en route. Drawn, however, from other sectors of the Empire's defensive perimeter, their departure left those areas in a weakened state. McCain's concept of Guadalcanal as a "sinkhole" for enemy air power posed a very real threat given the perilous state of Japanese naval aviation.

The Imperial Navy faced immense problems prosecuting a successful air offensive against Guadalcanal, many of its own making. The nearest fully operational airfields to the target remained the cluster of bases around Rabaul: Vunakanau Field (Rabaul West) for the bombers and the fighter strip at Lakunai (Rabaul East) set beneath a massive volcano. All lay at least 560 miles from Guadalcanal, entailing strike missions of eight hours or more. The auxiliary field at Buka, 400 miles from Guadalcanal, was used only sporadically for lack of support facilities.

The extremely long and fatiguing missions down the "Guadal Highway" (*Gadaru Gaitō*), as the Japanese nicknamed the Slot, adversely effected the Zero fighter escorts. To save fuel many pilots fought with their belly tanks attached, which reduced combat performance. Even so the fighter leaders set a maximum of 15 minutes over Guadalcanal. Most of the Rabaul Zeros, clipped-wing A6M3 Model 32s with 20 percent less range than the A6M2 Model 21s, could not even reach Guadalcanal and return. Work had only begun on the vital airstrip at Buin on southern Bougainville opposite Shortland Island and 300 miles from Guadalcanal. Until its completion set for late September, no Zero 32s could be used, and crippled aircraft enjoyed no refuge short of Buka.[14]

Despite Tsukahara's fervent calls for carrier strikes against Lunga, Combined Fleet no longer considered that an immediate option. They must be preserved for the anticipated carrier battles. On 28 August, the 3rd Fleet had loaned thirty *Shōkaku* and *Zuikaku* Zeros, but received only a bloody nose for its trouble. Four missions against Guadalcanal cost eleven Zeros (nine pilots), nine alone on 30 August in an especially adroit ambush by Major Smith's VMF-223.

Thus the destruction of Allied air power at Guadalcanal and also attacks against enemy ships fell to VAdm. Yamagata Seigō's 6th Air Attack Force (26th Air Flotilla) flying the long-range but highly vulnerable Mitsubishi G4M1 Type 1 land attack planes (*rikkō*). Against land targets they usually carried one 250-kilogram high-explosive "land" bomb and six 60-kilogram antipersonnel bombs (known to the Allies as "daisy cutters") or ten 60-kilogram bombs alone. The Japanese preferred mixed strike groups of eighteen or twenty-seven land attack planes drawn from all of the groups present, except for the 4th, whose survivors now flew only searches. Flight leaders from the different groups took turns commanding the strikes, which rarely comprised more than one *chūtai* per group.

Two 26th Air Flotilla groups, the Kisarazu and the Misawa, employed Type 1s over Guadalcanal. Commissioned 1 April 1942 in Japan, they counted a strong veteran cadre. On 7–8 August Capt. Sugawara Masao brought twenty-six Misawa Type 1s from Saipan to Rabaul. The 8 August fiasco cost seven, and in later raids against Guadalcanal and Port Moresby another five Type 1s were destroyed and two crash-landed. On 20 August nineteen Kisarazu Type 1 *rikkōs* reached Kavieng, New Ireland. Their first Lunga strike came five days later. Losses by 12 September amounted to four aircraft missing and three force-landed. Thus almost daily raids against Guadalcanal or Port Moresby cut *rikkō* operational strength by nearly 50 percent. Morale, however, remained high, with sufficient crews on hand to rotate missions and allow for periodic rest. On 2 September Lt. Andō Nobuo (NA 65-1938) brought a *chūtai* of ten land attack planes from Chitose Air Group (24th Air Flotilla) in the Marshalls. Four raids against Lunga cost two Type 1s shot down and two force-landed.

The stalwart Tainan Air Group wielded most of the Zero 21s capable of attacking Guadalcanal. Severely wounded Sakai Saburō had left for home on 12 August, and his much-admired *chūtai* leader, Lieutenant (jg) Sasai, fell on 26 August to VMF-223. On 2 September ten Zeros from the Chitose and 1st air groups filled only some of the gaps. From 9 August to 11 September the Tainan group and attached units lost thirteen pilots (eight over New Guinea, five over Guadalcanal). Much responsibility now fell on the shoulders of the senior *buntaichō,* Lieutenant Kawai, as HQ was reluctant to risk Lieutenant Commander Nakajima on many missions.

The 5th Air Attack Force's other fighter unit was the 2nd Air Group, the mixed force of Zero 32s and Type 99 carrier bombers. Lieutenant Inoue's Type 99s mostly succumbed on the 7 August Tulagi strike and later over Papua. Until 22 August Lieutenant Kurakane's Zeros defended Rabaul, then switched to New Guinea: first at Lae and then the new Buna airstrip. In late August and early September the 2nd, along with some Tainan Zeros, supported the unsuccessful invasion of Milne Bay, which cost at least seven Zeros and three pilots. Some pilots also flew Guadalcanal missions with the Tainan Air Group.

The 26th Air Flotilla provided Rabaul another fighter unit, the advance detachment of the 6th Air Group.[15] Likewise organized on 1 April 1942, the 6th participated in the Midway-Aleutians operation. Having absorbed a number of green pilots at Kisarazu, the whole group could not deploy to the Solomons. Therefore Lt. Kofukuda Mitsugi (NA 59-1931), the outstanding new *hikōtaichō,* led eighteen Zero 21s and two Kisarazu Type 1 *rikkōs* on a laudable (but not repeated) 5,000-kilometer overwater flight from Japan south to Rabaul via the island bases. Only thirteen Zeros actually made it there on 31 August. After assuming the 2nd Air Group's role as base defense and convoy cover, the 6th finally attacked Guadalcanal on 11 September. That day the converted carrier *Unyō* ferried ten Zero 32s to Rabaul (another arrived the day before).

Usually twelve to eighteen Zeros, split into two *chūtais* above and behind on either flank, offered the *rikkōs* direct escort. They had the unenviable task of dealing with the hit-and-run attacks by the Grumman Wildcats. The absence of radios in the land-based Zeros forced relatively inflexible escort tactics. Citing its limited range (50 miles) and poor reliability, the fighter groups had ripped out all the radio equipment, including the mast and aerial, to save 18 kilograms of weight. The lack of radios prevented close coordination between escorts and bombers and proved most detrimental in the Solomon air battles.[16]

Along with the *rikkōs,* Yamada's four-engine flying boats conducted arduous daily long-range searches. On 2 September Capt. Wada Saburō's Tōkō Air Group with eight Kawanishi H6K4 Type 97 flying boats joined the battered Yokohama Air Group. A mixed 14th and Yokohama detachment continued flying three experimental Kawanishi H8K1 Type 2 flying boats.

On 28 August the 8th Fleet created the "R-Area Air Force," equipped with seaplanes to make up for the lack of land bases. Newly promoted RAdm. Jōjima Takatsugu, CO of the 11th Seaplane Tender Division, formed the squadrons of four seaplane tenders into two ad hoc air groups (*hikōkitai*). Their twin-float, three-seat, Aichi E13A1 Type 0 reconnaissance seaplanes flew long-range searches and antisub patrols, while the two-man Mitsubishi F1M2 Type 0 observation biplanes acted as ersatz fighters for convoy escort and light bombing. To defend his air bases and anchorages, Jōjima relied on the *Kamikawa Maru*'s Nakajima A6M2-N Type 2 sea fighters, Zero 21s fitted with one large central float and two smaller stabilizing floats under the wings. They challenged enemy land-based bombers and search planes operating beyond enemy escort range, but hopefully also could cope with fighters if need be. (See table 10.5 for approximate plane strengths as of 12 September.)[17]

Jōjima assembled his forces in Shortland harbor, but earmarked Rekata Bay on Santa Isabel, only 135 miles northwest of Lunga, as his forward base. Base troops arrived there on 5 September. Because of the danger of Allied counterattacks, aircraft would tarry at Rekata only so long as needed before retiring to the safer waters of Shortland. Rekata's proximity to Guadalcanal meant that he could attack Lunga at will.

TABLE 10.5
R-Area Air Force Approximate Strength, 12 September 1942

		Type 0		Type 2
Air Group	Squadron	Observ.	Recon	Fighter
No. 1	*Chitose*	16	7	—
	Lt. Horihashi Takeshi[a] (NA 62-1934)			
	Kamikawa Maru	2	—	11
	Lt. Ono Jirō[b] (NA 64-1937)			
No. 2	*Sanyō Maru*	6	2	—
	Lt. Yoneda Tadashi[b] (NA 66-1938)			
	Sanuki Maru	6	—	—
	Lt. (jg) Watanabe Kaneshige[b] (NA 68-1940)			

[a] *Hikōtaichō*
[b] *Buntaichō*

12 SEPTEMBER

Fighting Five Christened at CACTUS

As the new boys, VF-5 drew the dawn alert and assembled before sunrise at the Pagoda. According to the morning routine, Marine and the few VF-5 mechanics warmed up the engines and checked magnetos. No order to take off came at 0500, so they hung around Air HQ. At 0810 Maj. Donald Kennedy in his jungle hideout at Segi in southern New Georgia heard aircraft evidently bound to the southeast. At 0830 twenty-three VF-5 Wildcats bounced through the grass to the runway, leaving only Smokey Stover's F-10 which, to his great consternation, failed to start. From the "cow pasture" nine F4Fs from 223 and 224 likewise made it aloft. The enemy strike never appeared on radar, so after 15 minutes Bayler recalled the CAP in shifts to refuel. Sailors from CUB-1 worked furiously to top off tanks. In the meantime the pilots took the opportunity to eat breakfast, one of only two meals they would get each day.

Spurred anew by aircraft crossing Vangunu to the south, Kennedy went back on the air at 1035. Fourteen minutes later, he heard more bandits over Blanche Channel off to his north. This time MAG-23 waited until the enemy showed up on radar at 1112, which at 59 miles out was much closer than usual. Condition YELLOW sounded at 1120. Those VF-5 pilots with F4Fs nearby ran to their planes, and jeeps delivered the rest. They restarted engines, which the ground crews had warmed up periodically. Not in any particular order as yet, they taxied to the west edge of Henderson Field and took off two at a time. The first aloft climbed in a wide spiral over the field, while following planes cut inside and joined up. Senior pilots worked their way ahead of divisions, while wingmen looked for section leaders. On occasion some VF-5 pilots formed on Marine F4Fs leaving the fighter strip. Once together the flights departed in steep, easterly climbs, opposite the direction of the incoming raid, and only at higher altitude reversed course to meet the enemy head-on. This time only twenty VF-5 F4Fs made it aloft, as Currie, Shoemaker, and Ens. William W. Wileman joined Stover as the angry possessors of balky airplanes. From Fighter 1 an even dozen Marine F4Fs took to the air.[18]

This day Base Air Force sent down twenty-six Mitsubishi Type 1 land attack planes from the 6th Air Attack Force under the able Kisarazu *hikōtaichō,* Lt. Nabeta Miyoshi (NA 60-1932). In December 1941 he had torpedoed the battleship *Prince of Wales.* Departing Rabaul at 0810, he deployed into the usual large Vee-of-Vees. His nine Kisarazu crews formed the 1st *Chūtai* in the center; the 2nd *Chūtai* on the left comprised eight Misawa aircraft under Lt. Nonaka Yusaburō (NA 64-1937), while to the right Lieutenant Andō's 3rd *Chūtai* numbered six *Chitose* and three Misawa Type 1s. Each *rikkō* lugged one 250-kilogram and six 60-kilogram bombs. At Lakunai, RAdm. Ugaki Matome, Combined Fleet chief of staff, bid farewell to fifteen escort pilots flying borrowed Zero 21 fighters. Lieutenant Kurakane's 1st *Chūtai* (nine 2nd Air Group) took station to the right, while moving up on the left was Lt. (jg) Kanemitsu Mukumi's 2nd *Chūtai* of three pilots from the 6th Air Group and three from the 2nd. He was another Eta Jima graduate (NA 68-1940) fresh from flight training.[19]

En route to Guadalcanal, Nabeta ascended to 8,500 meters (27,880 feet), with Zeros cruising above and a few thousand yards behind. They all settled down for the long flight in cramped quarters. One *Chitose* Type 1 turned back, leaving twenty-five *rikkōs*. In unusually high visibility over the central Solomons, the Japanese first eyeballed distant Guadalcanal at 1105, well before CACTUS radar returned the favor. Only ten minutes after Condition YELLOW, MAG-23 changed to RED. Sunlight glinting off silvery airplanes in the brilliant sky revealed the enemy northwest over the center of Iron Bottom Sound. East of Lunga, the still-climbing F4F pilots likewise spotted the "beautiful" Vee-of-Vees spread across a quarter-mile of sky, but they were still too low to think of intercepting. North of Lunga, Nabeta smartly executed a right turn to cross the coast and take aim at the airfield just beyond. He let down in a shallow dive toward 7,500 meters (24,000 feet) to gain speed for the bomb run and getaway.

If the late warning prevented fighter intercepts, the good visibility afforded Col. Robert H. Pepper's 3rd Defense Battalion a fine opportunity to shine. Emplaced at Henderson Field, Maj. James S. O'Halloran's Battery E with four 90-mm M1A1 AA guns enjoyed automatic fire control aided by the SCR-268 fire control radar's close-in altitude reading of the target. At 1148, the guns barked loudly against targets approaching from due north, estimated height 24,400 feet. Black bursts from the 23.4-pound projectiles first blossomed above and ahead of the silvery Vees, but Battery E swiftly corrected for the altitude of the descending bombers. Ground observers witnessed an orange flash beneath an aircraft on the left side. Its starboard engine smoking, PO1c Konno Takeji's Misawa *rikkō* dropped in distress from out of the rear of Nonaka's 2nd *Chūtai*. A few

One wing from Spec. Duty Ens. Takamatsu Naoichi's Kisarazu Type 1 land attack plane, destroyed on 12 Sept. 1942 by the 3rd Defense Battalion. In the left rear is a PBY-5A Catalina amphibian. (NA 80-G-16328)

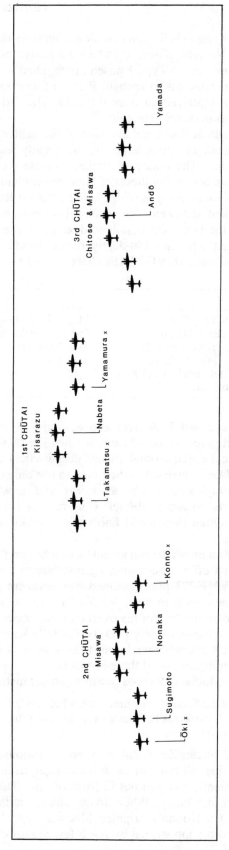

Japanese land attack plane formation, 12 September 1942.

seconds later another 90-mm shell exploded almost directly on the *rikkō* of Spec. Duty Ens. Takamatsu Naoichi, Kisarazu 2nd *Shōtai* leader in the center. Streaming flames and black smoke, his Type 1 nosed down, shed its wings in spectacular fashion, and disintegrated into a fireball. Pieces of wreckage, including parts of the crew, ended up scattered all over the field. The 3rd Defense Battalion claimed its two wings as personal souvenirs.[20]

Looking over the main field but still unaware of the fighter strip, the Japanese counted twenty-four small and three large aircraft, mostly wrecks dumped along the runway's south edge. The boneyard tricked Nabeta's enlisted bombardier into salvoing most of the bombs southeast of Henderson Field proper. One string detonated even farther south along the ridge held by the 1st Raider and Parachute battalions. Four men died and twenty-five suffered wounds, but the bombing was ineffective. Not even the boneyard sustained damage. Nabeta brought the land attack planes around to the left in a 180-degree turn to head back out to sea.

Smith's eight Marine and two VF-5 F4Fs charged hard for a massed attack:

1	2
Maj. John L. Smith (CO, 223)	Maj. John F. Dobbin (XO, 224)
2nd Lt. Willis S. Lees, III (223)	2nd Lt. Charles M. Kunz (224)
2nd Lt. Eugene A. Trowbridge (223)	Maj. Kirk Armistead (224)
2nd Lt. Kenneth D. Frazier (223)	1st Lt. Darrell D. Irwin (224)
Lt. (jg) Howard L. Grimmell, Jr. (VF-5)	
Ens. Harry A. March, Jr. (VF-5)	

From comfortably ahead and 5,000 feet above, Smith confronted the turning bombers in good position for overhead runs, his favorite tactic. The F4Fs could peel off one at a time and execute simultaneous near-vertical attacks without fear of collision. Smith and Galer instructed their men to use only overheads or, if not possible, very steep high-side passes as safest and most effective against bombers. They preferred to aim at the left wing root or engine to flame a fuel tank or kill the pilot. Often they could finish one bomber and quickly shift to others in the formation.

Smitty broke off for an overhead run against a bomber on the left side, and the other F4F pilots peeled off in succession against targets farther back. In this particular flurry, the VMF-223 pilots claimed five bombers (Smith two, Trowbridge two, Frazier one). Fifth to dive, VF-5's "Larry" Grimmell also singled out a land attack plane on the left for his overhead and noticed it pull up sharply and fall off in flames. Wingman Harry ("Dirty Eddie") March likewise tried an overhead, but could not say whether he hurt the enemy. Last to attack, John Dobbin's VMF-224 contingent tallied three bombers.

After their runs, the Marines followed Smith's general instructions:

> It was our policy to hit the bombers one time—the whole outfit—then pull up to the left then look around. If the Zeros had come over the top of the bombers and could attack us, we'd go away.[21]

On this occasion all fifteen Zeros did intervene in furious, but fruitless, pursuit. Adhering to doctrine, all but 2nd Lt. Bill Lees got clean away. He claimed one bandit, which evidently overran out in front of him. The Zeros chased the F4Fs too far to return in a hurry. While diving away, Smith, Trowbridge, and Frazier ran across PO1c Konno's crippled Misawa Type 1 lurching along at 10,000 feet and finished the job started by AA a few minutes before. Set ablaze,

Konno crashed near the Lunga River. No Marines bothered to claim this *rikkō;* no one from the Japanese strike group saw its fate.

Notwithstanding the many fighter claims, ground observers noticed only one bomber fall as a result of fighter attack, although others certainly were damaged. The victim was PO1c Yamamura Tsutomu, inside wingman in the Kisarazu 3rd *Shōtai* on the right center. He dropped out in flames as the formation recrossed the coast and headed out to sea. Frazier noticed this straggler escape north toward Tulagi. To the cheers of many Marines watching from Lunga Point, he harried the big airplane down to low level. Suddenly Yamamura pulled sharply into a stall. Another burst finished off the Kisarazu *rikkō*, which spun into the water with a "great backfire of ruddy flame and black smoke."[22] This hard-fought kill, Frazier's second of the day, gave him ten overall.

Only Grimmell and March of VF-5 regained altitude for a second pass. Recovering well ahead of the bombers, Grimmell swiftly reversed course for an opposite run against one, but this time saw no damage. Out over the channel, Nabeta turned left again, and most of VF-5 climbed in pursuit. New to this particular game, they, unlike the Marines, had not bothered to form up in one or two large groups, but headed out in separate flights. Retiring northwest at surprisingly high speed, the *rikkō* crews stoically filled the gaps in the tight Vees. No escorts lingered above, so VF-5 had their way with the bombers until Kurakane's Zeros could climb back into the fray. The eighteen VF-5 F4Fs moved in six separate groupings toward attack position:

1	2	3	4	5	6
Richardson	Simpler	Green	Crews	Clarke	Mankin
Eichenberger	Innis	Halford	Register	Wesolowski	
Roach	Kleinmann	Bright	Loesch	Morgan	
			Rouse	Nesbitt	

By the time the lead VF-5 flight began its runs, the *rikkōs* had descended to 21,000 feet. That offered Dave Richardson, Ike Eichenberger, and Mel Roach an advantage of only 500 feet for shallow high-sides against Andō's mixed *Chitose-Misawa* 3rd *Chūtai* on the right. No bombers fell to their guns, but Roach roughed up the right trailer, PO2c Yamada Shizuo's Misawa *rikkō*. Despite streaming white smoke Yamada held his perilous slot in formation. After his run, Richardson crossed over to the port side of the bombers, then slowed to permit his wingmen to join for a second pass. Eichenberger evidently followed, but Roach stayed on the right looking for more action.

The two wingmen never showed, so Richardson continued climbing alone. When well along into a high-side run from left of the bombers, tracers suddenly shot vertically past his cockpit and the trailing edge of the wing. A Zero that he never saw neatly ambushed him with an overhead attack. Many 7.7-mm slugs pierced the wings, then a 20-mm cannon shell ripped through the upper fuselage and detonated below and abaft the armor plate. Shrapnel peppered his legs, shattered glass in the instrument panel, and also cut the oil line, which spewed hot lubricant into the cockpit. Somewhat dazed, Richardson countered with a left diving turn, but another Zero happened to dive on past and pulled out below. Eager to retaliate, he pushed over for an opposite attack, but the enemy easily scooted out of reach. With both himself and his mount in a bad way, Richardson nosed down toward the field. The engine lost power, then cut out completely. Nevertheless, he made a fine landing, but once on the runway, he ground-looped

A VF-5 F4F in flight over Guadalcanal. (Capt. H. W. Crews)

because wounds prevented him from applying even pressure on the brakes. Marines gently lifted him out of the cockpit and drove him to the field hospital in the coconut grove.[23]

Like their division leader, Roach and Eichenberger tangled with the escort. Recovering from his first pass, Roach happened to see two Zeros below cavorting in a vertical figure-eight. He fired a quick squirt at one, but its wingman jumped his tail. Roach blew off all his remaining bullets at the first one and kept on going. Gunfire stopped Ike Eichenberger's engine and sent the F4F gliding without power. On the downwind leg of his approach, he stalled over the palms on the western fringe of Fighter 1 short of the main field. His wheels snagged a treetop that threw the F4F onto a captured steamroller the Seabees used to flatten the strip. Marines extricated the critically wounded pilot and rushed him to the hospital.

Simpler's division pitched in from right of the bombers and split their attacks. The skipper chose a flat-side and Innis a high-side, while Kleinmann essayed a shallow overhead against the rearmost bomber on the right (Yamada's Misawa Type 1, already mussed up by Roach). The first two pilots noticed no results from their tracers, but Kleinmann thought he smoked the trailer's port engine. Yamada dropped about 100 feet back from his slot in formation. Discouraged by the rapid speed of the bombers and a poor attack position, Innis and Kleinmann dived on out, but Simpler persevered. On his way back for a second go at the bombers, he saw two Zeros jump another Wildcat (possibly Eichenberger's) and rushed to help his teammate. One bandit turned up into him in order to scissor for an opposite attack, then both opponents broke off the action by mutual consent.

Leading his division, Frank Green maneuvered for a high-side from the right against the withdrawing bombers, but a Zero charged him on the way out. In his

words, "I left soon," which proved fortunate for a VF-5 teammate.[24] Green
spotted a Zero stalking a climbing F4F and warned the pilot, who turned out to
be March, Grimmell's wingman. Apprised of the danger, March turned sharply
right to scissor. Not eager to fight, the Japanese reversed course and climbed on
away. In his go at the bombers, Jim Halford, Green's wingman, rolled in too far
astern and was sucked flat behind them. At great risk from the tail gunners, he
snapped off a burst, then broke off to the left. From 2,000 feet above, a Zero's
quick high-side forced him to dive out. Two more wide-ranging Zeros "hopped"
Mark Bright before he could fairly get into battle. Looking around, he was
shocked to see another Zero actually flying wing on him. He dived away. Green's
division was out of action.

"Sandy" Crews first encountered the bombers from below and ahead, so he
led his people to the right and resumed climbing. The division strung out while
moving into attack position. Five or six Zeros tagged Dix Loesch and Will
Rouse, the 2nd Section, who spent their time sparring with two bandits around
21,000 feet. Cash Register fired into another Zero that had overshot and recovered ahead and below. This was the principal Japanese error repeated time after
time, often with dire results. Register claimed this bandit after he watched it spin
out of sight. A loud "crack-crack-crack" of gunfire startled Crews, intent on the
bombers. A Zero flashed past after making a low-side run. He countered by
turning into his opponent, then dived while the Japanese climbed. Another Zero
brushed him away before he could get at the bombers.[25]

While Kurakane's escort tangled with these fifteen or so VF-5 F4Fs, they left
the way open for more Wildcats to bounce the *rikkōs*. While climbing into attack
position, Wally Clarke's four F4Fs split up. He rolled into a high-side from left of
the bombers, and despite two balky outboard .50s, still blasted the *rikkō* of Res.
Ens. Sugimoto Mitsumi, the Misawa 2nd *Shōtai* leader. Sugimoto fell back toward PO1c Ōki Tetsugorō, his struggling left wingman already chopped by John
Smith. Clarke kept on diving and at 6,000 feet ran across another victimized
rikkō, a *Chitose* aircraft also roughed up by Smith's F4Fs. This time only three
Brownings responded. Three runs ran them dry of bullets, but the tough bird
chugged on. Clarke let it go and returned to base. The *Chitose* Type 1 limped to
Rekata and set down offshore.

John Wesolowski, Clarke's wingman, still lagged behind the bombers, but
George Morgan, 2nd Section leader, had moved out ahead. While setting up a
high-side run against the 2nd *Chūtai* on the left, he noticed two stragglers: Sugimoto and Ōki, victims of Smith and Clarke. Morgan passed up the obvious
cripple (Ōki) and put a good burst into Sugimoto. A Zero's 7.7-mm slug chinked
the armor plate behind his seat, as he pulled out. Determined to get the bombers,
Morgan gradually gained on them until two more Zeros chased him away for
good. Robert H. "JoJo" Nesbitt, AP1c, his wingman, submitted no report of his
activities that day.

The last VF-5 pilot to get into the fight was Paul Mankin, the skipper's wingman. His engine failed to deliver full power, which left him far behind the others.
Nevertheless the young NAP aggressively climbed alone and finally gained position above the bombers. Sugimoto and Ōki, the unlucky Misawa pair already
shot up by Smith, Clarke, and Morgan, limped along below the rest of their
mates. Mankin's high-side pass separated Ōki from his leader, but he held his run
too long and committed a cardinal error. Swinging his short-barreled 20-mm
Type 99 cannon on target, Sugimoto's tail gunner riddled Mankin's F4F through
the cowling, wings, and flaps. One fragment tore through the right rudder pedal

and lodged in the heel of his boot without injury. With a crisp high-side pass, a persistent Weasel Wesolowski dumped Ōki into the sea off Savo Island, but Sugimoto reached base.[26]

After his second attack, a head-on pass, Grimmell poured on the coal to overtake the bombers. March rejoined, but left when his fuel ran low. Soon Grimmell received a rare opportunity to surprise a Zero and calmly drew close to its tail before opening fire. Its startled pilot, PO2c Okazaki Torakichi, tried a spin and sharp wingover to evade, but to no avail, as the F4F's bullets set the aircraft smoking. Straightening out in a shallow dive, Okazaki ran for home. Grimmell pursued, but finally relented near Savo. From above Loesch and Rouse from Crews's division watched the obviously damaged Zero stream a white trail of gasoline. Using their own diving speed, the two F4F pilots latched onto Okazaki at 15,000 feet, but he remained too fast for them. Continuing to dive, they chased him 60 miles and finally called it quits over Indispensable Strait north of Florida Island. Okazaki was never seen again.

By ones and twos the VF-5 F4Fs returned to the bomber field after their first combat from CACTUS. Before they landed, the Seabees hurriedly filled bomb craters on the runway. A nose count revealed that Ike Eichenberger was missing. At the same time Simpler heard that an F4F had cracked up near Fighter 1, so he sent Crews to investigate. A surgeon shocked him with the terrible news that they had already buried Charles Eichenberger. Richardson's wounds earmarked him for evacuation.

CACTUS fighter claims totaled thirteen bombers, two Zeros, and two probables:

VMF-223	
Maj. J. L. Smith	2 bombers
2nd Lt. E. A. Trowbridge	2 bombers
2nd Lt. K. D. Frazier	2 bombers
2nd Lt. W. S. Lees	1 fighter
VMF-224	
Maj. J. F. Dobbin	1 bomber
Maj. K. Armistead	1 bomber
2nd Lt. C. M. Kunz	1 bomber
1st Lt. D. D. Irwin	1 bomber probable
VF-5	
Lt. W. E. Clarke	1 bomber
Lt. (jg) H. L. Grimmell	1 bomber
Ens. J. M. Wesolowski	1 bomber
L. P. Mankin, AP1c	1 bomber
Ens. F. R. Register	1 fighter
Ens. M. V. Kleinmann	1 bomber probable

With ninety-four rounds of 90-mm, the 3rd Defense Battalion claimed three bombers confirmed and two probables. In return no F4Fs went down outright, but two from VF-5 suffered heavy damage. During deadstick landings, one crashed (Ensign Eichenberger killed).

Actual Japanese casualties, six land attack planes, numbered the most since the 8 August disaster. Two Kisarazu Type 1s were seen to go down (Spec. Duty Ens. Takamatsu to AA, PO1c Yamamura to fighters), and two Misawa (PO1c Ōki and PO1c Konno) failed to return. One *Chitose* Type 1 ditched at Rekata Bay, and another flopped down at Buka. Ten others took hits (PO2c Ogawa Kinnosuke's Kisarazu totaled), and a Misawa crewman died. In return the crews notched eleven Grummans (including four unconfirmed). HQ considered the results of the bombing especially good. The 2nd Air Group escorts recorded fights with seventeen Grummans and claimed thirteen (including three unconfirmed) for the loss of PO2c Okazaki. PO2c Ishikawa Shirō's Zero took slight damage. Reading the reports, Ugaki complained in his diary that the Americans seemed to "bring up planes as fast as we shoot them down. It is a problem."[27]

The raid on the 12th, a typical Guadalcanal donnybrook, hammered home the tactical points Smith made the previous afternoon. The arthritic F4Fs did need at least 30 minutes to reach 28,000 feet and assure height advantage over the bombers. Simpler complained in his report, "The F4F-4 is too slow in climb to altitude and has insufficient ceiling and speed to deal with the modern bombers and fighters." Climbing in tight, compact formations such as the one Smith used kept the F4Fs together for massed attacks and somewhat discouraged the fighter escorts from diving in. Usually fighting in trios or pairs, the Zeros rarely surrendered altitude advantage.

VF-5 had trained for carrier defense, where it was critical to break up an enemy strike before it reached the ships. Conditions at CACTUS did not permit that. The Marines learned from bitter experience that more than one pass at the bombers risked a thrashing by the escort. Later in the campaign this did not necessarily apply. The bombers, especially after releasing payloads, cruised so fast that follow-up attacks became increasingly shallow, of low deflection, and more dangerous. Certainly VF-5's experiences vindicated Smith's warnings. In his action report Richardson opined it was "impracticable to make more than one run on the bombers and employ the speed gained in the attack to avoid the Zero." This would take VF-5 time to learn.

Aside from early warning the F4Fs fighting over CACTUS enjoyed additional advantages. Fuel limitations prevented the enemy fighters from prolonging any actions. The 1st MAW wrongly believed the Zeros operated from Buka, which at 400 miles was a great distance in its own right, but they later learned to their amazement that the enemy came the whole long way from Rabaul. The CACTUS fighters battled over their own turf, so to speak, to the great benefit of Dave Richardson and numerous others.

VF-5's second night on Guadalcanal definitely differed from the first. As before, the pilots set up their cots near the field and settled down for the night, but at 2100 without warning (the radar was out) an enemy cruiser float plane ("Louie the Louse") droned low over Lunga Point. It released a flare that descended with a "sickeningly yellow-green" glow. Something was up. The afternoon search had pegged a small force—light cruiser *Sendai* and destroyers *Shikinami*, *Fubuki*, and *Suzukaze*—about 200 miles up the Slot and bound for Lunga. Beginning at 2130 they pounded the field, the beach, and the surrounding bivouac areas for 20 minutes. Along with everyone else, VF-5 frantically sought cover in foxholes or shallow bomb craters. Sharing one hole with four or five others, some spare tires, and a box of ammunition, Crews noticed Loesch running for cover in a white terrycloth bathrobe, unusual night attire for CACTUS.[28]

Only a mile or so south of the field, Kawaguchi finally unleashed his night assault a day late against soon-to-be-dubbed "Bloody Ridge." The warships ceased fire for about a half hour to reverse course and resumed shooting at midnight. This session proved particularly bad. For 45 minutes they concentrated on the bivouac, airfield, and the ridge. Among others, the shelling killed two pilots from VMSB-232 (including Larry Baldinus, a hero of 25 August) and one from 231, but missed VF-5 personnel and aircraft. The desperate infantry battle so near kept most of the pilots awake for the rest of the night. In his diary Frank Green summed up their greatest worry: "The Japs would push the marines past my hole and I wouldn't know it." The defending raiders and parachutists held valiantly against Kawaguchi's men.

13 SEPTEMBER

More Fighters for CACTUS

The afternoon of 12 September, Turner formally recommended adoption of plans to transport the 7th Marines to CACTUS. He wanted to sail two days hence from BUTTON. TF-61 proceeded with its mission to bring Wildcats from BUTTON to CACTUS. Ten VB-8 SBDs with VF-72 pilots in the rear seats left the *Hornet*, while ten VF-71 pilots rode in six *Wasp* TBFs. That afternoon they returned with nineteen F4Fs, while the SBDs and TBFs fetched the Marines to fly them. Soon after takeoff from Santo, Ens. Philip F. Grant ditched his VB-8 SBD, injuring himself and his passenger, 2nd Lt. Eldon H. Railsback of VMO-251. Despite a broken arm, "Duke" Railsback pulled the dazed Grant from the cockpit and held his head out of the water until rescued by the *Gamble*. After a luxurious night on the CVs with all they could eat and long showers, the other Marines made ready to depart the next morning for CACTUS.[29]

Still bleary-eyed for lack of sleep, VF-5 turned out before dawn on 13 September on alert, greeted by tracers arcing in from the south. The fierce battle on Bloody Ridge wound down. While walking in the pitch-black night toward his F4F, Simpler stumbled into a machine-gun nest and received the ominous challenge, "What's the password, buddy?" That morning it was "Polly," replete with the "ell" sound that Japanese could not easily pronounce. However, Simpler could not pronounce it either, as no one had seen fit to vouchsafe the password to VF-5. He later wrote, "I was never as scared in the whole war as I was by that question." All he could do, conscious of the rifle pointed at him, was to reply carefully and clearly that he was a pilot looking for his plane. The Marine asked him about baseball and finally replied, "Okay, buddy."[30] At 0530 a dozen VF-5 F4Fs covered the takeoff of Maj. Harold A. Johnson's VMJ-253 R4D-1 transport plane taking the two admirals back to BUTTON. Their visit definitely gave them a taste of life at CACTUS.

Before dawn and 290 miles southeast of Guadalcanal, the *Wasp* launched Maj. Frederick R. Payne, XO of VMF-212, with nine F4Fs, including one from VF-71 substituted for a Marine fighter requiring minor repairs. At the same time nine under Capt. Carl M. Longley of VMO-251 left the *Hornet*. Without Railsback to fly it, another F4F-4 remained on board. SBDs escorted the Marines as far as San Cristobal. As the two flights neared Guadalcanal, Lieutenant Colonel Scollin came on the air to tell the "belly-tank fighters" to land on the sod strip a mile east of Henderson Field. Because their planes sported no tanks, Payne and Longley thought he meant someone else. Beginning at 0745 they landed at the main field as originally briefed. As each taxied up, he was sent to Fighter 1. There Bob Galer, also the MAG-23 LSO, amused himself by bringing them in with his paddles. Thus in the last two days CACTUS had received forty-two new, absolutely vital Wildcats.[31]

Reconnaissance in Force

Already once that morning Kennedy from his New Georgia hideout had reported hearing aircraft, but at 0829 he again warned CACTUS. No enemy planes subsequently appeared on radar, but MAG-23 was wary. At 0900 Colonel Wallace ordered a rare high-altitude CAP. From Fighter 1 Galer led five 224 F4Fs aloft, while Simpler's four departed the main field. About 0930 radar finally detected bogeys closing from the northwest. Clarke's VF-5 division manned four fighters at Henderson Field, and at the cow pasture Smith and three other VMF-223 pilots took the last operational 223 F4Fs. A few minutes later 2nd Lt. Hyde Phillips and 2nd Lt. Noyes McLennan of 223 grabbed the first pair of newly arrived Grummans just topped off with fuel. These ten Wildcats climbed at full power. At Fighter 1 Payne's flight crews awaited the refueling of the rest of their planes. Meanwhile Longley's men, not on alert, sampled CACTUS cuisine, "a rather thick soup of boiled rice with a few chunks of Spam or canned Vienna Sausage floating in it."[32]

The mid-morning Japanese foray was a reconnaissance in force rather than a bombing raid. On the basis of some confused messages reporting the capture of the airfield, Tsukahara ordered the Tainan Air Group to send Lt. Hayashi Hideo (NA 66-1938) with two Type 2 land reconnaissance planes and nine Zeros under Lt. Inano Kikuichi to ascertain the situation. Surprisingly Southeast Area and 17th Army both lacked direct radio communication with Kawaguchi. To remedy the situation, staff officer Maj. Tanaka Kōji rode in WO Ono Satoru's number 2 land recon plane. He had orders to land and establish contact if friendly troops occupied the airfield. Lieutenant Kofukuda's 6th Air Group prepared to operate from Lunga, with mechanics and logistics support to be brought in by transport planes. At the same time bombers stood ready to attack Taivu Point east of Lunga, thought to be occupied by the fleeing Americans. In Rabaul, at least, victory seemed imminent.[33]

After leaving Rabaul at 0630, the eleven aircraft eased up to 8,500 meters (27,880 feet) and approached Guadalcanal about 0940. West of Lunga the sharp-eyed Japanese spotted fighters (either Galer or Simpler) already on patrol at high altitude, but the CAP failed to reciprocate. Conscious of the need to protect his Army passenger, Hayashi delayed for an hour the scheduled close reconnaissance of the enemy airfield. Apparently this was a contingency plan. Perhaps he thought the Grummans were carrier-based and might soon withdraw.

Seeking the usual bomber formation, Wally Clarke climbed at full power while heading west.[34] His four VF-5 Wildcats strung out loosely by sections trying to keep in sight of each other. At 22,000 feet Mole Currie, his wingman, called it quits when a blown rubber gasket in his engine supercharger ruined high-altitude performance. Without realizing it, the others left him behind. Near to 1000, the Japanese noticed more Grummans climbing almost directly beneath. This time Inano set up an ambush by Warrant Officer Takatsuka with the 2nd and 3rd *shōtais,* while he and two wingmen stayed with Hayashi. Passing 25,000 feet, Clarke glimpsed six bandits diving straight in. Before defending himself he had time only to shout "Zero" over the radio.

It was shades of 7 August, and one of the three VF-5 pilots knew only too well what was happening. Don Innis, flying the trailing F4F, looked up at Zeros bouncing Clarke and Smokey Stover. The first attacker recovered out to the right, and Innis rolled after it, shot on target, and watched it smoke. Suddenly in his words, "the lightning hit the outhouse." From above another sharpshooting Japanese ripped the F4F with a full-deflection shot and either punctured the main fuel tank or severed a fuel line. A sheet of flame exploded from underneath the instrument panel and washed over Innis's face and body, leaving severe burns. Pushing back his canopy, he threw himself out of the still-climbing F4F. Clarke and Stover spiralled around the pilotless airplane until it dropped below 12,000 feet. Despite what appeared to be a torn or only partially opened chute, Innis safely reached the water after 20 harrowing minutes. For his own part Stover did not glimpse the Zeros until he dropped below 18,000 feet, but Clarke saw them well enough. He wondered if they got Currie too.

After they torched one Grumman, Takatsuka's six Zeros regrouped and drove Clarke and Stover from 12,000 feet down toward the cloud base at 6,000. Takatsuka, PO2c Matsuki Susumu, and PO3c Satō Noboru concentrated on Clarke, the leader, while the other *shōtai* (PO1c Ōki, PO1c Ōta Toshio, and PO3c Utō Kazushi) chased Stover. On the way down they peppered Smokey's tail. After making a high-side run, Utō overshot his target at 8,000 feet, the usual dangerous Japanese mistake. Before he could climb away, a strong burst from Stover's six .50s set his aircraft spinning in flames. With a "big flash" Utō plowed into a hilltop, where burning gasoline spread a "pool of flame," igniting a large grass fire.[35] Later Stover chanced to fly over the site (ten miles west of Lunga) and found the brush burning around the charred wreck.

Almost immediately after his first kill, Stover took a good head-on shot at one of Takatsuka's Zeros recovering from a run against Clarke. This time he caused its cowling to stream heavy white smoke. The target circled twice in manifest distress, but Stover did not see it crash. "White streaks" with "red ends" marking tracers zipped past his right wing, so he skidded out of the line of fire and took refuge in the low-lying cumulus clouds. Ōki and Ōta, the 3rd *Shōtai* survivors, remained a thousand feet above and kept him in the cloud bank by jumping him every time he tried to leave. Warily they offered Stover no further opportunities. Thus began an unusually long, low-level dogfight.

Nearby, "Sunshine" Clarke enjoyed his own good times playing tag with Takatsuka's three 2nd *Shōtai* Zeros (one already winged by Stover). After 20 minutes of evasive action, he happened to exit a cloud at 3,500 feet. Ahead a bandit was busy in a partial wingover. Closing unseen, Clarke scored quickly. While popping in and out of the clouds during his own fight, Stover chanced to see

Lt. (jg) Smokey Stover, an aerial self-portrait over Guadalcanal. (Capt. H. W. Crews)

Clarke's victim smack the ground. Soon after, Clarke disappeared in the clouds with two Zeros in hot pursuit.

After Clarke shot down the Zero, its undamaged teammate tore after him. He countered by abruptly turning to scissor, but unfortunately stalled and spun down to 400 feet before regaining control. The Japanese lunged again. Clarke repeated the counter, only to stall out a second time into a valley and nearly brush the trees. Now out of sky, a flat-out, low-level dash seemed his only chance to reach safety 10 miles east at Lunga. At full throttle (IAS 210 knots) under 100 feet and about 300 yards off shore, he streaked hell-bent for Henderson Field and its AA guns. Both 2nd *Shōtai* Zeros pursued, one glued to his tail. Three times it charged the straining Wildcat, only to fall back. Clarke was surprised the enemy pilot did not finish him then and there, but evidently the cautious Japanese worried about being jumped by other F4Fs. He broke off as Clarke reached Lunga Point and roared low over Henderson Field. Just after 1020 Clarke gratefully landed his shot-up Grumman at Fighter 1 and counted six holes in it. His two 2nd *Shōtai* pursuers went on east of Lunga before doubling back.

In the last 45 minutes, Smith's flight had reached 30,000 feet without spotting any enemy planes. Soon it seemed no one was coming, so he descended toward Lunga to land and refuel in time for the expected noon raid. His teammates were 2nd Lt. Robert Read, 2nd Lt. Conrad G. Winter, and 2nd Lt. Charles S. Hughes. From Galer's morning CAP, Maj. John Dobbin (XO, 224) and wingman 2nd Lt. Dean S. Hartley, Jr., joined him on the way down.[36] A few miles northeast of the fighter strip Smith dropped through a rain squall. Exiting at low level, he saw two Zeros flying westward at slow speed right over the trees. The Marines wondered if these bandits were lost, so far east were they. To Hartley one looked in trouble, battle-damaged although not smoking. Perhaps the pilot sought a clearing east of the mouth of the Tenaru River. Smitty quickly scored. Evidently trying to land, the first Zero crashed on a soggy meadow in sight of a patrol from Company L, 1st Marines. 223 later joked that Smith bagged this bird "on the first bounce."

After evading Smith's division, the second Zero climbed in the direction of Dobbin and Hartley, also very low. To Hartley it appeared this one had tried to cover the first. At 1,000 feet Dobbin overran, when the Japanese rolled adroitly right and quickly accelerated onto his tail. Nothing was wrong with this enemy plane. However, the pilot did not reckon on a wingman "in trail" on his section leader. Hartley dived close astern of the Zero, and three swift bursts exploded its cockpit as he flew past. So perished the last member of the 2nd *Shōtai*. Clarke accounted for the first, Smith finished off the second previously damaged by Stover, while Hartley destroyed the third.

A few minutes after Smitty's fight, Hyde Phillips and "Scotty" McLennan of 223 tangled with some Zeros near the field. Well before the usual noon raid, writer Dick Tregaskis settled at Lunga Point, and this time action came early and a lot closer to sea level. He saw:

> One Wildcat . . . come diving down like a comet from the clouds with two Zeros on his tail. He was moving faster than they, and as he pulled out of his dive and streaked across the water, he left them behind. They gave up the chase and pulled sharply back into the sky. We had a good view of their long, square-tipped [*sic*] wings, and the round red ball of the rising sun insignia, as they turned.

I watched two planes, one chasing the other, pop out of the tower of cloud, describe a small, precise semi-circle, and go back in again . . . A few moments later they made another circle, like two beads on the same wire.[37]

Phillips thought he finished one Zero, but another thoroughly shot up his plane. After the action McLennan flew up alongside, but inexplicably fell off on one wing and disappeared into the jungle southeast of the fighter strip. He never returned. Phillips and McLennan fought the Tainan 1st *Shōtai* of Inano, PO1c Okumura Takeo, and PO3c Mogi Yoshio. Along with Hayashi's two recon planes, they had marked time north of Guadalcanal until nearly 1030 before starting down at high speed toward Lunga. Hayashi and Ono split to check out the area at low altitude, while Inano dealt with the two F4Fs.

By 1030 Fighter 1 had refueled the rest of Payne's flight and some of Longley's. Five minutes later Ono's number 2 recon aircraft with staff officer Tanaka daringly buzzed Lunga at 400 meters without a shot in return and later reported over forty small aircraft parked on the field. Ten minutes later Hayashi in the number 1 aircraft observed no planes during a low pass. What happened during the overflights remains a mystery. Ground personnel took no notice of two big Nakajimas roaring overhead. In retrospect it appears that Ono spotted, among others, Payne's flight about to take off. Their engine noise masked his flyover. Hayashi evidently missed both fields. Otherwise it is inconceivable he failed to notice the many dispersed aircraft and the CACTUS boneyard on the south edge of Henderson Field. When clear of the area, the two crews radioed their contradictory findings.

The departure of Hayashi and Inano did not signal an end to the air battle. Until nearly 1050 (almost 30 minutes after Clarke left), Stover dueled Ōki and Ōta west of Lunga. When finally they pulled off, he gratefully withdrew, tested his torn-up mount, and returned to Henderson Field. The Wildcat was in pitiful shape: chewed wing (including one flap), rudder, stabilizer, and vacuum tank in the rear fuselage. However the armor plate was, Stover happily noted, "very good." This aircraft was not even his own F-10, but Melvin Roach's F-20, whose owner complained of its condition. From the number of hits old F-20 sustained, it is understandable why Ōki and Ōta thought they bagged four Grummans, never realizing they fought only one opponent that whole long time. In his short career, Ōta scored thirty-four kills, sixth highest in the Imperial Navy, and Ōki ended up with seventeen. Having survived the earnest attention of two of Japan's best, Smokey cockily commented in his report: "Enemy showed poor judgment and poor gunnery in combat. Their planes are very maneuverable and far superior to own when properly handled."

Meanwhile, Payne's eight VMF-212 and VMO-251 F4Fs hunted the enemy. Reaching high altitude, the flight experienced a tragedy all too common at CACTUS. At 24,000 feet 2nd Lt. Richard A. Haring abruptly pitched into a dive. His section leader, 2nd Lt. Jack E. Conger, shouted over the radio to warn him, but heard no response. Lack of oxygen must have rendered Haring unconscious. Its engine roaring at maximum RPM, the F4F plunged into the hills to the southwest of Lunga and raised a large pillar of smoke. A week later some of Snowy Rhoades's natives brought in Haring's effects from a wreck they located about 10 miles from the field.[38]

Two weeks before, VMF-224 had similarly lost two pilots and three F4Fs. The oxygen system on the F4Fs was difficult to service in the field. Often the primitive masks leaked. A pilot had to be alert and lucky to recognize the symptoms of oxygen deprivation before he passed out. Prior to CACTUS, most rookies gained very little high-altitude time. The Marines preferred the older, small white rubber nose mask worn in conjunction with a throat mike. VF-5 used the bulky Type D mask, which prevented the use of flight goggles. Further, the Type D contained the mike, which compelled VF-5 to rig up another on a cord for low-altitude use.

About the time Haring crashed, the last member of Payne's flight struggled to get airborne from Fighter 1. Shortly after liftoff, 2nd Lt. Oscar P. Rutledge of VMO-251 suddenly stalled, then whipped into a sharp "snap-roll" to the left. In the words of an eyewitness, Master Technical Sgt. Wendell P. Garton of VMO-251, "the nose went down, the left wing struck the ground, broke, and folded under the fuselage, which came to rest nearly inverted, lodged ten feet or so up a large tree."[39] Profuse bleeding from "Curley" Rutledge's ripped scalp caused rescuers to fear his injuries were fatal. However, aside from the severe cuts, he sustained only a concussion and a broken jaw. The Wildcat was totaled. Evacuated a few days later, he never remembered being at CACTUS, let alone the crash. Members of his squadron speculated that in his haste Rutledge, who was short in stature, might not have adjusted the rudder pedals and would not have been able to apply the full right rudder that the F4F's powerful leftward torque demanded.

The last of the CACTUS participants to return was VF-5's Stinky Innis. The *YP-239*, a part of the Lunga Naval Local Defense Force under Coast Guard Lt. Cdr. Dwight H. Dexter, fished him out of the channel and brought him back to Kukum at 1220. His brief combat inflicted second- and third-degree burns on the right side of his face, neck, both wrists, right arm, and both legs from ankles to knees, which demonstrated the need to be fully clothed to protect against flash burns. Like Richardson, Innis went to Efate for treatment.

Eleven of twenty-eight CACTUS fighter pilots fought a series of sharp actions against a "scattered" force believed to number fifteen Zeros. Claims totaled five: one each by Smith and Phillips of 223, Hartley (224), Clarke, and Stover of VF-5, who also received credit for a probable. In return, enemy action cost VMF-223 and VF-5 each an F4F (McLennan of 223 killed). Payne's flight missed the enemy, which was fortunate because their guns froze at 30,000 feet due to excess lubrication that MAG-23 armorers had no time to remedy. Haring of 212 died from equipment failure, while Rutledge (VMO-251) wrecked his F4F on takeoff.

At 1410 both land recon planes reached Rabaul without being intercepted by enemy fighters. After the debriefing, Base Air Force decided that Kawaguchi had not captured the enemy airfield, so no Zeros would be sent there to land. The five surviving Tainan pilots arrived at 1500 and reported fighting twenty Grumman fighters, claiming eight (Okumura three, Ōki two, Ōta two, and Inano one). They had successfully protected the land recon planes, but at the cost of Takatsuka, Matsuki, Satō, and Utō, another heavy blow to the group. Matsuki was an ace (eight victories), while Utō, a highly promising youngster (nineteen kills), had blossomed in the last few months. Steady Takatsuka (sixteen kills) was a stalwart leader ever since joining in June. Two years ago to the day (13 September 1940), both he and Ōki had scored kills during the Zero fighter's premier combat over Chungking. On that day thirteen Zeros claimed twenty-seven of thirty Chinese fighters without loss. Now things certainly had changed.[40]

Afternoon Raid

Back on the ground after the morning's excitement, the pilots tried to grab lunch or take a little rest. The ground crews finished gassing the F4Fs of Longley's flight, and at 1130 they took off to cover the landings of the other F4Fs. At 1320, before all the Wildcats could be refueled and rearmed, Condition YELLOW sounded again, when radar found bogeys at 122 miles. Pilots ran for any available planes. From Fighter 1 eleven Marine F4Fs made it aloft, including seven flown by the VMF-212 and VMO-251 newcomers. VF-5 at the main field launched nine. The usual mad quest for altitude ensued. Mark Bright and Dix Loesch each formed on a flight of Marines. Cash Register trailed them. Sandy Crews rounded up three squadron mates—Rouse, Stover, and Wileman—but Simpler found no one, so he went out alone. So did Junior Kleinmann, who discovered his oxygen had not been recharged after the morning flight. He delayed his climb until the enemy came closer.[41]

The incoming raid comprised twenty-seven land attack planes that departed Vunakanau airfield at 1000 under Lt. Nakamura Tomoo, the Misawa *hikōtaichō*. His 1st *Chūtai* numbered seven Misawa and two *Chitose* planes. Nine Kisarazu *rikkōs* under Lt. Mine Hiroshi (NA 63-1936) formed the 2nd *Chūtai* on the left, while Lieutenant Doki's newly arrived Kanoya flight made up the 3rd *Chūtai* on the right. Each Type 1 carried the customary payload of one 250-kilogram and six 60-kilogram land bombs. Lieutenant Kawai's 1st *Chūtai* of six Tainan Zeros took station above and behind their starboard quarter; WO Yamashita Sahei's six moved into the corresponding slot on the left side.[42]

Nakamura's mission was to bomb suspected American positions at Taivu Point well east of Lunga. Base Air Force knew of the 8 September landing at Tasimboko, but incorrectly believed that the Marines had moved in to stay. Because of the lamentable lack of communication with the Army troops ashore, Southeast Area command did not realize that the Americans pulled out the same day. In reality Kawaguchi's rear echelon occupied the designated target area. The strike approached at 7,500 meters (24,600 feet).

Again excellent visibility afforded the Japanese a faraway view of Guadalcanal at 1305. Only at 1400 as Major Galer's mixed Marine-Navy division of four F4Fs passed 25,000 feet did they see the wide Japanese Vee over the channel. Continuing to climb, Galer drew 3,000 feet above the enemy's right side. One right after another, the four Wildcats rolled into steep high-side runs against Doki's Type 1s on the right. As usual, the Zero escorts could not immediately counter them. Galer, Robert Read (223), and 2nd Lt. George L. Hollowell (224) each claimed a bomber on this pass; in fact they holed several Kanoya *rikkōs*, one of which dropped out of formation. In his excitement Bright, the trailer, chose the lead bomber for his high-side, forcing an especially awkward approach. He smoked the *rikkō*, but to avoid collision he exited through the narrow gap *between* two more bombers (leader and one wingman) in a trailing *shōtai*. He did not ever want to repeat that experience. Aware of fighters above, Galer's division dived out before Kawai's pursuing *chūtai* could catch them.

While Galer pounded the right side, Major Dobbin's Marine-Navy division of three F4Fs reached 26,000 feet to the left of the bombers. Settling for a high-side, Dobbin pushed over. At the same time Dix Loesch, the "tail-end Charlie," sighted three Zeros screaming in: Yamashita's *shōtai*. Jack Conger (212) followed Dobbin, but before Loesch could accelerate away in his dive, Yamashita was on him. His bullets sang past Loesch's head. One 7.7-mm slug tore into his right upper thigh, whose violent involuntary reflex jerked the rudder pedal, flipping the F4F into a tight spin. Gunfire also broke an oil line, which showered hot oil in the cockpit. Loesch shut down the engine to stop the oil bath, recovered at a lower altitude, and glided toward the field. Setting down skillfully without power and flaps, he deliberately ground-looped off the upwind edge of the runway into rough ground to get his crippled plane off the runway. One of Lieutenant Commander Mackenzie's Australians helped him out of the cockpit and into the shelter of a bomb crater.[43]

Meanwhile, Dobbin and Conger pressed their assault against Mine's Kisarazu *chūtai* on the left and claimed one bomber apiece. Actually they riddled the aircraft flown by WO Satō Susumu, the 2nd *Shōtai* leader, and his left wingman PO2c Hayashi Yoshitaka. While Conger admired his handiwork on Hayashi's stricken Type 1, his own thick, bullet-proof windscreen disintegrated, spewing fragments of plexiglass all over the cockpit. One splinter lodged in his left eye; the top of his head smarted, and his left foot went numb. From dead astern a Zero had sieved the F4F with 7.7-mm and 20-mm fire. One bullet nicked the headrest and creased Conger's flight helmet right down the middle. Another stuck in his left shoe. Without even a glimpse of his ambusher, he rolled over and dived straight down. Only when Conger thought his tail was clear did he pull out. He barely made it back to base with his windscreen a "mess of cracks," the propeller hit three times, and "a bunch of six-inch holes" in the rear fuselage. PO1c Kaneko Toshio, Yamashita's 2nd *Shōtai* leader, was the main culprit, but given the beating inflicted, his two wingmen, PO3c Nakaya Yoshi-ichi and Sea1c Nakazawa Tsuneyoshi, got in their licks as well.[44]

Thus two pilots from Dobbin's flight were lucky to be alive after a vigorous counterattack by Yamashita's six Zeros. One F4F was forced down and the other so badly damaged that it was just stripped for parts. Loesch did not realize the bombers were so close and never saw Dobbin attack. Instead he was angry that his flight leader had not immediately scissored the Zeros, rather than supposedly trying to escape. For his own part Dobbin concentrated upon the bombers and did not perceive the threat.

The two lead fighter divisions had forced one Kanoya land attack plane out of formation and damaged several others. Register followed with an overhead pass from 24,500 feet and blasted PO2c Hayashi's already stricken Kisarazu *rikkō* away from its fellows. Suddenly his engine sputtered when the main fuel tank ran dry, so he switched to the small reserve. About the same time Kleinmann (flying alone at 20,000 feet) found himself beneath the descending bomber formation; indeed, he almost climbed right through it. To avoid a collision, he rolled out and down, then slid up behind the same straggler beset by Register. Hayashi's stricken *rikkō* dipped down into a fast dive, stalked by Kleinmann from below and behind. The tail gunner held the F4F off with 20-mm tracers. Despite a smoking left engine, Hayashi leveled out at 13,000 feet going north.

Meanwhile, Register restarted his engine and reprised with a high-side run that finally set Hayashi's left engine on fire. Low on gas, he could not make certain of his victory. His fuel gave out, and he dead-sticked onto the main field. Kleinmann pursued the *rikkō* to low altitude. At 500 feet Hayashi dumped bombs in order to lighten his ship, but two more high-side attacks by Kleinmann finished him off. Surviving a more or less controlled ditching, Hayashi's crew reached Vatilau, an island northwest of Florida. There on the 18th a patrol from Company F, 2nd Marines, killed Hayashi and took the other six aviators prisoner.[45]

Attaining 26,000 feet, Crews, Rouse, Stover, and Wileman confronted the bombers from ahead and to their right. They sighted no enemy fighters, because Kawai was busy brushing Galer away. With high-sides or overheads, the four F4Fs attacked Doki's Kanoya Type 1s now letting down below 22,000 feet. Results were mostly inconclusive. Another lone warrior, 2nd Lt. Clair C. Chamberlain of VMF-212, rolled into a high-side pass from above the three tight bomber Vees, but a poor angle ruined his shot. Climbing for another run, he singled out the right-hand Vee and walked his tracers into the trailing Kanoya *rikkō,* but it would not go down. Not bothered by Zeros, Chamberlain resolved to try again.[46]

Two VMO-251 pilots who got away a little later than the others, 2nd Lt. Robert M. Livingston and Master Technical Sgt. Wendell Garton, saw F4Fs work over the incoming enemy bomber formation. At 12,000 feet, Garton noticed a Zero (probably 1st *Chūtai*) sneak in from above, so he reefed into a sharp climbing turn to scissor, but the enemy broke off and rejoined the bombers. In the process he separated from Livingston. For some reason Garton's particular F4F (BuNo. 03424) enjoyed superior high-altitude performance and sailed right by another Grumman also bent for the bombers.

Nakamura's brood, now twenty-five in number, surprised the CAP by going beyond Lunga without attacking. Fifteen miles east, they finally salvoed their bombs onto Taivu Point and their own troops. Knowing no reason why the Japanese would bomb that locale, CACTUS thought the enemy jettisoned their payloads. Chamberlain from VMF-212 enjoyed a much closer look at the bomb release than he liked. For his third run he crossed over to the left side and confronted the outside *rikkō* in the left Vee from underneath. Suddenly bomb bays yawned open and nearly pummeled him with their cargoes. While he evaded, one of Yamashita's Zeros charged close behind and filled his fuselage with slugs that bounced off his armor plate. Without ever seeing his adversary, Chamberlain rolled into a steep spiral. At 4,000 feet the engine quit, and he flopped into the channel. The life raft was shot full of holes, so from his fish-eye vantage point, it looked like a long swim to anywhere.[47]

The long Japanese run to the east and their withdrawal north over Malaita gave VF-5 and at least one Marine time for additional attacks despite the danger from the escort. Alone on the right side, Crews persevered until one of Kawai's Zeros forced him to dive away. Stover had an identical experience and likewise came back with a hole in his tail. From 20,000 feet Simpler saw two Zeros savage a lone F4F beneath them. Racing to the rescue he shot tracers into the fuselage of one, then scissored for a head-on run. Like many another F4F pilot, he was astounded how quickly in a series of twists and turns a Zero could "walk" around onto his tail. In a bad spot, he also had to dive away. Willie Wileman in the other Wildcat sustained heavy damage. While he was attempting an emergency landing on Henderson Field, his F4F crashed and burst into flames, injuring him critically.

Garton, the VMO-251 NAP, still climbed after the bombers that he observed make a left turn over Malaita and head away at 20,000 feet. Cutting inside their turn, he stalked them from a couple of miles to their left and leveled out at 26,000 feet. Finally at 1415 he dived from out of the sun with a high-side pass against the left trailer, a Kisarazu *rikkō.* In his words, "buck fever" caused him to open fire too soon and bracket the target with his tracers. Suddenly about seven or eight angry Zeros "popped out of the formation as though propelled by springs." Alone and heavily outnumbered, Garton rolled into a steep dive toward home, marking VMO-251's last chance for many weeks for air combat at Guadalcanal.[48]

That afternoon Nakamura's force lost PO2c Hayashi's Kisarazu land attack plane; Warrant Officer Satō from the same group limped to Rekata and ditched. Shot-up Kanoya Type 1s commanded by PO1c Tashiro Eibu and PO2c Toda Jirō (with two dead aircrew) took refuge at Buka. The *rikkō* crews tallied four Grummans (one unconfirmed), while the Tainan pilots claimed nine (two unconfirmed) of ten Grummans they fought. The Zeros sustained not so much as a single bullet hole.

CACTUS victory credits totaled seven bombers: one each by Galer, Dobbin, Hollowell (224), Read (223), Conger (212), and Register and Kleinmann of VF-5. Bright (VF-5) received credit for one damaged. Two F4Fs were lost. From 212 Chamberlain went missing, last seen in a high-speed dive, and Wileman of VF-5 crashed, badly hurt. Loesch (VF-5) and Conger both landed their battered Wildcats immediately. For the time being, VF-5 had no idea what happened to Loesch and Wileman. Despite the losses the 1st MAW felt excited about the raid's results: "For the first time today, [we] outnumbered Tojo in the air & he turned and fled."[49] Not surprisingly, the Japanese would not have agreed with this assessment.

The Third Night at CACTUS

Reassembling on the ground after their second combat that day, the VF-5 pilots were heartened to greet Chief Glenn Poston and nineteen enlisted specialists just arrived from BUTTON. Now a plane captain cared for each VF-5 F4F. "Buck" Poston's men found their work cut out for them. Two days of battle cost VF-5 four airplanes, with four others shot full of holes and one down for repairs. That left only fifteen flyable out of the original twenty-four. Repair and maintenance facilities were extremely primitive, as was everything else on Guadalcanal. Wrecks lying south of the field provided most of the spare parts. Marines from VMF-223 and VMF-224 and sailors from CUB-1 greatly assisted the VF-5 ground crews. All of these mechanics, armorers, radiomen, and other specialists devoted long, hard hours to keep the planes going. They likewise endured the hardships of life at CACTUS: climate, insects, the poor, infrequent meals, and lack of sleep, not to mention the enemy. All too often Condition RED interrupted their work with a mad scramble for shelter to escape the inevitable bombs.

Because they were vital to the air defense of BUTTON, Longley's eleven VMO-251 pilots (all but the injured Rutledge) had to depart the next morning. Payne's orders merely specified the ferrying of F4Fs to Guadalcanal, so he asked Wallace's permission for his flight to remain at CACTUS. He joined 223 as XO in place of Major Morrell, wounded on 5 September and evacuated. Other 212 pilots had fought in 223, and Smith certainly welcomed this new batch.

Late that afternoon the VF-5 pilots sat near their newly issued ready tent pitched on the lee (southwest) side of Pagoda Hill. MAG-23 also furnished a field telephone and a young Marine orderly/driver now remembered only as "Red." An unforgettable, tragic event unfolded before the entire air wing. At about 1740, ground observers suddenly noticed two strange monoplanes cruising eastward over the Lunga coast. Big central floats extending beyond the props revealed them as float-Zeros. Passing low over the beach, they drew some small arms fire. At the same time a VMSB-231 SBD from the afternoon search approached on its downwind landing leg at 300 feet with gear and flaps down. The Japanese leader charged directly behind the unsuspecting dive bomber turning left on final. Men on the ground saw the ambush coming, but could not warn the victims. In anger and frustration some yelled, jumped up and down, and fired pistols into the air. One Marine even threw a rock.

Concerned about a possible American air base on Malaita, Jōjima had sent the *Kamikawa Maru*'s Type 2 sea fighters down to protect Rekata. Taking off at 1510

Pagoda Hill, with the RADAR ONE antenna beyond on the left and the VF-5 ready tent in the left foreground. (NA 80-G-20673)

from Shortland, WO Kawamura Makio and PO1c Kawai Jirō flew a sweep over Lunga to see if Japanese ground troops had indeed captured the airfield. Now easing into a slight left bank, Kawamura cut inside as the SBD crossed in front. A short burst quickly inflicted fatal damage. The smoking Dauntless dropped off leftward and plowed into the bivouac area of the 1st Amphibious Tractor Battalion in the trees beyond the Lunga River. Its 500-pound bomb detonated in the flames. Kawamura thought he had knocked down a Grumman fighter. Recovering from his pass, he kept on going west, while Kawai strafed a jeep loaded with 224 pilots bound for a wash in the river. The two Japanese reached Rekata at 1810. The dead SBD pilot was 2nd Lt. Owen D. Johnson, whose radioman, Cpl. Horace B. Thomas, had been a VMSB-241 Midway survivor. Their deaths, a dramatic event long remembered by the eyewitnesses, numbered only two of many. The hardworking, unsung SBD crews faced danger in numerous other ways. Another member of that particular search, Ens. Emory S. Wages, Jr., of VS-3, radioed he was ditching 130 miles southwest of Guadalcanal. Neither he nor radioman, James Henry, Sea1c, ever turned up again.[50]

As did several others, Smokey Stover manned a plane to pursue the two, but he totaled his F4F on takeoff. To add insult to injury, someone purloined his Colt .45 automatic, which in his haste he had left behind. That evening at the coconut grove where VF-5 pitched their tents, a sarcastic John L. Smith tactlessly chided the squadron, declaring they would never make it in the Corps, that Marines never lost track of their weapons. The next day his pistol disappeared from his cockpit and caused quite a stir. A few days later Smith's .45 suddenly reappeared. Suspicion fell on VF-5, but nothing could be proven. Years later Smith again let Wally Clarke know how peeved he was about the humiliating loss of his personal Colt.[51]

Only ten minutes after the ambush, a large formation of planes approached the field at low altitude. Unannounced, Lieutenant Commander Kirn brought from BUTTON twelve more VS-3 SBDs plus Swede Larsen with six torpedo-armed VT-8 TBFs. While MAG-23 challenged the intruders by radio, nervous AA gunners trained their weapons. VF-5 picked up rifles and pistols. Just as everyone was about to cut loose, they recognized the aircraft as friendly. McCain had certainly followed CinCPac orders and committed as many planes from the stranded *Saratoga* Air Group as CACTUS could handle.

After dark on the 13th, Kawaguchi's infantry again bravely stormed Bloody Ridge, only to be repulsed with severe losses by the equally courageous Marine defenders. On both flanks of the perimeter, Marines also beat off secondary attacks. Five-inch guns from the defense battalion dueled with enemy warships in the channel. MAG-23 deployed ground crews from several squadrons as infantry to protect the bivouac area should the enemy break through. Mechanics piled sandbags beneath their planes and made ready to defend them. Deafened by the sound and dazzled by the flashes of howitzers booming near their tents, VF-5

Glenn Poston, ACMM, VF-5's leading chief, stands next to F-16 (BuNo. 5200) on Guadalcanal, mid-October 1942. The legend beneath the cockpit reads "The Mole," indicating the assigned aircraft of Ens. Benjamin Currie. (Capt. H. W. Crews)

spent another sleepless night, but that was infinitely preferable to having a rising sun flag hoisted over the Pagoda.

In the hospital dugout Dix Loesch endured a horrifying night in pain and with men dying all around him. Overworked corpsmen could not even treat all of the wounded Marines so "densely packed and partially stacked on each other" were they. Near to Loesch, William Wileman breathed his last. The only fighter pilot to fly in all three carrier battles (Coral Sea, Midway, and Eastern Solomons), he was also the second member of VF-5 to die on Guadalcanal.[52]

14 SEPTEMBER

Float-Zero Attack

Before first light an ambulance carried Dix Loesch and three other wounded men to Henderson Field for evacuation. A pair of VMJ-253 R4D-1 transport planes that had come in the previous day lay stranded until dawn. One flown by Capt. John L. Whitaker, Jr., rested on the west edge of the runway, preparing to take off. Before the patients could be removed from the ambulance, heavy gunfire from the southeast suddenly landed all around them. At 0530 about fifty Japanese from the 2nd Battalion, 4th Infantry Regiment, broke through the defenses on the Marine left flank and advanced near to the southwest corner of Fighter 1, where they fought at close quarter with Company C, 1st Engineer Battalion. Bullets directed westward at the engineers fell around the R4D on the southwest corner of Henderson Field. The corpsmen ran for dubious "cover" on the other side of the airplane, and only after Loesch's quite vocal complaints did someone drive the ambulance around there as well.

Soon the Marine engineers repulsed the attackers, although a Japanese officer and two soldiers infiltrated their lines and nearly killed Vandegrift. Firing around the R4D ceased. Overloaded with personnel and captured equipment being sent back for evaluation, Whitaker got away safely after daybreak. "Frightened down" by the memory of float-Zeros the evening before, he stayed at 50 feet, although he was nearly blinded by the rising sun reflected on the water. Sun or no sun, this maneuver was fortunate, however, because a sea fighter flown by Lt. Ono Jirō, the *Kamikawa Maru buntaichō,* prowled the skies over Lunga. At Efate Loesch's right leg was operated on, and he began his convalescence.[53]

About the time the first R4D departed, all three flyable P-400s of the 67th FS took to the air. Led by Capt. John A. Thompson, they raked Kawaguchi's retreating troops from low altitude and prevented them from regrouping. The Army pilots fought until they had expended all of the ammunition from their mixed batteries of 20-mm cannons, .30- and .50-caliber machine guns. Massive ground fire hit Thompson's P-400 and also 2nd Lt. Bryan E. Brown's. They glided a mile or so to the field for deadstick landings.

Alerted by Kennedy on New Georgia, MAG-23 again deployed a standing CAP. Five VF-5 F4Fs under Crews and five VMF-224 led by Galer circled at high altitude, seemingly in good position when at 0930 the Pagoda sounded Condition YELLOW. At 0921 coastwatcher Geoffrey Kuper on Santa Isabel had warned of three aircraft going southeast. From Fighter 1 Smith departed with eleven F4Fs, and from the main field came Simpler with nine more. A newly arrived VMJ-253 R4D captained by Maj. Walter Frear Kimball followed VF-5 aloft.[54]

MAG-23 expected the usual enemy bombing raid. In fact, the opposition proved to be three more *Kamikawa Maru* Type 2 sea fighters from Rekata: Lt. (jg) Kawashima Masashi (NA 67-1939), Warrant Officer Kawamura, and PO2c Ōyama Toshio. Jōjima sent them south at 0800 to reconnoiter Lunga and see who controlled the airfield. Kawashima scouted the area looking for signs of friendly troops, but found only death.[55]

Seven VF-5 F4Fs formed up at 3,500 feet east of Henderson Field, manned by Simpler, Wesolowski, Clarke, Rouse, Green, Stover, and Morgan. About to climb in earnest, Simpler happened to sight Kimball's R4D at 1,500 feet in dire straits. After the three bandits came in low over Lunga, one jumped the transport plane with a high-side attack. Simpler's own swift high-side forced the float-Zero to break off and defend itself. While shooting, he curved in astern, and his bullets tore into the fuselage and started it smoking. Then all but one gun quit, so the skipper rolled out to let his wingman take over. Weasel Wesolowski braved a head-on pass from the Type 2, which turned sharply toward him. It passed over, then both planes reversed course for another scissor. Before they could close, the bandit rolled over on its back past Wesolowski, who lost sight of it.

Third behind the skipper, Wally Clarke used his diving speed to run the float-Zero right down to the waves. Letting down as far as he dared, the Japanese reefed up into a wingover, but Clarke triggered a three-second burst and had the speed to stay on target. The Nakajima turned back over the coast and leveled off nose-high over the jungle. Only two guns responded for Clarke's second salvo, but they were sufficient. The target smoked, then abruptly dived into the ground with a fiery explosion. Clarke's wingman, Will Rouse, also loosed a few rounds at this airplane just before it crashed. He did not see Clarke shoot and naturally thought he himself finished it.

While the first sea fighter succumbed to Clarke, two VF-5 pilots flushed more game. Larry Grimmell and Jim Halford left after the skipper and had not climbed as high. South of the field they spotted two float-Zeros coming in at low level. Grimmell's high-side run caused the trailer to evade violently. He ended up astern of the nimble float plane, but could not hit it. Instead he kept outside of its turns to prevent it from escaping north out to sea. It ran into a low-level buzzsaw in the form of Simpler's other three F4Fs. Despite its burden of the huge center float and two wing floats, the Type 2 enjoyed superior low-speed maneuverability and easily rolled out of the way of the Wildcats eagerly trying to bag it. After Fog Green's long head-on run, the bandit whipped around in a tight Immelmann and almost collided with Stover, who closed within 50 feet and pulled the trigger. Two remarkable things happened. The guns of his borrowed Marine F4F would not fire, and the cockpit filled with thick, acrid smoke when an oil line ruptured, spilling lubricant onto the hot engine. By the time Stover pushed back his canopy, took a breath, and recharged his guns, teammate George Morgan torched the Nakajima. According to Morgan, it "blew up in my face," so close that he felt the heat of the fire. Rouse got a piece of this airplane, after he saw another F4F score. Bits of the Nakajima fluttered to the ground.

While the wingman fell to Morgan, Halford went after the leader, who turned south. Using his superior diving speed, he cut inside the twisting Nakajima and tailed in behind for a good burst. Over the "crater" (Mount Austen) he set the float-Zero on fire. The enemy swung north toward the sea, rolled his stricken mount, and bailed out northeast of Lunga. Halford pursued and killed the parachutist. Like many Japanese, he, too, gave no quarter. Later that year he described his feelings in the matter:

> It's true the Japanese go after American fellows who bail out. And we do likewise. After all, the planes are expendable, but the pilots aren't. If we let a Nip pilot get away, he may get us the next time.[56]

Other naval flyers certainly shared Halford's attitude. Much later Paul Mankin recounted discussions with Whitey Mehlig, VF-6 XO, over shooting enemy aviators who bailed out or strafing crews from planes that had crashed. Mehlig chivalrously averred he would never do so. Mankin did not agree:

> I never understood his point of view. I later learned of Mehlig's end [killed 21 February 1945 when two Kamikazes struck the CVE *Bismarck Sea*] and often thought was it a pilot that possibly had been shot down, bailed out and lived to fight another day.[57]

Circumstances dictated, however, that few Americans ever faced that choice. Averse to being taken prisoner, Japanese pilots rarely parachuted.

The exciting low-level melee over the field cost the R-Area Air Force its entire reconnaissance flight: Kawashima, Kawamura, and Ōyama. VF-5 reckoned they fought four enemy planes and parceled out credit to Clarke, Morgan, Halford, and Rouse. The only damage sustained in return was the burned-out engine of Stover's Marine F4F, which nevertheless brought him back safely. The float-Zeros proved no match for Wildcats.

The morning's action also made a strong impression on "Skip" Kimball's crew. On 25 September they returned with a thank-you note and a thoughtful gift: a quart of Australian "Green River" whiskey, which Kimball had reportedly purchased for $20. That evening VF-5 drank to the health of the R4D crews who regularly made the long, dangerous supply flights to CACTUS. An airline pilot and a Marine reservist since 1931, Kimball fatally crashed on 9 October during a night takeoff from Tontouta.[58]

Another Reconnaissance

Because Japanese search planes had spotted American carriers the previous day, Tsukahara held his land attack planes in reserve to protect Rabaul. Instead, eleven Model 21 Zeros flown by Lieutenant Kurakane's 2nd Air Group departed at 0945 for a fighter sweep against Guadalcanal, followed a quarter hour later by Lieutenant Hayashi's Type 2 land reconnaissance plane to evaluate the situation at Lunga. One Zero aborted immediately, then WO Wajima Yoshio, the 2nd *Chūtai* leader, ditched at Shortland. Two others made emergency landings at Buka, leaving only seven fighters for Guadalcanal.[59]

At 1315 without prior coastwatcher warning, MAG-23 called a Condition YELLOW alert, when radar detected Kurakane on the way in. Simpler took twelve VF-5 F4Fs aloft from Henderson Field, while Galer, Dobbin, and Payne led another dozen up from the fighter strip. On takeoff, Gene Trowbridge (an ace with 223) struck a fuel drum that threw his barely airborne F4F into Dean Hartley (224) taxiing along the runway. Trowbridge suffered severe injuries, and his F4F was wrecked. Above 20,000 feet the Marines tangled with an estimated ten Zeros. Galer and Dobbin claimed two, but 2nd Lt. Orvin H. Ramlo (223) took a bullet in the hip. From VF-5 only Green's division fought that afternoon. Several bandits scattered the F4Fs as they hunted through the clouds for bombers.

Kurakane claimed ten (three unconfirmed) of twenty Grummans encountered, but in return lost PO1c Magara Kōichi, a veteran with eight kills.

The 2nd Air Group fought and retired before Hayashi's reconnaissance plane approached Henderson Field from the south at 4,500 meters (14,763 feet). He instructed his pilot, PO1c Takahashi Jirō, to let down to 3,000 meters (9,842 feet) and circle the field. Unlike the previous day, the Type 2 drew Marine and VF-5 Wildcats like a magnet. Not having actually seen one before, the pilots were surprised by this new type of enemy aircraft, which Lieutenant Colonel Munn, 1st MAW intelligence officer, guessed was some sort of German Focke-Wulf bomber. From Green's division, Roach made two runs, the first a long overhead and the second a high-side against the camouflaged Nakajima. Takahashi responded by diving at very high speed toward a large cloud, but Roach raced close up the tail and emptied his guns before breaking off. His bullets seemed to hit, but he saw no effect and guessed incorrectly that the new twin-engine plane was armored. Bright enjoyed the height and position for no fewer than six runs, again without slowing the exceptionally speedy target. Halford claimed a probable. From the ground, Smokey Stover noted, "Everyone shot at him and finally got him smoking as he went into [a] cloud."[60]

Finally Frazier and Lees of 223 scored the kill. In excess of 200 knots they chased the strange aircraft over 50 miles and braved return fire from both its rear turret and the unique remote-controlled tail gun. One engine tore completely away before the shattered Type 2 finally succumbed. Hayashi and his crew perished. The Lunga reception committee bespoke eloquently of the real situation on Guadalcanal. From the many intercepts, CACTUS thought three Focke-Wulfs flew the mission and that one went down.[61]

All-out Attack

As the nearest source of air support for Guadalcanal, the R-Area Air Force was determined to do its best. That afternoon Jōjima committed most of his air strength for a strike led by the *Chitose hikōtaichō*, Lieutenant Horihashi. He received nineteen Mitsubishi F1M2 Type 0 observation seaplanes (eight *Chitose*, two *Kamikawa Maru*, four *Sanyō Maru*, and five *Sanuki Maru*), each armed with a pair of 60-kilogram land bombs. Four Nakajima A6M2-N Type 2 sea fighters from the *Kamikawa Maru* were to escort. Stopping at Rekata to refuel, only twenty-one aircraft (less two Type 2s not sent) departed around 1640 in three flights. Hoping to catch enemy fighters on the ground, Horihashi swung well south of Guadalcanal to sneak in over the mountains.[62]

At 1730 MAG-23 scrambled five VMF-224 and six VF-5 F4Fs after radar discovered something cooking. Above 7,000 feet a thick overcast dispersed them into several flights. The radar plot showed something strange about the approaching bogeys. Bayler warned that the enemy seemed to be circling southwest at 7,500 feet. From high altitude Simpler and Dobbin, the two flight leaders, dropped back through the clouds trying to find the enemy before sunset at 1815.[63]

While flying alone, Stover attained 24,000 feet before he heard Bayler's warning and dived. Breaking into the clear above 8,000 feet, he caught sight of two float-Zeros nearing the southwest coast. They were Lieutenant Ono and PO2c Ōmura Matsutarō coming in at 2,500 meters (8,200 feet). Ono countered by turning up into the F4F for head-on runs. Stover followed through with an opposite attack against the leader, but while he was recovering, the wingman came around in a wingover directly in front. This amounted to nearly a full-deflection shot, but Stover was equal to the challenge. Streaming smoke, Ōmura stalled while trying a slow roll, dropped in flames, and plowed into a hillside. Meanwhile, Ono evaded by heading west at high speed before turning back toward Lunga. He claimed one of two Grummans for the loss of his wingman.

At 1820 the nineteen Type 0s appeared at 2,000 meters (6,561 feet) just southeast of Lunga. In the deepening darkness most F4Fs missed the enemy, but over the field John Dobbin and George Hollowell of 224 spotted the two formations of float biplanes below 7,000 feet. They split up so each man could deal with one flight. Dobbin confronted Horihashi's lead *shōtai* of three *Chitose* Type 0s and flashed through a high-side run against one float plane that climbed, then fell off on one wing. WO Izumiyama Hiroshi in number 2 took an ineffective shot at the F4F, before Dobbin tore into the third float plane silhouetted in the sky above. Under the impact of his bullets, it likewise nosed up, then fell away to one side. In this attack he shot down the number 3 plane (PO2c Yamanaka Fujirō) and badly damaged Horihashi's number 1 aircraft. In turn Horihashi neatly credited himself and the missing Yamanaka with one Grumman apiece. Meanwhile, Hollowell bounced Lt. Yoneda Tadashi's flight and shot up Lt. (jg) Watanabe Kaneshige's *Sanuki Maru shōtai*. He certainly disrupted their attack and badly damaged PO2c Yamada Ichisaku's number 2 plane.

From 1825 to 1830 more than a dozen antiquated-looking biplanes in shallow glide attacks scattered small fragmentation bombs all over the CACTUS landscape. First in were about eight *Chitose* and *Kamikawa Maru* Type 0s, then Yoneda brought six more from the *Sanyō Maru* and *Sanuki Maru*. Four or five actually hit Henderson Field, but only finished off a P-400 consigned to the junk pile. Still, one bomb exploded about 90 feet from Green, who described how the concussion "shook" his "eye teeth." He fought the small fire ignited by the blast.[64]

Scanning the growing darkness, Dobbin happened to sight the *Chitose* 2nd *Shōtai* under Lt. (jg) Kuromaru Naoto (NA 67-1939) withdrawing north toward destroyers *Sterett* (DD-407) and *Hull* escorting two transports in mid-channel waiting to unload. The *Sterett*'s five-inchers forced him to sheer off. Returning to the field, he encountered Yoneda head-on and set the seaplane on fire, just as Simpler swooped in with a high-side. Its bright red flames lighted up the near darkness. Either Yoneda, the pilot, or WO Satō Yoshiharu, his observer, jumped, but horribly the man "burned while descending in his chute similar to a parachute flare."[65] Japanese aviators paid dearly for the lack of protected fuel tanks.

Tracers and shell bursts erupting over the darkened field alerted other F4F pilots to the enemy's presence. Stover cut across their line of retreat over the channel and in the fading light picked out an airplane at low altitude near Savo. Observing a biplane, he needed to come quite close before distinguishing it from a friendly Curtiss SOC float plane. This time in a "real dogfight," he chased his aerobatic antagonist through about five tight scissors while narrowly avoiding the rear gunner. Finally his superior firepower told. About five miles east of Savo, the biplane set down hard with about "ten bounces," but would not burn even after Stover expended all his ammunition. He felt certain this bird would never fly again.[66] However, Watanabe's own *Sanuki Maru* Type 0 (pilot Sea1c Takayasu Hiroshi) survived a long fight from 1840 to 1900 with a Grumman and reached base.

Climbing high above the overcast, Weasel Wesolowski of VF-5 also missed the actual bombing, but north of Savo he encountered about eight float biplanes, *Chitose* and *Kamikawa Maru* Type 0s, joining up at 5,500 feet. Light still creased the western horizon and silhouetted the formation, so Wesolowski bounced the trailer (PO2c Nishiyama Akio from the *Kamikawa Maru* Squadron) with an over-head attack. His first bursts set it on fire, then he pulled up behind the *shōtai* leader, Spec. Duty Ens. Shimura Mamoru, and shot until it also appeared to stream flames from beneath its cowling. Confident he finished off two aircraft, Wesolowski broke off and returned to base while the fading light still pointed the way. Other than Yamanaka (Dobbin's victim), all nine of Horihashi's flight reached Rekata. However, Wesolowski left nine bullet holes in Nishiyama's Type 0.

At 1945 Wesolowski touched down last of all at CACTUS. Total claims amounted to nine float planes (three each to Dobbin and Hollowell, Wesolowski two, and Stover one) and Stover's one float-Zero. Machine gunners from the 3rd Defense Battalion's Special Weapons Group reported downing two more enemy aircraft. Jubilation at CACTUS rang down the curtain on an exceptionally busy day. The Japanese had shot their bolt and failed. Bloody Ridge was generally quiet, as Kawaguchi's battered infantry stumbled back into the jungle.

Seventeen Type 0s and one Type 2 reached Rekata long after dark. Horihashi capsized while setting down off shore, and his Type 0 burned. PO2c Yamada's *Sanuki Maru* Type 0 suffered heavy damage, and he was wounded. In addition, two Type 0s (one *Chitose*, one *Sanyō Maru*) and one Type 2 failed to return. In return, the Japanese claimed five Grummans (including one unconfirmed) and numerous aircraft bombed on the airfield. Only seldom did Jōjima's flyers return to the unfriendly skies over Lunga. Thereafter they flew mainly searches and convoy protection for the Tokyo Express with many more brave fights against CACTUS aircraft. Before dawn on 15 September a *Sanyō Maru* Type 0 recon-naissance seaplane thoroughly checked out Lunga and reported that the Allies definitely held the airfield. That morning Base Air Force finally learned of the failure of the Kawaguchi Detachment.

CHAPTER 11

The Loss of the *Wasp*

As related previously, at dawn 13 September the *Wasp* and *Hornet* dispatched the eighteen Marine Wildcat reinforcements to Guadalcanal. That vital task accomplished, Rear Admiral Noyes stood eastward from San Cristobal toward Vanikoro to resume the original flanking position east of Santa Cruz. He was aware that carriers and a powerful battleship-cruiser force might be north of the Solomons. Ironically, he did not suspect that Japanese losses in August and early September rendered relative carrier air strengths in favor of TF-61's two carriers with 154 USN planes (69 VF, 59 VB, and 26 VT) to 129 Japanese on the *Shōkaku, Zuikaku,* and *Zuihō* (55 VF, 31 VB, 42 VT, 1 VR).

The morning searches from both sides gave results. Just after 1100, TF-61 learned that a PBY from Espiritu Santo had spotted two enemy cruisers immediately north of the Santa Cruz Islands. Noyes raced toward them for several hours while AirSoPac loosed strikes of B-17s and PBYs, but these "cruisers" proved to be phantoms. The Japanese were more successful. At 1110 Spec. Duty Lt. (jg) Mizukura Kiyoshi, a wily old hand who commanded a Rabaul-based Kawanishi Type 2 flying boat from the 14th Air Group Detachment, placed an American carrier force bearing 123 degrees and 345 miles from Tulagi. In fact, Mizukura's crew sighted a TF-61 carrier and joined the select few who lived to tell of it. Unfortunately for vice admirals Kondō and Nagumo, TF-61 moved southeast out of strike range and by dark cleared Vanikoro to the east.[1]

That evening ComSoPac formally implemented Turner's plan to transport the 7th Marines to Guadalcanal and incorporated the transports and escorts (Rear Admiral Wright's TF-64) as TF-65 under his personal command. They were to depart Espiritu Santo the morning of 14 September and reach Lunga two days later. Following Noyes's advice, Ghormley ordered the carrier neither to send planes to CACTUS nor to fly antisub patrols for the transports. TF-61's mission was to guard Turner's ships from enemy naval forces, particularly carriers, while the 1st MAW furnished close air cover around Guadalcanal. Ignorant of Turner's proposed track, Noyes accosted a passing PBY to pass on a message. In the meantime he reversed course west toward the channel between Vanikoro and Banks Island toward TF-65.

On 14 September the *Wasp* took the duty, flying routine CAPs and searches, while the *Hornet* held her strike group spotted on deck for swift launch. That day the *Wasp* was to see a major shift in command personnel: Cdr. Michael H. Kernodle, the air officer, would relieve XO Cdr. Fred C. Dickey, due for promotion and a new assignment. Newly promoted Commander Beakley, the air group commander, would become air officer, Lieutenant Commander Shands was to fleet up to group, while Lieutenant Commander Strickler became CO of VF-71. Because a battle threatened, Captain Sherman kept them in their old jobs for the time being.[2]

By 1000 TF-61 had returned south of Vanikoro, with Turner's TF-65 drawing up about 140 miles south of them. Noyes intended to operate about 100 miles northeast of the transports and interpose his carriers between them and any threat from the north. That threat soon appeared. At 1035 Noyes received the message, "Sighted enemy fleet Latitude 7°50′ Longitude 164°35′," from PBY 91-P-8 (Lt. Glen E. Hoffman) covering 334 to 341 degrees from Espiritu Santo. At 1020 Hoffman spotted Kondō's Advance Force northwest of Santa Cruz.[3] Like the other Japanese forces, Kondō eagerly sought the carrier that Mizukura had located the previous day.

At 1045 Hoffman's amplifying report came over as *four* enemy battleships and *seven* carriers on course 140 degrees, speed 17 knots. That placed this formidable force 325 miles north-northwest of TF-61 and closing. To forestall possible carrier strikes on Turner's transports, Noyes resolved to attack. At 1101 he changed course to 330 degrees and upped speed to 23 knots—all he and Sherman could risk from the *Wasp*'s suspect engines. The prospect of carrier battle loomed if the Japanese did not turn away.

At 1140 Hoffman corrected his original contact report to three battleships, four cruisers, four destroyers, and one transport, on 140 degrees, speed 18 knots. Sixteen minutes later TF-61 copied another PBY sighting report. Lt. (jg) Baxter E. Moore's 23-P-4 searching directly north (354–001 degrees) from Espiritu Santo located one Japanese carrier, three cruisers, and four destroyers about 200 miles north of Hoffman's contact. In fact, he had found Nagumo's Striking Force, but the *Shōkaku* launched six Zeros to intercept. Moore's harrowing last words sounded over the radio: "We're going down in flames."[4] The Japanese registered the kill at 1146, and no Americans survived.

Even without carriers, the powerful force ferreted out by Hoffman still represented a serious menace to Turner. Noyes opted for a "tactical scouting group" of *Wasp* SBDs armed with 500-pound bombs to search ahead of the *Hornet* strike group, locate possible targets for the *Hornet* flyers, then regroup and deliver their own attacks. The carriers would send follow-up strikes if the situation warranted.

At about 1315 TF-61 turned southeast into the wind. The *Wasp* launched a relief CAP of eight VF-71 F4Fs, four VS-71 SBDs for antisub patrol, and the scouting force of fourteen VS-72 SBDs under Lieutenant Commander Snowden to cover the sector 306 to 354 degrees from Ndeni. Simultaneously the *Hornet* dispatched the following strike:

CHAG	Cdr. Walt Rodee	1 TBF-1
VF-72	Lt. Cdr. Mike Sanchez	16 F4F-4s
VS-8 and VB-8	Lt. Cdr. Gus Widhelm	16 SBD-3s
VT-6	Lt. Edwin Parker	6 TBF-1s

Widhelm's Dauntlesses each carried one 1,000-pound bomb, while Parker's Avengers lugged two 1,000-pounders apiece in lieu of torpedoes. As Fletcher feared, conservative carrier tacticians opted for glide bombing rather than the much more deadly torpedo attack.

After the strike departed, Noyes resumed at 1340 a northwesterly course (300 degrees) at 20 knots to cut the distance to the enemy. He expected an air attack at any time. So did Rear Admiral McCain at Espiritu Santo, who ordered all ships but the seaplane tenders *Curtiss* (AV-4), *Mackinac,* and *McFarland* (AVD-14) to depart Santo immediately. Ray Davis's VB-6 flew a special afternoon search, while all the AirSoPac Army Martin B-26 Marauder medium bombers staged from New Caledonia to Espiritu Santo.

After two hours of nervous waiting, TF-61 intercepted a report at 1535 relayed by the *Curtiss,* because Japanese radio jamming prevented the carriers from receiving the PBY directly. Hoffman had noted at 1415 that the enemy ships reversed course to 005 degrees, 20 knots. The Japanese search had failed to sight the U.S. carriers, so Yamamoto ordered Kondō's entire Support Force to retire north to refuel. That unwittingly allowed Kondō to escape detection by the *Wasp* SBDs. Snowden's VS-72 crews went out almost 280 miles, but later calculations placed them just 50 miles short of the Advance Force. Rodee (USNA 1926) took the *Hornet* strike a full 225 miles, but likewise returned without finding any targets. However, Kondō did not escape a strike group of Army B-17 Flying Fortresses from Espiritu Santo. At about 1615 they bombed a "battleship" and claimed three hits. Actually they put a bomb alongside the CA *Myōkō.*

Aware that his strike headed back, Noyes turned southeast at 1600 into the wind. Beginning at 1648 the *Hornet* landed her thirty-nine planes, and the *Wasp* recovered her SBDs a half hour later. TF-61 closed shop after a day of blunted expectations, one of the great "almosts" of the Guadalcanal campaign. If carrier planes had pounded Kondō, Nagumo would have rushed to his aid and set the stage for a melee on the 15th. Privy to the latest CinCPac intelligence bulletin, which warned of the continued offensive against Guadalcanal, Noyes expected the danger to continue.

At 2300, 14 September, Noyes turned west at 16 knots to regain proper covering position for TF-65. A wary Turner decided to see what the 15th would bring before continuing the advance to Guadalcanal. He also waited for the cargo ship *Bellatrix* (AK-20) carrying vitally needed aviation gasoline for CACTUS. Noyes retained the *Wasp* as the duty carrier and reserved the *Hornet* for possible strikes. Perhaps the lack of belly tanks for VF-71's Wildcats, which prevented them from flying long escort missions, influenced his decision. Unlike the previous day, the morning of the 15th proved surprisingly quiet, as the enemy had steamed north out of range.

The first suspicious contact came at 1105, when the *Hornet*'s radar detected a "large" bogey bearing 275 degrees and 38 miles. The *Wasp* FDO, Lt. Frank G. Marshall, Jr., controlled the CAP, but her CXAM radar did not register intruders until they closed within 30 miles. He sent Lt. Downs Wright's VF-71 division west to investigate. About 18 miles out the four F4Fs encountered an enemy four-engine flying boat cruising at 1,800 feet. It was the Kawanishi Type 97 commanded by Lt. Yoneyama Shigeru (NA 64-1937), Tōkō Air Group *buntaichō.* This day he flew the 121-degree line from Shortland. He tried evading the fighters with a diving left turn, but Lt. (jg) John A. McBrayer, Wright's 2nd Section leader, closed in with an above-rear attack. Braving accurate gunfire from the side blister, he directed his bullets into the center of the mottled black wing near to the inboard engines. The big Kawanishi caught fire and plunged into the water. McBrayer chalked up VF-71's second aerial victory.[5]

Opinion differed as to whether the snooper had sighted TF-61. Shipboard watchers easily observed the dark pillar of smoke rising in the west. At any rate

Shortland never monitored a contact report from Yoneyama. Drawing near to where the Kawanishi splashed, at 1230 lookouts from the *Wasp* and her escorts observed two men floating on the water, so the *Helena* (CL-50) directed the *Farenholt* (DD-491) to investigate. She sighted wreckage and lowered a boat; the bodies of two Japanese aviators were discovered and their papers removed.

Leaving the *Farenholt* astern, TF-61 continued west on 280 degrees. At 1320 the *Wasp* and her screening ships (TF-18) turned southeast into the wind for flight operations, while five miles northeast Murray's *Hornet* group (TF-17) matched the maneuver. The *Wasp* dispatched fourteen VS-71 SBDs under Lieutenant Commander Eldridge on afternoon search and four from VS-72 for IAP. One SBD dropped on the *Hornet*'s flight deck a message from Noyes to Murray, stressing the vital need for all possible support to Turner and giving a new base course. A relief CAP of eight F4Fs (Lieutenant Commander Strickler and Lieutenant Rooney) followed the eighteen SBDs aloft, with Roland Kenton's F-12 the last to leave the *Wasp*'s flight deck.

The *Wasp* immediately landed eight VF-71 F4Fs (Russell's and Wright's divisions) and three VS-72 SBDs. Sherman ordered the SBDs struck below to the hangar deck and sixteen F4Fs brought up ready to take off. The *Wasp* was to be the reserve carrier on the 16th, so she needed to prepare the strike group before dark. Plane handlers pushed Russell's four F4Fs aft to Fly III abaft the island for fuel and made ready to strike below Wright's four, which had downed the Kawanishi. Thirty-seven aircraft crowded the hangar deck. Forward of the number 2 (center) elevator sat twelve F4Fs fueled and armed, four SBDs in the same condition, and the J2F amphibian duck secured without fuel or payload. One TBF armed with a torpedo but without fuel rested adjacent to the number 2 elevator, and nine more Avengers in the same condition were abaft the lift, along with six armed and gassed SBDs. Four more F4Fs hung as spares from the hangar overhead, two fore and two aft. The hangar deck crew prepared the twelve F4Fs to go up the number 2 elevator to the flight deck.

Flight operations completed for the time being, TF-61 turned starboard at 1342 to resume the base course of 280 degrees at 16 knots. Three minutes later while the *Wasp* still came about, her lookouts were horrified to see torpedoes churning directly toward the starboard bow. They were already too close to permit evasive action.

Unwittingly Noyes had penetrated the center of a scouting line of Japanese submarines arrayed from northeast to southwest. At 1250 Cdr. Kinashi Taka-ichi's *I-19* glimpsed an enemy task force 15 kilometers to the northeast and soon recognized one carrier. TF-61's dogleg to the southeast for flight operations drew the *Wasp* group right across Kinashi's bow. At the same time the *I-26* to the northeast spotted TF-17 as well, but too far away to attack. Not so for the *I-19*. With a spread of six torpedoes, Kinashi unleashed the single most devastating salvo of the war.[6]

While circling the carrier, Ens. Millard "Red" Thrash, a VF-71 CAP pilot, looked goggle-eyed at "two water spouts rearing high above the superstructure; smoke and flame bursting out amidships."[7] The first torpedo slammed into the *Wasp*'s starboard bow, ruptured aviation gasoline tanks, and let the sea into the five-inch gun handling room and powder magazines. A few seconds later the second fish struck the hull under the forward 1.1-inch gun mount just ahead of the island, tore open more aviation gasoline storage tanks, and flooded the bomb magazines. Twenty seconds later a third explosion traveled up the bomb elevator trunk and blew its armored hatch cover onto the flight deck. Gasoline vapor from leaking tanks triggered this blast, which many incorrectly thought came from another torpedo.

Tremendous shock and concussion reverberated throughout the ship. Tossed into the air, most of the aircraft dropped with such force that their landing gear collapsed. The F4Fs slung in the hangar overhead fell onto planes parked below, creating a horrible tangle of smashed metal and ruptured fuel tanks. Ahead of the number 2 elevator, leaking fuel ignited three SBDs. Thick, black smoke engulfed the hangar deck and hid the forward spaces, where falling F4Fs had squashed other Wildcats parked underneath. Burning gasoline ran into the starboard forward five-inch gun platform and touched off the ready ammunition. Below on the second deck, fires fed by aviation fuel lines fractured by the second torpedo spread inside and outside along the hull. Deep inside the ship another intense fire blazed from gasoline leaking out of buckled storage tanks. Within seconds the *Wasp* faced mortal danger. All lights in the forward half of the ship failed. The damaged forward fire mains lacked water pressure, which crippled fire fighting. She soon took on an 11-degree list to starboard.

About a dozen VF-71 pilots from Russell's, Leonard's, and Wright's divisions had been lounging in the squadron ready room on the starboard side near the island. Not on duty, the skipper's and Charlie Moffett's divisions had been forward in officer's country, resting in their rooms or relaxing in the wardroom—close to both torpedo hits. While Sam Forrer, for one, reclined in his bunk, a Pullman-type hinged affair, it closed three times in response to the three explosions. He was fortunate to escape.[8] The blast and subsequent blazes from the shattered fueling system killed several VS-72 pilots sleeping in their rooms. Jack Singer, the INS correspondent who flew the 24 August *Ryūjō* strike, was typing a story in the wardroom lounge when the first torpedo's impact hurled him fatally against a bulkhead. Eight black mess attendants, officer's cooks, and stewards from VF-71 died when the second torpedo blew up directly below the officer's galley. Intense flames quickly isolated officer's country and the area forward of the first torpedo hit, then spread through the crews' quarters to the portside five-inch gun platform. Cut off from the rest of the ship, the survivors hurried forward to the forecastle, but flames soon forced them over the side, where the *Duncan* (DD-485) closed in to pick them up. Among others, Lt. Frank M. Plake, a VF-71 A-V(S) officer, was commended for his part in getting men off the ship safely.

Monk Russell, the flight officer, took charge in the VF-71 ready room and brought the pilots up to the flight deck, where tall flames raged forward of the island. The fires cooked off the ready ammunition, five-inch, 1.1-inch, and 20-mm rounds, which scattered shrapnel all over the deck. To clear the island of the thick, black smoke, Sherman slowed to 10 knots, ordered left full rudder to place the wind on the starboard bow, then backed until the breeze blew from the starboard quarter. Engineers initiated counterflooding and soon reduced the list to 4 degrees.

Lt. Cdr. John J. Shea, assistant air officer, led the repair party on the flight deck, where the remaining F4Fs were in a shambles. Because the *Wasp* listed so quickly, several actually had rolled off the flight deck into the sea and floated tail up before sinking. Concussion had "caved in" the landing gear of the rest, and the fuel in their tanks posed a great menace. Russell divided his pilots among several parties of plane handlers pushing the crippled fighters over the starboard

The *Wasp* maneuvers to clear smoke from the flight deck, 15 Sept. 1942. (NA 80-G-13705)

quarter. When John McBrayer realized he was jettisoning the Wildcat in which he scored his victory, he relented and went over to another.

Forward on the *Wasp,* great fires grew out of control, punctuated by exploding bombs, ammunition, and gasoline. From his overhead vantage, Thrash described the horrible sight:

> Clouds of bright red fire erupted from both sides below the flight deck, billowing out 200 yards, leaving black smoke streamers and scattering little pools of fire on the water. Sprays of red, yellow, and green Very lights shot out like Roman candles.[9]

In the smoke-filled hangar, Lt. Raleigh C. Kirkpatrick, recently transferred from VF-71, and Lt. William H. Staples worked desperately to contain the inferno spreading from the tangle of smashed planes forward of the number 2 elevator, but crews could not approach them. Others enmeshed farther aft could not be separated to be pushed over the side. Gear and spare parts falling out of the overhead greatly imperiled the frantic repair crews, as did exploding bombs and bullets. "Ammunition going off weakened the bravest heart who wanted to fight the fire."[10] VF-71 personnel helped to combat the relentless flames that threatened the island.

At 1405 gasoline vapor touched off another huge explosion ahead of the island. A cloud of burning gasses swept over the bridge and blew the number 2 1.1-inch mount completely off its base. To watchers on the surrounding ships, it appeared everyone on the *Wasp*'s bridge, perhaps including both Noyes and Sherman,

Inferno on the *Wasp*, 15 Sept. 1942. (NA 80-G-16550)

must have died. Remarkably both men survived, but Noyes suffered burns. Sherman left the shattered bridge and retreated aft to Battle II.

Because the flight deck blazed forward of the palisades, Shea's flight deck repair party crossed over to the portside walkway ahead of the number 2 elevator, while Russell's men jettisoned all but one F4F, which was parked too close to the fire to risk moving. At 1410 another vapor explosion, this time directly under the number 2 elevator, tossed the elevator platform high into the air. It fell back and lay askew across the deck opening. Shea and his entire repair party perished, but Russell's VF-71 pilots escaped. Gasoline leaking from its tanks set the last F4F on fire.

In Battle II Sherman questioned his department heads and consulted the injured Noyes; then, at 1420, only 35 minutes after the first explosion, he reluctantly decided to abandon ship. As he later described, the carrier was "pretty well shattered from number two elevator well down and forward at least to the splinter deck."[11] The senior officers spread the word to the crew to assemble aft on the flight deck and prepare to evacuate over the stern. Along with others, VF-71 personnel helped move the injured. In the hangar Don Reeves joined a party throwing mattresses over the side to serve as ersatz rafts. Others stripped aircraft of rubber boats. Fuel oil and gasoline burning on the water surrounded the *Wasp* and endangered those swimming away.

The *I-19*'s salvo not only created the *Wasp* conflagration, but threatened other ships as well. Those torpedoes that missed the carrier plowed northeast through the rest of TF-18 toward Murray's TF-17 some five to seven miles away. At 1351 one fish slammed into the port bow of the *O'Brien* (DD-415) screening the battleship *North Carolina* and the *Hornet*. Fortunately no crew suffered injuries, but she sustained severe structural damage and later sank while en route to Pearl Harbor. A minute later another torpedo tore open a hole 32 by 15 feet in the *North Carolina*'s port bow, flooded the forward magazines, and killed five men. She took an immediate 5.5-degree list to port, but was not in any real danger. Her list quickly corrected, she could make 25 knots. (Later that evening Murray detached the wounded battleship and two destroyers directly to Tongatabu.) Murray quickly turned TF-17 away east to escape the sub-infested waters. Soon the *Wasp* was visible only as a pillar of smoke on the western horizon. He assumed temporary command of TF-61 and planned to head east until 0700 the next morning, before turning southeast for Santo.

At 1418, just as Sherman determined to abandon ship, RAdm. Norman Scott on the *Juneau* (CL-52) assumed tactical command of TF-18 and sent the *Aaron Ward* and *Duncan* (already loaded with *Wasp* forecastle survivors) to join cruisers *San Francisco, Salt Lake City,* and *Helena* churning at high speed around the stricken carrier. The *Juneau* and the *Farenholt, Lansdowne* (DD-486), *Laffey* (DD-459), and *Lardner* (DD-487) proceeded with the rescue of personnel.

Soon after 1420 the rest of the *Wasp*'s crew queued up on the flight deck and in an orderly fashion went down lines or jumped over the side. Fires raced through amidships spaces and shot upward through big holes in her hull, which glowed cherry red in some places. From overhead Thrash saw "hundreds of faces" in the oil-soaked water and worried about patches of flaming gasoline that threatened the swimmers. At about 1500 Noyes and finally Sherman left the *Wasp* and found their way to the *Farenholt*.

While Courtney Shands swam away, someone jumped 40 feet from the deck and landed directly onto his back. Despite his injuries, he helped a disabled man reach a nearby destroyer. On the way, despite all that had occurred, he enjoyed a laugh. Ray ("Tubby") Conklin from VF-71 swam up surprisingly fast despite also having a wounded man under tow. He offered to trade his bigger charge for the smaller man being assisted by the skipper, but Shands replied, "Nothing doing." Later he learned that Conklin "was putting water between himself and a big, hungry shark."[12]

The rescue was a time-consuming process. In the meantime Murray on the *Hornet* arranged to accommodate the *Wasp* planes still aloft. Captain Mason decided to free up her flight deck by sending fifteen VS-8 SBDs to look for surfaced enemy submarines ahead of TF-17 and to land at Espiritu Santo 200 miles away. With ships being torpedoed, a concerned Gus Widhelm arranged to fill the rear seat of Ens. Paul E. Tepas's SBD with his personal liquor supply. Consequently Tepas departed without a radioman. At 1539 the *Hornet* launched eight VF-72 F4Fs for CAP, five VT-6 TBFs for antisub patrol, and the fifteen SBDs to BUTTON.

In the meantime Strickler led eight VF-71 F4Fs east toward TF-17:

1st Division	2nd Division
Lt. Cdr. Robert L. Strickler (USNA 1932)	Lt. Carl W. Rooney (USNA 1934)
Ens. Norman V. Brown, A-V(N)	Ens. Roland H. Kenton, A-V(N)
Lt. (jg) Charles W. Tucker, A-V(N)	Lt. (jg) Raymond F. Myers, A-V(N)
Ens. Harold N. Riise, A-V(N)	Ens. Millard C. Thrash, A-V(N)

Watching the *Wasp* disappear astern, Thrash later spoke for all: "My last view of the flat-top was blurred with tears."[13] The flight reached the *Hornet* and landed safely along with the four VS-72 SBDs.

At 1632 the *Hornet* sent two VB-8 SBDs west to orbit over the *Wasp* and guide her afternoon search to TF-17. It was a wise precaution. By sections John Eldridge's fourteen VS-71 SBDs completed their searches and started back. The crews thought it strange they could not pick up the *Wasp*'s YE homing transmitter on their Zed Baker receivers, then the task force failed to appear where they expected to find it. Thinking the ships had not advanced as far as anticipated, the section leaders followed the old carrier doctrine of flying upwind and soon had TF-18 in sight. A shocked VS-71 circled the burning carrier for about 30 minutes and wondered about ditching, but the *Hornet* SBDs pointed them east toward TF-17. On the way Ens. Robert Escher ran low on gasoline, realized he might not make the *Hornet,* and turned back to TF-18. He suffered severe injuries while setting down on the water, but was rescued by the *Duncan.* Beginning at 1814 the *Hornet* recovered the other thirteen VS-71 SBDs as well as her own planes.

Ironically, while the *Wasp* planes reached safety, the *Hornet*'s own flight to BUTTON did not fare as well. Ten SBDs found Espiritu Santo without trouble, but the other five missed the big island in the haze and separated over Omba and Pentecost islands to the east. Paul Tepas correctly turned west but only made it as far as Gaua Island northeast of Espiritu Santo, where he ditched off shore and lost Widhelm's stash. Helped by friendly natives he reached Santo on 2 October.[14] Rescuers soon found the other four VS-8 crews on Pentecost Island. Thus the *Hornet* lost five SBDs, but no lives.

Aided by many spectacular explosions, fires worked their way rapidly aft on the abandoned *Wasp.* Her list increased to 15 degrees or more, and soon the sea entered the hangar deck forward. Scott gave the *Lansdowne* the melancholy task of sinking her. Like the *Lexington* at the Coral Sea, her fiery hulk lighted the night sky for many miles, posing a hazard to the other ships. Cdr. Ishikawa Nobuo's *I-15* spotted the burning carrier and confirmed *I-19*'s kill. Scott took the rest of TF-18 south at 25 knots. Beginning at 1807 the *Lansdowne* fired five torpedoes one at a time. Three ultimately hit, but the carrier seemed reluctant to give up. Fires raged throughout her length, and she drifted in a pool of flames. Finally, at 2000 the gallant *Wasp* sank by the bow. Of her crew and passengers, 194 died, including 10 members of VF-71:[15]

Quinten A. Blay, MAtt2c	Ernest G. Simpson, MAtt3c
William M. Brooks, MAtt1c	Robert L. Thom, AMM3c
Meryland Griffin, OS3c	Willie L. Wade, MAtt1c
Willie F. Kelly, OC3c	Willie J. Walton, Jr., MAtt1c
Jerome W. Kennon, AMM2c	Maurice Williams, MAtt2c

Wasp air losses numbered forty-six planes (twenty-four F4F-4s, eleven SBD-3s, ten TBF-1s, and one J2F-5), while twenty-five (eight F4F-4s, seventeen SBD-3s) reached the *Hornet,* where the *Wasp* orphans were well treated. Assigned the room of his old friend Ens. William E. Woodman of VS-8 (who had fetched up on Pentecost Island that evening), Roland Kenton of VF-71 helped himself to some of Woodman's clothes, and only years later remembered he never paid him back. Kenton's borrowing proved of little account, for in a little over a month, Woodman likewise lost everything else when the *Hornet* went down at Santa Cruz.[16]

The afternoon of 16 September, Murray sent the eight VF-71 F4Fs under Lieutenant Commander Strickler and Lieutenant Commander Eldridge's seventeen VS-71 and VS-72 SBDs west to BUTTON to join *Enterprise* and *Saratoga* aviators stranded there when their flattops were disabled. The *Wasp* aviators would play a significant role in the air defense of CACTUS. The same day the remnants of TF-18 arrived at BUTTON, where the ships off-loaded the seriously wounded and made ready to depart for Noumea. Word spread quickly throughout SoPac of the loss of the *Wasp*. At Efate Lt. Col. Joe Bauer confided to his diary: "Am wondering what will become of the boys at CACTUS."[17] He was not the only one.

CHAPTER 12

The Lull

THE 7TH MARINES REACH GUADALCANAL

Because the Japanese fleet units retired, the loss of the *Wasp* did not compromise the vital reinforcement of Guadalcanal. On 16 September Rear Admiral Turner's TF-65 loaded with the 7th Marines loitered northwest of Espiritu Santo waiting for things to settle down. Late that evening, after negative search reports from ComAirSoPac, he decided to proceed. Target date for arriving at Lunga was now 18 September. Rear Admiral Murray's TF-17 with the *Hornet* retired southeast toward Efate, while Rear Admiral Scott took the *Wasp* survivors to Espiritu Santo.

With the carriers out of the picture, AirSoPac and the 1st MAW at CACTUS provided total air support for TF-65. On 16 September B-17s discovered an enemy seaplane lair at Rekata Bay on Santa Isabel, which was the R-Area Air Force's forward base, long suspected as being there or at Gizo on New Georgia. At 0710 on the 17th, Lieutenant Commander Simpler of VF-5 departed with Paul Mankin, Howard Crews, and Harry March to scout the coasts of that long, narrow island. First they looked along Isabel's west coast, saw nothing of military value, then crossed the northern tip to start back down the east shore.[1]

Suddenly at Rekata, a small peninsula at the mouth of a river, Simpler beheld the enemy base: several buildings planted along the beach and a collection of wrecked aircraft. Rear Admiral Jōjima had already pulled the air contingent back to Shortland. Two land attack planes and one float biplane lay submerged offshore, another biplane had turned turtle on the beach, but a third, seemingly in good shape, stood out of the water. They were relics of the 14 September raid on Lunga. The four Wildcats endured tracers from several AA machine guns and at least one 25-mm cannon emplacement, but nevertheless, they shot up the real estate. Mankin set the intact seaplane on fire, but a 25-mm round nearly wrecked his starboard elevator and peppered the rudder with fragments. The skipper took two 7.7-mm slugs in the engine. All four Wildcats returned safely to base. Before landing, Simpler cautioned Mankin to keep up his speed so that he wouldn't stall. Years later in the Pentagon, he greeted the ex-NAP, "Have you had your tail feathers plucked lately?"[2]

Later that day VF-5 nearly lost an airplane and pilot during a scramble that proved to be a false alarm. Aircraft taking off from Henderson Field raised great clouds of dust. One F4F just getting airborne seemed to lose its way and swerved. Its left wing tore through the propeller and windscreen of Jim Halford's Wildcat taxiing westward along the north edge of the runway. Halford's right wing slapped the ground and ripped completely off. Miraculously uninjured, he jumped from his cockpit and doffed his shirt and pants to get all the bits of broken plexiglass out of his clothes. The other pilot (not VF-5) was likewise unhurt, but both aircraft were totaled.[3]

Eighteenth September was a red-letter day for CACTUS. Turner's transports anchored off Lunga and rapidly disembarked the 7th Marines to warm greetings. The Japanese tried hard to disrupt the festivities with twenty-seven land attack planes and thirty-seven Zeros, but stormy weather barred the way. Expecting an enemy attack, ship gunners tragically splashed 2nd Lt. Leland E. Thomas's VMSB-231 SBD, killing the pilot, but they were able to save the radioman. The ships quickly unloaded men and cargo and got underway within 15 hours, a "major achievement."[4]

That same day Simpler took four VF-5 F4Fs to escort a strike against Gizo in the central Solomons, but the weather front that vexed the enemy forced his return as well. On the way back Stover caught sight of Marine 2nd Lt. A. H. Smith's SBD crew, which had been downed the previous day, and reported their location.

Another Marine castaway also found the 18th to be exceptionally noteworthy. He was 2nd Lt. Clair Chamberlain of VMF-212 missing since the afternoon of 13 September. With little water and no food he finally touched ground around 0600 on the 14th at tiny, uninhabited Nugu Island in Nggela Channel about eight miles southeast of Florida Island. For the next four days he subsisted on coconuts and a few snails. The morning of the 18th Lieutenant Commander Kirn, CO of VS-3, happened to spot a figure waving furiously on Nugu's beach. He dropped a canteen and a bag of rations and advised MAG-23. About an hour later, Maj. Joseph N. Renner, 1st MAW assistant operations officer, brought a J2F-5 amphibian over to Nugu and found Chamberlain very weak from lack of food. Rough seas forced the underpowered Duck to make six tries to get aloft.[5]

THE *HORNET* ALONE

While Turner's TF-65 reinforced Guadalcanal, Murray's TF-17 with the *Hornet*, the sole remaining SoPac carrier, stayed near Espiritu Santo. Ghormley told Murray to avoid "Torpedo Junction," the waters south and east of San Cristobal. This would be impossible to do if enemy carriers actually showed up north of Guadalcanal. The next few weeks—until the *Enterprise* could return—would be especially dangerous for the weakened SoPac Striking Force.

The loss of the *Wasp* compelled Admiral Nimitz at Pearl Harbor to make a remarkable proposition that reflected his great concern for carrier strength in the South Pacific. On 18 September he offered Ghormley the newly commissioned (as of 15 June) auxiliary aircraft carrier *Copahee* (ACV-12) as a "combatant carrier" to be manned by the *Wasp* and other stranded carrier air personnel. She sailed on 5 September from Alameda bound for Noumea via Pearl Harbor and carried a full load of Marine replacement aircraft (thirty-nine F4F-4s, eighteen SBD-3s). The first of the *Bogue*-class carriers, only 494 feet long (442-foot flight deck) with a speed of 18 knots, her intended complement was twelve Grumman

Wildcats and nine Grumman TBF Avengers or twenty-four Wildcats alone. Nimitz conceded her crew was untrained for flight operations and that deck operations would be slow. After conferring with RAdm. Aubrey Fitch, incoming ComAirSoPac, Ghormley replied on 20 September that the *Copahee* would be more valuable for ferrying aircraft to CACTUS. "Her use as combatant carrier [in] this area not recommended," he concluded, but added that "effective combat use could be made" of three such auxiliary carriers.[6]

Ghormley's shriveled SoPac striking force now comprised the following heavy ships: Murray's TF-17 with the *Hornet*, heavy cruisers *Northampton* and *Pensacola*, and light AA cruisers *San Diego* and *Juneau*, and Scott's TF-64 with CAs *San Francisco*, *Minneapolis*, *Salt Lake City*, and *Chester* (CA-27), and the light cruisers *Boise* (CL-47) and *Helena*. They were a far cry from the halcyon days of August. On 20 September CinCPac strongly suggested that TF-17 seek refuge at Noumea as protection against submarines. The next day Admiral King cautioned about the employment of the SoPac carrier forces: "It is obvious protracted operations of our task forces on a strategically static basis in submarine infested waters is proving increasingly hazardous."[7] This was precisely the departed Fletcher's position.

Ghormley directed Murray to proceed to Noumea for the long-awaited opportunity to reprovision and rest. Fortunately the Japanese carrier force no longer appeared active in the South Pacific. On 26 September the *Hornet* dispersed her air group by sending thirty-two F4F-4s and twelve SBDs to Tontouta field northwest of Noumea and twelve SBDs to Efate, but retained VT-6 and the spare aircraft on board. She anchored at Noumea, already overcrowded with transports and cargo vessels waiting to be unloaded at SoPac's major supply base.

While the *Wasp* survivors regrouped at Noumea, CinCPac arranged to return them to the West Coast. Rear Admiral Noyes flew to Pearl Harbor to act as interim Commander, Air Forces, Pacific Fleet (ComAirPac), pending the arrival of VAdm. John H. Towers, while Halsey resumed the post of senior Pacific Fleet carrier commander. Noyes endured criticism from Ghormley for supposedly crossing and recrossing his previous track, thus risking detection by submarines. In October he pointed out that the submarine attack on the *Wasp* occurred "150 miles from nearest point of crossing an old track, and in an area which had not been entered or approached previously." Under the circumstances (the Japanese threat from the north), there was little else he could do. Of course, he operated where his mission demanded, and the *Wasp* was lost where TF-61 needed to be in order to protect Turner's convoy from hostile forces to the north. Exiled from combat as scapegoat for the loss of the *Wasp*, Noyes spent the rest of the war with the Board of Inspection and Survey. In criticizing Fletcher for not staying near to the transports and Noyes for closing his charges, some seemed to want to have it both ways.[8]

Captain Sherman and Commander Beakley joined the AirPac staff. The *Wasp* crew and air group personnel (less Lieutenant Commander Strickler's VF-71 and Lieutenant Commander Eldridge's VS-71 detachments) became the "Stinger Unit" under Cdr. (soon to be Capt.) Fred Dickey. Commander Kernodle and VF-71 CO Lieutenant Commander Shands remained on assignment in SoPac. Lt. Hawley Russell took over VF-71 in the Stinger Unit. Along with wounded from CACTUS, the *Wasp* survivors departed Noumea on 23 September on board the Dutch motor vessel *Brastagi* and finally reached San Diego on 21 October.[9]

LIFE AT GUADALCANAL

For the CACTUS Marine and naval fighter pilots, mid-September brought an unexpectedly quiet interval. Persistent bad weather shielded Guadalcanal from Base Air Force at Rabaul. Thus activity centered mostly around the runs ("Rat Transportation") of the so-called Tokyo Express of light cruisers and destroyers shuttling troops almost nightly from Shortland to Guadalcanal. This build-up of enemy ground forces posed a great threat to the 1st MarDiv. On 14 September McCain warned Vandegrift: "Your whole existence up there depends on hitting those Jap ships consistently *before* they get there, while they are there, or during departure." He recommended comprehensive searches, followed by day and night attacks by Marine and Navy SBDs and TBFs, supported by AirSoPac B-17s and PBYs operating out of Espiritu Santo.[10] In the next two weeks, the CACTUS F4Fs flew some escort missions, but encountered no enemy planes.

The Rekata raid proved to be VF-5's last aerial combat for ten days. Spared regular enemy air raids for a time, they had the leisure to examine the strange, remarkable surroundings into which they were thrust.[11] Despite the heat, the dust, the insects, and the enemy, the island certainly was scenic, as Frederick Mears of VT-8 described it:

> Guadalcanal is such a beautiful place . . . When we arrived the boys took us down to the beach and we looked across the golden sea to the islands of Florida, fringed by the distant outline of Malaita. At sunset we stood near the field on the edge of Lever Brothers Cocoanut Grove and watched the magic cloud covers above the mountains to the west.[12]

In late September 1942, VF-5 pilots (*l to r*) Cash Register, Junior Kleinmann, and George Morgan rest near the VF-5 ready tent, while Marines emplace 75-mm pack howitzers. VF-5 F4Fs are parked at the east end of Henderson Field. (Capt. H. W. Crews)

The long, tiring daily routine started with the predawn hike from the coconut grove north of the field down to the VF-5 ready tent pitched about 150 feet southwest of the Pagoda. Other than flying scheduled patrols or occasional scrambles, the pilots waited there on alert until dusk. Sitting around the tent on logs or ammunition cans, they amused themselves by talking, playing cards, writing home, or with numerous other diversions to wile away the hours not spent in the air. Several discovered a common fondness for singing and convened a group songfest, "harmonizing" on a nearby log. Harry March noted down the lyrics of favorite songs on a scrap of paper (a rare CACTUS commodity!) which he kept in his pocket. Often, however, because of the heat it was enough just to escape the sunlight.

The day's high points became breakfast at 0700 (0900 if a dawn patrol was flown) and dinner about 1630. During the busy time (12–14 September), the pilots had been lucky to get even one meal a day. For the first 10 days VF-5 patronized a Marine field kitchen near the remains of a hangar on the southern edge of the main field. Eating out in the open from their own mess kits, the pilots stood at long wooden tables and unsuccessfully battled flies in their food. Understandably, the cuisine was neither balanced nor particularly appetizing, despite the earnest efforts of their Marine cooks. Servings were hardly ample, and for pilots it was all too easy even to miss that because of flight duties. Mechanics servicing aircraft day and night experienced the same problem. CACTUS welcomed any new kinds of food, and ordinary standards of taste no longer applied. Frank Green, for example, devoured a can of Japanese peaches, which, according to his diary, "beats anything I have eaten." At the field Lister bags provided water that, although clean, was both warm and unpalatable due to the chlorine taste.

The nature of the food coupled with the lack of sanitary eating conditions soon led to "fluid drive" (dysentery), which forced frequent visits to the open head located on scenic Pagoda Hill. Even worse, some pilots became sick in their cockpits while flying or waiting on alert. Stamina and general health were badly affected, for some more swiftly than others. Mears noted, "The food and dysentery and malaria were what made people on Guadalcanal thin, I discovered."[13] For the diners, the food itself was not the only hazard. The day after the Battle of the Ridge, a sniper's bullet tore out a chunk of table planking close to where VF-5 stood. Along with everyone else, they hit the deck. A couple of Marines grabbed their weapons and disappeared into the jungle. Soon a burst of automatic fire signaled the all-clear. Eating conditions, at least, soon improved. By 22 September VF-5 enjoyed a screened-in mess tent and their own tableware.

Simpler quickly arranged to release from duty for a few hours each day one division of four or five pilots. The dwindling number of flyable aircraft soon ensured more pilots than planes anyway. Thus they could look forward to some free time at least every third or fourth day, usually more often. The favored leisure activity was a bath in the Lunga River, for the most part still a clear mountain stream. About a mile northwest of the field a large tree trunk stripped of its bark and made smooth sat in the river:

> This was handy for laying out your clothes and scrubbing them with soap. Sometimes we'd take off our clothes, pile them on the bank, and walk out into the stream with a bar of soap and have a good bath. Other times we'd wade into the river with our clothes on, get good and wet, soap the clothes while still on our bodies, rinse them off, wade out and walk back to base letting the clothes dry while being worn.[14]

Beards became fashionable in VF-5, mainly for lack of hot water for proper shaving. Cold-water shaving risked nicks that could easily become infected. Infrequent bathing, however, rendered beards rather uncomfortable in the wet tropical climate. George Morgan took over as squadron barber while waiting on alert at the ready tent. Even so, some VF-5 beards were rather spectacular. Lieutenant Colonel Bayler, who camped with Lieutenant Colonel Scollin near the VF-5 ready tent, thought they looked like "life-long members" of the hirsute House of David baseball team. "One wondered how they could sit in an airplane with helmet, goggles, throat microphone and oxygen mask over those whiskers."[15]

On 16 September Bill Robb flew in from Espiritu Santo with orders written inside a matchbook cover: "Bill, come to CACTUS. (signed) Leroy." He brought the bad news about the loss of the *Wasp,* and that elicited "plenty of cussing" over the faults of the high command. Without her the prospects of holding Guadalcanal looked bleaker. Robb took over operations, engineering, personnel, and served as squadron yeoman as well. He insisted upon having a desk inside the ready tent, and the pilots made him one. In addition, he served as chief "cumshaw" artist scrounging for needed materiel. Fighting Five personnel at Santo and Efate created a self-help network to forward to the advance echelon at CACTUS a wide range of food and supplies otherwise unavailable there. These "care packages" carried by MAG-25 R4Ds greatly raised morale and brought VF-5 through some mighty lean times. Such luxuries (by CACTUS standards, anyway) also proved invaluable as trade bait for essential items. For example, Robb exchanged fruit juice with the 1st Tank Battalion for Breeze engine starter cartridges (a sort of pelletless shotgun shell) used in their tanks. For the F4F-4s it was necessary to cut down a few grains on the charge. Bill Robb's

George Morgan cuts Weasel Wesolowski's hair in front of the VF-5 ready tent; Crud Blair is behind to the left. Photo taken about 29 September, only a few days before Morgan's death. (Capt. W. E. Clarke)

services were so highly valued that later Brigadier General Woods recommended him for the Distinguished Service Medal.[16]

On VF-5's first really quiet day, Simpler finally had the opportunity to make his formal call on Major General Geiger. He could be found in his "office," a wicker armchair in a corridor of the Pagoda. That edifice began to look deceptively substantial after being sided with boards. At first Simpler thought the general was dozing. As he quietly walked past, the older man surprised him: "Simpler, there is only one thing wrong with you." "What's that general? I will try to fix it." Geiger answered wryly, "You are not a goddamn Marine." Simpler felt this was "about as great a compliment as one could get from a Marine commanding general in a combat environment."[17]

VF-5 thought themselves well treated by the Marines, and Simpler got along extremely well with the wing and group staffs. The senior Marine officers looked upon VF-5 as a tangible symbol of the Navy's commitment to support the defense of Guadalcanal.

Early on the morning of 19 September, a bursting flare presaged another enemy ship bombardment, this time by the light cruiser *Sendai* and four destroyers. In the coconut grove, Simpler sat in a foxhole with Maj. John Smith, a former artilleryman, who commented on Japanese gunnery techniques. Fortunately, no shells fell near the VF-5 bivouac. As on other nights, some VF-5 pilots were sleeping near the ready tent to listen to Wally Clarke's Hallicrafter shortwave radio, which he had plugged into the Pagoda's line. Night provided the best reception, and at times they even tuned in San Francisco. Broadcasts from the States with their talk of AAF bomber exploits at the "fortress of Guadalcanal" grated on nerves at CACTUS. Howard Crews especially remembered a radio commentator boasting that MacArthur's B-17s had left Rabaul a "hollow, burning shell." Tell that to the Japanese.

When attacked that night the erstwhile radio listeners ran about 100 feet to the entrance of a small tunnel the Seabees were digging into the side of Pagoda Hill. First in, Cash Register stumbled over someone sleeping on an inverted life raft and soundly cursed until a flash of light revealed none other than Geiger. Characteristically the general took no offense and said nothing in reply to the ensign's profuse apologies.[18] This tunnel was soon enlarged into an underground communications center for the 1st MAW and MAG-23.

Later that morning Rear Admiral Fitch arrived on Guadalcanal for an inspection tour before taking over as ComAirSoPac from Rear Admiral McCain, who in turn would relieve Vice Admiral Towers as chief of the Bureau of Aeronautics in Washington. Very early in the campaign McCain had recognized the vital need for shore-based air power at Guadalcanal with its potential to harm the enemy and did his best with very limited resources to provide that air power. Fitch would do likewise. In addition to his reputation as a proven naval aviation commander he had skill as an organizer. Coming up in the admiral's party were Congressman Maas, an old acquaintance of VF-5's, and also the much-traveled Capt. John Wilkins, the carrier-qualified Army pilot who served briefly with VF-72 on the *Hornet*. Joining 223, Wilkins encountered his old friend Marion Carl, and the next day flew a strike against Rekata. He was on Guadalcanal only four days and returned to the States to command a P-38 Lightning fighter squadron. In November 1943 he was killed over Europe with the 20th Fighter Group. "Soldier" Wilkins was highly regarded by those Navy and Marine aviators with whom he flew.[19] Also on the 19th Claude Roberts, ACMM, brought a

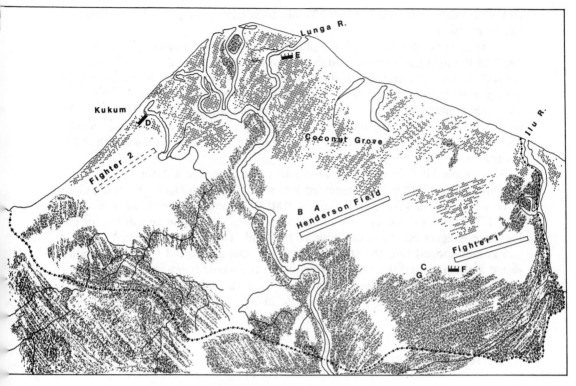

The Lunga airfields in late September.
Key A—Pagoda Hill
     B—RADAR ONE
     C—RADAR TWO
     D—Battery D (90-mm), 3rd Defense Battalion
     E—Battery E (90-mm), 3rd Defense Battalion
     F—Battery F (90-mm), 3rd Defense Battalion
     G—Secondary Control

party of fourteen VF-5 enlisted men from Efate. Tragically, half would be killed or wounded on the day they were to finally leave Guadalcanal.

Enjoying the pause in enemy raids, MAG-23 installed on 20 September a newly arrived SCR-270-B radar at the site of Bayler's "Secondary Control," the knoll south of Fighter 1. Dubbed RADAR TWO, it became the principal tool for CACTUS fighter direction. Joe Renner took over as FDO from Bayler, greatly assisted by the MAG-23 team of radar operators headed by Staff Sgt. Dermott H. MacDonnell, a very talented 21-year-old technician. He experimented with the tilt feature of the 270 to allow some estimate of altitude and could judge the approximate size and composition of incoming groups. RADAR ONE near the Pagoda reverted to the 3rd Defense Battalion to help control AA fire. Colonel Pepper now wielded Lt. Col. Kenneth W. Benner's entire Marine 90-mm AA group of twelve guns to protect both airfields.[20]

The first Marine F4F-7 photo plane (the old *Hornet* aircraft) reached Fighter 1 on 21 September to photograph terrain on Guadalcanal. Although qualified to fly the beast, Crews and Green stayed far away from it, happy to let Capt. Carl Longley of VMO-251 handle that chore. He and Maj. Michael A. Sampas, assistant W-2 under Lieutenant Colonel Munn, took many daring low-level photos of enemy positions.[21]

During rest periods several VF-5 pilots visited the front lines only a mile or so south of the field and experienced first-hand the grisly aftermath of the Battle of the Ridge. It was "souvenirs & stink galore," according to Green. They enjoyed talking with Marine raiders who, in Stover's words, were "thrilled to hear we were *real* fighter pilots," as if riflemen did not see combat. Twenty-second September brought "great trading of all kinds of Jap articles, guns, swords, money, medals." For swords the Marines charged up to $100. Rifles could be had for several candy bars, but pistols cost $30.[22]

Also on the 22nd a number of VF-5 pilots met danger of a different sort. That morning Simpler's four F4Fs escorted Renner's Grumman Duck up toward Gizo to recover Second Lieutenant Smith's VMSB-231 crew. After landing back at CACTUS, the VF-5 pilots took refuge from the pitiless noon sun in one of the Japanese hangars on the south edge of the field. Their first notice that an SBD had ground-looped into the structure was the sound of wood splitting. Simpler yelled a warning, and they ran outside just as the whole building collapsed. That afternoon VF-5 was surprised when Geiger himself took an SBD and bombed a target on western Guadalcanal. The "Old Man," too, had some frustrations to vent.

AVIATION RESOURCES FOR CACTUS

On 21 September Fitch took over as ComAirSoPac, and it is worthwhile to examine the combat planes he could actually commit to CACTUS. In one month of air operations (20 August–21 September), AirSoPac provided CACTUS a total of 153 aircraft. On 22 September Geiger's 1st MAW had eighty-seven planes either operational or repairable:

	Numbers Committed	Strength on 22 September	Total Losses
VMF-223, 224, VF-5	86 F4F-4s	43	43
VMSB-232, 231, Flight 300, VS-3	42 SBD-3s	27	15
67th FS	17 P-400s	9	8
VT-8	8 TBF-1s	8	0

That meant effective attrition of sixty-six planes (including some wrecks left at the field and salvaged later in the campaign).[23]

To support CACTUS from the nearby SoPac island airfields were another thirty-nine Grumman Wildcats (F4F-3P, F4F-3A, and F4F-4s), thirty Douglas SBD-3 Dauntlesses, six Grumman TBF-1 Avengers, ten P-400s and two P-39 Airacobras, ten Martin B-26 Marauder medium bombers, and about forty Boeing B-17E/-F Flying Fortresses (see table 12.1). Actual fighter strength was much weaker, as the F4F-3Ps and particularly the F4F-3As were not considered combat-worthy from wear and the lack of spare parts. The above figures include what remained of ninety-nine aircraft (thirty-two F4F-4s, fifty-three SBD-3s, and fourteen TBF-1s) with their trained crews from the three crippled or sunken flattops (*Enterprise, Saratoga,* and *Wasp*). So far twenty-four F4F-4s, twenty-nine SBDs, and eight TBFs reached CACTUS, and the rest were ready to go when needed.

TABLE 12.1
Support for CACTUS

ESPIRITU SANTO		
Fighters	VMO-251	13 F4F-3Ps, 2 F4F-4s
	VMF-212	13 F4F-3As
	VF-71	8 F4F-4s
Dive Bombers and Torpedo Planes	VS-71 and VS-72	17 SBD-3s
	VS-3	4 SBD-3s
	VB-6	8 SBD-3s
	VT-8	6 TBF-1s
Heavy Bombers	11th Bomb Group (H)	40 B-17Es,-Fs
EFATE	VMF-212	3 F4F-3As
TONTOUTA, NEW CALEDONIA	67th FS	10 P-400s, 2 P-39s
	69th Bomb Squadron (M)	10 B-26s

As for reinforcements, Lt. Col. Albert D. Cooley's green MAG-14, which comprised VMF-121 (Maj. Leonard K. Davis) and VMSB-141 (Maj. Gordon A. Bell), was en route from San Diego to the South Pacific. The personnel reached Noumea on the 22nd, while their twenty-one F4F-4 Wildcats and twenty-one SBD-3 Dauntlesses rode the aircraft transport *Hammondsport* (APV-2), slated to arrive at the end of the month. While the squadrons awaited their aircraft, several MAG-14 aviators went to CACTUS. In addition the *Copahee* brought thirty-nine F4F-4s and eighteen SBD-3s as spares for the 1st MAW. The 67th FS at Tontouta expected another thirty Bell P-39D and K Airacobras and fifteen Lockheed P-38F Lightning fighters diverted to them from Australia. No more single-engine planes currently moved in the long pipeline reinforcing SoPac.[24]

Guadalcanal inflicted a tremendous drain on the resources of AirPac. Noting Marine fighter losses at CACTUS, Admiral King requested from Gen. George C. Marshall immediate reinforcement by Army fighters and concluded bluntly, "The Navy is unable to meet this rate of attrition and continue to operate carriers." Fitch knew his call on the services of carrier aviators was limited. On 14 September, his last day as temporary ComAirPac, he asked RAdm. Charles A. Pownall, newly appointed Commander, Fleet Air, West Coast (ComFAirWest) at San Diego, for the immediate shipment to Hawaii of seventy fighters, fifty-five dive bombers, and nine torpedo planes. Pownall replied on 16 September that by 30 October he could ship only thirty-seven fighters, forty-nine dive bombers, and twenty-eight torpedo planes, unless he reduced Carrier Replacement Air Groups 11 and 12 and the West Coast Marine squadrons to less than one plane for every two pilots. That would severely curtail their training and delay their arrival in the fleet, which would have other repercussions. On the 19th, Vice Admiral Halsey, now temporary ComAirPac, decried in a message to CominCh "the dangerous shortage of trained carrier replacements," particularly fighter pilots, for the Pacific Fleet. He warned that "delay in this matter invites disaster."[25]

On 18 September Halsey had requested of AirSoPac the "earliest practicable return" of the carrier pilots and crews. He hoped to use "the least tired" to leaven the carrier replacement air groups. Fitch replied on the 22nd that they would be detached when "transportation and the military situation permitted." As things transpired these land-bound carrier aviators played a vital role in saving the island.[26]

The commanders addressed the increasingly complex administration and control of the CACTUS air bases. On 23 September Geiger took the opportunity of Lieutenant Colonel Cooley's presence to reorganize the 1st MAW advance echelon. Colonel Wallace, MAG-23 CO, received Fighter Command with VMF-223, VMF-224, VF-5, and the 67th FS. Cooley formed the Strike Command from VMSB-231, VMSB-232, Flight 300 (VS-5 and VB-6), VS-3, and VT-8. Henderson Field (Bomber Field No. 1) was being improved. The Seabees widened the field and by 25 September unloaded sufficient Marston mats to cover the entire runway. At the same time they began construction of Fighter Field No. 2 at Kukum immediately west of the Lunga River.

Taking advantage of aviation talent among former *Wasp* officers, AirSoPac ordered Cdr. Michael Kernodle, her air officer, and Lieutenant Commander Shands of VF-71 to CACTUS. Reporting on the 26th to Commander Compton, commanding the Naval Base, Kernodle took over construction, operation, and maintenance of the Advanced Air Bases, CACTUS-RINGBOLT (Guadalcanal and Tulagi).[27] Although not fully recovered from his injuries on the 15th, Shands became senior strike leader.

On the 23rd, the 1st Division opened a drive west toward the Mantanikau River to clear the immediate area of enemy troops and to deny them jumping-off points for a new offensive. Volley fire from a 75-mm pack howitzer battalion emplaced around the VF-5 ready tent caused the squadron to wonder when they would ever re-embark on a carrier. Stover, for one, noted "things are becoming too permanent around here." On the 24th Alex Barbieri came up from Efate with news that the squadron would soon be rotated back to the States.

The afternoon of 25 September Howard Crews with four VF-5 F4Fs escorted six SBDs and eight TBFs out past Gizo looking for enemy ships. Swede Larsen of VT-8 led the strike. Crews stayed with the bombers as long as fuel permitted and landed after dark at CACTUS. Larsen searched in vain for that day's Tokyo Express and ended up dumping his bombs on enemy positions at Cape Esperance. The mission underscored the vital need for fighter drop tanks. Without them the F4Fs simply lacked the legs to accompany the bombers past the central Solomons. Belly tanks, however, were in short supply at CACTUS.

Later that day VF-5 received word of the rescue of Hayden Jensen after an interesting adventure. On 19 September he had borrowed Lieutenant Colonel Bauer's personal SNJ trainer for a routine flight northwest from Efate to Espiritu Santo, but never made it. AirSoPac did not even know he was missing. On the 22nd Bauer flew to Santo to check the whereabouts of his SNJ, only to learn it never arrived. AirSoPac headquarters on the *Curtiss* ordered a search, which later that day found Jensen and his passenger, "T" "H" Latimer, CEM, safe on Epi Island about 75 miles northwest of Efate. Because of engine trouble they set down on the "main street" of what turned out to be a deserted village, hit a log, and nosed over. Later they found that the natives fled the island because of an outbreak of elephantiasis, not exactly comforting news.[28]

Eager for combat, Simpler led four F4Fs up to Rekata the morning of the 26th escorting Ens. Allard G. Russell's VS-3 SBD. The idea was for Russell to approach the seaplane base alone to decoy some of the nimble float biplanes aloft so that VF-5 could jump them. Around 0700 Russell neared Rekata from the north at 1,500 feet and behaved like a returning search plane, but no one took the bait. Simpler headed back to Lunga, while Allard bombed a suspected AA emplacement.[29]

JAPANESE AIR REINFORCEMENTS

From mid- to late September Base Air Force at Rabaul received strong air reinforcements to the tune of forty-three Type 1 land attack planes, thirty-eight Zero
fighters (the long-range Model 21s), and twelve Type 99 carrier bombers.[30] This
more than counterbalanced recent CACTUS air additions. On 16 September 1st
Air Attack Force (21st Air Flotilla) headquarters under RAdm. Ichimaru Rino-
suke reached Kavieng on New Ireland. He was a "fire-eater" (wings 1918), who
still limped badly from a 1926 plane crash. With him came most of the elite
Kanoya Air Group recently stationed at Sabang off Sumatra. They brought
twenty-three Type 1 land attack planes, including replacements for other groups,
and later operated eighteen *rikkōs* from Kavieng. The CO, Capt. Odawara Toshi-
hiko, was another of the handful of senior naval aviators. From the Kanoya
group's fighter squadron only the 1st *Chūtai* of nine Zero 21s, led by *hikōtaichō*
Lt. Itō Toshitaka (NA 60-1932), reached Rabaul for temporary duty with the
Tainan Air Group.[31] Eight more fighters with about nineteen additional pilots
arrived at the end of September.

The 3rd Air Attack Force (23rd Air Flotilla) in the Dutch East Indies loaned
portions of two more renowned groups. On 17 September the converted carrier
Taiyō (ex-*Kasuga Maru*) brought to Rabaul twenty-one Zero Model 21 fighters
(twenty-six pilots) from the 3rd Air Group under Lt. Cdr. Sakakibara Kiyoji, the
air officer. From the conquest of the Philippines and the East Indies, as well as
raids against Darwin, the 3rd enjoyed a reputation equal to that of the illustrious
Tainan Air Group. Several aces served at Rabaul, including the *hikōtaichō*, Lt.
Aioi Takahide (NA 59-1931). Long after the war he commanded the Japan Maritime Self Defense Force. His aggressive young *buntaichō*, Lt. (jg) Yamaguchi
Sadao (NA 67-1939), would see much action over Guadalcanal.[32] On the 22nd
twenty Type 1 land attack planes from the Takao Air Group under *hikōtaichō* Lt.
Makino Shigeji (NA 61-1933) reached Rabaul.

Five days later the *Taiyō* returned from the Philippines with nine Type 99s
from the 31st Air Group and three for the 2nd Air Group, along with three obso-
lete Mitsubishi A5M4 Type 96 carrier fighters [CLAUDE] and three even older
Aichi D1A2 Type 96 carrier bomber biplanes. The next day about 40 miles south
of Truk, the U.S. submarine *Trout* (SS-202) "smacked" the *Taiyō*'s stern, the
first carrier actually damaged by a U.S. sub.[33] Like the Allies, the Japanese
lacked sufficient aircraft transport ships, so they keenly felt her crippling.

The surviving aircrews from the 4th and Yokohama air groups gratefully departed for Japan and a well-deserved rest, while Lieutenant Andō's seven *Chitose* land attack planes returned on 23 September to the Marshalls. The Tainan
veterans could not be released from Rabaul. Constant flying and fighting also
wore down the 2nd Air Group and the *rikkō* groups of the 26th Air Flotilla, but
the biggest battle was about to commence. Base Air Force did rotate combat
assignments to provide some off-duty time. (See table 12.2 for composition of
Base Air Force in the Southeast Area as of 24 September.)[34]

Japanese plans for the second half of September centered around reinforcing
Guadalcanal with troops, heavy weapons, and supplies from the 17th Army,
completion of the vital new airfield at Buin in southern Bougainville, and destruction of Allied air strength in the Solomons. They thought American air strength at
Lunga numbered about forty small aircraft (fighters and carrier bombers) and ten
large and medium planes, with airfields on Espiritu Santo as the nearest support

TABLE 12.2
Base Air Force in the Southeast Area, 24 September 1942

Unit (Force)	Air Group	Operational Planes	Aircrew
	5th Air Attack Force		
	RAdm. Yamada Sadayoshi (CO, 25th Air Flotilla)		
No. 1	Tainan Air Group	8 Zero 21 fighters;	39
	Capt. Saitō Masahisa	1 Type 98 land recon;	?
		1 Type 2 land recon	?
	Attached: 3rd Air Group Detachment	20 Zero 21 fighters;	26
	Lt. Cdr. Sakakibara Kiyoji	4 Type 98 recon	?
	Kanoya Air Group Fighter Detachment	8 Zero 21 fighters	9
	Lt. Itō Toshitaka		
No. 3	2nd Air Group	16 Zero 32 fighters;	14
	Cdr. Yamamoto Sakae	5 Type 99 carrier bombers	?
No. 4	Tōkō Air Group	5 Type 97 flying boats	?
	Capt. Wada Saburō		
	Attached: Type 2 Flying Boat Detachment	1 Type 2 flying boat	?
No. 6	6th Air Group Advance Detachment	12 Zero 21 fighters;	30
	Lt. Kofukuda Mitsugi	13 Zero 32 fighters	
	6th Air Attack Force		
	VAdm. Yamagata Seigō (CO, 26th Air Flotilla)		
"A"	Kisarazu Air Group	15 Type 1 land attack planes	23
	Capt. Fujiyoshi Naoshiro		
"B"	Misawa Air Group	12 Type 1 land attack planes	23
	Capt. Sugawara Masao		
"C"	Takao Air Group Detachment	19 Type 1 land attack planes	20
	Lt. Makino Shigeji		
	1st Air Attack Force		
	RAdm. Ichimaru Rinosuke (CO, 21st Air Flotilla)		
	Kanoya Air Group (main force)	16 Type 1 land attack planes	18
	Capt. Odawara Toshihiko		

Total Operational Aircraft
48 Mitsubishi A6M2 Type 0, Model 21 carrier fighters [ZEKE]
29 Mitsubishi A6M3 Type 0, Model 32 carrier fighters [HAMP]
 5 Aichi D3A1 Type 99 carrier bombers [VAL]
 5 Mitsubishi C5M2 Type 98 land reconnaissance planes [BABS]
 1 Nakajima J1N1-C Type 2 land reconnaissance plane [IRVING]
62 Mitsubishi G4M1 Type 1 land attack planes [BETTY]
 5 Kawanishi H6K4 Type 97 flying boats [MAVIS]
 1 Kawanishi H8K1 Type 2 flying boat [EMILY]

air base to the target area. All of these operations prepared the way for a new ground offensive in mid-October. The Tokyo Express ran most evenings until 24 September, when the increasing threat of air attack compelled a temporary suspension.

To better utilize the new air strength now available, Vice Admiral Tsukahara directed on 18 September that Yamada's 5th Air Attack Force take control of all of the fighters as well as conducting searches. He pooled the long-range Zero 21s, so that each group, when assigned to a mission, could fill out its flight schedule.

Yamagata's 6th Air Attack Force handled its own land attack planes and those of Ichimaru's 1st Air Attack Force.

With more available Zero 21s, Yamada revamped escort tactics, now using as many as forty-two instead of twelve to eighteen. That permitted him to use the two standard escort assignments: direct escort (the "covering force" or *engotai*) as top cover in the usual way above and behind the land attack planes and the "air control force" (*seikūtai*) operating away from the bombers on a "free hunt" after the manner of the Luftwaffe's *Frei Jagd*. The air control fighters were to sweep ahead of the main body and knock out waiting interceptors. Unfortunately the direct escort still lacked a way to counter the steep dive-and-run attack tactics of the Grummans.

Base Air Force entertained high hopes for the effectiveness of their greatly augmented Zero escorts, but bad weather postponed the test. Heavy cloud cover or actual storms thwarted strikes against Guadalcanal on the 16th, 18th, 19th, and 24th. On 21 September twenty-seven *rikkōs* and thirty-seven Zeros struck Port Moresby. Tsukahara needed vital liaison on Guadalcanal for weather data, estimates of Allied air strength, targets, and damage assessments. In late September Lt. Cdr. Mitsui Kenji, former 4th Air Group air officer, and ten communication specialists went into the coastwatcher business on the slopes of Mount Austen overlooking the Lunga airfields. They were to keep Rabaul informed of American fighter activity.[35]

CHAPTER 13

The Attacks Resume

THE 27 SEPTEMBER RAID

Sunday morning, 27 September, VF-5 received welcome reinforcements in the form of the 6th Division (Hayden Jensen, Foster Blair, John McDonald, and John Kleinman) from Efate. Along with Chief Latimer they disembarked from a Marine R4D around 0700 to the roar of a Marine howitzer barrage from nearby batteries loosed against Japanese positions near the Mantanikau River. That showed how really close the enemy was. Now VF-5 had twenty-three pilots for nineteen F4F-4s (eighteen operational). John L. Smith's VMF-223 and Bob Galer's VMF-224 also profited from two weeks without enemy raids. On 26 September five pilots from Maj. Leonard Davis's newly arrived VMF-121 came up to CACTUS on temporary duty. On the 27th, VMF-223 was comprised of seventeen pilots (including three 212s and three 121s), and eleven operational F4F-4s; VMF-224 had sixteen pilots (including two 121s) and twelve operational F4F-4s.

After two frustrating weeks, the Japanese finally succeeded with a daylight strike against Guadalcanal. Vice Admiral Tsukahara's aviators received the crucial task of suppressing American air power to open the way for troops and supplies to the 17th Army on Guadalcanal. Crammed with men and weapons, the seaplane carrier *Nisshin* was to reach there on the 30th. She required protection at all costs. The Japanese were confident their recent powerful air reinforcements would soon assure control of the southern Solomon skies.

According to the new escort tactics, the strike group deployed in two elements. A dozen Zero fighters flown by Lieutenant Kurakane's 2nd Air Group departed Rabaul 15 minutes ahead of the main body to serve as the "air control force." At 1030 Lieutenant Nabeta of the Kisarazu Air Group led his nine Type 1 land attack planes and nine from Lieutenant Makino's Takao detachment making its first attack against Guadalcanal. Bad weather kept nine Kanoya Type 1s on the ground at Kavieng, so Nabeta deployed the Kisarazu *chūtai* directly ahead of the Takao *chūtai*. The "covering force" in direct escort comprised Lieutenant Aioi's entire 3rd Air Group Detachment of twenty-six Zeros. Two *chūtai* (seventeen Zeros) took the customary escort slots above and astern of the Type 1s, while the 3rd *Chūtai* climbed higher to serve as top cover. Thus thirty-eight Zeros, almost all of the available Model 21s, flew the mission.[1]

The new Japanese gambit began auspiciously when coastwatchers missed seeing Kurakane's dozen air control Zeros, thus creating a chance to ambush the defending Grummans. At 1315 Kurakane discerned Guadalcanal ahead on the horizon. Almost simultaneously the main body attracted the keen eyes of coastwatcher Donald Kennedy on New Georgia. At 1312 he warned of eighteen planes headed southeast, and two minutes later counted thirteen more aircraft above them.

Even before 1330—when Kennedy's message was relayed to the Pagoda— RADAR TWO had the bogeys bearing 310 degrees and closing. MAG-23 flashed Condition YELLOW at 1312, and the pilots raced to their parked Wildcats. From the cow pasture, Major Payne took nine VMF-223 and Major Galer eight VMF-224 F4Fs in mixed divisions. Fourteen VF-5 F4Fs under Lieutenant Commander Simpler got away from Henderson Field. Like the Marines they abandoned squadron order and sorted themselves out as best they could in four divisions:

1	2	3	4
Simpler	Crews	Green	Wesolowski
Currie	Grimmell	Halford	Mankin
March	Shoemaker	Bright	Register
		Roach	Nesbitt

The cargo ship *Alhena,* destroyer *Monssen,* and a batch of landing craft operated off Lunga. To guard them from torpedo attack, Joe Renner peeled off Sandy Crews and Fog Green with eight F4Fs to patrol directly over the channel.

Red, the Marine jeep driver, went tearing over to the coconut grove, where the 6th Division slept after their overnight flight, and brought Jensen, McDonald, Kleinman, and Blair back to the field. They took off well after the other fighters. Soon Blair's F4F began throwing oil when a cylinder head blew and forced him to return to Henderson Field. That left thirty-four F4Fs aloft.[2]

Fortunately for CACTUS, Kurakane's twelve air-control Zeros patrolling high over Lunga never did spot the climbing F4Fs. He stayed his 15 minutes and withdrew at 1345 without contacting the main body. Nabeta sighted Guadalcanal at 1330, and on the way in wingman PO1c Ueyama Tsunehito aborted, leaving 17 *rikkōs*. At 1353 the Takao crews observed a dozen Grummans below. They could not alert Kurakane or Aioi because the Zeros carried no radios.

Even so Nabeta almost reached Lunga before one division of Marines confronted him from ahead and about 2,000 feet above. They were:

> Maj. Kirk Armistead (224)
> 2nd Lt. Mathew H. Kennedy (224)
> 2nd Lt. Charles M. Kunz (224)
> 16 Capt. Marion E. Carl (223)
> 2nd Lt. Robert M. D'Arcy (224).

Armistead counted six Zeros strung out loosely well above and left of the bombers. Actually there were nine, the 2nd *Chūtai* led by Lt. (jg) Yamaguchi Sadao, while Aioi's 1st *Chūtai* with eight Zeros flew the corresponding slot to the right. Cruising at 8,500 meters (27,880 feet), the escort had strung out in loose formation. The 3rd *Chūtai*'s nine Zeros under Lt. (jg) Suzuki Usaburō (NA 68-1940) went higher, probably to 9,500 meters (31,160 feet).

The bandits Armistead could see posed no immediate threat, so the Marines peeled off to execute overhead runs against the left rear of the formation. As they dived, the 90-mm AA guns north of Henderson Field started blasting away at the bombers. Together Armistead and Carl shot the left trailing Takao Type 1 (PO1c

Asatobi Sueo) out in flames. At the same time Mathew Kennedy and Charles Kunz bounced Nabeta's Kisarazu *chūtai* flying ahead of Makino's Takao bombers. Kunz set afire the left trailer, PO1c Ogawa Kinnosuke's Type 1. Ground observers saw both stricken *rikkōs* fall. For the time being Ogawa straggled behind the formation, but Asatobi dropped straight into the water. Armistead's division claimed three bombers (one each to Kennedy and Kunz, one shared by Armistead and Carl). Kennedy's propeller pitch control malfunctioned (a common malady for F4F-4s), and he glided back for a safe deadstick landing at the fighter strip. Wary of Zeros lurking above, the others, with the exception of Carl, dived away from the fight.

About the same time Armistead attacked, a VMF-223 division reached the altitude of the oncoming bomber formation:

    12 Maj. Frederick R. Payne, Jr. (212-223)
    14 2nd Lt. Frank C. Drury (212-223)
    13 2nd Lt. Jack E. Conger (212-223)
    19 2nd Lt. Charles S. Hughes (223)

Payne rolled right to set up side attacks, but Yamaguchi's nine Zeros (the same *chūtai* seen by Armistead) quickly intervened. Payne told his pilots to scram, and the F4Fs scattered with the 2nd *Chūtai* in wild pursuit down to low altitude. One Mitsubishi latched onto Jack Conger's tail at 16,000 feet. "Straining and shuddering" in tight maneuvers, he countered his more nimble opponent by constant scissoring. Over the channel the two gradually worked their way down to 6,000 feet. Suddenly the Japanese dived beneath the F4F and inexplicably slow-rolled out in front. A good burst from Conger's guns sent it spinning away in distress, but a teammate retaliated with a 20-mm shell through the Wildcat's wing. With jammed guns, Conger escaped in the clouds.[3]

Shaking off the F4Fs, the fifteen land attack planes made their bomb runs against the field. At 1357 in the midst of black 90-mm shell bursts that damaged numerous aircraft, Nabeta's bombardier orchestrated a fine attack. Off duty for bathing, Smokey Stover from VF-5 watched with fascination the fighter contrails intersect the "double Vee of silvery bombers far up." Suddenly he realized the enemy had reached their release points and shouted a warning to the others as he threw himself to the dirt.[4]

At the same instant a mixture of 250-kilogram bombs and 60-kilogram "daisy cutters" exploded in a long string from Kukum to the Pagoda, set numerous fires, and holed five SBDs (one destroyed), five TBFs, and six F4Fs—a significant fraction of the available aircraft. Out riding a jeep on Henderson Field when the bombs detonated, Lieutenant Commander Shands tried to rescue the crew of a stalled plane. The concussion of a nearby blast threw him roughly into the seat and reinjured his bad back. Bombs also knocked out communications in 1st Mar-Div headquarters, which gravely affected ongoing Marine offensive operations at the Mantanikau. Nabeta later reported bombing four large and forty small aircraft on the ground.

After following Payne's F4Fs down, Yamaguchi and wingmen PO3c Nomura Shigeru and Sea2c Matsugeta Toshimi maneuvered to strafe the Lunga airfield. That tactic was popular with the air groups from the East Indies. They were the first Japanese to notice a second airfield in operation. From a foxhole next to the RECON truck parked near Fighter 1, Walt Bayler and Joe Renner, the two CACTUS FDOs, spotted the three Zeros barreling in. Renner ran to the radio truck, alerted the CAP, and kept sending reports until Lieutenant Colonel Scollin vehemently ordered him to take cover. Antiaircraft gunners claimed one raider, but all three strafers got clean away.[5]

Simpler's four F4Fs never had a chance to intercept the Japanese; neither did Galer with five Marine Wildcats. John Wesolowski led the other VF-5 division to 24,000 feet. He and his three companions drew close to the bomber formation about the time Yamaguchi's 2nd *Chūtai* jumped Payne's flight. Paralleling the fast-moving land attack planes as they flew east of Lunga, Wesolowski continued climbing for proper attack position. However Mankin, his wingman, grew impatient and rashly peeled off alone, but because he lacked sufficient altitude advantage, his dive was too shallow. Consequently, his overhead run never developed, and he ended up shooting while still on his back, a terrible angle. Not only did he miss, but his awkward maneuvering kinked the ammunition belts and jammed his guns.

From VF-5 only Paul Mankin actually threatened the bombers, and his run was no thing of beauty. The 2nd Section of Cash Register and JoJo Nesbitt broke off to follow him down. At this moment two of Aioi's 1st *Chūtai* Zeros intervened. Register countered by turning sharply starboard out of the way, while Nesbitt swung left. The lead Zero crossed in front of Register, who snapped off a full-deflection shot, certain he torched the bandit. No members of the 1st *Chūtai* went down. The second Japanese forced Register to run. A bit miffed at the way his teammates scattered, he complained in his report: "I consider myself fortunate to get back, since it is well known that Grumman's do not have much of a chance against 'Zero's' unless the Grumman's stick together and use team tactics." Actually Nesbitt lost contact when he evaded the first two bandits. A little later he drove off a Zero attacking another Grumman and covered its withdrawal. The quick skirmish division diverted Aioi's Zeros away from the land attack planes and left them untended.

As Mankin recovered at 12,000 feet from his abortive overhead, he was startled when two Zeros passed immediately ahead of him. Swiftly pulling the charging handles for all six guns, he attacked:

> I tore after one and the other disappeared, thank heaven . . . The one I went after was the closest I had ever been to a Japanese plane. I could easily see [the pilot's] head through the back of his canopy . . . For an instant I felt I was shooting a man instead of a plane. I was so close that with the pipper on his canopy the right outboard gun was the only one that fired, and the tracers were to the right of his canopy. He pulled up sharply and so did I, but by kicking a little left rudder I brought the line of fire on target. I knew there would be no bailing out.[6]

Smoke from the burning Zero filled Mankin's cockpit. Wesolowski happened to see the start of this altercation, but before he could get into effective range, the F4F shot down the Zero. Ken Frazier of 223 watched the flaming fighter fall all the way to the ground. Diving almost vertically at high speed, it passed by Register, who side-stepped what he thought was an attack and finished off what he believed was his second kill of the day. The Zero plowed into a grassy meadow about a mile south of Henderson Field. Guns no longer functioning, Mankin dropped in for a landing on the main field and was greeted by a Marine cheering section. For the 21-year-old NAP it was an unforgettable moment: "I had my fifth plane. I was an ACE."[7] His opponent, WO Yamanouchi Giichi, 2nd *Shōtai* leader in Yamaguchi's 2nd *Chūtai*, was highly experienced (wings 1935) and an old China hand. He met his death while climbing with a wingman seeking other members of the 2nd *Chūtai* who had swooped low after Payne's F4Fs.

After the initial combats, Simpler radioed for a high-altitude squadron rendezvous over the channel off Lunga. The scattered VF-5 pilots tried to comply. En route, Wesolowski regained 18,000 feet, when three Zeros dropped out of the sun. The leader had fired and flown on past, before the Weasel ever saw him. Two more bandits dived in, so he responded with a steep dive. Suddenly he overtook the lead Zero and shot until he saw a flash and the Mitsubishi apparently explode. He left the two Japanese wingmen behind in a harrowing high-speed dive. Wesolowski's opponents came from Aioi's 1st *Chūtai,* which quickly regrouped after sparring with his division a few minutes before. Instead of a kill, he apparently damaged PO2c Hashiguchi Yoshirō's Zero.[8]

Two VF-5 new arrivals also climbed toward the skipper's rendezvous. Having taken off later than the others, Jensen and McDonald never got high enough for a crack at the bombers. Instead, they patrolled 23,000 feet over Kukum, when about five of Aioi's Zeros showed up. McDonald eyeballed the intruders diving in from his left and radioed a warning to Jensen. Turning up into them to scissor, he unfortunately climbed too steeply and stalled. The first Zero handily evaded his head-on run by rolling out to the side. He also tried scissoring the next, but met with the same result. Suddenly a 7.7-mm bullet lanced into his cockpit from astern, grazed his neck, and shattered an instrument on the panel. Because of his Type D oxygen mask, McDonald could not wear goggles. Glass slivers temporarily blinded him. With a Zero crowding his tail, he was in a bad way.

Jensen saw his wingman get it and spin away, then it was his turn. Before he could counter, his "cockpit seemed to explode." From astern two 7.7-mm slugs wounded him and destroyed part of his plexiglass windshield. The F4F pitched into a steep dive. After regaining control, Jensen, with blood streaming down his face, used his speed to escape and rolled his ailerons to prevent a Zero from staying with him. He descended all the way to 4,000 feet, then cautiously circled in the clouds for a half hour before returning to base. When McDonald's vision cleared, he likewise found himself in a wild dive and aimed for a convenient cloud below. No Japanese pursued.

Only the rugged construction of their Wildcats saved Jensen and McDonald from more serious grief on their maiden CACTUS scramble. As Sandy Crews remarked in his diary, the Japanese merely "checked them out." Jensen's armor plate stopped at least four 7.7-mm rounds; other bullets holed his vacuum and auxiliary fuel tanks, as well as his right wing. McDonald found "one good hole" through his canopy and more bullet holes around the engine cowling and through the tail. The armor plate behind his seat had also saved his life. Both men were very impressed with the quality of the opposition, described by Jensen as "very high caliber." They were also quite exceptional given the generally poor enemy fighter tactics. He added that the Zeros "could not be shaken by us if they would chop their guns and sit on our tails." This is more proof that Japanese did not often dogfight, but preferred firing passes and follow-up attacks.

The combat was far from over. While his escorts chased F4Fs, Nabeta flew northwest back over the channel. At 1408, PO1c Ogawa's crippled Kisarazu Type 1 finally disappeared with no survivors. Soon Marion Carl caught up with the rest, counted fifteen bombers and at 1417 ripped the Takao *chūtai* in the rear. His overhead run knocked out the right engine of PO1c Satō Yoshimi's Type 1. The smoking *rikkō* left formation, but kept on going. Satō took refuge at Buka.

After diving out with Payne's division, Frank Drury (212) had 2nd Lt. Floyd A. Lynch (121) join on his wing. Overhead they noticed the contrails of fighters dogfighting, observed the bombers making their getaway, then climbed quickly toward Florida Island to cut across their line of retreat. After 60 miles the two overtook a formation of thirteen Type 1s beyond northeastern Florida. In addition to Carl's victim, another Takao *rikkō* (Res. Lt. [jg] Nagata Takeo, the 12th *Shōtai* leader) had pressed ahead alone to rush two wounded crewmen to base. At 1422, Drury's overhead shot Nagata's number 2, the outside plane in the left echelon (PO1c Oinuma Setsuzō), riddled the cockpit and wingroot, and wrecked the right engine. At 1535 Oinuma ditched at Rekata Bay. Aioi's escort never caught up with the three Marines.

Claims for the ten VMF-223 and -224 pilots actually engaged amounted to five bombers (Carl 1.5, Kennedy 1, Kunz 1, Drury 1, and Armistead .5) and one fighter to Conger. Fighting Five's six F4Fs tallied four Zeros: two to Register (his fourth and fifth kills), and one each to Wesolowski and Mankin (his fifth). For 282 90-mm rounds, the 3rd Defense Battalion tallied one bomber confirmed and one probable. No F4Fs went down, although six were shot up; two VF-5 pilots, Jensen and McDonald, were slightly wounded.

The Japanese estimated about twenty-one Grummans had intercepted the strike, and the Kisarazu gunners claimed one destroyed. Two land attack planes (one Kisarazu, one Takao) went down over the target, and another (Takao) ditched at Rekata. All fourteen surviving *rikkōs* sustained some sort of damage. Of twenty-six 3rd Air Group Zeros in close escort, only seventeen (Aioi's 1st *Chūtai* and Yamaguchi's 2nd *Chūtai*) actually fought. They claimed five Grummans (including two unconfirmed) and one unconfirmed carrier bomber, evidently a CACTUS SBD on afternoon search, but no intercepts are recorded. The reports offer no individual pilot credits. Warrant Officer Yamanouchi was missing in action. Another Zero suffered slight damage. Suzuki's 3rd *Chūtai* never sighted enemy planes, probably because they stayed too high. Neither did Kurakane's air control force. Thus the strongest fighter escort yet sent over Guadalcanal proved ineffective in protecting the bombers.

The 27th was also noteworthy for the evacuation of the last crews of the *Enterprise*'s Flight 300, having landed the evening of 24 August during the Battle of the Eastern Solomons. Turner Caldwell told correspondent Dick Tregaskis that he used to think there was no such thing as pilot fatigue: "Now I know what they [the flight surgeons] meant. There's a point where you just get to be no good; you're shot to the devil—and there's nothing you can do about it."[9] What was true for Caldwell's men certainly applied to the others. Simpler carefully watched his VF-5 pilots to assess the toll of combat, disease, and stress on their stamina.

THE GREAT BOMBER ROUT

The morning of 28 September brought a flurry of activity at Henderson Field. Around 0830 an AirSoPac B-17 operating from Espiritu Santo reported enemy ships in Manning Strait between Choiseul and Santa Isabel. Supposedly two transports and a destroyer swung at anchor, and another transport had run aground. Distance from Lunga was about 175 miles. Geiger quickly ordered a strike of eight SBDs and three TBFs escorted by Frank Green's four VF-5 F4Fs. As they started to attack, they discovered the "ships" to be three small islands. On the way back from the useless mission, the strike braved bad weather. In his diary Green uncharitably called the sighting a "typical Army report," as the AAF was renowned for wrongly identifying ship types.

Shot up in a raid on Tonolei harbor, 27 September, Capt. Glenn H. Kramer's B-17E
Flying Fortress (19122) from the 72nd Bomb Squadron takes refuge at Henderson Field.
Four Type 2 sea fighters from the *Kamikawa Maru* put one 20-mm shell into the ball
turret and another through the navigator's window in the nose. (NA 80-G-20684)

The 28th saw another day of heavy effort against Guadalcanal. The Misawa
buntaichō Lt. Morita Rinji (NA 63-1936) led twenty-seven land attack planes.
His 1st *Chūtai* of nine Misawa *rikkōs* took the lead, and the 2nd *Chūtai* with nine
Takao Type 1s under Lt. Kusuhata Yoshinobu (NA 64-1937) formed up on the
left. Lt. Naka Seiji (NA 66-1938) brought nine Kanoya Type 1s from Kavieng and
at 1000 eased into Morita's formation as 3rd *Chūtai* on the right. They departed
10 minutes later. Each Type 1 carried ten 60-kilogram bombs.[10]

The 5th Air Attack Force staff reversed the escort plan of the previous day. Of
forty-two assigned Zero Model 21s, Lieutenant Kofukuda with twenty-seven
(eighteen from the 6th and nine Kanoya) undertook air control duty far out ahead
of the main body, while Lieutenant Kawai's fifteen Tainan Zeros served as the
covering force in direct escort of the bombers. At 0930 Kawai took off from
Rabaul East and promptly contacted Morita's land attack planes as they climbed
toward 7,500 meters (24,600 feet). Taking station 1,000 meters higher than the
rikkōs, Kawai placed his 1st *Chūtai* of nine Zeros on the right, while the 2nd
Chūtai of six under Lt. (jg) Ōno Takeyoshi (NA 68-1940) took the left slot.
Young Ōno showed much promise and hopefully would prove a worthy successor to the fallen Lt. (jg) Sasai Junichi. Inexplicably Kofukuda's twenty-seven
air control Zeros (one soon aborted) left Lakunai Field only at 1010, much *later*
than the close escort.[11] This delay compromised the escort plan even before the
mission had fairly begun. Kofukuda ended up chasing the main body instead of
advancing ahead of it. A massive strike of sixty-six planes in two elements left
for CACTUS.

Near to 1300 as Morita's main body approached New Georgia, Kawai's Zero unexpectedly developed engine trouble and lost altitude. Obviously startled, the other eight 1st *Chūtai* pilots followed him down until he could turn control over to WO Yamashita Sahei, who led the flight back toward the bombers. Kawai barely made it to Buka, and his leadership would be sorely missed over Guadalcanal. Again the lack of aircraft radios in the Zeros adversely affected their combat performance. Kawai could not advise Morita, the bomber leader, Ōno his 2nd *Chūtai* leader, or Kofukuda with the air control Zeros.

Kennedy heard the enemy over Vangunu and alerted CACTUS at 1258, adding it "sounds like fair numbers." RADAR TWO detected the strike almost simultaneously, bearing 265 degrees and 136 miles. It looked as if the Japanese were aiming south of Guadalcanal instead of coming straight in. At 1310 with the YELLOW alert, thirty-five F4Fs began taking off. Twenty were Marine Grummans (ten each from VMF-223 and VMF-224 flying in mixed groups). Included in their number was Lieutenant Colonel Bauer, up early that morning from Efate on business. Delighted at the prospect of meeting a raid, he eagerly talked Galer into giving him a fighter. Fifteen VF-5 F4Fs (all the squadron had in operation) scrambled from Henderson Field.[12]

At about 1320 Morita spotted Guadalcanal ahead and off to his left, but continued on course until he had passed the island's southwest coast. Only then did he turn left to assume a direct northeasterly course to Lunga. Perhaps he took the southern detour to confuse the interceptors, but possibly he realized his escorts lagged behind and wanted to delay the final approach to the target until they caught up. On the way WO Kotani Takeo, the Misawa 3rd *Shōtai* leader, and wingman PO2c Motoyama Masaru aborted the mission. (Kotani here missed a rendezvous with death, but as the flag pilot on 18 April 1943 he died with Admiral Yamamoto.) That left twenty-five land attack planes, now directly protected only by Ōno's six Zeros. The stage was set for another classic air battle over Guadalcanal.

All Morita's gambit accomplished was to give CACTUS interceptors, warned by radar, even more time to get to high altitude. Major Renner, CACTUS FDO, matched the maneuver by advising the CAP that the enemy now approached from 235 degrees. The twenty Marine F4Fs turned southwest in two separate

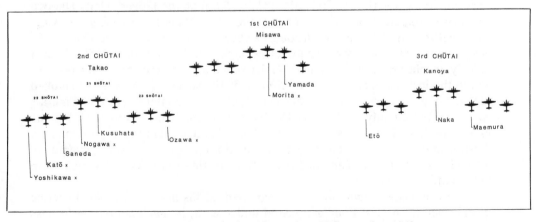

Japanese land attack plane formation, 28 September 1942.

groups, one small and the other quite large. John L. Smith led with a tight formation of seventeen Wildcats stepped down in column behind him:

1	2
16 Maj. John L. Smith (223)	13 Capt. Marion E. Carl (223)
2nd Lt. William V. Brooks (224)	2 2nd Lt. Cloyd R. Jeans (223)
19 2nd Lt. Willis S. Lees III (223)	12 Maj. Frederick R. Payne (212-223)
15 2nd Lt. Robert R. Read (223)	14 2nd Lt. Frank C. Drury (212-223)
18 2nd Lt. Charles S. Hughes (223)	2nd Lt. George A. Treptow (121-224)
10 2nd Lt. John S. P. Dean, Jr. (121-223)	

3
Maj. John F. Dobbin (224)
2nd Lt. Dean S. Hartley, Jr. (224)
Capt. Stanley S. Nicolay (224)
2nd Lt. Allan M. Johnson (224)
Capt. Darrell D. Irwin (224)
2nd Lt. Thomas H. Mann (121-224)

Slightly behind to the right and above were Major Galer (224), Lieutenant Colonel Bauer (212), and Capt. Howard K. Marvin (223 in number 6).[13]

Ably directed by Renner, the twenty Marine F4Fs at 28,000 feet attained a 4,000-foot advantage over the bombers ("in beautiful formation") while still many miles southwest of Lunga. Smith looked carefully for the escort. First he noticed three flights each of about eight Zeros at his same height, but far behind his quarry. They were Kofukuda's twenty-six air control Zeros. Six other Zeros (Ōno's Tainan *chūtai*) flew to the left of the bombers, but about 1,000 feet below. Yamashita's eight Tainan Zeros were not even in sight.

Using his favorite set-up against bombers, Smith led his seventeen F4Fs from right to left across the formation. At 1353 John Dobbin's trailing division peeled off for overheads against the Kanoya *chūtai* on the right. The six Marines claimed three bombers, and at the very least knocked one Kanoya Type 1 (PO1c Maemura Katsumi's number 2 in the 3rd *Shōtai*) out of formation and perforated several others. Dean Hartley, Dobbin's wingman, set himself up for an excellent run, but discovered to his intense disgust that he had not charged his guns and wasted his attack.

Rapidly closing from ahead of the bombers, Galer lined up for a tricky, swift opposite-course overhead against the Takao *chūtai* on the Japanese left. The two adversaries roared at each other at something like 400 knots. Dropping one wing, Galer half-rolled at the proper instant to execute a crisp, nearly vertical, overhead against PO2c Nogawa Kazuo, left wingman in the 21st *Shōtai*. The Type 1 quickly caught fire. Still in the dive, Galer rolled sharply and shifted his point of aim to the inside trailer in the 22nd *Shōtai*, PO1c Saneda Tamotsu, and smoked the right engine. Lower down at 20,000 feet, Galer encountered PO1c Maemura's Kanoya *rikkō* already shot up by Dobbin's division. It looked as if all but the pilot were dead, which was not the case. His side attack sent the Type 1 spinning down into the clouds at 10,000 feet but, far from finished, Maemura eventually ditched his battered airplane at Rekata Bay. In these attacks Galer racked up kills eight, nine, and ten.

Following Galer down, Joe Bauer experienced his first air combat. Reacting quickly before the last bombers passed underneath, he made an overhead pass against one in the left (22nd) Takao *shōtai*. Very likely his target was the outside plane, PO1c Yoshikawa Seihachi. Not much is known of Bauer's part in this

VMF-223, late September 1942. *Top row (l to r)*: Marvin, Frazier, Smith, Carl, Hughes, Kendrick. *Bottom row:* Read, Gutt, Lees, Winter, Jeans, Canfield. (Col. F. C. Drury)

battle, but it appears he made his run and regained altitude for a second go after the same target.

By the time "Marve" Marvin, the trailer, could set up his run, the bombers had slipped past. Below he glimpsed one of Ōno's Tainan Zeros, bounced it with a steep dive, and was certain it flamed. Another (most likely PO3c Moriura Toyoo) riddled his F4F with hits to the fuselage and wings. Fortunately the self-sealing fuel tank absorbed the bullets without leaking. Marvin took refuge in a convenient cloud and returned to base. Although he failed to destroy any Zeros, his surprise attack disrupted the Tainan 2nd *Chūtai* at a crucial moment, forcing the six Zeros to regroup before they could get back into the fight. Fresh from flight training in June, Ōno demonstrated the talent to be an excellent fighter leader, but in this desperate situation his inexperience showed.

Almost simultaneous with Galer's assault, Smith's 2nd Division under Marion Carl also rolled in against the Takao bombers. When Smith swung right to cross over the bombers, Carl cut inside of the turn and brought his five F4Fs into position for overhead runs against the left bomber division. He peeled off first against Yoshikawa, the left trailer already in trouble from Bauer's first pass, quickly scored, and riddled the *rikkō*.

Rex Jeans, Carl's wingman, turned right to parallel the target's flight path, then started his run. Appearing off his left wing was Bill Lees, who had dropped out of Smith's lead division. To make room for him, Jeans added throttle to "kick" his Grumman ahead over to the lead planes in the bomber formation

(Morita's Misawa *chūtai*), and rolled into his overhead. This placed him in excellent position against Morita's right wingman, PO2c Yamada Shizuo. A little later Jeans noticed this bomber straggle out of formation. In the meantime Lees took one of the bombers further back in the lead section of the left division. This was PO2c Nogawa's Takao Type 1, already perforated by Galer. After Lees attacked, Nogawa fell in flames.

Next from Carl's division, Fritz Payne selected an inside aircraft in the left (Takao) division—PO2c Saneda's *rikkō* already stricken on Galer's first run. Saneda had lost altitude and trailed the group. Payne pressed his firing pass to the limit and pulled out directly behind the bomber. Saneda's right engine smoked heavily, leading Payne to believe the target was about to break up. He could not watch it go down, because another bomber, the top of its fuselage thoroughly riddled, nearly collided with him. Turning swiftly, Payne snapped a burst at this interloper before he lost contact. This appears to have been Yoshikawa, already beset by Bauer and Carl. Eager for the kill, Bauer latched onto the. stricken bomber and expended nearly all his ammunition during a pursuit that only ended with the *rikkō*'s crash into the jungle not far from the field. Treptow, Payne's wingman, submitted no claims.

Jostled out of position, Frank Drury, Carl's other wingman, did not dive along with the others. It took a minute or so for him to regain station over the Takao *chūtai* on the left. By the time he rolled into his overhead, the whole left section broke up: Nogawa and Yoshikawa going down and Saneda in obvious trouble.

VMF-224, late September 1942. *Top row (l to r)*: Hollowell, Brooks, Musselman, Johnson, Kennedy, Kunz, Hartley, Marine Gunner Fuller. *Bottom row:* D'Arcy, Nicolay, Dobbin, Galer, Armistead, Irwin, Walter, Treptow. Number 15 is believed to be a VMF-224 aircraft. (Col. F. C. Drury)

VF-5 in front of its ready tent at Henderson Field, about 28 Sept. 1942. *Top row* (*l to r*): Grimmell, Robb, Bright, March, Wesolowski, Morgan, Clarke, Crews, Jensen, Stover, Rouse. *Center row:* Register, McDonald, Simpler, Kleinman. *Bottom row:* Nesbitt (*seated at l*), Green, Shoemaker, Kleinmann, Roach, Halford, Currie, Blair, Mankin. (Capt. H. W. Crews)

The 22nd *Shōtai* leader, PO1c Katō Kaeizō's *rikkō,* still flew its slot in the formation, so Drury went after it. He put a strong burst forward in the aircraft and perhaps hit the pilots, because Katō pulled up steeply, fell off into a wingover, and dived out of sight.

Smith and the balance of his division, Bill Brooks, Robert Read, Charley Hughes, and John Dean, were the last in. Denied elbow room for overheads by the many F4Fs attacking ahead, Smith settled for less desirable high-sides from the left. Nobody scored. To add injury to insult, cockpit dirt blew into his eyes and spoiled his aim.

The fourteen Marines who assailed the enemy's left flank claimed eight bombers and one fighter. To them it appeared that the whole side crumbled into smoking and burning airplanes. In a 1943 interview Galer described how on recovering from his pass, "you could look back up and there were wings, motors, and tail assemblies floating all around." Joe Bauer penned in his diary, "It was the greatest sight of my life to see the Jap bombers fall out of the sky."[14]

Galer and company knocked down far fewer than eight land attack planes, but nonetheless the effects on the Takao Air Group were catastrophic. In three minutes (1353–1355), four *rikkōs* dropped out of formation. Nogawa from the 21st *Shōtai* went down in flames, while Katō and Yoshikawa from the 22nd *Shōtai* simply fell away. Badly shot up, Saneda (number 3 in the ill-fated 22nd *Shōtai*), gradually faded back out of sight. From the Kanoya *chūtai* on the right, Maemura's Type 1 had departed courtesy of Dobbin's division. Rex Jeans worked over Yamada's aircraft in the Misawa 1st *Chūtai,* but it stayed in formation. Most of the Marines had glimpsed Zeros above. In their eagerness to avenge the land attack planes, Ōno's 2nd *Chūtai* chased some F4Fs away from the bombers.

Meanwhile, the fifteen VF-5 Grummans climbed at full power in two groups. Howard Crews led a compact formation of eleven in three divisions, because Simpler could not join up in time. Wally Clarke's division trailed the main body:

1	2	3	4
Crews	Grimmell	Simpler	Clarke
Kleinmann	Halford	Mankin	Nesbitt
Blair	Morgan	Kleinman	Stover
Wesolowski	Currie		March

Attaining 26,000 feet VF-5's main body neared the bombers just as the last of Smith's F4Fs made their unsuccessful passes. Crews took the eleven into successive high-side runs against the already battered left side of the bomber formation. He smoked the left engine of one *rikkō,* which Wesolowski later noted as having burned and fallen out of formation. Second was Junior Kleinmann who fired into one bomber which spun out of view. The unexpected appearance beneath of one of Smith's F4Fs compelled Crud Blair to roll out and shift his aim to the left outside (number 2) bomber, PO1c Etō Tetsuji, in the right (Kanoya) *chūtai.* Blair's bullets punctured the port engine and wingroot and killed Etō. The *rikkō* "practically did a flip flop" and dropped away from the others.[15]

Fourth to attack, Wesolowski counted two bombers set afire prior to his dive. Then he flamed his target's left wingroot as well. After his pass, the Weasel dived to 12,000 feet, where he happened to join Dobbin and Hartley of 224. Hartley still fumed at his inability to shoot at the bombers during his overhead pass and was not particularly pleased to see a darkly bearded VF-5 pilot, sans flight helmet, grinning broadly and showing three fingers. Happy over his fifth kill, the Weasel let the Leathernecks know what he and his squadron had accomplished. Hartley said later he was about ready then and there to gun down the smirking Navy pilot![16]

The high-speed Type 1s obliged the rest of VF-5 to nose down to retain good attack positions and diminished their altitude advantage. Larry Grimmell, fifth in line, started his run from only 1,000 feet over the formation. His target's wing disintegrated, pulling the Type 1 up into a wingover, before the *rikkō* fell off in flames and broke up. The next bomber he shot went down the same way.

Following Grimmell down, Jim Halford noticed some Zeros coming up behind the F4Fs—Kofukuda's 6th Air Group fighters which finally overtook Morita. Some moved closer to intervene. As he pushed over in his attack, a Zero that he never saw jumped him from above and peppered his fuselage and wing with about three 20-mm and seven 7.7-mm rounds. Two bullets lightly creased his neck, and shrapnel scored the glove on his left hand. The cockpit filled with black smoke and flying debris. He chopped his throttle, nosed over dead-stick when his engine stopped, and still followed through with a run against a land attack plane. One burst set it aflame. Halford held his dive to 15,000 feet, then restarted his engine without difficulty.

By the time number 7, George Morgan, took his turn, the remaining F4Fs held only a 500-foot advantage over the fast-stepping land attack planes. With a shallow high-side run, he massaged a *rikkō* and thought he got the tail gunner, if nothing else. Wingman "Mole" Currie finished the job by smoking that bomber's left engine. From the rear of the formation Simpler had watched his pilots make their high-sides in succession, then came his turn. His own bad luck continued.

The gun circuit malfunctioned and delayed firing until he had gone past the target. Behind the skipper, Paul Mankin executed a high-astern run against a trailing land attack plane and observed no effect; nor was Johnny Kleinman's attack successful.

During VF-5's assault, the bomber formation inexplicably salvoed its bombs near a jungle trail about ten miles west of Henderson Field. Most likely this error resulted from the loss of Morita's command plane, uncovered by the dispersal of the Takao *chūtai* on the left. As he recovered from his run, Crews saw one bomber roll over on its back and spin. Several VF-5 pilots obviously claimed this one airplane. The Japanese observers dropped on command from the lead plane, so when Morita's Type 1 careened out of formation, they evidently released their payloads. Soon the whole formation broke up. Lieutenant Naka later wrote that his Kanoya *chūtai* had dropped bombs while in a sharp turn and was not certain whether they even hit the airfield. Even so he tallied seven aircraft destroyed on the ground!

Although VF-5 claimed eight bombers in this phase of the intercept, Crews correctly counted only four dropping away in distress, "just like a Hollywood movie."[17] In addition to Morita, the other three *rikkōs* were: PO2c Ozawa Yoshihei from the Takao 23rd *Shōtai*, PO1c Etō's Kanoya (already damaged), and PO2c Yamada (Morita's previously damaged right wingman). Etō's crew later crashed at the uncompleted airfield at Buin. Yamada made it to Buka, but VF-5 was not finished with Ozawa.

Of the Marines, only Smith and Brooks, his wingman, regained altitude for another try. Crossing over to the right of the bombers, where Yamashita's Tainan Zeros had not yet caught up, they hit the right trailing section of Kanoya land attack planes. Each man claimed one bomber, but none of the 3rd *Shōtai*'s Type 1s took heavy damage. Brooks did not escape unscathed. Cannon fire from one of the Kanoya tail gunners struck his engine and set the Grumman smoking, forcing Brooks to land immediately.

In addition to observing the bombers, the fighter pilots carefully watched the fighter escorts, whose tactics seemed especially puzzling. The widely scattered Zeros appeared to fly simple line-astern formations behind their flight leaders. Crews thought them "more interested in acrobatics than intercepting our VF." Several even essayed slow rolls. Such runs as they did try usually started about 2,000 feet above lone Wildcats, with the Japanese rolling over into wingovers to dive for no-deflection stern shots. They proved quite ineffective. Other than Halford, the outmatched escort did not seriously bother VF-5. In his report Simpler commented, "Had [U.S.] Navy flyers been in the Zeros today, they would have slaughtered the Grummans."

While the main body pummeled the bombers, Clarke paralleled their course from a few thousand yards to the left and gained position for proper high-side runs. His 2nd Section of Smokey Stover and Eddie March peeled off early for what turned out to be shallow high-sides against the bombers and naturally failed to score. Diving past 16,000 feet, one Zero rather ineffectually lunged at Stover, put a 7.7-mm slug in his tail, and pulled out directly ahead. He responded with four quick but equally ineffective bursts. Evading with its "usual superior maneuverability," the Zero slanted away nearly vertically through a cloud, a good thing because Stover's guns no longer worked. About four minutes after the 2nd Section attacked, Clarke decided he was not going to get a good shot at the bombers, so instead he went after two Zeros below. No results appeared from his fire, so he kept on diving. Nesbitt, his wingman, followed but never saw the target. Clarke headed down to 7,000 feet and turned toward Savo to intercept cripples on their way out.

Five other VF-5 pilots likewise spiraled down to lower altitude and sought stragglers while headed west for the predetermined squadron rendezvous at 5,000 feet over Point Cruz. The rest chased the bomber formation for follow-up attacks. Bound and determined to get his first enemy plane, Simpler crossed over to the right of the bombers, just in time to greet Yamashita's 1st *Chūtai*, which had finally caught up. A Zero he never glimpsed blew 20-mm shells through his right wingroot and right horizontal stabilizer and shot numerous 7.7-mm bullets into the right fuselage. The skipper dived to safety and flew alone back to base. His opponent was Sea1c Nakazawa Tsuneyoshi, the only 1st *Chūtai* pilot credited with a confirmed Grumman kill.

Kleinmann and Blair joined at 10,000 feet and climbed together after the bombers. Over the channel they encountered about nine Misawa and Takao *rikkōs* still in formation trailed by one straggler (PO2c Ozawa of the Takao 23rd *Shōtai*) limping along about 1,000 feet below them. No escort was in sight. From ahead the two F4Fs made overhead passes against the cripple. Kleinmann's guns failed, but Blair's long burst tore into Ozawa's left engine and put the Type 1 into a violent left skid. Soon the bomber lost altitude and headed toward Tulagi. Blair reprised with a 180-degree turn and charged in from high above its tail, whose gunner lobbed orange 20-mm tracers in his direction. Blair shot off his remaining ammunition, and the bomber dropped steeply away. Beset by a Zero, he had to leave, but Wesolowski saw the Takao Type 1 splash.[18] Morgan and Currie tried to join in, but Zeros also ran them off.

While the bomber formation withdrew northwest past Florida, other CACTUS fighter pilots hunted cripples, a good many of which were far from finished. At 16,000 feet Fritz Payne of VMF-223 ran across a lone bomber "going downhill all the way to Savo." A miscalculated side attack put him directly behind, easy pickings for the tail gunner, who surprisingly never fired back. He lost the target in the clouds. Grimmell and Mankin of VF-5 joined at 15,000 feet, then let down toward the rendezvous. Mankin observed one *rikkō* seemingly in good shape (although Grimmell called it a "cripple") nose down in a shallow glide at 220 knots. Grimmell turned for an opposite ("roundhouse") attack as the Japanese went by, while Mankin raked its fuselage from fore to aft, but to no effect. At 5,000 feet the tough old bird escaped into a cloud layer.

Headed toward the Point Cruz rendezvous, Halford flew up alongside Crews at 7,000 feet, battle damage evident on his fuselage, especially the turtleback, where a gaping hole was all that remained of the raft compartment. Crews asked if he was all right and heard affirmative. Above them a westbound land attack plane lost altitude as it limped along the north coast. Very likely this was the same *rikkō* attacked by Grimmell and Mankin. Drawing near as the bomber dropped below 5,000 feet, Crews and Halford were rather surprised to see its mutilated right wingtip, bent upward at a 30-degree angle as the result of a midair collision. By the time they coordinated their runs from both sides, the Type 1 had descended so low that its propwash rippled the surface of the sea. During their attacks the *rikkō* exploded at 25 feet, and its flaming wreckage plowed into the water. Both men felt they were entitled to the victory, but neither wanted a half-kill to his credit. Back at the field they flipped a coin, and Crews won.[19]

On the way out the harried Tainan escort managed one victory. From Ōno's 2nd *Chūtai*, PO3c Moriura, who had already roughed up Marvin's 223 F4F, ambushed a lone VMSB-231 SBD flying a radar calibration test hop about a dozen miles west of Guadalcanal. The pilot was 2nd Lt. Dale M. Leslie, who had distinguished himself the previous day by establishing contact with the Marines cut off near Point Cruz. Moriura jumped the Dauntless at 3,000 feet and with two passes set it ablaze. The radioman, Pfc. Reed T. Ramsay (another VMSB-241 Midway veteran), was killed, but Leslie managed to bail out at 500 feet and rafted to the island's west coast. After five weeks behind enemy lines, he finally returned on 4 November to Lunga.[20]

The CACTUS fighter pilots were jubilant. Counting all the claims, they had accounted for no fewer than twenty-three of twenty-five bombers and one of an estimated thirty Zeros. Individual credits were:

VMF-223		
Maj. J. L. Smith	1 bomber	
Maj. F. R. Payne	1 bomber	
Capt. M. E. Carl	1 bomber	
Capt. H. K. Marvin	1 fighter	
2nd Lt. F. C. Drury	1 bomber	
2nd Lt. C. R. Jeans	1 bomber	
VMF-224		
Maj. R. E. Galer	3 bombers	
Lt. Col. H. W. Bauer	1 bomber	
Capt. S. S. Nicolay	1 bomber	
2nd Lt. W. V. Brooks	1 bomber	
Maj. J. F. Dobbin	0.5 bomber	
2nd Lt. A. M. Johnson	0.5 bomber	
Capt. D. D. Irwin	0.5 bomber	
2nd Lt. T. H. Mann	0.5 bomber	
VF-5		
Lt. H. W. Crews	2 bombers	
Lt. (jg) H. L. Grimmell	2 bombers	
Ens. F. J. Blair	2 bombers	
Ens. B. F. Currie	1 bomber	
Ens. J. A. Halford	1 bomber	
Ens. M. V. Kleinmann	1 bomber	
Ens. J. M. Wesolowski	1 bomber	

The bombers never came near enough to Henderson Field to engage the heavy 90-mm AA guns of the 3rd Defense Battalion (although light AA winged one Tainan Zero). In return CACTUS lost no Wildcats, but five (Marvin and Drury of 223, Brooks of 224, and VF-5's Simpler and Halford) were shot up. One VMSB-231 SBD (Leslie) went missing.

Japanese losses were many fewer than CACTUS believed, but the victory was stunning nevertheless. Five land attack planes: Morita's Misawa command plane and four Takao: PO2c Nogawa (21st *Shōtai*), PO1c Katō and PO1c Yoshikawa (both 22nd *Shōtai*), and PO2c Ozawa (23rd *Shōtai*) were shot down or missing. Two Kanoya Type 1s ditched or crash-landed: PO1c Maemura at Rekata Bay and the dead PO1c Etō's at Buin. Another *rikkō* had to be scrapped from battle damage. Thus the raid cost eight Type 1s and forty-one lives. The seventeen surviving land attack planes sustained damage as well. It was the third worst day (after 8 August and 12 November) for that type of aircraft in all of the Guadalcanal air battles. According to the Japanese, forty Grummans intercepted the strike, but only the Kanoya gunners claimed any (six). The fighter tally amounted to eleven Grumman fighters (including four unconfirmed) and one "Grumman" carrier bomber. One Zero was totaled, and four others took slight damage. The disparity of numbers and unfortunate initial positioning beneath and behind the bombers gave the close escort little chance to break up the interceptors. Inexplicably, Kofukuda's twenty-six air control Zeros exerted very little impact upon the battle; a dozen never even fought. No satisfactory explanation for their failure survives.

The great aerial victory helped make up for the reverses on the Mantanikau. At 1410 Macfarlan and Hay, coastwatchers perched on Gold Ridge far above Lunga, radioed that twelve planes had gone down, half of them bombers. In his diary 1st Lt. Chris Merillat at 1st Division headquarters described "everyone laughing & chattering" at the news. Vandegrift's heartening report reached Ghormley on the *Argonne* at Noumea, while he conferred with admirals Nimitz and Turner and generals "Hap" Arnold and Harmon.[21]

More good news for CACTUS was the arrival of six SBDs and four TBFs led by Lt. Cdr. John Eldridge of VS-71, including the first aircrews from the torpedoed *Wasp*. "Uncle John," as he was known to his squadron, proved to be an indomitable CACTUS warrior. That evening VF-5 was amused by Shoemaker and Roach, who constructed special rat traps for their tent in the coconut grove. Bets were placed as to who would capture more rodents. Certainly there was a plentiful supply of the varmints.

A briefing given that day by Rear Admiral McCain, ex-ComAirSoPac, for the CinCPac staff at Pearl Harbor would have greatly interested CACTUS. According to one listener's notes, the seemingly clairvoyant admiral stated, "The Japs are afraid of our F4F and will not attack consistently." He added, "It seems reasonable to suppose that we have now destroyed the cream of [the enemy's] naval air pilots." McCain stressed Guadalcanal could be held if fighter strength (pilots and aircraft) could be maintained at the present level. Ominously for CACTUS, he concluded, "Unfortunately, the requisite number of VF and trained pilots are not yet in sight."[22]

A CHANGE OF TACTICS

For Base Air Force the loss in the past two days of eleven land attack planes (nearly 20 percent of the effective force) and widespread battle damage to many others represented an especially heavy blow, with wide repercussions. Rear Admiral Ugaki compared Japanese claims with Lieutenant Commander Mitsui's observations on Guadalcanal, which noted that the same number of American interceptors landed as took off. Ugaki complained in his diary, "Why is it that results reported by our attack force and the reported number of planes taking off and landing on the island did not coincide, and only our loss was great?"[23]

On the evening of 28 September a distressed Tsukahara (already ill with malaria) convened a meeting between the staffs of Yamada's 25th and Yamagata's 26th air flotillas.[24] The large numbers of Zeros assigned to escort duty, thirty-eight one day and forty-two the next, did not prevent thirty-odd Grummans at Lunga from ripping through the land attack planes. Yamagata criticized Yamada's fighters for not showing "sufficient will" in cooperating with the *rikkōs* and decried their lack of skill. It was conceded that the Tainan close escort suffered from the unexpected absence of Kawai, who aborted the mission. Yamada's staff neatly turned the tables by pointing out that the "visiting fighters" (the 6th Air Group Detachment) from Yamagata's own 26th Air Flotilla had failed to protect the bombers. That morning Kofukuda's twenty-six air control Zeros departed late and only weakly supported the main body.

Blame having been apportioned, it was time to discuss possible solutions. Clearly, even heavily escorted daylight bombing raids were proving far too costly. For the next 10 days, the commanders would opt for limited night bombing attacks of only nuisance value against Guadalcanal. The task of dealing with enemy fighters fell solely to the Zeros. Yamagata's staff suggested a series of strafing attacks against the Lunga airfields, but Yamada disagreed. He knew from bitter experience that enemy coastwatchers and radar afforded the enemy fighters a warning of at least 30 minutes, making it virtually impossible to surprise Lunga.

How could they force the Grummans to fight under conditions more favorable to the Japanese? The defenders always rose to intercept bombing attacks. However, rather unsportingly they side-stepped the escorts in order to intercept the land attack planes. Yamada's staff thought the threat of a bombing raid was necessary to get the American fighters aloft and suggested fighter sweeps disguised as bombing missions. The *rikkō* decoys would turn around short of the target area. They anticipated much change for the better in early October once they improved facilities at Buka and completed the advance fighter base at Buin. Base Air Force could then employ the Zero 32s in conjunction with two large-scale strikes per day against Guadalcanal.

The morning of 29 September Base Air Force tried the new tactic of a bomber feint combined with a straight fighter sweep. Lieutenant Aioi led twenty-seven Model 21 Zeros from his 3rd Air Group (1st and 2nd *chūtais*) and the Kanoya Air Group Fighter Squadron (3rd *Chūtai*). From Kavieng nine Kanoya land attack planes joined at 1000. Sent to fool Allied coastwatchers, the *rikkōs* accompanied the fighters for two hours, but turned back over the central Solomons. Evidently the Japanese did not know where the coastwatchers lurked and thought they had gone past them. Aioi raced in hoping to catch the climbing Grummans unawares.

In the meantime, a radio message at 0845 had already roused CACTUS. Overlooking Buka, Jack Read reported fighters and bombers at 0730 "now going yours." Actually he only observed new aerial activity at Buka base. The previous day Commander Yamamoto brought twenty-one Zero 32s and five carrier bombers of his reinforced 2nd Air Group to cover the build-up in Shortland harbor for Express runs to Guadalcanal. Kennedy on New Georgia also noted aircraft overflights.

At CACTUS Condition YELLOW sounded at 0855. VF-5 scrambled fifteen F4Fs in a mad dash for altitude. As they reached 22,000 feet Renner radioed, "Navy fighters, pancake," which meant "Land, it was a false alarm." RADAR TWO failed to detect any incoming aircraft. Simpler used the occasion for some training in formation flying with a spiraling "snake dance" over the field, followed by a dive in column from 12,000 feet. Register burned out his engine and set down streaming smoke; Clarke's supercharger blew a rubber gasket, a perennial problem.[25] Chief Poston's machinists swarmed over both Wildcats to get them ready as soon as possible. Alongside the Marine mechanics, his men worked long hours, often overnight, and devotedly maintained VF-5's airplanes.

Early that afternoon, CACTUS radar, rather than coastwatchers, detected incoming raiders. At 1325 MAG-23 scrambled twenty Marine F4Fs from Fighter

1 and fourteen VF-5 F4Fs from Henderson Field.[26] VF-5 separated into two flights:

1		2
Simpler	Morgan	Green
Mankin	Bright	Rouse
Currie	Roach	McDonald
Wesolowski	Stover	Kleinman
Halford	Shoemaker	

The skipper's ten got off before Green and forged ahead. Looking for bombers, Simpler climbed through four layers of heavy overcast, the thickest between 17,000 and 18,000 feet. Soon he worried he would miss the enemy altogether if they slipped in underneath these clouds. Watching his plotting board, Renner warned the CAP that the enemy was close. Simpler, however, did not see them. At 1355 he decided to drop below the overcast.

Popping into the clear at about 17,000 feet, Simpler encountered six to eight Zeros that had just exited clouds about three miles ahead. They were Lieutenant (jg) Yamaguchi's 2nd *Chūtai* of nine 3rd Air Group Zeros. About 15 minutes before, the parade of twenty-seven Zeros had approached Guadalcanal, but clouds separated the three *chūtais* under Aioi, Yamaguchi, and the Kanoya's Lt. (jg) Baba Masayoshi (NA 67-1939).[27] Without radios they could not easily reassemble. Now Yamaguchi confronted the enemy in an old-fashioned dogfight over Lunga Point. The ten Wildcats and nine Zeros turned directly into each other, then the Japanese split up. Yamaguchi led six Zeros in a dive, while his top cover, PO1c Ōzumi Fumio's 3rd *Shōtai,* clawed for altitude advantage. Clouds, however, prevented Ōzumi's three from ever getting into action.

Wary of a trap, Simpler thought it best to chase the Zeros that dived. With an overhead run he drew close enough to crack the trailer with a good burst. Unfortunately the lead *shōtai* (Yamaguchi, PO3c Nomura Shigeru, and Sea2c Matsugeta Toshimi) craftily doubled back and regained altitude. While Simpler was busy, Yamaguchi swept out of the clouds above in a wide chandelle directly toward him. After radioing for help, Simpler tried his best to finish off the first target, but Yamaguchi came in too fast. Simpler ruefully admitted this Japanese "really let me have it." Simpler quickly rolled into a vertical dive and after gaining enough speed used his ailerons to shake off pursuers. Pulling out at low level, he sought out Henderson Field, looked carefully for enemy planes, then set down.

Excellent Japanese deflection shooting had punched three 20-mm cannon shells into Simpler's fuselage, tail, and wingroot, inflicting severe damage. One neatly removed a whole panel from the starboard elevator and, as he later learned, cut all but one of the elevator control wires. Several 7.7-mm slugs zipped through the cockpit and among other things severed the cord for the throat mike and scarred his shoulder holster. After landing Simpler felt an irritation on the top of his head. Removing his flight helmet, he noticed a hole about the diameter of a lead pencil and traces of blood. A 7.7-mm round had caressed his scalp![28] VF-5's skipper became renowned at CACTUS for two reasons: his intense quest for his first kill and his knack for returning from battle in badly shot-up airplanes. Some of the Marine fighter pilots with the big scores were a bit condescending, but VF-5 greatly respected their leader and vowed among themselves to see he got that first victory.

While Yamaguchi and company battled Simpler, other VF-5 pilots caught up with the 2nd *Shōtai* of PO1c Iwamoto Rokuzō, PO2c Nozu Yoshirō, and PO3c Ogawa Satoru. Mankin, Simpler's wingman, loosed a full-deflection shot at a twisting Zero, then lost contact with his leader and the enemy. Behind him Currie likewise lunged at a Mitsubishi below, also without success. The next three pilots, Wesolowski, Halford, and Morgan, were themselves overtaken by Bright, who had dived more steeply than they. "Hipockets" Bright eagerly chased a Zero that had turned left and dived. The target nosed into a high, steep wingover, but Bright had the speed to pull out, zoom up, and stay behind it. To counter, his opponent again dived and pulled into a zoom climb with the F4F in hot pursuit. Mel Roach tore after the same bandit with a high-side pass as it climbed, and the Zero countered with yet another wingover. Following it down, Bright and Roach individually cut inside the twisting fighter and fired short bursts all the way down. Smokey Stover chanced on the three combatants and joined in, only barely avoiding bands of tracers shot in profusion by both Bright and Roach. Under intermittent fire from all three Wildcats, the Zero smoked, then appeared to flame as it spun toward the water. Excited, Stover incautiously essayed a victory roll, then looked for his friends. The three knocked down Ogawa, who ditched and was later rescued.

At 8,000 feet Bright encountered another 2nd *Shōtai* fighter, who repeated the whole dive and wingover routine five or six times before escaping. Hipockets wondered why his opponent simply did not climb on away as Zeros certainly were capable of doing and generally did. Perhaps the maneuver was a trademark of the 3rd Air Group, who worked it against Curtiss P-40 Warhawks over Australia. After his brief encounter with a Zero, Currie tried latching onto Halford for company, but could not keep up with him. Suddenly a Zero making a steep wingover (Bright's opponent?) recovered right in front and climbed. The Mole quickly lined up a shot, but only three starboard guns responded. The unequal recoil slewed the F4F. Still some tracers seemed to hit, but Currie stalled, rolled out, and dived for base.

Other Zeros prowled the vicinity. After separating from the rest of Lieutenant (jg) Baba's Kanoya *chūtai,* PO1c Ōkura Tsumoru's 3rd *Shōtai* spotted three Zeros battling what looked like ten Grummans—the fight of Iwamoto's *shōtai.* Ōkura and his number 2, PO3c Abe Kenichi, charged to the rescue, but the number 3, Sea1c Iwakawa Ryōichi, withdrew because of oxygen trouble. Either Ōkura or Abe roared through a determined high-astern attack up Bright's tail at 5,000 feet. To Stover watching from a distance, the F4F appeared to be a goner, "duck soup."[29] Diving in to help his friend, Roach radioed a warning to Bright, who swiftly rolled out and down. Roach shot off all his remaining ammunition to chase away the Zero. Everyone agreed that Hipockets was very fortunate to survive this ambush.

One who did not escape was Dutch Shoemaker, one of Simpler's group. He dropped out of the climb with a smoking engine and radioed he was returning to base. Observers saw his F4F, wheels down, flying low along the beach east toward Henderson Field. After chasing Simpler, Yamaguchi's 1st *Shōtai* appeared at a terrible time. Shoemaker lacked altitude or speed with which to evade, and they struck swiftly. His crippled Wildcat dropped into the palms about three miles west of Lunga Point, then disintegrated in a long, fiery crash instantly killing the pilot. Joseph Shoemaker was not even scheduled to fly that mission. When the alert sounded, he and Cash Register, another standby pilot, eagerly sought F4Fs. Nesbitt said they could take his, so the two flipped a coin for it. Shoemaker "won." Harry March took his friend's death very hard and blamed Nesbitt, who was certainly the odd man out in VF-5.[30]

Fog Green's four-plane division, flying lower than Simpler's ten, missed the initial dogfight with Yamaguchi's six Zeros. While patrolling at 9,000 feet, they happened to see the flames ignited by Shoemaker's crash. Out toward Tulagi Green noticed an F4F at 3,000 feet duelling head-on with a Zero. From his perspective Stover saw one Wildcat battling three or four Zeros, "giving them hell."[31] Both Stover and Green's division hightailed it into the fight.

The lone Wildcat was Mankin's, and the four Japanese were Iwamoto and Nozu from Yamaguchi's 2nd *Shōtai* and Ōkura and Abe from the Kanoya 3rd *Shōtai*. Mankin had first dived after Abe, who evaded and tried to get on his tail with a loop. Instead, Abe overshot the F4F, which ended up behind him. Only by side-slipping did he avoid Mankin's bullets and escape the fight. Nozu's Zero flashed past Mankin after a head-on pass, and he noticed it was smoking. Diving steeply after the same bandit was Green, who surprised Nozu with an above-rear attack. Nozu rolled twice in succession out to one side, then essayed a loop to the right. Green used his diving speed to stay with the twisting Zero, kept firing, and saw a flash. The Mitsubishi fell off toward the water and splashed, leaving only a patch of burning gasoline. Both friend and foe thought Nozu a goner, but he bailed out and was later rescued by Japanese troops. Another Zero tried an overhead against Mankin, but missed. Stover charged its teammate, whose poor side attack badly underled the Grumman. The action broke off soon after.

In the dogfight over Lunga, the twenty Marine F4Fs never fought; neither did nineteen of twenty-seven Japanese. Thus the overcast played a definite role in this battle. Fighting Five claimed three Zeros (to Green, Bright, and Roach) and three damaged (by Simpler, Currie, and Mankin), but in return lost one F4F (Shoemaker, killed). The Japanese reported fighting thirty Grummans with fifteen destroyed (four unconfirmed), including one SBD. The four (one unconfirmed) credited to PO1c Ōkura and PO3c Abe were the Kanoya Air Group Fighter Squadron's first victories over Guadalcanal. From the 3rd Air Group, Yamaguchi's 1st *Shōtai* quite correctly claimed two Grummans (one unconfirmed): Simpler and Shoemaker. Iwamoto's 2nd *Shōtai* divided up the other nine kills (two unconfirmed), but at the cost of two Zeros missing, two totaled. Both PO2c Nozu and PO3c Ogawa survived.

PO3c Abe, for one, wondered both at the skill and aggressiveness of his opponents. He had been told that the Grummans would break off combat and dive when challenged, but their eagerness to fight proved a "frightening surprise." He also noted their teamwork, in that a Zero taking on a single Wildcat usually had its wingman dive in from behind.[32] Not surprisingly, Lieutenant Commander Simpler saw the fight from a different perspective. In his report he noted, "The number of times which the attacking 'Zero' pulls up in front of the attack are getting fewer and fewer. This was the only maneuver, aside from surprise attack, in which Grummans were ever able to shoot down 'Zeros.'"

That afternoon two search SBDs assailed four enemy landing craft off the small village of Visale near Cape Esperance. At 1820 Simpler, Mankin, Grimmell, and Halford left to escort three SBDs led by Capt. Elmer J. Glidden, the new CO of VMSB-231. Only 10 minutes elapsed before they located the boats. In the growing darkness the four F4Fs twice strafed barges apparently packed with troops, but it was difficult to gauge the effects. The light level of the old N2AN-illuminated gunsights hindered night vision. Grimmell's section separated from the skipper and returned alone. On Henderson Field MAG-23 set out markers to aid the night landings. Grimmell nosed over, but his F4F was repairable. Glidden likewise cracked up his SBD while landing.[33]

A VISIT BY CINCPAC

The last day of September a weather front closed down Japanese air operations from Rabaul and Buka. Headquarters postponed the *Nisshin's* proposed high-speed run to Guadalcanal until 3 October, but the regular Tokyo Express resumed the next day. Intermittent rain fell on CACTUS from 1100, but not enough to cancel routine searches and strafing missions by the Army P-400s. Fighting Five spent the day as usual at the ready tent, where Crud Blair diligently worked on his needlepoint.[34] That afternoon they learned that Admiral Nimitz was en route to the island. Glad CinCPac was coming, they wanted to show off the place. In his diary Stover remarked, "Everyone is praying for a raid."[35]

Actually, Nimitz wanted to see for himself if Guadalcanal could be held. Around 1600 in the midst of a rainstorm his B-17 arrived at Henderson Field after finding CACTUS with a *National Geographic* map.[36] Vandegrift and Geiger greeted the admiral, took him to see the Pagoda and the Ridge, and talked long into the night. Nimitz found little pessimism on CACTUS.

Word circulated that Nimitz would personally decorate members of the 1st MarDiv and the 1st MAW. In addition to Halford slated for a DFC earned at Midway, Wesolowski and Register were to receive the Navy Crosses recommended by Simpler. Bill Robb informed Wally Clarke and Smokey Stover that they, too, would be decorated for valor on 13–14 September. Before dawn on 1 October Simpler took his five pilots to division HQ for the ceremony. The recipients lined up to hear their citations read and have the medals pinned on by Nimitz. John L. Smith, Robert Galer, and Marion Carl received Navy Crosses. Twelve others received DFCs, including nine fighter pilots (five VF-5, four USMC, and one AAF). Clarke vividly remembered "Admiral Nimitz saying to me as he shook my hand, 'May your shooting eye always be true.' He seemed to look right through me with those deep blue eyes."[37]

VF-5 learned the admiral's party had not brought enough Navy Crosses, hence the lesser-ranked DFCs. However, VF-5's recommendations had coincided with a Navy (but not Marine) decision to limit award of the Navy Cross. Except one later awarded to Simpler, no VF-5 pilot received a Navy Cross for September and October 1942. With justification, the squadron felt their contribution to the defense of CACTUS was largely unrecognized.

Bad weather again prevented enemy raids and almost did in CinCPac as well. The B-17 could not get off the muddy field at 0630, so Nimitz's party waited until that afternoon, when two B-17s took them out. Flying back with Nimitz was Colonel Woods, Geiger's chief of staff, to organize the 1st MAW headquarters on Espiritu Santo. From VMF-212, Fritz Payne, Jack Conger, and Frank Drury returned to Efate for a rest. That day VF-5 did little flying. According to an All-Navy (AlNav) dispatch sent that day, all of the VF-5 ensigns, along with their contemporaries, were promoted to lieutenant (junior grade), but they did not learn the happy news for several weeks.

After dark, according to the new emphasis on night bombing, a land attack plane released a few bombs at Lunga. Around 0430 four more bombs shattered the stillness. This was the first actual appearance of "One Lung Charlie" or "Washing Machine Charlie," as the night intruder soon became known. Two

Type 0 reconnaissance seaplanes also appeared for one of Jōjima's rare harassments of Lunga. More common was "Louie the Louse," the cruiser seaplanes presaging a ship bombardment. The effect on MAG-23 was mostly irritation and lack of sleep. Fog Green noted in his diary, "I was in the foxhole before I was awake." The next morning, VF-5 laughed over their antics. In running to his slit trench "Mole" Currie had "overshot & fell two times & was still first. One's speed is judged by how close behind him we can get into the hole."[38]

AMBUSH

On 2 October the weather improved, but left a thick overcast at high altitude. At 1220, without prior warning, CACTUS radar detected incoming enemy planes at 120 miles. MAG-23 ultimately scrambled thirty-six F4Fs (ten VMF-223, twelve VMF-224, fourteen VF-5). Thirteen Marine F4Fs climbed fairly close together:

1	2
16 Maj. John L. Smith (223)	Maj. John F. Dobbin (224)
18 Capt. Howard K. Marvin (223)	2nd Lt. William V. Brooks (224)
19 2nd Lt. Willis S. Lees III (223)	Capt. Stanley S. Nicolay (224)
15 2nd Lt. Robert R. Read (223)	2nd Lt. Allan M. Johnson (224)
1 2nd Lt. Fred E. Gutt (223)	

3

Maj. Robert E. Galer (224)
2nd Lt. Dean S. Hartley, Jr. (224)
Capt. Darrell D. Irwin (224)
2nd Lt. Howard L. Walter (224)

2nd Lt. George Treptow (121, attached 224) chased the main body, while Lt. Col. Joe Bauer with four Marine F4Fs flew separately. That morning Bauer returned with three other VMF-212 pilots in tow. Off duty, Capt. Marion Carl's 223 division walked back to the field after washing in the Lunga River. When the alert sounded, they raced toward four F4Fs sitting idle on Fighter 1. Second lieutenants Ken Frazier, Charles Kendrick, and Charles Hughes took off together in VMF-224 planes, but Carl in balky number 13 from 223 climbed alone. VF-5 put fourteen Grummans aloft. The skipper had ten:

1	2
Simpler	Green
Nesbitt	Rouse
Halford	Bright
Currie	Morgan
Register	Stover

With Crews were four more in another formation.[39]

Based on information from his chief radar operator, Dermott MacDonnell, Joe Renner warned that many small planes appeared to be approaching at high speed—Zeros rather than bombers. MacDonnell correctly recognized small aircraft such as fighters by the "continuous jiggle" of their return on the scope.[40] This day Base Air Force essayed another fighter sweep, thirty-six Zeros under Lieutenant Kofukuda (6th Air Group) and nine Misawa *rikkōs* acting as decoy. They took off at 0910, but at 1000 the bombers and eight Tainan Zeros headed back to base. One 6th Air Group pilot, 18-year-old Sea2c Sugita Shōichi, aborted because of engine trouble. Later the third highest Navy ace with seventy kills, he would miss Base Air Force's biggest victory over the MAG-23 fighters.[41]

Warrant Officer Yamashita from Kawai's 1st *Chūtai* joined Ōno's nine in the 2nd *Chūtai*. Kofukuda also had seventeen 6th Air Group Zeros of his own 1st *chūtai* and the 2nd under Lt. (jg) Kawamata Katsutoshi (NA 67-1939). They charged in at high altitude (8,500 meters [27,880 feet]) and sighted Guadalcanal about 1210. Because of the overcast, Ōno's nine descended to hunt Grummans. This time the Japanese would cause the Marines some real problems, because they were a lot closer than CACTUS realized.

Out over the channel, Smith's thirteen Marine F4Fs ascended through several layers of clouds up to 25,000 feet. Trailing contrails from their wings, the lead division of five F4Fs emerged into the bright sunlight directly beneath Kofukuda's seventeen fighters. Smitty was shocked to see about eighteen bandits poised 2,000 feet above; Kawamata with six 2nd *Chūtai* Zeros had already peeled off to attack. Following Kofukuda's careful tactics, he motioned his 2nd *Shōtai* under Lt. (jg) Kanemitsu to stay high as top cover. Smith quickly nosed over to take his pilots back down into the safety of the clouds, but Kawamata personally finished Bill Lees almost immediately. He bailed out at high altitude, but was never seen again.

Before Smith could get away, another Zero peppered his wings and holed a vulnerable oil cooler. Dropping through the high clouds, he discovered three more Mitsubishis in formation below and bounced the trailer, which he thought he flamed before continuing to dive away. His targets were the Tainan 3rd *Shōtai*: PO1c Yasui Kozaburō, PO3c Mogi Yoshio, and Sea1c Yoneda Tadashi. None took any hits, but in reprisal, Yoneda shot at the F4F and claimed it. Damaged in the original ambush, Smith's engine overheated and ran rough, so he circled Fighter 1 waiting for the chance to land. The rest of his division likewise scrammed with Kawamata's six Zeros in hot pursuit all the way down to 8,000 feet. Marvin and Read fought no more, but later at 18,000 feet Fred Gutt latched onto a twin-engine (search?) bomber and pursued it past Savo.

John Dobbin's 2nd Division still rose through the high clouds, when four F4Fs dived past like maniacs. For a second he thought Smith was going after bombers below. Suddenly the sky above filled with eager Zeros, as well as Lee's "wrecked" number 19 and "plenty of tracers." Caught in an untenable situation, the 2nd Division also had no choice but to run away. They all escaped, but engine problems burdened Dobbin and Stan Nicolay as well.

Bringing up the rear, Bob Galer's division had attained 23,000 feet when it encountered upwards of a dozen Zeros above. Kofukuda went after these new interlopers with the six Zeros of his own 11th and the 12th *Shōtai* under Lt. (jg) Tanouchi Kennosuke (NA 68-1940), while WO Hirai Mitsu-uma and PO3c Ōshō-dani Sōichi (13th *Shōtai*) remained above as top cover for the *hikōtaichō*. The 11th *Shōtai* executed a series of fast high-side passes from the right, a "very systematic" attack that struck all of the F4Fs almost simultaneously. In deep trouble, Galer turned sharply right into the nearest bandits, but took only a brief head-on shot before Kofukuda was on him. The maneuver shook off Dean Hartley, "Slim" Irwin, and Howard Walter. Irwin and Walter dived immediately, but Hartley managed to rejoin his leader. The six Zeros stayed right with them and broke up to make individual firing passes in close succession. Galer and Hartley countered by scissoring, then split to make runs at Zeros shooting each other's tail, a sort of beam defense maneuver à la Jimmy Thach. To Galer it was "a case of having a hold of something we couldn't let go of."[42] Then Hartley was hit hard, had to break off, and made it safely to the field. Galer resumed scissoring his opponents as each came in one at a time.

Climbing alone out of sight of each other toward the scene of Smith's and Galer's fights were George Treptow (224) and Will Rouse (VF-5). No one saw Treptow go down; for the time being he went missing in action. Meanwhile, Rouse gained height more slowly than the rest of Simpler's F4Fs because his engine would not deliver the power even though set with full throttle on high blower. He ended up on his own. Above him it seemed about eight Zeros beat up a few F4Fs (Kofukuda's six versus Galer and Hartley). Not under immediate attack, he kept climbing, got above the action, and finally spotted two Zeros moving away from the others. He rolled into an overhead attack, but his guns would not fire. Even more worrisome, his engine rattled and vibrated roughly, then stopped altogether, while the cockpit filled with smoke. In the midst of his own misfortunes, Galer glimpsed one F4F dive past in close pursuit of a Zero that appeared to stream heavy smoke. Rouse was the culprit, but the smoke trail came from the F4F and not the Zero. He had to keep on diving, evaded the enemy by means of a "well placed cloud" and headed for home.

Galer's time was up. First he thought he finished a second Zero and dived for cloud cover. (None of Kofukuda's fighters was damaged.) Another parked on his tail and raked the F4F "from wingtip to wingtip, through cockpit and engine, which quit." One bullet even knocked the rudder pedal away from his foot. Using the rudder bracket to retain control, Galer successfully ditched without power near Mandoliana Island off Florida's southeast coast about a dozen miles southeast of Tulagi. It took him an hour to swim to the beach, where thoroughly exhausted, he collapsed on the sand. The action report noted why he was still around: *"Armor undoubtedly saved his life."* In return Kofukuda's pilots claimed no fewer than eleven fighters (seven shared). Galer and Hartley certainly made an impression on the 6th Air Group.

Out toward Tulagi and at 18,000 feet, Ken Frazier's three 223 F4Fs took some lumps. Their fight began well enough. Below, Frazier had spotted seven Zeros: five to his left about 4,000 feet down, and nearer, a pair perhaps 2,000 feet beneath him. They were the balance of Ōno's Tainan *chūtai* left after Yasui's three broke away to fight Smith. Frazier led his section into an overhead attack against the isolated pair flown by PO1c Ōki Yoshio and PO1c Okumura Takeo. They quickly spotted the diving F4Fs, did a split-S, and headed down. Charley Hughes pursued one Zero until he was certain he could not overtake it. Meanwhile, Frazier and "Red" Kendrick regained altitude advantage but could not regain position for another run. Passing through a cloud, Frazier lost contact with Kendrick, emerged above two more Zeros, made an ineffective overhead, and dived away. Hughes returned to the scene of the original fight, briefly tangled with two Zeros, then dived to safety. No one saw what happened to Kendrick. Some Japanese from this group also jumped Marion Carl climbing in the misbehaving Wildcat and sent him diving away before he could fire a shot.[43] In this particular fight Ōno and PO3c Moriura Toyoo notched one Grumman apiece.

Also looking for bombers, Simpler led his ten VF-5 F4Fs to high altitude. Rouse fell behind, then Stover dropped out when his supercharger blew a gasket. Probably George Morgan likewise suffered mechanical trouble and left formation. Attaining 27,000 feet over friendly ships in Sealark Channel, Simpler found no bandits, although Register, for one, happened see about eight enemy fighters (Ōno's Tainan *chūtai*) pass about 8,000 feet below. From radio chatter Simpler learned of the many fights at lower altitude, so he took the seven F4Fs still with him into a careful descent. Passing 20,000 feet he noticed near the water several Zeros ganging up on an SBD, hardly a fair fight. The Dauntless was flown by VMSB-141's 2nd Lt. Joseph M. Waterman, Jr., on antisub patrol over two ships in the channel. Most of Kawamata's six 6th Air Group Zeros took turns making runs against the twisting SBD.

By the time the VF-5 F4Fs spiralled down and divided by sections to attack, only Sea1c Kobayashi Yūichi, number 3 in Kawamata's own 21st *Shōtai,* had not departed. He paused to loop (seemingly in "exhilaration" according to one observer)[44] before heading west. It was a fatal delay. Simpler surprised the Zero with an above-rear run, shot into its fuselage while it looped again, and saw a bright flash. Streaming a thin trail of white smoke or gasoline, the *Reisen* rolled out and dropped close to the water. Kobayashi leveled out right above the waves and hightailed it westward. Simpler's guns malfunctioned; five of six no longer fired.

Wingman JoJo Nesbitt took over from the skipper as the Zero recovered from its dive and overtook it close to shore. Kobayashi responded by jinking violently. Nesbitt broke off after fruitlessly expending all of his ammunition. He explained his failure by describing his opponent as "very competent" and speculated (incorrectly) that this Zero featured self-sealing fuel tanks. Closing in from above for their turn were Jim Halford and Mole Currie, who saw the Zero pull away from Nesbitt. They pushed over to get on its tail. Halford opened up just as Kobayashi crossed the beach. He again tried evading tracers with tight S-turns over the treetops. Nonetheless Halford started the Zero smoking again before falling behind to rejoin Currie. Diving after the fleeing Zero, Cash Register used his speed to draw near for a low deflection shot. This time the target flamed up, leveled out, and dropped among the trees fringing the coast. Just before the airplane hit the ground, Kobayashi straightened up in his seat. A big explosion and fire marked the end of the only Zero lost that day.

After the VF-5 F4Fs regained some altitude, PO1c Ema Tomokazu, 23rd *Shōtai* leader in Kawamata's *chūtai,* bounced Halford and Currie from above and behind. Ema had to break off his run when Green and Bright intervened from starboard and 3,000 feet above with high-side runs. He responded with a scissor, made a head-on run with no results to either side, then scooted into a cloud. Simpler and the pilots with him fought no more that day. Ema later claimed a "Grumman" carrier bomber (Waterman) by cooperative action and one Grumman fighter, but two more put seven bullet holes in his aircraft.

Having fallen behind Simpler's formation, Stover continued slowly up to 24,000 feet. With a bum blower robbing him of power, it was a foolhardy gesture. Far above he could see four F4Fs circling as "top cover," either Bauer's Marines or the other VF-5 division led by Sandy Crews. Secondary control had warned both division leaders that the bombers might come in behind the fighters, so they kept a lookout. Neither saw enemy planes that day. Stover himself milled around for a time, heard word of fighting below, and dived in. East of Lunga he noticed three Marine F4Fs circling 4,000 feet above a grassy ridge. Led by Carl they were protecting Smith, who walked briskly away from his crashed Wildcat. He had flown eastward to escape Zeros reported lurking near Henderson Field. When the engine died, he bellied old reliable number 16 (BuNo. 02127, in which he made most of his kills) into a meadow about four miles east of the field. Carl's F4Fs orbited until he took cover in the trees. No Nip was going to strafe Smitty if they could help it.

It was grim at the Pagoda when the squadrons counted noses. From VMF-223 John Smith, Bill Lees, and Red Kendrick were missing, although Smitty was known to be hiking back through the jungle. The other Marine fighter squadron CO, Bob Galer of VMF-224, also failed to return. No one knew his whereabouts or George Treptow's. That made five Marines, four of whom had received decorations from Nimitz the previous day. Fighting Five anxiously awaited word on George Morgan, who was one of the best-liked men in the squadron. He was probably ambushed by Zeros while trying to get back to the field. Aside from the six missing CACTUS F4Fs, several others were shot up or sustained mechanical trouble. So far only VF-5 had scored, and the squadron gave credit to Simpler for his first kill.

To make matters even worse, two search SBDs also failed to return that afternoon. Out near the Russells, Lt. (jg) Herbert H. Perritte of VS-71 (radioman Irvin E. Newsome, Jr., ARM2c) and 2nd Lt. Edward Walton Ayres of VMSB-141 (radioman Pfc. E. R. Nelson) had run afoul of PO1c Okumura of the Tainan Air Group. At low altitude he chased them back toward Guadalcanal and thought he splashed both Dauntlesses. Actually Perritte and Ayres evaded, only to encounter Kofukuda with about ten 6th Air Group Zeros near Savo. This time the Dauntlesses did not escape. There were no survivors.[45]

While watching the air battle overhead, observers from the 5th Marines holding the west flank of the perimeter saw an F4F plow into the jungle about 400 yards from American lines. At 1400 a patrol returned with word that they had found the wreckage still containing the pilot's body. Wondering if he was George Morgan, Bill Robb from VF-5 volunteered to accompany another patrol to identify the pilot and destroy the IFF gear. They departed at 1530, promptly located the aircraft, and discovered it was George Treptow from VMF-224. His body could not be recovered. A brief survey of the wreck evidently failed to disclose any bullet damage, which led to the theory that Treptow died from oxygen failure, but no one knew for sure.[46]

A tired John Smith reached the bivouac area late that evening to the cheers of his pilots. He told of his combats and reported one Zero destroyed. As he worked his way back through dense jungle and across the Tenaru River, he had come across the shattered remains of an F4F, which he thought might be Scotty McLennan's, missing since the morning of 13 September. Close to dark Smitty started across a grassy field, where none other than Col. Clifton B. Cates, CO of the 1st Marines, awaited him. The colonel had sent out several patrols looking for the fighter leader, then personally went to the likeliest spot for Smith to re-enter the perimeter. To Cates, he seemed most perturbed about leaving behind his black "lucky baseball cap," the symbol of Marine fighter pilots at CACTUS. That evening a patrol from the 1st Marines destroyed the F4F and retrieved his cap.[47] Of the other missing pilots, Smith could only say he had seen another F4F crash on a ridge east of his own landing site. Late that evening MAG-23 also learned that Bob Galer was safe on Tulagi.

Back at base Kofukuda's and Ōno's pilots were very pleased with the day's outcome, which seemed to vindicate the fighter-sweep tactic and provided sweet revenge for 28 September. Kofukuda's dozen Zeros really did a number on the thirteen CACTUS F4Fs they ambushed, forcing all to dive away. The fight was another classic example of the value of altitude superiority and surprise. Japanese claims amounted to seventeen Grumman fighters (two unconfirmed): fourteen (two unconfirmed) by the 6th Air Group and three by the Tainan Air Group. In addition Okumura, a Tainan pilot, claimed two carrier bombers destroyed, as did the 6th Air Group with shared victories. The 6th Air Group lost one fighter (Sea1c Kobayashi) and another totaled. While landing at Buka, PO3c Mogi's Tainan Zero cracked up when its landing gear collapsed. Another Tainan fighter was also written off due to battle damage.

TURNING THE TABLES

For 3 October Tsukahara planned another fighter attack with land attack planes as decoys. The main force again comprised twenty-seven Zeros, this time led by Lieutenant Itō of the 751 Air Group Fighter Squadron. (Two days before, the Kanoya Air Group became the 751 Air Group, foreshadowing a general renumbering of all air groups in November.) Itō received eighteen Zeros from his 751 Group, while the 3rd Air Group provided nine more under the redoubtable Lieutenant (jg) Yamaguchi. Fifteen unarmed *rikkōs* served as decoys. At 0905 the forty-two aircraft departed Rabaul. Within sight of the Russells the land attack planes reversed course. Racing toward Lunga, Itō's twenty-seven fighters completed their climb to 8,500 meters (27,880 feet) and again hoped to catch the enemy below them.[48]

The morning of 3 October things were still rather subdued at Henderson Field, but morale soon enjoyed a real boost. Galer showed up in a J2F-5 and found everyone "a little upset"; they were about to attend a mass to be held for their CO. The previous afternoon Galer had met friendly natives on Mandoliana Island, who paddled him over to the Marine outpost at Bungana southeast of Tulagi. From there he got a ride to Tulagi. He claimed two Zeros on 2 October before another got him. That raised that day's tally to four (Galer two, Smith one, Simpler one).

Bogeys suddenly appeared on RADAR TWO at 145 miles, and MacDonnell estimated their altitude as 12,000 feet. The Pagoda sounded Condition YELLOW at 1154. Two minutes later Kennedy on New Georgia warned that at 1140 he had heard planes going overhead. Twenty-nine Wildcats (five VMF-223, nine VMF-224, and fifteen VF-5) departed their respective fields. Included in their number was Lieutenant Colonel Bauer. He asked permission to fly a 223 fighter, and Smitty referred him to Marion Carl, the 223 flight leader that day. Somewhat surprised that the decision was his, Carl replied, "Hell, yes!"[49] Because of the previous day's ambush, the fighters aimed for 30,000 feet and above. To Renner the radar plot indicated the enemy strike had split up. He informed the fighters that one group circled at 100 miles.

At 1230 Itō approached Lunga at high altitude. Nine/tenth cumulus cloud cover blanketed the area. Consequently the Japanese failed to sight any Grummans, which because of the early warning already neared 33,000 feet. The clouds hid the Zeros as well. Itō made one pass over Lunga at high altitude, then decided to go down to 4,000 meters (13,123 feet). During the descent Yamaguchi's 3rd *Chūtai* separated from the others. At 14,000 feet, the 2nd *Chūtai* under Lieutenant (jg) Baba also disappeared into the murk. Thus the strike split into three flights and, lacking radios, each was out of contact with the others.

Yamaguchi leveled out at 3,000 meters (9,842 feet) and through breaks in the clouds discovered he was east of Lunga. He decided to turn left over the channel and head northwest hoping to find either enemy planes or the 751's Zeros. The 3rd *Chūtai* flew a loose Vee formation:

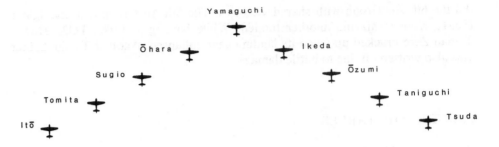

At 1238 Yamaguchi signaled for a 180-degree left turn. Coming onto the new northwesterly heading, several pilots glanced back in horror to behold dark-blue Grummans hurtling down at them.

This day the ambushers were Marion Carl's five Marine F4Fs.[50] From 34,000 feet, they happened to sight through gaps in the clouds Yamaguchi's nine Zeros (Carl thought about eleven) cruising far below. Flying behind Carl were Ken Frazier (223), Joe Bauer (212), "Ike" Winter (223), and Floyd Lynch (121). Carl quickly called Bauer on the radio, but heard no response. He then led the division into a spiral, which greatly increased speed, and took care that he kept diving from out of the sun. As it happened, Lynch missed his signal and lost sight of the others. Carl and company executed one of the most effective fighter attacks of the entire campaign, equivalent to VMF-223's other great fighter victory on 30 August against Lieutenant Shingō's carrier Zeros.

By the time the 3rd *Chūtai* spotted the F4Fs screaming in from above and behind, Carl was less than 1,000 feet away. He singled out the right trailer in the lead group of five and blasted PO1c Ōzumi's Zero at 100 yards. It exploded in flames for his sixteenth kill. Pulling out of his steep dive, he found that his guns had jammed. Next Frazier barreled in from behind and to his right. The surprised Japanese planes maneuvered violently. Frazier took a Zero on his left, the one immediately behind Carl's victim, and triggered a burst. At the sight of tracers, PO2c Taniguchi Jōji nosed up sharply to evade, but at 50 yards, Frazier blew off one wing. He ducked to avoid debris, but one piece cracked his plexiglass windshield.

Frazier dived to the right, then pulled out to regain altitude for another run. In front another Zero tried to jump an F4F's tail: Yamaguchi going after Carl, but he glimpsed the Grumman coming and reefed up into a tight loop. Pulling the stick into his lap, Frazier matched the maneuver, used his speed to stay with the swift Zero, and ended up close on Yamaguchi's tail. The Zero fell out obviously damaged, and Frazier raised his tally to 12.5 kills. Meanwhile, Carl dived to get clear and fix his jammed guns.

Third to attack was Bauer, a consummate fighter pilot enjoying his first crack at Zeros. He made the most of it. The enemy formation quickly broke up. A group of five Zeros (PO3c Ōhara Giichi, PO3c Ikeda Mitsuji, PO1c Sugio Shigeo, PO2c Tomita Masashi, and Sea1c Itō Kiyoshi) swung off to the left. Bauer's high-rear attack on Itō, the trailer, swiftly inflicted hits, and the Zero dropped away. He pulled up and stalked the next victim in the column. The ad hoc leader of the pack (possibly Ōhara) executed a climbing left turn, and the other three followed. Bauer cut inside the new trailer (Tomita) and shot before his steeply climbing F4F could stall. His bullets must have hit Tomita, who cut loose with his guns into clear sky. He went down in flames. The effort cost Bauer most of his firepower, when five of six .50s quit.

Winter, the last man in, confronted three burning Zeros (Ōzumi, Taniguchi, and Tomita), the handiwork of those who preceded him. He ducked sharply to avoid narrowly a collision with Carl's victim (Ōzumi), but noticed another Zero (Sea1c Tsuda Gorō) pull up almost directly in front. Trying to bag it, he climbed sharply and almost stalled. Nevertheless, he got on the Zero's tail at 100 yards, but missed. Tsuda did a wingover and dived out. Winter snapped off a close shot (25 to 50 yards), certain he flamed the Zero, but Tsuda got away. Winter also dived and soon joined up with Carl.

The first pass of Carl's division was a whopping success. Four Marines knocked down five Zeros from the 3rd Air Group. Three went down (Ōzumi, Taniguchi, and Tomita), and only Ōzumi bailed out. Yamaguchi crashed on the north coast of Guadalcanal, where Japanese Army troops soon rescued him. Itō limped northwest as far as Gizo in the New Georgia group and ditched. Carl and Winter fought no more that day.

Meanwhile "One-Gun" Bauer kept chasing Ōhara, Ikeda, and Sugio. No F4Fs were in sight. "They all shoved right away leaving me to play with the Zeros all by myself," the colonel later scribbled in his diary. "Play" with them he certainly did. He harried the last plane in the column, very likely the experienced Sugio trying to get the lead. The other two Zeros countered with the familiar climbing left turn, which Sugio followed in close succession. Again Bauer cut inside the turn and climbed steeply after them. Before his F4F stalled out, he shot into the trailer with his one gun. Sugio dropped out and got away safely. Bauer lunged six or seven times at the two remaining Zeros, which responded in the same way. Neither tried to get on his tail, so deeply must they have been demoralized. Finally he realized how far he had pressed his luck with only one gun and very little ammunition, so he disappeared into the clouds to work on his other Brownings.

Baba's 2nd *Chūtai* from the 751 Air Group witnessed part of Yamaguchi's fight, as the combatants swirled in the clouds below. He led his wingmen PO2c Sawada Tomotsugu and PO2c Honda Minoru into the fight. Baba and Sawada briefly chased two Grummans (Carl and Winter), but soon lost track of both the enemy and the rest of the *chūtai* in the whiteness. Honda ended up on his own. Floyd Lynch, the fifth man in Carl's division, had circled alone at 30,000 feet after the other F4Fs disappeared. Finally far below he spotted a loose column of six or seven Zeros at about 14,000 feet. They were six, the balance of Baba's 2nd *Chūtai* now led by PO1c Ōkura Tsumoru, 2nd *Shōtai* leader. Lynch rocketed down against the trailer, Sea1c Suematsu Shin. In his steep overhead, he failed to realize how fast he was going and his first shots missed. Pulling out abruptly, he found himself at 350 knots easily overtaking the target from directly astern. A quick burst blew Suematsu's Zero apart. Nosing down to avoid the debris, Lynch dived on out of the fight. The 2nd *Chūtai* never saw the Grumman pick off the straggling Suematsu.

Ōkura's own 2nd *Shōtai* spotted no more enemy planes that day, but it appears that PO2c Iwata Toshikazu and PO3c Fujita Tamotsu, the balance of 3rd *Shōtai*, may have doubled back to find Suematsu. While trying to recharge his guns, Bauer exited a cloud and below found Iwata wonderfully set up for ambush. His high-side run set the Mitsubishi aflame for his fourth victory of the flight and fifth overall. As with Suematsu no Japanese saw Iwata perish.

After his two kills, Frazier was alone. Passing through an open space, he carefully watched for Zeros, then aimed toward some convenient clouds. Suddenly 20-mm shells crashed through the bottom of number 10's fuselage and cut the fuel line. Frazier made it into the clouds, but his engine caught fire and soon stopped. Realizing he was over enemy territory, he turned out to sea and made ready to abandon his burning mount. His unseen opponent was PO2c Honda, Baba's number 3, who had lost contact with the rest of the 1st *Shōtai*.

Looking around after the kill that made him an ace, Bauer happened to see two parachutists drift down toward the coast. One, much lower, was Japanese, most likely PO1c Ōzumi, Carl's victim. Ken Frazier was the other. He had flown his burning Wildcat north a couple of miles out to sea, then with much effort tried to escape the cockpit. Finally he had to roll on his back and drop out. Fearful of being strafed in midair, he intended to wait and pull the ripcord close to the water. However, the parachute opened almost immediately. While rocking beneath the white canopy, he heard a "snap-crack" and saw a Zero making a run on him. "Shaken out of my skin by the sight and sound of tracer bullets whizzing past within inches of my head," Frazier thought his time had come.

Bauer saw the whole incident. "Infuriated" by the strafer, he charged "with much gusto" after the interloper. The first pass started the Zero smoking heavily. It turned and dived for the water, but Bauer pursued and fired several more bursts. Finally he noticed his fuel was just about gone and regretfully broke off the fight. Trailing black smoke, the Zero disappeared northward at low level. Bauer's opponent appears to have been Honda, the only pilot from the 751 Group who claimed any kills (two) and only his mount was shot up (six hits). He reached Buka. A skilled and aggressive pilot seeing his first combat, Honda survived the war with seventeen kills to his credit.[51]

Fortunately Ken Frazier also survived his brief acquaintance with Honda. Very grateful for his rescue, he reached the water safely and floated in his life vest. Bauer raced back to Fighter 1 and landed on fumes. So excited was he that he left the blower set on high and the auxiliary fuel pump running. (Ordinarily they were turned off below 15,000 feet because at low altitude they caused flames to issue from the exhaust, which threatened the engine.)[52] The colonel immediately grabbed another plane and flew back to the spot where he saw the pilot splash. He found Frazier and zoomed overhead.

Observers on board the *Nicholas* (DD-449) had seen Frazier parachute at 1320 a good distance away, but to them it looked as if he reached the beach. At 1340 MAG-23 requested the *Nicholas* to rescue the pilot. Near where he splashed, she loosed 30 rounds of five-inch at a "Zero" buzzing around. That was Bauer, who did not seem to notice. He waited until the *Nicholas* lowered a whaleboat and retrieved Frazier at 1410. The tincan treated a wound in his right leg and that evening delivered him to the naval base at Lunga.[53]

The excitement at CACTUS was far from over. Frustrated at not getting into action, Itō's 1st *Chūtai* (751 Air Group) hunted through the clouds. For a brief time they caught sight of a fight north of the field, but by the time they closed in, both friends and foes departed. Itō orbited the airfield twice, but shed his 3rd *Shōtai* (PO1c Imahashi Takeru) in the clouds. He finally gave up and at 1325 took his six Zeros home without firing a shot.

Rather impetuously, Imahashi decided to leave his calling card by strafing the Lunga airfield. He led PO2c Shimizu Takeo and PO3c Takahashi Junichi around south of the target. In close column, they streaked in just over the treetops and crossed the perimeter. Every gun that could bear opened an intense AA fire.

Turning left, the Japanese shot the length of Henderson Field and the boneyard, their shells bouncing off the steel Marston matting. The *shōtai* paid a terrible toll. Imahashi plowed into the ground just west of the field; Shimizu took three hits, and Takahashi, his plane heavily smoking, departed with nine. They both made it back to base and claimed a large aircraft set on fire. To Simpler the foolhardy attack seemed "without other objective than to measure the effectiveness of our antiaircraft fire." The next day several VF-5 pilots hiked out to the wreckage of Imahashi's fighter, one of the few actually to fall near Henderson Field, and salvaged a piece of the wing, including the red "meatball," which they divided up as souvenirs.[54]

From the CAP only Carl's division fought that day. Their cunning, deadly ambush elicited claims of nine Zeros and one probable: Bauer (four plus one probable), Frazier two, and one each to Carl, Winter, and Lynch. They won a tremendous victory for the 1st MAW and took revenge for the previous day. Bauer earned great admiration for his skill, leadership, and devotion to his teammates. Two days later Geiger presented "Coach" with a Japanese rising sun banner to mark his achievements. Bauer gave it to MAG-23. Even though the other F4Fs had not fought, they suffered numerous mechanical failures, illustrating the great strain on men and materiel at CACTUS. Of Armistead's seven VMF-224 F4Fs that reached 33,000 feet, five dropped out (two with blown supercharger gaskets and one from oxygen failure). Blair crashed with a burned-out engine, leaving VF-5 with sixteen Wildcats (eleven flyable).[55]

Returning from his flight, 2nd Lt. Rex Jeans of VMF-223 happened to fly low over the downed F4F Smith reported east of his own crash site. Jeans thought he saw some movement, so Smith gave him permission to hike there and investigate. Charley Hughes, another VMF-223 pilot, volunteered to accompany him behind enemy lines. Together with a captain and a platoon of the 1st Marines, they set out that afternoon. Fighting Five waited with interest, still hoping George Morgan might turn up. Jeans and Hughes reached their goal about five miles southeast of the field and discovered a VMF-224 flipped over on its back. Red Kendrick of 223 was still strapped in the cockpit; he died on impact. Much liked, he was well known to the 1st MAW for his "Ode to the Marines," sung to the tune of "On the Road to Mandalay." They buried him by his plane and burned the F4F. Neither George Morgan nor Bill Lees of 223 was ever found. Simpler's tribute to Morgan applied equally to Lees and Kendrick: "A cool, resourceful and highly courageous pilot."[56]

The two Zero flights headed for different bases. At Buka Itō collected fifteen from the 751 Air Group, while the four 3rd Air Group Zeros flew directly to Rabaul. The pilots survived a very sobering and puzzling encounter that demonstrated that, unlike the previous day, the overcast made a fickle ally. Eight Zeros (three 751 Air Group, five 3rd Air Group) failed to return. Six were shot down and only one pilot, PO1c Ōzumi, remained. Chuting into the channel, he contacted friendly troops and finally reached Rabaul on the 26th. Lieutenant (jg) Yamaguchi crash-landed on Guadalcanal, and Sea1c Itō ditched at Gizo. In addition, two other Zeros had to be scrapped from battle damage. Claims totaled seven Grumman fighters (two unconfirmed) destroyed in aerial combat and one large plane burned on the ground.

Despite MAG-23's stunning aerial victory, the seaplane tender *Nisshin* completed her high-speed run to Guadalcanal that night and unloaded troops and materiel for the Lunga offensive. Her last CAP, six Zero 32s from the 2nd Air Group at Buka, had to ditch. Thus the total loss for 3 October was sixteen Zeros, the worst single day for land-based fighters in the Guadalcanal campaign. For the next several days Base Air Force eschewed air strikes against Guadalcanal in order to regroup and cover subsequent trips by the *Nisshin*. She was well underway before dawn on 4 October, and later that morning a strike group of seven SBDs and four TBFs from CACTUS caught up with her 140 miles up the Slot. They scored no hits. The skies over Henderson Field were untroubled by enemy aircraft. That day Simpler advised Geiger that VF-5 was becoming worn out and recommended that the squadron be evacuated in the near future.

The 3 October fiasco made a profound impression on Lieutenant Itō, who was appalled at the increasing fighter losses. Later in October he prepared a controversial special briefing for his pilots, which stressed that they were "national assets" and should not waste their lives taking unfounded risks in battle. He warned of danger posed by the cooperative defensive tactics of the Grummans. However, when Rear Admiral Ichimaru received an advance copy, he forbade Itō from delivering it. From the old school, Ichimaru valued fighting spirit and individual pilot skills over teamwork and caution. Imperial Naval fighters must shoot down the enemy no matter what the cost. That was fitting, for their anthem, "Fall Like a Cherry Blossom," could be loosely translated as "Die Like a Hero."[57]

CHAPTER 14

"Doggone ball of weather": The *Hornet*'s Bougainville Raid

On 1 October Vice Admiral Ghormley decided to risk his sole carrier, the *Hornet,* for the first time since the disastrous loss of the *Wasp.* The sheltered waters of Tonolei and Faisi harbors, an area 25 miles across between southern Bougainville and Shortland, served as the main staging area for the fast warships of the Tokyo Express. They posed great danger to CACTUS. That evening at Noumea the SoPac operations officer surprised Rear Admiral Murray with a question: "How would you like to do an operation against Buin and Faisi?" He replied, "That's exactly what we're here for; that's the only employment for the carriers in this area: to go up and hit them and get out."[1]

The next day TF-17 received formal orders to attack the Buin-Faisi-Tonolei area on 5 October, then retire southeast "at best speed consistent with fuel limitations."[2] That morning bombers from Major General Kenney's Fifth Air Force would also pound airfields at Buka and Kieta to pin down enemy planes.

Surprisingly Ghormley ordered AirSoPac to provide B-17 Flying Fortresses as fighter cover from 0800 to 1200 over TF-17. Rear Admiral Fitch disagreed with using heavy bombers as fighters and suggested that instead they top off their tanks at Henderson Field and strike Buka and Kieta, while MacArthur's heavies plastered Rabaul. He conceded the B-17s possessed "excellent defensive qualities," but stressed they were incapable of intercepting enemy planes and totally useless in defending a carrier. Nevertheless, at ComSoPac's insistence he would try to put some over the *Hornet* the morning of the raid.[3]

The morning of 2 October, Murray met with his ship captains to discuss their first offensive operation of the campaign. Several problems became evident. The task force would be operating within easy attack range of enemy planes based at Rabaul and Buka. The nearly constant southeasterly trade winds, characteristic of the Coral Sea in certain seasons, dictated launch courses away from the target. Therefore the ships would have to go in as close as possible. Murray decided to run in at high speed to southwest of Buin, launch at dawn, then recover the strike while withdrawing southeast. At noon on the 2nd, TF-17 with the *Hornet,* heavy cruisers *Northampton* and *Pensacola,* light AA cruisers *San Diego* and *Juneau,* and six destroyers departed Noumea.[4]

During the *Hornet*'s sojourn in port, she had kept on board VT-6's TBFs along with the inoperable and spare aircraft. At Tontouta Field near Noumea were thirty-two of Lt. Cdr. Mike Sanchez's VF-72 Grumman F4F-4 Wildcats and twelve Douglas SBD-3 Dauntlesses from VS-8 led by Lt. Cdr. Gus Widhelm.

That afternoon the F4Fs and all but one of the SBDs flew out to the *Hornet*, but there was no sign of Lt. "Moe" Vose's twelve VB-8 dive bombers due from Efate. So as not to break radio silence, Murray sent two SBDs back to Tontouta to radio orders for Vose to meet TF-17 the next afternoon northwest of New Caledonia. The two courier planes returned the morning of the 3rd, but again Vose's SBDs did not show up. In fact they could not get away because of bad weather, as the *Hornet* finally learned on 4 October. In the meantime Cdr. Marcel E. A. Gouin's Air Department brought four F4Fs and six SBDs down from the hangar overhead, and squadron personnel also readied two spare TBFs. Thus operational air strength comprised thirty-six fighters, eighteen dive bombers, and fifteen torpedo planes.

TF-17 held a steady northwesterly course. At 1000 on 4 October, when about 300 miles south of Guadalcanal, the destroyers, reduced to five after the *Anderson* (DD-411) left the previous day, slowed to 19 knots to conserve fuel. The five heavy ships pressed ahead at 28 knots toward the 0430, 5 October, launch point 120 miles southwest of Buin. On the way in, TF-17 sighted no enemy planes, but at 1145 a bogey appeared on radar bearing 335 degrees, distance 80 miles. Despite a vaguely worded intercept of a possible Japanese sighting report copied earlier that morning, Murray believed he had eluded detection.

Following the doctrine practiced since training exercises in Hawaii, the *Hornet*'s air plan envisioned two deckload strikes. With eighteen SBDs and eight F4Fs, the first wave would strike Tonolei harbor on southern Bougainville, while the second wave of fifteen TBFs and eight F4Fs hit Faisi, a small island southeast of Shortland. At 0430, 5 October, the *Hornet* made ready to launch

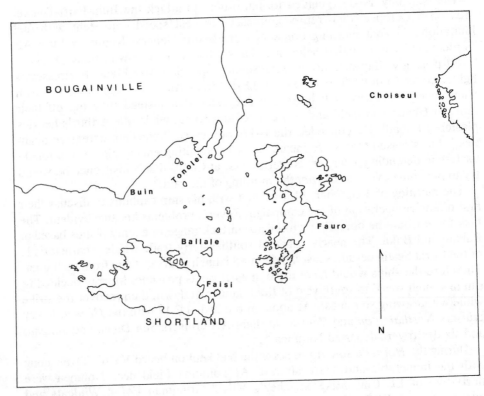

Shortland Harbor.

aircraft. Weather conditions were hardly ideal for her first night takeoffs. The quarter moon and low clouds obscured the horizon. To aid pilot orientation Murray deployed the *San Diego* and *Juneau* (acting as plane guards) off the carrier's port bow and starboard beam. Along with the *Hornet,* they showed truck lights, but the two heavy cruisers did not illuminate.

Spotted on the flight deck were eight VF-72 F4Fs for the first CAP and twenty-six aircraft of the first strike: Lieutenant Commander Widhelm's eighteen VS-8 and VB-8 SBDs (armed with one 1,000-pound bomb each) and eight escort F4Fs:

Division #1	Division #9
Lt. Cdr. Henry G. Sanchez	Lt. John C. Bower, Jr.
Lt. (jg) William V. Roberts, Jr.	Lt. (jg) Robert H. Jennings, Jr.
Lt. Thomas C. Johnson	Lt. (jg) Robert E. Sorensen
Ens. Philip E. Souza	Ens. Roy B. Dalton

In the darkness all aircraft managed to rendezvous except for Phil Souza, who joined the CAP fighters by mistake.

Taking his departure at 0500, Widhelm swung the strike around to approach Bougainville from the west. He aimed for Tonolei, an inlet about four miles long. The extra time required for this detour would help coordinate his attack with the second strike under Cdr. Walter F. Rodee (USNA 1926) bound for Faisi near Shortland. Things proceeded well until Widhelm's flyers confronted a massive weather front punctuated by severe thunderstorms. In places the ceiling fell to 200 feet and quickly fragmented the strike. Ten SBDs split into several groups, failed to find the target area, and turned back. One even ended up over Gizo Island far to the south. Jack Bower's fighter division, joined by Tom Johnson, likewise aborted. Only eight dive bombers and two F4Fs found the target.

The violent thunderstorms separated Mike Sanchez's VF section from Widhelm's SBDs. At 0610 he and wingman Willie Roberts approached Tonolei harbor at low level. The *Hornet* aerographers opined that the weather over the target would be clear, but that did not come to pass. Despite sunrise, visibility there was equally poor—rainy with a cloud base in places below 1,000 feet. Sanchez waited nearly 10 minutes for the SBDs, and when they failed to show, he decided to check out Faisi 20 miles south. On the way he encountered what looked like a large heavy cruiser (actually the seaplane carrier *Nisshin*), which challenged the strange aircraft with her truck light. Cleverly following Japanese identification procedure described by CinCPac intelligence, Sanchez rocked his wings and turned left. She did not open fire.

Ahead of Sanchez and Roberts loomed two lines of flying boats moored at Faisi, advance base of the Tōkō Air Group. From 250 feet Sanchez strafed one group of six Type 97s, while Roberts tackled four more. Barreling in extremely low, they walked their tracers from one target into another. Their second run drew AA fire from positions on Faisi and Shortland. Apparently none of the flying boats were fueled, or at least they did not flame, and Sanchez estimated they probably destroyed four. Breaking away from the moored planes, he pounced on a small destroyer or gunboat and with three runs expended the rest of his ammunition. He observed no return fire from that vessel. Gathering Roberts, he started back toward the *Hornet* and after 30 miles broke into clear skies.

Only five SBDs, led by Lt. (jg) Frank E. Christofferson (VB-8), reached Tonolei. Because of the low ceiling, they tried shallow glide-bomb runs down

Lt. Cdr. Henry Sanchez, VF-72 CO. Photo taken September 1943 at Jacksonville. (NA 80-G-398922)

through the clouds hoping to spot a target when they popped out, but climbed back into the whiteness if no ships materialized below. From a number of such harrowing dives, Christofferson's flight believed they scored one hit on a heavy cruiser, a possible on a transport or cargo vessel, and a near miss against a 10,000-ton cargo ship. Like Sanchez, they saw no enemy planes.

Cutting around the storm by heading north, Gus Widhelm and two VS-8 wing-men emerged in the clear way up near Buka Passage off northern Bougainville. They paralleled the island's long east coast until they saw the small airfield at Kieta, which they mistook for Buin. The three SBDs cratered the runway, but observed no signs of inhabitation, let alone resistance.

After the first wave got away without incident, plane handlers brought the second strike up from the *Hornet*'s hangar deck. It comprised fifteen TBFs (including CHAG Rodee and fourteen from VT-6) and eight VF-72 F4Fs:

Division #4	Division #5
Lt. Edward W. Hessel	Lt. Robert W. Rynd
Lt. (jg) Thomas J. Gallagher, Jr.	Ens. George L. Wrenn
Lt. Claude R. Phillips, Jr.	Lt. (jg) Kenneth C. Kiekhoefer
Lt. (jg) John R. Franklin	Lt. (jg) Dupont Paul Landry

Rodee's command TBF carried no payload, but the VT-6 Avengers each lugged four 500-pound bombs. Murray felt the weather rendered takeoffs with torpedoes too hazardous. Developing engine trouble on its takeoff run into the darkness, one TBF struggled at low altitude perilously close to the *Northampton*. She turned on her lights, and the pilot swerved just in time. Mason computed launch time for both waves at 55 minutes (0430–0524), a little ahead of schedule, and was proud of their first night launch.

Bound for Faisi, Rodee's second strike traversed the same bad weather that had bedeviled Widhelm and fared about the same. Three F4Fs and eight TBFs (including CHAG) lost contact and returned because of low visibility and storms, a "doggone ball of weather," as Rodee complained.[5] Descending beneath 800 feet, Lt. E. B. Parker's seven VT-6 TBFs pressed on to Faisi, accompanied by Red Hessel's five F4Fs. Reaching the target area about 0650, the *Hornet* flyers discovered what they thought were two light cruisers, four destroyers, one transport, and one seaplane tender, but no enemy aircraft.

Yet Japanese planes either patrolled aloft or were scrambling. PO1c Kawai Jirō's two *Kamikawa Maru* Type 2 sea fighters flew CAP, and two Type 0 observation seaplanes from the *Sanyō Maru* patrolled for subs. Low visibility and the large area to be covered prevented interception of the first strike, but as Parker and Hessel approached Faisi, from 0655 to 0700 three more sea fighters and five Type 0s hurriedly took to the air. While Hessel's five Wildcats slanted in for a strafing run against a cruiser and a destroyer, PO2c Tanaka Takeshi's Type 0 observation plane from the *Kamikawa Maru* lifted off and happened to fly beneath the incoming F4Fs. Hessel's quick burst caused the biplane to snap-roll and drop toward the water. Bob Rynd (the orphan from Division #5) and Claude Phillips, the 2nd Section leader, also fired before it disappeared from view. Tanaka survived a rough ditching four miles southeast of Ballale Island, but his observer, Sea1c Nakagawa, died.[6]

Weather at Faisi forced five TBFs to make glide-bomb attacks similar to Christofferson's at Tonolei, but in this case the Avenger pilots needed up to four runs apiece, as each wielded four 500-pound bombs. Torpedo Six finally claimed a hit and a near miss on a 10,000-ton cargo ship and one certain and two possible hits on a *Kamikawa Maru*–class converted seaplane tender.

The other two TBFs proceeded individually to Tonolei, where Lt. (jg) John E. McInerny (a former VF-8 pilot) scored a hit on a cargo ship. On his first run, Ens. Johnny Cresto toggled one of his bombs against a cargo ship, only to be jumped by four enemy float planes. Two *Sanuki Maru* Type 0s led by Lt. (jg) Watanabe Kaneshige stayed with the TBF only a short time, but Kawai's two Type 2 sea fighters proved much more persistent. One float-Zero roared in from ahead, while the other tried to box Cresto in. Both then chased the TBF south over Shortland island. Finally gunners Wesley H. Harris, AMM3c, and Albert H. Miller, ARM3c, thought they splashed one pursuer (actually it withdrew), but lost the second adversary in a cloud. Cresto gamely returned for three more bomb runs for three near misses against the cargo ship.[7]

The Japanese estimated that beginning about 0600, twenty-two dive bombers and six Grumman fighters attacked the Buin-Shortland area. One Type 0 observation seaplane from the *Kamikawa Maru* Squadron went down, and enemy fighters shot up five flying boats on the water (three of them badly damaged). The "heavy cruiser" so often noted by the attackers was actually the *Nisshin,* while the converted seaplane tender *Sanuki Maru* was evidently the "10,000-ton AK" and her fellow seaplane tender (AVS) *Sanyō Maru* the smaller cargo vessel. They took no hits, but the destroyers *Minegumo* and *Murasame* sustained "medium" and "minor" damage respectively. Fortunately for the *Hornet* flyers scattered by weather that prevented effective fighter escort, the Japanese air defense proved disjointed and fragmentary. Only five of eleven float planes aloft ever fired their guns. A rain-soddened field had prevented nine Zero 32s from the 2nd Air Group from staging to Buin on 4 October.[8]

At 0524 after the last strike plane lifted off, TF-17 headed southeast at 25 knots. The *Hornet* recovered some of the attack planes that returned prematurely, then at 0700 reinforced her CAP with twelve F4Fs. At 0813 the destroyers hove into sight on schedule, and soon afterwards she safely recovered all of her strike planes where and when Murray expected. If the raid failed to meet all expectations, at least no Americans died. Admiral Nimitz later congratulated Murray for a skillfully planned operation.

The 1st MAW tried to support the *Hornet*'s raid by a dawn strike against Rekata Bay to prevent any float planes from getting aloft and possibly sighting TF-17. Well before sunrise eleven SBDs and five TBFs departed Henderson Field and in the darkness overflew five Japanese destroyers on the return leg of a normal Express run to Guadalcanal. Weather of the kind encountered by the *Hornet* planes fragmented the attack, so that only eight SBDs and three TBFs actually found the target. Over Rekata Lieutenant Commander Eldridge, the strike leader, ran afoul of three Type 0 observation seaplanes led by WO Ōta Haruzō of the *Kunikawa Maru* Squadron giving air cover for the five tincans. Ōta shot up Eldridge's SBD, which later ditched off the southern tip of Santa Isabel. A Grumman J2F-5 Duck fetched the crew back to CACTUS.

The rest of the morning the *Hornet* rotated her CAP, drawing on all thirty-six Wildcats to defend the task force. Controlling them was the FDO, Lt. Allan Foster Fleming. Originally the *Hornet*'s flight deck officer, he took over air operations after Midway, until, as he later wrote, "I bitched so much about the failure of fighter direction at Midway that they said, 'Well, you do it.' " That summer he attended the Fighter Director School at Pearl and worked closely with VF-72, who greatly appreciated his skill and philosophy in that difficult job. Events proved him an outstanding carrier fighter director, so much so he did not escape that duty until 1946, when he had become perhaps the most experienced FDO in the fleet.[9]

Around 1100 the CAP checked out a flight of B-17s, the AirSoPac strike against Shortland. At 1154 the CXAM radar discovered a bogey bearing 325 degrees, distance 42 miles, and closing at about 1,500 feet. Fleming had deployed the fourteen F4Fs aloft on three levels (5,000 feet, 10,000 feet, and 15,000 feet). He alerted the low patrol, Bob Rynd's division, and sent them out 32 miles to make the intercept. At 1204 Rynd spotted a twin-engine bomber approaching rapidly from ahead, withheld fire to make certain it was hostile, then rolled into a high-side run from the left. His first bursts set the port engine on fire. The other three pilots, George Wrenn, Claude Phillips, and Paul Landry, followed their leader's attack. None noticed any return fire, and the task force copied no enemy radio message. The crippled search plane plunged into the water about 21 miles from the task force. It was PO1c Fukushige Yoshinori's Misawa Type 1 land attack plane, one of five searching the B and C sectors southeast of Rabaul. When destroyed, the *rikkō* was still on the outbound leg of C2.[10]

Fukushige's demise resulted from a pinpoint intercept by the FDO and the CAP. A second soon ensued. At 1239 the *Hornet*'s radar picked up another unidentified contact, this one due south, again at 42 miles. The intruder flew course 330 degrees, speed 190 knots at 1,500 feet—evidently another search plane, but this time on its return leg. Fleming alerted his high patrol, four former VF-8 pilots led by Jock Sutherland, and loosed them southwest along 210 degrees to cut off the bogey's retreat. The F4Fs descended and split to cover a thick cloud layer at 2,500 feet. At 1249 Sutherland with the lower section flushed the game and shouted "Tally ho," while the upper section, lieutenants (jg) Dave Freeman and Al Dietrich, dived in. The quarry, another Type 1 land attack plane, nosed down and headed away surprisingly fast. Boring in from astern, Lt. (jg) Henry "Hank" Carey, Sutherland's wingman, finally holed its port engine, and the rest of the pack caught up. The tough bird evaded many lunges, but at last its fuselage caught fire. One crewman jumped before the aircraft exploded on the sea about 30 miles from the ships. Sutherland's F4Fs finished PO2c Yamada Shizuo's Misawa Type 1 on the C1 return leg. Having survived two close calls with VF-5 on 12 and 28 September over Guadalcanal, Yamada's luck had run out.[11]

No word from Fukushige or Yamada reached base, but their failure to return pointed to a carrier task force 300 miles southeast of Bougainville. Vice Admiral Tsukahara reserved his striking force to counterattack the next day should it remain within range and postponed the *Nisshin*'s planned high-speed run to Guadalcanal to make sure the coast was clear. Other than demonstrating the *Hornet*'s high level of training, that delay proved to be the principal benefit of TF-17's Bougainville raid. Murray had no intention of remaining in range on 6 October, but continued southeast.

The evening of the 6th, Ghormley ordered TF-17 to fuel the next day off New Caledonia and be prepared for more action. Meanwhile AirSoPac sent Vose's stranded VB-8 SBDs from Efate to Tontouta Field. On 7 October they finally returned to the *Hornet,* joined by five former *Wasp* SBDs to make up for the operational losses in September. Ghormley instructed TF-17 to operate between New Zealand and Australia, but Nimitz would have much preferred the ships anchored at Espiritu Santo, from where they could sortie at short notice. Ghormley's chosen operating area placed TF-17 "too far south to be used offensively." More positively, he informed Ghormley that TF-16 with the *Enterprise* would depart Pearl on 16 October for the South Pacific, and that the *Saratoga* should be ready about 10 November.[12]

CHAPTER 15

Sparring with the Tokyo Express

On 5 October, Roy Simpler started his evacuations by sending Howard Crews and Ben Currie to Espiritu Santo. From Santo he welcomed Lt. Carl ("Pat") Rooney and lieutenants (jg) Charles Tucker, Ray Myers, and Roland Kenton from VF-71. After 15 September they had helped defend Santo while awaiting orders. Learning only four could go to CACTUS, Lieutenant Commander Strickler had everyone draw straws to determine the lucky ones. MAG-23 sent Rooney to the "Navy Squadron," VF-5's usual Marine moniker. For Myers it was old-home week. Fighting Five was his regular squadron, and he well knew the few old hands who remained.[1]

On 5 October VF-5 flew two escort missions. The first was a fruitless foray to Santa Isabel, while late that afternoon Wally Clarke's four F4Fs accompanied six SBDs under Lt. (jg) Allard "Slim" Russell of VS-3 after some destroyers struck previously by Lou Kirn, who claimed one sunk. At 1800 they located four destroyers bearing 280 degrees and 110 miles from Lunga, fought no enemy aircraft, but scored no hits either.

Surprisingly, the next two days at CACTUS were relatively quiet, with VF-5 handling routine dawn CAPs. On 7 October a welcome reinforcement of eleven Army Bell P-39Ks and Ds reached Henderson Field. They came from the 339th FS activated four days before from the valiant 67th. At the same time Swede Larsen returned for his second tour with two more VT-8 TBFs.

With the departure of Mark Bright and Harry March on 6 October for BUTTON, VF-5 now comprised twenty-one pilots, eight relatively fresh. (See table 15.1 for their credited aerial victories to date.) Only sixteen F4F-4s, not all flyable, remained. Since 11 September VF-5 lost four pilots killed, three wounded, and eight F4Fs. Maj. John L. Smith's VMF-223 now numbered ten pilots and eight Wildcats and Maj. Robert Galer's VMF-224 fourteen pilots and nine F4Fs. Three pilots from VMF-121 and three from VMF-212 augmented their strength.

Five destroyers crammed with troops for the coming offensive mounted the 7 October Tokyo Express run to Guadalcanal, while early on the 8th, the large seaplane tender *Nisshin* and five destroyers finally departed Shortland for her fast run to Guadalcanal. In addition to troops and supplies, the *Nisshin* portered heavy weapons needed so desperately on Guadalcanal. Scrappy as ever, Rear Admiral Jōjima's R-Area Air Force provided close air support for the final leg of the trip. After a month's steady combat, operational air strength dwindled to five Nakajima A6M2-N Type 2 sea fighters from the *Kamikawa Maru* Squadron,

TABLE 15.1
Fighting Five Credited Aerial Victories as of 6 October 1942

1st Division		3rd Division	
Lt. Cdr. Leroy C. Simpler (USNA 1929)	1.0	Lt. Walter E. Clarke, A-V(N)	3.0
Lee Paul Mankin,[a] AP1c, USN	5.0	Lt. (jg) Wildon M. Rouse,[a] A-V(N)	3.0
Lt. (jg) John M. Wesolowski, A-V(N)	5.0	Lt. (jg) Elisha T. Stover, A-V(N)	3.0
Robert H. Nesbitt,[a] AP1c, USN	—	Lt. (jg) M. V. Kleinmann, Jr., A-V(N)	2.0
5th Division		6th Division	
Lt. Frank O. Green, A-V(N)	1.0	Lt. Hayden M. Jensen, USN	5.0
Lt. (jg) Francis R. Register,[a] A-V(N)	5.0	Lt. (jg) Foster J. Blair, A-V(N)	2.0
Lt. (jg) H. L. Grimmell, Jr.,[a] A-V(N)	3.0	Lt. (jg) John M. Kleinman, A-V(N)	2.0
Lt. (jg) Melvin C. Roach, A-V(N)	1.0	Lt. (jg) J. B. McDonald, Jr., A-V(N)	2.0
VF-71 Division		Spare	
Lt. Carl W. Rooney (USNA 1934)	—	Lt. (jg) James A. Halford, Jr.,[a] A-V(N)	3.5
Lt. (jg) Roland H. Kenton, A-V(N)	—		
Lt. (jg) Charles W. Tucker, A-V(N)	—		
Lt. (jg) Raymond F. Myers, A-V(N)	—		

[a] Attached from VF-6

twelve Mitsubishi F1M2 Type 0 observation seaplanes from the *Chitose, Sanuki Maru, Sanyō Maru,* and *Kunikawa Maru,* and nine long-range Aichi E13A1 Type 0 reconnaissance seaplanes from the *Chitose* and *Sanyō Maru* squadrons. Air units drawn from other ships provided two more Type 0 observation seaplanes, two Type 0 reconnaissance seaplanes, and nine antiquated Kawanishi E7K2 Type 94 reconnaissance seaplanes [ALF].

On rainy 8 October a team of four Navy fighter directors, under Lt. Lewis C. Mattison, A-V(S), joined the 1st MAW. A graduate of the first class of Cdr. John H. Griffin's Fighter Director School at Pearl Harbor, Mattison penned a vivid description of his initial impressions of a wettened CACTUS:

> It was just about the last outpost in the world. I'll never forget the bleak aspect of the place when we came in under the lowering clouds, circled over the mud holes and lopsided tents of the Marines across the Lunga River, and finally put down in the slop of Henderson Field.[2]

Their welcome at the Pagoda was less than enthusiastic. Joe Renner, acting CACTUS FDO, was not certain how to use his inexperienced but eager controllers, and the Marines needed a little time to become acquainted with their abilities and to work them into the system. That day Lt. Cdr. Courtney Shands, VF-71's former CO, left CACTUS suffering from his badly injured back and dengue fever. He spent 106 days on the sick list before resuming active duty back in the States.[3]

The rainstorms postponed a planned fighter sweep by twenty-seven Zeros guided by nine land attack planes. However, they also hindered air support for a new Marine drive across the Mantanikau toward Point Cruz to deny the Japanese key terrain needed for their assault against Lunga. Headquarters had to delay operations until the 9th. Despite the weather, persistent MAG-14 search planes directed a strike of seven SBDs against the five destroyers retreating about 180 miles up the Slot and discovered the *Nisshin* force on its way in. That afternoon

Major General Geiger hurriedly arranged for another strike. Fred Mears of VT-8 described what it was like to await word of these impromptu missions:

> Pilots of the attack group on stand by in the afternoon as a rule were nervous until the afternoon scouting flight made contact. They smoked and fidgeted more than the others. What they wanted to know all afternoon was "how many today."[4]

By 1745, the five incoming Japanese ships, if they maintained reported course and speed, would be 125 miles northwest of Lunga.

Ready to go were seven SBDs (two VS-71, five VMSB-141) led by VS-71's XO, Lt. Porter W. Maxwell, and Lieutenant Larsen's four VT-8 TBFs. Eleven VF-5 F4Fs under Simpler would escort them. They departed Henderson Field at 1655 and flew westward into the setting sun. Soon two F4Fs (John McDonald and John Kleinman) had to turn back from lack of oxygen. That left eight stepped down in pairs behind Simpler: Myers and Roach, Green and Tucker, Rooney and Register, Jensen and Blair. The F4Fs gradually worked up to 19,000 feet, with the SBDs a few thousand feet below and the TBFs at 10,000.[5]

Around 1745 as expected, the strike sighted ahead the wakes of several ships southeast of New Georgia. Unbeknownst to the CACTUS aviators, the Nisshin's CAP of nine Zero 32s from the 2nd Air Group had just turned back. Reaching Buin after dark, seven of nine cracked up on the primitive field. Losses in the past eleven days of Zero 32s from Buka and Buin totaled about twenty: six ditched, seven crashed, and six or seven bombed on the ground. The remnants of the 2nd Air Group gratefully withdrew to Rabaul, leaving inhospitable Bougainville to Lieutenant Kofukuda's 6th Air Group.

As the CACTUS dusk strike drew nearer, the enemy force appeared to comprise a heavy cruiser surrounded in horseshoe formation (open end to the fore) by five destroyers. Actually the "cruiser" was the Nisshin. On her port bow and quarter respectively were the Yūdachi and the Harusame of the 2nd Destroyer Division; the 9th Destroyer Division's Asagumo and Natsugumo held identical slots on the starboard side, while the special AA destroyer Akizuki steamed directly astern. Eight Type 0 observation seaplanes, divided into three shōtai, patrolled overhead at different altitudes. Lieutenant (jg) Watanabe with three float planes from the Sanuki Maru and two Sanyō Maru had departed Shortland at 1500, while the Chitose shōtai of three under WO Suzuki Hisamukita followed 40 minutes later.[6]

By 1800, the sun nearly touching the horizon "froze the sea with the metallic enamel of light," according to Mears.[7] Simpler advised Larsen and Maxwell that he would strafe destroyers and draw fire. He eased down through a light overcast (top at 16,000 feet) against the enemy's starboard flank. The SBDs let down toward their pushover points, while the TBFs followed for high-speed torpedo attacks from the port side.

Diving past 14,000 feet, Simpler encountered the high CAP, the 2nd (Sanyō Maru) shōtai of PO1c Imaki Kaneyoshi and PO3c Yoshimura Yoshirō. They had spotted the whole American strike group and correctly counted seven carrier bombers and four torpedo planes with nine Grumman escorts. Imaki broke off to Simpler's left and kept diving, so he sent Ray Myers and Mel Roach after that bird. Meanwhile, Yoshimura reefed into an opposite run against Simpler to no effect, then both he and Simpler dived away. Simpler continued his planned strafing attack, his tracers "bouncing off the topside" of the tincan Asagumo off the Nisshin's starboard beam. He withdrew flat out at low level in order to evade AA fire and the two bandits. At the same time Myers and Roach pursued Imaki below 10,000 feet with long overhead runs, but the Type 0, using its vaunted maneuverability, easily rolled out of the lines of tracers. Recovering much lower, the two F4Fs split up.

The main body of six F4Fs missed the opening skirmishes and continued its descent. In the meantime Maxwell's dive bombers and later Larsen's torpedo planes made their runs. The SBDs claimed one bomb hit and three near misses against a *Kinugasa*-class heavy cruiser. In the midst of fierce AA fire, VT-8 executed what Mears described as "a torpedo attack the likes of which I never hope to make again."[8] The Avengers descended in fast, shallow dives toward the *Nisshin*'s port quarter. Particularly annoying were AA bursts and tracers from the *Akizuki* and *Harusame*. Letting down to 200 feet, the pilots fired their fish from about 1,000 yards off the "CA's" port bow. The crews noticed the splash from one torpedo hit by Lt. (jg) Albert K. Earnest (one of two VT-8 pilots to survive torpedo attacks at Midway), but it must have been a near miss from a bomb. The *Nisshin* sustained no damage, although two fish passed as near as 20 meters. Earnest described the flak as worse than Midway.

Strike planes recovering low over the water drew undesired attention from the CAP. Imaki and Yoshimura regained contact near the water and joined the other six Type 0s to harass the SBDs. One pilot frantically radioed that six Zeros chewed his tail. Hearing that cry for help, the six F4Fs immediately dived in. Spiralling through a hole in the clouds, Fog Green, Charlie Tucker, and Pat Rooney emerged above a Type 0 seaplane cavorting at between 2,000 and 3,000 feet. It was Warrant Officer Suzuki, the *Chitose shōtai* leader, whose pilot was PO1c Katō Junji. Green attacked, but the biplane flipped out of the way. Next Tucker tried an overhead run, but Katō scissored by turning directly up into the descending Wildcat. Tucker had to dive almost vertically to prevent colliding and blacked out as he leveled off. By the time he regained his wits, his opponent had disappeared. Rooney also essayed an overhead, but with no visible effect on the feisty float plane.

Green and Rooney climbed above their nimble adversary and reefed through two more runs apiece. Jensen wisely refrained from attacking, figuring enough F4Fs were already involved, but Crud Blair rushed in with a high-side pass against Suzuki now flying below 1,500 feet. Finally, on Green's third attempt his tracers tore into Katō's cockpit and set the forward fuselage ablaze. The Type 0 nosed down sharply, with Suzuki jumping out of the rear cockpit just before the flaming biplane exploded on the water. It left a burning patch of gasoline. Neither Suzuki nor Katō survived.

Nearby, other F4Fs battled the balance of the *Chitose shōtai*. Having dived in behind Rooney at the beginning, Cash Register chased a different plane than the one selected by his section leader. His side run turned into a head-on, when the wily Type 0 swung up into the diving Grumman. He came round for a full-deflection shot and tailed in behind the Japanese for a close burst. The biplane commenced spinning, leading Register to think he got it, but the third biplane kept him too busy to watch. His opponent was apparently PO1c Kawazoe Nari-futa's *Chitose* number 2 aircraft, damaged in the fuselage, but not finished.

Mel Roach had seen Green, Tucker, and Rooney fly rings around the biplane that Green finally splashed. Another appeared to Roach's right. After much twisting and turning, he finally managed to get on its tail, but flashed right past when the Type 0 abruptly slowed, seemingly aflame. Suddenly his own cockpit filled with thick smoke and hot oil, compliments of the Japanese he had just shot. Sea1c Nakamura Akira, pilot of PO2c Yagi Masaaki's *Chitose* number 3 aircraft, reported downing one dive bomber, then battling a Grumman, which he shot down but not before taking many hits in return. Nakamura soon set the crippled Mitsubishi down on the water, and he and Yagi were rescued.

Realizing his predicament, Roach immediately turned southwest for tiny Buraku Island, located about halfway between New Georgia and the Russells. He radioed the skipper that he was making for Buraku and heard someone reply, "OK." Two more enemy planes threatened from below, so he firewalled the throttle to get away while he still could. Soon the engine stopped, and the prop slowly spun in the wind. Dropping fast in the darkness, Roach released his tail hook, unbuckled his safety belt, tightened his chest strap, and carefully awaited touchdown. As soon as the tail hook slapped the waves, he cracked full flaps and bellied into the sea for an excellent night ditching. The F4F remained afloat long enough for him to clamber out on one wing, open the compartment behind the cockpit, and break out the rubber boat. "The Roach" would paddle all the way to San Francisco if need be.

After strafing the destroyer, Simpler also heard the cry for help. Ahead and off to port he spotted two float planes working over an SBD, but both retreated after he triggered a long-range burst. Looking around he noticed that the attacks on the ships had ended, and that it was getting quite dark. Green's victim burned brightly as a beacon on the water, so Simpler radioed VF-5 to rendezvous above it. While the F4Fs were busy with the *Chitose shōtai*, Watanabe's *Sanuki Maru shōtai* and Yoshimura from the *Sanyō Maru* had ganged up on the SBDs. They claimed no fewer than seven (including one unconfirmed shared). However, no Dauntlesses went down.

Soon after the first fight, Yoshimura neatly turned the tables on Blair, who had been happily chasing the biplane. With a quick chandelle to the left, Sea1c Ōkubo Shigeji (Yoshimura's pilot) whipped around, pulled up straight into the F4F, shot up its right wing, and jumped its tail, "making a monkey out of me," as Blair wrote in his diary. He was not the first to be surprised by the F1M2's "tigerish" performance, so different from the U.S. float jobs. At the same time Green fended off overheads by Watanabe's eager Type 0s. At just the right instance to counter, he pulled up sharply into his attackers as they fired and left their tracers astern. Meanwhile, Rooney expended all his remaining bullets in a futile attempt to bag the fourth Type 0.

Exiting a cloud, Charlie Tucker beheld all three fights. Jensen with a timely high-side run surprised Blair's assailant, Ōkubo, who evaded with a split-S right to wave-top level. Tucker fired at him as well, then joined up on Jensen. Together they fought two more of the seemingly endless supply of enemy float biplanes with a flurry of head-on runs in close succession. The second one swung furiously left after passing Jensen and missed Tucker by only 50 feet. He was certain he put twenty or thirty rounds right into this bird, which went "flip-flopping down," but Jensen saw it recover lower down and scoot away. Blair lunged at one of the pair, but the light from his tracers blotted out the pipper in his illuminated gunsight. The two biplanes disappeared into the darkness. Dogfight number 2 was over.

Simpler called for another rendezvous over the burning plane, and this time five F4Fs joined: Rooney, Jensen, Green, Register, and Tucker. Three others were missing. Roach was already rowing hard for Buraku, while Blair never got the word. Neither did Myers who had not rejoined following the first action. After he separated from Roach, he pursued a lone *Chitose* float plane low over the water—PO1c Kawazoe already damaged by Register. Alarmed by the Grumman, Kawazoe ran toward the protection of *Nisshin*'s AA, but before he could get there, Myers fired at long range. Kawazoe pulled up sharply, but Myers shot as the biplane rolled over on its back. He lost sight of it soon after. Actually, friendly AA ventilated the Type 0, but Kawazoe made it back to Shortland. Not finding his teammates, Myers vented his frustration by strafing a destroyer before turning alone for home.

VF-5 claimed three float planes (to Green, Roach, and Register), one probable (Register), and no fewer than ten damaged. Two SBD radiomen reported downing enemy planes: Lyle H. Faast, ARM2c, of VS-71 with Lt. (jg) Chester Zalewski, and from VMSB-141 Pvt. Edward J. O'Connor, who flew with 2nd Lt. Henry F. Chaney. Roach's ditched F4F was the 1st MAW's only loss in the battle area. In turn the R-Area Air Force claimed three enemy fighters and nine dive bombers (including one unconfirmed) for one missing *Chitose* Type 0 (Suzuki), one *Chitose* Type 0 (Yagi) ditched due to battle damage (crew rescued), and three others shot up. In addition PO1c Imaki (*Sanyō Maru*) suffered a severe wound. The Japanese also marked the fight as memorable, with much praise for the crews who saved the *Nisshin*.[9]

Unfortunately, the YE homing equipment at Henderson Field did not function well. According to Lou Kirn of VS-3, the transmitter was "not radiating properly."[10] To help retrieve night flights, the 1st MAW switched on a searchlight unless enemy planes actually prowled overhead, which was often the case. That night most of the aircraft came back together and landed safely.

Two VF-5 pilots found their own way back home. Noticing Guadalcanal in the moonlight about seven miles northeast, Blair soon reached the field, but had a hard time getting down when control kept turning the lights on and off. He ended up rolling off the runway into the mud and wrecked the aircraft.[11] Myers likewise had turned south too early, but unlike Blair he could not find the island. Eventually he happened upon 1st Lt. Louis R. Norman's lone VMSB-141 SBD, which signaled him to join up on course 180 degrees. Myers assumed the Marine knew his way home, but soon decided no. Realizing they were already too far south, he tried to get Norman to turn left, but the Marine stolidly signaled, "Dead ahead." Finally Myers switched to 020 degrees and soon spotted the big island. Landing downwind on Henderson Field, he ran out of fuel taxiing up the runway.[12]

At the VF-5 ready tent, Simpler counted noses and discovered that Roach was missing. The squadron was fairly certain he ditched and resolved to find him the next day. Myers asked permission to go out the next morning to look for the missing Marine SBD crew south of Guadalcanal. Near midnight the *Nisshin* and her escorts unloaded their cargo. A few more missions like this, and 17th Army would be ready for the big push against Lunga.

That evening Vandegrift learned he would be getting direct naval support to prevent a repeat of the *Nisshin*'s trip. Rear Admiral Scott's TG-64.2 with two heavy cruisers, two light cruisers, and five destroyers left BUTTON on 7 October to operate north of Rennell Island in position to attack the next big Express. Rear Admiral Murray's TF-17 with the *Hornet* also moved within supporting range south of Guadalcanal, while Rear Admiral Willis A. Lee's TG-17.8 with the new battleship *Washington* (BB-56), a light (AA) cruiser, and two destroyers protected a CACTUS "*Nisshin* mission." Early on 9 October Rear Admiral Turner sailed from Noumea with seven ships carrying the Army's 164th Infantry Regiment and a new ground detachment for the 1st MAW.

Henderson Field bustled before dawn on 9 October. In addition to the usual searches, Geiger prepared a sendoff for the retiring *Nisshin* force. Back from his

5 October dunking off Santa Isabel, John Eldridge of VS-71 led nine SBDs escorted by six P-39 Airacobras from the 339th FS under Capt. John W. Mitchell. The Army's 75-gallon belly tanks gave the Airacobras the range to accompany the dive bombers farther than the CACTUS F4Fs. At 0655 Eldridge confronted *Nisshin* and her five escorts 150 miles up the Slot near New Georgia, but failed to hit any of the swift warships. The P-39s played tag with four Type 0 observation seaplanes and three float-Zeros. Neither side took any losses in air combat, but AA bagged one SBD. The AAF pilots were quite impressed with the maneuverability of their float opponents. Fortunately for Eldridge, his strike attacked and retired about 10 minutes before the first CAP of nine 2nd Air Group Zeros arrived from Buka.

Fighting Five provided the routine dawn patrol of four F4Fs, while Wally Clarke, Smokey Stover, and Will Rouse departed on special search for the missing Mel Roach. First they checked Buraku, the likeliest location, but Roach still paddled his raft in the waters north of there. Myers also went out alone looking for Norman's SBD crew missing south of Guadalcanal, but he found no trace of them.

That morning Base Air Force unleashed against Guadalcanal the usual fighter sweep of twenty-seven Zeros led by Lieutenant Aioi. Nine land attack planes accompanied them part way. At 1158 CACTUS radar reported bogeys bearing 294 degrees and 140 miles. MAG-23 arrayed for defense fifteen F4Fs from VMF-223 and VMF-224, eight P-39s and twelve F4Fs from VF-5. They disappeared up into the heavy cloud cover blanketing the area. Soon one of Simpler's Wildcats dropped out with mechanical trouble. At 22,000 feet Green also had to abort, as his engine just did not produce enough power. From behind the formation, he noticed another F4F not only lose altitude, but fly erratically. At the same time Simpler glanced back only to see one of his boys "flopping around." It was Charlie Tucker in F-11. Simpler warned all of his pilots to check their oxygen systems, but for Tucker it was already too late. Flying on Tucker's wing, Myers saw that his chin had fallen to his chest. He soon lost F-11 in the clouds. Green followed the errant Wildcat down into the overcast, but when he broke into the clear, it splashed south of Guadalcanal.[13]

Fighting Five felt pretty certain that Tucker lost consciousness due to oxygen starvation, but the exact cause remains a mystery. Careful and conscientious, experienced in high-altitude flying, Charles Tucker had definitely checked his oxygen gear before takeoff. Already an attorney specializing in maritime law, he was also a poet. In 1944 his father, the Reverend Louis Tucker, published a collection of his works entitled *Poems of a Fighter Pilot*.[14]

For nearly a half hour Aioi's twenty-seven Zeros (nine each from the 3rd Air Group Detachment, the Tainan Air Group, and the 751 Air Group Fighter Squadron) patrolled Lunga and Tulagi at high altitude, but started back at 1245, while the CAP F4Fs still climbed. After the debacle on 3 October, the Japanese knew better than to descend and risk being ambushed. Ironically, the CACTUS fighter pilots anxiously hunted the enemy, but missed them in the clouds. Tucker was the only fighter loss that day.

That afternoon Jensen led eight VF-5 F4Fs northwest toward New Georgia for another look-see for Roach. Over the west coast of Buraku Blair happened to sight a flare. Certain Roach fired it, he returned post-haste to Henderson Field with hopes of getting a J2F amphibian aloft to rescue him. Lieutenant Colonel Scollin, however, vetoed another mission because he thought the slow Duck could not return before dark. Roach would wait at least one more night.[15]

The big event that day at CACTUS proved to be the arrival at 1500 of the first new squadron of Wildcats since VF-5 came in nearly a month before. Led by Maj. Leonard Davis, twenty VMF-121 F4Fs trooped in from the escort carrier *Copahee* because they lacked the auxiliary tanks necessary to stage from Espiritu Santo to Guadalcanal. Capt. Joseph J. Foss, the XO, was destined to be the highest scoring CACTUS fighter pilot. VMF-121 was an eager, confident bunch, but very inexperienced. While waiting to land, Foss noticed "hundreds of pockmarks . . . foxholes and slit trenches, and many wrecked planes ranged around the field." VMF-121 received about the same reception as had VF-5 back on 11 September, except now after a month at CACTUS, Simpler's men understood why the Marines had been so happy to see *them*. After setting down on Henderson Field, Foss noticed "rough-looking fellows with beards came running out of the woods to meet us. They cheered almost hysterically, climbed onto the Wildcats, and seemed almost ready to kiss us."[16] John L. Smith informed the new arrivals they had landed in the wrong place, but at Fighter 1 the greeting was equally sincere.

In addition to Tucker, VF-71 suffered another tragic loss on 9 October. That evening Bob Strickler returned from a CAP to the Turtle Bay fighter strip at Espiritu Santo. Short of the runway his F4F suddenly dropped into the jungle, and he died instantly. Howard Crews took over the VF detachment of Mark Bright, Ben Currie, and Harry March of VF-5, Red Thrash, Harold "Norm" Riise, and Ens. Norm Brown from VF-71.[17]

That same evening the Tokyo Express made an especially noteworthy run, delivering Lt. Gen. Hyakutake Harukoshi, 17th Army CO, from the light cruiser *Tatsuta*. Before dawn on 10 October, the 1st MAW dispatched a very large strike group: fifteen SBDs (Lieutenant Commander Kirn), six TBFs (Lieutenant Larsen), eight P-39s (Captain Mitchell), and fifteen F4Fs (223 and 224, led by Major Smith). The Wildcats were along to strafe and draw fire away from the strike planes. Near New Georgia they spotted two light cruisers and four destroyers. Two Type 2 sea fighters from the *Kamikawa Maru* Squadron and two *Sanuki Maru* Type 0 observation seaplanes flew CAP. Evidently thinking they were merely torpedo planes, the four Japanese bounced the fifteen Wildcats, but the Leathernecks "cleaned" them up, accounting for all four and claiming ten kills in the process (including Smith's nineteenth and last victory). The strike planes, however, scored no hits against the six warships, but lost one SBD and one P-39. Eldridge followed up the first strike at 1120 with nine SBDs and twelve VMF-121 F4Fs, but also failed to damage the enemy. At least they faced no aerial opposition.

Also at dawn on 10 October, an impatient McDonald and Blair took off to escort Maj. Michael Sampas in the J2F amphibian to check out Buraku. After Sampas set down just off the reef, out from the island swam a bedraggled Roach, looking "more tired than injured." His first words were "Last night I was converted."[18] Upon his return to Henderson Field, he related quite a story. After ditching the evening of 8 October, he spent the rest of the night in the raft, which weathered a number of squalls. In the morning he found himself surrounded by sharks, but early that afternoon reached Buraku, a small island about 18 miles west of the Russells. It stuck up out of the sea "like a rock." Uninhabited and unappealing, Buraku featured some coconut trees, but was mainly scrub brush and mangroves.

Safely ashore, Roach was resting when he saw two F4Fs fly over. He waved and shot off the flare that Blair had seen. Certain he had been found, he sat down on the beach and took off his shoes. Glancing inland, however, he felt something was amiss:

> Suddenly I noticed that a clump of bushes . . . had changed position since I last looked at it. It was getting dark, but I was sure it had moved, and then I noticed that two other clumps had also shifted. As I watched they all moved silently again, toward me.[19]

Now he deeply regretted leaving his shoulder-holstered .45 Colt back at Henderson Field, as he had only his pocket knife and the Very pistol with three cartridges. He fired a flare at one of the mobile bushes, and the bright glare revealed a Japanese crouching behind it. Two others jumped up brandishing bayonets and started encircling him, so he took to his heels, abandoning his rubber boat, food, and water. Cutting his bare feet on the coral, he ran "like hell" seeking some sort of cover. At a nearby cove was a coral ledge at water level, and in the center a large hole. Roach jumped into the hole and disappeared out of sight.

The Japanese waited outside eating the rations they plundered from the raft. Not so comfortable was Roach, who discovered himself in some sort of "alligator hole," fortunately unoccupied. As the tide came in, each incoming wave completely submerged his refuge, forcing him to take a deep breath every time the sea rose, then breathe when the water level finally dropped below his head. It was the longest night of his life. After dawn he finally heard engine noises and peeked out as Sampas brought the J2F down outside the reef. The aircraft scared off the Japanese. Finding the coast was clear, Roach crawled out of the hole, ran to the beach, and swam out to the Duck. Again his bare feet suffered from the sharp coral, but no matter, he was safe.

Roach took a great deal of good-natured kidding from his squadron mates, who were happy to see the rotund pilot safely back at base. He suspected the three Japanese were downed aviators but, more likely due to the bayonets, they were soldiers, possibly survivors of the barge attacks in late August and early September. If so, they were probably quite glad to get the emergency rations.

CHAPTER 16

CACTUS in Peril

GETTING READY FOR THE BIG PUSH

Beginning 11 October the Japanese set into motion plans for the final combined land, sea, and air offensive to gain Lunga airfield. Ironically, because of recent reinforcements Roy Geiger's 1st MAW had never been as strong. It is worthwhile to examine the two opposing air forces and describe their resources for some of the toughest times yet on Guadalcanal.

The 1st MAW on Guadalcanal operated through two group headquarters. Colonel Wallace's MAG-23 numbered about forty-five flyable Grumman F4F-4 Wildcats in Duke Davis's VMF-121, Bob Galer's VMF-224, and Roy Simpler's VF-5, reinforced from VMF-212 on Efate and VF-71 at Espiritu Santo. John Smith's battle-hardened VMF-223 prepared to leave for a well-earned rest, although some pilots stayed on for a time with 224. The AAF fighter contingent under Maj. Thomas Hubbard comprised nine Bell P-39D and K Airacobras and three Bell P-400s of the valiant 67th and 339th fighter squadrons of the 347th Fighter Group created on 3 October. Unsupercharged engines rendered the P-39s little better for high-altitude work than the old P-400s, but they excelled in ground attack. From Lieutenant Colonel Cooley's MAG-14, three squadrons, VS-3 (Lieutenant Commander Kirn), VS-71 (Lieutenant Commander Eldridge), and VMSB-141 (Maj. Gordon A. Bell) flew the sixteen flyable SBDs, while VMSB-232 and VMSB-231 prepared to depart. Swede Larsen's old dependables in VT-8 boasted six TBFs. B-17 heavy bombers from Colonel Saunders's 11th Bombardment Group shuttled through CACTUS for strikes and searches farther up the Slot. The 1st MAW was powerful yet brittle, due to the vulnerable Lunga air base and the lack of replacements in the forward area. The Japanese would soon tax the 1st MAW to the limit.

Base Air Force presented a new look. First of all, on 8 October VAdm. Kusaka Jinichi relieved the ill Vice Admiral Tsukahara in command of the Southeast Area and presided over a reorganization of Base Air Force.[1] Vice Admiral Yamagata of the 6th Air Attack Force regained control over his fighter component, Capt. Morita Chisato's 6th Air Group, which finally reassembled on 7 October at Rabaul. That day the light carrier *Zuihō* had dispatched thirty Mitsubishi A6M3 Model 32 Zero fighters led by the senior *buntaichō*, Lt. Miyano Zenjirō (NA 65-1938), but north of New Ireland, severe weather cost four planes (three pilots killed). The entire 6th Air Group prepared to operate from Buin, beginning 10 October, to protect Shortland and fly CAP over Express runs. Buin and improvements at the Buka field now permitted the long-awaited "two-a-day" strikes against Lunga. (See table 16.1 for organization of Base Air Force in the Bismarcks-Solomons area as of 10 October.)

On 11 October several interconnected naval operations against Guadalcanal were put in the works. The big seaplane carriers *Nisshin* and *Chitose*, crammed with troops, equipment, and supplies, sailed that day from Shortland with six escorting destroyers. To ease their way, RAdm. Gotō Aritomo's Support Force with three heavy cruisers and two destroyers would bombard Lunga airfield after midnight on 12 October. These operations anticipated an even more ominous move: the "High Speed Convoy" of six Army transports to land troops and supplies on X-Day (15 October) to bring the 17th Army up to strength. On 11 October a substantial portion of the Combined Fleet departed Truk in support, including Vice Admiral Kondō's Advance Force (2nd Fleet), with the carriers *Hiyō* and *Junyō,* and Vice Admiral Nagumo's Striking Force (3rd Fleet) built around the carriers *Shōkaku, Zuikaku,* and *Zuihō.* Only the 1st MAW prevented the enemy from reconquering Guadalcanal.

To counter, Vice Admiral Ghormley deployed the four SoPac task forces. Scott's TG-64.2 of four cruisers and five destroyers moved northward toward Rennell Island. With the 164th Infantry Regiment on board, Turner's reinforcement convoy (joined by Lee's TG-17.8 with the new battleship *Washington*) closed Guadalcanal from the southeast. At the same time Murray's TF-17 with the *Hornet* operated in the Coral Sea west of New Caledonia. Upon learning of the incoming Express, Turner took his convoy eastward to await a clear avenue

TABLE 16.1
Base Air Force in the Bismarcks-Solomons Area, 10 October 1942 (with approximate operational strength)

Unit (Force)	Group	Aircraft
	5th Air Attack Force RAdm. Yamada Sadayoshi	
No. 1	Tainan Air Group Attached: 3rd Air Group Detachment 751 Air Group Fighter Squadron[a]	50 Zero 21s
No. 3	2nd Air Group	8 Zero 32s, 7 Type 99 VBs
No. 4	Tōkō Air Group Attached: 14th Air Group Detachment	6 Type 97 VPs
	6th Air Attack Force VAdm. Yamagata Seigō	
"A"	Kisarazu Air Group	
"B"	Misawa Air Group	Total 45 Type 1 LAs
"C"	753 Air Group Detachment[b]	
"D"	6th Air Group	28 Zero 32s
"E"	31st Air Group	9 Type 99, 3 Type 96 VBs
	1st Air Attack Force RAdm. Ichimaru Rinosuke	
	751 Air Group[a] (without Fighter Squadron)	18 Type 1 LAs

[a] On 1 October the Kanoya Air Group was redesignated 751.
[b] On 1 October the Takao Air Group was redesignated 753.

to Lunga. It seemed the odds were far from favorable against what appeared to be the strongest threat yet to the tenuous hold on Guadalcanal.

TWO-A-DAY AIR STRIKES

On 11 October Base Air Force loosed two air strikes within an hour of each other against Guadalcanal, hoping to catch the American fighters off balance. The tactic would continue to cause the 1st MAW much consternation. A fighter sweep by eighteen Tainan Zeros (two soon aborted) under Lieutenant Commander Nakajima departed Rabaul at 0910, accompanied by nine land attack planes as far as the Russells. Forty-five minutes behind came the second strike comprising forty-five Type 1 land attack planes: twenty-seven from the 6th Air Attack Force (nine Kisarazu, nine Misawa, and nine 753) and eighteen from the 751 Air Group (1st Air Attack Force). Given the special occasion, Lt. Cdr. Uchida Tomoyuki, the Kisarazu air officer (hikōchō), led the formation, by far the strongest bomber strike sent against Guadalcanal. Lieutenant Itō's escort numbered twenty-nine Zero 21s from the 5th Air Attack Force: nine 751, twelve 3rd (Lieutenant [jg] Yamaguchi), and eight 2nd under Lt. (jg) Futagami Tokitane (NA 68-1940). Thus ninety planes bore down on CACTUS.[2]

Strangely, no coastwatchers detected the inbound aircraft. At 1224 the Pagoda called Condition YELLOW, when RADAR TWO unexpectedly picked up two flights 138 miles northwest. From Fighter 1 and Henderson Field thirty-nine F4Fs (fifteen VMF-121, sixteen VMF-223 and 224, and eight VF-5) scrambled, followed by nine P-39s and three P-400s. Heavy cloud cover obscured the skies over Lunga. The P-39 ceiling was 19,000 feet, and the P-400s stayed much lower. Several small flights of CACTUS F4Fs hunted the enemy at high altitude. Condition RED followed at 1254, but a few minutes later Nakajima's sixteen Tainan Zeros roared down on Lunga, where they tangled with eight VMF-121 F4Fs led by Major Davis. PO1c Nishizawa Hiroyoshi, the celebrated ace, forced 2nd Lt. Arthur N. Nehf's F4F to ditch in the channel. All sixteen Zeros returned to base and claimed two Grummans (one unconfirmed).

Around 1345 Uchida's second wave of forty-five land attack planes and twenty-nine Zeros turned up over Lunga, but clouds obscured the airfields. Most aircraft turned back without attacking, but Lt. Cdr. Nishioka Kazuo (NA 58-1930), the 751 hikōtaichō, took his eighteen Type 1s below the overcast and bombed Lunga with uncertain results. Actually his 180 60-kilogram bombs pummeled the jungle several miles southeast of Fighter 1. After missing Nakajima's Zeros in the clouds, about a dozen F4Fs from VMF-224 and VMF-223 under Major Galer were descending to land when suddenly Renner warned of more incoming bombers. Regaining altitude, Galer encountered at 1357 what appeared to be twenty bombers and four Zeros—Nishioka's flight and some of the escort. Although nearly out of gas (Galer himself had only eight gallons), the Marines made one pass. They tallied nine bombers and all four Zeros. In fact, they crippled one 751 Type 1 land attack plane (PO1c Tashiro Eibu) and badly damaged three others (one totaled). Part of the escorting 3rd Air Group claimed three (one unconfirmed) of fifteen Grummans without loss.

Galer's flight had to land instantly, and one F4F quit from fuel starvation before it could taxi off the runway. Capt. William C. Sharpsteen, flying a P-39D from the 339th, saw Tashiro's rikkō level out at 12,000 feet and harried the straggler until it fell out of control, crashed, and burned.[3] Itō's 751 squadron claimed two enemy fighters (both unconfirmed) and did shoot down 1st Lt. Howard L. Stern's P-39.

The two raids cost the 1st MAW Stern's P-39 and Nehf's 121 F4F. In the confusing actions the CACTUS fighters claimed eleven bombers and four Zeros destroyed. The 1st MAW was very fortunate that weather adversely affected both the Japanese bombers and the escorts. The first double raid must be judged a failure. VF-5 never contacted the enemy, but was reduced to twelve F4F-4s, exactly half the original number. During that morning's dawn patrol John McDonald's prop shifted into high pitch, causing him to make a forced landing. The F4F flipped over on its back and injured McDonald's head.

That day the redoubtable pair of VMF-223 aces, John Smith and Marion Carl, left Guadalcanal. Their vital contribution to its defense, both flying and leadership, is incalculable. They would be sorely missed. Twelve SBDs arrived from Espiritu Santo, and fifteen B-17s stayed the night at Henderson Field, making it seem crowded for a change. Gotō's cruiser bombardment had the potential of inflicting heavy damage to the 1st MAW.

Six 6th Air Group Zero 32s flew the late afternoon CAP over the inbound *Nisshin* force, but five pilots died after they became lost in the clouds. Bad weather and poor fields had slammed that hard-luck outfit (ten Zeros and nine pilots in the last four days), and more rough times lay ahead. The *Nisshin* and *Chitose* and six destroyers reached Guadalcanal at 2245 and unloaded their cargoes on the north shore. Near to midnight Gotō's Support Force, with three heavy cruisers and two destroyers, approached Savo Island for a swift run down to bombard the Lunga airfields.

Unknown to Gotō, the stage was set for the first major surface action since the 9 August Battle of Savo Island. Scott's TG-64.2 (two heavy cruisers, two light cruisers, and five destroyers) ambushed his three columns by "crossing the T." At 2346 they fired the opening shots of the Battle of Cape Esperance, and within 35 minutes Scott had won the U.S. Navy's first night victory in the South Pacific. The heavy cruiser *Furutaka* and destroyer *Fubuki* sank; damaged Japanese ships included flagship *Aoba* on whose bridge Gotō was killed. In return the light cruiser *Boise* and the destroyer *Duncan* took heavy damage. Unfortunately Scott never knew the location of the *Nisshin* force, which completed unloading and soon withdrew back up the Slot. By dawn on 12 October, all the ships capable of steaming had quit the battle area. TF-17 with the *Hornet* moved northwest toward Rennell Island to support CACTUS.[4]

Around midnight distant gun flashes and bright explosions had alerted CACTUS of a naval battle in progress northwest. Before dawn Lieutenant Colonel Cooley personally led a strike of eleven Marine and five VS-71 SBDs, escorted by eight P-39s and sixteen VMF-121 F4Fs under Major Davis. Near the Russells, the Marine Dauntlesses attacked destroyers *Shirayuki* and *Murakumo*, which the *Nisshin* force had detached to rescue survivors of Gotō's fight. They sustained no hits, but the 1st MAW was not done with them. Detached by Cooley to search farther up the Slot, John Eldridge with the five VS-71 SBDs unsuccessfully bombed the destroyer *Hatsuyuki* off Santa Isabel. Lou Kirn of VS-3 with seven SBDs and six TBFs, escorted by Major Dobbin's fourteen Marine F4Fs, later discovered the *Shirayuki* and the *Murakumo* near New Georgia. This time the Japanese were not so fortunate. Ripped open by a torpedo, the *Murakumo* went dead in the water.

While Cooley's first strike took off, VF-5 flew a four-plane dawn patrol. Checking out the waters northwest of Guadalcanal, Simpler and Clarke happened upon the abandoned *Duncan* near Savo. Although she drifted without power with two big holes in her hull, one under the bridge and the other well forward, and her "bow end looked cooked," Simpler thought she was "floating beautifully." He tried making radio contact without success, and then returned to base to advise that she could be saved. The skipper of the destroyer *McCalla* (DD-488) agreed. Before dawn he had sent a salvage party on board. The fires abated, but she took in water astern and only lasted until noon, despite valiant efforts by the *McCalla*'s crew.[5]

That afternoon, Geiger hurled his third strike against the enemy warships to the northwest. Eldridge led eleven SBDs, Larsen's lone VT-8 TBF, four P-39s, and also eight VF-5 F4Fs:[6]

1st Division	2nd Division
Lt. Hayden M. Jensen	Lt. (jg) Ray F. Myers
Lt. (jg) Foster J. Blair	Lee P. Mankin, AP1c
Lt. Carl W. Rooney	Lt. (jg) Roland H. Kenton
Lt. (jg) John M. Kleinman	Robert H. Nesbitt, AP1c

Southeast of New Georgia and about 165 miles from Lunga, they came across what appeared to be a heavy cruiser circled by one light cruiser and two destroyers. In fact, all were tincans, the crippled *Murakumo* attended by the *Shirayuki,* and the *Natsugumo* and *Asagumo* sent back by the *Nisshin* force.

Larsen signaled Jensen to support his lone torpedo attack against the "cruiser" floating dead in the water, but all the Dauntlesses ganged up on the hapless *Natsugumo*. To draw AA fire away from the TBF, Jensen led his 1st Division against the side opposite to Larsen's attack. While shooting up the *Murakumo*, he noticed only two guns firing back. Low over the water, he shifted to the *Natsugumo* 2,000 yards off the *Murakumo*'s port bow. She had already stopped and clearly was sinking. Near misses by seven 1,000-pound bombs had torn open her hull and knocked out all power. Boring in from astern, the 1st Division shot up her bridge and deck, then headed on out.

Ray Myers never heard Larsen's order to strafe the "cruiser." While circling overhead at 14,000 feet, he noticed a huge column of black smoke rise from the *Murakumo*, then led his division into a long, steep, high-speed strafing run against the screening ships. After barely clearing the "cruiser's" mast, at bridge level the four F4Fs tore after a nearby destroyer. Black five-inch AA bursts and 25-mm tracers appeared all around. One gun crew had it in for Roland Kenton. As he streaked away at low level, their shell bursts followed right behind. Smoke and the tropic heat made him wonder if his F4F had caught fire. Paul Mankin, for one, "just hated" AA fire and preferred dueling with Zeros. For his own part, Larsen gratefully noted the "excellent" support of the fighters.[7] Erstwhile rescuer *Natsugumo* sank very quickly after the attack, while the *Shirayuki* later torpedoed the *Murakumo*. They marked the first two destroyers sunk since late August by the 1st MAW.

With the waters ahead now secure, Turner's reinforcement convoy steamed west to reach Lunga the next morning, while Lee remained southeast off San Cristobal. VF-5 welcomed its own reinforcement in the person of Dave Richardson, who arrived in an R4D from Espiritu Santo. Recovered from his wounds, he eagerly resumed his post as squadron XO. Elated at the results achieved on the 12th, Ghormley sent Vandegrift a "well done," and added, "Your hard hitting flyers are making many protruding teeth rattle." Unfortunately, Combined Fleet arranged for more than a few Allied teeth to rattle on Guadalcanal.[8]

BOLD WATERS FOR A CARRIER TASK FORCE

Westward of Rennell Island, snoopers bothered Murray's flagship *Hornet* the morning of 12 October as the ships steamed southward.[9] At 1000 her CXAM radar detected a bogey 35 miles due north. Al Fleming, the fine FDO, alerted two old VF-8 veterans, lieutenants (jg) George Formanek and Richard Z. Hughes, and sent them north while climbing to 13,000 feet. A few thousand feet below, there appeared a Kawanishi Type 97 flying boat (PO1c Katō Fumio) from the Tōkō Air Group. Both F4Fs flashed through consecutive high-sides from the right and set ablaze its wing and port inboard engine. While Katō nosed down for speed, Formanek's second high-side torched the other port engine. The big Kawanishi spiraled down to a massive explosion. Katō never got a message off to base.[10]

Task Force 17 barely recovered from the first sighting, when at 1155 the *Northampton*'s radar showed a contact at 60 miles, bearing 150 degrees. Little did they know that the bogey, PO1c Takazawa Hirotsugu's Kisarazu Type 1 *rikkō*, had spotted and reported TF-17's location over a half hour before. Fleming again turned to his 10,000-foot CAP, this time Lt. (jg) Robert E. Sorensen and Ens. Roy B. Dalton. At 1210 Takazawa saw danger coming, turned away and let down in fast glide, hoping to use speed (up to 230 knots) to escape. At 1220 Sorensen and Dalton finally overtook the *rikkō* at 7,000 feet. Dalton rolled into a left high-side run, while Sorensen charged in from astern and below. At first their tracers inflicted no damage, but Dalton's second high-side set the left wing on fire. The *rikkō* descended in a shallow dive all the way to the water.[11] With the day's adventures over, TF-17 steamed southeast until 2045, then reversed course northwest toward the assigned area in the waters northwest of Rennell. Enemy snoopers beware, because the *Hornet* exacted a stiff toll.

After an all-night run to get into position, Murray again patrolled west and south of Rennell Island. At 0600 on the 13th he began the usual southward run and planned, if nothing turned up, to make a fueling rendezvous with the oiler *Guadalupe* set for the next day 300 miles south. Another of the ubiquitous midday bogeys appeared at 1145 on the *Hornet*'s radar. This one bore 025 degrees, distance 29 miles. As usual Fleming tabbed his medium-level CAP, this time XO Al Emerson, Lt. (jg) William J. Moran, and Ens. James O. ("Sleepy") Weimer. While bustering north, they noticed far below a twin-engine bomber almost hugging the waves.

Emerson led the division into a spiraling attack, and only when the F4Fs closed nearly into shooting range did the bomber crew react. PO1c Koga Mamoru of the Misawa group, flying the C4 search line, flashed a sighting report and increased speed. Firing from long range (600–800 yards), Moran silenced several gunners and started the starboard engine smoking. Meanwhile, Emerson and Weimer split up to bracket both sides. Koga set down the burning aircraft in tolerable fashion near Rennell, and the crew climbed out onto a wing. Overhead Emerson watched: "They did look kind of pitiful there, not being able to decide whether to drown or burn to death." Suddenly the wreck exploded, killing all the

Japanese. Back on board, Emerson's friend, artist Tom Lea, observed him visibly "upset by the necessity for killing."[12]

Koga and his men had done their job. Their last radio message warned of an enemy carrier 70 miles southwest of Rennell. However, TF-17 moved south out of range toward the fueling rendezvous south of Guadalcanal. Search planes also spotted Lee's TG-17.8 with the massive *Washington*. The Japanese tried to puzzle out the American deployment.

CALM BEFORE THE STORM

The 13th of October augured favorably for the 1st MarDiv. Turner's reinforcement convoy disembarked the 164th Infantry Regiment and fresh ground crews for the 1st MAW. More troops now held the perimeter, while Geiger wielded more than ninety aircraft. Morning searches by CACTUS SBDs were refreshingly negative. VF-5 prepared for eventual evacuation by sending Alex Barbieri to Espiritu Santo to bring the VF-5 detachment to Efate, where the squadron was to reassemble.

For 13 October Kusaka planned another double strike. The first wave comprised twenty-seven land attack planes (nine each from the Kisarazu, Misawa, and 753 groups) led by Lieutenant Makino of the 753 Air Group Detachment; on the way at least three aborted. Lieutenant Aioi's escort numbered eighteen Zeros (nine 3rd Air Group and nine 751). Two hours behind the lead strike, Lieutenant Commander Nishioka brought fifteen land attack planes (one soon aborted) from the 751 Air Group and Lieutenant Kawai's eighteen Tainan Zeros. If fighters opposed the first wave, the second might catch them refueling on the ground; at least that was the hope.[13]

At 1115 Donald Kennedy on New Georgia warned CACTUS of a flight of enemy planes, and RADAR TWO detected them at 1130. Colonel Wallace's MAG-23 scrambled no fewer than forty-two F4Fs (twenty-two VMF-121, eleven VMF-224, nine VF-5), seven P-39s, and six P-400s. Despite the warnings, the Japanese seemed to close faster than usual and reached Lunga at 1202. Makino passed right over Turner's transports. From 7,500 meters (24,600 feet) his twenty-four Type 1s executed an unopposed, highly effective bombing run against both airfields and reported blasting twenty small aircraft on the ground. Actually they destroyed one B-17, slightly damaged twelve other planes, and spectacularly torched a cache of 5,000 gallons of aviation gasoline. The whole Seabee detachment turned out to repair the field, replacing torn Marston matting and filling bomb craters. Due to a lack of shovels, many men used their helmets to move dirt.

Only four F4Fs from Duke Davis's VMF-121 flight even intercepted the raiders, and that fully a half hour after the bombing. VF-5 only sighted the distant enemy bomber formation withdrawing. At 1230, Davis dived against the 753 *chū-tai*. Lieutenant (jg) Baba's 3rd *Chūtai* of six Zeros (three 751, three 3rd Air Group) chased them away, but not before 2nd Lt. William B. Freeman winged PO2c Negishi Genji's 753 *rikkō*. Baba covered the straggler on the way out. A little later, 2nd Lt. Joseph L. Narr single-handedly jumped the escort and crippled Sea1c Itō Manri's 3rd Air Group Zero. With his F4F shot up in return, Narr set down in the water unhurt off Lunga, but Itō later died while ditching his fighter at Rekata. Negishi's land attack plane had just enough left in it to reach base.

Radar tagged the next wave at 1335. This time twelve VMF-121 F4Fs gained attack position above, but ran afoul of the Zero escort. At 1400 Nishioka's fourteen land attack planes approached at 8,000 meters (26,240 feet) and reported bombing thirty aircraft on the ground. Actually they inflicted only "slight" damage according to the 1st MAW. Five of Kawai's eighteen Tainan Zeros got into action, claiming five (including two unconfirmed) of ten Grummans. PO1c Yasui Kozaburō, PO3c Yanami Nobutaka, and Sea1c Yoneda Tadashi bounced Joe Foss and three other 121 F4Fs while they sought altitude advantage out to the left of the bombers. One Zero overran after a pass against Foss, who thought he bagged that bandit for his first victory, but the Mitsubishi was undamaged. The Yasui *shōtai* proceeded to teach Foss a lesson. They knocked out his oil cooler, which froze the engine, and ran the ailing F4F all the way back to Lunga. Fortunately Foss had the height and speed to make it. With the propeller windmilling, he dropped in at Fighter 1 "like a rocket ship," bounced along the dirt, and barely halted short of the stumps bordering the Ilu River.[14]

Claims by CACTUS against both raids totaled two Zeros (by Narr and Foss) and three bombers (one by Freeman, two by 90-mm AA guns). Both missions cost Base Air Force one Zero ditched at Rekata, and several *rikkōs* damaged. Kusaka was highly pleased at the reported results, which seemed to show the enemy was wavering. Along with most of the CACTUS fighters, VF-5 had not fired a shot except to test guns. More impressive was what they found back at Henderson Field: "Someone had sent us a carton of Coca-colas and they acquired some ice so we had an ice-cold 'Coke' when we got back from our flight, the most appreciated luxury we ever had up there."[15] It was the proverbial calm before the storm.

That afternoon and evening two very ominous events hinted of trouble brewing for CACTUS. Two hundred miles northwest of Guadalcanal, an SBD on the afternoon search spotted three transports and three destroyers approaching at 15 knots. They were part of the High Speed Convoy, the force of six transports escorted by eight destroyers from Rear Admiral Takama's 4th Destroyer Squadron. The heavily laden APs carried seven infantry battalions plus heavy weapons, including tanks, for the 17th Army.

At 1818 an artillery shell exploding just off the west edge of Henderson Field shattered the stillness at Lunga. This was the first of many shots by a pair of 15-cm howitzers of the 4th Field Heavy Artillery Regiment. From concealed emplacements southwest of Kokumbona, they kept up an intermittent barrage for about 45 minutes while registering on target. One shell raised a splash 25 yards from Turner's flagship *McCawley*. Three destroyers, the *Nicholas*, *Sterett*, and *Gwin* (DD-433), shelled Point Cruz in retaliation.

When the first round landed, Roy Geiger was chatting with Simpler in front of the VF-5 ready tent. Suddenly men dived for the safety of a nearby dugout, but ended up in a heap at the entrance. Simpler "wiggled loose" and looked around for the general. Retracing his steps, he saw Geiger "standing at the rear of the tent, a mosquito protecting head piece on, and his fingers in his ears waiting for the next salvo." Simpler said, "General, you know that you should seek shelter as fast as possible in such a danger." Geiger replied, "Yes I know, but I am not going to let a goddamn Jap cause me to get my last clean uniform dirty."[16] Soon dubbed variously "Millimeter Mike," "Pistol Pete," or "Mountain Joe," the artillery proved only a foretaste of what soon would descend upon CACTUS.

BOMBARDMENTS

On 12 October Combined Fleet decided to ease the High Speed Convoy's approach by means of a battleship bombardment of Lunga to knock out enemy air strength. Kondō's Advance Force sent RAdm. Kurita Takeo's 3rd Battleship Division (the *Kongō* and *Haruna*) and Rear Admiral Tanaka's 2nd Destroyer Squadron (light cruiser *Isuzu* and nine destroyers) south at high speed. The *Kongō* readied special 14-inch AA incendiary shells, while her sister *Haruna* loaded high-explosive shells. Both battlewagons also used normal armor-piercing rounds and some subcaliber 12-inch shells. They would put the men of CACTUS through an ordeal faced by few other Allied troops during the war.

Near midnight on 13/14 October, Kurita roared down from the north past Savo. At 0130 his float planes dropped three bright flares: red over the western edge of the runway, white above the Pagoda in the center, and green over the eastern part of the field. Three minutes later the *Kongō*'s first 14-inch salvo thundered, as the special shells, leaving fiery trails, slammed into the perimeter west of Henderson Field. Upon detonation they "spewed forth hundreds of tiny cylinders, open at both ends and spitting fire."[17] The *Haruna* followed suit at 0135. Gunnery officers soon adjusted to rake the runway, the aircraft dispersal areas north of the field, and the bivouac areas northeast in the coconut grove.

Taking cover in the handiest dugout, slit trench, or depression, those on the receiving end soon realized this was no caress by five-inchers, but something totally new, a brilliant display of deadly fireworks. No less than 150 men, many from VF-5, crowded into the Pagoda tunnel and the underground operations room. A veteran of the 67th FS later wrote:

> They had hardly hit the foxholes before the air was filled with a bedlam of sound: the screaming of shells, the dull roar of cannonading off shore, the whine of shrapnel, the thud of palm trees as they were severed and hit the ground, and in the lulls from the big noises, the ceaseless sifting of dirt into the foxhole.[18]

Lou Kirn of VS-3 noted, "You feel so utterly helpless . . . feel, rather than hear, salvos being walked right over your position." Soon aviation gasoline supplies, aircraft, and ammunition dumps began exploding. Lieutenant Colonel Bayler later wrote of the "ghastly blaze of light." Elated Japanese observers described the Lunga airfield as a "sea of fire."[19]

At 0213 Kurita drew out of range to the east and reversed course back toward Lunga. This time his two battlewagons used the less-effective AP shells. When the bombardment finally ceased at 0256, the total number of shells fired reached 973. Just to keep things lively, two land attack planes from Rabaul occasionally dropped bombs on targets illuminated by the many fires. Two more *rikkōs* relieved them later that morning and kept up the harassment until near dawn.

Kurita's bombardment torched nearly all of the aviation gasoline held at CACTUS and set afire or riddled with shrapnel most of the planes at Henderson Field. Only seven of thirty-nine SBDs could fly immediately after the ordeal. VT-8 was completely out of business with no operational TBFs. Just four P-400s and two P-39s were ready to go. The previous afternoon eight B-17s led personally by Colonel Saunders, CO of the 11th Bomb Group, had taken refuge at Henderson Field after a tough Buka mission. They expected a quiet night, but didn't get one. The bombardment knocked out two and damaged a third Fortress.

Fighting Five lost four F4Fs, which left eight (six flyable). From the Pagoda tunnel Major Renner beheld a horrible scene of burning aircraft, including a VF-5

Wildcat parked 100 yards away. It threatened another F4F 50 feet beyond. Heat from the nearby fire caused gasoline to stream from the undamaged F4F's overflow valve. He swiftly organized a party to push that Wildcat out of danger, then checked out Henderson Field. Thirteen large craters tore the Marston matting on the runway. Armor-piercing shells had burrowed as deep as 15 to 20 feet, but fortunately left quite narrow holes. VF-5's ready tent sported a neat hole from a shell that had passed through and detonated near the tent occupied by Scollin and Bayler. Scattered around the whole area were jagged pieces of shrapnel and baseplates of 14-inch shells. Fighter 1 came through better than the main field. Of thirty Marine F4Fs, eighteen still flew.[20]

The coconut grove, where the pilots lived, was a mess from shell bursts in the treetops. The "entire floor of the grove was littered with fallen trees, palm fronds, coconuts whole and shredded, and assorted debris from tents and buildings." Partially destroyed coconut trees had a nasty habit of falling on men who worked to clean up beneath them. The VF-5 tents were "cut to ribbons."[21] The pilots just sifted the living sites for personal belongings, then moved on. Forty-one men died from the bombardment, and many were wounded. VF-5 was very fortunate to suffer no serious casualties. Only Roland Kenton was hurt, having cut an eye from running into a clothesline. Other squadrons were not so lucky. A direct hit on their dugout killed Maj. Gordon Bell, the VMSB-141 CO, and four of his officers (including the XO and the flight officer), along with Lieutenant Kephart from VS-71.[22]

At 0500 Combined Fleet declared the enemy air force at Lunga to be no more. Yamamoto loosed the 2nd and 3rd fleets to hunt down and destroy Allied naval forces in the southern Solomons. The 1st MAW reeled, but was far from gone. At 0540, to his great surprise Lieutenant Commander Mitsui on Mount Austen saw several SBDs lift off Henderson Field for the morning search. Simpler followed to check out the area, while two Marine F4Fs took off from Fighter 1 for the customary dawn patrol. The 17th Army's two 15-cm howitzers pounded the west half of Henderson Field. During the day four P-400s tried unsuccessfully to knock out elusive Millimeter Mike.

With Henderson Field rapidly becoming untenable, Colonel Saunders was anxious to get his five flyable B-17s safely back to Espiritu Santo. Only about 1,800 feet of runway were clear. Around 1700, while the B-17s warmed up their engines, seven VF-5 pilots (Jim Halford, Cash Register, Mel Roach, John McDonald, Jack Wesolowski, Junior Kleinmann, and Paul Mankin) received orders to depart CACTUS as soon as possible. It was the beginning of the evacuation of VF-5. With no R4Ds available, Register climbed on board a B-17 to ask if there was room for the party. Before he could get to the cockpit, the pilots gunned their engines, dodged two big craters, and lifted off. Register had his ride to Santo. The other six men went out in the remaining B-17s and Geiger's PBY-5A.[23] Later another Flying Fort got away on three engines and reached Espiritu Santo, but the two stranded at Henderson Field never flew again. However, their partially filled tanks proved a valuable source of aviation gasoline, for the 1st MAW was critically short of fuel.

The morning search revealed the full strength of the High Speed Convoy, six transports and eight destroyers, only 140 miles northwest. To Vandegrift and Geiger it looked like the big push at last. The commanding general inspected battered Henderson Field and discovered his aviation strength much reduced. Talking over the situation with Geiger, he drafted a message to ComSoPac stressing the "urgent necessity that this force receive maximum support of air and surface units."[24] The scuttlebutt among the aviators was that the CO had sent out a "virtual S-O-S." Finally realizing the Pagoda had to go, Geiger ordered it razed as too handy a point for enemy observers to register their guns. Radio equipment went into the Pagoda Hill tunnel, while aviation headquarters relocated near Secondary Hill in the woods south of Fighter 1.

On New Georgia Donald Kennedy warned of incoming enemy planes, so at 0945 the 1st MAW sounded Condition YELLOW, followed at 1003 by RED. From Henderson Field, VF-5 scrambled five F4Fs, while Fighter 1 sent aloft sixteen from VMF-121 and four VMF-224. No contact creased RADAR TWO's scope, which behaved a bit erratically after the bombardment (the old RADAR ONE machine no longer functioned). Renner gave the all-clear at 1042. However, no one bothered to lower the black flag; it was Condition RED all day. Renner parked the RECON BASE truck at Secondary Hill, and Lew Mattison's FD team camped alongside. On landing, Richardson ground-looped F-13, leaving VF-5 with four operational F4Fs.

Base Air Force repeated the tactic of two strikes timed an hour apart. Leaving Rabaul at 0810, the first wave comprised forty-five planes: twenty-seven land attack planes (as usual, nine each Kisarazu, Misawa, and 753) under Lieutenant Nabeta, escorted by Lieutenant Itō's eighteen Zeros (nine 751, six Tainan, and three 3rd). En route one Kisarazu *rikkō* aborted, leaving twenty-six. They climbed to high altitude.[25]

Probably because of malfunctioning radar, the 1st MAW called YELLOW alert too late. Only at 1157 did twenty-five F4Fs begin taking off: twelve VMF-121 under Joe Foss, nine VMF-224 led by Bob Galer, and four VF-5 under Hayden Jensen. To clear the fields, most of the operational Airacobras and SBDs followed them off. Before the F4Fs could gain much height, the first wave arrived. Nabeta's twenty-six land attack planes approached from the west-southwest and at 1213 bombed both airfields from 7,500 meters (24,600 feet). On the heavily cratered main field they counted fifty aircraft and bombed thirty small and thirteen large planes, mostly wrecks. The 3rd Defense Battalion's 90-mm crews claimed one bomber and four probables. In turn the escort reported fighting eight enemy carrier bombers, two fighters, and two bombers withdrawing toward Malaita, and claimed one Grumman. Available records do not indicate the identity of their opponents. The Zeros stopped at Buka to refuel. The first wave suffered no losses; neither did the 1st MAW.

At 1303 the second wave hove into sight. It comprised Lt. Doki Osamu's twelve land attack planes from the 751 Air Group, escorted by Lieutenant Kurakane with fifteen Zeros (nine 2nd, six 3rd).[26] Nearing Lunga, Doki let down from 8,000 meters (26,400 feet) at high speed. This time some F4Fs waited overhead, eager to deal out punishment. Galer led nine VMF-224 Grummans against the enemy and claimed five bombers and two Zeros (including his fourteenth and final kill). The intercept was a great success. From 1302 to 1306 the Japanese reckoned that fourteen Grummans ripped through Doki's 1st *Chūtai* and shot down three *rikkōs* (PO1c Ibaraki Akifumi, PO1c Maruo Tokujirō, and PO1c Yusa Takao). From Lt. Naka Seiji's 2nd *Chūtai*, PO1c Iida Noboru's Type 1 took such damage that it dropped from formation. The escort under Kurakane and Yamaguchi proved completely ineffectual in preventing the attacks.

The land attack *chūtais* split up to bomb the two airfields from 7,000 meters (22,900 feet). At 1307 Naka's five released their payloads against three large planes on Henderson Field. A minute later Doki's three from the 1st *Chūtai* struck at ten small aircraft visible at Fighter 1. Then came VF-5's turn. At 1310, right after the bombing, Jensen, Clarke, Myers, and Richardson claimed five bombers with high-side runs: two to Jensen (his sixth and seventh kills) and one each for the others.[27] Actually two 751 land attack planes sustained heavy damage. PO1c Funakawa Hisayoshi (1st *Chūtai*) took hits in the right engine, limped all the way to Buka, and flopped down at 1610. Lt. (jg) Ueda Shigeru (NA 67-1939), 2nd *Shōtai* leader in the 2nd *Chūtai*, set down in the shallows off Rekata, where the crew counted fifty-three bullet holes. Because some Zeros remained overhead, the VF-5 pilots dived away. While descending, Myers watched a stricken bomber (previously crippled by the Marines) fall as if "suspended by a string," then explode in midair. From below he tried another run against Naka's surviving four, fired on several bombers, then did a split-S and followed the rest of the troops on out.[28]

Unable to climb with the rest of his flight, Joe Foss ambushed a Zero that had dived low in pursuit of a 224 Grumman and claimed it. Several of his pilots busied themselves chasing a speedy Tainan J1N1-C Type 2 land recon plane that was checking out Lunga between raids. They shot out its right engine. WO Ono Satoru dumped the fuel in that wing, but gunfire set it ablaze. He dived to try to extinguish the flame, which a rather thrilling descent finally snuffed out. Ono made it to Buin, but understandably Master Sgt. Joseph J. Palko of VMF-121 thought he had downed an enemy bomber.

Claims by CACTUS against the second raid amounted to eleven bombers and three Zeros shot down, one bomber and one Zero probable. The 3rd Defense Battalion reversed its tally from the first raid: four confirmed bomber kills and one probable. The 1st MAW lost 2nd Lt. Koller C. Brandon from Foss's flight. In fact all the Zeros returned to Rabaul but, rather chastened, their pilots submitted no claims. The 751 Air Group lost three land attack planes shot down or missing, one ditched at Rekata, one force-landed at Buka, and several others damaged. CACTUS proved it could still fight back aloft.

After the departure of the seven pilots, the rest of VF-5 encamped on the lee side of a hill just south of Fighter 1. Due to the ministrations of Millimeter Mike, they lost two more F4Fs at Henderson Field, leaving just six at Fighter 1. At least VF-5 had airplanes. Temporarily out of commission, VT-8 handed out the small arms and prepared to fight alongside the Marines should the Japanese invade Lunga. For fear of revealing Fighter 1 to further ship bombardments, Geiger canceled SBD night operations that would require setting out landing lights for their return.

That afternoon and evening CACTUS twice struck Takama's High Speed Convoy. At the cost of 2nd Lt. Paul S. Rutledge and Technical Sgt. Alexander Thomson (VMF-121) and one P-39 (1st Lt. Edgar E. Barr, later returned), a tincan suffered only minor damage. Six Zero 32s from Buin met the second attack, then ditched at Rekata. The 6th now counted only fourteen Zeros, having suffered horrendous noncombat losses the previous week. Nevertheless the Japanese were jubilant. The High Speed Convoy had weathered all attacks and would reach Guadalcanal that night.

Lt. Cdr. Ray Davis, with eight SBDs of Bombing Six, arrived at CACTUS just before dark to reinforce the five operational dive bombers. At Espiritu Santo, Rear Admiral Fitch requested twenty more SBDs from AirSoPac for Guadalcanal and even suggested that the *Hornet* provide ten more for CACTUS. During the day, pilots from Lt. Col. Joe Bauer's VMF-212 ferried SBDs from Efate to Santo, then rode back in an R4D to fetch their own fighters. They chomped at the bit to get to CACTUS. Fitch was scraping the barrel trying to get as many airplanes as he could to Geiger. He arranged for the converted seaplane tender *McFarland* to load 200 drums of aviation gasoline and twelve torpedoes for Guadalcanal.[29]

That evening Ghormley studied the situation, formulated plans, and advised CinCPac of developments. ULTRA provided not a glimmer of Japanese strength, movements, or intentions, something the admiral's critics rarely take into account. From actual sighting reports he learned of several powerful enemy task forces in the Solomons area. Six transports, one light cruiser, and seven destroyers (the High Speed Convoy) neared Guadalcanal and would land troops that night. Covering them were what he believed to be one battleship, three light cruisers, and four destroyers, actually Mikawa's bombardment force. Ghormley also knew a strong force of carriers protected by battleships, cruisers, and destroyers lurked 400 miles northeast of Guadalcanal. Closer in northeast at 225 miles was an advance force of cruisers and destroyers. AirSoPac had sighted portions of Kondō's 2nd and Nagumo's 3rd fleets which threatened the supply line between BUTTON and CACTUS.

Ghormley warned Nimitz that "the situation is critical." To counter these forces, he had only Murray's TF-17 with the *Hornet* and two surface task groups led by Lee and Scott. Murray was refueling northwest of New Caledonia, when he received orders to rush north toward Guadalcanal and late on 15 October move into position to deal with enemy ships descending from the north. Ghormley planned to unite Lee and Scott and use them on the 16th to deter further landings on Guadalcanal. For 15 October CACTUS was on its own.[30]

The night of 14/15 October the 1st MarDiv turned into their holes wondering if the convoy would deliver the long-feared counterlanding against the Lunga beaches. Instead, about midnight Takama disembarked troops, weapons, and supplies at Tassafaronga. At Cape Esperance Mikawa dropped off two CLs and four DDs as a regular Express run, then continued toward Lunga with heavy cruisers *Chōkai* and *Kinugasa* and two destroyers. About 0150 they cut loose with their eight-inchers for a 30-minute bombardment of Henderson Field. For the 1st MAW it was rough, but not anywhere near as severe as the previous night. On their ridge southeast of Fighter 1, VF-5 was not badly shaken.

15 OCTOBER

Ashore

Before dawn Vandegrift radioed Ghormley that no landings had indeed occurred at Lunga. However, as dawn broke six transports had anchored "brazen and bold"[31] about 15 miles west, a gauntlet thrown at the feet of the 1st MAW. Takama risked daylight air attack to rush as many men ashore as he could. He hoped Mikawa's bombardment had neutralized the enemy air force at Lunga, and that 17th Army artillery would successfully interdict the airfield. The Japanese took elaborate steps to protect the convoy. Before dawn six Type 0 observation seaplanes under WO Matsuoka Chikara flew down from Rekata, and at 0800 Lieutenant Kofukuda's twelve Zero 32s arrived from Buin. Eleven *Junyō* Zeros were en route from Kondō's 2nd Carrier Division northeast of Guadalcanal. Other flights were scheduled to relieve these aircraft.[32]

Search planes from BUTTON spotted the night Express, as well as Mikawa's bombardment force, but the immediate problem at hand was the six transports off the beach just west of Kokumbona covered by destroyers steaming between Savo and Guadalcanal. Geiger's aviators were eager to plaster these fat targets right within sight of Lunga. At Fighter 1 VF-5 had three F4Fs in commission along with perhaps twenty Marine Wildcats, but only three SBDs could fly, although crews labored hard to repair more. The SBDs had to taxi over rough dirt the mile or so from Henderson Field to Fighter 1. Only one made it. Even though he could not retract his wheels or extend his flaps, 1st Lt. Robert M. Patterson of VMSB-141 made the first of a series of pennypacket assaults, whose exact sequence cannot now be determined.

Pat Rooney and Smokey Stover of VF-5 flew the first fighter strike of the day.[33] Taking off about 0800, they quickly attained 7,000 feet. Black AA bursts chased them even before they pushed over west of Point Cruz to strafe three transports anchored in line off the beach. Barreling in "below masthead height," they shot into the slab-sided vessels, roughed up a landing barge, then recovered inland, where they turned right toward rugged Cape Esperance and flew through a valley. The two F4Fs reversed course to have a another go at the same targets, this time from the opposite side.

Recovering from his second run, Stover zoomed back to 7,000 feet bound for Lunga. Suddenly he spotted a Type 0 observation seaplane diving at him from behind. It was the *Sanuki Maru*'s Q-178, flown by PO1c Sakuma Kiichi with Sea1c Yoshimitsu Shigeru as observer. They were well acquainted with VF-5, having fought both the 14 September and 8 October battles. Stover countered by turning sharply and climbing, but Sakuma clung to his tail. At 8,000 feet, Stover confronted his pursuer with a long, nearly head-on attack. Sakuma shot first, but the 7.7-mm tracers "dribbled off to the right." At 500 yards Stover replied with four .50s, also underled his target, and missed. As if mesmerized, neither pilot pulled out of his run in time to avoid colliding. Stover's right wing sliced through one of the biplane's fabric-covered right wings and tore away the wing strut. He retained control and brought the F4F around for another run. Only one gun responded, and he was not certain he hit anything, but Sakuma was finished. He spun away, and Rooney watched the crash.

A pair of 6th Air Group Zeros trailed the two F4Fs back to the field. At 0820 3rd Defense Battalion spotters noticed two Zeros with square-tipped wings similar to those on the Wildcats for the first direct observation by CACTUS of the A6M3 Model 32 Zero (later called HAP, then HAMP by the AAF). As Stover touched down on Fighter 1, his damaged right wing slowly sagged and tore the right flap nearly off. Caught in the jagged metal of a foot-long gash marring its leading edge was a "yard square strip of black fabric containing part of a blood-red Rising Sun, edged with a gray circle,"[34] a souvenir of a fight remarkable even by CACTUS standards. Stover treasured the canvas for the rest of his life. Aside from the collision, his F4F also survived four 25-mm AA hits.

Against the 1st MAW raids that morning, the air defense was strangely ineffective despite strong fighter support. Except for Sakuma, none of the thirty-eight Japanese aircraft on patrol before 1000 fought American aircraft. The key factor was the inability of the ships to alert fighters of incoming attacks.

The acute shortage of aviation gasoline at CACTUS abated somewhat when the 1st MAW staff located a cache of 465 drums thoughtfully buried several weeks before by Colonel Woods. In addition R4Ds from VMJ-253 and C-47s from the AAF's 13th Troop Carrier Squadron regularly risked artillery fire to bring twelve drums apiece and roll them out onto Henderson Field. From Tulagi YP boats transported 200 more drums. The gas crisis still loomed, and CACTUS awaited the arrival of the *McFarland*. Fitch advised Ghormley that it was no longer possible to stage B-17s through CACTUS for strikes farther up the Solomons. He strongly suggested that Kenney's Fifth Air Force in New Guinea and Australia assault Rabaul, Buka, and Kahili (Buin) to relieve enemy pressure on CACTUS.

Two of the several late-morning attacks were especially notable. The first originated from CACTUS. The previous afternoon Maj. Jack R. Cram, Geiger's pilot, brought in the general's personal PBY-5A amphibian with a torpedo slung under each wing. CACTUS control tried to get him to land on Fighter 1, but he insisted on setting down at Henderson despite Millimeter Mike's interference. No TBFs could fly, and nothing else at CACTUS even carried a torpedo. The morning of the 15th, Cram volunteered to make a torpedo attack with the PBY even though patrol squadrons executed strikes only at night without fighter opposition. Cram knew numerous Zeros protected the target, but he was determined to go. Geiger reluctantly agreed. When Cram went around saying goodbye to the other pilots, Simpler offered advice on the technique of aiming torpedoes.

At 1015 Cram joined a strike of twelve SBDs, two P-39s (with 500-pound bombs), four P-400s (with 100-pound bombs), and five VMF-121 F4Fs under Duke Davis. They headed out to the southwest and circled all the way around to attack the ships from the north. Beneath them Cram cut inside of their turn, continued all the way around to head southeast, and started in from 6,000 feet. From Buka a patrol of six Tainan and three 3rd Air Group Zeros under Lieutenant (jg) Ōno furiously intercepted the strike. While the SBDs dived in from 10,000 feet, Cram accelerated to 240 knots and released his first fish from 500 yards out. Its load unbalanced, the PBY lurched to starboard, so he kicked the nose to the right and lined up against another transport. Cram reported hitting one ship, and the other CACTUS attackers apparently scored at least another. At any rate the *Sasago Maru* was set afire and became a total loss. After getting a near miss on a transport, Captain Sharpsteen in a 339th P-39 ambushed and flamed a Zero, very likely Sea1c Iwase Jisuke.[35] The SBDs (which also claimed two Zeros) paid a heavy toll: three VMSB-141 flown by 2nd Lt. Anthony J. Turtora, 2nd Lt. Dante Benedetti, and 2nd Lt. Robert C. Le Blanc were lost.

From Buka Warrant Officer Yamashita's eight Tainan Zeros joined the action at 1030. PO1c Ōta (a top-scoring ace), PO2c Sakurai Chūji, and Sea1c Sugawara Yōzō took after Cram's PBY now chugging at low level east toward Lunga. Ōta for one thought he finished the Consolidated, but the others stayed with it. With Sakurai right on his tail, Cram roared low over Henderson Field into the midst of fierce AA. 2nd Lt. Roger A. Haberman of VMF-121 happened to be circling Fighter 1 about to land his heavily smoking Wildcat. Wheels down and coming on final, he extended the turn and shot at Sakurai as he went by. Swinging around again, he blew up the Zero for his first kill. Cram set the battered Catalina on Fighter 1, while Sugawara strafed and headed on out. Haberman quickly joined those congratulating Cram for his magnificent attack.[36]

The second vital strike originated at BUTTON and comprised Major Maniere's nine B-17s from the 11th Bomb Group, the "Grey Geese." The *Nankai Maru* completed unloading and departed at 1145. Five minutes later, as the Flying Forts overflew CACTUS Lew Mattison watched as "everyone ran out of the holes & out on the field & cheered them."[37] Despite fierce attacks by several intercepting Zeros, they fatally damaged the transport *Azumasan Maru*. The Japanese claimed two B-17s; the 11th Bomb Group thought they downed three or four Zeros, but neither side lost anything in this exchange. Yamashita overstayed his time limit and crash-landed at Buin, while three Tainan teammates ditched, all were rescued.

Base Air Force's daily contribution to the woes of CACTUS occurred at 1245. Lieutenant Makino, the 753 *hikōtaichō*, led twenty-three land attack planes (nine Misawa, eight Kisarazu, and six 753). Their fine bomb run at 7,500 meters (24,600 feet) against both fields inflicted "some damage to planes and runways," according to the MAG-23 Record of Events. About seven VMF-121, three 224, and VF-5's last two operational F4Fs had insufficient warning and got off too late. None secured a shot at the bombers, which were opposed only by 90-mm AA that claimed four bombers, plus one probable, and actually holed numerous land attack planes.

Lieutenant (jg) Baba's mixed *chūtai* of eight Zeros (five 751, three 3rd) escorted Makino's strike.[38] They left Rabaul at 0700 and stopped at Buka to refuel before joining their charges. With plenty of fuel, they were ready to fight as the *rikkōs* departed. At 1220, just after the bombing, Baba broke off to bounce about seven scattered Grummans he spotted below. East of Lunga Dave Richardson and Will Rouse from VF-5 had only reached 20,000 feet, when Baba's 3rd *Shōtai* of PO2c Sakai Tadahiro, PO3c Ōhara Giichi, and PO3c Morioka Tatsuo (all 3rd Air Group) pounced on them. Rouse went down immediately with a severed oil line. The engine froze, and he ditched dead-stick just off the mouth of the Tenaru River. Two Marine F4Fs covered him all the way to the water. Despite scalp and knee injuries, he escaped the sinking Wildcat, but neglected to retrieve his life raft, thinking he would not need it. Farther from shore than he realized, he almost did not survive the choppy seas. In the meantime Richardson fired at a Zero that had overshot its attack and claimed it for VF-5's last score. He returned safely.[39]

From the CACTUS interceptors, only VMF-224 and VF-5 made contact. Richardson and 1st Lt. William Watkins (212, attached 224) each claimed a Zero, for the loss of Rouse and 2nd Lt. Hugo A. Olsson (121 in a 224 F4F), both rescued. VF-5 lost another F4F while under repair, when a bomb scored a direct hit, leaving only four Wildcats (one flyable). Baba's escort Zeros fought seven Grummans and claimed five (including four unconfirmed) without loss.

Around 1300 Baba's fighters joined Lieutenant (jg) Futagami's nine 2nd Air Group Zeros protecting the transports, but even so at 1315 they could not prevent CACTUS SBDs from pounding transport *Kyūshū Maru*. She had to be beached as a total loss at Bunina Point, not far from Kokumbona. Of the *Sasago Maru* and the *Azumasan Maru*, one sank in deep water and the other washed ashore. Thus pressure exerted by the 1st MAW and Saunders's B-17s forced Takama to withdraw the *Sado Maru* and the *Sakaido Maru* before they could completely unload. Search planes watched them "milling around" in the waters north of Savo. Takama hoped to return after dark, but the 17th Army warned him off. Balancing the numbers of troops and cargo put ashore with three ships lost, the High Speed Convoy was judged only a partial success.[40]

That afternoon VF-5 continued its evacuations. Wally Clarke, Frank Green, Smokey Stover (clutching his celebrated souvenir), Larry Grimmell, Johnny Kleinman, Will Rouse, and Bob Nesbitt boarded an R4D bound for BUTTON. The last four VF-5 enlisted men from the original party (Edward E. Popovich, AMM1c, Carl J. Duracher, AMM2c, Philip F. Belger, AMM3c, and John H. Lynch, ARM3c) went with them. About an hour after takeoff, gunfire rocked the Douglas. Thinking themselves under attack by an enemy search plane, the passengers grabbed Thompson submachine guns provided for defense and poked them out the side windows. Actually four U.S. destroyers fired a salvo at the low-flying plane, fortunately not hitting anything. For VF-5, the incident was particularly ironic. Clarke summed up their feelings: "What an ending this might have been to our successful tour on Guadalcanal."[41]

At CACTUS Simpler remained with six pilots (Richardson, Jensen, Rooney, Myers, Kenton, and Blair), Bill Robb, and thirty-three enlisted men. Through his old friend "Toby" Munn, he arranged to see Geiger and informed him VF-5 was finished, out of men, airplanes, and equipment. They had given their all. In fact, he remarked with a smile, all he had left was his pair of binoculars and then promptly lifted them over his head and presented them to the general.[42]

Air operations on 15 October cost the Marines three F4Fs, three SBDs, and one P-39 (the Japanese lost six Zeros and one Type 0 observation seaplane), but the 1st MAW was still in business, a major victory in itself. Vandegrift and Geiger conferred with Cdr. Mike Kernodle, commanding the Guadalcanal naval air base. They stressed that Japanese control of the seas and skies around Guadalcanal permitted them to bomb and shell Lunga at will. If this continued, the 1st MarDiv "will be unable indefinitely to hold these positions." The 1st MAW could no longer strike back with any regularity, as "offensive air operations [are] limited now to strikes from Espiritu Santo." That afternoon Kernodle delivered these realistic assessments to Fitch.[43]

At Sea

On 15 October important events occurred in the waters around Guadalcanal. At 0530 TF-17 completed fueling northwest of New Caledonia and bent on more knots to reach the designated launch point for the next day's dawn strike. George Murray hoped to find the enemy ships that had savaged Guadalcanal still within strike range of the *Hornet* Air Group.[44]

Early that afternoon the *Hornet*'s radar gained the seemingly inevitable contact with a Japanese search plane, this day 30 miles due south. WO Yaguchi Toshihito's Kawanishi Type 97 flying boat from the Tōkō Air Group plodded on its return leg bound for Shortland. Al Fleming mustered his troops and sent George Formanek and Dick Hughes southward at 4,000 feet. Everyone was getting to be an old hand at this. Ahead and off to starboard Formanek sighted the Kawanishi flying boat and led his wingman into high-side runs from the left. Yaguchi fled toward the water. After his first attack, Formanek crossed over to the right side and pressed his run all the way in to 50 yards. At 1245 the Kawanishi exploded in midair, just as Hughes commenced his second run. Yaguchi never contacted base.[45]

The rest of the day TF-17 narrowed the range to Guadalcanal and by dark was about 150 miles southeast of San Cristobal. To support TF-17, Ghormley directed Lee and Scott to rendezvous at 1600 northwest of Espiritu Santo. Lee was to take over as CTF-64 and operate south and west of Guadalcanal, hopefully to ambush a run of the Tokyo Express.

Ghormley worried about powerful Japanese carrier forces well east of Guadalcanal, particularly as ULTRA gave no warning of their approach. Kondō and Nagumo tirelessly searched for the U.S. fleet thought to be southeast of Guadalcanal. Early that afternoon an R-Area Air Force Type 0 reconnaissance seaplane located an American "convoy" southeast of San Cristobal, leading carriers *Shōkaku* and *Zuikaku* to attack the fleet tug *Vireo* (AT-144) towing a PAB barge, escorted by the destroyer *Meredith* (DD-434). They quickly sank the DD, but did not bother the tug, whose crew had taken refuge on the doomed *Meredith*. SoPac did not confirm the loss until the next day when a PBY sighted the drifting tug.

Because they failed to contact significant enemy forces on the 15th, Kondō and Nagumo retired to fuel from their oilers. Fitch's flyers from BUTTON spotted the enemy carriers while their planes pounded the *Meredith*. Nagumo's ostensible threat to BUTTON caused quite a stir, particularly as no one knew he was about to withdraw. Fitch sent five B-17s to attack and arranged for five radar-equipped PBYs for a night strike. Howard Crews and his VF-5 contingent stood on alert along with Bauer's twenty VMF-212 F4Fs just in from Efate. That evening a false alarm thoroughly stirred up the island. No enemy planes appeared, but BUTTON remained ready to meet a possible dawn air attack.

16 OCTOBER

The Hornet's Raid

For the third night in a row, the Imperial Navy serenaded CACTUS with heavy-caliber shells. From 0025 to 0125 heavy cruisers *Myōkō* and *Maya*, supported by Tanaka's 2nd Destroyer Squadron, pounded the airfield areas, and also, by error, the very site where VF-5 chose to sleep. As Blair wrote in his diary, "Tonight we all went up to the front to stay hoping to get away from the shelling and I'll be damned if they didn't follow us again." The pilots had squatted on a ridge southeast of Fighter 1 and right on the front-line perimeter. Suddenly flares dropped by enemy float planes illuminated the top of their hill rather than the one overlooking the fighter strip. Apparently its grassy crest looked like a runway to Japanese observers. The ships "worked over the ridge quite thoroughly," and left VF-5 with a "very healthy respect for shore bombardment." While no one in the squadron was harmed, nine Marines died on the hill. The 5th Cruiser Division expended 926 eight-inch and 253 five-inch shells and reported five separate fires. Pleased with their night's work, they withdrew north. As disconcerting to VF-5 as the shelling were the Marines, who intermittently fired their weapons at enemy troops at the bottom of the slope. Among others Hayden Jensen and Roland Kenton "spent the night huddled together with only our feet sticking out of the tin helmets the Marines gave us." To Kenton, "Certainly it was a night well etched in my memory."[46]

At dawn the 1st MAW wielded a force of nine F4Fs, eleven SBDs, and seven Army P-39s and P-400s, a far cry from just a few days before. Among the four VF-5 F4Fs, only one was flyable. That day Geiger enumerated the total damage inflicted by the bombardments and bombings of the last three days and nights:

	Destroyed	Repairable	Needing Major Overhaul
F4Fs	6	3	—
SBDs	13	13	10
TBFs	5	—	3
P-39s	4	—	—
	28	16	13

The morning searches from CACTUS proved negative. At dawn Joe Foss took six VMF-121 F4Fs to strafe enemy landing boats at the beaches west of Kokumbona. Most of the day's air operations would be directed there.

The boneyard on the edge of Henderson Field, mid-October 1942. The overturned F4F in front is 81, a VMF-223 replacement wrecked on 9 September. A VS-5 SBD (identified by the *S* on the fin) sits ahead of an 11th Bomb Group B-17. (Col. F. C. Drury)

At Fighter 1 Geiger turned to Simpler and observed, "I don't think we have a goddamn Navy." He replied, "We have one, general, and I think I can find it." Geiger told him to scout the area, locate friendly naval forces, and return. Simpler departed for his quest in VF-5's sole flyable F4F, flew along the south coast, then headed further into the Coral Sea. Turning westward he went as far west as the Russells and swung back toward San Cristobal. Just as he thought about returning, a task force loomed ahead. Carefully approaching so as not to be mistaken for a bandit, he flew close to the carrier, which had only a few aircraft on deck. Without breaking radio silence, he requested permission to come on board, but she refused. Finally he turned northwest for CACTUS, and nearing the airfield he saw Navy TBFs working over the two beached transports west of Lunga. "This answered the general's question," Simpler later wrote.[47]

The task force was TF-17; the carrier was the *Hornet*.[48] Most definitely she attacked Japanese ships and shore installations. From 95 miles south of Guadalcanal, Murray launched his first strike at 0620 comprising Commander Rodee's command TBF, sixteen VS-8 and VB-8 SBDs led by Lieutenant Commander Widhelm, and 8 VF-72 F4Fs:

Division #2	Division #6
Lt. Alberto C. Emerson (XO)	Lt. (jg) Frederick W. Luebke
Ens. James O. Weimer	Lt. (jg) Ernest L. McClintock
Lt. (jg) Andrew J. Lowndes	Lt. (jg) Van H. Morris
Lt. (jg) William J. Moran	Lt. (jg) Bascomb Montgomery

Once aloft, Fritz Luebke detached his 2nd Section (Morris and Montgomery) to cover CHAG's TBF. The strike first checked west of Guadalcanal for enemy ships and looked over the Russells without sighting any targets. Gus Widhelm then pushed north to Rekata Bay on Santa Isabel against the R-Area Air Force's advance base, where they estimated eight float-Zeros, five Type 0 biplanes, and three twin-float reconnaissance seaplanes were anchored off shore. The *Hornet* planes dived in from several directions. Al Emerson's five F4Fs strafed the float-Zeros on the water and reported setting two on fire; others doubtless sustained bullet damage but probably were not fueled. The SBDs plastered shore installations as well as aircraft. Only Andy Lowndes encountered a float plane in the air, but it showed no inclination to fight. He chased it out of the area. By 1000, Rodee's strike group had knocked out everything seen of military value and claimed a dozen float planes. All aircraft returned to the *Hornet* and started landing around 1100. Emerson and his pilots much appreciated the belly tanks that gave them four-and-a-half hours aloft with a reserve of 20 gallons.

The *Hornet*'s second strike took off at 0705 with fourteen VT-6 TBFs under Lieutenant Parker, escorted by eight VF-72 F4Fs:

Division #7	Division #8
Lt. Warren W. Ford	Lt. Louis K. Bliss
Lt. (jg) Robert S. Merritt	Lt. (jg) Robert E. Holland
Lt. (jg) Morrill I. Cook	Lt. (jg) George Formanek
Lt. (jg) Henry A. Fairbanks	Lt. (jg) Richard Z. Hughes

Six Avengers carried torpedoes; the other eight each lugged four 500-pound bombs. "Iceberg" Parker led the strike to Cape Esperance on the west tip of Guadalcanal. With no enemy ships in sight, like Rodee he searched northwest past the Russells and flew all the way up to Astrolabe Bay on New Georgia.

On the way out Warren Ford developed magneto trouble. His engine began throwing oil, so he turned back. According to doctrine his division accompanied him. They flew back to Guadalcanal before taking a direct course to the ship. On the north coast at the mouth of what their maps wrongly called the "Kukum River," they noticed something suspicious and reversed course. It was VF-72's chance to participate in a favorite CACTUS diversion: barge-hunting. Ford led his four F4Fs in strafing attacks and sank four landing barges (two large and two small). Eager for more, he rounded Cape Esperance and discovered another nest of barges on the west coast. The F4Fs shot up several more *daihatsus* and AA machine guns, then returned to the *Hornet*.

A few minutes after Ford's division left the TBFs, George Formanek concluded that he and wingman Dick Hughes should also turn back because of dwindling fuel. They made it safely to TF-17. "Ken" Bliss and wingman Bob Holland stayed with VT-6. At Astrolabe Bay Parker found no targets and retired. Like Ford, he, too, returned via Cape Esperance. The only targets of note were the two beached transports burning after attacks the previous day. Parker directed two divisions of four bomb-armed TBFs to finish off the hapless Marus. Each Avenger made four shallow dives (one for each 500-pounder); claims totaled six hits. Regretting they had nothing to attack, the rest of the strike headed back home.

Sixteen VF-72 CAP Wildcats defended the *Hornet* during both strikes. Half were aloft: the high CAP (25,000 feet) under skipper Mike Sanchez and Jack Bower's medium CAP at 10,000 feet. Tom Johnson, 2nd Section leader in Sanchez's division, experienced control stiffness with his ailerons, so he signaled his

T-16 (BuNo. 00468) from the *Hornet*'s VT-6 flies over a burning Japanese transport on the northwest coast of Guadalcanal, 16 Oct. 1942. (USN)

plight and received permission to exchange station with Bob Sorensen's section flying with Bower.

While descending, Johnson and wingman Phil Souza learned at 0942 that radar detected a bogey bearing 260 degrees and 37 miles. The Type 97 flying boat flown by the Tōkō Air Group *buntaichō*, Lt. Hinata Yoshihiko (NA 66-1938), radioed base of an enemy task force on course 300 degrees and 60 miles southeast of Guadalcanal. Far below, Frank Christofferson's VB-8 SBD on IAP had already latched onto the huge snooper. In five determined attacks he fired off all his ammunition only to take decisive retaliation from the 20-mm tail stinger. He flopped down in the water near the destroyer *Morris* (DD-417), which rescued him and his radioman unharmed.

At 8,000 feet Johnson and Souza scouted southwest, missed the bogey in the thick clouds, and headed back. Soon Souza sighted approaching from ahead at 5,000 feet below what he later called "the biggest airplane I had ever seen." It was Hinata who had just downed Christofferson. He called "Tally ho" and dived for a high-side run from the left. The Type 97 responded with tracers the size of "red ping pong balls." Johnson followed, but attacked from an unfavorable angle. After his third high-side run, Souza lost contact with the Kawanishi in a cloud but, as he broke into the clear, its large greenish-brown parasol wing filled his sights directly ahead. Joining Souza for the coup-de-grce was Lt. (jg) Robert H. Jennings diving in from the medium CAP. Under the impact of their bullets the Type 97 exploded in a flash of flame. "Engines with their propellers still spinning" dropped off the wing. The Kawanishi fell in two burning pieces about 18 miles from the task force, with smoke from both blazes remaining visible for a long time.[49]

During that CAP Sanchez was startled to see in the distance one cruiser and three merchant vessels off San Cristobal. Other pilots confirmed what looked like a landing force with small boats ferrying cargo ashore. At 1045 the *Hornet* landed the second CAP, and Sanchez hurriedly reported the sighting. From planes returning from both waves, Mason quickly organized a strike. At 1230 Widhelm took twelve SBDs, four TBFs, and eight F4Fs (divisions under Sanchez and Bower) eastward with great anticipation after the frustration of not finding any juicy targets that morning. To his great embarrassment Sanchez discovered the ships to be "large offshore rocks." Widhelm, who did not get along particularly well with him anyway, sarcastically dubbed the event the "Battle of Sanchez Rocks" and rode the VF-72 skipper unmercifully about the error. In Sanchez's defense, the other pilots with him that morning were convinced they had sighted an enemy force invading San Cristobal. In a way, the "Battle of Sanchez Rocks" about summed up the results of the *Hornet*'s 16 October raids. Targets proved disappointingly meager. If stronger enemy forces had been there, the *Hornet* would have hit them hard.

On his way back to Guadalcanal, Simpler came across the *McFarland*, the old four-piper converted into a seaplane tender and now laden with 40,000 gallons of much-need aviation gas (avgas). Before the day was done, he would get to know her quite well. Landing at Fighter 1 after well over three hours, he discovered that orders had come through for the evacuation of VF-5. Dave Richardson, Hayden Jensen, Bill Robb, Ray Myers, Foster Blair, and Chief Poston with twenty enlisted men were to board an R4D, while he and the remainder with the squadron gear, such as it was, would go out on the *McFarland* that evening.[50] The move was part of a massive evacuation of most MAG-23 personnel, including the VMF-223 ground crew, VMF-224 (all but Major Galer), VMSB-231, and VF-5. Lieutenant Colonel Cooley, commanding MAG-14, relieved Colonel Wallace, and MAG-23 departed for good—a real milestone in the Guadalcanal campaign.

Simpler turned over his four surviving Grumman F4F-4 Wildcats (BuNos. 5045, 5121, 5180, and 5200) to VMF-121. To Geiger and Scollin he gave something almost equally welcome, VF-5's last two bottles of liquor. The staff told him to gather up his twelve remaining enlisted men under Ray F. Malone, ACOM, and report to the naval operating base for passage. The party set to leave by transport plane waited at the field for the R4Ds to come in. Somewhat bewildered at staying at CACTUS were Pat Rooney and Roland Kenton, part of the VF-71 contingent formerly on temporary duty with VF-5. The 1st MAW had asked that they remain behind, as three more VF-71 pilots, lieutenants (jg) Norm Riise and Red Thrash, and Ens. Norm Brown, were expected that day from BUT-TON. Rooney's division would fly with Duke Davis's VMF-121.

At 1320 the *McFarland* anchored about 300 yards off Lunga and began unloading the twelve torpedoes and the gas drums on deck. At the same time she pumped more fuel from storage tanks into drums located on a 100-ton sectional pontoon barge tied up on her starboard side. A tank lighter lay alongside to port. Small boats brought out 160 passengers, mostly MAG-23 ground crews and hospital patients (*not* all "war neurotics" wrongly described in several sources).[51] Simpler took his dozen men on board. Climbing to her bridge he greeted her captain, Lt. Cdr. John C. Alderman, an old friend. He hoped by dusk to be free of the hazardous waters off Guadalcanal. Until then everyone was wary of a raid, as it was "Tojo Time." This day, however, Base Air Force launched an unsuccessful search-and-destroy mission against the American carrier force detected the previous day. At 1410 CACTUS called an alert, and Alderman got underway. Soon the all-clear sounded, and he resumed unloading his important cargo.

At 1350 the *Hornet* launched her fourth strike of the day, five SBDs, nine TBFs (seven with bombs, two with torpedoes), and eight VF-72 F4Fs:

Division #4	Division #3
Lt. Edward W. Hessel	Lt. John F. Sutherland
Lt. (jg) Thomas J. Gallagher	Lt. (jg) Henry A. Carey
Lt. Claude R. Phillips	Lt. (jg) David B. Freeman
Lt. (jg) John R. Franklin	Lt. (jg) Alfred E. Dietrich

On the north coast of Guadalcanal, they sought the enemy forces discovered by Ford near the so-called Kukum River, but could find no targets there at all. Red Hessel went down to 300 feet to entice enemy fire, but ended up strafing a grass hut near the beach. For want of a better target, the SBDs and TBFs obliterated the hapless structure and some nearby tents, while Jock Sutherland shot what looked like some camouflaged barges. A lone machine gunner bravely replied and suffered for his efforts. The *Hornet* planes reached the ship at 1650, and TF-17 soon withdrew southeast. Rodee summed up well the mood of all: "It is regretted that more suitable targets were not available." After refueling, TF-17 would await the arrival of TF-16 with the *Enterprise*.

McFarland *Bombed*

At 1700 with half the *McFarland*'s cargo discharged, Simpler noticed F4Fs scramble from Fighter 1: eleven VMF-121 led by 1st Lt. Edwin C. Fry. He warned Alderman to check with MAG-14 to see if there was an alert, but base replied the Wildcats were "practicing new tactics." To that VF-5's skipper snorted, "They do not schedule training flights here."[52] At 1605 Kennedy on New Georgia had warned CACTUS of hearing a "fair number" of enemy planes bound southeast for Guadalcanal. Also worried by a report of a periscope sighted westward in Sealark Channel, Alderman got the *McFarland* underway at 1715 headed east at five knots with gas barge and lighter still tied alongside.

About a half hour later Simpler happened to glance skyward at a Japanese dive bomber already screaming in against the *McFarland*. It was Res. Lt. Kitamura Norimasa, flight leader of the 31st Air Group. At 1500 his nine Type 99 carrier bombers and twelve 6th Air Group Zeros (Lt. [jg] Kawamata Katsutoshi) departed Buin in search of the enemy carrier reported off Guadalcanal by Hinata.[53] Following doctrine each *kanbaku* lugged only two 60-kilogram bombs, an almost worthless payload. After searching the northern Coral Sea, Kitamura returned by way of Lunga. There at 1730 he spotted a "medium-sized oiler." Fry's F4Fs did not intercept them.

Simpler suggested to Alderman that he cut the lines and order full engine power. Alderman gave the orders. A VMF-223 enlisted man, Cpl. Raymond O. Erickson, grabbed an ax and severed the line to the fuel barge. When the first bomb exploded amidships close aboard the port side, the *McFarland* had moved about three-quarters of her length ahead of the barge. Subsequent bombs mostly fell astern as she accelerated away, but one of the last, however, struck her squarely portside on the fantail and set off at least one depth charge. The massive explosion blew off the stern with heavy loss of life among her passengers and crew and also torched 20,000 gallons of avgas packed in drums on the barge drifting off her starboard quarter, instantly incinerating the twelve men on board. Rudderless, the *McFarland* settled to port, and Alderman needed her engines to steer. Louis Zakhar, GM3c, manning her number 3 20-mm gun, flamed Res. Ens. Kawaga Atsushi's Type 99, which flew into the water. Kitamura led the eight other carrier bombers low over the water and strafed positions on Kukum beach before turning west for home.[54]

Revenge was close at hand. Lt. Col. Joe Bauer with nineteen VMF-212 F4Fs, seven SBDs, and four R4Ds arrived after the long flight from BUTTON. Almost all the fighters had landed before the attack, and the rest circled at low altitude. The VF-5 contingent boarded one R4D that was ready to depart only ten minutes after landing. It had taxied to the end of the runway, when the black flag was raised. Fighting Five piled out of the Douglas and took cover at the edge of the runway.[55] Circling at 3,000 feet Bauer spotted a line of dive bombers about 500 yards apart and withdrawing at 200 feet over the channel. Very little fuel remained to him, and the two 58-gallon wing tanks (one still full, as he could not transfer its load) burdened the Wildcat. Nevertheless, he firewalled his throttle in pursuit. On shore Joe Renner saw him work his way from rear to center of the string and burn three Type 99s in succession, the last only 50 feet above the water out near Savo. Bauer thought he bagged four; actually he destroyed the entire 3rd *Shōtai* of WO Iwami Kenzō, PO3c Tokuoka Masahiro, and PO3c Ozeki Mitsuo. He remarked that if he had had the gas, he would have splashed all of the "hawks." This magnificent performance, along with his gallantry on 3 October (four Zeros destroyed), earned Bauer the Congressional Medal of Honor.[56]

The 31st Air Group's Type 99s reached Buin at 2030, and PO2c Kitagai Ichirō cracked up on landing. Kitamura claimed four hits and four damaging near misses that set the oiler on fire, but he lost four carrier bombers shot down and one wrecked. The surviving crews saw splashes, but no enemy fighters, and thought unusually fierce AA downed the four planes. Fortunately for Bauer, Kawamata's escort Zeros were busy at high altitude sparring with the four B-17 heavy bombers that escorted VMF-212. They never engaged Fry's VMF-121 flight, which lost one F4F (2nd Lt. John H. Clarke) forced down by mechanical trouble.

The gallant *McFarland* made for Tulagi harbor 19 miles north, but by 1950 she was dead in the water eight miles short of her goal. Tank lighters embarked the wounded and all the passengers. Just before midnight the *YP-239* towed her into the harbor, where she remained until November. Total casualties were nine killed, twenty-eight wounded, and eighteen missing. For the faithful MAG-23 ground crews, it was a tragic way to exit CACTUS. Fighting Five lost missing: Rider W. Berge, AOM2c; Dennis V. Cornelius, AMM2c; Charlie A. Bagwell, Jr., AMM3c; Archie J. Parker, AOM3c; and William J. Wright, AMM3c; severely wounded Ray Malone, ACMM, and Leo Nieme, PR3c. The party on the R4D reached Efate safely late the night of the 16th.

VMF-212 leaders and F4F-3A on Efate, summer 1942 (*l to r*): Fritz Payne, Chick Quilter, Lieutenant Martin (flight surgeon), Joe Bauer, Doc Everton. (Col. F. C. Drury)

Events on 16 October helped precipitate another change of command. Worried by the sighting of enemy carriers north of Espiritu Santo, Ghormley hurried TF-17 east of there to attack enemy carriers if favorable opportunities afforded. To remain undetected, Murray was to proceed south of Efate, although he had planned to take the *Hornet* north of Guadalcanal. Around 1600 Ghormley informed King and Nimitz of the "all out enemy effort against CACTUS, possibly other positions also. My forces totally inadequate meet situation. Urgently request all available reinforcements possible." This message, presaging decisive battle for Guadalcanal, sealed Ghormley's fate.[57]

CARRIER STRIKE

Vice Admiral Kondō required one last task of the Advance Force before it retired north to refuel. Worried that the Americans were reinforcing Guadalcanal, he received permission to loose RAdm. Kakuta Kakuji's 2nd Carrier Division (*Hiyō* and *Junyō*) the next morning against the Lunga anchorage. They would make the first carrier strike on Guadalcanal since the ill-fated *Ryūjō* on 24 August.

The 2nd Carrier Division had only reached Truk on 9 October after training in the Inland Sea. Converted passenger liners, the *Hiyō* (Capt. Beppu Akitomo) and *Junyō* (Capt. Okada Tametsugu) each displaced nearly 27,000 tons fully loaded, but their relatively short flight decks (690 feet) and slow speed (25 knots only under exceptional conditions) hurt their effectiveness as combat carriers. Authorized strength for each air group was forty-eight planes (twenty-one Zero fighters, eighteen Type 99 carrier bombers, and nine Type 97 carrier attack planes). In early October the *Hiyō* possessed all forty-eight, but the *Junyō* lacked three Zeros.[58]

Hurriedly organized in May 1942, the *Junyō* Air Group participated in the Aleutians operation. The group commander, Lt. Shiga Yoshio (NA 62-1934), the *Kaga* fighter CO at Pearl Harbor, also commanded the *Junyō* Carrier Fighter Squadron. His fighter *buntaichō* was well-traveled Lt. Shigematsu Yasuhiro, newly back from the *Shōkaku*. The *Junyō* squadron counted many experienced fighter pilots, including eight who served at Midway. Lt. Yamaguchi Masao (NA 63-1936), a Pearl Harbor and Coral Sea veteran, led the *Junyō* Carrier Bomber Squadron. Ex-*Sōryū* Lt. Itō Tadao (NA 65-1938) commanded the newly formed *Junyō* Carrier Attack Squadron. Formed in July 1942, the *Hiyō* Air Group was a twin to the *Junyō*. Lt. Kaneko Tadashi (NA 60-1932), the group leader/fighter squadron commander, was likewise a highly experienced fighter pilot who fought from the *Shōkaku* at Pearl Harbor and with the 6th Air Group from the *Akagi* at Midway. Lt. Fujita Iyōzō (NA 66-1938), the fighter *buntaichō*, had served with the *Sōryū* from Pearl Harbor through Midway, and brought with him seven more *Sōryū* veterans. Leading the *Hiyō* Carrier Bomber Squadron, Lt. Abe Zenji (NA 64-1937), an ex-*Akagi buntaichō*, came over from the *Junyō* in July. Lt. Irikiin Yoshiaki (NA 65-1938) commanded the *Hiyō* Carrier Attack Squadron. Like the *Junyō*, the *Hiyō*'s fighter squadron included many veterans, but the *kanbaku* and *kankō* crews less so.[59]

While Kakuta moved south, American radio intelligence intercepted some of his orders. For the first time since 7 August, HYPO actually deciphered portions of some messages in timely fashion, but the cryptanalysts never realized they were dealing with carrier planes, specifically *Hiyō* and *Junyō*, which they still placed in Japan. At 0110, 17 October, Ghormley warned Vandegrift that eighteen fighters and eighteen bombers would attack shipping off Lunga. Another message noted at 0325 that enemy planes might depart Buin at 0700 and Buka 30 minutes later. Before dawn the 1st MAW scrambled twenty-five F4Fs.[60]

The enemy indeed was coming in. At 0515 and 180 miles north of Lunga, the 2nd Carrier Division launched eighteen Zero fighters and eighteen Type 97 carrier attack planes (each carrying one 800-kilogram bomb): from the *Hiyō*, nine Zeros commanded by Lieutenant Kaneko and nine Type 97 VTs commanded by Lieutenant Irikiin; from the *Junyō*, nine Zeros commanded by Lieutenant Shiga and nine Type 97 VTs commanded by Lieutenant Itō.[61] They departed at 0530 in two groups, but soon engine trouble sent WO Ōtawa Tatsuya's carrier attack plane back to the *Junyō*. By 0700 Florida Island hove into sight. Approaching at medium altitude, apparently at 3,000 meters (9,845 feet), the groups expected to make horizontal bombing runs against anchored transports. Instead they found the destroyers *Aaron Ward* and *Lardner* busily shelling the supply dumps near Kokumbona.

Lieutenant Irikiin led the *Hiyō* group after one warship, which he identified as a *Honolulu*-class light cruiser. At 0727 his four 1st *Chūtai* Type 97s released their big 800-kilogram bombs, followed two minutes later by the 2nd *Chūtai* (Lt. [jg] Endō Tetsuo NA [67-1939]) with five more. Five-inch AA fire blasted PO1c Sai Gorō's *kankō* down in flames and damaged PO1c Toyama Kiyosuke's aircraft. After scoring no hits, seven *Hiyō* carrier attack planes withdrew north, while Toyama limped to Buin.

Irikiin's force got off easy. A few minutes later Lieutenant Itō aimed his eight *Junyō* Type 97s against the second ship, but ran into a buzzsaw in the form of

Major Davis's eight VMF-121 Wildcats. At 0732 the Marines jumped what they thought were land-based dive bombers. Within two minutes three Type 97s (PO2c Abe Keiji, PO2c Sashō Hisashi, and PO2c Konno Kiyoshi) slanted down toward the sea, and those flown by Lt. (jg) Kuno Setsuo (NA 67-1939), the 2nd *Chūtai* leader, and WO Yashirō Shichirō took severe damage. At 0735 the remaining three *kankōs* (Itō, PO1c Shikakuma Kumekichi, and PO1c Ōkono Mitsuji) dropped their payloads against the destroyer without success, but the Wildcats retaliated by destroying all three planes. The *Junyō* Carrier Attack Squadron suffered virtual annihilation—six aircraft destroyed (including the CO's) and two damaged (Lieutenant [jg] Kuno killed).

Appalled at the loss of the carrier attack planes, Shiga's *Junyō* Zeros tore into the scattered Marine F4Fs, as did Kaneko's *Hiyō* Zeros. They shot down 2nd Lt. Wiley H. Craft, but 2nd Lt. "Big Bill" Freeman badly wounded PO1c Harada Kaname, a *Hiyō* ace. Harada ditched at Rekata and was invalided out of the service.[62] The other seventeen Zeros claimed thirteen Grummans without additional loss.

By 1025 the *Hiyō* and *Junyō* strike groups circled their respective carriers. Of eighteen carrier attack planes, only eight returned, including Warrant Officer Ōtawa who aborted the mission. Seven (six *Junyō,* one *Hiyō*) splashed and three (two *Junyō,* one *Hiyō*) crash-landed at Buin. VMF-121 compiled its first big score, and the claims of eight "dive bombers" (*sic*) proved very close to the mark: two each to Major Davis, 2nd Lt. Roger Haberman, and 2nd Lt. Joseph Narr; one each to 1st Lt. Gregory K. Loesch (a cousin of Ens. Richards "Dix" Loesch lately with VF-5) and 2nd Lt. Wallace G. Wethe, while 2nd Lt. William Freeman claimed two Zeros. The 2nd Carrier Division's torpedo attack capability suffered crippling losses even before the anticipated decisive carrier battle, but CACTUS never perceived the enemy planes as carrier-based.

Ironically, after an excellent start in the morning the 1st MAW ineffectually met subsequent Japanese attacks that day. Aerial success seemed so transitory at Guadalcanal. The 17th was only the beginning of a seven-day period that would see consecutive air attacks against CACTUS, as the 17th Army prepared its great offensive against the airfield.

FIGHTING FIVE'S VALEDICTORY

Beginning 17 October VF-5 reassembled at Efate after its eventful tour at CACTUS (11 September–16 October 1942). In a sense a phantom squadron, VF-5 contributed mightily to the defense of Guadalcanal, although it never received proper recognition of that fact. The big Navy squadron brought twenty-four F4F Wildcats and ultimately thirty-two experienced pilots to CACTUS at a time when Marine fighter strength ebbed. Credited with 45 kills (12 fighters, 21 medium bombers, 5 float-Zeros, and 7 float planes), Japanese records indicate VF-5 actually accounted for some 22 enemy planes (7 fighters, 8 land attack planes, 4 float-Zeros, and 3 float planes). During the same period, victory credits for VMF-223, VMF-224, and VMF-121 totaled 100 planes, while enemy sources point to the real tally as about 38 (12 of 31 fighters, 15 of 47 medium bombers, 3 of 4 dive bombers, 1 of 2 reconnaissance planes, 2 of 3 float-Zeros, and 5 of 13 float planes). VF-5 lost six pilots killed or missing in action and four wounded and evacuated. Combat cost seven F4Fs, operational accidents six, and seven sustained bombs or shells on the ground.[63]

In an analytical action report and with detailed interviews, Lieutenant Commander Simpler distilled the vital lessons from VF-5's battle experiences on Guadalcanal.[64] They were especially important, for VF-5 saw the most protracted combat of any carrier fighting squadron. For the first time Navy VF fought from a land base rather than a flattop, and Simpler considered that "far more intense and difficult for VF" than shipboard service. He found it necessary to watch his pilots carefully to see the effects of the "stress of continued action." The lack of adequate sleep and living conditions at Guadalcanal proved crucial: "A man's 'guts' is directly proportional to how rested he is—nothing more or less." Simpler also elucidated his basic philosophy of command, which he followed to the letter at CACTUS:

> In wartime, a squadron commander has got to be a squadron commander; he can't be wishy-washy; he has to take responsibility freely. He's got to assert himself always and never send anyone where he wouldn't go himself.

He described in detail the familiar drawbacks of the Grumman F4F-4 Wildcat, namely low climb rate, slow speed, and insufficient range. He added the interesting observation:

> The common practice is to judge a fighter by the number of planes it destroys. This is most misleading. Any fighter's worth is determined by the number of enemy planes who escape to return again.

Under this criterion the noble Wildcat indeed proved deficient at CACTUS.

Simpler's action report received favorable endorsements up the chain of command from ComSoPac to CominCh in Washington. Rear Admiral Fitch (1 December 1942) described it as an "excellent presentation," and Admiral Halsey (20 December 1942) called it "timely, well concerned and most informative." On 17 January 1943 VAdm. John Towers, ComAirPac, noted "the effectiveness

Lt. Cdr. Leroy Simpler, CO of VF-5, February 1943. (NA 80-G-40830)

of our carrier squadrons in combat operations from advanced shore bases is gratifying." Certainly their training and fundamental doctrine appeared sound. Yet he was concerned about the misuse of specialist pilots, noting that they operated from ashore only from "grave necessity." He desired the carrier pilots be reserved for sea duty if at all possible. On 22 February Rear Admiral Spruance, Pacific Fleet Chief of Staff, seconded Towers's comments and stressed the need to conserve carrier pilots. He considered the "performance at Guadalcanal of Fighting Squadron Five, under the command of Lieutenant Commander Simpler, . . . highly commendable."

PART IV

The Battle of Santa Cruz

CHAPTER 17

The "Hottest Potato"

INTRODUCING FIGHTING TEN

In September when the battered *Enterprise* docked at Pearl Harbor, she found Carrier Replacement Air Group Ten (CRAG-10) under Cdr. Richard K. Gaines (USNA 1925) waiting to deploy on board. Formed on 1 March 1942 at NAS San Diego, CRAG-10 was, along with its twin CRAG-9, the first of the carrier air groups given separate numbers rather than a ship's name. That spring, Replacement Bombing Ten (VRB-10), Replacement Scouting Ten (VRS-10), and Replacement Torpedo Ten (VRT-10) proceeded with their organization. The formation of Replacement Fighting Ten (VRF-10) was delayed until the return of its prospective commander, Lt. Cdr. James H. Flatley, Jr., from the South Pacific. He was worth the wait.

One of the most impressive individuals in naval aviation, Jimmy Flatley was a dynamic, yet thoughtful leader with strong religious convictions, who exerted a powerful impression upon those with whom he served. A 1929 Annapolis graduate, he earned his wings in 1931 and accumulated much experience in fighters (VF-5B 1931–34, VF-6B 1936–37). Beginning in July 1939, he instructed at NAS Pensacola and played an important role in the creation of the pilot training program at NAS Jacksonville. In September 1941 he gladly reported as VF-2 XO under Lt. Cdr. Paul Ramsey on board the *Lexington,* but returned to the West Coast in February 1942 before seeing any combat. In April he headed south to take command of VF-42 on the *Yorktown,* but became temporary XO due to a mix-up of orders. After accounting for three enemy fighters on 7–8 May in the Battle of the Coral Sea, Flatley headed back to the States to form VRF-10.[1]

On 3 June, the day after Flatley arrived at San Diego, VRF-10 was commissioned with six pilots and three F4F-4s, along with two training planes. Flatley dubbed his new squadron "The Grim Reapers" and adopted as its insignia a flying skeleton wielding a large scythe for "Mow 'em Down!" VRF-10 incorporated a number of Coral Sea SBD veterans, including Lt. Thomas E. Edwards (USNA 1937) and Lt. (jg) John A. Leppla from VS-2, lieutenants Frederick L. Faulkner and Stanley W. Vejtasa (VS-5), and Lt. Albert D. Pollock from the *Lexington*'s Air Department. They helped season a large crop of green ensigns fresh from ACTG.[2]

Flatley's "Grim Reapers" enjoyed an especially close association with VRT-10, the "Buzzard Brigade," led by his Annapolis classmate, Lt. Cdr. John A.

VF-10, 23 Oct. 1942. *Top row (l to r)*: Greene, Harman, Coalson, Boren, Kilpatrick, Rhodes, Reding, Mead, Leppla, Kona, Fulton, Davis, Pollock. *Center row:* Feightner, Slagle, Gordon, Long, Faulkner, Caldwell, Billo, Blair, Edwards, Packard, Kanze, Voris, Ruehlow. *Bottom row:* Barnes, Leder, Dowden, Harris, Vejtasa, Miller, Wickendoll, Eckhart, Kane, Axelrod, Witte, Reiserer, Flatley. (NA 80-G-30070)

Collett. In honor of the Grim Reapers, the amused torpedo pilots called themselves "The Moppers," their insignia a buzzard flying a mop and the words "Mop 'em up!" Collett himself was an innovator in high-speed torpedo attack tactics. Later at Pearl Harbor, he purloined the first air search radar-equipped Grumman Avenger to reach the fleet and planned to use its ASB-1 radar for night and other low-visibility attacks.[3]

That summer CRAG-10 experienced great difficulty training because of the few available planes. Finally on 8 August the group, minus aircraft, shipped out from NAS Alameda to Pearl Harbor. From stocks at Pearl, VRF-10 drew aircraft and moved over to NAS Maui for a period of extended tactical training alongside Lieutenant Commander O'Hare's VF-3. Jimmy Thach's old pupil gradually won Flatley over to the idea of flying four- rather than six-plane flights and taught him the beam defense maneuver. The squadron also became the first to practice "coordinated drilling" with the Fighter Director School on Oahu.[4]

In early October VF-10 (along with the rest of CRAG-10) streamlined its enlisted echelon by transferring all but fifteen chiefs and senior petty officers. Henceforth the mechanics, armorers, plane captains, and other specialists would be ship's company rather than members of individual squadrons. By mid-October VF-10 numbered thirty-eight pilots. Lt. Cdr. William R. ("Killer") Kane (USNA 1933), another aggressive and talented leader, became XO on 8 October after gratefully escaping a long tour of duty with NAS Pearl Harbor. Flight officer Lt. Stanley E. Ruehlow (USNA 1935), a former VF-8 pilot, gladly left VF-3 when he learned VF-10 would go into action. Also joining was former VF-2 NAP Howard Packard, AP1c, who fought with VF-6 at Midway and in the Eastern Solomons. Despite a badly injured back, Lt. (jg) Gordon Firebaugh desperately wanted to go as well, but the flight surgeons would not let him out of bed. Despite his many rookies, Flatley soon molded VF-10 into a team.

Now CAG-10 (unofficially but happily dropping the replacement "R") made ready to embark on the *Enterprise*. First of the new groups to deploy on a big carrier, Ten's progress would be closely watched. Fully repaired, "The Big E" sported an augmented AA armament, including sixteen 40-mm Bofors guns in four quadruple mounts in place of 1.1s. Along with the other squadrons, VF-10 delivered spare aircraft (in its case four F4F-4 Wildcats) to the carrier and operated thirty-two planes. On 10 October the *Enterprise* got underway for a short shakedown to carrier-qualify Air Group Ten. Having done his "darnest" to train CAG-10, group LSO Lt. James G. Daniels III turned over his charges to his old friend, Lt. Robin Lindsey, the senior *Enterprise* LSO. CAG-10 came through magnificently. Two days with 274 landings saw not a single mishap. Lindsey handed the paddles back to Daniels with "They're all yours." On the 12th, Captain Davis gave the group a "well done." CAG-10 was going to war.[5]

With the presence at Pearl of VAdm. John Towers as the new ComAirPac, a rejuvenated VAdm. Bill Halsey resumed command of TF-16 with his beloved *Enterprise* as flagship to redeploy to the South Pacific to re-form TF-61, the SoPac Striking Force. To get acquainted with the situation in the South Pacific, he joined an inspection team of senior officers led by Pacific Fleet chief of staff

Air Group Ten's leaders, 23 Oct. 1942 (*l to r*): Lt. Cdr. James A. Thomas (VB-10), Lt. Cdr. James R. Lee (VS-10), Cdr. Richard K. Gaines (group commander), Lt. Cdr. John A. Collett (VT-10), and Lt. Cdr. James H. Flatley, Jr. (VF-10). (NA 80-G-30072)

RAdm. Ray Spruance. On 14 October they left on a big Consolidated PB2Y flying boat for a series of stops, to include Guadalcanal. Meanwhile, Rear Admiral Kinkaid would bring TF-16 to the South Pacific, where he would turn command over to Halsey and relieve Rear Admiral Murray as commander of TF-17 on the *Hornet*.[6]

The morning of 16 October TF-16 sailed from Pearl Harbor. The *Enterprise*'s air group comprised:

CAG-10	Cdr. Richard K. Gaines	1 TBF-1 (1)[a]
VF-10	Lt. Cdr. James H. Flatley, Jr.	36 F4F-4s (24)
VB-10	Lt. Cdr. James A. Thomas	22 SBD-3s (15)
VS-10	Lt. Cdr. James R. Lee	22 SBD-3s (15)
VT-10	Lt. Cdr. John A. Collett	14 TBF-1s (12)

[a] Number in parentheses is number of aircraft operating.

Embarked aircraft totaled ninety-five: thirty-six fighters, forty-four dive bombers, and fifteen torpedo bombers, including eight SBDs and two TBFs earmarked as AirSoPac replacements.[7]

THE NEW COMSOPAC

Early on the evening of 15 October at Pearl Harbor, Admiral Nimitz wrestled with the very difficult decision whether or not to relieve the ComSoPac. Japanese ground forces on Guadalcanal had received strong reinforcements, three days of naval bombardment severely crippled the 1st MAW, and the main body of the Japanese fleet rampaged southeast of the Solomons. All indications pointed to another big enemy offensive. That evening he read Vice Admiral Ghormley's message that declared his forces "totally inadequate" to meet the expected Japanese attack. To Nimitz it sounded as if Ghormley might already have written off Guadalcanal, so he swiftly received CominCh permission to name Halsey as the new ComSoPac.[8]

The afternoon of 18 October Halsey learned of his new assignment after his flying boat set down in Noumea harbor. He responded with the famous retort: "Jesus Christ and General Jackson! This is the hottest potato they ever handed me!"[9] Kinkaid retained TF-16, and as the senior carrier task force commander (CTF) he would form TF-61 with the *Enterprise* and the *Hornet*. The change of command provided a strong boost to morale at CACTUS. With the highly aggressive Bill Halsey at the helm, things would happen soon.

Halsey knew SoPac's resources to meet the impending Japanese land-sea-air onslaught were barely adequate at best. Nowhere was this better illustrated than in AirSoPac. By 18 October it was obvious that another crisis in air strength threatened. Just prior to his relief, Ghormley dispatched an "urgent request [for] all aviation reinforcements possible." On 17 October CinCPac echoed ComSoPac's plea in a message to King: "Greatest urgency is augmentation air strength Guadalcanal, Efate, and Espiritu Santo."[10]

Ghormley and Nimitz were absolutely correct. Air losses for Major General Geiger's 1st MAW at CACTUS between 22 September and 18 October escalated dramatically (see table 17.1).[11] The CACTUS maelstrom had sucked in both the available carrier planes and the reinforcements that reached AirSoPac in September.

TABLE 17.1
Air Losses for 1st Marine Air Wing at CACTUS, 22 September–18 October 1942

	Strength 9/22	Numbers Committed 9/22–10/18	Strength 10/18	Effective Loss 9/22–10/18
F4F-4s	43	39	32	50[a]
SBD-3s	27	57	27	57
TBF-1s	8	6	4	10
P-400s	9	4	6	7
P-39s	0	12	5	7
	87	118	74	131

[a] Loss figures include both aircraft actually destroyed and those rendered unflyable by damage or lack of spare parts.

The so-called CACTUS Air Force faced great peril. Unlike in September, the air reserves were nearly depleted, as the air bases in immediate support of CACTUS had been considerably weakened, lacking even the minimum forces required for their own defense. At the various bases, approximate strength was as follows: At Espiritu Santo, VMO-251 had thirteen F4F-3Ps and three F4F-4s; VS-3 had eight SBD-3s; and the 11th Bomb Group had forty B-17s. At Efate, VMF-212 rear echelon and VF-5 had twenty-one F4F-4s, and at Tontouta, New Caledonia, the 347th Fighter Group had ten P-400s and twelve P-39s.

Aviation reinforcements then en route to the South Pacific comprised personnel of Lt. Col. William O. Brice's MAG-11: VMF-112 (Maj. Paul J. Fontana), VMF-122 (Maj. Elmer E. Brackett, Jr.), VMSB-132 (Maj. Joseph Sailer, Jr.), and VMSB-142 (Maj. Robert H. Richard).[12] On 15 October, MAG-11 sailed on the SS *Lurline (Mumu)* from San Diego bound for Noumea. They brought no planes with them, but were to fly what they found already in the South Pacific. That would not be much. The only replacement aircraft actually en route directly to AirSoPac were the ten (eight SBDs and two TBFs) shipped on the *Enterprise,* but their delivery date was uncertain. At Tontouta the 339th FS assembled the first of fifteen Lockheed P-38F twin-engine fighters, but they were not expected to be ready before early November.

Nimitz had cut the Navy and Marine squadrons in the Hawaiian Islands to the bone. They were as weak as in May 1942 before the Battle of Midway. While the *Saratoga* underwent repairs at Pearl Harbor, her air group trained ashore (air strength as of 18 October): CSAG one TBF-1, VF-6 eleven F4F-4s, VB-3 and VS-6 thirty-three SBD-3s, and VT-3 twelve TBF-1s. She was expected to be ready in early November. Meanwhile, her squadrons, particularly VF-6, required additional aircraft to come up to authorized strength. At the same time, Lieutenant Commander O'Hare's VF-3 retained no airplanes at all. Only nine other F4F-4s remained in Hawaii, mostly under repair. Three Marine fighting squadrons (213, 214, and 221) numbered only fourteen old F4F-3s and one F4F-7 between them, and VMSB-233 and VMSB-234 only sixteen SBD-1s and -2s, and seven SBD-3s. The only Marine squadron capable of deployment was VMSB-131 with twelve TBF-1s under Lt. Col. Paul Moret (USNA 1930).

On 17 October Nimitz proposed sending AirSoPac two Army fighter squadrons (the 44th from Oahu with twenty-five P-40F Warhawks and from Christmas Island the 12th with twenty P-39Ds) and Moret's VMSB-131. He warned King, "No other air support can be furnished Ghormley from Hawaii at this time without dangerous weakening of defense elements." Two ships bound for Pearl from Alameda—the new auxiliary carrier *Nassau* (ACV-16) and the aircraft transport *Kitty Hawk* (APV-1)—were bringing a cargo of twenty-two F4F-4s and twenty SBD-3s to Pearl. The *Nassau*'s air component was VGS-16 (Escort Scouting Squadron 16) under Lt. Cdr. Charles E. Brunton (USNA 1929) with a nominal strength of twelve F4F-4s and nine TBF-1s. Nimitz released all twenty Dauntlesses for the South Pacific. The two ships could depart Pearl around the 27th with the 44th FS and VMSB-131 and pick up the 12th FS on the way.[13]

Other than what CinCPac could scrape out of Hawaii and Christmas, no other aircraft reinforcements were currently in the pipeline for AirSoPac. Set to leave San Diego in early November was the escort carrier *Altamaha* (ACV-18) with VGS-11 (eighteen F4F-4s, six TBF-1s) under Lt. Cdr. Charles H. Ostrom (USNA 1930). Her cargo was yet to be determined.

On 20 October Geiger delivered his own hot potato to Halsey and Fitch: "Past experience required 50% replacement SBDs and F4Fs every 10 days. Should Jap pressure continue, CACTUS will require 18 F4Fs and 18 SBDs with 100% reserve flight crews every 10 days." Essentially Espiritu Santo possessed no aircraft reserve, as its planes were not adequate even to defend the place. The same day Fitch informed Towers, the new ComAirPac, of the serious situation and desired aircraft replacements, particularly TBFs, of which CACTUS currently had none operational. On the 22nd he brought up the "critical shortage" of fighters in SoPac in a message to Fleet Air West Coast at San Diego, responsible for loading the *Altamaha*. He wanted as many F4F-4s as possible, even if that meant stripping other units, and he needed them ready to fly off the carrier, not disassembled. Fitch would get his way. When the *Altamaha* sailed on 3 November, she carried fifty F4F-4s for SoPac, in addition to VGS-11 with eighteen F4Fs and six TBFs. However, she would need nearly three weeks to reach the South Pacific. Meanwhile, Fitch tried to persuade Nimitz to put some F4Fs on the *Nassau* as well, but because of the need to fill VF-6, he released none.[14]

This digression of squadron lists and aircraft numbers demonstrates that in essence AirSoPac was on its own until at least the second week of November. Much could happen in that interval. Another bombardment such as endured on 14 October might wipe out air strength of the 1st MAW at CACTUS, leaving few planes to replace them. With regard to aircraft, CACTUS indeed hung by a shoestring. On 21 October King sent Nimitz a summary of aircraft allocation approved by the JCS. A powerful force it was, but for CACTUS in October and November, only promises of things to come.[15]

"WHEN YOU SEE ZEROS, DOGFIGHT 'EM!"

On 16 October the tiny VF-71 detachment joined the newly arrived VMF-212 contingent as part of Major Davis's VMF-121, while Lt. Col. Joe Bauer took over the CACTUS Fighter Command. Lt. Carl Rooney and Lt. (jg) Roland Kenton had flown with VF-5 from 5 October until the 16th, when lieutenants (jg) Harold "Norm" Riise and Millard Thrash, and Ens. Norman Brown arrived from Espiritu Santo. Now Rooney led a VMF-121 division comprised of his men and three Marines. The Navy flyers joined the Marines at Fighter 1, sharing all of the dangers, thrills, and difficulties.[16] They did not fly on the 17th, when the Marines dealt with the 2nd Carrier Division's abortive strike, but they fought during one of the busiest weeks of air fighting at CACTUS.

The VF-71 detachment, late October 1942. Standing (*l to r*) Red Thrash, Pat Rooney, and Roland Kenton; *kneeling:* Norm Brown. Evidently Norm Riise, the missing member, is the photographer. (Capt. R. H. Kenton)

Base Air Force operational air strength on 18 October numbered approximately thirty-six Zero 21s, nineteen Zero 32s, forty-nine Type 1 land attack planes, thirteen Type 99 carrier bombers, one land recon plane, and five flying boats. That day they essayed another of their patented two-pronged air strikes. Vice Admiral Kusaka's staff considerably underestimated Lunga air strength at only fifteen fighters, ten carrier bombers, and a half-dozen B-17 heavy bombers. This day another so-called air control mission or fighter sweep comprised the lead Japanese element. At 0740, Lieutenant (jg) Baba led aloft six Zeros from his 751 Air Group and three from the 3rd Air Group from Rabaul.[17] They stopped off at Buka to top off tanks. After they departed, a coastwatcher, apparently Jack Read at Buka, radioed of twelve fighters headed southeast.

The report reached CACTUS at 1030. About a half hour later, Joe Bauer assembled his pilots. Exceptionally pugnacious even for a fighter leader, he elucidated his air fighting philosophy. "Be an aggressor. You're out there to shoot down enemy planes." He strongly felt the Wildcat could take the measure of the Zero by carefully turning into enemy attacks and scissoring for head-on runs, where the F4F enjoyed superior firepower: "Have complete faith in your armor and confidence in your ability to shoot down the enemy when you get him in your sights." He would not tolerate only one run against enemy fighters and diving out. His credo was "When you see Zeros, dogfight 'em!"[18]

After the Coach's fight talk, thirty-two F4Fs scrambled in two big flights: one mostly of VMF-212 and VF-71 pilots (divisions led by Fritz Payne, Capt. Loren

D. ["Doc"] Everton, Rooney, and Kenton) and the other all VMF-121 under Joe Foss. On takeoff, 2nd Lt. Edward P. Andrews in Foss's flight died when he ground-looped into a parked aircraft. After takeoff the flights did not assemble, but started out in separate divisions.

At 1210 the 1st MAW unexpectedly monitored a transmission from Donald Kennedy on New Georgia warning of planes going southeast at 1155, "sounds like fair number." That was part two of the strike, about a half hour behind the fighter sweep. Lieutenant Nabeta, veteran of many Guadalcanal strikes, led fifteen Type 1 land attack planes (six Kisarazu, nine Misawa). His direct escort, originally nine Zeros, suffered two aborts, including the leader, Lieutenant (jg) Ōno of the Tainan Air Group. PO1c Sugio Shigeo of the 3rd Air Group filled the lead slot with a wingman from the 3rd and five Tainan fighters.[19]

CACTUS sounded Condition RED at 1220, but the fighter sweep had already struck. At 1215 Baba's Zeros evidently surprised one of Foss's climbing divisions and shot down 2nd Lt. Lowell D. Grow (VMF-121). He ditched offshore behind Japanese lines and returned to the perimeter on 4 November. 2nd Lt. Wallace Wethe (VMF-121) claimed a Zero, probably by a defensive countermove. Joe Foss and company soon extracted revenge. Eying three Zeros below, eager to be ambushed, the eight Marines "slid gently down behind"[20] a shōtai of three 751 Zeros: PO2c Sawada Tomotsugu, PO2c Honda Minoru, and PO3c Fujita Tamotsu. Foss picked off the fighter on the left, which spun away in flames. The rest of Baba's six Zeros mixed in among the F4Fs for a wild dogfight. Foss tailed in behind one Mitsubishi and set it smoking, but could not confirm his kill. Another Zero latched onto his tail, but he scissored and nailed it with a head-on shot.

Against Baba's flight, the Leathernecks claimed five Zeros (Foss two, 2nd Lt. Cecil J. "Danny" Doyle two, and 2nd Lt. William P. Marontate one). Sawada and Sea2c Gotō Mitsuo went down immediately. Surviving a holed fuel tank, PO3c Fujita limped up to Santa Isabel and ditched. After wandering around the island, he ran afoul of 1st Lt. Wallace Dinn of the 67th FS, shot down on 28 October in a raid against Rekata. Friendly natives helped Dinn to collar the unhappy Fujita and bring him back to Lunga on 4 November.[21]

During Foss's fight, Nabeta's bomber formation and Sugio's Zeros neared Guadalcanal. Payne's division first spotted the rikkō about 15 miles up the channel and intercepted with a series of overhead attacks. Despite claims of three bombers, no land attack planes fell at this time. At 1250 the fifteen Type 1s salvoed their bombs west of Henderson Field into the pioneer battalion bivouac (seven killed and eighteen wounded). Reporting a big fire on the airfield, Nabeta turned the formation left toward the channel.

Doc Everton's five VMF-212 F4Fs reached 26,000 feet astern of the bombers, saw Payne's attacks, but could not join in. Continuing to climb, they flew into the midst of Sugio's Zeros drifting along behind the bombers and executing slow rolls. Everton and two pilots dueled with fighters, claiming three, but 1st Lt. Jack Conger and 1st Lt. George F. Bastian persevered after the trailing chūtai, Lieutenant Nonaka's nine Misawa Type 1s. At 1255 Conger rolled into a high-side run against Res. Ens. Sugimoto Mitsumi's rikkō leading the left shōtai (22nd) in the trailing Vee. Watching his tracers "carving up" the target, Conger closed within 200 feet when the bomber suddenly disintegrated in a fiery explosion. Conger ducked beneath, but "Blackie" Bastian could not avoid some of the wreckage. After several close shaves over Guadalcanal (including 12 September against

VF-5), Sugimoto did not beat the odds. Conger worked over the retreating bombers, then nailed a Zero in a head-on pass.[22]

While Conger roughed up the left side of the Misawa *chūtai,* Rooney's flight tackled the right. Only Lt. (jg) Red Thrash scored. He torched the right outside trailer, PO2c Azuma Shūichi's land attack plane, just as Joe Foss was about to blast it. This time Foss flashed through debris. Azuma set his stricken Type 1 down in the channel, and only two crewmen, PO3c Ōta Rikirō and Sea2c Katō Masatake, survived to become POWs. For his own part Thrash was a "cheerful, zany, and intelligent fellow," "well remembered" by VF-71 for creating a sort of primitive crash helmet by cutting holes in the side of an M1 helmet liner to permit earphones to be worn.[23]

Cheated by Thrash of Azuma's bomber, Foss shifted to the next target up the echelon and smoked the *shōtai* leader, WO Gotō Shinji. Following through, he dived under the left side of the formation for a "belly shot at the last plane,"[24] PO1c Katō Sadao's number 2 in the 22nd *Shōtai.* Its left engine burst into flame, dropping the plane away from the others. Katō's Type 1 ditched farther up the Solomons, killing four of the crew. Nonaka's Misawa 2nd *Chūtai* lost three land attack planes blasted out of formation. Other F4Fs tangled with Sugio's Zeros and possibly some from Baba's fighter sweep as well. Norm Brown of VF-71 and 2nd Lt. Thomas Mann of VMF-121 shared credit for a VF destroyed, and 1st Lt. Robert F. Flaherty of VMF-212 destroyed one as well. Two Zeros chased "Pop" Flaherty down to the waves and forced him into the water near Savo. Found by the natives, he returned on the 23rd to Lunga.

At the cost of two F4Fs (Grow and Flaherty, both rescued), the 1st MAW claimed thirteen Zeros and seven bombers. In return the Japanese reported downing twenty-four Grummans (including five unconfirmed) for the loss of three 751 Air Group Zeros from the fighter sweep and from the strike three Misawa land attack planes and a Tainan Zero (Sea1c Sugawara Yōzō, recovered by friendly forces).

Although the 18th witnessed a spirited free-for-all with the honors to CACTUS, the 19th proved less sanguine. At 1015 a radar warning of approaching bogeys caused Bauer to send Rooney aloft with eight Navy and Marine F4Fs. They never made contact with Lieutenant Kawamata's nine 6th Air Group Zero 32s, which prowled Lunga from 1015 to 1135 before returning to Buin. Despite missing combat, Rooney's division suffered a loss when 2nd Lt. Floyd Lynch's VMF-121 F4F inexplicably rolled over at 18,000 feet and plunged into the sea. The others thought him another victim of oxygen failure.

At 1300 a second contact appeared on radar, so sixteen Marine F4Fs under Maj. Charles J. Quilter II (VMF-212) took to the skies. Unfortunately, the enemy already lurked overhead. Leading another 6th Air Group fighter sweep from Buin, Lieutenant Miyano discovered Grummans set up neatly below. Before Quilter's pilots could react, the nine clipped-wing Zero 32s were on them— shades of 2 October. 2nd Lt. Charles M. ("Mel") Freeman of VMF-212 watched helplessly as a Mitsubishi slow-rolled onto the tail of another Wildcat. All of the F4Fs dived away. Miyano personally claimed the only two Grummans chalked up by the flight. He blasted one F4F at 20,000 feet, and Staff Sgt. James A. Feliton (VMF-121) parachuted 15 miles east of the perimeter. He walked in two days later. Fragments from Miyano's 20-mm explosive rounds tore into 1st Lt. Clair Chamberlain's shoulder, and the plucky VMF-212 pilot (who had survived being shot down on 13 September) was evacuated because of wounds. Feliton and 1st Lt. Edwin Fry (VMF-121) both claimed Zeros, but all the Japanese returned to base. Learning what befell Quilter's flight, Bauer was livid. "Why didn't you stay and fight?" he roared, and threatened to ship out the whole lot. Their colonel's righteous anger left the CACTUS fighter pilots burning for revenge against the Japanese.[25]

On the 20th, after a "blessed quiet night," according to Foss, the 1st MAW confronted an especially complicated Japanese plan of attack: a double fighter sweep followed by an escorted bomber raid. From Buin Lieutenant (jg) Kawamata took aloft at 0850 fifteen Zero 32s from the 6th Air Group, reported inbound at 1017 by Kennedy. In response Bauer loosed Foss's seven VMF-121 F4Fs at 1025 and eight more led by Major Davis. He shrewdly retained Doc Everton's eight Wildcats in reserve for immediate takeoff. This new tactic he devised with Lt. Col. Ray Scollin, acting 1st MAW operations officer, to beat the sweeps.

Halfway between Lunga and Savo, Foss's VMF-121 flight tangled with Kawamata's fifteen Zeros. Foss took out two Mitsubishis, before a third smoked his engine and sent the Wildcat into a long glide back to the field. Roger Haberman and Bill Marontate each notched a Zero, but the flight lost 2nd Lt. Eugene A. Nuwer, last seen diving with a Japanese chewing his tail. In turn Kawamata claimed eight of twelve Grummans at the cost of Sea1c Tamai Sadamu.[26]

While Foss engaged Kawamata, Bauer launched Everton's flight (reduced to seven F4Fs when one dropped out). In the meantime, the second fighter force closed Lunga. Lieutenant Yamaguchi led twelve Zeros (nine from his 3rd Air Group and three Tainan) which had departed Rabaul at 0800. They jumped Davis's flight at 1130 over Guadalcanal and claimed three Grummans (one unconfirmed), but neither side suffered any casualties. At 1140 Everton's seven VMF-212 F4Fs ran directly into the actual raid, nine land attack planes from the 753 Air Group cruising at 26,000 feet. Handily evading Lieutenant (jg) Futagami's escort of thirteen Zeros (seven 2nd Air Group, six Tainan), the Marines all flashed through one pass against the bombers, then split up. Part chased the *rikkōs* who dropped their bombs north of Henderson Field, while the rest sparred with Futagami and Yamaguchi. "Still mad" at Bauer's rebuke, first lieutenants John King and John Massey and 2nd Lt. Mel Freeman harassed the withdrawing strike all the way up to Santa Isabel. After shooting two Zeros, King took damage and ditched near Santa Isabel. He soon met up with coastwatcher Geoffrey Kuper (Firebaugh's benefactor), who reported him safe that day.[27]

Against the second fighter sweep and the strike itself, VMF-212 reported downing three bombers and five fighters, for the loss of one F4F (King safe). In turn all twenty-five Zeros returned (as did the whole 753 Air Group) and claimed ten Grummans (two unconfirmed) besides.[28] Thus the day's tally for the 1st MAW Fighter Command numbered nine Zeros and three bombers, but the Japanese actually came out ahead, one Zero for two F4Fs. Yet CACTUS certainly would have snorted at the Base Air Force assessment of the day: "In comparison with the past, Guadalcanal enemy air activity has decreased."[29]

Coastwatcher alerts punctuated the morning of 21 October. Finally at 1040 CACTUS received notice from Kennedy on New Georgia that 10 minutes before some thirty-five enemy planes in three groups had passed over. This day Base Air Force reversed the usual pattern of attack by sending the bombers in first: nine Kisarazu land attack planes (Lieutenant Nabeta) and thirteen Zeros (eight Tainan, five 2nd Air Group) under Lieutenant (jg) Ōno. Thirty minutes later came the inevitable sweep—twelve Zeros (nine 751, three 3rd Air Group) led by Lieutenant Itō.[30]

Fighter Command scrambled virtually all flyable F4Fs, seventeen in two big flights commanded by Fritz Payne and Pat Rooney. Barely reaching high altitude, Payne, 1st Lt. Frank Drury, and Mar. Gun. Tex Hamilton of VMF-212 dueled Ōno's escort. One Zero traded head-on bursts with Payne, who thought he finished it. Drury felt the same after an opposite attack against another. Suddenly a third Japanese Zero flashed past Drury, who reefed into a tight climbing turn and blazed away until his F4F shook in a stall. The Zero emitted a cloud of smoke, the pilot's helmet flew off, followed by a "lot of white stuff." The smoking fighter disappeared below. Looking around, Drury noticed an American parachutist, Tex Hamilton, who hung limply in the harness. He dropped into the jungle southeast of Lunga and did not survive. Payne's flight had fought the Tainan Zeros, whose only loss was PO1c Ōta Toshio. Ōta's teammates saw him score his thirty-fourth kill (the only one credited that day to the Japanese) before going down. It seems certain he shot down Hamilton, only to fall to Drury. The top Imperial Navy ace to die in the Guadalcanal campaign, his death greatly sorrowed the Tainan Air Group. At 1115 the nine land attack planes bombed the area around Fighter 1, killing nine and wounding forty-four. The 3rd Defense Battalion reported one bomber down and another damaged.[31]

Rooney's flight plus the team of Conger and Bastian (VMF-212) tangled with Itō's sweep after the bombers withdrew. Six Zeros fought Conger and Bastian at 10,000 feet. With two Marines protecting each other's tails before Bastian was wounded and dived out, each man claimed one Zero. So did Rooney and Norm Brown together, but the enemy shot down Technical Sgt. Emmet L. Anderson (VMO-251), who did not survive. All of Itō's dozen Zeros reached home.

After the losses and wear-and-tear of the past several days, the 1st MAW vitally needed the reserve F4Fs at Efate. To ferry them in, Fitch tapped VF-5, which had reassembled at Efate. Simpler led twelve Wildcats to Espiritu Santo, added 2nd Lt. Jacob A. O. Stubb (VMF-121) in another, and started for CACTUS. Just short of San Cristobal, Lt. (jg) Will Rouse suffered engine trouble and landed in the water. The others watched him take to his raft, but he was never found. A fine young pilot (VF-6 and VF-5) with three kills to his credit, Rouse had cheerfully volunteered for the ferry mission. With the twelve fresh F4Fs, Bauer's Fighter Command now counted thirty flyable Wildcats. That evening the VF-5 contingent rode an R4D back to Efate.[32]

Twenty-second October brought some variety. Bad weather aborted the usual Rabaul cast of characters, but did not prevent the arrival of carrier bombers from Buin. In a reprise of the 16 October mission that crippled the *McFarland,* Reserve Lieutenant Kitamura led six Type 99 carrier bombers from his 31st Air Group and six more from the 2nd Air Group, escorted by Lieutenant Kofukuda's twelve Zero 32s.[33] They looked for Allied ships off Lunga spotted by Japanese observers. After milling around in the clouds, the Type 99s made for the DD *Nicholas,* but ran the gauntlet of Marine F4Fs, who claimed five VBs over the harbor. About five or so VB executed shallow dives against the tincan, but scored no hits. Kitamura lost one carrier bomber destroyed, another crashed (crew killed) at Gatukai Island in the New Georgia group, and two returned badly damaged. Kofukuda's Zeros never engaged the Wildcats.

Two unrelated events enlivened Fighter 1 that day. The Japanese howitzers dubbed Millimeter Mike succeeded in lobbing shells only 500 feet shy of the fighter strip in welcome for Lt. Gen. Thomas Holcomb, the Commandant of the Corps, and Maj. Gen. Ralph J. Mitchell, Director of Marine Corps Aviation.

FDO Lew Mattison described a typical shelling as it appeared from his roost south of Fighter 1:

> You would see a puff down around the strip or over by the coconut grove, and a cloudy smoke and dust rise; sometimes the breeze would start blowing it away and you would see men running (either from it or toward it) before you heard the beginning of the scream; then it would go, down and down and down, and finally the crash![34]

Early the next morning three F4Fs covered the PBY-5A carrying Holcomb, Vandegrift, and Mitchell to Noumea to confer with ComSoPac.

At 1050 on the 23rd, CACTUS radar and the invaluable Kennedy on New Georgia simultaneously announced enemy planes. Bauer scrambled twenty-eight F4Fs (flight leaders Davis, Payne, Foss, and Rooney) and four P-39s, the last of which barely got off when Condition RED sounded at 1114. Base Air Force had recourse to a typical attack pattern: a fighter sweep from Buin with twelve Zero 32s from the 6th Air Group (Lieutenant Kofukuda) set to arrive just ahead of a Rabaul-based force of sixteen land attack planes (eight Misawa, eight Kisarazu) under Lieutenant Nakamura and seventeen Zeros (six 751, six Tainan, five 2nd Air Group) led by Lieutenant (jg) Baba.[35]

The resulting air battle broke in utter mayhem, dogfights all over the sky. Joe Bauer described it best: "God Almighty, that was a great fight!"[36] Defending Wildcats mauled the fighter sweep, shooting down three Zeros and hitting another so hard it had to ditch at Rekata (killing the pilot). The four dead were Lt. (jg) Kanemitsu Mukumi, PO1c Suzuki Gunji, PO3c Tagakagi Shimpei, and PO3c Fukuda Hiroshi.

Four VF-71 pilots—Rooney, Brown, Kenton, and Thrash—ganged up on Nakamura's Misawa 1st *Chūtai,* and Rooney flamed PO2c Nishizawa Jintarō's *rikkō.* Lew Mattison watched the stricken bomber "float gently down leaving a feathery white plume of smoke to the last." Then a "hell of a dogfight" broke out to the northeast at low level.[37] Marines cost the strike escort stalwart Lieutenant (jg) Baba and also Sea2c Mitsunaga Hachirō from the 751 Air Group.

Marine Fighter Command boasted twenty Zeros and two bombers destroyed, and three other bombers heavily damaged ("smokers"). Top scorer was Joe Foss with four Zeros, while Pat Rooney of VF-71 received credit for both bomber kills and one "smoker." In return only one F4F suffered heavy damage and seven others were readily repaired. The total Japanese loss came to six fighters and one bomber. CACTUS reacted jubilantly to the big victory, which vindicated Bauer's aggressive tactics. Some Marine pilots felt they stayed right with dogfighting Zeros, which indicated to them a great decrease in Japanese pilot skills.[38] It was a wonderful way to cap a hectic week. Millimeter Mike seemed unimpressed with the celebrations and shelled the officer's bivouac and Fighter 1. That night the Japanese launched a tank-infantry assault up the coast road and over the mouth of the Mantanikau, which the Marines beat back with heavy losses. More was in store for CACTUS.

The period between 18 and 23 October saw claims by the 1st MAW amounting to fifty fighters, twelve bombers, and five dive bombers, for the loss of seven F4Fs. In turn Base Air Force tallied forty-one Grummans (six unconfirmed) for twelve Zeros, four land attack planes, and two carrier bombers. Greatly overestimating his successes, each adversary decided that he came out ahead in one of the wildest weeks of CACTUS air fighting. Now the Japanese were preparing the coup-de-grâce.

CHAPTER 18

The Big October Offensive Unfolds

OPENING MOVES

After Vice Admiral Halsey took over as ComSoPac on 18 October, his first priority centered on ending the grave threat to the 1st MarDiv on Guadalcanal. To this aggressive commander, prompt action seemed in order. Two weeks later, on 31 October, he recalled the situation in a letter to Admiral Nimitz: "I had to begin throwing punches almost immediately. As a consequence quick decisions had to be made."[1] He certainly did not shrink from them.

For the past few months, radio intelligence from the cryptanalysts at Pearl Harbor (HYPO), Washington (NEGAT), and Brisbane (BELCONNEN) availed little on Japanese plans and fleet movements. In particular, information on enemy carriers appeared both sparse and vague.[2] The flattops that had threatened Espiritu Santo and panicked Ghormley had faded away. Nothing appeared on the immediate horizon against CACTUS, although the troops that the Japanese "High Speed Convoy" had delivered at such cost certainly would show up soon. Attention centered on the coastal route and the Mantanikau River. Major General Vandegrift assessed the greatest danger as an enemy thrust east along the coast, possibly coordinated with a counterlanding on the Lunga beaches by troops convoyed from Buin.

Over the next few days, Halsey and his staff considered ways to employ So-Pac's enhanced naval power soon to comprise the two carriers *Enterprise* and *Hornet* and two fast battleships *Washington* and *South Dakota* (BB-57). Coming down from Pearl Harbor, Rear Admiral Kinkaid set the rendezvous for 24 October northeast of the New Hebrides between his TF-16 with the *Enterprise* and *South Dakota* and Rear Admiral Murray's TF-17 (*Hornet*). Bloodied on 20 October when the *Chester* took a fish, Rear Admiral Lee's TF-64 with the *Washington* temporarily withdrew to Espiritu Santo for fuel. He would sail again on the 23rd.

Kinkaid, Murray, and Lee learned of Halsey's audacious plan on 22 October. It ordered Kinkaid's newly reorganized TF-61 to "sweep around north of Santa Cruz" into waters not cleaved by American carriers since the 24 August Battle of the Eastern Solomons. Beginning about 25 October, TF-61 would pass north of Santa Cruz, search aggressively beyond air-support range of Espiritu Santo, then continue southwest toward San Cristobal. Southeast of Guadalcanal, Lee's TF-64 would join in position to counter threats against CACTUS. In the 31 October letter to Nimitz, Halsey professed that he intended for TF-61 to "sweep" past Santa Cruz only if "no enemy comes down," that is, with no powerful Japanese forces obviously poised north of the Solomons. Unfortunately, he never specified that contingency to Kinkaid.[3]

According to Halsey's plan, Japanese action would determine the next move of the combined task force. If no offensive or reinforcement convoy immediately endangered Guadalcanal, he proposed a daring spoiling attack, a massive reprise of the *Hornet*'s 5 October raid against the great nest of enemy shipping in the Buin, Tonolei, and Faisi triangle off southern Bougainville. Should conditions be favorable, Halsey even thought of loosing Lee with battleships and cruisers to bombard the harbor. Given the propinquity to Japanese air bases at Rabaul and Buka, not to mention Buin, such a slugfest would present the carriers with real problems both protecting themselves and providing fighter support for the bombardment force.

After sending the preliminary Santa Cruz "sweep" orders to Kinkaid, ComSoPac learned on the 22nd from CinCPac intelligence of another Japanese move against Guadalcanal expected in the next day or two. The cryptanalysts had pieced together references to a "Y-Day," but could not predict when or where. Halsey regretfully informed Vandegrift that no SoPac task forces could immediately intervene. The next morning even more indications arrived of an imminent enemy offensive. Decrypts revealed to CinCPac at least eight Japanese I-boats designated to "form scouting line in Solomons area." That foreshadowed a "sweep for BLUE [U.S.] forces." Later in the day CinCPac analysts placed no fewer than ten submarines in the Solomons and New Hebrides and advised of an enemy thrust against Guadalcanal slated for the next two or three days.[4]

CinCPac intelligence definitely placed in the South Pacific only two (*Shōkaku* and *Zuikaku*) of the enemy's supposed five combat carriers. Evidence still indicated that 2nd Carrier Division's *"Hitaka"* (*Hiyō*) and *"Hayataka"* (*Junyō*) remained in home waters. Of course these two flattops had actually come south in early October. Traffic analysis vouchsafed no definite information on the *Zuihō* at all. Projecting the optimum strength for a Japanese offensive, OP-20-G in Washington estimated four Japanese carriers (with 72 fighters and 132 dive bombers and torpedo planes) might be near the Solomons, but did not identify them. Despite this fresh intelligence, Halsey did not cancel or modify Kinkaid's orders for the Santa Cruz "sweep."[5]

Enemy activity on the 23rd was widespread. That morning an AirSoPac PBY (91-P-3, patrol plane commander [PPC] unknown) encountered a large Japanese task force about 650 miles north of Espiritu Santo. Late that evening Lt. (jg) Donald L. Jackson's Catalina night tracker (91-P-14) located two groups of enemy ships: a CA, a CL, and two DD operating ten miles ahead of another force that included one carrier. Three PBYs armed with torpedoes hunted them in the moonlight. Later at 2030, 24 October, Lt. (jg) George A. Enloe in 51-P-8 tallied a possible hit on a heavy cruiser.[6] These contacts certainly confirmed the presence of strong Japanese naval forces perched north of Santa Cruz. That same evening a noisy tank-infantry attack blundered across the mouth of the Mantanikau River. The 1st MarDiv repulsed the intruders with heavy losses. SoPac remained watchful and wary.

The evening of 23 October also witnessed the famous meeting at Noumea between Halsey and Marine generals Holcomb and Vandegrift. Vandegrift himself best described the high point:

> Gray eyebrows bristling, the compactly built Halsey drummed the desk a moment with his fingers. He abruptly turned to me. "Can you hold?"

"Yes I can hold. But I have to have more active support than I have been getting."

He nodded. "You go back there, Vandegrift. I promise to get you everything I have."[7]

The next few days Halsey amply backed his words with deeds.

Tom Kinkaid's TF-16 completed a fast and uneventful trip to the South Pacific. On 19 October destroyers *Lamson* (DD-367) and *Mahan* (DD-364) departed for a swift diversionary foray through the Japanese-held Gilbert Islands. Following the policy of seasoning carrier captains, Capt. Osborne B. Hardison relieved Captain Davis on the *Enterprise* two days later. Also on board was Capt. Andrew C. McFall, set to replace the *Hornet*'s Captain Mason, already selected for rear admiral. The afternoon of the 21st proved not so sanguine for VF-10 CO Jimmy Flatley. During exercises on deck, a pilot accidentally stomped on his right foot and broke a bone. Flatley would not let a mere break impair his performance. Like the rest of VF-10, he was raring to go.

On 23 October while refueling from the oiler *Sabine,* TF-16 took the opportunity to transfer part of Halsey's old staff to proceed immediately to Noumea. One was Cdr. Leonard Dow, his staff communications officer, but also the *Enterprise* FDO since before the outbreak of the war. Poor communications had plagued SoPac from the very beginning, so Halsey definitely desired his expert

Air Group Ten staff, 23 Oct. 1942. *Top row (l to r):* Lt. (jg) Zimmerman, radio officer; Lt. "Hampy" Barnes, air intelligence officer; Cdr. Richard Gaines, group commander; Cdr. John Griffin, FDO; Lt. Hightower, flight surgeon. *Bottom row:* Lt. James Daniels, group LSO; Lt. Robin Lindsey, *Enterprise* LSO; Lt. "Hod" Proulx, *Enterprise* Asst. LSO. (Capt. J. G. Daniels)

on the spot. He later informed Nimitz that he "debated for a long time" before ordering Dow to Noumea, but felt his presence vital for the proper functioning of his communications.[8]

Halsey readily released Ham Dow because Cdr. John H. Griffin, the respected head of the Fighter Director School on Oahu, rode the *Enterprise* as a member of Kinkaid's staff. Griffin possessed great theoretical knowledge of fighter direction, including training by the RAF, but had yet to control fighters in a carrier battle. The present conditions of radio silence allowed no opportunity for live exercises with the immediate FD staff (radar operators and plotters) and the VF-10 pilots. Lt. John Baumeister, Jr., the previous *Enterprise* radar officer and like Dow an old hand, left prior to this cruise, and his understudy lacked experience. In addition some key *Enterprise* radar personnel were also transferred. By shifting personnel, the admirals underestimated the complexity of radar detection and fighter direction. As events transpired, deep flaws became manifest in the CXAM-1 radars on both the *Enterprise* and the *Hornet*.[9]

At 1245, 24 October, TF-16 (*Enterprise, South Dakota,* one CA, one CL-AA, seven DD, and an AO) contacted Murray's TF-17 (*Hornet,* two CA, two CL-AA, and six DD) 250 miles northeast of Espiritu Santo. As officer in tactical command (OTC), Kinkaid reestablished TF-61, but in accordance with earlier practice he retained two single carrier task forces and instructed Murray to operate five miles southeast of TF-16. As before, the two carriers alternated the daily duty of providing searches and patrols. Kinkaid specified that unless directed the duty carrier should retain the radar guard and fighter director control. Under the circum-

Ens. Lyman Fulton's VF-10 Wildcat F-17 (BuNo. 5229) about to take off from the *Enterprise*, 24 Oct. 1942. In battle on 26 October, Ens. James Dowden flew F-17. (NA 80-G-30005)

stances, the two admirals could not confer in person as to the upcoming mission and carrier operations in general. Murray certainly felt the lack. As events would show, he distrusted the standard practices and held his own ideas about handling carriers.

Following the ComSoPac orders, the newly reconstituted TF-61 rang up 23 knots bound for the waters north of Santa Cruz. That also kept the carriers clear of I-boats prowling the New Hebrides–Santa Cruz channel. Kinkaid awaited fresh information from AirSoPac searchers to help decide his future moves, although the quiet radio network on the 24th seemed to indicate the enemy force might have retired north out of range. Despite concerns about Japanese intentions, TF-61 continued its headlong dash into perilous waters.

JAPANESE PLANS

An examination of Japanese Army and Navy plans for the big October offensive against Guadalcanal underscores just how dangerous were these particular waters. On 15 October, the High Speed Convoy had completed disembarking troops and weapons for the 17th Army. To mask his main effort, Lieutenant General Hyakutake used a series of diversionary stabs east along the coastal corridor past the Mantanikau. At the same time nine battalions of the 2nd Division disappeared south into the jungle for a wide eastward sweep across the Lunga River. The night of 22 October ("Y-Day") these troops were to emerge from the forest for a surprise assault against the Lunga airfield.[10]

Admiral Yamamoto coordinated Combined Fleet operations with the 17th Army's timetable. Vice Admiral Kondō's Support Force (his Advance Force and Vice Admiral Nagumo's Carrier Striking Force or *Kidō Butai*) already loitered on station north of the Solomons well out of Allied air search range. Once the Army captured the airfield, Kondō would destroy U.S. naval forces supporting Guadalcanal. (See table 18.1 for the Support Force configuration.) From Shortland, Vice Admiral Mikawa's 8th Fleet was to land troops at Koli Point, east of Lunga, and support the 17th Army's mop-up of the American forces.

While marking time before the 17th Army's attack, the Support Force fueled and prepared its scheduled southward sprint. However, the morning of 21 October, an engine-room fire crippled carrier *Hiyō*, Rear Admiral Kakuta's flagship.

TABLE 18.1
Vice Admiral Kondō's Support Force

Advance Force ←————————100 to 120 miles————————→ Striking Force	
(2nd Fleet—Kondō)	(3rd Fleet—Nagumo)
2 CVL (*Hiyō, Junyō*)	2 CV (*Shōkaku, Zuikaku*)
(80 planes)	1 CVL (*Zuihō*)
2 BB, 4 CA	(158 planes)
1 CL, 12 DD	1 CA, 8DD
	Vanguard Force (Abe)
	2 BB, 3 CA, 1 CL, 7 DD
Mission	
Pass east of Malaita, thence south of Guadalcanal	Operate east of Kondō thence southeast of Guadalcanal

A day of emergency repairs restored her speed to 16 knots, too slow to conduct regular air operations and stay with the Advance Force. On 22 October Kakuta reluctantly shifted to the *Junyō* and released the *Hiyō* and two destroyers to Truk. She provided the *Junyō* three Zeros, one Type 99 carrier bomber, and Lieutenant Irikiin's five Type 97 carrier planes to rebuild the *Junyō* Carrier Attack Squadron. On the 23rd she launched Cdr. Mieno Saburō, the air officer, with Lieutenant Kaneko's sixteen Zeros and Lieutenant Abe's seventeen carrier bombers to join the Base Air Force at Rabaul. These aircraft would be sorely missed afloat.

Meanwhile, the wretched terrain delayed the 2nd Division's move into position south of the Lunga airfield, compelling 17th Army on the 21st to postpone the assault 24 hours to the night of the 23rd. To resynchronize their movements with the Army, Support Force ran north until noon the next day before swinging south again. Expecting the long-awaited seizure of the airfield, Kondō's Advance Force would at dawn on the 24th be only 200 miles northeast of Lunga, with Nagumo's Striking Force about 100 miles further east.

Thus on 23 October the Support Force again pounded southward. Japanese search planes failed to sight any U.S. ships ahead, but as related above an American search plane scouted both Nagumo's Vanguard Force under Rear Admiral Abe and his main body carriers. Even more disturbing, the 17th Army again delayed the assault on the airfield for 24 hours, this time to the night of 24 October. In another "piston maneuver," the whole Support Force reversed course so as not to proceed too far south and risk its premature disclosure.

The evening of 23 October Combined Fleet headquarters at Truk pondered the implications of the 17th Army's repeated postponements. On 21 and 22 October Japanese search planes dogged an enemy battleship force southeast of Guadalcanal: Lee's TF-64 retiring to Espiritu Santo for fuel. Yamamoto and his staff considered whether they might be bait to lure the Japanese south into a trap waiting to be sprung by U.S. carriers lurking eastward off their left flank. Japanese naval radio intelligence warned that an American carrier force had departed Pearl Harbor some days ago and could soon reach the battle area. The evening of 23 October, Combined Fleet designated Support Force positions set for the morning of 25 October in order to exploit the expected capture of the airfield. Yamamoto also warned his commanders to search diligently for enemy carriers, particularly southeast toward Santa Cruz.

Even such caution proved insufficient for Nagumo and his outspoken chief of staff, RAdm. Kusaka Ryūnosuke, who knew full well that on the 23rd the American searchers had marked the Striking Force. Early on 24 October while they considered their options, enemy flying boats delivered an unsuccessful night torpedo attack against Rear Admiral Abe's Vanguard Force out ahead of Nagumo's carriers (Lieutenant [jg] Enloe's fish nearly brushed the heavy cruiser *Chikuma*). At Kusaka's urging, Nagumo altered the Combined Fleet plan by retiring even farther north than ordered before reversing course again. In effect Nagumo set back a whole day Yamamoto's timing for the 3rd Fleet's southerly shift.

Holding radio silence, Nagumo continued northwest for most of the 24th and only that afternoon informed the other commanders. To the west Kondō's Advance Force had already started south, opening the distance to the Striking Force. Belatedly learning of Nagumo's change of plan, he had no choice but to conform to the intricate duet for which the plans called. At Truk Combined Fleet command reacted with great displeasure to Nagumo's action. Chief of Staff Ugaki even called the move "outrageous" and "arbitrary." At 2147 he ordered

Kondō and Nagumo to adhere to the original plan as closely as possible. "Do not hesitate or waver!" he wrote in his diary.[11] Thus at 2300, 24 October, and about ten hours behind schedule, Nagumo finally turned south and boosted speed to 26 knots. At the same time screaming troops from the 2nd Division hurled themselves against the defenses protecting the Lunga airfield. The October offensive had truly begun.

25 OCTOBER

"Dugout Sunday"

On the rainy night of 24/25 October the left wing of the reinforced 2nd Division stormed the thinly defended perimeter south of Henderson Field. Somehow word filtered back to 17th Army headquarters that their soldiers had hacked their way through to the airfield. At 0130, 25 October, Hyakutake jubilantly announced the victory to the Combined Fleet. Navy commanders pressed plans to exploit the success. They were all wrong. The valiant Marine and Army defenders held the line.

By dawn the ground fighting died down for the time being, but Japanese shelling continued. To the west, Mikawa's 8th Fleet Force gathered strength for its mission to cut off the defeated Americans at Lunga by landing troops at Koli Point across their escape route. At Fighter 1 the 1st MAW floundered in thick black mud, which even rendered their tents uninhabitable. Conditions at the field contributed to their "foul humor." Lieutenant Colonel Bauer's Fighter Command numbered twenty-seven operational F4F-4s, but no one was certain any could lift off the morass.[12]

The SBDs on morning search did get away from Henderson Field and at 0700 spotted trouble in the form of three bold enemy destroyers only 35 miles northwest. Beginning at 0715, coastwatchers up the line radioed of enemy planes bound for Guadalcanal. The first interloper was Capt. Kirita Hideo's sleek Mitsubishi Ki-46 Type 100 command reconnaissance plane [DINAH] from the Japanese Army Air Force's 76th Independent Air Squadron, which brazenly buzzed Henderson Field expecting to see a rising sun flag. Instead AA transformed the squadron commander's plane into junk alongside the runway—the first Imperial Army aircraft lost in the Southeast Area. Heretofore the Imperial Navy had provided all the air support. About 10 days later someone at CACTUS noted that the flying helmets snatched from the dead crew by souvenir hounds sported the Army star and warned SoPac of the presence of Imperial Army planes in the region.[13]

In addition to the usual bomber raid, set for the late afternoon, Base Air Force arranged for twenty-eight Zeros divided into four hourly flights from Rabaul to conduct patrols over Lunga. The staff told the pilots to circle the airfield for two hours, then land if they could see that friendly troops definitely controlled the area. The first flight comprised Lieutenant (jg) Yamaguchi's nine 3rd Air Group Zeros. Coastwatchers gave warning of his approach. Indeed they kept up a steady stream of reports of incoming planes.

At Fighter 1 Bauer tapped Joe Foss, who would get his Wildcats aloft if anyone could. At about 0945 Foss led five other VMF-121 pilots out to their planes. Conditions forced them to start from the eastern (downwind) edge of the field and take off without flaps in hopes of avoiding the worst of the mud. Once airborne,

Foss and his teammates barely reached 1,500 feet before six of Yamaguchi's Zeros intervened. The Marines held them at length up to 6,000 feet, where the battle started in earnest. Foss claimed two Zeros and 2nd Lt. Danny Doyle a third, but enemy bullets flamed 2nd Lt. Oscar M. Bate's F4F. He bailed out and walked back to the field. Actually two Zeros, flown by PO1c Iwamoto Rokuzō and PO2c Maeda Naoichi, succumbed to Foss's flight. Later the other seven Japanese dueled with seven VMF-121 F4Fs led by Major Davis, who got up about 1000. In that action nobody went down.[14]

Around 1030 with the skies momentarily clear, Bauer loosed his third flight: six VMF-212 pilots under 1st Lt. Robert F. Stout. One F4F stuck firmly in the mud, and engine trouble sent another back. The other four pilots soon found work over the channel between Lunga and Tulagi. The destroyers *Akazuki*, *Ikazuchi*, and *Shiratsuyu* had chased the APDs *Trevor* and *Zane* (DMS-14) east into Nggela Channel, sank the fleet tug *Seminole* (AFT-65) and the *YP-284*, and dueled with shore batteries at Lunga. Along with the 3rd Defense Battalion's five-inchers, VMF-212's ardent strafing forced the tincans to make smoke and retire behind it so precipitously that many shore observers thought they foundered.

Short of ammunition and preparing to land, Stout's four F4Fs clashed directly over Lunga with the number 2 patrol, Lieutenant (jg) Futagami's eight 2nd Air Group Zeros. While Futagami's lead *shōtai* of three Zeros busily strafed the airfield, 1st Lt. Jack Conger flamed the trailer, then overtook the other two bandits out over the beach. He put a good burst into the nearer one, but did not see its fate. Ground observers later informed him that his second victim plowed into the ground. Now out of ammo, Conger ended up in a head-on run at 1,500 feet against the leader, very likely Futagami himself. At the last second, Conger determined to slice off the Zero's tail with his prop ("a crazy thing to do," he later remarked). Instead he tore the enemy's fuselage in half, but the Wildcat lurched downward as well. Conger's parachute barely flapped open before he struck the water hard. Alone he had accounted for the whole 1st *Shōtai*: Futagami, PO3c Morita Toyoo, and Sea1c Ubukata Naoshi.

"Cowboy" Stout called over the radio: "Three Zeros on my tail, and I'm out of guns."[15] Despite that he landed successfully, as did Frank Drury. At the same time 1st Lt. Lawrence Faulkner torched another Zero. While floating off Lunga, Conger narrowly missed being struck by the flaming Mitsubishi, which splashed only 100 feet away. Its erstwhile occupant parachuted down 20 yards away. He was 19-year-old PO2c Ishikawa Shirō, the 3rd *Shōtai* leader, burned on his hands and face. Faulkner needed three tries at the field before he shook Ishikawa's wingman, Sea1c Nagano Kiichi, and landed safely. A Higgins boat came out from Lunga to pick up Conger, who suggested they capture the enemy pilot as well. Despite Ishikawa's attempt to shoot him, Conger dissuaded several Marines from finishing off the young Japanese, bashed him on the head with a jerry can, and brought him dazed but alive to Lunga.

VMF-212 and the 2nd Air Group fought one of the classic air actions of the Guadalcanal campaign. At the cost of one F4F, Conger received credit for two Zeros and Faulkner for one. The 2nd Air Group lost three pilots killed and one missing (POW). In return Nagano claimed four Grummans (one unconfirmed) and PO3c Kawasaki Katsuhiro two more. In a letter home Nagano vividly summed up the battle: "It would not be an exaggeration to say that this was one day in which I was reborn. It is one day I will never forget."[16]

Around 1130, Foss, the irrepressible Bate, and the VF-71 contingent took to the skies over Lunga: Capt. Joseph Foss (VMF-121), 2nd Lt. Oscar Bate (VMF-121), Ens. Norman Brown (VF-71), Lt. Carl Rooney (VF-71), and Lt. (jg) Millard Thrash (VF-71). Norm Brown joined the leader's wing. "I want to see how you do it [i.e., shoot down Japanese]," he radioed Foss as they departed. "We were able to show him a little excitement,"[17] Foss later explained. The third fighter patrol numbered six Tainan Zeros (with claims):[18]

1st *Shōtai*		2nd *Shōtai*	
WO Yamashita Sahei	1 VF (1)	PO1c Okumura Takeo	2 VF
PO2c Nakaya Yoshiichi	2 VF	PO3c Gotō Tatsusuke	MIA
Sea1c Yoshimura Keisaku	MIA	Sea1c Yamamoto Suehiro	1 VF

Several of these pilots have received much notice in these pages. Already an ace, Yamashita shot down Ens. Dix Loesch (VF-5) on 12 September, while Okumura, the tough *Ryūjō* survivor, ended up as fifth-ranking Imperial Navy ace with thirty kills. Barely 20 years old but with nine kills to his credit, Yoshimura had battered Gordon Firebaugh's VF-6 Wildcat on 7 August, so long ago. The Tainan pilots were exhausted from months of incessant combat. They departed Rabaul at 0730, stopped at Buka to refuel, and took off at 1015. From his roost overlooking Buka, coastwatcher Paul Mason informed CACTUS of six Zeros "going yours via west coast."[19]

At 1245, while Yamashita's *chūtai* anxiously searched the skies over Lunga, the combined Marine-Navy flight stalked them from above. Foss described the Japanese as "sailing along with splendid calm and indifference." Diving in, he drew close to blast one Zero, whose exploding engine nearly smashed Brown's Wildcat. "Things weren't so easy after that." The remaining Japanese tore into the F4Fs before they could regain height. After a fast run, one Zero overshot Foss, who jumped its tail for some "liberal treatment" and blew the Mitsubishi out of the sky. To his surprise (and no doubt to the other pilot as well), the Japanese emerged seemingly unhurt and bailed out. Brown also claimed a Zero during this flurry. A few minutes later some of the F4Fs circled low over Fighter 1 to land. Despite being low on fuel and ammunition, Foss warily swung south over Mount Austen to look over the situation before coming in. To his horror he saw two Zeros about to ambush a lone Wildcat flying straight and level. Too far away to intervene, Foss shouted a warning over the radio. Wrapped by Japanese fire, the Grumman dropped so convincingly that the lead Zero essayed a "triumphant slow roll." Foss later learned the pilot recovered from the shock-induced spin and set down safely. He did not have time to watch, for the two bandits took after him. Losing them in a cloud, he turned the tables and blasted one Zero into "a million little jagged worthless pieces." Out of bullets, Foss ducked into Fighter 1.[20]

This spirited fight, certainly VF-71's wildest, proved archetypical of the Guadalcanal campaign as a whole. The Americans claimed four Zeros and did finish the two flown by Gotō and Yoshimura. Yamashita later ditched his battered fighter farther up the Slot. In turn the Japanese notched five Grummans (one unconfirmed) on their tally, but actually only bruised two of the sturdy Wildcats, whose pilots lived to fight again. The fight also spawned two humorous anecdotes. Norm Brown teased Foss: "You don't fight fair. You get up so close to the Zeros that it would be impossible for anybody to miss. Why, you actually leave powder burns on 'em." Later Foss told his friend Danny Doyle that for the first time the Japanese had put no bullets in his plane. Startled, Doyle pointed to a neat row of holes in Foss's turtleback. "What do you call those?" he wanted to know.[21]

The four Tainan survivors departed around 1305, the same time Lieutenant Commander Eldridge's four SBDs plastered the second of Mikawa's surface forces having the temerity to invade the waters around Guadalcanal in daylight. Ultimately four strikes that afternoon so crippled the light cruiser *Yura* that she was scuttled. Understandably Mikawa postponed the landing at Koli Point.

The fourth and final fighter patrol, Lieutenant (jg) Ōno's five Tainan Zeros, roared over Lunga around 1400. That coincided with the daily raid of sixteen Type 1 land attack planes escorted by twelve Buin-based *Hiyō* Zeros under Lt. Fujita Iyōzō. Major Davis's eleven Marine F4Fs tangled with them over the field in a dizzy succession of air actions impossible to sort out. The CAP claimed four bombers and five Zeros without any casualties in return. One fighter pilot, PO3c Morimura Toyoo, failed to return from Ōno's patrol, while the strike lost two *rikkōs* (one Kisarazu, one 753 Air Group) and one *Hiyō* Zero (PO2c Ogino Kyōichirō). On the way in Ogino suffered mechanical trouble and crashed at Gizo, only to be captured later by Donald Kennedy's natives. Taken to New Georgia, he committed suicide on the first anniversary of the Pearl Harbor attack in which he took part.[22]

About 1550, Lieutenant Shiga's strike group of twelve Type 99 carrier bombers and twelve Zeros from the carrier *Junyō* with Kondō's Advance Force assailed Lunga. In response to a direct order from Combined Fleet, Kakuta had dispatched the twenty-four planes at 1435 from about 200 miles northeast of Guadalcanal. The *Junyō* flyers happily bombed and strafed Henderson Field without loss. In fact they only disturbed some wrecks in the boneyard south of the main runway.[23]

Shiga's strike was the last of the hectic 25th. During the day the 1st MAW lost two F4Fs destroyed (Bate and Conger, both safe) and four perforated by enemy bullets. Six more Wildcats took damage either from accidents or from the muddy field. That left only eight F4Fs immediately flyable. Total air claims numbered twenty Zeros and five bombers, while AA added four Zeros and one bomber. That day the Japanese hurled eighty-two aircraft in six waves against CACTUS. Fourteen (eleven Zeros, two land attack planes, and one Army observation plane) failed to return. Two other Zeros were totaled. Yet even more than the loss endured, Base Air Force seemed to lose heart in the face of stiff CACTUS resistance. Yamada's battle report complained, "Employing positive tactics, the enemy has recently reinforced their fighter strength."[24] Never afterward did the Zeros appear as numerous or aggressive over Lunga.

Shadow Boxing

While massive land and air battles raged at Guadalcanal, the only direct participation by the main fleets maneuvering hundreds of miles off shore comprised the *Junyō*'s afternoon strike. Just what were Kondō and Nagumo, Kinkaid and Lee doing on 25 October?

Overnight on the 24th/25th, Kondō's Support Force bore down on the Solomons to exploit the anticipated capture of the Lunga airfield. His own Advance Force (with the *Junyō*) operated about 120 miles southwest of Nagumo's Striking Force (*Kidō Butai*) with the three carriers *Shōkaku*, *Zuikaku*, and *Zuihō*. While the ships prepared searches to blanket the waters south and east of the Solomons, they received the jubilant word at 0500 of the successful assault against Lunga. Now they hunted Allied ships supposedly rushing to aid the stricken Lunga garrison.

By 0730 both Kondō and Nagumo knew that the happy news of victory at Lunga was fraudulent. No triumphant rising sun flags fluttered over the long-contested airfield. Defiant Lunga still bristled with aircraft that threatened Japanese ships, and the Allied naval command was not preoccupied trying to rescue its troops. With recourse again to the "piston," Support Force immediately swung around to the north to draw out of strike range of Lunga. Now they depended on the eyes of their search crews, but a plague of enemy snoopers soon bedeviled both Kondō and Nagumo.

From BUTTON, Fitch's AirSoPac undertook the vital roles of search, tracking, and strikes. His dawn search of ten PBYs and six B-17s covered the northern semicircle from BUTTON out 650 to 800 miles. Acting as an advance base, the converted seaplane tender *Ballard* deployed to Vanikoro, southernmost of the Santa Cruz Islands, to service flying boats. Fitch's flyers soon produced important sightings. Around 0930, 1st Lt. Mario Sesso's B-17 flying the 325-degree line from BUTTON ran across Kondō's Advance Force. After surviving a mauling by PO1c Sawada Mankichi's three *Junyō* Zeros which killed his bombardier, Sgt. Eldon M. Elliott, Sesso raised base at 0948. He placed an enemy task force bearing 325 degrees and 525 miles from BUTTON and headed due east. Fitch quickly alerted twelve B-17s for strike missions.[25]

Just 10 minutes after Sesso's message, PBY 91-P-14 (Lt. [jg] Warren B. Matthew) searching the sector 332 to 338 degrees spotted Abe's Vanguard Force operating south of Nagumo's carriers. The only message of his vouchsafed to base located eight enemy ships at 7° S, 163° E. A pair of pugnacious Mitsubishi Type 0 observation seaplanes from the battleship *Kirishima* chased Matthew through the clouds, and by the time he finally evaded them, 91-P-14 sported

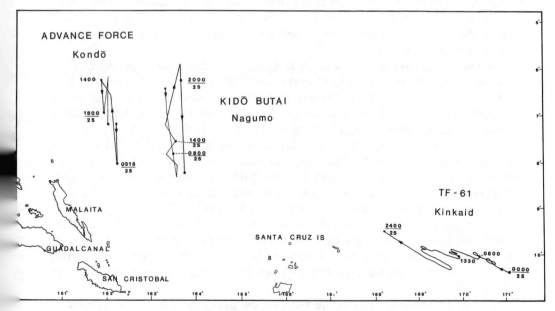

Task force operations, 25 October 1942.

seventy-six new holes, including hits in the port engine. Unluckily the *Curtiss* and TF-61 never heard his subsequent reports of enemy course changes.[26]

Almost simultaneous with Matthew's contact came one that drew SoPac's full attention. Flying the adjacent sector (338–344 degrees), Lt. (jg) Robert T. Lampshire's 24-P-7 radioed at 1000 of finding "unidentified task forces." The *Ballard* soon rebroadcast another of Lampshire's reports which noted two BB, two CL, and four DD at 8°05' S, 164°20' E. While scouting the enemy force, Lampshire saw a carrier (the *Zuihō*) launching fighters. At 1103, he added two more carriers to those previously reported. The enemy held course 145 degrees, speed 25 knots. Indeed, to Nagumo's great displeasure, Lampshire had exposed the main body. He decided to head north again once he completed air operations.[27]

The AirSoPac search reports intruded upon an otherwise uneventful morning for Kinkaid's TF-61 with the *Enterprise* and the *Hornet*. Obedient to SoPac's original orders, he proceeded northwest toward Santa Cruz at 22 knots. The *Enterprise* assumed the normal patrols and searches, while the *Hornet* prepared a deckload strike on alert. Later that morning *Enterprise* crews delivered three spare SBDs and two TBFs to the *Hornet*. To their dismay, she soon re-spotted the deck with her strike group and, rather rudely, would not break the spot to return the *Enterprise* men to their ship. At 1025 Kinkaid monitored a rebroadcast from the *Curtiss* of Sesso's 1000 report of two BB, two CA, two CL, and four DD poised about 150 miles northeast of Guadalcanal. Fully 375 miles northwest of TF-61 they were far out of strike range. For the time being, Kinkaid awaited word of enemy carriers.[28]

The new aircraft gave the *Hornet* Air Group a total of 85 aircraft (38 fighters, 31 dive bombers, and 16 torpedo bombers). To facilitate deck handling, she operated 33 fighters, 24 dive bombers, and 16 torpedo planes. The *Enterprise*'s Air Group Ten now comprised 36 fighters, 41 dive bombers, and 13 torpedo planes, with 29 VF, 27 VSB, and 13 VTB available to fly. Both carriers retained numerous spare F4Fs and SBDs for which they possessed available crews, although the *Hornet,* at least, consigned only weary SBDs to the hangar overhead. The upcoming battle demonstrated this policy to be ill-conceived, especially with regard to fighters. On the 24th, Halsey forbad the carriers from sending any of their spare aircraft to reinforce island bases ashore, unless "special circumstances make such action unavoidable."[29]

While Lt. (jg) William K. Blair was flying CAP, his electric propeller pitch control malfunctioned—the old ailment of the F4F-4s. The prop froze in full high pitch, which greatly reduced power and made it impossible for Blair to fly straight and level with his gear down. After he signaled the *Enterprise* for a deferred forced landing, Captain Hardison agreed at 1119 to let him try the hazardous recovery. Under stress, Blair forgot to drop his hook; the LSO's spotter missed it as well. The Wildcat failed to snag a wire, bounced, and crashed through the wire barriers straight into the SBDs parked forward. The impact knocked one VB-10 airplane overboard and crumpled three more Dauntlesses, as well as wrecking F-14. Thus the accident cost five planes. Blair emerged unhurt, but four plane handlers sustained injuries. Crommelin's airdales hastened to untangle the mess and rerig the torn barriers, but the flight deck would be tied up for some time—a matter of real concern because of the enemy to the west. Hardison ordered the battered F4F and two of the smashed SBDs pushed over the side.[30]

As her crewmen sorted out the mess on the deck, the *Enterprise* received at

1150 via the *Curtiss* one of Bob Lampshire's updated reports, which placed two carriers and supporting forces about 130 miles northeast of the first (Sesso's) contact. Making 25 knots, the enemy carriers held course 145 degrees, that is, toward TF-61. In flag plot Kinkaid and his staff bent over the chart. These juicy targets bore 287 degrees and 355 miles from TF-61, and at 250 miles northeast of CACTUS this force could support a possible amphibious landing from the ships known to be standing northwest of Guadalcanal. Likewise studying the morning sighting reports at Noumea, Halsey immediately sent the categorical order to Kinkaid and Lee: "Strike, Repeat, Strike. ComSoPac sends Action CTF61 and 64."[31] That set the stage for the Battle of Santa Cruz.

Rapidly cutting down the range, the near head-on approach of TF-61 and its opponent rendered feasible an afternoon strike if the Japanese continued to come on. However, TF-61 flight operations necessitated turning nearly 180 degrees from its base course to steam southeast into the wind and greatly slowed the rate of advance to the northwest. That forced Kinkaid to close well within maximum range before actually launching his strike.

Kinkaid raised speed to 27 knots in a dash toward the target. For some unexplained reason, he preferred to send the *Enterprise*'s inexperienced Air Group Ten on the afternoon attack instead of using the *Hornet*'s deckload strike already waiting in reserve. Possibly VF-10's 58-gallon wing tanks were a factor. They allowed these Wildcats to fly a little further than the *Hornet*'s fighters with only the smaller belly tanks. At any rate the decision proved highly questionable in light of Air Group Ten's subsequent performance.

Again ferreted out by the enemy, Nagumo ran north to resume his assigned position. At 1300, after sending four *Zuikaku* Type 97 carrier attack planes on a search, the *Kidō Butai* main body, soon followed by Abe's Vanguard, retired north out of possible attack range. The *Zuikaku* provided the Vanguard two more carrier attack planes for antisub patrol and three Zeros under Lt. (jg) Araki Shigeru (NA 67-1939) to chase away snoopers.

At 1415 while Nagumo headed away, Base Air Force announced discovery of a powerful American force of two battleships, four heavy cruisers, one light cruiser, and no fewer than twelve destroyers about 30 miles east of Rennell Island. Actually the ships were Lee's TF-64 with the new BB *Washington,* the *San Francisco,* two CL(AA), and six destroyers moving up from Espiritu Santo with the idea of circling northwest around the Russell Islands to derail the Tokyo Express. Kondō wanted the *Kidō Butai* to strike that force if possible but, after calculating the range to the battleships (340 miles), Nagumo demurred. He anticipated no combat the rest of 25 October, but someone else did.

Kinkaid and Hardison decided upon an afternoon search of six pairs of SBDs to check the waters ahead from 280 to 010 degrees out to 200 miles. They would scout out targets for a strike group of sixteen F4Fs, twelve SBDs, and seven TBFs (including Gaines, CAG-10) scheduled to depart an hour later on the median line of the search (325 degrees). Kinkaid intended the attackers to fly out only 150 miles and then, if not informed of suitable targets, to return and land before dark. Somehow these orders became garbled in transmission, leading some of the pilots to believe the outward leg was 200 miles.

At 1336 the *Enterprise* dispatched twelve VS-10 SBDs under Lt. Cdr. James R. Lee (USNA 1928) on search and prepared the thirty-five-plane strike group.[32] Further confusion ensued. Nowhere near the number of assigned planes got off in the launch that began at 1408. The VF-10 contingent comprised only eleven

F4Fs, each equipped with a wing tank. Ensigns M. Philip Long, Donald Gordon, and Lynn E. Slagle from Fritz Faulkner's REAPER 8 missed the rendezvous and returned to the ship. Thus the bobtailed VF-10 escort numbered:

REAPER 4	REAPER 7
Lt. Cdr. William R. Kane (USNA 1933)	Lt. Stanley W. Vejtasa, USN
Lt. Frederick L. Faulkner, A-V(N)	Ens. Edward L. Feightner, A-V(N)
Lt. Frank Don Miller (USNA 1939)	Ens. James H. Dowden, A-V(N)
Ens. Maurice N. Wickendoll, A-V(N)	Ens. William H. Leder, A-V(N)

Lt. Cdr. James Thomas (USNA 1932), VB-10 CO, slipped into the lead slot with only five VB-10 SBDs instead of a dozen, followed by VT-10 XO Lt. Albert P. ("Scoofer") Coffin (USNA 1934) with six torpedo-armed TBFs. Caught in the prop wash of the plane ahead while on its takeoff run, Lt. (jg) George D. Welles's Avenger dipped its right wing for a sickening scrape along the port edge of flight deck. Despite a bent wing tip, the imperturbable TBF seemed OK, so Welles took the mission. Originally Jack Collett in radar-equipped T-1 was to lead the flight, but the flight surgeon refused to release his ailing radar operator. Gaines flew tail-end Charlie in the special CAG TBF without payload.

At 1425, after the last plane departed, the strike group completed a rapid rendezvous and climbed toward the afternoon sun. Enjoying excellent visibility, the fighters worked up to 17,000 feet, while the SBDs and TBFs cruised somewhat lower. As the senior squadron commander, Thomas led the strike according to ComCarPac's July dictum that CAGs serve only as strike evaluators.[33] He headed out on 287 degrees, nearer to the bottom of the search sector than the median, and evidently assumed the enemy had continued closing at high speed and would be farther south than originally thought.

Air Group Ten's first offensive mission was already frustrated, although the crews themselves were ignorant of it. Around 1430, 1st Lt. John H. Buie's second flight of six AAF strike B-17s overtook Abe's Vanguard Force retiring north at 25 knots. At 1510 they executed a level bomb run from 15,000 feet against the battleship *Kirishima* but achieved no hits. Araki's three *Zuikaku* Zeros picked up the gauntlet and claimed one B-17, but all aircraft returned safely. Sounding over the search network at 1510, Buie's contact report informed SoPac that the enemy ships were withdrawing north. Thus Kinkaid knew his strike would never catch up with them. He was irritated that AirSoPac trackers had not informed him earlier, which would have saved him from sending the strike. Given his orders to proceed only 150 miles and return promptly if no enemy appeared, Kinkaid deemed it unnecessary to break radio silence and recall his planes.

At 150 miles Thomas sighted no enemy ships, but with what Kinkaid later described as "excess zeal" to find the enemy,[34] he pressed ahead another 50 miles. Even then, only after flying an additional 80-mile dogleg to the north did Thomas finally swing southeast back toward TF-61. Soon the planes ran short of sunlight and gas. The *Enterprise* had scheduled their return at 1735, about sundown, but they would be late. Meanwhile she landed the search SBDs between 1712 and 1802. All that time the task force ran southeast into the wind, drawing them 20 more miles away from the returning strike planes. As the evening wore on, the task force grew increasingly worried about the overdue group. Kinkaid warned the *Hornet* to prepare to land *Enterprise* aircraft.

Thomas and Gaines kept the SBDs and F4Fs at 17,000 feet until dark. Evidently they thought this was necessary to retain the *Enterprise*'s YE homing signal (line-of-sight) tuned on their Zed Baker receivers, but in fact they could have let down gradually and still rode the YE beam. High altitude especially imperiled the VF-10 pilots, who ran low on oxygen. Several of them had trouble transferring the fuel from their auxiliary wing tank because of poor suction. "Swede" Vejtasa, for example, ruined his gloves by pumping out the whole tank by hand.

The evening turned hazy with no visible horizon before moonrise. Fritz Faulkner, flying in Kane's flight, eased up alongside his leader and signaled him to turn. Listening carefully to the YE signals, Faulkner, an experienced ex-SBD pilot, had plotted the correct course home. Often, the Zed Baker homer proved less reliable closer to the task force, but Faulkner was certain he knew the way. Thinking Kane passed him the lead, he changed course. Looking around a few minutes later, he discovered himself completely alone. Nobody had followed him. In fact, Faulkner's homing technique was accurate. The *Enterprise* appeared dead ahead. He immediately landed, the only one to get back so far.

The rest of the group was not so fortunate. Hindered by low clouds, they searched the seas on a "pitch black night" and kept formation by watching the "reddened exhaust stacks" of the surrounding planes. At 1814 and what later proved to be about 40 miles northwest of TF-61, Lt. Don Miller's F4F lost power and fell back through the formation. He gave a farewell wave to Ens. Edward ("Whitey") Feightner, who later saw him bail out. Miller's wingman, Ens. Maurice Wickendoll, followed F-32 down and observed it splash. In the darkness he could not determine whether the pilot survived. Miller never returned. The squadron attributed his loss to fuel problems and speculated that he perhaps could not transfer fuel from his wing tank.

Descending low over the water, the group reached Point Option, the position where they expected to find the carriers. When the SBD pilots jettisoned their 1,000-pound bombs, one exploded on the water. Its flash revealed an oil slick to a sharp-eyed Vejtasa, who remembered that when he took off the ship had been leaking oil a bit. Figuring he knew her location, he took the lead. This time the fighters followed and soon spotted silver ship wakes ahead.

Although Vejtasa brought VF-10 home after 1830, the pilots now had to land at night, the first time for many of them. Soon Thomas and the rest of the group appeared as well. The *Enterprise* blinkered to the circling planes that fighters should come in first. Waving illuminated wands, LSO Robin Lindsey brought VF-10 on board, but the landings took a long time, with many wave-offs. Waiting on deck for someone to lift his hook, Vejtasa noticed some confusion behind when another F4F landed almost simultaneously with his own plane. It was Whitey Feightner making his first night landing. Fortunately he caught a wire that stopped him from plowing into Vejtasa's tail.[35]

In the low visibility, planes cut each other out of the landing circle. Time finally ran out for one VB-10 pilot, who ditched at 1905. Four minutes later another, Ens. Jefferson H. Carroum, came in high, disregarded Lindsey's wave-off, spectacularly slammed into the island with a sheet of flame, and crushed the tail of Ens. Robert D. Gibson's VB-10 SBD. Fortunately no one was hurt, but both SBDs were strikes.[36] Clearing the flight deck used more valuable minutes. Finally coming in, Scoofer Coffin's TBF faltered in the groove and splash just astern of the carrier. The landings went on until 1925, with lucky George Welles the last to come on board. His bent right wing tip caused him no trouble. At 1927 the last two TBFs in the landing circle, flown by Lt. (jg) Robert S. Nelson and Ens. George R. Wilson, ran out of gas and went into the water. Ultimately two

SBDs (flown by ensigns Dan H. Frissell and Paul M. Halloran) and the three TBFs ditched, and destroyers rescued all of the crews but one VT-10 aircrewman, Arthur M. Browning, Sea1c.

The unsuccessful *Enterprise* search/strike mission cost two lives, plus one F4F, four SBDs, and three TBFs either ditched or damaged beyond repair. As in the Battle of Midway, a controversy erupted between the pilots and the TF-61 staff as to whether the task force had advanced far enough on its Point Option course. The pilots complained the *Enterprise* was not where they expected, but Kinkaid disagreed, pointing out that the strike itself went too far west before starting back. Jim Flatley personally felt TF-61 should have run toward the target at high speed in order to get really close and launch a moonlight strike. The nearly full moon, once it did rise, shone brightly. In fairness to Kinkaid, he based his decisions on information not privy to Flatley or the other air commanders.

NIGHT MOVES

After the *Enterprise* landed her planes, a quiet interlude permitted the principal players to regroup and prepare for battle the next day.

At Guadalcanal the 17th Army troops renewed their ferocious assault on the perimeter and also stormed Marine positions near the Mantanikau River. For the 2nd Division it was to be the last, supreme effort, but the defenders rose to the occasion. The Marines and soldiers held, and CACTUS was safe. Although feisty as ever, Geiger's 1st MAW dwindled to twelve F4F-4s, eleven SBD-3s, three P-39s, and three P-400s in operation.

Returning north, Kondō and Nagumo separately formulated plans and set launch points for the dawn search on 26 October. In essence they were going to try the whole thing over again by steaming south at the proper time and hoping the Army finally succeeded. At 1900 Kondō's Advance Force with the *Junyō* swung around to 180 degrees, while to the northeast Nagumo's *Kidō Butai* conformed about an hour later. Abe's Vanguard Force pushed ahead to take station about 60 miles ahead of Nagumo's main body. The three carriers spotted their CAP, search, and first strike wave deckload on their flight decks, while the *Shōkaku* and *Zuikaku* gassed and armed their second wave strikes on their hangar decks.

Anxiously overseeing the operation from on board the giant battleship *Yamato* anchored at Truk, Yamamoto took the opportunity at 2218 to have Chief of Staff Ugaki summon the forces to battle. They believed strong American naval forces would appear the next day southeast of Guadalcanal and expected the Support Force to crush them. Ugaki urged search pilots to do their utmost to find the enemy. The long-sought decisive battle appeared at hand.[37]

At Espiritu Santo, Fitch took vigorous measures both to defend the island and to find and assail the enemy. Worried about a possible Japanese air strike, he ordered VF-5 at Efate to bring all available F4F-4s to Santo and the 347th Fighter Group to stage in twelve P-39s from Noumea. At the time VF-5 prepared to return to the States as ordered. Indeed, Dave Richardson, Hayden Jensen, Wally Clarke, and Frank Green had already left by air for Pearl Harbor. After dark Simpler reached BUTTON with eight F4Fs, but over Bomber No. 1, they mixed in with B-17s back from the strike. Bob Nesbitt totaled his mount on the new bomber field, still under construction. That left eleven operational F4F-4s at BUTTON, and Fitch hoped to fly some of them to CACTUS the next day should

Japanese naval forces withdraw. To follow up the afternoon strikes, he dispatched a PBY night tracker and later (1730) sent five PBYs, armed with torpedoes or bombs, to search the sector 325 to 350 degrees out to 500 miles. They especially sought enemy carriers. Fitch slated ten PBYs and six B-17s for a dawn search to depart at 0330, 26 October.[38]

Twenty-five October proved particularly hard on Air Group Ten: twelve aircraft (two F4Fs, seven SBDs, and three TBFs) lost to all causes. In addition three SBD and two TBF crews were marooned on the *Hornet*. That day VF-10 lowered four F4Fs from the hangar overhead and put them in commission, giving Flatley thirty-one Wildcats. That night they also brought down the three remaining F4Fs, but did not have the time to prepare them. VB-10 and VS-10 faced the same problem. *Enterprise* operational plane strength now numbered only thirty-one fighters, twenty-three dive bombers (ten VB, thirteen VS) and ten torpedo planes, with an additional three F4Fs and eleven SBDs either as spares or not flyable. Crommelin called his pilots to the wardroom for an excellent, earnest fight talk never forgotten by those present. He explained the situation and stressed what had to be done. While he spoke, the loudspeaker announced to a "mighty roar" that all but one of the ditched pilots were safe. "Uncle John's" final comment to his assembled pilots equally raised morale: "If you get back to the ship and into the groove, we'll get you aboard!"[39]

With the full moon rising, Kinkaid kept the *Hornet* at full readiness to launch Lieutenant Commander Widhelm's moonlight strike of eight F4Fs, fifteen SBDs, and six TBFs should the AirSoPac night search locate carriers within 150 miles of TF-61. At 2115 he came around northwest on 305 degrees, speed 22 knots. Less than thrilled with their assignment to strafe enemy flight decks full of planes, the VF-72 escort pilots knew they faced almost certain ditching in the dark. Although one could even read a newspaper in the moonlight, there was no guarantee that clouds might not settle in. The prospect of ditching a Wildcat at night was not encouraging, for VF-72, unlike VF-10, had not yet received the new seat-pack life rafts attached to the parachute harnesses.[40]

To VF-72's relief, the *Hornet* finally received orders to cancel the night strike and stand down. It became obvious the Japanese would not be within range that night. Murray suggested to Kinkaid that because his pilots would get little rest, perhaps the *Enterprise* might again take the duty (and thereby fighter direction) the morning of the 26th. That offered the added advantage of keeping the *Hornet*'s flight deck spotted for launch, loaded and cocked, so to speak.

The shadow boxing on 25 October positioned the carrier forces of Imperial Japan and the United States for desperate battle on the morrow. The great Japanese land offensive enticed the naval forces of Halsey's South Pacific Area into a more climactic encounter than perhaps he intended. As he wrote a week later, "The yellow bastards have been playing us for suckers."[41] In his mind at least, TF-61's planned sweep north of Santa Cruz was to occur only if enemy carriers did not venture south from Truk. Now in response to the obvious threat to CACTUS and just plain excitement over the chance to destroy enemy carriers, he forgot such caution. Instead of keeping them south of Guadalcanal to counter direct threats against CACTUS, he committed Kinkaid's *Enterprise* and *Hornet* (two-thirds of America's surviving fast carriers) into battle northeast of the Solomons near the limit of Allied land-based air support. The opponents would turn out to be four enemy flattops. The opposing operational carrier plane strengths: 137 U.S. (64 VF, 47 VB, 26 VT) versus 194 Japanese (76 VF, 60 VB, 57 VT, 1 VR) reflected the odds in favor of Japan, not to mention great Japanese superior-

TABLE 18.2
Opposing Carrier Air Strength, Dawn, 26 October 1942

Striking Force (*Kidō Butai*)—VAdm. Nagumo Chūichi
1st Carrier Division—VAdm. Nagumo

Shōkaku	Capt. Arima Masafumi	
Air Group Commander	Lt. Cdr. Seki Mamoru[a]	
Carrier Fighter Squadron	Lt. Shingō Hideki[a]	22 Zero VF (18)
Carrier Bomber Squadron	Lt. Cdr. Seki	21 Type 99 VB (21)
Carrier Attack Squadron	Lt. Cdr. Murata Shigeharu[a]	24 Type 97 VT (24)
Carrier Reconnaissance Unit		1 Type 2 VR (1)
Zuikaku	Capt. Nomoto Tameteru	
Air Group Commander	Lt. Takahashi Sadamu[a]	
Carrier Fighter Squadron	Lt. Shirane Ayao[b]	21 Zero VF (20)
Carrier Bomber Squadron	Lt. Takahashi	24 Type 99 VB (22)
Carrier Attack Squadron	Lt. Imajuku Shigeichirō[b]	20 Type 97 VT (20)
Zuihō	Capt. Obayashi Sueo	
Air Group Commander	Lt. Satō Masao[a]	
Carrier Fighter Squadron	Lt. Satō	19 Zero VF (18)
Carrier Attack Squadron	Lt. (jg) Tanaka Ichirō[b]	6 Type 97 VT (6)

Advance Force—VAdm. Kondō Nobutake
2nd Carrier Division—RAdm. Kakuta Kakuji

Junyō	Capt. Okada Tametsugu	
Air Group Commander	Lt. Shiga Yoshio[a]	
Carrier Fighter Squadron	Lt. Shiga	20 Zero VF (20)
Carrier Bomber Squadron	Lt. Yamaguchi Masao[a]	18 Type 99 VB (17)
Carrier Attack Squadron	Lt. Irikiin Yoshiaki[b]	7 Type 97 VT (7)

Task Force 61—RAdm. Thomas C. Kinkaid

Task Force 16—RAdm. Kinkaid
Enterprise—Capt. Osborne B. Hardison

CAG-10	Cdr. Richard K. Gaines	1 TBF-1 (1)
VF-10	Lt. Cdr. James H. Flatley, Jr.	34 F4F-4s (31)
VB-10	Lt. Cdr. James A. Thomas	14 SBD-3s (10)
VS-10	Lt. Cdr. James R. Lee	20 SBD-3s (13)
VT-10	Lt. Cdr. John A. Collett	9 TBF-1s (9)

Task Force 17—RAdm. George D. Murray
Hornet—Capt. Charles P. Mason

CHAG	Cdr. Walter F. Rodee	1 TBF-1 (1)
VF-72	Lt. Cdr. Henry G. Sanchez	38 F4F-4s (33)
VB-8	Lt. James E. Vose	15 SBD-3s (14)
VS-8	Lt. Cdr. William J. Widhelm	16 SBD-3s (10)
VT-6	Lt. Edwin B. Parker	15 TBF-1s (15)

[a]*Hikōtaichō*
[b]*Buntaichō*

ity in other warship classes. The Japanese carrier air groups included many veteran aviators, while Air Group Ten counted nearly all rookies.

At the risk of second-guessing an aggressive commander eager to get at the enemy, ComSoPac's carrier counterattack now looks like a dangerous, almost foolhardy gesture. However, Halsey strongly believed the carriers must fight in order to save Guadalcanal, and he confidently affirmed they would beat anything the enemy could send against them.

CHAPTER 19

Pounding the *Shōkaku* and *Zuihō*

THE DAWN SEARCH

The night of 25/26 October five radar-equipped PBY Catalinas prowled the key waters northeast of Guadalcanal. There was much to find in the bright moonlight. Two powerful Japanese fleets awaited the final seizure of the hated Lunga airfield before rampaging among Allied ships thought to be rushing to the aid of the beleaguered Guadalcanal garrison. The Japanese admirals rightly suspected an American carrier task force might attack their eastern flank. Thus came to pass the Battle of Santa Cruz.

The skillful AirSoPac search crews soon found what they sought. At 1201 the *Enterprise* monitored a message from PBY 51-P-8 flown by Lt. (jg) George S. Clute of VP-11. It placed "the enemy" about 300 miles northwest of TF-61— much too far for the proposed *Hornet* moonlight attack. Twenty-four minutes later Clute reported attacking heavy cruisers with results unknown. In fact his torpedo had narrowly missed the destroyer *Isokaze* screening Rear Admiral Abe's Vanguard Force about 20 miles south of Vice Admiral Nagumo's carriers. At first Nagumo wondered whether enemy search planes also sighted his carriers, but after 0250 he entertained no doubt on that score. In a lumbering glide bombing run Lt. Glen Hoffman's 91-P-3 laid the nearest of four 500-pound bombs 300 meters off the *Zuikaku*'s starboard side. Dropping a brilliant flare to blind AA gunners, Hoffman exited in spectacular fashion.[1]

The effect on Nagumo was equally spectacular. Convinced he had tripped the long-feared trap, the admiral hastened out of flag plot to the *Shōkaku*'s bridge and personally ordered the task force to reverse course at 0330. Mindful of what befell him at Midway, Nagumo disarmed and degassed the strike planes in the *Shōkaku* and *Zuikaku* hangars. That would delay the dispatch of the second wave. Now he would run north, send his search out before dawn, locate the U.S. carriers, and strike as soon as possible. At 0415 while the main body retired north, Abe's Vanguard reached the scheduled point 250 miles northeast of Guadalcanal, where seven *Tone* and *Chikuma* recon seaplanes left to search south beyond the island. Abe reversed course to follow the main body.

After 0400 the flight decks of Nagumo's three carriers bustled with activity, as figures carrying red-shaded flashlights moved among the dark aircraft. The 1st Carrier Division prepared a comprehensive eastward search 050 to 230 degrees to 300 miles by four *Shōkaku*, four *Zuikaku*, and five of the six *Zuihō* Type 97 carrier attack planes. They took off at 0445, an hour before sunrise.[2] Deckloads totaling 22 CAP fighters and 70 planes for the first strike wave perched on the three carriers:

	VF	VB	VT	VR
Shōkaku	13	—	20	1
Zuikaku	16	22	1	—
Zuihō	18	—	1	—
	47	22	22	1

Tense and expectant, aircrews remained by their aircraft, while Nagumo, wearing "snow-white gloves," fidgeted on the *Shōkaku*'s bridge.[3] At 0520 the *Zuihō* launched the first CAP, three Zeros led by the group commander, Lt. Satō Masao (NA 63-1936), the former *Kaga* fighter CO.

Before dawn TF-61 steamed northwest on course 305 degrees. While the *Hornet* remained on alert, the *Enterprise* as duty carrier prepared the dawn search, IAP, and CAP. Shortly after 0500, Kinkaid came around into the southeasterly breeze, and by 0512 the seven VF-10 F4Fs of Stan Ruehlow's REAPER 3 and REAPER 9 (Lt. Macgregor Kilpatrick [USNA 1939]) left to fly the first CAP in the darkness. Eight pairs of SBDs (six VB-10, ten VS-10) covered the western quadrant 235 to 000 degrees out to 200 miles. Each lugged one 500-pound bomb. Last aloft four SBDs (one VB-10, three VS-10 with VB-10 crews) flew antisub patrol around the task force.[4] TF-61 assumed a Point Option course of 270 degrees. At 0551, just after sunrise, the *Hornet* added seven (soon bumped up to eight) VF-72 F4Fs: Al Emerson's BLUE 5 and Lt. (jg) Frederick "Fritz" Luebke's BLUE 21 divisions.

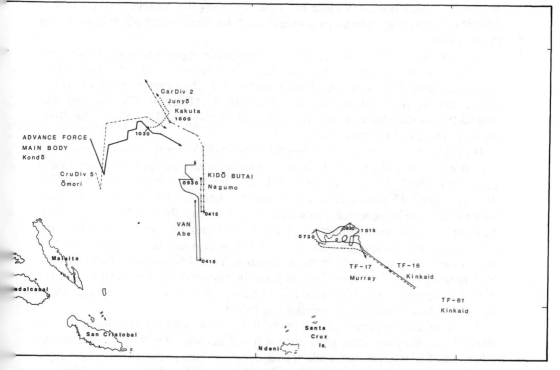

Task force operations, 0000–1200, 26 October 1942.

While his search took off, Kinkaid in his old, torn khaki shirt, trousers, and gleaming polished shoes watched from his flag bridge.[5] At 0512 he finally learned of Hoffman's attack from a routine rebroadcast by the *Curtiss*. At 0310 91-P-3 had radioed, "One large carrier, six other vessels on a southerly course, speed 10."[6] After the battle Kinkaid and Halsey discovered that several TF-61 ships logged Hoffman's original message at 0415, but they thought the *Enterprise* copied it as well. ComSoPac did not exaggerate when he called the incident a "serious communication delinquency."[7] Kinkaid later remarked that had 91-P-3's contact arrived in timely fashion, he would have reduced the size of his search, which consumed valuable dive bombers. At the time he had no reason to believe the enemy had discovered TF-61. His chief of staff, Capt. Edward P. ("Country") Moore, and the other aviators on the staff urged the admiral to loose the *Hornet* planes immediately on a search/strike mission. More cautious than the previous day and mindful of the losses suffered, Kinkaid disapproved and gave up TF-61's last chance to catch the enemy carriers with planes on deck.[8]

The *Enterprise* dawn searchers turned up several important contacts. About 85 miles out, VB-10's XO, Lt. Vivien W. Welch, and Lt. (jg) Bruce A. McGraw, flying due west (sector 266–282 degrees) noticed a Type 97 carrier attack plane approaching from ahead, obviously on the same mission. Passing three miles to starboard was the *Shōkaku* number 2 plane on the 125-degree line from the *Kidō Butai*. Welch later endured some criticism for not breaking off his mission and finishing off the enemy snooper, wrongly thought to have located TF-61. Continuing on course, the two SBDs discovered a powerful enemy force (Abe's Vanguard Force) at 0617. Welch radioed the position of two battleships, one heavy cruiser, and seven destroyers bearing 275 degrees, 170 miles from TF-61 and headed north at 20 knots. Kinkaid received the message at 0639; it confirmed that enemy ships remained close by. After covering the balance of their sector, Welch and McGraw again let pass unmolested the same search plane now also on its return leg.

Bothered by enemy carrier planes, Abe prudently upped speed to 30 knots and turned left to 300 degrees to flee the likely direction of attack. His precautions proved justified. Patrolling the adjacent sector (282–298 degrees) north of Welch, lieutenants (jg) Howard Burnett and Kenneth R. Miller of VS-10 found Abe around 0645 and rolled in from 14,000 feet. Their 500-pounders missed the *Tone*, but AA fire pinked Burnett's plane.[9]

Handling the sector north of Burnett (298–314 degrees), VS-10 skipper Lt. Cdr. Bucky Lee and Lt. (jg) William E. Johnson chanced upon Nagumo's main body about 0645. Circling 15 miles out, Lee reported one carrier, course 330 degrees, speed 15 knots. In the next quarter hour he ferreted out two more flattops but despite repeated messages never heard a "Roger" from base. Now Kinkaid's search had pinpointed all three of Nagumo's carriers, but Lee and Johnson did not escape unscathed. At 0650 lookouts excitedly pointed out two enemy carrier bombers lurking on the horizon. The *Shōkaku* immediately scrambled nine fighters, including four previously assigned the first strike, and the *Zuikaku* responded with eight more. That raised the total CAP to twenty, including Satō's three *Zuihō* fighters already on patrol.

A pair of Zero fighters caught up with Lee and Johnson at 2,200 feet. Lee claimed one with his fixed guns after it holed his windshield, and Johnson the other. The SBDs separated while trying to take refuge in the clouds. Two Japanese latched onto Lee and trailed him for 40 miles, foiling his plan to rendezvous the search SBDs to attack the enemy carriers, but other crews learned of the contact and headed that way. Emerging from the overcast, Johnson smoked a second Zero, but beat it when about five more showed up. From immediately north of Lee, lieutenants (jg) Leslie J. Ward and Martin D. Carmody of VS-10 circled east of Nagumo, hoping to get into attack position. They drew close enough to see two carriers across an open space, but ran afoul of the CAP chasing Johnson. Unable to fight their way through the alert fighters, Ward and Carmody turned back, but not before seeing three Zeros go down in distress (the first to Ward's radioman Nick Baumgartner, Jr., ARM3c, then one each to Carmody and his radioman John Liska, ARM2c).[10]

It appears that seven fighters intercepted the four SBDs and claimed two. They comprised Lieutenant Satō's *Zuihō shōtai*, another trio from the *Shōkaku* led by Spec. Duty Ens. Abe Yasujirō, and a loose *Shōkaku* wingman, PO3c Yano Shigeru. Although no Zeros went down, several expended much of their ammo.

LAUNCHING THE STRIKES

Based on Lee's 0650 report, the TF-61 staff plotted enemy carriers bearing 300 degrees, distance 185 to 200 miles. Their northerly course meant increasing range. Kinkaid ordered the *Enterprise* to strike and blinkered the same message to the *Hornet* about five miles south. At 0708 TF-61 changed course to 330 degrees at 27 knots to close the target until ready to launch the first attack planes. Within three minutes Murray learned from a flag hoist on the *Northampton* of a suspicious radar contact bearing 200 degrees, 28 miles. The interloper circled southeast and closed to 20 miles. This warning of a possible enemy search plane did not reach Kinkaid, although at 0737 the battleship *South Dakota* incautiously broke radio silence on TBS to warn of intercepted Japanese voice transmissions.

The twenty-nine planes (eight F4Fs, fifteen SBDs, and six TBFs) of the *Hornet*'s original moonlight strike rested on deck, while her hangar held the second wave of eight F4Fs, nine SBDs, and ten TBFs (including the group commander's Avenger). The first-wave crews spent a long night with little rest. Now at 0714 the ready room teletypes clattered word of an enemy carrier bearing 302 degrees, distance 196 miles. Captain Mason ordered the crews to seek flattops and settle for other capital ships only if they could not be found. The ticker tapes ended: "Pilots man planes—Good luck."[11] Carrying their plotting boards, the pilots scrambled out of their ready rooms and strode across the flight deck.

Murray brought TF-17 around into the wind, then from 0732 to 0743 the *Hornet* dispatched her first deckload of twenty-nine planes. The irrepressible Lieutenant Commander Widhelm led seven VS-8 and eight VB-8 SBDs, escorted by VF-72's Division 1 (Lieutenant Commander Sanchez) with four F4Fs. Lieutenant Bower's Division 9 (four F4Fs) accompanied Lieutenant Parker's six VT-6 torpedo planes. Each Wildcat sported one 42-gallon belly tank. The second wave manned their planes on the hangar deck and started engines. Murray resumed his base course of 330 degrees, and plane handlers brought the second wave up to the flight deck. Fear of imminent Japanese attack prompted the *Hornet* to dispatch the two groups separately. Accordingly, Widhelm departed with the first group at 0755 on course 300 degrees for an outbound leg of 210 miles. The ship expected him back by 1100.

At 0747 the *Enterprise* turned into the wind and quickly dispatched her second CAP of eleven VF-10 F4Fs (REAPER 2 under Dave Pollock, Bill Kane's

REAPER 4, and Thomas "Bobby" Edwards's REAPER 5). Ens. Gerald V. Davis, one of Pollock's pilots, remained behind due to engine trouble. Because "The Big E" already handled search and CAP, Hardison assigned to the strike only twenty-one Air Group Ten aircraft under Dick Gaines, the CAG-10, whose TBF carried no payload. Preparations, such as they were, strongly suggest a last-minute improvisation as much to clear the flight deck of planes as to hit the enemy. The main striking power rested with nine VT-10 TBFs under skipper Lt. Cdr. Jack Collett. The Air Department hurriedly assigned Lt. (jg) George Glen Estes to lead a token force of three VB-10 SBDs flown by VS-10 crews. Jimmy Flatley limped out on his broken foot to his Wildcat to fly the escort with the eight fighters of his own REAPER 1 flight and Jack Leppla's REAPER 6. Each F4F lugged one 58-gallon wing tank.

Around 0750 the *Enterprise* launched Flatley's eight F4Fs, all but one of the TBFs (Gaines and Jack Collett) and finally Estes' three SBDs. Because mechanics had not finished replacing his damaged right wing, Lt. (jg) George Welles of VT-10 could not depart along with the rest. That left Gaines with twenty planes, including nine TBFs. While taxiing up to the launch officer, each pilot saw two placards. One announced, "*Proceed* without Hornet," that is, do not join with the *Hornet* planes. That contravened Kinkaid's verbal orders for the *Enterprise* strike to rendezvous with the *Hornet* gang if feasible. The second placard announced the enemy's speed at 0730 as 25 knots.[12]

Because Ens. Millard W. Axelrod's F4F propeller malfunctioned, the *Enterprise* sent Ens. Edward B. Coalson to take his place in REAPER 1. With Estes leading the parade, Gaines signaled the departure shortly after 0800 on 304 degrees with a navigational leg of 210 miles. Widhelm's first wave passed by the *Enterprise* planes completing their rendezvous at 2,000 feet. Flatley thought not combining the two strikes to be a serious error.

Ten minutes after her first strike departed, the *Hornet* turned back into the wind, and within two minutes the lead aircraft rolled down her flight deck. Striking power for the second wave rested with Lt. John J. Lynch's nine SBDs (six VB-8, three VS-8), each armed with one 1,000-pound bomb, and nine VT-6 TBFs (four 500-pound bombs apiece) led by VT-6 XO Lt. Ward F. Powell. Arming the Avengers with bombs instead of the far more powerful torpedoes represented an overcautious decision on the part of Murray and Mason. Eight VF-72 F4Fs of Warren Ford's Division 7 and Jock Sutherland's Division 3 made up the escort, and each wore a belly tank. Just after takeoff, Robert Merritt dropped out of Ford's division when his oil pressure suddenly failed, badly overheating the engine. The *Hornet* lacked time to launch an additional fighter, so only seven F4Fs flew the mission. Last to go, group commander Rodee carried no bombs in his TBF. Tom Lea described the procedure for launching the "Sea-Hag":

> His specially marked, fully-manned plane appears suddenly on the empty deck, brought up from the hangar deck on an incredibly fast elevator. It is like Toscanini being magically lifted to the podium by unseen angel hands—a winged, roaring Toscanini about to lead a chorus of warhawks.[13]

Rodee took his departure at 0810 on 305 degrees. He was to return at 1130, a half hour later than Widhelm. TF-61's fragmented strike was en route.

Kidō Butai

Even while his CAP chased the two troublesome carrier bombers, Nagumo received the word he long awaited. At 0658 the *Shōkaku* monitored a sighting report placing one enemy *Saratoga*-class carrier and fifteen other ships bearing

125 degrees, distance 210 miles. Although the call sign was that of the *Shōkaku* number 1 aircraft (140-degree line), WO Ukita Tadaaki's *Shōkaku* number 4 plane on the 110-degree line actually sent the message. Ukita first discovered ships at 0612, but low visibility prevented positive identification, so he turned north to shadow and cautiously confirmed the sighting. While snooping TF-17, his plane appeared on the *Northampton*'s radar. Ukita confused matters by inadvertently using the wrong call sign. Despite doubts about the accuracy of the enemy position report, Nagumo, only too aware from Midway of the folly of delay, did not hesitate. He ordered the 1st Carrier Division to launch its first strike wave, but hedged his bets by sending the *Shōkaku*'s fast Yokosuka D4Y1-C Type 2 carrier reconnaissance plane to check out the 140-degree search line.

After being briefed, the aircrews ran to their aircraft and enjoyed a warm send-off by cheering men lining the decks. First the *Shōkaku* dispatched the Type 2 on its precautionary mission, then at 0710 four escort Zeros (Lt. Miyajima Hisayoshi [NA 66-1938]) and Lieutenant Commander Murata's twenty torpedo-armed Type 97 carrier attack planes started down her flight deck. Murata commanded the whole first strike wave. The *Zuihō* followed at 0715 with five CAP Zeros and her contribution to the strike: nine escort Zeros under Lieutenant Hidaka and one Type 97 carrier attack plane minus payload for contact work. Last of all, at 0725 the *Zuikaku* sent skyward eight escort Zeros (Lieutenant Shirane), twenty-one Type 99 carrier bombers (one other aborted) led by the group commander, Lieutenant Takahashi, and one Type 97 carrier attack plane as a tracker. Murata gathered Hidaka's fighters and left at 0730—25 minutes ahead of TF-61's strike. Takahashi's *Zuikaku* contingent departed 10 minutes later and soon caught up with them. Thus the 1st Carrier Division's initial wave comprised sixty-four aircraft: twenty-one fighters, twenty-one dive bombers, and twenty-two torpedo planes (two minus fish).

With flight decks free, the *Shōkaku* landed Abe's fighter *shōtai* for ammo and fuel, then along with the *Zuikaku* brought the armed second-wave aircraft up on deck. At the same time the *Zuihō* landed group commander Satō's Zero. Overhead twenty-one Zeros prowled the skies, but neither they nor the *Shōkaku*'s radar prevented an especially irritating attack perpetrated by two wide-ranging VS-10 SBDs. Lt. Stockton Birney Strong and Ens. Charles B. Irvine checked their assigned sector (330–345 degrees), then swung southwest toward Welch's battleship-cruiser contact now almost 150 miles away. En route they had the great good luck to copy Bucky Lee's carrier sighting report. After his failure to bomb the *Ryūjō* while on a similar mission on 24 August, Strong was determined to smack this carrier force.

Eighty miles into their detour, the two SBDs came upon part of Nagumo's main body slithering underneath the intermittent cloud cover. While climbing to 14,000 feet, Strong stalked a flattop. After achieving complete surprise the two pilots pushed over at 0740 against what they thought was a *Shōkaku*-class carrier and claimed two hits. Actually their victim was the light carrier *Zuihō* steaming 8,000 meters to port of the *Shōkaku*. One 500-pounder blew a 15-meter hole far aft on her flight deck, which torched a stubborn fire that destroyed all three Zeros parked astern and wrecked her arresting gear. The *Zuihō* could no longer recover aircraft. The sneak attack caused great consternation to the *Kidō Butai*.

Pulling out low over the water, Strong and Irvine ran afoul of three *Zuikaku* Zeros (Lt. [jg] Yoshimura Hiroshi [NA 68-1940]) eager to avenge the assault on the *Zuihō*. The 17th *Shōtai* tailed the two SBDs for 45 harrowing miles, but lost Sea1c Nakagami Kōichi's Zero without downing a Dauntless in return. Both radiomen, Clarence H. Garlow, ARM1c, in Strong's plane and Elgie P. Williams,

ARM3c, with Irvine, claimed Zeros. Thus Strong and Irvine crippled one Japanese flattop and lived to tell of it. During Yoshimura's pursuit, Garlow keyed the heartening message to TF-61 announcing two hits on a carrier, but only a few ships received it. Later Captain Hardison thought so much of the feat that he recommended Birney Strong for a Medal of Honor.[14]

Fearing another Midway debacle when enemy "helldivers" unexpectedly appeared above, the flight deck crews of the *Shōkaku* and *Zuikaku* immediately ceased fueling and pushed all the refueling carts over the side, then redoubled their efforts to get the second wave aloft as soon as possible. Shortly after 0800 the *Shōkaku* made ready to dispatch the five Zeros led by Lieutenant Shingō, the squadron commander, Abe's three CAP Zeros, and Lieutenant Commander Seki's twenty Type 99 carrier bombers. However, on the *Zuikaku,* the air officer grabbed all available personnel, including the flight crews themselves, for a feverish slinging of torpedoes onto fourteen available carrier attack planes. Meanwhile at 0754 the *Zuikaku* landed her four Type 97s from the search and set aside two of them to be serviced for the strike.

Nagumo and his staff pondered whether to delay the *Shōkaku* takeoffs at least half an hour so her planes could accompany the *Zuikaku* force or to split the strike and send Seki ahead on his own. Ever reminded of the bitter lessons of Midway, Nagumo ordered Seki to depart as soon as possible. At 0810 the flagship launched the first plane, and the group quickly formed for departure at 0818. Later PO1c Yamashita Toshihira's Type 99 aborted, leaving Seki with nineteen carrier bombers. Taking advantage of the *Shōkaku*'s clear deck, two Type 97 carrier attack planes from the morning search set down.

Well south of Nagumo's main body, Abe's Vanguard Force held course 300 degrees at 30 knots. From southwest of Abe's ships, Vice Admiral Kondō's Advance Force (less two heavy cruisers and two destroyers recovering search planes) bent on 24 knots on 070 degrees toward Nagumo. This move also cut down the distance to the enemy, so Kondō's own carrier, the *Junyō,* would strike from long range against the American carrier force. At 0740 Kondō (overall commander of the Support Force) ordered Abe to attack the enemy carrier force located by the *Shōkaku*'s search, so he rounded up his ships, spread southwest to northeast across 50 kilometers of ocean. By 0925 the Vanguard had come around to 090 degrees at 24 knots, soon increased to 26. They did not form up in line abreast as before, but gathered in two groups. Abe directly controlled the battleships *Hiei* and *Kirishima,* heavy cruiser *Suzuya,* and the 10th Destroyer Squadron (*Nagara* and four destroyers), while to the southeast was Rear Admiral Hara's 8th Cruiser Division (*Tone* and *Chikuma*) with destroyers *Tanikaze* and *Urakaze.*

The Ambush of Air Group Ten

Riven into three separate flights, the seventy-five aircraft of TF-61's air attack force droned northwest toward Nagumo's carriers. In the lead, Widhelm's fifteen *Hornet* SBDs and Sanchez's four VF-72 F4Fs slowly worked up to 12,000 feet. Intermittent cloud cover soon obscured the second element of his force: six TBFs led by VT-6 CO Parker and Bower's four VF-72 Wildcats. With Bower keeping station a thousand feet above, Parker elected to remain under 1,000 feet, hugging the waves as if he still flew the old VT-5 TBD Devastators. In this case he underestimated the ability of the TBFs, which were perfectly capable of staying close to SBDs.

Flying the trailing Wildcat in Widhelm's strike group, Ens. Phil Souza kept a good lookout in the hazy sky. Near to 0830 and perhaps 75 miles northwest of TF-17, he noticed planes a few miles away to starboard. They were already abeam and about to slide past in the direction of the *Hornet*. So fleeting was the encounter that most of the SBD crews never saw the strangers, but Souza recognized Japanese. He called "Hey Johnny!" to his section leader Tom Johnson and also alerted Sanchez, who quickly warned TF-61 of incoming bandits: "24 dive bombers RED BASE. Approach. Standby for bombing attack."[15] He never heard an acknowledgment. Souza and Sanchez had passed part of Nagumo's first attack group headed southeast, specifically Lieutenant Commander Murata's twenty *Shōkaku* carrier attack planes closely escorted by four *Shōkaku* and nine *Zuihō* fighters slightly above. They cruised a few thousand feet higher than the *Hornet* planes. At the same time the *Shōkaku* crews warned Nagumo of fifteen inbound enemy bombers. Far above Murata, Takahashi's twenty-one *Zuikaku* carrier bombers and Shirane's eight *Zuikaku* Zeros never saw the *Hornet* strike.[16]

A few miles to the east the small *Enterprise* strike of twenty planes nearly paralleled Widhelm's course, but lagged five minutes behind him. Glen Estes' three VS-10 SBDs set the pace with a shallow climb at 115 knots. Behind them VT-10 had formed up in two four-plane divisions: skipper Jack Collett's 1st Division on the right, and behind and to the left the 2nd under Lt. Macdonald Thompson (USNA 1937). To maximize the defensive firepower of the four turrets and the four tunnel guns, each TBF division assumed a new style diamond-shaped "box-step down formation," with three Avengers in a Vee and the fourth directly astern and below them. Jim Flatley's REAPER 1 flight of four VF-10 F4Fs took station on the right and Jack Leppla's REAPER 6 to the left—each slightly ahead and 1,000 feet above their respective VT-10 divisions. Throttles set at 140 knots for maximum range, the Wildcats gently weaved in wide S-turns toward and away from the TBFs to cut down their actual rate of advance. At 120 knots Collett's TBFs did the same so as not to nuzzle the tails of the slower SBDs. Dick Gaines, the CAG-10, trailed the group from slightly above.[17]

By 0835 Air Group Ten had put 60 miles of ocean between them and the *Enterprise*. The SBDs and Collett's TBFs climbed past 6,000 feet and headed higher, while the eight F4Fs weaved a thousand feet above. In his solitary slot high astern, Gaines reached 9,000. Following strict radio discipline, several crews had yet to turn on radios or test their guns. Nobody heard Sanchez's alert or realized that enemy planes threatened them.

From 14,000 feet, Hidaka, leading the *Zuihō* escort, spotted another batch of enemy planes coming in, this time almost dead ahead. Already itchy at the trigger when Widhelm passed by, he could not resist attacking these new interlopers on his own initiative, despite the risk of weakening Murata's escort. He evidently anticipated only a swift attack to break up the American attack before rejoining Murata. Signaling his flight, Hidaka deployed the nine Zeros into a long string:

14th *Shōtai*	15th *Shōtai*	16th *Shōtai*
Lt. Hidaka Saneyasu	Lt. (jg) Utsumi Shūichi[a]	WO Kawahara Masaaki
PO1c Mitsumoto Jirō	PO1c Kawasaki Masao[a]	PO1c Kondō Masaichi
PO3c Takagi Shizuta[b]	PO3c Matsumoto Zenpei[b]	Sea2c Nakamura Yasuhiro

[a] Missing in action
[b] Killed in action

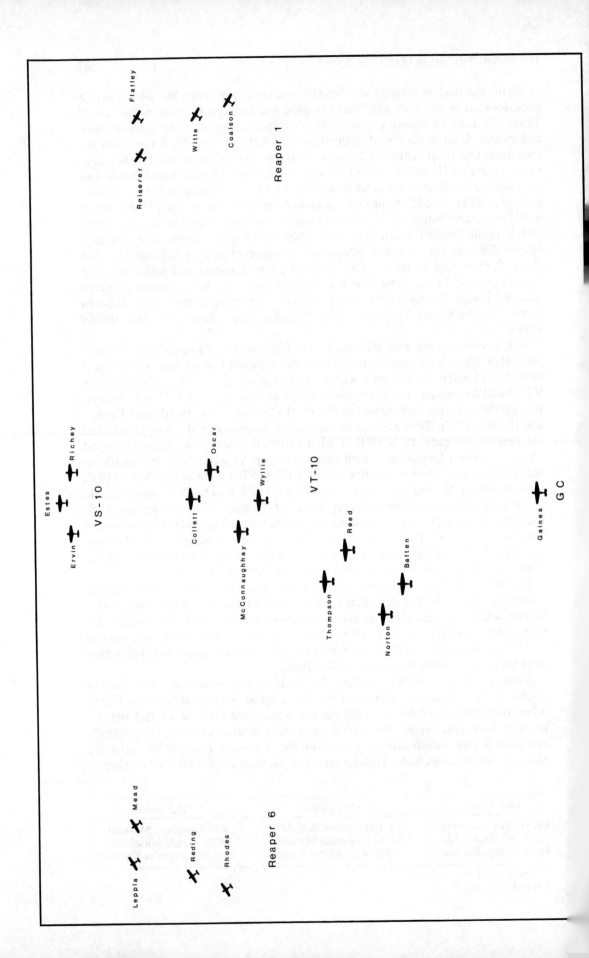

Taking advantage of altitude superiority, Hidaka cleverly set up his ambush to swoop in from out of the sun. A wide 180-degree left turn brought him around to behind the enemy strike group. Rolling into a very steep high-rear run, Hidaka took careful aim against the lead TBF. Bands of red tracers and cannon shells streaking through their formation took VT-10 totally by surprise. Gunfire swiftly set T-1's cockpit and engine ablaze, forcing Collett out onto the right wing. Lt. (jg) Raymond G. Wyllie, in the number 4 slot behind the lead Vee, saw him jump. Seated in the little compartment beneath the turret, Collett's radioman, Thomas C. Nelson, Jr., ARM1c, was startled to feel the Avenger quiver. He glanced out the glass port to starboard and noticed "sheer horror" on the face of Ens. Robert E. Oscar, Collett's wingman. T-1 fell off on its right wing and spiraled toward the water. Quickly buckling on a chute, Nelson kicked open the side door, and threw himself into the slipstream, which whisked off a shoe. A passing Zero spat tracers at him, but he reached the water unhurt. Stephen Nadison, Jr., AM1c, the turret gunner, never left the airplane, while Jack Collett's fate remains unknown.[18]

Most of the VT-10 crewmen never even saw the attacks of Hidaka or PO1c Mitsumoto Jirō, but the third member of the 14th *Shōtai* bore the brunt of retaliation. Training their turrets slightly to their left, the gunners quickly got on target with their single .50s. Lines of tracers converged on PO3c Takagi Shizuta as he dived in from the starboard quarter. Absorbing bullets, the Zero blossomed into flame at 100 yards and veered sharply left. Failing rapidly, Takagi still managed to rake the right wing of Lt. Marvin D. Norton's T-7 on the outside of Thompson's 2nd Division. While shooting back, Norton's turret gunner, Robert W. Gruebel, AMM3c, watched as the Zero "pulled up about 50 or 75 feet above the flight and exploded in a fireball"[19] directly over Lt. (jg) Richard K. Batten's T-11

VT-10, 23 Oct. 1942. *Top row (l to r)*: Rapp, Wyllie, Reed, Oscar, Wilson, Nelson, Batten, Welles. *Bottom row:* Kemper, West, Norton, Coffin, Collett, Thompson, McConnaughhay, Boudreaux. (NA 80-G-30015)

trailing the formation. Debris gouged one of Batten's elevators, but he kept on going. The squadron credited Batten's turret gunner, Rexford B. Holmgrin, AM2c, with the kill. In turn those Japanese following Takagi witnessed his spectacular demise.

One of the 15th *Shōtai* pilots, either Lt. (jg) Utsumi Shūichi (NA 68-1940), PO1c Kawasaki Masao, or PO3c Matsumoto Zenpei, smashed up Ens. John M. Reed's T-10 on the right of the 2nd Division. Busy operating the turret, Murray Glasser, ARM3c, noticed pieces of the greenhouse canopy blow past his head. When Reed shouted "Bail out! Bail out!" over the intercom, Glasser needed no further urging to abandon. Dropping into the radio compartment, he tossed a chest-pack parachute to the radioman, Morse Grant Harrison, ARM3c, grabbed another for himself, then "opened the hatch, backed out, pulled the ripcord, and floated on down."[20] He was the only one to get out before T-10 blew apart. Charles E. Shinneman, ARM3c, the tunnel gunner in Thompson's T-8 flying at the head of the 2nd Division, glimpsed its "engine coming by our wing tip, the prop still spinning."[21] While Glasser chuted in, one Zero splashed beneath his feet. Like Nelson, he ended up alone on the ocean, with only his Mae West to keep him afloat.

The 16th *Shōtai* of WO Kawahara Masaaki, PO1c Kondō Masaichi, and Sea2c Nakamura Yasuhiro concentrated on the rear of the 2nd Division. From his perch ahead and above Batten's T-11, Shinnemann watched holes, "like live coals in a piece of paper," appear inboard on its port wing. Suddenly the aileron stood straight up, as hydraulic fluid burned out in the wing. Holmgrin, T-11's turret gunner, "hollered" over the intercom: "Mr. Batten, our wing is on fire!"[22] Other crews heard Batten respond on the radio: "Get ready to jump, I'll put her in the water. V11 landing in the water. I am on fire."[23] After dropping out of formation, his stalwart Grumman Avenger shed the aileron, but stubbornly continued flying. The destroyed hydraulic system jammed the bomb-bay doors which prevented him from jettisoning the torpedo. Alone, Batten turned back toward the task force.

On the left, REAPER 6 finally became aware of the wolves raiding the henhouse. Apparently Leppla glimpsed only the last few fighters making up the tail end of Hidaka's attack, so he looked to bounce these bandits as they pulled out below and behind. Alerting REAPER 6 to drop wing tanks, he reefed into a hard right turn back toward the TBFs. When Ens. Willis B. Reding, 2nd Section leader, pulled the tank release handle, his engine lost fuel suction, and the F4F dropped like a brick. Although his tank would not release at all, wingman Ens. Raleigh E. ("Dusty") Rhodes loyally spiraled above until Reding regained power. Distracted by their predicaments Reding and Rhodes ended up level with the TBFs. From above Ens. Albert E. Mead, Leppla's wingman, saw his own drop tank narrowly miss first one F4F, then another. REAPER 6 forfeited cohesion at the outset. Leppla and Mead swooped after the last of the Zeros recovering from the first pass on VT-10, yet more bandits tore into them from above and behind. They were Hidaka and PO1c Mitsumoto from the 14th *Shōtai*, who had climbed after finishing Collett. Although left alone, Reding and Rhodes in their faltering mounts were too distracted to fight. REAPER 6 had to shift instantly from attack to defense. Neither section could help the other against the swarming *Zuihō* pilots.

Out to the right and above the TBFs, Flatley's REAPER 1 turned back in after completing the outward leg of an S-turn and beheld a horrifying tableau. Three TBFs, including Mopper Leader (his Annapolis classmate), spun away in flames, and numerous Zeros beat up REAPER 6 now well astern. Only one enemy fighter remained within REAPER 1's immediate grasp. After completing his pass, PO3c Matsumoto, number 3 in the 15th *Shōtai*, boldly winged around for a head-on pass against the lead TBFs. At Flatley's command, REAPER 1 shed its drop tanks, then rolled into a diving turn against the interloper. In succession, the skipper, Lt. (jg) Russell L. Reiserer, Ens. Roland R. ("Cliff") Witte, and Ens. Edward Coalson, snapped full-deflection shots at the Zero, which nosed skyward. Expecting this counter, Flatley led the flight into a tight zoom climb outside and above the twisting target. Coming out over the top, they barreled down into successive high-astern attacks at long range. Streaming smoke, Matsumoto kept straight and level. With a series of high-sides, REAPER 1 dropped the Mitsubishi into the sea. Flatley marked the kill shared by the whole flight.

Someone from the 16th *Shōtai* saw Matsumoto go down, but the Japanese never learned what befell the two remaining 15th *Shōtai* pilots, Lieutenant (jg) Utsumi and PO1c Kawasaki. One of the pair returned for a second go against the remnants of VT-10's 2nd Division. In the meantime "Doc" Norton (USNA 1939) had checked over his battered T-7. With the right wing riddled and hydraulics also gone, he, too, could not go on. Signaling his intention to Thompson, he dropped out. That left Thompson all alone behind the 1st Division and a tempting target. Not long afterward Thompson called over the intercom, "Zero coming up underneath us!" Charging in from below and astern, the Japanese missed, as his tracers fell behind the target. Incautiously he drew too close to the Avenger and Shinneman's single .30-caliber stinger before deciding to break off:

> At that time [the Zero] was underneath and behind us and was a sitting duck as he drifted away. I put about a half canister of .30s into his cockpit. He drifted away and fell off on a wing below us out of sight.[24]

Other VT-10 aircrew likewise saw Shinneman's tracers stitch through the Zero's fuselage. Now two of three 15th *Shōtai* pilots were dead.

After his victory, Flatley quickly assessed the situation, but regretfully realized that he could not rush to Leppla's aid. The mission demanded top priority. Leaving his men in such peril was one of the hardest things Flatley ever had to do. Thompson gathered four TBFs behind the SBDs, which, along with Gaines, the Zeros never bothered. The battered strike group now comprised only five TBFs (including Gaines), three SBDs, and four F4Fs.

In two separate fights REAPER 6 battled the remaining six Zeros. The 14th *Shōtai* of Hidaka and Mitsumoto concentrated on Jack Leppla and Al Mead by alternating head-on and stern attacks against the two beleaguered Grummans. From the outset Leppla fought with only one working Browning, having signaled Mead that sad fact when they tested their guns a few minutes before. Mead was surprised his leader did not assume the beam defense position invented by Lieutenant Commander Thach and recently introduced to VF-10 by Butch O'Hare. He stayed right with Leppla, who, perhaps wounded early in the fight, "seemed to fly straight ahead and I don't believe fired a shot." Mead added, "I shot for both of us and believe I got three."[25] Actually he finished off the third member of the ill-fated 15th *Shōtai*—either Utsumi, a recent flight school graduate, or the veteran Kawasaki. Unseen by either Hidaka or Mitsumoto, one of those two had joined the battle, but after recovering from a run carelessly slow-rolled or looped within Mead's reach and met his demise. Meanwhile, gunfire relentlessly showered the two Wildcats, as the much more nimble *Zuihō* fighters literally flew rings around them. "Popcorn popping" was how Mead described the boom of 7.7-mm slugs ripping through his empennage to impact on the stout armor plate behind his seat. Soon bullets riddled his cockpit and shattered his instruments. A shard from an exploding 20-mm shell tore his ankle.

Finally a head-on pass from either Hidaka or Mitsumoto ended Al Mead's aerial combat career. Engine bruised and failing, he dropped toward the water. Leppla's F4F still struggled in level flight. Mead thought his leader must be dead in the cockpit. Fighting his own battle some distance away, Dusty Rhodes last glimpsed an F4F in dire circumstances with a Zero tucked close on its tail and another screaming in from ahead. No one saw Leppla jump, and he died fighting. Executing a deadstick ditching into the waves, Mead evacuated his battered Grumman before it sank. He inflated the small raft attached to his parachute pack and floated in the strange silence now surrounding him.

Meanwhile, Kawahara, Kondō, and Nakamura of the 16th Shōtai latched onto the hapless Reding and Rhodes. Their swift passes quickly shredded the two Wildcats before they could join and fight as a team. A 20-mm cannon shell squarely in the instrument panel and many 7.7-mm holes through the fuselage knocked out Reding's radio, electrical system, and the circuits to fire his six .50s. At the same time Rhodes's wing tank streamed bright flames until the gasoline burned off. Japanese slugs also transformed his Wildcat into a mess. The instrument panel showed mostly gaping holes, and the Mark VIII reflector gunsight dangled from its mounting cable, which made no difference because Rhodes could not fire his six Brownings either. Bullets even tore away the goggles pushed up on his forehead. Amazed the Wildcat still chugged along, he hoped "he could get this one back to show the guys."[26]

Once Reding and Rhodes got back together, they put on a grand display of defensive weaving according to the Thach doctrine. Deploying abreast, each watched the other's tail. When a Zero dived after the tail of his teammate, the other turned sharply toward the first F4F as a warning. The pilot under attack responded by scissoring his teammate now roaring toward him for a good shot at the bandit. In this case Reding and Rhodes could not even fight back, but their maneuvers seemed to baffle the 16th Shōtai. The Japanese repeatedly reacted in surprise when erstwhile victims inexplicably evaded just at the right moment and received support from another Grumman countering from head-on or the side.

Weaving for about five minutes under constant assault Reding and Rhodes gradually lost height to about 2,500 feet. Rhodes's engine trailed smoke, then seized and stopped altogether with a rigid prop. Nosing down, he hoped to ride his mount to the water and ditch, but more bullets severed the rudder cables, freeing the rudder pedals to slide abruptly "to the firewall." In an uncontrollable aircraft and nearly out of altitude, Rhodes remembered that his instructor at flight school stressed, "never attempt a bail out under 500 feet." At this point he had no choice:

> I had thought about that statement and what to do if one had to bail out at such a low altitude. I pushed the remains of the canopy aft, unsnapped the seat belt then stood up, kicked the stick and pulled the ripcord simultaneously. I was catapulted clear of the aircraft, and the parachute opened almost immediately, snapping my shoes off. At the bottom of the first swing I hit the water.[27]

Safely on the sea, Dusty Rhodes released his chute straps and popped his life raft, and only then noticed a wound in his leg.

Reding saw his wingman take to the silk. Now suddenly on his own with three Zeros jockeying for the kill, he pushed his stick forward and hurtled toward the water as fast as he could go. One particular Japanese kept him company until the Grumman pulled out at 100 feet and used what power remained to hightail it toward TF-16. Doubtless low on ammunition, the Zero relented. From his fish-eye view, Tom Nelson watched Reding exit and one pursuer fly back overhead, while Rhodes observed all three of his erstwhile tormentors, one smoking, draw off to the northwest. Suddenly he, too, noticed the quiet after the roaring engines and gunfire. Nelson, Glasser, Mead, and Rhodes bobbed individually in a lonely sea many miles from rescue.

The ambush gave the Reapers and the Moppers a cruel introduction to combat. Three F4Fs and two TBFs went down; five men died and four others faced an uncertain future on the sea. Two TBFs and one F4F turned back, while a shaken and much weakened strike group pressed on. Dropping wing tanks prematurely severely restricted Flatley's options. Official victory credits amounted to three Zeros for VF-10 (Leppla, Mead, and one shared by REAPER 1), two to Holmgrin, and one to Shinneman of VT-10.

Scattered in the fighting and short of fuel and ammunition, the five surviving *Zuihō* pilots bore tales of battling six Grummans and eight Douglas carrier bombers and neatly claimed all fourteen planes. In return they paid a heavy price: Takagi and Matsumoto shot down, Utsumi and Kawasaki missing, while another Zero (Hidaka or Mitsumoto) sustained heavy damage in the fight with Mead. Instead of rejoining Murata's carrier attack planes, the long, bitter brawl finally forced Hidaka to limp home. Due to Murata's subsequent fate, some Japanese strongly questioned the ambush with recriminations long outlasting the war.[28]

From left of and behind the *Enterprise* planes, the second *Hornet* strike group witnessed the fight. In the half hour after their departure, they slowly climbed to 10,000 feet. The SBDs and TBFs flew in one formation led by Rodee's command TBF, while the VF-72 fighter escort deployed above and out on both flanks. On the right covering VT-6, Jock Sutherland enjoyed an especially good view of the oncoming enemy strike group. Wingman Hank Carey sounded "Tally ho!" Feinting a head-on approach, Lieutenant Miyajima's four *Shōkaku* Zeros scared some VT-6 crews on the right by closing to within 700 yards before breaking off to follow Murata. For their own part the *Hornet* crews sadly watched only two men parachute from the stricken TBFs. Rodee could not help. Neither he nor Murata could afford any more diversions; each sought the other's carriers.

Widhelm Finds the Enemy Ships

Aside from Murata's warning of incoming enemy planes, the *Shōkaku*'s radar also registered the *Hornet* first strike group at 0840, bearing 135 degrees, distance 145 kilometers (78.2 miles). This was a fine performance by the inexperienced Japanese radar team. The CAP numbered twenty-three fighters (see table 19.1). From Nagumo's flag plot, the fleet FDO deployed the CAP at different altitudes to guard against both dive bombing and torpedo attacks—another expensive lesson learned at Midway. The staff preferred to keep most fighters within sight of the carriers, probably due to the poor aircraft radios. Only Warrant Officer Okamoto's three *Zuihō* Zeros ventured south toward the Vanguard Force, apparently to deal with enemy search planes bothering Abe.

At the time of the radar contact, the *Zuikaku* finally completed preparations to launch her second wave: seventeen carrier attack planes (sixteen with torpedoes) under Lt. Imajuku Shigeichirō and WO Shigemi Katsuma's four Zeros. While

TABLE 19.1
Japanese Combat Air Patrol, 0910, 26 October 1942

Shōkaku (9 Zeros)		*Zuikaku* (7 Zeros)	
Lt. (jg) Kobayashi Hōhei	2	Lt. (jg) Araki Shigeru	3
Spec. Duty Ens. Abe Yasujirō	3	Lt. (jg) Yoshimura Keisaku	2
PO1c Ōmori Shigetaka	4	PO1c Itō Junjirō	2

Zuihō (7 Zeros)	
WO Okamoto Shigeru	3
PO1c Yamamoto Akira	2
PO1c Moriyama Gonji	2

turning into the wind, the *Zuikaku* and two destroyers separated from the rest of Nagumo's force. Imajuku departed at 0900.

Simultaneous with these flight operations, two American search planes approaching from different directions happened to sight the *Kidō Butai*. From the southeast, Lt. (jg) Enos L. Jones in a VP-24 PBY flying boat glimpsed a "large cargo vessel" (actually the *Zuikaku*) escorted by two destroyers. The *Curtiss* failed to copy his contact report. Three harmless *Zuikaku* carrier attack planes forming up overhead chased the Catalina out of the area.

Closing from the southwest, Lt. (jg) George F. Poulos in 11-P-8 maneuvered within visual range of the enemy ships until he recognized at least one carrier, then withdrew to send his contact report. It noted position and the enemy's composition: one carrier, three heavy cruisers, and four destroyers, course 050 degrees, speed 18 knots. Atmospherics or Japanese jamming (they certainly guarded most American frequencies) affected reception and forced his radioman to repeat many times. Finally at 0925 the *Curtiss* acknowledged the transmission. Meanwhile, Poulos started back north to amplify the contact, but also ran afoul of the outbound *Zuikaku* strike. He barely radioed, "Enemy CV aircraft," before Shigemi's four escort Zeros jumped him. Certain they splashed the PBY, they swiftly rejoined the carrier attack planes. Poulos had to retire. Several times his PBY and others rebroadcast the original sighting report, but only in mid-afternoon did TF-61 copy it.[29]

About 20 minutes after passing the enemy strike group, Gus Widhelm noticed ship wakes ahead. They were the *Tone* and *Chikuma* (Rear Admiral Hara's 8th Cruiser Division) escorted by the *Tanikaze* and *Urakaze*. For the last 40 minutes the Vanguard Force had steamed east on 090 degrees at 26 knots toward the American task force, but during high-speed maneuvering Hara lost contact with the rest of Abe's ships. By 0850, Hara was only 150 miles northwest of TF-61. At the same time Nagumo's main body retired north to increase the distance to the enemy carriers.

After scanning the area, Widhelm radioed escort leader Mike Sanchez at 0850: "Gus to Mike: Do you see carriers?" The reply came over as "Mike to Gus: No carriers in sight out here. Let's return."[30] That answer did not please Widhelm at all, who was convinced, as were his companions on the strike, that Sanchez actually spoke those craven words. (A week later at Noumea, Gus even took a swing at Sanchez, but the poor man was unjustifiably defamed. The culprit was a Japanese attempting radio deception. That day the enemy had successfully intercepted both the U.S. search/attack and fighter direction frequencies.)

Widhelm hunted far bigger game than some cruisers. Continuing on 300 degrees, he soon left Hara astern. Twenty miles beyond the first group of enemy

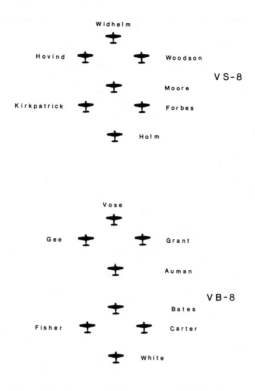

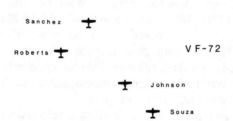

Formation of the top echelon, first *Hornet* wave.

ships, another task force appeared in the haze well off to his left. Intending to climb a little for a better look, Widhelm radioed Sanchez at 0905: "Gus to Mike: I'm going up. Help me dive bomb." He wanted fighter cover to support his attack. Soon he surveyed a mixed group of two battleships and some cruisers and destroyers and reported the two battlewagons. They comprised the main body of Abe's Vanguard Force, namely the *Hiei* and *Kirishima* of the 11th Battleship Division, the *Suzuya* (flagship of Rear Admiral Nishimura's 7th Cruiser Division), light cruiser *Nagara* (flagship of Destroyer Squadron 10), and the four destroyers *Makigumo*, *Akigumo*, *Yūgumo*, and *Isokaze*. At 0910 the *Isokaze* warned the other ships of intruders.

Deployed in standard cruise formation, Sanchez's VF-72 Division 1 with four

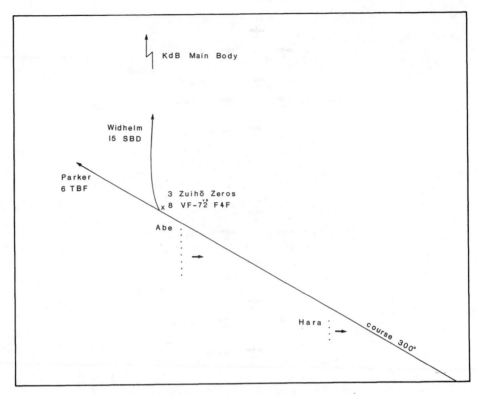

KdB   Main Body

Widhelm
15 SBD

Parker
6 TBF

3 Zuihō Zeros
x 8 VF-72 F4F

Abe

Hara

course 300°

The first *Hornet* wave makes contact, 0850–0915

F4Fs cruised at 12,000 feet—behind and slightly *below* the fifteen VS-8 and VB-8 SBDs. The *Hornet* planes all shuffled along at 120 knots. While passing east of the battleship-cruiser formation, one SBD crew piped up at 0910: "Tally ho dead ahead; Tally ho down below two Zeros." Warrant Officer Okamoto and his two *Zuihō* wingmen, PO1c Seki Kazuo and Sea1c Maki Masanao, swiftly climbed over their opponents, then crossed left to right over Widhelm's formation. Confronting the VF-72 F4Fs with great tactical superiority, Okamoto rolled into a high-side run to take out the Grumman fighters flying astern of the dive bombers. Some SBD crews watched the Zeros come around, but the Japanese had already dived before VF-72 became aware of them.[31]

Flying the last F4F on the right, Phil Souza realized with a sick feeling that he was the immediate object of Japanese desire. The dreaded Zeros impressed him by their appearance ("beautiful and shiny") and by the expertise of their long high-side approach. Pulling the release lever for his 42-gallon belly tank (it failed to drop), he jammed the throttle forward, then warned Tom Johnson, his section leader, to scissor the incoming attackers. Souza essayed a sharp climbing right turn into the lead Zero, but the F4F flew too slowly to maneuver crisply. In his diving turn, Okamoto compensated superbly for deflection and riddled Souza's right wing and fuselage. The impact of numerous 20-mm cannon shells exploding on its right wing actually pushed old F-25 into a violent snap-roll to the right, but that at least sent Souza away from further harm. As Okamoto pulled out ahead and below the formation, Sanchez evidently took a shot, which forced the Zero to continue diving.

When the next Grumman inexplicably remained in level flight, Seki in the second Zero modified his dive to jump directly on its tail. Taking advantage of

Ens. Phil Souza in the cockpit of his VF-72 F4F, with Howard Schumacher, AMM1c, early 1943. (Cdr. P. E. Souza)

the excellent angle, he swiftly raked Johnson's F4F, then, like Okamoto, recovered below and ahead of the target. Coming out of his involuntary roll, Souza chanced to find Seki almost directly in his sights. One long burst from his six .50s exploded the Mitsubishi like a bomb. At the same time Johnson pitched out of control and rode the Wildcat all the way to the water. About to stall, Souza finally noticed that his F4F behaved strangely. Okamoto's caress had jammed the right aileron in the up position. Despite full aileron tab, Souza kept the stick far to the left just to fly level.

Maki, the third assailant, drew down against the next F4F—Willie Roberts, Sanchez's wingman, who must have tried diving away. Below and to his left Souza happened to see a Zero shoot up the tail of a Grumman. Closing, he fired. The target flashed and trailed smoke, but kept on going, so Souza was not certain he finished it. At any rate, all the Japanese disappeared after only one devastating pass through Division 1, which killed Tom Johnson (also Seki, his assailant) and badly hurt Willie Roberts. Souza flew up alongside Roberts's battered F4F, which showed numerous holes and a stream of gasoline. The cockpit seemed bathed in blood from a fearful wound in Roberts's left shoulder. At 0915 Souza advised, "Let's get out of here." The only way home he knew was the reciprocal bearing of the outbound leg. Meanwhile, Sanchez fruitlessly scouted the area, looking for his division and also the SBDs.

Okamoto and Maki happened to spot more enemy aircraft below—the four VF-72 F4Fs of Jack Bower's Division 9 cruising 2,000 feet over Parker's TBFs. The two *Zuihō* pilots set up another ambush and crippled Bower's plane, seen to dive into the water. At low altitude Bob Jennings, Bob Sorensen, and Roy Dalton swiftly regrouped and avenged their leader. Sorensen and Jennings each claimed a probable Zero, and one of them did kill Okamoto. Meanwhile, Parker pressed on unmolested by Zeros. Indeed he never saw enemy fighters and only later noticed the absence of his escort. The three F4Fs rejoined at low altitude near Abe's force, and Sorensen led them toward home plate.

Okamoto's interception cost VF-72 two Wildcats and pilots and two others badly damaged (one pilot gravely wounded). It also separated the escort from its charges, as no F4Fs went beyond the Vanguard Force. Low speed and poor tactical deployment meant defeat for VF-72. Maki, the sole surviving Japanese participant, did not see his *shōtai* leader go down but, with eight bullets in his Zero, he later landed on the *Junyō*. For his *shōtai* he claimed three Grummans for two Zeros and pilots. The only CAP element to report fighting Grummans, the Okamoto *shōtai* did a fine job, but at a heavy price.[32]

Crippling the Shōkaku

Seeing Okamoto's three *Zuihō* Zeros rip through the *Hornet* escorts, Gus Widhelm alertly evaded with a right turn north toward some clouds. At sea level Parker missed the maneuver and kept his six VT-6 Avengers pointed on course 300 degrees out beyond the Vanguard Force. The two components of the *Hornet* first wave did not regain contact until they met back over TF-61.[33]

Widhelm's impromptu turn proved to be the key decision of the whole attack. Five minutes later, after passing through the clouds, he noticed more ship wakes and smoke perhaps 25 miles ahead and off his left. He radioed, "Contact bearing about 345." Soon he discerned one carrier and several destroyers and, not far from the first, another, smaller flattop that billowed thick, black smoke. Widhelm had found flagship *Shōkaku* and the light carrier *Zuihō* still burning after Strong's bomb hit 90 minutes before. Nearby but hidden by the overcast, the *Zuikaku* completed the launch of her second strike. Several times Widhelm tried raising the second *Hornet* strike perhaps 60 miles astern. Rodee never heard him, but the *Enterprise* strike leaders certainly did. Widhelm announced enemy carriers: "I have one in sight and am going after them."[34]

On the northern edge of the clouds Widhelm's fifteen dive bombers encountered opposition at 0918 in the form of four *Shōkaku* Zeros flown by PO1c Ōmori Shigetaka, PO1c Kodaira Yoshinao, PO3c Komachi Sadamu (all 13th *Shōtai*), and Sea1c Itō Tomitarō (18th *Shōtai*). Similar to VT-10, the *Hornet* SBDs flew in diamond-shaped sections of four, but deployed in a column stepped down to the rear—far superior in firepower and control to the usual Vee-of-Vees.

A veteran of *Akagi*'s CAP at Midway, Ōmori, the 13th *Shōtai* leader, knew from bitter experience the danger posed by enemy carrier bombers. Determined to break up their attack, he rolled into a nearly vertical head-on slice through the SBD formation, while the others opted for side and overhead attacks directed mainly against the planes on the right and in the rear. Within two minutes, two *Zuihō* Zeros, PO1c Yamamoto Akira and PO1c Mukai Tasuke, latched onto the intruders. Widhelm used various defensive maneuvers to foil the aim of the relentless CAP pilots. In the rear seat, George D. Stokely, ARM1c, carefully watched the individual Zeros as they flashed in from behind and warned what type of run they were making. With high-siders Widhelm countered with a turn toward the attacker. Against the rarer overhead runs, he nosed down to evade. Inevitably the SBD formation loosened up. To the rear the VB-8 planes drifted off to the right in response to Widhelm's repeated right turns and reversals back on course.

Testing the enemy commander's nerve, Ōmori reprised his first attack with a second unusual diving head-on run against the leader. Widhelm had no worry on that score. As the Zero closed in, he walked .50-caliber tracers into its cowling and at 100 yards exploded its engine. Ōmori pushed over to ram, but at the last instance Widhelm ducked beneath the burning Mitsubishi, which disintegrated above the formation. From their vantage points, Ōmori's teammates felt certain he crashed the lead bomber at the cost of his own life. They much admired his fighting spirit. The quiet, conscientious Ōmori received a posthumous double promotion two ranks to special duty ensign.[35]

As the SBDs overhauled the *Shōkaku* from astern, five *Zuikaku* Zeros tore into them: 14th *Shōtai*—Lt. Araki Shigeru, PO1c Kamei Tomio, and Sea1c Egawa Yoshitake; 18th *Shōtai*—PO1c Itō Junjirō and PO3c Takayama Takashi. Thus a dozen fighters battled Widhelm's SBDs. Kobayashi's and Abe's five *Shōkaku* Zeros stayed low to guard against torpedo attack, while Yoshimura's pair (17th *Shōtai*) flew direct cover over the *Zuikaku*. The Japanese had most definitely learned to layer their CAP.

The *Kidō Butai* knew enemy planes bore down on them, but two events provided momentary distraction. At 0910 came the long-awaited word that their own first strike was attacking an American carrier. About the same time the high-speed Type 2 carrier reconnaissance plane buzzed the *Shōkaku* after checking out the 140-degree line. A bum radio prevented it from reporting its findings. Before bringing it on board, the *Shōkaku* launched a Type 99 carrier bomber (PO1c Ishiyama Kenjirō) as another contact plane. Evidently, due to mechanical trouble the D4Y1-C ditched just astern. While the *Amatsukaze* picked up the crew, her lookouts spotted approaching carrier bombers.[36]

One cagey *Zuikaku* Zero (a silver airplane sporting two red fuselage bands) hovered over the right side of the SBD formation, "stalking us," according to VB-8 pilot Lt. (jg) Kenneth B. White, the Tail-end Charlie. Widhelm also saw it poised balefully, but then another high-side attack distracted him. Waiting just for this moment, the *Zuikaku* pilot rolled into a swift overhead against the leader. Lt. (jg) Clayton Evan Fisher from VB-8 noticed the "sickly blue flashes" of its 20-mm cannons. The run was a beauty, as shells and bullets punctured Widhelm's left wing, tail, and engine. Oil pressure dropped alarmingly, and the powerplant streamed black smoke that trailed through the whole formation. His air time now measured in minutes, Widhelm added power to hold formation, but the engine quickly overheated. He was in deep trouble, but he was not the only one. Soon after, White dropped out when a Zero detached the left aileron and holed his left arm. He drifted down into the clouds, dumped his bomb, and escaped.

Another *Zuikaku* pilot attacking about this time left a lasting impression upon everyone who saw his end. From behind the SBDs, PO1c Kamei Tomio (14th *Shōtai*) dived in very fast, made his firing pass, then tried the usual recovery to soar back for another run. He never made it. Pulling too many Gs, the Zero shed one wing without flame or smoke, then part of the other. To Lt. (jg) Roy P. Gee of VB-8, it was the "darndest thing" he ever saw. Stripped of its airfoils, the fuselage knifed into the water. Kamei never bailed out.

About 0925 and still a few miles short of the pushover point, Widhelm's engine froze despite his earnest coaxings, leaving its prop rigid in front of the cowling. For several minutes his men had wondered how long the stricken Dauntless

Lt. Cdr. William "Gus" Widhelm, CO
of VS-8, late 1942. (NA 80-G-33758)

could hold out. Glancing over at his leader, wingman Lt. (jg) Ralph B. Hovind
saw Widhelm rage at not being able to lead the final descent against the carrier.
About the time Widhelm finally relinquished the lead slot, he loosed his anger
over the radio, letting all and sundry know what he thought of Sanchez and the
lack of fighter support. Other *Hornet* aviators heard his outburst and admired the
broad range of his vocabulary. Eavesdropping as he shepherded Roberts back
home, Phil Souza thought the whole thing "very hilarious." Widhelm ditched the
battered Dauntless, then he and Stokely took to their life raft hoping to see the
Hornet flyers plaster the big flattop. Tom Lea well described Widhelm's sterling
qualities:

> He was born to fly; he was born to lead men; he was born to fight. He was the stuff
> of which heroic tradition was made . . . . In all things he stuck his square chin out
> and dared the world to take a poke at it.[37]

After Widhelm dropped out, tactical command passed to Moe Vose, but the
formation had already dispersed as VB-8 drew up abreast and to the right of
VS-8. During the final approach, several more SBDs took heavy damage. A Zero
massaged Fisher's Dauntless with 20-mm shells and among other things knocked
out the hydraulic system. Fisher sought refuge in the clouds. This time a fighter
followed and inflicted even more damage. Only the skill of radioman George E.
Ferguson, ARM3c, kept the bandit at length. Near to the dive point, Lt. Fred L.
Bates looked down and saw VB-8 wingman Lt. (jg) Phil Grant fall away, his
Dauntless torn by bullet strikes. An ammo belt ripped from the rear twin .30s
briefly hung on its horizontal stabilizer. Grant faded rapidly out of sight, and no
one saw what happened to him and radioman Floyd D. Kilmer, ARM2c. Thus
during the approach two of fifteen SBDs (Widhelm and Grant) went down and
two (White and Fisher) were forced to withdraw prematurely.

At 0927 five VS-8 SBDs on the left finally reached the pushover point against
the *Shōkaku* twisting below at over 30 knots. Soon Vose's five VB-8 Dauntlesses
came in from the south. "The skies were filled with white and yellow smoke," as
the ships cut loose with AA.[38] For the *Shōkaku* it was a replay of the 8 May
Coral Sea attack, only worse. Captain Arima avoided the initial three or four
bombs, but in close succession several thousand-pounders struck home. After a

VB-8, Aug. 1942. *Top row (l to r)*: Friesz, White, Christofferson, Lynch, Tucker, Vose, Bates, Auman, Wood. *Bottom row:* Cason, Grant, Gee, Adams, Barrett, Nickerson, King, Carter, Fisher (USN via J. C. Sawruk)

charred chunk of wooden flight deck plopped into Bates's cockpit, courtesy of a hit by Vose, he added his bomb to the inferno raging amidships on the great carrier. Another bomb had hit aft knocking out AA guns and crews. The shattered deck prevented flight operations, and severe fires destroyed her center elevator and much of the hangar as well. In contrast to Midway, flames cooked off no negligently stored bombs or torpedoes, but did apparently engulf one of the two Type 97 carrier attack planes parked on deck. Although fires burned out of control for five hours, the *Shōkaku* could still steam at 31 knots. She faced mortal danger only if the Yankees attacked again.

After their daring recoveries, the *Hornet* SBDs still battled the Zeros that followed them down. Their numbers included *Zuihō* pilots PO1c Moriyama Gonji and PO3c Tochi Hajime, who had roughed up the search SBDs. While Lt. Ben Moore (VS-8), Lt. (jg) Donald Kirkpatrick (VS-8), and Roy Gee (VB-8) withdrew together, one Japanese pilot ("a real hot shot") riddled all three in succession. One 20-mm shell penetrated the pilot's armor, lacerated Moore's neck, and made a mess of the cockpit and windscreen. The radioman, Ralph Phillips, ACRM, was hit in the arm. The Japanese also wounded Kirkpatrick's gunner, Richard T. Woodson, ARM2c. His guns dry, the enemy pilot briefly flew wing on Gee and smartly tossed him a salute before breaking off. A similar thing happened to Ralph Hovind. Other SBDs took battle damage on the way out, but none succumbed. After barely missing the destroyer *Teruzuki* with his bombs, Lt. (jg) Stanley R. Holm got in some licks of his own firing his last few rounds of .50-caliber at the heavy cruiser *Kumano*. The SBDs proudly claimed four to six hits on the enemy carrier and fifteen Zeros downed by joint action. The only radioman given direct credit for a Zero was James Black, Jr., ARM3c, in Holm's plane. In due course Vose collected nine SBDs into loose formation, but the other four pilots separately found their way home.

Now with two carriers out of action, the *Kidō Butai* risked a knockout blow if the remaining *Hornet* and *Enterprise* strikes could score. In the battle against

Widhelm's SBDs, the CAP claimed sixteen carrier bombers for the loss of Ōmori and Kamei shot down and PO3c Tochi later ditched.

Northwest of Abe's Vanguard Force, Edwin Parker's six VT-6 torpedo-armed TBFs never copied Widhelm's sighting reports—another instance of horrible U.S. communications so evident in this battle. After covering 210 miles on 300 degrees, Parker scouted west and north 50 more miles, searching the horizon in vain for enemy carriers. Unwittingly he ended up too far south and west to sight Nagumo. Fuel becoming critical, Parker decided to have a go at the battleships and cruisers he had passed by.

AIR GROUP TEN VERSUS THE *SUZUYA*

Reduced by ambush to four F4Fs, five TBFs, and three SBDs, Air Group Ten pressed ahead in hopes of finding the Japanese carriers.[39] The fighters and TBFs completed their climb to 10,000 feet, while Dick Gaines (CAG-10) went even higher. In the lead Glen Estes with three SBDs at 9,000 feet lost sight of the *Hornet* first wave in the many scattered cumulus clouds. From the rear Jim Flatley noticed the second *Hornet* strike group on his port quarter and at about 0855 unsuccessfully urged Gaines or Thompson, leading VT-10, to join them for mutual protection. Disgusted at the pennypacket strike groups launched by both carriers, Flatley felt strongly that one large force accomplished much more than several small ones.

Between 0915 and 0920 Flatley and Thompson eavesdropped on Widhelm's reports to Rodee of an enemy carrier, but neither realized that the *Hornet* first strike had turned north instead of continuing northwest. Although they saw Hara's ships off in the distance, Thompson already noticed Abe's main body to the west: "There is another group of ships 270 way over there. Let's go." He swung toward them; Flatley and Gaines followed. One of them remarked, "Did you pick up that other task group? I have lost them."[40] At the same time Estes and his two SBD wingmen missed their turn to the west and kept flying northwest toward a very large cumulus cloud mass.

Thompson soon approached the Vanguard Force main body: *Hiei, Kirishima, Nagara, Suzuya,* and four destroyers, but unfortunately no carriers. He led the group out beyond the Vanguard Force and in particular checked out the seas behind a bank of towering white cumulus clouds, but sighted nothing. T-1's ASB-1 aerial search radar might have proved invaluable in this situation. By radio Thompson asked REAPER LEADER if his F4Fs could persevere another 90 miles, but Flatley demurred. Because they dropped wing tanks nearly an hour before, the VF-10 pilots retained insufficient fuel for an extended search.

At 0930, Thompson reversed course to attack the nearest capital ship, a heavy cruiser on the western flank of the enemy force. At the same instant, Widhelm's *Hornet* SBDs pounded the *Shōkaku* over the northern horizon. While Gaines circled overhead taking pictures, Thompson led the four TBFs into a high-speed torpedo attack against the *Suzuya*'s port side. As the ship turned away to starboard at top speed, VT-10 drew close enough to fire their fish at 0937. Only two torpedoes released, and both missed. Lt. James McConnaughhay (USNA 1939) later had to dump his, but Ray Wyllie quickly returned for a second go, this time from off the starboard bow. The sleek cruiser handily evaded that missile as well. Flatley's four F4Fs did their best to support VT-10 by strafing the cruiser and drawing fire, but inflicted little damage. The *Suzuya* ceased fire at 0938, when the nine *Enterprise* aircraft withdrew southeast.[41] On the way back, Air Group Ten missed Hara's 8th Cruiser Division to the east. Discouraged by the air attacks, Abe pressed northwest away from the American carriers.

ATTACKS ON THE 8TH CRUISER DIVISION

Around 0915 Glen Estes' three VS-10 SBDs sighted Hara's small force of the *Tone*, *Chikuma*, *Tanikaze*, and *Urakaze*, spared by Widhelm's first *Hornet* strike. They continued searching the area for juicier targets. Walt Rodee's second *Hornet* strike group (seven F4Fs, nine SBDs, and ten TBFs), the only U.S. force still intact, appeared five minutes later and endured some AA potshots from Hara's force while taking a good look at the ships.[42]

On the flight out, Rodee's crews unfortunately heard the infamous "Mike to Gus" message that so enraged Gus Widhelm. Heading the nine SBDs, Lieutenant Lynch never copied Widhelm's subsequent contact reports and reasoned that if Widhelm, with his 20-minute head start, missed carriers, they must have steamed north out of range. He advised Rodee that if not otherwise ordered he would attack the cruisers. Hearing no reply, Lynch led the SBDs and Warren Ford's three VF-72 F4Fs against the *Chikuma*. Rodee and escorts, Dave Freeman and Al Dietrich, likewise broke formation to return to the cruiser force, but

The *Chikuma* maneuvering to evade attack, 26 Oct. 1942. The four eight-inch gun turrets of this class of heavy cruiser are all located forward of the bridge. Photo taken from Cdr. Walt Rodee's TBF. (NA 80-G-30614)

Ward Powell's nine bomb-armed VT-6 TBFs, accompanied by Jock Sutherland and Hank Carey from VF-72, maintained the original northwest course. Thus the second *Hornet* strike fragmented as well, reflecting the bane of American carrier aviation.

From 0926 to 0931, exactly the same time the *Hornet* first-wave SBDs bombed the *Shōkaku* some 50 miles north, Lynch's dive bombers pushed over against the much less important *Chikuma*. Ford's top cover encountered no aerial opposition, while Rodee photographed the attack to evaluate the damage. First Lynch's six VB-8 SBDs sliced downward, then Lt. Edgar E. Stebbins's VS-8 section. The *Chikuma,* like sister *Tone,* presented an unusual appearance with all four eight-inch turrets located forward of the bridge, leaving room astern for a sort of flight deck for float planes. At 0926 one VB-8 thousand-pounder exploded on the port side of her bridge and knocked out the main battery directors. Five minutes later a VS-8 bomb smashed the starboard half of the superstructure. The two heavy hits demolished the bridge, wounded Capt. Komura Keizō, killed the XO, and inflicted severe casualties on the crew. Splitting up, Lynch's SBDs headed back at low level. Ford also took his fighters home. They had pounded a heavy cruiser, but poor communications and a lack of perseverance prevented the bombing of something that really mattered—an enemy flight deck.[43]

After peeking behind the cloud mass to the northwest, Estes turned the three VS-10 SBDs back south toward Hara's force and the wounded *Chikuma*. After Lynch's Dauntlesses departed, Estes, Lt. (jg) Henry Ervin, and Lt. (jg) John F. Richey dived at 0939 against what *Enterprise* air intelligence later guessed was the fast battleship *Kongō*. Actually two of the three 1,000-pound bombs landed close aboard to starboard of the unlucky *Chikuma*. One opened a "big hole" in her side, which let water into the starboard fireroom and reduced her speed. Although the SBDs had faced no appreciable AA on the way in, the Japanese let them have it low over the water. Even worse, three wide-ranging Zeros from the *Kidō Butai* CAP lunged against the trailer, Richey, whose radioman, Jay B. Pugh, ARM3c, thought he splashed one fighter. In the quick skirmish neither side sustained loss. A few minutes later Estes spotted a lost F4F flying somewhat erratically, "all over the sky." It was Mike Sanchez, who surprised Estes by nonchalantly lighting a cigarette. After getting his bearings, Sanchez disappeared ahead.[44]

While Lynch and Estes plastered the *Chikuma,* Ward Powell's 2nd Division of VT-6 and two VF-72 escorts pressed northwest at 10,000 feet, but found no fresh targets. At 0945 more of the enemy CAP turned up, but only *Zuikaku* pilots PO1c Itō Junjirō and Sea1c Takayama Takashi noticed the Americans. Itō screamed in with a head-on run, forcing Powell's 2nd Division to adroitly open formation to let him pass by. He claimed one torpedo plane out of the ten he thought present and withdrew. Takayama followed with an opposite attack of his own and vaulted the TBFs. Swinging wide to follow up with a high-side run, he crossed below and in front of the two Wildcats flown by Jock Sutherland and Hank Carey cruising 4,000 feet above and behind the Avengers. Swiftly sighting in, Sutherland cut loose at 400 yards with an excellent full-deflection shot and held the proper angle until the Zero exploded only 100 yards ahead. He even had to brave the debris. His marksmanship impressed Carey tremendously.

By coincidence, both VT-6 divisions—Parker's 1st at low altitude and Powell's 2nd at medium height—converged almost simultaneously against Hara's two cruisers. Disappointed after a fruitless search, Parker returned the way he came, missing Abe's battleship force, but rediscovering the ships he first

TABLE 19.2
Task Force 61 Strike Groups

Hornet 1st Strike
Dive Bombers

1st Division (VS-8)	2nd Division (VB-8)
S-1 Lt. Cdr. William J. Widhelm[a]	B-1 Lt. James E. Vose, Jr.
Lt. (jg) Ralph B. Hovind	S-19 Lt. (jg) Roy P. Gee
Lt. (jg) William E. Woodman	B-12 Lt. (jg) Philip F. Grant[a]
Lt. Ben Moore, Jr.	B-7 Lt. (jg) Forrester C. Auman
S-2 Lt. (jg) Donald Kirkpatrick, Jr.	(8-)B-8 Lt. Fred L. Bates
Lt. (jg) James M. Forbes	(10-)B-8 Lt. (jg) Clayton Evan Fisher[b]
S-6 Lt. (jg) Stanley R. Holm	S-22 Lt. (jg) William D. Carter
	B-13 Lt. (jg) Kenneth B. White

Torpedo Planes (VT-6)

Lt. Edwin B. Parker, Jr.[b]	Lt. (jg) Karl B. Satterfield
T-7 Lt. (jg) Rufus C. Clark[a]	Lt. (jg) John M. Armitage
Evan K. Williams, AP1c	Lt. (jg) Jack Kopf, Jr.[b]

Escort Fighters (VF-72)

Division 1	Division 9
F-13 Lt. Cdr. Henry G. Sanchez	Lt. John C. Bower, Jr.[a]
Lt. (jg) William V. Roberts, Jr.[b]	F-12 Lt. (jg) Robert H. Jennings
Lt. Thomas C. Johnson[a]	F-17 Lt. (jg) Robert E. Sorensen[d]
F-25 Ens. Philip E. Souza[c]	F-21 Ens. Roy B. Dalton

Enterprise Strike
Torpedo Planes (VT-10)
GC Cdr. Richard K. Gaines

1st Division	2nd Division
T-1 Lt. Cdr. John A. Collett[a]	T-8 Lt. Macdonald Thompson
T-2 Ens. Robert E. Oscar	T-10 Ens. John M. Reed[a]
T-3 Lt. James W. McConnaughhay	T-7 Lt. Marvin D. Norton[b]
T-4 Lt. (jg) Raymond G. Wyllie	T-11 Lt. (jg) Richard K. Batten[b]

T-6 Lt. (jg) George D. Welles[b] (tookoff alone at 0840)

Dive Bombers (VS-10 crews)

B-2 Lt. (jg) George Glen Estes, Jr.
B-9 Lt. (jg) Henry N. Ervin
B-19 Lt. (jg) John F. Richey

Escort (VF-10)

REAPER 1	REAPER 6
F-26 Lt. Cdr. James H. Flatley, Jr.[g]	F-8 Lt. (jg) John A. Leppla[a,c]
F-18 Lt. (jg) Russell L. Reiserer[g]	F-13 Ens. Albert E. Mead[a,c]
F-29 Ens. Roland R. Witte[g]	F-25 Ens. Willis B. Reding
F-15 Ens. Edward B. Coalson[g]	F-34 Ens. Raleigh E. Rhodes[a]

Hornet Second Strike
Torpedo Planes
GC Cdr. Walter F. Rodee
2nd Division (VT-6)

Lt. Ward F. Powell	Lt. (jg) Humphrey L. Tallman[b]
T-12 Lt. (jg) Frank A. Elam[b]	Lt. (jg) Robert M. Weeks
Ens. Fred D. Hoover, Jr.[b]	Ens. John Cresto[b]

Lt. (jg) John E. McInerny, Jr.
Lt. (jg) John E. Boudreaux [VT-10]
Lt. (jg) Jerome A. Rapp, Jr.[b] [VT-10]

TABLE 19.2 (cont.)

Dive Bombers
2nd Division (VB-8)

B-11 Lt. John J. Lynch	B-16 Lt. (jg) Frank E. Christofferson
B-5 Lt. (jg) Joe W. King	B-14 Lt. (jg) Thomas J. Wood
B-6 Lt. (jg) J. Clark Barrett	B-4 Lt. (jg) Henry J. Nickerson

Section (VS-8)

S-4 Lt. Edgar E. Stebbins
B-9 Lt. (jg) Philip J. Rusk
S-12 Lt. (jg) Albert H. Wood

Escort (VF-72)

Division 7	Division 3
F-31 Lt. Warren W. Ford[d]	F-37 Lt. John F. Sutherland[f]
Lt. (jg) Morrill I. Cook, Jr.[a]	F-28 Lt. (jg) Henry A. Carey, Jr.[d]
F-4 Lt. (jg) Henry A. Fairbanks[e]	F-35 Lt. (jg) David B. Freeman, Jr.[d]
	F-23 Lt. (jg) Alfred E. Dietrich[d]

[a]Shot down/missing in action
[b]Ditched
[c]Claim: 1 VF
[d]Claim: 1 VB
[e]Claim: 2 VB
[f]Claim: 1 VF, 2 VB
[g]Claim: 1 VF shared

sighted an hour before. At 0951 the six TBFs executed a torpedo strike against flagship *Tone,* which responded with violent maneuvering at top speed. Five pilots dropped their fish (as the *Tone* correctly reported) and claimed three hits. However, all missed the target. It appears that Parker was unable to fire his torpedo. After attacking the *Tone,* the VT-6 crews noticed far to the north a towering cloud of black smoke—the burning *Shōkaku.* With payloads expended, the 1st Division headed home.

The nine bomb-armed TBFs of the 2nd Division flew about 30 miles beyond Hara's ships before Powell decided further searching to be useless. Turning back, he selected the already battered *Chikuma* for a glide-bombing attack and personally put a third bomb, this time a 500-pounder, through a torpedo mount aft. The blast set afire an Aichi Type 0 reconnaissance seaplane on the starboard catapult. Burning furiously from all the attacks, the *Chikuma* lost 192 dead and 95 wounded, but could still make 23 knots. From his life raft, Widhelm got a good look at her limping north and described her stern turrets as "melted," not realizing these CAs featured no turrets aft.

Torpedo Six sustained no loss in the attack and claimed five bomb hits on a heavy cruiser. Lt. (jg) Humphrey L. Tallman (another former VF-8 pilot) separated when all four 500-pound bombs failed to release. He followed with a lone attack against either the *Urakaze* or *Tanikaze* and reported a hit on a light cruiser. During the bombing runs, Sutherland and Carey supported the TBFs by strafing the destroyer nearer to the *Chikuma* and shot up her bridge, but observed no return fire. That brought back memories of a very similar strafing run on 4 June at Midway, when they shot up the *Mogami* and *Mikuma.* At 0959, with the completion of the attack, the two F4Fs joined seven TBFs, but Lt. (jg) Jerome A. Rapp, Jr., and "Hump" Tallman flew back alone.

By 1000 the crews from the three U.S. strikes all headed home, no doubt wondering what occurred in their absence. Kinkaid shot his bolt for this battle. Committed piecemeal with poor coordination due to shocking failures in communications, the seventy-five planes failed to yield results commensurate with their numbers. As the Japanese had hoped, the Vanguard Force drew the most attention. If not for Birney Strong and Gus Widhelm, no Japanese carriers would have sustained damage. United States fighter escorts proved largely ineffective, continuing a trend evident in all of the carrier attacks to date. Immediate losses for the TF-61 strike groups totaled five F4Fs, two SBDs, and two TBFs. For various reasons other planes would ditch later. The carrier *Shōkaku* and the heavy cruiser *Chikuma* sustained heavy damage. Five CAP Zeros failed to return and one ditched, while Hidaka's *Zuihō* escort, acting in a CAP role, lost four.

CHAPTER 20

"*Hornet* hurt"

THE DEFENSE PREPARES

As the last strike planes disappeared westward, TF-61 immediately switched from offense to defense. Kinkaid planned to hold his Point Option course northwest toward the enemy and meet the expected counterblow with every available fighter and gun barrel.

Cdr. John Griffin, the new *Enterprise* FDO (REAPER BASE), retained seven F4Fs (REAPER 2—Pollock and REAPER 5—Edwards) 10,000 feet over TF-16 and placed Kane's REAPER 4 (four F4Fs) southward between the two task forces. To conserve their fuel and oxygen, he did not deploy the CAP higher than 10,000 feet for the time being. Unaware the enemy had spotted TF-61, he anticipated that radar would give ample warning to send the fighters higher when necessary. Strangely, no one informed him of Kinkaid's visual message blinkered at 0811 to the rest of TF-16 stating his belief (possibly based on the *South Dakota*'s notice of intercepted aircraft radio transmissions) that the Japanese had located the task force. Ultimately, Griffin's decision to keep the CAP at 10,000 feet proved disastrous, but the blame rested mainly in a stunning failure of the carrier radars to pick up enemy strikes at hitherto normal detection ranges.

For the *Enterprise* (TF-16) and *Hornet* (TF-17), the first task at hand was to refuel CAP fighters now aloft for nearly three hours and to augment their numbers. With her flight deck open for business, "The Big E" landed Ensign Axelrod's malfunctioning escort F4F at 0816 and the seven REAPER 3 (Stan Ruehlow) and REAPER 9 (Mac Kilpatrick) Wildcats. Because VF-10 lacked enough operational planes for all of its divisions, these pilots reluctantly relinquished their mounts—Ruehlow's planes to Swede Vejtasa's REAPER 7 and Kilpatrick's to Fritz Faulkner's REAPER 8. Crommelin added one to round out Faulkner's flight to four. In addition, Jerry Davis in F-2 was ready to go, while Ruehlow and Kilpatrick manned the two spare fighters. After the fueling detail topped off all tanks, the eleven Wildcats (equipped with one 58-gallon wing tank apiece) started taking off at 0830 to circle TF-16 at 10,000 feet.

About 10 miles southwest, the *Hornet* likewise attended to the vital reservicing of VF-72's CAP. At 0814 she landed "Moose" Merritt's oil-starved Wildcat from the second strike, then at 0822 launched the eight F4Fs of her second CAP—divisions 4 and 5 led by Red Hessel and Bob Rynd. Allan Fleming, the *Hornet* (BLUE BASE) FDO, sent them scurrying to 10,000 feet over TF-17. Next the *Hornet* took on board her first CAP of seven F4Fs. One Wildcat's landing gear collapsed on deck. Fritz Luebke's Division 6 turned over their mounts to Ken Bliss's Division 8, and the 2nd Section (Andy Lowndes and Bill Moran) of Al Emerson's Division 2 likewise had to stay behind. In the meantime, Merritt climbed into the spare F4F to increase Emerson's rump Division 2 to three. The seven fighter pilots waited for the signal to go, while Commander Gouin's Air Department struck the two inoperable F4Fs below to the hangar deck.

About 0830, Sanchez's distant warning of incoming enemy planes ("Stand by for dive bombing attack") sounded loudly, if not clearly, at TF-61. At 0837, before Emerson could get away, Kinkaid broke radio silence on the TBS to order the *Hornet:* "Launch all planes immediately. Jap planes coming in."[1] Snatches of frantic transmissions from Air Group Ten hinted at the fierce battle raging 60 miles northwest. At 0840 the *Enterprise* hurriedly sent Lt. (jg) George Welles aloft to clear the deck of a fueled and torpedo-armed Avenger. Crommelin intended him merely to mark time until it was safe to return, but in the haste of the launch nobody passed on the word. In the absence of definite orders, Welles polled his crew, Earl B. Bjerke, AM2c, and Lee F. Hollingsworth, ARM3c, to see what they should do. Hollingsworth later wrote, "We all voted to go kill something." They bravely sortied alone to take on the Japanese fleet.[2] With all her operational aircraft aloft, the *Enterprise* resumed the westward base course toward the enemy.

The TF-16 CAP numbered twenty-two VF-10 F4Fs, half of which circled at 10,000 feet, with the rest slanting up toward that height. Eight VF-72 F4Fs neared 10,000 feet over TF-17. The *Hornet* turned southeast into the wind to launch seven more under Emerson (BLUE 5) and Bliss (BLUE 29), then resumed 330 degrees. Thus Kinkaid wielded thirty-seven fighters, enough to break up the attack, but only if deployed on time to the right place.

Radars in both carriers should have picked up the approaching bandits at 75 miles or more, but they remained clear. Listening in "The Big E" 's radar plot, Griffin heard someone, thought to be a nearby aircraft or ship, warn of dive bombers "off to port." (The transmission actually originated from one of the beleaguered Air Group Ten strike planes.) As TF-16 was steaming northwest on 330 degrees, that message seemingly placed intruders to the south. Nothing appeared on the radar screen, but Griffin thought it useful to repeat the warning to the CAP aloft. At 0842 he broke radio silence on the fighter direction circuit to tell REAPER 5, REAPER 2, and the BLUE CAP: "Look for Hawks [VB] on port bow and port quarter. Angels [altitude] probably high." He added, "Look south of REAPER BASE." Cloud cover or violent maneuvers often made estimating bearings relative to the carrier very difficult, so the pilots especially disliked them and later severely criticized the FDO for using them. In fact, the radio logs show that Griffin rarely relayed information couched in relative bearings, and did so only when he had nothing better to send.[3]

On the basis of intercepted *Hornet* strike transmissions, Murray warned at 0843 on TBS of an attack coming in from 275 degrees. To Kinkaid, TF-16 appeared more in the path of a likely enemy strike, so at 0844 he informed Murray that REAPER BASE would handle fighter direction. Normally, the *Enterprise,* as the the duty carrier, would retain control of the CAP. The VF-72 pilots greatly resented this arrangement because they had the utmost confidence in their own experienced FDO, Al Fleming.

The minutes ticked past menacingly with Griffin growing increasingly concerned. Very likely a raid was building to the west, but the *Enterprise*'s radar screen inexplicably remained clear. So did the *Hornet*'s. At 0847 Griffin recalled

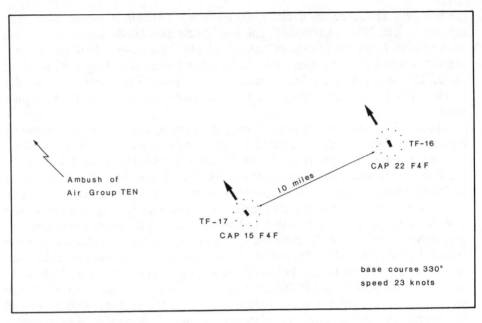

TF-61 situation, about 0840.

REAPER 4 from its post halfway between the two task forces and told Kane to watch for planes to the southwest. The next minute he decided, in the absence of radar contacts, that it was vital to alert the *Hornet* high CAP to "protect BLUE BASE." Likewise puzzled because no enemy contacts disturbed the *Hornet*'s radar screen, Fleming repeated REAPER BASE's warning and told Hessel and Rynd to orbit overhead. What was happening?

Actually, the CXAM radars on board both carriers malfunctioned badly and in effect blinded the FDOs. The enemy indeed bore down on TF-61. Neither Griffin nor Fleming knew that at 0841 the excellent CXAM radar team on Rear Admiral Good's flagship *Northampton* with TF-17 had detected bogeys bearing 295 degrees, distance 70 miles and closing. No doubt confident the carriers already had the contacts, Good forwarded her sightings by flag hoist to TF-17 rather than announcing them immediately over TBS. Consequently that vital information only reached Fleming after some delay, and Griffin in the *Enterprise* never learned of it at all.

At 0853 sharp-eyed members of Murata's *Shōkaku* Carrier Attack Squadron spotted ahead and to their left ship wakes of an American task force. Drawing closer, they recognized one carrier, two cruisers, and four destroyers. Cloud cover obscured TF-16 to the east of them. The twenty Nakajima B5N2 Type 97 carrier attack planes cruised at 14,000 feet accompanied by two unarmed Type 97s from the *Zuikaku* and the *Zuihō*. Only Lieutenant Miyajima's four *Shōkaku* Zeros escorted, for Lieutenant Hidaka's nine *Zuihō* Zeros never rejoined. Above at 17,000 feet group commander Lieutenant Takahashi led twenty-one Aichi D3A1 Type 99 carrier bombers from the *Zuikaku* Carrier Bomber Squadron, while behind and 4,000 feet above, Lieutenant Shirane's eight *Zuikaku* Zeros watched for Grummans.

Murata instructed his radioman, PO1c Mizuki Tokunobu, to send "*To-tsu-re* [Assume attack formation]." At Pearl Harbor Mizuki had ridden with Cdr. Fuchida Mitsuo and tapped out the famous message "*Tora Tora Tora* [Tiger, Tiger,

Tiger]" announcing the complete surprise of the U.S. Pacific Fleet. Now Murata was about to sting the Americans again. Out of fighter range, the two contact planes peeled off to observe the strike results and look for fresh targets.[4]

Two minutes after the Japanese sighted TF-17, Fleming finally had something on radar. At 0855 he dispatched Hessel and Rynd westward on 260 degrees (M.) against "a fairly large bogey" 35 miles ahead. At the same time the *Enterprise* radar finally registered its first contact, bogeys bearing about 255 degrees, 45 miles. Griffin shifted REAPER 2 and REAPER 5 15 miles west of base at Angels 20 and added, "Large group now 20 miles from base." The raid was developing quickly.

Bustering westward with eight VF-72 F4Fs, Red Hessel knew from the Air Group Ten radio chatter with its grim talk of parachutes and planes going down in flames that this was the real thing. Believing that 10,000 feet was certainly not enough altitude, he started climbing. It was a significant decision. At 0859 wingman Tom Gallagher ("who could see like an eagle") sang out, "BLUE 14 Tally ho, dead ahead Angels 17." Fleming immediately responded, "What have you got? To Red from Al, what is composition of Tally ho?" Gallagher replied, "I think they are Hawks, Angels 17."[5]

Out in front of VF-72 the distant specks resolved into the whole Japanese strike group: fifty-five planes poised in a "compact, formidable looking column" of fighters, dive bombers, and torpedo planes. Bound to the southeast, the Japanese crossed from starboard to port ahead of the F4Fs. Fleming acted swiftly to get Hessel some help. Within a minute of Gallagher's report, he dispatched the rest of the BLUE CAP, Emerson and Bliss, out on 250 (M.) toward bogeys 20 miles southwest and at 17,000 feet or above. These seven F4Fs clawed for al-

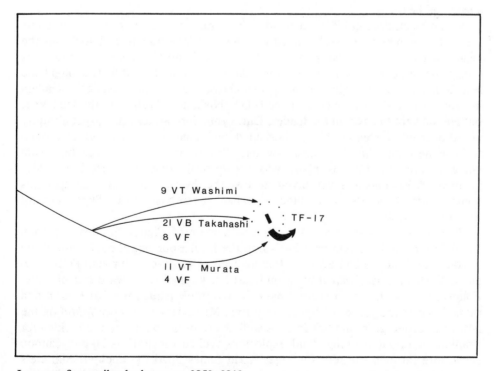

Japanese first-strike deployment, 0850–0910.

titude. Thus the *Hornet* belatedly committed her CAP to battle. In turn Griffin urged REAPER 7 (Vejtasa) and REAPER 8 (Faulkner), "Climb, climb!"

Intermittent cloud cover prevented the *Zuikaku* contingent from seeing the target until 0858. At that moment Mizuki keyed the letters "*To-to-to* [All forces attack]"—a most welcome sound for Japanese listeners far and wide. Cheated of enemy carriers at Pearl Harbor, Midway, and Eastern Solomons, Murata made the most of his unparalleled opportunity for the first coordinated Japanese torpedo and dive-bombing attack since the Coral Sea battle. Choosing "Attack Method B," he had divided the carrier attack planes for simultaneous torpedo attacks from both bows of the carrier. To evade the eight Grummans barreling in from ahead, he nosed down into a shallow, high-speed dive toward the enemy task force. From the rear of the column, nine Type 97s of the 2nd *Chūtai* under Lt. Washimi Gorō (NA 65-1938) broke off to the north. Murata took the 1st *Chūtai*'s eleven *kankōs,* covered by all four *Shōkaku* Zeros, southward against the opposite flank. Theoretically they would trap the carrier no matter how she wriggled.

FIRST CONTACT

From 17,000 feet Takahashi's twenty-one *Zuikaku* carrier bombers dipped down into a gradual descent toward the eventual pushover point at 12,000. They flew a column of three seven-plane *chūtai:* Takahashi's 1st, the 2nd under Lt. Tsuda Toshio (NA 63-1936), and the 3rd led by Lt. Ishimaru Yutaka (NA 66-1938). Shirane's eight Zeros occupied the usual Japanese escort slot well above and behind the bombers—poor position from which to block fighters charging in from ahead and below.

As the black dots in his windshield swiftly transformed themselves into dark-green dive bombers, Hessel singled out the lead Vee hoping to knock out the leader at its apex and disrupt the whole attack. With Gallagher tucked on his right wing, he banked sharply left for a flat-side run at 15,000 feet, brought the lead *kanbaku* into his sights, then zoomed above to attack position again. Gallagher roughed up the left outside plane (PO2c Nishimori Toshio) in the lead Vee, but Hessel kept his eye on the leader. During his third attack, the target abruptly nosed over into a steeper dive and escaped into some clouds. His quarry proved to be none other than Takahashi, whose "frantic maneuvers saved him from being shot down, but his plane was so seriously damaged that the rudder jammed."[6] Takahashi never dived against the *Hornet,* but later dumped his bomb. During Hessel's short vendetta, Gallagher ran Nishimori's Type 99 out of formation as well.

Fanning out to starboard, Hessel's 2nd Section of Claude Phillips and John Franklin followed the two lead F4Fs into the fray. Bouncing the left side of the middle Vee (Tsuda's 2nd *Chūtai*), Phillips walked his tracers through PO2c Tsuchiya Yoshiaki's *kanbaku* trailing outboard. It lurched downward out of view. Following through with a second pass, he overtook Ishimaru's 3rd *Chūtai* and riddled one of the planes of Spec. Duty Ens. Murai Hajime's 27th *Shōtai* on the left. The second go-round left Phillips well astern of the bombers and looking for Franklin. Without warning, loud explosions racked the F4F as 20-mm cannon shells tore through the rear fuselage. Acrid fumes filled the cockpit. Shirane's own 11th *Shōtai* Zeros joined battle with a vengeance. Dreading fire, Phillips pushed back his canopy and made ready to abandon, but the smoke soon cleared. To his horror he saw Franklin under savage attack. Reefing hard around after one assailant's tail, Phillips rapidly slowed, but nevertheless rolled into a quick head-on run that brushed the Japanese off Franklin. Holed in numerous places and with its rudder in shreds, the Wildcat pitched into a steady dive toward the water. Phillips disengaged and followed, hoping to see Franklin bail out, but the aircraft plunged into the sea near the task force. John Franklin was the first VF-72 pilot to die in battle. His own airplane in bad shape, Phillips limped off at low altitude. For this phase of the action he later claimed two dive bombers.[7]

Ishimaru's 3rd *Chūtai* in the rear also fell prey to Bob Rynd's four F4Fs barreling in from behind Hessel's division. With a shallow side attack, Rynd singled out one dive bomber, but the hawk adroitly rolled out of the way with a skill that impressed Rynd's wingman, Ens. George Wrenn. From above and behind, WO Osanai Suekichi's 12th *Shōtai* surprised Rynd. One overeager Zero overshot out ahead. Eager to bag that interloper, Rynd pursued by climbing steeply. Wrenn tried to follow, only to lose airspeed alarmingly fast. Nosing over, he picked up speed, but a Zero buzzed his tail, forcing him to keep diving. Wrenn's impromptu escape placed him in great position to wreak havoc on torpedo planes far below. The 12th *Shōtai* likewise hustled Rynd out of the fight, but not before he claimed two dive bombers (one probable).[8]

Last of the VF-72 fighters to intercept the *Zuikaku* carrier bombers, Rynd's 2nd Section of "K. C." Kiekhoefer and Lt. (jg) Paul Landry barely rolled into their first run against the hapless 3rd *Chūtai* before PO1c Noda Mitsutomi's 13th *Shōtai* (the last two top-cover Zeros) appeared. Even so, while Noda and wingman PO1c Nagahama Yoshikazu worked in behind them the two F4Fs smoked one Type 99. Beneath the dive-bomber formation, the two F4Fs split up. Against a Zero that flashed in front of his guns, Kiekhoefer replied with a strong burst. It smoked, rolled over in evident distress, and fell away. Victim of the second Japanese, Landry dived out of control straight toward the sea. Meantime, his assailant chased Kiekhoefer toward the refuge of a cloud.[9]

Beset by the eight F4Fs of BLUE 13 and 17, the *Zuikaku* Carrier Bomber Squadron disintegrated. Takahashi's erratic flight caused the 1st *Chūtai* to drift off to the north as they tried to stay with their crippled leader. Tsuda's six undamaged 2nd *Chūtai* Type 99s forced their way through the gap, trailed by PO2c Tsuchiya's *kanbaku,* roughed up by Phillips. They escaped the VF-72 F4Fs. Not so fortunate was Lieutenant Ishimaru's 3rd *Chūtai,* in which at least two *kanbakus* suffered heavy damage. Like the 1st *Chūtai,* CAP pressure crumbled the 3rd.

While the Zeros ripped through the other F4Fs, Hessel and Gallagher tagged a lone Type 99 ahead, whose pilot aggressively scissored for an opposite approach. Both sides held the run to the limit, but at the last instant before colliding Hessel pushed over and Gallagher pulled up. The Japanese split the difference. Coming back around, Hessel watched the *kanbaku* abruptly nose over into a vertical dive all the way to the sea. Evidently the enemy pilot had died or passed out during the head-on run. Hessel learned a valuable lesson: Don't try to bluff a dead man. Out of ammunition and shot up, he descended toward the *Hornet* hoping to land and rearm, while Gallagher tangled with more 3rd *Chūtai* Type 99s, which repaid him with bullets. Ditching his battered F4F near the task force, Gallagher broke out his life raft before the Wildcat sank. Each pilot received credit for one dive bomber destroyed and two probables.[10]

The eight BLUE 13 and 17 F4Fs claimed four dive bombers and one fighter, as well as seven dive-bomber probables. Perhaps three carrier bombers (all 3rd *Chūtai*) went down, and three others sustained severe damage. The cost was heavy: three F4Fs (Franklin, Landry, and Gallagher). Shirane's Zeros drove the others out of the fight.

After avoiding most of the first CAP wave, Tsuda's 2nd *Chūtai* soon encountered the second. The radar plot showed the enemy swinging south of TF-17, so at 0904 Fleming steered the seven VF-72 F4Fs of Al Emerson's BLUE 5 and Ken Bliss's BLUE 29 left to 225 degrees (M.). Flying last in the loose formation, Dick Hughes, another pilot gifted with excellent eyesight, noticed a small flight of dark-green dive bombers crossing ahead to the north and 1,000 feet below. By the time he could alert Bliss, they slipped past. The four BLUE 29 F4Fs turned around, but Emerson in the lead never got the word. Bliss overtook only one dive bomber—PO2c Tsuchiya's damaged Type 99 trailing the other six of Tsuda's 2nd *Chūtai*. It immediately dived when the F4Fs tailed in behind. With a series of wingovers and other talented flying, PO3c Katō Motomu, Tsuchiya's pilot, led Bliss's division on a merry chase down toward the ships. That dismayed Hughes, who knew more hawks lurked at high altitude. Passing 5,000 feet, Bliss, with an assist from wingman Robert Holland, finally set the Type 99 streaming thick, black smoke. George Formanek also thought he gunned down the cavorting Aichi, but Hughes never fired. The fight dispersed BLUE 29 at fairly low altitude west of the screen.[11]

Greatly worried whether his second wave ever found the enemy, Fleming kept calling Emerson after 0905 and finally said, "Hey Rube" (return to base if he found no enemy planes). At 0910 Emerson replied no contact, but Bliss exulted, "Have shot down one hawk, don't see any more around." By this time Tsuda's carrier bombers and Murata's torpedo planes had begun their runs against the *Hornet*. Her defense now rested on AA fire, VF-10 pilots roaring down from the northeast, and a formidable VF-72 wingman, George Wrenn.

As the Japanese strike closed TF-17, Griffin on the *Enterprise* tried desperately to sort out the situation. About the time VF-72 first made contact, he asked Fleming whether his radar showed more than one flight of bogeys. Fleming replied, "Negative, one group spread out." Finally realizing that all the Japanese had circled south after TF-17, Griffin loosed REAPER 2 and 5 with seven VF-10 F4Fs southwest along 230 degrees (M.) to orbit at 10 miles, nearly as far as TF-17. He expected them to help defend *Hornet,* but reserved the other REAPERS for TF-16. Four minutes later he queried Fleming as to the altitude of the bogeys and heard, "Angels 7" (7,000 feet). Therefore Griffin cautioned the CAP, "Look south of base." Given that low altitude he anticipated a torpedo attack and alerted Kane (REAPER 4), Vejtasa (REAPER 7), and Faulkner (REAPER 8): "Look for fish." However, REAPER BASE no longer controlled his CAP. At least twenty-one of the twenty-two VF-10 fighters (the lone exception perhaps Ens. Jim Dowden) now raced southwest toward TF-17.

THE *HORNET'S* ORDEAL

When enemy planes first appeared, Kinkaid brought both carrier task forces around to 120 degrees to steam into the light southeasterly wind. Attaining 28 knots, TF-17's screen of two heavy cruisers, two light AA cruisers, and six destroyers deployed in a circle 4,000 yards in diameter around the *Hornet*. Lookouts searched the skies, generally clear but punctuated with patches of cumulus clouds. They knew all too well the Japanese were coming. Because TF-17 had drawn ahead, Kinkaid ordered TF-17 at 0902 to close TF-16 now a dozen miles to the northeast. A minute later Murray complied by swinging left to 040 degrees. Subsequently, he held mainly northerly courses.

At 0905 the *Hornet* lookouts finally sighted enemy aircraft—seven dive bombers in a long string closing from the west. They were Tsuda's *Zuikaku* 2nd *Chūtai,* about to be reduced by one when Bliss cut out Tsuchiya's trailing plane. Intermittent clouds obscured them from the gunnery directors, but at 0909 the *Hornet*'s five-inchers opened up at 10,500 yards. Lacking the *Enterprise*'s vastly improved AA capability, Captain Mason depended as much upon evasive maneuvering, whipsawing at 28 knots to avoid bombs and torpedoes, as defensive firepower tried to knock down enemy planes. A combined dive bomb–torpedo attack, such as Murata expertly coordinated, reduced AA effectiveness by dividing the guns among many widely scattered targets.[12]

Slanting down, Tsuda's six carrier bombers met no fighters and faced relatively lessened AA fire. At 0910 in close succession they pushed over into careful, deliberate descents and emerged at 5,000 feet from beneath a cloud. The first three Type 99s (Tsuda's own 24th *Shōtai*) plunged steeply from astern of the *Hornet,* but the last three planes dived in at increasingly shallow angles (down to 45 degrees) as the target steamed away from them. Tsuda's bomb churned a

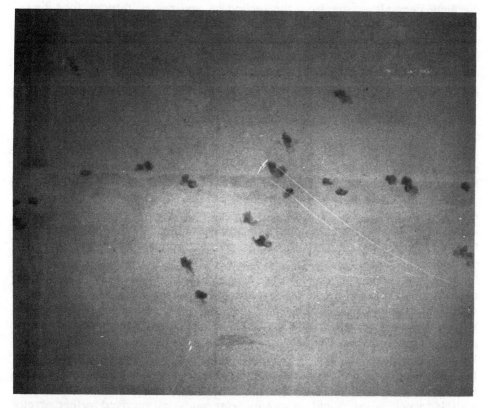

Lt. (jg) Shimada Yōzō's stricken *Zuikaku* carrier bomber after bombing the *Hornet.* Seconds later Shimada bailed out from the rear seat and ultimately survived, but his pilot, PO1c Taka Asatarō, crashed. Photo taken from the *Pensacola.* (NA 80-G-33929)

geyser of water to starboard alongside the *Hornet*'s bow. Wingman PO2c Miya-kashi Katsuhi's 250-kilogram "ordinary" (semi–armor piercing) bomb holed the center of the flight deck opposite the island and penetrated three decks to blow apart the forward messing compartment and inflict hideous wounds to a repair party.[13] The next aircraft fell victim to AA fire. Its bomb still attached, PO2c Kitamura Ichirō's Type 99 plowed into the sea only 30 feet from the carrier's starboard bow.

The 25th *Shōtai*, led by Lt. (jg) Shimada Yōzō (NA 68-1940), achieved hits two and three in close order. Shimada's pilot, PO1c Taka Asatarō, delivered his 242-kilogram "land" bomb onto the *Hornet*'s flight deck aft only 20 feet in from the starboard edge. A huge sheet of reddish flame erupted from an 11-foot hole through the deck planking, killing thirty men in the nearby starboard after gun gallery. An SBD-3 Dauntless triced in the overhead crashed to the hangar deck. Avenging 20-mm tracers cut off Shimada's escape. Zooming almost vertically and streaming blue smoke from its engine, the *kanbaku* stalled, but gained enough altitude for Shimada to bail out from the rear seat. He floated down not far from the heavy cruiser *Pensacola*, while the stricken Type 99 with Taka still on board plunged into the sea 1,000 yards from her starboard bow. Miraculously, Shimada witnessed (à la George Gay) the *Hornet*'s ordeal and survived to be picked up the next morning by the *Isokaze*.[14]

Either PO3c Hirayama Akitatsu or PO3c Yano Shōichi, numbers 3 and 4 in the 25th *Shōtai*, secured the third hit by circling ahead to approach the carrier from high off her port bow. The semi–armor piercing bomb sliced into the center of the flight deck aft not far from the second hit and passed through four decks before exploding in the CPO messroom. It also caused heavy loss of life. Last to attack from the 2nd *Chūtai* was Tsuchiya's Type 99 crippled by Bliss. Limping in from astern of the *Hornet*, the smoking Type 99 never reached the target. Katō, the pilot, jettisoned his bomb, but immediately followed his payload into the carrier's wake. Bliss remembered that the "plane and bomb made separate water impacts."[15]

The 2nd *Chūtai* of the *Zuikaku* Carrier Bomber Squadron scored three times against the *Hornet* at the cost of two aircraft (Kitamura and Shimada) finished by AA, one (Tsuchiya) to fighters. Tsuda, Miyakashi, Hirayama, and Yano escaped at low level after a superb exhibition of dive bombing. For the *Hornet,* shaken by three bombs, more woe soon followed.

Led by the incomparable Murata Shigeharu, the eleven Type 97s of the *Shō-kaku* Carrier Attack Squadron's 1st *Chūtai* curved south of TF-17 while coordinating their torpedo attack with Lieutenant Washimi's 2nd *Chūtai* sweeping in from the north. Out ahead of Murata, Miyajima's four *Shōkaku* Zeros suddenly spotted Kiekhoefer's F4F escaping trouble above. One of Miyajima's pilots, very likely number 4, PO3c Horiguchi Shunji, peeled off to surprise the lone F4F from behind. When tracers zipped past his head, Kiekhoefer popped open his flaps, which caused the much swifter Zero to overshoot the target and recover out ahead. It passed so near that Kiekhoefer clearly picked out the "bright band around its fuselage" that denoted a *Shōkaku* plane. He triggered a burst, but only his right outboard .50-caliber functioned. When the Japanese swiftly scissored for a head-on run, Kiekhoefer dropped his left wing as if to ram. The bluff forced the Zero to reef away into a steep climb, allowing the F4F to break off. Apparently Horiguchi never caught up with his teammates, but survived further adventures over TF-17.[16]

Meanwhile, Miyajima's three Zeros flushed more Wildcats—Bliss's BLUE 29 division regrouping below 5,000 feet after torching Tsuchiya's *Zuikaku* carrier bomber. Alerted only by the sound of gunfire, Bliss was startled when a spent 7.7-mm slug buried itself halfway in his instrument panel. To his surprise, his adversary slipped on past and somewhat leisurely pulled out ahead. Bliss snapped off a burst and quickly flamed the Mitsubishi, which was fortunate because his guns quit firing, evidently out of ammunition. His victim was WO Hanzawa Yukuo, the veteran 18th *Shōtai* leader. When Bliss later ditched his battered Wildcat, he was shocked by the damage Hanzawa's bullets had caused. Among other things, the life raft had been blasted out of its compartment behind the cockpit. Bliss surmised that his opponent mistook it for the pilot abandoning the F4F and fatally let down his guard. At the same time, Miyajima and wingman Sea1c Ishida Masashi riddled Formanek's F4F. Despite his wounds, Formanek set down in the water. The destroyer *Russell* (DD-414) hauled him on board at 0925. Miyajima later described how his *chūtai* battled some Grummans on the way in and claimed three for the loss of Hanzawa.[17]

Murray's course reversal some minutes before placed Murata's *chūtai* in the unenviable position of attacking the carrier from astern rather than from ahead. Wheeling in toward the carrier, now turning away to the northeast, the eleven carrier attack planes spread out from a column of *shōtais* into a ragged, very loose right echelon. Well separated, the other three *shōtais* pivoted around Murata's own 40th on the extreme left in the following order: the 41st under Lt. (jg) Suzuki Takeo (NA 67-1939), the 42nd (WO Shibata Masanobu), and behind and farthest to the right, WO Nakai Taneichi's 49th *Shōtai*. In the long, shallow dives, the Nakajimas accelerated to high speed and strived to get ahead of the carrier's starboard beam. Mason tightened his turn to keep her stern toward the incoming torpedo planes.

Coming in first, the 40th *Shōtai* of Murata, WO Matsushima Tadashi, and PO1c Kawamura Zensaku penetrated the screen between the *Northampton* and the destroyer *Anderson*. They let down to 300 feet and closed the *Hornet*'s starboard quarter. One pilot fired his brightly painted fish within 1,500 yards of the carrier, but ran afoul of black five-inch AA bursts and lines of red tracers. His *kankō* burst into flames and spun into the water. The other two pressed within 1,000 yards before releasing their torpedoes, then banked right in a sweeping turn to parallel the target's course and pull off ahead. Suddenly AA tagged the second Nakajima, igniting its left wing tank. Leaving a fiery trail like a "flaming meteor," it rolled violently to port and disappeared in a huge splash off the *Hornet*'s starboard side. Despite streaming two thin trails of grey smoke, the third *kankō* kept on chugging past the target. Thus perished the crews of Murata's number 1 and Matsushima's number 2 aircraft, while Kawamura's number 3 plane exited on ahead.[18]

Despite the poor angle, the pilots of the lead *shōtai* had aimed their weapons with precision. At 0914.5 one torpedo struck the *Hornet*'s starboard side amidships beneath the 1.1-inch batteries abaft the island. Twenty seconds later a second detonated in the engineering spaces aft on her starboard side, while the wake of the third torpedo barely missed the bow. Both hits combined to inflict immense damage. The forward engine room and two firerooms swiftly flooded; all power and communications failed including fighter direction; this reduced her to a darkened hulk with a 10.5-degree starboard list. The *Hornet* soon lost headway and glided to a stop.[19]

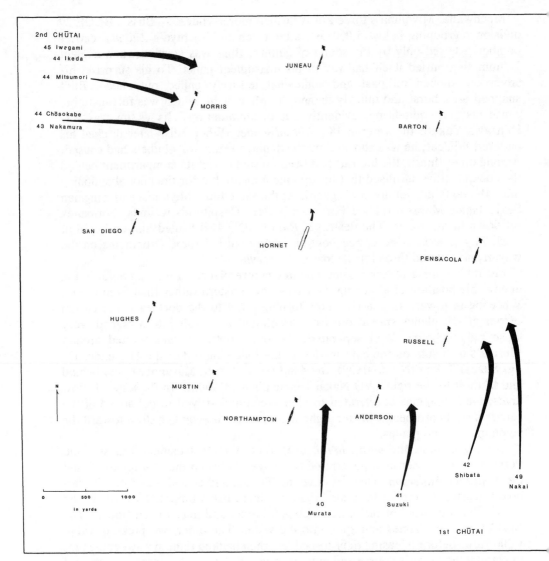

The *Shōkaku* torpedo attack on TF-17, 0912.

One of the outstanding naval aviators of the war, the happy-go-lucky Murata had conducted his last and finest torpedo attack. His friend Cdr. Genda Minoru described him in the following terms: "Murata knew no fear, he was calm and cold as a rock in zero weather, was never nervous, and under the worst of circumstances always smiling."[20] The Imperial Navy posthumously promoted him two ranks to captain and also honored him on 20 November 1943 with a special Combined Fleet citation.

Suzuki, PO1c Okazaki Yukio, and PO1c Kurita Kōkichi of the 41st *Shōtai* comprised the second attack element. Their three *kankōs* appeared about a minute behind Murata and turned in toward the target from astern of the *Anderson*. Some 20-mm AA fire ripped Okazaki's aircraft, causing him to dump his torpedo

The end of a Samurai. Lt. Cdr. Murata Shigeharu's *Shōkaku* Type 97 carrier attack plane (with elaborately marked tail) smokes before splashing in flames to starboard of the *Hornet*. Photo taken from the *Pensacola*, 26 Oct. 1942. (NA 80-G-33944)

only 75 yards beyond the destroyer's stern and veer sharply left. The flaming Type 97 splashed close aboard the *Northampton*'s port bow. The other pair fired their fish from far abaft the *Hornet*'s beam and missed her to starboard as she continued to turn away. Following through, Suzuki and Kurita crossed behind her stern to withdraw up along her port side.

If the lead half-dozen *kankōs* faced great difficulty getting into a good attack position against the carrier, the five remaining Type 97s, at the end of Murata's game of crack the whip, had no chance at all. Curving in close abeam of the heavy cruiser *Pensacola* off the *Hornet*'s starboard side, the 42nd *Shōtai* (WO Shibata Masanobu, PO2c Kodama Kiyomi, and PO2c Miya Tatsuhiko) strived to get ahead of the carrier. Struck by AA, Kodama jettisoned his torpedo and fell back trailing smoke. Meanwhile Shibata and Miya released their payloads from well abaft the carrier's beam and banked left. Their fish passed ahead of the carrier. They escaped, but Kodama did not fare as well. Crossing ahead of the *Pensacola,* his aircraft blossomed flames and splashed.

Sucked out of position in the rear, the 49th *Shōtai* of WO Nakai Taneichi and PO2c Kobayashi Yoshihiko split up. Nakai followed the 42nd's crews inside the screen and passed the *Pensacola*'s port quarter. Sizing up the situation, he decided the cruiser was a more feasible target than the carrier. He evidently

Lt. Cdr. Murata Shigeharu (*Maru Magazine* via Michael Wenger)

fired his torpedo from off her port beam. At the same time Kobayashi ended up outboard of the others, with the *Pensacola* looming between himself and his target. He also chose the heavy cruiser. That meant pressing even farther east before cutting in against her starboard beam. Perceiving the danger, Capt. Frank L. Lowe ordered right full rudder and swung the *Pensacola* sharply toward her assailant. Kobayashi's *kankō* burst into flames 1,000 yards out, but he gamely attempted to crash the ship. The Type 97 missed her bow by only a few feet before raising a huge splash 100 feet to port. Noting the splash near the cruiser's port bow, Nakai assumed his own fish had struck home.[21]

Thus AA fire downed five Type 97s (Murata, Matsushima, Okazaki, Kodama, and Kobayashi) from the *Shōkaku* 1st *Chūtai*. Of eight torpedoes actually launched against the *Hornet,* only two found her, and the *Pensacola* avoided at least one more. At 0915 a jubilant Japanese radioman informed base, "Enemy *Saratoga* large fire."[22] Nagumo happily received these tidings only minutes before Gus Widhelm's *Hornet* SBDs ruined the mood by pummeling the *Shōkaku* with four 1,000-pound bombs.

FOLLOW-UP ATTACKS

By running group leader Takahashi out of formation, Red Hessel and Tom Gallagher briefly dispersed the *Zuikaku* 1st *Chūtai*, but soon Lt. (jg) Yoneda Nobuo (NA 68-1940), the 22nd *Shōtai* leader, gathered the six remaining Type 99 carrier bombers (one damaged). They cut north around to the port side of the task force, but the detour placed them directly astride the first of several VF-10 CAP flights bustering southwest from TF-16. Ascending past 12,000 feet, Vejtasa's four REAPER 7 F4Fs noticed Yoneda's column of five dive bombers, trailed by a sixth (PO2c Nishimori previously ruffled by Gallagher), emerge ahead from out of the sun. Even while gliding down toward their pushover points, the hawks still enjoyed an altitude advantage of several thousand feet over the F4Fs. Suddenly Nishimori angled down toward REAPER 7, perhaps hidden from him by the clouds. With a deft wingover Vejtasa rolled into a short high-side run and torched the straggler. Meanwhile, Yoneda's five Type 99s cleared the F4Fs by 2,000 feet or more bound for the task force.[23]

Next on the scene, Fritz Faulkner's REAPER 8 with four F4Fs spotted Yoneda's five carrier bombers as they began their final dives over TF-17. Scrambling after the hawks, Faulkner, Phil Long, and Ens. Gordon F. Barnes lost contact slicing through a cloud. Only Mac Kilpatrick actually latched onto a *kanbaku*, but could not stay with it long.

Perhaps a minute behind Tsuda's *Zuikaku* 2nd *Chūtai* and with Murata's torpedo runs in progress, Yoneda's five 1st *Chūtai* carrier bombers swarmed in against the *Hornet*'s port side from about 12,000 feet. On their way south two

Shōkaku Type 97 carrier attack planes flown by PO2c Kodama Kiyomi (*l*) and PO2c Miya Tatsuhiko (*r*) attack from astern of the *Hornet*. Photo taken from the *Pensacola*. Seconds later Kodama crashed ahead of the *Pensacola*. Miya also failed to return to base. (NA 80-G-33950)

orphaned VF-10 pilots, "Wick" Wickendoll and Whitey Feightner, from Lieutenant Commander Kane's REAPER 4 had lost contact investigating what turned
out to be *Enterprise* search SBDs. Regaining altitude, they happened upon two
enemy planes in the final stage of bombing the *Hornet*. Wickendoll's guns would
not fire, so he relented and Feightner followed.[24] Four Type 99s from the 1st
Chūtai bombed the *Hornet*, scored no hits, then withdrew low over the water.
Among them were PO2c Maeno Hiroshi and his pilot, Sea1c Ōkawa Toyonobu,
the sole *Zuikaku* crew to return from the 24 August attack on the *Enterprise*. This
day Ōkawa survived, but Maeno did not.

Maeno's *shōtai* leader, WO Satō Shigeyuki (PO1c Yasuda Kōjirō, observer),
made the most spectacular attack of the battle.[25] At 0914 his Type 99, already
with flame blossoming on its underside, appeared high above the *Hornet*'s starboard quarter. Perhaps dead or dying, Satō did not release his bomb but kept
coming directly at the carrier. He did not miss. His starboard wing carried away
the signal halyards and creased the edge of the *Hornet*'s stack, then the fuselage
caromed off the island and exploded in flames. Ruptured fuel tanks sprayed the
signal bridge with burning gasoline, while the wrecked airplane smashed into the
flight deck and nearly penetrated all the way to the number 2 (VS-8) ready room
directly beneath. Several squadron members barely escaped with their lives,
when fire from the airframe embedded in the ceiling spread to the upholstery and
torched the compartment.[26]

Fortunately for the Americans, Satō's 250-kilogram bomb proved to be a dud,
not properly armed. Later it rolled around in a passageway outside the ready
room. Contrary to U.S. reports, the aircraft did not carry a pair of underwing
60-kilogram bombs. None of the carrier-based *kanbaku* did. Instead, the underwing containers held aluminum powder to be dropped on the water as a marker
to aid the post-attack rendezvous. Damage control wrongly thought that one of
these nonexistent 60-kilogram bombs had detonated.[27] The impact and burning
fuel alone were sufficient to kill or maim many men, and fires blazed for two
hours. On the signal bridge, seven signalmen died from the flames that destroyed
all of the flags. Others in the island, including correspondent Charles McMurtry,
suffered severe burns. In the nearby VF-72 ready room, Luebke, Lowndes,
Montgomery, McClintock, Morris, and Moran were not hurt.

American observers noticed two stripes somewhere on the tail of the suicide
aircraft and wrongly assessed the pilot was a "squadron commander." Actually
all *Zuikaku* aircraft sported the two bands around the rear fuselage which denoted their particular ship. Subsequent writers have exaggerated this mistake by
ascribing the aircraft to Lieutenant Commander Seki, the *Shōkaku* Air Group
commander, who never attacked the *Hornet*. Evidently no one from the Japanese side witnessed the crash.[28]

A classic sequence of photos depicts the plunge of Satō's *Zuikaku* carrier
bomber into the *Hornet*'s island. Also visible are Suzuki's and Kurita's two
41st *Shōtai* Type 97s flying alongside the *Hornet*'s port side, as well as PO3c
Horiguchi's lone *Shōkaku* Zero busily strafing the carrier's starboard bow. On
his way north Horiguchi raked the destroyer *Morris* on the *Hornet*'s port
beam, and a 20-mm shell killed Lt. Cdr. Lee S. Pancake on the gun director
platform.[29]

While Murata's 1st *Chūtai* assailed the *Hornet* from the south, Lieutenant
Washimi's 2nd *Chūtai* with nine Type 97 *kankōs* approached from the north.
Unlike Murata, Washimi encountered determined fighter opposition, but enjoyed
no protecting Zeros. With Washimi's 43rd on the extreme right as guide, the

WO Satō Shigeyuki's stricken *Zuikaku* Type 99 carrier bomber about to strike the *Hornet*. In the center is Lt. (jg) Suzuki Takeo's *Shōkaku* Type 97 *kankō* withdrawing after firing its torpedo at the carrier. (NA 80-G-33947)

other two *shōtais* deployed leftward from a column to a loose echelon in the following order: the 44th under Lt. (jg) Chōsokabe Akira (NA 67-1939), and Spec. Duty Ens. Iwagami Rokurō's 45th behind on the far left. The nine Japanese pivoted eastward for torpedo runs against the carrier's port side.

Don Gordon and Jerry Davis from REAPER 8 found themselves at 15,000 feet and southwest of TF-17. Suddenly "Tally ho" resounded over the radio. Directly beneath their right wing five enemy torpedo planes dropped past 7,000 feet: the right and center elements of the 2nd *Chūtai*'s echelon wheeling in against the *Hornet*. Nosing down, the two F4Fs swung around almost 180 degrees to take on the lead plane, which had drawn a thousand yards or more ahead of the others to its left. Their quarry was indeed Washimi's Type 97, which angled down and pulled out low over the water. Diving in at high speed, Gordon misjudged range and the deflection angle in a low-side run from the right, but his tracers surprised Washimi, who countered with a tight right turn away. That set up Davis for a good shot from astern. The smoking Type 97 veered off away from the ships, and the two F4F pilots let it go.[30]

In the meantime Mac Kilpatrick of VF-10 had latched onto the next *kankō* over, Washimi's number 2 in the 43rd, PO2c Akiyama Hiroshi. With uncertain lunges he began "pecking away" at the Nakajima. His bullets neutralized the rear gunner, Sea2c Ōguri Kazuo, who slumped, leaving his 7.7-mm Lewis machine gun sticking almost straight up. Akiyama evaded by dropping to 50 feet.

Fresh from winging Washimi, Gordon and Davis roared in behind Akiyama, but failed in their first breathless rush. With another slashing attack up the Nakajima's unprotected tail, Gordon torched the Type 97 barely 10 feet over the waves. None of the VF-10 pilots saw it go down, as shell bursts and tracers from the screening ships forced all three to sheer off, but Akiyama did perish. Kilpatrick learned the lesson, forcibly demonstrated by "Flash" Gordon, that air combat required decisive action for a quick kill.[31]

After escaping Shirane's *Zuikaku* Zeros, George Wrenn from Rynd's BLUE 17 division discovered himself in extraordinarily good position over six torpedo planes—the left and center sections of the 2nd *Chūtai*—slicing down toward the task force. Screaming in, he overhauled Iwagami's 45th *Shōtai* on the extreme left, matched its turn, and with a shallow high-side run from the left ripped PO2c Suzuki Katsu's outboard plane. To his surprise the target did not scissor, but banked left (south) toward the other Type 97s. That cleared its field of fire aft. Trying to hold the proper deflection, Wrenn almost rolled into inverted flight, but his bullets quickly silenced all return fire. Charging directly up the unprotected tail, he shot until Suzuki's *kankō* smoked and fell away. Wrenn swiftly targeted the next torpedo plane, now crossing ahead neatly set up for a side approach. That was PO1c Sano Gonari's in the middle of the 45th *Shōtai*. Good deflection shooting set the Type 97 ablaze. Thick AA from the screening cruisers and destroyers soon dissuaded Wrenn from chasing more torpedo planes, and he reluctantly braved the towers of water blasted out of the sea by five-inch shells dropping in front of him. His plane badly damaged, Suzuki never attacked the task force, but turned back to the *Kidō Butai*. Sano's doomed aircraft swung sharply left intending to crash the CL(AA) *Juneau*, only to be blasted into the water close aboard by her formidable portside battery.[32]

Ens. George Wrenn, VF-72 ace. Photo
taken September 1943 at Jacksonville.
(NA 80-G-399224)

Around 0914, while Yoneda's Type 99s and the last of Murata's torpedo planes completed their attacks, five 2nd *Chūtai* Type 97s flooded the skies around the destroyer *Morris* on the *Hornet*'s port bow. Remaining relatively high, 200 to 300 feet, they curved left to take on the carrier from ahead. First in, PO2c Nakamura Toshiaki (sole remaining plane from the 43rd *Shōtai*) and Chōsokabe (the 44th *Shōtai* leader) passed astern of the *Morris*. PO1c Mitsumori Yoshio (44th) hurdled the tincan, but fierce AA fire quickly pitched him into the sea. PO2c Ikeda Hiroshi (number 3 of the 44th *Shōtai*) and Iwagami, leader of the 45th, cut ahead of the *Morris*. Shipboard observers watched the four dark-green torpedo planes "dodge sideways" out of the path of red tracers and hurtle shell splashes to release their fish from 300 to 800 yards sharp off both the *Hornet*'s bows. No torpedoes struck home. On the way out one radioman used his 7.7-mm gun to rake the starboard side of the *Mustin* (DD-413). All four Type 97s successfully escaped the vicinity. Three of their torpedoes churned south through the task force and nearly smacked the *Northampton*'s stern as she hurriedly swung hard aport. So far three Type 97s splashed—two of them victims of Grumman fighters that subsequently crippled two more. In this instance the CAP did a fine job ruining a torpedo assault.

Ripped apart by BLUE 13 and 17, Ishimaru's 3rd *Chūtai* of the *Zuikaku* Carrier Bomber Squadron lost three Type 99s before Shirane's top cover rescued the remaining four. Cautiously gathering the survivors, Ishimaru circled well south of the task force before finally turning in against the carrier. Even so, he ran afoul of still another VF-10 flight hunting the enemy. By 0912 Dave Pollock's REAPER 2 with three F4Fs had gone about 10 miles beyond the *Hornet*. From 22,000 feet the pilots looked back toward the ships and observed black AA bursts, smoke, and bright red streaks from planes falling in flames.

With no bandits visible nearby, Pollock was loath to relinquish altitude superiority and dive in. Suddenly he found much closer game, what looked like three (actually four) dive bombers sneaking past at 16,000 feet. His "Tally ho" sounded at 0914. By the time REAPER 2 closed within effective range, Ishimaru had already canted down against the *Hornet*. Pollock singled out the second plane, knocked out the rear gunner at 300 yards, then cut loose at point-blank range with all six Brownings. At 13,000 feet fire erupted from underneath the *kanbaku* and sent it spinning in flames. Distracted when his wing tank did not release, Ens. Steve Kona, joined by Ens. Lyman "Squeak" Fulton, caught the third Aichi 12,000 feet over the *Hornet*. They stayed with the Type 99 for 5,000 harrowing feet in the midst of tracers, but finally let it go.[33]

Ishimaru and his two wingmen pressed their runs against the *Hornet* without success. For them escape proved as perilous as attack. North of TF-17 Kona and Fulton essayed a couple of passes at the retreating *kanbakus* with no evident damage, then sparred with a lone Zero (possibly Horiguchi from the *Shōkaku* torpedo escort). The two F4Fs quickly scissored into Jimmy Thach's beam defense maneuver and soon lost the bandit in low-lying clouds.

Meeting REAPER 7 spelled the doom of Ishimaru's little force. Vejtasa's flawless long diving approach flamed an enemy dive bomber at low altitude. Stan Ruehlow, REAPER 3 CO leading the 2nd Section, did likewise. Neither Japanese pilot had deviated from level flight before sustaining fatal damage. Ens. William "Hank" Leder, Ruehlow's wingman, claimed the third carrier bomber, but in fact he missed Ishimaru, the only member of the 3rd *Chūtai* to leave TF-17 behind. Meanwhile, Vejtasa likewise could not dump his wing tank and had to restart his engine when it sputtered from loss of fuel suction. Gasoline spraying from the right wing indicated either a holed fuel tank or a loose line. Only after he pulled the release lever several times did the balky tank finally drop away.[34]

In the wake of Ishimaru's unsuccessful assault, two crippled stragglers menaced the *Hornet*. At 0917, a carrier bomber trailing smoke appeared in a shallow descent from off her stern. It may have been Pollock's victim from the 3rd *Chūtai*. Gunfire tore into the *kanbaku* as it seemed to float down in flames. Still retaining some control in his death dive, the pilot aimed for the carrier's port quarter. By this time she had nearly coasted to a stop on a northwesterly heading. The shallow glide forced him to lob his bomb, which fell about 50 yards ahead of the *Hornet*. Courageously fighting his faltering controls, the Japanese pulled out over her starboard bow and reversed course over the *Northampton* in "a lazy glide" back toward the *Hornet*. Despite every gun that could bear, he crossed ahead of her bow, banked sharply, and sliced through the hull just ahead of the port forward gun gallery. The burning fuselage slanted down through the gallery deck into the forward elevator pit, where it ignited a nasty fire.[35]

A minute later a *Shōkaku* 2nd *Chūtai* carrier attack plane, almost certainly Washimi's own, matched the *kanbaku*'s suicidal desire against the carrier. Badly shot up by Davis and Gordon of REAPER 8, Washimi had sheered off to the west of the task force and evidently dumped his torpedo to stay aloft. Now from the northwest (dead ahead of the *Hornet*), the aircraft bore down on the stopped carrier, but could not stretch its fleeting flight time far enough to crash the *Hornet*. The Type 97 fell short of her port bow.

Miyajima and Ishida, two *Shōkaku* escorts, skirmished briefly with Wickendoll and Feightner of REAPER 4, when the two VF-10 pilots tried ambushing a pair of Zeros. Before the F4Fs could shoot, both Japanese looped to get in behind them. Lacking the speed to match their maneuver, Wickendoll led Feightner into a sharp turnaway, then reversed course to meet the enemy head-on. By that time both Zeros disappeared. Miyajima later claimed one of two Grummans he encountered on the way out from the enemy task force.[36]

After launching torpedoes against the *Hornet*'s starboard beam, six surviving *Shōkaku* 1st *Chūtai kankōs* had traversed the task force in pairs or singly only to confront a lurking Grumman. North of TF-17, George Wrenn assaulted one torpedo plane with a head-on run at wave-top level and raked the second with a full-deflection shot as it passed by. He claimed the pair, but both Japanese escaped. His try for kill number 4 of the mission almost ended his own life, when the F4F barely avoided digging a wing tip in the water. East of TF-17, Claude Phillips in a shot-up VF-72 F4F jumped a lone torpedo plane chugging north toward TF-16 and claimed a probable. Evidently Robert Holland did the same. Newly returned from the search, Lt. (jg) Howard Burnett, a highly aggressive VS-10 pilot, was anxious to repeat his success on 24 August when he bagged a dive bomber. Even closer to TF-16 than the others, he knocked down a *Shōkaku* Type 97 carrier attack plane retiring at low level. Almost certainly this was PO2c Miya Tatsuhiko from the 1st *Chūtai*'s 42nd *Shōtai*. One of the other crews saw Miya ditch at 0920. The reports listed his crew as "failed to return," rather than "self-exploded battle death," as with all the others. Burnett and his radioman strafed the crew as the Japanese abandoned the sinking aircraft.[37]

At a rendezvous point north of TF-17, Lieutenant (jg) Suzuki assembled the five surviving 1st *Chūtai* carrier attack planes and retired north, while the five remaining 2nd *Chūtai kankō* ended up southwest of the task force. On the way out one *Shōkaku* crew noticed a second U.S. carrier force northeast of the one they attacked and at 1020 relayed the word back to Nagumo. They placed the second carrier bearing 020 degrees, 15 miles from the first, on course 000 degrees, speed 24 knots. It is possible this message was garbled in transmission or receipt, as at least one Japanese force recorded the position as 045 degrees, 40 miles from the first carrier force. That would be a significant error. Even so, TF-16 soon drew much more Japanese interest.[38]

FIGHTER ACTIONS WEST OF TASK FORCE 17

After Shirane's eight *Zuikaku* Zeros dispersed the five surviving BLUE 13 and 17 F4Fs, other fighter combats broke out west of TF-17. Attaining 20,000 feet, Al Emerson's three BLUE 5 F4Fs overran the battle area without seeing any enemy aircraft and turned around. Soon they spotted planes ahead and below. A cool, confident fighter leader, "Silver" Emerson asked wingmen Sleepy Weimer and Moose Merritt whether they were ready to go and chuckled when both assented somewhat unintelligibly. Rocking his wings, he led the flight down and bagged one Mitsubishi on the first pass. The Wildcats split up when the Zeros scattered. Discovering one bandit racing up Weimer's tail, Merritt fired until it fell away, then Emerson opportunely reappeared to blast another Zero off Merritt's tail. During the scuffle the F4Fs lost considerable height, then reassembled.[39]

REAPER 5's 2nd Section of Lt. (jg) James D. Billo and Ens. James E. Caldwell witnessed some of this fight. Bobby Edwards had led the flight toward 20,000 feet while steering 210 (M.) from TF-16, but his electric propeller control suddenly shifted to full high pitch and overheated the engine. Unable to keep up, he dropped out, accompanied by wingman Bill Blair. Billo and Caldwell kept on going. Ahead at 12,000 feet they observed what looked like seven or eight Zeros beating upon a lone F4F. Yet the Wildcat appeared to destroy two enemy planes. Closing in, Billo burned one Zero with a steep overhead pass, but another bandit forced him to dive on out. Near the water he used S-turns to shake any pursuers, but no Japanese followed. Billo evidently saw Emerson fighting Zeros and mistook Merritt and Weimer for more bandits.[40]

At 0925 a pilot announced on the radio, "Going into the water." Someone responded with "Good luck," to which the first replied, "I hope they pick me up."[41] Off to one side Billo noticed a pilot parachute past 2,000 feet, but was too far away to identify him. Given the circumstances he was almost certainly Jim Caldwell, who fell to Shirane's Zeros and was never rescued. Regaining altitude, Billo joined the three BLUE 5 F4Fs over TF-17. He tried to get the leader to follow and find more Zeros, but Emerson must have felt the action was over. The *Hornet* needed fighter protection, so Billo stayed on.

Air combat near TF-17 soon claimed another VF-10 victim. After their futile intercept of Ishimaru's 3rd *Chūtai*, Steve Kona and Lyman Fulton of REAPER 2 heard REAPER BASE warn, "Torpedo attack coming in." They hurried northeast toward the *Enterprise*. Halfway there, Fulton suddenly broke off about 0928 and hightailed it back toward TF-17. He may have heard the warnings of another wave coming in. Trying to overtake his wingman, Kona soon lost sight of the F4F in the clouds. He circled the *Hornet* for five minutes and raced northward again. Perhaps Fulton fell prey to Zeros.[42]

In their several combats, Shirane's 1st *Chūtai* Zeros estimated fighting no fewer than thirty Grummans and tallied fourteen. Their actual kills included John Franklin and Paul Landry of VF-72, Jim Caldwell and likely Lyman Fulton of VF-10. In return, Shirane lost his wingman PO2c Hoshiya and also WO Osanai

Suekichi, the highly regarded leader of the 12th *Shōtai*. It is impossible to state with any certainty who shot down whom. Unable to join up with any of the strike planes, Shirane set his own course back to base.

SUMMING UP THE FIRST STRIKE

The Japanese strike group comprised twelve fighters, twenty-one carrier bombers, and twenty carrier attack planes, total fifty-three aircraft (not counting two reconnaissance planes). The survivors claimed:

Sunk	Aircraft shot down
1 carrier (6 bombs, 2 torpedoes)	4 Grummans by *Shōkaku* Zeros
1 heavy cruiser (1 torpedo)	14 Grummans by *Zuikaku* Zeros
1 destroyer (suicide crash by VT)	2 Grummans by *Zuikaku* VB
Heavily Damaged	
1 destroyer (suicide crash by VB)	

Success cost dearly in what was the last and finest coordinated carrier attack executed by the Imperial Navy. It appears the CAP destroyed five *Zuikaku* carrier bombers before they could dive against the *Hornet*. Antiaircraft fire blasted four more, and CAP F4Fs bagged two others on the way out. Thus eleven carrier bombers fell in the target area, and several others left badly shot-up. On the way in, fighters splashed one of the twenty *Shōkaku* torpedo-armed Type 97 carrier attack planes and crippled several others. During the actual runs, AA finished eight Nakajimas, including three that missed suicide attacks against ships, and on the way out from the task force an SBD dropped another Type 97. Three Zeros (two *Zuikaku*, one *Shōkaku*) also went down.

Therefore Japanese losses in the target area numbered twenty-four: three fighters, eleven carrier bombers, and ten carrier attack planes. Two more Zeros, six carrier bombers, and six carrier attack planes later ditched from battle damage or lack of fuel while waiting to come on board the *Zuikaku* and the *Junyō*. Thus only fifteen of the fifty-three first-wave attack aircraft (seven Zeros, four carrier bombers, and four carrier attack planes) touched down on friendly flight decks.

TF-17's air protection comprised fifteen VF-72 and twenty-one VF-10 F4F fighters, but only thirty-two (fifteen VF-72, seventeen VF-10), plus one VS-10 SBD, fired their guns at the enemy. (See table 20.1 for air combat claims and casualties.) Three 250-kilogram bombs, two torpedoes, and two crashed aircraft left the *Hornet* adrift without power or propulsion, unable to move or conduct air

TABLE 20.1
Task Force 17 Air Combat Claims and Casualities

	VF		VB		VT		
	Confirmed	Probable	Confirmed	Probable	Confirmed	Probable	Losses
VF-72	5	0	5	9	4	2	4 (2 pilots)
VF-10	1	0	5	3	1	3	2 (2 pilots)
VS-10	0	0	0	0	1	0	0

TABLE 20.2
Task Force 61 CAP Situation, 0840

Radio Call	Task Force 17 (*Hornet*—VF-72)	Claims 0900–0930 Confirmed	Probable
	2nd CAP (aloft)		
Division 4			
BLUE 13	F-9 Lt. Edward W. Hessel (USNA 1937)	1 VB	2 VB
14	Lt. (jg) Thomas J. Gallagher, Jr.,[a] A-V(N)	1 VB	2 VB
15	F-18 Lt. Claude R. Phillips, Jr., A-V(N)		2 VB, 1 VT
16	Lt. (jg) John R.Franklin,[b] A-V(N)	—	—
Division 5			
BLUE 17	F-11 Lt. Robert W. Rynd (USNA 1938)	1 VB	1 VB
18	F-27 Ens. George L. Wrenn, A-V(N)	4 VT	—
19	F-29 Lt. (jg) Kenneth C. Kiekhoefer, A-V(N)	1 VF	1 VB
20	Lt. (jg) Dupont Paul Landry,[b] A-V(N)	—	—
	3rd CAP (about to take off from the *Hornet*)		
Division 2			
BLUE 5	F-32 Lt. Alberto C. Emerson, USN	2 VF	—
6	F-5 Ens. James O. Weimer, A-V(N)	—	—
26	Lt. (jg) Robert S. Merritt, A-V(N)	1 VF	—
Division 8			
BLUE 29	F-7 Lt. Louis Kenneth Bliss (USNA 1938)	1VB, 1 VF	—
30	F-10 Lt. (jg) Robert E. Holland, Jr., A-V(N)		1 VT
31	Lt. (jg) George Formanek, Jr.,[a] A-V(N)	1 VB	1 VB
32	F-2 Lt. (jg) Richard Z. Hughes, A-V(N)	—	—
	Task Force 16 (*Enterprise*—VF-10) 2nd CAP (aloft)		
REAPER 2	F-28 Lt. Albert David Pollock, Jr., USN	1 VB	—
	F-24 Ens. Steve Kona, A-V(N)	—	2 VB
	F-3 Ens. Lyman J. Fulton,[b] A-V(N)	—	—
REAPER 4	F-6 Lt. Cdr. William R. Kane (USNA 1933)	—	—
	F-20 Lt. John C. Eckhardt, Jr. (USNA 1938)	—	—
	F-9 Ens. Maurice N. Wickendoll, A-V(N)	—	—
	F-31 Ens. Edward L. Feightner, A-V(N)	—	—
REAPER 5	F-35 Lt. Thomas E. Edwards, Jr.	—	—
	F-1 Lt. (jg) William K. Blair, A-V(N)	—	—
	F-23 Lt. (jg) James D. Billo, A-V(N)	1 VF	—
	F-10 Ens. James E. Caldwell, Jr.,[b] A-V(N)	—	—
	3rd CAP (aloft)		
REAPER 7	F-19 Lt. Stanley W. Vejtasa, USN	2 VB	—
	F-22 Lt. Leroy E. Harris (USNA 1939)	—	—
	F-16 Lt. Stanley E. Ruehlow (USNA 1935)	1 VB	—
	F-21 Ens. William H. Leder, A-V(N)	1 VB	1 VB
	F-17 Ens. James H. Dowden, A-V(N)	—	—
REAPER 8	F-7 Lt. Frederick L. Faulkner, USN	—	—
	F-11 Ens. Merl Philip Long, A-V(N)	—	—
	F-33 Ens. Gordon F. Barnes, A-V(N)	—	—
	F-5 Ens. Donald Gordon, A-V(N)	1 VT	1 VT
	F-2 Ens. Gerald V. Davis, A-V(N)	—	1 VT
	F-12 Lt. Macgregor Kilpatrick (USNA 1939)	—	1 VT

[a]Shot down, later rescued
[b]Shot down, missing in action

TABLE 20.3
1st Carrier Division, 1st Strike (Lt. Cdr. Murata Shigeharu)

Zuikaku Carrier Bomber Squadron (21 Type 99 VB)
1st *Chūtai*

21st *Shōtai*	22nd *Shōtai*	23rd *Shōtai*
Lt. Takahashi Sadamu (P)	Lt. (jg) Yoneda Nobuo (O)	WO Satō Shigeyuki[a] (P)
PO1c Suzuki Toshio (P)	PO2c Nishimori Toshio[a] (P)	PO2c Maeno Hiroshi (O)
PO2c Shigesaka Isamu (O)		

2nd *Chūtai*

24th *Shōtai*		25th *Shōtai*
Lt. Tsuda Toshio (P)		Lt. (jg) Shimada Yōzō[a] (O)
PO2c Miyakashi Katsuhi (O)		PO2c Tsuchiya Yoshiaki[a] (O)
PO2c Kitamura Ichirō[a] (O)		PO3c Hirayama Akitatsu (O)
		PO3c Yano Shōichi (P)

3rd *Chūtai*

26th *Shōtai*	27th *Shōtai*	28th *Shōtai*
Lt. Ishimaru Yutaka[c] (P)	Spec. Duty Ens. Murai Hajime[a] (O)	WO Okamoto Kiyohisa[a] (P)
PO1c Bekku Toshimitsu[a] (O)	PO1c Katō Kiyotake[a] (P)	PO1c Miyabara Chōichi[a] (P)
Sea1c Yokota Masutarō[a] (O)		

Close Escort
Zuikaku Carrier Fighter Squadron (8 Zeros)
1st *Chūtai*

11th *Shōtai*	12th *Shōtai*	13th *Shōtai*
Lt. Shirane Ayao	WO Osanai Suekichi[a]	PO1c Noda Mitsutomi
PO2c Hoshiya Yoshisuke[a]	PO2c Kai Takumi	PO1c Nagahama Yoshikazu
Sea1c Kurata Nobutaka	Sea1c Nisugi Toshitsugu	

Shōkaku Carrier Attack Squadron (20 Type 97 VT)
1st *Chūtai*

40th *Shōtai*	41st *Shōtai*
Lt. Cdr. Murata Shigeharu[a] (P)	Lt. (jg) Suzuki Takeo (P)
WO Matsushima Tadashi[a] (O)	PO1c Okazaki Yukio[a] (P)
PO1c Kawamura Zensaku (O)	PO1c Kurita Kōkichi (O)

42nd *Shōtai*	49th *Shōtai*
WO Shibata Masanobu (O)	WO Nakai Taneichi (P)
PO1c Kodama Kiyomi[a] (O)	PO2c Kobayashi Yoshihiko[a] (O)
PO2c Miya Tatsuhiko[c] (O)	

2nd *Chūtai*

43rd *Shōtai*	44th *Shōtai*	45th *Shōtai*
Lt. Washimi Gorō[a] (P)	Lt. (jg) Chōsokabe Akira (O)	Spec. Duty Ens. Iwagami Rokurō (P)
PO2c Akiyama Hiroshi[a] (O)	PO1c Mitsumori Yoshio[a] (O)	PO1c Sano Gonari[a] (O)
PO2c Nakamura Toshiaki (O)	PO2c Ikeda Hiroshi (O)	PO2c Suzuki Katsu (O)

Close Escort
Shōkaku Carrier Fighter Squadron

17th *Shōtai*	18th *Shōtai*
Lt. Miyajima Hisayoshi	WO Hanzawa Yukuo[a]
Sea1c Ishida Masashi	PO3c Horiguchi Shunji

Contact Planes (Type 97 VT)
Zuikaku Lt. (jg) Sakumuki Tsugimi (O)
Zuihō WO Tanaka Shigenobu[b] (O)

Note: Aircraft commanders: P = pilot; O = observer
[a]Shot down or missing in action (ditched planes not given in Japanese records)
[b]Subsequently shot down
[c]Died after ditching

operations (trapped on board were eight F4F-4s and seven SBD-3s inoperable or spares). The flooding of two firerooms and the forward engine room brought on a starboard list of 10.5 degrees, soon reduced by counter flooding to about 2 degrees. Stubborn fires raged on the signal bridge, flight deck, the number 2 ready room, the hangar deck amidships, and farther below decks in the CPO quarters, the GSK storeroom, the 02 deck portside, and in the number 1 elevator pit. No pressure in the water mains compelled the use of massive bucket brigades. To remain afloat in the teeth of further Japanese attacks, the *Hornet* desperately needed VF support from TF-16.

CHAPTER 21

"The Big E" Survives

THE SECOND WAVE FINDS TASK FORCE 16

Seki's Shōkaku *Carrier Bombers*

From about a dozen miles northeast of TF-17, Rear Admiral Kinkaid's TF-16 clearly witnessed the hits on the *Hornet,* while Japanese aircraft set ablaze in midair appeared like "fireflies" suddenly lighting up.[1] To prevent the same thing from happening to the *Enterprise,* Kinkaid turned southeast at 27 knots and sought concealment in rain squalls. Soon TF-17 shrank to a distant pillar of smoke. No one knew for certain the *Hornet*'s condition, but indications were not good. By 0930 the majority of the twenty SBDs (seven VB-10, thirteen VS-10) from the search and IAP waited to come on board the *Enterprise.* All were low on fuel, and five had suffered battle damage.

At 0931 Jim Daniels, the Air Group Ten LSO, started bringing in SBDs. CAP Wildcats also entered the landing circle. Bobby Edwards of VF-10 brought the first F4F in safely, despite a prop frozen in full high pitch. Next came Mac Kilpatrick with an overheating engine and Steve Kona hoping for fuel and ammunition. From VF-72 Red Hessel, Bob Rynd, and K.C. Kiekhoefer touched down in their shot-up F4Fs. Claude Phillips's first attempt (with no flaps) elicited a wave-off for excess speed, but on his second approach he gratefully took the cut for a "hot" but safe touchdown.[2] By 0948 Daniels recovered all twenty SBDs and seven F4Fs. The *Enterprise* closed down to re-spot her flight deck. More aircraft wanted to land, notably four VF-72 F4Fs, six VF-10 F4Fs (including "Chip" Reding), and the two riddled VT-10 TBFs.

At 0941 Kinkaid radioed Rear Admiral Good, TF-17 cruiser commander on the *Northampton,* asking whether the *Enterprise* should land the *Hornet* "chickens" (aircraft). The disheartening reply was "affirmative."[3] While the cruisers and most of the destroyers protectively circled the wounded flattop, the *Morris, Mustin,* and *Russell* moved alongside to help fight fires. At 0948 the *Hughes* (DD-410) rescued Tom Gallagher of VF-72, shot down by a *Zuikaku* carrier bomber. Good planned for the *Northampton* to tow the *Hornet* to safer waters. He desperately required fighter support, but the four F4Fs (Al Emerson's BLUE 5 plus Jim Billo from VF-10) could not stay overhead for long. The *Enterprise* could not help; her effective CAP numbered only eleven F4Fs.

Kinkaid sent at 0949 a short but accurate assessment to ComSoPac: "*Hornet* hurt." At the same time Halsey, chafing from the sidelines of a major battle,

Plane handlers re-spot the *Enterprise*'s flight deck while landing F4Fs and SBDs around 0940 on 26 Oct. 1942. In the center is Lt. Robert Rynd's F-11 (BuNo. 02001) from VF-72 and to its right VS-10 Dauntless S-9 flown on IAP by Lt. (jg) F. R. West of VB-10. (NA 80-G-30033)

advised his task force commanders: "Operate from and in positions from which you can strike quickly and effectively. We must use everything we have to the limit." Unfortunately for SoPac "everything" would not be enough.[4]

The *Enterprise* needed to clear her flight deck to handle the *Hornet* aircraft as well as her own. After debriefing VB-10 pilots Welch and McGraw for the position of the enemy Vanguard Force, Captain Hardison proposed that Lieutenant Commander Thomas take an unescorted strike of ten VB-10 crews as soon as possible (preferably around 1000) to pound that enemy force, then fly to Henderson Field.[5] TF-16 came right to 200 degrees, heading southwest so as not to open the range too far for the returning strike groups. After re-spotting "The Big E" 's flight deck, her Air Department rearmed and refueled SBDs both on the flight deck and in the hangar. Some VF pilots were angered to see their F4Fs struck below deck. The *Enterprise* also hoped to recycle some of the CAP aloft by landing F4Fs immediately after Thomas's SBDs took off, and then refuel, rearm, and relaunch them. With that in mind, Jack Griffin told REAPER 8 at 0952 to pancake, so Fritz Faulkner brought his three F4Fs down to low level. By 1000 only eight F4Fs patrolled at any substantial altitude over TF-16: Bill Kane's REAPER 4 (in two separate sections) and four F4Fs of REAPER 7 (Swede Vejtasa). The next strike group already had TF-16 in its sights.

As related previously, the 1st Carrier Division sent its second strike wave in two separate flights of dive bombers and torpedo planes. Far in the lead, nineteen

Aichi Type 99 carrier bombers under Lieutenant Commander Seki, the *Shōkaku* group leader, escorted by Lieutenant Shingō's five Zeros, cruised at 5,000 meters (16,140 feet). The *Zuikaku*'s contribution of seventeen Nakajima Type 97 carrier attack planes and four Zeros lagged about 45 minutes behind.

Even before the Japanese admirals monitored the first strike's 0920 sighting report, they decided one or more American carriers lurked near the one assailed by Lieutenant Commander Murata. Alerted by voice transmissions intercepted from enemy FDOs, Vice Admiral Nagumo informed all forces at 0927, "There appear to be two carriers, one as yet unknown, estimated south of *Saratoga*'s position, 8-35 S, 166-45 E." On the *Junyō* Rear Admiral Kakuta came to the same conclusion. At 0928 he warned, "Enemy force is in two groups of at least 10 ships centering around large carriers." Checking out the area, the *Zuikaku* Type 97 contact plane, commanded by Lt. (jg) Sakumuki Tsugimi (NA 67-1939), piped up at 0937: "Another large enemy force, one carrier, one light cruiser, six destroyers, speed 20 knots, position 8-37 S, 166-37 E, 0730 [Z-9]." Because of the excellent search and shadowing work, Seki knew he had plenty to do.[6]

The first inkling in TF-16 of Seki's approach appeared about 0930, when Good informed Kinkaid of bogeys bearing 315 degrees, 76 miles. The *Northampton*'s radar team continued its excellent work. About seven minutes later Good reported bogeys at 290 degrees, 35 miles. At 0945, the *South Dakota*'s SC-1 radar registered many bogeys bearing 325 degrees, distance 55 miles. The intruders first creased the *Enterprise* A-type radar scope at 0953, bearing 340 degrees and 45 miles.

About the same time Seki spotted off to his right the TF-17 screen circling the crippled *Hornet,* but quickly identified Murata's handiwork. However, the second carrier, reported 15 miles north of the first, was not in sight—evidently having retired east or southeast. Pressing on, Seki soon located TF-16 and at 1000 warned of a new carrier force 090 degrees and 20 miles from the stopped carrier. The *South Dakota*'s radar reported multiple bogeys at 25 miles, while the *Enterprise*'s own radar showed planes to the north and circling east. Maj. Bankson T. Holcomb's Mobile RI Unit on the *Enterprise* soon translated snatches of Japanese radio traffic for Kinkaid.[7] Closing the U.S. task force from the north, the *Shōkaku* flyers recognized an *Enterprise*-class carrier with twenty planes on deck and astern a new *South Dakota*–class battleship. At 1108 Seki gave the order: "All forces attack."[8]

Meanwhile, Jack Griffin, REAPER BASE FDO, continued to battle a confusing situation. In the last hour numerous bogeys appeared on radar, and he was uncertain of both the situation and the exact disposition of his own CAP. Subsequent analysis has shown it to be:

---

8 F4Fs on station over TF-16		
	REAPER 4A	Kane, Eckhardt
	REAPER 4C	Wickendoll, Feightner
	REAPER 7	Vejtasa, Harris; Ruehlow, Leder
13 F4Fs circling at low altitude		
	REAPER 2	Pollock, Dowden
	REAPER 5B	Blair
	REAPER 8	Faulkner, Long, Barnes; Gordon, Davis
	REAPER 6C	Reding (returned from the strike badly damaged)
	BLUE CAP	Bliss, Holland, Hughes, Wrenn (not together)

Aware of possible danger brewing astern (to the north), Griffin relied primarily on Kane's REAPER 4 and never used REAPER 7's call, although Vejtasa's four

F4Fs patrolled 10,000 feet over base. At 0959 he sent Kane northwest on 330 degrees (M.) and five minutes later told him to orbit, adding, "Bogey north of you." Griffin warned all REAPERs to look north for bogeys coming from that direction, and at 1006 retrieved Kane, telling him to "look behind you to east and northeast."[9]

During the enemy's approach, TF-16 experienced a curious and tragic distraction. Two TBFs and one F4F, crippled survivors of the Air Group Ten ambush, had returned. Dick Batten extinguished the fire in his Avenger, but still could not dump the torpedo. Hoping to land, at 0959 he approached the *Enterprise* from astern, but she could not take him on board. Two minutes later Batten ditched T-11 off her port quarter and 1,500 yards ahead of the destroyer *Porter* (DD-356). After nosing over on touchdown, the crew scrambled to escape and break out their life raft. The *Porter* moved in to make the rescue, slowed and stopped near the raft off her starboard bow.

Suddenly in the midst of a routine pickup a *Porter* lookout shouted, "Torpedo wake on the port bow!" While orbiting at low altitude, Albert "Dave" Pollock and Jim Dowden of VF-10 noticed a porpoising torpedo circling counterclockwise to starboard ahead of the *Porter*. They dived to strafe and touch off its warhead, making two passes at 300 feet, but only managed to scare the ships and loose a torrent of AA fire onto their heads. The torpedo curved around the *Porter*'s port side and at 1004 slammed in amidships between the number 1 and 2 firerooms. White smoke from her boilers shot into the air, and she drifted dead in the water. Those present thought a Japanese submarine scored, but actually none was even there. The culprit was Batten's rogue T-11 Mark XIII aerial torpedo which finally broke loose during ditching and ran in an irregular circle until it smote its crew's benefactor. The destroyer *Shaw* (DD-373) stood by her unfortunate companion, while TF-16 steamed on. Finally Kinkaid ordered her to rescue survivors and sink the *Porter,* which she did at 1208.[10]

Warned of imminent air attack by radar and Holcomb's radio intercepts, Kinkaid altered course further right to 235 degrees. The screen comprised the heavy cruiser *Portland* 2,500 yards off the *Enterprise*'s port bow, the CL(AA) *San Juan* in the corresponding slot off her starboard bow, the massive *South Dakota* 2,500 yards astern, and the six remaining destroyers. To fill the gap left by the *Porter* and *Shaw,* Kinkaid ordered the *Conyngham* (DD-371) to drop back from the head of the task force to the *Enterprise*'s starboard quarter. Meanwhile, the other destroyers took equal intervals in a 1,500-yard radius around the carrier. Caught in the midst of preparing her own strike of ten SBDs, the *Enterprise* had as yet only one Dauntless spotted aft on her flight deck. Some others, already fueled and armed with 500-pound bombs, were still parked forward, while hangar deck crews readied several more SBDs for the mission. Now "The Big E" risked grave danger of fire and explosions should bombs torch these vulnerable planes on her own deck.

Because REAPER 4 had obviously missed the bogeys in the clouds, Griffin summoned Kane back at 1007. At the same time he informed all REAPERS, "Look out for bogeys approaching from north and northeast, angels probably low," and at 1011 told the fighters overhead to orbit three to five miles northeast of base. Keeping Kane busy, Griffin sent him southeast on 150 to cut inside the circling enemy planes. Three minutes later he relented with "Return to base," and added, "Look for bogeys northeast. They are astern of BB [*South Dakota*]."

Unfortunately, Griffin's efforts availed nothing for the defense of TF-16. He committed virtually all of the CAP to the northeast, but gave no orders to climb. The pilots were unsure whether they faced "hawks" (dive bombers) or "fish"

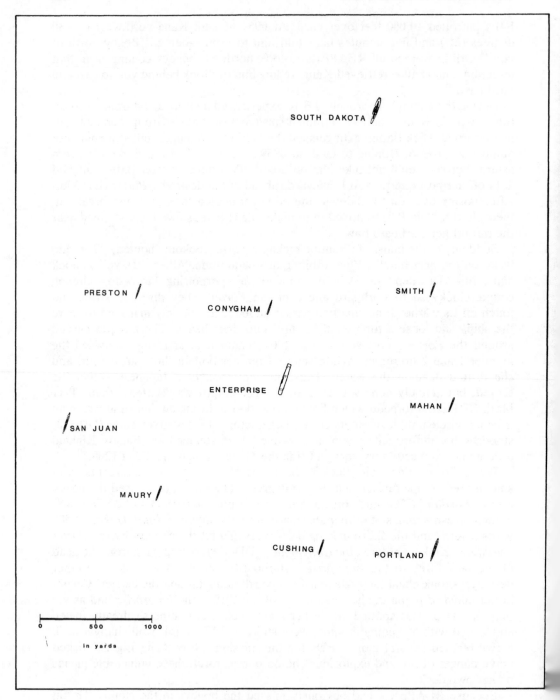

TF-16 formation, 1010.

(torpedo planes), but Griffin confronted the same dilemma because the bogeys appeared so close to the ships. He relied on CAP sighting reports for information, but thus far no fighters had spotted the enemy.

Seki deployed his force into line-astern to attack from up sun against the carrier's starboard side. In the lead he had seven *kanbaku* (his 20th *Shōtai* and Lieutenant Yoshimoto's 3rd *Chūtai*), covered by Shingō's five escort Zeros.

Spreading out astern were Lieutenant Arima's 1st *Chūtai* (seven Type 99s) and, last of all, the 2nd *Chūtai* (five aircraft) under Lt. Yamada Shōhei. Most of the CAP F4Fs milled around well below them. Pollock for one only reached 12,000 feet, and eight more F4Fs (including REAPER 7 and REAPER 8) operated under the same handicap. Unscathed, the dive bombers swept on toward the *Enterprise*. Only REAPER 4's Wick Wickendoll and Whitey Feightner managed to intercept Yamada's Type 99s before they reached the pushover point. With only his left outboard gun working, Wickendoll managed four passes, but the uneven recoil skidded the Wildcat during firing. At the same time Feightner shot on target and flamed his first hawk. The hapless *kanbaku* pitched into a fiery dive witnessed by other *Shōkaku* crews as well as by the *Portland*. She reported at 1014 that an enemy plane splashed 4,000 yards off her bow.[11]

At 1015 *Enterprise* lookouts spotted the string of dive bombers only after the leader had pushed over unopposed by fighters. Scattered clouds at about 6,000 feet had obscured their approach. On station ahead and starboard of the *Enterprise,* the destroyer *Maury* loosed the first five-inch shells directed against the attackers. "The Big E" quickly added the weight of her powerful AA battery, including the sixteen new 40-mm Bofors guns, while Hardison turned radically away to port to evade bombs.[12] In response to sightings by lookouts, Griffin warned the CAP, "REAPERS look for planes in dives. REAPERS from base: Look for bogeys diving on port bow." At 1015 the *South Dakota* cut loose a tornado of gunfire against the dive bombers coming in high from astern against the carrier's starboard quarter.

Despite the lack of warning, AA fire grew extremely heavy. Mott described the dives: "As each plane came down, a veritable cone of tracer shells enveloped it. You could see it being hit and bounced by exploding shells."[13]

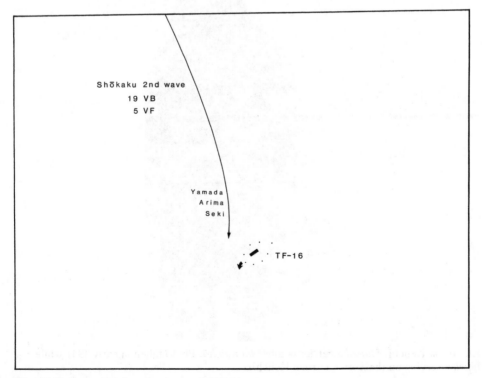

The *Shōkaku* carrier bombers assault TF-16, 1015.

From directly behind the group command *shōtai*, Yoshimoto watched Seki take repeated shell hits as he dived in steeply from high off the *Enterprise*'s starboard bow. The *hikōtaichō*'s Type 99 slowly rolled over on its back, "flame shot out of the bomber and, still inverted, it continued diving toward the enemy ship."[14] The *kanbaku* seemed to disintegrate before the wreckage plunged into the sea. Seki's bomb raised a pillar of water close amidships off the *Enterprise*, as Hardison put her into a radical left turn.

None of the other six pilots scored any hits either, due (according to Mott) to the volume and accuracy of the AA fire, which ruined their aim if it did not kill them outright. Scooting out at low altitude, they also braved a gauntlet of machine-gun and cannon tracers. The unprecedented barrage also destroyed the Type 99s of PO2c Itaya Yoshimi (20th *Shōtai*) and from the 3rd *Chūtai*, PO1c Someno Fumio (a 24 August veteran) and Sea1c Hiroso Goichi. Shingō's escort Zeros descended low to draw fire away from their charges, as the *South Dakota* noted that some enemy planes deliberately flew alongside at wave-top height. The Zeros sought to cover the Type 99s on the way out, but did not regain contact. They never engaged the CAP, which was busy elsewhere.

Arima's *chūtai* attacked from astern of the rapidly turning *Enterprise* about two minutes after Seki. He noticed no defending fighters, but AA fire seemed much more severe than on 24 August. Numerous aircraft, including the group

Lt. Arima Keiichi, *Shōkaku* carrier bomber *buntaichō*. Photo taken in early 1941 while he was serving on the *Soryū*. (Arima Keiichi)

commander's, burst into flames from the furious barrage. From his post in sky control, Benny Mott spotted the leader of the second group emerging from a cloud at 8,000 feet and aiming for the starboard quarter. To his gunners he bellowed over the bullhorn: "Four o'clock—four o'clock—get him!"[15] The formidable AA did not deter Arima's pilot, PO1c Furuta Kiyoto, from going low and securing his hit. At 1017 the 250-kilogram "ordinary" bomb punched through the center of the flight deck only 20 feet from the forward edge. Leaving only a small hole, it dropped clear of the deck, sliced through the forecastle, and detonated in midair near the port bow. The concussion blew one VB-10 SBD off the bow, killing Sam D. Presley, AMM1c, who had bravely manned its rear twin .30s. Set afire, a VS-10 SBD leaked burning gasoline onto the flight deck, but plane handlers quickly pushed it over the bow and put out other small fires. The bomb blast also roughed up the 1.1-inch AA mount recently installed on the forecastle and wounded the battery officer, Ens. Marshall Field, Jr. Otherwise bomb damage was remarkably minor.[16]

Behind Arima came the rest of the 1st *Chūtai,* and Yamada's flight followed them. Because the target kept swinging directly away from them, these Type 99s made increasingly shallower dives. In the teeth of intense AA the pilots angled down from different bearings and altitudes. A minute after Arima's hit, a second 250-kilogram semi–armor piercing bomb landed 10 feet abaft the number 1 elevator in the center of the flight deck forward and detonated inside the ship with two distinct explosions. The first swept through the hangar, killing and injuring many men, set afire three SBDs (two VS, one VB) trussed in the overhead, and threatened five more being armed and gassed nearby. Hangar personnel courageously lowered the three burning aircraft and jettisoned them along with three more from VS-10. The three VF-10 F4Fs just brought down from the overhead sustained no damage. The second explosion resounded on the second deck, wiped out Repair Party II, wrecked staterooms in officer's country, and ignited a fire in the number 1 elevator pit.

Despite his gun problems, Wickendoll stuck with the enemy and confronted one of Yamada's dive bombers about to push over. Following all the way down to 4,000 feet, he knocked out the rear gunner, but relented when flames streamed from his own airplane. While disposing of his burning wing tank, Wickendoll missed seeing the fate of his erstwhile target. Two other VF-10 F4Fs intercepted the 2nd *Chūtai* during its dives. Bill Blair (REAPER 5B) caught one Type 99 at 12,000 feet, stayed with it down to 9,000, and later saw it splash in flames. He thought AA fire might have done the job. Prodded by the *South Dakota*'s massive secondary batteries, Don Gordon (REAPER 8C) cranked up his wheels and climbed at full power out of the landing circle. Beneath 10,000 feet he discovered two hawks diving at him. Successive quick lunges at both Japanese failed, and AA forced Gordon to pull out. Climbing once again he latched onto a third Aichi and shot until his six .50s ran dry. This time the target smoked, staggered at 4,000 feet, and exploded, credit either AA or Gordon. Surviving Japanese remembered that Grummans finished two carrier bombers on the way in, so in addition to Feightner someone tagged a hawk.[17]

At 1020 one of the last bombs slapped the sea only 10 feet from the *Enterprise*'s starboard quarter. Its heavy concussion rocked her like a rowboat and opened underwater seams. The planes parked in Fly I forward lifted clear of the deck, and Kona's F-24 F4F farthest forward on the starboard side "waddled" over the side. A VB-10 SBD located aft in Fly III bounced sideways across the flight deck and perched precariously in the starboard 20-mm gun gallery. This certainly surprised stranded VF-10 pilot Howard Packard, who happened to be standing on its wing firing his Colt .45 pistol at recovering dive bombers. Along with several others he tried unsuccessfully to push the rogue SBD over the side. Finally LSO Robin Lindsey grabbed a rammer for a five-inch gun and levered it under the left wing. Hardison saw what he was doing and put the *Enterprise* into a violent turn to port. "That did the trick and over the side she went," Packard later recounted.[18]

Dick Hughes of VF-72's BLUE 29 division challenged the *Shōkaku* carrier bomber that had scored the near miss. From low level he watched the *kanbaku* release its bomb and pull out, then overtook it out near a destroyer that fired impartially at both planes. The Type 99 turned sharply into Hughes to scissor, but when he pulled the trigger, only one gun responded. As the bomber flashed past, its rear gunner blazed away at Hughes. The two planes scissored indecisively three more times. Finally Hughes compensated for the slewed recoil and walked his tracers into its engine. The Type 99 ended as a burning patch on the sea.[19]

Griffin rallied his CAP at 1017 with "Hey Rube—Looks like hawks—Close in quick!" However, only four F4Fs (Wickendoll, Feightner, Blair, and Gordon of VF-10) fought dive bombers before or during their runs, and Hughes (VF-72) engaged one immediately afterward. A dozen eager F4F pilots never joined battle because they were out of position—an extremely frustrating situation. Only Feightner and Hughes submitted claims for two dive bombers destroyed.

Of the twelve carrier bombers of the *Shōkaku* 1st and 2nd *chūtais*, it appears CAP fighters got two before and during the dives, AA finished three others, and the sixth fell to a fighter after pulling out. The dead included Yamada, the highly regarded Pearl Harbor veteran, and Lt. (jg) Miyauchi Haruo (NA 68-1940), the young 25th *Shōtai* leader. Counting Seki's lead *chūtai*, losses therefore totaled ten *kanbaku* (three to F4Fs, seven to AA). Three of the dead crews had also bombed the *Enterprise* on 24 August. The Japanese thought six bombs had pounded an *Enterprise*-class carrier. At 1030 one crew radioed that a carrier burned and listed to starboard. Arima reported the bombing completed and quipped, "Good health to two enemy carriers."[20]

Just as on 24 August, the redoubtable Seki led the force that hurt "The Big E," but this day success came at the cost of his life. His pilots secured two hits and one near miss. Although not crippling, the damage inflicted on the *Enterprise* caused heavy loss of life: forty-four killed and many more wounded. The number 1 elevator remained locked in the up position, and its future functioning seemed uncertain. Of the thirty-one SBDs (twelve VB-10, nineteen VS-10) on board during the attack, nine (three VB, six VS) went over the side because of fire or damage. One VF-10 F4F also fell into the sea.

For aviators caught on board their flattop during an attack, the experience was unnerving. The VB-10 war diary offers a vivid description of what it was like for once to be on the receiving end of bombs:

> The squadron ready room was piled in some cases two and three deep . . . It was a grim time. The ship rocked with its own firing, the near misses and direct hits from the enemy and its violent maneuvering. In the ready room the squadron heard the attack, felt it, and waited anxiously for the next portentous announcement from the public address system . . . ventilation and air conditioning turned off in the ready room—steel helmets, sweat, life preservers, and anxiety sitting heavily on the

squadron squeezed together on the deck, awaiting the next explosion, the next violent shudder of the ship.

Things were much the same in the VF-10 ready room, where Mac Kilpatrick later described the "acrid dust cloud" raised by the amidships hit.[21]

Immediately after the bombing, the second battle-damaged VT-10 TBF, Doc Norton's T-7, also ditched. During the attack he had tried to stay out of trouble. While avoiding potshots from the *South Dakota* (described as a "volcano" or a "ring of fire"), George Wrenn of VF-72 was surprised to see an enemy dive bomber tear after a fleeing TBF (Norton). He pursued the pair, lost them in a low cloud, cut around to the other side, but no one emerged. Instead, Norton's rapidly failing airplane headed for the *Enterprise* and dropped its tail hook, requesting a deferred forced landing. The stars on its wings gave the TBF no immunity from AA fire, and Norton could not stay aloft long enough to land on the carrier. At 1020, when he set down inside the task force, lookouts on board the *South Dakota,* the *Conyngham,* and the *Smith* (DD-378) mistook the sinking Avenger for a surfacing submarine and opened fire. Norton and his crew only barely escaped injury to be rescued by the *Preston* (DD-379).[22]

At the same time the *Shōkaku* main body approached TF-16, WO Tanaka Shigenobu's *Zuihō* Type 97 carrier attack plane stalked the crippled carrier to the north. Despite not having any payload, Tanaka decided to disrupt the towing operation now well underway. At 1009 he swooped low in a shallow glide bomb-

Lt. Doc Norton's TBF T-7 under AA fire from TF-16, about 1020, 26 Oct. 1942. Norton gives the signal for deferred forced landing (wheels up, hook down). He ditched a minute or two later. (NA 80-G-33342)

ing run and dropped a target indicator or navigational marker that narrowly missed both the *Hornet* and the *Morris* off her starboard side. Escaping AA fire, Tanaka remained in the vicinity of TF-17 to continue his contact work. The *Northampton* moved away and the destroyers cast off. Lt. Cdr. H. A. I. Luard, a Royal Navy observer on board the *Hornet,* noted how the tincans departed, "with more speed than finesse, trailing hoses, wires and rigging behind like a dish of spaghetti." Tanaka did well, for his bluff considerably delayed towing efforts.[23]

The *Shōkaku* second wave last fought about 30 minutes after hitting the *Enterprise.* Shingō's five Zeros found no opponents over TF-16, as no F4Fs came near them. About 50 miles northeast, they flushed a PBY returning from the morning search. Seeing a flock of angry fighters, Lt. (jg) Norman S. Haber (VP-24) immediately firewalled his throttles and dived as low as he dared. With repeated runs, the five persistent *Shōkaku* pilots thoroughly perforated the Catalina's tail (including all of the rudder and elevator controls), and wounded two crewmen. In turn Haber's gunners claimed one Zero and actually punctured two fighters. Shingō went on his way certain he downed the flying boat, but Haber escaped in the clouds after a courageous fight. All nine surviving *Shōkaku* carrier bombers rendezvoused, for Haber counted them. His own adventures, however, were far from over.[24]

TABLE 21.1
1st Carrier Division, Second Strike (Lt. Cdr. Seki Mamoru)

Shōkaku Carrier Bomber Squadron (19 Type 99 VB)		
20th *Shōtai*	27th *Shōtai*	28th *Shōtai*
Lt. Cdr. Seki Mamoru[a] (P)	Lt. Yoshimoto Kazuo (P)	Spec. Duty Ens. Saitō Chiaki (O)
PO1c Imada Tetsu (O)	PO1c Someno Fumio[a] (O)	Sea1c Hiroso Goichi[a] (O)
PO2c Itaya Yoshimi[a] (O)		
1st *Chūtai*		
21st *Shōtai*	22nd *Shōtai*	23rd *Shōtai*
Lt. Arima Keiichi (O)	Lt. (jg) Saitō Toshiji (O)	WO Tanaka Yoshiharu (P)
PO1c Koitabashi Hiroshi (O)	PO2c Tsuchiya Ryōroku[a] (O)	PO2c Sugano Masanari[a] (P)
PO2c Honda Yoshimaru[a] (O)		
2nd *Chūtai*		
24th *Shōtai*	25th *Shōtai*	26th *Shōtai*
Lt. Yamada Shōhei[a] (P)	Lt. (jg) Miyauchi Haruo[a] (O)	WO Shimizu Tsukushi (O)
PO3c Mochizuki Isaku (P)		PO2c Sueyasu Kazuhito[a] (O)
Close Escort		
Shōkaku Carrier Fighter Squadron (5 Zeros)		
11th *Shōtai*	16th *Shōtai*	
Lt. Shingō Hideki	PO1c Matsuda Jirō	
PO1c Taniguchi Masao	PO2c Sasakibara Masao	
Sea2c Suzuki Taiji		

Note: Aircraft commanders: P = pilot; O = observer
[a] Shot down or missing in action over TF-16 (planes that ditched not indicated in records)

The Zuikaku *Carrier Attack Planes*

With the disappearance of the *Shōkaku* strike group, by 1030 only a portion of TF-16's CAP retained the fuel or ammunition to remain effective. Kinkaid pondered a message from Good standing by the stricken *Hornet:* "JOE [*Hornet*] stopped burning. Request fighter coverage."[25] Unfortunately TF-16 was in no position to render assistance. Concerned about dive bombers possibly lurking off the *Enterprise*'s port quarter, Griffin told the CAP to climb. Eleven F4Fs responded to his call:

REAPER 2	Pollock, Holland (VF-72)
REAPER 4	Kane, Eckhardt
REAPER 7	Vejtasa, Harris, Ruehlow, Leder
REAPER 8	Faulkner, Long, Barnes

Another fourteen F4Fs circled TF-16 at low altitude:

REAPER 4	Wickendoll, Feightner
REAPER 5	Blair, Billo
REAPER 7	Dowden
REAPER 8	Gordon, Davis
REAPER 6	Reding (from strike)
BLUE 5	Emerson, Weimer, Merritt
BLUE F4Fs	Bliss, Hughes, Wrenn

Trying to reorganize the CAP, Griffin queried Kane and Pollock, but not Vejtasa and Faulkner, perhaps not realizing they were there. He certainly had work for those he contacted. At about 1035, the *Enterprise*'s radar had picked up a contact bearing 330 degrees (M.)—friendly or not, the operator could not say. At 1040 the contact resolved into a large bogey bearing 330 degrees. Griffin alerted his workhorse, REAPER 4, telling Kane to investigate the contact at Angels 12, and likewise headed REAPER 2 (Pollock) northwest. Others, too, were anxious to fight. Unbidden, Vejtasa took REAPER 7 out on 330 (M.). West of TF-16 a squall line consolidated rapidly. Meanwhile, Faulkner, Long, and Barnes (REAPER 8) spiraled down from high altitude westward over the ships to look for torpedo planes. On the way Faulkner lost sight of Barnes's F4F.[26]

More enemy aircraft indeed were inbound—the *Zuikaku*'s contribution to the second wave. Lieutenant Imajuku's seventeen Type 97 carrier attack planes (sixteen with torpedoes and WO Suzuki Naoichirō's unarmed contact plane) from his *Zuikaku* Carrier Attack Squadron, escorted by four *Zuikaku* Zeros under WO Shigemi Katsuma, a *Ryūjō* veteran, had departed about 50 minutes after Seki's carrier bombers. They worked up to 4,000 meters (13,123 feet). At 1035 Imajuku observed a heavily damaged carrier tended by escort ships (TF-17) and beyond the rain clouds two minutes later caught sight of wakes of another enemy force. Soon the *Zuikaku* flyers identified an *Enterprise*-class carrier, a *South Dakota*-class battleship, two cruisers, and eight destroyers. At that time TF-16 steamed southwest on 235 degrees. Eager to sink the undamaged carrier, Imajuku pressed on.[27]

On the *Enterprise* Griffin pondered the nature of the opposition reflected in the radar plot. At first the bogeys appeared to be at medium or high altitude, but something hinted at a possible torpedo attack. At 1044 he warned his fighters of bandits bearing 330 degrees (M.), distance 15 miles: "Look out for fish [torpedo planes]. Look out for fish. Fish bear about 330 degrees from base."[28] This time he was able to position the CAP ahead of the incoming enemy planes.

While the new attack developed to the west, an F4F unexpectedly bellied into the water off the *South Dakota*'s starboard quarter. The *Maury* cut out of formation and reversed course to rescue the pilot seen floating in his life vest well astern. He was Gordon Barnes, who had dropped out of REAPER 8 a few minutes before. Lt. Cdr. Gelzer L. Sims anticipated a normal pickup.[29]

Intercepting the 2nd *Chūtai*

While closing TF-16 in a shallow glide, Imajuku formulated his tactical plan. He would take the eight *kankōs* of his 1st *Chūtai* directly against the carrier's starboard bow, while the 2nd *Chūtai* of eight Type 97s under Lt. Yusuhara Masayuki (NA 66-1938) cut around astern to assault her port side. From the head of the column, Imajuku split off the 1st *Chūtai* with a wave of encouragement for the others. Just after the 1st *Chūtai* separated, part of the CAP sighted the incoming raiders about 10 miles northwest of the ships. Noticing planes a few thousand feet below, Hank Leder of Vejtasa's REAPER 7 called, "Tally ho nine o'clock down." He and section leader Stan Ruehlow dived in from 13,000 feet against two Zeros which apparently accelerated ahead of the rest to meet them.

A minute or so later Swede Vejtasa and Lt. Leroy E. ("Tex") Harris (USNA 1939) saw what looked like eleven dark-green torpedo planes deployed in a column and descending at 250 knots or more. Actually they were Yusuhara's eight

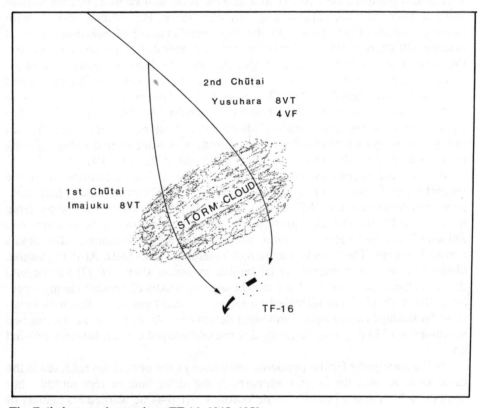

The *Zuikaku* torpedo attack on TF-16, 1045–1050.

2nd *Chūtai kankōs* with perhaps a few Zeros nearby. The Japanese aimed for the clouds through which the fighters had just climbed. The two F4Fs roared steeply down through a very fast high-side run from the left of WO Yaegashi Haruzō's 46th *Shōtai* in the rear. Accelerating to 350 knots, the Wildcats still retained enough aileron control to do some maneuvering, one of its strong points. Once in range Vejtasa blasted one Type 97 and Harris another. Together they torched PO1c Toshida Ken'ichirō's trailing *kankō*.[30]

Meanwhile, the 2nd *Chūtai* also ran afoul of REAPER 2's Dave Pollock and Bob Holland (VF-72), who had no ammunition. They discovered several torpedo planes approaching about 8,000 yards to the right and diving 1,000 feet below. The Japanese started to fan out by sections. Noticing Vejtasa and Harris at work on the left side, Pollock singled out one in the rear with an overhead pass, but Holland warned that his opponent was a Zero, not a torpedo plane. More anxious to intercept aircraft capable of hurting his carrier, Pollock broke off prematurely and resumed the run against torpedo planes farther down.[31]

Plunging straight into the dark storm clouds rather than dropping beneath, the 2nd *Chūtai* lost height very swiftly, as individual Type 97s loosened formation. While recovering from his long high-side pass, Vejtasa saw his friend Pollock catch another Nakajima at 4,000 feet. The evidence points to his target as PO3c Kikuchi Yasuo, number 3 in the lead 44th *Shōtai*. Pollock stormed up its tail to point-blank range and shot off all his remaining bullets. The target smoked, then disappeared into the whiteness.

Vejtasa reprised his first run by chasing the whole 45th *Shōtai* of three Type 97s down through the murk. From directly astern he triggered two short bursts against the number 2 plane, PO1c Tamura Heiji. Shifting his aim over to the leader, Spec. Duty Ens. Kanada Kazumasa, Vejtasa saw pieces fly off the *kankō* and thought he shot off the rudder. PO1c Yamauchi Kazuo, the number 3, essayed a shallow evasive turn, but Vejtasa responded with a long squirt and likewise thought he torched the Nakajima. He noticed no return fire during any of his attacks. Although he felt certain he finished all three aircraft, they kept on going toward the task force.

After dipping down through the clouds, Pollock saw a flaming victim strike the water. Very likely this was Toshida from the 46th *Shōtai*, destroyed as a result of Vejtasa's first run. Shipboard observers noticed the bright, fiery trail of the one victim of the CAP as it smacked the water about five miles astern of the task force. Still enmeshed in the clouds, Vejtasa himself caught sight of a lone torpedo plane above, almost certainly Kikuchi's previously damaged by Pollock. After his low-side run missed, Vejtasa tailed in behind as the *kankō* descended rapidly toward the water. Thus it appears that while intercepting the 2nd *Chūtai* the CAP had destroyed one Type 97 (Toshida), crippled a second (Kikuchi), forced a third to abort the attack altogether (seen by Vejtasa), and shot up several of the remaining five Nakajimas.

The 1st *Chūtai* Goes In

While Vejtasa and company roughed up Yusuhara's 2nd *Chūtai* to the north, Imajuku's unescorted 1st *Chūtai* slipped underneath the squall line to threaten TF-16 from the west. To defend against fighter attack, Imajuku let down to wave-top level while still far out from the ships and bored in against the *Enterprise*'s starboard side as she held course 235 degrees. The eight Type 97s opened up in loose *shōtai* order, as they wheeled around from west to southwest of the ships. Imajuku's 41st *Shōtai* held the lead, followed by the 42nd under Lt. (jg) Itō Tetsu

Lt. Stanley W. Vejtasa, the renowned VF-10 ace, 27 Apr. 1943. (NA 80-G-67547)

(NA 67-1939) and in the rear, Spec. Duty Ens. Suzuki Nakakura's 43rd with two *kankōs*.

Out ahead of the 1st *Chūtai,* some F4Fs, low on fuel and ammunition, marked time at 500 feet awaiting the signal to land. They included VF-72's George Wrenn and Jim Dowden from VF-10. Skimming the waves at 10 feet, Imajuku in the lead plane swept past Wrenn, who turned onto his tail. Adding to Imajuku's woes, he neared the *Maury* from sharp off her port bow, and she brought her 20-mm cannons to bear. While maneuvering to pick up the fighter pilot who ditched a few minutes before, Sims, her CO, noticed six torpedo planes (41st and 42nd *shōtais*) coming in from dead ahead. He reluctantly sheered away from the man in the water to regain his place in the screen and take them on.

Beset by Wrenn shooting from astern and the *Maury*'s 20-millimeters, the Type 97 suddenly shed its port wing. The fuselage rolled over and dipped the starboard wing tip into the waves. Wrenn, the *Maury*'s gunners, and one of the *Enterprise*'s port forward five-inchers all claimed the kill (Wrenn's fifth kill of the flight). Dowden also claimed a probable VT. On the *Maury* Sims worried about the pilot (Gordon Barnes of VF-10) left in the water and later learned he was never recovered. He strongly recommended that all ships prepare life rafts to toss to men spotted in the water. CinCPac agreed.[32]

At 1046 the rest of the Type 97s pressed their attacks against fierce AA fire. PO1c Kawada Tadayoshi, number 2 in the 41st *Shōtai,* flashed past the *Maury*'s port side, launched his torpedo against the *Enterprise* from abaft her starboard beam, and turned away. The missile missed the target. At the same time PO1c Kawabata Ōyoshi in the last 41st *kankō,* sought a better angle from which to attack the carrier. Nearly brushing the *Maury* to starboard he flew parallel to the task force's course to gain position out ahead.

Flying relatively close together, Itō's 42nd *Shōtai* executed an excellent joint attack from off the *Enterprise*'s starboard bow. Expertly advised by the navigator, Cdr. Richard W. Ruble ("They don't come steadier than Ruble," wrote an admiring Eugene Burns),[33] Captain Hardison conned the *Enterprise* from her navigating bridge wings. Seeing three closely spaced white torpedo tracks nearly abreast of each other churning in from starboard, he immediately ordered right full rudder to turn sharply starboard to swing inside them. Her rapidly swinging bow permitted "The Big E" to comb the wakes to starboard. The three *kankōs* crossed ahead of the *Enterprise* and escaped, flying along her port side directly toward the *South Dakota* ablaze with gun flashes.

Unable to gain proper position against the carrier, the veteran Suzuki and PO1c Yukawa Nagao of the 43rd *Shōtai* turned sharply left to take on the *South Dakota* pounding up astern of her. Assaulting the battleship's starboard side, Yukawa released his fish and banked away, but Suzuki bored in although set afire by AA. At 1048 he lobbed his torpedo like a bomb against the *South Dakota*'s stern. The 18-foot cylinder sailed right over the main deck from starboard to port and flopped into the water about 20 yards off her quarter. Suzuki's mangled Type 97 splashed 200 yards beyond. The *Preston*'s lookouts saw Yukawa's torpedo miss the "*SoDak*"'s port quarter. Confident, however, of fatal damage to the battleship, Yukawa swung northwest away from the ships.[34]

Hardison next reversed the *Enterprise*'s rudder to swing hard aport and avoid the battered destroyer *Smith* coming up from her port quarter. He came left again onto a new base course of 135 degrees. All this time PO1c Kawabata from Imajuku's 41st *Shōtai* had marked his target while he flew out ahead of the task force to starboard. Finally swinging in, he fired his torpedo from dead ahead of the carrier. Her lookouts did not spot the wake until it was within 800 yards. Hardison applied hard right rudder, and as the *Enterprise*'s stern came left, the torpedo bubbled past only 100 yards off her starboard side. Valiantly brought back into service after the bombing attack, Ensign Field's forecastle 1.1-inch mount tagged Kawabata after he dropped his fish. The Type 97 actually survived a sort of controlled crash into the sea, and while the *Enterprise* passed a few hundred

Two *Zuikaku* Type 97 carrier attack planes from the 42nd *Shōtai* head toward the *South Dakota* after firing torpedoes at the *Enterprise*. Photo taken to port from the *Enterprise*'s island. (USN)

yards close aboard, two crewmen scurried out onto the wreckage. Mott pointed out the Japanese survivors over the bullhorn, and to his horror the starboard automatic AA batteries erased them in a torrent of shell splashes.[35]

Thus six *kankōs* from the 1st *Chūtai* had assailed the carrier's starboard bow and beam and two likewise braved the battleship's massive starboard battery, but none scored. Three succumbed to AA and an F4F; the five survivors passed around the ships to exit northward.

The 2nd *Chūtai* Attacks

During the 1st *Chūtai*'s charge from starboard of TF-16, six *kankōs* (including one cripple) from Yusuhara's 2nd *Chūtai* emerged one at a time or in pairs from out of the storm to the north. The black clouds rendered the dark-green Type 97s quite hard to discern as they threatened the task force from astern.

In the lead was the Type 97 (very likely Kikuchi's of the 44th *Shōtai*) Vejtasa was pursuing. He decided this bandit flew too high and was in poor position to threaten the carrier. Furthermore, AA fire from the *South Dakota* and other warships burst thickly around, so he sheered off. Either Vejtasa or the AA had tagged this *kankō*, for it suddenly burst into flames. Still lugging his torpedo and diving plenty fast, the pilot (Sea1c Takei Kiyomi) realized he could not reach the *Enterprise*, but gazed instead at the *Smith* off her port quarter. To the amazement of onlookers, the burning aircraft overtook the *Smith* from abaft of her starboard beam and at 1047 plowed into the shield of the number 2 five-inch gun mount. The fuselage exploded as it fell onto the number 1 mount and dropped over the side, leaving behind the torpedo warhead rolling back and forth on the forecastle. Six minutes later it detonated with a terrific blast under the number 1 gun. Meanwhile, gasoline sprayed from ruptured fuel tanks ignited a bad fire. Battered by the suicider, the *Smith* fell off sharply to starboard, forcing the *Enterprise* to move out of her way.[36]

Five other 2nd *Chūtai* Type 97s stuck doggedly to the original plan by trying to gain proper position off the carrier's port bow. Hardison adroitly kept "The Big E" 's stern pointed at them. Massive AA gunfire concentrated upon the Japanese while they tried improving their poor approach angle. Finally one frustrated *kankō* pilot (Sea1c Ōba Rinzō of PO1c Yamauchi's number 3 of the 45th *Shōtai*) simply overhauled the carrier from dead astern. His tormentors included, strangely enough, the two LSOs. Just prior to the attack, plane handlers spotted a half dozen SBDs aft to remove them from the fires up forward. Manning the two rearmost parked Dauntlesses, Lindsey and Daniels swung out the twin .30s and blazed away. Only a few yards short of the fantail, their bullets may have reached the enemy pilot, who pulled up sharply, dropped his fish in the climbing turn, rolled awkwardly into a steep wingover, and splashed in flames close astern of the *Portland*. Enjoying his first chance to retaliate since he destroyed an enemy land attack plane on 1 February, Daniels described his backseat antics as "the most fun I've had."[37] The other four *kankōs* launched their fish from off the *Enterprise*'s port quarter. One torpedo passed to port while the carrier combed its wake, and the remainder never threatened the target. All four attackers escaped to the south, although the *Enterprise* gunners thought they downed two of them.

Shortly after this attack, the *Portland* suffered quite a thrill while her engineers tried to correct a sudden steering malfunction. A few minutes before, Itō's 42nd *Shōtai* had fired three torpedoes against the *Enterprise*'s starboard bow, but she had adroitly evaded them. Now nearly at the end of their run they struck the "*Sweet Pea*"'s starboard side, but all three were duds. Reviewing the incident, Halsey later remarked it was nice to see the enemy's materiel fail, too.[38]

At 1052 the ships ceased fire when the surviving *kankōs* drew out of range. However, several Wildcats loitering at low altitude west of the task force blocked the line of retreat. At wave-top level two 1st *Chūtai* carrier attack planes headed toward VF-10 pilots Whitney Feightner, Swede Vejtasa, and Don Gordon. Noticing Feightner take after the nearer one, Vejtasa joined the chase and emptied his guns (remarkably he had bullets left!) into the straining Type 97. To escape the tracers its pilot skidded violently—about the only feasible evasive maneuver at that height. The plane caught fire, but stoically flew on. Feightner broke off at that point and never saw what happened, but Vejtasa watched it stagger another five miles and splash. This was Vejtasa's fifth torpedo plane in this fight (seventh kill overall for the mission). George Wrenn happened to see it succumb, remembered the victor's side number (F-19), and later congratulated Vejtasa on board the *Enterprise*. It is fitting they talked because, credited with five torpedo planes apiece, they had become the bane of the 3rd Fleet's carrier attack squadrons.[39]

While Feightner and Vejtasa finished one Type 97, Gordon went after the other. Hoping to squeeze some more bullets from his apparently empty guns, he lined up for a head-on run. The enemy pilot had been glancing over his left shoulder back toward the ships and suddenly looked around to see the Grumman filling his windshield. Instinctively he dropped his left wing to roll out of the way but dug its tip in the sea and cartwheeled to destruction. The three VF-10 pilots had destroyed two *kankōs* from Itō's 42nd *Shōtai*.[40]

Thus the combat over TF-16 cost eight of sixteen *Zuikaku* Type 97s, including the squadron leader, Lieutenant Imajuku. It appears the 1st *Chūtai* lost one downed straightaway by an F4F and AA (Imajuku) and two more to AA. Fighters destroyed two more on the way out. In addition to one forced to abort before the attack, Yusuhara's 2nd *Chūtai* lost three planes: one before release to an F4F, one that crashed the *Smith,* and the third to *Enterprise* AA.

The Japanese survivors later decided that three *kankōs* fell during the high-speed approach—one supposedly disintegrating from excessive speed! They claimed two torpedo hits on the *Enterprise*-class carrier (severe damage), two on the battleship (sunk), and one against a heavy cruiser (also sunk). In addition they witnessed the suicide dive onto the destroyer. A Japanese radioman notched one of fourteen Grummans believed to have intercepted the squadron. All four escorting Zeros survived a tussle with reportedly ten fighters and claimed seven (including one unconfirmed). Actually their opponents were Ruehlow, Leder, Pollock, and Holland, none of whom went down. After Shigemi separated from wingman PO3c Ōishi Yoshio, he opted for Buin. Perhaps his homing receiver was damaged, or, remembering 24 August, he did not want to return to a burning flight deck. At any rate he reached Buin after a long flight, while Ōishi returned safely to the *Kidō Butai*. PO2c Ōkura Shigeru and Sea1c Doi Shizuo (2nd *Shōtai*) likewise sought the carrier to the northwest.

The *Enterprise* very fortunately did not take one or more torpedo hits, which could have spelled disaster at this juncture. The intervention by Vejtasa and company proved crucial for her defense. They shattered the 2nd *Chūtai* and disrupted timing between the two attacking elements. The ship noted five torpedoes launched from starboard and four from port. Most were released from perhaps 75 feet of altitude and between 1,000 and 2,000 yards from the target, but a few runs came much closer. Described in the *Enterprise* report as showing "obvious skill and great determination,"[41] the *Zuikaku* Carrier Attack Squadron deserved better from their courageous attack.

CAP claims were:

		VT	Probable
VF-10	Vejtasa	5	1
	Harris	1	1
	Pollock	1	—
	Feightner	—	1
	Ruehlow	—	1
	Dowden	—	1
	Gordon	1	—
VF-72	Wrenn	1	—
		9	5

RETURNING STRIKE GROUPS

The two *Hornet* and one *Enterprise* strike groups did not fly out together, certainly did not attack in concert, nor did they return together. In fact, the planes straggled back in small groups—their crews hoping to roost on open flight decks. The *Hornet*'s loss of power silenced her YE homer; her distant aviators heard

TABLE 21.2
1st Carrier Division, Second Strike (Lt. Imajuku Shigeichirō)

Zuikaku Carrier Attack Squadron (17 Type 97 VT)
1st *Chūtai*

41st *Shōtai*	42nd *Shōtai*	43rd *Shōtai*
Lt. Imajuku Shigeichirōa (O)	Lt. (jg) Itō Tetsua (P)	Spec. Duty Ens. Suzuki Nakakuraa (O)
PO1c Kawada Tadayoshi (O)	PO1c Nagashima Masayoshia (O)	PO1c Yukawa Nagao (O)
PO1c Kawabata Ōyoshia (O)	PO2c Satō Masatoshia (O)	

2nd *Chūtai*

44th *Shōtai*	45th *Shōtai*	46th *Shōtai*
Lt. Yusuhara Masayuki (P)	Spec. Duty Ens. Kanada Kazumasa (O)	WO Yaegashi Haruzō (P)
PO1c Yoshii Shirō (O)	PO1c Tamura Heiji (O)	PO1c Toshida Ken'ichirōa (P)
PO1c Kikuchi Yasuoa (O)	PO1c Yamauchi Kazuoa (O)	

Contact Plane
WO Suzuki Naochirō (O)

Close Escort
Zuikaku Carrier Fighter Squadron (4 Zeros)
15th *Shōtai*
WO Shigemi Katsuma
PO3c Ōishi Yoshio
PO2c Ōkura Shigeru
Sea2c Doi Shizuo

Note: Aircraft commanders: P = pilot; O = observer
a Shot down or missing in action (ditched planes not indicated in records)

only an ominous "growl" on that frequency. The *Enterprise*'s YE signal worked fine.

First to start back from the target area were two badly damaged VF-72 F4Fs that had escorted the *Hornet* first wave. Phil Souza accompanied Willie Roberts, who was gravely wounded and flying an even more shot-up Grumman. They lost track of both friendly and enemy planes. Lacking navigational data, Souza set course about 0915 for home by taking the reciprocal bearing of the outbound leg and guided Roberts through widely scattered clouds down to 2,000 feet. After about 45 minutes, five enemy torpedo planes approached head-on at nearly the same altitude—Lieutenant (jg) Suzuki and the other four survivors from the *Shōkaku* 1st *Chūtai* fresh from their attack on the *Hornet*. When Souza smoked a Type 97 with an opposite run, he was surprised that the Japanese rear gunner suddenly jumped up as the F4F went by. He never saw whether the plane splashed, but quickly rejoined his wounded teammate. Although Warrant Officer Nakai's *kankō* did not go down, the radioman, PO2c Nakano Toshio, died in the rear cockpit.[42]

A few minutes after the fight, Souza and Roberts met up with their squadron CO, Mike Sanchez. Soon they spotted TF-17 in the distance. Sanchez executed the proper recognition turns and at 1029 radioed, "BLUE 1, we are coming in." The *Hornet* looked in bad shape, stopped and listing to starboard. The *North-*

ampton again worked ahead to tow her, while the other screening ships circled counterclockwise. Their gunners were still touchy after the surprise mock attack by Tanaka's *Zuihō* carrier attack plane 20 minutes before and took no chances. At 1029 the *Juneau* reported two planes at 326 degrees, then employed her massive five-inch battery. Other ships followed suit. An exasperated Souza exclaimed on the radio, "Christ sake stop shooting at me. I haven't a hell of a lot of gas."[43]

That stopped the AA fire, but the end had come for Willie Roberts. Despite his wounds and severe bleeding, he courageously returned to the task force. The battered F4F ran out of fuel, and Roberts set down a few miles short of the ships. He escaped his sinking Grumman and pulled his dye marker, but quickly disappeared while Souza helplessly circled overhead trying to catch the attention of the destroyers.

After taking a good look at the stricken *Hornet*, Souza flew southeast toward TF-16 and arrived just as the *Zuikaku* torpedo planes attacked. Powerless to intervene, he could only watch the suicide crash into the *Smith*. (In 1961 he happened to mention his propinquity to the *Smith*'s former XO, who responded vehemently, "Then why didn't you do something?") Sanchez and Souza joined the landing circle around the *Enterprise* and hoped they could get on board before their fuel ran out.

Little is known about the VF-72 first-wave torpedo escort, other than that Bob Sorensen, Bob Jennings, and Roy Dalton reached TF-16 safely. At some time on the return leg, Sorensen claimed a dive bomber and Dalton a probable, but it is not known whether they were returning *Zuikaku* or *Shōkaku* carrier bombers. The evidence points to the former. On the flight back, enemy fighters ambushed Lieutenant Ishimaru, CO of the *Zuikaku* Carrier Bomber Squadron's ill-fated 3rd *Chūtai*, and killed his observer, WO Azuma Tōichi. Not unlike Willie Roberts, the wounded Ishimaru limped to the *Kidō Butai*, landed in the water, but died soon after on the *Amatsukaze*.[44] Thus all fourteen men of the 3rd *Chūtai* fell in battle.

The SBDs and F4Fs from the *Hornet*'s second wave, which pummeled the heavy cruiser *Chikuma*, straggled back in several small groups. Around 1045 the lead flight of about six SBDs spotted TF-17 but, uncertain as to what to do, they circled the stricken carrier. Warren Ford of VF-72 noticed a strange plane hanging around the *Hornet* as if observing her condition. It turned out to be a Japanese dive bomber, PO1c Ishiyama's *Shōkaku* carrier bomber sent out as a contact plane almost two hours before. Ford set its left wingroot on fire, forcing the crew to bail out. That was the last Ford saw of them, but the destroyer *Isokaze* rescued both men the next morning.[45]

Meanwhile, Lieutenant Parker's six VT-6 TBFs from the first wave joined the procession over TF-17 at 1055. Noting so many planes overhead, Rear Admiral Good on the *Northampton* sent by blinker light: "Go to *Enterprise*." Three F4Fs, seven SBDs, and six TBFs swung southeast toward TF-16. So by mistake did the *Juneau*, unintentionally weakening the *Hornet*'s AA protection. However, her error proved fortunate for VB-8's Evan Fisher, one of Gus Widhelm's first-wave SBD pilots. He found TF-17, but halfway to TF-16, he ditched at 1112 near the *Juneau*. George Ferguson, the wounded radioman, pulled Fisher from the sinking Dauntless, and the cruiser quickly rescued both men.[46]

Led by Edgar Stebbins, three VS-8 SBDs from the *Hornet* second wave took a straight course back to TF-17, but kept on going after what they saw. Around

1045 a "spectacular show" of black AA bursts blossomed on the horizon, followed a few minutes later by the tempting sight of two enemy torpedo planes. Stebbins and Lt. (jg) Philip J. Rusk turned to chase them, but the pair split up. One headed toward Lt. (jg) Albert H. Wood in the third SBD, giving him a better chance to intercept. He fired short bursts with his two .50s, and endured fire ("puffs of black smoke") from the Japanese rear gunner. One .50 jammed, but as Wood pulled off to clear it, his adversary plunged into the water, leaving a fiery patch of gasoline on the surface. The victim was the remaining plane from Itō's 42nd *Shōtai* (1st *Chūtai*) and the ninth *Zuikaku* carrier attack plane lost on the mission. Stebbins gave Wood "thumbs up" for good work.[47]

About 1110 Walt Rodee arrived over TF-17 with eight Avengers from Ward Powell's 2nd VT-6 Division and four VF-72 escort F4Fs led by Jock Sutherland. They soon struck out for TF-16. Returning alone, the last VT-6 pilot, Hump Tallman, survived a rough time with some of Lieutenant Shirane's first-wave escorts when Zeros jumped the TBF at 10,000 feet. Before Tallman could dive away, his radioman, Francis J. Chantiny, ARM1c, was wounded. He reached TF-16 about the same time as Powell. The *Zuikaku* fighter pilots claimed two dive bombers destroyed on their return flight, one of which was this TBF.[48]

The last *Hornet* planes to appear were the eleven VS-8 and VB-8 SBDs that had plastered the *Shōkaku*. Homing on "The Big E" 's YE signal they encountered numerous enemy aircraft on their way back. For the most part neither side seemed ready to pick fights, but VB-8's Lt. (jg) William D. Carter and Ralph Hovind of VS-8 tackled enemy dive bombers and thought they at least inflicted some damage.

Near to TF-17, Lt. (jg) Forrester C. Auman of VB-8 sighted an enemy torpedo plane coming toward him at 500 feet. In a diving opposite attack, Auman stitched a stream of bullets across its fuselage and flew up alongside the Type 97, so his radioman, Samuel P. McLean, ARM3c, could shoot his twin .30s. The enemy replied with his 7.7-mm Lewis gun. Auman broke off for home without seeing the torpedo plane splash, but there is strong evidence that he shot down Warrant Officer Tanaka's *Zuihō* contact plane. Its last known message went out at 1040: "Remaining enemy strength is two cruisers, nine destroyers, position 8-37 S., 166-37 E. One carrier is stopped."[49] Tanaka had shadowed TF-17 with the stricken *Hornet,* while Sakumuki from the *Zuikaku* dogged TF-16. At 1106 TF-17 lookouts reported a burning plane bearing 270 degrees, distance nine miles—very likely Auman's kill.

THE *JUNYŌ* STRIKE AGAINST TASK FORCE 16

Even while Nagumo's *Kidō Butai* fought and retired northwest, another combatant entered the lists. Kakuta's *Junyō,* with Kondō's Advance Force, pounded northeast toward Nagumo. Anxious to attack as soon as possible, Kakuta instructed the *Junyō* to launch her first wave at 0905 at an estimated 280 miles. Led by the group commander, Lt. Shiga Yoshio, the attackers numbered twelve Zeros and seventeen Type 99 carrier bombers under Lt. Yamaguchi Masao.[50] With the *Junyō*'s strike, the Japanese had hurled 138 aircraft (42 fighters, 57 carrier bombers, 36 carrier attack planes, and 3 contact planes) against the American carriers, almost twice as many planes as Kinkaid sent in return.

Four CAP Zeros followed the twenty-nine planes aloft, while the *Junyō*'s hangar readied the second strike of seven Type 97 carrier attack planes. Lieutenant

Irikiin, the torpedo squadron leader borrowed from the *Hiyō*, would command them. Engine trouble brought Lieutenant Shigematsu's Zero back from the first strike. He stalked up and down the flight deck while mechanics prepared another fighter, then took off alone to make the mission—his third against the American carriers in as many battles.[51]

Continuing northeast toward Nagumo's carriers, Kondō heard at 0945 of the *Shōkaku*'s woes and Nagumo's retreat to the northwest. He also intercepted reports from the first strike group indicating heavy damage to the Americans. Consequently he flung the Advance Force southeast after the battered enemy and at 1018 detached Kakuta with the *Junyō* and two destroyers to join Nagumo's command. Before Kakuta could depart, lookouts from the battleship *Haruna* excitedly pointed out ten large enemy planes. The *Junyō* scrambled four Zeros and Irikiin's six Type 97s to clear the flight deck, but it proved a false alarm. She recovered Irikiin and resumed preparations for her second strike. Sea1c Maki's errant *Zuihō* CAP Zero, the only survivor of Okamoto's battle with the VF-72 escorts, followed them on board. At 1045 Kakuta set off to join Nagumo.

By 1058 it became evident to TF-16 that the *Enterprise* escaped the torpedo planes without taking further damage, but her CAP had just about shot its bolt. So had the radar. After the *Zuikaku* torpedo attack, "The Big E" 's big CXAM radar antenna ceased rotating. Lt. Dwight M. B. Williams, the radar officer, hastened up through Mott's sky control and bravely climbed all the way up the mast to the array, which he found out of alignment. To fix the motors, he lashed himself to the antenna. Thinking the radar was repaired, someone below gave the order to turn on the power, which, in Mott's words, sent him into "merry-go-rounds with the now rotating antenna." Soon the whirling bedspring ceased, and a rather shaken Brad Williams eased his way safely down to the island.[52]

Temporarily blinded, Griffin told the fighters at 1058, "Remain close to base; no definite bogeys now." That was about all the eighteen F4Fs (thirteen VF-10, five VF-72) could do. Nearly out of ammunition and critically low on fuel, they patronized the *Enterprise*'s landing pattern. Vejtasa spoke for all when he asked permission to pancake. About the only CAP section capable of fighting was Kane and Lt. John C. Eckhardt (USNA 1938) (REAPER 4), hitherto not engaged. Soon the *Hornet* strike planes filtering in from the west joined the CAP. Until about 1120 approximately ten VF-72 F4Fs from both strikes, ten SBDs (mostly second wave), and sixteen TBFs entered TF-16's crowded landing circle.

After 1100, John Crommelin's *Enterprise* flight deck team struck below a few SBDs. Not trusting the damaged number 1 elevator, they used numbers 2 and 3 located aft in the recovery and run-up areas. For a time, even number 2 jammed in the lowered position, a frightening development, but finally after almost 90 minutes delay, the *Enterprise* reopened for business at 1115. Air Group Ten LSO Jim Daniels waved in several F4Fs: from VF-72 Sanchez, Emerson, and Weimer for certain, and very likely Sorensen, Jennings, and Dalton, as well as VF-10's Dowden. Worried about his frozen right aileron, Phil Souza of VF-72 was not at all certain he could land, but Daniels brought him in without ado. The F4F was a sight, with gaping 20-mm shell holes all along the right wing. Before it could be struck below, TF-16 came under surprise attack from the *Junyō* flyers.

By 1100 the *Junyō* strike had been aloft nearly two hours, as Shiga sought an enemy carrier task force not previously attacked. He had already sighted at 1040 the *Hornet* dead in the water and a "battleship" (the *Northampton*) bringing her under tow. Not satisfied, Shiga pressed on. Overcast skies hindered his search.

He thought of settling for the "battleship," but around 1100 suddenly copied a vital message. Via the destroyer *Arashi*, Nagumo transmitted (and the *Junyō* rebroadcast) the location of the second enemy carrier force as 300 degrees and 30 miles from the first. Shiga knew that to be incorrect, but thought another enemy carrier force must be nearby.[53]

With the radar out, REAPER BASE had no real warning of Shiga's approach and certainly did not realize the enemy was so close. The *South Dakota*'s SC radar found planes bearing 285 degrees and 45 miles, but that vital information never reached Griffin. At 1110 the *Portland* warned of many bogeys 25 miles west, but Kinkaid replied they were friendlies. Bothered by bogeys on her radar screen, the *South Dakota* mistakenly fired at one batch of *Hornet* planes.

Finally at 1115 the *Enterprise*'s now-functioning radar registered a large group of planes only 20 miles off. Griffin advised the CAP of bogeys approaching from the north and added, "They may not be friendly." His next orders were more definite, "All planes in air prepare to repel attack," but he cautioned them not to approach the ships too closely. Suddenly at 1119 the *South Dakota* cut loose again at aircraft astern of the carrier, evidently friendlies. Yet someone spotted enemy planes, too. Griffin announced, "Bandits reported above clouds. All planes in air standby to repel attack approaching from north. Above clouds. Above clouds."

At 1121 almost on cue, a swarm of dive bombers spilled out of the clouds above the *Enterprise*. Aft on her flight deck the crowd of men around Souza's battered Wildcat took to their heels in dismay, while Brad Williams was still up on the radar array.

Spotting ships from the TF-16 screen through a momentary break in the clouds, Lieutenant Yamaguchi led his nine 1st *Chūtai* carrier bombers down into the murk and disappeared. Somewhat startled, Shiga's Zeros and the eight Type 99s of the 2nd *Chūtai* under Lt. Miura Naohiko (NA 66-1938) tried to follow the *kanbaku hikōtaichō*, but immediately lost contact. At 1120 a hollow space revealed an enemy force almost directly below. Shiga rocked his wings and signaled his Zeros to drop tanks, while Miura prepared to attack.[54]

Greatly hampered by thick clouds and a ceiling in some places as low as 500 feet, Miura's eight carrier bombers slanted down in close succession at shallow angles (about 45 degrees) against the stern of the *Enterprise*. Given the slow speed of the *kanbakus* once they popped their dive brakes, Shiga had to loop his Zero merely to stay near them. Pulling out, he almost clipped a destroyer's stack before AA drove him into a nearby cloud. The flattened dives rendered Miura's Type 99s very vulnerable to AA fire, particularly from the deadly 40-mm Bofors guns. No F4Fs intercepted the leader, but gunfire soon torched Miura's *kanbaku* and also blew off the tail of PO1c Yabuki Katsuyoshi's Type 99 next in line. Their bombs splashed quite close together astern of the *Enterprise*. Third to dive, PO2c Kataoka Yoshiharu released his bomb and, without visible flames, his Type 99 plunged straight into the water. The entire 25th *Shōtai* had perished.

Following Miura down, WO Honmura Masataka, leader of the 26th *Shōtai*, scored the only success. His 250-kilogram bomb glanced off the carrier's port bow near the waterline and exploded underwater less than 10 feet from the hull. The concussion dished in plating, opened voided areas to the sea, and knocked out for good the mechanism controlling the number 1 elevator. Neither his two wingmen nor the two of WO Nakako Masahiko's 27th *Shōtai* secured any hits.

Parked aft on deck while "The Big E" twisted and turned to evade attacking bombers, Souza's torn-up F-25 bounced and rocked, then broke loose. The rogue

Commander Rodee's TBF captures TF-16 under attack by *Junyō* carrier bombers. Note the thick cloud over the *Enterprise* that hindered the Japanese pilots. (NA 80-G-304525)

Wildcat slid on its belly (due to its collapsed landing gear) toward the starboard five-inch gun gallery, but plane handlers quickly dumped the aircraft over the side. Souza regretted the loss of the excellent pair of sunglasses he had left on its gunsight.[55]

The brief 2nd *Chūtai* attack cost three Type 99s to the unusually fierce AA fire. Certain that he and his teammates scored three times with medium damage to the enemy carrier, Honmura led the five survivors out at low level, where they stirred up a nest of American planes in the landing circle. In the meantime, Kinkaid at 1126 chided the *South Dakota,* "You are reported firing on friendly planes." However, Griffin warned, "Friendly planes, turn to your right. Hawks reported diving astern." Just as eager to fight, the *Junyō* Zeros regrouped to support their charges (details of that melee appear below).

As things settled down, George Wrenn of VF-72 realized that if the flattop did not take him on his first try, he would run out of gas. It did not look good when the *Enterprise* turned sharply, but Daniels gave him a Roger. After touch-down, the F4F rolled perilously near the deck edge when the ship heeled sharply to one side, and green water loomed below. A plane handler lifted Wrenn's hook, and he taxied forward. No one came out to chock his wheels, so he sat uneasily in his cockpit. Again bombs fell on TF-16, but this time the *Enterprise* was not the target.[56]

Hunting through the rain clouds, Yamaguchi's 1st *Chūtai* finally regained contact at 1129 with part of the enemy force, but not the carrier. While maneuvering to evade Miura's surprise attack, TF-16 had spread out over the sea. Because of the poor visibility, the nine *kanbakus* split up in a confused, disjointed attack from many directions. Yet this time the low ceiling of the dark cloud mass (1,000–1,500 feet) greatly hindered recognition and direction by the AA gunners. Also proving a distraction were Kinkaid's TBS orders: "Do not fire at chickens [U.S. planes]. Bogeys coming in now, also friendly aircraft."

One at a time Yamaguchi and three teammates dropped through the rainclouds after the battleship *South Dakota*. They broke into the clear only 1,000 feet over the battlewagon's port bow. The first three 250-kilogram bombs fell either to port or starboard of the *South Dakota*, but the last one burst squarely on the flat, heavily armored top of 16-inch turret number 1. Bomb splinters wounded Capt. Thomas L. Gatch standing exposed on the catwalk forward of the armored conning tower. The explosion caused no real damage, but as a consequence the battleship temporarily lost steering control and blundered through the formation, forcing the *Enterprise* to turn away. No other enemy planes appeared, and she quickly ceased fire.[57]

Off the carrier's starboard bow, the *San Juan* absorbed the rest of the 1st *Chūtai* attack a minute or so later. Five Type 99s led by Lt. (jg) Katō Shunkō (NA 68-1940) swooped down individually against the *San Juan*, ordinarily a dangerous thing to do because of her massive AA battery. However, under the circumstances, fire control had only a few seconds to get on target before the

Near miss against the *Enterprise* during the *Junyō*'s attack, 26 Oct. 1942. (NA 80-G-33340)

Ens. Phil Souza's F-25 (BuNo. 5246) from VF-72 slides on the *Enterprise*'s deck during the *Junyō*'s attack, 26 Oct. 1942. Battle damage had jammed the right aileron in the up position. (NA 80-G-42561)

dive bombers dumped their payloads. The five-inch barrage burst deep in the clouds at 3,000 feet, well above the hawks, and even the deadly 20-mm could not score. Around 1132 waterspouts from three quick near misses showered the cruiser, then a 250-kilogram semi–armor piercing bomb slapped the water close aboard the port side and damaged the hull. The fifth and last 250-kilogram semi–armor piercing bomb sliced through her stern on the starboard side, passed all the way through the thinly armored hull, and detonated beneath the ship. In addition to flooding several compartments, the concussion jammed the rudder hard right. She churned in circles, but at 1141 she regained control.[58]

The 1st *Chūtai* claimed one hit on a heavy cruiser (medium damage) and two on a light cruiser (heavy damage) accurate with the exception of mistaking a BB for a CA. Under adverse circumstances AA destroyed no 1st *Chūtai* Type 99s, but they proved easy meat for American planes waiting to land on the *Enterprise*. The CAP F4Fs were largely *hors de combat*, low on fuel and out of bullets. Unlike 24 August, the F4F-4's reduced ammunition capacity (240 rounds per gun) elicited scathing descriptions such as "glaring deficiency" and "extremely embarrassing."[59] For the most part only the VF-72 second-wave escorts retained the ammunition and fuel to fight. SBDs and (in one instance) a TBF also mixed in with the retreating *Junyō* planes.

It is impossible in most instances to determine who fought whom and the specific results. Apparently fourteen carrier bombers (five 2nd *Chūtai*, nine 1st *Chūtai*) survived the attacks against the ships. In subsequent air actions, the 2nd *Chūtai* lost one shot down and another badly damaged (observer killed), while four 1st *Chūtai* aircraft (including Yamaguchi) went down in this phase of the battle. Thus a total of five Type 99s fell to U.S. planes. United States Navy claims were:

VF-72	7 VB, 2 VB probable, 1 VF probable
VF-10	1 VB
VB-8	3 VB
VS-8	1 VB

Obviously, with twelve dive bombers claimed, different U.S. aircraft fought the same Japanese planes. It was a confusing low-level combat against scattered targets. At this late date it is possible only to offer some personal accounts of the action.

During Miura's surprise assault against the *Enterprise*, Warren Ford's rump VF-72 division orbited at 300 feet outside the screen. Antiaircraft fire soon separated the three F4Fs. Drawing near the *South Dakota*, which was blasting indiscriminately at every plane within range, Ford noticed a dive bomber pull out very low and make off at high speed. He gave chase, but above at 2,000 feet a few Zeros worked over an F4F, "flying rings around it." Ford joined that fracas, but not at VMax because only the fuel in his belly tank remained. Both Zeros released their prey and eagerly swooped down in after the erstwhile rescuer. After scissoring for a head-on shot against the leader, Ford stalled before he could deal with the second bandit. Using simultaneous runs from astern and ahead, the two Japanese effectively trapped him. A 20-mm shell slammed the armor plate behind his seat and loosed bolts that whizzed around the smoke-filled cockpit. Fearing a fuel-tank fire, Ford lifted both feet on top of the instrument panel (he never thought he could do that), pushed the stick forward, and dived. Some low clouds provided much needed relief, and he emerged among some TBFs.[60]

Number 3 in Ford's division was Al Fairbanks. Along with Jim Billo from REAPER 5, he took out after PO3c Shizuno Ryūnosuke's Type 99 from Miura's 2nd *Chūtai* and downed it. The two F4Fs started back toward the task force, but discovered another *kanbaku* coming out, this one from Yamaguchi's 1st *Chūtai*. They split up to bracket the target, and the sharpshooting Fairbanks scored again.[61]

In his shot-up mount, Ken Bliss of VF-72 chased right down to the wave tops one 1st *Chūtai* dive bomber that had attacked the battleship. Only the right outboard .50-caliber gun fired, and the uneven recoil threw off his aim. Despite silencing the rear gunner, Bliss could not finish off the airplane.[62] The only other CAP pilot who fought the *Junyō* carrier bombers was REAPER 4's John Eckhardt. Misdirected during three raids, he finally got his chance and claimed one dive bomber.

Newly returned from escorting the second-wave TBFs, Jock Sutherland's four VF-72 F4Fs intercepted both *Junyō* attacks. In close succession Sutherland shot down two dive bombers, while Dave Freeman and Al Dietrich each claimed one VB destroyed and one probable. Hank Carey saw Miura's 2nd *Chūtai* assail the *Enterprise*, whose 40-mm AA chopped the first few dive bombers into the sea. He pursued one survivor into the midst of the *South Dakota*'s AA fire, far more of a threat than the enemy rear gunner, and shot it down. A whole *shōtai* of three Zeros showed up to avenge their comrades. A 20-mm shell punched through Carey's armor plate into the main fuel tank and detonated with a terrifying blast, but F-28 chugged along seemingly unaffected. After winging a Zero, Carey evaded the others. Perhaps he was the one Ford helped escape.[63]

Two F4Fs disappeared during the attack. Over TF-16 since 0930, Jerry Davis of the VF-10 CAP evidently developed some sort of engine trouble and was last seen clearing the immediate area when the ships cut loose at the *Junyō* carrier bombers. The squadron felt AA probably got him, but possibly he flew the F4F Ford saw under Zero attack. Several pilots noticed a man floating in a life raft, and Dick Hughes of VF-72 tried unsuccessfully to entice a destroyer to come out after him. Very likely this was Davis, whose parachute harness sported the new life raft.[64]

The second MIA was VF-72's Morrill Cook, a VF-8 vet credited with two Zeros at Midway. Unlike the depleted CAP, he could fight when the *Junyō* carrier bombers unexpectedly turned up. About five minutes after the attack, some VF-10 pilots, including Swede Vejtasa, observed an F4F pilot bail out at 7,000 feet and flop into the water a dozen miles northwest of TF-16. Again no ship went to the rescue. Very likely the unfortunate individual was Cook, as it is doubtful Davis would have gone out that far.[65]

The *Hornet* SBDs, like their escorts, saw heavy action against the *Junyō* attackers. From the second wave, VB-8's Lt. (jg) Thomas J. Wood claimed two dive bombers withdrawing low over the water. Teammates Lt. (jg) J. Clark Barrett and Lt. (jg) Joe W. King gave their radiomen, William Berthold, ARM3c, and Wilson C. Lineaweaver, ARM3c, shots at a dive bomber, later declared a kill. Several *Junyō* Zeros riddled the right wing of Joe Auman's first-wave SBD, and he was very lucky to survive. Stebbins, Rusk, and Al Wood from VS-8 observed a full *shōtai* of three Type 99s dive bomb either the *South Dakota* or the *San Juan*. Stebbins slowly overtook the trailing Japanese, who countered by dipping lower and lower. Just as he was about to shoot, the Type 99 dropped its wing into the waves and cartwheeled in spectacular fashion. That surprised Stebbins almost as much as the two Japanese, for he never fired a shot.[66]

Lt. (jg) Rufus C. Clark, a VT-6 pilot in the first wave, also hunted enemy planes. Several other VT-6 crews saw Clark disappear in the midst of black shell bursts. The TBF definitely fell victim to *Junyō* Zeros, which claimed one "TBD" torpedo plane. Like so many other TBF drivers, Clark was a frustrated fighter pilot. His original posting was to VF-42.[67]

Excepting Jim Flatley's four VF-10 F4Fs, the *Junyō* attackers offered the *Enterprise* strike group no offense, although a VS-8 crew could not say the same thing of them. All three radiomen in Glen Estes' VS-10 section blazed away at a "Zero," which turned out to be Stan Holm's SBD. Estes later apologized to

Holm, but privately he was miffed that the gunners not only failed to recognize a friendly plane but missed the target to boot![68]

Flatley's four REAPER 1 F4Fs and the VT-10 TBFs only arrived as the last *Junyō* attack went in against TF-16. The fighters took station at 4,000 feet clear of AA fire and in position to cover several SBDs below. At 1135 Flatley noticed Zeros prowling above, a good incentive to test Jimmy Thach's special defensive tactics. He radioed Russ Reiserer on his wing and the 2nd Section of Cliff Witte and Ed Coalson: "Let's line abreast. Keep sharp look out. If you see anything start weaving . . . Cliff, stay on line abreast and keep your eyes open."[69] Flatley and Reiserer made up one element, Witte and Coalson the other. In the clouds Shiga had lost contact with the carrier bombers and the other Zeros, but finally saw F4Fs and attacked alone. Very low on fuel, Flatley was reluctant to fight on more than 50 percent power, and the strafing cost most of his ammo.

Despite these limitations, Flatley and Witte worked the weave very well. Shiga made three or four runs, then pulled off, seemingly baffled by the intricate defense. In a postwar interview, he remarked, "That teamwork was very good."

TABLE 21.3
2nd Carrier Division, First Strike (Lt. Shiga Yoshio)

Junyō Carrier Bomber Squadron (17 Type 99 VB)		
1st *Chūtai*		
21st *Shōtai*	22nd *Shōtai*	23rd *Shōtai*
Lt. Yamaguchi Masao[a] (P)	Lt. (jg) Katō Shunkō (O)	PO1c Tajima Kazuo (O)
PO1c Seiwa Yoshijirō[a] (O)	PO2c Nishiyama Tsuyoshi (O)	PO2c Honmura Haruo[b] (O)
PO3c Yamanoi Kaku[a] (O)	PO2c Nakao Tetsuo[a] (O)	PO3c Nakatsuka Hisayoshi[c] (P)
2nd *Chūtai*		
25th *Shōtai*	26th *Shōtai*	27th *Shōtai*
Lt. Miura Naohiko[a] (O)	WO Honmura Masataka (O)	WO Nakako Masahiko[c] (P)
PO1c Yabuki Katsuyoshi[a] (O)	PO1c Yanagihara Fusao (O)	PO2c Satō Masahisa (O)
PO2c Kataoka Yoshiharu[a] (O)	PO3c Shizuno Ryūnosuke[a] (O)	
Close Escort		
Junyō Carrier Fighter Squadron (12 Zeros)		
1st *Chūtai*		
11th *Shōtai*	13th *Shōtai*	
Lt. Shiga Yoshio	WO Kitahata Saburō	
PO1c Satō Tadaaki	PO2c Ishii Shizuo	
Sea1c Banno Takao	Sea1c Sanada Eiji	
2nd *Chūtai*		
15th *Shōtai*	16th *Shōtai*	
Lt. Shigematsu Yasuhiro	WO Ono Zenji	
PO1c Muranaka Kazuo	PO2c Hasegawa Tatsuzo	
Sea1c Kotani Kenji	PO3c Bandō Makoto	

Note: Aircraft commanders: P = pilot; O = observer
[a] Shot down or missing in action
[b] Killed on ditching
[c] Ditched

He noted that whenever he got on the tail of a Grumman, another roared after him. The interviewer aptly summarized the skirmish: "No runs, no hits, and no errors."[70] In his reports for Santa Cruz, Flatley christened the defensive tactic as the "Thach Weave": "This maneuver, which is offensive as well as defensive, was conceived by Lieut.-Comdr. J.S. Thach. It is undoubtedly the greatest contribution to air combat tactics that has been made to date." Flatley did a great deal to popularize and refine the famed weave.[71]

Shiga's fight with Flatley was not the last air combat that day near TF-16. At 1200 two *Junyō* Zeros flushed Norm Haber's badly damaged PBY, whose redoubtable crew had fended off Lieutenant Shingō's five *Shōkaku* Zeros. Limping south at 1,000 feet toward Espiritu Santo, Haber spotted two fighters diving in from ahead and starboard. Their pilots went through the motions with a couple of perfunctory passes, but soon broke off after claiming a kill. Again Haber remained aloft, bound for further adventures over TF-16. Henceforth air action shifted back to TF-17 and the hapless *Hornet*. The *Junyō* escort claimed twelve Grummans (including four unconfirmed), one "TBD," and one PBY. In return they lost no aircraft.[72]

CHAPTER 22

Defeat and Retreat

THE JAPANESE REGROUP

After the *Hornet* dive bombers departed, Vice Admiral Nagumo's *Kidō Butai*, with the *Shōkaku*'s buckled flight deck burning fiercely and the *Zuihō*'s tender stern still smoking, recoiled to the northwest at 28 knots. Both stricken carriers displayed red flags, which forbade flight operations. Starting about 1000 the *Zuikaku* recovered some of the seventeen Zeros overhead and at 1025 redeployed three *Zuihō* and three *Shōkaku* Zeros aloft as relief CAP. When more fighters landed, Sea2c Sugano Katsuo, a green *Shōkaku* pilot, died when his Zero bounced overboard, flipped upside down, and immediately sank. Fifty miles astern, Rear Admiral Abe's Vanguard Force retired northwest until Vice Admiral Kondō brought him back around to pursue the Americans. When Abe saw the sad condition of the *Chikuma*, at 1108 he detached her and two destroyers for Truk.

The last U.S. attacker remains to be accounted for here. Lt. (jg) George Welles of VT-10 left the *Enterprise* at 0840, just as the Japanese first strike appeared on radar. Flying alone, he and his crew boldly crossed nearly 300 miles of ocean before spotting the distant ship wakes of the *Kidō Butai* around 1100. Cautiously approaching at 5,000 feet, he sent a voice contact report (never received), and busily counted ships, none of which were carriers. At 1105 a roving ad hoc reception committee of three *Shōkaku* Zeros (PO2c Yamamoto Ichirō, PO3c Komachi Sadamu, and Sea1c Itō Tomitarō) discovered the lone TBF and forced Welles to jettison his torpedo and run. One 20-mm shell knocked out the TBF turret, and a 7.7-mm slug ricocheted off Welles's headrest and grazed his scalp. Nevertheless he escaped in the clouds and got his bearings for the long flight home. The Yamamoto *shōtai* thought they engaged three enemy torpedo planes during the spirited chase, but claimed none. In return one Zero took slight damage.[1]

Heartened at the *Junyō*'s imminent arrival, Nagumo considered more attacks against the enemy. His staff digested the many confusing reports and decided there were three American carriers: one cripple drifting without power, and two others, to the northeast and east of her respectively. Consequently Nagumo radioed at 1132: "Cancel assumption that there is an enemy carrier south of the first carrier."[2] That let TF-16 and the *Enterprise* off the hook, as the Japanese looked east rather than southeast of the *Hornet*. Because one enemy flattop appeared to be sinking, Nagumo told Kakuta to concentrate on the other two *Yorktown*-class carriers.

To mount follow-up strikes, the *Kidō Butai* needed aircraft from the earlier waves. Thirty-three planes (ten carrier bombers, nine carrier attack planes, and fourteen fighters, including Hidaka's five *Zuihō*), many of them damaged, staggered back from the first wave. Also five *Zuihō* carrier attack planes from the dawn search and a *Shōkaku* carrier bomber (an abort) waited to land. Because the *Shōkaku*'s transmitters malfunctioned, she could not advise her aviators of her crippled condition. They wasted time and fuel looking for her. At 1140, the *Zuikaku* started the time-consuming process of landing all the planes. Meanwhile she directed some to seek out the *Junyō* coming from the southwest.

By 1230 the *Zuikaku* brought on board ten fighters, eight carrier attack planes, and one *Shōkaku* carrier bomber. At the same time the *Junyō* landed, in addition to six of her own CAP Zeros, two *Zuikaku* fighters, four *Zuikaku* carrier bombers, and one *Shōkaku* carrier attack plane. A total of thirteen first-wave aircraft ditched: five *Shōkaku* carrier attack planes, two Zeros (one *Shōkaku*, one *Zuikaku*), and six *Zuikaku* carrier bombers. The latter included Lieutenant Ishimaru, who died on the *Amatsukaze*, and also Lieutenant Takahashi, the group commander. Fighting the controls of his crippled Type 99 for nearly six hours, Takahashi had the good fortune to stumble across one of the Japanese fleet oilers and set down nearby. During the landings the *Junyō* drew close to the *Kidō Butai*, so Nagumo detached the *Zuikaku* and five destroyers to operate with her. Because the *Shōkaku*'s damage was largely confined topside, Captain Arima desperately urged Nagumo to accompany the force into battle and absorb attacks, but he would not hear of it. Unable to shift his flag to the *Zuikaku* before she separated, Nagumo remained on board the *Shōkaku*. Now the *Junyō* and *Zuikaku* were free to launch follow-up strikes.

TASK FORCE 16 RETIRES

By the time the enemy third wave pulled away from TF-16, Kinkaid knew he had to break off the battle or risk the *Enterprise*. Both of his carriers had sustained damaged, one severely, but their planes had to be recovered as soon as possible. He felt he could render no fighter support to Murray's TF-17 with the crippled *Hornet*, especially since he believed the enemy retained one or two undamaged carriers. As confirmation, TF-16 later learned that Lieutenant (jg) Poulos's PBY shadowed a carrier force on 090 degrees. Considering his options, Kinkaid made his decision "without hesitation."[3] At 1135 he informed Murray and ComSoPac: "I am proceeding southeastward toward ROSES. When ready proceed in the same direction."[4]

A few minutes later TF-16 copied a message to ComSoPac sent by Good:

> *Hornet* attacked by ORANGE carrier planes at 0911L . . . Several bomb hits one or more torpedo hits. Now dead in the water and burning somewhat. *Northampton* preparing take in tow. Have lost touch with Kinkaid.[5]

The *Northampton* finally began towing the *Hornet*, only to have the line snap at 1108. While they rigged another line, Murray and his staff took the *Russell*'s whaleboat over to the *Pensacola*. At 1155 Kinkaid sent Good his valedictory for TF-17: "If Murray safe direct him to take charge salvaging operations. Have been under continuous air attack. Otherwise you take charge."[6]

In the meantime the *Enterprise* worked quickly to clear her flight deck and resume landing planes. As of 1140, no fewer than seventy-three aircraft from both the *Hornet* and Air Group Ten waited to come on board "The Big E": twenty-eight F4Fs (nine VF-72, nineteen VF-10); twenty-four SBDs (twenty-one *Hornet,* three *Enterprise*); twenty-one TBFs (fifteen *Hornet,* six *Enterprise*). All were very low on fuel. Their loss would be catastrophic.

TF-16 had already witnessed a graphic example of what would soon happen if the aircraft did not land. Unable to get on board the *Enterprise* when division leader Al Emerson and Sleepy Weimer landed prior to the last attack, Moose Merritt's engine died from fuel starvation. He used the wobble pump to keep going, buzzed the destroyer *Preston,* and ditched ahead. The tincan coasted up and took him on board at 1135.[7]

The damaged *Enterprise* faced real problems in attempting to recover so many planes. Crommelin's Air Department had already parked some fifteen to twenty F4Fs and SBDs forward on the flight deck. With the number 1 elevator frozen in the up position, it would take too long to strike them below via the other two elevators, both of which sat in the landing and run-up areas needed by the aircraft coming in. Once the landings commenced, the flight deck would rapidly fill with planes, including many SBDs with nonfolding wings. Soon they would crowd over the folded barriers, rendering any accident disastrous. Great responsibility rested on the shoulders of LSOs Robin Lindsey and Jim Daniels.

TF-16 steamed southeast into the wind, and at 1139 the *Enterprise* reopened for business under the liabilities mentioned above. Daniels started bringing in aircraft, but not quickly enough to suit pilots anxiously watching their gas gauges. As VB-8's Ken White put it, the landing circle seemed to extend "from Maine to Florida," with pilots "eager to get in before their engines sputtered from lack of fuel and they went into the drink."[8] In their frustration some planes crowded others out of the circle. Daniels tried to give priority to the F4Fs and SBDs with hurt crews, but the TBFs would have to wait. He gave a good many wave-offs to planes coming in before others cleared the arresting gear.

First to land were *Enterprise* and *Hornet* CAP fighters, mostly running on reserve fuel or an empty gas gauge. Jim Billo of VF-10 received two wave-offs because of planes in the gear, but the second meant a water landing because he lacked the gas for another go-round. Passing the *Enterprise*'s island, he cranked up his wheels and stalled down off her port bow. When the F4F plowed into the waves, its canopy slammed shut. Only after a desperate struggle did Billo win free to the surface, where he inflated the raft attached to his parachute pack. Russ Reiserer saw the Wildcat splash and buzzed overhead until he got the *Preston*'s attention. At 1208 Billo met her skipper, Cdr. Max C. Stormes, who remarked dryly that if he had known Billo was a pilot, "he would not have bothered." Stormes was only teasing but, leery of I-boats, the destroyermen were a little touchy over the torpedoing of the *Porter* while undertaking a similar act of mercy. The stalwart *Preston* picked up eleven aviators that afternoon. Unfortunately she sank in the great 15 November night battle, and many of her crew perished, including Stormes.[9]

From VF-10 Lieutenant Commander Kane and Lieutenant Eckhardt (both REAPER 4), and Lieutenant (jg) Long (REAPER 8) went into the water about the same time as Billo. At 1150 the *Maury* recovered Kane (whose F4F had taken some AA damage along the line), while the *Cushing* (DD-376) picked up the other two. At 1159 Lieutenant Bliss of VF-72 tried contacting the carrier to warn he had no flaps, and the *San Juan* forwarded the message. Invited by the *Enterprise*

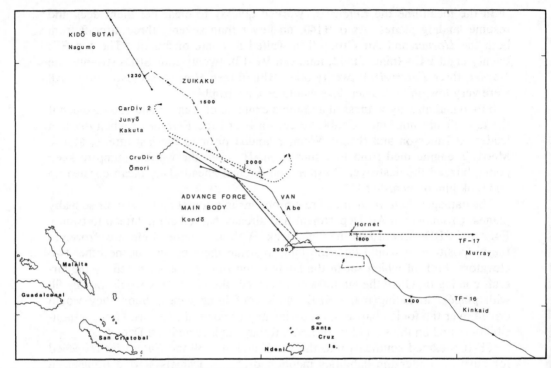

Task force operations, 1200–2400, 26 October 1942.

to come in, he took a wave-off, then set down about 200 yards ahead of the *Mahan*, which brought him on board at 1210.[10] Only these five F4Fs ditched during the actual landings.

Prior to 1200 the *Enterprise* landed six VF-10 CAP F4Fs and several *Hornet* planes, then recovered most of the surviving VF-10 escorts: three from Flatley's REAPER 1 and Chip Reding from ill-fated REAPER 6. For a time Daniels even landed planes with an open number 2 elevator amidships lowering aircraft to the hangar deck. After he touched down, Don Gordon was guided onto the center elevator and immediately taken down, fully aware that if the next plane jumped the barrier, it would squash him at the bottom of the well. Reaching the hangar deck, he gratefully taxied forward and cut his switches. More SBDs landed along with the VF-72 escorts. An SBD forced Warren Ford out of the landing circle, but he yielded gracefully when he saw that virtually its whole canopy (aside from the windshield) was shot away. It was Benny Moore's from VS-8. Ford came around again and got down straightaway. After the F4F was parked forward, he saw corpsmen patching up Moore in the corridor leading to the VF-10 ready room. Just about out of gas, Hank Carey signaled for deferred forced-landing. Three aircraft crowded the groove (Carey's in the middle), but Daniels chose him to come in.[11]

Once the SBDs started coming on board, the flight deck rapidly congested. Soon aircraft spread abreast of the island, and finally plane handlers had rolled them over the three folded wire barriers. Since 0930 Jim Daniels had landed without mishap over sixty planes, some badly shot-up. Now senior LSO Robin

Lindsey took over for the last thirty or so with no barriers to catch them in the event of a crash. As the deck filled, Lindsey brought the planes in farther and farther aft, with fewer arresting wires available.

An admiring Daniels described Lindsey as a virtuoso at his profession:

He played those pilots like a master, slowing them down, easing the tension by signalling a Roger—"Everything OK"—then bringing them in slowly and carefully—no wave offs allowed—until he got everyone aboard.[12]

Soon Lindsey had only the number 1 and 2 wires. As he later reminisced, the bridge ordered, "That's all, knock it off brother." However, Crommelin let it be known from PriFly that although he put out the red flag—no more landings—the ship *would* continue steaming into the wind. "Crommelin had kept his word to his embattled pilots."[13]

Both LSOs remembered Crommelin's inspired words the previous night to the air group, "If you get back to the ship and into the groove, we'll get you aboard!" Lindsey took "Uncle John" 's hint to land planes so long as there was room on deck. Daniels bet him a dime for every plane he could bring in on the number 1 wire. Soon the debt rose to 80 cents for five SBDs and three F4Fs from Vejtasa's REAPER 7. Delayed while overseeing Billo's rescue by the *Preston,* Reiserer found only one other F4F in the landing circle and almost no deck upon which to land. After coming in, he taxied forward only a few feet before nearly touching the tail of the plane ahead. At 1222 Lindsey gave the cut to Swede Vejtasa, who smartly hooked the number 1 wire. After lifting his hook, the flight deck crew chocked his Wildcat right on the spot. That was all the room there was. Vejtasa walked over to thank Lindsey, who laughingly collected ten dimes from Daniels.[14]

LSOs Lindsey and Daniels, their pilots, and Crommelin's *Enterprise* flight deck crew had accomplished a tremendous feat: forty-seven planes (twenty-three F4Fs, twenty-four SBDs) landed in the last 43 minutes under harrowing conditions without a mishap. Only five F4Fs, but no SBDs, ditched. With full flight deck, "The Big E" shut down temporarily to strike planes below and make room for the twenty-one TBFs still aloft. At 1235 TF-16 changed course to 123 degrees, 27 knots, to resume its retreat.

Even if she could not land them, "The Big E" managed to keep some TBFs entertained. Shortly after 1200 her radar picked up a bogey, and everyone worried about a possible enemy intruder. Using F4Fs for CAP was out of the question. Almost all had landed, and those still aloft flew on fumes. At 1205 Jack Griffin used the search frequency to entreat "any SBD with fuel to investigate bogey," but had no takers. Five minutes later he called, "Any REAPER fish answer," and instructed "any" TBF to check out bogeys bearing 030 degrees, distance 25 miles. About six Avengers responded against the contact now swinging around to the east. It was certainly a novel use of torpedo planes for CAP, especially since these TBF-1s featured only a single .30-caliber "peashooter" firing forward.[15]

Shortly Griffin issued a recall, when the bogey turned out to be a PBY flying boat. As in August, the *Enterprise* entertained considerable suspicion that Japanese might be flying a rogue Catalina. However, it was none other than Norm Haber's battered Catalina that had fought seven Zeros to a standstill. He sighted the destroyer *Porter* about to sink, then TF-16 itself. Four hours later Haber set down at Espiritu Santo without rudder or elevator control. 24-P-6 sported about 144 bullet holes (78 from rear blisters to the tail). Haber and crew survived a remarkable mission. Their courage and skill exemplified the superb AirSoPac search crews.[16]

On the *Enterprise*'s flight deck a massive re-spot sorted out the F4Fs and SBDs all mixed together. Plane handlers struck below as many SBDs as possible and rearmed fighters. Jim Daniels left the LSO platform to go below deck, but in the hangar he discovered the "unbelievable horror" wrought by the second Japanese bomb hit. The dead and dying lay all around. One sailor in particular he never forgot:

> I recognized a fo'castle bos'n with only one arm and no legs and fingers that seemed to dig into the steel deck, slowly and painfully pull himself to an opening on the starboard side. One of the corpsmen spoke to me thinking I might make a move to help, and cautioned me to just let him alone and let him pull himself over the side. He would die anyway. In a very few minutes he made his last trip off the "E."[17]

His death symbolized the sacrifice, 240 killed, borne by the TF-61 ships' companies in the Battle of Santa Cruz. That was well over twice as many American lives as were lost on Guadalcanal repulsing the 17th Army's four-day ground assault against the 1st MarDiv perimeter.[18]

At 1225, with fires totally extinguished, the Air Department finally reopened the gasoline system purged with carbon dioxide. Below decks the fighter pilots tried to relax, but that was impossible. The ready rooms were crowded. All Vejtasa wanted was a drink of water, but the water fountains had failed due to battle damage. After someone provided dungarees to replace a torn flight suit, George Wrenn found the gedunk stand and some ice cream. Soon the call sounded for fighter pilots to man planes. Hustling through the island, Wrenn confronted a grizzled chief who because of the dungarees thought a seaman had run amok. The chief threw him against a bulkhead, but when Wrenn identified himself as a VF-72 pilot, he tossed the bemused ensign out onto the flight deck.[19]

Overhead the TBFs were running out of time. Considering the *Enterprise*'s packed flight deck, CHAG Walt Rodee realized ruefully he was not particularly needed and used his extra fuel to reach Espiritu Santo. About 1500 he landed at the bomber strip. The others lacked that option. Hump Tallman's battered VT-6 TBF was the first to run out of fuel. He ditched successfully, and at 1238 the whole crew came on board the hardworking *Preston*. At 1240 the *Enterprise* told group commander Dick Gaines, "Hang on 20 to 25 minutes, and we will take you on." He replied, "That is about the time I have left."[20]

Between 1251 and 1305 "The Big E" sent aloft a mixed CAP of twenty-five F4Fs in divisions led by Mike Sanchez, Al Emerson, Red Hessel, and Claude Phillips (all VF-72), Dave Pollock and Bobby Edwards of VF-10. They were the first aircraft she launched since 0830. Afterward Crommelin's men frantically re-spotted the deck forward to make room for the TBFs, and at 1318 the LSOs received clearance to land planes. Seven VT-6 Avengers and two from VT-10 touched down, and at 1322 Gaines made it ten. In the interval, eight other TBFs (six VT-6, two VT-10) went into the drink; all the crews were rescued by destroyers and the *Juneau,* which joined TF-16 at 1226. Still in-bound was George Welles of VT-10 coming back from the *Kidō Butai.* Thus of the seventy-three aircraft aloft at 1139, fully fifty-seven made it on board the *Enterprise,* fourteen ditched, one had yet to arrive, and one went south.

About 30 minutes after the TBFs came on board, the *Enterprise*'s radar registered a bogey bearing 40 miles, perhaps one of the Japanese contact planes that swept the waters round the stricken *Hornet*. At 1400 another contact appeared at 40 miles, closing fast. Griffin deployed the CAP when it appeared that TF-16 would be attacked. From the confusion on the flight deck, Crommelin wrung five F4Fs under Ruehlow and Ford, but the re-spot prevented Welles's TBF from landing on board. After Lindsey gave him a wave-off, he set down in the water. The *Maury* rescued the three-man crew at 1403. Ruehlow and Ford got away at 1417 and heard, "REAPER BASE under attack!" "Bogeys approaching 020, 7 miles!" "Fish dead astern, 6 miles!" The Japanese never showed up, because they were not present in the first place. It soon became evident the radar contacts were false. Kinkaid reduced speed to 23 knots.

The *Enterprise* resumed refueling thirteen SBDs (four of her own and nine *Hornet*) for VB-8 and VS-8 crews to relieve the congestion on deck by flying to Espiritu Santo. Lieutenant Lynch of VB-8 led them aloft at 1507, and Rodee greeted them around sundown at the Santo Bomber Strip No. 1. After the ferry flight departed, the *Enterprise* again laboriously re-spotted the flight deck to land about eighteen F4Fs at 1520. An even dozen fighters protected TF-16, now sailing beyond range of possible Japanese strikes, but none guarded TF-17 and the crippled *Hornet*. Aircraft remaining on the *Enterprise* numbered eighty-four: forty-one F4F-4s, thirty-three SBD-3s, and ten TBF-1s, counting inoperable and spare planes.

At 1540 Kinkaid warned Halsey that the *Enterprise* suffered more severely than previously indicated and summarized damage to other ships in TF-16. He requested an oiler meet him "as soon as practicable" northeast of Espiritu Santo. The message crossed one from Halsey ordering all SoPac TF commanders to "retire to southward."[21] Kinkaid disengaged, but Murray's TF-17 had not. Would the Japanese permit the *Hornet* to escape?

That evening, after the last CAP landed on the *Enterprise,* a weary bunch of pilots assembled in the fighter ready room. Eleven VF-10 pilots had not returned to the ship, but it was known that some were on board destroyers after having landed in the water. For the twenty members of VF-72 there were quarters to find and personal gear to be scrounged, for none of them arrived with so much as a toothbrush. Characteristically, Jimmy Flatley greeted the newcomers by gently anointing them with holy water as they rested in the upholstered seats. When Jock Sutherland pointed out he was not Roman Catholic, Flatley smiled, "It won't do you any harm."[22]

Flatley worried deeply about his "discouraged and dejected" pilots. The CAP participants regarded the battle as an almost unmitigated disaster, a personal insult eased only by the sterling performance of a few like Swede Vejtasa. The CAP destroyed the enemy planes they actually intercepted, but all too often other Japanese just passed overhead. Their ire centered on the fighter direction, which elicited a storm of complaints. Late that night Crommelin and Flatley hunted up Ens. George Givens, one of the junior FDOs attached to ship's company, and ordered him to bring the fighter direction battle plot and radio logs to the wardroom. While six inches of water sloshed from side to side on the deck, they pelted Givens with questions such as: "Why this? Why that?" as he tried to explain the various contacts and the FDO responses.[23] This episode was only Round 1 of what would become, once the participants submitted their action reports, perhaps the most bitter controversy of the battle.

THE JAPANESE PURSUE

Following the course of the battle from massive *Yamato* anchored in Truk Lagoon, Admiral Yamamoto urged his fleet commanders at 1300 to pursue and destroy the retreating American carriers. Both Rear Admiral Kakuta on the *Junyō* and the *Zuikaku*'s Captain Nomoto readied follow-up air strikes, while to the southeast the battleships, cruisers, and destroyers of Vice Admiral Kondō's Advance Force and Rear Admiral Abe's Vanguard Force raced after the enemy.

At 1306 the *Junyō* dispatched her second wave: the strike leader was Lt. Irikiin Yoshiaki, with eight Zeros (five *Junyō*, two *Zuikaku*, and one *Zuihō*), led by Lt. Shirane Ayao (*Zuikaku*), and seven Type 97 carrier attack planes (six with torpedoes) led by Lieutenant Irikiin. The fifteen planes departed at 1313 on 120 degrees to search 260 miles. To the north the *Zuikaku* independently mounted the 1st Carrier Division's third attack wave at the same time: the strike leader was Lt. (jg) Tanaka Ichirō (*Zuihō*), with five Zeros (three *Zuikaku*, two *Shōkaku*) led by Lt. (jg) Kobayashi Hōhei (*Shōkaku*); two Type 99 carrier bombers (one *Shōkaku*, one *Zuikaku*) led by PO1c Hori Kenzō (*Zuikaku*); and seven Type 97 carrier attack planes (five *Zuihō*, two *Zuikaku*—six with 800-kilogram bombs) led by Lieutenant Tanaka. That two very junior officers led the *Zuikaku* strike epitomized the great loss in aviation leaders suffered by the Japanese.

With flight decks clear the two Japanese flattops recovered more aircraft that limped back from earlier attack waves. From 1320 to 1400 the *Zuikaku* landed five Zeros (one from her second wave and four *Junyō*, including Lieutenant Shigematsu), Lieutenant Arima's seven *Shōkaku* carrier bombers, Lieutenant Yusuhara's six *Zuikaku* carrier attack planes, and one *Shōkaku* carrier attack plane from the morning search. At the same time the *Junyō* brought on board Lieutenant Shiga with eight Zeros, Lieutenant (jg) Katō's six Type 99 carrier bombers, and one stray *Zuikaku* Zero (Sea1c Nisugi Toshitsugu) from the first wave. Two *Zuikaku* Zeros, two *Shōkaku* and two *Junyō* carrier bombers, and one *Zuikaku* carrier attack plane set down in the sea.

Lt. Cdr. Okumiya Masatake, Kakuta's air staff officer, described the return of the *Junyō* first-wave remnants:

> We searched the sky with apprehension. There were only a few planes in the air in comparison with the numbers launched several hours before. . . . The planes lurched and staggered onto the deck, every single fighter and bomber bullet holed . . . As the pilots climbed wearily from their cramped cockpits, they told of unbelievable opposition, of skies choked with antiaircraft shell bursts and tracers.

When Katō, the youngest aviation officer on board and the only surviving carrier bomber leader, reported to Captain Okada, he appeared "so shaken that at times he could not speak coherently."[24]

The *Zuikaku* reinforced her CAP, but Nomoto decided not to cull a fourth strike wave from his battered air group. However, the aggressive Kakuta, "a hard but courageous taskmaster," directed Shiga to lead another strike as soon as serviceable planes could be readied. Support Force called for a night surface action, and Kakuta wanted to land one more blow before dark. In the *Junyō*'s wardroom, Okumiya informed the badly shaken Katō of his orders, but was shocked to hear him say, "Again? Am I to fly *again* today?"

Lieutenant Shiga jumped to his feet and shouted across the room. "Ton-chan [Katō's shipboard nickname]; this is war! There can be no rest in our fight against the enemy . . . We cannot afford to give them a chance when their ships are crippled . . . We have no choice . . . We go!'' Katō pulled himself together and replied, ''I will go.''[25] The *Junyō*'s third wave of six Zeros and four Type 99 carrier bombers departed at 1535.

THE LOSS OF THE *HORNET*

For a time after 1200, TF-17 was left alone. TF-16 had disappeared over the southern horizon, taking the fighters with it. Even so, things began looking up. The heavy cruiser *Northampton* busily rerigged the tow line to the stricken *Hornet* parted two hours before during the sneak dive-bombing attack. Finally at 1330 she drew up the slack and worked the tow up to three knots, while the *Hornet* engineers labored to bring some boilers on line to add speed. By proceeding directly east toward Tongatabu, Murray planned to bypass sub-infested waters to the south. Meanwhile, the *Hornet*'s wounded sailors and air group personnel continued transferring to the *Russell* and *Hughes*. Towing speed increased to six knots. Ominously, several Japanese search planes watched the whole proceedings, and no fighters were present to shoo them off. Not realizing what had befallen the *Enterprise,* many from TF-17 felt betrayed because of the lack of VF support.

At 1345, the *Northampton*'s CXAM radar revealed a new threat, a large group of bogeys bearing 310 degrees, 103 miles, and closing. That was Irikiin's *Junyō* second strike of eight Zeros and seven carrier attack planes. To the radar plotters the planes appeared to ''mill around for some time'' to the northwest. Actually Irikiin and company sought the two damaged American carriers they were told lurked in those waters. At 1400 the U.S. radars picked up Tanaka's *Zuikaku* group also at 310 degrees and 110 miles likewise searching north of TF-17.

The *Russell* cast off at 1440, taking with her the last of the so-called excess personnel. It proved to be good timing, because Irikiin abandoned the area he had searched the past hour and turned south. Radar showed the enemy closing. At 1513 Irikiin finally sighted an obviously damaged carrier listing to starboard and decided to finish her off. Murray cast off the *Northampton*'s tow and took a protective circular formation around the *Hornet*.

From about 6,000 feet Irikiin's six Type 97 carrier attack planes pushed over into a high-speed torpedo attack against the carrier's starboard side. All of the ships' guns, even main batteries, frantically tried to disrupt the attackers. In the center Irikiin passed over the *Russell* crammed with *Hornet* Air Group personnel and aimed his torpedo for the *Hornet*'s starboard beam. It struck aft near one of Murata's torpedo hits and ensured the *Hornet* would never again move under her own power. Her list increased to over 14 degrees. As with Murata, success extracted a terrible price, when AA fire caught Irikiin as he pulled up. The aircraft veered right and plowed into the water ahead of the *Northampton*. The other five *Junyō* torpedo planes failed to score, and gunfire likewise splashed WO Yokoyama Takeo's Type 97 on the *Hornet*'s port side. The survivors claimed three hits on the carrier and one on a heavy cruiser. On the flight back two *Junyō* Zeros flown by the veteran PO1c Suzuki Kiyonobu and Sea2c Nakamoto Kiyoshi separated from the main body and were not seen again. Thus the strike cost two Zeros as well as the two *kankōs*. Three other Zeros later ditched.

His flagship wounded anew, Murray again asked Kinkaid for fighter support, but TF-16 could not comply. As a result of the list, Captain Mason ordered his crew to prepare to abandon ship. Meanwhile, the *Zuikaku* third strike had split up. First to locate TF-17, PO1c Hori's mixed pair of carrier bombers dived at 1541 and badly rocked the *Hornet* with a near miss. Her list now attained 18 to 20 degrees. Mason felt he could wait no longer. Two minutes after Hori's attack, he reluctantly told his men to abandon ship. At 1555 Tanaka's tight formation of six Type 97 horizontal bombers appeared off the *Hornet*'s port quarter at 8,000 feet and simultaneously dropped their 800-kilogram bombs in a close pattern. One big land bomb detonated on the flight deck aft, causing surprisingly little damage, and the rest raised a huge splash astern. Tanaka decided that the carrier he badly damaged had to be different from the other two previously attacked.

After Tanaka's attack, Mason hurried the evacuation from the *Hornet* and at 1627 was the last man to leave her. Of 118 men killed in the attacks on the *Hornet,* VF-72 lost nine:[26]

Frank Calhoun OC3c	Tommy H. Matlock, AMM3c
Virgile E. Daniel, Sea1c	Herbert J. Meirick, AMM3c
Walter F. Ellis, SC3c	Virgil E. Powell, Jr., Sea1c
Olander Goss, MAtt3c	Joaquin J. Taimanglo, OC3c
Rodrick J. Martin, Sea1c	

While the screening ships picked up survivors, at 1650 Shiga's third *Junyō* strike with four carrier bombers and six Zeros located an enemy task force with one crippled carrier. Katō's flight pushed over at 1710. One 250-kilogram bomb pene-

A *Junyō* carrier attack plane launches its torpedo against the *Hornet*. (NA 80-G-33965)

trated the *Hornet*'s flight deck and exploded in the hangar forward of the island. A large fire blazed for 15 minutes, then died down. After pulling out, one Type 99 roared right over a boat filled with *Hornet* survivors and refrained from strafing, so to the men in the launch AA fire proved more of a hazard. Shiga and Katō reached the *Junyō* safely after dark. They claimed four hits for four bombs dropped.

At 1740 Murray detached Cdr. Arnold True with the *Mustin* to sink the *Hornet*, while the rest of TF-17 withdrew east at 27 knots. The end of the gallant flattop contributed no less a saga than her fight during the day. Beginning at 1803 the *Mustin* fired eight torpedoes into her side, and apparently four detonated, but the carrier showed no evidence she was about to sink. Several Japanese float planes watched the proceedings. Murray sent the *Anderson* to help finish off the *Hornet*. She scored six hits with eight torpedoes, seemingly without effect. Finally the two tincans poured 430 rounds of five-inch into the valiant flattop, and by 2030 when they departed, the *Hornet* blazed throughout her length. Riding the *Mustin*, Mason felt certain she would soon sink, but that knowledge did not make it any easier to leave her that way.[27]

While the *Hornet* endured her last agony, the Japanese commanders puzzled over the plethora of contact and action reports from returned plane crews. How many American carriers were there, and what happened to them? Their best initial guess was three. However, after interrogating the crews of several newly returned contact planes, Captain Nomoto of the *Zuikaku* became skeptical. At 1628 he reported that none of his aviators had actually seen three separate enemy carriers and felt certain no additional carriers remained within 50 miles of the one under tow. Two hours later Kakuta assessed all three enemy carriers as sunk or severely damaged.

In hopes of mopping up a couple of wrecked carriers, at 1904 Kondō directed the Support Force warships to conduct a night battle by scouting on a line oriented from the east to the southwest. At the same time he ordered Kakuta's carriers to head north and be prepared to search and attack the next morning. With the return of the third attack waves, Kakuta on the *Junyō* and Nomoto on the *Zuikaku* finally assessed their battered air strength. Between them the two carriers numbered 97 planes, no less than 106 fewer than that morning:

	Junyō	*Zuikaku*
Carrier fighters	12	38
Carrier bombers	12	10
Carrier attack planes	6	19
	30	67

The battered *Shōkaku* retained four Zeros and one carrier attack plane, while another of her carrier attack planes (Lt. Iwaki Kentarō [NA 65-1938]) and a *Zuikaku* fighter reached Buin. Even more crucial, so many able officers were missing and feared dead, including two group and four squadron commanders.

After analyzing the many reports, Yamamoto stated at 1950 that the enemy indeed committed four carriers to battle. One already sank (along with two battleships), and the other three were badly damaged. Nagumo later concurred. Yamamoto described the Americans as in "disorderly flight" and ordered Kondō to pursue until he was certain the enemy had withdrawn out of reach.[28]

Around 2100 the destroyers *Makigumo* and *Akigumo* closed the abandoned *Hornet* and learned her identity from her hull number. To the north, the *Junyō* saw the glow of her fires on the horizon, a heartwarming experience for Kakuta. Obviously the American derelict could not be saved or even boarded, so the Japanese fired four more torpedoes into her side. The gallant *Hornet* finally disappeared at 0130, 27 October—U.S. Navy Day.[29]

After passing the burning *Hornet,* Kondō decided to break off the night pursuit at 2300 if no more enemy ships turned up. Sending his two operational carriers north to regroup, he planned to search the area in the morning, then contemplate his next move.

Early the morning of 27 October Rear Admiral Fitch's AirSoPac night raiders tried their best to even the score in carrier losses. The evening of the 26th three radar-equipped PBYs departed Espiritu Santo to hunt Japanese carriers. Near midnight Lt. (jg) Donald L. Jackson's 51-P-6 scented game in the form of one carrier, one battleship, and three cruisers and destroyers. Actually he located Kakuta's *Junyō* group bound for a rendezvous with the *Zuikaku*. Scouting around, he soon found both carriers headed north. At 0100 Lt. Melvin K. Atwell in 91-P-3 bombed what he reported as a heavy cruiser, in fact the destroyer *Teruzuki* screening the *Zuikaku*. One of his four 500-pounders exploded close off her starboard beam and killed or wounded nearly fifty of her crew, but her speed remained unimpaired. Thirty minutes later Jackson made a torpedo run against a large carrier and claimed a hit.[30]

Quickly evaluating the rather equivocal radio decrypts, U.S. naval intelligence identified Jackson's target as the *Zuikaku* and decided she indeed was damaged. Actually they detected the alarums raised when Jackson's torpedo barely missed the *Junyō*. In this battle the AirSoPac B-17 Flying Fortresses and the lumbering PBY Catalinas certainly impressed the Japanese, as reflected in grudging praise in the 2nd Destroyer Squadron's action report: "Furthermore, it must be said, even though they are the enemy, that this [duty] was admirably performed."[31]

BREAKING OFF THE BATTLE

By 27 October it became obvious that the 17th Army's Lunga offensive had failed, and because of its battered carrier air groups Combined Fleet could do nothing immediately to threaten Guadalcanal. That morning Kondō's Support Force scouted for the enemy northwest of the Santa Cruz area, but finally turned north for Truk. During the day the lookouts carefully searched the water for downed Japanese aircrew and did locate three. At 0825 near where the *Hornet* sank, the *Isokaze* with Rear Admiral Abe's Vanguard Force recovered three grateful carrier bomber crewmen (two wounded), who witnessed the loss of the *Hornet:* Lieutenant (jg) Shimada from the *Zuikaku* and PO1c Ishiyama's *Shōkaku* crew.[32] Not only Japanese populated the surface of the sea, but also four castaways from the *Enterprise,* last noted the morning of the 26th when they entered the water. It is useful here to discuss their experiences in the order in which the enemy found them.[33]

On 27 October the Japanese first spotted Murray ("Mick") Glasser, a VT-10 aircrewman. He floated only in a Mae West without any drinking water, but had the foresight to keep his helmet and goggles, which protected him somewhat from the remorseless sun. Also fortunately, he was entertained by porpoises instead of threatened by sharks. The morning of the 27th Glasser noticed ships approach, and a destroyer sent a boat for him. She brought him on board at 0652. His treatment was relatively benign according to Japanese standards. The enemy

CO even apologized for the quality of food, explaining that the destroyer had been at sea for a long time. Although Glasser identified his ship as the *Hornet,* a holster marked "USS ENT" later gave him away. He fended off the worst questioning by pleading his status as a young, lowly enlisted man who knew little. The only nasty trick occurred that evening, when under interrogation the Japanese went through a mock execution ceremony, but the CO relented.

Fortunately, Glasser did not realize the destroyer was the notorious *Makigumo,* part of the 10th Destroyer Division (DesDiv) screening the Vanguard Force. In June at Midway her crew had murdered the two aviators from the *Enterprise*'s VS-6, Ens. Frank H. O'Flaherty and Bruno P. Gaido, AMM1c, picked up after the great attack on the Japanese carriers. This time perhaps their glee at sinking the *Hornet* mellowed them.[34]

Of the four *Enterprise* aviators, Ens. Al Mead of VF-10 enjoyed the best gear, having ditched his Wildcat and secured the survival package with water and tools in addition to his seatpack life raft. Despite his wounded ankle, he was ready to paddle as far as necessary to reach safety. That afternoon a PBY (possibly Norm Haber's) passed close by on its return leg, but Mead's flare fizzled when he ignited it. A dye marker also produced no joy. The next morning a destroyer appeared over the eastern horizon, but as it closed, Mead decided she "looked wrong," with no hayrake radar antenna. More ships followed. Seeing a man floating in the water, the destroyer *Kazegumo* from DesDiv 10 stopped at 0730 and lowered a boat. Drawing near, its disappointed crew realized their prize catch was American, not Japanese. One of them simply clubbed Mead over the head with a boat hook and hauled the unconscious aviator into the boat. On board the tincan, they dumped Mead into an empty bathtub in the crew's quarters and kept him under guard. His captors tried interrogating him, but their English was so poor that "all they were able to do was beat me up."

Fellow VT-10 radioman Tom Nelson was in the same fix as Glasser, with no raft or canteen, just a leaky vest that he kept having to inflate. After a "long night" bobbing on the waves, there arose a "beautiful dawn" on the 27th. He soon saw the whole Vanguard Force, but they did not find him immediately, so he noticed the enemy ships making a series of squares criss-crossing the area. By 0825 when the destroyer *Yūgumo* (also 10th Division) cruised up alongside, the crew knew of downed enemy aviators in the area. Recognizing Nelson as an American, they only tossed down a rickety rope ladder and unceremoniously hauled him on board. Interrogation was immediate. Only when the parched and sunburned aviator answered a question was he given a sip of tea. Like Glasser, he tried passing himself off as a *Hornet* crewman, but a prescription on an *Enterprise* form later ended that ruse. As Nelson related, just name, rank, and serial number quickly soured his captors. "I soon adopted a policy of lying about how well they did" by greatly exaggerating U.S. losses. The Japanese pushed him to explain terms, such as "boogy at 10,000," taken from intercepted radio messages they had copied down in fractured English. His treatment on board the destroyer, while not pleasant, proved heavenly compared to what later befell him.

Ens. Raleigh ("Dusty") Rhodes of VF-10 had parachuted from his F4F not too far from the others, but unaccountably he never saw the enemy ships the morning of 27 October. Like Mead, he rode a seatpack life raft, but bullet holes rendered it nearly useless, even when patched. That became particularly worrisome as Rhodes bled from a leg wound. Sharks trailed him intermittently on the 27th. That afternoon the masts of Kondō's Advance Force marched from south to north across the horizon, and lookouts from the destroyer *Kagerō* in Tanaka's

2nd Destroyer Squadron noticed another man bobbing on the water. She closed in, stopped, and tossed a rope to the weakened aviator alongside. Not until Rhodes looked up to the rail did he realize the tincan was Japanese. As with Mead, his interrogators knew too little English for effective questioning. Despite the "USS *Enterprise*" clearly stenciled on his Mae West, the Japanese evidently believed for a time he came from the *Hornet*.

On 27 October, Nagumo succeeded in boarding the carrier *Zuikaku* and led the *Kidō Butai* back to Truk. The next day Abe's Vanguard Force rejoined. Watchful for submarines, the entire Support Force entered Truk on 30 October and anchored. Preceding them by two days were the two wounded carriers *Shōkaku* and *Zuihō*. With her severely buckled flight deck, scorch marks and burn spots from the fire, and lone Type 97 carrier attack plane parked aft, the *Shōkaku* looked particularly forlorn. Despite that the 3rd Fleet "seemed proud of themselves for their success and blamed the Combined Fleet command for the failure of land warfare on Guadalcanal."[35]

Well to the south, an early morning collision on 27 October between the battleship *South Dakota* and the destroyer *Mahan* marred the getaway of Kinkaid's TF-16. Alarmed by a submarine scare, the task force initiated an emergency turn, but the two ships turned toward each other. The *Mahan*'s bow slammed into the battlewagon's starboard quarter. That came as a big surprise to Lt. Ken Bliss, a rescued VF-72 pilot sleeping on a transom in the tincan's wardroom. The shock bashed his head into a nearby bulkhead and loosed furniture that flew around the compartment. That and fire in the adjacent passageway sent him scurrying on deck thinking the tincan had swallowed a torpedo. For him, this was the "scariest part of the whole operation."[36] The *South Dakota* suffered relatively little damage, but the *Mahan* lost her whole bow. Fortunately she could limp south to base.

By dawn on the 27th, TF-16 drew northeast of Espiritu Santo, with the remnants of TF-17 closing from astern. At 0604 the *Enterprise* sent eight TBFs 200 miles astern to look for signs of pursuit. Lt. (jg) John E. Boudreaux of VT-10 failed to return. After evading an aggressive enemy dive bomber out near the limit of his search, Boudreaux became lost in the clouds and ditched. For three days he and his crew drifted in their life raft, but safely reached Aoba Island in the New Hebrides.[37]

After Murray's cruisers and destroyers hove into sight late that morning, Kinkaid continued south toward New Caledonia and safe haven at Noumea. On the 28th, the task force cheered the news of the rescue of VS-8 CO Gus Widhelm and his radioman George Stokely. That morning a sharp-eyed VP-23 PBY (PPC Lt. [jg] William T. O'Dowd) spotted their raft about 25 miles north of where they went down two days before. The same day Halsey alerted MAG-25 to prepare a camp for eighty carrier planes, pilots, and crews at Tontouta field 40 miles northwest of Noumea. The next day four F4Fs under Lieutenant Commander Sanchez and Lieutenant Welch of VB-10 landed at Tontouta. The majority of Air Group Ten (Commander Gaines with one torpedo bomber, thirty-two fighters, and eighteen dive bombers) followed on the 30th, and TF-16 anchored that afternoon at Noumea.

Lt. Claude Phillips, a VF-72 pilot who took refuge on the *Enterprise*, noticed a whaleboat coming alongside:

> Riding in the stern alone was RADM Murray, a dejected looking figure in rumpled khakis apparently on his way to RADM Kinkaid. I knew it was a sad day in his life and it was a sight that I still recall with too great clarity and sadness.[38]

George Murray had his first meeting with his task force commander, but after the abandonment of the *Hornet,* there was little to say. In this bitter defeat the "what ifs" were almost too painful to voice.

COUNTING THE COSTS

At the end of October and securely in port, both the Support Force and TF-61 licked their wounds and evaluated the gains and losses wrought in the recent slugfest north of the Solomon Islands. The Battle of Santa Cruz (dubbed the "Naval Battle of the South Pacific" by the jubilant, if battered, Japanese) ended in an American tactical defeat. Only the escape of the *Enterprise* with her own and most of the *Hornet*'s aircraft prevented disaster. Yet the Allies retained the strategic advantage because of the 17th Army's failure to capture the Lunga airfield and destroy the 1st MarDiv on Guadalcanal. In consolation TF-61 also savaged the Japanese carrier air groups.

It is interesting to look at the respective claims of the Imperial Japanese and the U.S. navies for the Santa Cruz battle, particularly as neither side had any real notion of the strength of the other. The Japanese consistently overestimated the numbers of their foe. Imperial General Headquarters and Combined Fleet decided that four enemy carriers fought the battle and that all four sank, along with two battleships. That put the total carriers sunk since the outbreak of the war as eleven, with four others damaged. (Obviously the Americans must have had a lot of carriers.) Interrogations of the *Enterprise* POWs revealed that the *Enterprise* and *Hornet,* along with the new battleship *South Dakota* and supporting cruisers and destroyers, had departed Pearl Harbor on 16 October. They also provided the names and hull numbers of carriers 1 to 10, information already much published in the United States. The Japanese knew the carrier their destroyers torpedoed was the *Hornet.* In his diary Rear Admiral Ugaki explained why the Japanese thought they sank the same carriers so many times:

> The enemy builds and christens second and third generations of carriers, as many as we destroy. No wonder they do not need to change the names and numbers, but at present most of them are certain to be missing numbers.[39]

On 31 October, Nagumo reported the results of a conference on the *Zuikaku* investigating the great victory. It assessed as sunk the following: three large carriers (one finished off by her own destroyers), one battleship featuring a "dragon" (cage) mast, one cruiser, one destroyer, and one unidentified warship (large cruiser or above). Three cruisers and three destroyers were thought to have sustained heavy damage. Japanese aircraft destroyed fifty-four-plus enemy planes over the American carriers and ten more protecting the *Kidō Butai,* while Nagumo's AA finished five and Abe's Vanguard ten—grand total seventy-nine American planes, not counting those lost when their carriers sank. That clean sweep seemed to simplify matters in the South Pacific.[40]

A subsequent Japanese analysis reduced Allied strength at Santa Cruz to three carriers, one battleship, eight cruisers, and eighteen to twenty destroyers, of which all three carriers, the battleship, two heavy cruisers, and one destroyer went down. Two of the enemy carriers were definitely the *Hornet* and the *Enterprise,* but the third remained unidentified (not the *Saratoga,* according to Nagumo). Interestingly, Japanese radio intelligence "confirmed" the presence of three carriers by eavesdropping the U.S. FD frequency. The analysts noted call

signs "Red Base," "Blue Base," and "River Base." Of course BLUE BASE
was the *Hornet* and REAPER BASE the *Enterprise,* but in the heat of action
both pilots and the FDOs occasionally reverted to RED BASE, "The Big E"'s
former call sign. "River" was the most the Japanese could make out of the
unfamiliar term "Reaper."[41]

To achieve their supposed decisive victory, the Japanese paid an appalling
cost in men and planes, if not actually in ships. The carriers *Shōkaku* and *Zuihō*
sustained sufficient damage to require lengthy repairs in the homeland, as did the
battered *Chikuma.* Simple statistics reveal the grievous wounds suffered by the
four Japanese carrier air groups. Aircraft losses comprised:

	Present on 10/26	Shot down	Ditched/ crashed	Bombed on ships	Total lost	Remaining
Fighters	82	15	9	3	27	55
Bombers	63	30	11	0	41	22
Attack planes	57	22	7	1	30	27
Recon planes	1	0	1	0	1	0
Total	203	67	28	4	99	104

Aircrew losses were crushing:

	Killed		Section leaders and above[a]	Pilots killed
	Pilots	Observers		
Fighters	16	—	6	20%
Bombers	30	32	9	49
Attack	22	45	8	39
Total	68	77	23	

[a] Both pilots and observers

Most of the group and squadron commanders perished, and leaders of the caliber
of Murata and Seki could not easily be replaced. In this regard the "Naval Battle
of the South Pacific" truly became a pyrrhic victory for Japan.[42]

On 2 November the 3rd Fleet effectively bowed out of the Guadalcanal Campaign, when Combined Fleet detached the flattops *Shōkaku* and *Zuihō* for repairs
in the homeland. Rather surprisingly the unhurt *Zuikaku* also joined them, departing on the 4th. Combined Fleet sent her back to rebuild and train the 1st
Carrier Division air groups, but she could have participated in further operations
with an air group organized around the beached *Hiyō* flyers.[43] With the *Hiyō*
immobilized at Truk, only the *Junyō* remained operational in the South Pacific.
By 9 November her reinforced air group comprised twenty-seven Zero fighters
(mainly reinforced by the *Zuihō* Fighter Squadron), twelve Type 99 carrier
bombers, and nine Type 97 carrier attack planes. The *Zuihō* also left her carrier
attack squadron ashore at Truk for the *Hiyō.*

Obviously Combined Fleet felt the U.S. carriers were no longer a factor in the
defense of Guadalcanal—had not the Imperial Navy sunk all those in the South
Pacific? Now Yamamoto was loath to pit the remnants of his carrier aviators
against land-based planes. An exhausted Nagumo rode the *Zuikaku* north and
would soon receive a new posting as commandant of the Sasebo Naval District.
For a year he had wielded the single most powerful naval force in the Pacific, and
his fortunes, good and bad, reflected the course of the war for Japan.

In turn, Kinkaid's TF-61 encountered some difficulty proving that they fought as many carriers (four) as they actually did. On 30 October Kinkaid provided a summary of damage inflicted by his carriers on 26 October:

Air Group Ten	Hornet Air Group
2 hits on a *Shōkaku*-class CV 2 hits on a *Kongō*-class BB 26 planes shot down 25 planes by TF-16 AA	4–6 hits on a *Shōkaku*-class CV 5 hits on a *Tone*-class CA 4 hits on a second *Tone*-class CA 3 torpedo hits on a *Nachi*-class CA 41 planes shot down 23 planes by TF-17 AA

Kinkaid added that 150-plus planes (the air groups of four carriers) comprised the enemy strikes on the 26th and that about 133 actually attacked (49 against the *Hornet* and 84 versus the *Enterprise*).[44]

Interestingly, the potency of AA at the battle became a bone of contention between veterans of the *Enterprise* and the *South Dakota*. Some sources (but significantly not the *South Dakota*'s action report) ascribed twenty-six kills to the battlewagon alone.[45] Without going into detail it is possible, based on all available sources, including Japanese, to offer a reasoned estimate of relative effectiveness of AA versus the CAP in destroying Japanese planes. Counting only aircraft believed destroyed in the vicinity of the two U.S. task forces, the ratio between CAP and AA kills counting all the raids was twenty-nine by aircraft to twenty-five by AA (see table 22.1).That the fierce AA did not actually finish nearly as many Japanese aircraft as estimated in no way diminished its role in ruining the attacker's accuracy.

United States naval intelligence could not definitely place four combatant carriers (let alone five) in the South Pacific. As related previously they knew only of the *Shōkaku* and *Zuikaku,* the former believed damaged by bombs on the 26th and the latter possibly hit early the next morning by a torpedo from a PBY. Only gradually did they realize the presence of the *Zuihō* and, ultimately, the *Junyō* from a Japanese aviator's notebook captured on the *Smith.*

Battle losses included the carrier *Hornet* and the destroyer *Porter,* with damage to the carrier *Enterprise,* battleship *South Dakota,* the light AA cruiser *San Juan,* and the destroyer *Smith.* In addition the destroyer *Mahan* suffered extensive damage in her collision with the *South Dakota.* Actual U.S. plane losses from 25 to 27 October were extremely heavy:

	Start	Shot down	Ditched/ crashed	Lost on ships	Total	Remaining
F4F-4s	74	13	10	10	33	41
SBD-3s	72	2	8	18	28	44
TBF-1s	29	3	16	0	19	10
	175	18	34	28	80	95

Fortunately aircrew losses were fewer, as the two carrier air groups had come through nearly intact with a good share of their planes. This was a great victory in itself since, unlike the Japanese, SoPac would make much use of them (see table 22.2). The two fighting squadrons had by far taken the heaviest pilot casualties.

TABLE 22.1
Japanese Air Losses and Probable Causes, 26 October 1942

	Destroyed by AA			Destroyed by aircraft			
	VF	VB	VT	VF	VB	VT	Total
Versus TF-17	0	4	8	3	7	3	25
Versus TF-16	0	10	3	0	9	7	29

Writing on 31 October to Nimitz, Halsey declared he would not send the wounded *Enterprise* or the other damaged vessels back to Pearl Harbor for repairs "unless absolutely necessary." Instead, he resolved to "patch up what we have and go with them." As for his beloved "Big E," she would fight if necessary with reduced air strength, as "half a loaf is better than none." The letter concluded with the new SoPac policy:

> We are in need of everything we can get, planes, ships, escort vessels, so on ad nauseum. You are well aware of our needs and this is not offered in complaint or as an excuse, but just to keep the pot boiling. We are not in the least downhearted or upset by our difficulties, but obsessed with one idea only, to kill the yellow bastards and we shall do it.

An impressed Nimitz noted in the margin: "This is the spirit desired."[46]

Simply put in light of Halsey's determination to keep fighting, the "Naval Battle of the South Pacific" (to give the victors their due in naming the battle) merely reduced effective Japanese carrier superiority in the South Pacific from four versus two all the way down to parity: the unhurt *Junyō* with a battered air group versus the damaged *Enterprise* with air group intact. Of the two antagonists, Halsey was by far more likely to commit his lone carrier to battle at Guadalcanal than Yamamoto.

The impact of the battle off Santa Cruz lasted far longer than just November 1942. On the morning of 26 October, during the attack on the *Enterprise*, Kinkaid remarked with pardonable hyperbole to AP correspondent Eugene Burns: "You're seeing the greatest carrier duel of history. Perhaps it will never happen again."[47] In one sense, Kinkaid was absolutely correct. The Japanese carrier force never again enjoyed the numerical superiority and leaven of veteran aviators than the one assembled in October 1942 off Santa Cruz. Although their

TABLE 22.2
U.S. Navy Carrier Aviator Losses, 26 October 1942

	Pilots		Aircrew		(Section Leader and above)	Pilots lost to op. planes
	KIA	POW	KIA	POW		
Fighters	12	2	—	—	4	16%
Dive bombers	1	0	1	0	0	2%
Torpedo planes	3	0	5	2	1	10%
	16	2	6	2	5	

carrier fleet grew bigger, it certainly did not become more effective. The same cannot be said for the USN. Combined with greatly augmented numbers of ships, the much improved planes (notably the Grumman F6F Hellcats and Vought F4U Corsairs), more sophisticated technology, and increasingly stronger doctrine and tactics transformed the USN's carriers into perhaps the single most efficacious weapon system of World War II.

BATTLE LESSONS

The action reports compiled by the various U.S. commanders shortly after the battle bristled with complaints and recommendations, some more shrill than others. A defeat such as suffered at Santa Cruz compelled a total re-examination of basic doctrine and assumptions. Perhaps the most important concerned carrier deployment, which ultimately influenced both attack and defense.

When Kinkaid reassembled TF-61 on 24 October, he assumed the standard carrier dispositions used since Midway. Each surrounded by her own screen, the two flattops operated in easy visual signaling range five miles apart and were to remain together even in the event of enemy attack. Kinkaid felt this arrangement allowed for maximum coordination of the two air groups in sharing routine duties (CAP, search) as well as in attack and defense. Ideally, one FDO could mass the CAPs of both carrier task forces, and the two TF commanders could coordinate their strikes. The Battle of Santa Cruz did not alter his basic philosophy. Apparently Kinkaid did not consider placing both carriers in the same formation, as he preferred the individual carriers and escorts maneuver independently under attack.

Murray, commanding TF-17, did not share Kinkaid's regard for the current wisdom, although now it is difficult to say exactly what his prebattle ideas were. Certainly he felt the lack of opportunity to discuss carrier tactics with Kinkaid before the battle. His action reports and endorsements stress the need, when enemy contact is made, to separate the individual carrier task forces by at least 25 to 50 miles to get out of visual range of each other. Then they would operate independently under the overall direction of a commander based ashore, who did not have to maintain radio silence. Thus he firmly believed the carriers should control their own fighter direction, CAPs, and strikes.

Opinion at the SoPac level, as well as the *Enterprise* herself, tended to agree with Murray. That was not surprising since it reflected Halsey's and Murray's thought evolved during their long association on "The Big E," that is, separation rather than concentration in the face of "imminent attack," although what constituted imminent attack was not explained. That tactic was predicated upon operating under one's own shore-based air umbrella and required much better air search and strike coordination to work properly. Some of the reports commented favorably on the Japanese use of a vanguard of warships deployed well ahead of the main body, and Jimmy Flatley specifically advocated the use of destroyers as radar pickets, an idea employed to great advantage later in the war.[48]

Thus carrier deployment was far from settled. Perhaps Lieutenant Commander Luard, the Royal Navy observer on the *Hornet,* best summed up the difficulty at Santa Cruz by noting that the TF-61 deployment seemed to "retain all the disadvantages of concentration with none of its advantages."[49]

The reports described fighter direction in broad terms as "inadequate" (Flatley), "ineffective" (Sanchez), a "disappointment" (Hardison), and "confused and disorganized" (Halsey). The VF pilots felt they had the numbers to crush enemy attacks, but that their efforts were wasted. Understandably—given the controversial nature of the battle—there seemed to be more of an effort to assess blame than to understand what exactly happened. For example, Commander Griffin, the *Enterprise* FDO, compiled a detailed battle report with supporting documents that honestly analyzed the shortcomings of fighter direction at Santa Cruz. Yet when he submitted it for inclusion in the *Enterprise* battle report, he was informed rather tartly that it was not needed.[50] Only Kinkaid summarized its findings in his endorsements of other reports, and these comments were basically ignored. Virtually all of the reports were compiled before anyone other than Griffin had a chance to consult with his colleague Al Fleming, who was recovering from severe wounds received during the attack on the *Hornet*.[51]

In general the reports identified three particular areas of concern. The first was the lack of warning of incoming enemy planes provided the CAP and the consequent inability to deploy the CAP on time in the proper places. Therefore the actual fighter interceptions (when they even occurred) took place too close to the ships to give the CAP time to whittle down the opposition. They needed to attack the enemy at least 20 miles out.

Prior to the first raid, the *Hornet* and *Enterprise* strike groups encountered the Japanese attackers 60 to 75 miles northwest of TF-61 and sounded the alarm. Certain of the pilots involved (such as Sanchez) certainly stressed to angry listeners that these warnings were disregarded or mishandled. The *Hornet* people contrasted unfavorably the quality of the *Enterprise*'s fighter direction with their own highly regarded Fleming. Of course, the failure by *both* FDOs Griffin and Fleming to give adequate warning stemmed primarily from the unexpectedly poor performance of the *Enterprise* and *Hornet*'s CXAM radars (maximum range 45 miles despite the enemy's altitude).[52] That was not realized or acknowledged by most of the commentators. The poor state of radio communications with many distant messages garbled in receipt also contributed to the problem.

The second area of complaint concerned the height at which the CAP was deployed prior to action. Counting on the long-range warning hitherto afforded by carrier radars, Griffin deliberately kept the fighters at 10,000 feet in order to save fuel and oxygen. As he and many others stressed, that decision was especially unfortunate, primarily due to the performance of the Grumman F4F-4 Wildcat, which desperately needed replacement by the F4U-1 Corsair. Describing the Wildcat as a "very clumsy interceptor," Dave Pollock of VF-10 commented, "The F4F4 is a heavily loaded airplane and cannot climb and zip around from place to place and up and down."[53] Most of the time Griffin had no positive indication of the enemy's altitude because the radar only detected bogeys relatively close to the ships. Consequently the CAP rarely enjoyed the altitude superiority vital for successful attacks. Almost all the commentators, including Griffin, recommended that at least a substantial portion of the CAP climb to 20,000 feet when raids were expected.

The third particular complaint concerned Griffin's handling of the CAP. Many pilots accused him of poor technique in using relative bearings ("port bow" "starboard quarter," etc.) based on the *Enterprise*'s present course, which quickly changed as she maneuvered. Analysis of the fighter net transmissions rarely show the use of relative bearings and only when Griffin could offer nothing better. Yet the pilots certainly remembered those instances and harped on them.

In January 1943 Griffin returned to the Fighter Director School (which soon joined an expanded Fleet Radar Center) on Oahu, and Fleming later rejoined the fleet as a senior FDO. They carried with them the bitter lessons of Santa Cruz and built upon them to train a whole generation of fighter directors who helped to orchestrate the great fighter victories of 1943–45. In that regard, as many others, the sacrifice at Santa Cruz was not in vain.

Likewise a real start had been made on improving fighter escort tactics, never really successful in all of 1942. Flatley realized that the "Thach Weave," as he christened it, offered the best way to protect the bombers and bring the fighters through without heavy losses. He advocated placing the fighters out ahead and above the strike aircraft and deploying the four-plane flights in line abreast, one section somewhat beneath the other. If the escort was attacked, they could go into the weave immediately. If the bombers were jumped first, the escort VF would dive in to interpose themselves between intercepting fighters and their charges. After countering, the escort would begin weaving over the formation.

> Just your presence over the formation with two units (sections or 4-plane flights) weaving so that someone is always heading toward each flank, will detour the enemy and will keep you in a position to take head-on shots.[54]

In 1943 these tactics and continuing improvements prevented the type of bomber losses sustained in the first year of the war and destroyed many Japanese interceptors.

PART V

The Naval Battle of Guadalcanal

CHAPTER 23

Holding the SoPac Line

PATCHING "THE BIG E"

Soon after the wounded *Enterprise* dropped anchor off Noumea, experts from the repair ship *Vestal* and about seventy Seabees swarmed on board to assist her crew in effecting bomb damage repairs. Only minor restoration of the affected areas below deck (which included the ravaged officer's country) could be done, while they concentrated on removing the bulge in the hangar deck forward. Once the hangar deck was level, work could commence on the fractious number 1 elevator. Unable to drydock the carrier, the repair crews could do little for the crumpled sideplating dished in by the mining effects of the near misses. Not only the bomb damage came under scrutiny, but also the balky CXAM-1 radar. An extensive overhaul of the apparatus led to replacement of the damaged wave guides. Vice Admiral Halsey expected to complete the current schedule of repairs by 21 November, enabling the *Enterprise* to handle sixty-six planes (thirty fighters, twenty-seven dive bombers, and nine torpedo bombers). On 6 November a personal letter from Halsey to Admiral Nimitz described his plans for "The Big E":

> I hope to operate her fully, and with a full equipment of planes. If we do get away with it, and I fully believe we shall, I think a splendid job has been done under the conditions pertaining here.[1]

On 31 October, about 3,000 *Hornet* and *Porter* survivors crowded into a tent camp constructed by the Army near Noumea. Visiting the next day, Halsey was "delighted" at the "spirit of the officers and men." He decided to retain the entire *Hornet* Air Group, pilots as well as ground personnel, "until the situation clarifies."[2] By 1 November all of the Air Group Ten personnel had settled in on a hillside about three miles from Tontouta field, where the aircraft were based. Living in tents under rather rustic conditions gave all hands a chance to brush up on their "Boy Scout training." With the luxury of a 36-hour notice before re-embarking on board the *Enterprise*, Commander Gaines established a daily routine with work and flying in the mornings and afternoons off. A mountain stream three miles away ran "cool, deep and crystal clear," and the bracing weather offered a good change of pace from tropical heat. The more aggressive pilots hunted the elusive mountain deer. "After prolonged effort," a VT-10 pilot returned with "the tiniest deer in the world which he brought down with his .45 while the trusting little animal was looking at him with soft friendly eyes."[3]

At Tontouta VF-10 welcomed back those pilots who ditched at Santa Cruz and rode destroyers back to Noumea. About the only thing that troubled the squadron's idyllic existence in the New Caledonian mountains occurred on 5 November when "Axel" Axelrod ventured into soft ground while taking off and flipped the Wildcat onto its back. Fortunately he suffered only minor injuries, and VF-10 retained thirty-five F4F-4s at Tontouta.

THE QUESTION OF BRITISH CARRIER SUPPORT

On 27 October, in the wake of the defeat at Santa Cruz, Halsey requested that CinCPac look into the possibility of immediate reinforcement by one or more carriers from Adm. Sir James Somerville's British Eastern Fleet based in the Indian Ocean. Given the grave situation after the loss of the *Hornet* and the possible crippling of the *Enterprise,* Nimitz strongly endorsed the idea to Admiral King, not known for a high opinion of his British allies.[4]

Although the initial planning for the Solomons Campaign envisioned some sort of diversionary operations by Somerville's ships against the Dutch East Indies, nothing had come of it. Instead, the fleet supported the occupation of Madagascar and generally remained well away from trouble. By November Somerville retained only one carrier, whose superb combat record in the Mediterranean reflected her name: HMS *Illustrious.* Completed in August 1940, she displaced 28,000 tons (speed 30.5 knots), but her overall length of 740 feet was considerably less than her American counterparts. Yet in January 1941 her armored flight deck allowed her to survive no fewer than eight heavy bomb hits. However, such protection cost air strength. Lacking a deck-park capability and serviced by only two small lifts, the *Illustrious* carried only forty-seven aircraft: twenty-three Martlet IIs (Wildcats), six Fulmar II two-seat fighters, and eighteen antiquated Swordfish biplane torpedo bombers.[5]

Despite reservations about operating British and U.S. carriers together, King quickly brought up the matter with the British. He consulted RAdm. Denis Boyd, RN, the Eastern Fleet carrier commander (fortuitously in Washington) before Boyd was to proceed to Pearl Harbor to study U.S. carrier operations. CominCh agreed to use *Illustrious* in the Pacific "when and if made available." On 7 November he opined it would be best for her to proceed to Pearl to re-equip with Grumman TBF Avengers and warned that USN squadrons in SoPac must augment her air strength.[6]

Wondering about his possible new acquisition, Halsey decided the *Illustrious* needed to be refitted with U.S.-style wire flight deck barriers and furnished with American LSOs and key flight deck personnel to run the air group. He also recommended American rather than British aircraft torpedoes (a dubious idea given their poor performance). If this were accomplished, Halsey felt she would require only two weeks training, although he warned any contemplated reinforcement by USN squadrons must come from Pearl. Whether such a major revamping of carrier doctrine might not be welcomed by the British did not figure in his 11 November dispatch to Nimitz. At the same time, Nimitz consulted with his air commander Vice Admiral Towers, just joined by Rear Admiral Boyd from Washington. They proposed re-equipping the *Illustrious* with thirty-six fighters and sixteen Avengers, although six SBD Dauntless dive bombers could be substituted for nine fighters. Nimitz preferred keeping British pilots. Only in an emergency would he consider it wise to work up the air group in the South Pacific.[7]

The British were receptive to the idea of sending carriers to the Pacific. On 5 November Adm. Sir Dudley Pound, First Sea Lord, had proposed to Prime Minister Winston Churchill the loan of both the *Illustrious* and sister *Victorious* to the Americans in return for the *Ranger* to serve with the British Home Fleet. This would "do more to security of Indian Ocean than by retaining in this area a weak Eastern Fleet." Unexpectedly King demurred, saying that he needed the *Ranger* in reserve for carrier qualifications.[8]

SoPac's unexpected decisive November victory permitted such a delay in providing carrier support. In the end the Americans received the *Victorious*. In January 1943 she refitted at Norfolk before heading out to Pearl for a two-month work-up. With four squadrons numbering thirty-six Martlet IVs and fifteen Tarpon I torpedo planes (TBF Avengers), she sailed in May from Pearl and teamed up with the *Saratoga* for the New Georgia invasion before leaving for home.

CHANGING OF THE GUARD AT CACTUS

The first week of November brought massive alterations in the 1st MAW at CACTUS, when the exhausted Navy squadrons finally left the South Pacific. Lt. Cdr. Roy Simpler's VF-5 assembled at Noumea waiting for orders to leave for home, but it took Lieutenant Robb, the smooth-talking VF-5 A-V(S) officer, to persuade Brig. Gen. Louis Woods, the 1st MAW chief of staff, to allow the squadron to embark on the ex–luxury liner *Lurline*. Woods later reminisced that he had no authority to issue such orders to VF-5, but did so anyway because he admired that "damn fine outfit."[9] On the ship the pilots met up with Don Innis and Dix Loesch, back from convalescing at Auckland, New Zealand. Sailing on 7 November with many Navy and Marine CACTUS veterans, the *Lurline* reached San Diego on the 18th. VF-5 was finally decommissioned in early January 1943.

Next to leave CACTUS was the small VF-71 contingent. Lieutenant (jg) Kenton departed Guadalcanal on 28 October, his 24th birthday, and the others (Lieutenant Rooney, lieutenants [jg] Riise and Thrash, and Ensign Brown) left on 3 November. The closest call after the furious 25th of October had come the evening of 2 November, during a fruitless dusk scramble. Pounding rainstorms in the increasing darkness made it difficult to find the field. Finally, off Lunga, Red Thrash's engine gobbled the last of its fuel and suddenly cut out. He had to bail out immediately and barely missed Joe Foss's wing, but made it to the beach safely.[10]

On 8 November the last of the Navy dive-bombing squadrons, VS-71 (under Lt. Porter Maxwell since Lieutenant Commander Eldridge's death on 2 November) and Lt. Cdr. Ray Davis's VB-6 took their leave. VT-8, manning the TBF Avenger torpedo planes, were the only remaining Navy flight crews at CACTUS. Within a few days virtually all of VMF-212 likewise departed, except for a few pilots and Lt. Col. Joe Bauer, who remained in charge of the CACTUS Fighter Command. In addition stalwart VMF-121 and VMSB-141 also rotated out some of their pilots for rest.

To replace the tired squadrons at CACTUS, AirSoPac gradually fed in crews from Maj. William R. Campbell's VMO-251 at BUTTON and newly arrived MAG-11 squadrons, VMSB-132 (Maj. Joe Sailer), and VMF-112 (Maj. Paul Fontana). They came up on 1 and 2 November. On the 7th, Maj. Louis B. Robertshaw (USNA 1936), VMSB-132 XO, brought eight ex-*Hornet* SBDs from

BUTTON to Guadalcanal. The others would fly planes off the auxiliary carrier *Nassau*.

REINFORCING CACTUS

During the first week of November, the way appeared clear for Rear Admiral Turner to land strong reinforcements at Guadalcanal. The 1st MarDiv sealed off a Japanese force that landed at Koli Point east of the perimeter and to the west pursued the retreating 17th Army back across the Mantanikau River. (See table 23.1 for deployment of the main SoPac task forces as of 7 November.) That day Turner issued his OpPlan A23-42, which arranged for Scott, Callaghan, and his own TG-67.1 to reach Guadalcanal on 11 and 12 November and unload troops and supplies as quickly as possible.

With Turner's preparations well underway, Halsey decided to make his long-anticipated visit to CACTUS. He flew north on 7 November to Espiritu Santo, where he spent the rest of the day with Rear Admiral Fitch. The AirSoPac situation now appeared favorable. (See table 23.2 for air strength, not counting Air Group Ten and the Army fighters at Tontouta.)[11] In reserve ComSoPac retained fifteen new P-38 Lightning fighters and eleven B-26 Marauder medium bombers on New Caledonia and another ten B-26s at Fiji. Soon the planes on the auxiliary carriers *Nassau* and *Altamaha* would also arrive.

Early the next morning Halsey departed for Guadalcanal, and a grateful Vandegrift later described his presence "as a wonderful breath of fresh air," which greatly raised morale. The irrepressible admiral took a good look at Henderson Field and Fighter 1, as well as the new Fighter 2 strip being completed across the Lunga west of Kukum. Concerned about the physical toll of two months at Guadalcanal on Major General Geiger, his top Marine air commander, Halsey had ordered Brigadier General Woods to take over as Senior Naval Aviator, CACTUS. Both generals briefed him about the aviation situation. Disappointed but exhausted, Geiger prepared to leave for a short rest before joining Fitch at BUTTON to coordinate the growing Marine aviation presence in SoPac.[12]

At dawn on the 9th Halsey took leave of his host after a "most interesting and instructive" sojourn at Guadalcanal. He lunched at Espiritu Santo and spent the night at Efate. The next morning the flag PBY-5A Catalina set down in Noumea

TABLE 23.1
Deployment of Main SoPac Forces, 7 November 1942

	at Espiritu Santo
TG-62.4	TG-67.4
RAdm. Norman Scott	RAdm. Daniel J. Callaghan
CL(AA) *Atlanta*, 4 DD	CAs *San Francisco, Pensacola*,
3 AP/AK	CL *Helena*, 6 DD
	at Noumea
TG-67.1	TF-16
RAdm. Richmond Kelly Turner	RAdm. Thomas C. Kinkaid
CA *Portland*, CL(AA) *Juneau*	*Enterprise*
4 DD, 4 AP/AK	BBs *Washington, South Dakota*
	CA *Northampton*, CL(AA) *San Diego*
	8 DD

TABLE 23.2
AirSoPac Air Strength, 7 November 1942

	Aircraft (Operational)
CACTUS 1st MAW Advance Echelon	
Grumman F4F-4 Wildcats	42 (39)
Douglas SBD-3 Dauntlesses	24 (17)
Grumman TBF-1 Avengers	3 (3)
Bell P-39 Airacobras	4 (3)
Bell P-400 Airacobras	3 (2)
Espiritu Santo	
Grumman F4F-4 Wildcats	9 (7)
Grumman F4F-3P Wildcats	13 (11)
Douglas SBD-3 Dauntlesses	18 (10)
Consolidated PBY-5 Catalinas	31 (20)
Bell P-39 Airacobras	12 (12)
Boeing B-17 Flying Fortresses	46 (37)
Lockheed Hudsons (RZNAF)	10 (10)
New Caledonia (Plains des Gaics)	
Martin B-26 Marauders	11 (5)
North American B-25 Mitchells	4 (3)

Note: AirSoPac air strength with the exception of Air Group Ten and the USAAF at Tontouta

harbor, where a concerned Capt. Miles R. Browning, the chief of staff, waited with word of yet another major Japanese push against Guadalcanal.[13]

PREPARING FOR THE NEW ENEMY OFFENSIVE

As early as 4 November naval intelligence forecast "important enemy moves in southern Solomons," but an ULTRA flash from Admiral Nimitz received the morning of 10 November at Noumea electrified ComSoPac. Unquestionably the greatest radio intelligence breakthrough since the Battle of Midway, naval cryptanalysts had deciphered significant portions of a Combined Fleet operations order issued on 8 November. It offered "excellent indications of major operation assisted by CV striking force slated to support Army transports to Guadalcanal." This appeared to be the major counterlanding over the Lunga beaches, ever the greatest worry of the American commanders. The operation involved the usual cast of characters: the 3rd (CV Striking) Fleet which retained at least light carriers *Zuihō* and *"Hayataka"* (*Junyō*) plus some converted flattops, the land-based 11th Air Fleet, and the 8th Fleet covering the transports. The decrypts named "Z-Day" for the landing, although intelligence had yet to determine the exact date. Land-based air strikes against CACTUS would begin on Z−3 Day, with the carriers joining on Z−1. Nimitz closed: "While this looks like a big punch, I am confident that you with your forces will take their measure." Confirming the build-up, a photo mission on the 9th by the Fifth Air Force uncovered a rich harvest of enemy ships at Shortland.[14]

Halsey examined his options.[15] Turner, Scott, and Callaghan were already at sea, with Scott expected to reach CACTUS the next morning. Halsey decided to let Turner go ahead with the reinforcement plan, especially as CinCPac soon

The *Enterprise* at Noumea, 10 Nov. 1942. (NA 80-G-30547)

passed on OpNav's estimate that Z-Day was 13 November.[16] Despite the supposed risk of carrier strikes on Z−1 Day, he thought the 1st MAW and Callaghan's and Scott's forces offered adequate cover for Turner's transports to unload and clear out before the crucial 13th.

Halsey considered his main battle force to be Rear Admiral Kinkaid's TF-16 with the damaged *Enterprise* and new battleships *Washington* and *South Dakota*. By "great good luck," SoPac had already placed "The Big E" and her air group on a precautionary 24-hour sailing notice and completed repairs on the *Washington*'s engines. That afternoon Halsey summoned Kinkaid to headquarters to discuss the role of the damaged carrier in defending Guadalcanal. His initial idea, communicated to Fitch, was to send TF-16 to Espiritu Santo for the initial stage of the enemy offensive, base her air group there, and see what the situation held.[17] To reinforce Kinkaid, he instructed Callaghan to detach RAdm. Mahlon Tisdale's flagship *Pensacola* and two destroyers to return to Santo, refuel, and sail on his order to join TF-16. As events would prove, this was an important diminishment of Callaghan's force, but Halsey never intended TG-67.4 to take on the enemy single-handedly. That evening he placed the *Enterprise* on a one-hour notice to begin 0900, 11 November. The actual sailing orders followed at 0802 on the 11th. They instructed TF-16 to depart Noumea at 1100 on 11 November, and by 0800, 13 November, be 200 miles south of San Cristobal and prepared to strike targets near CACTUS. Clearly Halsey planned to disrupt the enemy landings and possibly send the battleships in that night. Thus TF-16 would not stop at Espiritu Santo.[18]

Around 1800 on 10 November, a bugle roused the Air Group Ten camp at Tontouta, and Commander Gaines alerted the aviators and ground crews to prepare to re-embark the next day. That day VF-10 had received a welcome reinforcement of ten familiar faces from VF-72 led by Lt. Warren Ford to bring the squadron up to strength. Eight were VF-8 veterans. The spare pilots and ground personnel packed the baggage for a hair-raising night drive over poor roads the 44 miles to Noumea harbor and the *Enterprise*. They barely made it.

The morning of the 11th the air group assembled at Tontouta field to fly out to the *Enterprise*. Jimmy Flatley's VF-10 took thirty-five F4F-4s aloft. The ship, however, did not sail when the group expected, so the planes returned to Tontouta for fuel. Because of a knee badly wrenched the previous day hunting deer, Lt. Bobby Edwards of VF-10 had to be lifted from his cockpit. To his intense displeasure, the swollen leg forced his immediate transfer to the Army base hospital. His F4F remained at Tontouta for lack of a pilot. However, Edwards would be heard from during the upcoming battle.[19]

At 1100 TF-16 sailed from Noumea, only about 24 hours since SoPac learned of the impending enemy offensive. It is difficult to imagine given the situation that the *Enterprise* could have departed any sooner. Chosen repair personnel remained on board to continue work on her number 1 elevator. If it remained inoperable, VT-10's TBF Avengers would be sent to a land base. According to the VB-10 war diary, "Air Group Ten came aboard in a ragged, dirty condition," happy to be free of their jungle hideaway. Obviously with repair crews bustling about, they knew the carrier was not 100 percent restored. The *Enterprise* wielded the following strength:

Tontouta airfield, 10 Nov. 1942. VF-10 F4Fs take off past VT-10 TBFs and R4D and C-47 transports. P-39s are parked to the right. (NA 80-G-29319)

Air Group Ten		
CAG-10	Cdr. Richard K. Gaines	1 TBF-1
VF-10	Lt. Cdr. James H. Flatley, Jr.	37 F4F-4s
VB-10	Lt. Cdr. James A. Thomas	15 SBD-3s
VS-10	Lt. Cdr. James R. Lee	16 SBD-3s
VT-10	Lt. Albert P. Coffin	8 TBF-1s

The Japanese would indeed feel the sting of these seventy-seven planes from a carrier they thought no longer existed.

JAPANESE PLANS AGAINST GUADALCANAL

As previously noted, Imperial General Headquarters in Tokyo assessed the "Naval Battle of the South Pacific" (the Battle of Santa Cruz) as an overwhelming Japanese victory, which substantially destroyed U.S. naval power in the region. That opened the way for another major offensive to retake Guadalcanal. As Richard B. Frank pointed out in his *Guadalcanal,* Tokyo took much stock in incautious Allied news reports that announced ship losses, including a carrier, and hinted at deteriorating morale at Guadalcanal. The press accounts were real enough and bedeviled Halsey at Noumea, who believed the leaks originated in Australia.[20]

Reeling from its repulse at Lunga, Lieutenant General Hyakutake's 17th Army nevertheless anticipated resuming the offensive, now postponed to late December, after a massive influx of fresh troops, including the 51st Division. The priority changed to rushing additional support troops, weapons, and supplies to lay the groundwork for the attack. Vice Admiral Mikawa's 8th Fleet (Outer South Seas Force) organized a special Tokyo Express run to Guadalcanal. The night of 7/8 November eleven destroyers delivered to Tassafaronga 1,300 troops, including Lt. Gen. Sano Tadayoshi, commander of the 38th Division. The force escaped damage from Lunga-based enemy planes, a good omen for the Japanese. Believing a strongly escorted convoy would be superior to a series of destroyer runs, the Combined Fleet staff put together on 7 November a complex operation designed to assemble as many fast transports as possible and deliver the cargo on 13 November (Z-Day). The next day newly promoted Vice Admiral Ugaki issued the op order recovered in so much detail by U.S. cryptanalysts.

Sailing south on 9 November from Truk, Vice Admiral Kondō's Advance Force (2nd Fleet) controlled the main fighting strength: the *Junyō* (sole operational carrier in the Southeast Area), four fast battleships, three heavy cruisers, two light cruisers, and nineteen destroyers organized into four main task groups. They drew up north of the Solomons. A vital part of Combined Fleet's plan involved reprising the massive ship bombardments of October to destroy or neutralize air power based at Lunga, believed the last bastion of enemy strength in the area. The night of Z−1/Z-Day (12/13 November), Vice Admiral Abe's two battleships were to pulverize Henderson Field, and Vice Admiral Mikawa's 8th Fleet with four heavy cruisers, one light cruiser, and six destroyers was set to mop up the night of Z-Day. Meanwhile, Rear Admiral Tanaka's convoy of eleven transports and eleven destroyers assembled at Shortland for the trip to Guadalcanal. Passengers included more troops from the 38th Division (but only two battalions of infantry), specialist and service units, while the cargo comprised massive food supplies, ammunition, and craft to land them.[21]

Through cryptanalysis, U.S. naval intelligence picked up key elements of the enemy plan, but understandably erred in interpretation. Halsey foresaw an assault landing at Lunga, a cataclysmic struggle for Guadalcanal itself, for which they would battle with everything they had. Not realizing Nagumo's 3rd Fleet had withdrawn, leaving only the *Junyō*, SoPac thought two carriers would execute the Z−1 day attack against U.S. air power at Lunga. However, Combined Fleet arranged for a battleship bombardment by Kondō, followed on Z-Day by another caress by Mikawa's cruisers. In fact they never envisioned this operation as the decisive battle to wrest control of Guadalcanal from the Americans. Instead it was to be another reinforcement operation, a super "Tokyo Express," to set the stage for the eventual grand offensive in December. Combined Fleet neither expected nor was prepared to commit the last ship or plane to see this operation to completion. Such a difference in perception of the operation's goals and SoPac's willingness to fight greatly affected the course of the battle. Things looked grim, but Halsey's warriors felt confident they could handle whatever the enemy sent down.

A NEW LOOK FOR BASE AIR FORCE

With almost all the Japanese carriers out of the picture, air support for the Guadalcanal operation, such as it was, fell mainly upon CACTUS's old adversary, Vice Admiral Kusaka's Base Air Force (11th Air Fleet).[22]

On 1 November the Imperial Navy initiated a comprehensive administrative reorganization devised by some orderly minded bureaucrat. The land-based air groups all received intricate numerical designations in place of names, foreshadowed in October with the numbering of the Kanoya (751) and Takao (753) air groups. The first or hundreds number denoted the principal type of plane flown, such as single-engine carrier fighter (200s), carrier attack plane or carrier bomber (500s), land attack plane (700s), flying boat and seaplane fighter (800s), and fleet cooperation (900s). The second digit identified the particular naval district that administered the group (0, 1, or 2: Yokosuka; 3 or 4: Kure; 5, 6, or 7: Sasebo; and 8 or 9 Maizuru). The last digit denoted the group itself. If odd, the air group originally bore a name; if even, just a number. Thus the Tainan Air Group became the 251 Air Group: the 2 denoted carrier fighters, the 5 identified Sasebo Naval District, and the 1 (an odd number) signified a previous name rather than a number. (See table 23.3 for the the groups and detachments within Base Air Force as of 1 November.)

In addition to new designations, Base Air Force greatly changed personnel in the two weeks following the great October offensive. Old units left, and others took their places. On 31 October Lieutenant Makino's 753 Air Group land attack detachment (ex-Takao) left to rejoin the 23rd Air Flotilla in the Dutch East Indies, followed on 8 November by Lieutenant Commander Sakakibara's 202 Air Group fighters. The most significant departures occurred on the 10th and 11th. The headquarters of Rear Admiral Yamada's 5th Air Attack Force (25th Air Flotilla) finally left for Japan, followed by twenty-odd surviving fighter pilots of Captain Saitō's redoubtable 251 Air Group. No group fought harder over New Guinea and Guadalcanal.

The first major reinforcement comprised the main body (twenty-seven Type 1 land attack planes) of Capt. Ōhashi Fujirō's *Chitose* (later 703) Air Group. They flew in on 27 October to Rabaul from the 24th Air Flotilla in the Marshalls. On 9

TABLE 23.3
New Designations for Air Groups in Base Air Force, 1 November 1942

Fighters	Land Attack Planes
202 Air Group (ex-3rd)	703 Air Group (ex-*Chitose*)
204 Air Group (ex-6th)	705 Air Group (ex-Misawa)
251 Air Group (ex-Tainan)	707 Air Group (ex-Kisarazu)
253 Air Group (ex-751 [Kanoya] Air Group VF Squadron)	751 Air Group[a] (ex-Kanoya)
Carrier Bombers	Flying Boats
582 Air Group[b] (ex-2nd)	802 Air Group (ex-14th)
	851 Air Group (ex-Tōkō)
Fleet Cooperation	
954 Air Group (ex-31st)	

[a]Numbered as of 1 October 1942
[b]Included carrier fighters

November the newly repaired escort carrier *Taiyō* ferried to Rabaul the main body (twenty-one Zero 32s and five Zero 21s) of the 252 Air Group. Formerly the fighter squadron of the Genzan Air Group (22nd Air Flotilla), the 252 came into existence on 20 September at Tateyama Air Base in Japan. The CO was Capt. Yanagisawa Yoshitane (wings 1925), with Lt. Suganami Masaji (NA 61-1933), the aggressive former *Sōryū* fighter leader, as *hikōtaichō* and Lt. Yamamoto Shigehisa (NA 66-1938), a *Shōkaku* Coral Sea veteran, as *buntaichō*. On 10 November the *Unyō* delivered the 956 Air Group with ten Type 99 carrier bombers to replace the battered 954 Air Group transferred out to re-form.

As of 11 November, VAdm. Kusaka Jinichi's Base Air Force comprised approximately sixty Zero 21s, forty-five Zero 32s, thirty-seven Type 99 carrier bombers, and fifty-seven Type 1 land attack planes, not all flyable (see table 23.4).

PRELIMINARY SKIRMISHES, 11 AND 12 NOVEMBER

At 0530, 11 November, Norman Scott's TG-62.4 arrived at Lunga and quickly unloaded the Marine aviation specialists and vital supplies. Warned by searches, Base Air Force arranged for an antishipping mission from Buin. Newly promoted Lt. Cdr. Kaneko Tadashi led eighteen Zeros from his own *Hiyō* and the 204 Air Group to protect Lt. Abe Zenji's nine *Hiyō* Type 99 carrier bombers. Warned by radar at 0905, the 1st MAW massed twenty-one Grumman F4F-4 Wildcats from VMF-121, VMF-212, VMO-251, and VMF-112 to meet them. However, thick clouds over Lunga shielded the strike from the CAP. Braving fierce AA from the flagship *Atlanta,* Abe's pilots scored three near misses alongside the transport *Zeilin* (AP-9), which flooded a hold, and also slightly damaged two other transports. In return four Type 99s went down and another force-landed, mostly due to AA fire. The clouds assisted Kaneko's escorts' efforts to ambush six F4Fs (killing four pilots: second lieutenants Joseph L. Narr, Roy M. A. Ruddell, and Robert F. Simpson, all of VMF-121, and Master Technical Sgt. William H. Coahran, Jr., of 112), for the loss of two *Hiyō* Zeros (PO2c Yoshiwara Isamu and PO2c Morita Toshio).[23]

Already en route from Rabaul, Raid II lugged bombs for Lunga instead of torpedoes, because Japanese coastwatcher warnings had not come in time to change the mission. Lt. Watanabe Kazuo (NA 61-1933) of the 703 Air Group led twenty-five Type 1 land attack planes protected by twenty-six Zeros under Lieutenant Itō of the 253 Air Group. At 1127 the *rikkōs* came in high against Lunga, missed Henderson Field, but cratered the coconut grove and Fighter 1. About seventeen F4Fs intercepted, and their spirited pursuit downed four land attack planes (two 703, two 705). Perhaps because of the clouds, most of the Zeros did not engage, and they suffered no loss. The only Marine casualties occurred when two F4Fs collided, killing Master Technical Sgt. Joseph J. Palko of VMF-121.[24]

After the interruption, Scott resumed unloading the transports. Around 1800 he withdrew east to Indispensable Strait, where along with the *Atlanta* and three destroyers he joined Callaghan's incoming TG-67.4 for a pair of night sweeps around Savo Island to cover the arrival of Turner's convoy. After dawn on the 12th, the four transports recommenced offloading the 182nd Infantry Regiment and other troops at Lunga. Out in the sound, Callaghan's and Scott's two heavy cruisers, three light cruisers, eleven destroyers, and two destroyer minesweepers offered close protection. Newly arrived Lt. Cdr. Emura Kusao, formerly the *Sanyō Maru*'s air officer, eagerly counted the assemblage of ships and alerted Rabaul of three battleships, three cruisers, eleven destroyers, and five transports.

Kusaka hurriedly ordered an attack. Beginning around 1000, Lt. Cdr. Nakamura Tomoo, the veteran 705 (Misawa) Air Group *hikōtaichō*, left Rabaul with seventeen torpedo-armed land attack planes (one soon aborted), escorted by thirty Zeros under the 252 Air Group *hikōtaichō*, Lieutenant Suganami. That set

TABLE 23.4
Base Air Force Organization, 11 November 1942

1st Air Attack Force (21st Air Flotilla)	RAdm. Ichimaru Rinosuke	Rabaul
751 Air Group (Type 1 *rikkōs*)	Capt. Odawara Toshihiko	Kavieng
253 Air Group (Zero fighters)	Cdr. Kobayashi Yoshito	Rabaul and Kavieng
582 Air Group Main Force (Zero fighters)	Capt. Yamamoto Sakaė	Rabaul
252 Air Group Main Force (Zero fighters)	Capt. Yanagisawa Yoshitane	Rabaul
6th Air Attack Force (26th Air Flotilla)	VAdm. Yamagata Seigō	Rabaul
705 Air Group (Type 1 *rikkōs*)	Capt. Sugawara Masao	Rabaul
707 Air Group (Type 1 *rikkōs*)	Capt. Fujiyoshi Naoshiro	Rabaul
204 Air Group (Zero fighters)	Capt. Morita Chisato	Buin
582 Air Group Carrier Bomber Squadron (Type 99s)	Lt. Cdr. Inoue Fumito	Buin
703 Air Group Main Force (Type 1 *rikkōs*)	Capt. Ōhashi Fujirō	Rabaul
956 Air Group (Type 99 carrier bombers)	(CO unknown)	Rabaul
Hiyō Air Group (Zero fighters and Type 99 VB)	Cdr. Mieno Saburō	Buin
Flying Boat Force	Capt. Wada Saburō	Rabaul and Shortland
851 Air Group (Type 97 flying boats)	Capt. Wada	
802 Air Group Detachment (Type 2 sea fighters)	(CO unknown)	

up a reprise of the disastrous 8 August mission against the same wily opponent. Warned at 1317 by coastwatcher Paul Mason at Buin, Turner soon got underway and gathered his screen to greet the raiders from the center of Sealark Channel. Nakamura appeared on the CACTUS radar at 109 miles, and Lt. Lew Mattison's controllers gave continuous warning of his approach but, hidden by thick clouds, the crafty Nakamura circled northeast of Lunga over Florida Island.

The 1st MAW CAP flew in two elements. At 29,000 feet Capt. Joe Foss circled with eight Marine F4Fs and eight Army P-39 Airacobras, while Maj. Paul Fontana, CO of VMF-112, with eight more newly scrambled F4Fs climbed past 5,500 feet. At 1415 Nakamura's sixteen *rikkōs,* with Suganami's fighters on their right wing, suddenly emerged east of Florida from out of the clouds at 500 feet in a steep, high-speed dive. Yelling "Let's go gang!," Foss led the sixteen fighters in a hell-raising dive east toward the enemy. The windshield in 2nd Lt. Frank Clark's P-39 fogged so rapidly in the moist warm air near the water that he became disoriented and plowed into the sea.[25]

Seeing incoming planes in two formations, Turner swung broadside ahead of the first (actually Suganami's Zeros), only to present his stern adroitly to the real torpedo planes. First Fontana's Wildcats tangled with the fast *rikkōs,* and Foss's F4Fs and the P-39s joined the fierce low-level (50 feet or less) melee smack in the midst of five-inch shell bursts and 20-mm tracers. The result was a slaughter second only to 8 August. Only a few of Nakamura's pilots ever fired their torpedoes. The only damage to the ships, and it was not crippling, occurred when one burning Type 1 "side swiped stern to bow"[26] the *San Francisco,* Callaghan's flagship. Ships' gunners enthusiastically claimed no fewer than forty-three enemy planes, while the CAP chalked up seventeen bombers and seven fighters for three Marine F4Fs (pilots safe) and the one Army P-39. To FDO Mattison Lt. Col. Joe Bauer exulted, "We did fine! Had one of the best days we've had!"[27] At 1525 Turner's jubilant transports returned to their Lunga anchorage and resumed unloading. By 1830 they had landed about 90 percent of the personnel and much of the cargo. Emura radioed to Kusaka that unhappy development and that the weather closed over Guadalcanal's north coast.

Nakamura's sixteen attack planes suffered near annihilation: eleven shot down or crash-landed, and all of the rest (including the abort) so badly damaged as to be written off. Of seven 705 Type 1s, only one reached base; three went missing and the other three (including Nakamura) took refuge at Buin. Only one of nine *rikkōs* from the 703 Air Group landed back at Rabaul. Six disappeared and two others, including Res. Lt. (jg) Fukuchi Yoshihiko, force-landed at Guadalcanal. PO2c Itō Isao's 582 Air Group Zero also failed to return. Results did not appear commensurate with the sacrifice. The survivors claimed damage to three transports and an escorting destroyer, although Emura on shore witnessed no hits. The appalling losses on 12 November seemed to break the back of the land attack plane contingent, and Kusaka sent none to raid Lunga during the next two crucial days. He strongly distrusted the quality of replacement bomber crews provided in the last several weeks.

CACTUS also celebrated massive aircraft reinforcements, mainly as a result of the arrival the previous day at Espiritu Santo of the escort carrier *Nassau.* Marine and *Hornet* pilots had ferried twenty SBDs (one ditched), twelve TBFs, and six F4Fs ashore to Santo. On the 12th, ten SBDs led by Maj. Robert Richard (VMSB-142), six VMSB-131 TBFs under Lt. Col. "Pat" Moret, and Maj. Elmer Brackett's six VMF-122 F4Fs flew to CACTUS. Maj. Dale Brannon, former CO of the 67th FS and now leading the 339th, arrived with eight long-awaited twin-engine Lockheed P-38F Lightning fighters. Heavily armed with one 20-mm cannon and four .50-caliber machine guns in the nose, the P-38Fs greatly outperformed Grumman F4F-4 Wildcats as pure interceptors. Capable of 352 knots (395 MPH) at 25,000 feet, they attained 20,000 feet in 8.8 minutes.

From search contacts Turner already knew of enemy ships bound for Guadalcanal. At 1035 Capt. Frank J. Puerta's B-17 sighted two battleships or heavy cruisers, one cruiser, and six destroyers, 270 miles north of Santa Isabel or about 335 miles north of Guadalcanal. They closed on course 180 degrees. A subsequent message gave their speed as 25 knots. Another B-17 detected five destroyers 110 miles north of Santa Isabel, most likely headed for the first group. The searchers had indeed located Abe's Bombardment Force racing south to plaster the Lunga airfield. The Japanese commanders did not expect the American ships at Lunga to stay and fight, but they had a big surprise coming.

Even before Nakamura's air strike, Kelly Turner had ordered TF-67 to withdraw that night eastward through Indispensable Strait. The transports and escort left directly for BUTTON, while the remaining thirteen warships, a Support Group under Dan Callaghan, were to "return to CACTUS tonight and strike enemy ships present." Turner felt impelled to oppose and delay the incoming Japanese force unexpectedly discovered by AirSoPac.[28]

During the 12th Kinkaid's TF-16 pounded northwestward cutting down the distance to Guadalcanal but, still far to the south, the *Enterprise* could not intervene. Tisdale's *Pensacola* and two destroyers left Espiritu Santo to join TF-16 the next day. In the late afternoon 2nd Lt. William E. Hronek's VMSB-132 search section placed two carriers and two destroyers south of New Georgia and only 150 miles west of Guadalcanal. Lieutenant Colonel Moret led twelve SBDs and seven TBFs after this force, but impending darkness and poor weather turned them back early. Turner, at least, tended to discount the accuracy of the CV sighting. At 1804 Kinkaid learned from CACTUS radio of the two supposed carriers northwest of Guadalcanal. From 575 miles away, TF-16 could not strike them that day or offer any immediate help to Turner. Nor could Kinkaid altogether discredit the reports of carriers, although like Turner he believed them "improbable."[29]

At dark Turner withdrew his ships eastward through Indispensable Strait and sent Callaghan's Support Group back to protect CACTUS. Only warned on 10 November of the Japanese offensive, Halsey could not position his main battle force to meet the incoming Japanese, so on his own volition Turner threw Callaghan's Support Group into the breach. Against an enemy whose strength was uncertain and might number as many as two BBs or CAs, one cruiser, and eleven DDs, Callaghan wielded heavy cruisers *San Francisco* and *Portland*, the light cruiser *Helena*, the two light AA cruisers *Atlanta* (Norm Scott's flagship) and *Juneau*, and destroyers *Cushing, Laffey, Sterett, O'Bannon* (DD-450), *Aaron Ward, Barton* (DD-599), *Monssen*, and *Fletcher* (DD-445). Early the next morning, they would battle a foe superior in numbers and firepower and forestall a possibly calamitous pounding of the 1st MAW, but only at the cost of several ships and hundreds of lives. It proved to be the key decision of the campaign.[30]

CHAPTER 24

The Death of the *Hiei*

Shortly after midnight on 13 November, RAdm. Dan Callaghan gallantly interposed his two heavy cruisers, three light cruisers (two AA), and eight destroyers between CACTUS and Vice Admiral Abe's incoming bombardment force of two battleships, one light cruiser, and eleven destroyers. The resulting slugfest, which broke out at 0145 near Savo Island, saw some of the fiercest naval night combat of the war at ranges that would have delighted John Paul Jones.

Heavier Japanese guns and greatly superior torpedoes battered the Allied force. One Japanese destroyer (*Akazuki*) and two American ones (*Laffey*, *Barton*) went down almost immediately; many other ships suffered hideous damage. The destroyers *Cushing*, *Monssen*, and *Aaron Ward* lay dead in the water southeast of Savo, while the crippled cruisers *Portland* and *Atlanta* limped a bit closer to Lunga. Both Callaghan on the *San Francisco* and Norm Scott on the *Atlanta* died from shell fire, leaving Capt. Gilbert C. Hoover to command the mobile remnants: his *Helena*, the torn-up *San Francisco* and *Juneau*, and the destroyers *O'Bannon*, *Sterett*, and *Fletcher*. After passing Lunga, Hoover turned southeast along the coast of Guadalcanal toward San Cristobal.

The Americans triumphed in spirit. Shocked at the fierce opposition, Abe promptly canceled the bombardment. More than eighty-five shells struck flagship *Hiei*, and one eight-incher flooded the steering room aft and badly affected control. Other than the wounded battleship, the only other Japanese warship in serious trouble was the destroyer *Yūdachi*, dead in the water perilously close to the enemy ships. The *Kirishima* and most of the destroyers pulled off to the north to get clear of the area before daylight and rejoin Kondō's Advance Force.

At 0344, a shocked Admiral Yamamoto postponed the Z-Day arrival of the convoy at Guadalcanal one day to 14 November and turned Tanaka's transports back to Shortland for the time being. However, he retained the scheduled bombardment for the night of the 13th/14th by Mikawa's cruisers and ordered Kondō to follow up with another shelling the next night. The problem became air support for the *Hiei*, lying just off the enemy's lair at Lunga and certain to draw all of the enemy's attention on 13 November.[1]

The only buffers for the crippled *Hiei* against the unhurt enemy air force at Lunga were Rear Admiral Kakuta's carrier *Junyō* with Kondō 200 miles north of the Solomons and the fighters of distant Base Air Force. The *Junyō* Air Group numbered twenty-seven Zero fighters, twelve Type 99 carrier bombers, and nine Type 97 carrier attack planes, not all operational. Vice Admiral Kusaka's Base Air Force groups at Rabaul, Kavieng, and Buin comprised some fifty-seven Zero

21 and forty-five Zero 32 fighters, along with approximately thirty-two Type 99 carrier bombers and forty Type 1 land attack planes. On 13 November approximate fighter strength at the two crucial bases numbered: at Rabaul, the 252, 253, and 582 air groups, with thirty-five Zero 21s and twenty-one Zero 32s; at Buin, the 204 Air Group with twenty-four Zero 32s and the *Hiyō* Air Group with thirteen Zero 21s. The *Hiei* was not as well protected as these figures imply. Not all of these planes were operational, and other commitments existed for those that were. In addition to CAP missions, the 252 Air Group at Rabaul provided nine fighters to protect an ammunition convoy to Lae, while nine Buin-based Zeros undertook a search for enemy activity elsewhere in the Solomons.[2]

The bright flashes and the boom of distant heavy guns, followed by the enemy's unexpected retirement, caused the 1st MAW to be extremely grateful to be spared what could have been a devastating bombardment. Brigadier General Woods wielded the following operational force:

MAG-14 Lt. Col. A. D. Cooley	
VMF-112, 121, 122	19 F4F-4 Wildcats
VMSB-132, 141, 142	23 SBD-3 Dauntlesses
VMSB-131, VT-8	8 TBF-1 Avengers
347th Fighter Group	18 P-39 Airacobras, 8 P-38 Lightnings

The Marine flyers arose before dawn to scout the situation. Seven search SBDs fanned out in the three sectors: the west (New Georgia), northwest (Santa Isabel), and north (Malaita). After sunrise Major Sailer, VMSB-132 CO, took three Dauntlesses on a "special tracking mission" toward Savo and beheld the tableau of hurt and dying warships. Nearest to Lunga the *Atlanta* listed with her crew crowded on deck. Next, the *Portland* circled without obvious damage except at the stern. South of Savo drifted three friendly destroyers. About four miles southeast of Savo, the Marine flyers watched another ship suddenly explode and quickly sink. She was the *Yūdachi*, finished off by the pugnacious *Portland*. The wounded giant *Hiei* had lurched a few miles north of Savo, where her rudder finally jammed. She circled at five knots. Sailer noticed a bad fire forward and the rear turret guns seemingly askew. The destroyer *Yukikaze* stood by. The search discovered four destroyers moving to join the *Hiei* and only 20 miles north of Savo the *Kirishima* and three more destroyers.[3]

The damaged battleship lurking only 30 miles from CACTUS posed special danger to the 1st MAW. At Henderson Field, Woods swiftly readied a strike. At 0615 Major Richard's six VMSB-142 SBDs departed first and climbed to altitude. Arming his bomb, Richard inadvertently dumped his payload into the water. Taking off later, seven F4Fs led by Major Campbell of VMO-251 escorted six TBFs (two soon aborted) under Capt. George E. Dooley, the VMSB-131 operations officer. To his disgust, MAG-14 had co-opted Lt. Col. Pat Moret, 131's CO, for staff duty. Around 0655 RADAR TWO picked up an estimated ten enemy fighters at 42 miles, so Lt. Col. Joe Bauer immediately loosed 2nd Lt. Archie G. Donahue's three VMF-112 CAP F4Fs at high speed toward Savo.[4]

Early that morning two separate carrier forces, one hundreds of miles to the north and the other even further south also took great interest in the waters immediately northwest of Guadalcanal. Kakuta's light carrier *Junyō* received orders to support Abe's retreating Bombardment Force. In addition to searches and CAP, she launched at 0530 eight Zeros led by a familiar warrior, Lt. Shigematsu Yasuhiro, to cover the *Hiei*. Bad weather prompted the *Junyō*'s Captain Okada to send along two Type 97 carrier attack planes as guides.[5]

By 0500, Kinkaid's TF-16 with the *Enterprise,* as ordered, reached the waters 250 miles directly south of San Cristobal and some 270 miles south-southeast of CACTUS. Still concerned about the carriers spotted the previous afternoon by the VMSB-132 search, Kinkaid sent ten SBDs out 200 miles ahead to cover the waters in the immediate vicinity, spotted a strike group on deck until they reported back, and kept a CAP of eight F4Fs aloft. The search results and continuing problems with "The Big E" 's forward elevator would determine the next move.

Kinkaid and Captain Hardison finally decided that the *Enterprise*'s forward elevator could not be trusted. Testing risked it freezing in the down position, which would prevent flight operations. They now implemented the contingency plan to send VT-10 ashore. John Crommelin briefed Lt. Scoofer Coffin and his pilots for an "offensive sweep" to Guadalcanal. Handing out some simple, hastily inked maps to Henderson Field, he laid out a course of 345 degrees out to 285 miles. That allowed a look west of Guadalcanal before the strike landed at CACTUS. Coffin would take all nine TBFs, eight with torpedoes, and the ninth (the borrowed CAG plane) loaded with three 500-pound bombs. In turn Lt. Cdr. Jimmy Flatley received orders to send six wing tank–equipped VF-10 F4Fs as escort. He chose Lt. Jock Sutherland's flight, plus a section led by Lt. (jg) Robert Holland. Pretty certain by 0700 that the morning search was negative, Kinkaid gave the go-ahead for the strike. Coffin's force took off without incident and at 0722 departed northwest.[6]

In the meantime Richard's strike maneuvered for the best attack position over the *Hiei* north of Savo. Clouds and smoke made it difficult at times to pick out the enemy ships. The Marines showed up at an opportune time and distracted the battleship from finishing off the immobile *Aaron Ward* in retaliation for the sinking of the *Yūdachi.* Around 0710 VMSB-142 started down against the massive warship. Master Technical Sgt. Donald V. Thornbury's thousand-pounder detonated directly on her superstructure amidships, and the others scored four near misses along her port side.

No fighters intercepted the Dauntlesses either on their way in or out, but that did not mean none prowled out there. Sweeping in from the north, Shigematsu's eight *Junyō* fighters first spotted Savo about 0700 and passed the *Hiei.* Patrolling the area, they came upon a flight of enemy planes. Five Zeros, Shigematsu's 1st and CPO Mukai Tasuke's 3rd *shōtais,* peeled off for a fierce little dogfight at low altitude against Donahue's three VMF-112 Wildcats. Enthusiastically sitting on the tail of one Zero, 2nd Lt. Thomas H. Hughes, Jr., fired all his bullets, but could not finish it off. Donahue's extended pursuit finally blasted the bandit into the water. His victim was the veteran Mukai (wings 1935), on detached duty from the *Zuihō.* Fighting alone, the third member of VMF-112, 2nd Lt. Howard W. Bollman, enjoyed a good shot at a fighter and claimed it, but his Wildcat took numerous bullets in return.

Under cover of the dive-bombing attack, Dooley set up a high-speed torpedo approach with his four remaining Avengers. Heading in around 0715, he noticed the fighter melee break out ahead. Suddenly he had his own worries. WO Ono Zenji's 2nd *Shōtai* of three Zeros noticed about five enemy torpedo planes and latched onto the TBFs. Evidently 131 expected little fighter opposition, for after someone yelled "Zeros!" an exasperated Marine added, "Hell! The air is full of 'em right around me." 1st Lt. Douglas Bangert's Avenger suffered special punishment, ripped by 20-mm cannon shells that wounded a crewman. With his .50-caliber turret gun, Technical Sgt. John L. Dewey drove off the assailant.[7]

Help for Dooley's flight was close at hand. From 12,000 feet Major Campbell's seven escort F4Fs neatly ambushed Ono's scattered *shōtai*. From a series of low-level dogfights, the Marine fighter pilots tallied nine Zeros:

VMF-121	
1st Lt. John P. Sigman	2.0 VF
2nd Lt. Donald C. Owen	1.5 VF
1st Lt. Otto H. Bruggeman, Jr.	1.0 VF
VMF-112	
2nd Lt. Wayne W. Laird	1.5 VF
2nd Lt. Archie G. Donahue	1.0 VF
2nd Lt. Howard W. Bollman	1.0 VF
VMO-251	
2nd Lt. Herbert A. Peters	1.0 VF

The highly regarded Ono and CPO Hasegawa Tatsuzō died in battle; from the 2nd *Shōtai* only PO2c Banno Takao (a *Shōhō* Coral Sea and *Ryūjō* Eastern Solomons veteran) survived. Meanwhile, Dooley pressed his attack against the *Hiei*, which countered with fierce AA, including the experimental Type 3 fourteen-inch special incendiary-shrapnel rounds that acted like big shotgun shells, raising many small splashes of water ahead of the Avengers. Dooley and 1st Lt. William C. Hayter each felt confident they scored against the battlewagon, while the 1st MAW assessed one torpedo hit for VSMB-131. Back at CACTUS Bangert's plane went into the scrap pile.

Bollman from 112 joined on Campbell's wing, but soon his oil pressure gave out. Avoiding a Zero, he ditched near Savo. An hour's swim brought him to shore and the company of friendly natives, and on 18 November a Higgins boat fetched him back to Lunga unharmed. Marine claims totaled ten fighters, for the loss of one F4F. In turn, Shigematsu's flight lost three Zeros and pilots for claims of two Grumman fighters (one unconfirmed). This proved to be the most spirited fighter action of the day.

As the action heated up, the long-range air search from Espiritu Santo approached the end of the outward legs and found elements of Kondō's Advance Force, including the *Junyō*, near Ontong Java 225 miles north of Guadalcanal. At 0750 1st Lt. Robert M. Creech's B-17 Flying Fortress (72nd Bomb Squadron) placed one carrier, one battleship, and three destroyers about 225 miles north of Guadalcanal. Ten minutes later 1st Lt. Robert E. Hawes from the same squadron located three heavy cruisers and a destroyer only 27 miles south of Creech's contact. Both groups of ships retired north at high speed. Rear Admiral Fitch loosed the ready B-17s at BUTTON against the carrier force. Another search B-17 sighted Tanaka's convoy retiring northwest to Shortland, verifying the accuracy of CinCPac's estimate of enemy plans thrown out of kilter only by Callaghan's gallant action.[8]

While the air command digested the search reports, the 1st MAW furiously rearmed and refueled its strike planes for a second go against the *Hiei* and the *Yukikaze*, joined by the AA destroyer *Teruzuki* and the 27th Destroyer Division (*Shigure*, *Yūgure*, and *Shiratsuyu*). Joe Sailer led nine SBDs (seven 132, two 142), seven F4Fs under Capt. Robert B. Fraser, VMF-112 XO, and George Dooley's three TBFs (another aborted) after the crippled battleship. No bombs struck home during their 0915 attack, but 1st Lt. William W. Dean received credit for a possible torpedo hit against her port side. Fraser's Wildcats strafed to divert AA fire away from the Avengers. The raiders never encountered the second *Junyō* fighter patrol, Lt. (jg) Watanabe Torio's six Zeros guided by a Type 97 *kankō*. On the way south Watanabe had sparred with one of the search B-17s and reached the *Hiei* about 0800, but departed after an uneventful patrol just prior to Sailer's arrival. The flight back north was no picnic. In decreasing visibility Watanabe and wingman CPO Kubota Wataru separated from the others and finally ditched near a friendly destroyer. Aided by two Type 97s thoughtfully provided for that purpose, the experienced CPO Sawada Mankichi brought the other six fighters back to the *Junyō*.

After the second assault against the *Hiei,* an erroneous contact introduced an unneeded measure of farce to the proceedings. The coastwatcher on San Cristobal (ZGJ4), Capt. Michael Forster, BSIPDF, sounded the alarm for three enemy carriers and two destroyers seen prowling the southeast coast of Guadalcanal.[9] In fact, he had spotted Hoover's distant cruisers and destroyers retiring south. Not daring to ignore the report, especially in light of the previous day's sighting, Woods sent Major Fontana with seven F4Fs, eight SBDs, and two TBFs to comb the suspected waters. At 1410 a no doubt exasperated Fontana went out again with eight F4Fs and six SBDs on another unfortunate waste of effort for the second of two CACTUS wild-goose chases that day.

While CACTUS worried about mythical carriers, the *Enterprise*'s offensive sweep neared western Guadalcanal. Ten miles east of Savo they encountered what looked like one battleship and a supporting cast of cruisers and destroyers headed in (albeit slowly) to bombard Henderson Field. Climbing to 5,000 feet, Coffin carefully used clouds to screen his approach and at 1020 confronted the battlewagon from ahead. He divided the squadron for high-speed torpedo runs from both sides of the target, taking the port side himself and sending Thompson's 2nd Division around to starboard. At the same time John Boudreaux took the CAG TBF higher for a nerve-wracking solo bomb run against the *Hiei*.

With no Zeros in sight, Jock Sutherland's six VF-10 F4Fs slanted down to strafe and draw fire. Circling slowly, the *Hiei* responded with her main battery firing ahead of the torpedo planes and a host of 12.7-cm and 25-mm AA guns. For several of the pilots, VF-8 Midway veterans and those with VF-72 at Santa Cruz, shooting up Japanese warships seemed old hat. Hank Carey remembered, "My God what a wall of fire they put up as we made our attack over the top of those torpedo planes."[10] Dropping their fish at 200 feet and about 200 knots, Coffin's division reported hits ahead and astern to port, and Macdonald Thompson's pilots a third blast starboard amidships. Boudreaux's bomb run proved unsuccessful. Skeptical of the reliability of the Mark XIII torpedoes, Lt. (jg) George Welles thought the water spouts they produced resulted from low-order detonations rather than full-size explosions. To him the *Hiei* seemed unaffected by VT-10's efforts. "Anyhow after the attack she was sailing along just as majestically as before. We must not have even damaged her paint job."[11]

The Air Group Ten crews encountered no fighter opposition, although on the way out some bandits appeared way off above the clouds: six Zero 32s from the 204 Air Group under Res. Lt. (jg) Morisaki Takashi. The first air support provided by Base Air Force, they left Buin at 0930 and hastened to Savo, but arrived too late to protect the *Hiei*.[12]

Coffin led his jubilant crews east toward CACTUS and at 1045 landed on Henderson Field as an unexpected but highly welcome reinforcement. The *Enterprise* pilots were amazed by the aircraft boneyard alongside the main runway, now grown to epic proportion. While ground crews swarmed over the Avengers, Woods and Cooley hurried up to greet them. The general told VT-10, "Boys, I don't know where you came from, but you look like angels dropping out of heaven to us." Continuing tongue-in-cheek, the unofficial "History of the Buzzard Brigade" related: "And the boys did look good, with their khakis fresh from the ship's laundry, faces smooth-shaven, and smelling faintly of hair oil and shaving lotion. By sunset perspiration, dust, and blood had altered this natty appearance considerably."[13]

Beginning about 1100, three more air attacks went in against the *Hiei*. The irrepressible VMSB-131 raiders (unofficial insignia Satan riding a torpedo) eagerly rearmed, and three Marine TBFs sortied, this time alone, for their third assault against the *Hiei*. Dooley, Bangert, and 1st Lt. James E. Maguire, Jr., thought they gained two torpedo hits among them. CACTUS records never registered the mission. The Marine Avengers noticed Zeros circling far above, but the 204 Air Group did not see them.

Diverted from the CV contact to the battleship, fourteen B-17s in two flights under Maj. Donald E. Ridings, CO of the 72nd Bomb Squadron, passed over at 14,000 feet and at 1110 dropped sixty-eight 500-pounders against the slowly circling battleship as she trailed a large oil slick. Photos verified one hit. Morisaki's Zeros never intercepted the big bombers either.

Around noon Joe Sailer returned with six Marine SBDs (four 132, two 141) and six TBFs (four VT-8, two VMSB-131) under the redoubtable Swede Larsen, escorted by Major Campbell's dozen Wildcats. Against fierce AA their well-coordinated strike chalked up according to 1st MAW reports three 1,000-pound bomb hits (by Sailer, 2nd Lt. Charles E. Kollman [132], and 2nd Lt. John O. Hull [141]) and two torpedo hits (by Larsen and 2nd Lt. Martin B. Roush [131]). On the way out they sparred briefly with Morisaki's fighters and suffered no loss.[14]

A lull descended over the *Hiei* drama beginning about 1215. United States sources show that six waves of twenty-one dive bombers (four hits), one TBF with bombs, fourteen B-17s (one hit), twenty-five torpedo planes (eight hits according to 1st MAW), thirty-five fighters, and an unknown number of P-39s had assailed the battleship. Between 0730 and 1230, the Japanese had counted some sixty enemy planes which scored a total of three bomb hits and numerous near misses, but *no* torpedo hits. Exploding on contact, the heavy bombs had wreaked havoc with the *Hiei*'s tender superstructure, while close misses inflicted underwater hull damage (with three boilers knocked out of service) and a slight list to port. Yet her crew made real progress repairing the damage aft to regain steering control and contained the fires still raging forward of the foremast.[15]

The *Hiei*'s next CAP flight had to come all the way from Rabaul, some 530 miles. Lt. Yamamoto Shigehisa arrived about 1230 with six Zeros from the 252 Air Group and patrolled overhead until 1405. Ferocious storms with pelting rain had materialized over the Slot and blocked the path back to Buin. For over an hour Yamamoto's men unsuccessfully fought the weather, but finally relented and found their way to Rekata base, where they ditched at 1605. Yamamoto suffered severe injuries, which invalided him back to Japan.[16]

The seventh and fatal strike against the *Hiei* showed up just after Yamamoto's flight departed and before the next CAP appeared. It comprised eight Marine SBDs (six 132, two 141) under 2nd Lt. John H. McEniry, Jr., of VMSB-132, Lieutenant Coffin's six VT-10 TBFs, and fourteen F4Fs under Joe Foss (121) and Bob Fraser (112). Low clouds from the worsening weather ruined the dive bombing, but Coffin's Avengers bored in against heavy gunfire and claimed three torpedo hits (two to starboard by Coffin and Welles, one to port). While strafing the big warship, Foss was treated to a "wonderful" event amidships, a torpedo detonation "which shot water, steam, fire, and debris high into the air."[17] Still distrusting his weapon (other pilots saw two fish simply strike the BB's side and sink), Welles never realized that very likely his torpedo had struck the *Hiei*'s stern and made all the difference.

Before this attack, Abe had expected the *Hiei* to regain steering control shortly, as the pumping of the steering room proceeded well. However, about twelve carrier attack planes (the Japanese counted some F4F escorts as torpedo planes) unfortunately put two torpedoes into her starboard side. The one that Foss saw explode near amidships struck her forward under the 14-inch turret ahead of the pagoda bridge. The second hit aft and holed the starboard engine room and ended efforts to pump the steering room dry. Now the old battleship increasingly took on water and listed to starboard. It soon became evident she was doomed.[18]

The fifth CAP patrol for the *Hiei* reached the skies over Savo only after the fifth CACTUS strike had gone. Nine *Junyō* Zeros under the group commander, Lieutenant Shiga, had left the carrier at 1310 with Lieutenant Tsuda's three Type 99 carrier bomber guides. The only item of note during their patrol occurred at 1443 when Shiga chased away a lone "Grumman" from over Savo. The encounter is unrecorded from the CACTUS side, but likely involved one of the afternoon search SBDs. With the weather really turning rotten, Shiga broke off the patrol shortly thereafter and landed back on board at 1610. The *Junyō* closed down for the day.[19]

Tired of the incessant attacks and the *Hiei*'s increasing debility, Abe on the *Yukikaze* ordered at 1530 that the crippled battleship be scuttled. However, Capt. Nishida Masao and many of his officers hoped to regain power and steering. He delayed abandoning ship, while some of his officers urged him to make for Guadalcanal. At Truk the Combined Fleet staff also wrangled with the problem of what to do with the wounded giant.

Despite the weather, Base Air Force sent a sixth and last CAP patrol to the *Hiei*. WO Tsunoda Kazuo of the 582 Air Group recorded in his memoirs a moving account of his experiences,[20] which well illustrates the improvisational nature of the day's fighter missions. Around noon, Tsunoda reported to group headquarters at Rabaul, where Capt. Yamamoto Sakae briefed him of the situation. Yamamoto thought the damaged *Hiei* had retired northwest from Guadalcanal, possibly as far as Manning Strait between Santa Isabel and Choiseul, and warned Tsunoda the weather might deteriorate. Even so, he told Tsunoda to patrol two hours over the *Hiei* or at least until she safely disappeared into squalls. He could expect no relief, and could choose a base on which to land after completing his mission. Under no illusions as to Tsunoda's chances, Captain Yamamoto, unusually grave, showed "tears in his eyes."

Accompanied by a Type 1 land attack plane from the 705 Air Group as guide, Tsunoda's six Zeros departed Rabaul about 1300. By the time they passed Manning Strait and paralleled the long south coast of Santa Isabel, heavy dark clouds, squalls, and fog obscured the skies. The *rikkō* broke off for home, while Tsunoda checked the area. No ships hove into sight; blocked by a towering wall of clouds, the *Hiei* lay a further 80 miles southeast near Savo.

Reluctantly Tsunoda abandoned his mission and retraced his way northwest into a growing mass of horrible weather, the same barrier that had thwarted Yamamoto Shigehisa's 252 flight. Thunderstorms that he could not possibly fly over or through closed the way ahead. Soon pelting rain and low ceiling forced the pilots all the way down to 10 feet over the churning water. They held close formation just to keep in sight of each other, and the flight became very harrowing, especially for the rookie wingmen.

Finally, from where he later estimated as 10 kilometers east of Kolombangara, Tsunoda decided he would not reach Buin. In typical Japanese fashion, he wanted to find Guadalcanal and end it all in glorious battle. Lacking a radio to warn his flight and loath even to take his eyes off the horizon only meters ahead, he started a gentle right turn to reverse course. The maneuver startled his inexperienced number 3, LdgSea Wakasugi Ikuzō, tucked in just behind his right wing. Suddenly Wakasugi's Zero nosed down into the sea with a big flash. Its fuselage broke in half, and Tsunoda glimpsed its tail dart upward out of sight in the clouds. Quite shaken, he reproached himself for Wakasugi's death ("I killed him by my mistake"). Despite the odds he brought the balance of the flight safely to Buin and refueled before continuing that evening to Rabaul.

About 1745 the indomitable Major Sailer led eight SBDs (four 132, four 141) from CACTUS against the *Hiei* and her consort of destroyers. Two Dauntlesses had to turn back, probably fortunately for them. The weather so socked in the skies over Savo that only the persistent Joe Sailer found a target (he thought a light cruiser) and attacked. He reckoned a hit either on her deck or immediately alongside. When last seen by the Americans, the battleship drifted dead in the water, being evacuated by her crew. The same type of weather that finished Wakasugi also killed the two VMSB-141 crews of second lieutenants William J. Knapp, Jr., and Amedeo Sandretto. It also deterred bomb-armed P-39s seeking the battleship. During the day the 67th FS flew several four-plane patrols over the target.

After dark Nishida finally removed his crew and abandoned the *Hiei*. Sometime during the night she sank unobserved by friend or foe—the first Japanese battleship lost in the war. American pilots reported hits by no fewer than eleven torpedoes (not counting one probable and two unofficial), four 1,000-pound and one 500-pound bombs, but the Japanese confirmed only three bomb and two torpedo hits. Like sisters *Kongō, Kirishima,* and *Haruna,* the *Hiei* was designed about 1910 as a battlecruiser. Completed in 1914, she underwent modernization in the 1920s and '30s with additional underwater protection. However, her capacity to absorb damage was not nearly as high as more recently designed ships. The *Hiei* could not possibly have taken more than a few torpedoes without quickly sinking.

Of the other cripples, the heavy cruiser *Portland* and destroyer *Aaron Ward* were towed to Tulagi, but the crew scuttled the light AA cruiser *Atlanta* off Lunga that evening. During the day the destroyers *Cushing* and *Monssen* also disappeared beneath the waves. The 1st MAW lost one F4F (pilot recovered) and two SBDs (crews missing). The aircraft, at least, were more than made good by a reinforcement of Capt. Robert L. Faurot's eight AAF P-38F Lightnings from the 39th FS (35th Fighter Group). Guided by one B-17, they flew directly from Milne Bay to CACTUS, where they landed at Fighter 1. Three Marine F4Fs also came in from BUTTON. Five VMSB-131 TBFs flew down that afternoon to BUTTON for torpedoes and would be back the next day.

The 1st MAW certainly demonstrated it could strike at will targets close to its base. Due to a lack of planning and coordination, hasty improvisation, and the unexpectedly bad weather, Japanese fighters proved totally ineffective in protecting the *Hiei*. No fewer than a dozen Zeros succumbed to all causes. The *Junyō*'s twenty-three fighter sorties cost three shot down (pilots killed) and two ditched (pilots rescued). Base Air Force sent eighteen Zeros from Buin and Rabaul and lost seven ditched (one pilot killed, one badly injured). All in all, Japan experienced an extremely frustrating Friday the 13th.

MAIN FLEET MOVEMENTS ON 13 NOVEMBER

While the *Hiei* held center stage, other important cast members moved on the periphery, preparing the next act of the drama.

Forced to postpone Z-Day to 14 November, Combined Fleet devised new schedules for the several commands. At 0630 on the 13th, Vice Admiral Mikawa, 8th Fleet commander, sailed from Shortland with four heavy cruisers, two light cruisers, and four destroyers bound for the northern route above the Solomons and a night bombardment of Lunga. Shielded by bad weather, he was not molested during the day. At the same time Rear Admiral Tanaka's transport convoy retired temporarily to Shortland to regroup, and sailed again at 1730 aiming down the center of the Slot. All day Vice Admiral Kondō's Advance Force had stood off 200 miles or more north of Guadalcanal, while the *Kirishima* and the rest of Abe's force (less the *Hiei* and her consorts) rejoined that evening. They planned to shell Lunga the night of the new Z-Day (14/15 November).

Early on the morning of the 13th, after sending off Lieutenant Coffin's "offensive sweep" of eight VT-10 TBFs and six VF-10 F4Fs to Guadalcanal, Rear Admiral Kinkaid's TF-16 worked northward toward San Cristobal. Sub scares and repeated course changes to the southeast to conduct flight operations slowed the advance. Plane strength on the *Enterprise* now counted thirty-one fighters and thirty-one dive bombers. That morning Rear Admiral Tisdale brought the heavy cruiser *Pensacola* and two destroyers, raising TF-16 to one carrier, two battleships, two heavy cruisers, one light AA cruiser, and ten destroyers. In the *Enterprise* and Rear Admiral Lee's two new battleships *Washington* and *South Dakota*, Kinkaid controlled SoPac's main fleet assets. That morning he monitored the sightings north of Guadalcanal, which included one carrier and the damaged battleship off Savo. Still to be explained were the two carriers located the previous afternoon west of Guadalcanal.

At Noumea Halsey slowly grasped the magnitude of the losses sustained early that morning by TF-67.4. Ominously, nothing came from Callaghan and Scott, and it would be a few days before Halsey knew for certain they were dead. Around 0705 Hoover advised that the *Helena, San Francisco, Juneau,* and three destroyers, all damaged, were retiring south of Guadalcanal. He requested air cover. Halsey also learned from Pearl that the enemy had postponed Z-Day. Although not positive, CinCPac intelligence thought that the new date was the 14th. Nimitz added that the delay might mean "main body Combined Fleet will participate."[21]

Even while ComSoPac deliberated, TF-16 experienced more excitement. Around 1045 the *Enterprise*'s CXAM radar detected a bogey 50 miles ahead. Commander Griffin, the FDO, broke radio silence to send Lt. Swede Vejtasa's REAPER 7 out on 025 degrees (M.). At 1100 the four F4Fs bounced a Shortland-based Kawanishi Type 97 flying boat commanded by PO1c Maemura Tadayoshi of the 851 Air Group. Before plunging into the ocean, Maemura only got off the codeword "HI," meaning "enemy plane encountered." Vejtasa had poured his bullets into the center portion of the wing, setting it ablaze. Next, in his words, the other pilots "cut the plane into doll rags." He awarded equal credit for the VP's destruction to Lt. Tex Harris, Ens. Chip Reding, and Ens. Hank Leder, as well as himself.[22]

At 1110 Halsey directed Kinkaid north to support the damaged TF-67 warships withdrawing southeast from Guadalcanal. However, TF-16 was to remain south of latitude 11°40′ S (roughly level with Rennell Island and about 60 miles

A pair of deadly 40-mm quadruple mounts on the *Enterprise*, 13 Nov. 1942. In the upper right corner is F-38, a repainted VF-72 Wildcat assigned to VF-10. (NA 80-G-30536)

south of San Cristobal) and outside of visual range of possible enemy observers at Rennell and Indispensable Reef. Halsey gave Kinkaid the option of organizing his task force as he desired, a sure clue that at this juncture he did not contemplate detaching Lee's battleships to operate separately. Clearly Halsey anticipated that TF-16 would move north toward San Cristobal or Guadalcanal and operate that afternoon from somewhere just south of the line he set.[23]

Convinced the doomed flying boat had pinpointed his location, Kinkaid provided ComSoPac at 1159 his 1100 position (160 miles south of San Cristobal) and stated he was "proceeding north as directed," that is, supporting Hoover's withdrawing ships. Unknown to SoPac the *I-26* torpedoed the *Juneau,* which virtually disappeared after a massive explosion. Kinkaid advised Halsey of Coffin's TBF strike to Guadalcanal and the reason for it—the *Enterprise*'s still unreliable number 1 elevator. Of the most worry were the reports of enemy carriers to the west and north of Guadalcanal and the lack of any follow-up. "Request continuous information enemy carrier." Under the circumstances Kinkaid did not consider it wise to continue north toward Halsey's limit, but for the time being remained to the south in the same general area.[24]

Maemura never disclosed TF-16's location, but another 851 Air Group Type 97 flying boat indeed spotted TF-16. At 1000 WO Satō Tomosaburō informed base of an enemy carrier force 200 miles south of San Cristobal. Although not specifically revealed in the reports, Kinkaid may have learned of these sighting messages from Major Holcomb's RI Unit on board the *Enterprise.* Certainly

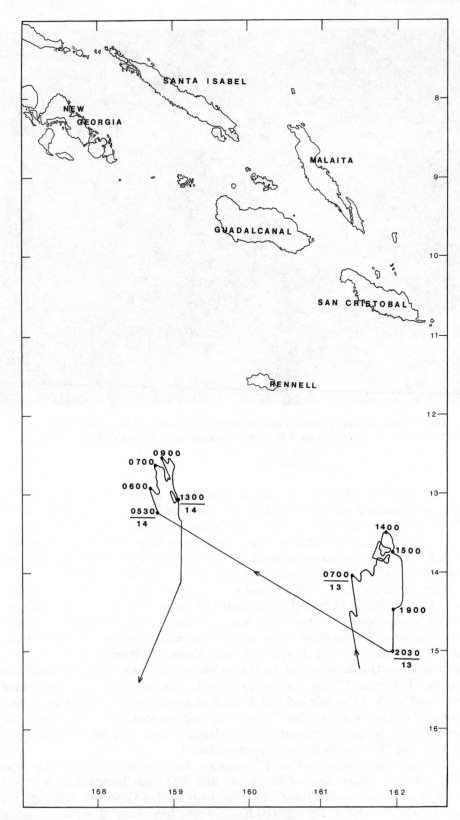

TF-16 track, 13–14 November.

nerves were on edge when at 1352 "The Big E" 's radar detected bogeys bearing 295 degrees, 39 miles. The carrier scrambled twelve F4Fs to reinforce the dozen already aloft, but the contact never materialized.[25]

Apparently, as of the afternoon of 13 November, Halsey had not yet decided how to counter the estimated Z-Day offensive against Lunga, especially if the main body of Combined Fleet would actually participate. At 1432 he advised Kinkaid that the morning searches were negative with regard to enemy carriers, and in his opinion no CVs were southwest of Savo. Around 1500 Halsey received a vitally important CinCPac intelligence bulletin noting that the commander of the 3rd Fleet (Vice Admiral Nagumo's carrier striking force) was no longer thought to be in the Southern Area. That placed the remaining enemy carriers, possibly three, under 2nd Fleet command. Nimitz concluded, "Expect surface attack on Guadalcanal airfield night 13/14 Nov. with landing attempt from transports early 14th."[26]

With such a positive statement of the enemy's dire threat to CACTUS, Halsey could no longer lay in the weeds waiting for the Japanese to come to him. The situation called for bold decisions, something in which he excelled. Nagumo's absence hinted that the Japanese carriers might not pose as much of a threat as before. (At Pearl Capt. James M. Steele, head of War Plans on the CinCPac staff, opined that day there was "an even chance no CV's will be involved in the Z-Day push.") Halsey certainly expected Kinkaid's TF-16 to be close to the northerly limit he set (latitude 11°40' S) and therefore not far from Rennell and San Cristobal. Shortly after 1600 he alerted Kinkaid to prepare Lee's battlewagons and four destroyers to form a separate force. On ComSoPac order only, it would rush north to the waters east of Savo and intercept an enemy bombardment force that night. The actual order came through an hour later, directing Lee's new TF-64 to prevent the shelling of Guadalcanal and withdraw by daybreak.[27]

For two hours TF-16 had steamed straight south, so by 1600 Kinkaid drew some 180 miles south of San Cristobal and fully 360 miles southeast of Savo Island. He instantly realized he could not comply with Halsey's new orders, as TF-16 obviously was nowhere near where ComSoPac thought it was. Now Lee was much too far south to reach Guadalcanal in time. To warn ComSoPac, but not to give away his exact position to enemy radio direction finders, Kinkaid sent the destroyer *Mustin* 50 miles east to radio a message. In the meantime he went ahead and detached Lee's TF-64.[28]

While Kinkaid arranged Lee's departure, he received more orders from Halsey directing TF-16 to a dawn position on the 14th about 125 miles southwest of Guadalcanal. ComSoPac attempted to position his carrier to strike the transports early the next day. Unfortunately TF-16 was so far south that even an overnight speed run could put the *Enterprise* no closer than 90 miles south of the designated position. At 2049 Kinkaid changed course to 300 degrees, speed 23 knots (later 25 knots), toward the assigned waters off Guadalcanal.[29]

Kinkaid's cautionary message stating that Lee's battleships could not possibly reach Savo before 0700 the next morning struck the SoPac flagship *Argonne* like a bomb. Halsey later recorded his "great disappointment" (no doubt a euphemism for a fiery outburst) and his worry over what a bombardment might do to the 1st MAW. Late that evening he ruefully informed Major General Vandegrift at CACTUS, "Sorry—Lee cannot comply—too far." Central to this failure to meet the expected Japanese attack was a misunderstanding between Halsey and Kinkaid as to the proposed movements of TF-16. In retrospect Halsey should have been more specific as to where he desired Kinkaid to be. As for Kinkaid's motives, the reports mention continuous flight operations that unexpectedly slowed the *Enterprise*'s northward speed of advance, but it seems clear that Kinkaid deliberately kept far to the south. Three weeks before he had suffered greatly from a head-long assault into the teeth of the Japanese forces; now he felt good reason to be more cautious.[30]

As darkness settled over SoPac, many shared Halsey's "apprehension" as to the fate of CACTUS, especially if they were privy to the fact that Lee's battleships would not even reach Guadalcanal that night. They expected the decisive battle the next day. If the enemy transport force fought its way through to Lunga, possibly thousands of Japanese troops might swarm over the beaches. A young Marine dive-bomber pilot, 2nd Lt. John McEniry of VMSB-132, remembered the dramatic night briefing by Brigadier General Woods, who concluded, "We lay the fate of Guadalcanal in your hands and know that each of you will do his best."[31] Ironically, the Japanese themselves shared no belief they were about to wage the decisive battle of the entire campaign. Even more than with the green Marine dive-bomber and torpedo crews at CACTUS, the fate of Guadalcanal rested with Admiral Yamamoto and whether he would commit all of his forces.

CHAPTER 25

"A dive and torpedo bombers' paradise"

MIKAWA'S CRUISER FORCE

Another Bombardment

The Marines, bluejackets, and soldiers around Henderson Field dreaded few things more than a bombardment by heavy ships. Yet early on the morning of 14 November 1942, neither they nor the rest of Vice Admiral Halsey's SoPac command could do anything to stop one. Under cover of bad weather all the previous day, Vice Admiral Mikawa's 8th Fleet had closed Guadalcanal from the north. At 0010 out near Savo, Rear Admiral Nishimura's Support Force with the heavy cruisers *Suzuya* and *Maya*, light cruiser *Tenryū*, and three destroyers separated from the main body and raced toward Lunga. Ten minutes later a seaplane dropped two green flares over Henderson Field, and everyone present knew the jig was up. Beginning at 0125, the two cruisers launched 989 eight-inch shells into the perimeter for a 31-minute bombardment. Some at CACTUS thought the battleship they assailed on the 13th had been towed into gun range.

Thus at least part of Air Group Ten would be treated to a favorite CACTUS tourist attraction. That evening Jock Sutherland's VF-10 flight had renewed its acquaintance with Ens. William A. Noll of Lt. Lew Mattison's FD team and heard many tall tales of life at Guadalcanal. Even so, Sutherland slept in a tent near Fighter 1 rather than the recommended foxhole closer to the front-line Marines. Suddenly heavy shells started dropping in, likened by 2nd Lt. John McEniry of VMSB-132 to the sound of "a freight train going overhead."[1] To Sutherland's dismay, most of the ordnance seem to strike near the fighter strip and its environs. He ran for shelter and later discovered his cot in shreds. Three other REAPERS shared a dugout with Noll, who diverted them with accounts of the October shellings.[2]

The men of the 347th Fighter Group bore the brunt of the assault. The 67th's history bemoaned that the Japanese seemed to wish their annihilation, as all but one salvo struck near their quarters. "The men kneeling in their foxholes could hear trees falling, tents collapsing, shrapnel cutting through their airplanes nearby." Shell fragments holed fifteen of sixteen operational P-39s and P-400s parked on the right side of Fighter 1, leaving only one P-400 (the "oldest, most bent up klunker") untouched. Yet most of them could be repaired. Other than that, the 1st MAW largely escaped significant damage. All the aircraft at Henderson Field (including the P-38s) emerged unscathed. Two big holes pocked Fighter

Fighter Field No. 1 with Henderson Field (Bomber Field No. 1) beyond. Photo taken by an *Enterprise* plane on 16 Nov. 1942. (NA 80-G-29351)

1. In addition to the Airacobras, two F4Fs burned, three other Wildcats and an SBD were badly perforated, and seventeen more F4Fs suffered light damage. Aircraft immediately available that morning (counting the *Enterprise* detachment) numbered fourteen F4F-4s, sixteen SBD-3s, nine TBFs, three P-39s, and seven P-38s.

The CACTUS flyers eagerly prepared for revenge against their assailants. At 0500, 40 minutes before dawn, four VMF-112 Wildcats led by 2nd Lt. James L. Secrest taxied around the obstacles at Fighter 1, helped by a light held by VMF-121 ground officer 2nd Lt. Henry O. DeFries, and departed on CAP. Six VMSB-132 SBDs followed them aloft to search the three sectors (New Georgia, Isabel, and Malaita), seeking the bombardment group. Unlike the previous day, the rising sun revealed crystal-clear skies over the Slot, and the visibility proved exceptional. No battleship could be seen, but out past Savo a huge oil slick 3,000 yards in diameter pointed to the overnight demise of one.

At 0630 two outbound SBDs in the B sector (Isabel), flown by second lieutenants William Hronek and Horace C. Baum, found the culprits near the south coast of New Georgia. To the Marines they looked like two light cruisers and five destroyers bearing 280 degrees, distance 140 miles from Lunga, course 280 degrees, speed 16 knots. Indeed the search had located Nishimura's Support Force (two CAs, one CL, three DDs) racing to overtake Mikawa's main body (CAs *Chōkai, Kinugasa,* CL *Isuzu,* and one destroyer) not far ahead. The word galvanized the 1st MAW, which needed to strike fast before the ships passed beyond normal attack range (200 miles) out near Vella Lavella. Around 0700, Maj.

Joe Sailer departed with six VMSB-132 SBDs, six VMSB-131 and VT-10 TBFs led by Capt. Dooley, and Capt. Joe Foss with eight VMF-121 Wildcats. For some reason this contact report never reached the other SoPac commands, notably Rear Admiral Fitch's AirSoPac or Rear Admiral Kinkaid's TF-16. However, they also went gunning for Mikawa's warships.

Task Force 16 Intervenes

Overnight on the 13th/14th, Vice Admiral Halsey carefully considered possible enemy moves against CACTUS. Dan Callaghan threw off the original Japanese timetable that had called for landings the night of 12/13 November. On the 13th a search plane had spotted the convoy lurking off Shortland. Halsey thought it would now reverse course and approach Guadalcanal under the cover of the weather front to invade CACTUS on the 14th. "Acting on this hunch, and ignoring the very doubtful presence of a CV," he positioned his two task forces to counter.[3]

During darkness TF-16 hastened northwest at 25 knots to take station southwest of Guadalcanal. At 0518 Kinkaid received a message from ComSoPac directing TF-16 to proceed north, operate 100 miles south of the Solomons, and attack transports coming down from Shortland. Rear Admiral Lee's TF-64 with the two new battleships would take a parallel position only 50 miles off the island chain. Halsey added, "Supplement BUTTON and CACTUS searches by your own as necessary to locate and destroy transports." In compliance, Kinkaid changed course at 0532 to 350 degrees. Now about 200 miles south-southwest of Guadalcanal, TF-16 headed into a band of squalls and low visibility—"bad waters again"—into an "obscure" situation. Maddeningly, the TF-16 staff heard nothing more of the carrier contacts the previous day or of the condition of Henderson Field.[4]

The *Enterprise* wielded sixty-two planes: thirty-one VF-10 fighters and thirty-one dive bombers from VB-10 and VS-10. Kinkaid decided to allocate as few search SBDs as feasible for adequate coverage. That permitted a larger strike group, which he hoped to launch as soon as possible before retiring southward away from danger. Heavy rains postponed the dawn takeoffs, but at 0608 eight F4Fs got away for CAP, followed by ten search SBDs (six VB-10, four VS-10) and three more VB-10 Dauntlesses for antisub patrol. Two planes independently covered ahead an arc 285 to 315 degrees to 200 miles, while four pairs handled the crucial northwest and northerly sectors (315–015 degrees) out to 250 miles. The pilots were briefed to fly to CACTUS rather than back to the carrier if so ordered. Meanwhile, TF-16 cut back to 22 knots and settled down to await the word.

The first contact report arrived much sooner than expected. At 0707 Lt. William I. Martin (USNA 1934), VS-10 XO leading the section out the 000-degree line, warned of a flight of ten unidentified aircraft at low altitude about 140 miles north of the task force.[5] In response, TF-16 assumed the 1-Victor formation ready for attack. Martin's bogeys never materialized, likely an optical illusion since the Japanese certainly had no planes out there. Yet Kinkaid knew it was only a matter of time before the enemy found him. Consequently he ordered the strike group launched on a search-attack mission north-northeast against targets certain to be found off Guadalcanal. The strike numbered seventeen SBD dive bombers (eleven VS-10, six VB-10 with 1,000-pound bombs) under VS-10 CO Lt. Cdr. Bucky Lee, escorted by Lt. Cdr. Jimmy Flatley with ten VF-10 F4Fs.

VS-10, 23 Oct. 1942. *Top row* (*l to r*): Burnett, Ramsay, Carmody, Ward, Strong, Miller, Mohr, Finrow, Irvine, Ervin, Waters. *Bottom row:* Edwards, Lucier, Estes, Johnson, Richey, Lee, Martin, Boardman, Frohlich, Edmondson, Bloch, Dardis. (NA 80-G-30074)

Commander Crommelin instructed Lee to head north, monitor the search net for sighting reports, and select the juiciest target within range. As with the search, the option remained whether to return to the ship or land at CACTUS. Flatley's escort comprised:

REAPER 1	REAPER 7	REAPER 3
Lt. Cdr. James H. Flatley	Lt. Stanley W. Vejtasa	Lt. Stanley E. Ruehlow
Lt. (jg) Russell L. Reiserer	Lt. Leroy E. Harris	Lt. (jg) Roy M. Voris
Ens. Roland R. Witte	Ens. Willis B. Reding	
Ens. Philip E. Souza	Ens. William H. Leder	

The strike took off beginning at 0737, with a relief CAP of twelve F4Fs. At 0757 Kinkaid came around to 180 degrees, 25 knots, to "clear area to south." Obviously he thought his role on the 14th was over.[6]

While climbing to high altitude on the way north, Bucky Lee's strike group made enemy contact out toward Rennell, which reduced fighter strength to eight. About 60 miles from the ship, what looked like two "float-Zeros" suddenly appeared below the F4Fs on the starboard side. To the second section of REAPER 7 (ensigns Chip Reding and Hank Leder), these bandits apparently threatened the SBDs at 10,000 feet. The two Reapers peeled off to bounce them, but the Japanese escaped in the clouds. Unable to find the rest of the group, the two VF-10 pilots ended up on their own. Their quarry was actually an Aichi E13A1 Type 0 reconnaissance seaplane flown by a wily veteran, Lt. (jg) Ikeya Nobuo, of the *Chitose* squadron. Departing Shortland at 0555, he later encountered about twenty small enemy aircraft and survived an "air battle" with two. Continuing his search for the enemy, he soon struck paydirt.[7]

Battering Mikawa's Cruisers

After some searching, Joe Sailer's CACTUS strike (six VB, six VT, eight VF) overtook the cruiser raiding force up near Rendova off New Georgia, where Mikawa and Nishimura had just rendezvoused. He alerted base to four CA and three DD bearing 280 degrees, distance 170 miles from CACTUS. Equally favorable was the lack of enemy fighters. Around 0830 Sailer led the assault against an "*Atago*-class" cruiser and claimed a 1,000-pound bomb hit on the bow. Next, 2nd Lt. Robert E. Kelly of 132 placed his ordnance directly on the bridge, and the other pilots reported three near misses.[8] The *Kinugasa* was VMSB-132's victim. One heavy bomb struck the forward part of the bridge near the 13-mm machine-gun mounts, sliced through the superstructure, and exploded on the lower deck below the waterline. In addition to blowing out big sections of the hull, the blast killed both Capt. Sawa Masao and the XO, leaving the torpedo officer in command. Shrapnel set afire the forward gasoline storage, which burned fiercely for 30 minutes. Severe flooding soon induced a 10-degree list to port. The *Kinugasa* was in deep trouble.[9]

At the same time that Sailer's dive bombers were hitting the *Kinugasa*, Captain Dooley led the six TBFs against a "*Mogami*-class" heavy cruiser, actually Mikawa's flagship *Chōkai*. She depended on speed and firepower rather than fancy maneuvers to evade. Against her port side three Marine Avengers claimed

VT-10 TBF passes the heavy cruiser *Suzuya* on the morning of 14 Nov. 1942. (NA 80-G-30516)

two hits (by Dooley and 2nd Lt. Ervin W. Hatfield), while from VT-10 Lt. James McConnaughhay, Lieutenant (jg) Boudreaux, and Ensign Oscar all thought their fish struck the starboard side. The raiders felt they left two CAs in sinking condition, but the *Chōkai* was undamaged.[10] All of the CACTUS strike planes returned safely to Henderson Field.

Even as Sailer pounded Mikawa, the first of the *Enterprise* searches also had the 8th Fleet in sight. Lt. (jg) Robert D. Gibson (a VB-6 veteran) and Ens. Richard M. Buchanan of VB-10 covered the sector 330 to 345 degrees.[11] At about 0750, through translucent skies they noticed white ship wakes far to the northwest. Slowly drawing closer, the two SBDs attained 17,000 feet and sought some scattered cloud cover south of the ships. Gibson's first voice contact report, sent at 0810, came through garbled, so his radioman, Clifford E. Schindele, ARM2c, keyed messages informing the search net at 0815 of nine ships, including a possible converted carrier, off New Georgia and headed west. Too far off to see the Marine attacks, Gibson continued shadowing and amplified his reports. One received at 0844 by the *Enterprise* noted "2 BB, 2 CA, 1 CV (garble), 4 DD, course 290, 08-45, 157-10."

Doubtless because Gibson's messages mentioned possible carriers, the *Enterprise* showed special interest in his target. At 0844 the ship radioed Bucky Lee asking if he knew of it as well. He replied that he had everything but the position, and Crommelin provided it. Therefore at 0845 Hardison ordered Lee to attack that force, now over 270 miles from TF-16, and take his planes to Guadalcanal. Unfortunately Jimmy Flatley was not privy to this confabulation, as no one had thought to change the coils and tune his radio (and those of the other F4Fs) to the search-attack frequency. At 0845 Lee swung left and northwest to 330 degrees to close Gibson's contact. Through cumulus clouds Air Group Ten glimpsed distant Guadalcanal some 50 miles northeast and also saw TF-64 steaming northwest.

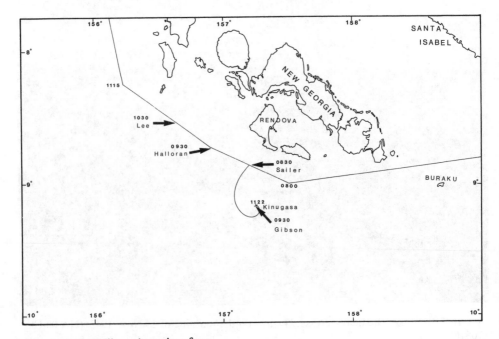

Air attacks on Mikawa's cruiser force.

For over an hour Gibson and Buchanan observed Mikawa's ships from a nest of clouds to the south. Base had acknowledged his messages, so Gibson felt free to attack. Coming in about 0915, he selected a lone "*Nachi*-class" CA already leaving an oil slick. Instead of withdrawing west with the rest of Mikawa's force, she had slowly swung all the way around in a big circle and resumed a northwesterly heading. A destroyer was in attendance and another approached. Gibson's quarry was the stricken *Kinugasa* accompanied by the *Makigumo* and *Kazegumo*. Counterflooding had righted the cruiser, but she still took on water. The two SBDs dived against the *Kinugasa* from astern. Gibson logged a hit forward on the superstructure and Buchanan another portside amidships. Actually both 500-pound bombs fell short, but nonetheless proved fatal to the target. Their concussion knocked out her steering and greatly increased flooding to port. No longer able to maneuver, the *Kinugasa* was doomed.[12] The Dauntlesses encountered accurate AA, and Buchanan's B-8 survived an eight-inch dud that passed through its tail. After advising the ship, they started east to Henderson Field after an outstanding, aggressive search.

While Gibson and Buchanan attacked the *Kinugasa,* two more VB-10 searchers appeared over Mikawa's force—ensigns Robert A. Hoogerwerf and Paul M. Halloran covering the sector 315 to 330 degrees just to the south. On their dogleg to the northeast, they spotted at 0923 south of Rendova the wakes of two cruisers, one light cruiser, and four destroyers steaming northwest at 25 knots. Heading in, they noticed one of the heavy cruisers (the *Kinugasa*) low in the water and burning, circled by two destroyers. Ten miles west were the light cruiser and a destroyer, and five miles south of that pair the undamaged heavy cruiser and a destroyer also westbound.

At 17,500 feet Hoogerwerf and Halloran separated, each to take on one group of enemy ships. Tackling the "undamaged CA," Hoogerwerf dived against the *Suzuya,* Nishimura's flagship, for a near miss, but she sustained no damage. He last saw Halloran going after the "CL," which soon gave off thick, black smoke from a direct hit. Halloran never returned. Later investigation revealed his target as the heavy cruiser *Maya*. Dropped from astern, his 500-pound missed, but his starboard wing struck the mainmast and pitched B-14 into the superstructure near the number 2 (port) 12-cm high-angle gun mount. Gasoline from the crumpled SBD set off the ready ammunition, which wrecked the port HA and AA gun mounts and the searchlights. Fire also threatened the torpedo mounts, which compelled the ship to jettison sixteen fish. Although still combat-worthy, the *Maya* lost thirty-seven men killed and twenty-four wounded.[13]

Thus the pugnacious *Enterprise* search already finished off one heavy cruiser and roughed up another at the cost of one SBD and crew. Gibson and Buchanan reached CACTUS without incident and later flew strikes on the convoy. Hoogerwerf returned to the *Enterprise,* where he received some heat for not radioing word of his contact and attack back to the ship.

Coming in, Bucky Lee's strike shed more planes. Around 0930, he changed course further left to 300 degrees to aim west and ahead of the retreating Japanese and cut them off from their base. The SBDs cruised at 15,000 feet, with six fighters (Flatley's REAPER 1 and half of Vejtasa's REAPER 7) 3,000 feet above on the starboard side and two (Ruehlow and Voris of REAPER 3) to the left. Perhaps too attentive in looking for Zeros, Flatley's batch missed Lee's second turn and kept going on 330 degrees. They lost sight of the SBDs, and the different radio frequencies prevented a greatly frustrated Flatley from contacting Lee.

Now only Stan Ruehlow's fighter section stayed with the dive bombers for the time being, and he anxiously watched his dwindling fuel.

Shortly after 0930 low fuel forced Ens. Leonard Robinson of VB-10 to drop out, and soon Ruehlow and Voris did the same. That left Lee with only sixteen Dauntlesses. Two "float-Zeros" (every aggressive small enemy seaplane was a "float-Zero") essayed a run against the VS-10 formation, only to be deterred by John A. Moore, ARM3c, in Ens. Leonard Lucier's S-6, who claimed one bandit. Most likely they were seaplanes launched by the cruisers themselves, as no R-Area Air Force aircraft from Shortland or Rekata were involved. About the same time (around 0950) Lee sighted southwest of Rendova the heavily damaged *Kinugasa* afire and with a pronounced list. The two escorting destroyers cut loose with the range estimated accurately but insufficient deflection. Lee passed them by, looking for better targets.

Around 1015 and 25 miles beyond the stricken cruiser (fully 330 miles from TF-16), he found his goal. Far ahead under a large white cloud appeared the high-speed wakes of an estimated two CA, four CL, and four DD pointed northwest: Mikawa's main force of CAs *Chōkai*, *Suzuya*, and *Maya*, CLs *Isuzu* and *Tenryū*, and two destroyers. Yet no carrier was in evidence. Approaching the target, Lee directed Lieutenant Commander Thomas's five VB-10 SBDs against the heavy cruisers and Lt. Birney Strong's second VS-10 division (five SBDs) after the light cruisers. Lee personally took VS-10's 1st Division (six SBDs) a little farther on seeking the supposed carrier.

After 1030 VB-10's dives on the *Chōkai* elicited a thick but ineffective AA barrage. The first two 1,000-pounders fell wide of the twisting cruiser, then Ens. Edwin J. Stevens's bomb detonated 30 feet off her starboard side. After another miss, Ens. Jeff Carroum scored a near miss 10 feet off the starboard bow. The concussion from both close misses flooded some compartments and shut down number 4 and 6 boilers for a time. The *Chōkai* still made 29 knots and continued toward Shortland, while VB-10 swung southeast for CACTUS over 200 miles away.

Strong selected the *Isuzu*, and the last two of his VS-10 pilots to dive, lieutenants (jg) Howard Burnett and John H. Finrow, claimed direct hits. Although not struck by enemy bombs, the *Isuzu* likewise suffered from explosions right alongside that buckled hull plates, allowing water to pour in the number 2 and 3 firerooms and affecting steering control. Nevertheless she kept on going. Lee's own 1st Division did not fare as well against the CL *Tenryū*. After checking the seas a little farther west under the cloud, he determined no carrier was nearby and returned to the ships. Climbing back to 7,500 feet, he initiated a quick series of dives against the light cruiser for four near misses. The *Tenryū* sustained no damage.

Mikawa's force continued its fast retreat to Shortland to refuel before heading back out to support the convoy. The *Kinugasa* did not join them. Her list so increased that at 1122 she suddenly rolled over to port and sank with fifty-one of her crew. Thus the 8th Fleet lost one heavy cruiser sunk, one heavy cruiser and one light cruiser damaged. Mikawa estimated some sixty planes had pummeled his force. Believing that the bombardment must have neutralized Lunga at least to some extent, he thought his assailants came from a carrier and worried over the ability of Base Air Force to deal with her. In fact, only forty planes (twenty-six dive bombers, six torpedo planes, and eight escorting fighters) had harried the 8th Fleet. They claimed two heavy cruisers sunk, one heavy and one light cruiser damaged, at the cost of one *Enterprise* SBD missing. Both Thomas and

Lee saw the *Kinugasa* in extremis, and their reports lent credence to 1st MAW's tally.

Around 1315 the sixteen *Enterprise* SBDs landed at Henderson Field. The VF-10 fighter escorts did not have such an easy time. Because they could not copy the search network, they knew of neither the objective nor the orders to fly to CACTUS. The fuel situation gave Ruehlow and Voris no choice but to try for Henderson Field. They made it without incident. After losing track of the SBDs, Flatley kept northwest on 330 degrees hoping to rejoin them over the target. At about 1015 and within sight of Gakutai (easternmost of the New Georgia group), he relented and swung back southeast toward the *Enterprise*. At least he knew roughly where she might be. Chip Reding and Hank Leder, the two VF-10 pilots who separated from the strike group out near Rennell, anxiously searched the sea and finally discerned the ship wakes of Lee's TF-64 southwest of Guadalcanal. So as not to break radio silence, Leder swooped low over the battleship *Washington* and dropped a note: "Please point your ships in the direction of our carrier." The admiral graciously complied and turned south. Off went the two F4F pilots, fully aware they faced an ordeal finding home plate.[14]

TANAKA'S CONVOY

The second great air battle on 14 November raged over the inbound Japanese convoy. It is necessary to go back to 0630 and resume discussion of the CACTUS morning search. After sighting Nishimura's Support Force scurrying west, second lieutenants Hronek and Baum of VMSB-132 on the B Sector search came upon a second highly significant discovery, this time in the center of the Slot off New Georgia. At 0700 Hronek reported one CV, two CA, and one BB, bearing 300 degrees, distance 150 miles from Lunga, course 1200, speed 15 knots.[15]

Within a few minutes two separate searchers confirmed the general location of the enemy force and identified it as the much-awaited invasion convoy. At 0715 while flying Sector C (New Georgia), second lieutenants Walter A. Eck and Andrew Jackson, also from 132, spotted two BB, one CL, and eleven DD out very close to Hronek's contact. Fifteen minutes later a New Guinea–based RAAF Hudson patrol bomber identified twelve transports in the Slot off New Georgia and positioned behind the massive covering force already discovered. To the Allied commanders this looked like the big grab for Guadalcanal. The adrenaline certainly flowed at CACTUS, which swiftly rebroadcast the B and C sector findings.

The object of so much concern was the Outer South Seas Force Reinforcement Force commanded by Rear Admiral Tanaka, CO of the 2nd Destroyer Squadron. The 17th Army's so-called 2nd Ship Group under Maj. Gen. Tanabe Suketomo (38th Division) comprised eleven modern ex-merchantmen:

No. 1 *Butai*	Speed	Tonnage	No. 2 *Butai*	Speed	Tonnage
Nagara Maru	14	7,198	*Yamazuki Maru*	13	6,438
Hirokawa Maru	16	6,872	*Yamaura Maru*	14	6,798
Sado Maru	16	7,180	*Kinugawa Maru*	11	6,936
Canberra Maru	16	6,477	*Shinanogawa Maru*	12	7,504
Nako Maru	14	7,145	*Brisbane Maru*	10	5,425
			Arizona Maru	11	9,685

Although three ships, the *Sado Maru*, *Arizona Maru*, and *Hirokawa Maru* were considered "AA ships" with six 13-mm AA machine guns, the others also carried a number of 13-mms. In addition to 7,000-odd troops and many tons of ammunition and supplies, the transports bore the burden of seventy-six large and seven small landing craft mounted on deck. The No. 1 *Butai* was to unload at Tassafaronga, the slower No. 2 *Butai* at Aruligo Point near Cape Esperance. Eleven destroyers provided the escort:

DesDiv 15	DesDiv 24	DesDiv 31	Recovery Unit
Hayashio (F.)	*Umikaze*	*Takanami*	*Amagiri*
Oyashio	*Kawakaze*	*Naganami*	*Mochizuki*
Kagerō	*Suzukaze*	*Makinami*	

The convoy departed Shortland the previous evening and deployed into one long column at 10 knots aimed directly down the Slot. Confidence grew as the ships learned of Nishimura's pounding of the Lunga airfields.[16]

At 0849 the active *Enterprise* morning search also turned up the convoy. Two VS-10 crews, lieutenants (jg) Martin D. Carmody (in S-13) and William E. Johnson (in B-6), handled the 345- to 000-degrees sector north of Gibson. "Red" Carmody's contact report came over the air as "many enemy transports, 2 CA, 3 CL, 6 DD," and its position, course, and speed corresponded with the other sightings. Eager to attack once they fulfilled the search mission, the two SBDs pushed over around 0900 against a large transport. Carmody's bomb fell short, but he thought Johnson might have scored. The ships sustained no damage at this time. Strafing a destroyer on the way out, Carmody headed for convenient low-hanging "SBD clouds," but Johnson never made it.

Off in the distance Carmody's radioman, John Liska, ARM2c, saw a plane strike the water, and Carmody noticed Zeros strafing not far away. Their opponents were the 1st CAP, Lt. Miyano Zenjirō's six Zero 32s from the 204 Air Group based at Buin. They shot down B-6, but either Johnson or his radioman, Hugh P. Hughes, Jr., ARM3c, took PO2c Hoshino Kōichi's Zero with him. Perhaps the strafing Carmody witnessed was Miyano's attempt to alert Japanese destroyers to Hoshino's plight. Like the downed Americans, he was never found. Tanaka reported that his air cover destroyed two enemy carrier bombers. Miyano's five fighters soon pulled off for Buin, while Carmody aimed south for the *Enterprise*.[17]

The second CAP patrol, Lt. (jg) Iwaki Manzō's six *Hiyō* Zeros from Buin, arrived over the convoy not long after Carmody's attack and soon found work harassing a B-17 Flying Fortress from Espiritu Santo. She was "Typhoon McGoon" flown by Capt. James E. Joham of the 98th Bomb Squadron. Beginning around 0930 six enemy fighters (described as three with fixed landing gear and three "ME109s" from "carriers") executed numerous runs against the B-17, whose gunners claimed five of six. The *Hiyō* flight suffered no damage. During their onslaught, Joham radioed the sighting of "2 CVs, 23 other ships," later amplified as two forces: one CV, two CA, two CL, and seven DD bearing 300 degrees, 150 miles from CACTUS and one CV, two BB, two CA, two CL, and five DD 10 miles closer to Guadalcanal. He apparently landed his shot-up B-17 at Henderson Field for quick repairs before returning to Santo.[18]

While Iwaki played tag with "Typhoon McGoon," Tanaka's lookouts glimpsed a fearful distant sight. In the unusually clear weather, sunlight reflected off a formation of enemy planes far to the south. Tanaka ordered each *butai* of

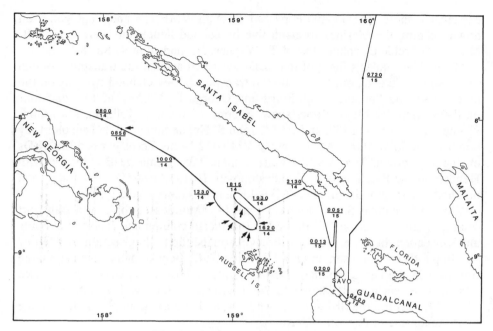

The destruction of Tanaka's convoy.

transports to separate and turn away. At the same time the destroyers spread into a screen and laid smoke. The apparition that so frightened the convoy was Bucky Lee's *Enterprise* strike, which continued westward after Mikawa's cruisers on the other side of New Georgia.

At CACTUS Woods quickly assembled a real threat to the convoy. The 1st MAW ground crews labored to refuel and rearm aircraft returning from searches and the strike on the cruisers. Around 1100 the first of thirty-eight planes bumped down the runways at Henderson Field and Fighter 1. Joe Sailer led ten SBDs (eight from VMSB-132, two from VMSB-142) and Major Richard nine, including Gibson and Robinson from VB-10, while Lieutenant Coffin took seven VT-10 TBFs. Captain Fraser's eight VMF-112 F4Fs and 1st Lt. Martin E. Ryan's four P-39s served as escort. They headed northwest in several flights out beyond the Russells. En route the SBDs ascended to 12,000 feet and the fighters 1,000 feet above them. Around 1245 they located about 100 miles from Lunga what Sailer described as three groups of transports (four or five to a group) accompanied by two CL and eight or nine DD.

Tanaka's lookouts already had the raiders in sight. The evidence indicates the convoy had redeployed into three columns, with the five ships of the No. 1 *Butai* on the right (south), the first three ships of the No. 2 *Butai* in the center, and on the left (north) the remaining three vessels of the No. 2 *Butai*. Tanaka's eleven destroyers spread out to screen their charges.

The third patrol, Lieutenant Iizuka's six Zeros from the 253 Air Group, circled the transport force. Departing Rabaul at 0630, they had stopped at Buka to top off fuel. Sighting approaching carrier bombers, Iizuka climbed to gain altitude advantage, then dived in. 2nd Lt. James G. Percy, leading one of the two Wildcat divisions, saw six Zeros barreling in from ahead and alerted Fraser. All eight Marines turned up into their opponents for head-on attacks. After a flurry of exchanged shots, the Japanese passed through VMF-112 and kept going on down, leading the Marines to claim five by second lieutenants Percy, John B. Maas, Jr., Archie Donahue, Joseph F. Wagner, Jr., and John R. Stack.[19]

Meanwhile, Sailer's flight of ten SBDs swarmed against the transport column to the south. Singling out two 8,000-ton transports, they claimed two hits on the first (by second lieutenants McEniry and George B. Herlihy of 132) and four on the second (by Major Robertshaw, Second Lieutenant Kollman, Mar. Gun. Kenneth D. Gordon of 132, and 1st Lt. John S. Henderson of 142). Together they bombed the *Sado Maru*. After evading VMF-112, some Zeros jumped the SBDs on the way down. Two VMSB-142 radiomen, Pfc. Talmadge B. Johnson with Henderson and Pvt. Travis L. Huddleston with 1st Lt. Arthur O. Hellerude, each notched a Zero shot down, and VMSB-132 left two more smoking.[20]

Coming in behind Sailer, Richard's six 142 Dauntlesses took on a transport ("larger than the '*Lurline*' ") in the left (northern) column and reported five hits and subsequent heavy explosions. Bob Gibson led the trailing section with fellow VB-10 pilot Len Robinson and Staff Sgt. Albert C. Beneke of 142 against a large transport in the center column. Despite fighter interference, they reported two hits and one near miss.[21] The No. 2 *Butai* suffered no damage from either attack. The P-39s covered the SBDs on the way out, and 2nd Lt. Emil Novak took some lumps in a game of tag with a Zero.

Watching the convoy break up as individual ships maneuvered to evade bombs, Scoofer Coffin's VT-10 TBFs showed up a few minutes after the SBDs. For their divisions Coffin and Macdonald Thompson each picked an undamaged transport in the southern column. Latching onto Coffin's lead division on the way in, a Zero bothered trailer Lt. (jg) Dick Batten with a head-on run. Diving in, Fraser "virtually disintegrated" the offending fighter. Coffin's four TBFs reported two hits on the port side of one transport (probably the *Nagara Maru*), and Thompson's three chalked up one hit to starboard of the other (likely the *Canberra Maru*). The torpedo crews characterized AA as "moderate." A piece of shrapnel tore through George Welles's windshield and plopped into his lap, while Coffin's TBF took some holes in the tail. Their assailant, the *Takanami*, steamed at the head of the No. 1 *Butai*. She claimed a carrier attack plane shot down at 1300.[22]

Every aircraft from the first CACTUS strike against the transports returned to base. Claims amounted to six transports severely damaged or sinking and eight Zeros destroyed. In turn the destroyer crews counted eight B-17s (not even present), eight fighters, seven torpedo planes, and seventeen carrier bombers attacking between 1250 and 1302. The Americans smashed the No. 1 *Butai*. An appalled Tanaka noted the *Canberra Maru* and the *Nagara Maru* listing from one or more torpedoes in their tender sides. Evidently damaged in the stern by bomb near misses, the *Sado Maru* had lost steering control. At 1325 Tanaka detached the Recovery Unit (destroyers *Amagiri* and *Mochizuki*) to tend to the crippled vessels and pressed southeast with the remaining eight transports and nine destroyers. The placid sea permitted the *Amagiri* and *Mochizuki* to rescue some 1,562 men from the sinking *Canberra Maru* and *Nagara Maru*. Later they escorted the stricken *Sado Maru* (a survivor of the 15 October High Speed Convoy) back to Shortland, where she subsequently sank.

Iizuka's flight took heavy losses, three of six missing in action: veteran CPO Ōkura Tsumoru (2nd *Shōtai* leader) and wingman PO1c Tanaka Minoru, and PO1c Hikuma Meiji from the 1st *Shōtai*. The three survivors departed at 1310; PO2c Kawasaki Katsuhiko (2nd *Shōtai*) took refuge at Buka, but Iizuka and wingman PO3c Abe Kenichi reached the Vunakanau bomber field at 1700. They claimed two Grummans destroyed, one Grumman and one Grumman carrier attack plane unconfirmed from thirty-three enemy planes encountered. Unfortunately for Tanaka no CAP would arrive overhead for the next 90 minutes.

Carrier Interlude

At 0757, after Kinkaid dispatched Bucky Lee's strike group, TF-16 retired southeast at 25 knots. Getting clean away would not be easy. At 0825 the *Enterprise*'s CXAM radar registered a bogey 42 miles astern, but it stayed at low altitude on the northern horizon. From the CAP of twenty VF-10 F4Fs, Commander Griffin sent the four of Lt. Macgregor Kilpatrick's REAPER 5 45 miles northeast on 025 degrees (M.). Rather unusually, the bogey intermittently dipped below the radar beams, but the *Enterprise* lookouts spotted sunlight glinting off the distant aircraft and kept the FDO informed of its bearing.

At 0852 Kilpatrick and Lt. (jg) Bill Blair discovered a flying boat hugging the waves about 30 miles northeast of TF-16. Their high-side pass quickly exploded the Kawanishi, and smoke from its funeral pyre appeared off the *Enterprise*'s port quarter. At 0853 Kilpatrick offered his memorable quip, "Bogey found and downed." The victim was a Type 97 flying boat from the 851 Air Group commanded by no less than Lt. Cdr. Wada Ryū (NA 58-1930), the *hikōtaichō*. There were no survivors, and Shortland never copied any messages from Wada, although he likely sent some. Kinkaid did not know for certain whether the snooper reported TF-16's location.[23]

The rest of the morning proceeded smoothly. The *Enterprise* changed to the Point Option course of 345 degrees to be ready to recover any search planes that might return rather than fly to CACTUS. By 1100 she landed three search SBDs and turned due south to clear out. To ComSoPac, Kinkaid summarized the main events and outlined his plans: "Retiring south to fuel DDs tomorrow. If there is an air group available Guadalcanal can return to pick it up but not advisable."[24] Clearly he sought to keep the *Enterprise* out of harm's way.

Kinkaid did not realize that another wily Japanese had successfully snooped TF-16. At 1040 Lieutenant (jg) Ikeya, flying the *Chitose* Type 0 reconnaissance seaplane that had eluded Reding and Leder, radioed the R-Area Air Force to report one carrier, two battleships, and five cruisers and destroyers. Deciphering the message, CinCPac analysts flashed an ULTRA at 1221 to SoPac task force commanders. After a long mission, Ikeya finally returned to Shortland at 1730.[25]

Around 1130 the *Enterprise* brass was surprised to see Jimmy Flatley's six VF-10 escort fighters turn up from the first strike. They landed along with Red Carmody's VS-10 search SBD. Hardison and Crommelin quickly organized a second strike group against the transports northwest of Guadalcanal, and Flatley was eager to lead it. During preparations, Reding and Leder, the two wayward escort pilots, showed up at 1234 low on fuel after a harrowing search for home plate and gratefully landed on board.

Hardison allocated twelve F4Fs to Flatley's strike, leaving seventeen:

REAPER 1	REAPER 2	REAPER 8
Lt. Cdr. James H. Flatley	Lt. Albert D. Pollock	Lt. Frederick L. Faulkner
Lt. (jg) Russell L. Reiserer	Ens. Edward L. Feightner	Ens. M. Philip Long
Ens. Roland R. Witte	Ens. Steve G. Kona	Ens. Donald Gordon
Ens. Philip E. Souza	Ens. Edward L. Coalson	Ens. Lynn E. Slagle

VB-10, 23 Oct. 1942. *Top row (l to r)*: Wakeham, Griffith, Hoogerwerf, Goddard, Gibson, Halloran, Buchanan, Nelson, Allen, West, Carroum. *Bottom row:* Wiggins, Buell, Frissell, Robinson, Stevens, Dufficy, Leonard, Welch, McGraw, Thomas. (NA 80-G-30069)

Lt. (jg) Ralph H. Goddard led five VB-10 SBDs and three VS-10 under Lt. (jg) William C. Edwards. The strike began taking off at 1305 with orders to attack the convoy and land at CACTUS.[26] After they departed, TF-16 turned south at 27 knots. The weather closed in as the ships neared a storm front 300 miles south of Guadalcanal. At 1400 the *Enterprise* landed the CAP and secured from flight quarters.

On 14 November SoPac's one carrier contributed thirty-one dive bombers, nine torpedo planes, and twenty fighters to the defense of Guadalcanal. What did the Support Force's one carrier accomplish? Along with Vice Admiral Kondō's Advance Force, the *Junyō* stood off north of the Solomons. That morning her sole contribution to the battle involved a reconnaissance mission to Tulagi evidently to scout out the situation for Kondō. Lt. (jg) Katō Shunkō departed at 0900 with three Type 99 carrier bombers and nine Zeros under WO Kitahara Saburō. At 1040 they spotted two warships in Tulagi harbor and correctly identified the larger as a *Portland*-class heavy cruiser—actually the *Portland* and the destroyer *Aaron Ward*, both crippled in the great night battle of the 13th. At 1240 Katō's force landed back on board the *Junyō*. That was all in that battle for the normally aggressive Rear Admiral Kakuta.[27]

The Convoy Battle Resumed

The increasing enemy air strength at Lunga amazed Lieutenant Commander Emura, who radioed that afternoon that upwards of forty carrier bombers, forty fighters, and three large planes had landed there. Never had the hard-pressed 1st MAW ground echelon worked as hard as on 14 November in a ceaseless effort to refuel and rearm aircraft. The second CACTUS convoy strike got away in several waves. Around 1430 Lieutenant Commander Lee with three VS-10 and two VMSB-132 Dauntlesses located Tanaka's transports northwest of the Russells. No defending fighters appeared over the convoy, as the SBD pilots pushed over from 10,000 feet and claimed two hits (by Lee and John Richey of VS-10) on two transports. By 1445 they cleared out and scooted back to CACTUS.

Lt. Bill Martin, VS-10 XO, followed with eight VS-10 SBDs escorted by Lt. Jock Sutherland's eight Wildcats (six VF-10, one VMF-112, and one VMF-122). Easily finding the convoy plodding southeast toward the Russells, Martin decided to search beyond to determine if any carriers indeed lurked nearby. Around 1450 he turned back after the convoy and dived from 16,000 feet. VS-10 claimed four hits by Martin, Lt. (jg) Joseph Bloch, and ensigns Leonard Lucier and Max D. Mohr against two targets. Again no enemy fighters intervened. Ens. Charles Irvine's solo dive chalked up one hit on an AP.

Lieutenant Suganami, *hikōtaichō* of the 252 Air Group, led the six Zeros of the fourth transport CAP directly from Rabaul.[28] Arriving about 1440, they were too late and too low to catch any SBDs before they dived. Much bigger adversaries were in the offing around 17,000 feet, seven B-17 Flying Fortresses under Maj. Allan Sewart, CO of the 26th Bomb Squadron. They were the first of two flights that had left BUTTON around 1048 to bomb Captain Joham's two imaginary carriers. En route, Rear Admiral Fitch changed their target to the convoy reported by CACTUS. Climbing furiously, one of Suganami's pilots, PO1c Miyazaki Isamu, could not help but admire the "beautiful formation" of enemy heavy bombers.[29] Before the Zeros could reach them, Sewart's bombardiers loosed twenty-eight quarter-ton bombs, whose splashes bracketed one transport and evidently scored one hit. Suganami's men sparred with the B-17s as they retired and claimed four, but no Fortresses went down.

While Suganami fought the B-17s, the next (fifth) CAP patrol reached the scene. They were Warrant Officer Tsunoda's eight Zeros (another aborted) from the 582 Air Group. Again Tsunoda's memoirs provide a vivid look at the convoy battle from the Japanese viewpoint.[30] Early that morning Captain Yamamoto ordered him to fly air cover over the convoy expected that afternoon to be east of the Russells. To accomplish that, the flight had to circle the convoy for one hour (1500–1600) at 4,000 meters (13,123 feet). The CO described the situation as grave; the convoy had to get to Guadalcanal at all costs, despite Allied planes that staged in from Australia and New Guinea. Tsunoda's flight stopped off at Buka and departed around 1245.

Out over the Slot, Tsunoda marveled over the difference in the weather from the previous day. Instead of black, foreboding clouds, the blue sky was unusually bright and clear over the sparkling sea. Twenty minutes from the battle area, he was surprised to see five distant thin plumes of white smoke, rising as if from incense sticks, and wondered if he was too late. Closing in around 1440, he discerned five ships burning, likely confusing some destroyers laying smoke for ships in distress. In the distance Suganami's Zeros ("red dragonflies") swarmed after Sewart's B-17s. Tsunoda chased the Fortresses as well and did not think any of their bombs struck home. While climbing he noticed far to the east more batches of enemy planes, appearing like "silver powder scattered in the blue sky." Now he attempted to restrain his men from pursuing the B-17s, but rallied only three of the other seven.

From overhead Suganami's *chūtai* noticed "a dozen Grummans," actually Jock Sutherland's VF-10/VMF escort flight patrolling near the water. In turn Sutherland had observed Zeros chasing the B-17s far above. Thinking the enemy fighters might strafe the ships, Suganami dived swiftly, scattering the Wildcats in a wild low-level dogfight. Cutting out one Zero, Sutherland whacked it hard and thought he dropped it. His wingman Hank Carey in "an old klunker of a Marine Wildcat" had trouble keeping up when Jock surprised him by reefing up in a tight turn. To Carey it was like being at the end of "crack the whip." A Zero flashed in from starboard in a high-side pass and with good deflection shooting set Carey's cockpit on fire with a 20-mm shell. A 7.7-mm slug stabbed his right thigh. Thinking it was high time to exit, he pushed back the canopy, but then found he could stamp out the fire with his glove and kept on flying.[31] Miyazaki was not Carey's particular assailant. The Japanese was amazed how fast the Grummans pulled off. Finally he latched onto one's tail just over the water and hoped the American would err by bringing his nose up. No such luck. Miyazaki gave up the fruitless pursuit. All of Sutherland's flight returned; only Carey took much damage. In turn they tallied two Zeros, one to Sutherland, the other to 2nd Lt. Ernest A. Powell of VMF-122. Actually no one from Suganami's flight went down, and they claimed four of ten Grummans besides.[32]

After 1500 a little lull occurred in the action, which permitted Tanaka to assess the situation. He estimated that between 1430 and 1450 twenty-four enemy carrier bombers and eight B-17s had bombed the convoy and set on fire one transport, the *Brisbane Maru* from the No. 2 *Butai*. He assigned the *Kawakaze* to stay with her. Her crew and passengers soon abandoned ship, and the tincan picked up 550 men. In the meantime, Tanaka resumed his advance with seven transports and eight destroyers.

By 1515 the two combats had scattered Suganami's Zeros and, desperately low on fuel, they headed northwest for the predesignated rendezvous. The last to arrive, Miyazaki was greatly relieved to see the other five pilots circling ahead. With his *chūtai* complete, Suganami shocked his men by signaling that he was going alone back to the target area. CPO Nakajima Bunkichi, the 2nd *Shōtai* leader, anxiously requested to accompany his leader, but Suganami made a negative sign. Nakajima tried again, but Suganami ended all discussion with a "strong gesture," leaving Nakajima no choice but to take the flight home. The five pilots dolefully watched their leader disappear to the southeast. Perhaps Suganami Masaji, the proud ex-*Sōryū* fighter leader who fought at Pearl Harbor and Midway, sought to atone for the delay in reaching the convoy and the heavy damage sustained during his watch. He never returned from the mission.[33]

From high altitude Tsunoda and three of his 582 pilots observed the low-level dogfight, but were not sure what was happening. Before they could close, the action dissipated. Around 1515, while Tsunoda climbed back to 2,000 meters (6,562 feet), a new group of enemy aircraft approached high from the south. They were the twenty planes of the *Enterprise* second strike group. At 22,000 feet Flatley's twelve VF-10 F4Fs held station 4,000 feet above the eight SBDs. Around 1500 they noticed the convoy up toward Santa Isabel, so Flatley turned west in a long approach to take position astern of the ships. He counted about nine transports and five or six destroyers, but in the distance three or four more ships burned. Some Zeros already patrolled at high altitude (the four 582 fighters who chased Sewart's B-17s), but they did not seem eager to fight. The *Enterprise* flyers missed Tsunoda's other four fighters frantically climbing to interpose themselves between these new attackers and the ships.

Near to 1530, after swinging around from the west and astern of the convoy, Flatley personally assigned targets to the VSB pilots. On final approach the SBDs let down to 15,500 feet, while the fighters followed from above. Goddard's five VB-10 SBDs in the lead fanned out over the nearest transports on the Japanese right, mostly the remnants of No. 1 *Butai,* and dived against three. They claimed a hit on each, but the vessels sustained no damage. Despite the proximity of the escort, Edwards's three VS-10 SBDs suffered interception by the four 582 Zeros. Two radiomen, both Coral Sea veterans, retaliated with claims of three fighters destroyed (two to Wayne C. Colley, ARM2c, in Edwards' S-4 and one to Raymond E. Reames, ARM2c, in Lt. [jg] Robert F. Edmondson's B-7). The fighters could not break up the attack, as Edwards worked his way over to the Japanese left flank, the outer column of the No. 2 *Butai.* Edwards, Red Carmody, and Edmondson selected different transports, and each reported a direct hit. They had executed the most successful individual strike of the day, scoring against the *Shinanogawa Maru* in the lead and the *Arizona Maru* at the rear of the column. Near to the water only one Zero disputed the withdrawal of the SBDs by jumping Ens. Nelson E. Wiggins (VB-10) at 300 feet. With the help of Colley in S-4, Wiggins's radioman, Claude V. Mayer, ARM3c, drove off the bandit.

While the Dauntlesses went in, Flatley's three flights peeled off in order: his REAPER 1, Pollock's REAPER 2, and Faulkner's REAPER 8 in the rear. They slanted down to support the attack and possibly strafe ships if no enemy fighters intervened. Desperately climbing so steeply that he risked stalling, Tsunoda anxiously watched the twelve Grummans deploy into three separate flights. He thought the fighters carried bombs and threatened the ships (evidently he never saw the SBDs). Maneuvering head-on against Fritz Faulkner's diving REAPER 8, he took aim at the trailer, Ens. Lynn Slagle, who also lined up a shot at the lead Zero. Slagle's slugs tearing through Tsunoda's wings and fuselage resounded like someone "smacking a fuel drum," but he took no notice. With "indescribable joy," he concentrated completely on defending the ship below. To the enemy pilot he silently screamed, "Hit me, hit me, then you can't drop your bombs!" The battered Zero finally stalled, rendering its controls ineffective. From the corner of his eye, Tsunoda glimpsed the black shadow of the Grumman pass by. In turn "Rip" Slagle last saw the Zero drop away trailing smoke.[34] Tsunoda observed to his great satisfaction that the ship below him remained undamaged. He had fulfilled his duty.

Meanwhile, Flatley's and Pollock's flights witnessed the "terrible picture of destruction" wrought by VS-10. Seemingly packed with troops, several transports suffered devastating direct hits and near misses. The F4Fs circled at 10,000 feet, then broke off in pairs to strafe different transports. Roaring in, each pilot cut loose with his six .50s at 4,000 feet and fired intermittently until pulling out at 1,500. Machine-gun bullets churned the surface of the sea. Flatley's flight followed with a run against a destroyer. Antiaircraft fire blew off Phil Souza's empty wing tank without harming the plane.[35]

Becoming separated while shooting up a transport, Ens. Ed Coalson from Pollock's REAPER 2 ran afoul of four Zeros drawn low to chase SBDs. Two raced in from ahead and below, the other pair closed from below and behind. Using the speed accumulated in his dive, Coalson adroitly looped, dropped back down, and flamed one of the Japanese crowding his tail. His opponent, LdgSea Honda Hidemasa from the 582's 2nd *Shōtai,* survived a ditching nearby.

In addition to Honda, Tsunoda also went down. The duel with Slagle left his Zero vibrating violently as he withdrew northwest. Both fuel and oil tanks were holed, and the engine streamed black smoke. Fearing the aircraft might explode, he opened his canopy and hurriedly buckled on his parachute harness. Finally the engine stopped altogether, creating an eerie silence. As he turned southeast to windward, he thought how well this fighter had served him, at full throttle for the last hour. He eased into the water with little shock and quickly escaped the sinking Zero. Tsunoda ended up close to the Recovery Unit tending to the stricken *Sado Maru* and climbed on board the *Amagiri,* crammed with 550 survivors.

While Flatley's raiders attacked, the second wave of eight B-17s led by Maj. Donald Ridings, CO of the 72nd Bomb Squadron, already closed quickly. Approaching the convoy at 20,000 feet, they enjoyed a good view of the *Enterprise* attack and particularly admired one direct hit scored on a zigzagging enemy ship. She stopped instantly, full of fire and smoke, and started sinking. Not bothered by AA or fighters, the bombardiers unloaded thirty-two 500-pound bombs against the transports, but could notch only a few near misses. When Halsey learned the altitude from which the fifteen B-17s bombed, much higher than he expected, he was livid. To Nimitz he described their performance as "worse than disappointing."[36]

After Ridings attacked, PO1c Yokoyama Takeshi, the 582's 2nd *Shōtai* leader, gathered a few Zeros for some ineffective runs against the withdrawing B-17s. Despite losing Tsunoda, the 582 flight stayed on until 1600 (as scheduled) before turning for home. Yokoyama's three Zeros reached Buin at 1715, three others touched down at 1745 at Buka. Total claims came to six (three unconfirmed), but the 582 Air Group lost two aircraft (both pilots rescued). In turn, no American planes went down. Flatley pointed his Air Group Ten flyers southeast toward Henderson Field, while the B-17s retraced the 700 miles to Espiritu Santo.

The Japanese recorded no damage from the eight B-17s, but the *Enterprise* attack, perceived as three carrier bombers between 1532 and 1538, cost the No. 2 *Butai* the *Shinanogawa Maru* and the *Arizona Maru,* both burning from bomb hits. The destroyers *Naganami* and *Makinami* stood by to pick up survivors and eventually recovered 1,592 men. Tanaka's lookouts incorrectly reported that the energetic CAP destroyed all three offending Douglasses.

A Tragic Mission

At 1500 CinCPac broadcast a rocket to all task force commanders: "Looks like all out attempt now underway to recapture Guadalcanal regardless losses."[37] That certainly was no news to CACTUS, whose planes ceaselessly droned in and out of Henderson Field and Fighter 1. Around 1530 Lieutenant Commander Thomas, VB-10 CO, led seven VB-10 SBDs out to strike the convoy. Once aloft he looked around for his fighter escort, but no F4Fs showed up. Heading northwest, he delayed his climb; by the time the target appeared, the SBDs had attained only 9,000 feet. In the distance transports milled around about 10 miles north of the Russells. Two cripples could be seen burning off to the northwest, one or two others steamed west, three or four floated dead in the water, but four or five others continued in toward Guadalcanal. Still hoping for an escort, Thomas procrastinated and only reached 12,000 feet before closing the target from the southwest. Hoping to dive from 15,000 feet or more, the other pilots greatly resented their CO's hesitation to climb to high altitude and attack immediately. At the same time Tanaka had learned of enemy ships sighted by search planes southwest of Guadalcanal and temporarily changed course away to the northeast toward Santa Isabel.[38]

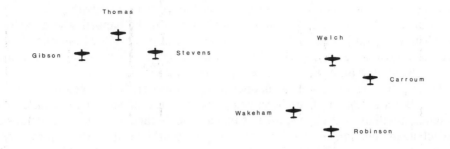

Thomas's indecisiveness gave Japanese lookouts and the CAP plenty of warning. The sixth patrol, six *Hiyō* Zeros under Lieutenant Commander Kaneko, the group leader, departed Buin at 1430 and reached the convoy around 1535. Now at 1620 they perceived the danger and were in good position to intervene.[39] The VB-10 flight flew in formation stepped down behind the leader (see figure).

About five miles from the ships, Kaneko's six Zeros charged in from the left of the SBDs. It appears that Kaneko and wingman CPO Tanaka Jirō started working over the lead section with high-sides mostly against Lt. (jg) Bob Gibson in B-3 on the left and to a lesser extent Ens. Edwin J. Stevens's B-10. At the same time WO Mori Mitsugu's four Zeros beat up Lieutenant Welch's section.

Sandwiching Lt. (jg) J. Donald Wakeham's B-12 and Len Robinson's B-11 tucked close together, Mori roared in with a low opposite run, while another Japanese flew up Robinson's tail. Robinson fired his twin .50s at the head-on assailant and saw tracers striking home. Mori's Zero took about ten hits, headed on down, and soon ditched. So swift was Mori's fight that he never triggered his 20-mm cannons, but claimed one carrier bomber when he later saw Robinson fall. At the same time a stream of gunfire from astern laced into Robinson's left wing and also Wakeham's right wing. Robinson eased off a bit and noticed that Wakeham's radioman, Forest G. Stanley, ARM1c (a decorated VB-2 Coral Sea veteran), abruptly ceased fire, possibly wounded.

The sharpshooter behind Robinson's SBD also blasted a 20-mm shell into its engine, igniting some oil or gasoline. Trailing smoke, B-11 dropped out of formation. Robinson's adroit rear assailant, PO2c Motegi Shigeo (number 3 in Mori's 2nd *Shōtai*), was far from finished with the stricken SBD. Side-slipping in his dive, Robinson extinguished the cowling fire and restarted his engine, but from directly behind, Motegi blazed away. Robinson retained his bomb to increase his diving speed, but even a gut-wrenching pull out at 2,500 feet failed to shake the Zero shooting up his tail. Neither did a split-S down to 300 feet. Robinson hedge-hopped south over the Russell Islands, hoping the palm-studded hills might brush off the Mitsubishi, to no avail. Finally he nosed up toward some low clouds. Motegi gracefully relented, rocked his wings, and returned north toward the convoy. He had expended all 110 20-mm cannon shells and also 600 7.7-mm rounds, but submitted no victory claims. Some sixty-eight holes perforated B-11, but it reached Henderson Field, a testimony to the aircraft and to Robinson's skill as a pilot.

After Robinson dropped out, the two VB-10 sections separated when Thomas and Welch went after different targets. With repeated passes, Kaneko and Tanaka kept up the pressure on Thomas's section. Gibson later described how the Zeros would "sit, belly-exposed for a second or two, high over the SBD's tail, then turn and make a high-side run on the portside and withdraw . . . to starboard.'' After recovering from one such run, Kaneko happened to cross behind Thomas's tail, when radioman Gordon C. Gardner, ACRM (another VB-2 veteran), gave the Zero's exposed belly a good rip. The Mitsubishi ''burst into flames, went over on its back, and fell into the sea.''[40]

Tanaka Jirō never saw what happened to his leader, but stayed on Gibson. Finally B-3's radioman, Cliff Schindele, smacked the persistent Zero hard and watched it withdraw trailing smoke. Tanaka soon ditched his stricken Mitsubishi and claimed four carrier bombers. In fact he nearly finished B-3, ailing from twenty-seven-plus shell hits. Forced into a spin, Gibson recovered lower down and limped back to CACTUS. Now free of fighter interference, Thomas and Stevens successively attacked the same transport on the southern edge of the convoy and reported two direct hits. They both reached Henderson Field.

Welch's section was not so fortunate. While the three SBDs worked their way north of the convoy, *Hiyō* pilots CPO Morishima Hideo and PO2c Nishimori Kikuo stayed right with them. The evidence shows that Lieutenant Suganami, the 252 Air Group *hikōtaichō,* joined the relentless attacks over the convoy. Ens. Jeff Carroum (the only survivor from the three Dauntlesses) remembered that two Zeros made opposite or beam runs, while a third came in from directly ahead. Welch selected a large transport crowded with troops in the center of the task force. Carroum lost track of Wakeham before the dive and Welch afterward, but claimed two hits for Welch and himself.

Withdrawing south at very low altitude, Carroum passed close to three destroyers firing tracers hot and heavy. One burst struck his engine, causing it to stream smoke and throw oil back onto the windshield. Only 100 feet above the sea, the engine suddenly quit, and Carroum made a rough water landing. Both he and Robert C. Hynson, ARM3c, escaped the sinking SBD, but the raft went down with the plane. They started swimming toward the Russells a dozen miles south. The next morning Hynson's strength gave out, and he disappeared. After a tremendous effort, 73 hours in the sea without any drinking water, Carroum dragged himself ashore the evening of 17 November. Helped by friendly natives, he evaded the Japanese and reached Tulagi on the 26th.[41]

Of Welch and Wakeham nothing is known. They and their radiomen, Harry C. Ansley, ARM1c, and Forest Stanley, ARM1c, never returned. Although Morishima and Nishimori claimed three carrier bombers between them, it is doubtful they alone accounted for Welch and Wakeham. Nishimori only expended forty 20-mm shells and Morishima none. The strong possibility exists that Suganami finished at least two SBDs, but was not done fighting yet.

Despite attacking ''assiduously'' according to Rear Admiral Tanaka, the VB-10 mission scored no hits according to Japanese records. In return the flight suffered the heaviest casualties of all the USN and USMC squadrons on the 14th: three SBDs shot down (five men dead) and two badly damaged. The CAP lost three *Hiyō* Zeros and one pilot killed, Lieutenant Commander Kaneko, a highly respected veteran flight leader. Morishima, Nishimori, and Motegi left the battle area about 1710 and reached Buin at 1815. They and the two downed pilots, Mori and Tanaka, claimed a total of eight carrier bombers.

''Coach Is Down''

In the late afternoon the exhausted 1st MAW mounted yet another series of strikes against the convoy. At Fighter 1 FDO Lew Mattison summed up the heated atmosphere at CACTUS. He acknowledged the reports of sinking transports, but added it "seems too good." "Skepticism, fear, hope and optimism play tag around the hilltop."[42] The ground crews prepared seventeen Marine and Navy SBDs (nine 132, two 141, five 142, and one VS-10) under the redoubtable Joe Sailer, three VT-10 TBFs with bombs led by Scoofer Coffin, and fourteen Marine F4Fs under Major Fontana (112) and Captain Foss (121). Twice that day Combined Fleet urged 17th Army to bombard and neutralize the airfields. Despite the severe shell shortage, Millimeter Mike cut loose around 1600 against Henderson Field and Fighter 1 with two 150-mm howitzers joined by some 75-mm mountain howitzers. The VMF-112 war diary noted, "Inspite [sic] of this, operations proceeding normally but nerves were on edge, and no one whistled or ran."

While the pilots received their final briefing under shellfire, Lt. Col. Joe Bauer told Foss, "I'm not going to let you fellows have all the fun."[43] He hurriedly donned his flight gear and grabbed a fighter. As the strike planes taxied in position to take off, the twelve VF-10 F4Fs from the *Enterprise* second wave began landing at Fighter 1. Flatley happened to recognize Joe Bauer ready to go and ran over to talk to his old friend (one class behind him at Annapolis). Climbing up on the F4F's wing, he shouted over the engine noise:

Where are you going, Joe? I thought they'd make you a ground officer around here.

Bauer replied, showing how much this day in particular both exhilarated and frustrated him:

That's the trouble. I'm tired of seeing the boys off all day while I stay behind. I'm going to see for myself what the convoy looks like.[44]

While Flatley and Bauer briefly conversed, Ens. Cliff Witte of VF-10 enjoyed a happy reunion with an old friend, 2nd Lt. Art Nehf of VMF-121. He asked about an odd-looking puff of dust billowing at the eastern edge of the runway. When another appeared closer, Nehf surprised him by dropping flat on the ground. Witte finally realized the enemy was shelling the airfield. Revving engines had blanketed the sounds of Millimeter Mike.[45]

Bauer, Sailer, and Coffin gathered their respective flights and headed northwest in separate formations. Soon the setting sun revealed the enemy ships "in disarray." The seventh and last fighter patrol had just come on station: six square-winged Zero 32s of the 204 Air Group led by another illustrious fighter leader, Lt. Cdr. Kofukuda Mitsugi. They arrived around 1715 from Buin, the same time Tanaka's lookouts sighted more incoming enemy planes. For the first time during the day, aircraft from the R-Area Air Force also a played a role in the defense. At 1630 Lt. (jg) Koyanagi Shōichi (NA 68-1940) of the *Kunikawa Maru* led eight Mitsubishi Type 0 observation seaplanes (two *Kunikawa Maru*, two *Hiei*, three *Sanyō Maru*, and one *Sanuki Maru*) down from Rekata and reached the convoy about a half hour later.[46]

Of the escort, only Paul Fontana's eight VMF-112 F4Fs encountered air opposition on the way in, what they later estimated as eight Zeros and at least as many float planes. Staff Sgt. Thomas C. Hurst swung sharply for a head-on pass against an aircraft closing the formation. His opponent turned out to be a *Sanyo Maru* Type 0, whose engine started smoking. Suddenly it pulled up sharply (a "suicide maneuver" according to Hurst) and knocked a wing off the Wildcat at dire cost to itself. Hurst bailed out about 10 miles northwest of the Russells. After 47 hours in the water, he was helped by natives, and later met up with Jeff

Carroum of VB-10. Japanese lookouts marked the collision at 1723 and saw both aircraft splash. Fontana described the sky over the convoy as "one mass dog-fight." VMF-112 tallied six float planes and two Zeros for one F4F (pilot res-cued): Maj. Paul Fontana one VOS, one VF; 2nd Lt. James Secrest one VOS, one VF; 2nd Lt. Edward K. Pedersen two VOS; and one VOS each to 2nd Lt. Leon L. Clark and Staff Sergeant Hurst.[47]

Joe Sailer's incoming SBDs drew most of the actual fighter opposition. Two VMSB-132 radiomen (Cpl. Orville C. Simmons with 2nd Lt. George Herlihy and Pfc. Franklin N. Pearlt with 2nd Lt. Charles Kollman) claimed enemy planes. The four survivors of Kofukuda's flight later spoke only of fighting carrier bombers. The 1st MAW credited Sailer's force with five hits on two transports, Sailer and Herlihy of 132 on one, second lieutenants Austin Wiggins, Jr., and Albert L. Clark and Master Technical Sergeant Thornbury of 142 against the other, and by Second Lieutenant Kollman of 132 on a light cruiser. According to Tanaka, the transport *Nako Maru* from the No. 1 *Butai* absorbed bombs that ignited severe fires punctuated by exploding ammunition. Even so, the *Suzukaze* picked up 1,100 survivors before leaving the *Nako Maru* adrift and abandoned.

For the last attack of this long, long day, Coffin's three VT-10 Avengers came in for a horizontal bombing run at 1738. From 6,000 feet they aimed their bombs in the midst of shell bursts against two transports already dead in the water. Coffin and Thompson each claimed a 500-pound hit. Tanaka thought four B-17s made the level bomb run and assessed no damage. While jinking to escape AA fire on the way out, the third pilot, Lt. (jg) Jerry Rapp, heard turret gunner Clarence T. Wall, AM3c, announce a Zero on their tail. Wall triggered only one burst from his single .50-caliber machine gun before it jammed, but he was dead on target. The Japanese rolled over and dived into the water. Both Rapp and Coffin saw the splash.[48]

During the SBD attacks, Bauer, Foss, and 2nd Lt. Thomas W. Furlow circled the south edge of the convoy watching for Dauntlesses in distress.[49] Finally they decided to strafe the two nearest bombed transports, the *Shinanogawa Maru* and the *Arizona Maru*, whose decks teemed with men abandoning ship. Small boats surrounded the stricken vessels, while the destroyers *Naganami* and *Makinami* stood by. Bauer and Furlow selected one of the slab-sided merchantmen, Foss the other, and all gave them a good pasting.

Near to sunset the three Marine F4Fs reassembled low over the water. Sud-denly lines of red tracers zipped past from behind. Two Zeros had stalked them. The first to react, Bauer turned sharply for a head-on shot and swiftly blew up the lead Mitsubishi. Foss noticed the colonel zoom the kill site. Meanwhile he and Furlow pursued the wingman to the northwest back over the convoy. Hedge-hopping ships, they could not overtake him after a long chase. On the way south to rejoin Bauer, the two aroused a tincan loosing a blizzard of AA. She was the *Makinami*, which claimed a carrier bomber shot down at 1750.

A dozen or so miles north of the Russells, Foss noticed a ripple on the water near to where Bauer shot down the Zero. It appeared as if a plane had just splashed and sank. He perceived Joe Bauer swimming in the middle of the distur-bance. Circling low overhead, Foss opened the door of the compartment behind the cockpit, but the raft inside would not release. Responding to the next low pass, Bauer leapt out of the water, waved, and emphatically pointed southeast: "Go home!" Watching his leader buzz the water, Furlow never did see anyone in the sea. Foss tried unsuccessfully to penetrate the static to alert CACTUS. Unable to do anything else, the two F4Fs ran home at full power.

Thus the dusk strike left one more transport, the *Nako Maru,* mortally damaged. Two Marine F4Fs went down, leaving both pilots in the water. The R-Area Air Force reported fighting more than ten fighters and carrier bombers and claimed one. Five Type 0s (three damaged) reached Rekata at 1820, but three failed to return: one from the *Hiei* missing, one *Sanyō Maru* lost when it rammed an enemy plane, and another *Sanyō Maru* set on fire and forced down. Returning crews observed four parachutes in the battle area and the one seaplane land in the water. At 1740 the destroyer *Kagerō* brought on board the surviving crewman of the *Sanyō Maru* aircraft that had ditched. The seventh CAP lost two 204 Air Group Zeros, flown by PO1c Matsumoto Sanae and PO2c Nagata Toshio. One Zero (probably Nagata's) fell to Clarence Wall of VT-10 and the other (most likely Matsumoto's) to Joe Bauer. The four surviving 204 Air Group pilots of the seventh CAP (1st *Shōtai* Lieutenant Commander Kofukuda and LdgSea Nishiyama Shizuka; 2nd *Shōtai* CPO Okazaki Masayoshi and LdgSea Shimokawa Masaaki) reported attacking fifteen carrier bombers between 1720 and 1740 and claimed two (one unconfirmed). They arrived at Buin beginning about 1815.

What happened to Joe Bauer? The war diary of the 2nd Destroyer Squadron apparently provides the answer. In the entry for 1753, which described the last action of the long day of air attacks, Japanese observers noted that one friendly fighter shot down a carrier bomber. That was three minutes after Foss and Furlow passed the *Makinami* and before they could have returned to the scene of the first fight. It now seems that another Zero lurked in the vicinity and finished Bauer long after the 204 Air Group fighters left. Yet the victor never returned to report his kill. It is difficult to avoid the conclusion that an avenging Suganami Masaji, who lacked the fuel to reach any Japanese base, indeed shot down Bauer.

Swiftly reaching Henderson Field, Foss ran over to aviation headquarters and yelled to Maj. Joe Renner, "Coach is down." They prepped the Grumman J2F-5 amphibian and taxied the clumsy biplane to the end of the field. Unfortunately ten Martin B-26 Marauder medium bombers coming in from Noumea tied up the runway while they landed. Finally the way was clear, and the Duck got away around 1850 with Bob Fraser (112) and 2nd Lt. Samuel B. Folsom (121) as escorts and droned northwest into the darkness. By the time they passed the Russells, the last glow of the sun had departed. Low clouds obscured the "pitch black" sky, except where about five transports burned brightly. The Duck found no trace of Bauer. Renner suggested to Foss that they set down on the sea and wait for dawn, but Foss felt a naval battle was brewing and declined. After a harrowing night flight, the Duck landed safely at Henderson Field.[50]

Meanwhile Art Nehf, one of the fighter pilots, brought the final report of the enemy north of the Russells vouchsafed Woods that night: two transports dead in the water, two burning, with both groups being circled by four destroyers. Eight miles west seven vessels, believed to be two light cruisers and five destroyers, were still pointed toward Guadalcanal. South of the Russells two more ships, evidently destroyers, also headed southeast.[51] CACTUS knew the battle was far from over.

Summing Up the Convoy Battle

Darkness descended upon a totally exhausted 1st MAW at Lunga. The incessant pace wore out both the air and ground crews. Even food was scarce because the 1st MAW had dragooned the cooks and messmen to help rearm and refuel planes. The newly arrived Air Group Ten aviators scrounged up a sparse meal of Vienna sausage and Spam, then sought quarters. For the old hands of VT-10 (one day more at CACTUS than the others), Lieutenant Colonel Cooley brought a case of brandy, and some bourbon was "mysteriously produced."[52]

Mulling over the many reports generated that day, the 1st MAW estimated five transports sunk and three burning. However, four more, with escorts, still came on. Ten waves, including the *Enterprise* dawn search, battered the convoy, with sixty-one SBD sorties (claiming forty hits), ten by TBFs (seven with torpedoes claiming four hits, three reporting two 500-pound bomb hits), fifteen by B-17s (one hit), and forty-two F4F escort sorties, as well as numerous P-39 attacks. Victory credits totaled twenty-six Zeros and six float planes; losses amounted to two F4Fs and five VB-10 SBDs (including one flown by a VS-10 crew). From Air Group Ten twenty VF, eleven VB, fifteen VS, and nine VT actually reached the island. That evening CACTUS air strength (1st MAW and Air Group Ten) was probably more powerful than any previous time (totals do not include planes effectively inoperable but later repaired or salvaged):

> 24 of 39 F4F-4 Wildcat fighters
> 16 of 32 SBD-3 Dauntless dive bombers
> 13 of 15 TBF-1 Avenger torpedo bombers
> 0 of 1 P-400 Airacobra fighters
> 10 of 10 P-39K Airacobra fighters
> 13 of 16 P-38F Lightning fighters
> 9 of 10 B-26 Marauder medium bombers

The total included five VMSB-131 TBFs, under the new CO, Capt. Jens C. Aggerbeck, Jr., back from BUTTON with torpedoes. Ground crews worked through the night to ready as many aircraft as possible.

A day of savage air attacks had pared Tanaka's 2nd Transport Convoy down to four undamaged transports: the *Hirokawa Maru* (sole survivor of No. 1 *Butai*), *Yamazuki Maru, Yamaura Maru,* and *Kinugawa Maru,* covered by five destroyers: *Hayashio* (Tanaka's flagship), *Oyashio, Kagerō, Umikaze,* and *Takanami.* They were the ships that Nehf had seen bound for Guadalcanal. Bombs left the *Brisbane Maru, Shinanogawa Maru, Arizona Maru,* and *Nako Maru* dead in the water. Four destroyers, the *Kawakaze, Naganami, Makinami,* and *Suzukaze,* had or were still recovering some 3,240 survivors from these ships. They would soon rejoin Tanaka. Torpedoes had sunk the *Canberra Maru* and the *Nagara Maru.* With 1,062 of their passengers crowded on board, the destroyers *Amagiri* and *Mochizuki* shepherded the crippled *Sado Maru* to Shortland. Tanaka estimated that 106 enemy planes assailed his ships and set the loss at 450 men. Base Air Force provided forty-five Zeros for the CAP. They claimed thirty enemy planes (including six unconfirmed) at the cost of twelve fighters (eight pilots). The R-Area Air Force lost three Type 0 observation seaplanes (five men).

THE SECOND NIGHT BATTLE

After dark a few *Enterprise* aviators, including George Welles, ascended a hill near Henderson Field for "a clear view of the bay, and Savo, and Tulagi. We were hoping to see a little night action from the surface fleets, but nothing was stirring."[53] In fact they went to bed a little early. Another big action was brewing. At RADAR TWO, Lew Mattison assessed the odds of a second bombardment as 50–50.

Near the Russells, Tanaka's "sorry remnant" of four transports and five destroyers moved toward Guadalcanal under direct Combined Fleet orders to continue the operation. Leaving behind the *Junyō* and (inexplicably) the fast battleships *Kongō* and *Haruna*, Kondō's Advance Force (battleship *Kirishima*, heavy cruisers *Atago* and *Takao*, two light cruisers, and nine destroyers) bore down from the north toward Savo to blast a path open for the convoy and shell the Lunga airfields. From a series of air search reports, Kondō expected at most opposition from four cruisers and two destroyers pinpointed during the day coming around from southwest of Guadalcanal. Other planes erred by placing a carrier and possibly some battleships 50 miles south of Guadalcanal, but Kondō felt they could do nothing to harm him during the night. Late that evening Tanaka was greatly relieved to see the "stalwart guardians" of the Advance Force slide in ahead of him.

Kondō's opponents were far more powerful than he realized: the new battleships *Washington* and *South Dakota*, which along with destroyers *Walke* (DD-416), *Benham* (DD-397), *Preston*, and *Gwin* comprised Lee's TF-64. A virtual magnet for Japanese search planes, they cut around the western tip of Guadalcanal in obedience to Halsey's orders to be east of Savo by midnight. After 1600 Halsey and Lee knew from the submarine *Flying Fish* (SS-229) that TF-64 confronted at least four heavy cruisers, a light cruiser, and ten destroyers, very likely to blast CACTUS and smooth the way for the surviving transports. On the basis of a partially deciphered message from C-in-C 8th Fleet (Mikawa), ULTRA warned Halsey, Lee, and Vandegrift of a force to arrive near Savo around 2330.[54]

Far to the south, Kinkaid's TF-16 secured the *Enterprise*'s CAP at 1400 and sought concealment in squalls 300 miles south of Guadalcanal. Warned around 1700 by ULTRA of a supposed enemy sighting, Kinkaid changed course to avoid an expected enemy strike. Actually the Japanese had misidentified TF-64, so the enemy had no idea of his position.

After dark, Lee swept around Cape Esperance and to the north of Savo looking for the convoy or the bombardment force. He circled all the way around Savo before heading west back past Cape Esperance. Through a judicious use of radar (so lacking on 13 November), he spotted Kondō's oncoming ships and opened fire at 2317. The massive 16-inch battleship shells came as a big surprise to the Japanese. An hour's fierce combat southwest and west of Savo cost Kondō the *Kirishima* and the destroyer *Ayanami*, while Lee lost three gallant destroyers, the *Walke*, *Benham*, and *Preston*. The *South Dakota* suffered severe damage. The heavy forces from both sides retired, Lee to the southwest and Kondō north. At 0043, 15 November, Kondō informed Tanaka that the enemy battleships had withdrawn and ordered him to press on and beach his transports at Tassafaronga. At 0052 Kondō canceled the Lunga bombardment and left Tanaka totally on his own.

Thus ended what Richard Frank has rightly called "a clear cut American victory,"[55] but one not as yet perceived by anxious watchers at CACTUS. In his diary Mattison vividly described the distant naval action as an "extraordinary display of red shells, on various trajectories, from just over coconut trees to high lob, 15 to 20 in air at once in each stream." At least one ship disintegrated in a massive explosion. He voiced the uncertainty faced by all after the brilliant flashes and dull booms faded away:

A hundred stories were rife about what was happening; nobody knew; the Navy told nobody nothing, which of course was necessary for fleet security, and we just sat ashore biting our nails and wondering who was getting blown up and bracing our nerves for anything.[56]

CACTUS did not realize that they, too, were on the brink of total victory. Analyzing fragmentary reports from back at Pearl Harbor, Nimitz correctly assessed the significance of 13 and 14 November:

As the day ends it seems most probable that while we have suffered severe losses in ships and personnel, our gallant shipmates have again thwarted the enemy. If so, this may well be *the* decisive battle of this campaign.[57]

CHAPTER 26

Mopping Up

BEACHING THE TRANSPORTS

After the night battle Tanaka "extracted" his ships from a squall and turned southeast at 11 knots for Tassafaronga. The original plan called for the ships to begin unloading at midnight and with luck complete the operation by dawn. Now badly behind schedule and suspecting an enemy carrier lurking south of Guadalcanal, he agreed with the necessity of running his fine transports aground to give their crews time to disembark the passengers and offload supplies.

Around 0400 the four transports *Hirokawa Maru, Kinugawa Maru, Yamaura Maru,* and *Yamazuki Maru* and their nine escorting destroyers glided past Savo and aimed for the anchorage on Guadalcanal's north coast. Three transports beached themselves at about the same time and near to 0500 the last slid into the darkened shore. In a line from west to east about a dozen miles long the landing points were:

1. Aruligo Point (*Yamazuki Maru*)
2. Doma Cove (*Yamaura Maru*)
3. and 4. Close together at the mouth of the Bonegi River near Tassafaronga (*Kinugawa Maru* and *Hirokawa Maru*)

Confusing matters for CACTUS would be the hulk of the *Kyūshū Maru,* beached a month before (15 October) off Bunina Point between Doma Cove and Tassafaronga. The transports immediately disgorged troops and piled supplies on the shore nearby. Of the survivor-laden destroyers, only the *Suzukaze* landed any men. Fearing air attack, Tanaka soon rounded up his tincans and steamed past Savo toward the waters north of Santa Isabel.[1]

By 0500 in the dim light of the approaching dawn, the airfields at Lunga bristled with activity. Maj. Joe Renner in the J2F Duck and Capt. Joe Foss with eight Marine F4Fs took off first, eager to be over the Russells at sunrise to locate Lt. Col. Joe Bauer and Staff Sgt. Tom Hurst, the two Marine fighter pilots forced down the previous evening. The search SBDs followed them aloft. At the same time the new Fighter 2 airstrip, located near shore at Kukum and just west of the Lunga River, became operational. A number of P-39s had shifted there to disperse fighter strength, but now they were even closer to Millimeter Mike. Before dawn 1st Lt. James T. Jarman from the 67th FS readied a flight of four P-39s when Japanese artillery pieces opened fire on Lunga. Evidently lights from taxiing aircraft drew their attention to Fighter 2. Periodic shelling that day all over the airfield complex made life interesting for the 1st MAW.

On the way out Renner's flight passed over the transports, and Foss radioed of one vessel "full of men" underway seven miles west off the western end of the island.[2] Evidently he saw the last ship just before she grounded at Aruligo Point. By dawn the rescue force was out near the Russells over the four abandoned transports. Carefully checking out the waters where they last saw Bauer, they found no trace of the colonel. To westward near Buraku (Mel Roach's refuge), they encountered two Mitsubishi Type 0 observation seaplanes from the *Sanuki Maru* which had left Rekata at 0530. The flight leader was Lt. (jg) Watanabe Kaneshige, acting CO of the *Sanuki Maru* squadron and stalwart veteran of many air battles chronicled in these pages. CPO Yamamoto Kusuhiro commanded the second Type 0.

Seeing enemy planes, Renner dropped low over Buraku to evade. He later said that if the opposition had been Zeros, "I was going to land the damned Duck and jump into the water." In the face of overwhelming opposition, Watanabe and Yamamoto separated. Foss quickly smoked one Type 0, while seven F4Fs pursued the other, which eventually fell to 2nd Lt. Oscar Bate, also VMF-121. Looking back, Foss saw his target lurch away. Despite its sharp turn into the charging Wildcat, Foss scored with a full-deflection burst and dropped the float plane toward the water. Its rear gunner kept firing on even as the biplane exploded on the sea. No Japanese survived the action. Renner and Foss returned greatly disappointed at not finding Coach Bauer. Late that afternoon Captain Fraser of 112 escorted the Duck out again to the Russells looking for downed aircrews, but found no survivors. Joe Bauer was later presumed dead, a tremendous loss for the country.[3]

As the sun came up, CACTUS spotters clearly picked out the two nearest transports beached off Tassafaronga, as well as the one at Doma Cove. Sandwiched in between was the *Kyūshū Maru* at Bunina Point. During the day both ground and air observers thought her hulk was one of the four transports beached that morning. Gunners from the Army's Battery F, 244th Coast Artillery, lugged two 155-mm guns down to the beach at Lunga and cut loose at the nearest transport 19,500 yards away. A half hour later Marine five-inchers from the 3rd Defense Battalion joined in and soon, with deliberate salvos, all of the guns dropped shells on target.[4]

Aside from artillery, repeated air strikes soon dealt out more destruction on Tanaka's "remnants." At 0555 Maj. Joe Sailer led eight Marine SBDs against the two vessels at Tassafaronga, where they noted "much Japanese activity," including shore-based AA guns. They pounded both targets with three direct hits. Three VS-10 SBDs under Lieutenant (jg) Ramsay next lifted off from Henderson Field, followed by Lt. Scoofer Coffin in a lone TBF. The Dauntlesses climbed while Coffin went straight in. On the way he narrowly avoided Lieutenant Horihashi's flight of eight Type 0 observation seaplanes (six *Chitose*, one *Sanuki Maru*, one *Kunikawa Maru*). They were the only direct cover proffered the transports that day by any Japanese aviation command. Coffin completed his attack unscathed, but only one of four 500-pound bombs even released. In turn, Horihashi intercepted Ramsay's VS-10 section at 12,000 feet, but could not prevent their dives. The Japanese departed soon after. Unopposed by aircraft, an additional sixteen SBDs and twelve P-39s executed attacks between 0725 and 0930 against the transports. Then a new character entered the lists.

Around 0830 Major General Vandegrift ordered Lt. Cdr. Raymond S. Lamb's destroyer *Meade* (DD-602) at Tulagi to shell the transport grounded at Doma Cove.[5] She got underway at 0914 and raced across the sound at 25 knots. Lamb contacted an SOC Seagull spotter plane (Lt. John A. Thomas [USNA 1937]) from the *San Francisco,* which had done good duty on the 13th over the *Hiei.* The *Meade* pinpointed all four transports (correctly ignoring the hulk of the *Kyūshū Maru*) and assessed the westernmost one (the *Yamazuki Maru* at Aruligo Point) as burning so fiercely as to be virtually destroyed. (As later photos show her in remarkably good shape, one wonders if her captain essayed a ruse.) Between 1012 and 1054 the *Meade* fired 600 rounds of five-inch against the ship at Doma (which broke in half) and the two at Tassafaronga. Thereafter she rescued survivors from the *Walke* and *Preston.* Inexplicably, Thomas's SOC crashed with no survivors. The *Meade*'s shelling caught the fancy of CACTUS and higher commands, but her unimpeded maneuvering occurred only because of American fighter superiority over Guadalcanal.

With all four transports in poor shape, attention at CACTUS shifted at least briefly to other matters. Second lieutenants McEniry and Herlihy of VMSB-132 discovered Tanaka's destroyers (reported as four CL, nine DD) withdrawing at high speed north of Isabel. Kondō's forces were already out of range. Woods and Cooley evidently considered these swift and elusive targets not worth a Parthian shot. Instead they decided to prevent any salvage of the four abandoned transports *Brisbane Maru, Nako Maru, Arizona Maru,* and *Shinanogawa Maru* floating north of the Russells and 100 miles northwest of Lunga. The 1st MAW sent four torpedo-armed TBFs (two VT-8, two VT-10) led by the redoubtable Lt. Swede Larsen, escorted by six Marine F4Fs under Maj. William Campbell (VMO-251). Departing around 1020, they remained at low altitude.

The strike crossed "seventy miles of wreckage . . . along the groove—debris of ships, corpses, oil streaks, life rafts, and an occasional burning hulk."[6] About 80 miles northwest of Savo appeared two transports (*Arizona Maru* and *Shinanogawa Maru*) dead in the water and relatively close together. Two more (*Brisbane Maru* and *Nako Maru*) could be seen beyond. Lt. (jg) George Welles and Ens. Bob Oscar of VT-10 peeled off to take the nearer pair. Despite torpedo runs under perfect conditions, the fish proved to be duds. Welles even saw Oscar's missile strike the target's stern and sink. In the meantime Larsen's run missed one of the other transports, but Lt. (jg) Lawrence S. Engel scored a direct hit amidships. The two TBFs stayed overhead until that vessel sank, then rejoined Welles and Oscar. Apparently they saw another transport go under as well, evidently succumbing to previous damage. That left two wrecks still afloat.

From Espiritu Santo fourteen AAF B-17 Flying Fortress groups sortied in two groups against targets in the CACTUS area. Maj. Don Ridings turned his six back without wasting bombs when seeing the condition of the transports beached at Guadalcanal. With his seven (another aborted), Capt. Walter Y. Lucas of the 98th Bomb Squadron sallied out beyond the Russells, where he claimed a 500-pound bomb hit on one of the derelicts. Later that afternoon 2nd Lt. Robert R. Finch of VMSB-142, flying the Isabel search sector, put another bomb into one of the two transports. Evidently one vessel went down that night, but the last drifted eastward four more days before sinking off Malaita.

The 1st MAW was not finished with the beached transports. The P-39s kept busy all day bombing and strafing the ships and surrounding dumps. At 1145 Coffin's four VT-10 TBFs worked them over with a mixture of bombs and ersatz

Japanese transports burning on Guadalcanal's north coast (Point Cruz in left foreground), 15 Nov. 1942. (NA-80-G-30529)

incendiaries dubbed "Molotov bread baskets." That afternoon Lt. (jg) Bob Gibson's three VB-10 SBDs went out to bomb the transport at Doma Cove, whose bow was still exposed. Gibson achieved a close miss, while one of the wingmen, Lt. (jg) Ralph Goddard, sought an AA battery reported near Tassafaronga. Not finding it he bombed instead what looked like a supply dump and elicited a huge explosion with thick black smoke rising to 2,000 feet. The area burned vigorously for 16 hours, the "greatest sight ever seen on Guadalcanal," according to CACTUS radio.[7]

What did Tanaka's Outer South Seas Force Reinforcement Force accomplish, aside from expending eleven fine vessels? Under punishing air and artillery attacks, the four beached transports and the destroyer *Suzukaze* deposited about 2,000 men ashore, mainly infantry, along with 260 boxes of shells and some 1,500 bags of rice, only about four days' rations for the destitute 17th Army. That was almost negligible given the desperate situation.

THE LAST AIR BATTLE

During the morning the 1st MAW kept a regular CAP over Lunga, but contacted no enemy planes. For the VF-10 pilots at Fighter 1, the morning was quiet except

for occasional artillery shells that fell all around the 1st MAW HQ area. At 1230
Lt. Cdr. Jimmy Flatley led eight F4Fs aloft as relief CAP:

REAPER 1	REAPER 2
Lt. Cdr. James H. Flatley, Jr.	Lt. Albert D. Pollock
Lt. (jg) Russell R. Reiserer	Ens. Edward L. Feightner
Ens. Roland R. Witte	Ens. Steve Kona
Ens. Philip E. Souza	Ens. Edward B. Coalson

1st MAW Operations told him not only to cover Lunga, but also to patrol out in
the direction of Cape Esperance and Savo to protect the *Meade* and others rescu-
ing survivors from the two sunken destroyers.[8]

The first alert of Base Air Force's only appearance that day sounded at 1418.
The Australian radio station at Lunga copied a transmission from station DEL,
Lt. Alexander N. A. Waddell, RANVR, who had reached northern Choiseul
Island on 19 October. He advised that eleven float planes had gone southeast at
1345.[9] What he actually saw was the second wave of a mini two-pronged strike
from Buin. The first group, Lieutenant Itō's air control force of six 253 Air Group
Zeros, departed Buin at 1230. The second wave was an antishipping strike (possibly in response to the *Meade*) of seven *Hiyō* Type 99 carrier bombers led by Lt.
(jg) Kurihara Ichiya (NA 67-1939), escorted by a mixed *chūtai* of 252 and *Hiyō*
air group fighters.

1st *Shōtai*	2nd *Shōtai*	3rd *Shōtai*
Lt. (jg) Mitsumori Kazumasa[a]	CPO Takahashi Munesaburō[b]	CPO Mita Gen[b]
PO1c Nahara Yasunobu[a]	PO2c Futaki Masami[b]	LdgSea Ueno Masahiro[b]
PO2c Oda Tōru[a]		

[a] 252 Air Group
[b] *Hiyō* Air Group

These fourteen planes left Buin at 1330 and took the northern route over
Choiseul and Isabel beyond the top edge of the Slot.[10]

Itō's six Zeros had Guadalcanal in sight by 1445 and gained altitude as they
closed the target area. A little before 1500 they appeared on RADAR TWO at 65
miles and an estimated 20,000 feet. Lew Mattison instructed Flatley's two flights,
now getting very low on fuel, to climb to 20,000 feet and keep watch in the
direction of the Russells. The 1st MAW also scrambled seven ready VF-10 F4Fs
from Fighter 1:

REAPER 3	REAPER 8
Lt. Stanley E. Ruehlow	Lt. Frederick L. Faulkner
Lt. (jg) Roy M. Voris	Ens. M. Philip Long, Jr.
Ens. Lynn E. Slagle, Jr.	Ens. Donald Gordon
	Ens. James H. Dowden

The two flights got away separately and turned left toward Savo with orders to
climb toward the raid. That afternoon Bobby Edwards arrived at Henderson
Field on a transport plane. Despite a swollen knee, he had taken "French leave"
from the hospital at Tontouta field and "thumbed a ride" to CACTUS. Legend
has it that when he learned of VF-10's impending scramble, he purloined a jeep
at Henderson Field and sped over to Fighter 1. There he grabbed an armed and

fueled Marine F4F and took off in the direction of the fight.[11] That gave VF-10 sixteen pilots aloft: eight on station at high altitude and eight (not all together) furiously climbing.

Itō evidently stayed only a short time beyond the Russells and turned back almost immediately. At 1512 RADAR TWO logged a contact bearing 314 degrees and already 112 miles out. It is possible that Itō's force was intended only to be a decoy to grab enemy attention while Kurihara and Lt. (jg) Mitsumori Kazumasa (NA 68-1940) sneaked in from the north. At 1526 Geoffrey Kuper (ZGJ6) on southern Santa Isabel warned of the drone of a large number of enemy planes heading southeast at 1515. Consequently the 1st MAW sounded Condition RED at 1535.[12]

Itō's decoy mission, if indeed it was, worked perfectly. Neither Flatley's eight F4Fs high over Savo nor the seven under Ruehlow and Faulkner immediately spotted the fourteen enemy planes cutting in behind and below them. Around 1540 Kurihara looked over the Tassafaronga anchorage, but saw no enemy ships. The pugnacious Meade had departed over an hour before. He decided to abort the mission, but before the Japanese could turn away, they ran afoul of Bobby Edwards trailing the rest of the F4Fs. It appears that about 18 miles west of Lunga he climbed right into the Japanese formation and holed one carrier bomber (he thought it was a Zero). Kurihara's seven Type 99s (one damaged) kept on going, retraced their route to the north, and got clean away.

All seven of Mitsumori's Zeros jumped Edwards in close succession. He even remembered the correct number of his assailants and thought he winged one or two of them. In the process he fired off all his ammunition, but ended up with a couple of Zeros crowding his tail. The other Japanese stayed above the fight as top cover. Stan Ruehlow's REAPER 3 showed up overhead in the nick of time. They noticed the dive bombers with Zeros above and below, but from their height did not see Edwards beset by more bandits. Spotting his teammates, Edwards radioed words to the effect: "Hey, take this lug off my neck. I'm out of ammunition."[13]

Diving in from about 20,000 feet, Ruehlow's three F4Fs tore into the top cover and retained the speed and position for several runs against individual Zeros. Ruehlow, Voris, and Slagle all felt confident they scored. They broke up the enemy formation and eased the pressure off Edwards. Pulling out of his third run, "Butch" Voris suffered a 20-mm shell through the upper left side of his canopy. Slanting down, it penetrated his instrument panel, and exploded beneath with a great deal of smoke and noise. Fragments peppered his right thigh. His assailant stayed right with him, so Voris dropped into a tight spiral and rolled his ailerons when he gained sufficient speed. He shook the Zero over Savo and turned toward home. In the short, sharp melee, the four VF-10 pilots each claimed one fighter and added four probables (two by Edwards, one by Ruehlow, and one by Slagle). In turn Mitsumori tallied one of nine Grummans in return for one Zero missing (Hiyō pilot LdgSea Ueno Masahiro) and three damaged.[14]

Ueno had ended up at about 18,000 feet, well over the fight, but unwittingly flew directly under Flatley's REAPER 1 flight at 20,000. From radio chatter Flatley knew something was happening. He never saw the actual melee, only the lone fighter below. Warning his flight, he pushed over in a dive, followed in order by Reiserer, Witte, and Souza. Flatley's steep overhead missed the nimble Zero, as did Reiserer's. More successful, Witte shot tracers into the Mitsubishi's cockpit and pulled off to the side to make another run only to see his target suddenly disintegrate. Last in, Souza had noticed Ueno's Zero climb and tailed in behind for a good shot. At his first bursts the *Reisen* "exploded like a bomb." Avoiding the wreckage, he saw what appeared to be the pilot's body, but no parachute. Thus Witte and Souza each thought they bagged one Zero, but together they finished Ueno—the only loss for Base Air Force that day.[15]

While the air battle took place nearby, REAPER 2 leader Dave Pollock experienced trouble with the propeller pitch control in his borrowed Marine Wildcat and glided back toward Lunga. He did not make it, but flopped into the water off the Mantanikau River. Wingman Whitey Feightner followed and covered him as Marines hurriedly rafted out from the beach after him. Feightner discouraged a Zero from interfering and also strafed some enemy positions firing from shore. Aside from a cut from slamming his forehead into the gunsight when he ditched, Pollock was okay.[16]

CACTUS restored Condition GREEN at 1557, and at the same time Maj. Paul Fontana departed Fighter 1 with eight Marine F4Fs (including one VF-10 Wildcat substituted for the one Edwards took) as relief CAP. Around 1615 Flatley's REAPER 1 and the rest of REAPER 2 landed with empty fuel gauges. Edwards came in shortly thereafter and found Flatley and a Marine major waiting to talk to him. The Marine told Edwards he "appreciated" his "aggressiveness," but added, "I needed that plane for my next flight." An embarrassed Edwards could not reply. The Marine later told Flatley, "We need more like him in the air."[17]

Kurihara's strike proved to be a watershed event—the last daylight strike against Guadalcanal until 25 January 1943, when the Japanese finally prepared to evacuate their decimated forces from that horrible island. Against eleven Zeros, the eight VF-10 pilots tallied six confirmed and four probables without loss. In turn, Mitsumori's seven claimed one Grumman in return for one pilot missing and three aircraft damaged.

Ironically, while VF-10 fought, Maj. Dale Brannon's twin-engine P-38 Lightnings from the 339th FS finally flew their first combat mission. Snoopers beset Lee retiring south of Guadalcanal with battleships *Washington* and the *South Dakota,* which streamed oil. Halsey and Lee anticipated possible enemy strikes on TF-64 and requested fighter cover from the 1st MAW. Late that afternoon two flights of four P-38s headed out 110 miles southeast to cover the two battleships, but at 1700 found only what they reported as one destroyer trailing oil. Forty miles beyond, a weather front forced them to return. The P-38s would have to wait a long time before the Japanese again appeared over Guadalcanal in daylight.[18]

WINDING DOWN

After an overnight run to the south, TF-16 labored through choppy seas about 400 miles south of Guadalcanal. At 0707, 15 November, Kinkaid advised ComSoPac that the *Enterprise* would not, after all, retrieve her air group from Guadalcanal. He expected to arrive at Noumea the morning of the 17th unless otherwise ordered. A few hours later CinCPac informed the task force commanders that the Japanese had retired from Guadalcanal waters, at least temporarily. Halsey concurred and later wrote Nimitz in characteristic language, "I felt comparatively assured, that after the beating he had taken, the monkey would withdraw." At first he had hedged his bets by instructing Lee's TF-64 battleships to rendezvous with four newly arrived destroyers and take station by 2200 near Savo. After 1200 he relented and told both Lee and Kinkaid to break off for Noumea. The afternoon search confirmed that all Japanese naval forces had indeed departed the lower Solomons.[19]

The morning of the 15th, Lt. Swede Vejtasa and Ens. Chip Reding of VF-10 flew what was supposed to be a routine delivery of dispatches from TF-16 to ComSoPac. Departing the *Enterprise* at 0910, the two F4Fs soon ran into the same weather front, squalls, and low visibility that would bedevil their comrades staging south from CACTUS. Unaware of an incorrectly swung compass, Vejtasa turned southeast far short of the proper point and ended up north of New Caledonia. After nearly six hours and desperately low on fuel, they gratefully sighted a suitable flat spot on Uvea in the Loyalty Islands some 80 miles north-northeast of Tontouta. Greeted warmly by the French resident commissioner, they availed themselves of his radio to announce their plight to Noumea. Asked for authentication, Swede dryly replied, "Anyone with the name of Vejtasa needs no further identification." SoPac agreed and sent a seaplane to fetch the dispatches. The next day a PBY returned with gasoline, allowing Vejtasa and Reding to continue their interrupted journey to Tontouta.[20]

That afternoon Woods radioed Kinkaid to advise that CACTUS would forward the *Enterprise* planes to BUTTON "as rapidly as conditions warrant."[21] Around 1400 Lieutenant Commander Lee took twelve VS-10 SBDs and Lieutenant Coffin eight VT-10 TBFs south to Espiritu Santo. All of the Army B-26 Marauders likewise departed to ease crowding at the fields. Just after takeoff, Lt. Jim McConnaughhay's sputtering engine put his Avenger into the water off Lunga without injuring the crew. Lt. (jg) George Welles left on his own, but aborted because of bad weather. On the way south, squally skies caused lieutenants (jg) Red Carmody and John Richey of VS-10 to become lost. Both planes ditched independently off Espiritu Santo, but all four aviators were safe. The following Air Group Ten planes remained at CACTUS (not all operational): twenty VF-10 F4Fs, eleven VB-10 SBDs, three VS-10 SBDs, and two VT-10 TBFs. Losses in the past two days comprised five SBDs shot down (nine men killed), two SBDs and one TBF ditched, two F4Fs damaged.[22]

On the 16th Welles got away for BUTTON, while the pugnacious Bobby Edwards and Russ Reiserer flew VF-10's last combat mission of the battle. That afternoon they strafed likely targets around the four hulks. The next day the remaining Air Group Ten personnel left Guadalcanal, mostly by transport plane. Jimmy Flatley turned over fifteen VF-10 Wildcats to MAG-11 and led the five remaining fighters south to BUTTON. VB-10, VS-10 and VT-10 left all of their aircraft either at CACTUS or BUTTON. With the *Enterprise* at Noumea as of the afternoon of the 16th, Air Group Ten gradually reassembled at Tontouta, awaiting new planes and training until the day they would go out again.

A TALE OF TWO CONVOYS

The Guadalcanal reinforcement operation (11–15 November) cost Imperial Japan two battleships, one heavy cruiser, three destroyers, and eleven transports, and about sixty-four aircraft. In their postmortem on 22 November at Truk, Japanese commanders estimated they had destroyed two battleships, nine cruisers, and nine destroyers, as well as damaging numerous other ships—a "commendable result." Yet the upshot was the delivery of almost insignificant numbers of troops and supplies to the 17th Army on Guadalcanal. Lieutenant General Hyakutake's besieged troops looked upon the convoy as their last chance to resume the offensive, only to have that hope "shattered." In his diary Vice Admiral Ugaki cited two big failures. The first was not dealing with the enemy carrier task force that appeared on 13 November south of the Solomons. He had wanted to postpone the convoy's advance one day more from the 14th to the 15th, but could not "due to difficulties of maintaining our air strength." The second concerned the inability to neutralize the Lunga airfields either by ship bombardments or by 17th Army artillery. In the end Allied air power and the "fervent fighting spirit of the American forces" proved just too strong for a Combined Fleet unwilling to commit all its forces to battle.[23]

In contrast, U.S. losses in defending Guadalcanal and preserving CACTUS air strength amounted to two light AA cruisers and seven destroyers with most of their crews and thirty-six aircraft. Their claims comprised two battleships, two heavy cruisers, four light cruisers, four destroyers, and twelve transports sunk and numerous other vessels damaged. The key to Allied success was the prevention of two deadly battleship bombardments of Henderson Field and its satellite airstrips. The afternoon of 15 November Vandegrift offered a special tribute to Dan Callaghan, Norm Scott, and their valiant crews. Their sacrifice permitted the 1st MAW and Air Group Ten to execute devastating daylight air strikes against Japanese ships within 200 miles of CACTUS. In turn, the Japanese failed to commit their air power, except for the rather feeble air protection afforded Tanaka's convoy. Halsey noted, "The plane attack by the Nips was anything but impressive."[24]

Nothing sums up this battle better than the contrast between Turner's two convoys which successfully landed nearly all their passengers and cargo on 11–12 November at Lunga and Tanaka's pathetic results on 14–15 November. Now the future looked brighter at Guadalcanal, and the eventual end of the campaign appeared in sight. The victory also relieved the gloom and doom in Washington. On 26 November the president announced the richly deserved promotion of William Halsey to admiral to date from the 18th.

Understandably not revealed at the time was the enormous contribution of ULTRA, its first big victory since Midway. On 16 November CinCPac sent accolades to the various codebreakers at Pearl, in Washington, and in Australia: "Once again radio intelligence has enabled the fighting forces of the Pacific and Southwest Pacific to know when and where to hit the enemy." Admiral King added, "Well done."[25] The drought of radio intelligence was over. Never would U.S. naval commanders have as little enemy information to go on as between August and November 1942, something that must be considered when assessing VAdm. Robert Ghormley's lackluster performance as ComSoPac.

THE CONTRIBUTION OF AIR GROUP TEN

While the Air Group Ten pilots and aircrewmen filtered back to Tontouta field, the A-V(S) officers labored mightily to interview them and compile squadron action reports for a basic assessment of the group's role in the victory. Given the great deal of cooperation with the 1st MAW in the many strikes, even the *Enterprise*'s own report could not precisely quantify Air Group Ten's part in the battle. Captain Hardison credited the group with sinking one *Nachi*-class CA, and probably finishing off one *Kongō*-class BB, one CA, one CL, and two transports, while inflicting damage on numerous other vessels. Aircraft claims totaled seventeen, including ten (two VP, eight VF) credited to VF-10. In turn the group lost five VB-10 SBDs (four VB-10 and one VS-10 crews), from which only Ens. Jeff Carroum survived.

The reports echoed praise for the performance of Air Group Ten. A proud Hardison called them "undoubtedly the most valuable carrier air group in the service," "veterans tried and seasoned by actual combat, whose skill, determination and valor are outstanding."[26] Lieutenant Colonel Cooley attested to the "fine cooperation and spirit shown by the naval units temporarily attached to Group 14."[27] Perhaps Bill Halsey summed it up best: "The splendid work of the ENTERPRISE air group while temporarily based at CACTUS is noted with extreme pleasure." In a 29 November letter to Nimitz he enclosed the *Enterprise* claims and added, "It sounds fantastic but I am convinced it is true."[28]

Both Kinkaid and Hardison expressed approval over the employment of the *Enterprise* and Air Group Ten in this battle as opposed to the Santa Cruz slugging match. This time the carrier operated in the rear well within land-based air support and waited for the enemy to come calling. "The Big E" launched her strikes, shuttled the planes to a land base, then pulled out in timely fashion before absorbing a counterattack. According to Kinkaid, "This time the air group on the carrier was utilized more effectively than ever before."[29] He held the November operation as a model for the use of carriers in the constricted waters of the Solomons, where the enemy enjoyed an extensive air search network. Halsey concurred.

CinCPac did not altogether agree with Kinkaid's conservative use of the *Enterprise,* which sent her far south the evening of 14 November, preventing any kind of pursuit of the fleeing Japanese. In the general report of 18 February 1943 Rear Admiral Spruance, the chief of staff, suggested she might have remained closer to Guadalcanal to retrieve at least a portion of her group late on the 14th or early on the 15th. With the support of the *Washington* and the TF-16 heavy cruisers, she might have pursued the cripples and stragglers withdrawing toward Buin.

Leaving aside the might-have-beens, the record shows that the contribution of the *Enterprise* and Air Group Ten was decisive to the aerial victory and second only to two night surface battles that prevented battleship bombardments of CACTUS. Her thirty-one dive bombers, nine torpedo planes, and twenty fighters more than doubled the offensive power of the 1st MAW, and the results were commensurate with their strength. Air Group Ten finished off the *Hiei* and the *Kinugasa* and sank or crippled at least four of the transports on the 14th. Indeed, just the presence of the lone carrier caused the Japanese great consternation and froze much of Base Air Force's bomber strength, held in reserve until she could be located and attacked. The fear of a nearby carrier compelled Kondō to withdraw early on the 15th and led to the order to Tanaka to beach his transports. SoPac could scarcely have won the battle without the *Enterprise* and her aviators. The same can be said of the carriers for the whole Guadalcanal Campaign.

Conclusion

THE END AT GUADALCANAL

Following the defeat of the great convoy, the nature of the Solomons campaign changed, although that was not immediately apparent to both sides. Although the Japanese persevered with the Tokyo Express runs and tried to hold off the surging U.S. ground forces on Guadalcanal, neither side wished to commit its much-reduced carrier forces unless absolutely necessary. In fact, Admiral Halsey controlled the only remaining big carriers in the Pacific Fleet, the *Saratoga* and the *Enterprise*. They would not be reinforced until the first of the new *Essex*-class CVs completed shakedown in spring 1943. At the same time AirSoPac enjoyed about as much land-based aviation as its forward fields could handle. Now with Base Air Force eschewing daylight raids on Guadalcanal, the action shifted farther up the Slot. Thus for the remainder of the battle for the island, the carrier air groups saw very limited combat. They assumed a strictly peripheral role, a force to counter any large-scale efforts by the Combined Fleet, especially by its replenished carrier groups. That did not occur.

Given the temporary lull in the action, Halsey planned to build up CACTUS as quickly as possible and enhance its facilities. Fresh Army and Marine troops relieved the exhausted 1st MarDiv to complete the conquest of Guadalcanal. The naval situation was improving. The *Enterprise* would be ready to go at the end of November, while the refurbished *Saratoga* hastened south. SoPac would also have the two auxiliary carriers *Nassau* and *Altamaha,* to be joined in early 1943 by the converted fleet oilers *Suwannee* (ACV-27) and *Chenango* (ACV-28) fresh from the TORCH landings in North Africa. Their flight decks were 60 feet longer than the *Bogue*-class, and they were considered more combat-capable.

Combined Fleet and 17th Army enjoyed no such respite. Indeed, on 16 November an event occurred which, when combined with the stinging defeat the day before at Guadalcanal, changed the whole complexion of the campaign. For the past two months Guadalcanal had riveted Japanese attention, with very few resources spared for New Guinea. In the meantime, General MacArthur's Australian troops pushed the Japanese back north over the rugged Owen Stanley Mountains toward their base at Buna on the Papuan coast. On the 16th a Japanese lookout on the coast a few miles southeast of Buna excitedly warned of a small group of coastal vessels. They accompanied troops from the U.S. Army's 32nd Division advancing up the coast. Unbeknownst to the Japanese, the Allies had transported strong forces over to the southeast approaches of Buna. Now suddenly they threatened the heart of the Japanese hold over Papua. Vice Admiral Ugaki chided his Army colleagues, "How careless they were."[1]

Worried more about Buna, uncomfortably closer to Rabaul than his deteriorating stronghold in the Solomons, Vice Admiral Kusaka committed much of Base Air Force to stave off imminent defeat in New Guinea. At the same time 17th Army diverted troops intended for Guadalcanal. Until Buna's fall in January 1943, the Japanese centered their efforts there and postponed for the foreseeable future any general offensive against Guadalcanal. Instead they worked to improve the supply situation in the Solomons and constructed more forward air bases, notably at Munda on New Georgia, only 170 miles from Lunga. Air strength from the homeland increased, but the low quality of replacement fighter pilots and bomber crews greatly dismayed the air commanders at Rabaul. If Japanese air power regained control of the skies over the southern Solomons and isolated the enemy forces, Imperial General Headquarters thought Guadalcanal could be recaptured. That never came to pass. Instead, the Japanese decided to cut their losses. On 8 February, at the end of a brilliantly executed plan of withdrawal, the last Japanese destroyer, packed with starving soldiers, departed Guadalcanal, never to return. The next day SoPac declared the long ordeal at an end.

EXEUNT OMNES

Although the purpose of this two-volume history is to chronicle the decisive first year (December 1941 to November 1942) of U.S. naval fighter operations in the Pacific War, it is both useful and fitting to sketch what happened to the principal characters.

One of the first to bow out of the theater was RAdm. Thomas Kinkaid. On 16 November RAdm. Frederick C. Sherman, the outspoken former captain of the *Lexington* at Coral Sea, arrived at Noumea. He seemed the obvious choice to supplant Kinkaid as CTF-16 on "The Big E." Halsey stressed to Admiral Nimitz that this was no reflection on Kinkaid, who did a "fine job," but that "it would be inexcusable to have a man of Sherman's air experience not utilized on the *Enterprise* when he is available."[2] After Kinkaid, nonaviators never again led carrier task forces in battle. On 24 November he received one of the SoPac cruiser striking forces being formed, but events soon took him away from the theater. After a well-deserved rest, he assumed command of the North Pacific amphibious forces gathering to reconquer Attu and Kiska in the Aleutians. On 25 October 1944 at the head of the 7th Fleet, MacArthur's Navy, Kinkaid again had to deal with Halsey's impetuous nature, this time during the climactic Battle of Leyte.

During the balance of November, with the *Enterprise* docked at Noumea, Air Group Ten trained at Tontouta. After a few brief training cruises, the carrier again sortied to battle the Japanese. On 30 January 1943 south of Rennell, Lt. Cdr. Jimmy Flatley's VF-10 splashed seven of eleven land attack planes from Lieutenant Commander Nishioka's 751 Air Group in a valiant but vain attempt to save the crippled heavy cruiser *Chicago*. Subsequently Ens. Lewis W. Gaskill shot down PO2c Nakajima Tetsuo's 705 Air Group Type 1 *rikkō* on 8 February to chalk up the final aerial victory of the Guadalcanal Campaign. Thus the fighting squadrons managed to be at the conclusion as well as the beginning of the long ordeal.

On 13 February Flatley turned the Grim Reapers over to his able XO, Lieutenant Commander Kane, and proceeded back to the States to take command of Air Group Five being organized for the new *Yorktown* (CV-10). As before, he worked his special magic, transforming largely inexperienced aviators into the air warriors who introduced the *Essex* (CV-9), *Yorktown,* and the CVL *Independence* (CV-22) into battle that summer. Later, as operations officer for VAdm. Pete Mitscher's fast carrier task force in October 1944 off the Philippines and again in 1945 in the Okinawa Campaign, he influenced the course of carrier warfare at the highest levels.

Fighting Ten continued its superb record as one of the Navy's finest squadrons. Changing over to Grumman F6F-3 Hellcats for its second tour (December 1943–July 1944) on "The Big E," VF-10 participated in the capture of the Marshalls, raids on Truk, Palau, and Hollandia, and in the Marianas Turkey Shoot. Unique for a naval fighting squadron, VF-10 then exchanged its F6Fs in September 1944 for its third wartime fighter type, Vought F4U-1 Corsairs. Lt. Cdr. Wally Clarke (ex-VF-5) led the Reapers on board the *Intrepid* (CV-11) for combat off Okinawa. VF-10's final wartime score amounted to 217 kills.

Drawing a new crop of ensigns, Lt. Lou Bauer re-formed Fighting Six in the fall of 1942 around a few veterans, notably NAPs Dick Gay, Hal Rutherford, Don Runyon, and Red Brooks, as well as Vince de Poix and Ram Dibb. The Shooting Stars took VF-5's place in the *Saratoga* Air Group. Back in southern waters by late November, VF-6 chafed at the lack of opportunity to engage enemy planes because of Halsey's firm policy of keeping his few carriers largely out of harm's way. The sole exception occurred in early February. In a performance reminiscent of VF-72's October vendetta against the snoopers, the Shooting Stars destroyed one Type 1 *rikkō* on the 2nd, two on the 3rd, and another on the 4th for their only victories for the entire tour. Otherwise the high point of the deployment occurred between 20 June and 24 July, when "Bauer's Flowers" operated from the HMS *Victorious* in support of the invasion of New Georgia. On 15 July 1943 VF-6 swapped squadron designations with Lt. Cdr. Butch O'Hare's VF-3 and became Fighting Three.[3] That September VF-3 returned to the States and was re-formed a month later. In October 1944 the reorganized VF-3 embarked on the *Yorktown* for the Philippines Campaign and the capture of Iwo Jima.

Fighting Five and Fighting Seventy-one were decommissioned shortly after they returned to the States, and their pilots dispersed to other duty. Only VF-72 saw further combat before its demise. In mid-November SoPac divided the Blue Wasp squadron, half to reinforce VF-10 and the balance under Lt. Cdr. Mike Sanchez to season Lieutenant Commander Brunton's VGS-16 on board the *Nassau.* Later that month Lt. Warren Ford's contingent left the Reapers for similar duty with Lt. Cdr. "Whitey" Ostrom's VGS-11 on the *Altamaha.* In this way Halsey hoped the experienced pilots might assist the two baby flattops in becoming combat-ready more quickly. It became obvious that the diminutive *Bogue*-class ACVs would be more suitable for antisubmarine or aircraft transport duty.

In early February 1943 VF-72, now under Lt. Al Emerson, joined the beached squadrons from the *Nassau, Altamaha,* and the *Copahee's* VGS-12 at Henderson Field. AirSoPac worried about the Japanese naval build-up, not realizing that the enemy planned to evacuate Guadalcanal rather than reinforce it. The afternoon of 4 February the new arrivals flew their first strike mission against incoming destroyers off New Georgia 200 miles up the Slot. In sorties that totaled twenty SBDs, thirteen TBFs, eight P-39s, four P-38s, and twenty-five F4Fs, the CACTUS flyers claimed fifteen Zeros at the substantial cost of two SBDs, four TBFs, one P-40, and three F4Fs.[4] Victory credits included four by VF-72 old hands Lt. Red Hessel (one), Lt. (jg) Bob Sorensen (one), and Ens. Bob Jennings (two). On the 12th the aggressive Emerson failed to return from a strike against Munda, a great loss to the Navy. Hessel took the remaining Blue Wasps back to the States, where in March 1943 VF-72 ceased to exist.

THE ACHIEVEMENT AND THE LEGACY

The taking and holding of Guadalcanal, the first Allied amphibious offensive of the war, represented a watershed in the Pacific War. Striking rapidly before the Japanese could consolidate their defenses in the southern Solomons, SoPac secured a toehold from which it repulsed blow after blow from an enraged enemy. Intense attrition whittled down both sides, but finally the Japanese had to give in and withdraw. Never again would they go on the offensive in the Pacific. The whole array of sailors, ground troops, aviators, and logistical support personnel shared credit for the victory.

The U.S. Navy's carrier fighting squadrons took particular pride in their own contribution during the first fourteen crucial weeks, from 7 August to 15 November 1942. At heavy cost VF-5, VF-6, and VF-71 provided fighter support during the initial two days of the amphibious invasion, the first time they attempted such a difficult endeavor. In August and October, VF-5, VF-6, VF-72, and VF-10 fought two desperate carrier slugging matches whose level of ferocity was seldom equaled until the Kamikaze onslaught of 1944–45. Beached when their carriers were sunk or heavily damaged, VF-5 and VF-71 joined the 1st MAW at besieged Henderson Field, pitching in during one of Marine aviation's proudest exploits. Sharing the primitive conditions, the Navy pilots helped their fellow Marine and AAF fighters blunt the Japanese air onslaught. Nowhere else did aviators fly for months from a squalid airfield perched precariously on the front lines and subjected to almost incessant bombing and shelling. Finally in November VF-10 swooped down on CACTUS from the one wounded but operational flattop to take part in the defeat of the enemy's last big push.

Between 7 August and 15 November 1942, while operating from the carriers or land-based at Guadalcanal, VF-5, VF-6, VF-71, VF-72, and VF-10 claimed 193 aircraft destroyed in aerial combat:

	Claims	Estimated Actual Score
Fighters	54	25
Dive bombers	62	32
Medium bombers	40	20
Torpedo planes	15	7
Flying boats	9	9
Float planes	8	5
Float fighters	5	4
	193	102

Other Japanese aircraft damaged in combat with Navy Wildcats either crash-landed or had to be written off, but the exact number cannot be determined. A total of 185 VF pilots, of whom only 30 had previously fired their guns in anger, served in the five squadrons during their combat deployments. Thirty-one were killed during the campaign.[5] At the same time the five squadrons operated 178

Grumman F4F-4 Wildcats and lost 108 to all causes, including the sinking of the *Wasp* and *Hornet*.

In strictly fighter-versus-fighter combat, the ratio of loss was approximately thirty-one Navy F4Fs (twenty-three pilots killed) to twenty-five Zeros. The raw statistics do not tell the whole story. After the disaster on 7 August (nine F4Fs lost to two Zeros), the fighter battles tended to even out. Following the universal axiom of fighter combat, those with altitude advantage tended to dominate the skies. Distant warning by radar and coastwatchers proved decisive in giving the slowly climbing Wildcats time to ascend over their opponents. Even so, much of the U.S. Navy's success depended on deflection shooting, particularly in defensive countermoves after the Zeros made their firing passes and pulled out ahead. Their stoutly protected Wildcats kept their pilots alive until they could score and brought them back home again.

By all accounts the 1942 combats proved to be quite exceptional for the U.S. Navy's fighting squadrons. Later in the war other units ran up far more impressive totals of enemy planes destroyed, but the newcomers soared in Vought F4U Corsairs or Grumman F6F Hellcats. Unlike the Wildcats, these fighters greatly outperformed the Zero. To borrow a phrase from the Battle of Britain (which in so many aspects the Guadalcanal air battles resembled), America's "Few" of 1942 (the Marine, Navy, and AAF fighter pilots) withstood Japan's own precious "Few."

The quality of Japanese naval pilots who fought in 1942 differed markedly from the vast majority encountered later in the war. During the crucial battles of 1942, Coral Sea, Midway, and the Guadalcanal Campaign, the U.S. Navy's fighter pilots faced the best aviators the Imperial Navy would ever wield. Land- and carrier-based operations in the Southeast Area (including New Guinea) between 7 August and 15 November 1942 cost the Imperial Navy 119 fighter pilots either killed or taken prisoner. In the attacks directed against Guadalcanal between those dates the Japanese fighter squadrons claimed 392 American aircraft (almost all Grummans) at the cost of 87 Zeros (66 pilots). At the same time, during operations afloat in the two carrier battles and against snoopers Zero pilots claimed 90 American planes for 19 *Reisen* (17 pilots killed).

Due in no little measure to the severe losses inflicted during the Guadalcanal Campaign by Marine, Navy, and USAAF fighter pilots, the number of experienced Japanese pilots declined greatly. Replacements proved to be inadequately trained, and the worsening war situation forced the Japanese to commit masses of green pilots to battle with disastrous results. By mid-1943 most of those thrown into combat were little more than students with minimum flight training. After the defeats in the Marianas and the Philippines, Kamikaze tactics became the Imperial Naval Air Force's only alternative to surrender.

By contrast, so many well-trained U.S. Navy pilots became available in 1943 that during 1944 pilot training had to be cut way back. The amount of time allocated for U.S. naval flight training also increased substantially. In February 1942 the Bureau of Aeronautics lengthened the training period from seven to over eleven months. Thus more than a year would pass from commencement of training to the new pilot's first operational posting. In 1942 some U.S. carrier aviators had entered combat units after serving as few as nine or ten months in the Navy. That would never happen again. In January 1943, BuAer added two months of "War Training Service" to help season the masses of aviation cadets. By the end of the war, fighter pilots received up to *two years* of training before joining their first combat squadrons.

In terms of carrier aviation alone, the improved strategic situation in the South Pacific allowed the recently created carrier air groups on the newly arrived *Essex*-class CVs and the smaller *Independence*-class CVLs to work up gradually for battle. CinCPac eased them into combat with raids on Marcus (31 August 1943), Tarawa (19 September), and Wake (5 October). By contrast, the Japanese carrier air groups had enjoyed no such recess. Repeatedly committed to land bases, these elite squadrons played a prominent role in the unsuccessful April 1943 I-Gō air offensive against Guadalcanal and other actions that summer. In addition, constant losses inflicted on the land-based groups forced the transfer of veteran carrier pilots to bolster their ranks. Ultimately Japanese carrier aviation never recovered from the casualties suffered in 1942.

As in the first six months of the war, the Guadalcanal Campaign demonstrated the effectiveness of U.S. naval fighter doctrine, particularly deflection shooting and team tactics. The hasty mounting of the invasion prevented much opportunity for the squadrons to absorb combat lessons from the early battles, particularly when most of the veteran pilots headed stateside. Fortunately, the system required no major revamping. Perhaps the weakest aspect was fighter direction, due to inexperience and the limitations of the equipment. Based on the lessons learned at Guadalcanal, fighter direction improved dramatically in 1943. The "angel on the yardarm," as former FDO Cdr. John Monsarrat dubbed fleet radar, proved as vital as the new fighters in protecting the new fast carrier task forces. Nearly as important, the careful organization and intricate timing required to control the hundreds of aircraft embarked on the carriers originated from such endeavors as Rear Admiral Noyes' Guadalcanal invasion air support OpPlan 2-42 (4 August 1942). This pioneering effort became the prototype for the highly integrated carrier task forces that supported the many Pacific invasions that followed.

Also a part of the legacy of Guadalcanal was the sprinkling among the new fighting squadrons and in the training command of (in the words of VF-17's former CO Capt. Tom Blackburn) the "blooded veterans" of 1942. Those who were ensigns or jaygees at Guadalcanal soon found themselves leading flights of rookies. They helped spread the word, and the best among them became indispensable to their skippers and greatly enhanced the combat effectiveness of their new units.[6] Twenty-five-year-old Guadalcanal hands perished before the end of the war, either in combat or accidents. Almost immediately after the campaign the more senior leaders had fleeted up out of the squadrons for other duties, and it took time for the more junior officers to work their way into command. However, by March 1945 Guadalcanal veterans led no fewer than five of TF-58's seventeen VF squadrons off Okinawa: Lt. Cdr. Edward Hessel's VF-82 on the *Bennington* (CV-20), Lt. Cdr. Macgregor Kilpatrick's VF-5 (*Franklin* [CV-13]), Cdr. James Southerland's VF-83 *(Essex)*, Lt. Cdr. Walter Clarke's VF-10 (*Intrepid*), and Cdr. Carl Rooney, CAG-46 and CO, VF-46, on the *Independence*.

A great deal of what Jimmy Flatley wrote in February 1943 as a farewell to his Grim Reapers applies equally well to all of the U.S. Navy fighter pilots who fought during the first year of the Pacific War:

> I want you to know that I take my leave with deep regret. No squadron commander, anywhere, has ever had a gang like you serving with him. I'm so darn proud and fond of every one of you that my heart's about to bust.
> Take care of yourselves. Stick together and don't forget to respect that airplane . . .

One parting word of advice. There is a definite tendency on the part of every one of you to throw caution to the winds every time you meet the enemy. We've been lucky so far. But it's dumb. We've spent hours and hours on tactics, designed not only to destroy, but also to protect ourselves. Keep that thought foremost in your minds. Rip 'em up and down, but do it smartly.[7]

In all of World War II no one did their job more "smartly" than the fighter pilots of the United States Navy.

APPENDIX 1

The Significance of the Captured Zero

During the first month of the Pacific War, the Mitsubishi Type 0 Carrier Fighter, Model 21, came as a distinct and disastrous surprise to the Allies. Greatly outperforming its Allied antagonists, the Zero ensured Japanese air superiority from Pearl Harbor to Singapore. Despite some hints in prewar intelligence bulletins, relatively little was known about the seemingly ubiquitous wonder-fighter. It enjoyed fast speed, phenomenal climb, and strong armament. The U.S. Navy's own carrier fighters first encountered Zeros on 7 May 1942 at the Coral Sea and also fought them at Midway. On the whole the Navy VF pilots did well, mainly due to their tactics which emphasized the strong points of their Grumman F4F Wildcats.

By July 1942 Allied air intelligence believed two types of Zeros existed. The first, based mainly on encounters in the Far East, was the so-called Mitsubishi Zero fighter. Thought first to have appeared in 1940 over China, this mythical version featured an elliptical wing and a profile markedly different from the actual aircraft. An improved model, the "O1 Modification," supposedly entered service in 1941. The second, more modern version was the "Mitsubishi-Nagoya," or more commonly, the "Nagoya Zero Fighter," also called the "00" ("Zero-Zero") or "Zero-2." The term *Nagoya* derived from identification plates recovered from crashed aircraft and referred to "Mitsubishi Heavy Industries, Inc., Nagoya Aircraft Plant." Its profile closely resembled the actual Mitsubishi A6M2 Type 0 Model 21 carrier fighter.

On 10 July 1942 a VP-41 PBY commanded by Lt. William N. Thies noticed a small Japanese aircraft crashed on a marshy meadow on uninhabited Akutan Island 25 miles northeast of Dutch Harbor in the Aleutians. Subsequent examination revealed a Zero lying on its back in mud and water, with the pilot dead in the cockpit. A victim of AA during the 4 June raid on Dutch Harbor, PO1c Koga Tadayoshi from the *Ryūjō* had attempted a wheels-down landing, but sheered off his landing gear and died instantly when his plane turned over in the muck. His teammates circling overhead had decided not to destroy the aircraft.[1]

On 14 July ComPatWing 4 announced to BuAer and CinCPac the exciting discovery of an "only slightly damaged" Zero, which "with care and some luck expect [to] salvage in flyable condition." Delighted, Washington radioed back on the 16th, "Ultimate assembly and flight test of airplane of highest importance." OpNav specifically desired to know whether the fighter sported any pilot armor. On 18 July Lt. Cdr. Paul Foley, Jr. (USNA 1929), VP-41's CO, described the new find as a "Nagoya Zero Fighter" manufactured in February 1942. It featured

Lt. Cdr. Eddie Sanders taxis the captured Zero fighter at San Diego, September 1942.
(NA 80-G-12777)

no armor or self-sealing fuel tanks. In addition, its integral wing construction
precluded rail shipment to an East Coast facility. Foley followed on 22 July with
a detailed report to OpNav. In the meantime, the aircraft was brought to Dutch
Harbor and on 12 August reached NAS San Diego, where reconditioning was
expected to take about six weeks.[2]

On 22 August BuAer assigned the Zero project to Cdr. Frederick M. Trapnell
(USNA 1923), chief of the flight test section at NAS Anacostia, and his deputy,
Lt. Cdr. Eddie R. Sanders (USNA 1930), who arrived first in mid-September.
The assembly and repair section did a wonderful job preparing the captured
Zero. However, certain necessary modifications proved slightly detrimental to
the original performance.[3]

After a few familiarity hops, Sanders began formal flight tests on 26 September. By the 29th he drew up a preliminary assessment for Trapnell. Quite impressed with the Japanese machine, he felt that aside from the lack of protection,
it was a "carefully constructed and well equipped fighter." He added a "summary of pertinent points for F4F comparison," which he qualified as being based
on incomplete calibration. He found the Zero to be slower than the F4F-4 Wildcat by at least several knots (this would be much disputed by USN fighter pilots).
The Zero enjoyed a high rate of climb and maneuverability, particularly at lower
speeds, but its ailerons greatly stiffened as speed increased. At 200 knots its rate
of roll was slightly less than the F4F, while above 250 knots Sanders found fast
rolls to be "physically impossible." Another detrimental factor involved quick
pushovers into Negative G, which caused the Zero's engine to cut out momentarily. All in all, Sanders believed the F4F could accelerate more quickly in a
dive and roll or twist at high speed so that the Zero could not readily follow.[4]

Sanders's important memo went to RAdm. Charles A. Pownall, ComFAir-West, who forwarded it on 1 October to ComAirPac in Hawaii. Lt. Cdr. James Flatley, CO of VF-10, undoubtedly studied it before the *Enterprise* sailed on 15 October from Pearl Harbor. Copies reached the South Pacific by airmail, where in early November after leaving CACTUS, Lt. Cdr. Roy Simpler and some of the other VF-5 pilots discovered the memo.

On 31 October Trapnell forwarded to BuAer the formal preliminary report which described flight tests between the captured Zero and the F4F-4 Wildcat and the F4U-1 Corsair. In general the results echoed Sanders's memo, but noted that the Zero was indeed faster than the F4F-4 in speed and climb rate between 1,000 and 19,000 feet. Success by F4Fs against the Zero, Trapnell concluded, depended on "mutual support, internal protection, pullouts, or turns at high speed."[5] On 4 November the Navy's Aviation Intelligence Branch issued a comprehensive report based on his findings, and the AAF soon followed suit with evaluations of the Zero against the P-39D, P-40F, P-38F, and P-51 Mustang.

The capture and flight tests of Koga's Zero is usually described as a tremendous coup for the Allies in that it revealed the secrets of that mysterious aircraft and led directly to its downfall. According to this viewpoint, only then did Allied pilots learn how to deal with their nimble opponents. The Japanese could not agree more. The brilliant aviation strategist Genda Minoru believed that at Guadalcanal, "Japan commanded complete air supremacy as long as our Zeros were in the air over the area."[6] Okumiya Masatake considered the capture of Koga's Zero to be "no less serious" than the "debacle at Midway." He thought it "did much to hasten" Japan's final defeat.[7] It was rumored that the design of the Grumman F6F Hellcat benefited directly from this inside information, but that was not the case.

Yet those naval pilots who fought the Zero at Coral Sea, Midway, and Guadalcanal without the benefit of the test reports would beg to differ with the contention that it took the dissection of Koga's Zero to create the tactics that beat that fabled airplane. To them the Zero did not long remain a mystery plane. Word quickly circulated among the combat pilots as to its particular attributes. Indeed on 6 October while testing the Zero, Trapnell made a highly revealing statement: "The general impression of the airplane is exactly as originally created by intelligence—including the performance."[8]

In the spring of 1942, even before they fought the Zero, USN VF pilots profited from the experiences of those brave souls who had. They knew not to dogfight the nimble Mitsubishi product. As demonstrated in *The First Team,* the U.S. Navy's deflection shooting and mutual support tactics already provided the foundation for success, despite the inferior performance of the rugged F4F-4 Wildcat. The Navy pilots even deduced the Zero's main drawback, loss of control at high speed. On 8 May in the Coral Sea battle, Lt. (jg) Richard G. Crommelin of VF-42 shook Zeros on his tail by using sharp turns during high-speed dives.[9] Word soon got around that Zeros would not follow F4Fs in corkscrew dives (VF-5 at Eastern Solomons, 24 August 1942). Thus before ever learning of Koga's Zero, the Navy and Marine fighter pilots knew relatively well what they could and could not do against Zeros. They set up their attacks carefully, fought under favorable conditions whenever possible, and took full advantage of enemy mistakes.

Actual combat conditions and maneuvers used by both F4Fs and Zeros proved much different than the understandably artificial conditions under which the evaluations were made in the States. The test pilots did not utilize typical

Japanese tactics. At this stage of the war the Japanese generally did not dogfight or chase tails. Rather they executed steep firing passes and climbed away in hit-and-run fashion. Thus extended dives in tail chases were not common. Roy Simpler commented: "Incidentally, if you had a Zero any place around, the safest place for him was right on your tail. That back armor would hold up beautifully; they could shoot at you all day long back there—and that's not an exaggeration!"[10]

Fighting Zeros close in, the CACTUS Marines raised the so-called pincushion tactics to a fine art. They felt the F4F's qualities rendered these extraordinary tactics "quite practicable." In October 1942 Lt. Col. Harold W. ("Joe") Bauer, Maj. Leonard K. Davis, and Capt. Joseph J. Foss stressed how much more rugged and better armed was the F4F in comparison to a Zero, in their words "a fertile target." When under attack the key for the F4F was to scissor and turn into the incoming Japanese for a head-on pass. If a Zero jumped his tail, the F4F pilot was to "cut the throttle, slip, skid, and otherwise kick it around until the Zero overruns, then 'pour the coal on' and 'let 'em have it.'" Under no circumstances was the F4F to turn tail and run. That was the recipe for disaster.[11]

After fighting what he thought were "Nagoya" Zeros at Santa Cruz and over Guadalcanal, Jim Flatley for one incorrectly considered them to be different airplanes than the older "Mitsubishi" Zeros he battled in May at the Coral Sea. The "Nagoyas" showed "poor aileron control at high speeds."[12] Of course they were the same A6M2 Type 0 Model 21s. The key might be Flatley's further observation: "The ability of the enemy VF pilots encountered in the vicinity of Guadalcanal is considered to be much inferior to the pilots encountered earlier in the war."[13]

That decline in Japanese pilot skill and experience as a result of attrition proved far more detrimental to Imperial Japan than the so-called secrets revealed by Koga's Zero. Where the captured Zero proved most useful was in evaluation against new fighters which had not yet seen combat against it, to assist their pilots in understanding its performance and design philosophy.

APPENDIX 2

List of U.S. Navy Fighter Pilots

Pilots in Fighting Squadrons Five, Six, Seventy-one, Seventy-two, and Ten, Embarked Operationally, 7 August–15 November 1942

Name	Age[a]	Rank[b]		Squadrons	Enlisted
1) Achten, Julius A.	27	Mach.	USN	VF-6,5,6	1935
2) Allard, Clayton	25	Mach.	USN	VF-6	1936
3) Altemus, John P.	26	Lt. (jg)	USNR	VF-5	1941
4) Axelrod, Millard W.	26	Ens.	USNR	VF-10	1941
5) Barnes, Doyle C.	30	Ens.	USN	VF-6	1933
6) Barnes, Gordon F.	23	Ens.	USNR	VF-10	1941
7) Bass, Horace A., Jr.	26	Ens.	USNR	VF-5	1941
8) Bauer, Louis H.	30	Lt.	USN	VF-6	1931
9) Billo, James D.	22	Lt. (jg)	USNR	VF-10	1941
10) Blair, Foster J.	22	Lt. (jg)	USNR	VF-5	1941
11) Blair, William K.	26	Lt. (jg)	USNR	VF-10	1941
12) Bliss, Louis K.	26	Lt.	USN	VF-72	1934
13) Boren, Albert G.	24	Ens.	USNR	VF-10	1941
14) Bower, John C., Jr.	26	Lt.	USN	VF-72	1938
15) Brewer, Charles E.	29	Gun.	USN	VF-6,5,6	1934
16) Bright, Mark K.	23	Lt. (jg)	USNR	VF-5	1941
17) Brittain, Alexander F., Jr.	23	Lt. (jg)	USNR	VF-71	1941
18) Brooks, George W.	29	Ens.	USN	VF-6	1935
19) Brown, Herbert S., Jr.	24	Lt.	USN	VF-5	1938
20) Brown, Norman V.	26	Ens.	USNR	VF-71	1941
21) Caldwell, James E., Jr.	22	Ens.	USNR	VF-10	1941
22) Capowski, Thaddeus J.	25	Lt. (jg)	USNR	VF-71	1941
23) Carey, Henry A., Jr.	22	Lt. (jg)	USNR	VF-72,10	1941
24) Clarke, Walter E.	27	Lt.	USNR	VF-5	1939
25) Coalson, Edward B.	22	Ens.	USNR	VF-10	1941
26) Conklin, Raymond F.	26	Lt. (jg)	USNR	VF-71	1941
27) Cook, Earl W.	26	Ens.	USNR	VF-6	1941
28) Cook, Morrill I., Jr.	23	Lt. (jg)	USNR	VF-72	1941
29) Crews, Howard W.	28	Lt.	USN	VF-5	1937
30) Currie, Benjamin F.	22	Lt. (jg)	USNR	VF-5	1941
31) Dalton, Roy B.	25	Ens.	USNR	VF-72	1941
32) Daly, Joseph R.	24	Lt. (jg)	USNR	VF-5	1941
33) Davis, Gerald V.	24	Ens.	USNR	VF-10	1941
34) Davy, Charles D.	23	Lt. (jg)	USNR	VF-5	1941
35) de Poix, Vincent P.	26	Lt.	USN	VF-6	1935
36) Dibb, Robert A. M.	22	Lt. (jg)	USNR	VF-6,5,6	1941
37) Dietrich, Alfred E.	23	Lt. (jg)	USNR	VF-72,10	1941
38) Disque, Robert M.	24	Lt. (jg)	USNR	VF-6	1941
39) Dowden, James H.	26	Ens.	USNR	VF-10	1941
40) Dufilho, Marion W.	26	Lt.	USN	VF-5	1934
41) Eckhardt, John C., Jr.	26	Lt.	USN	VF-10	1934
42) Edwards, Thomas E., Jr.	27	Lt.	USN	VF-10	1933
43) Eichenberger, Charles E.	22	Ens.	USNR	VF-5	1941
44) Elin, Michael	23	Lt. (jg)	USNR	VF-71	1940
45) Emerson, Alberto C.	33	Lt.	USN	VF-72	1931
46) Fairbanks, Henry A.	21	Lt. (jg)	USNR	VF-72,10	1941
47) Faulkner, Frederick L.	28	Lt.	USNR	VF-10	1937
48) Feightner, Edward L.	22	Ens.	USNR	VF-10	1941
49) Firebaugh, Gordon E.	31	Lt. (jg)	USN	VF-6	1929

	Decorations[c] 8/42–11/42	Confirmed Victories			Remarks
		To 6/42	8/42–11/42	Total[d]	
1)	—	0.5	1.0	1.5	NAP; Ret. 1964 as Lt.
2)	—	0.0	0.0	0.0	NAP; K. 3 Aug. 42
3)	—	—	0.0	1.0	Lt. Cdr. USNR
4)	—	—	0.0	0.0	Lt. Cdr. USNR
5)	—	2.0	1.0	3.0	NAP; MIA 24 Aug. 42
6)	—	—	0.0	0.0	MIA 26 Oct. 42
7)	—	1.0	0.0	1.0	MIA 24 Aug. 42
8)	NC	0.0	1.0	1.25	USNA 1935; Ret. 1965 as Capt.
9)	AM	—	1.0	3.25	Lt. Cdr. USNR
10)	SS	—	2.0	2.333	Lt. Cdr. USNR
11)	AM	—	0.0	5.0	Ret. 1957 as Cdr.
12)	AM	—	2.0	2.0	USNA 1938; Ret. 1959 as Capt.
13)	—	—	0.0	0.0	Ret. 1968 as Cdr.
14)	SS	—	0.0	0.0	MIA 26 Oct. 42
15)	DFC	0.0	3.0	3.0	NAP; Ret. 1959 as Capt.
16)	NC, DFC, 2 AM	0.0	4.0	9.0	KIA 17 June 1944 in VF-16
17)	—	—	0.0	1.5	D. 12 Apr. 44
18)	DFC	—	2.0	2.25	NAP; Ret. 1956 as Capt.
19)	—	—	0.0	0.0	Ret. 1959 as Capt.
20)	AM	—	2.0	2.0	Ret. 1958 as Lt. Cdr.
21)	AM	—	0.0	0.0	MIA 26 Oct. 42
22)	—	—	0.0	0.0	Ret. 1949 as Lt. Cdr.
23)	DFC, AM	0.0	3.0	7.0	Lt. Cdr. USNR
24)	2 DFC, 3 AM	—	4.0	7.0	Ret. 1959 as Capt.
25)	—	—	1.25	1.25	K. 18 Apr. 43 in VF-10
26)	NC, AM	—	0.0	0.0	K. 24 Jan. 52 in VF-24
27)	—	—	0.0	0.0	MIA 7 Aug. 42
28)	SS	2.0	0.0	2.0	MIA 26 Oct. 42
29)	SS, DFC, AM	—	2.0	2.0	Ret. 1963 as Capt.
30)	2 AM	—	2.0	2.0	Lt. Cdr. USNR
31)	2 DFC	—	0.5	0.5	K. 4 Jan. 58 as Cdr.
32)	NC	0.0	2.0	2.0	Lt. Cdr. USNR
33)	—	—	0.0	0.0	MIA 26 Oct. 42
34)	—	—	0.0	0.0	Ret. 1955 as Lt. Cdr.
35)	AM	—	1.0	1.0	USNA 1939; Ret. 1974 as VAdm.
36)	DFC	1.0	2.0	7.0	K. 29 Aug. 44
37)	AM	0.0	1.0	1.333	Ret. 1956 as Lt. Cdr.
38)	DFC	—	3.0	3.0	Ret. 1968 as Cdr.
39)	—	—	0.0	0.0	Lt. Cdr. USNR
40)	NC, DFC	0.0	2.0	2.0	USNA 1938; MIA 24 Aug. 42
41)	—	—	1.0	1.0	USNA 1938; Ret. 1949 as Cdr.
42)	SS	0.0	1.0	1.0	USNA 1937; K. 30 Jan. 43 in VF-10
43)	AM	—	1.0	1.0	KIA 12 Sept. 42
44)	—	—	0.0	0.0	Ret. 1962 as Lt. Cdr.
45)	DFC, AM	—	2.333	2.333	MIA 12 Feb. 43 in VF-72
46)	2 AM	0.0	2.0	3.0	Lt. Cdr. USNR
47)	—	0.0	0.0	0.0	Ret. 1959 as Capt.
48)	—	—	1.0	9.0	Ret. 1974 as RAdm.
49)	DFC	—	3.0	2.0	NAP; Ret. 1957 as Capt.

Name	Age[a]	Rank[b]		Squadrons	Enlisted
50) Flatley, James H., Jr.	36	Lt. Cdr.	USN	VF-10	1925
51) Ford, Warren W.	26	Lt.	USN	VF-72,10	1933
52) Formanek, George, Jr.	23	Lt. (jg)	USNR	VF-72	1940
53) Forrer, Samuel W.	25	Lt. (jg)	USNR	VF-71	1941
54) Franklin, John R.	23	Lt. (jg)	USNR	VF-72	1941
55) Freeman, David B., Jr.	24	Lt. (jg)	USNR	VF-72,10	1941
56) Fulton, Lyman J.	20	Ens.	USNR	VF-10	1941
57) Gallagher, Thomas J., Jr.	22	Lt. (jg)	USNR	VF-72	1941
58) Gates, Clark H.	24	Lt. (jg)	USNR	VF-71	1941
59) Gay, Theodore S., Jr.	34	Lt. (jg)	USN	VF-6	1926
60) Gordon, Donald	22	Ens.	USNR	VF-10	1941
61) Gray, Richard	29	Lt.	USN	VF-5	1932
62) Green, Frank O.	24	Lt.	USNR	VF-5	1939
63) Grimmell, Howard L., Jr.	24	Lt. (jg)	USNR	VF-6,5	1940
64) Gunsolus, Roy M.	21	Lt. (jg)	USNR	VF-5	1941
65) Halford, James A., Jr.	23	Lt. (jg)	USNR	VF-6,5	1941
66) Hall, William M.	22	Lt. (jg)	USNR	VF-71	1941
67) Hamilton, Fred C.	25	Lt. (jg)	USNR	VF-71	1940
68) Harman, Walter R.	22	Ens.	USNR	VF-10	1941
69) Harmer, Richard E.	30	Lt.	USN	VF-5	1931
70) Harris, Leroy E.	27	Lt.	USN	VF-10	1935
71) Hartmann, Henry E.	24	Lt. (jg)	USNR	VF-6	1941
72) Haynes, Leon W.	28	Lt. (jg)	USNR	VF-5	1941
73) Hessel, Edward W.	29	Lt.	USN	VF-72	1933
74) Holland, Robert E., Jr.	27	Lt. (jg)	USNR	VF-72,10	1941
75) Holt, William M.	24	Lt. (jg)	USNR	VF-5	1940
76) Hughes, Richard Z.	23	Lt. (jg)	USNR	VF-72,10	1941
77) Huss, Frederick L.	21	Lt. (jg)	USNR	VF-71	1941
78) Innis, Donald A.	26	Lt. (jg)	USNR	VF-5	1941
79) Jennings, Robert H., Jr.	21	Lt. (jg)	USNR	VF-72	1941
80) Jensen, Hayden M.	31	Lt.	USN	VF-5	1938
81) Johnson, Douglas M.	22	Lt. (jg)	USNR	VF-6	1941
82) Johnson, Thomas C.	30	Lt.	USNR	VF-72	1938
83) Jorgensen, John B.	22	Lt. (jg)	USNR	VF-71	1941
84) Kane, William R.	31	Lt. Cdr.	USN	VF-10	1929
85) Kanze, Robert F.	26	AP1c	USN	VF-10	1936
86) Kenton, Roland H.	23	Lt. (jg)	USNR	VF-71,5	1941
87) Kiekhoefer, Kenneth C.	22	Lt. (jg)	USNR	VF-72	1940
88) Kilpatrick, Macgregor	26	Lt.	USN	VF-10	1935
89) Kleinman, John M.	22	Lt. (jg)	USNR	VF-5	1941
90) Kleinmann, Mortimer V., Jr.	22	Lt. (jg)	USNR	VF-5	1941
91) Kona, Steve G.	25	Ens.	USNR	VF-10	1941
92) Landry, Dupont P.	24	Lt. (jg)	USNR	VF-72	1941
93) Lankau, Earl H.	26	Lt. (jg)	USNR	VF-71	1940
94) Laskey, Norman J.	26	Lt. (jg)	USNR	VF-71	1941
95) Leder, William H.	24	Ens.	USNR	VF-10	1941
96) Leonard, George S.	28	Lt.	USNR	VF-71	1938
97) Leppla, John A.	26	Lt. (jg)	USNR	VF-10	1940
98) Lindsey, Charles W.	23	Lt. (jg)	USNR	VF-6	1941
99) Loesch, Richards L., Jr.	24	Lt. (jg)	USNR	VF-6,5	1941

	Decorations[c] 8/42–11/42	Confirmed Victories			Remarks
		To 6/42	8/42–11/42	Total[d]	
50)	DFC	2.0	2.0	4.0	USNA 1929; Ret. 1958 as VAdm.
51)	AM	1.0	1.0	2.0	USNA 1937; Ret. 1957 as RAdm.
52)	DFC, 2 AM	1.0	2.5	4.5	KIA 23 Apr. 44 in VF-30
53)	NC, AM	—	0.0	2.5	Ret. 1962 as Capt.
54)	AM	—	0.0	0.0	MIA 26 Oct. 42
55)	2 AM	0.0	1.0	1.0	Ret. 1965 as Capt.
56)	AM	—	0.0	0.0	MIA 26 Oct. 42
57)	2 AM	—	1.0	1.0	Ret. 1970 as Capt.
58)	—	—	0.0	0.0	Ret. 1968 as Capt.
59)	2 AM	0.0	1.0	1.0	NAP; Ret. 1955 as Capt.
60)	2 AM	—	2.0	5.0	Ret. 1967 as Capt.
61)	2 AM	0.0	2.0	2.0	USNA 1936; Ret. 1960 as Cdr.
62)	DFC	—	2.0	2.0	Ret. 1960 as Cdr.
63)	DFC, AM	0.0	3.0	4.0	Ret. 1968 as Cdr.
64)	—	0.0	0.0	0.0	Ret. 1962 as Lt. Cdr.
65)	DFC, AM	0.5	3.0	3.5	Ret. 1959 as Cdr.
66)	NC	—	1.0	1.0	Ret. 1958 as Capt.
67)	AM	—	0.0	0.0	K. 19 June 45
68)	—	—	0.0	6.0	Ret. 1966 as Capt.
69)	DFC	—	1.0	3.0	USNA 1935; Ret. 1965 as Capt.
70)	AM	—	1.25	9.25	USNA 1939; Ret. 1966 as Capt.
71)	—	—	0.0	0.25	Lt. Cdr. USNR
72)	AM	0.5	1.0	1.5	Lt. Cdr. USNR
73)	—	—	1.333	3.333	USNA 1937; Ret. 1967 as Capt.
74)	AM	—	2.0	2.0	KIA 4 Apr. 44 in VC-36
75)	DFC	0.0	0.0	0.0	MIA 7 Aug. 42
76)	DFC, AM	0.0	1.5	3.5	Ret. 1962 as Cdr.
77)	—	—	0.0	0.0	K. 18 June 43 in VC-37
78)	—	—	0.0	0.0	K. 20 June 44
79)	DFC, AM	—	0.5	9.5	K. 30 June 54 as Lt. Cdr
80)	NC, DFC, 3 AM	—	7.0	7.0	D. 6 June 49 as Lt. Cdr.
81)	AM	—	1.0	1.0	Lt. Cdr. USNR
82)	SS	—	0.0	0.0	MIA 26 Oct. 42
83)	—	—	0.0	0.0	Ret. 1961 as Cdr.
84)	—	—	0.0	6.0	K. 6 Feb 57 as Capt.
85)	—	0.0	0.0	2.392	NAP; Ret. 1965 as Cdr.
86)	NC	—	0.0	0.0	Ret. 1973 as Capt.
87)	3 AM	—	1.0	1.0	Ret. 1962 as Lt. Cdr.
88)	DFC	—	1.0	4.5	USNA 1939; Ret. 1947 as Cdr.
89)	DFC	—	2.0	3.0	K. 18 Feb. 44
90)	SS	0.0	2.0	2.0	Lt. Cdr. USNR
91)	—	—	0.0	3.0	Ret. 1968 as Cdr.
92)	SS, AM	—	0.0	0.0	MIA 26 Oct. 42
93)	AM	—	0.0	1.0	Ret. 1967 as Cdr.
94)	AM	—	0.0	0.0	Lt. Cdr. USNR
95)	AM	—	1.25	2.25	K. 5 Sept. 43 in VF-10
96)	AM	—	0.0	0.0	Ret. 1960 as Cdr.
97)	—	4.0	1.0	5.0	MIA 26 Oct. 42
98)	AM	—	1.0	1.0	Lt. Cdr. USNR
99)	—	—	0.0	0.0	Lt. Cdr. USNR

Name	Age[a]	Rank[b]		Squadrons	Enlisted
100) Long, Merl Philip	24	Ens.	USNR	VF-10	1941
101) Lowndes, Andrew J. III	28	Lt. (jg)	USNR	VF-72	1941
102) Luebke, Frederick W.	25	Lt. (jg)	USNR	VF-71	1940
103) Mankin, Lee Paul	21	AP1c	USN	VF-6,5	1937
104) March, Harry A., Jr.	23	Lt. (jg)	USNR	VF-6,5	1941
105) Mayo, Robert A.	21	Lt. (jg)	USNR	VF-71	1941
106) McBrayer, John A., Jr.	27	Lt.	USNR	VF-71	1939
107) McClintock, Ernest L., Jr.	24	Lt. (jg)	USNR	VF-72	1941
108) McDonald, John B., Jr.	24	Lt. (jg)	USNR	VF-5	1941
109) Mead, Albert E.	22	Ens.	USNR	VF-10	1941
110) Mehlig, John L.	27	Lt.	USN	VF-6	1933
111) Merritt, Robert S.	22	Lt. (jg)	USNR	VF-72,10	1941
112) Meyer, Arnold S.	26	Lt. (jg)	USNR	VF-71	1941
113) Miller, Frank D.	26	Lt.	USN	VF-10	1935
114) Moffett, Charles S.	27	Lt.	USN	VF-71	1934
115) Montgomery, Bascomb	26	Lt. (jg)	USNR	VF-72	1941
116) Moran, William J.	23	Lt. (jg)	USNR	VF-72	1941
117) Morgan, George J., Jr.	28	Lt. (jg)	USNR	VF-5	1941
118) Morris, Van H.	23	Lt. (jg)	USNR	VF-72	1941
119) Myers, Raymond F.	26	Lt. (jg)	USNR	VF-71,5	1941
120) Nagle, Patrick L.	25	Ens.	USN	VF-6	1936
121) Nesbitt, Robert H.	25	AP1c	USN	VF-6,5	1934
122) O'Leary, Harold M.	21	AP1c	USN	VF-6	1939
123) Packard, Howard S.	24	AP1c	USN	VF-6,5,6,10	1937
124) Phillips, Claude R.	26	Lt.	USNR	VF-72	1939
125) Pollock, Albert D., Jr.	27	Lt.	USN	VF-10	1938
126) Presley, Wayne C.	26	Lt. (jg)	USNR	VF-5	1941
127) Price, Robert L.	23	Ens.	USNR	VF-5	1941
128) Purcell, Thomas M., Jr.	27	Lt. (jg)	USNR	VF-71	1941
129) Reding, Willis B.	22	Ens.	USNR	VF-10	1941
130) Reeves, Don G.	22	Lt. (jg)	USNR	VF-71	1941
131) Register, Francis R.	24	Lt. (jg)	USNR	VF-6,5	1941
132) Reid, Beverly W.	25	Mach.	USNR	VF-6	1935
133) Reiplinger, Frank J.	22	Lt. (jg)	USNR	VF-5	1941
134) Reiserer, Russell L.	22	Lt. (jg)	USNR	VF-10	1941
135) Rhodes, Raleigh E.	24	Ens.	USNR	VF-10	1941
136) Rhodes, Thomas W.	26	Rad. Elec.	USN	VF-6	1937
137) Richardson, David C.	28	Lt.	USN	VF-5	1932
138) Riise, Harold N.	27	Lt. (jg)	USNR	VF-71	1941
139) Roach, Melvin C.	24	Lt. (jg)	USNR	VF-5	1941
140) Roberts, William V., Jr.	24	Lt. (jg)	USNR	VF-72	1941
141) Rooney, Carl W.	31	Lt.	USN	VF-71,5	1930
142) Rouse, Wildon M.	22	Lt. (jg)	USNR	VF-6,5	1941
143) Ruehlow, Stanley E.	30	Lt.	USN	VF-10	1931
144) Runyon, Donald E.	29	Ens.	USN	VF-6	1934
145) Russell, Hawley	29	Lt.	USN	VF-71	1935
146) Rutherford, Harold E.	37	Lt. (jg)	USN	VF-6	1924
147) Rynd, Robert W.	27	Lt.	USN	VF-72	1934
148) Sanchez, Henry G.	34	Lt. Cdr.	USN	VF-72	1926
149) Senft, David V.	22	Lt. (jg)	USNR	VF-71	1941

	Decorations[c] 8/42–11/42	Confirmed Victories			Remarks
		To 6/42	8/42–11/42	Total[d]	
100)	—	—	0.0	3.0	Ret. 1954 as Lt. Cdr.
101)	—	—	0.0	0.0	K. 12 Jan. 43 in VF-72
102)	—	—	0.0	0.0	Ret. 1960 as Cdr.
103)	2 DFC, AM	—	5.0	5.0	NAP; Ret. 1958 as Capt.
104)	—	—	2.0	4.0	D. 3 Feb. 46 as Lt. Cdr.
105)	—	—	0.0	0.0	Lt. Cdr. USNR
106)	DFC, AM	—	1.0	1.0	Lt. Cdr. USNR
107)	—	—	0.0	0.0	Ret. 1963 as Cdr.
108)	DFC	—	2.0	2.0	Ret. 1944 as Lt.
109)	AM	—	1.0	1.0	POW; Lt. Cdr. USNR
110)	—	—	0.0	0.0	USNA 1937; KIA 21 Feb. 45
111)	AM	0.0	1.0	3.0	Ret. 1962 as Cdr.
112)	—	—	0.0	2.0	Ret. 1953 as Cdr.
113)	—	—	0.0	0.0	USNA 1939; MIA 25 Oct. 42
114)	—	—	0.0	0.0	USNA 1938; Ret. 1968 as Capt.
115)	—	—	0.0	3.0	Lt. Cdr. USNR
116)	—	—	0.5	0.5	Ret. 1975 as VAdm.
117)	—	—	1.0	1.0	MIA 2 Oct. 42
118)	—	0.0	0.0	0.0	Lt. Cdr. USNR
119)	—	—	1.0	1.0	Ret. 1968 as Cdr.
120)	—	0.0	0.0	0.0	NAP; MIA 7 Aug. 42
121)	—	—	0.0	0.0	NAP; Ret. 1964 as Lt.
122)	—	—	0.0	0.0	NAP; Lt. Cdr.
123)	DFC	0.0	2.0	2.0	NAP; Ret. 1957 as Cdr.
124)	AM	—	0.583	0.583	Ret. 1961 as Capt.
125)	DFC, AM	—	2.0	2.0	K. 7 Nov. 52 as Lt. Cdr.
126)	AM	0.333	1.0	3.333	MIA 16 Sept. 43 in VF-38
127)	DFC	—	0.0	0.0	MIA 7 Aug. 42
128)	—	—	0.0	4.0	Lt. Cdr. USNR
129)	AM	—	0.25	1.875	Ret. 1966 as Cdr.
130)	NC, AM	—	0.0	0.0	K. 25 Aug. 43 in VF-12
131)	2 DFC, 2 AM	—	6.0	6.0	K. 16 May 43 in VF-21
132)	—	2.0	0.0	2.0	NAP; MIA 24 Aug. 42
133)	—	—	0.0	0.0	Ret. 1962 as Cdr.
134)	AM	—	0.25	9.25	Ret. 1969 as Capt.
135)	AM	—	0.0	0.0	POW; Ret. 1961 as Cdr.
136)	2 AM	0.0	2.0	3.0	NAP; Ret. 1965 as Cdr.
137)	DFC	—	3.0	3.0	USNA 1936; Ret. 1972 as VAdm.
138)	2 AM	—	0.0	0.0	Lt. Cdr. USNR
139)	DFC	1.0	2.0	3.0	KIA 12 June 44 in VF-15
140)	SS, AM	—	0.0	0.0	MIA 26 Oct. 42
141)	DFC, AM	—	2.5	3.5	USNA 1934; Ret. 1961 as Capt.
142)	DFC, AM	—	3.0	3.0	MIA 21 Oct. 42
143)	—	0.0	2.0	2.0	USNA 1935; Ret. 1965 as Capt.
144)	NC, DFC	0.0	8.0	11.0	NAP; Ret. 1963 as Cdr.
145)	AM	—	0.0	4.0	Ret. 1961 as Capt.
146)	—	0.0	0.0	0.0	K. 12 Jan. 43 in VF-6
147)	—	—	1.583	1.583	USNA 1938; Ret. 1968 as Capt.
148)	LM, DFC, 2 AM	—	0.0	0.0	USNA 1930; Ret. 1959 as RAdm.
149)	—	—	0.0	0.0	Ret. 1963 as Cdr.

Name	Age[a]	Rank[b]		Squadrons	Enlisted
150) Seybert, James A., Jr.	24	Lt. (jg)	USNR	VF-71	1941
151) Shands, Courtney	36	Lt. Cdr.	USNR	VF-71	1923
152) Shoemaker, Joseph D.	22	Ens.	USNR	VF-6,5	1941
153) Simpler, Leroy C.	37	Lt. Cdr.	USN	VF-5	1925
154) Slagle, Lynn E., Jr.	21	Ens.	USNR	VF-10	1941
155) Smith, James C.	26	Lt. (jg)	USNR	VF-5	1940
156) Sorensen, Robert E.	25	Lt. (jg)	USNR	VF-72	1940
157) Southerland, James J., II	30	Lt.	USN	VF-5	1931
158) Souza, Philip E.	23	Ens.	USNR	VF-72,10	1941
159) Starkes, Carlton B.	27	Lt. (jg)	USNR	VF-5	1940
160) Steiger, Earl H.	23	Lt. (jg)	USNR	VF-71	1941
161) Stepanek, Edward G.	25	Lt.	USNR	VF-5	1939
162) Stephenson, William J., Jr.	24	AP1c	USN	VF-6	1940
163) Stover, Elisha T.	22	Lt. (jg)	USNR	VF-5	1940
164) Strickler, Robert L.	32	Lt. Cdr.	USN	VF-71	1928
165) Sumrall, Howell M.	30	Mach.	USN	VF-6,5,6	1934
166) Sutherland, John F.	27	Lt.	USNR	VF-72,10	1938
167) Tabberer, Charles A.	26	Lt. (jg)	USNR	VF-5	1939
168) Thrash, Millard C.	25	Lt. (jg)	USNR	VF-71	1941
169) Trimble, Richard B.	24	Lt. (jg)	USNR	VF-71	1941
170) Tucker, Charles W.	24	Lt. (jg)	USNR	VF-71,5	1940
171) Tumosa, Stanley W.	20	AP2c	USN	VF-6	1939
172) Vejtasa, Stanley W.	28	Lt.	USN	VF-10	1938
173) Voris, Roy M.	22	Lt. (jg)	USNR	VF-10	1941
174) Vorse, Albert O., Jr.	28	Lt.	USN	VF-6	1933
175) Wallace, Clark A.	27	AP1c	USN	VF-6	1932
176) Warden, William H.	24	Mach.	USN	VF-6	1936
177) Weimer, James O.	21	Ens.	USNR	VF-72	1941
178) Wesolowski, John M.	23	Lt. (jg)	USNR	VF-5	1941
179) Wickendoll, Maurice N.	24	Ens.	USNR	VF-10	1941
180) Wileman, William W.	25	Ens.	USNR	VF-6,5	1941
181) Wilkins, John C.	29	Capt.	USAAF	VF-72	1938
182) Witte, Roland R.	24	Ens.	USNR	VF-10	1941
183) Wrenn, George L.	27	Ens.	USNR	VF-72	1941
184) Wright, Spencer D.	29	Lt.	USN	VF-71	1938
185) Wright, Wilson G., III	26	Lt.	USN	VF-71	1935

	Decorations[c] 8/42–11/42	Confirmed Victories			Remarks
		To 6/42	8/42–11/42	Total[d]	
150)	—	—	0.0	1.0	Ret. 1973 as Capt.
151)	NC, AM	—	0.0	0.0	USNA 1927; Ret. 1961 as RAdm.
152)	—	—	1.0	1.0	KIA 29 Sept. 42
153)	NC, 2 DFC	—	1.0	1.0	USNA 1929; Ret. 1959 as RAdm.
154)	—	—	1.0	1.0	Lt. Cdr. USNR
155)	—	0.0	0.0	0.0	MIA 24 Aug. 42
156)	DFC	—	1.5	2.5	K. 1958 as Cdr.
157)	DFC	—	2.0	5.0	USNA 1936; K. 12 Oct. 49 as Cdr.
158)	2 AM	—	2.5	2.5	Ret. 1965 as Cdr.
159)	NC, DFC	0.0	5.0	5.0	Ret. 1962 as Cdr.
160)	—	—	0.0	0.0	KIA 13 July 43 in VC-13
161)	—	—	0.0	0.0	Ret. 1951 as Lt. Cdr.
162)	—	—	0.0	0.0	NAP; MIA 7 Aug. 42
163)	DFC, AM	0.0	4.0	4.5	MIA 17 Feb. 44 in VF-5
164)	—	—	0.0	0.0	USNA 1932; K. 9 Oct. 42
165)	AM	0.5	1.0	1.5	NAP; Ret. 1957 as Capt.
166)	DFC, 2 AM	0.0	3.0	3.0	Cdr. USNR
167)	DFC	—	0.0	0.0	MIA 7 Aug. 42
168)	DFC, 3 AM	—	0.5	0.5	K. 1954 as Lt. Cdr.
169)	—	—	0.0	0.0	Lt. Cdr. USNR
170)	AM	—	0.0	0.0	KIA 9 Oct. 42 in VF-5
171)	—	—	0.0	0.0	NAP; KIA 19 Mar. 45 in VF-5
172)	NC	1.0	7.25	8.25	Ret. 1970 as Capt.
173)	—	—	1.0	7.0	Ret. 1963 as Capt.
174)	DFC	2.0	3.0	11.5	USNA 1937; Ret. 1959 as RAdm.
175)	—	—	0.0	0.0	NAP; Ret. 1955 as Lt. Cdr.
176)	—	—	0.0	0.0	NAP; Ret. 1966 as Lt.
177)	DFC, 2 AM	—	0.333	0.333	Ret. 1966 as Cdr.
178)	DFC, 2 AM	—	5.0	7.0	Ret. 1963 as Cdr.
179)	AM	—	0.0	0.0	K. 6 Mar. 51 as Lt. Cdr.
180)	—	1.0	0.0	1.0	KIA 13 Sept. 42
181)	—	—	0.0	0.0	MIA 7 Nov. 43 in 20th FG
182)	DFC	—	1.25	3.25	Ret. 1962 as Lt. Cdr.
183)	NC, 2 AM	—	5.25	5.25	Ret. 1954 as Cdr.
184)	NC, AM	—	0.0	0.0	Ret. 1970 as Capt.
185)	AM	—	0.0	1.0	USNA 1939; Ret. 1960 as Cdr.

[a] Age as of August 1942
[b] Highest rank attained by 15 November 1942
[c] Decorations: NC = Navy Cross; SS = Silver Star; LM = Legion of Merit; DFC = Distinguished Flying Cross; AM = Air Medal (additional awards possible due to incomplete records)
[d] Total victories based on research by Frank Olynyk

APPENDIX 3

Bureau Numbers of Fighter Aircraft

Squadrons Embarked July–November 1942
1) Fighting Squadron Five
Cruise on the *Saratoga,* 7 July–2 September 1942

36 F4F-4s:	5050, 5121, 5125, 5127, 5129, 5133, 5137, 5141, 5154, 5163, 5185, 5190, 5191, 5192, 5195, 5196, 5198, 5199, 5200, 5201, 5202, 5205, 5207, 5233, 5240, 5241, 5242, 02014, 02017, 02044, 02066, 02068, 02072, 02078, 02080, 02081
1 F4F-7:	5263

Losses: 20 July: 5240 (Ens. R. M. Gunsolus)
  7 Aug.: 5137, 5154, 5192, 5202, 02072, 02080
  8 Aug.: 02044 (Ens. F. J. Blair)
  24 Aug.: 5133, 5190, 02066 (aerial combat), 02078 (Lt. R. E. Harmer) jettisoned
Received 25 Aug. from VF-6: 5045, 5051, 5052, 5054, 5055, 5056, 5067, 5070, 5073, 5075, 5084, 5114, 5180, 5183, 5234, 5259, 02125
To VF-71 (*Wasp*), 26 Aug.: 5114, 5183, 5259, 02125

Remaining on the *Saratoga,* 2–21 September (VF-5 Detachment)

9 F4F-4s:	5051, 5052, 5054, 5055, 5067, 5129, 5163, 5205, 5233
1 F4F-7:	5263

Ashore at Efate and Espiritu Santo, 2–11 September

28 F4F-4s:	5045, 5050, 5056, 5070, 5073, 5075, 5084, 5121, 5125, 5127, 5141, 5180, 5185, 5191, 5195, 5196, 5198, 5199, 5200, 5201, 5207, 5234, 5241, 5242, 02014, 02017, 02068, 02081

To VF-71 (*Wasp*), 5 Sept.: 5056, 5070, 5199, 02068

At Guadalcanal, 11 September–16 October

24 F4F-4s:	5045, 5050, 5073, 5075, 5084, 5121, 5125, 5127, 5141, 5180, 5185, 5191, 5195, 5196, 5198, 5200, 5201, 5207, 5234, 5241, 5242, 02014, 02017, 02081

Losses: 12 Sept.: 5234 (Ens. C. E. Eichenberger)
  13 Sept.: 5242 (Ens. D. A. Innis)
    5241 (Ens. W. W. Wileman)
    5185 (Lt. [jg] E. T. Stover)
  17 Sept.: 02014 (Ens. J. A. Halford)

29 Sept.: 5141 (Ens. J. D. Shoemaker)
2 Oct.: 5084 (Lt. [jg] G. J. Morgan)
3 Oct.: 5198 (Lt. [jg] F. J. Blair)
8 Oct.: 02017 (Lt. [jg] M. C. Roach)
5127 (Lt. [jg] F. J. Blair)
9 Oct.: 5191 (Lt. [jg] C. W. Tucker)
11 Oct.: 5125 (Lt. [jg] J. B. McDonald)
13 Oct.: 5050, 5073, 5196, 02081 to bombs and shells
14 Oct.: 5201, 5207 to shelling
15 Oct.: 5195 (Lt. [jg] W. M. Rouse)
5075 bombed

Transferred to 1st MAW, 16 Oct.: 5045, 5121, 5180, 5200

2) Fighting Squadron Six
Cruise on the USS *Enterprise,* 15 July–10 September
36 F4F-4s: 5045, 5049, 5051, 5052, 5054, 5055, 5056, 5063, 5067, 5068,
5070, 5071, 5073, 5075, 5077, 5082, 5084, 5092, 5114, 5126,
5149, 5166, 5179, 5180, 5183, 5193, 5222, 5224, 5228, 5234,
5235, 5236, 5243, 5259, 02062, 02083
1 F4F-7:   5265
Loss 15 July: 5149 (H. M. O'Leary, AP1c)
Received 15 July: 02125 (from MAG-23)
Losses: 3 Aug.: 5224 (Mach. C. Allard)
7 Aug.: 5068 (Mach. P. L. Nagle)
5071 (Ens. E. W. Cook)
5082 (W. J. Stephenson, AP1c)
5228 (Mach. J. A. Achten)
5235 (Mach. W. H. Warden)
5236 (Lt. [jg] G. E. Firebaugh)
24 Aug.: 5049 (Ens. D. C. Barnes)
5179 (Ens. R. L. Loesch) jettisoned
02083 (Mach. B. W. Reid)

Transferred to VF-5 (*Saratoga*), 24–25 August
17 F4F-4s: 5045, 5051, 5052, 5054, 5055, 5056, 5067, 5070, 5073, 5075,
5084, 5114, 5180, 5183, 5234, 5259, 02125
To VMO-251, 26 Aug.: 5265 (F4F-7)

Returned on the USS *Enterprise* to Pearl Harbor
9 F4F-4s: 5063, 5077, 5092, 5126, 5166, 5193, 5222, 5243, 02062

3) Fighting Squadron Seventy-one
Cruise on the USS *Wasp,* 30 June–3 September
30 F4F-4s: 4061, 4062, 4063, 4067, 4068, 4070, 4073, 4074, 4076, 5031,
5032, 5033, 5041, 5098, 5099, 5100, 5102, 5103, 5108, 5120,
5135, 5136, 5156, 02132, 02133, 02144, 02145, 02147, 02148,
02150
Losses: 7 Aug.: 4076 (Lt. W. G. Wright)
5103 (Lt. [jg] F. C. Hamilton)
02133 (Ens. T. J. Capowski)
August: 5031 (date and cause unknown)

Received from VF-5, 26 Aug: 5114, 5183, 5259, 02125
  5 Sept.: 5056, 5070, 5199, 02068
Left ashore at Tontouta, 8 Sept.: 4061, 4068

Cruise on the USS *Wasp*, 8–15 September
  32 F4F-4s: 4062, 4063, 4067, 4070, 4073, 4074, 5032, 5033, 5041, 5056,
               5070, 5098, 5099, 5100, 5102, 5108, 5114, 5120, 5135, 5136,
               5156, 5183, 5199, 5259, 02068, 02125, 02132, 02144, 02145,
               02147, 02148, 02150
Received from Espiritu Santo, 12 Sept.: 5176
Sent to CACTUS, 13 Sept.: 5100

Lost on the USS *Wasp*, 15 September
  24 F4F-4s: 4063, 4073, 4074, 5033, 5041, 5056, 5070, 5098, 5099, 5102,
               5108, 5114, 5135, 5136, 5156, 5176, 5183, 5199, 5259, 02068,
               02125, 02132, 02145, 02148

Transferred to the USS *Hornet*, 15 Sept. 1942, and subsequently sent to
Espiritu Santo:
  8 F4F-4s: 4062, 4067, 4070, 5032, 5120, 02144, 02147, 02150
Loss at Espiritu Santo, 9 Oct.: 5032 (Lt. Cdr. R. L. Strickler)

Transferred to MAG-14, 16 Oct. 1942:
  7 F4F-4s: 4062, 4067, 4070, 5120, 02144, 02147, 02150

4) Fighting Squadron Seventy-two
Cruise on the USS *Hornet*, 17 August–26 October
  37 F4F-4s: 5090, 5110, 5112, 5124, 5130, 5169, 5181, 5184, 5186, 5188,
               5197, 5208, 5209, 5210, 5211, 5212, 5213, 5214, 5215, 5226,
               5227, 5238, 5246, 5248, 5254, 02000, 02001, 02002, 02003,
               02004, 02006, 02012, 02045, 02058, 02065, 02067, 02069
  1 F4F-7:   5268
Transferred to VMO-251, 10 Sept.: 5268 (F4F-7)
Received from Espiritu Santo, 12 Sept.: 03455
Sank on the *Hornet*, 26 Oct.: 5112, 5248, 02004, 02006, 02058, 02065,
                          02067, 03455
Losses: 26 Oct.: 5130 (Lt. [jg] W. W. Roberts)
                 5181 (Lt. T. C. Johnson)
                 5188 (Lt. J. C. Bower)
                 5197 (Lt. [jg] J. R. Franklin)
                 5208 (Lt. [jg] D. P. Landry)
                 5209 (Lt. L. K. Bliss)
                 5210 (Lt. [jg] R. S. Merritt)
                 5215 (Lt. [jg] G. Formanek)
                 5226 (Lt. [jg] T. J. Gallagher)
                 5227 (Lt. [jg] M. I. Cook)
                 5246 (Ens P. E. Souza) jettisoned

Transferred to VF-10
  19 F4F-4s: 5090, 5110, 5124, 5169, 5184, 5186, 5211, 5212, 5213, 5214,
               5238, 5254, 02000, 02001, 02002, 02003, 02012, 02045, 02069

5) Fighting Squadron Ten
Cruise on the USS *Enterprise,* 16–31 October

    36 F4F-4s: 5043, 5063, 5077, 5078, 5079, 5092, 5105, 5107, 5126, 5138,
                            5139, 5144, 5147, 5148, 5153, 5168, 5171, 5175, 5177, 5193,
                            5194, 5203, 5204, 5229, 5243, 5245, 02040, 02042, 02102,
                            03417, 03421, 03429, 03432, 03509, 03517, 11611

       Losses: 25 Oct.: 5138 (Lt. [jg] W. K. Blair)
                      5204 (Lt. F. D. Miller)
            26 Oct.: 5043 (Ens S. Kona)
                      5078 (Ens. R. E. Rhodes)
                      5079 (Ens. J. E. Caldwell)
                      5107 (Ens. A. E. Mead)
                      5148 (Ens. M. P. Long)
                      5153 (Ens. L. Fulton)
                      5177 (Lt. Cdr. W. R. Kane)
                      5194 (Ens. G. V. Davis)
                      5245 (Ens. G. F. Barnes)
                      02040 (Lt. [jg] J. A. Leppla)
                      02102 (Lt. J. C. Eckhardt)
                      03432 (Lt. [jg] J. D. Billo)

     Received from VF-72 on 26 Oct.
       19 F4F-4s: 5090, 5110, 5124, 5169, 5184, 5186, 5211, 5212, 5213, 5214,
                            5238, 5254, 02000, 02001, 02002, 02003, 02012, 02045, 02069
       Losses: 30 Oct.: 5212 (strike for parts; later rebuilt)
              5 Nov.: 5171 (Ens. M. W. Axelrod)

     Cruise on the USS *Enterprise,* 11–16 November
       38 F4F-4s   (one of these left ashore at Tontouta): 5063, 5077, 5090,
                           5092, 5105, 5110, 5124, 5126, 5139, 5144, 5147, 5168, 5169,
                           5175, 5184, 5186, 5193, 5203, 5211, 5213, 5214, 5229, 5238,
                           5243, 5254, 02000, 02001, 02002, 02003, 02012, 02042, 02045,
                           02069, 03417, 03421, 03429, 03509, 11611
       15 F4F-4s   (left behind with VMF-121 on 15 Nov.): 5124, 5144, 5147,
                           5168, 5169, 5193, 5203, 5211, 5243, 5254, 02000, 02001,
                         02003, 03429, 03509
       Lost at Guadalcanal 13–14 Nov.: 5168, 5254
       23 F4F-4s   (remaining with VF-10): 5063, 5077, 5090, 5092, 5105, 5110,
                         5126, 5139, 5175, 5184, 5186, 5213, 5214, 5229, 5238, 02002,
                         02012, 02042, 02045, 02069, 03417, 03421, 11611

APPENDIX 4

Fighting Colors, Insignia, and Markings

During the summer and fall of 1942, the U.S. Navy's carrier squadrons retained the same basic drab utilitarian patterns of aircraft camouflage, insignia, and markings finally formalized in mid-May 1942. At that time the Navy removed the red ball in the center of the national insignia, as well as the colorful red and white striped rudders.

Given the primary mission of operating over water, camouflage schemes for carrier aircraft continued to utilize a deep blue gray on the upper surfaces and light gray on the lower surfaces. Sunlight and harsh conditions contributed to a rapid fading of the finish. The national insignia was a white five-pointed star inside a blue circle, which appeared on the upper and lower surfaces of both wings and both sides of the rear fuselage. The wing circles were generally 50 inches in diameter, but the size and placement of the fuselage insignia varied considerably. The smallest were used by VF-71, whose 20-inch circles set well aft on the fuselage were relics of the late 1941–early 1942 painting scheme applied at the Grumman factory. Other VF squadrons preferred fuselage circles about as large as those used on the wings. The tail of each carrier aircraft featured three specific pieces of information, generally in black letters and numerals one inch high, one inch wide, with a quarter-inch stroke. On the rudder was the model designation, which for that particular mark of Grumman Wildcat was "F4F-4." In line with the bureau number on the vertical fin was the aircraft's individual acceptance serial number or "bureau number." Placed just above the bureau number on the fin was the service designation "NAVY."

Beyond the fundamentals of camouflage and insignia, the carrier air groups and even squadrons differed in the manner in which they marked their planes. Unfortunately even less photographic evidence for naval fighter aircraft markings exists for the second half of 1942 than for the first, and some procedures must be surmised from later practices.

The greatest variation in markings concerned the individual aircraft identification (or "side") numbers within the squadrons. They could be either black or white numerals and were placed in various locations on the fuselage and wings. Some carrier squadrons combined the fuselage side numbers with the letter indicating the class of squadron (*F* for fighting, *B* for bombing, *S* for scouting, and *T* for torpedo). Thus F-12 would be the number 12 aircraft of the fighting squadron. Prewar regulations also added the squadron number ahead of the class letter (e.g., 5-F-12 for the number 12 aircraft of VF-5), but for security reasons all the

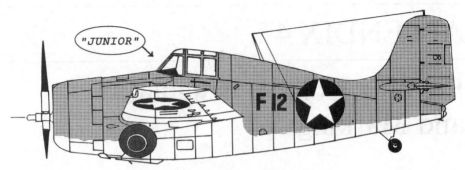

Grumman F4F-4 Wildcat, BuNo. 5192.

combat squadrons had deleted them by mid-June 1942. While at sea carrier fighter pilots usually did not have a permanently assigned aircraft but for each mission took whatever aircraft the flight officer allocated to them. Examination of numerous VF pilot flight logs show that they rarely flew the same aircraft from day to day.

Lacking squadron records that detailed marking procedures, it is only possible here to describe briefly the styles of markings used in the fighting squadrons of the five carrier air groups which fought at Guadalcanal.

Grumman F4F-4 Wildcat, BuNo. 5192, F-12 (Fighting Five) as flown on the afternoon of 7 August 1942 by Lt. James J. Southerland II, USN. Launched from the *Saratoga,* "Pug" Southerland shot down a Japanese land attack plane for the first aerial victory of the Guadalcanal Campaign. A few minutes later he had to bail out after an epic fight with four Zeros led by PO1c Sakai Saburō of the Tainan Air Group. The Navy had accepted this particular Wildcat on 1 April 1942, and VF-5 took delivery a week later. Listed as lost in action on 7 August, BuNo. 5192 was formally stricken from the Navy inventory on 30 September 1942.

Fighting Five's plane numbers were black numerals placed aft on the side of the fuselage, on the bottom of the engine cowling, and on the top of both wings just outboard of where they folded. Of the five VF squadrons, only VF-5 retained the F-designator for the class of squadron and put it next to the fuselage number. In a rare example (for the USN) of individuality, Lt. Cdr. Roy Simpler permitted the pilots to paint their nicknames in black letters beneath the cockpits. The mechanics likewise added in small letters the names of their own girlfriends on

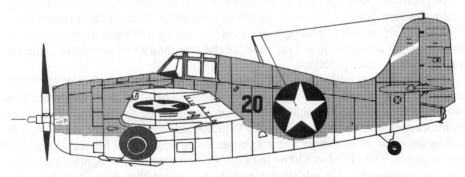

Grumman F4F-4 Wildcat, BuNo. 5075.

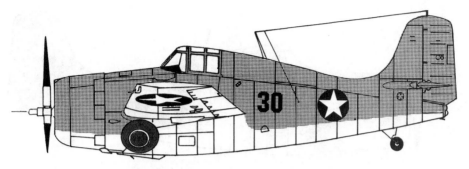

Grumman F4F-4 Wildcat, BuNo. 02148.

the engine cowlings. Therefore F-12, nominally assigned to Ens. Mortimer C. Kleinmann, Jr., featured his nickname "Junior" beneath the cockpit.

Grumman F4F-4 Wildcat, BuNo. 5075, F-20 (Fighting Six), as flown on 24 August 1942 by Mach. Donald E. Runyon, NAP, USN. Defending the *Enterprise* from Japanese attack during the Battle of the Eastern Solomons, Runyon shot down three dive bombers and a Zero fighter in this Wildcat. Delivered on 10 February 1942 from the Grumman factory on Long Island, BuNo. 5075 was assigned to VF-6 on 1 April and participated in the Tokyo Raid and in the Battle of Midway. On 25 August this F4F was transferred to VF-5 on the *Saratoga,* and in September it went to Guadalcanal. It is believed that VF-5 changed the number of this particular F4F to F-38 because the squadron already had an F-20. Bombed on 15 October at Henderson Field, BuNo. 5075 was formally stricken on 9 November 1942. Runyon, the U.S. Navy's top scoring fighter pilot during the second half of 1942, flew BuNo. 02125 (F-32) on 7 August (two VB destroyed) and BuNo. 02062 (F-36) on 8 August (one medium bomber and one Zero destroyed).

For its plane numbers, VF-6 applied black numerals on the fuselage and on the top of the wings. The presence of small white numbers on the side of the engine cowling is inferred from photos taken after November 1942 during VF-6's subsequent cruise on the *Saratoga*. Like other *Enterprise* squadrons, VF-6 also favored a stripe on the vertical tail to assist the LSOs in determining the aircraft's attitude during carrier landings.

Grumman F4F-4 Wildcat, BuNo. 02148, F-30 (Fighting Seventy-one), as flown the morning of 7 August 1942 by Lt. Cdr. Courtney Shands, USN. While leading the predawn strike against Tulagi, Shands strafed and burned four float-Zeros and one flying boat. VF-71 took delivery of BuNo. 02148 on 27 June at NAS San

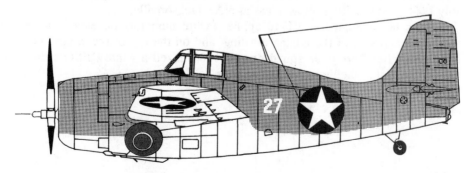

Grumman F4F-4 Wildcat, BuNo. 02069.

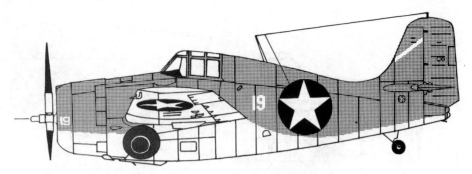

Grumman F4F-4 Wildcat, BuNo. 03417.

Diego, two weeks after its acceptance by the Navy. This F4F flew from the *Wasp* until she was lost on 15 September 1942 and was declared a strike on 30 November 1942.

Plane numbers in VF-71 were black and, in addition to those on the rear fuselage, they appeared at the bottom of the engine cowling and on the top of the wings.

Grumman F4F-4 Wildcat, BuNo. 02069, F-27 (Fighting Seventy-two), as flown on 26 October 1942 by Ens. George L. Wrenn, A-V(N). Operating from the *Hornet* during the Battle of Santa Cruz, Wrenn destroyed five torpedo planes in two separate Japanese attacks. After the *Hornet* was crippled, he took refuge on the damaged *Enterprise*. Accepted by the Navy on 22 May 1942, BuNo. 02069 reached Oahu in early June and on the 15th was issued to VF-8. Five days later it ended up in VF-72. On 30 October VF-10 took over BuNo. 02069 as a replacement for losses at Santa Cruz and kept it until May 1943. Returned to the United States for overhaul, BuNo. 02069 served in the operational training command until it was declared a strike on 31 August 1944.

Opting for white numerals, VF-72 placed its plane numbers on the side of the fuselage and on the leading edge of both wings.

Grumman F4F-4 Wildcat, BuNo. 03417, F-19 (Fighting Ten), as flown on 26 October 1942 by Lt. Stanley W. Vejtasa, USN. While defending the *Hornet* and *Enterprise* during the Battle of Santa Cruz, "Swede" Vejtasa shot down two dive bombers and five torpedo planes in two separate waves. After being delivered on 24 June 1942 to the Navy at NAS New York, BuNo. 03017 was issued on 18 August to VRF-10 in Hawaii. It served with the Grim Reapers until February 1943, when it was reassigned to MAG-11. Sent that September to the West Coast for overhaul, BuNo. 03017 ended up in the operational training command. On 29 July 1944, it was written off as a loss at NAS Jacksonville.

For its plane numbers, VF-10 applied white numerals on each side of the fuselage, each side of the engine cowling, and on the top of the wings. In common with other *Enterprise* squadrons, VF-10 utilized a white "LSO stripe" on the vertical tail to facilitate carrier landings.

APPENDIX 5

Fighting Five Nonflying Personnel

CACTUS, September–October 1942

Arrival Date	Name	Rank	Departure Date
10 September	Edward L. Bell	AMM1c	14 October
	Philip F. Belger	AMM3c	15 October
	Carl J. Duracher	AMM2c	15 October
	Anthony Jay	AMM3c	14 October
	John H. Lynch	ARM3c	15 October
	Edward E. Popovich	AOM1c	15 October
13 September	Joseph W. Buddi	AMM1c	16 October
	Francis B. Farris	AMM2c	16 October
	Tee R. Hadley	AMM2c	16 October
	Walter J. Harvey	AMM2c	16 October
	Marvin J. Henion	AMM3c	16 October
	Irvin J. Howe	PhM1c	16 October[a]
	William H. Johnston	AMM3c	16 October
	William H. McDonald	AM2c	16 October
	John W. Moore	AOM3c	16 October
	Lester S. Owenby	AMM3c	16 October
	Leonard J. Perkins	AMM1c	16 October
	Wesley R. Poole	AMM1c	16 October
	Glenn C. Poston	ACMM	16 October
	Donald H. Robb	AMM3c	16 October
	Charles E. Savo	AMM2c	16 October
	John Stefanou	AMM2c	16 October
	Burton R. Tabbert	AMM1c	14 October
	Robert G. Tyrell	AMM1c	16 October
	Theodore P. Winfield	AOM3c	16 October
	Otto F. Wrbas	AMM2c	16 October
16 September	William S. Robb	Lt., A-V(S)	16 October
19 September	Charlie A. Bagwell, Jr.	AMM3c	16 October[a] (KIA)
	Jimmie R. Becraft, Jr.	AOM3c	16 October
	Rider W. Berge	AOM2c	16 October[a] (KIA)
	Dennis V. Cornelius	AMM2c	16 October[a] (KIA)
	Archie J. Ferguson	AOM2c	16 October
	Joel A. Gabel	AMM2c	16 October[a]
	James D. Harvell	AOM1c	16 October[a]
	Joseph P. Lodolce	AMM2c	16 October[a]
	Ray F. Malone	ACOM	16 October[a] (WIA)
	Leo Nieme	PR3c	16 October[a] (WIA)
	Archie J. Parker	AOM3c	16 October[a] (KIA)
	Claude Roberts	ACMM	16 October

Arrival Date	Name	Rank	Departure Date
	William J. Wright	AMM3c	16 October[a] (KIA)
	John O. Yarwood	AOM3c	16 October[a]
24 September	Alexander F. Barbieri	Lt., A-V(S)	13 October
27 September	"T""H" Latimer	CEM	7 October (injured)

[a]On board the USS *McFarland* when bombed on 16 October.

Notes

1 THE NEW MISSION

1. RAdm. W. N. Leonard corresp.
2. Message CominCh to CinCPac 231255 of June 1942; King followed up the next day with more detailed plans: CominCh to CinCPac 242303 of June 1942.
3. CinCPac to ComSoPac 230017 of June 1942.
4. ComSWPac to JCS, CinCPac 080731 of June 1942.
5. VAdm. William Ward Smith, *Midway: Turning Point of the Pacific*, 61. In 1928 Fletcher attempted to join naval aviation, but failed the physical; see Dr. Clark G. Reynolds, *Admiral John H. Towers: The Struggle for Naval Air Supremacy*, 284. No friend of Fletcher, despite being classmates, Towers also complained that in the late 1930s Fletcher "persistently denigrated naval aviation," or perhaps Towers's vision of it. Often Towers could not tell them apart. Also on Fletcher see my two-part article "Frank Jack Fletcher Got a Bum Rap" in *Naval History* 6:2 (Summer 1992) 22–27, and 6:3 (Fall 1992) 22–28.
6. On the SBD and TBF, see two of Barrett Tillman's books: *The Dauntless Dive Bomber of World War II* and *Avenger at War*. In *Wings of the Navy,* Capt. Eric Brown, RN, has written a series of summaries of Allied carrier aircraft with marvelous comments based upon flying of all of them.
7. On the F4F-4, see my *The First Team*, 138–40, 441–47. One of the Corsair's test pilots, Boone T. Guyton, covers the long development of the F4U in *Whistling Death*.
8. Frank L. Greene, *History of the Grumman F4F "Wildcat,"* 15. See also National Archives, Record Group 313, ComCarPac, VF4F-7: ltr. ComCarPac (Admin) to BuAer, etc. F4F-7, Restrictions and Operational Information (19 May 1942) and ltr. Fleet Air Tactical Unit, Pacific Fleet, to Chief, BuAer, F4F-7 Photo Airplane (29 Sept. 1942).
9. The basic source is Capt. James M. Shoemaker's detailed report: ComCarPac (Admin) to ComCarPac, Resume of ComCarPac (Admin), Activities since 14 June 1942 (16 July 1942), in NA RG 313 ComNavAirPac, A16-3. See also Aircraft Status Reports in RG 313 ComCarPac, A4-1.
10. Details on U.S. carriers from Norman Friedman, *U.S. Aircraft Carriers: An Illustrated Design History*.
11. RAdm. Leroy C. Simpler corresp.
12. Capt. Howard W. Crews, "Flags, Umbrellas and Mumus," an unpublished vignette, in Crews papers.
13. For a recent account of the Med missions, see Christopher Shores and Brian Cull, *Malta: The Spitfire Year 1942*, 195–252.
14. War diaries, USS *Wasp* and VS-71, NHC.
15. Thomas F. Gates, "Track of the Tomcatters: A History of VF-31," part 1: "Fighting Six—The Shooting Stars, 1935–42," *The Hook* 12:3 (Fall 1984) 13–28; part 2: "Fighting Six at Guadalcanal," *The Hook* 12:4 (Winter 1984) 17–29.

16. Capt. Gordon E. Firebaugh, corresp. and phone interviews.
17. Cdr. Henry G. Sanchez to CNO (Aviation History Unit Op-33-J): Fighting Squadron 72, History of (22 July 1945).
18. CinCPac to ComCarPac 131445 of July 1942; also corresp. with VAdm. William J. Moran, who flew with Wilkins in VF-72.
19. Frederick Mears, *Carrier Combat*, 66.
20. Ens. John P. Altemus diary.
21. Aircraft Loss Report, 5 July 1942 (Ens. S. Hopfensperger), in RG 313, ComCar-Pac, VF4F-4/L11-1.
22. CinCPac to ComCarPac 030221 of July 1942.
23. ComCarPac (Admin) to CinCPac 062315 of July 1942.
24. RAdm. A. O. Vorse corresp.
25. Altemus diary.

2   SOUTH TO GUADALCANAL

1. CominCh to CinCPac 022100 of July 1942 series.
2. CinCPac Greybook, 743, Estimate for offensive for the capture and occupation of Tulagi and vicinity, 6 July 1942.
3. CinCPac to CTF-11 062229 of July 1942.
4. ComSoWesPacFor to CominCh, CinCPac 081012 of July 1942 series.
5. CominCh to ComSoPac 102100 of July 1942; CinCPac Greybook, 19 July 1942.
6. War diaries, TF-18 and *Wasp*.
7. VS-71 war diary.
8. CTF-18 to CinCPac 140510 of July 1942.
9. CTF-18 to CinCPac 182230, 210802 of July 1942; Capt. Roland H. Kenton corresp.
10. USS *Saratoga* war diary, which is the best source for TF-11 movements.
11. Clark G. Reynolds, *The Saga of Smokey Stover*, 33, a fine narrative with the text of Stover's diary.
12. Lt. (jg) Frank O. Green diary.
13. Ibid.; Altemus diary.
14. Green diary; ComSoPac to CinCPac 160612 of July 1942; CominCh to CinCPac 151300 of July 1942.
15. Foster J. Blair diary, 19 July 1942. VF-5 dubbed everyone with nicknames and painted them on their planes. Blair acquired the sobriquet "Crud" from a skin infection on his face suffered during the voyage from San Francisco to Pearl; Blair diary, 29 May 1942.
16. ComSoPac to TF-11, -16, -18, -44, etc. 170602 of July 1942, Summary of SoPac Op Plan 1-42.
17. Green diary; Altemus diary; Blair diary.
18. War diaries, TF-16 and USS *Enterprise*.
19. C. J. Dobson war diary, 8 July 1942, via Robert J. Cressman.
20. Capt. Henry A. Rowe, phone conv. On fighter direction in general see BuAer Interviews: Cdr. L. J. Dow (29 Sept. 1942); Lt. H. A. Rowe (2 March 1943). ltr. CominCh to CinCPac, Notes on Fighter Direction from Carriers (4 Aug. 1942); CSP 1291 Confidential Fighter Director Vocabulary, in Lt. Col. H. W. Bauer Papers, Marine Corps Historical Center (MCHC).
21. Mears, 87.
22. Because of the proximity to the date line, various sources date the conference to 25 or 26 July; this date is from the *Saratoga* deck log. For the background of the conference, see my "Frank Jack Fletcher Got a Bum Rap," part 2.
23. A. A. Vandegrift, *Once a Marine*, 120; Altemus diary.
24. Only existing notes are Callaghan's in VAdm. Robert L. Ghormley's unpublished memoir "The Tide Turns," 65–69, NHC. See also VAdm. George C. Dyer, *The Amphibians Came to Conquer*, 1:299–305.
25. ComAmphibSoPac to CTF-11 200135 of July 1942.
26. Turner to Fletcher, 25 July 1942, quoted in Dyer, 1:307–8.
27. See excerpts of Fletcher interview in Dyer, 1:390–95; Cdr. Oscar Pederson, "Historical Presentation Solomon Islands Campaign," Lecture, Army-Navy Staff Col-

lege, 22 Oct. 1943; Adm. Thomas C. Kinkaid, "Four Years in the Pacific," 207, an uncompleted memoir in Kinkaid Papers, Naval Historical Center (NHC) (hereafter Kinkaid memoir). In his *They Call It Pacific,* 323–24, correspondent Clark Lee recorded a revealing conversation with a junior officer on Fletcher's staff. After chiding the Navy for not charging in and relieving Wake and the Philippines despite possible ship losses, Lee asked, "How about this present mission whatever it is? Are we going to risk this carrier?" The reply was: "Not if we can help it."

28. Vandegrift, 120.
29. Dyer, 1:301.
30. CominCh to CinCPac 242303 of June 1942.
31. MAW-2 to CinCPac 220613 of July 1942; CinCPac to ComSoPac 222211 of July 1942.
32. ComAirSoPac to ComSoPac 020854 of August 1942.
33. Turner to ComSoPac 210335 of July 1942; ComAirSoPac to ComSoPac 211021 of July 1942; ComAirSoPac to BuAer 250811 of July 1942.
34. What later (July 1943) came to be known as escort carriers (CVE) were first designated aircraft escort vessels (AGV), changed to auxiliary aircraft carriers (ACV) in August 1942.
35. CinCPac to ComSoPac 222111 of July 1942.
36. CTF-61 Operation Order No. 1-42 28 July 1942; *Wasp* war diary; phone conv. with Capt. Robert M. Bruning.
37. Altemus diary; Green diary; *Enterprise* war diary; War Information Bulletin No. 145, 29 July 1942.
38. ComSoPac to CTF-61 020240 of August 1942.
39. Dyer, 1:300.
40. Lt. Col. H. W. Bauer diary, Bauer papers.
41. Mears, 97. Aircraft Trouble Report (Mach. C. Allard), 3 August 1942, in RG 313 ComCarPac VF4F-4/L11-1.
42. CTG-61.1 (Air Support Force) Op Plan 2-42 (4 Aug. 1942); Green diary.
43. ComAirSoPac to ComSoPac 041436 of August 1942.
44. ComAirSoPac to all CTFs 052357 of August 1942.
45. Japan, Self Defense Force, War History Office, *Senshi Sōsho,* 49:429–30. Search radii in August (400 miles) were considerably shorter than those flown in May (650–700 miles).

3   "SOCK 'EM IN THE SOLOMONS!"

1. Basic sources for naval operations in the invasions of Guadalcanal and Tulagi, 7–8 Aug. 1942, are the ship action reports and war diaries in the NHC. Important secondary sources in addition to those specifically cited in the bibliography include the O.N.I. Combat Narrative, *The Landing in the Solomons 7–8 August 1942* (Washington, 1943) and U.S. Naval War College, *The Battle of Savo Island August 9, 1942* (Newport, 1950).
2. Primary sources for carrier air operations are the carrier action reports and their many enclosures, including air group and squadron reports: CO USS *Saratoga* to CinCPac, Report of Action Tulagi-Guadalcanal Offensive 7–8 Aug. 1942 (19 Aug. 1942); CO USS *Enterprise* to CinCPac, Operations in Support of Occupation of Tulagi-Guadalcanal 7–8 Aug. 1942, Report of (24 Aug. 1942); and CO USS *Wasp* to CinCPac, Capture of Tulagi-Guadalcanal Area 7–8 Aug. 1942 (14 Aug. 1942). Also important are documents, correspondence, and interviews with participants.
3. Kinkaid memoir, 222.
4. His class number and year of graduation from the Imperial Japanese Naval Academy at Eta Jima.
5. For the Yokohama Air Group Sea Fighter Squadron see Izawa, Yasuho, "Nihon Kaigun Suijo Sentokitai," *Koku Journal A.J. Cyclone* No. 7 (March 1977 Special Issue) 116–17.
6. Lt. G. W. Pepper, A-V(S), USNR, Air Intelligence Officer, to CO, Report of Operations of WASP Air Group over Tulagi-Gavutu Area—7 Aug. 1942, with Enclosed

U.S. Aircraft-Action with Enemy (ACA) Reports: Flight 101: Shands, Wright, Gates, Moffett.

7. Lt. Frank Marvin Plake, USN, in *St. Louis Post-Dispatch*, 28 Oct. 1942. Plake was one of VF-71's A-V(S) officers.

8. VS-71 war diary, 7 Aug. 1942.

9. Message log in *Senshi Sōsho*, 49:441.

10. Reports by 1st Lt. Eugene T. Boardman, USMCR, September 1942, who interrogated prisoners from Satō's detachment and translated his diary. Copies in the papers of Prof. Edward M. Coffman, University of Wisconsin–Madison; 2nd Marines Record of Events Aug.–Sept. 1942.

11. Cdr. VF-5 to CO USS *Saratoga,* Report of Combatant Flight Operations Conducted In Guadalcanal-Tulagi Area, 7–8 Aug. 1942 (12 Aug. 1942); VF-5 ACA Report, 7 Aug. 1942 (Simpler).

12. Clark Lee, in *St. Louis Post-Dispatch*, 16 Sept. 1942.

13. *Senshi Sōsho,* 49:499.

14. On 5th Air Attack Force, 25th Air Flotilla war diary, August 1942, Detailed Action Report, 7–11 Aug. 1942, in CNO, OpNav, OP29 Naval History, Japanese World War II Naval Records seized in Post-War Japan, in Japanese on microfilm JD86 (NHC); Washington Document Center (WDC) 161730 "Records of the 25th Air Flotilla sent to Navy Board of Merit 1 Aug.–31 Aug. 1942," "Extracts of 25th Air Flotilla 1 Aug.–31 Aug. 1942." Japanese Monographs No. 120, "Southeast Area Naval Air Operations, January to August 1942."

15. For the history of the 4th Air Group, see Iwaya Fumio, *Chūkō,* 262–81. This is a general history of the Japanese naval medium bomber units. On the formations and tactics of land attack units in general, I am indebted to Dr. Izawa Yasuho, who has contacted on my behalf Mr. Iki Haruki, a highly experienced *rikkō* leader and president of the association of former land attack crews.

16. For the Type 1 *rikkō* see Bunrin-Do's "Mitsubishi Type 1 Attack Bomber," in *Famous Airplanes of the World,* No. 155 (May 1986), and Rene J. Francillon, *Japanese Aircraft of the Pacific War,* 378–87.

17. Masatake Okumiya and Jiro Horikoshi, *The Zero Fighter;* and Robert C. Mikesh and Rikyu Watanabe, *Zero Fighter.*

18. Ikuhiko Hata and Yasuho Izawa, *Japanese Naval Aces and Fighter Units in World War II,* 132–36.

19. For the 2nd Air Group see Hata and Izawa, 157–58; for the Zero A6M3 Zero 32 see the books cited in n. 17 above.

20. Basic Japanese sources for the 7 August mission are the two unit combat logs (*kōdōchōsho*): 4th Air Group, 7 Aug. 1942, and Tainan Air Group, 7 Aug. 1942 (in War History Office in Japan); also *Senshi Sōsho,* 49:442–44. There are accounts by two Japanese participants. Sekine Shōji, an observer in the 4th Air Group, wrote *Honoo no Tsubasa* and covers the 7 August mission on pp. 122–46. There are several accounts by Sakai Saburō: with Fred Saito and Martin Caidin, *Samurai;* Masatake Okumiya and Jiro Horikoshi, *Zero,* 180–203; and the Japanese version of his memoirs, *Ōzora no Samurai.* See also the pictorial biography of Sakai: Henry Sakaida, *Winged Samurai.*

21. CinCPac to CTF-61, CTF-62 062325 and 062336 of August 1942.

22. G. Hermon Gill, *Royal Australian Navy,* 2:132; ComSoWesPacFor to ComSoPac 070927 of August 1942. For the coastwatchers who played a vital role in the whole Solomons campaign, see especially Eric Feldt, *The Coast Watchers,* and Walter Lord, *Lonely Vigil.*

23. *Saratoga* Air Group 7 Aug. 1942 summary in Altemus diary.

24. Sources for SCARLET 2 and SCARLET 8 include: VF-5 ACA reports for Lt. H. S. Brown Jr., Ens. D. A. Innis, and Ens. F. J. Blair; Lt. James J. Southerland II, Statement, 27 Aug. 1942 (published in a slightly censored version as "One of the many personal adventures in the Solomons," *U.S. Naval Institute Proceedings* [April 1943] 539–47); narrative by Capt. H. S. Brown, Jr., "April to October 1942 Revisited by Pete—A Fighting Five Pilot" (14 Nov. 1981) (hereafter Brown narrative); Lt. (jg) Joseph Raymond Daly, "Shot Down in Flames," *Cosmopolitan* (April 1943) 51, 88. In addition, Foster Blair in his diary recorded the initial statements of Brown and Innis, as well as his own. Taken down by the squadron yeoman just after the pilots landed, these accounts are more detailed than the

subsequent ACA reports. Altemus diary also has VF-5 mission summaries with a few details not subsequently included in the action reports.

25. Lt. Cdr. L. C. Simpler, BuAer interview (26 Feb. 1943).
26. Southerland statement.
27. Brown narrative.
28. Simpler, BuAer interview.
29. Daly, "Shot Down in Flames," 51; also corresp. with Joseph Daly.
30. Sekine, 130.
31. In his statement, Blair noted he counted twenty-five bombers before his last attack and saw only two others go down before—Blair diary.
32. Daly, "Shot Down in Flames," 51.
33. A rumor arose that Bill Holt had been rescued and was somehow lost subsequently, perhaps on the ill-fated destroyer *Jarvis,* but this cannot be substantiated. Smokey Stover noted in his diary on 26 Aug. 1942 (Reynolds, *Saga of Smokey Stover,* 51) that the word from Guadalcanal (via a *Saratoga* SBD pilot) was that he had been picked up, "but we have heard nothing official or reliable." Unfortunately the rumors led to Holt's family being given false hopes of his survival before he was officially listed as missing in action. Frances Willis, a friend of Bill Holt's, and her husband James have undertaken exhaustive research on his career.
34. For this fight see the several Sakai accounts and Southerland's statement (27 Aug. 1942). The author was the first to identify Sakai's opponent: see "Saburō Sakai over Guadalcanal," *Fighter Pilots in Aerial Combat,* No. 6 (Fall 1982) 1–11.
35. Southerland statement.
36. VS-71 ACA Report, Flight 120 (Eldridge).
37. VS-71 ACA Report; Tainan Air Group *Kōdōchōsho,* 7 Aug. 1942.
38. CO VB-6 to CinCPac, Report of Action on 7 and 8 Aug. 1942 (22 Aug. 1942); on Sakai's fights with the SBDs, see especially Sakaida, 74–84, based on interviews with participants.
39. Cdr. VF-6 to CinCPac, Report of Action 7–8 Aug. 1942 (23 Aug. 1942); and corresp. with Capt. Howell Sumrall and Lt. J. A. Achten.
40. Sekine, 135–36.
41. Sources on Flight 321: VF-6 Report (23 Aug. 1942), Interview of Lt. (jg) Gordon E. Firebaugh by lieutenants C. C. Colt and G. J. Burck; corresp. with Capt. Gordon Firebaugh, Capt. Paul Mankin, and Lt. William Warden; phone conv. with Cdr. Thomas W. Rhodes; ltr. Cdr. Robert M. Disque to Eric Hammel (n.d.), in Hammel Papers, NHC; Tainan Air Group *Kōdōchōsho,* 7 Aug. 1942.
42. Disque to Hammel, in Hammel papers.
43. Mankin corresp.
44. Ibid.
45. *Senshi Sōsho,* 49:452.
46. Quoted in Dyer, 1:391.
47. *Enterprise* (VF-6) to CinCPac 122231 of August 1942.
48. Simpler corresp.; Brown narrative.
49. Blair diary, 7 Aug. 1942, with the full text of these invaluable statements.
50. Cdr. W. G. Wright III, corresp.; deck log, USS *Lang.*
51. *Saratoga* war diary, 7 Aug. 1942.
52. On 2nd Air Group's mission, see 2nd Air Group *Kōdōchōsho,* 7 Aug. 1942.
53. On this fight see VF-6 Report (23 Aug. 1942) and the individual VF-5 ACA reports, 7 Aug. 1942: Richardson, Gray, Jensen, Dufilho, Starkes, Bright, Davy; Blair's diary (7 Aug. 1942) recorded initial statements by Gray, Jensen, Dufilho, Green, Starkes, and Bright which are more detailed and useful than their subsequent reports.
54. USS *Mugford* Action Report (12 Aug. 1942).
55. VF-5 claims: Starkes 3, Jensen 2, Dufilho 2, Bright 1.5; VF-6: Runyon 2, Vorse 1, Packard, 1, March 1, Shoemaker 0.5.
56. Kinkaid memoir, 226.
57. Correspondence with Lt. Cdr. T. J. Capowski.
58. Cdr. USS *Enterprise* Air Group to CO USS *Enterprise* (10 Aug. 1942), Narrative and Comments concerning the Tulagi-Guadalcanal Air Action and Landing Force Operations of 7–8 Aug. 1942. See also VF-6 Action Report (23 Aug. 1942).
59. Southerland statement; corresp. with Capowski, Firebaugh, and Warden; ltr.

ComAirSoPac to ComSoPac (5 Oct. 1942) based on an interview of Warden by Lt. C. C. Colt.

60. CTF-62 to ComSoPac, CTF-61 071030 of August 1942.
61. CTF-62 to ComSoPac, CTF-61 071517 of August 1942.
62. For the Allied Air Force based in Australia, see George C. Kenney, *General Kenney Reports,* 51–61; Steve Birdsall, *Flying Buccaneers: The Illustrated Story of Kenney's Fifth Air Force* (New York, 1977), 12–13.
63. John H. Mitchell, *On Wings We Conquer,* 123–43.
64. Kenney, 61; *Senshi Sōsho,* 49:455. For the deciphered message, RG 457, SRH-012 *The Role of Communication Intelligence in the American-Japanese Naval War,* Volume III (21 June 1943) 610.

4   D PLUS ONE

1. Sources for 8 August operations are the same as cited in chap. 3, plus Adm. Arthur J. Hepburn, USN (Ret.) to CinCPac, Report of Informal Inquiry into Circumstances Attending the Loss of USS VINCENNES etc. on August 9, 1942, in Vicinity of Savo Island (13 March 1943).
2. VS-72 ACA Report, 8 Aug. 1942; Snowden thought his opponent was a single-seat float fighter.
3. CTF-16 to CTG-61.1 072058, CTG-61.1 to CTF-16 072120, CTG-61.1 to *Saratoga* 072225, all August 1942, in *Saratoga* war diary, 8 Aug. 1942.
4. *Saratoga* to CTG-61.1 072246, CTG-61.1 to CTU-61.1.1 072315, both of August 1942, in *Saratoga* war diary, 8 Aug. 1942.
5. 25th Air Flotilla war diary, August 1942, Detailed Action Report, 7–11 Aug. 1942 (see chap. 3, n. 13); WDC 161730 Records of the 25th Air Flotilla sent to the Navy Board of Merit, 1–31 Aug. 1942 (see chap. 3, n. 13); *kōdōchōshos,* 4th, Misawa, and Tainan air groups, 8 Aug. 1942.
6. Gill, 2:136; Lord, 48–49.
7. Altemus diary, 8 Aug. 1942; Green diary, 8 Aug. 1942.
8. Report by Lt. (jg) P. B. Grosscup and Lt. (jg) W. D. Sheldon to Lt. Cdr. Lester Armour (22 Sept. 1942). See also ships' action reports and O.N.I. Combat Narrative, *The Landing in the Solomons.*
9. VS-71 ACA Report Flight 104 (Lt. Cdr. J. Eldridge, Jr.), 8 Aug. 1942.
10. Richard Tregaskis, *Guadalcanal Diary,* 52–53.
11. VF-6 Action Report, 23 Aug. 1942; 4th Air Group *Kōdōchōsho,* 8 Aug. 1942.
12. Green diary, 8 Aug. 1942.
13. Altemus diary, 11 Aug. 1942; also Blair diary, 8 Aug. 1942.
14. 080400 CTF-61 to CTG-61.1 in *Saratoga* war diary, 8 Aug. 1942.
15. A postwar interview of Capt. Leroy Simpler by Roger Pineau of Samuel E. Morison's historical staff (ltr. 19 Feb. 1949, S. E. Morison Office Files, Box 27, NHC) offers an insight into Fletcher's "state of mind," as Denis Warner and Peggy Warner note in their *Disaster in the Pacific,* 77–78. Reporting to the admiral that afternoon following his fruitless race to intercept the Japanese strike, Simpler advised that he had not caught up with the enemy. Fletcher replied that "he was lucky in not having been engaged and that it was just as well." A shocked Simpler later related his great displeasure that his commanding officer was so pessimistic. Yet given the heavy losses of the previous day (related in chap. 3) with the F4F's apparent impotence against land-based Zeros (which Morison and the Warners, among others, brush off as insignificant), Fletcher's attitude is more understandable. Mirroring his first name, Fletcher had a tendency to speak his mind at all times, not a leadership trait that helped whip up fighting spirit.
16. For Fletcher's thoughts see Dyer, 1:390–95.
17. CTF-61 to CTG-61.1 080425 and CTG-61.1 to CTF-61 080515, both of August 1942, in *Saratoga* war diary, 8 Aug. 1942.
18. CTF-61 to ComSoPac, CTF-62, CTF-63 080707 of August 1942. Then Yeoman 1c Thomas I. Newsome was the admiral's talker on duty in flag plot on the *Saratoga.* He has strong recollections of the lengthy meeting the afternoon of 8 August among Fletcher, Ramsey, and the CTF-61 staff to discuss TF-61's withdrawal. According

to Newsome, no one raised any violent objection to the proposal to retire the carriers. Newsome interview.

19. *Saratoga* war diary, 8 Aug. 1942; message is 0717Z/8 Aug. 1942 MELBOURNE to Any Or All US Men-O-War. In their *Disaster in the Pacific* (19–22, 252–54), Denis Warner and Peggy Warner demonstrate that the two RAAF Hudson search planes (flown by Sgt. W. J. Stutt and Flying Officer M. W. Willman) spotted Mikawa's incoming force and immediately radioed their findings. Several senior officers in certain ships in TG-61.1 and TG-61.2 knew of the messages. Although highly critical of Fletcher's role in the Guadalcanal landings (unfairly in this author's opinion), they admit (234) there is no evidence that Fletcher knew prior to 1845. Kinkaid wrote that he did not receive the sighting report until much later that night: CTF-16 to CinCPac, Recent Operations of TF-16 (10 Sept. 1942).

20. TF-62 to ComAirSoPac 081055 of August 1942.

21. Ltr. CTF-11 to ComSoPac (9 Sept. 1942); message CTF-18 to CTF-11 082225 of August 1942, in *Saratoga* war diary, 9 Aug. 1942.

22. Daly, "Shot Down in Flames," 88.

23. Capt. Howard Crews corresp.; Joseph Daly later wrote a memoir entitled *Luck Is My Lady*.

24. Kinkaid memoir, 231.

25. RAdm. Samuel Eliot Morison, *History of United States Naval Operations in World War II*, Vol. 5, *The Struggle for Guadalcanal August 1942–February 1943*, 58, citing a letter from Vice Admiral Sherman dated 14 February 1949. Regarding Fletcher's decision to retire the carriers on 8 August, Sherman felt "no reason to be apprehensive over a temporary withdrawal. It was not until after the night action that the situation became critical." S. E. Morison Office Files, NHC.

26. *Wasp* action report; ltr. CTF-11 to ComSoPac (9 Sept. 1942). S. E. Morison noted a conversation on 14 Nov. 1943 with RAdm. Carlton Wright, Fletcher's cruiser commander, in which Wright stressed the "terrible" communications in TF-11. He explained the *Saratoga* depended on the *Minneapolis* for much of the radio and TBS traffic, but even he "knew nothing of what went on at Guadalcanal, though occasionally [he] picked up scraps of TBS." Of Savo, Wright concluded that "Frank Jack certainly wouldn't have pulled out had he known what had happened." S. E. Morison Office Files, NHC.

27. CTF-18 to CTF-61 082139 of August 1942 in *Saratoga* war diary, 9 Aug. 1942.

28. CTF-62 to CTF-61 081941 of August 1942, in ibid.

29. Fletcher to ComSoPac 090206 of August 1942.

30. CTF-61 to ComSoPac 090415 of August 1942; also ltr. CTF-11 to ComSoPac (9 Sept. 1942). Fletcher to Ghormley 090315 of August 1942.

31. ComSoPac to CinCPac 090834 of August 1942.

32. For a sample, see Naval War College Analysis (see chap. 3, n. 1); Morison, *The Struggle for Guadalcanal;* Dyer, vol. 1; Herbert Christian Merillat, *Guadalcanal Remembered*, 67–72; Richard B. Frank, *Guadalcanal*, 93–94; and Warner and Warner.

33. Morison, *The Struggle for Guadalcanal*, 28.

34. Noyes on 8 August, in *Saratoga* war diary, 8 Aug. 1942; Kinkaid when interviewed in 1963 by George Dyer in Dyer, 1:394.

35. Ltr. ComCruPac (VAdm. F. J. Fletcher) to CinCPac, Subject: Carrier Task Forces, some lessons learned in operating of (24 Sept. 1942).

36. Ltr. Cdr., Air Force, Pacific Fleet (VAdm. W. F. Halsey) to CinCPac, Subject: Carrier Task Forces, some lessons learned in operating of (9 Oct. 1942).

37. ComSoPac endorsement (24 Jan. 1943) of CTF-11 (RAdm. D. C. Ramsey) to CinCPac, Operations of Carrier Task Forces (31 Dec. 1942).

38. Ltr. CTF-11 to ComSoPac (9 Sept. 1942).

39. Ibid.

40. Ltr. ComCruPac to CinCPac (24 Sept. 1942).

41. Southerland statement; corresp. with Capowski, Firebaugh, and Warden; ltr. ComAirSoPac to ComSoPac (5 Oct. 1942); Lord, 64–79, 154–78.

42. Lt. Cdr. F. A. Rhoades, RANVR, *Diary of a Coastwatcher in the Solomons*, 22–23.

43. Southerland statement.

44. *Senshi Sōsho*, 49:499–500.

45. Not until October at Pearl Harbor when Firebaugh received orders to VF-10 was
his back X-rayed. The doctors discovered he had two cracked vertebrae and placed
him in a body cast for 14 weeks. He did not leave the hospital until February 1943:
Firebaugh corresp.

5 THE WAITING GAME

1. CG 1st MarDiv to ComSoPac 100915, CTF-62 to CTF-61, ComSoPac 101220, both
of August 1942.
2. ComSoPac to CTF-61 110206 of August 1942.
3. Cdr. Oscar Pederson, "Carrier Operations," Lecture, Army and Navy Staff College, 4 Nov. 1943.
4. CinCPac to ComSoPac 102147 and 112209 of August 1942.
5. CominCh to CinCPac 112030, 121750; CinCPac to CominCh 122337, all of August
1942.
6. 1st MarDiv to ComSoPac 102023 of August 1942; Altemus diary.
7. Aircraft Trouble Reports (Lt. [jg] H. L. Grimmell and Lt. A. O. Vorse), 13 Aug.
1942, RG 313 ComCarPac VF4F-4/L11-1.
8. For background of Solomons counteroffensive, see *Senshi Sōsho*, 49:446–51,
508–9, 514–16; also Matome Ugaki, *Fading Victory: The Diary of Admiral Matome
Ugaki 1941–1945*, 177–84.
9. On rebuilding the carrier forces: *Senshi Sōsho*, 43:637–45, 49:545–47.
10. For Eta Jima class, naval flight training class and fate of all Japanese aviation
leaders, see *Kaigun Kūchū Kimmusha (Shikan) Meibo* ("Registry of Naval Aviation Duty Naval Officers"), issued in 1954 by the *Kaikō Kai* (Naval Air Society),
photocopy furnished by Dr. Izawa Yasuho. For more specific information on Japanese naval fighter pilots, see Hata and Izawa. The *kōdōchōshos* for the carriers
help to identify the changing squadron personnel.
11. Rikihei Inoguchi and Tadashi Nakajima, *The Divine Wind* (Annapolis, 1958), 35.
12. RG 457, SRMD-002 War Plans Section Comments on ComIntel Summaries, 15 and
21 Aug. 1942.
13. ComSoPac to CominCh, CinCPac 161146 of August 1942.
14. CTF-61 to ComCarPac 171007 of August 1942.
15. CTG-2.6 to ComAirSoPac, CinCPac 130240, ComAirSoPac to ComSoPac 140402,
both of August 1942. See also Robert J. Cressman, "The President's Escort Carrier: A History of USS *Long Island* (CVE-1)," *The Hook* (Spring 1984) 21–30.
16. Blair diary; Capt. Howard W. Crews diary.
17. CinCPac to ComSoPac 172047 of August 1942, Info CTF-61.
18. CinCPac to ComSoPac 180215 of August 1942, Info CTF-61; ComSoPac to CTF-61
180916 of August 1942.
19. 14th Air Group *Kōdōchōsho*, 20 Aug. 1942. For searches in general from 20 to 25
August, see 25th Air Flotilla (5th Air Attack Force), Detailed Action Report, 12–25
Aug. 1942, in microfilm JD86; partial translation in WDC 160140.
20. VS-71 ACA Report, 20 Aug. 1942; 14th Air Group *Kōdōchōsho*, 20 Aug. 1942.
21. 14th Air Group *Kōdōchōsho*, 20 Aug. 1942; *Senshi Sōsho*, 49:537–40.
22. CinCPac to ComSoPac 200247 of August 1942, Info CTF-61.
23. ComGenCACTUS to ComSoPac 202019 of August 1942.
24. ComAirSoPac to CTF-61 201920 of August 1942; *Saratoga* war diary, 21 Aug.
1942.
25. Yokohama Air Group *Kōdōchōsho*, 21 Aug. 1942; VS-72 ACA Report, 21 Aug.
1942; Reynolds, *Saga of Smokey Stover*, 46; Blair diary.
26. CG 1st MarDiv to ComSoPac 210900 of August 1942; Fletcher to ComSoPac
211120 of August 1942.
27. Maj. John L. Smith, BuAer Interview (10 Nov. 1942); Tainan Air Group *Kōdōchōsho*, 21 Aug. 1942; VMF-223 war diary. For CACTUS air operations, the basic
source is Cdr. Forward Echelon, MAG-23 to CO MAG-23, Report of Action of the
Forward Echelon of Marine Aircraft Group Twenty-three during the period 20
August 1942 to 30 August 1942 (17 Sept. 1942)—hereafter MAG-23 Report of
Action.

28. Cdr. VF-6 to CinCPac, Report of Action 22 Aug. 1942 (24 Aug. 1942); 14th Air Group *Kōdōchōsho*, 22 Aug. 1942.
29. Reynolds, *Saga of Smokey Stover,* 47.
30. Fletcher to ComSoPac 220900, ComSoPac to CTF-61 220910, both of August 1942.
31. Basic sources for 23 August operations include: CTF-61 (ComCruPac) to ComSo-Pac, Preliminary Report of Actions, August 23–24, 1942 (6 Sept. 1942); *Saratoga* war diary, 23 Aug. 1942.
32. Lee, *They Call It Pacific,* 339; he flew the mission and described it on pp. 339–44; also Cdr. *Saratoga* Air Group, Narrative of Operations on August 23, 1942 and the Morning of August 24, 1942 (5 Sept. 1942).
33. CinCPac to all CTFs 190145 (Bulletin 156), 220251 (Bulletin 159), and 230345 (Bulletin 160) of August 1942.
34. See CTF-11 to CinCPac, Endorsement of the *Saratoga's* Report of Action against Enemy (Japanese) Forces in the Solomon Islands Area on August 24, 1942 (24 Sept. 1942); CinCPac to all CTF (Intell. Bull. 161) message 240223 of August 1942.
35. CG 1st MarDiv to CTF-61 231040 of August 1942; Lee, *They Call It Pacific,* 346–47.

6 SINKING THE *RYŪJŌ*

Primary sources for the Battle of the Eastern Solomons: CinCPac to CominCh, Solomon Islands Campaign, Action of 23–25 August 1942 (24 Oct. 1942) with enclosed action reports of ships and squadrons, including:

CO USS *Enterprise* to CinCPac, Action of August 24, 1942, including Air Attack on USS *Enterprise,* Report of (5 Sept. 1942), with war damage, air group, squadron, and fighter director reports included.

CO USS *Saratoga* to CinCPac, Report of Action against Enemy (Japanese) Forces in Solomon Islands Area on August 24, 1942 (10 Sept. 1942), including group and squadron reports, and Tactical Situation and Chronological History of Events—August 24, 1942.

CTF-61 (ComCruPac) to ComSoPac, Preliminary Report of Actions, August 23–24, 1942 (6 Sept. 1942), with 2nd Endorsement by ComAirSoPac, and Tabular Record of Combat Reports.

TF-16 Chronological Order of Events 0500–2400, 24 Aug. 1942.

War diaries: ComAirSoPac; TF-16; USS *Enterprise;* USS *Saratoga.*

Senshi Sōsho, 49:563–91; Yokosuka Air Group, Battle Lessons Investigation Committee, Greater East Asia War Battle Lessons (Aviation), Chapter 8, Second Solomons Sea Battle, Naval Battle of the South Pacific (3 May 1943). *Kōdōchōshos, Shōkaku, Zuikaku, Ryūjō,* Yokohama Air Group, and Misawa Air Group (24 Aug. 1942).

25th Air Flotilla Detailed Action Report, 12–25 Aug. 1942, in JD86 microfilm; 7th Cruiser Division Detailed Action Report, 24–25 Aug. 1942, and 8th Cruiser Division Detailed Action Report, 24 Aug. 1942, both in JD16 microfilm; 2nd Destroyer Squadron Detailed Action Report, 13–31 Aug. 1942, in JD26 microfilm.

1. Message *Kidō Butai* #18 (0630/24) in Yokosuka Air Group, Greater East Asia War Battle Lessons, Chapter 8, Appendix, 7–8.
2. Search rosters from research of James C. Sawruk in AirSoPac records and contacts with participants.
3. ComAirSoPac war diary, 24 Aug. 1942.
4. Lee, *They Call It Pacific,* 350.
5. ACA Report 24 Aug. 1942 (Ens. G. C. Burkey and Lt. [jg] W. J. Gentz); *Ryūjō Kōdōchōsho* (24 Aug. 1942).
6. TF-16 Chronological Order of Events.
7. CTF-11 to CinCPac (24 Sept. 1942), *Saratoga's* Report of Action, 5.
8. All quoted dialogue from the FD circuit in chapters 6, 7, and 8, unless otherwise noted, is from USS *Saratoga* Fighter Net Radio Log and Radar Plot for Engagement against Japanese on August 24, 1942, enclosure to *Saratoga* Report of Action (times converted from Z − 11.5 to Z − 11).
9. VF-5 ACA reports by Lt. D. C. Richardson, Lt. (jg) F. O. Green, Ens. F. J. Blair, and Ens. D. A. Innis; Green diary; Blair diary; Yokohama Air Group *Kōdōchōsho* (24 Aug. 1942).

10. TF-16 Chronological Order of Events.
11. Misawa Air Group *Kōdōchōsho* (24 Aug. 1942); VF-5 ACA reports: Lt. R. Gray, Ens. L. W. Haynes, Ens. M. K. Bright.
12. Green diary.
13. The *Ryūjō* Air Group *Kōdōchōsho* is exceptionally detailed; see also a memoir by an aviation mechanic on board the ship, Saitō Yoshio, "The Destruction of the Carrier *Ryūjō* in the 2nd Solomons Sea Battle," in *Maru Special, The Life and Death Struggle of Guadalcanal*, 44–75, photocopy provided by Osamu Tagaya and partially translated by D. Y. Louie.
14. Sources on the 24 August attack include the MAG-23 Forward Echelon Report of Action (17 Sept. 1942); VMF-223 war diary; 1st MarDiv, D-2 Journal (MCHC); Tregaskis; Maj. John L. Smith's personal notebook (in John L. Smith papers held by his family); Maj. Gen. Marion Carl's unpublished memoir (furnished by Barrett Tillman); 2nd Lt. Deltis Fincher's battle report; interviews and/or phone conversations with participants Fred Gutt, Brig. Gen. Rivers Morrell, Col. Robert R. Read, Col. John King, and Col. Dale Brannon; *Ryūjō Kōdōchōsho* (24 Aug. 1942).
15. CO Third Defense Battalion to Commandant, U.S.M.C., Report of Third Defense Battalion Operations at Guadalcanal (7 March 1943).
16. Tregaskis, 158.
17. Ibid., 157.
18. Ibid.
19. Cdr. VT-3 to CO USS *Enterprise*, Report of Action—August 24, 1942 (29 Aug. 1942).
20. Cdr. VS-5 to CO USS *Enterprise*, Operations of Scouting Squadron FIVE in Area Northeast of Solomons during Period 9–25 August 1942, Report of (31 Aug. 1942).
21. Capt. Tameichi Hara, *Japanese Destroyer Captain*, 109.
22. Del Wiley's story is chronicled in his fine memoir *Wiley's Island or Island Blong Wiley*.
23. Cdr. *Saratoga* Air Group to CO USS *Saratoga*, Narrative Report of Action with Enemy on August 24, 1942, in Solomon Islands Area (29 Aug. 1942); Cdr. VB-3 to CO USS *Saratoga*, Narrative Report of Action against Enemy on August 24, 1942, in Solomon Islands Area (27 Aug. 1942); Cdr. VS-3 to CO USS *Saratoga*, Narrative Report of Action with Enemy on August 24, 1942 in Solomon Islands Area (26 Aug. 1942); Cdr. VT-8 to CO USS *Saratoga*, Narrative Report of Action with Enemy on 24 August 1942 in Solomon Islands Area (27 Aug. 1942).
24. In addition to the VT-8 report, see Jack Singer, "Jack Singer's Last Despatch Is Thrilling Account of Bomber, Torpedo-Plane Attack on Japanese Ships," *Honolulu Advertiser*, 23 Sept. 1942. Singer flew the mission in the middle seat of Harwood's TBF.
25. CSAG report (29 Aug. 1942).

7 RIPOSTE—THE *KIDŌ BUTAI* ATTACK ON TASK FORCE 61

1. Dialogue on Fighter Net as previously cited (chapter 6, n. 8); for *Enterprise* fighter directors Lieutenant Commander Dow and Lieutenant Rowe, see their Memorandum Report of Fighter Direction during Enemy Attack on *Enterprise*, 24 August 1942, enclosed with *Enterprise* action report; Cdr. VF-6 to CO USS *Enterprise*, Report of Action—24 August 1942 (1 Sept. 1942).
2. *Senshi Sōsho*, 49:567. No *kōdōchōshos* or air group reports exist for most of the cruisers; Fukuyama's identity came from Imperial Naval casualty lists examined by Dr. Izawa.
3. Cdr. VB-6 to CO USS *Enterprise*, Report of Action, August 24, 1942 (31 Aug. 1942).
4. Interview with WO Komachi Sadamu, 9 May 1992.
5. Ibid.
6. Richardson slightly damaged his F4F (F-11) upon landing on the *Enterprise*, so he took his wingman Blair's F4F, leaving Blair to go when F-11 could be repaired— Blair diary, 24 Aug. 1942. The divisions became mixed because the *Enterprise* did not adhere to VF-5 flight organization; see Cdr. VF-5 to CO USS *Saratoga*, Narra-

tive Report of Action with Enemy on August 24, 1942, in Solomon Islands Area (24 Aug. 1942). Thus Richardson (SCARLET 7) ended up with Dufilho and Haynes from Gray's SCARLET 5.

7. Vorse was not so sure of its identity, either—Vorse corresp.
8. TF-16 Chronological Order of Events.
9. Pederson, "Carrier Operations" lecture.
10. Cdr. John M. Wesolowski corresp.
11. Blair diary, 24 Aug. 1942.
12. VF-6 report; corresp. with RAdm. Vorse, Capt. Howell Sumrall, and Lt. Cdr. Richards L. Loesch; and Warrant Officer Komachi interview.
13. Sumrall corresp.
14. Shigematsu's activities, along with the rest of the *Shōkaku* Air Group, appear in a sketch in Yokosuka Air Group, Greater East Asia War Battle Lessons, Chapter 8, that is reproduced in *Senshi Sōsho,* 49:570.
15. VF-5 ACA reports Richardson, Haynes.
16. VF-5 ACA reports Gray, Green; Green diary.
17. *Kōdōchōshos, Shōkaku* and *Zuikaku* (24 Aug. 1942)—the *Shōkaku*'s is particularly detailed with observations as to the fate of each missing airplane; interview and corresp. with Arima Keiichi.
18. VF-5 ACA reports Harmer, McDonald, Crews, Currie; Captain Crews interviews, corresp.
19. Ltr. George P. Givens to Eric Hammel (16 Aug. 1982), in Hammel papers.
20. Mears, 111.
21. VF-6 report.
22. *Enterprise* Report, photo caption ENT 1087-H; Lt. Cdr. Elias B. Mott II, the assistant gunnery officer up in sky control, felt the heat of its flames; see Cdr. E. B. Mott Narrative (22 March 1944).
23. Furuta graduated in July 1936 (32nd Pilot Class), and from Pearl Harbor to Midway he served as the pilot for Lt. Chihaya Takehiko (NA 62-1934), CO of the *Akagi* Carrier Bomber Squadron.
24. Arima corresp.; CO USS *Enterprise* (CV-6) to Chief, Bureau of Ships, War Damage Report (5 Sept. 1942), for the extent of the damage.
25. Lt. Robin M. Lindsey Narrative (17 Sept. 1943), 11.
26. For the attacks on the battleship, see CO to CinCPac, USS *North Carolina*—Action of August 24, 1942, Report of (26 Aug. 1942); VF-6 report.
27. Lindsey narrative, 11.
28. VF-5 ACA reports Jensen, Starkes, Kleinman; Cdr. Carl Starkes corresp.
29. VF-6 report; corresp. with Cdr. Donald E. Runyon and Cdr. Howard S. Packard.
30. Green diary.
31. VF-5 ACA Report Eichenberger.
32. Translated Item #251, 12 Dec. 1942. "Outline of a (forced) landing on Malaita in the Solomon Islands, excerpts from a personal diary 24 Aug.–3 Nov. 1942."
33. Lindsey narrative, 11.
34. Lt. Cdr. Leroy C. Simpler Narrative (8 March 1943).
35. VF-5 ACA Report Presley.
36. VF-5 ACA reports Stover, Kleinmann; Reynolds, *Saga of Smokey Stover,* 49.
37. VF-6 report; Achten corresp.
38. Ltr. Cdr. Robert M. Disque to Eric Hammel (n.d.), in Hammel papers.
39. Corresp. Paul W. Knight with Eric Hammel, in Hammel papers.
40. Disque to Hammel, in Hammel papers.
41. VF-6 report.
42. VS-5 report; corresp. Glen Estes with James C. Sawruk.
43. VT-3 report; Mears, 113; corresp. with Charles R. Beatty.
44. Narrative by Lt. Cdr. Louis J. Kirn, 3 June 1943, 5–6.
45. VS-3 report, in *Saratoga* action report.
46. VF-6 report; VF-5 report; VF-5 ACA Report Bright.
47. Phone conv. with Cdr. Thomas Rhodes.
48. Corresp. Capt. Paul Mankin with Thomas F. Gates; also corresp. and phone conv.
49. CEAG to CinCPac, Report of Action in the Solomon Islands Area, Aug. 22–25, 1942 (2 Sept. 1942) 16. Emphasis in original.
50. Mankin corresp.

51. Arima corresp.; Crow's account in Eric Hammel, *Guadalcanal: The Carrier Battles*, 201–2, where he claimed all three planes.

8   MUTUAL RETREAT

1. Dialogue on the Fighter Net as cited in chap. 6, n. 8.
2. TF-16 Chronological Order of Events.
3. Aircraft Trouble Report (Ens. R. M. Disque), 24 Aug. 1942, in RG 313, ComCarPac, VF4F-4/L11-1.
4. Loesch corresp.
5. VT-8, VB-3 reports, NHC.
6. *Shōkaku Kōdōchōsho*, 24 Aug. 1942; corresp. Edward Velazquez with James C. Sawruk.
7. Corresp. Capt. Rubin H. Konig with James C. Sawruk.
8. Arima corresp.
9. Komachi interview.
10. Translated Item # 251; see also 2nd Marines Record of Events November 1942; part of I Company reached Malaita on 2 November and on 5 November wiped out a party of starving Japanese, killing twenty and taking one POW.
11. Hara, 113–14.
12. CTF-61 to ComSoPac 241014 of August 1942.
13. ComSoPac to CG 1st MarDiv 241400 of August 1942.
14. For TF-18's actions, see Capt. Forrest Sherman to CinCPac, Movements of USS *Wasp*, August 25, 1942 (14 Nov. 1942); VS-71 war diary, and war diaries of screening ships.
15. Yokohama Air Group *Kōdōchōsho*, 25 Aug. 1942.
16. VS-71 ACA reports; VS-72 ACA Report 25 Aug. 1942.
17. CinCPac to ComSoPac, CTF-61 242125 of August 1942.
18. VS-71 ACA Report, 25 Aug. 1942; 14th Air Group *Kōdōchōsho*, 25 Aug. 1942.
19. CTF-16 to CTF-61 242325 of August 1942.
20. Interview with Capt. Walter Clarke and Cdr. Frank Green; Blair diary, 25 Aug. 1942.
21. CTF-61 to ComSoPac 250646 of August 1942.
22. See Fletcher's report: CTF-61 to ComSoPac, Preliminary Report of Action August 23–24, 1942 (6 Sept. 1942); Pederson, "Carrier Operations" lecture.
23. Combat Intelligence Unit, Traffic Intelligence Summary, 24 Aug. 1942, in RG 457, SRH-12, 4:800–801.
24. Pederson, "Carrier Operations" lecture; RG 457 SRH-036 Radio Intelligence in World War II Tactical Operations in the Pacific Ocean Areas, January 1943, 256–57, 0008/10 Nov. 1942 Navy Minister to All Commands.
25. CinCPac to CominCh (24 Oct. 1942).
26. Memorandum Report of Fighter Direction during Enemy Attacks on *Enterprise*, 24 Aug. 1942.
27. VF-5 report.
28. USS *Saratoga* Report of Action (10 Sept. 1942), 2.
29. Endorsement CTF-61 to CinCPac, Action of August 24, 1942, including Air Attack on USS *Enterprise*, Report of (25 Sept. 1942) 1.
30. Endorsement CTF-11 to CinCPac, *Saratoga's* Report of Action (24 Sept. 1942).
31. CTF-16 to CinCPac, Recent Operations of Task Force SIXTEEN (10 Sept. 1942), which is a lengthy analysis of carrier doctrine and operations.

9   "LET'S NOT LET THIS OFFENSIVE DIE ON THE VINE"

The chapter title comes from: CinCPac to CominCh, ComSoPac 252241 of August 1942.
1. Aside from the war diaries and other general sources, a very important source for carrier operations and with many appended documents is "Record of Proceedings

of an Investigation conducted by Rear Admiral J. F. Shafroth United States Navy by order of the Commander-in-Chief Pacific Fleet to inquire into the facts connected with the sinking of the U.S.S. *Wasp*," 4 Jan. 1943 (hereafter *Wasp* investigation).

2. ComSoPac to CTF-61 271026 of August 1942.
3. Cdr. David V. Senft corresp.; VF-71 ACA Report 27 Aug. 1942; Ens. William M. Hall Navy Cross citation; 14th Air Group *Kōdōchōsho*, 27 Aug. 1942.
4. Important sources on TF-17 include the TF-17 war diary; *Hornet* war diary (in existence until 31 Aug. 1942).
5. See Tom Lea, "Aboard the U.S.S. *Hornet*," *Life* (March 22, 1943), 50–61, for fine portraits of Murray, Mason, and other *Hornet* officers.
6. Ibid., 56
7. CTF-17 to CinCPac (14 Oct. 1942), first endorsement to the *Hornet*'s Report of Action October 5, 1942 (8 Oct. 1942); Murray, BuAer interview (25 Nov. 1942). Later when VF-72 operated thirty-six planes, two were allocated to escort the air group commander's TBF.
8. Ltr. RAdm. George D. Murray to CinCPac (25 Aug. 1942).
9. ComSoPac to CominCh 290310 of August 1942.
10. CG 1st MarDiv to ComSoPac 290905 of August 1942.
11. ComSoPac to CTF-61 291442 of August 1942.
12. CO USS *Saratoga* to CinCPac, Action Report on Torpedoing of USS *Saratoga*, 31 Aug. 1942 (10 Sept. 1942). Crews diary, Green diary.
13. CinCPac to CominCh, Solomon Islands Campaign—Torpedoing of *Saratoga*, *Wasp* and *North Carolina* (31 Oct. 1942).
14. ComSoPac to CTF-61 310242 of August 1942; CTF-61 to ComSoPac 310930 of August 1942.
15. ComAirSoPac to ComSoPac 310402 of August 1942.
16. W. F. Craven and J. L. Cate, *The Army Air Forces in World War II*, Vol. 4, *The Pacific: Guadalcanal to Saipan*, 46; ComSoPac to OpNav 031000 of August 1942.
17. ComAirSoPac to CinCPac, CominCh 310402 of August 1942.
18. ComSoPac to CinCPac 010305, CTF-62 to CinCPac 0111230, both of September 1942.
19. CinCPac to CominCh 012331 of September 1942.
20. Gen. H. H. Arnold, *Global Mission* (New York, 1949), 337.
21. Ltr. Fletcher to Nimitz (24 Sept. 1942).
22. Ltr. Halsey to Nimitz (9 Oct. 1942).
23. Endorsement of *Enterprise* Report (25 Sept. 1942).
24. ComSoPac to CTF-17 030706 of September 1942.
25. TF-17 war diary; USS *Hornet* Conf. Memo (8 Sept. 1942); Alexander R. Griffin, *A Ship to Remember*, 178–80; *Senshi Sōsho*, 83:87.
26. CTF-17 to ComSoPac 070217 of September 1942.
27. CTF-17 to ComSoPac 080953 of September 1942.
28. Ltr. Turner to Noyes (9 Sept. 1942) with tentative draft of Op Plan A15-42; messages CTF-18 to CTF-62 090445, CTF-62 to CTF-18 090600, both of September 1942; ltr. Noyes to Ghormley (9 Sept. 1942).
29. ComSoPac to TF-17, -18, -62, -63 091016, ComSoPac to CTF-17, -18, -62, -63 091032, both of September 1942.

10 THE JAPANESE OFFENSIVE

The primary source for 1st MAW operations is: CO MAG-23 to CNO, Report of Action of Marine Aircraft Group 23 (VMF-223, VMF-224, VMSB-231, and VMSB-232) with *Enterprise* Flight 300 (six pilots of VS-5 and five pilots of VB-6), VF-5, VS-3, VT-8, and the 67th Fighter Squadron, USA, attached, for the period 31 August to 15 Sept. 1942 (6 Oct. 1942).

1. Howard Crews vignette, "The War in the Pacific as Seen from the Trenches at Hollywood and Vine," in Crews papers; Crews interview. For VF-5 on a day-to-day basis, see VF-5 war diary, August–November 1942.

2. Capt. Richard G. Hubler and Capt. John A. DeChant, *Flying Leathernecks,* 51; see also Roger Willock, *Unaccustomed to Fear: A Biography of the Late General Roy S. Geiger,* a fine, sympathetic portrait.

3. Lt. Col. Dennis Byrd, USMC (Ret.), who was Dick Mangrum's radioman, has done exhaustive research on VMSB-232 at Guadalcanal; his book *Tip of the Spear* will soon be published.

4. 67th Fighter Squadron Operations Reports and History, NA RG 18; 347th Fighter Group Records, NA RG 18; interview with Col. Dale D. Brannon, USAF (Ret.); also a fine study by a veteran of the 67th—Robert Lawrence Ferguson, *Guadalcanal: The Island of Fire, Reflections of the 347th Fighter Group.*

5. Basic sources for VMF-223 and VMF-224 are their war diaries; Richard Wilcox, "Captain Smith and His Fighting 223," *Life* (7 Dec. 1942) 120–30; Smith personal notebook (in possession of Smith family); and the extensive research and wide contacts of Rex Hamilton, a VMF-223 veteran who has organized the VMF-223 reunions.

6. See Commander Compton's report: CO Advance Naval Base CACTUS-RINGBOLT to ComAirSoPac, Aviation Unit CUB One, Employment of (27 Sept. 1942); also narrative by Lt. George W. Polk, 2 Feb. 1944, and the fine *Saga of the Sixth: History of the Sixth U.S. Naval Construction Battalion* (privately published, n.d.).

7. Maj. John L. Smith, BuAer interview (10 Nov. 1942); Maj. R. E. Galer and Maj. F. R. Payne, BuAer interview (6 Jan. 1943).

8. From the growing literature on coastwatchers, see especially Feldt, *The Coast Watchers* (the Australian edition and not the greatly abridged New York edition) and Lord, *Lonely Vigil.* The D-2 Journal of the 1st MarDiv gives the daily message traffic between the coastwatchers and CACTUS.

9. See above all Lt. Lewis C. Mattison, USNR, Report of Fighter Direction at CACTUS, October 8, 1942–January 1, 1943 (n.d.), in Lt. Gen. Louis E. Woods Papers, MCHC, and Capt. Lewis C. Mattison Papers (Mattison family). This comprehensive report also offers much background on operations prior to 8 October; also Master Technical Sgt. Dermott H. MacDonnell, Report on Radar Operations at CACTUS (16 Dec. 1942), in Mattison papers; Ens. William A. Noll, BuAer Interview (23 March 1943). Lieutenant Mattison kept a marvelous diary of his experiences on Guadalcanal from 8 October 1942 to mid-January 1943, which will be much cited in the following chapters. Lieutenant Colonel Bayler offered interesting anecdotal recollections of his time at CACTUS in *Last Man Off Wake Island.*

10. Ens. Harold L. Buell diary, 11 Sept. 1942, from Commander Buell. He has written a superb memoir of his World War II experiences: *Dauntless Helldivers.*

11. ComSoPac to CTFs 100255 of September 1942.

12. General sources on Base Air Force include *Senshi Sōsho,* 83:78–82; 25th Air Flotilla war diary and Detailed Action Report, 26 Aug.–14 Sept. 1942, microfilmed in JD86; Japanese Monograph No. 121, Outline of Southeast Area Naval Air Operations, Part VIII (27 Aug.–15 Sept. 1942); unit *kōdōchōshos.*

13. *Senshi Sōsho,* Vol. 83, interpolating figures on 78 with known losses.

14. *Senshi Sōsho,* 83:37; Kunio Yanagida, *Reisen Moyu,* 1:468–69; interviews and corresp. with Mr. Ishikawa Shirō, formerly of the 2nd Air Group, who flew fourteen combat missions against Guadalcanal.

15. Hata and Izawa, 148–50.

16. Japanese Monograph No. 118, Operational History of Naval Communications, December 1941–August 1945, 298; for the characteristics of the aircraft radio/telephone Set No. 1, see pp. 137, 179.

17. *Senshi Sōsho,* 83:47–48, with corrections from squadron reports: *Chitose Kōdōchōsho;* 2nd *Hikōkitai* (*Sanyō Maru* and *Sanuki Maru*) Detailed Battle Report; XAV *Kamikawa Maru* Air Unit Detailed Action Report, 4 Sept.–25 Oct. 1942, in JD11 microfilm. Lt. Takano Hiroshi (NA 65-1938), the *Sanuki Maru buntaichō,* was killed on 8 September in a dusk attack on Tulagi.

18. For the 12 September air fighting, see Cdr. VF-5 to CominCh, Action Reports—Combat in Guadalcanal Area (n.d., received 25 Nov. 1942), hereafter VF-5 combat reports; this document includes all of the individual VF-5 pilot ACA reports for the period 11 Sept.–16 Oct. 1942 and is invaluable for reconstructing the air battles.

For 12 September ACA reports by Simpler, Richardson, Crews, Clarke, Grimmell, Green, Wesolowski, Innis, Loesch, Bright, Morgan, Register, Roach, Halford, March, Kleinmann, Rouse, and Mankin. For USMC in addition to the war diaries, see 2nd Lt. E. A. Trowbridge, Report of Action with Enemy (12 Sept. 1942), one of a number of action reports written by USN air intelligence officers in September and October 1942 and compiled in Commander Air Force, Pacific Fleet, memorandum of combat reports and summaries involving U.S. fighters (19 Dec. 1942) (hereafter ComAirFor combat reports).

19. *Kōdōchōshos*, Kisarazu, Misawa, Chitose, and 2nd Air Group (12 Sept. 1942); Ugaki, 209–10.

20. On AA guns, see 3rd Defense Battalion Action Report; also "Talk given by Lt. Col. Kenneth W. Benner, USMC . . . at Noumea" (6 Oct. 1942); Benner commanded the 90-mm AA Group.

21. Smith, BuAer interview.

22. Tregaskis, 222.

23. Corresp. VAdm. D. C. Richardson with Thomas F. Gates.

24. Green diary.

25. Crews interview.

26. Corresp. Capt. Paul Mankin with Thomas F. Gates.

27. Ugaki, 210.

28. Crews interview.

29. VMO-251 war diary; corresp. Col. E. H. Railsback, USMC.

30. Simpler corresp.; see also Allen Raymond, "Tojo Meets A Wildcat," *Popular Science* (August 1943) 100.

31. Corresp. Brig. Gen. F. R. Payne, USMC, and Lt. Col. Carl M. Longley, USMC; for VMF-212 see the very important unpublished manuscript from the papers of Col. Frank C. Drury, USMC: Frederick Faust, "The Squadron," based upon extensive interviews conducted in 1943. Faust wrote numerous westerns under the name "Max Brand," and was killed at Anzio in May 1944 as a war correspondent in Italy.

32. Corresp. with Lt. Col. Wendell P. Garton, USMCR.

33. Tainan Air Group *Kōdōchōsho*, 13 Sept. 1942; for the Type 2 land recon plane, see Robert C. Mikesh and Osamu Tagaya, *Moonlight Interceptor: Japan's "Irving" Night Fighter* (Washington, 1985), 21–25.

34. VF-5 combat reports 13 Sept. 1942: Clarke, Stover, Innis, Clarke; interview with Capt. W. E. Clarke.

35. Reynolds, *Saga of Smokey Stover*, 59.

36. Phone conv. with Col. Robert R. Read, USMC, and Conrad G. Winter, and corresp. and interview, Col. Dean S. Hartley, USMC.

37. Tregaskis, 225–26.

38. Corresp. with Brig. Gen. Payne, Col. Jack E. Conger, USMC, and Col. Drury.

39. Garton corresp.

40. Hata and Izawa, 91, 98, 258, 267, 271.

41. VF-5 combat reports 13 Sept. 1942: Simpler, Crews, Stover, Kleinmann, Loesch, Bright, Register. ComAirFor combat reports: Hollowell, Read, Galer.

42. *Kōdōchōshos*, Misawa, Kisarazu, Kanoya, and Tainan Air Group (13 Sept. 1942).

43. Loesch corresp.

44. Conger corresp.; Faust, "The Squadron," 99–101.

45. Memo by Lt. Roger Kent, Naval Air Combat Intelligence, on questioning of [six] Japanese aviators (26 Sept. 1942) by Col. Buckley (1st MarDiv D-2) and Capt. Moran (D-2 language officer). Although no names are given, comparing the crew list from the Kisarazu *Kōdōchōsho*, 13 Sept. 1942, with the crew stations of the prisoners show that Hayashi, the senior observer commanding the aircraft, must have been the casualty.

46. Col. C. C. Chamberlain, USMC corresp.; Faust, "The Squadron," 104–5.

47. Faust, "The Squadron"; also clipping in *Rochester Post Bulletin*, 8 Oct. 1942, with Chamberlain's diary written on driftwood.

48. Garton corresp.

49. 1st MarDiv, D-2 Journal, 13 Sept. 1942.

50. *Kamikawa Maru* Air Unit Detailed Action Report, 4 Sept.–25 Oct. 1942 on microfilm, JD11, NHC. This document does not give full names of all the pilots; Dr.

Izawa Yasuo supplied their given names from IJN casualty lists. Interviews with numerous American eyewitnesses at Henderson Field.

51. Clarke interview.
52. Loesch corresp., phone conv.
53. Corresp. Loesch, Dr. John L. Whitaker; Richard Frank's *Guadalcanal*, 240, identifies the Japanese attackers.
54. VF-5 combat reports 14 Sept. 1942: Simpler, Clarke, Green, Stover, Grimmell, Wesolowski, Morgan, Rouse, Halford; Green diary; Reynolds, *Saga of Smokey Stover*, 60–61; VMJ-253 Muster Roll, September 1942.
55. *Kamikawa Maru* Air Unit Detailed Action Report, 4 Sept.–25 Oct. 1942.
56. Undated clipping from *Dinuba Sentinel*, provided by Mrs. Janis Halford.
57. Corresp. Captain Mankin with Thomas F. Gates, 25 Sept. 1981.
58. VMJ-253 Muster Roll, October 1942.
59. *Kōdōchōshos*, 2nd and Tainan Air Groups (14 Sept. 1942).
60. VF-5 combat reports, 14 Sept. 1942: Bright, Roach; Reynolds, *Saga of Smokey Stover*, 61.
61. Summary in 1st MarDiv, D-2 Journal, 14 Sept. 1942.
62. *Chitose Kōdōchōsho* (14 Sept. 1942); *Kamikawa Maru* Air Unit Detailed Action Report, 4 Sept.–25 Oct. 1942; R-Area Air Force, 2nd *Hikōkitai* (*Sanuki Maru* and *Sanyō Maru*) Detailed Battle Report, 14 Sept. 1942.
63. VF-5 combat reports, 14 Sept. 1942: Simpler, Crews, Stover, Wesolowski; ComAirFor combat reports: Dobbin, Hollowell, D'Arcy, Hartley, Brooks; Reynolds, *Saga of Smokey Stover*, 62.
64. Green diary.
65. Simpler report.
66. Reynolds, *Saga of Smokey Stover*, 61.

11   THE LOSS OF THE *WASP*

Basic sources for this chapter include: the *Wasp* investigation; CTF-61 to ComSoPac, Report of Operations 8–18 Sept. 1942 (21 Sept. 1942); Memo, RAdm. Leigh Noyes to CinCPac (5 Oct. 1942); CO USS *Wasp* to CTF-18, Loss of USS *Wasp*, Preliminary Report (18 Sept. 1942); CO USS *Wasp* to Secretary of the Navy, Loss of *Wasp* (24 Sept. 1942), with numerous enclosed reports and statements; Navy Dept., Bureau of Ships, USS *Wasp* (CV-7) Loss in Action—15 Sept. 1942—South Pacific (15 Jan. 1944).

1. 14th Air Group *Kōdōchōsho*, 13 Sept. 1942.
2. Statements in *Wasp* investigation.
3. ComAirSoPac war diary, 14 Sept. 1942; details in Hoffman's lengthy citation for the Silver Star, 21 Jan. 1943 (hereafter Hoffman citation), via James C. Sawruk, who is the expert on SoPac flying boat operations.
4. ComAirSoPac war diary, 14 Sept. 1942.
5. Tōkō Air Group *Kōdōchōsho*, 15 Sept. 1942; *Wasp* to *Hornet* 150103 of September 1942. That message and others also mention destruction of a "two-motored job," but no such attack took place.
6. For an excellent reconstruction of the torpedoing of the *Wasp*, see Capt. Ben W. Blee, USN (Ret.), "Whodunnit?" *U.S. Naval Institute Proceedings* (July 1982) 42–47; *Senshi Sōsho*, 83:125–26.
7. As told to Spencer Held, "Death of the *Wasp*," *Flying* (September 1944) 110.
8. Lt. (jg) David V. Senft, "When the *Wasp* Went Down," *Liberty* (9 Jan. 1943) 9.
9. Held, 110.
10. Statement by Lt. (jg) Joseph J. Bodell, Jr., in *Wasp* action report (24 Sept. 1942).
11. *Wasp* report.
12. Senft, 48; Held, 112.
13. Held, 112.
14. ComAirSoPacFor to ComSoPac, Interview of Ens. Paul E. Tepas, VS-8 (5 Oct. 1942); on Widhelm's "stash," private communication from VS-8 pilots via James C. Sawruk. For an SBD to fly without a radioman was a highly unusual event.
15. MAtt, Mess Attendant; OC, Officer's Cook; OS, Officer's Steward.

16. Kenton corresp.
17. Bauer diary, 16 Sept. 1942.

12 THE LULL

Principal source for CACTUS air operations is MAG-23 Report of Action, September 16–October 16, 1942; for VF-5: VF-5 war diary.
1. VF-5 combat reports, 17 Sept. 1942: Simpler, Crews, March, Mankin; principal source for 1st MAW air operations is Cdr. MAG-23 Report of Action, September 16–October 16, 1942.
2. Ltr. Capt. Paul Mankin to Thomas F. Gates (25 Sept. 1981); Crews interview; Simpler corresp.
3. Ltr. J. A. Halford to Janis M. Boone (future Mrs. Halford) (17 Sept. 1942); it is not possible at this time to identify the pilot of the other aircraft.
4. ComAmphibSoPac to ComSoPac, Report of Operations to Land the 7th Marines (27 Sept. 1942).
5. Chamberlain corresp., with text of his ad hoc diary kept on the island; undated interview (1943) with Maj. J. N. Renner, MCHS, via Robert J. Cressman; Hubler and DeChant, 95.
6. CinCPac to ComSoPac 182239, ComSoPac to CinCPac 210226, both of September 1942.
7. CinCPac to ComSoPac 202147 of September 1942; CominCh to CinCPac 201755 of September 1942.
8. RAdm. Leigh Noyes to CinCPac, Report of Operations 8–18 September 1942 (5 Oct. 1942); Noyes biographical file, NHC.
9. CO USS *Wasp* (Cdr. Fred C. Dickey) to Chief of Naval Personnel, Officers—Availability of (21 Oct. 1942), in Dickey Papers from Fred C. Dickey, Jr.
10. Ltr. McCain to Vandegrift (14 Sept. 1942), Woods Papers, MCHC.
11. Sources on CACTUS life, VF-5 diaries and recollections of participants.
12. Mears, 122.
13. Ibid., 131.
14. Crews corresp.
15. Bayler and Carnes, 354–55.
16. Simpler corresp.; Green diary; ltr. Senior Marine Aviator Present to SecNav, Recommendation for Lt. William S. Robb, A-V(S) (10 Nov. 1942), in Woods papers.
17. Simpler corresp.
18. Howard Crews vignette, "A Generalized Judgment."
19. On Wilkins, Moran corresp., Maj. Gen. Marion Carl interview.
20. Mattison Fighter Direction Report, Mattison papers.
21. Longley corresp.
22. Reynolds, *Saga of Smokey Stover,* 64; Green diary.
23. Figures from a study of all available sources, including RG 313, ComCarPac, A4-1 Aircraft Status Reports.
24. ComAirPac to *Copahee* 150327; CinCPac to ComSoPac 182105; ComAirPac to CominCh 190131: all of September 1942.
25. Memo CominCh to Chief of Staff U.S. Army 17 Sept. 1942. Messages ComAirPac to ComFAirWest 142009; ComFAirWest to ComAirForPac 161816; ComAirPac to CominCh 190131: all of September 1942.
26. ComAirPac to ComAirSoPac 180246; CinCPac to ComSoPac 190307; ComAirSoPac to ComAirPac 221107: all of September 1942.
27. Ltr. Compton to Fitch (27 Sept. 1942), in Turner Papers, NHC.
28. Bauer diary; Green diary; Blair diary.
29. VF-5 war diary; VS-3 ACA Report 26 Sept. 1942.
30. *Senshi Sōsho,* 83:146–47; 25th Air Flotilla Detailed Action Report, 15 Sept.–27 Oct. 1942, in JD86; Japanese Monograph No. 121.
31. Hata and Izawa, 160–61.
32. Ibid., 123–27, 339 (on Aioi), 312–13 (on Yamaguchi).
33. *Taiyō* Detailed Action Report, 28 Sept. 1942, in JD10 microfilm.

34. Okumiya and Horikoshi, *Zero,* 209. Japanese Monograph No. 121, Southeast Area Naval Air Operations Part IX (16–30 Sept. 1942); 25th Air Flotilla Detailed Action Report Summary, 1 April–9 Nov. 1942, in JD86 microfilm.
35. *Senshi Sōsho,* 83:149; Japanese Monograph No. 118, 298–99.

13 THE ATTACKS RESUME

Principal sources: MAG-23 Report of Action, 16 September–16 October 1942; 25th Air Flotilla war diary and Detailed Action Report, 15 Sept.–27 Oct. 1942, in JD86 microfilm; Japanese Monograph 121.
1. *Kōdōchōshos,* Kisarazu, Takao, 2nd, and 3rd air groups, 27 Sept. 1942.
2. Blair diary, 27 Sept. 1942. For 27 September air battle, see VF-5 combat reports: Jensen, Wesolowski, McDonald, Register, Mankin, Nesbitt; ComAirPac combat reports: Armistead, Kennedy, D'Arcy, King, Carl, Payne, Drury, Lynch, Conger, Hughes, Frazier.
3. Faust, "The Squadron," 106–8.
4. Reynolds, *Saga of Smokey Stover,* 69.
5. Renner, undated interview, 4.
6. Ltr. Mankin to Gates.
7. Ibid.
8. In addition to Wesolowski's report, see his recent account in Eric Hammel, *Aces against Japan,* 65–67.
9. Tregaskis, 250.
10. *Kōdōchōshos,* Misawa, Kanoya, and Takao air groups, 28 Sept. 1942.
11. *Kōdōchōshos,* 6th, Kanoya, and Tainan air groups, 28 Sept. 1942.
12. VF-5 combat reports, 28 Sept. 1942: Simpler, Crews, Clarke, Grimmell, Stover, Wesolowski, Kleinmann, Blair, Currie, Halford, Mankin, Nesbitt. ComAirFor combat reports, 28 Sept. 1942: Currie, Blair, Halford.
13. ComAirFor combat reports, 28 Sept. 1942: Galer, Bauer, Marvin; Carl, Jeans, Treptow, Drury, Payne, Smith, Lees, Brooks, Read. Maj. John L. Smith's notebook for side numbers.
14. Galer [and Payne], BuAer interview (6 Jan. 1943); Bauer diary, 28 Sept. 1942.
15. Blair diary, 28 Sept. 1942.
16. Hartley corresp.
17. Crews interview.
18. Blair diary, 28 Sept. 1942.
19. Crews interview.
20. Hubler and DeChant, 114.
21. 1st MarDiv, D-2 Journal (28 Sept. 1942); H. C. Merillat, 157; message Com1stMar-Div to ComSoPac 280502 of September 1942.
22. CinCPac Greybook, 27 Sept. 1942.
23. Ugaki, 219–30.
24. *Senshi Sōsho,* 83:149–51, based on notes taken by Cdr. Shibata Bunzō of the 26th Air Flotilla staff.
25. Reynolds, *Saga of Smokey Stover,* 70.
26. VF-5 combat reports, 29 Sept. 1942: Simpler, Green, Stover, Currie, Bright, Roach, Mankin. ComAirFor combat reports, 29 Sept. 1942: Bright, Roach.
27. *Kōdōchōshos,* 3rd and Kanoya air groups, 29 Sept. 1942.
28. Simpler corresp.
29. Reynolds, *Saga of Smokey Stover,* 72.
30. Ibid., 73.
31. Ibid., 72.
32. Abe's account in Yanagida, 1:468–71.
33. VF-5 combat reports, 29 Sept. 1942: Simpler, Grimmell, Halford, Mankin.
34. He purchased the embroidery at Efate to "occupy my mind so that I don't shortly go nuts." Blair diary, 14 Sept. 1942.
35. Reynolds, *Saga of Smokey Stover,* 73.
36. H. Arthur Lamar, *I Saw Stars,* 9. Lamar was Nimitz's flag lieutenant.
37. Clarke corresp.

38. Green diary.
39. VF-5 combat reports, 2 Oct. 1942: Simpler, Green, Register, Halford, Currie, Bright, Rouse, Nesbitt. ComAirFor combat reports, 2 Oct. 1942: Smith, Read, Marvin, Gutt, Dobbin, Nicolay, Johnson, Brooks, Carl, Frazier, Hughes, Galer, Hartley, Irwin, Walter. VMF-223 side numbers from Major Smith's notebook.
40. MacDonnell radar report (16 Dec. 1942), Mattison papers.
41. *Kōdōchōshos,* 6th and Tainan air groups, 2 Oct. 1942.
42. Brendan Gill, whose column, "A Reporter At Large–Where They Wanted to Be," *New Yorker* (March 13, 1943) 34–35, featured a long interview with Maj. Galer.
43. Carl interview.
44. Mears, 125.
45. VS-71 war diary, 2 Oct. 1942; VMFB-141 history, March 1942–Jan. 1945.
46. 5th Marines Record of Events; VF-5 war diary.
47. Clifton B. Cates, "My First at Guadalcanal, 7 August to 22 December 1942," Cates Papers, MCHC.
48. *Kōdōchōshos,* 751 and 3rd air groups, 3 Oct. 1942.
49. MG Marion Carl, USMC, Oral History, MCHC.
50. ComAirFor combat reports, 3 Oct. 1942: Carl, Watkins, Frazier, Bauer, Lynch, Winter.
51. Hata and Izawa, 269.
52. Faust, "The Squadron," 118–20.
53. USS *Nicholas* war diary, 3 Oct. 1942.
54. CO VF-5 to CominCh, Report of Air Operations Against the Japanese, Guadalcanal Area, September 11 to October 16, 1942 (11 Nov. 1942); Green diary.
55. Faust, "The Squadron," 121–22. ComAirFor combat reports, 3 Oct. 1942: Armistead. Blair diary, 3 Oct. 1942.
56. On Jeans and Hughes, information from Rex Hamilton, VMF-223 historian. He also furnished a clipping describing Kendrick's father recovering the body in 1946; on Morgan, Cdr. L. C. Simpler, Memo for Cdr. Morrison, "Pilots of VF Squadron Five, Killed in Action," from files of Ships History, NHC, via historian Robert J. Cressman.
57. Abe Kenichi in Yanagida, 1:471–72.

14 "DOGGONE BALL OF WEATHER"

1. Murray, BuAer interview.
2. ComSoPac to CTF-17 011430 of October 1942.
3. ComAirSoPac to ComSoPac 020050 of October 1942.
4. Basic sources for the 5 October raid include: CTF-17 to CinCPac, Report of Air Raid on Buin-Faisi-Tonolei, Bougainville Island (14 Oct. 1942); CO USS *Hornet* to CinCPac, Report of Action, October 5, 1942 (8 Oct. 1942).
5. Lea, "Aboard the U.S.S. *Hornet,*" 54.
6. Capt. E. W. Hessel corresp.; *Kamikawa Maru* Air Unit Detailed Action Report.
7. 2nd *Hikōkitai* (*Sanuki Maru*) Detailed Battle Report; *Kamikawa Maru* Air Unit Detailed Action Report.
8. *Senshi Sōsho,* 83:174–75.
9. RAdm. Allan F. Fleming corresp.
10. Misawa Air Group *Kōdōchōsho,* 5 Oct. 1942.
11. Ibid.
12. ComSoPac to CTF-17 060734 of October 1942; CinCPac Greybook, 6 October 1942; CinCPac to ComSoPac 070021 of October 1942.

15 SPARRING WITH THE TOKYO EXPRESS

1. Kenton corresp.; phone conv. with Cdr. Raymond F. Myers.
2. War diary of Lt. L. C. Mattison, USNR, Oct. 3, 1942–Jan. 16, 1943, 4, from Capt. Lewis C. Mattison.

3. ComSoPac to CinCPac 160313, ComAirSoPac to CinCPac 160830, *both* of October 1942; corresp. with Mrs. Elizabeth Shands.
4. Mears, 130.
5. VF-5 combat reports, 8 Oct. 1942: Simpler, Jensen, Rooney, Green, Myers, Register, Tucker, Roach, Blair. War diaries, VS-71 and VT-8.
6. *Nisshin* Detailed Action Report, 11 Sept.–3 Nov. 1942, in JD10 microfilm, NHC; 2nd *Hikōkitai* (*Sanyō Maru* and *Sanuki Maru*) Detailed Battle Report, 8 Oct. 1942; *Chitose Kōdōchōsho*, 8 Oct. 1942.
7. Mears, 138.
8. Ibid.
9. *Senshi Sōsho*, 83:183.
10. Kirn narrative, 3 June 1943.
11. Blair diary, 8 Oct. 1942; VF-5 war diary.
12. Myers phone conv.; VMSB-141 Muster Roll, October 1942.
13. Simpler, BuAer interview; Simpler corresp.; Green interview.
14. Book in possession of Cdr. Frank O. Green.
15. Blair diary, 9 Oct. 1942.
16. Walter Simmons, *Joe Foss: Flying Marine*, 30. This memoir is especially accurate and exciting.
17. Crews diary, interview.
18. "Castaway U.S. Flier Held at Bay by Japs on Islet in Solomons," clipping in Altemus diary, 134; also Blair diary, 10 Oct. 1942.
19. "Castaway U.S. Flier Held at Bay by Japs on Islet in Solomons."

16   CACTUS IN PERIL

Basic source: MAG-23 Report of Action, September 16–October 16, 1942; thereafter continued by MAG-14 as "MAG-23 war diary."
1. *Senshi Sōsho*, 83:175–76.
2. *Kōdōchōshos*, Tainan, Kisarazu, Misawa, 2nd, 3rd, 751, and 753 air groups, 11 Oct. 1942.
3. Galer [and Payne], BuAer interview (6 Jan. 1943); Capt. William C. Sharpsteen, 339th Fighter Squadron, Report, "Combat Experiences at CACTUS," 26 Oct. 1942 (hereafter Sharpsteen report).
4. Charles Cook, *The Battle of Cape Esperance*; Frank, 296–307.
5. Simpler, BuAer interview (26 Feb. 1943).
6. VF-5 combat reports, 12 Oct. 1942: Jensen, Rooney, Blair, Kleinman, Myers, Kenton, Mankin, Nesbitt.
7. Corresp. with Myers and Kenton; ltr. Mankin to Gates; VT-8 war diary, 12 Oct. 1942.
8. ComSoPac to ComGenCACTUS 121400 of October 1942.
9. CO USS *Hornet* to CinCPac, Report of Action, 12–13 October 1942 (17 Oct. 1942), includes VF-72 action reports for 12–13 Oct. 1942.
10. Tōkō Air Group *Kōdōchōsho*, 12 Oct. 1942.
11. Kisarazu Air Group *Kōdōchōsho*, 12 Oct. 1942.
12. Lea, "Aboard the U.S.S. *Hornet*," 56; Misawa Air Group *Kōdōchōsho*, 13 Oct. 1942.
13. *Kōdōchōshos*, Kisarazu, Misawa, Tainan, 3rd, 751, and 753 air groups, 13 Oct. 1942.
14. Simmons, 34–36.
15. Reynolds, *Saga of Smokey Stover*, 77.
16. Simpler corresp.
17. Bayler and Carnes, 280.
18. 67th FS History, 41.
19. Bayler and Carnes, 279; Kirn narrative, 3 June 1943; *Senshi Sōsho*, 83:213.
20. Renner, undated interview, 4–5.
21. Bayler and Carnes, 282; Simpler corresp.
22. VMFB-141 history; VS-71 war diary.
23. Clipping dated 10 Jan. 1943 in J. A. Halford papers.

24. CG 1st MarDiv to ComSoPac 141942 of Oct. 1942.
25. *Kōdōchōshos*, Kisarazu, Misawa, Tainan, 3rd, 751, and 753 air groups, 14 Oct. 1942.
26. *Kōdōchōshos*, 2nd, 3rd, and 751 air groups, 14 Oct. 1942.
27. The four pilots reported downing five bombers, but each claimed only one; they flipped a coin to see who should get credit for the odd one, and Jensen won. Blair diary, 17 Oct. 1942.
28. Myers phone conv.; Blair diary, 17 Oct. 1942.
29. ComAirSoPac to ComSoPac 140138 of October 1942.
30. ComSoPac to CinCPac 141410 of October 1942.
31. Hayden Jensen in clipping, Altemus diary.
32. *Kōdōchōshos*, 6th Air Group, *Chitose*, and *Junyō*; 2nd *Hikōkitai* Detailed Battle Report.
33. VF-5 combat reports, 15 Oct. 1942: Rooney, Stover.
34. Simmons, 46.
35. Sharpsteen report, 26 Oct. 1942.
36. Cram's report in SoPacFor NACI Air Battle Notes from the South Pacific, No. 4 (23 Nov. 1942); Colonel Haberman's recent account in Joe Foss and Matthew Brennan, *Top Guns*, 73–74.
37. Mattison war diary, 7.
38. *Kōdōchōshos*, 3rd and 751 air groups, 15 Oct. 1942.
39. VF-5 combat reports, 15 Oct. 1942: Richardson, Rouse.
40. CG 1st MarDiv to ComSoPac 150415 of October 1942.
41. Clarke corresp.
42. Lt. Gen. John C. Munn, USMC, Oral History, MCHC, 67–68.
43. ComAirSoPac to ComSoPac 150921 of October 1942.
44. CTF-17 to CinCPac, Action Reports, 15–16 October 1942 (21 Oct. 1942).
45. CO VF-72 Action Report, 15 Oct. 1942; Tōkō Air Group *Kōdōchōsho*, 15 Oct. 1942.
46. Blair diary, 17 Oct. 1942; Simpler corresp.; Kenton corresp.
47. Simpler corresp.
48. CO USS *Hornet* to CinCPac, Report of Action, 16 Oct. 1942 (18 Oct. 1942), with the air group and squadron reports; CO USS *Hornet* to CinCPac, Report of Action, 16 Oct. 1942 (20 Oct. 1942).
49. Tōkō Air Group *Kōdōchōsho*, 16 Oct. 1942; Cdr. Philip E. Souza corresp.
50. Simpler corresp.; Blair diary, 17 Oct. 1942.
51. CO USS *McFarland* to CinCPac, Report of Action (15 Dec. 1942); Charles Rawlings, "The *McFarland* Comes Home," *Saturday Evening Post* (13 March 1943), 11. According to Rex Hamilton and others from VMF-223, the Marine and USN ground crew still greatly resent this calumny.
52. Simpler corresp.
53. *Kōdōchōshos*, 6th and 31st air groups, 16 Oct. 1942.
54. *McFarland* Report of Action (15 Dec. 1942); Rex Hamilton interview.
55. Blair diary, 17 Oct. 1942.
56. Bauer's combat report in NACI-ComAirSoPac Air Battle Notes from SoPac No. 3 (1 Nov. 1942); Maj. J. N. Renner, BuAer interview (17 July 1943); Faust, "The Squadron," 146–50.
57. ComSoPac to CTF-17 160032 of October 1942; ComSoPac to CinCPac 160440 of October 1942.
58. Hansgeorg Jentschura et al., *Warships of the Imperial Japanese Navy, 1869–1945*, 52–53; Hata and Izawa, 61–62, 64.
59. The *Hiyō* and *Junyō* kōdōchōshos illustrate the change in air group personnel.
60. ComSoPac to ComGenCACTUS 16140, ComSoPac to CACTUS, CTF-17 161625, both of October 1942. RG 457 SRNS-0186 CNO Intelligence Summary, 16 Oct. 1942; MAG-23 war diary, 17 Oct. 1942.
61. *Kōdōchōshos*, *Hiyō* and *Junyō*, 17 Oct. 1942.
62. Hata and Izawa, 343.
63. VF-5 war diary; Cdr. VF-5 to ComAirPac, Fighting Squadron Five, Tabular Report of Pilot and Plane Requirements during Operations Period July 7, 1942–October 16, 1942.
64. Cdr. VF-5 to CominCh, Report of Air Operations against the Japanese, Guadal-

canal Area, September 11 to October 16, 1942 (11 Nov. 1942); Simpler, BuAer interview (26 Feb. 1943) and narrative (8 March 1943).

17   THE "HOTTEST POTATO"

Principal source for CACTUS air operations: MAG-23 war diary, 17–23 October 1942.

1. For Flatley's earlier career, see *The First Team, passim.*
2. VF-10 war diary; VAdm. J. H. Flatley Papers in possession of Flatley family, including original sketch of "The Grim Reaper"; in general, Stanley Johnston, *The Grim Reapers,* based on extensive interviews with Flatley and other members of the squadron, and a fine new history: Peter Mersky, *The Grim Reapers: Fighting Squadron Ten in WWII.*
3. "History of the Buzzard Brigade" (unpublished); corresp./interviews with VT-10 veterans who have a strong reunion association organized by Thomas C. Nelson.
4. VF-10 war diary, August–November 1942.
5. Capt. James G. Daniels III, diary, interview, and corresp.
6. E. B. Potter, *Bull Halsey,* 158; CinCPac to CTF-16 110045 of October 1942.
7. ComAirPac to ComAirSoPac 160136 of October 1942.
8. CinCPac to CominCh 160937; CominCh to CinCPac 170245: both of October 1942.
9. FAdm. William F. Halsey and Lt. Cdr. J. Bryan III, *Admiral Halsey's Story,* 109.
10. ComSoPac to CinCPac 171230, CinCPac to CominCh 172359, both of October 1942.
11. Compiled from all available sources.
12. War diaries, VMF-112, VMF-122, VMSB-132, VMSB-142.
13. CinCPac to CominCh 172359, ComAirSoPac to ComSoPac 210212, both of October 1942.
14. Messages all of October 1942: ComMarWing 1 to ComAirSoPac 200407; ComAirPac to ComAirSoPac 210212; ComAirPac to ComFAirWest 212300; ComAirPac to ComAirSoPac 212350; ComFAirWest to ComAirPac 222253. *Altamaha* war diary.
15. CominCh to CinCPac 211630 of October 1942.
16. Activities of the VF-71 Detachment are covered, albeit briefly, in VMF-121 war diary, October–November 1942; also Kenton corresp.
17. *Kōdōchōshos,* 3rd and 751 air groups, 18 Oct. 1942.
18. ComAirFor combat reports, Summary of Operations at CACTUS 16–30 Oct. 1942; Simmons, 54, 80–81. Faust, "The Squadron," is by far the best source on Bauer's personality and philosophy.
19. *Kōdōchōshos,* Kisarazu, Misawa, Tainan, and 3rd air groups, 18 Oct. 1942.
20. Simmons, 55.
21. Hq 347th Fighter Group, Combat Report of 1st Lt. Wallace S. Dinn, Jr., 339th Fighter Squadron (6 Dec. 1942); I MarAmphibCorps, POW Interrogation of "Fujiden Yasuo" (3 Dec. 1942). Like many Japanese POWs, Fujita used a pseudonym to his interrogators.
22. Faust, "The Squadron," 156.
23. Senft corresp.
24. Simmons, 56.
25. 6th Air Group *Kōdōchōsho,* 19 Oct. 1942; Faust, "The Squadron," 169–71.
26. 6th Air Group *Kōdōchōsho,* 20 Oct. 1942.
27. Faust, "The Squadron," 171–78.
28. *Kōdōchōshos,* Tainan, 2nd, 3rd, and 753 air groups, 20 Oct. 1942.
29. 25th Air Flotilla Detailed Action Report, 15 Sept.–27 Oct. 1942, message 1703/20 Oct. 1942 5th Air Attack Force Battle Report No. 194, in JD86 microfilm.
30. *Kōdōchōshos,* Kisarazu, Tainan, 2nd, 3rd, and 751 air groups, 21 Oct. 1942.
31. Faust, "The Squadron," 179–84; interview with Frank Drury; Hata and Izawa, 246–47, for Ōta.
32. VF-5 war diary; Blair diary, 22 Oct. 1942.
33. *Kōdōchōshos,* 2nd, 6th, and 31st air groups, 22 Oct. 1942.
34. Mattison war diary, 14.
35. *Kōdōchōshos,* Kisarazu, Misawa, Tainan, 2nd, 6th, and 751 air groups, 23 Oct. 1942.
36. Faust, "The Squadron," 188.

37. Mattison war diary, 9.
38. Faust, "The Squadron," 187–92.

18 THE BIG OCTOBER OFFENSIVE UNFOLDS

1. Personal ltr. Halsey to Nimitz (31 Oct. 1942), in Fleet Adm. C. W. Nimitz Papers, NHC. Halsey's long letters to his boss offer the best indication of what he was thinking during the crucial months of October and November 1942.
2. RG 457, SRNS-180 CNO Summaries, 10 Oct. 1942.
3. ComSoPac to CTF-16, -17, -64 220042 of October 1942; ltr. Halsey to Nimitz (31 Oct. 1942).
4. Messages all of October 1942: CincPac to ComSoPac 220350; ComSoPac to Com-GenCACTUS 220558; CinCPac to ComSoPac 222040; CinCPac to ComSoPac 230405.
5. RG 457, SRMN-009 CinCPac Fleet Intelligence Summaries, 22 Oct. 1942, 23 Oct. 1942; SRNS-0193 OpNav Estimate 0193, 23 Oct. 1942.
6. ComAirSoPac war diary, 23 Oct. 1942.
7. Vandegrift, 184.
8. ComSoPac to CTF-16 192354 of October 1942,; ltr. Halsey to Nimitz, 31 Oct. 1942.
9. Interview with Capt. John H. Griffin.
10. For Japanese plans in general, see Senshi Sōsho, 83:238–74; Frank, 337–51, 368–72.
11. Ugaki, 245.
12. Basic sources for CACTUS air operations on 25 October: war diaries, MAG-23, VMF-121.
13. Simmons, 78; message ComSoPac to CinCPac 080525 of November 1942. Capt. Shinohara Hideo took over the chūtai after Kirita failed to return. Akimoto, Minoru, "Ki-46 Type 100 Command Reconnaisance Plane," Part 3, Koku-Fan (April 1982) 137.
14. Simmons, 79–80; 3rd Air Group Kōdōchōsho, 25 Oct. 1942.
15. Mattison war diary, 11.
16. Faust, "The Squadron," 193–207; interviews with Colonel Conger and Ishikawa Shirō, who were reunited in April 1990 at the Admiral Nimitz Museum in Fredericksburg, Texas. Quote by Nagano in Hata and Izawa, 257.
17. Simmons, 74.
18. Tainan Air Group Kōdōchōsho, 25 Oct. 1942.
19. 1st MarDiv, D-2 Journal, 25 Oct. 1942.
20. Simmons, 74–76.
21. Ibid., 76–77.
22. Kōdōchōshos, Tainan, Hiyō, Kisarazu, and 753 air groups, 25 Oct. 1942; Item #323 (S-64) Diary of PO2c OGINO, Kyoichiro (or Yasuichiro), entries dated 25 Oct. to 10 Nov. 1942 (4 Feb. 1943); 1st MarDiv, D-2 Journal, 13 Nov. 1942.
23. Junyō Kōdōchōsho, 25 Oct. 1942.
24. Message 0031/26 Oct. 1942 CO, 5th Air Attack Force to CO, Base Air Force, Battle Report #199 (Oct. 25, 1942), in 25th Air Flotilla Detailed Battle Report, 15 Sept.–27 Oct. 1942, in JD86 microfilm.
25. For an account by Sesso, see Ira Wolfert, Battle for the Solomons (New York, 1943), 108–10. Messages from ComAirSoPac war diary, 25 Oct. 1942.
26. Lt. (jg) Warren B. Matthew to Cdr. B. Paschal, Ops. Off. (1 Nov. 1942), Action with Enemy, 25 Oct. 1942, furnished by Commander Matthew to James Sawruk.
27. ComAirSoPac war diary, 25 Oct. 1942; VP-24 detachment diary, 25 Oct. 1942, in Dr. Norman S. Haber papers; corresp. with James C. Sawruk.
28. For TF-61 operations on 25 October, see TF-16 war diary; CTF-61 to CinCPac, Report of Carrier Action North of the Santa Cruz Islands, 26 October 1942 (20 Nov. 1942).
29. Air strengths from analysis by James Sawruk and the author of all action reports and available documents, including Aircraft Status Reports (in RG 313, ComCarPac, A4-1) and the Bureau Number Cards (National Air and Space Museum); message ComSoPac to CTF-16, -17 231349 of October 1942.
30. War diaries, VF-10, VB-10; Capt. James G. Daniels corresp.

31. ComSoPac to CTF-61 242350 of October 1942. The erroneous "Attack Repeat Attack" from *Admiral Halsey's Story* (p. 121) is a paraphrase.
32. Sources on the 25 October dusk strike include: VF-10 war diary, 25 Oct. 1942; Cdr. VF-10 to CO USS *Enterprise,* Fighting Squadron Ten Action Reports for October 25 and 26, 1942 (31 Oct. 1942); VB-10 war diary, 25 Oct. 1942; Cdr. VT-10 to CO USS *Enterprise,* Action, October 26, 1942—Report of (30 Oct. 1942); "History of the Buzzard Brigade" (VT-10), (1943); Unpublished memoir by George B. Welles (from his son Jeffrey Welles via James Sawruk); interviews or corresp. with Capt. S. W. Vejtasa, Capt. F. L. Faulkner, RAdm. E. L. Feightner (VF-10); Thomas C. Nelson (VT-10).
33. ComCarPac to Carriers, Pacific, Air Group Commanders, Duties of (10 July 1942), in RG 313 ComAirPac, A16-3.
34. CTF-61 Report (20 Nov. 1942).
35. Vejtasa thought that Ens. Edward L. Coalson was the offender, but he did not fly that mission.
36. Lindsey narrative.
37. *Senshi Sōsho,* 83:282.
38. AirSoPac Operations Book, 25 Oct. 1942; Crews diary, 25 Oct. 1942.
39. Daniels corresp.; Eugene Burns, *Then There Was One,* 112–13.
40. Souza corresp.
41. Ltr. Halsey to Nimitz (31 Oct. 1942).

19   POUNDING THE *SHŌKAKU* AND *ZUIHŌ*

General sources on the Battle of Santa Cruz:
  CinCPac to CominCh, Solomon Islands Campaign, Battle of Santa Cruz—26 October 1942 (6 Jan. 1943). Enclosed with this report are nearly all of the relevant reports, including task forces, task groups, ships, groups, and squadrons, as well as message logs. Filed separately is CO USS *South Dakota* to CominCh, Action Report, October 26, 1942, off Santa Cruz Islands (2 Nov. 1942). Also vital are the war diaries of ComSoPac, ComAir-SoPac, TF-16, *Enterprise,* VF-10, and VB-10.
  Principal Japanese sources include: *Senshi Sōsho,* 83:286–316; Yokosuka Air Group Battle Lessons, Chapter Eight, 2nd Solomons Sea Battle and the Naval Battle of the South Pacific (3 May 1943); *Kōdōchōshos, Shōkaku, Zuikaku, Zuihō, and Junyō,* 26 Oct. 1942; 7th Cruiser Division War Diary and Detailed Action Report, 11–30 Oct. 1942, and 8th Cruiser Division War Diary and Detailed Action Report, 26 Oct. 1942, both in microfilm JD16; 2nd Destroyer Squadron War Diary and Detailed Action Report, 11–26 Oct. 1942, in microfilm JD26, portions translated as: Battle of Santa Cruz: Information from Japanese Sources, Despatches from DesRon 2 Combat Report 11–30 October 1942, (n.d.); WDC 161270 CO Striking Force to CinC 2nd Fleet (27 Oct. 1942); WDC 160985 10th Destroyer Division Combat Report No. 2, 25–27 October 1942.
  1. ComAirSoPac war diary, 26 Oct. 1942; corresp. Cdr. George S. Clute and Capt. Glen Hoffman with James Sawruk; Hoffman citation.
  2. Principal source for all Japanese air operations are the carrier *kōdōchōshos.*
  3. Hara, 128.
  4. Cdr. VS-10 to CO USS *Enterprise,* Report of Action, October 16 to October 26, 1942 (29 Oct. 1942); Cdr. VB-10 to CO USS *Enterprise,* Report of Action, October 26, 1942 (30 Oct. 1942).
  5. Burns, 119–20.
  6. Search messages from ComAirSoPac war diary, 26 Oct. 1942.
  7. Endorsement by ComSoPac (30 Nov. 1942) of CTF-61 to CinCPac, Report of Carrier Action North of the Santa Cruz Islands, 26 October 1942 (20 Nov. 1942).
  8. Griffin interview.
  9. In addition to VS-10 report (29 Oct. 1942), see also Air Force, Pacific Fleet, Scout Bombers in Action (2 Jan. 1943) (hereafter AirFor Scout Bombers), which contains individual reports by Burnett and Miller.
 10. VS-10 report; AirFor Scout Bombers, reports by Lee, Johnson, Ward, and Carmody; RAdm. M. D. Carmody interview.
 11. From notes taken by VS-8 pilot Don Adams in the squadron ready room and furnished to James Sawruk.

12. A photo exists of the two placards being presented to a VT-10 TBF.
13. Lea, "Aboard the U.S.S. *Hornet*," 54.
14. VS-10 report; Burns, 141–44; VAdm. James H. Flatley, Jr., "The Bravest Man I Knew," *Shipmate* (December 1978).
15. Message log in CTG-17.2 (ComCruDiv 5) to CinCPac, Action Report of Air Action Fought North of Santa Cruz Islands, October 2, 1942 (2 Nov. 1942); this comprehensive log covers virtually all forms of commmunication (fighter net, search and attack frequency, coded despatches, TBS, visual, etc.) used during the battle; other vital message logs include Excerpts from the *Pensacola* Log of Fighter Director Circuit, 10/26/42, filed with CO USS *Hornet* to the Secretary of the Navy, Report of Action, October 26, 1942, and Subsequent Loss of USS *Hornet* (30 Oct. 1942); and FDO [Cdr. John H. Griffin] to CO USS *Enterprise,* Report on Fighter Direction on October 26, 1942 (6 Nov. 1942), with enclosures included extracts from the TBS, Fighter Net (6390 kc.), and Search and Attack (6970 kc.) logs maintained in the *Enterprise's* Radar Plot. All messages quoted come from these logs.
16. Souza corresp.; Cdr. VF-72 to CTF-17, Action Report of October 26, 1942 (2 Nov. 1942). Radio traffic in ComCruDiv 5 message log.
17. On Air Group Ten's mission, see: CAG-10 to CinCPac, Report of Action, October 26, 1942, in Santa Cruz Islands and Stewart Islands Area (2 Nov. 1942); VF-10 report (31 Oct. 1942) includes Comments on Air Action of Air Group Ten Attack Force on October 26, 1942 by Leader of Escort VF, and Report of Action on October 26, 1942, by Ens. Willis B. Reding, USNR; VS-10 report (29 Oct. 1942); VT-10 report (30 Oct. 1942); Johnston, 129–33; Burns, 126–27; Edward P. Stafford, *The Big E,* 157–59 (interview of R. E. Rhodes); Hammel, *Guadalcanal: The Carrier Battles,* 358–59, account of M. D. Norton; corresp. with Lt. Cdr. A. E. Mead, Cdr. R. E. Rhodes, Capt. R. L. Reiserer, Cdr. R. R. Witte (all VF-10); Cdr. Glen Estes (VS-10); VT-10: T. C. Nelson, Michael Glasser, Thomas Powell, and additional interviews via William Shinneman, brother of Charles Shinneman, who kindly shared his research with me. *Zuihō Kōdōchōsho,* 26 Oct. 1942.
18. Nelson corresp.
19. Dr. Robert Gruebel interview, via William Shinneman.
20. Michael Glasser corresp.
21. Charles Shinneman interview, via William Shinneman.
22. Burns, 126.
23. ComCruDiv 5 message log.
24. Shinneman interview, via William Shinneman.
25. Mead corresp.
26. Stafford, 158.
27. Rhodes corresp.
28. Dr. Izawa Yasuho, personal communication.
29. AirSoPac war diary, 26 Oct. 1942; George Poulos narrative, March 1982 (via James Sawruk).
30. *Hornet* message log recorded by Don Adams, VB-8; see also J. J. Lynch, Lt. USN to CTF-17, Action October 26, 1942 in Solomons Area Against Japanese Forces— Report of (28 Oct. 1942); Souza corresp.
31. Cdr. VF-72 to CTF-17, Action Report of October 26, 1942 (2 Nov. 1942); VF-72 history, NHC; Souza corresp.; *Zuihō Kōdōchōsho.*
32. On 3 March 1943 Maki rammed an enemy plane off Lae and earned a posthumous double promotion; Hata and Izawa, 382.
33. Sources for *Hornet* first-wave SBDs and TBFs include: Cdr. VS-8 and VB-8 [Lt. Cdr. W. J. Widhelm and Lt. J. E. Vose] to CO USS *Hornet,* Action Report of 26 October 1942 with enemy Japanese fleet—Solomon Islands Area (2 Nov. 1942); Cdr. VB-8 to CO USS *Hornet,* Action on 26 October 1942 (29 Oct. 1942); Cdr. VT-6 to CO USS *Hornet,* Action Report for October 26, 1942 of 1st Division of VT Planes (2 Nov. 1942); NACI-ComSoPac Air Battle Notes from the South Pacific Nos. 1–25 (12 Oct. 1942–5 Oct. 1943), reprinted February 1944: interview with Widhelm (19–22); interview with rearseat men of *Hornet's* Dive Bombers, 22–27; corresp. James Sawruk with VS-8: Ralph Hovind, William Woodman, Donald Kirkpatrick, James Forbes, Stan Holms, James Black, Richard T. Woodson; VB-8: Roy Gee, Forrest C. Auman, Fred Bates, Evan Fisher, William Carter, Kenneth B. White; VT-6: Evan K. Williams.
34. ComCruDiv 5 message log.

35. Hata and Izawa, 303–4.
36. Hara, 130.
37. Lea, "Aboard the U.S.S. *Hornet*," 55.
38. Yanagida, 1:533–34.
39. See note 17 above.
40. ComCruDiv 5 message log.
41. *Suzuya* Action Report, 26 Oct. 1942, in microfilm JT1, NHC.
42. *Hornet* second-wave sources: Lynch VB-8 report (28 Oct. 1942); XO VT-6 to CO USS *Hornet*, Action Report on October 26, 1942, Second Division of VT Planes (28 Oct. 1942); VF-72 report; VF-72 war diary; corresp. James Sawruk with Edgar Stebbins (VS-8), Al Wood (VS-8), J. Clark Barrett (VB-8), Ward Powell (VT-6), Humphrey Tallman (VT-6); NACI-ComSoPac Air Battle Notes Nos. 1–25; VF-72: Warren Ford, John Sutherland, Henry Carey, family of David B. Freeman.
43. Japanese sources include 8th Cruiser Division Detailed Action Report, 26 Oct. 1942, in JD16 microfilm; *Chikuma, Tone* Action Reports, 26 Oct. 1942, in reports in microfilm JT1; U.S. Strategic Bombing Survey, *Interrogation of Japanese Officials*, 2:461, for interrogation of RAdm. Komura; Ugaki, 254.
44. Corresp. Estes with Sawruk.

20 "*HORNET* HURT"

1. ComCruDiv 5 message log.
2. Ltr. Lee F. Hollingsworth to James Sawruk; on T-6's operations see also the unpublished Welles memoir.
3. For CAP operations in general, see message logs cited in chap. 19, n. 15 above; VF-10 report, VF-72 report, and especially John Griffin's report: FDO to CO USS *Enterprise*, Report on Fighter Direction on October 26, 1942 (6 Nov. 1942), provided by Captain Griffin.
4. *Kōdōchōshos, Shōkaku* and *Zuikaku*, 26 Oct. 1942.
5. Hessel corresp.
6. Okumiya and Horikoshi, *Zero*, 263, citing Takahashi; Okumiya errs seriously in ascribing the first wave to Seki and the second to Murata; actually Murata led the first wave against the *Hornet*, while Seki later attacked the *Enterprise*. Also Okumiya's strengths for each wave are incorrect.
7. Capt. Claude Phillips corresp.
8. Cdr. George Wrenn corresp.
9. Lt. Cdr. Kenneth C. Kiekhoefer corresp.
10. Hessel corresp.
11. Capt. Kenneth Bliss narrative (n.d.) in Eric Hammel Papers, NHC; Cdr. Richard Z. Hughes corresp.
12. CO USS *Hornet* to SecNav, Report of Action, October 26, 1942, and subsequent loss of USS *Hornet* (30 Oct. 1942), with enclosured reports by ship's departments.
13. For damage to the *Hornet*, see USS *Hornet* (CV-8) Loss in Action Santa Cruz, 26 October 1942, War Damage Report No. 30 (8 July 1943).
14. USS *Pensacola* war diary; WDC 160985 10th Destroyer Division Combat Report No. 2, 25–26 Oct. 1942.
15. Bliss narrative.
16. Kiekhoefer corresp.
17. Bliss narrative.
18. Communications Officer [Lt. Cdr. Oscar H. Dodson] to CO USS *Hornet*, Report of Action, October 26, 1942 (30 Oct. 1942). Aside from eyewitnesses on the *Hornet* and screening ships, the *Pensacola*'s photographer took a series of photos extremely valuable in reconstructing the 1st *Chūtai*'s attacks.
19. *Hornet* Report of Loss.
20. Gordon Prange, *At Dawn We Slept*, 197.
21. CO USS *Pensacola* to CinCPac, Report of Engagement with Enemy Aircraft on October 26, 1942 (31 Oct. 1942).
22. Message 0718/26 Oct. 1942 (Z-9). Unless otherwise noted, Japanese radio messages cited in chapters 20, 21, and 22 come from the log in 2nd Destroyer Squadron

Detailed Action Report, 11–30 Oct. 1942, in microfilm JD26, and the partial translation by the U.S. Pacific Fleet.

23. Narrative of Events by Lt. S. W. Vejtasa, USN, leader of one combat patrol on 26
Oct. 1942, in VF-10 report; see also Burns, 136–37.

24. Report of Action on Oct. 26, 1942 by Ens. Maurice N. Wickendoll, in VF-10
report.

25. Satō's identity is postulated by accounting for all the other members of the 1st
Chūtai; see *Zuikaku Kōdōchōsho,* 26 Oct. 1942.

26. One pilot was Lt. (jg) Ivan Swope, who described the attack in a wartime interview
now in the Sawruk papers.

27. The *kōdōchōshos* are explicit on armament; for the navigational markers and the
250-kilogram bombs, see OpNav 30-3mm, Handbook of Japanese Explosive Ordnance (15 Aug. 1945), 246–47, 94–95.

28. Misled by Okumiya and Horikoshi (*Zero,* 261–62), Thomas G. Miller Jr., *The Cactus Air Force,* 162, has Seki crashing into the *Hornet.*

29. CO USS *Morris* to CinCPac USS *Morris* (DD417)—Action North of Santa Cruz
Islands on October 26, 1942—Report on (30 Oct. 1942).

30. Report of Action 26 Oct. 1942 by Ens. Donald Gordon, USNR, in VF-10 report;
also account in Eric Hammel, *Aces against Japan,* 69–70.

31. Ibid.; Cdr. Macgregor Kilpatrick phone interview.

32. Wrenn corresp.; CO USS *Juneau* to CinCPac, Report of Action on October 26,
1942 (30 Oct. 1942).

33. Narrative of Events by Lt. A. D. Pollock, USN, leader of one combat patrol on 26
Oct. 1942; Report of Action on 26 Oct. 1942 by Ens. Steve G. Kona, both in VF-10
report.

34. Vejtasa narrative.

35. *Hornet* Action Report (30 Oct. 1942); *Hornet* Loss in Action Report (30 Oct. 1942);
CO USS *Northampton* to CinCPac, Report of Action with Enemy (31 Oct. 1942).

36. Wickendoll report; *Shōkaku Kōdōchōsho,* 26 Oct. 1942.

37. Wrenn corresp.; Phillips corresp.; VS-10 report; Burnett's report in ComAirPac
Scout Bombers.

38. Messages in 2nd Destroyer Squadron Detailed Action Report; Yokosuka Air
Group, Battle Lessons, Chapter Eight, 2nd Solomons Sea Battle and the Naval
Battle of the South Pacific (3 May 1943) has sketches of enemy ship positions as
interpreted at different times by the Japanese.

39. Cdr. Robert S. Merritt interview.

40. Cdr. James D. Billo has furnished a copy of his combat report for 26 Oct. 1942.

41. ComCruDiv 5 message log.

42. Kona report.

21 "THE BIG E" SURVIVES

1. Mott narrative (22 March 1944).

2. Phillips corresp.

3. ComCruDiv 5 message log.

4. CTF-16 to ComSoPac 252249, ComSoPac to CTF-61, -64 252250, both of October
1942.

5. VB-10 war diary, 26 Oct. 1942.

6. Messages from 2nd Destroyer Squadron Detailed Action Report: 0727/26 Oct. Cdr.
Kidō Butai to CinC 2nd Fleet; 0728/26 Oct. *Junyō* to all planes; 0737/26 Oct.
Zuikaku plane to Cdr. KdB.

7. Mott narrative.

8. *Shōkaku Kōdōchōsho,* 26 Oct. 1942.

9. For messages on the fighter director circuit, see sources cited in chap. 19, n. 15.

10. James Sawruk research; CO to CinCPac, USS *Porter*—Report of Torpedoing (31
Oct. 1942), examines the question with statements from ship's officers and Lieutenant (jg) Batten, who believed the TBF's torpedo did not break out of the airplane; *Senshi Sōsho,* 83:292, categorically states no I-boats were in the area; in
discussing the event with former ordnancemen who armed TBFs with torpedoes,

they stated that the torpedo, which Batten tried fruitlessly to jettison, might have rested on the bomb-bay doors and could have broken loose upon ditching.

11. Arima corresp./interview; Wickendoll report; clipping in Feightner papers.
12. *Enterprise* report.
13. Capt. Elias B. Mott, "The Battles of Santa Cruz and Guadalcanal: Stopping the Japanese Offensive," *The Hook* (August 1990) 44.
14. Okumiya and Horikoshi, *Zero*, 262.
15. Mott, "The Battles of Santa Cruz and Guadalcanal," 44.
16. *Enterprise* report; Burns, 122–23, 133
17. Wickendoll report; for Blair, see Cdr. VF-10 to Air Officer, USS *Enterprise*, Damage Inflicted on Enemy and Suffered by VF-10 from October 16 to 26, 1942, inclusive—Report of (28 Oct. 1942) in Billo papers; Gordon report.
18. Packard corresp.
19. Cdr. Richard Z. Hughes phone interview.
20. Messages in 2nd Destroyer Squadron Detailed Action Report: 0832/26 Oct. 3rd Fleet aircraft; 0837/26 Oct. *Shōkaku* plane.
21. VB-10 war diary, 26 Oct. 1942; Kilpatrick phone interview.
22. VT-10 report; Norton's account in Hammel, *Guadalcanal: The Carrier Battles;* Wrenn corresp.
23. Reports call the intruder a dive bomber, but photos taken at the time clearly show it to be a Type 97 *kankō;* Japanese records contain nothing on the incident, because Tanaka never returned to base. Report by Lt. Cdr. H. A. I. Luard, RN, on attachment to U.S. Pacific Fleet (n.d., but forwarded by CinCPac dated 8 Jan. 1943).
24. Corresp. with Dr. Norman S. Haber, who provided a copy of the ComPatWing 1 recommendation for awards for this mission. Dr. Haber has become friends with General Shingō's daughter, Sumiko Shingō, who lives in the United States.
25. TG-17.2 to CTF-61 252250 of October 1942.
26. Faulkner phone interview.
27. *Zuikaku Kōdōchōsho*, 26 Oct. 1942.
28. *Enterprise* message log enclosed with Griffin's report (6 Nov. 1942).
29. CO USS *Maury* (DD401) to CTF-16, Report of Action Against Japanese Carrier Based Planes Attacking Task Force Sixteen on October 26, 1942 (3 Nov. 1942).
30. Vejtasa narrative.
31. Pollock narrative.
32. Wrenn corresp.; *Maury*'s report.
33. Burns, 120.
34. CO USS *South Dakota* to CominCh, Action Report, October 26, 1942, off Santa Cruz Islands (2 Nov. 1942); CO USS *Preston* to CinCPac, Report of Action Enemy Air Attack Against Task Force Sixteen on 26 October 1942 (31 October 1942).
35. Mott, "The Battles of Santa Cruz and Guadalcanal," 45.
36. CO USS *Smith* to CinCPac, Action Report USS *Smith*, October 26, 1942 (2 Nov. 1942). The *Smith*'s crew recovered a notebook belonging to one of the dead Japanese. On 4 November it gave Kinkaid first notice of the *Junyō*'s presence in this battle. In January 1943 aircraft codes that it also contained proved vital in deciphering enemy transmissions. For the notebook see 040252 of November 1942 CTF-16 to CinCPac; Ronald Spector, ed., *Listening to the Enemy*, 80.
37. Daniels diary, 26 Oct. 1942; Daniels corresp.
38. CO USS *Portland* to CinCPac, Air Attacks Upon the USS *Enterprise* by Japanese, October 26, 1942—Report of (30 Oct. 1942), and ComSoPac endorsement; see also Heber A. Holbrook, *The History and Times of the U.S.S. Portland*, 166–68, where the evidence indicates only one dud may have struck the ship.
39. Vejtasa narrative; clipping in Feightner papers.
40. Gordon report; also account in Hammel, *Aces against Japan*, 71–72.
41. *Enterprise* report, 10 Nov. 1942.
42. Souza corresp.; *Shōkaku Kōdōchōsho*, 26 Oct. 1942.
43. ComCruDiv 5 message log.
44. VF-72 report; VF-72 history; Okumiya and Horikoshi, *Zero!*, 263; Hara, 132–33, who says the pilot who died came from a fighter, but no fighter pilots died after ditching.
45. Ford corresp.; *Shōkaku Kōdōchōsho*.
46. *Juneau* report (see chap. 20, n. 32); Fisher corresp. with Sawruk.

47. Stebbins corresp. with Sawruk; Wood corresp. with Sawruk.
48. Tallman corresp. with Sawruk.
49. 2nd Destroyer Squadron Detailed Action Report, 0928/26 Oct. from *Zuihō* aircraft; Auman corresp.
50. *Junyō Kōdōchōsho,* 26 Oct. 1942.
51. Okumiya and Horikoshi, *Zero,* 264.
52. Mott, "The Battles of Santa Cruz and Guadalcanal," 45; Burns, 138–39.
53. Okumiya and Horikoshi, *Zero,* 269–70; *Junyō Kōdōchōsho,* 26 Oct. 1942.
54. Shiga's memoir in Yanagida, 1:530–32.
55. Souza corresp.; F-25's antics appear on motion-picture film taken from the carrier's bridge.
56. Wrenn corresp.
57. *South Dakota* report.
58. CO to CinCPac, Report of Action, USS *San Juan,* October 26, 1942, Forwarding of (31 Oct. 1942).
59. Flatley in VF-10 report.
60. Ford corresp.
61. Billo combat report.
62. Bliss narrative.
63. Carey corresp.
64. VF-10 report; Hughes phone interview.
65. VF-72 report; Vejtasa narrative.
66. VB-8 report; Stebbins corresp.
67. VT-6 report.
68. Estes corresp. with Sawruk.
69. ComCruDiv 5 message log.
70. USMC Hq MAG-22, n.d. Spec. Intel. Report on a Japanese Naval Aviator's War Experience from Pearl Harbor on [Lt. Cdr. Shiga Yoshio].
71. VF-10 report.
72. Haber corresp.; *Junyō Kōdōchōsho.*

22   DEFEAT AND RETREAT

1. Welles memoir; ltr. Hollingsworth to Sawruk; *Shōkaku Kōdōchōsho,* 26 Oct. 1942.
2. 2nd Destroyer Squadron Detailed Action Report, message 0932/26 Oct. Cdr. KdB to Cdr. 2nd CarDiv, CinC 2nd Fleet.
3. TF-16 war diary, 26 Oct. 1942.
4. CTF-61 to CTF-17 260035 of October 1942.
5. CTG-17.2 to ComSoPac 252340 of October 1942.
6. CTF-61 to CTG-17.2 260055 of October 1942.
7. Merritt interview.
8. White corresp. with Sawruk.
9. Billo corresp. with author.
10. Bliss narrative.
11. Gordon's account in Hammel, *Aces against Japan,* 72; Ford phone interview; Carey corresp.
12. Daniels corresp.
13. Ibid.; Lindsey narrative.
14. Daniels corresp.; Capt. Russell L. Reiserer phone interview; Vejtasa phone interview.
15. ComCruDiv 5 message log.
16. Haber corresp.
17. Daniels corresp.
18. Casualty figures in Frank, 364–65, 401.
19. Vejtasa phone interview; Wrenn corresp.
20. ComCruDiv 5 message log.
21. CTF-16 to ComSoPac 260440, ComSoPac to all SoPac CTFs 260450, both of October 1942.
22. Cdr. John F. Sutherland phone interview.

23. Ltr. Givens to Eric Hammel (5 Sept. 1982), in Hammel Papers, NHC.
24. Okumiya and Horikoshi, *Zero!*, 265, 267.
25. Ibid., 267, 268.
26. Frank, 639; VF-72 muster roll, October 1942. MAtt, Mess Attendant; OC, Officer's Cook; SC, Ship's Cook.
27. *Hornet* Report; *Hornet* War Damage Report; *Northampton* Report (see chap. 20, n. 35).
28. 2nd Destroyer Squadron Detailed Action Report, message 1750/26 Oct. Chief of Staff Combined Fleet to all Cdrs, GA Operation.
29. 2nd Destroyer Squadron Detailed Action Report; 10th Destroyer Division Combat Report; *Senshi Sōsho*, 83:304–5.
30. ComAirSoPac war diary, 27 Oct. 1942; James Sawruk research on PBY operations.
31. Messages: CinCPac to all CTF 270347 of October 1942, Intell Bulletin puts *Zuihō* north of Santa Cruz; NERK to COMB 280430 of October 1942. 2nd Destroyer Squadron Detailed Action Report, 11–30 Oct. 1942.
32. WDC160985 10th Destroyer Division Combat Report No. 2, 25–27 Oct. 1942 (10 Nov. 1942).
33. Corresp. with Mead, Rhodes, Nelson, and Glasser; narratives by Nelson and Glasser; Stafford, 178–81, based on long interview of Rhodes; WDC160985 10th Destroyer Division Combat Report No. 2, 25–27 Oct. 1942, gives the times of pickup for the first three; *Senshi Sōsho*, 83:306, gives pickup by *Makigumo* and *Kagerō;* Ugaki, 252–53.
34. Robert E. Barde, "Midway: Tarnished Victory," *Military Affairs* 47:4 (December 1983).
35. Ugaki, 255.
36. Bliss narrative.
37. "History of the Buzzard Brigade."
38. Phillips corresp.
39. Ugaki, 252–53.
40. WDC 161270 Message 1110/27 Oct. Cdr. KdB to CinC Combined Fleet, 2nd Fleet; 2nd Destroyer Squadron Detailed Action Report messages 1928/28 Oct. Cdr. AdB to CinC Combined Fleet, 0220/31 Oct. Cdr. KdB to CinC Combined Fleet, 2nd Fleet.
41. Yokosuka Air Group Battle Lessons; *Senshi Sōsho*, 83:307–8, 310–11.
42. Based on a study of the carrier *kōdōchōshos;* data from Michael Wenger shows that the Pearl Harbor veterans who died at Santa Cruz numbered four VF pilots, thirteen VB pilots, and fourteen VB observers, and nine VT pilots and twenty-two VT crewmen.
43. According to Abe Zenji, CO of the *Hiyō* Carrier Bomber Squadron, there was no thought of putting the *Hiyō*'s aircraft on board the *Zuikaku:* Abe interview, 7 Dec. 1991.
44. See message 280433 of October 1942 CinCPac Intelligence Bulletin (in RG 457, SRMN-013), which shows the U.S. Navy had no idea the *Junyō* was in the battle; CTF-61 to ComSoPac 300629 of October 1942.
45. Mott, "The Battles of Santa Cruz and Guadalcanal," 45; Capt. W. J. Frazier's rebuttal in *The Hook* (Spring 1991) 89–90.
46. Ltr. Halsey to Nimitz (31 Oct. 1942).
47. Burns, 122.
48. VF-10 report; for initial tests in placing FDOs on destroyers, see John Monsarrat, *Angel on the Yard Arm,* 39–40.
49. Luard report.
50. Griffin interview. His report, cited above many times, is absolutely invaluable for an understanding of the CAP in the Santa Cruz battle.
51. For *Hornet* fighter direction, see also Cdr. CAG-10 to CinCPac, Memorandum "Fighter Director Methods," by Lt. (jg) John A. McGlinn, Jr. (15 Dec. 1942). McGlinn was one of Fleming's assistants.
52. Griffin interview; CTF-61 endorsement to *Hornet* Air Group Report (8 Nov. 1942).
53. Pollock narrative.
54. VF-10 report (31 Oct. 1942).

23 HOLDING THE SOPAC LINE

1. Ltr. Halsey to Nimitz (6 Nov. 1942), Nimitz papers; *Enterprise* war diary.
2. Ltr. Halsey to Nimitz (6 Nov. 1942).
3. Quote, VT-10 "History of the Buzzard Brigade"; see also war diaries, VB-10 and VF-10.
4. ComSoPac to CinCPac 262320, CinCPac to CominCh 270251, both of October 1942.
5. Norman Friedman, *British Carrier Aviation: The Evolution of the Ships and Their Aircraft,* chap. 7.
6. CominCh to CinCPac 081515 of November 1942.
7. ComSoPac to CinCPac 110954, CinCPac to CominCh 120031, both of November 1942.
8. Arthur J. Marder et al., *Old Friends, New Enemies,* 191–92.
9. Lt. Gen. Louis Woods, USMC, oral history, 176.
10. VMF-121 war diary; Simmons, 88.
11. ComAirSoPac to CinCPac 062351 of November 1942.
12. Vandegrift, 195; Willock, 230.
13. Ltr. Halsey to Nimitz (17 Nov. 1942), Nimitz papers. In *Admiral Halsey's Story,* 124, Halsey wrongly dated his return to Noumea a day early, 9 November, and is followed by most of the other historians. This makes his battle preparations seem rather dilatory; see Frank, 491.
14. CinCPac to ComSoPac 092107; also NERK Canberra to COMB 100951; Com-SWPac to all CTFs 091921: all of November 1942.
15. Ltr. Halsey to Nimitz (17 Nov. 1942).
16. CinCPac to ComSoPac 100622 of November 1942; RG 457, SRNS-0211 CNO Summary 10 Nov. 1942.
17. ComSoPac to CTF-63 100430 of November 1942.
18. ComSoPac to CTF-16 100952, ComSoPac to CTF-16 102102, both of November 1942.
19. Johnston, 160–61; VF-10 war diary.
20. Frank, 405.
21. Ibid., 428–29; Ugaki, 259–64.
22. 11th Air Fleet war diary, November 1942; *Senshi Sōsho,* 83:331–36.
23. MAG-23 war diary, 11 Nov. 1942; *Kōdōchōshos, Hiyō* and 204 Air Group.
24. MAG-23 war diary; *Kōdōchōshos,* 703 and 705 air groups.
25. MAG-23 war diary; Simmons, 121–24; U.S. Pacific Fleet, NACI Air Battle Notes from the South Pacific, No. 4 (23 Nov. 1942), "25 Jap Planes Attack US Shipping." *Kōdōchōshos,* 253, 582, 703, and 705 air groups.
26. CTF-67 to ComSoPac 130140 of November 1942.
27. Mattison war diary, 24.
28. Cdr. Amphibious Force Pacific Fleet to ComSoPac, Report of Operations of Task Force 67 and Task Group 62.4, Reinforcement of Guadalcanal, November 8–15, 1942, and Summary Third Battle of Savo (3 Dec. 1942).
29. CTF-16 to CominCh, Operations of Task Force SIXTEEN in the Action for the Defense of Guadalcanal 12–15 November 1942 (23 Nov. 1942).
30. Frank, 433–34, 491.

24 THE DEATH OF THE *HIEI*

General sources used for TF-16 and the 1st MAW in the Naval Battle of Guadalcanal, 13–15 November 1942: ComSoPac war diary; TF-16 report (23 Nov. 1942); TF-16 war diary, 12–16 November 1942; CO USS *Enterprise* to CinCPac, Report of Action 13–14 November 1942 (19 Nov. 1942) (with air group and squadron reports, cited individually); ComAirSoPac to ComSoPac, Action Report—Task Force SIXTY-THREE 10–16 November 1942 (30 Nov. 1942); ComAirSoPac war diary; CO MAG-14 to CG, FMAW, Report of Action on November 13, 14, and 15 (18 Nov. 1942); MAG-23 war diary, 13–15 November 1942; individual squadron war diaries (cited individually).

Japanese sources: *Senshi Sōsho*, 83:353–98; 11th Air Fleet Summary of Air Operations in the Southeast Area, 13–15 Nov. 1942; 2nd Destroyer Squadron War Diary and Detailed Action Report, 3–15 Nov. 1942, in microfilm JD27; unit *kōdōchōshos;* Ugaki, 260–82; Tanaka, "The Struggle for Guadalcanal," in Evans, 187–96.

1. Frank, 436–51.
2. Summary of Air Operations in the Southeast Area, 13–15 Nov. 1942 (via Dr. Izawa Yasuho); unit *kōdōchōshos*.
3. VMSB-132 war diary.
4. War diaries, VMSB-142, VMF-112, and VMSB-131; 1st MarDiv, D-2 Journal, 13 Nov. 1942.
5. *Junyō Kōdōchōsho*, 13 Nov. 1942.
6. Cdr. VT-10 to CO USS *Enterprise*, Action, November 13, 14, 15, 1942—Report of (19 Nov. 1942); Cdr. VF-10 to CO USS *Enterprise*, Report of Action, November 10–17, 1942 (21 Nov. 1942).
7. Hubler and DeChant, 130–31.
8. AirSoPac war diary, 13 Nov. 1942; W. M. Cleveland (ed.), *Grey Geese Calling*, 391–92.
9. 1st MarDiv, D-2 Journal, 13 Nov. 1942.
10. Carey corresp.
11. Welles memoir.
12. 204 Air Group *Kōdōchōsho*.
13. "History of the Buzzard Brigade."
14. VMSB-132 war diary; VMFB-141 history.
15. Text of Abe's Summary Action Report, No. 2 (14 Nov. 1942) in Ugaki, 272–73.
16. 252 Air Group *Kōdōchōsho*, 13 Nov. 1942; Hata and Izawa, 115.
17. Simmons, 125; Foss wrongly thought VMSB-131 flew the mission rather than VT-10.
18. Ugaki, 273.
19. *Junyō Kōdōchōsho*.
20. Kazuo Tsunoda, *Shura no Tsubasa* ("Winged Battle"), 109–13.
21. CinCPac to CominCh 121929, *Helena* to ComAirSoPac 122005, both of November 1942.
22. VF-10 report; Foss and Brennan, 89; 851 Air Group *Kōdōchōsho*, 13 Nov. 1942.
23. ComSoPac to CTF-16 122301 of November 1942.
24. CTF-16 to ComSoPac 122359 of November 1942.
25. 851 Air Group *Kōdōchōsho*, 13 Nov. 1932.
26. Message CinCPac to all CTF 130305 of November 1942 (Intelligence Bulletin); RG 457, SMRN-013.
27. RG 457, SRMD-002 "War Plans Section Comments on Combined Intelligence Summaries," 12 Nov. 1942. Messages ComSoPac to CTF-16 130505, ComSoPac to CTF-16 130552, both of November 1942.
28. Kinkaid to ComSoPac 130701 of November 1942.
29. ComSoPac to CTF-16 130642 of November 1942.
30. Ltr. Halsey to Nimitz (17 Nov. 1942); message ComSoPac to CG 1st MarDiv 131008 of November 1942.
31. Col. John Howard McEniry Jr., USMCR, *A Marine Dive-Bomber Pilot at Guadalcanal*, 60.

25   "A DIVE AND TORPEDO BOMBERS' PARADISE"

1. McEniry, 61.
2. Johnston, 171–72.
3. Ltr. Halsey to Nimitz (17 Nov. 1942).
4. ComSoPac to CTF-16 131730, ComSoPac to CTF-64 131740, both of November 1942.
5. Cdr. VS-10 to CO USS *Enterprise*, Battle Report, November 14–15, 1942 (20 Nov. 1942).

6. CTF-16 report (23 Nov. 1942); for strike see *Enterprise* report (19 Nov. 1942) and squadron reports (VF-10, VB-10, VS-10).
7. *Chitose Kōdōchōsho,* 14 Nov. 1942.
8. VMSB-132 war diary; McEniry, 64.
9. *Kinugasa* Action Report, 14 Nov. 1942, in microfilm JT1, NHC; Dr. E. Lacroix's excellent treatise, "The Development of the 'A-Class' Cruisers in the Imperial Japanese Navy, Part VI," *Warship International,* No. 3 (1983) 239, errs in ascribing no damage to VMSB-132's attack.
10. VT-10 report; VMSB-131 war diary; *Chōkai* Action Report, 14 Nov. 1942, in microfilm JT1.
11. Cdr. VB-10 to CO USS *Enterprise,* Report of Action, November 14–15, 1942 (20 Nov. 1942).
12. *Kinugasa* Action Report, 14 Nov. 1942.
13. *Maya* Action Report, 14 Nov. 1942, in microfilm JT1; Lacroix, "The Development of the 'A-Class' Cruisers in the Imperial Japanese Navy," 239.
14. Burns, 153–54.
15. VMSB-132 war diary.
16. Main sources on the convoy: 2nd Destroyer Squadron Detailed Action Report, 3–15 Nov. 1942, JD27 microfilm; Tanaka in Evans, 190–93; Frank, 428.
17. VS-10 report; Carmody interview; 204 Air Group *Kōdōchōsho,* 14 Nov. 1942.
18. AirSoPac war diary; Cleveland, 318; *Hiyō Kōdōchōsho,* 14 Nov. 1942.
19. 253 Air Group *Kōdōchōsho,* 14 Nov. 1942; VMF-112 war diary; James Percy's account in Foss and Brennan, 153–54.
20. VMSB-132 war diary.
21. VMSB-142 war diary; VB-10 report.
22. 2nd Destroyer Squadron Detailed Action Report, 3–15 Nov. 1942; VT-10 report; Welles memoir; VMF-112 war diary.
23. *Enterprise* report (19 Nov. 1942); VF-10 report; Kilpatrick phone interview; 851 Air Group *Kōdōchōsho,* 14 Nov. 1942.
24. CTF-16 to ComSoPac 140122 of November 1942.
25. *Chitose Kōdōchōsho;* message CinCPac to all CTFs 140121 of November 1942.
26. Reports, VF-10, VB-10, VS-10.
27. *Junyō Kōdōchōsho,* 14 Nov. 1942.
28. 252 Air Group *Kōdōchōsho,* 14 Nov. 1942.
29. Miyazaki's account in Yanagida, 1:564–66.
30. Tsunoda, 113–21; 582 Air Group *Kōdōchōsho,* 14 Nov. 1942.
31. Barrett Tillman, *The Wildcat in WWII,* 129–30.
32. VF-10 report; Intelligence Section, 1st MAW, CACTUS, Summary of Fighter Operations, November 11–15, 1942.
33. Yanagida, 1:566.
34. VF-10 report; Lt. Cdr. Lynn Slagle phone interview.
35. Souza corresp.
36. Cleveland, 392; ltr. Halsey to Nimitz (17 Nov. 1942).
37. Message CinCPac to all CTFs 140359 of November 1942; RG 457, SRMN-013, 14 Nov. 1942.
38. VB-10 report; Cdr. VB-10 to CO USS *Enterprise,* Report of Action November 14–15, 1942, Supplementary Report (4 Dec. 1942); H. L. Buell, 157.
39. *Hiyō Kōdōchōsho,* 14 Nov. 1942.
40. VB-10 report (20 Nov. 1942); for Kaneko, see Hata and Izawa, 355–56.
41. Cdr. VB-10 to CO USS *Enterprise,* Air Combat Intelligence Officer, VB-10 to Air Combat Intelligence Office, Intelligence Center, POA, Crash Landing and Subsequent Rescue of Ens. J. H. Carroum (10 Dec. 1942); Burns, 157–63.
42. Mattison war diary, 26.
43. Simmons, 127.
44. Johnston, 186.
45. T. Miller, 197; Witte phone interview.
46. 204 Air Group *Kōdōchōsho,* 14 Nov. 1942; sea-plane strengths from air unit reports in: Carrier Records of Meritorious Service, May–November 1942 (includes sea-plane tenders), in microfilm JD183, NHC.
47. VMF-112 war diary; Hubler and DeChant, 115–16.

48. VT-10 report; Capt. J. A. Rapp phone interview.
49. For Bauer's last fight, see Simmons, 127–28; Faust, "The Squadron," 244–46, citing ltr. of Foss to Mrs. Bauer; Hubler and Dechant, 97; Brig. Gen. Joe Foss interview; Col. T. W. Furlow phone interview.
50. Renner, undated interview, 5–6; Hubler and DeChant, 97–98.
51. 1st MarDiv, D-2 Journal, 14 Nov. 1942.
52. "History of the Buzzard Brigade."
53. Welles memoir.
54. RG 457, SRMD-002, 14 Nov. 1942.
55. Frank, 486.
56. Mattison war diary, 27.
57. CinCPac Greybook, 13 Nov. 1942.

26 MOPPING UP

1. 2nd Destroyer Squadron Detailed Action Report, 3–15 Nov. 1942, JD27 microfilm.
2. 1st MarDiv, D-2 Journal, 15 Nov. 1942.
3. Simmons, 128–29; Renner, undated interview, 5–6; Hubler and DeChant, 98–99; *Sanuki Maru* Detailed Battle Report, 15 Nov. 1942.
4. VMSB-132 war diary; VS-10 and VT-10 reports; *Chitose Kōdōchōsho*, 15 Nov. 1942.
5. CO USS *Meade* to CinCPac, Report of Action against Enemy Transports located on Guadalcanal Island on November 15, 1942 (19 Nov. 1942).
6. Ira Wolfert, *Torpedo 8*, 126.
7. 1st MarDiv, D-2 Journal, 15 Nov. 1942.
8. VF-10 report.
9. 1st MarDiv, D-2 Journal, 15 Nov. 1942; Halsey later wrote that the failure of these float biplanes to reach Guadalcanal prevented "a clay pigeon show for our splendid pilots," ltr. Halsey to Nimitz (17 Nov. 1942).
10. *Kōdōchōshos*, 252, 253, and *Hiyō* air groups, 15 Nov. 1942.
11. Burns, 156.
12. 1st MarDiv, D-2 Journal, 15 Nov. 1942.
13. Burns, 156.
14. Cdr. R. M. Voris phone interview; Slagle phone interview. Voris denied the story in T. Miller (p. 263) of Ruehlow calling him off a Zero and later yelling for help. It appears to have been confused with Edwards asking for assistance.
15. Souza corresp.; Witte phone interview.
16. RAdm. Edward M. Feightner interview.
17. Burns, 156.
18. MAG-23 war diary, 15 Nov. 1942.
19. Messages CTF-16 to ComSoPac 142007 of November 1942; CinCPac to all CTFs, Intell. Bull. 150239. RG 457 SRMN-002 14 Nov. 1942; ltr. Halsey to Nimitz (17 Nov. 1942).
20. VF-10 war diary; Mersky, 50.
21. Senior Aviator at Guadalcanal to CTF-16 150205 of November 1942.
22. ComAirSoPac to ComSoPac 151226 of November 1942, with Lee summary.
23. Ugaki, 270, 281–82.
24. Ltr. Halsey to Nimitz (17 Nov. 1942).
25. RG457, SRH-306, citing message CinCPac to ComSoPac, ComSoWesPac, CominCh, OpNav, Belconnen, Com14, CETYH 170139 of November 1942.
26. Memorandum 15 Nov. 1942 in TF-16 war diary.
27. CO MAG-14 to CG FMAW, Report of Action on Nov. 13, 14, and 15 (18 Nov. 1942).
28. First Endorsement (Dec. 15, 1942) to ComAirSoPac Action Report—Task Force Sixty-three 10–16 Nov. 1942 (30 Nov. 1942); ltr. Halsey to Nimitz (29 Nov. 1942).
29. CTF-16 report.

CONCLUSION

1. Ugaki, 277.
2. Ltr. Halsey to Nimitz (17 Nov. 1942); for the new lineup see ComSoPac to all CTFs 230612 of November 1942.
3. The move was intended to reconcile the air groups and squadron numbers, as O'Hare's squadron was to be part of Air Group Six (intended for the *Enterprise*— CV-6) and Bauer's squadron in Air Group Three on the *Saratoga* (CV-3).
4. Their opponents were twenty-nine Zeros, mostly from the *Zuikaku*, and the only loss was the veteran WO Shigemi Katsuma.
5. Comparable figures for USMC fighter pilots from 21 August to 15 November 1942 were (with estimated score based on a study of Japanese records):

	Credits	Estimated score
Fighters	170.5	61
Medium bombers	121.5	40
S/e bombers	40.0	17
Float biplanes	27.0	9
Float Zeros	12.0	8
Flying boat	1.0	1
Recon. plane	1.0	1
	373.0	137

Between those dates 134 Marine fighter pilots (not counting those solely on ferry duty) served at CACTUS, and 30 were lost to all causes. Only seven had previously seen combat, having survived the slaughter of VMF-221 on 4 June at Midway.
6. Hal Buell in *Dauntless Helldiver,* 183–86, relates a conversation with Wade Mc-Clusky which superbly elucidates the importance of the 1942 combat veterans.
7. Full text in Johnston, 221.

Appendix 1. The Significance of the Captured Zero

1. Jim Rearden, *Cracking the Zero Mystery,* chap. 8.
2. ComPatWing 4 to BuAer, Info CinCPac 142326 of July 1942; OpNav to Cdr. Alaskan Sector, ComPatWing 4 162214 of July 1942; Cdr. Patrol Squadron 41 to OpNav, CinCPac, Cdr. Northwest Sea Frontier 180900 of July 1942.
3. CO NAS San Diego to Chief, BuAer, Japanese Fighter—Status of (15 Aug. 1942).
4. Memorandum for Flight Test Officer, U.S. Naval Air Station San Diego (29 Sept. 1942); Endorsement by ComFAirWest to Commander, Air Force, Pacific (1 Oct. 1942).
5. Flight Test Officer, NAS Anacostia, D.C., to Chief, BuAer, Japanese Nagoya Type Zero Fighter, Preliminary Tests, Report of (31 Oct. 1942).
6. Jiro Horikoshi, *Eagles of Mitsubishi,* 140.
7. Okumiya and Horikoshi, *Zero,* 160, 163.
8. Memorandum for Files, Japanese Model Zero-2 Airplane (6 Oct. 1942).
9. Lt. (jg) R. G. Crommelin VF-42 ACA Report (8 May 1942).
10. Simpler, BuAer interview.
11. ComAirPac, Memorandum of Combat Reports and Summaries involving U.S. Fighters (19 Dec. 1942): Observations of Marine Pilots at Guadalcanal October 16–October 31, 1942; Foss, BuAer interview (26 March 1943).
12. VF-10 report (31 Oct. 1942).
13. VF-10 report (19 Nov. 1942).

Sources

Of all of the campaigns of the Pacific War, the six-month battle for Guadalcanal has certainly generated the most published accounts. Two books, one recent and the other over 20 years old, are this author's particular favorites. Virtually all of the works on Guadalcanal emphasize one of the three aspects (sea, land, and air) of this intricate campaign. The only work that provides proper coverage to all three areas from both the Allied and Japanese points of view is Richard B. Frank's magisterial *Guadalcanal*. Perceptive, well written, and meticulously documented, *Guadalcanal* is the standard upon which future works will be judged. His book has proved invaluable while researching every stage of this effort.

The second is *The Cactus Air Force* by the late Thomas G. Miller, Jr. This compact, spirited history of the airmen who fought for Guadalcanal sparked my interest in this area and led directly to the present work.

DOCUMENTS

The documentary sources reside in several locations. The Operational Archives Branch of the Naval Historical Center in the Washington Navy Yard contains the U.S. Navy action reports, war diaries, interviews, tactical publications, and biographical files cited in the notes, as well as selected Japanese documents, both translated (WDC numbers) and on microfilm (JD [untranslated] and JT series). The center also has the personal papers of Fleet Admiral Chester W. Nimitz and admirals Thomas C. Kinkaid and Richmond Kelly Turner. In the Marine Corps Historical Center located adjacent to the Naval Historical Center repose the invaluable 1st Marine Division Final Report for Guadalcanal, war diaries, histories, and muster rolls of Marine Corps aviation groups and squadrons, as well as oral histories and/or personal papers of several Marine Corps officers.

The U.S. National Archives feature several record groups vital to this research. Record Group (RG) 18 has U.S. Army Air Force documents relating to the 11th Bomb Group (Heavy) and 347th Fighter Group (67th and 339th fighter squadrons). Deck logs of U.S. naval vessels and muster rolls of ships and squadrons are in RG 24. RG 38 contains Message Files of Commander-in-Chief, U.S. Fleet, relating to the South Pacific, and on microfilm the voluminous Commander-in-Chief, U.S. Pacific Fleet Secret and Confidential Message Files. RG 72 comprises the records of the Bureau of Aeronautics. RG 313, the so-called

Flag Files, contains valuable administrative files of Commander, Carriers, Pacific Fleet (filed under Commander, Aircraft, Battle Force), Commander, Air, Pacific Fleet, Commander, South Pacific Area (message files only), and Commander, Aircraft, South Pacific Area. Filed by year, they are organized according to the Navy Filing Manual, 1941 edition. Especially important headings are A4-1 (Aircraft Status Reports), A16-3 (Combat Reports), and the individual aircraft types, such as VF4F-4. RG 457 has the radio intelligence materials released by the National Security Agency.

Through the kindness of Dr. Izawa Yasuho, Dr. David C. Evans, and Osamu (Sam) Tagaya, the author secured copies of numerous documents in Japanese from the War History Office of the Japanese Self Defense Force.

PARTICIPANTS CONTACTED

Abe Zenji *Hiyō*
Lt. Julius A. Achten VF-6
MGen. Arthur H. Adams VMJ-253
Lt. Cdr. John P. Altemus VF-5, Personal diary
MGen. Norman J. Anderson VMJ-253
Arima Keiichi *Shōkaku*
Capt. Louis H. Bauer VF-6
Charles R. Beatty VT-3
Capt. Forrest R. Biard HYPO
Lt. Cdr. James D. Billo VF-10
Col. Dale D. Brannon 67th FS
Capt. Charles E. Brewer VF-6
Capt. Herbert S. Brown VF-5
Capt. Robert M. Bruning *Saratoga*
Cdr. Harold L. Buell VS-5, VB-10, Personal diary
Lt. Col. Dennis Byrd VMSB-232
Lt. Cdr. Thaddeus J. Capowski VF-71
Lt. Cdr. Henry A. Carey, Jr. VF-72, VF-10
MGen Marion E. Carl VMF-223
RAdm. Martin D. Carmody VS-10
John Carr VMF-223
Col. Clair C. Chamberlain VMF-212
Capt. Walter E. Clarke VF-5
Martin Clemens, Coastwatcher
Col. Jack E. Conger VMF-212
Capt. Howard W. Crews VF-5, Personal diary
Lt. Cdr. Joseph R. Daly VF-5
Capt. James G. Daniels III Air Group Ten, Personal diary
Col. Jefferson J. DeBlanc VMF-112
VAdm. Vincent P. de Poix VF-6
Col. Frank C. Drury VMF-212
Carl J. Duracher VF-5
Capt. Frederick L. Faulkner VF-10
RAdm. Edward L. Feightner VF-10
Lt. Col. Wallace Fields 19th Bomb Group, Personal diary
Capt. Gordon E. Firebaugh VF-6

RAdm. Allan F. Fleming *Hornet*
RAdm. Warren W. Ford VF-72, VF-10
Brig. Gen. Joseph J. Foss VMF-121
Lt. Col. William B. Freeman VMF-121
Col. Thomas W. Furlow VMF-121
Brig. Gen. Robert E. Galer VMF-224
Lt. Col. Wendell V. Garton VMO-251
Michael Glasser VT-10
Cdr. Frank O. Green VF-5, Personal diary
Capt. John H. Griffin *Enterprise*
Fred E. Gutt VMF-223
Dr. Norman S. Haber VP-24
Col. Roger A. Haberman VMF-121
Rex Hamilton VMF-223
Capt. Richard E. Harmer VF-5
Capt. Leroy E. Harris VF-10
Col. Dean S. Hartley, Jr. VMF-224
Capt. Edward W. Hessel VF-72
Col. George L. Hollowell VMF-224
Cdr. Richard Z. Hughes VF-72, VF-10
Ishikawa Shirō 2nd Air Group
Capt. Roland H. Kenton VF-71, VF-5
Lt. Cdr. Kenneth C. Kiekhoefer VF-72
Cdr. Macgregor Kilpatrick VF-10
Komachi Sadamu *Shōkaku*
Lt. Col. Allan M. Johnson VMF-224
Col. John H. King, Jr. VMF-212
RAdm. William N. Leonard VF-42
Lt. Cdr. Richards L. Loesch VF-6, VF-5
Lt. Cdr. M. Philip Long VF-10
Col. Carl M. Longley VMO-251
Capt. L. Paul Mankin VF-6, VF-5
Capt. Lewis C. Mattison CACTUS, Personal diary
Col. Grant W. McComb VMJ-253
Lt. Cdr. Albert E. Mead VF-10
Herbert Christian Merillat 1st MarDiv
Cdr. Robert S. Merritt VF-72, VF-10
VAdm. William J. Moran VF-72
Brig. Gen. Rivers J. Morrell, Jr. VMF-223
Cdr. Raymond F. Myers VF-71, VF-5
Thomas C. Nelson VT-10
Thomas I. Newsome CTF-61 staff
Col. Stanley S. Nicolay VMF-224
Brig. Gen. Frederick R. Payne VMF-212
RAdm. Oscar Pederson CTF-61 staff
Bernard W. Peterson VT-3
Capt. Claude R. Phillips, Jr. VF-72
Thomas A. Powell VT-10
Col. Eldon H. Railsback VMO-251
Capt. Jerome A. Rapp VT-10
Col. Robert R. Read VMF-223

SOURCES

Capt. Russell L. Reiserer VF-10
Cdr. Raleigh E. Rhodes VF-10
Cdr. Thomas W. Rhodes VF-6
VAdm. David C. Richardson VF-5
Capt. Henry A. Rowe *Enterprise*
Cdr. Donald E. Runyon VF-6
Sakai Saburō Tainan Air Group
RAdm. Henry G. Sanchez VF-72
Cdr. David V. Senft VF-71
RAdm. Leroy C. Simpler VF-5
Lt. Cdr. Lynn E. Slagle VF-10
Cdr. Philip E. Souza VF-72, VF-10
Cdr. Carlton B. Starkes VF-5
Richard T. Stith, Jr. VMJ-253
Capt. Howell M. Sumrall VF-6
Cdr. John F. Sutherland VF-72, VF-10
Capt. Stanley W. Vejtasa VF-10
Cdr. Roy M. Voris VF-10
RAdm. Albert O. Vorse VF-6
Lt. William H. Warden VF-6
Cdr. John M. Wesolowski VF-5
Dr. John L. Whitaker VMJ-253
Delmar D. Wiley VT-3
Lt. Col. Conrad G. Winter VMF-223
Lt. Cdr. Roland R. Witte VF-10
Cdr. George L. Wrenn VF-72
Capt. S. Downs Wright VF-71
Cdr. Wilson G. Wright III VF-71
Families of
Lt. Col. Harold W. Bauer VMF-212, Personal diary
Lt. Cdr. Foster J. Blair VF-5, Personal diary
Capt. Louis K. Bliss VF-72
RAdm. Fred C. Dickey
VAdm. James H. Flatley, Jr. VF-10
Capt. David B. Freeman VF-72, VF-10
Cdr. James A. Halford VF-6, VF-5
Capt. William R. Kane VF-10
Capt. Gregory K. Loesch VMF-121
RAdm. Courtney Shands VF-71
Maj. Gen. Shingō Hideki *Shōkaku*
Col. John L. Smith VMF-223, Personal diary
Cdr. James J. Southerland II VF-5
Lt. Elisha T. Stover VF-5, Personal diary
Via James C. Sawruk
Capt. Forrester C. Auman VB-8
J. Clark Barrett VB-8
Capt. Fred L. Bates VB-8
James Black, Jr. VS-8
Cdr. George S. Clute VP-11
Cdr. George G. Estes VS-10
Cdr. Clayton E. Fisher VB-8

Capt. James M. Forbes VS-8
Capt. Roy P. Gee VB-8
Lt. Cdr. Robert D. Gibson VB-10
Capt. Glen E. Hoffman VP-91
Lee F. Hollingsworth VT-10
Capt. Stanley R. Holm VS-8
Cdr. Ralph B. Hovind VS-8
Capt. Donald Kirkpatrick VS-8
Cdr. George F. Poulos VP-11
Capt. Ward F. Powell VT-6
Capt. Edgar E. Stebbins VS-8
Capt. Ivan L. Swope VS-8
Capt. Humphrey L. Tallman VT-6
Capt. Richard J. Teich VP-91
Cdr. Kenneth B. White VB-8
Evan K. Williams VT-6
Capt. Albert H. Wood VS-8
Capt. William E. Woodman VS-8
Richard T. Woodson VS-8
Family of George D. Welles VT-10

BOOKS

Agawa, Hiroyuki. *The Reluctant Admiral: Yamamoto and the Imperial Navy.* Tokyo: Kodansha, 1979.

Bayler, Lt. Col. Walter L. J. and Cecil Carnes. *Last Man Off Wake Island.* Indianapolis: Bobbs & Merrill, 1943.

Belote, James H. and William M. Belote. *Titans of the Seas.* New York: Harper & Row, 1975.

Blackburn, Tom. *The Jolly Rogers.* New York: Orion Books, 1989.

Brown, David. *Carrier Operations in World War II.* Volume 1. *The Royal Navy.* London: Ian Allan Ltd., 1974.

Brown, Capt. Eric, RN. *Wings of the Navy.* London: Jane's, 1980.

Buell, Harold L. *Dauntless Helldivers.* New York: Orion Books, 1991.

Buell, Thomas B. *Master of Sea Power: A Biography of Fleet Admiral Ernest J. King.* Boston: Little, Brown, 1980.

Burns, Eugene. *Then There Was One: The U.S.S. Enterprise and the First Year of War.* New York: Harcourt, Brace, 1944.

Cleveland, W. M. (ed.). *Grey Geese Calling: A History of the 11th Bombardment Group Heavy (H) in the Pacific, 1940–1945.* Askov, Minn.: American Publishing, 1981.

Cook, Charles. *The Battle of Cape Esperance.* New York: Crowell, 1968.

Craven, W. F. and J. L. Cate, *The Army Air Forces in World War II.*
Volume 1. *Plans and Early Operations (January 1939 to August 1942).* Chicago: University of Chicago Press, 1948.
Volume 4. *The Pacific: Guadalcanal to Saipan (August 1942–July 1944).* Chicago: University of Chicago Press, 1950.

Daly, Joseph R. *Luck Is My Lady.* New York: Vantage, 1989.

DeChant, John A. *Devilbirds.* New York: Harper, 1947.

Dull, Paul S. *A Battle History of the Imperial Japanese Navy (1941–1945).* Annapolis: Naval Institute Press, 1978.

Dyer, VAdm. George C. *The Amphibians Came to Conquer: The Story of Admiral Richmond Kelly Turner*. 2 vols. Washington, D.C.: GPO, 1971.

Elliott, John M. *The Official Monogram U.S. Navy and Marine Corps Aircraft Color Guide*. Volume 2. *1940–1949*. Sturbridge, Mass.: Monogram Aviation Publications, 1989.

Evans, David C. (ed.). *The Japanese Navy in World War II*. 2d edition. Annapolis: Naval Institute Press, 1986.

Ewing, Steve. *USS Enterprise (CV-6): The Most Decorated Ship of World War II*. Missoula, Mont.: Pictorial Histories, 1989.

Feldt, Eric. *The Coast Watchers*. Melbourne: Oxford University Press, 1946.

Ferguson, Robert Lawrence. *Guadalcanal: The Island of Fire, Reflections of the 347th Fighter Group*. Blue Ridge Summit, Pa.: Aero, 1987.

Feuer, A. B. *Coast Watching in the Solomon Islands: The Bougainville Reports, December 1941–July 1943*. New York: Praeger, 1992.

Foss, Joe and Matthew Brennan. *Top Guns: America's Fighter Aces Tell Their Stories*. New York: Pocket Books, 1991.

Francillon, R. J. *Japanese Aircraft of the Pacific War*. London: Putnam, 1970.

Frank, Richard B. *Guadalcanal*. New York: Random House, 1990.

Friedman, Norman. *British Carrier Aviation: The Evolution of the Ships and Their Aircraft*. Annapolis: Naval Institute Press, 1988.

_____. *U.S. Aircraft Carriers: An Illustrated Design History*. Annapolis: Naval Institute Press, 1983.

Garrison, Ritchie. *Task Force 9156 and III Island Command: A Story of a South Pacific Advanced Base During World War II, Efate, New Hebrides*. Boston: Nimrod Press, 1983.

Gill, G. Hermon. *Royal Australian Navy*.
Volume 1. *1939–1942*. Canberra: Australian War Memorial, 1957.
Volume 2. *1942–1945*. Canberra: Australian War Memorial, 1968.

Gillison, Douglas. *Royal Australian Air Force 1939–1942*. Canberra: Australian War Memorial, 1962.

Great Britain, Colonial Office. *Among Those Present: The Official Story of the Pacific Islands at War*. London: H.M.S.O., 1946.

Great Britain, Naval Intelligence Division. *Pacific Islands*.
Volume 3. *Western Pacific (Tonga to the Solomon Islands)*. London: H.M.S.O., 1944.
Volume 4. *Western Pacific (New Guinea and Islands Northward)*. London: H.M.S.O., 1945.

Greene, Frank L. *History of the Grumman F4F "Wildcat."* Bethpage, N.Y.: Grumman, 1962.

Griffin, Alexander R. *A Ship to Remember: The Saga of the Hornet*. New York: Howell, Soskins, 1943.

Griffith, BGen. Samuel B. II. *The Battle for Guadalcanal*. Philadelphia: J. P. Lippincott, 1963.

Guyton, Boone T. *Whistling Death*. New York: Orion Books, 1990.

Halsey, FAdm. William F. and J. Bryan III. *Admiral Halsey's Story*. New York: Whittlesey House, 1947.

Hammel, Eric. *Aces against Japan*. Novato, Calif.: Presidio Press, 1992.

_____. *Guadalcanal: The Carrier Battles*. New York: Crown Publishers, 1987.

_____. *Guadalcanal: Decision at Sea*. New York: Crown Publishers, 1988.

_____. *Guadalcanal: Starvation Island*. New York: Crown Publishers, 1987.

Hara, Capt. Tameichi. *Japanese Destroyer Captain*. New York: Ballantine Books, 1961.

Hata, Ikuhiko and Yasuho Izawa. *Japanese Naval Aces and Fighter Units in World War II*. Annapolis: Naval Institute Press, 1989.

Hayes, Grace Person. *The History of the Joint Chiefs of Staff in World War II: The War Against Japan*. Annapolis: Naval Institute Press, 1982.

Holbrook, Heber A. *The History and Times of the U.S.S. Portland*. Dixon, Calif.: Pacific Ship and Shore, 1990.

Holmes, W. J. *Double-Edged Secrets*. Annapolis: Naval Institute Press, 1979.

Horikoshi, Jiro. *Eagles of Mitsubishi*. Seattle: University of Washington Press, 1981.

Horton, D. C. *Fire Over the Islands*. London: Leo Cooper, 1970.

Hough, Lt. Col. Frank O., Major Verle E. Ludwig, and Henry I. Shaw, Jr. *Pearl Harbor to Guadalcanal. History of U.S. Marine Corps Operations in World War II*. Volume 1. Washington, D.C.: GPO, 1958.

Hoyt, Edward P. *How They Won the War in the Pacific: Nimitz and His Admirals*. New York: Weybright and Tally, 1970.

Hubler, Capt. Richard G. and Capt. John A. DeChant. *Flying Leathernecks*. Garden City, N.Y.: Doubleday, Doran, 1944.

Iwaya, Fumio. *Chūkō*. Tokyo: Genshobō, 1976.

Japan. Self Defense Force. War History Office. *Senshi Sōsho* (War History Series).
Volume 43. *Middowē Kaisen* (Midway Sea Battle). Tokyo: Asagumo Shimbunsha, 1971.
Volume 49. *Nantōhōmen Kaigun Sakusen, 1 Gatō Dakkai Sakusen Kaishimade* (Southeast Area Naval Operations, 1, To the Beginning of Operations to Recapture Guadalcanal). Tokyo: Asagumo Shimbunsha, 1971.
Volume 83. *Nantōhōmen Kaigun Sakusen, 2 Gatō Tesshumade* (Southeast Area Naval Operations, 2, To the Withdrawal from Guadalcanal). Tokyo: Asagumo Shimbunsha, 1975.

Jentschura, Hansgeorg, et al. *Warships of the Imperial Japanese Navy 1869–1945*. London: Arms & Armour Press, 1977.

Johnston, Stanley. *The Grim Reapers*. New York: Dutton, 1943.

Kaigun 705 Kōkai Kai-in Kyōchō. *Dai 705 Kaigun Kōkūtai Shi* (The 705th Air Group). Tokyo: Kaigun 705 Kōkai, 1975.

Kaikōkai. *Kaigun Kūchū Kimmusha (Shikan) Meibō* (Naval Aviation Association, Register of Naval Aviation Duty Officers). Tokyo: Kaikōkai, 1954.

Kenney, George C. *General Kenney Reports*. New York: Duell, Sloan, and Pearce, 1949.

Kreis, John F. *Air Warfare and Air Base Air Defense*. Washington, D.C.: GPO, 1988.

Kūshō Shingō Hideki Tsuisoroku (Record of Reminiscences of Air General Shingō Hideki). Tokyo: privately published, 1986.

Lamar, H. Arthur. *I Saw Stars*. Fredericksburg, Tex.: Admiral Nimitz Foundation, 1985.

Larkins, William T. *U.S. Navy Aircraft 1921–1941, U.S. Marine Corps Aircraft 1914–1959*. New York: Orion Books, 1988.

Layton, RAdm. Edwin T. *"And I Was There."* New York: Morrow, 1985.

Lee, Clark. *They Call It Pacific*. New York: Viking, 1943.

Lord, Walter. *Lonely Vigil: Coastwatchers of the Solomons*. New York: Viking, 1977.

Lundstrom, John B. *The First South Pacific Campaign: Pacific Fleet Strategy, December 1941–June 1942.* Annapolis: Naval Institute Press, 1976.

_____. *The First Team: Pacific Naval Air Combat from Pearl Harbor to Midway.* Annapolis: Naval Institute Press, 1984.

McEniry, Col. John Howard, Jr. *A Marine Dive-Bomber Pilot at Guadalcanal.* Tuscaloosa: University of Alabama Press, 1987.

Marder, Arthur J. *Old Friends, New Enemies: The Royal Navy and the Imperial Japanese Navy, Strategic Delusions 1936–1941.* Oxford: Oxford University Press, 1981.

Marder, Arthur J., Mark Jacobsen, and John Horsfield. *Old Friends, New Enemies: The Royal Navy and the Imperial Japanese Navy, The Pacific War 1942–1945.* Oxford: Oxford University Press, 1990.

Mears, Lieut. Frederick. *Carrier Combat.* New York: Doubleday, Doran, 1944.

Merillat, Herbert Christian. *Guadalcanal Remembered.* New York: Dodd, Mead, 1982.

Merillat, Capt. Herbert L. *The Island: A History of the Marines on Guadalcanal.* Boston: Houghton Mifflin, 1944.

Mersky, Peter. *The Grim Reapers: Fighting Squadron Ten in WWII.* Mesa, Ariz.: Champlin Museum Press, 1986.

Mikesh, Robert C. and Rikyu Watanabe. *Zero Fighter.* New York: Crown, 1981.

Miller, John, Jr. *Guadalcanal: The First Offensive.* Washington, D.C.: GPO, 1949.

Miller, Thomas G., Jr. *The Cactus Air Force.* New York: Harper & Row, 1969.

Mingos, Howard. *American Heroes of the War in the Air.* New York: Lanciar, 1943.

Mitchell, John H. *On Wings We Conquer.* Springfield: G.E.M., 1990.

Model Art Co., Ltd. *Shinju Wan Kōgekitai* (Pearl Harbor Attack Force). Tokyo: Model Art, 1991.

Monsarrat, John. *Angel on the Yard Arm: The Beginnings of Fleet Radar Defense and the Kamikaze Threat.* Newport, R.I.: Naval War College Press, 1985.

Morison, RAdm. Samuel Eliot. *History of United States Naval Operations of World War II.*
Volume 4. *Coral Sea, Midway and Submarine Actions May 1942–August 1942.* Boston: Little, Brown, 1949.
Volume 5. *The Struggle for Guadalcanal August 1942–February 1943.* Boston: Little, Brown, 1950.

Morton, Louis. *Strategy and Command: The First Two Years.* Washington, D.C.: GPO, 1962.

Musicant, Ivan. *Battleship at War: The Epic Story of the U.S.S. Washington.* San Diego: Harcourt, Brace, Jovanovich, 1986.

Newcomb, Richard F. *Savo: The Incredible Naval Debacle off Guadalcanal.* New York: Holt, Rinehart & Winston, 1961.

Newton, Wesley Phillips and Robert R. Rea. *Wings of Gold.* Tuscaloosa: University of Alabama Press, 1987.

Okumiya, Masatake and Jiro Horikoshi. *Zero!* New York: Dutton, 1956.

_____. *The Zero Fighter.* London: Cassell, 1958.

Olynyk, Frank J. *USAAF (Pacific Theater) Credits for the Destruction of Enemy Aircraft in Air-to-Air Combat World War 2.* Aurora: privately printed, 1985.

_____. *USMC Credits for the Destruction of Enemy Aircraft in Air-to-Air Combat World War 2.* Aurora: privately printed, 1981.

————. *USN Credits for the Destruction of Enemy Aircraft in Air-to-Air Combat World War 2*. Aurora: privately printed, 1982.

Orita, Zenji. *I-Boat Captain*. Canoga Park, Calif.: Major Books, 1976.

Peterson, Capt. Bernard W., USMCR Ret. *Briny to the Blue: Memoirs of WWII*. Scottsdale, Ariz.: Chuckawalla Publishing, 1992.

Polmar, Norman. *Aircraft Carriers*. New York: Doubleday, 1969.

Potter, E. B. *Bull Halsey*. Annapolis: Naval Institute Press, 1985.

————. *Nimitz*. Annapolis: Naval Institute Press, 1976.

Prange, Gordon. *At Dawn We Slept*. New York: McGraw-Hill, 1981.

Rearden, Jim. *Cracking the Zero Mystery*. Harrisburg, Pa.: Stackpole Books, 1990.

Reynolds, Clark G. *Admiral John H. Towers: The Struggle for Naval Air Supremacy*. Annapolis: Naval Institute Press, 1991.

————. *Famous American Admirals*. New York: Van Nostrand Reinhold, 1978.

————. *The Fast Carriers: The Forging of an Air Navy*. New York: McGraw-Hill, 1968.

————. *The Saga of Smokey Stover*. Charleston: Tradd Press, 1978.

Rhoades, Lt. Cdr. F. A. *Diary of a Coastwatcher in the Solomons*. Fredericksburg, Tex.: Admiral Nimitz Foundation, 1982.

Sakai, Saburō, with Fred Saito and Martin Caidin. *Samurai!* New York: Dutton, 1957.

————. *Ōzora no Samurai*. Tokyo: Koninsha, 1967.

Sakaida, Henry. *Winged Samurai*. Mesa, Ariz.: Champlin Museum Press, 1985.

Sekine, Shōji. *Honoo no Tsubasa*. Tokyo: Koninsha, 1976.

Sherrod, Robert. *History of Marine Corps Aviation in World War II*. Washington, D.C.: Combat Forces Press, 1952.

Shores, Christopher. *Duel for the Sky*. Garden City, N.Y.: Doubleday, 1985.

Shores, Christopher and Brian Cull. *Bloody Shambles*. London: Grubb Street, 1992.

————. *Malta: The Spitfire Year 1942*. London: Grubb Street, 1991.

Simmons, Walter. *Joe Foss: Flying Marine*. New York: Dutton, 1943.

Sims, Edward H. *Greatest Fighter Missions*. New York: Harper, 1962.

Smith, VAdm. William Ward. *Midway: Turning Point of the Pacific*. New York: Crowell, 1966.

Solomon Islands College of Higher Education. *The Big Death*. Suva, Fiji: Fiji Times, 1988.

Spector, Ronald H. *Listening to the Enemy: Key Documents on the Role of Communications Intelligence in the War with Japan*. Wilmington: Scholarly Resources, 1988.

Stafford, Cdr. Edward P. *The Big E: The Story of the U.S.S. Enterprise*. New York: Random House, 1962.

Tillman, Barrett. *Avenger at War*. New York: Scribner's, 1980.

————. *Corsair: The F4U in World War II and Korea*. Annapolis: Naval Institute Press, 1979.

————. *The Dauntless Dive Bomber of World War II*. Annapolis: Naval Institute Press, 1976.

————. *Hellcat: The F6F in World War II*. Annapolis: Naval Institute Press, 1979.

————. *The Wildcat in WWII*. Annapolis: Nautical & Aviation, 1983.

Tregaskis, Richard. *Guadalcanal Diary*. New York: Random House, 1943.

Tsunoda, Kazuo. *Shura no Tsubasa*. Tokyo: Koninsha, 1989.

Ugaki, Matome. *Fading Victory: The Diary of Admiral Matome Ugaki 1941–1945*. Pittsburgh: University of Pittsburgh Press, 1991.

U.S. Navy. *Building the Navy's Bases in World War II*. 2 vols. Washington, D.C.: GPO, 1947.

U.S. Navy. Bureau of Navigation/Bureau of Naval Personnel. *Register of Commissioned and Warrant Officers of the U.S. Navy and U.S. Marine Corps*. Washington, D.C.: GPO, 1941–45.

_____. *Register of Commissioned and Warrant Officers of the U.S. Naval Reserve*. Washington, D.C.: GPO, 1941–44.

U.S. Strategic Bombing Survey, *Interrogation of Japanese Officials*. 2 vols. Washington, D.C.: GPO, 1946.

Vandegrift, A. A. *Once a Marine*. New York: Norton, 1964.

Warner, Denis and Peggy Warner. *Disaster in the Pacific: New Light on the Battle of Savo Island*. Annapolis: Naval Institute Press, 1992.

Wiley, Delmar D. *Wiley's Island or Island Blong Wiley*. Privately published, 1986.

Willock, Roger. *Unaccustomed to Fear: A Biography of the Late General Roy S. Geiger*. Princeton: privately published, 1968.

Wolfert, Ira. *Torpedo 8*. Boston: Houghton Mifflin, 1943.

Yanagida, Kunio. *Reisen Moyu*. 2 vols. Tokyo: Bungei Shunji, 1984.

Y'Blood, William T. *The Little Giants: U.S. Escort Carriers Against Japan*. Annapolis: Naval Institute Press, 1987.

Zero Fighter Pilots Association. *Kaigun Sentōkitaishi* (History of Naval Fighter Squadrons). Tokyo: Genshobō, 1987.

Zimmerman, Maj. John L. *The Guadalcanal Campaign*. Washington, D.C.: GPO, 1949.

Index

About the Author

John B. Lundstrom is curator of the Nunnemacher Arms Collection at the Milwaukee Public Museum. A member of the museum staff since 1967, he earned a master's degree in diplomatic and military history in 1974.

His first two books were also published by the Naval Institute Press. *The First South Pacific Campaign: Pacific Fleet Strategy, December 1941–June 1942* came out in 1976, and *The First Team: Pacific Naval Air Combat from Pearl Harbor to Midway* appeared in 1984. He is currently at work on the naval aviation chapters of a history of U.S. airpower in World War II, as well as conducting research for a book on the Battle of the Coral Sea.